SEMIOTICA INDICA

SEMIOTICA INDICA

Encyclopaedic Dictionary of Body-Language in Indian Art & Culture

H.L. Shukla

Volume I

Aryan Books International
New Delhi

SEMIOTICA INDICA
Encyclopaedic Dictionary of Body-Language
in Indian Art & Culture

ISBN: 978-81-7305-044-2 (Vol. I)
978-81-7305-046-6 (Set)

First Published: 1994

Reprinted: 2022

Published by:

Aryan Books International
Pooja Apartments, 4B, Ansari Road, New Delhi-110 002 (India)
Tel.: 23287589, 23255799; Fax: 91-11-23270385
E-mail: aryanbooks@gmail.com
www.aryanbooks.com

Printed in India

PREFACE

This book is meant to provide some basic ideas, concepts and material for the study of nonverbal communication in India. It draws on work from semiotics but revolves around the core concept of communication.

The book covers much of the literature in Sanskrit and modern Indian languages on nonverbal communication and organizes it in a fashion useful for three purposes: (a) to provide "an ancient overview" of the nonverbal communication; (b) to map nonverbal continuity in India from Bharata's time to the present day; and (c) to provide a conceptual base into which new findings may be integrated.

This Encyclopaedic Dictionary of nearly 6000 terms relating primarily to social semiotics was compiled as much for my own benefit as for anyone else's. Quite frankly, I was becoming increasingly overwhelmed by the proliferation of terms that has inevitably accompanied the development of semiotics and other disciplines of relevance to linguistic analysis since the 1980s; and I was becoming increasingly frustrated by the semantic problems in the terminology that have resulted. And while there are dictionaries of critical terms and linguistic terms in the market, there is not even a single reference work for guidance in the close analysis of nonverbal communication that incorporates terms from paralanguage, kinesics, haptics, oculesics, olfaction, gustation. proximics, chronemics, speech behaviour, discourse analysis, communication theory — in a word *semiotics.*

I hope this volume provides enough groundwork for readers to pursue some of the topics raised in more depth, and especially to 'decode' one of the most ubiquitous and tenacious forms of communication and ideology in Indian society. I hope this volume contributes in some way to that topic and will help people become more aware of the images and values perpetuated by body semiotics, and the forms and structure which carry and determine what they mean.

This book is also a trip into the ancient past. On remote islands and interior parts of India there are people who are extremely backward in terms of civilization. Until recently they did not have their written languages and did not know metals. The life of these primitive people has much in common with the life of our Vedic ancestors. In order to gain a better understanding of their life I went to the places of Central India where they still live. I tried to win their trust gradually learning their languages and adopting their way of life and thereby gaining an opportunity to study their nonverbal behaviour. It was as if I found myself in the distant past. The study of the backward people's life enabled me to better understand how our Vedic and Puranic ancestors lived.

I am obliged to Verrier Elwin, Richard Lannoy, Kapila Vatsyayana, S N Ghosal Shastri, Sadashiv A Dange, N N Bhattacharya, S K Ramachandra Rao and others whose works are used by me in connection with the translation of the texts wherever necessary. Many other authors and friends also helped me in various ways by providing illustrations and sending me information connected with different entries. I am indebted to them. The line-drawings are by Bhasha and Abhisheka. I thank them for their sense of involvement. I must thank M/s Aryan Books International of Delhi, who accepted and carried out the publication of this book so willingly.

H. L. SHUKLA

Probable Chronology of the Works and Authorities Referred to

Ṛgveda = 6000 B.C. - 3000 B.C.

Brāhmaṇas = 1500 B.C. - 1000 B.C.

Rāmāyaṇa = 1500 B.C. - 1000 B.C.

Mahābhārata = 1000 B.C. - 900 B. C.

Upaniṣads = 1000 B.C. - 600 B.C.

Sūtras = 800 B.C. - 300 B.C.

Gautama Buddha = 563 B.C. - 483 B.C.

Pāṇini = 500 B.C.

Bhāsa = 450 B.C.

Kauṭilya = 300 B.C. - 100 B.C.

Aśoka = 268 B.C. - 232 B.C

Aśvaghoṣa = 1st c. A.D.

Nāṭyaśāstra = 2nd c. B.C.

Brahmayāmala Tantra = 2nd c. B.C. - 5th c. A.D

ManuSmṛti = 2nd c. B.C. - 2nd c. A.D.

Patañjali = 150 B.C.

Kālidāsa = 1st c. B.C. - 4th c. A.D.

Kāmasūtra = 1st c. A.D.

YājñavalkyaSmṛti = 100 A.D. - 300 A.D.

BṛhaspatiSmṛti = 100 A.D. - 400 A.D.

Matsya Purāṇa = 300 A.D.

Vāyu Purāṇa = 3rd or 4th c. A.D.

Nārada Smṛti = 4th c. A.D.

Viṣṇudharmottara = 450 A.D. - 650 A.D.

Abhinayadarpaṇa = 500 A.D.

Tantras = 5th c. A.D. onwards

Kāśikā = 662 A.D.

Paumacaria 677 A.D. - 760 A.D.

Purāṇas earlier than 7th c. A.D.

Bharata Kośa = 700 A.D.

Kāmandaka Nītisāra = 700 A.D.

Gauḍavaho = 725 A.D.

Kuṭṭinīmatam = 755 A.D. - 786 A.D.

Varāha Purāṇa = 800 A.D.

Rājaśekhara = 900 A.D.

Nala Campū = 915 A.D.

Daśarūpaka (Dhanañjaya) = 974 A.D. - 995 A.D.

Abhinavagupta = 990 A.D. - 1020 A.D.

Vāmana Purāṇa 9th or 10th c. A.D.

Dhanika = 1000 A.D.

Kāvyaprakāśa = 1050 A.D. - 1150 A.D.

Nāṭakalakṣaṇa ratnakośa (Sāgaranandī) = 1100 A.D.

Bhoja (Śṛṅgāraprakāśa) = 1100 A.D.

Kumārapālacarita = 1100 A.D.

Nāṭyadarpaṇa = 1093 A.D. - 1175 A.D.

Aparārka on Yāj. Smṛti = 1125 A.D.

Someśvara's Mānasollāsa = 1127 A.D.

Rājataraṅgiṇī = 1148 A.D. - 1150 A.D.

Naiṣadhacarita = 1150 A.D. - 1200 A.D.

Bhāvaprakāśa = 1175 A.D. - 1250 A.D.

Ruyyaka (Nāṭaka mīmāṁsā) = 1200 A.D.

Hemacandra (kāvyānuśīlana) = 1200 A.D.

Abhinayadarpaṇa (Nandikeśvara) = 12th c.A.D. - 13th c.A.D.

Saṅgītaratnākara (Sārṅgadeva) = 1210 A.D. - 1247 A.D.

Pratāparudrīya = 1275 A.D. - 1325 A.D.

Sāhityadarpaṇa = 1300 A.D. - 1340 A.D.

Śiṅgabhūpāla = 14th c. A.D.

Aśokamalla = 14th c. A.D.

Jagaddhara (commentator) = 1300 A.D. - 1450 A.D.

Rūpagosvāmī = 15th c. A.D.

Caitanya = 1486 A.D. - 1533 A.D.

Nāṭyapradīpa (Sundara Miśra) 1700 A.D.

ABBREVIATIONS

A	:	Arthaśāstra
AB	:	Abhinayabhāratī
AD	:	Abhinayadarpaṇa
AK	:	Amarakośa
AS	:	Aśvaśāstra
AY	:	Āyurveda
BP	:	Bhāvaprakāśa
BT	:	Brahmayāmala Tantra
C	:	Chandaḥśāstra (prosody)
D	:	Darśana Śāstra (philosophy)
DR	:	Daśarūpaka
G	:	Gajaśāstra (elephant-lore
HC	:	Harśacarita
J	:	Jyotiṣaśāstra (astronomy and astrology)
K	:	Kāmaśāstra (erotics)
Kr	:	Kṛṣiśāstra (agriculture)
Mbh	:	Mahābhārata
MR	:	Mudrārākṣasa
NC	:	Naiṣadha carita
ND	:	Nāṭyadarpaṇa
NLR	:	Nāṭakalakṣaṇaratnakośa
NP	:	Nāṭyapradīpikā
NS	:	Nāṭyaśāstra
Raghu	:	Raghuvaṁśa
Ram	:	Rāmāyaṇa
S	:	Saṅgītaśāstra (music)
SD	:	Sāhitya darpaṇa
SK	:	Śākuntalam
SM	:	Smṛtiśāstra
SR	:	Saṅgītaratnākara
Sy	:	Śyainikaśāstra (hawking)
T	:	Tantraśāstra
U	:	Udbhid-vidyā (botany)
V	:	Vāstuvidyā (architecture)
VD	:	Viṣṇudharmottara
VK	:	Vikramorvaśīya
VS	:	Veṇīsaṁhāra
Vy	:	Vyākaraṇa (grammar)
Fig. – (X)	:	Fig. for Entry No. X

INTRODUCTION

Modern India is perhaps unique, historically, in that its twentieth -century existence is still fashioned on traditions laid down thousands of years ago. Yet it has by no means trapped in the rigid mould of an archaic civilization, in fact, its present evolution in the industrial field shows to what an extent its national equilibrium and coherence are based on an admirable continuity. The slow pace at which changes of all kinds have taken place in India is the necessary accompaniment of this continuity, and reflects accurately the rhythm of rural life, which has always provided the essential framework of the country's structure.

For all these reasons we have been obliged to choose an exceptionally lengthy period, almost eight thousand years, in order to give necessary breadth of detail to the present study. There has been no escaping these extended time limits in this instance: any attempt to shorten the period would have resulted inevitably in an incomplete impression of nonverbal communication in India.

This is a survey of Indian semiotics from the *Ṛgveda* (6000 B.C.) to the present day sketching the theoretical (*śāstra*) and practical (*prayoga* = *loka*) approaches of the leading semioticians with respect to their differing objectives : classifying the *śāstra* and *loka* ; establishing the philosophical sign system for canonical representation of human thought; devising *Purāṇas* for the creation of new ideas; gaining insight into the conditions of human knowledge; increasing the efficiency of *sāhitya, saṅgīta, citra, vāstu, āyurveda, jyotiṣa, darśana* and the various branches of the arts; extending communication into *āgama, nigama, tantra, yonija* and *ayonija* species. The underlying world-view has crystallized in certain concepts, reflecting the understanding of body and soul, of space and time, of *indriya* and *atīndriya*, of the part and the whole, of the body and senses. So far most indological or semiotic research has been done in single disciplines or in limited area, but a serious investigation into the inter - relatedness of all these fields is still a desideratum. A semiotic approach is the first prerequisite to understanding the relationship between the ancient sciences and the various branches of the arts. Considering that semiotic research itself is semiosis, we present here the compilation of different signs from Vedic period to the modern age.

Cultural Semiotics

The science that deals with the dynamics of signs is called semiotics. The science of semiotics or the theory of signs and symbols studies the language of animals, our own human language, and the numerous and diversified language systems of signs and symbols like road signs, signal systems, displays, maps, diagrams and the like. The process through which signs function is called semiosis.

In ancient India Sanskrit scholars laid special stress on the pragmatic nature of signs. While dealing with *yuktiśāstra, Mahābhārata* (V. 30.49) resorts to its pragmatic interpretation. Later on *Daśarūpaka* (1.43) commenting on *kāryayukti* explains that it is the "study of appropriateness or suitability of action or sign in a drama". These seminal ideas of *Mahābhārata* and *Daśarūpaka* were further nurtured in the *yuktidīpikā* with an outline of five broad sub-fields of semiotics pertaining to the secret codes. The meanings, however, have undergone some change as the term semiotics is now used for the study of signs in general. Although major contributions to the study of signs have emerged from the West, we should credit the major impetus toward the emergence of this concept to the influence of work conducted a millennium ago by Dhanañjaya (an Indian dramaturgist who wrote *Daśarūpaka*). Classical Indian arts were rife with symbols and signification prior to Dhanañjaya (974 - 995 A.D). Some of these arts mentioned by Kauṭilya (300 B.C. - 100 B.C.), Bharata (2nd B.C.), Vātsyāyana (1st c. A.D.) and Bāṇabhaṭṭa are as follows:

(i) *ālāpayojanam* : art of discourse design.

(ii) *kāvyasamasyā pūrṇam* : art of completing a verse whose one part has been supplied.

(iii) *calitayoga* : tricky and critical communication to delute others.

(iv) *tarkakarma* : art of disputation.

(v) *deśabhāṣājñāna* : knowledge of dialects.

(vi) *nimittajñāna* : art of signs and omens.

(vii) *pratimālā* : art of reciting verses beginning with the letter with which one recited by one's adversary ends.

(viii) *prahelikā* : art of riddles.

(ix) *mlecchitavikalpa* : art of speaking by changing the forms of words, learning of various foreign codes, symbolic scripts and speeches.

(x) *vācikā* : art of oral communication; also known as *vāk-dīkṣā.*

(xi) *vaināyikī* : art of submission or discipline.

(xii) *saṁvādana* : art of entertaining in conversation.

(xiii) *sarvabhāṣākauśalam* : art of knowing all the languages.

(xiv) *sarvalipikauśalam* : art of knowing all the scripts.

Today, semiotics is vast beyond measure. Umberto Eco, who himself holds a professorship of semiotics, has conservatively listed multiple sub-fields; zoosemiotics, olfactory signs (codes of scents), tactile communication, codes of taste, paralinguistics (supplementary codes during speech events), medical semiotics, kinesics and proximics (gesture codes), musical codes, formalized languages, written languages, unknown alphabets, secret codes, natural languages, visual communication, systems of objects, plot structure, text theory, cultural codes, aesthetic texts, mass - communication and rhetorics (*A Theory of Semiotics*, 1976, 9-14). Even then there are many ancient arts or codes which are still to be enumerated as sub-fields of semiotics.

It is necessary to specify the object of study of semiotics in our approach. As students of linguistics, we are interested in semiotics to help us in making progress toward greater comprehension of what people are doing when they communicate. As Roland Barthes (1964) pointed out, any social object can become the sign of its own function. Social systems of use- such as kinshop systems, manners, clothing, shelter and any system of object and/or actions - have a semiotic, communicative aspect. The symbolic or conventional use of language has been readily indentified in *Dharmaśāstras* in such acts as greetings, leave ṭakings, introductions, memorized rituals, marriage proposals and other different rites. Etiquette books are concerned with conventional expressions and polite phrases. *Manu* (3.18) points out differences between phrases, which express real condition and conventional phrases. Conventional signs and gestures are freely used in all our institutions.

The universality of symbolic speech acts and NV act is yet to be explored. There are suggestions that palm-presentation is universal among humans and some other primates. Other possibilities of universal symbolic acts are hand-raising and eye avoidance. The hand-raising has been ritualized in parliamentary proceedings when a speaker (chair person) does not want to give the floor to a member of parliament.

Verbal and nonverbal expressions of status (reflecting the economic systems) and male/female differences are the most important features of differentiation in the dynamics of human interactions.

Very intense emotions are usually dealt with euphemistically by means of symbolic acts. Direct speech is not the modality of such communications as "I hate you". Even "I love you", said in so many words, can be meaningless. Insulting and obscene gestures replace speech act as a means of rejecting and repelling in the interactional behaviour. There is no other way to understand the deep -rooted culture of this country other than semiotics. Since expression and content, differences and significance are dialectically united, there is need for the formation of a new science and hence *yuktiśāstra* or semiotics which has its long tradition in this country. To know the Indian system of symbolization, therefore, is to know the culture of the Indian people who created it.

Semiotics is an approach which has adopted some concepts and tools of analysis from structural linguistics, which attempts to uncover the internal relationships which give different languages, their forms and functions. Although language is a basic model, semiotics has cast its net wider, and looks at any system of signs whether the substance is oral, written, visual, aural, verbal or nonverbal or the complex mixture. Thus, speech, myth, folktales, novels, drama, comedy, mime, paintings, cinema, comics, news items and advertisements can be analyzed semiotically as systems of signification similar to languages.

This approach involves a critical shift from the simple interpretation of objects and forms of Indian communication to investigations of the organization and structure of cultural artefacts of India, in particular, to enquiry into how they produce meaning. It is argued that the meaning of Indian culture is not something there, statically inside the Great Tradition, waiting to be revealed by a correct interpretation. What Indian culture means depend on its continuity - how it operates, how signs and its ideological effects are organized—internally within its continuous flow, and—externally in relation to its production.

In order to clarify the contribution that semiotics (structuralism) can make to the analysis of Indian culture as signs and sign systems, I will describe some of the basic features and concepts of the structural model that may be applied to Indian culture.

Structuralism (and I am taking this word to be more or less synonymous with semiotics) usually makes a distinction between the systematic and social part of *signifying practices/structural systems* - the material, conditioning and determining aspects of culture - and the resulting *individual signifying practice*.The former is usually referred to as *langue* (*bhāṣa*) and it consists of structural rules and conventions, which are independent of the individual use of them. The individual use is called *parole* (*vāk*), and is the manifestation of the selected, combined and articulated elements of *langue* (language). In language itself, the distinction between *langue* and *parole* (speech) is perhaps more clear-cut than in a system like nonverbal (NV) communication. Nevertheless it could be argued that NV is a *parole* - the ordered combinations of NV signs into messages - and that verbal communication is the means (codes) which allow the messages to function. *Langue* conditions and is conditioned by *parole* and consists of a diverse set of social constraints, references, images, formal techniques and rhetorical figures which the NV communication draws upon.

A second distinction, which is important for understanding how sign systems work, is that made between the two parts which make up the sign, be it visual or verbal. A sign is made up of the *signifier,* a material vehicle, and the *signified,* a mental concept or reference. A signifier has potential but not actual meaning whereas the signified is the concept or meaning which the signifier refers to. The two are materially inseparable, although it is useful to distinguish between them for the purpose of analysis in order to see how the sign works.

The important thing to remember about signs is that their meaning can only be assessed in relation to their structure and their structural relationships with other signs. A sign not only means in and for itself but also through its place in other signifying systems. The signified does not exist except as a function of a particular signifying system. Meanings are organized in "chains" of signification and signifieds can become signifiers for further chains of signification.

Culture, like language, is a system of distinct signs. It is a system of differences and oppositions which is crucial in the transfer of meaning. The most obvious way of creating a distinction between cultural artefacts and make one stand out from the rest is to give it a distinctive image.

Icon, Index and Symbol

Signs being the bedrock of communication, may be divided into three broad categories :

(a) Iconic signs (natural signs)

(b) Indexical signs (copy signs)

(c) Symbolic signs (conventional signs).

Iconic signs are nonconventional signs manifested through objective nature, independent of human will. These include weather signs, climatic symptoms, geographical contour of an area, animal signs, smells, odour, taste, medical symptoms and other signs pertaining to behaviour of the elements of nature. Photographic images look like the thing, place or person being represented. This makes them iconic signs, and the signifier - signified relationship one of the resemblance or likeness. A portrait of a person is an obvious example of an iconic sign, because the picture resembles that person.

Indexical signs are very akin to iconic signs. They are duplicated by means of which a message regarding the original is encoded. Indexical signs indicate their entities through existential relationship in situations of usage, frequently take on conventional associations such that they are used when the signalled entity does not occur contiguously in the utterance situation. A little boy who pretends to hit his finger while pounding with a toy hammer and screams "Ouch" is not indexing a real pain, but rather symbolizing a nonexistent pain in conventional manner. The school teacher who shouts "Fire" during a fire - drill is not drawing attention to a fire in the situation of his or her utterance but is using a conventional index in simulating what would happen in the event of a real fire. And the boy who cries, "Wolf" uses a cultural convention in conveying a danger that does not actually exist in the context of his shouting.

Not only are these indexes that function as symbols, but there are others that function both as indices and symbols. These are known as referential indexes (Silverstein, 1976). To return to our example, "I gave you the bribe", it may now be noted that the personal pronouns *I* and *you* operate simultaneously as referential symbols and situated indexes. The signal referential values in the proposition coded in the sentence (first person reference "gives to", second person referent) at the same time they indicate that the speaker of the situated utterance was the giver and the hearer was the receiver. The school teacher who shouts "fire" and the boy who cries "wolf" are also using referential indexes. In both examples, the speaker indicates the presence of danger in the situation of utterance (even when the danger is fictitious), and refers to a specific danger entity.

Thus, some signs go beyond the mere description of a person (iconic) or things are used indexically to indicate a further or additional meaning to the one immediately and obviously signified. For example, the costume a person is bearing may denote iconically the mode of dress worn by a person or character in an ad, but at the same time stand indexically for a social position or profession. A character's movements may simultaneously represent some (dramatic) piece of action and indicate his or her frame of mind, habits or livelihood. A woman in ads is often represented indexically by bits of her body - hips, eyes, head, hands or legs - which signify not only in themselves but also her own being. They can also signify a commodity - lip-stick, eye make-up, shampoo, nail-polish, etc. - thus suggesting that women are commodities also.

If one wants to convey the idea of heat, he or she could show beads of sweat on a person's brow. As with all indexical signs, there is a sequential or causal connection between signifier and signified.

A great number of signs with which man manipulates are symbolic. Being a social being, man is surrounded by a multitude of various symbolic signs that have become the part of his cultural heritage.

The relationship between signifier and signified in some signs is arbitrary based neither on resemblance nor on any existential link. In other words, the signifier does not resemble or cause the signified, but is related to it only by convention or 'contract'. This kind of sign is called a symbol. A lotus is a symbol of love or passion not because a lotus (*līlākamala*) looks like love or passion or even because the flower causes it. It is just that members of some cultures have over the years used the lotus in certain circumstances to mean love. In many cases the symbols used to convey meanings or ideas are not entirely arbitrary: the symbol for Justice, a pair of scales, for instance, could not be replaced by any other symbol. In other words there are the rudiments of a 'natural' bond between signifier and signified in many symbols.

Symbolic signs may be grouped under the following categories:

(a) Non-linguistic visual, tactile and behavioural signs (architectural signs, paintings, sculpture, musical codes, rites, rituals, ceremonies, manners, etiquettes, kinesic movements, proximics, signs of various signalling systems including colours and lights, non-linguistic communication signs used by tribals).

(b) Linguistic signs and symbols (cultural symbols expressed in language, dream symbols, neurotic symbols, literary symbols, signs and symbols used in folklore like myths, folktales, folksongs, legends, fables, proverbs, abuses and the like).

(c) Paralinguistic signs (suprasegmental features).

(d) Archaeological codes (that help in decoding historical data).

(e) Audible signs (musical signs).

Syntagmatic and paradigmatic sign relations

Before discussing the code-system, I need to introduce another pair of semiotic concepts. De Saussure proposed a distinction between the *syntagmatic* relation between elements in a language, and *paradigmatic* relations. Syntagmatic relations are the permissible ways in which elements succeed each other or combine together in a chain of discourse. These elements have nothing in common and are brought together by virtue of 'combinatory (syntactic) rules'. A syntagm is defined by its opposition to that which follows or precedes it.

In NV communication the syntagm is the body or series of body as that appear before us — a chain of visual, verbal and aural signs. In order to discover the paradigm and eventually the rules of a body signification, we have to break up the syntagmatic chain and isolate (for the purposes of analysis) a distinctive unit, in order to find the roots of its meaning. A unit or sign thus identified, for example a person with the crown, can then be (theoretically) classified according to its paradigmatic relations, which in this case consist of all other functionally similar objects: turban, *dhotī*, hair-dress, hairband, etc. Obviously the 'crown' is chosen in the marriage ceremony because of its particular associations. It recalls a system of meaning beyond the immediately of the syntagmatic text. Paradigmatic structures facilitate the associative and connotative use of terms: they assume a code or coding. A crown is understood by virtue of its relation and opposition to turbans, hair-dresses, hair-bands, etc. but it is connotative due to a 'deeper' paradigmatic relations. Connotation relies on the viewer's cultural knowledge of a system which can relate 'crown' to feelings of nobility, masculinity, divineness, individuality, etc.

Paradigmatic relations are those which belong to the same associative set by virtue of the function they share. So a sign is in a paradigmatic relation with all other signs which can also occur in the same context but not at the same time. An example from Barthes's (1967) might help to clarify these concepts: In the garment/fashion semiotic system, the paradigmatic order is 'A set of pieces; parts or details which cannot be worn at the same time on the same part of the body, and where variation corresponds to a change in meaning of the clothing: toque - bonnet - hood, etc'. The syntagm consists of the 'juxtaposition in the same type of dress of different elements: skirt-blouse-jacket' (*Ibid*). A linguist, Roman Jakobson, extended the idea of paradigm and syntagm to the notions of metaphor and metonymy: metaphors belong to a paradigmatic order and metonymy to a syntagmatic order. Metaphor is a matter of the selection of elements from an associative plane; metonymy is concerned with combination at a horizontal level (Jakobson, 1971.67).

Denotation and Connotation

The concepts of denotation and connotation are two of the most important in semiotic analysis (although they are not exclusive to semiotics) Roughly speaking, denotation and connotation refer to first and second levels of meaning in a sign. The term denotation refers to the literal meaning of a sign; to what is 'objectively' present and easily recognized or identified. Connotation is a term used to refer to meanings which lie beyond denotation but are dependent on it. Connotative readings of signs are introduced by an audience/viewer/reader beyond the literal meaning of a sign and are activated by means of conventions or coded. Roland Barthes elaborates these concepts in *Elements of Semiology,* where he says 'the first system (denotation) becomes the plane of expression or signifier of the second system (connotation) ..... the signifiers of connotation... are made up of signs (signifiers and signifieds united) of the denoted system' (1967. 91). We the expectators can only join up or make sense of these two systems by our knowledge of cultural codes and associative meanings without which the second system, connotation, is not possible. A lotus, for example, means on the denotative level, a flower. The signified can become signifier (vehicle) of another signified at another level. Depending on the context, the lotus can connote lore or passion.

Readers or spectators have actively to introduce cultural codes in order to interpret a sign by uniting signifier and signified. Cultural meaning is constructed not just by the discrete signs but by the ordering of events. It uses objects which are signifieds of ideological systems and thought that already exist and then makes them signifiers of another structure. Denotation is still dependent on a context of meaning and association.

We should not forget that ideology also works throughout the linguistic message. This level 'fixes the floating chains of signifieds in such a way as to counter the terror of uncertain signs' (Barthes 1964.37). All images are made of a number of 'floating' signs and subject to a variety of interpretations.

Codes

The concept of code is central to semiotic analysis. The formation and understanding of messages (encoding and decoding) is made possible by codes — a set of rules or an interpretative device known to both transmitter and receiver, which assigns a certain meaning or content to a certain sign. We recognize the signifier, long blonde hair for example, as a sign of feminity when we interpret it through the code of feminity as the signifier of a certain signified, woman. Within that code there is a sub-code which assigns this long - blonde - haired woman a particular meaning — a particular kind of 'healthy sexuality'. Codes are forms of social knowledge which are derived from social practices and beliefs although they are not laid down in any stature. Codes organize our understanding of the world in terms of 'dominant meaning patterns', patterns which vary from culture to culture and from time to time but which we largely take for granted and which are uppermost in our minds when we interpret things or think about them.

It is necessary to establish a clear and working differences between several kinds of signs in order to cover the whole spectrum of semiotics (the verbal, the nonverbal aspects).

For this we feel that there is a growing need for the cooperation of the plastic artists and his critics, the musician and the musicologist, if a thorough analysis is to be made of such manifestations far from the merely impressionistic accounts which in other conditions, are the only possible ones.

In conclusion, we feel that semiotics is paving the way to a plural world in which pluralism may be able to contribute rather to the common human achievement than to the destruction of knowledge, wealth and power, or the developments of Good and Evil which pose as two monstrous relatives unable to show any possible chance of blending.

Semiotics of Nonverbal Communication

Avāciki - *Sañcāriki* : nonverbal communication. The noted tāntric book *Śāradātilaka* has formulated the concept of *vāciki i.e.* initiation with *mantras.* The reverse of it is *avāciki.* Thus NV communication is communication through any means other than language. NV communication includes para language, kinesics, expressive gestures, costume and make up, haptics, oculesics, olfaction, gustation, hearing, proximics, and chronemics. In fact whole actions and sequences of action can be communicated. This is why Vātsyāyana in his *Kāmasūtra* has designated it as *kriyāvikalpa* which is an art to achieve one's objectives by diverse actions. Vātsyāyana believes that the NV factor of action precedes and supports verbal activity. Action, according to him, is a universal language (of love).

All animals perform actions and most do little else. A great many also make artefacts — constructed or manufactured objects — such as nests, webs, beds and burrows. Among the monkeys and apes there is also some evidence of abstract thinking. But it is only with man that artefaction and abstraction have run riot. This is success of his story. With his massive brain, man has increasingly internalized his behaviour through complex processes of abstract thought — through language. Throughout it all, he has remained a creature of action — a gesticulating, posturing, moving, expressive primate.

Unlike Vātsyāyana, Bharata has used the term *abhinaya. Abhinaya* is also an action that sends a visual signal to an on-looker. To become a gesture, an act has to be seen by someone else and has to communicate some piece of information (message) to them. It can do this either because the gesturer deliberately sets out to send a signal — as when he bends his head — or it can do it only incidently - as when he sneezes. The head-bend is a primary gesture (*abhinaya*), because it has no other existence or function. It is a piece of communication from start to finish. The sneeze, by contrast, is a secondary, or incidental gesture (*ceṣṭita*). Its primary function is mechanical and is concerned with the sneezer's personal breathing problem. In its secondary role, however, it can not help but transmit a message to his companions, warning them that he may have caught a cold.

Gestures transmit messages. So this book deals with actions, about how actions become gesture, and about how gestures transmit *sandeśa* (messages).

A message is a sign system of the source's intentions. Messages do not mean anything in and of themselves. The meaning exists in the heads of the sender and receiver. In communicating, we try to find those signs (verbal as well as NV) which capture the meaning we intend and which we think will evoke a like response in the minds of our receivers.

Semioticians seem to be in agreement that a sign (*cihna*) is an object of some sort that "stands for something else" (Pierce 1931 - 1958, de Saussure 1916, Morris 1938, Barthes 1964, Eco 1976). There seems to be little disagreement about the constituting features of the sign (a) it must be 'something'. (b) it must represent (c) it must be based on a convention.

It is necessary to specify the object of study of semiotics in our NV approach. While verbal features of Sanskrit have been considered, now it is useful to evaluate the semiotic systems of meaning - the NV 'languages' and their interaction — drawn from the cultural matrix of India embedded into different *śāstras, vidyās* and *kalās.* For our present purposes, I will consider only the Non Verbal dimensions. Two levels of analysis may be undertaken. The first is relatively straightforward and mechanical. On the basis of Sanskrit texts following fields emerge in NV semiotics:

(1) Paralinguistics (supplementary codes during speech events)
(2) Kinesics (body language gesture code)
(2) Expressive Gesturology (physical sensation)
(4) Systems of objects (*āhārya*)
(5) Haptics (tactile communication)
(6) Oculesics (visual communication)
(7) Olfaction (codes of smell)
(8) Gustation (codes of taste)
(9) Auscultation (audible communication and musical codes)
(10) Proximics (spatial code)
(11) Chronemics (temporal code)

These NV dimensions are present in most of the texts, and are either reflected faithfully or altered strategically to impart meaning. Aesthetics is also a critically important 'language' employed in NV communication, as it serves to organize our perception of the cultural document. Sanskrit works address these surface features, and have profoundly suggestive implications for message encoding. The second level of analysis necessarily unfolds on a deeper, more fundamental plane, but here it does not fall under our semiotic framework. We know that culture is a communication, and that culture is composed of primary message systems which include interaction, association, subsistence, bisexuality, territoriality, temporality, learning, play, defence, and exploitation. Each of these categories is enmeshed in every other. Each category can be used to understand every other, and ultimately to produce a comprehensive picture of Indian culture. Vātsyāyana has categorized the following arts with the semiotic load:

(1) *Uttarakalā* 'arts used after coition'.

(2) *Udakakrīḍā* 'aquatic arts'.

(3) *Aindrajāla* 'art of jugglery'.

(4) *Kusuma - taṇḍula - vali - vikalpa* 'greeting and entertaining guests with betels and decoration of houses with colours and flowers'.

(5) *Kriyākalpa* 'art of action'.

(6) *Grathan - granthana - kalā* 'art of garlanding, selecting and compiling beautiful and precious things and thoughts' (*Śukranītisāra*).

(7) *Taṇḍula -prasūna -vali - vikāra - kriyā* 'art to prepare squares etc. in the temples with rice and flowers'.

(8) *Durvācaka-yoga* 'knowing with cheats and rogues'.

(9) *Deva-toṣaṇa-kalā* 'art of pleasing gods' (*Śukra*)

(10) *Nāṭakadarśana-kalā* 'art of seeing plays'.

(11) *Nāṭakākhyāyikādarśana-kalā* 'art of attending dramas and variety shows'.

(12) *Puṣpaśakaṭikā-kalā* 'art of preparing flower-carts'.

(13) *Puṣpāstaraṇa-kalā* 'art of decoration of halls and assemblies with flowers and foliage'.

(14) *Bhojyavikāra-kalā* 'art of cookery'.

(15) *Mānasī-kalā* 'art of observation'.

(16) *Mālā-grathana-kalā* 'art of preparing garlands'.

(17) *Meṣa-kukkuṭa-lāvaka-yuddhavidhi* 'art of fighting of cock, bull and ram'.

(18) *Yantramātṛkā-kalā* 'art of framing mystical diagrams'.

(19) *Yantramālikā-kalā* 'art of charms and amulets'.

(20) *Vāyasa-vidyā* 'art of the interpretation of crow's cries'.

(21) *Śayanaracanā-kalā* 'art of preparation of beds for different times and seasons'.

(22) *Śayanopacāra-kalā* 'arts performed on the bed, sixteen in number'.

(23) *Śukanirutajñāna* 'art of parrot-speech' (*Kādambarī*).

(24) *Śuka-Sārikā-pralāpana-kalā* 'art of teaching parrots and startlings to speak'.

The former views socio-cultural knowledge as revealed through performance of speech acts which are bound in real time and space, and which are restrained in form and content by culturally specific norms and values. The latter posits abstract semantic constructs (frames, scripts, schemata, etc.) by which actors apply their knowledge of the world to the interpretation of an encounter. The former approach examines the impact of social norms on communication, while the latter examines the cognitive functioning of contextual and other knowledge. The data from Indian culture has also been gathered on the basis of these two approaches.

Types of nonverbal Communication

Those who have written about the NV communication in the West are not in agreement on the categories we should use for analysis. I think the easiest way to classify non-speech communication is best demonstrated in the concept of *yukiśāstra* in *Mahābhārata,* and later it was scientifically developed in *Arthaśāstra, Nāṭyaśāstra* and *Kāmasūtra.* In the following pages we have presented an integrated approach to the NV categories. Our data entry in the dictionary is based on these categories.

1 **Pāṭhakriyā**: paralinguistics. Other communication systems are superimposed on the linguistic one, augmenting and modifying the messages communicated by language in speech. One such system overlapping the *vācika* (verbal communication) of Bharata, can be called *pāṭhakriyā* —the paralanguage. Paralanguage significantly interacts with language in spoken discourse in ways Bharata is keen to study. It includes all of the sounds coming from our mouth and nose that are not directly part of language. For the most part they accompany speech (*e.g.* drawling, whispering, shouting), but they can also convey messages in place of speech (*e.g.* shushing, whistling, hissing etc.). Vātsyāyana in his *Kāmasūtra* has subdivided these paralinguistic features into four types of arts: (a) *Samavācya-samapāṭhya-kalā* : art of repeating what has been said by another person, though one does not know the language. (b) *Vācana-kalā* : art of reciting. (c) *Durvācakayoga* : art of speaking in such a manner that it should not be understood easily. (d) *Mānasī-kāvyakriyā* : art of versification in mind.

In this respect paralanguage has been regarded as a nonverbal, but vocal system, along with prosodic features, such as pitch and loudness. Any characteristic paralinguistic features would be noises that do not function as phonemes (*i.e.* in building words), but nonetheless do communicate a 'meaning' or 'attitude' in speech: *e.g.* giggles, snorts, exclamation of disgust, disapproval, boredom, etc. We can now conveniently distinguish four separate sub-grouping:

(i) First there is the voice-set, the physically and physiologically determined characteristics of an individual's voice that serves as background for evaluating meaningful paralinguistic variations. One's voice set identifies him as a particular individual, and can give the listener information about his sex, age, body build, and even location.

Against a background of voice set, the listener measures two other aspects of paralanguage: vocal segregates and voice qualities.

(ii) *Vocal segregates* or gestural segregates : The many vocalizations we make that are expressive but not really a part of language. We make *sītkāra* to indicate that it is cold, grunt "yes" "no", make several varieties of tongue clicking for approval or disapproval, imitate a cock, or hiss at a bad movie. Gestural segregates such as a nod or shake of the head, a pointing finger, a good-bye wave of the hand, crossed legs, finger snapping, slapping the thigh, clapping or a friendly wink have varying degrees of culturally determined meaning. These all interact with vocal segregates, as they can convey some rather specific messages. They can be executed and described with reference to gesture qualities noted above. Above all they convey information that can amplify, emphasize, or modify linguistic and paralinguistic messages as well as information which can be transmitted in the absence of any vocal communication. As with the vocal — auditory mode of communication, the gestural — visual mode is always manifested in a social context, and it is the total context which provides the means necessary for interpretation of any message.

(iii) *Voice qualities* or gesture qualities include the loudness, pitch, and length variations superimposed on syllable nuclei that in same languages make referential distinctions. If they are distinctive referently, then they are part of the linguistic system. Where they do not play in the linguistic system, they are free to signal paralinguistic information. Other voice qualities that can accompany speech are whinning, yawning, moaning, whispering, snickering, sobbing, whimpering, giggling, laughing and crying, as well as qualities inter-locking these—tempo (from fast to slow), rhythm (from smooth to jerk), resonance (from thin to full bodied) and others. Voice qualities can tell the listener if we are nervous, confident, angry, exuberant, irritated, or calm. That is they are indicators of our emotional state among other things. Such information, naturally is very important for the interpretation of *vāciki* (vocal messages).

(iv) *Temporality*: A second major way content free speech may be conceptualized in terms of its temporal characteristics ( ), that is, in terms of the variables of utterance, interruption (including simultaneous speech), and reaction time latency (Matarazzo and Wiens, 1972). Other content–free measure include quantity of speech, verbal productivity, and rate of speech. Silences, including hesitations and pauses can also be described as "nonverbal" speech phenomena that are important aspects of interpersonal communication. All these aspects of speech can be considered temporal characteristics of speech in that they are defined in terms of units per time interval. Disturbances of speech and dysfluencies are the remaining kinds of content–free speech that are considered (Harper, Weins and Matarazzo, 1978.21).

2. **Āṅgikābhinaya:** Kinesics. Popularly known as *āṅgika abhinaya* (body language), it includes gesture, postural shifts, and movements of the hands, head, feet and legs. According to *NS* of Bharata, *āṅgikābhinaya* (body language) consists of facial expression and movements of concerned limbs. *Aṅgas pratyaṅgas* and *upāṅgas* are employed in *āṅgikābhinaya.* Each movement of the limbs is indicative of a distinct mood or thought.

The subject of several classification systems, *āṅgika* (kinesics) has been defined ın a variety of ways. (a) According to Bharata's *NS*, it is divided into three types, namely, *śārīra* (of the limbs), *mukhaja* (facial) and *ceṣṭākṛta* (movement of the different parts of the entire body). (b) Indian philosophers are not in agreement with the Indian theatrics (*NS*) on the categories for NV communication. They have classified non-speech communication on the basis of the channels used to pick up the "messages". The *pañcendriyāṇi* (five senses); then would give the categories for analysis. The only problem with this system, however, is that one important kind of non-speech communication does not fall neatly into one of the five categories. We shall have to deal with it separately. In spite of this flaw in the system, let us look at five NV communication: (1) *Sparśana* (touching), (II) *āsvādana* (tasting), (III) *ghāṇa* (smelling), (IV) *śravaṇa* (hearing) and (V) *darśana* (seeing). (c) The palmists have their own classification and denotation according to *Sāmudrikaśāstra.*

The Western kinesics whether defined in terms of Birdwhistell's (1970) kinemes, kinemorphs and allokines; Ekman's (1975) emblems, illustrator, regulators and adaptors; or Mehrabian's (1972) forward, sideways lean, arm or leg position asymmetry, trunk swivel movements and gesticulations; the system is designed to assign meaning to movements and to provide a framework for research (Druckman and others, 1982.64) Though recognised as a new approach, Western system lacks in determining the relative significance of different NV behaviours. Moreover, the approach does not confront the issue of verification: one cannot be certain that this is the best-fitting model or the "correct" one (Weitz, 1974). Alerted to these problems, we will have to go back to Bharata to solve them. Bharata's initial treatise inspired a number of researchers to look seriously at these channels of communication and ushered in the NV revolution. Sanskrit dramas were written on the principles of *āṅgikābhinaya* of Bharata.

In Act IV, of *Abhijñāna Śakuntalam,* when Śakuntalā leaves *āśrama* all the verses demand *āṅgikābhinaya* constantly: a great part of Kaṇva's speech is full of movement, and the vision of creepers, plants, streams, etc, is built up only through words and *abhinaya* (gesture). The seventh act builds up a vision of the sky and the king and Mātali riding across the sky only through gestures. Bharata prescribes the appropriate gait for moving in the sky and says: "gait of a character moving through the sky is to include the aerial *cārī* and looking downwards: he is to move from *samapāda sthāna* with simple steps. The gait of one who descends from the sky is also to be of this kind (*NS*, XII. 92-95).

Examples of this kind could be multiplied : the actor has to walk in a certain way, a special *sthāna, cārī or maṇḍala* to establish his locale: so signs, symbols or announcements are necessary and once the *sūtradhāra* (director) has left the stage, it is through stylized movement with precise and stylized use of the space of the stage that the full meaning of drama is communicated to the audience. From these examples it is clear that by the time Kālidāsa wrote his dramas, the rules of gesticulation were perfectly understood and practised : the writer needs to offer no explanation for what he is doing : he is following an absolutely known and prevalent convention of the body language.

There is in Sanskrit drama always a situation which depends for its successful portrayal not on the words but on the *āṅgikābhinaya,* and this situation is the climax or turning point of a play. The Sanskrit dramatist never makes the body language an accessory to the verbal (*vācika*); he consciously uses this stylized technique of kinesics in order to achieve the most effective stage spectacle. In Act IV of *Ratnāvalī* of Harśa, the most popular piece of kinesics relates to the rising of flames in the palace. The king enacts putting off his cloak, rushing into the fire, and being overpowered by smoke. With quick movements and jumps, the king tells up of his entering into fire; and then through the quivering movement of the *tripatāka-hasta* he suggests flames and fires. This sequence is followed up by a sharp stroke of the *patāka-hastas* indicating the warding off the smoke. Ratnāvalī is rescued. She enters the stage in fetters, is released, and the illusion of fire and everything is explained by Yaugandharāyaṇa : and on this note of reconciliation and happiness the play ends.

Indian society has entirely stored in its body-memory the basic principles of its culture which was abbreviated in NS and is prevalent among them in mnemonic form. This is more true of preliterate societies of India which lack any other recording and objectifying instrument, so that inherited knowledge survived only in its embodied state. It is quite in order therefore, that gestures of obeisance should figure so prominently in the Hindu *Dharmaśāstra* as the key to better life. Why, for instance, must a youth leave his seat and greet an older man?' 'For, says, *Manu* (II.120), 'the vital airs of a young man mount upwards to leave his body when an elder approaches', but by rising to meet him and saluting he recovers them. There are many verses in that text devoted to the virtues of rising, prostrating, clasping of feet, etc, as indicative of subordinate (or respect-giving) status. And the authority of this body-language derived not only from sacerdotal prescriptions but also from the power of state. Thus according to Abul - Fazl, kings make regulations for the manner in which people are to show their obedience. This was also meant to promote a 'true humility' under the feudal setup and it still remains engraved in the bodies of the people.

Gestural communication, often called kinesics, also has its analogue to language. That is, in some societies or social groupings within societies communication takes place through a gesture language. Sleeman has already analyzed the sign language of the *Ṭhugas* in Madhya Pradesh. American sign language, for example, is the language for the deaf. *Ṭhugī* in Madhya Pradesh utilized a vocabulary of gestural signs which combined in rule-governed ways to form gestural statements. Possessing a vocabulary and syntax, a gesture language can be considered to coordinate with, rather than necessarily, subordinate to, a language proper. It performs similar functions, slightly differently expressed.

2.b. **Āsana:** posturics. From early childhood, each of us has been almost harassed by admonitions regarding "correct" posture, and not without some justification. Whether walking, standing, sitting or lying down, the body is all too frequently abused, twisted, distorted into all sorts of unproductive and even ugly shapes. We may recognize the postural differences between people who are happy or distressed, healthy or chronically ill, pensive or angry. Posture can be static or active and sometimes corresponds to expression. Poses can be composed, relaxed, leisurely, passive, leaning, seductive, snuggling. Bodies can be vertical or horizontal. An individual can use another to act as a shield or as an object to lean against, or rest hands or legs on. Pose is also related to social position and status, hence villagers are often seen in a lower position than city-dwellers, for instance sitting at their feet.

2:c. ***Gaṭi*** : art of training of movement. Śukrācārya in his *Śukranītisāra* evolved a new art of *āṅgikābhinaya* (kinesics) in order to train the correct speed and action. It is known as the art of *gatiśikṣā*, which includes movements of the body. Here, in *Śukranītisāra*, that thought in that direction, speed and range of gross bodily action also serve as signs of certain mental states and dispositions.

Walking to and from the speaker's platform, shifting weight from side to side or back and forth, and pacing about the platform are all examples of bodily movement. The speaker who slips sheepishly out of his chair, shuttles to the platform, and settles into a slouch is hardly seem confident. Contrast the speaker who rises with dignity and moves with purpose and ease. He stands erect but relaxed at the lectern. Such a speaker wins his audience's attention and confidence.

The only rule governing total physical behaviour is that movement be purposeful. Random movement may relieve tension but it detracts from the speaker's ideas. Anytime a speaker moves on the platform it should be for a good reason. A step forward may indictate "Here comes the main point". A step to the side may accompany a transition. A step to rear may invite the audience to relax and think over what has been said.

Body movement may be quite functional, *i.e.* simply related to what the actor is doing—cleaning the kitchen floor, making beds and gardening etc. These movements may be exaggerated, ridiculous or child-like, calling into question the competence of the performer. Bodies, particularly women's, are often not treated seriously, either through 'ritual subordination'(that lowering the body in front of others more superior, lying or sitting down, ritually bending the knee or lowering the head) or through puckishness and clowning.

3. ***Sāttvikābhinaya*** : expressive gestures. These are gestures of the type which all men, everywhere, share with one another, and which other animals also perform. They include the important signals of *mukhaja-abhinaya* (facial expression), so crucial to daily human interaction. Bharata (*NS*) calls them *sāttvika abhinaya* which means graceful gesticulation or physical sensations. *Sāttvika abhinaya* is a particular state of mind which is influenced by the contemplation of happiness and grief of others. Out of such mental states arise certain effects, which are termed as *sāttvika bhāvas.*

Kālidāsa is also a master of *sāttvikābhinaya*, and the drama as it has come down to us, employs the *sāttvikābhinaya* to a very large extent. The blossoming of Śakuntalā's love is manifested by this type of *abhinaya* and is an excellent illustration of the *bhāvas*, *anubhāvas* and *vibhāvas* of Sanskrit dramatic theory.

All primates are facially expressive and among the higher species the facial muscles become increasingly elaborate, making possible the performance of a whole range of subtly varying facial signals. In man this trend reaches its peak, and it is true to say that the bulk of NV signalling is transmitted by human face.

These natural gestures are usually spontaneous and very much taken for granted. These are the gestures that nearly everyone performs nearly everywhere in the world. Bharata has given an elaborate description of these gestures.

4. ***Āhāryābhinaya*** : The object language, props and setting. The way we decorate our bodies with clothing and surround ourselves with material goods, can also communicate.

Take the simple matter of clothing. It's fine to say that the way a person dresses shouldn't affect our judgment of him? Perhaps it shouldn't. But Bharata indicates that most of us place a lot of stock in a person's dress, particularly in the early stages of an association. A simple thing like eye-glasses can create a strong impression. In experiments, subjects frequently perceived those who wore glasses as more intelligent and industrious than those who didn't wear glasses.

Your home style and decorations, your choice and care of an automobile, also aid others in making judgments about you. You need only to look at advertisements for home furnishings or cars to see that admen know the symbolic value of the items they are "pushing".

Bharata all knew this and he has given the concept of *āhāryābhinaya* to explain the communicative value of the object language.

Costume and make up, decoration and ornaments come under this fourth type of NV communication. Bharata prescribes different kinds of dresses, ornaments and precious stones for human body. He also cautions the actors against wearing too many ornaments for, they may hinder their free movement.

Human beings and human activities are complex and diverse. It is impossible either to categorize them or to generalize about them. The decoration of the body is an exception. A people may be both painted and tattooed, and the motive for this may be simultaneously sexual, social and magical.

In India, the decoration of the body changes according to occasion or status. Without elaborate clothing and other devices, a whole language of body art has developed in which feelings, aesthetic sense and cultural attitudes are expressed by colourful designs, intricate tattooing, oils, fragrances and hairstyles. I shall consider *Kāmasūtra*-based body art primarily as a symbolic statement in which the decoration transmits messages about groups or individuals. By transforming the natural body into a cultural body, the individual subordinates himself to the common social values of his group. The body may even become a kind of model of society, which aesthetically communicates customs and role relationships from individual to individual.Vātsyāyana in his *Kāmasūtra* has mentioned some of the following body arts:

(a) *aṅgarāga-kalā* : The art of pointed body. Body art, like any other art form, ranges from the frivolous to the serious. Among the ascetics of India the body is painted and otherwise decorated for a number of reasons. Sometimes it is purely cosmetic-body art for body art's sake. Women care for their skin and their hair, washing and oiling them and making their preparations from turmeric and flour known as *ubṭan* (in Hindi). All fragrant powders and things are mixed and pounded together and mixed, then rubbed into the body and hair to make them shine.

(b) *Ullekhya-kalā* : *The tattooed body art.* While body painting is an ephemeral art, removable and renewable, tattooing is an indelible, permanent art which cannot be removed without ugly scarring or elaborate over-tattooing. To display absolute commitment of a role, ancient Indian people needed tattoo.

(c) *Karṇapatrabhaṅganirmāṇa* : The mutilated body art, drawing lines or figures or mutilation for ornamentation.

(d) *Saṁvāhana-śilpa* : The art of massaging. It is also known as *saṁvāhana-kauśala.*

(e) *Mardanādi-śilpa* : The art of rubbing the body.

(f) *Utsādana-kauśala* : The art of rubbing and kneading the body.

(g) *Daśana-rāga-kalā* : The art of colouring of teeth, also known as *dantarāgādinirmāṇa.*

(h) *Keśamardana-kalā* : Proficiency in braiding.

(i) *Keśa śilpa* : The art of hair-dressing.

(j) *Vastrarāga-kalā* : The art of colouring the garments. Accordingly clothes are a kind of uniform that unwritten rules stipulate according to the occasion and the circumstances.

(k) *Vastragopana-kalā* : The art of preservation of clothes.

(l) *Bhūṣaṇa-yojana* : The art of adorning with ornaments.

(m) *Rūpanirmāṇa-kauśala* : The art of turning ugly persons into handsome one.

(n) *Dhāraṇa-mātṛkā* : The art of changing oneself by mere wearing something.

(o) *Śekharāpīḍa yojana* : Art of adornment with chaplets etc.

(p) *Vicitra-vidhāna* : The art of changing the sex.

(q) *Bahurūpadhāritva* : The art of assuming various forms.

(r) *Nepathya-racanā* : Costumes; also known as *nepathya-prayoga.* Very little psychological study has been made of the choosing, display and interpretation of Indian costume. By wearing costume and other accoutrements, according to Bharata, must be taken as a semiotic activity, a statement-making act, displaying something for interpretation and correlatively, as chosen. Traditionally, one selects a costume from the wardrobe. If one is sixteen or seventeen, the problem of shoes may reach cosmic dimensions, why? Teenagers know what the rest of us have forgotten: the costume is a message which is publicly available for all to read. If there is a semantics and syntax of costume, then there must be a semiotics of it. The first step in pursuing that semiotics should be the putting together of a lexicon and a grammar, an exploration of the local rules of consistency and contradiction and so on. But then to carry this into individual modes of symbols, one simply applies the competence—performance distinction. The semiotic programme of research needs that distinction to bring an individual functioning to a last stage. If some one has set before the mirror thinking about costume, certain rules, conventions, interpretations, aesthetic and presentational standards have crossed and recrossed the mind of the brooder. There must be, of course an individual dimension.

Body decoration, then, is to be looked at as device for making statements, and given the attention to choice of decoration by certain categories of persons, those public statements must be interpreted as being made intentionally, on the basis of careful thought, cosideration and judgement. In short, if public objects have semantic loading, private processes must have semiotic and not just causal status.

Correlatively, if body art can be interpreted, if a hermeneutics of modes is possible, so body art can be meant, and the semantic principles that lie behind choosing and meaning what one adorns must be co-ordinated with those which lie behind its interpretation by the roots of one's social milieu. Only a competence-performance structuring of semiotics this could be properly studied.

Though NV communication is associated mainly with 'actors', yet Bharata did not forget that there are other visual elements—stage props and other objects (like grass), the setting (including weather), and of course the environment. You might think that meaning of an inanimate object or place is fairly straightforward. But physical objects can convey meanings to us in both literal or objective ways and also more subtly by suggestion and association. Objects are cultural as well as physical. Their appearance, shape, size and colour are the intentional result of a series of conscious choices and decisions made by human beings. The look of a thing is rarely accidental. The furniture we use, the rooms we live in, the meals we eat, our activities and everyday household objects implicitly or explicitly embody meanings.

Props are often used and can be as prominent as the person or relatively significant. Props can be selected because they help to demonstrate a person's choice. They are more likely to appear with a signifying as well as a functional role to play. Prop is intended to convey a special meaning; taste and quality. In this way the prop has both a functional and a symbolic meaning.

Some props occur so frequently in a person that they have gained a conventionalized or symbolic value; they stand for what is regarded as being desirable wealth, love, power, luxury, security. An elephant was used as a prop signified wealth and power. So is the car in modern days. Certain breeds of cows and horses appear frequently, so are the houses. Dogs usually signify loyalty and devotion, parrots and *mainas* were used as symbols of fastidiousness and luxury. Drinks are symbols of good taste. *Madhuparka* has strong connotations of masculinity. Books symbolize sound educational taste, while spectacles are meant to suggest cleverness.

NV cues do not always contain *settings*; even those with persons have non-specific backgrounds. Like objects, settings are carriers of meaning and rarely value-free. They act as a context which qualifies the background. Sometimes peoples and objects personalize the form. The more defined, obtrusive or cluttered the background, the more it will affect the main action or purpose of the NV communication. The setting may be quite vague and hazy or it can be a collection of specific props, but as far as impact goes the whole may be greater than the sum of the parts. Outdoor settings generally have a different meaning in comparison to indoor settings.

Clothes, according to Bharata, are obviously extremely important carriers of meaning. They can range from the formal to the informal and can be smart, sophisticated, glamorous, elegant, trendy or comfortable and casual. They can of course sum up a look.

Hair is one of the most potent symbols in cultural communication. Female hair in particular is considered to be seductive and narcissistic, meaning an object of love or self-admiration. The colour, length, texture and style of a person's hair are important qualifiers of their overall appearance.

In addition to vocal—auditory and visual—gestural channels of communication which Bharata and his followers have analysed, we transmit some information that is perceived through the senses of touch (*haptics*), seeing (*oculesics*), smelling (*olfaction*), tasting (gustation) and hearing (music). Most obvious of such things as kissing, spanking, wearing perfume, shaking hands, and hugging. We can probably think of many more to add to this, such as *proximics*, *chronemics*, and *orientations*. One day, perhaps, these communicative modes will be studied as closely as vocal and gestural communications have been in the past. These communication modes may be presented as follows:

5. **Sparśana** : haptics. This is an area in Indian *Dharmaśāstras* and *Tantras* that has been widely studied though it has been relatively unstudied by Bharata and his followers. However, the reader should not forget the concept of *hastasiddhi* given by *Yuktidīpikā* which has graped the deep significance of "touch by hand", particularly "touch of each other with their hands". The hands are called the "two chasers of disease, which stroke the patient with a gentle touch" (*RV*, X.137.7 and X. 60.2). *Yuktidīpikā* has understood how important it is to keep the person related to the world in which he lives. *Kulārṇava-Tantra* has focused upon the study of touching behaviour and it has outlined essentially a structural approach to *tacesics* which is known as *sparśa-dīkṣā*. But these references are not enough to integrate ideas that are useful for empirical investigation.

Western scholar Kauffman has proposed a "processual model" by which touching behaviour can be predicted based upon a person's past experience, present situational factors and motivational characteristics. Her goal, however, is to identify "tacemes", "tacemorphs" and "tacemorphic constructions", an approach similar to the linguistic-kinesic analogy developed by Birdwhistell.

Touching implies interpersonal involvement, but the meaning of that involvement can range from affirmation to "put down". It is complicated by social norms regarding who has permission to touch whom and what is considered to be an appropriate context for such behaviour. The meaning of a touch is affected by (1) what part of the body touched the other person, (2) what part of the body is touched, (3) how long the touch lasts, (4) how much pressure is used, (5) whether there is a movement after contact has been made, (6) whether anyone else is present, (7) if others are present, who are they, (8) the situation in which it occurs and the mood created by the situation and (9) the relationship between the persons involved.

Touching can convey liking, power and sexuality, and accordingly it has three broader subcategories in Indian culture, which have been evolved as *vidyā* or *kalā* :

(a) *Saṁsargavidyā* : the art of association (*Arthaśāstra*).

(b) *Āśleṣa-siddhi* : power of embracing (*Yuktidīpikā*) and

(c) *Kāmaśāstra* or *Kāmakalā* or *Ratikalā* : the art of love and sex (*Kāmasūtra, Śukranītisāra*). Vātsyāyana has discussed the *karmāśraya-kalā* which is based on action and numbers twenty-four.

Heslin (1974) has specified five kinds of situations/relations involving touching. Ranging from the most distant to the most intimate, they are (i) Functional/professional, (ii) social/polite, (iii) friendship/warmth, (iv)love/intimacy, (v) sexual arousal.

Some touches carry no personal messages. The doctor touches in order to examine, the hairdresser to cut hair, and the tailor to measure. But most communicate sometimes much more powerfully than words. A touch lends support, asserts that we are together or shows appreciation, affection, or attraction. By "control touches" we guide and steer people, or call for their attention and participation. Touching has ritual meaning during the marriage ceremony—sealing a bondage.

Social rules that ban overly familiar or overbearing touches closely regulate these touches : how much and where on the body people touch implies how intimate their relationship is, and how power is distributed between them. We have to touch strangers, superiors, inferiors, mere acquaintances, friends and intimates each in the right way. Higher status people in India intimate touching lower status people and therefore for males it is a dominance signal rather than an affiliative one.

The finger brought to the mouth or face can signify thoughtfulness but of a dissociated kind; women and children are often seen with the tips of their fingers in the mouth. Finger to finger touching similarly implies dissociation. Women more than men are seen touching, or delicately fingering objects, tracing their outline, caressing their surfaces. This ritualistic touching is different from functional touching like grasping or holding. Hand holding can be a significant gesture and often is used to allow the man to protect or direct the woman. Auto-touch (self touching) is again something that women do more than men; it conveys the impression of narcissism, admiring one's own body and displaying it to others, so that everyone can share the delicate and precious thing. Sometimes the act of touching is displayed onto things—sun, or water on the naked body when swimming. The feel of clothes against the skin is conveyed as a pleasurable thing.

6. ***Cākṣuṣa*** : Oculesics. *Cākṣuṣaśāstra* is the science of visual behaviour which deals with the direct mutual glance in the given environment. *Cākṣuṣaśāstra* also appears to provide information at several different communicational levels in social interactions. The established terminology for visual behaviour in Sanskrit is related with vision and glance. *Yuktidīpikā* deals with the *dṛṣṭi-siddhi* *i.e.* power of vision. There is an elaborate description of *dṛṣṭi-siddhi* in *Mahābhārata.* In relation to *dṛṣṭi-siddhi,* we can also note the overall impact and impression created by an object, action or space. The overall impression of an object will depend on how many of the elements appear in it and how large they are. In the *Mālatī-Mādhavam* of Bhavabhūti, Mādhava describing Mālatī to Makaranda, tells us of various *dṛṣṭis* (glances). They announce different types of communications.

The *Cākṣuṣī-dīkṣā* or *dṛk-dīkṣā* described in *Kulārṇava-Tantra* is a type of gaze behaviour. Eventually when the persons were initiated they used to sit close together, gazing deeply into each other's eyes for long periods of time, with only occasional glances away. It can be said that a direct stare indicates ntensely active feelings of an amorous, hostile, or fearful kind, while a deflected gaze is linked with shyness, casual superiority, or downcast submissiveness. Since there are basically only two kinds of gazing—away and downwards—it is left up to the accompanying facial expressions to signal which of the three major moods are involved—love, anger, or fear.

Even at the *Yuktidīpikā's* hypothesized initiated level of meaning, our understanding of the persons and objects before us is not completely natural, innocent or intuitive. Although we take for granted the process of seeing and observing the people, things or events in our environment, visual perception is not altogether straightforward. To start with, our vision is unlike that of a camera; it is not a passive operation. We actively exploit, select and organize sensory stimuli in the visual field. Our eyes usually see the essentials of an object and what we see is rarely determined by the look of an object in front of us. We know this because it has been found that even the simplest images are interpreted and reproduced differently in different cultures. Seeing has more to do with learning and knowledge than with the unambiguous transfer of images to the brain. When we see persons or things we know what is there. We observe an image we 'read' it rather than just absorb it, and it is therefore accurate to talk of visual 'literacy'. There are several perceptual exercises such as visual illusions and puzzles and unfamiliar representations which demonstrate the general way in which our brains deal with the information it receives, how we are selective about what we see and how our previous learning and experience constrains our perception. Looks are related to the overall class age, style and impression created by a person. Looks, needless to say, are conventionally 'good looks'—handsome men, beautiful women, children, kindly old folk.

7. ***Sugandhayojana*** : art of use of perfumes, *olfaction*. We get interesting messages through smell. We get the delicious perfume and begin to feel hungry. Delicious smells are themselves very much communicative. We need not taste some food to get a message that it is spoiled; smelling the stuff may be enough for us.

Vātsyāyana in his *Kāmasūtra* has for the first time given the concept of olfaction by the term *sugandhayojana* and has treated it as an art-form. He has enumerated odour differences between males and females, to which the tribes still respond but which now play only a comparatively minor role in our society, unlike their role in other primate species. These odours are produced by special scent glands in the skin, especially in the armpit region and the crotch and vagina. The hairs in these regions act as scent traps to retain the odours and intensify them. When people shave their armpits, the natural odour is reduced. In the past ladies produced natural female odour which was a form of gender signalling in the period of Vātsyāyana. Now it is fading away due to shaving of the secret parts.

The use of perfumes in ancient India was a communicative technique. The art of preparation of scents was known to *Kāmasūtra* and *Agnipurāṇa* as *gandhayukti-kalā* .*Amarakośa* has enumerated six types of fragrances.

The *Gṛhyasūtras* mentions the rite of the smelling of the son's head.

Body odour is something modern. Non Verbal communications rarely talk about it. It is one of those taboo subjects that is avoided in every day conversation, but it was very much studied by Vātsyāyana in his *Kāmasūtra*. Smell was, also an important feature of daily life in ancient India. The major effect of a perfume containing musk was to increase the sexual arousal of the women who used to wear it. It still does.

8. ***Asvādana*** : gustation, tasting. The art of preparing and tasting various drinks, drugs and wines was known to Vātsyāyana as "*pānaka-rasa-rāgāsava-yojana*. We get different types of messages from taste. When a child tastes a hearty meal prepared by the mother, it gets an affectionate message. In the olden days wives used to please their husbands with gustatory delight which was a message of love. One may get message of warning through taste as well. We get the message "the milk is spoiled" through taste. There is an elaborate description of the types of taste in ancient literature. The literary critics have also talked about the taste of poetry.

9. *Śravaṇa* : hearing. We get two kinds of messages through hearing : sound and silence. We have already discussed paralanguage—the vocal characteristics that are part of speech communication. We are not talking here about the speech sounds, but our main concern is the musical sounds which convey messages. These musical tones are very much effective in changing the moods of person within a hidden message. Abhinava (*NS*, Vol.IV, pp. 360-61) has illustrated the use of *ākṣepikī drutā* in the change of mood of Rāma in the *Udāttarāghava from* that of love to that of heroic after listening to thc words of Rāvaṇa, and *Vilambitā* in the change of mood of Aśvatthāmā in the *Veṇīsaṁhāra* from that of heroic to that of pathetic, after listening to the speech from behind the curtain. The *ND* (pp. 172-3) also has given illustrations of *dhruvās* from the classical dramas, *e.g.*, the *prāveśikī* indicating the entry of Viśvāmitra in the *Anargharāghava of* Murāri in which there is the description of the sunrise; the *prāveśikī* indicating the entry of Prince Candragupta in the *Devīcandragupta* of Viśākhadatta (who gesticulates feigned madness) in which the moonrose is described; *naiṣkrāmikī* indicating exit of Candragupta in the same play, leaving for the place; *ākṣepikī*, the same illustration from the *Udātta-Rāghava* cited by Abhinava.Rājaśekhara (*Bālabhārata*, 1-14) has put in *dhruvā* in his plays. He says (verses 880,883,927) "It (the *dhruvā*) announces or communicates the respective characters, delights the hearts of the audience and establishes the emotional continuity". The symbolism of the *dhruvās* with their meaningful content enriched by the melodious music served as the fitting background to the performance.

Apart from the music, many other nonhuman sounds are used for signals. In our school, bells signal the beginning and end of class periods. Bells may also indicate the worship of the god in a temple. We can use buzzers for signals too.

Just as the presence of sound communicates information to us, so also the absence of sound (silence) communicates information to us.

10. *Dik* : *proximics. Dik-kāla* space and time, the tāla-concept of Bharata, one of the most pervasive concepts of the Indian tradition, evades every clear definition, though the literature is full of attempts to describe it. Sanskrit grammarians have conceptualized the space both as close and far away. *Samīpatā* (nearness) and *dūratā* (distance) is again *kālakṛta* (temporal) and *deśakṛta* (spatial). Pāṇini while analyzing *Sāmīpya* has given the same concept. The *kāśikā-vṛtti* explains the concept of *sāmīpya* as *pratyāsatti* (close proximity), which can be of two kinds, *viz.* (a) *Kālakṛta* (in point of time) and (b) *deśakṛta* (in point of space).*Sāhityadarpaṇa* (3.108) also presents *sannidhi* (closeness) both in place and time. Thus, they have discussed the manner in which individuals use physical and temporal space in their close and distant behaviours. Thus, according to Indian tradition, man consciously structures microspace—the proximity and distance between men-in the contact of daily transactions, the organization of space in his environment, and ultimately the universal space—*deśāntaragataḥ jitakleṣo bhavati.*

Edward T. Hall has long been fascinated by man's reaction to the space about him, by how he utilizes that space and how his spatial use communicates certain facets and signals to other man. As Hall studied man's personal space, he coined the word *proximics* to describe his theories and observations about zones of territory and how we use them.

Man's use of space, Hall believes, has a bearing on his ability to relate other people, to sense them as being close or far away. Every man, he says, has his own territorial needs. Hall has broken these needs down in an attempt to standardize the science of proximics and he has come up with four distinct zones in which most men operate. He lists these zones as (a) intimate distance, (b) personal distance, (c) social distance and (d) public distance. As we might guess, the zones simply represent different areas we move in, areas that increase as intimacy decreases.

Culture is still a guiding factor in all body language, and this is particularly true of body zones. In India, crowding together is a sign of warm and pleasant intimacy. In certain situations, Indians prefer crowding. To the Indian, privacy exists in terms of his house. He regards this area as his own and resents intrusion into it. The fact that he crowds together with other people does not negate his need for living space. Westerners see space as the distance between objects. To Americans, space is empty. The Indians see the shape and arrangement of space as having a tangible meaning. This is apparent not only in our art, but in our gardens as well, where units of space blend harmoniously to form an integrated whole. The Hindus, in their closeness, preserve a formality and an aloofness. They manage to touch and still keep rigid boundaries. The Muslim pushes these boundaries aside. Along with this closeness, there is a pushing and a sharing in the Muslim world that Hindus find distasteful. To a Hindu the body is sacred. To the Muslim violation of the body is a minor thing. However, violation of the ego by insult is a major problem.

(a) *Intimate distance* : Intimate distance can either be *close*, that is actual contact, or *far*, from six to eighteen inches. The close phase of intimate distance is used for making love, for very close friendships and for children clinging to a parent or to each other. When you are at *close intimate distance* you are overwhelmingly aware of your partner. For this reason, if such contact takes place between two men, it can lead to awkwardness or uneasiness. It is most natural between a man and woman on intimate terms. When a man and a woman are not on intimate terms the close intimate situation can be embarrassing.

Between two women in our culture, a close intimate state is acceptable, while in the Muslim culture such a state is acceptable between two men. Men will frequently dine together in Muslims. Hindus have the concept of *paṅktipāvana*.

(b) *Personal distance* : The second zone of territory charted by Hall is called the personal distance zone. Here, too, he differentiates between two areas, a *close* personal distance and a *far* personal distance. The close area is one and a half to two and a half feet. You can still hold or grasp your partner's hand at this distance. As to its significance, he notes that a wife can stay within the close personal distance zone of her husband, but if another woman moves into this zone, she presumably has designs on him.

The far phase of personal distance, Hall puts at two and one half to four feet and calls this the limit of physical domination. You cannot comfortably touch your partner at this distance, and it lends a certain privacy to any encounter. Yet the distance is close enough so that some degree of personal discussion can be held. When two people meet in the street, they usually stop at this distance from each other to chat. At a party they may tend to close in to the close phase of personal distance.

There have been many studies attempted to find out just how the reaction to invasion of personal space is related to personality. Introverts tend to keep people at a greater conversational distance than the extroverts.

There is, in the whole business of invasion, a strong sexual link. A girl moving into territory encounters a different set of signals than if she were moving into a woman's territory. There is more acceptance and the possibility of flirtation makes the man less likely to resent the intrusion. The same situation reversed, however, generally puts a woman on her guard.

The crowding in buses is only bearable, because the riders tend to think of each other as non-persons. The reverse is also true.

Corresponding to ethnic or social distance, there was also notion of physical space in the colonial India which figured prominently in every tribal rebellion and constituted an important element of its territoriality. Its function was to enable the insurgents to assert their own identity in terms of what they claimed to be their home-land. As with the category of ethos, antagonism towards the *pardesī* provided it with its negative determination. It had its roots in the undoubted fact of the expropriation of the *Ādivāsīs.* "They have taken away from us our trees, fiches, lands and Jāgīrs", said Singrai, the Kol. The massive alienation of tribal lands to outsiders in the years preceding the insurrection which he led, testified to the truth of indictment and was indeed officially acknowledged.

But the notion of *deśa* (original home) was more than a mere zero sign of rebel consciousness. Territoriality expressed as a sense of physical space had also a positive side to it. For them the river was the frontier by which the realm of insurgency defined itself—a sort of geographical sign.

(c) *Social distance* : Social distance too has a *close* phase and a *far* phase. The close phase is four to seven feet and is generally the distance at which we transact impersonal business. It is the distance we assume, in business, we meet the client from our own town or the office manager. It is the distance the housewife keeps from the delivery boy. You assume this distance at a casual social gathering, but it can also be a manipulative distance.

A boss utilizes just this distance to dominate a seated employee—a secretary or a receptionist. The *far* phase of social distance, seven to twelve feet, is for more formal social or business relationships. The "big boss" in colonial India had a desk large enough to distance him from his employees. On the positive side, this distance allows a certain protection. Elaborate techniques from gun salutes to precedence at official receptions were manipulated by the officials to keep the princes during colonial period at an appropriate distance. The maintenance of a proper distance between English class and the public populace seemed socially appropriate by political necessity. Those who threatened to bridge the distance aroused great concern. Indian princes as members of ruling class but not of the ruling race were seen threatening the social hierarchy carefully manipulated by the official elite to accord with the structure of power. This threat was perceived towards the end of the 19th century when princes were acquiring a western education and western tastes. It they married English women or if they moved in high society in Europe, it was feared that they would learn to infringe the distance separating them from the ruling class. Their designs upon white women were seen as an important reason for restricting their visits to Europe. All members of the ruling race were supposed to keep this distance.

In India itself, the tribal or the scheduled caste's consciousness was indistinguishable from its recognition of its ethnic self. The tribe remained the boundary for man, in relation to himself as well as to outsiders.

The distance we keep in social interactions is important because it affects the impressions that others develop. Changing your distance can express a desire for non-involvement, or it can heighten or reduce your influence over another person. Distance is also useful because it affects how we use eye contact, touch, orientation and other elements of body language.

Social distance creates the concept of dominance and subordination in a society. Members of the dominant groups ascribe to themselves the qualities needed for the tasks which they wish to monopolize. They are unable to perceive such qualities in persons of subordinate groups, who are excluded from positions in which they can demonstrate such qualities. Persons of subordinate groups, on the other hand, are perceived as born with the qualities appropriate to activities involving obedience and subordination and as they are confined to such activities, they duly demonstrate that they do indeed possess these qualities. Such reasoning is vitiated by its circularity, but it is repeated in various forms by members of the dominant elite to justify their position. Within the dominant group women are perceived as subordinate group but towards all other subordinate groups they are expected to display attitudes disappropriate to the dominant group. In particular, they must show distance for any relationship that might bridge the social distance between the dominant group and the subordinate groups.

(d) *Public distance* : Hall cites public distance as the farthest extension of our territorial bondage. Again there is a *close* phase and a *far* phase, a distinction which may make us wonder why there aren't eight distances instead of four. But actually, the distances are arrived at according to human interaction, not to measurement.

The *close* phase of public distance is twelve to twentyfive feet, and this is suited for more informal gatherings, such as teacher's address in a room full of students. The *far* phase of public distance, twentyfive feet or more, is generally reserved for politicians where distance is also a safety or a security factor, as it is with animals. Certain animal species will let you come only within this distance before moving away. The *far* public sphere of the politician or the actor on a stage contains a number of body language statements which are used to impress the audience not necessarily to tell the truth. At this distance the actors gestures must be stylized, affected and far more symbolic than they are at closer—public, social or intimate distances.

One of the things that is inherited genetically is the sense of territory—*bhūmi.* Robert Ardrey has written a fascinating book, *The Territorial Imperative*, in which he traces this territorial sense through animal kingdom and into the human. one of the most frightening plays of modern times is home. It postulates a world of the future where the population explosion has caused all notion of territory to be discarded. All men live in cells in a gigantic metal hive enclosing the entire planet. They live out their lives, whole families confined to one room, without ever seeing sky or earth or another cell. In this prophetic horror story, territory has been completely abolished.

We don't know how much space is necessary to any individual man, but what is important in our study of body language is what happens to any individual man when this shell of space or territory is threatened or breached. How does he respond and how does he defend it, or how does he yield?

We each possess these zones with us and we react in different ways to the breaking of these zones. These are all elements of NV communication. This guarding of zones is one of the first basic principles. Sanskrit dramatists seem to follow the same. The impression of distance is created through zonal treatment and stylized walking on the stage, (e.g., In Act III of *Śānkuntalam* the distance between Śakuntalā and Duṣyanta).

Proximity signals arouse personal and intimate feelings. That is people take up position closure to those they like and know well than they do to strangers. The actual size of zone which people maintain around their persons depends on situational factors, but it also depends on culture. But again, we have to remember that NV behaviours operate together and with verbal behaviour, both to reinforce and to compensate for each other. For example, when people disclose intimate information about themselves, often they will avert the gaze and turn the body away. Enforced close proximity may result in a reduction in eye contact. Proximity, — eye contact and touch taken together—seems to reflect sex differences in style of interaction. For example, women have a more "immediate" and personal style to judge by the fact that they talk more, gesture more, gaze more, orient the body in more varied ways than men do and respond more positively to touch.

11. ***Kāla*** : *Chronemics.* We have examined ten types of Non Verbal communication. But there is one important type of Non Verbal communication that does not fit into this classification system. We do not perceive this particular type of communication through one of the senses. If we perceive it at all, we do so through several of the senses. Time after all, involves relationships. The way we perceive times communicates. The study of time in modern linguistics is called chronemics, a term introduced by Poyatos (1972).

Cultures differ in the ways they perceive time—in their use of time and the importance they attach to time.

A correlate of Non Verbal language of *dik* is a sense of *kāla.* As such this also enters the subjective determination of territoriality as one of its elements and helps a man to defend his territory. Expressed in its most generalized form as a contrasted pairs of times (then/now), a good past is negated by a bad present, its function is to endow the struggle against the alien with the mission of recovering the past as a future.

Indians look back to an age of relatively greater affluence and purer ethical conduct. The decline since then is said to have been caused by factors of two different kinds—those which are internal to the Indians itself (*purāṇamityeva*) and those for which the responsibility lies with the external (*navamīti*) factors.

A sense of time expressed in terms of a then/now distinction may be said to have been implicit everywhere in India. The termination of an unbearable present is regarded as the means of recovering the past. A tendency to look back in time and to anticipate the future marks Indians strikingly different from other peoples. This is the element of *depth* in time. The distinction between past and present acquires a decisive indeological function in the village India. Codified in the form of the antinomy *Sat-yuga/Kali-yuga*, it derives from the same time from the Hindu myth of four *yugas* (epochs). Whatever its origin, the opposition between two *vugas figures* prominently in the religious discourses and rituals.

The contrast between two *yugas* is used to encourage people not to reject inglorious present but also to fight for a better future and *Satyuga* is the blueprint for the future. History is filled with actions,events, and concepts giving testimony to the notion Indian needs to have a quality of depth to his consciousness, he needs to know that he extends beyond any given moment that he has roots, and he has growing space (his future). The walls of cities prophesize the end of *Kaliyuga* in chiliastic terms:

Kaliyuga jāyegā, Satyuga āyegā (*Kaliyuga* will pass away, *Satyuga* is ahead).

Another feature of the broader category is *kālacakra* (time is cycle). It refers to expected repetition of acts, events, thoughts, phenomena and the like which furnishes the sense of gradual modification.

Related to the features of *yuga* and *cakra* in Indian time is the element of *krama* (motion or order). *Krama is* most easily identified in perceived regularity of relationships, be they among physical or psychological entities. *Kāmasūtra* has given the concept of *samayamātṛkā* for the measurement of time.

In addition to *yuga*, *cakra* and *krama*, time manifests itself in *laya* (rhythm). In point of fact, *laya* is a factor in *yuga*, *cakra* and *krama* as they are applied to every day situations. It is so much a part of the naturalness of a man that its absence may easily result in the rejection of anything from objects to ideas which is non-rhythmical or out of phase with the individual observer. While it may not be instinctive, the sense of *laya* lies deeply embedded in the human organism as it does in his animal and plant companions.

Now we may consider the communicative power of time in our relationships. people who "have no time" for we make us feel unimportant. Those who are close to us "we drop in any time". The man who makes an excuse to "cut the conversation" communicates that he is not much interested in developing an on-going relationship.

Lateness also communicates. Keeping someone waiting three minutes usually requires no apology and creates no offence. Keeping someone waiting for 45 minutes is an insult which requires an apology. People sometimes use lateness to gain attention. Some people always arrive late because they want to be special or important. Of course, the constantly late person may not realize that he uses lateness to communicate.,

Thus, the Non Verbal (tacit) component of time is temporal because it is the framework within which communication occurs and is, itself, a factor in the sharing of meaning.

Semiotica Indica : the NV dictionary

Within the perspective of the long history of NV communication in India, a case can now be made for the adequacy of the modern science known as semiotics. As a matter of fact, viewing the ancient body and body language together offers more hope of resolving admittedly difficult problems of communicative interpretation than does the arbitrary application to either kinesics or notions of NV communication in the West. But a prerequisite of this approach is that the traditional approach of the Indian body language be taken seriously as criticism, as an attempt to understand a kind of NV communication in its form and aim.

The question of a universal NV language is possible only in historical terms. The false universality of the present may lead the more enthusiastic social scientist to propose values and ideals for all time. In fact, even his analysis assumes, and is dated by the communicative ideas of his age. It appears quite unfruitful, given the enormous differences in the dimensions of time and taste, to expect Indian communication to have explored problems whose relevance is a product of recent past and of a different spirit. It is in the realm of its assumptions that one civilization or civilized tradition is different from another.

This Dictionary appears to offer more hope for understanding the peculiar behaviour of what was certainly one of the most brilliant of Indian traditions and also how it works at present. In doing so, we have studied the social understanding of signs from *Vedic* people to modern tribal folk, referring to the changes and development within centuries and by different social strata.

Semiotica Indica attempts to identify precisely what it means to be a social animal — to uncover the central features of our cultural skills and abilities. Drawing extensively on the original texts and field - trips, it seeks to provide fresh insights how we inherit those interactions and to provide ideas for improving our culture. It must be stressed, however, that *Semiotica Indica* is not a "cook book". There are no simple recipes for a complete and fulfilled social existence. There are, however, certain principles that Indian society in the past uncovered and which have shown to be effective in a range of settings and contexts.

The head-words in Sanskrit, numbered for subsequent references in the indexes, are ordered in the Devanāgarī - tradition. The head-word is followed by its primary meaning, explained by the *śāstric* tradition and elaborated with *grāmya* (rural) or *āraṇyaka* (tribal) currents of the country. Thus, the first meaning presented is from the Great Tradition and the extended meaning, encompasses the Little Traditions. This method of juxtaposing *Śāstra* and *Loka* under the same banner for the first time will enhance our knowledge to unravel the roots of Indian culture with its branches and sub-branches labelled as *grāmya* and *āraṇyaka.* If we look upon the vocables in broad perspective, we discern that the tribe and the non-tribe were complementary and the existence of one was the pre-requisite of the existence of the other. Thus, the division of Indian culture into three major cultural substructures (elite, folk, tribal) is not expected to result in three neatly cut-off segments, clearly distinguishing from each other. Each word in the dictionary tells its own story. The entry would provide the conceptual tool for classification of the varieties of adaptation in culture at different levels of differentiation and adaptation.

In presenting the present dictionary the hope is that it will help us to take a comprehensive view of the NV communication in India. We shall be able to locate the past about which we are talking, with the help of this frame. Moreover, the frame should facilitate communicative studies of different aspects to NV behaviour—between various oral interactions in India, and with corresponding behaviours in cultures of other countries.

In short, the present work is not a stereotyped dictionary. It is, in fact, a practical study of Sanskrit Semiotics, incorporating the modern ethnic behaviour through ancient texts, which gives an insight into the inspired flashes of the modern semioticians together with an idea of vast sweep of ancient Sanskrit scholars.

There are bound to be omissions, not all deliberate and planned. As any dictionary-maker knows, the selection of material ultimately depends upon personal idiosyncracy, taste and fancy, which differ from person to person. I have done, my best (single - handed and without any type of assistance from any agency) to maintain the functional character of this compilation and will consider my labours amply rewarded if people find it useful as well as necessary.

अं – Aṁ

1 अंश

Aṁśa : (a) portion, part, share; (b) pain. *'Śaṅke aṁśam kena tāmyati'*, *Kirāta*. 15.10. (a) shoulders of the *vedī* (*uttaravedī*); the two corners on the eastern side: *uttara* or the north-eastern corner and *dakṣiṇa* or the south-eastern corner. (b) it also symbolizes the sacrificial share which belongs to gods and kings. (c) prominent note of a *rāga* (SR).

2 अंशकरी-मुद्रा

Aṁśakarī-mudrā : kissing gesture. "Enjoy a happy dance with wavy and loose hairs. Make loud kissing sounds with lips in a typsy air and kiss appropriate parts of the body especially hands and feet and ultimately retreat back playfully from former position" (BT). *aṁśa* means part of the whole. It is subdivided into *kalā* - a portion of a part, and *kalāṁśa* - a part of a portion.

3 अंशुक

Aṁśuka : A technical term in the architecture which means a moulding of pedastal, generally placed between a cyma and a corona (*kapota*).

4 अंशुमती-मुद्रा

Aṁśumatī-mudrā : radiant gesture. "Place your hands on the mouth, styling them like buds of flowers and style other fingers there in a befitting manner. This is called the *aṁśumatī-mudrā*, what assures rise to one's own good fortune". (BT).

अ – A

5 अकडम-चक्र

Akaḍama-cakra : one of the tables for the determination of suitability of a *mantra* for the *Sādhaka*.

6 अकद्वद

Akadvada : just in speech, applauding.

7 अकर्तव्य

Akartavya : not to be done, improper act.

8 अकृतप्रवेश

Akṛta-praveśa : not permitted to enter (*A*, 4.10.7).

9 अक्का

Akkā : 'mother' *Kāśikāvṛtti* (Dravidian borrowing), Marathi akā f. 'respectful term for elder sister or any elderly woman'.

10 अक्षत

Akṣata : uninjured, unhusked grain; *akṣatā* 'virgin' Rice-grains, coloured with saffron or virmilion, placed on the forehead of an idol; also on the foreheads of bride and bridegroom at their marriage. Rice-grains are also used on other auspicious occasions (Garg, 1992. 310).

11 अक्षत-तिलक

Akṣata-tilaka : The ceremony of putting a few grains of rice on the forehead of an image or of a Brāhmaṇ when invited to an entertainment.

12 अक्षमाला

Akṣamālā : rosary, a string of beads; also known as *Japamālā* (q.v.) *akṣa* like *rudrākṣa* is seed. Three varieties of rosaries are distinguished : (1) *varṇa-mālā*: representing the fifty letters of the Sanskrit alphabet from *'a'* to 'kṣ', the latter constituting the *meru* (the final letter); (2) *akṣa-mālā*:: made up of beads, seeds or berries like the seeds of the lotus-plant (*Kamalākṣa*), seeds of the grass known as *kuśa*, seeds of *putra-jīva*, berries of *rudrākṣa*, beads made from the *tulasī*-plant, sandal-wood, conch-shell, elephant's tusk or from precious stones (ruby, coral, gem etc.); and (3) *kara-mālā*: finger-joints or *parva* of the right hand being employed in lieu of beads.

The number of beads in a rosary is prescribed to be 108 for success in all endeavour.

The symbolic meaning of rosary indicates the spiritual orientation of a person. It can be seen in the right hand of religious persons. Often, the hand carrying the rosary will also be in the *Vyākhyāna-mudrā*.

13 अक्षय

Akṣaya : imperishable, the episode of *akṣaya-pātra* occurs in *Mbh* (*vana*.3). Every day this *pātra* (pot) never got empty till the meals of Draupadī were over. This type of vessel has become a proverbial and found many echos.

14 अक्षयतृतीया

Akṣayatṛtīyā : A festive rite observed on the third bright day of *Vaiśākha* month. Pacification of the manes is a speciality of this day. Among special gifts are mentioned things that are necessary in the hot season that follows - such as water-jars, water-pitcher, umbrellas, shoes and the like; even gold and a piece of land are prescribed as gifts (*Bhaviṣya-Purāṇa, Uttarakāṇḍa*, 30.1-16). This day is called *akṣayya*, as things given as gifts on this day are believed never to be in shortage-*asyām tithau kṣayam upaiti na hutam na dattam, tenākṣayā* (*Ibid.* 19).

The tribal version of this festive rite is *akhtaī* in Halbi, which falls usually on the second fortnight of April, by a ceremonial *pāraḍ* (hunting) for fish. All the men go into the forest to gather the leaves, roots, and fruits used for poisoning fish, then they poison the selected and previously dammed rivulet or small tanks; after the stupefied fish have been collected and divided, each family cooks and eats the fish with the new mangoes, and the head of the family goes to the source of their usual water-supply and offers water in a new *hāṇḍī* with a little grain in the name of ancestors. In Gondi this is called the ceremony of *uparihānā hānāl* (offering water to the clan - god and the Departed).

15 **अक्षर**

Akṣara : (a) one of the forms of *Brahman*, the others being *kāla* (time), *karma* (action) and *svabhāva* (nature) according to *vallabhites*. (b) a letter (c) imperishable. (d) it is a term applied to the syllable *AUM* and equated with *Brahman*, and hence with the whole world. (e) *ākṣarā* is a personification of speech (*RV*, 7.15.9; 7.36.7). (b) *akṣarapallī* was a practice of writing by syllables, found in epigraphs prior to the common adoption of the decimal system. (g) *ākṣarā* in now a translated form of English syllable. Syllable, according to David Crystal (1985.342) is a unit of pronunciation typically larger than a single sound and smaller than a word.

16 **अक्षरन्यास**

Akṣara-nyāsa : writing.

17 **अक्षरभूमिका**

Akṣara-bhūmikā : writing tablet, slate. Comp. *nyastākṣarāmakṣarabhūmikāyām*, (*Raghu.* 18.46).

18 **अक्षरमुष्टिका**

Akṣara-muṣṭikā : finger-speech, speaking by means of finger-signs.

19 **अक्षरमुष्टिवाक्कथनकला**

Akṣaramuṣṭivākkathanakalā : telling the written matter in cipher, putting a missing letter in a poem and poetic symbolism, one of the 64 arts in *Kāmasūtra* (1.3.16).

20 **अक्षरसंघात**

Akṣara-saṁghāta : syllables to serve the purpose of equivocation (*NS*).

21 **अक्षसूत्र**

Akṣasūtra : rosary of *rudrākṣa*. The string of beads carried by saints and religious minded persons, meant for chanting. It is also known as *akṣa-mālā* which is made of *akṣa*--seeds and is commonly known as *rudrākṣa*. There are usually 108 beads in this rosary. (b) in the Tāntric works, Devanāgarī alphabets froma to *kṣa* are known as *akṣasūtra* (*Gautamīya Tantra*).

22 **अक्षरास्फुट**

Akṣarāsphuṭa : whispering, *khusur-pusur* in Hindi.

23 **अक्षि**

Akṣi : which graps or sees objects, the eye; *akṣikampa*: twinkling (*Raghu.* 15.67); *akṣivikūṇitam*: a side look; *akṣivikūśitam*: a look with eyelids partially closed; *akṣiśravas*: serpent; *akṣisūtram*: the line of the eye (with reference to idols); *akṣispandanam*: eye-twitching.

The most fundamental primary mode of interpersonal encounter is the interaction between two pairs of eyes and what is mediated by this interaction. For it is mainly here, throughout the wide ranges of social encounter, that people actually meet in the strict sense (Heron, 1970.244) .References to the significance of eyes abound in Sanskrit literature as well as in modern Indian languages and dialects. Both what you do and how you do it tell others about the kind of person you are. Not merely the act of approaching a prospective partner in a crowd (*bhare bhavan*) but an intense 'eye - speech' (*nainan hī so bāt*) expresses the intimacy of the persons involved. Ellsworth and Ludwig (1972. 375) have stated: 'Visual behaviour appears to provide information at several different communication, at levels in social interaction. As a dependent variable, it has been used to measure stable individual and group differences, the regulation of the flow of conversation, and the search for feedback in an interaction. As an independent variable, it has been shown to influence emotional responses and cognitive attributions'. The moon is said to have born from the eye of Atri (*Agni. P* .183.13). Even fever was produced from the third eye of Rudra - Śiva (*Garuḍa*, P 1.147.1)

24 **अक्षिकूट**

Akṣikūṭa : edge of the eye-socket. It creates a type of secretive Eyes Point. If I wish to warn you that someone has just entered the room, out of your line of vision, I may glance quickly in its direction, pause with an intense stare for a fraction of a second, then return my gaze to you again to see if you have understood. The chances are that I will have to repeat this special glance several times before you get the message. This is deliberate and intensified version of the ordinary Eye Glance action, but it requires delicate handling (Morris, 1985. 65).

25 **अक्षिनिकाण**

Akṣi-nikāṇa : closing the eyes, eye-cover: *akṣinikāṇam jalpati*. It is a type of gaze avoidance where eye contact does not occur. It may also be termed as gaze omission. The eye-cover act is shown most often by individuals who are depressed, particularly if their depression involves withdrawal and shame. The eye-cover act will often be preceded or followed by turning away from the other interactant, and sometimes by crying. Observers who see only the eye-cover act will infer shame and general unhappiness. Certainly the overall context, the physical setting, the age, body size and role of the person showing the act, and the rest of the Non Verbal and verbal behaviours modify the meaning of such an act, much as the verbal context, voice, tone and speaker characteristics modify the meaning of a word; however, the act, like the word, has a distinct set of meanings different from the meanings associated with another act.

26 **अक्षिभ्रुव**

Akṣibhruva : 'the eyes and the brows' —Pāṇini.

27 **अक्षिसम्पर्क**

Akṣi-samparka : eye-contact. The eyes have frequently been described as "windows to the soul", and in some respects, at least, this appears to be true. In particular, much is revealed by the amount and pattern of others' eye contact with us. First, we often use such information as a rough indicator of their overall affective state: the more they gaze at us, at least up to a point, the more positive we assume they feel. Indeed, when others avoid our gaze we usually conclude that they feel guilty, are harbouring negative thoughts, or are generally depressed.

Second, and perhaps of even greater importance, we use the amount and pattern of others' gaze as evidence of their feelings towards us.

The eyes too clearly show the love and hatred of the breast, as in the clear glasses faces fair and ugly are expressed:

नैना देत बताय सब हिय को हेत अहेत ।
जैसे निर्मल आरसी भली बुरी कह देत ।।

Sharp women and brave men play their hundred thousands slay. No veil ever can conceal their eyes incessant:

चतुर नार औ सूरमा करे लाख में चोट।

नैन छिपाए न छिपे, पट-घूंघट की ओट ।।

28 **अक्ष्याकृतिविज्ञान**

Akṣyākṛti-vijñāna :sign of the eye. A person whose eyes are curved inside and reddish, is full of pleasure, happy; one whose eyes are like a cat is sinful; with eyes like honey and yellowish in colour he is crooked; one who is squaint-eyed is cruel; one whose eyes are greenish is cunning; one having oblique (*Jimha*) eyes is brave; one whose eyes are deep is sure to be a lord; large eyes portend the person to be a minister; if dark eyes, he is fortunate; if of round eyes, he would be sinful (*Garuḍa P*). Persons having cat-eyes indicate moderate temper.

The winks of the eyes are divided into two, three, four and five a moment. They indicate respectively good position, happiness, lordship and long pious life.

Eyes like lotus, fish and deer are supposed to be an ideal beauty in Sanskrit literature - *nīlotpalākṣī, mīnākṣī* and *mṛgākṣī.*

Curiously enough the eyes which are so important to non-tribes, are almost ignored by the tribes. This may have an entirely practical cause. I do not remember even having seen a central Indian tribe with beautiful eyes.

Blurred and brown - eyed men, according to central Indian villagers, are often very unreliable. They become very cunning. One should avoid both blurred and brown-eyed men as a safeguard to one's interest.

29 **अखण्ड**

Akhaṇḍa : indivisible, entire. *akhaṇḍa-deśa* "indivisible space'. *akhaṇḍa-kalā* 'indivisible time'. *akhaṇḍārtha* 'each word has its own meaning and yet, both of them refer to one entity, a literal expression of non-duality'.

30 **अखण्डत्व**

Akhaṇḍatva : the theory of indivisibility of the sentence propogated by Bhartṛhari. (*Vākyapadīya* II. 55).

31 **अख्खल**

Akhkhala : an exclamation of joy; a paralinguistic feature (*RV.* 7.103.3).

32 **अगम्या गमन**

Agamyā-gamana : illicit intercourse. *Agamyā* is a woman with whom sexual intercourse should not be established, such as preceptor's wife, king's wife, step-mother and her daughter, female-disciple, disciple's wife, son's wife, pregnant woman, mother-in-law, sister, brother's wife, etc. (*Brahmavaivarta.* 2.27). According to *Anaṅgaraṅga* (8.40) such women are: a virgin, a female religious mendicant, a chaste wife of an enemy, wife of a friend, a deceased woman, wife of a pupil, outcaste woman, a mad woman, wife of kins, and old woman, wife of the preceptor, a pregnant woman, an unknown woman, a vicious woman, a woman whose complexion is entirely yellow, a very dark complexion woman.

33 **अगुणीभूत**

Agunibhūta : not become subordinate.

34 **अग्नि**

Agni : fire, god of fire, the chief god of *Ṛg Veda. Agniparīkṣā* is a fire ordeal by the accused walking through a fire (*Rām*). *Agnipradakṣiṇā* is the circumambulation of the fire at the marriage ceremony. The bridegroom leads the bride three times round the fire (and the water pot) in such a manner as to their right sides are always turned towards the fire, opposite of *prasavya* (*Garga*, 221).

Certain taboos are mentioned in respect of fire. Water and fire should not be carried together (*Agni P.* 155.27). One should not ask fire from his neighbour. The house-fire should not be extinguished. It should be kept burning covered with ashes in the *gorasī* (fire-pot). Fire of the funeral pyre was used for sorcery.

35 **अग्निमन्थ**

Agnimantha : 'producing fire by friction' (*Suśr*) is an art in the Hill Maria Society of Bastar. The Hill Marias have their own way of fire-making which materially differs from that prevalent among other tribes like the Kamārs of Raipur district and the Baigas of Mandla. The Hill Marias of Abujhmark make fire with the help of a fire saw, as mentioned in the *Suśruta*. The fire-saw consists of two flat pieces of bamboo each about one and a half inches long. One of the pieces has a node at one end and the other end is split into two equal parts. This piece is known as *nogho* meaning hearth. The Hill Marias say that this is the 'mother' of the fire. A small roundish stone is inserted between the parted splints of the piece. The node prevents breaking up of the bamboo pieces. The split piece is kept over a big stone and some dry leaves are put below the bamboo.

Two persons sit opposite each other on either side of the stone and one of them keeps the split bamboo pressed to the stone with his foot so that it does not move. This piece is sawed with the help of the second piece known as *Kāṇḍā*. Each of the two persons holds one end of this second piece with both of his hands. The saw is moved slowly in the beginning and the speed is gradually increased. Because of the friction of the two pieces, the saw dust drops on the dry leaves below and, being hot because of the friction, it finally lights the dry leaves. Some dry grass is put over it and the fire produced is blown by breath. The dry grass catches fire very soon.

The whole operation just takes about five to seven minutes or so. The fire is preserved and smouldering pieces of wood are continuously kept burning the *ghotul* day and night and the villagers take this fire home by lighting dry wood (K.C. Dubey).

36 **अग्निमुद्रा**

Agni-mudrā : Fire-God gesture. gesture symbolizing the Fire-God of the Vaiṣṇava cult. Fingers on the tip of the thumb in a waving style symbolize the Fire-God (*VD*).

37 **अग्निवेला**

Agnivelā : time for kindling sacrificial fire.

38 **अग्निसंस्कार**

Agnisaṁskāra : burning of the dead. The sacrement of fire, the worship of fire as the completion of any essential rite; the burning of the dead body of a Hindu (*Garga Saṁhitā*, 22).

39 **अग्निहस्त**

Agni-hasta : gesture of the Fire-God. *Tripatāka* with the right hand and *kāṅgula* with the left; indicates *agni*, the Fire-God (*VD*).

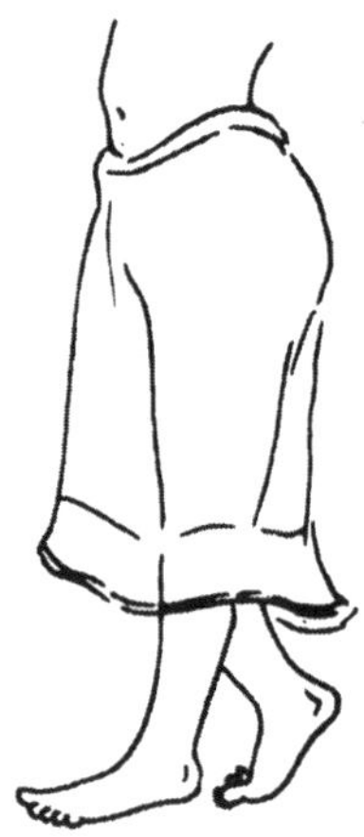

Fig. – (40)

40 **अग्रग-पाद**

Agraga-pāda : forepart of the toes of the feet touch the ground, going speedily with fore-feet. It is used to indicate walking across the muddy earth; also known as *agraga-caraṇa* (*SR*, IV. 7. 324) (Fig. 40).

41 **अग्रग-हस्त**

Agraga-hasta : going forward at a high, low or mid level.

42 **अग्रतल-सञ्चर-पाद**

Agratala sañcārapāda : the heel up, the big toe bent and other toes shrunk; the crossed foot movement; when only the big toe touches the ground and the rest of the foot is lifted up as in the Western classical ballet; it is used to urge, to break, to observe, a particular pose in a dance-drama; to kick, to strike the ground and to walk indicating a heel - sore (*NS*, X. 40-51). In *Mālavikāgnimitra* (V), the

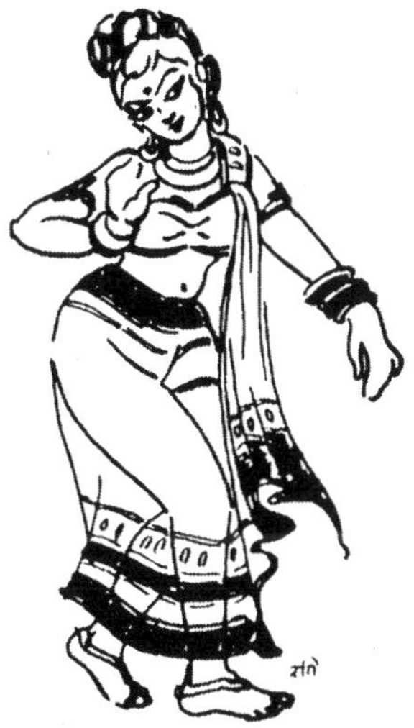

Fig – (42)

dwarf enters the stage with one foot in *agratala sañcāra* position and the other in the *añcita* one. Some of the Mathurā railing figures are in this position.

Thus in this movement the heels are raised up, the big toe extended and the other toes bent. It is used in urging, pounding, standing posture, pressing, striking the ground, moving round, throwing away, various *recaka* movements and walking on forepart of the foot due to the wound in heel. (Fig. 42).

43 **अग्रपूजा**

Agrapūjā : the highest or first mark of reverence (*Rāmāyaṇa*).

44 **अग्रभूमि**

Agrabhūmi : stage or place to be obtained.

45 **अग्रसर**

Agrasara : going in front or taking the lead.

46 **अग्रहस्त**

Agrahasta : the forepart of the hand or arm; *agrahastena gṛhītvā prasādayinām (Ratnāvalī,* III).

47 **अग्राक्षि**

Agrākṣi : pointed vision, side-look (*Rāmāyaṇa*).

48 **अग्रासन**

Agrāsana : first seat of honour (*Mudrārākṣasa* 1.2).

49 **अघ**

Agha : mischief, guilt, misdeed, wickedness, impurity, pain. All of us feel guilt sometimes. It is a normal, inborn, human emotion, and, like, other emotions, it serves a purpose. Guilt is a way of controlling wild and primitive feelings that would threaten our existence or even that of civilization if we acted on them. The capacity to feel guilty does not vary among different cultures, but each society has its own code of behaviour from which the ingredients of guilt arise.

Guilt is a complex feeling that we should not atone for something we have either done or thought of doing. It has developed as a source for preserving society by giving humans the means to deal with constant temptation to put their own interests and immediate gratification before the needs of the community. To be effective, such a force must be very strong, and it is therefore not surprising that guilt is probably the most oppressive of all emotions. However, within limits, it is valuable both to the individual and to society. Guilt causes personal impurity and a Hindu woman seeks ritual purification by bathing in the sacred water or Ganges or by other means. Women tend to report more feelings of guilt than men. The reason probably lies in their psychological makeup.

Shame and guilt are closely related, but there is a clear difference between them. With both, we feel bad about ourselves because of something we have done. However, shame occurs when our transgressions are observed by others, where as guilt, which may involve the same disagreeable emotion, does not need to involve the judgements of others. The feeling of shame is related to public humiliation or embarressment about a misdeed or to real or imagined inadequacy in ourselves. Guilt, on the other hand, arises because you have violated someone's trust or confidence in you.

50 **अघमर्षण**

Aghamarṣaṇa : removing sins. The rite of driving out sin. It consists in taking water in the right hand formed in the shape of cow's ear, holding it near one's nose, breathing out from he nose on the water - with the idea of driving away sin from oneself - to the accompaniment of three verses from *Ṛgveda* (X. 190. 4 - 3) and then casting the water away to one's left on the ground (*Manu,* XI. 259-60).

51 **अघोरमुद्रा**

Aghora-mudrā : evil-gesture. At the fold of both the palms, put the left ring-finger to the right and the left middle-finger to the right - middle and curve the two thumbs. When it takes the shape of a lance, turn it reversely to the head. This is the *aghora - mudrā* that wipes out all bad omen; a type of protective gesture (*VD*). *Aghora* is one of the five forms of Śiva, black in colour, terrible in nature and is presiding deity of the southern region.

52 **अङ्क**

Aṅka : lap. (a) *aṅke nidhāya karabhoru yathāsukham te* (*Śāk.* 3.20). (b) mark, act. *aṅka* in the *nāṭaka* (act) is also derived from *aṅka* (mark), as it is characterized by various sentiments. (c) a type of *rūpaka* which is also known as *utsṛṣṭikāṅka.* The story here is either well-known or otherwise. The males participating in it are other than the divine ones. The sentiment of pathos is mostly found here. After the fight is over, there are many bewildered movements and lamentations by women. It has only *bhāratī* style.

53 **अङ्कन**

Aṅkana : marking. A marked category is signalled by adding something to an unmarked category. Social events are marked in our society by things like refined speech, fancy food, and explicit rules of etiquette. Social events in a tribal house are marked by, among other things, the degree of penetration required for an outsider to reach their setting. Animals are marked. Things are marked and even persons are marked. Marking rules rewrite the code meanings in accordance with context and social expectations.

54 **अङ्कपाली**

Aṅka-pālī : close-embrace; *aṅkbār* in Bengali and Hindi dialects. In Bagheli it is boud with *bheṅṭ,* such as *bheṅṭ-akbār, aṅga lagānā* to embrace (Hindi). The following *doha* prohibits to embrace other's wife:

> *par nārī painī curī koī mat lagāo aṅga.*
> *das sir rāvaṇ ḍhah gaye is nārī ke saṅga.*
>
> "A sharp sword is another's wife
> let none her form embrace.
> Rāvaṇa's ten heads the foefeit paid
> A woman in the case".

55 **अङ्कुर**

Aṅkura : sprouting; a division of the *ceṣṭākṛta* part of *āṅgikābhinaya,* a type of physical gesticulation. It is one of the three types of gesticulation seen in the *abhinaya* of drama. In the technique of communication through gestures when temperament is employed to recapitulate past events, whether by mere illusion to a past event or by portrayal of the whole episode through *abhinaya,* it is called *aṅkura* (*NS,* XXII. 44). Kālidāsa has used the *aṅkura-* technique in *Śākuntalam* (I). What the King does, as an observer - narrator of the scene in another section of the stage, is known as "sprouting" employing hand and facial gestures only.

The *aṅkura* is defined as *sūcanā, i.e.* it is suggestive. Dr. Ghosh translates it as "pantomiming through gestures" is the *aṅkura. Aṅkura,* according to the *NS* is the suggestive gesticulation like the sprout that indicates the future tree. When one skillfully represents by gestures like *sūcā* the words which one has in his mind is called *aṅkura.*

Abhinava (*NS,* III. 170-175) explains *aṅkura* by illustrating the gesticulation by Sāgarikā in Act I of *Ratnāvalī,* when she enacts collecting flowers after saying, "I shall also collect flowers and worship Madana". This gesticulation of collecting flowers peculiar to Sāgarikā would be different from an ascetic. According to *SR* (VII. 38) in *sūcī* the gesticulation by hand would precede the speech, while in *aṅkura,* follow the speech.(Fig. 55)

56 **अङ्कुश-मुद्रा**

Aṅkuśa-mudrā : occurs in *BT* but unexplained. (a) It literally means the gesture of an elephant-goad; *aṅkuśa* is a sharp hooked instrument employed in controlling the elephants. The goad symbolizes suppression. (b) one of the *mudrās* used in the worship of Gaṇeśa. It is also used in the worship of Śakti as stated above. In this *mudrā,* the middle fingers should be kept straight and both the forefingers be anchored with each other at the middle joints. The forefingers should also be bent a little, pulling each other.

57 **अङ्ग**

Aṅga : (a) major limbs of gesticulation; head, chest, waist, breast, sides, hips, thighs, hands and feet constitute the major limbs. (b) the body; the word *aṅga* meaning body has many synonyms such as *śarīra, kalevara, gātra, vapu, saṁhanana, varṣman, vigraha, kāya, deha, mūrti, tanū* and *tanu* (*Amarakośa* 2.6). In the context of *abhinaya, aṅga* is used constantly in *Nāṭyaśāstra* and never is *śeha* or *Śarīra* or any other word used. There is one solitary reference to śārīra *abhinaya* as one of the three varieties of *āṅgika abhinaya.* The famous verse of *Saṅgītaratnākara* (7.1) describing Śiva's body, speech, mind and ornaments in cosmic terms is notable here:

> *āṅgikam bhuvanam yasya vācikam sarvavāṅmayam*
> *āhāryam candratārādi tam namaḥ sāttvikam-Śivam*

"We bow down the *Sāttvika Śiva,* whose *āṅgika* (bodily movement or body itself) is the universe, whose *vācika* (verbal expression is (manifested as the) the expanse of verbal communication (and), whose *āhārya* (acquired costumes, ornaments, makeup etc.) is the moon and sun."

It can be seen that the movements of the five major limbs would come under the *śārīra* division.

(b) one of the paralinguistic features, one of the six *pāṭhyaguṇas* discussed by Bharata in his *NS*. *aṅga* as a *pāṭhyaguṇa* may again be divided in six units. They are the following: (I) *viccheda* is separating due to pause, (II) *arpaṇa* is recitation which as it were, fills the auditorium with graceful modulation of voice, (III) *visarga* is finishing a sentence, (IV) *anubandha* is the absence of separation between words or not taking breath while uttering them, (V) *dīpana* is gradual augmentation of notes, charming in three voice registers and (VI) *praśamana* is the lowering of the notes of high pitch without making them discordant. *arpaṇa, viccheda dīpana* and *praśamana* are to be used in the comic and erotic texts; *dīpana* and *anubandha* in the heroic text. (c) In iconography *aṅga* or *avayava* means major limbs or members of the body; the head, the torso, the arms and the legs. They are distinguished from the minor parts of the limbs (like the eyes, mouth, nose and ears in the head, or the fore-arm, or hand in the arm), called *upāṅgas*. The expression is sometimes used as a general term for the body.

In *Śaiva āgama,* the expression *aṅga* (division) refers to head (*śiras*), mouth (*vaktra*) and heart (*hṛdaya*), while *pratyaṅga* includes chest (*vakṣa*), neck (*kaṇṭha*), breasts (*stana*), arms (*bāhu*), navel (*nābhi*), genitals or vulva (*guhyāṅga*), stomach (*udara*), eyes (*netra*), nose (*nāsikā*), mouth (*āsya*), ears (*karṇa*), hands (*pāṇi*), feet (*pāda*) and fingers (*aṅguli*). (d) we can read something about another's emotions from their body. We may judge by gestures and postures whether our neighbour are having a tensely aggressive or relaxed and friendly conversation. Body language is mainly facial, but

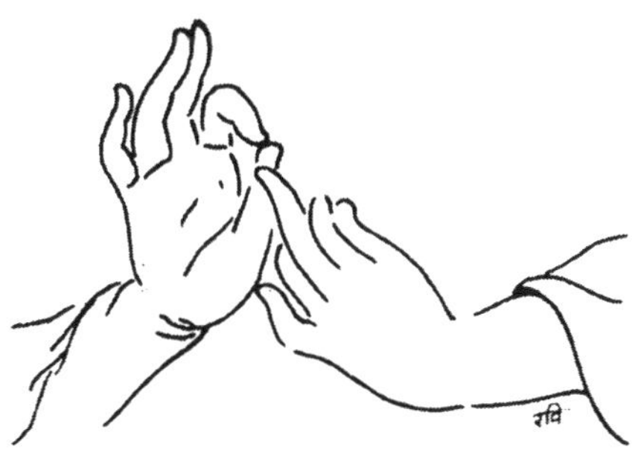

Fig. –(55)

58 **अङ्गदूषण**

Aṅgadūṣaṇa : the defects of the limbs (*Mānasasāra*, LXIX. 1-73). Sinful men suffer defect or deformity of appearance or have some visible marks to indicate that they have committed sins either in this life or in the previous one (*Vaśiṣṭha* 1.18; XX.6, XXI.43-44; *Viṣṇu,* XLV; *Yājñavalkya,* III. 207-215). He who steals a Brāhmaṇ's gold will have diseased nails; a *surā* - drinker will have black teeth; a slayer of a Brāhmaṇa consumption and a violator of a *guru's* bed will have a diseased skin. There are other deformities for other sins. An informer will have a foul - smelling nose, a calumniator a stinking breath, a grain -hief deficiency of limbs and grain - adulterator will have redundant limbs. Again, a man who steals cooked food will have dyspepsia, a man who steals the *Vedas* learns them without necessary permission will be born dumb, a stealer of clothes will have white leprosy and the stealer of a horse will be born as lame. A man who steals a limp will be born as blind, he who puts it out will be born as one-eyed, injury characterised as *jātibhraṁśakara* (causing loss of caste). An adulterer will have swellings in his limbs. The deformities may be of the body as well as of the mind. Idiots are born due to sins committed in the previous births.

Soft and attractive limbs are appreciated in Sanskrit literature, such as *komalāṅgī, sundarāṅgī.*

59 **अङ्गन्यास**

Aṅganyāsa: automanipulation is a self-touching activity such as hand-to-face, hand-to-neck, hair-preen, scratch and so on; which is a common behavioural reaction to aversive social situations in Sanskrit dramas. Certain automanipulations, notably hand-cover-mouth has been interpreted firmly as an expression of negative reaction. Self-touching activity occurs most frequently in contact situations, in settings where interaction is more likely to be initiated or prolonged.

The automanipulations can be interpreted as signals of a more ambiguous social attitude. They appear to express strong avoidance tendency in the performer. They occur most frequently among subjects who, for a variety of reasons, find it necessary to interact and actually deal with a stranger. They may be correlated with gazing - at sustained physical proximity, and approach. Hand-to-neck, hand - behind - head, scratch, touch - eye, and so on, occur when subjects become involved inadvertently or accidentally in relationship with strangers. The relationships typically are brief and do not include smiling, touching, and related conversation. The self-touch behaviours, in some ways inappropriate to the social context, might be interpreted as displacement activities performed in response either to conflicting tendencies of approach/avoidance or to thwarted avoidance. In both cases the automanipulations appear to express a strong avoidance tendency in the performer.

(b) *Ātmasparsa-vyavahāra* : auto-contact behaviour. Auto-contact behaviour occurs whenever we touch our own bodies. It contrasts with allo-contact, which occurs when we touch someone else's body. The most common form of auto-contact can best be called a self-intimacy, and apart from cleaning and shielding actions, which respectively groom and protect the body, this category accounts for the majority of all touching actions that we direct towards ourselves. The most common actions are those in which the hand comes up to touch the head. Masturbation is a specialized form of sexual contact. Here the use of the hand as a substitute for a partner is obvious enough.

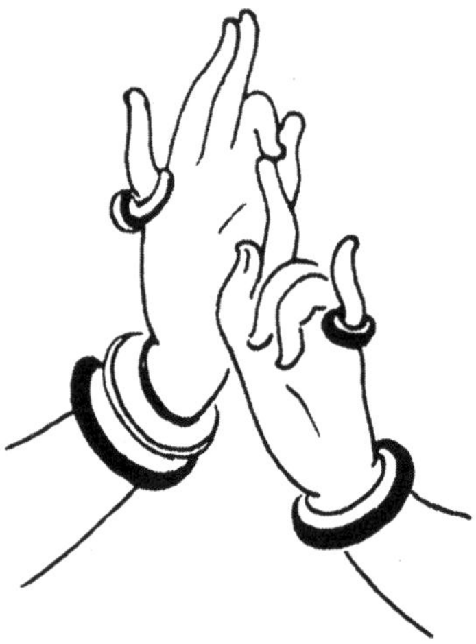

(Fig. 59)

60 **अङ्गप्रदर्शन**

Aṅgapradarśana : body display. (a) Hill Māriās of Bastar are slantly clothed as men and women. The private parts of men are hardly concealed under the very scanty loin - cloth and the upper part of the women are bare. The Hill Marias are completely oblivious of these parts and do not pay any attention to them. It is clear that to them the human body is just body and there is nothing shameful about it or its particular part. They do not suffer from inihibitions of any kind.

This is clear from the fact that they take their bath naked and pay no attention to whoever may be standing there. While the present writer was coming from Kaccāpal to Kutul, he halted for a little rest on the banks of the Kursod stream. The three Hill Marias of Kaccāpal who were accompanying him with the luggage went to the stream and in full view of the writer, took off their loin-cloth and started bathing completely nude in a complex, unconcerned and detached manner.

Similarly in village Marhoda, the writer went for a bath in the evening in Korugunda stream which flows down about five hundred yards or so from Marhoda. Pharsa kosa, son of Irpa, the village *Leske*, accompanied him. The writer had just started bathing when he looked back and found Kosa taking bath completely nude. Kosa even talked to the writer standing just like that and without any feeling of shame. After bath which is quick affair, Kosa went non-chalantly to the bank, picked up and put his loin - cloth.

Again in village Dhobe, the writer went to the Adro stream for a bath and about ten villagers accompanied him. As soon as the writer started bathing, all the ten Hill Marias took off their loin-cloths and started bathing. Women also bathe with their loin-clothes removed, but keep on the *mudāṅg* and the cloth attached to it.

One illustration from observation may be given here to prove that the Hill Marias regard body just as body and nothing else and they unhesitatingly enjoy playing with the body. At Dodimarka village a man came to the present writer's camp with his son who was just about three years old. The man sat on the cot and the child lay on the cot. Another young boy aged about 20 years also sat on the cot and in the very presence of the father and of about twenty villagers present, he started playing with the penis of the child and stimulating it. When the male organ of the child started throbbing, he and all of them laughed and the father of the child also enjoyed it.

(b) a wanton woman or a lustful woman exposes her bosom to attract the prey. She is known as *uchāl - chakkā* in Hindi.

61 **अङ्गभङ्ग**

Aṅgabhaṅga : yawning or opening wide of the body, collaspse of the body. Displacement yawning when bored or frustrated seems to be almost universal for mankind. Yawning is a type of 'boredom signal'. If disinterest fails to make its usual impact, a stronger response displays open boredom. A favourite signal employed here is the mock-yawn.

62 **अङ्गभङ्गिमा**

Aṅgabhaṅgimā : gestures and postures (used in Bengali). (Fig 62)

63 **अङ्गभाव**

Aṅgabhāva : bodily position; (a) a stylized form of communication suggested by the reciprocal arrangement of the parts of body in gesture, facial expression, movement or stance. It plays a cardinal role in dance, drama and sculptural symbolism, as also in ritual, meditative and occult practices. (b) the expression *bhāva* is used in the texts of

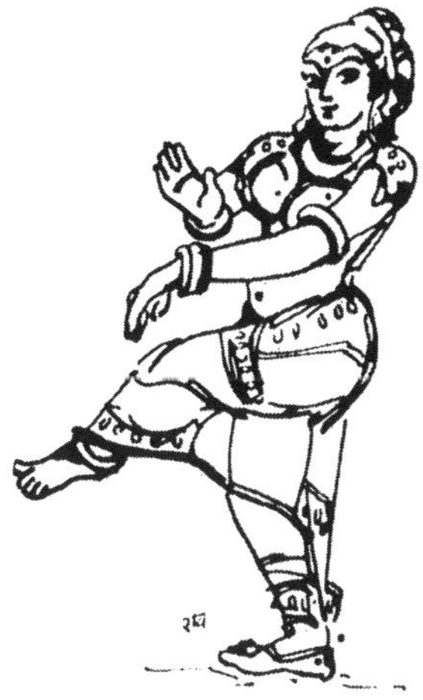

Fig. – (62)

Śaivāgama in the sense of mental disposition, contemplation or the act of relating. More specifically, it suggests the reciprocal involvement of the two principles, one indistinct, inarticulate, and devoid of details (*niśkalā*) and the other distinct, articulate and having details *(sakalā)*. The former is the pure, undifferentiated, and incorporeal Absolute, technically *Śiva-tattva* (a unitary principle), while the latter is the divine manifestation of the glory of the former in the terms of the phenomenal universe (called *Maheśa tattva*) illustrated iconographically in the twenty-five *līlā-mūrtis* of Śiva.

The combination (*viz.* mutual projection) of the two principles is called *Sadāśiva tattva,* expressed in five aspects; Śiva, Īśa, Brahma, Iśvara and Īśāna. Each of these aspects appearing in an act of contemplation is a *bhāva*; and each of the aspects, articulate as they are when impregnated with the inarticulate *Śiva-tattva* is known as '*Sāda*' (attempt at articulation). (fig. 63)

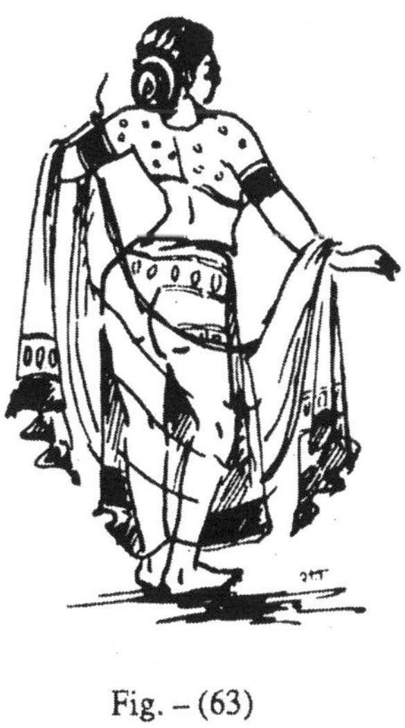

Fig. – (63)

64 **अङ्गमुद्रा**

Aṅgamudrā : position of the body; both the fists are said to be upstretched and alternately got released and bound up again (*Garuḍa,* I.II. 26).

65 **अङ्गरचना**

Aṅgaracanā : make-up. Bharata has discussed the technique of make-up (*NS*, III. 125) in detail, which includes painting of body and dress, colour design, and the application of beards, etc. The painting should be effected first and then the dresses according to habitation and condition should be put on. The four original colours are black, blue, yellow and red. The derivative colours are to be prepared by mixing them proportionately. They are *pāṇdu* (yellowish white); *kapōta* (pigeon-colour-white and blue); *padma* (lotus colour - white and red); *harita* (green - yellow and blue); *kaṣāya* (violet - blue and red); *gaura* (yellowish red - red and yellow). By mixing three or four colours many other shades may be prepared. In the mixture, the ratio of the strong colour to the weak should be one to two; in the case of blue it should be one to four, for blue is the strongest of all colours. Thus knowing these rules of colours, the body should be painted. When one's own form is thus covered, with the change of dress, it is called *vartanā, i.e.*, change of personality of the dramatic characters according to dramatic conventions. By the colours, together with the dress, one's original complexion is to be concealed and the form is so created that it resembles the particular character. Just as a creature enters another body giving up his own and resorts to the nature of the other one, so also the man covered with dress and make-up takes up the role of the other whose dress he has put on. The different characters are to be painted as follows: In Bhāratavarṣa, the kings should have lotus colour, yellowish white or dark blue; happy men should be of yellowish red. Those practising wicked acts, possessed of evil spirits, engaged in penance, those whose work entails extreme physical work and those of inferior birth like *dhīvara, ḍomba,* etc. should be painted black. The sages should have the colour of *badara* (plum) and those engaged in penance should be black.

In the furious sentiment (*NS*, XII. 50-51) the body should be dripping in blood, mouth should be moistened with it and pieces of flesh in the hands. The demonic character should have huge physical frame with many heads and many hands, holding weapons of various kinds. In the case of the sentiment (*NS*, XII. 138) of laughter, the *Vidūṣaka* should be covered with tattered clothes or skin or smeared with lamp back, ashes or reddish—ochre. The teeth should be big; hunch in the black, lameness, distorted face, baldness etc. may be employed. Lifeless objects, *e.g.*, mountain, place, mechanical contrivances, shield, armour, banner, rivers and various weapons should have bodily form according to necessity with suitable dress and speech as per the dramatic convention (*e.g.* weapons of Viṣṇu in *Bālacarita* of Bhāsa, rivers in *Uttararāmacarita*).

Again, *Muni-kanyās* were to have a costume suitable for their dwelling in forests, the *gandharva* - women were to have sapphires to decorate them, white teeth and black clothes (*NS*, XXI. 61). When representing women separated from their husbands, their dress was to be dusty and their hair bound up in a single plait (*NS*, XXI. 75).

The colours of the costumes too, varied according to the convention. Thus monks were dressed in ochre coloured robes, the *Pāśupatas* were to have variegated robes (*NS*, XXI. 110). Warriors were to be shown in martial attire with armour, bow and quiver. Kings were to have crowns of which three varieties have been mentioned. Ministers and merchants were represented as wearing turbans (*Ibid)*.

66 अङ्गराग

Aṅgarāga : cosmetics, a slented compic application perfumed unguents to the body; *puṣpagandhena aṅgarāgena* (*Raghu*, 12.27, 6.10); *stanāṅgarāgat* (*Kumārasaṁbhava* 5.11.). Cosmetics or *aṅgaracanā*—has been subjected to endless forms and styles over the centuries. Ancient cosmetic boxes reveal the minute attention that was paid by early Indians to their facial make-up, and ancient paintings show us with remarkable clarity, some of the results of their labours.

Make-up does several things to human face. It may disguise it as Kauṭilya formulated, or protect it from the sun; it may make it look younger and healthier, or it may label it as belonging to a particular social category; it may signal aggressiveness or sexuality. As with hair-adornments, there have been periods when any form of make-up has been spurned as 'unnatural', and others when to be without it would be tantamount to indecent exposure.

In tribal societies make-up plays an important role in establishing the status of the individual within the community, and gives him a cultural 'badge'. It may also be thought of as protective, defending the wearer against imagined evils, but in reality this amounts the same thing, since the true protection it affords is that of group membership.

In ancient societies an underlying motive in using make-up was protection, not against evil but against the sun. Like modern sunbathers with their sun-lotions, the ancient Indians protected their body and faces against the damaging glare of the sun's rays by the application of ashes (*bhasma)* all over the body. In the passage of time, their interest to cosmetics grew beyond the purely protective and became highly decorative in its detailed application. *Kāmasūtra*, for instance, has accepted cosmetics as an art.

There is therefore little (in comparison to *Kāmasūtra*) that is new in the world of facial adornment. All that has happened over the centuries is that our culture has approved or disapproved - exaggerated or restricted - to varying degrees, the cosmetic activities of *Kāmasūtra* and tribal peoples. Sometimes the more elaborate application of cosmetics was confined to one particular class - the courtesans - while at others it spread from royalty downwards. Tragically, in the colonial period, the chemistry of make-up became increasingly dangerous and frequently damaged the faces it was meant to improve.

Another facial device belonging to the modern India is the more drastic phenomenon of cosmetic surgery. Apart from making modern faces look younger and healthier, and therefore more appealing, the application of careful make-up means three things: time, materials and services. All these three mean affluent status. On this basis make-up has always been, and always will be, a facial signal saying 'I have money to burn'. (Morris, 1985).

67 अङ्गविद्या

Aṅgavidyā : kinetic art. It is the study of how body language, movements of the knees, feet and trunk are related to communication. It is an ancient science of foretelling good or evil of the body language according to *Arthaśāstra* (1.12) and *Bṛhat Saṁhitā* (51).

The concept of kinetics is new in the West. From GK *kineo* meaning 'move', developed the concept of kinetics. in semiotics describing the communication system of gestures and motion, *i.e.* 'body language but simply to work out a text. The word is also used to describe the study of this.

Kinetics was first systematically analysed in the 1950s by the anthropologist Bird-whistell, who showed how much of our body behaviour was conventionalized and socialized.

Aṅgavidyā was the science of prognostication or foretelling good or evil by the movements of limbs, gait, voice, etc. mentioned in early Buddhist, Brahminical and Jain works. Varāhamihira states that one well-versed in this science is respected by all. This is also the name of Chapter 51 of *Bṛhat Saṁhitā*, which gives full details of this science. Thus it corresponds to modern kinetics or kinetic art.

More popularly known as "body language" kinetics includes gestures, postural shifts and movements of the hands, head, feet and leg. The subject of several classification systems, kinetics has been defined in a variety of ways. Whether defined in terms of Bird-whistell's (1970) kinemes, kinemorphs and allokines; Ekman's emblems, illustrators, regulators and adapters, or Mehrabian's (1972) forward, sideways lean arm or leg position ásymmetry, trunk swivel movements, and gesticulations, the system is designed to assign meaning to movements and to provide a framework for research. These systems have indeed been heuristic: going from conceptual categories to coding rules, each of these investigators has produced results that enhance our knowledge of the role of kinetics in communication.

It is only recently, with the advent of video recordings, that Discourse Analysts have begun to take serious interest in those aspects of face-to-face interaction which are not verbalized, or even vocalized, but which are an integral part of communication. Just as linguistic study can be divided into descriptive and historical linguistics, kinesics can be broken down into *pre-kinesics* (physiological determinants), *micro-kinesics* (units of measurement) and *social kinesics* (patterns of movements in terms of their social functions). The *kineme* is regarded as the smallest set of body movements with differential meaning, analogous to the linguistic unit referred to as the phoneme. Along with both smaller and larger units, the *kineme* provides the basis for extraordinary detailed descriptions of each body part in terms of its width and extent, or velocity. Not simply content with measurement, however, Birdwhistell (1970) provided a system for classifying types of non-verbal communication and a vocabulary for discussing a wide variety of body movements.

Poyatos (1977) has briefly suggested a chart in relation to Birdwhistell's linguistic-kinesic analogy; but it would be particularly interesting to attempt to elaborate a kinemic alphabet, not necessarily for its application to a literary relatively refined transcription system, since it would show: internally, the speech organs (teeth, lips, tongue, - tip, blade, front, back etc, - and externally, the facial moving parts - eyebrows [high, middle, low, knit], eyelids [raised, lowered], pupil [dilated, contracted], mouth, etc.

Poyatos (1977) has attempted to offer a morphological and functional classification of kinesic behaviour. He has differentiated *gestures* (conscious or unconscious body movements made mainly with the head, the face alone, or the limbs, learned or somatogenic, and serving as a primary communication tool, dependent or independent from verbal language, either simultaneous to or alternating with it, and modified by the conditioning background - smile, eye movements, a gesture of beckoning, a tic), *manners* (although similar to gestures, more or less dynamic body attitudes that, while somatogenically modified, are mainly learned and socially codified according to specific situations, either simultaneous to or alternating with verbal language - the way one eats, greets others, coughs), and *postures* (conscious or unconscious positions of the body, more static than gestures, learned or somatogenic, either simultaneous to or alternating with verbal language, modified by social norms and by the rest of the conditioning background, and used less as a communicative tool, although they may reveal affective states and social statues - sitting, standing). Poyatos has defined kinesics as: "the systematic study of psycho-muscularly - based body movements and/or their resulting positions, either learned or somatogenic, of visual, visual - acoustic, and tactile or kinesthetic perception, that whether isolated or combined with the linguistic - paralinguistic structures and with the situational context, possess communicative value, either in conscious way or out of awareness. When applied to its analysis the methodology of linguistic structuralism, kinesics has revealed the smallest discrete element, the *kineme* (analogous to the phoneme), made of various *alokines. kinemes* combine into morphological constructs called *kinemorphs* and *kinemorphemes*, and these in turn form kinesyntactic structures. Birdwhistell has also reported certain suprasegmental elements, namely *kinemes* of stress and juncture, as appearing in the linguistic - kinesic stream, and has also studied the relationship between linguistic pitch and body movement.

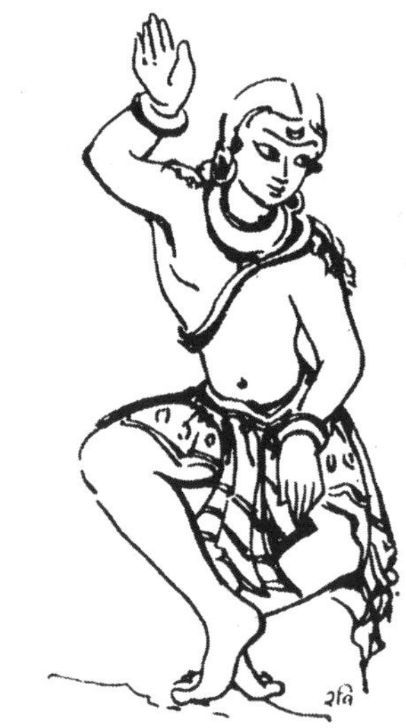

Fig. – (67)

Paralanguage and kinesics complete, then, the basic triple structure one must analyze in narration. In the case of *kinesics*, the narrative text will reveal the ability of the writer to desynchronize it from the other two as little as possible (since a description must necessarily precede or follow the verbal expression), the ratio between kinesic repertoires and linguistic and paralinguistic ones, and which types of kinesic behaviours are consciously used as communicative vehicles in the story.

Each culture also develops special systems of gesture and movement for specific, often ritualistic purposes. *Kinetic art* is sometimes used to describe those art forms where body prime, centres of meaning. *Aṅgavidyā* has been used in the same sense.

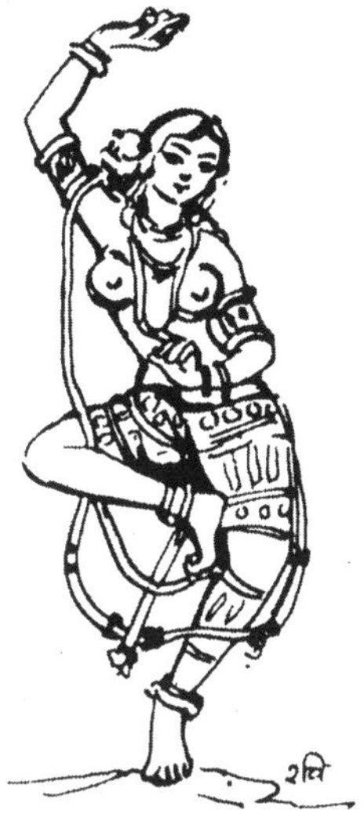

Fig.– (68)

68 **अङ्गवैकृत**

Aṅgavaikṛta : gesture or expression of the face leading to a knowledge of internal thoughts. The question of nature versus nurture as the origin of behaviour is very much present in *aṅga-vaikṛta*. Nature (genitics) may give up our bodies, but in a very real sense we learn its *vikṛti*. We learn to manipulate our bodies to convey emotions and this is *aṅgavaikṛta*. (Fig. 68)

69 **अङ्गसंस्कार**

Aṅgasaṁskāra : embellishment of person; personal decoration, doing whatever serves a fine personal appearance such as bathing and rubbing the body. There are thousands of ways in which the Indian seeks to adorn his/her body and enhance its display qualities. It is the efficiency of the ratio of action-effort to display-impact that ensures that *aṅga-saṁskāra* will be with us for a longer period.

70 **अङ्गसङ्ग**

Aṅgasaṅga : Body-contact tie-signs. It is displayed whenever the bond between two people expresses itself in the form of physical touching of one by the other when this happens, what we see is the attraction process of the bonding overcoming the natural inclination of each individual to defend his personal space. Because there is a basic conflict between 'keeping your distance' and 'making contact', the result is that there are many varieties and degree of friendly touching.

(a) In the villages of northern Abujhmārh (Bastar) bordering the Muria tract and in the villages of mixed multi-clan nature, girls also attend Ghotul. But in the Muria region every girl has to go to Ghotul compulsorily. Here girls are paired off with boys belonging to *akomāmā* clans. The girls comb the hair of their partners, massage their arms and legs, dance with them and initiate them or get initiated by them, as the case may be, into the contact ties of sex.

(b) one of the four-fold divisions of contemplation in *Śaivāgama*. *Saṅga* means disposition of the iconic forms characterized by weapons and emblems like trident (*triśūla*, symbolizing the three *guṇas* of *prakṛti*, i.e. sattva, rajas and tamas); battle-axe (*paraśu*, symbolizing power or *Śakti*), sword (*khaḍga*, symbolizing valour or *pratāpa*).

71 **अङ्गस्पर्श**

Aṅgasparśa : fitness for bodily contact, being touched by others, bodily contact, being touched by others, bodily contact, conditions under which a person will permit another to touch him, body contact, touch-taboo has penetrated in our culture. Most of us learn it in our childhood. Making us describe our ancestors in our text books as his our forefather did not get closure to his fellows than a foot or so, ignoring the vast literature that teaches us tactile behaviour. Touching was proclaimed as a horrible behaviour. There is the story of mura in *Purāṇas*. Mura practised penance and won a boon from Brahma that whomsoever he would touch should die. (*Vāmana Purāṇa* 34. 30-48).

72 **अङ्गहार**

Aṅgahāra : gesticulation, movement of the limbs, dance-movement; a long sequence of movements (Nāṭyaśāstra IV). Two or three *mātṛkas* constitute, on *aṅgahāra*. There are thirty-two *aṅgahāras* enumerated in Indian classics. *Aṅgahāras* are divided into two classics: (I) *Karaṇa* - being the unit of movement having subclasses as *cārī, recaka, bhramarī, utpluta* and *nṛtta hasta*. (II) *Karaṇa* second is a sequence of movements. In *Rāmāyaṇa* (SK, 10.36) it is used for pose as a generic term. It indicates the posture of the sleeping queens of *Rāvaṇa*. *aṅgahāri* is a synonymous term. *aṅgahāra* depends upon *Karaṇas* and the latter consists of different arrangements of hands and feet.

The term *aṅgahāra* means the movement of *aṅgas* (limbs) in a particular manner. Some explain it as a movement pertaining to *Hara* (i.e., Śiva) and demonstrated by limbs (*aṅga*). According to Sāraṅgadeva, the graceful movement of the limbs to proper places, composed of groups of *mātṛkas* (i.e. combinations of two *Karaṇas*) is called *aṅgahāra*. The number of *aṅgahāra* is infinite. Sāraṅgadeva mentions thirty-two as important among them.

The only rule governing total physical behaviour is that *aṅgahāra* may be purposeful.

73 **अङ्गाङ्गिभाव**

Aṅgāṅgibhāva : reciprocal relationship of limbs and body. The relation of a limb to the body, of the subordinate to the principal, or of that which is helped or fed to the helper or feeder.

74 **अङ्गिका**

Aṅgikā :woman's bodice. The *Skanda Purāṇa* (IV.4.9) mentions a *Kañcuk* a(Synonym of *aṅgikā*) infilled with cotton to be donated in one of the vows in the month of *Māgha*.

75 **अङ्गुल**

Aṅgula : The iconographic technique of analysis of human form in the term of *aṅgula* measurement; a unit of body measurement; *āṅgula* is the basis of *tāla* and can further be divided and subdivided into *yava, likhyā, rōmāgāra*, reṇu and *aṇu* (ray of the Sun) as the minutest unit. Different texts work out the exact proportions for the total height of the image (*Bṛhat Saṁhitā* LVII-LVIII; *Mānasāra* LXV; *Sāmarāṅgaṇa Sūtradhāra*, vol.I; *Viṣṇudharmottara Prāṇa*, III, 34).

Aṅgula was a measure equal to 8 barely corns. 12 *aṅgulas* made one *vitasti* (span), 24 *aṅgulas* were equal to 1 *hasta* (cubit). Kauṭilya has defined one *aṅgula* as equal to 8 *yavas* (barely of middle size) or 3/4th of an inch.

76 **अङ्गुलि**

Aṅguli : finger; different fingers are designated as follows: *aṅguṣtha*: thumb; *tarjanī:* forefinger; *madhyamā* middle finger; *anāmikā*: ring finger; *kaniṣṭhā: the little finger.*

aṅguli is the finger of the hand or member of the foot. In Iconography, the five fingers are: *aṅguṣtha* (thumb), *prādeśikā* or *tarjanī* (fore-finger), *madhyamā* (middle finger), *anāmikā* (ring-finger) and *kaniṣṭhikā* (little finger). The length of the finger, especially the middle finger, is a unit of measurement. The distance between the tip of the thumb and the tip of the fore-finger when the palm is fully extended is known as *prādeśa;* hence the expression *prādeśika.*

Finger - beckon is a common gesture all over India. Finger - crossing is a symbolic gesture. Fingertips kiss is becoming popular in the urban areas. The man kisses his fingertips and then fans them out, flinging them towards the girl. Fingers are also ritualized. In *Buddhāṣṭamī Vrata* eight hand-fuls of rice, collected by leaving the first two fingers, are to be locked (*Garuḍa Purāṇa* 1.132. 4-5). Cow-dung for the ritual use is collected with similar manner, but with the middle finger and thumb (*Bhaviṣya P.* 53.92).

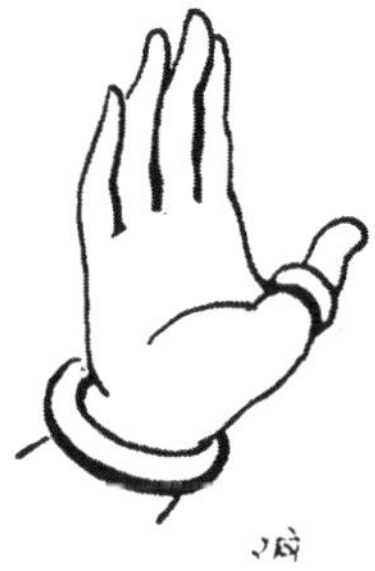

Fig. (78)

77 **अङ्गुलिपर्वन्**

Aṅguli-parvan : finger-joint.

78 **अङ्गुलिमुद्रा**

Aṅguli-mudrā : finger pose; includes *varada, abhaya, tarjanī, bhūmisparśa, jnāna* and *viṣmaya mudrās.* (Fig. 78)

79 **अङ्गुलिसन्देश**

Aṅguli-sandeśa : making signs with fingers; cracking or snapping the fingers as a sign; also known as *aṅguli-moṭanam* and *aṅguli-sphoṭanam,* and *aṅguli-samajñā.* To drive one's finger into the privities is known as *ungalī karṇā* in Hindi. *aṇḍakhī phuṭātor*: to crack the finger means to curse someone in the tribal dialect of Halbi. (Fig. 79)

80 **अङ्गुलि-स्फोटन**

Aṅguli-sphoṭana : Cracking the fingers.

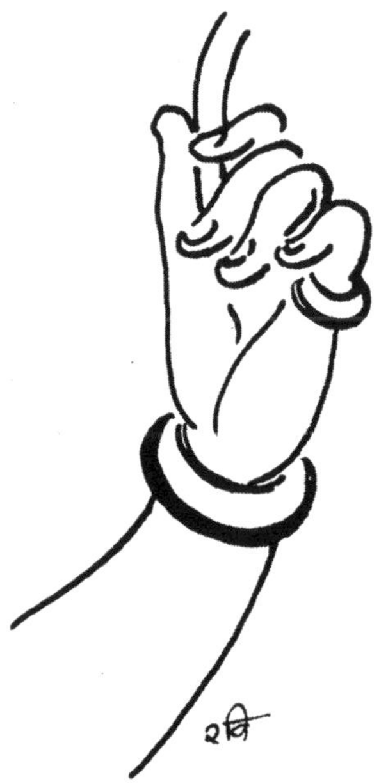

(Fig. 79)

81 **अङ्गुलीयक**

Aṅgulīyaka : ring. Vālmīki was quite aware of a script eventhough there is no proof for it being used for the composition of books. We come across a reference to the script while he tells about the ring where letters are inscribed. *Rāmanāmāṅkitam cedam paśya devyaṅgulīyakam.* (*Sund. Kāṇḍa,* 36.2)

82 **अङ्गुल्याकृतिविज्ञान**

***Aṅgulyākṛti-vijñāna*:** signs of the finger. If the fingers are slender, it is the sign of intelligence (*Garuḍa*). If they are flat, it is an indication of subservience. If they are bony thick, they indicate moneylessness. If thin, it is the sign of subjection. If the fingers are separated, it is a sign of poverty; if they are joined and close together, it is a sign of wealth.

In an another context, the making of the crackling sound from the fingers is termed inauspicious (*Matsya*,186.40-41).

83 **अङ्गुल्याभरण**

Aṅgulyābharaṇa : (a) ornaments of the fingers (*NS*), males: *vetikā* (golden ring) and *aṅguli mudrā* (rings with various designs). (b) females: *kaṭaka, kalāpi, śaṅkha, hastapatra* and *mudrāṅgulīyaka.*

84 **अङ्गुष्ठ**

Aṅguṣṭha : thumb. It has different symbols. *aṅgūṭhā cūmnā* in Hindi means to lick the thumb, *i.e.* to flatter. *angūṭhā/ ṭhengā dikhānā* means to show ones thumb in derision, or as if implying sexual intercourse.

The *thumb* is the symbol of soul according to *Matsya Purāṇa* (71.34). Thumb point (*aṅgūṭhā dikhānā*) is a derisive signal in India. Thumbs-up for life and thumbs-down for death. Thumb-sucking among children is fairly transparent in its relation to sucking at the breast, and its frequency increases and decreases with the rise and fall of moment-by-moment tensions; but once the adulthood has been reached we have to put away childish things. Thumb also symbolizes penis according to *Agni Purāṇa* (8.31-37).

85 **अच्**

Ac : (a) term for vowels in *Vyākaraṇa.* (b) to bend, go.

86 **अचेलक**

Acelaka : a class of ascetics which preferred to remain naked.

87 **अज-मुद्रा**

Aja-mudrā : gesture of Aja. *ardhapatāka* twisted upward, touching the body, placed by the side to indicate *Aja,* the mythical ruler (Mirror of Gesture, p. 47).

88 **अज्जुका**

Ajjukā : In Sanskrit dramas, the courtezans were addressed as *ajjukā* by the servants (*NS.* XVII. 65-94).

89 **अञ्चन**

Añcana : bending of the body (*A*, 3.19.6) comp. *romāñca* *'thrill* of hair'.

90 **अञ्चित**

***Añcita*:** (a) the bending position of any part of the body (*NS.* IV. 84), flexing of the body-part, charming gait. (b) a special kind of kiss in which the parts below the breasts or armpits are tenderly kissed (*Kāmasūtra* 2.3.23). (c) *ancita hasta-mudrā* 'bent cupped hand' is a hand-pose, where the fingers are all turned towards the palm. It is a *Naṭarāja-mudrā.*

91 **अञ्चितकरण**

Añcita karaṇa : the feet are in *añcita* and then a *svastika* is performed, hands move in *vyāvartita* and *parivartita* movement: in the final pose one hand is near the nose (NS. IV. 836-846, IX. 276-278). The *karihasta* hand is in *vyāvṛtta* and *parivṛtta* alternately and then bent upon the tip of the nose. It is used in elation due to one's own superiority or excellence, in the presence of others.

92 **अञ्चितग्रीवा**

Añcita grīvā : taking place when the head is turned back; inclined to a side and stretched; a type of neck movement, cf. *utkṣipta* head movement thrown back but the neck movement indicates an extreme position (*NS.* VII); a neck with the turned back head. It suggests hair-dressing, looking upward and hanging to death. (*NS*, VIII. 164-171).

93 **अञ्चितपाद**

Añcita pāda : when only the heels touch the ground and the rest of the foot is lifted up; heels on the floor, fore-foot raised and toes extended; *añcita* indicates a wound on the fore-foot, turn to every direction and to exhibit various poses of a *brahmacārin's* style in dance (*NS*, X 40-51).

94 **अञ्चित-बाहु**

***Añcita bāhu*:** the curved arm (*NS*, IX. 205-206).

95 **अञ्चित-भ्रू**

Añcita bhrū : the two-way movement of the eye-brow, viz. both *kuñcita* and *recita* (NS, VIII. 122-123). It occurs in *Buddhacarita* (2.31).

96 **अञ्चित-शिरस्**

Añcita Śiras : head with a slight sideways bent; when the neck is bent on one side; a slightly bent neck as to bend a little. It is used to suggest sickness, anxiety, pathos, swoon and intoxication (*NS*, VIII. 17-18).

97 **अञ्जलि**

Añjali: the folded hands; (a) the two hands held side by side and slightly hollowed; a cavity formed by folding and joining the open hands together (*Veṇī-Saṁhāra* Act I), *navāri añjalinā pibet* (*Manu*, 4.63). When two hands in the *Patākā* style are joined together, it is called the *añjali-hasta*. It is used to salute Gods, revered persons and friends and relatives. For divine beings, it should touch the head; for respected ones it touches the face or the foreheads; for friends and relatives, it is placed by breast and for the rest, there is no definite indication (*NS*, IX. 121-123). (b) *anjali* is one of the forms of respectful obeisance.

98 **अञ्जलिपुरुष-मुद्रा**

Añjali-puruṣa-mudrā : thumbs of the both hands joined together and the little finger joined with the other little finger (*VD*).

99 **अञ्जलिबद्ध**

Añjalibaddha : folding hands together and raising them to the head in salutation; *praṇāmāñjali (Uttararāmacarita* 3.4). (Fig. 99)

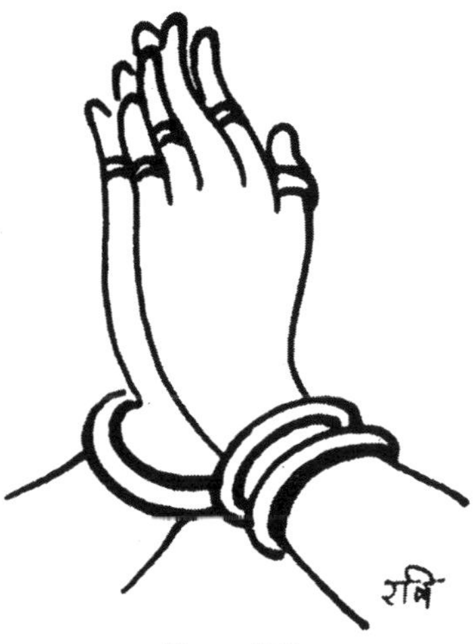

Fig. – (99)

100 **अञ्जलिमुद्रा**

Añjali-mudrā : a gesture in dance, worship and scultpture where both open hands are folded and joined (*saṁyukta-hasta*) to form a slight hollow or cavity to mark a reverential attitude or supplication. Thus, in this gesture the two hands are clasped against the chest, palm to palm, and extended upwards with all fingers erect or slightly bent. It is also known as *Sarvrarājendra-mudrā* or the *sampuṭāñjali*.

101 **अञ्जलिहस्त**

Añjali-hasta : both hands gesture like full-blown lotus. The *añjali* is a gesture of honour and respect. In *Vikramorvaśīya*, the king holds his hands in *anjali-hasta*. In Amarāvatī scupltures femal figure has a pair of *annali-hasta* above her head. Thus in the *annali-hasta*, both the hands are in *patāka* with palms joined together. To represent great gods it is held on head; respectable elders near one's face; and friends on breast. No fixed rules are prescribed in the case of women. Now salutation with single hand is in practice. This may be on account of the impact of British - rule. It has now replaced the *añjali*.

102 **अटवी**

Aṭavī : Apart from the settled communities in towns and villages, *Arthaśāstra* refers to forest tribes, called *aṭavī* or *āṭavika*. It is stated that they were entrenched in jungle fastness and can be a source of great danger to the state. They are said to be well-organized and brave, practically autonomous and without any scruples in the matter of looting and killing: pratirodhakāḥ pramattasyāpa haranti, alpāḥ kuṇṭhāḥ sukhā jnātum gṛhītum ca svadeśasthāḥ prabhūtā vikrāntāścāṭavikāḥ prakāśayodhino apahartāro hantāraśca deśānām rājasadharmmāṇa iti (A, B. 4.43). Infact, the danger of the state from forest tribes is declared to be only less serious than from an enemy. A forest chieftain is often mentioned as one of those who are capable of seizing the throne from the ruler: āṭavikānarthamānābhyāmupagṛhya rājyamasya ghātayet (A, 12.3.17). Nevertheless, troops recruited from forest tribes, that is *aṭavī-bala*, form one of the six kinds of troops that may be at the disposal of the ruler. Such troops are apparently under the command of their own chieftains, and it is recognized that they are likely to be more interested in plunder than in the house: āryādhiṣṭhitamamitrabalamaṭvībalācchreyaḥ (A, 9.2.18.20). It is clear that the separateness of forest tribes from civilized society is regarded something irrevocable.

103 **अटवी-बल**

Aṭavī-bala : tribal force. It refers to forest tribes such as *Śabaras, Goṇḍas, Pulindas, Bhillas* and others. These were under their own chiefs. It seems that the enemy and forest troops were not to be paid regular wages, for it is stated that they should be maintained with *kupya*, minor produce, or that in alternative, they should be allowed to keep what plunder they may get in the fighting. This troop, infact, looked forward to plunder, and if there was no plunder to be had, it is said, they may prove dangerous (*A*, 9. 2. 19-20).

104 **अट्टहास**

Aṭṭahāsa : loud laughter. It is known as *ṭhahākā* in Hindi. *Thahākā* is characterized by loud bursts of vocalization through a wide-open mouth. Each burst comes in a long, forceful exhalation at the end of which the subject sometimes chokes. Then comes a deep, whinning inhalation and the next burst. The laugher's head is thrown back so that he loses sight of the person or object that is making him laugh. At the same time he experiences an accelerated heart-beat, tears and a flushed face.

105 **अड्डिता-चारी**

Aḍḍitācārī : feet in *samapāda, agratala sañcāra* foot runs against the side of the *samapāda* foot; also *aḍḍita maṇḍala.* one *agratalasañcāra* foot is rubbed against the forepart or the back of the other (*NS*, X.23).

106 **अणु**

Aṇu : (a) the minutest unit of *aṅgula*, a type of measurement of human body in sculpture; fine, minute, atom. (b) *Aṇu* has certain yogic connotation being the back-formation of certain words such as *Śivāṇu, hṛdayāṇu, gavāṇu, mūlāṇu, sarāṇu, bhāṣyāṇu, kavacāṇu, sāstrāṇu, āyudhāṇu.* Thus the concept of *aṇu* is a symbolic ritual which occurs only in the *Agni Purāṇa* (75.27).

107 **अतिकर्षण**

Atikarṣaṇa : encroachment on the road (*A*, 3.10.6).

108 **अतिक्रान्त**

Atikrānta : passed, gone beyond, transgressed.

109 **अतिक्रान्त अवेक्षण**

Atikrāntamavekṣaṇa : past looking, reference to a past statement (A, XVI).

110 **अतिक्रान्त करण**

Atikrānta karaṇa : feet as in the *pārśvakrāntā cārī* : but this is an extreme position of the infolded knee; one hand rests on the thigh and the other is held in *musṭi* on chest. The commentary adds that resting hand is in *ardhacandra* (*NS*, IV. 133b-134a, x.32). After performing *atikrāntā cārī*, the foot is extended in front with hands in conformity with the foot. It is employed in gaits.

111 **अतिक्रान्ता-चारी**

Atikrāntā cārī : The moving about on the sky can be shown by a number of *cārīs* ; *atikrāntā cārī* is one of them. Feet in *samapāda kuñcita* ; *kuñcita* foot taken up to the knee level approximately and then placed forward four *tālas* ; *nata jānu, atikrānta karaṇa* and *maṇḍala.* In *Vikramorvaśiya* (I), the king portrays the speed of chariot by taking a round of the stage in fast, and then the *apsarās* enact descending the mountain. This is performed in the *atikrāntā cārī* ; the body is held up; in descending the mountain one foot is in the *atikrāntā cārī* and the other in *anncita* position. Urvaśī appears on the chariot leaning on the arm of the king and the king's descriptions of the earth and its movements are supported by their enacting. Urvaśī and the king rub against each other as they alight from the chariot and, as they enact this, the chariot enacts the stopping of the vehicle. The rest of the act has many examples of the chariot's movement.

Abhinava (*NS*, X.10) explains this *cārī* in the following manner:"The *kuñcita* foot is taken to the base level of the other foot and then dropped forward four *tālas.*"

112 **अतिचार**

Aticāra : transgression, misconduct in general (*A*, 4.13), acts of misconduct. These include such offences as approaching an elder's wife with carnal intentions, and having sex-relations with a woman of another *varṇa* - offences to which *Smṛtis* refer. Other *aticāras* are of miscellaneous character, such as making a person eat what is unfit for consumption or drink what is undrinkable, entering another man's house with or without weapon, failing to warn persons to get out of the way when felling a tree or leading an untamed animal or throwing a stone, stick, etc., failure of cart-driver to take precautions against injury to passers-by, causing injury to others by means of magic, and so on (A, 4.13).

113 **अतिथि**

Atithi : guest. (a) one not staying permanently at another's house. (b) a Brāhmaṇa guest who stays for one night only (*Smṛti*). (c) son-in-law Bihar state.

114 **अतिथि-सत्कार**

Atithi-satkāra : hospitality. In ancient India, the *gṛahasta* was responsible, too, for performing the rites of hospitality to which distinguished guests were entitled. Those rites were back to the Vedic age, and as time went on, the gradually increasing emphasis on ritual codification made them over more important.

When a guest was expected, the chair which was to be offered to him was got ready, and a special beverage (*madhuparka*) composed of sugar, ghee, curd, herbs and honey, was prepared (Upadhyaya, B.S., *India in Kālidāsa*, Allahabad, 1947, p.211). This was a sort of hydromel consumed on great occasions: women were given it to drink when five months pregnant, the eldest son's lips were moistened with it at the time of his birth, the student was offered it when he left his *guru* to become a *snātaka*, the suitor just before he went to ask for the hand of a girl in marriage, and the bridegroom when he arrived at the home of his future father-in-law on the morning of the wedding.

As soon as the guest appeared at the dwelling's main entrance gate, his host went out to meet him (*Raghuvaṁśa* 5.2) in an appropriate manner. A great number of different forms of salutations existed, depending up on the exact relationship between the two parties: an inferior bowed his head before his superior; but in the case of venerable persons, such as his teacher, his father or mother, he touched their feet respectively; the superior responded by reciting to him a formula of blessing. This is still a current practice. Hsuan-Chuang (Beal, *op.cit.*I, p.85) mentions nine different forms of salutations. When someone addressed a request to a superior, he joined his hands together in front of his chest. Brothers and individuals of the same social status, embraced each other or shook hands (Upadhyaya, *op.cit,*. pp. 209-10). In actual practice, a guest was automatically considered a superior and honoured accordingly.

As soon as he had been escorted inside the house, he was led to the cushion or rattan chair which had been set in portion for him. In Vedic times the cushion was a heap of grass (Renou and Filliozat, *op.cit.*I, 1209). A servant brought him water to refresh his feet. Then he was offered water to drink. Finally he was presented with a bowl containing hydromel. He was required to accept it with both hands and to place it by his side, on the ground, without drinking from it. Soon afterwards, he stirred the mixture three times in succession, by making a circular motion in the liquid with the thumb and index finger of the right hand, pressed together. He consumed the ritual drink in three mouthfuls (or a single mouthful, according to other texts) and then drank a little water. Similar rites are still practiced in Indian tea ceremony.

If the guest was a brāhmaṇa or a king, the ceremony was completed by an important rite. He was raised solemnly towards a cow and it was offered to him as a present. In the Vedic age, the animal was slaughtered in his honour, as the scapegoat for his sins, and actual purification was thus achieved. In later times, the sacrifice became entirely symbolic; At that time the custom was that the *gṛhastha* held out a knife to his guest, who handed it back to him, reciting this formula: "She is the mother of the Rudras, the daughter of the Vasus, the sister of the Ādityas, the womb of immortality. Do not kill the innocent cow; she is the very goddess of Earth I say this to those who understand me." Then he added: "My sins have been slain. Let her go, let her drink water and graze."

The reception ended with a meal that included meat, a food which was eaten by a brāhmaṇa, and the host supervised its preparation in person. The *gṛhastha* took leave of his guests by rising from his seat first in their presence, following the code of courtesy that is still in use today.

The *atithi-yajña* is a part of a householder's duty and is counted among the *Mahāyajñas.* According to *Purāṇas* and *Smṛtis,* a guest is one who is constantly on the move. An unknown person who comes to one's house, is also called an *atithi.*A guest who returns from one's house disappointed, takes away the merits of the householder and gives instead all the sins. For a guest it should not be thought whether he is learned or a fool. A guest is to be fed according to one's capacity.

115 अतिदेश

Atideśa : substitution, extended application. By this principle, a thing applicable at one place may be applicable at another. For example, *gotra,* though applicable in the case of Brāhmaṇas only may be applicable, by *atideśa,* in the case of kṣatriyas etc. also. Again the word 'son' denotes the male issue of a person, yet by *atideśa,* the word may refer to the male issue of one's co-wife also.

atideśa is the process or method by which the details prescribed in connection with one sacrifice are transferred to another. The seventh chapter of *Pūrvamīmāmsā Sūtra* deals with the general question of the extension or transference of details in general to *Aindrāgna* and other sacrifices (*Yaj.* 1.236; *Pārāśara* VII. 18-19).

Atideśa-vākya is an assimilative proposition.

116 अतिपातक

Atipātaka : a class of sins comprising adultery with one's mother, daughter and daughter-in-law (*Smṛti*). There is no penance for such great sin except entering fire according to *Viṣṇu Dh. S.* (XXXIV. 1-2). These are included in the *Mahāpātaka* list by *Manu* (XI. 58) and *Yāj* (III. 233-34). (Fig. 116)

117 अतिभङ्ग

Atibhaṅga : a type of *deflected stances* (*bhaṅga*); a pose; (a) it denotes greater deflection from the plum line and is used to depict the demonic mood. The maximum deviations are allowed to the different parts of the body in the *atibhaṅga*: the bend of the knees, the deflection of the hips, the extension of the side, and the movements of the head can all take place at the same time in the *atibhaṅga.* Some of the contortionist sculpture and the *acrobatic* feats of the Indian dancing were possible by the principle of *atibhaṅga.* Used in a restrained manner, it resulted in the powerful stances of Durgā and Śiva. (b) one of the four *flexions* or bodily attitudes in which the standing icons (*sthānaka*) are represented (see

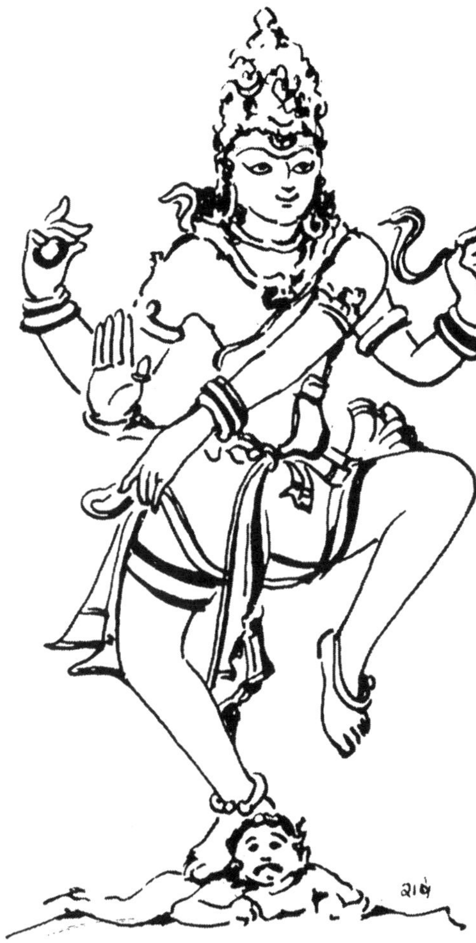

Fig. – (116)

bhaṅga). It is a variety of three-bend (*tri-bhaṅga*) attitude, employed to depict superhuman vigour and action. The upper part of the body (the torso) is made to swing to the right or left, with an arm forcefullly stretched out, clutching a weapon (like bow or sword). The attitude can be seen in deities engaged in fight or in deities roused to anger. Some forms of the dancing Śiva are instances of this posture.

This is really an emphasized form of the *tri-bhaṅga,* the sweep of the *tri-bhaṅga* curve being considerably enhanced. The upper portion of the body above the hips, or the limbs below, are thrown to right or left, back-wards or forwards, like a tree caught in a storm.

118 **अतिभाषा**

Atibhāṣā : language of the super human (*NS*, XVIII. 26-65); one of the four varieties of language occurring in Sanskrit plays; *atibhāṣā* belongs to deities.

119 **अतिवाद**

Ativāda : (a) excessive praise (A, 4.1.59). (b) harsh speech *(Amarakośa).*

120 **अतिव्याप्ति**

Ativyāpti : fallacy of including what is not intended to be included. For example, if we define 'cow' as a quadruped having two horns, they will include buffaloes etc.

121 **अतिहसित**

Atihasita : excessive laughter. The second of the two types of the *adhama hāsya.* It is roaring laugh, the meanest type of laughter indulged by ruffians. The whole body is rudely shaken into distorted movements and a loud noise accompanies the laugh. It is beyond the control of the laughing person and indicates absence of culture and decorum. It is the symbol of the inferior types of people. It is one of the six *anubhāvas* of *hāsa.* In it eyes are expanded and tearful. It represents excessive sound and sides are covered with hands. (It is a roaring laugh. It is beyond the control of the laughing person and indicates absence of culture and decorum.)

122 **अतीन्द्रिय**

Atiṅdriya : beyond the senses, trans-sensuous, infra-sensible, *trancendental..* (Fig. 122)

123 **अत्ता**

Attā : the mother of the courtezan is to be addressed as *attā* by the servants in Sanskrit dramas (*NS,* XVII. 65-94).

124 **अत्यन्तप्रौढवचः**

Atyanta-prauḍha-vacaḥ : pompous speech: quality of the Bull-man (*Pañcasāyaka,* 2.10).

125 **अदर्शन-पथ**

Adarśana-patha : what is beyond vision. Comp. *adarśanapatham gataḥ*

126 **अद्‌भुत**

Adbhuta : the sentiment of astonishment, surprise; The art of wonderful sentiment. When an image or scene, or a sketch suggests a hair-startling sensation, other than those of the furious, the heroic and the disgustful and inspires a sense of wonder, or a surprise; it is the art-culture of wonderful relish (*Visṇudharma,* III. 43.9). It is aroused by determinants such as sight of heavenly beings or events, attainment of desired objects, entry into a superior mansion, temple, audience hall, seven storeyed palace or divine chariots and seeing illusory and magical acts. It is to be represented by the consequents such as wide opening of eyes, looking with fixed gaze, horripilation, tears (of joy), perspiration,

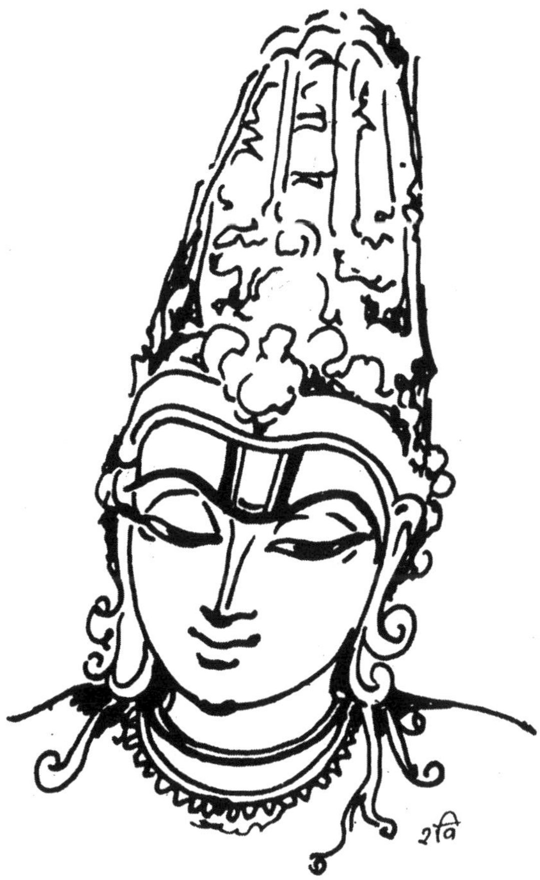

Fig. – (122)

joy, uttering words of approbation, making gifts, crying incessantly *'hā ha'* waving the hand, mouth and movement of fingers and the like. Transitory psychological states are cessation of bodily movement, weeping, perspiration, choking voice, horripilation, agitation, hurry, inactivity, death and the like, Bharata states two kinds of the marvellous sentiments celestial and joyous. Celestial is due to seeing of heavenly sights and joyous is due to joyful happenings.

127 **अद्‌भुता-रसदृष्टि**

Adbhutā-rasadṛṣṭi : the glance suggests wonder with eyelashes shut slightly; eye-balls express the thought of charm and wonder (*NS*, VIII. 27-51). Eyelashes are slightly curved at the end, pupils raised in wonder and the eyes widened. It is used in the marvellous sentiment.

128 **अद्वारासङ्ग**

Advārāsaṅga : unrestricted entry *(A*, 1.19.26).

129 **अधमा प्रकृति**

Adhamā prakṛti : the inferior type of men are of harsh speech, bad character, bad constitution, dull, irascible, hurting, disloyal to friends, fault-finding, back-biting, aggressive in speech, ungrateful, lazy, lacking determination, between those who deserve and those who do not deserve respect, flirtatious, quarrelsome, infamous, sinful and snatching other people's wealth (*NS,* XXIV. 5-7).

The inferior women are similar to inferior men (*Ibid,* XXIV. 11-12).

130 **अधर**

Adhara : lower lip, lips; enacted according to emotions such as *visargs* (protruding lips, spread out) or *samudga* in *sṛṅgāra; kampana* (trembling) in *bhayānaka; visarga or vivartana* (narrowing) in *hāsya; samudgaka* (contracting) in *karuṇa, visarga or sama in adbhuta; kampana or sandaṣṭaka* (bitting by teeth) or *vinigūhana in raudra; vivartana in bībhatsa.* Lips are classified according to muscular possibilities. The *Saṅgītaratnākara* adds a few more movements of lips such as *udvṛtta, āyata* and *recita.* According to *NS*(VIII. 142-143) there are six types of lip movements: *vivartana* (twisting of lips in an awry fashion), *kampana* (tremulous lips), *visarga* (protruding lips), *vinigūhana* (drawing the lips inside), *sandaṣṭaka* (lip bitten by the teeth) and *samudga* (pouting of lips).

The fleshy lips of our species are not merely for infantile sucking or for kissing (other species also do), but appear to be a visual signal; rather than a tactile one. Vātsyāyana has worth recorded that like labia (*bhagoṣṭha*), the lips become redder and more swollen during sexual arousal and, like them, they surround a centrally placed orifice. The Muria legend about the vagina supports this conjecture. Lips have been artificially reddened with lipstick for thousands of years and this suggests their role of 'genital echo'. Moistening of the lips, or the wearing of glistening lipstick, adds an extra hint of genital lubrication. Also, the positioning of phallic-shaped objects so that they appear to be ready to pass between the lips is a device often employed by commercial advertising.

adhāra-rāga is a dye for the lips—a lipstic— which has been mentioned in *Brahmavaivarta Purāṇa* 53. 17-24). Kṛṣṇa applied *adhāra-rāga* as per the wish of Rādhā.

131 **अधर-चुम्बन**

Adhara-cumbana : Kissing the lips; Aśvaghoṣa (*Saundaryananda,* 8.35) drinks the lips of women: *nipīyate adharaḥ. Māgha* (10.52) has also explained the kissing behaviour of a lover: "A lover having dragged the hair of his beloved in embrace drinks the lips of his beloved who has closed her eyes and whose face is bent down due to shame". Nala having seen Damayantī, longs her lips in *Naiṣadha-carita* (9.117, 18.59): *tavādharāya spṛhyāmi; adharam dhyāyāmi te.* There are many references of *adhara-pānam* in Sanskrit literature.

Kissing the lips has a ritual significance in planting trees. The performer causes his wife to sit on his lap, after bath on the fifth day of menstruation, and makes to kiss her with a *mantra:*

भार्यामृतुमतीं स्नात्वा पञ्चमेऽहनि सत्तमाः ।
उत्सङ्गे स्थापयित्वाच चुम्बयेन्मन्त्रयेत्ततः ॥

(*Bhaviṣya Purāṇa* 1.10.28)

This is obviously for the germination of seed, and comparing the symbolic conception mentioned in the text, it is a charm.

132 अधरलक्षण

Adhara-lakṣaṇa : signs of lips. If reddish like the *bimba* and clear, Kingship; if broken, uneven and dry, poverty (*Garuḍa*); if lotus-petal-like, wealth; if thick, sorrow (*Brahma*, 26.47.).

Lips like a *bimba* fruit are appreciated in Sanskrit literature: *bimboṣṭhī, raktādharī.* Compare *bhagoṣṭhī* and try to understand the comparability of the lips with the sexual echo.

133 अधरोत्तर

Adharottara : higher becoming lower, reversal, upside down, topsy-turvy, losing and winning, earlier and later. Comp. '*Śrutam bhavadbhir adharottaram*', (*Śākuntalam* 5.24). The concept of *adharottara* in the violence of the state was first presented by *Manu* (7. 20-21). He records "If the king did not exercise his power of punishment (*daṇḍa*) relentlessly enough, the crow would eat the sacrificial cake, the dog licks up the food put out for ritual oblation and no right of ownership (*svāmyam*) would be there for anyone to retain - in short, we are warned, "the lower would become the higher - *pravarteta adharottaram*. This concept of the inversive process was systematized later by Srinivas into the theory of Sanskritization, but Srinivas lacks that vision which Manu had presented thousands of years before. Sanskritization is one way process (lower becoming higher) but *adharottarīkaraṇa* functions in both the ways, higher becoming lower and *vice versa.*

134 अधिकरण

Adhikaraṇa : ground, substratum. A complete argument treating of one subject. (a) According to the followers of Mīmāṁsā and *vedānta*, a complete *adhikaraṇa* consists of five members: *viṣaya, saṁśaya, pūrvapakṣa, uttara and siddhānta.* (b) locative case in grammar.

135 अधिपाणि कपोलौ

Adhipāṇi kapolau : hands on the cheeks, showing anxiety (Bhāravi, *Kirāta* 9.43). It is an auto-contact behaviour, where a little comfort is suggested. Cheek support is a way to finding minor comfort in a stressed social world.

136 अधिबल

Adhibala : out-vying; a dialogue between two persons in emulation, each of which outdoes the other in his remarks. Bharata defines that when somebody else's words and those of one's ownself, in course of dialogue, lead to their mutual modification, it is *adhibala.* Abhinava adds that it is so called because in mutual dialogue one tries to outdo the other by making his stand firm. It is one of the thirteen constituents of *vīthī.*

137 अधिष्ठान

Adhiṣṭhāna : (a) seat, base, standing place, residence (A, 1.16.10); prominent position (A, 10.3.42); anything on which it is erected (*Mānasāra*, XIV. 1-442); especially the foundational tier (*tala*) of the ornate superstructure over the sanctum known as *vimāna.* (b) The four qualities in the *acalā* stage towards the attainment of Bodhisattvahood. They are *satya* (truth), *tyāga* (renunciation), *upasama* (remission) and *prajñā* (wisdom). (c) substratum - that which itself remaining unperceived and changeless gives the appearance of reality to an illusion based on it (*Vedānta*). (d) a seat of administration. (Fig. 137)

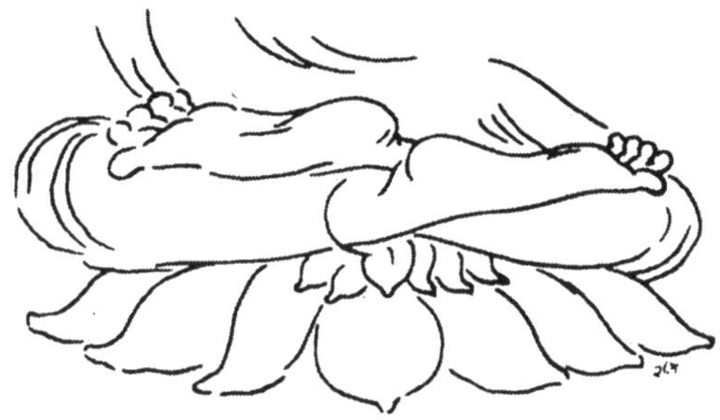

Fig. – (137)

138 अधि स्पर्श

Adhi-sparśa : Vedic usage, to press with force, to place in proximity (to eliminate excess of inter-space).

देवयजनगर्तयोर्मध्ये शकटस्य गमनाय यावदन्तरं पर्याप्तं तावदेवान्तरं कर्त्तव्यं सोऽयमधिस्पर्शः

139 अधोगत शिरसू

Adhogata śiras : face is turned down, head going downwards; bending down the head to lock at a thing on the ground. It suggests grief, shame, disgrace, salutation, etc. (*NS*, VIII. 17-18).

140 **अधो मस्तक**

Adho-mastaka : having the head downwards.

141 **अधोमुख**

Adhomukha : the down-facing, lowering of head, down towards ground, *adhomukha* head is used in bashfulness etc. Śakuntalā lowers her head in this manner to the king's loving attention. Bharata's term for this movement is *adhogata* or *adhomukha* (*NS*, VIII. 36), both are similar movements. The *naṭa* movement of the neck or *adhogata* position of the head is suggested in Amarāvati sculpture. One of the three movements of hands. All these (including the *uttāna* and the *pārśvagata*) styles of hands are to be exhibited with the expression of eyes, eye-brows and appearances of the face.

142 **अधोमुख-बाहु**

Adhomukha bāhu : the down-facing arm (*NS*, IX. 205-206).

143 **अधोवदनहस्त**

Adhovadanahasta : Fingers downwards on the vertical plane.

144 **अधोवर्म**

Adhovarma : The name of the lower eyelid.

145 **अध्यग्नि**

Adhyagni : a kind of *strīdhana* given to a girl at the time of her marriage before the nuptial fire (*Smṛti*).

146 **अध्यर्धिका चारी**

Adhyardhikā cārī: Foot on *samapāda añcita* position, a *tāla* and a half apart: sideways direction : a movement ending in a posture is indicated, *adhyardha maṇḍala;* scenes from the Rānīgumphā and Udayagiri caves in Orissa represent this movement. Here the left foot follows the right, and is at a distance of one *tāla* from the first (*NS*, X.17). In Amarāvatī *stūpa*, the woman steps forward in this movement, with her left foot at the back of the right, and placed two *tālas* apart. The left foot is at the back of the right and then the right to be moved a *tāla* and half, or the left foot is placed near the heel of the right foot. The right foot is drawn to its own side and placed obliquely.

147 **अध्यवाहनिक**

Adhyavāhanika : a kind of *strīdhana* given to a girl at the time of her marriage before the nuptial fire (*Smṛti*); wealth which is obtained by a wife at the time of departure from her parents' house to her husband's house.

148 **अध्यास**

Adhyāsa : false attribution, superimposition, projection, wrong supposition, e.g. nacre mistaken for silver (a philosophical term). The process of the imaginary attribution of something where it does not exist. In psychological terminology it is similar to projection. From a religious viewpoint it is a form of symbol worship. The objective approach to the symbol is known as *sampad,* while the subjective is known as *adhyāsa.*The former is like the visualization of the deity or idea in a thing, may be an image or symbol, while in the case of the latter, though the thing exists and is used and a means of concentration, the main emphasis is on the mind of the worshipper and on the deity or idea that is chiefly concerned (*Vedānta Kalpataru,* 1.1.4)

Some people cope with unacceptable aspects of their own make-up by projecting unpleasantness onto someone else. We all have a bad side - e.g. selfish and aggressive urges - but we do not like to recognize it. It is quite common to see people projecting their own faults onto others - convincing themselves that it is boss who is being unreasonable (not themselves who are incompetent), or their partner who is constantly fantasizing about having affairs (and not themselves who have a roving eye). Those who do this a great deal are prone to criticizing or blaming others.

149 **अध्याहार**

Adhyāhāra : supplying words not stated. For example in *rathastham* (Vāmanam dṛṣṭvā punarjanma na vidyate, the words *sthitasya janasya* have to be supplied between *dṛṣṭvā* and *punarjanma* for grammatical accuracy; supplementing with another word, *padānta-pūraṇa.*

150 **अनङ्ग**

Anaṅga : meaning 'devoid of body'. It is one of the names of *Kāmadeva* (cupid), the Indian god of beauty and love. It also means the sex. The bodiless one. He had been so called because he was reduced to ashes by Śiva.

151 **अनङ्गक्रीडा**

Anaṅga-krīḍā : amorous sport, sexuality. The development of sexuality is of prime importance in psychoanalytic theory of Vātsyāyana. Later on Freud described the infant as a polymorphous pervert, by which he meant that any form of bodily stimulation is pleasurable to it. Gradually, however, this changes up to about one year of age. This sexual pleasure is centred on the mouth - this is the oral stage. Later, at around the age of toilet training, the anus becomes the centre of excitation - the anal stage. At about the age of five eroticism is centred on the penis and clitoris (the phallic stage). The child then enters the latency period when all sexuality is repressed. At puberty it awakens, and the adult genital stage is reached, characterized by adult love and sexual satisfaction. This includes oral, anal and phallic components, and is characterized of a mature healthy person who has passed through all the normal developmental phases (Wilson, 1989, 79).

152 **अनङ्गलेख**

Anaṅga-lekha : love-letter.

153 **अनङ्गविद्या**

Anaṅgavidyā : sexology. There are hundreds of texts on sexology in Sanskrit right from *Kāmasūtra* to the present day writings. For example Kalyāṇamalla (1460-1530) wrote *Anaṅgaraṅga* which runs in ten chapters. The work contains classification of men and women, days and time most congenial for sexual excitement and pleasure, ways and means of producing orgasm, ingredients and aphrodisiacs for both men and women, depilatory chemicals, stiffening the loose and sagging breasts and numerous other topics of erotics. The work also covers the eight kinds of heroines, a longish section on palmistry, and an extended account of various *bandhas* (postures for congress). Some chapters deal with social matters, such as marriage, selection of a bride, the social customs to be observed by the bride, etc. (Fig. 153)

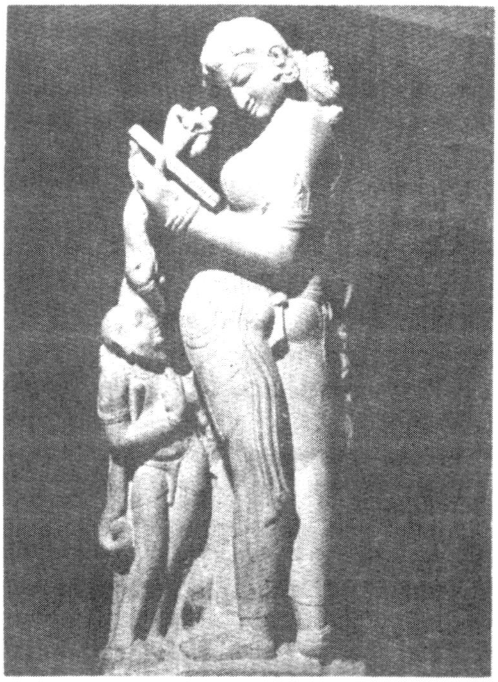

Fig. – (153)

154 **अनन्त-मुद्रा**

Ananta-mudrā : gesture of infinite. (a) Place both of the palms flat, inter-woven all other fingers mutually and put the thumb at the end of the little-finger; this is *ananta* (*VD*). (b) It is considered ritually and spiritually the base of the universe which holds *dharma, jñāna, vairāgya* and *aiśvarya* - the four desirable ends of any worship, or spiritual cultures.

Ananta meaning 'endless' (or infinite), it is one of the names of Viṣṇu, and also a name of the mythical dragon, Śeśa.

155 **अनन्तशयन-मुद्रा**

Ananta śayana-mudrā : gesture symbolizing Lord Viṣṇu lying on Śeṣa. Fingers of the *makara* - hand extended on upper tips (*VD*).

'Gesture of reclining on Ananta', iconic representation of Viṣṇu which shows him recumbent on the folds of the great snake, with the hoods serving as a canopy over his head.

156 **अनध्याय**

Anadhyāya : non-study. Suspension of study caused by a number of factors, e.g. disturbance in village, conflagration, *amāvāsyā, paurṇamāsī* of certain months, storm, rainfall, eclipse, earth-quake, etc. (*Smṛti*). The subject of *anadhyāya* is discussed in the *Gṛhya* and *Dharma-sūtras* and in almost all *Smṛtis* (*Manu:* 2.105). It is said that a student should not study in the shade of a Śleṣmātaka tree, a Śālmalī tree, Madhūka, Kovidāra and Kapittha tree (*Kūrma* II. 14. 29). Certain days are taboo for study; likewise when a fellow student dies or a teacher passes away, non study is prescribed. It is said that these days prescribed for non-study are infested with goblins, and the latter would kill any one who studies on these days (*Ibid.* II. 14.7). But the taboo for study (*anadhyāya*) is not applicable to the ancillary texts, or the texts on law, *Dharmaśāstras* etc; *anadhyāya* should be observed in the case of the Vedic text: (Fig. 156)

अनध्यायस्तु नाङ्गेषु नेतिहासपुराणयोः ।
न धर्मशास्त्रेष्वन्येषु पर्वण्येतानि वर्जयेत् ॥

(*Kūrma,* II. 47.80)

157 **अनध्याय-महोत्सव**

Anadhyāya-mahotsava : great festival of intermission from study. '*anadhyāya-mahotsavam khelantau sambhāvayāvaḥ*' *Uttara-rāmacarita* 4.6).

158 **अनपशब्द**

Anapaśabda : having words grammatically correct.

159 **अनवेक्ष**

Anavekṣa : without looking with care.

160 **अनशन**

Anaśana : abstinence from the food, having no food; post-independence pressure tactics for the fulfilment of a demand. It is also called *upavāsa.*

Anaśana or fasting is a mark of mourning to be undertaken by the relatives of the deceased.

161 **अनागत-अवेक्षणम्**

Anāgata-avekṣaṇam : looking to future, reference to future statement (A, XV. I). Literally *anāgata* means unarrived. Knowledge of the past and future can be gained by *samyama* on the three *pariṇāmas.* It can be equated with the modern futurology. The student of yoga is very conscious of the pain that may arise in the future since the past is already over and the present will turn into past in a moment. What is avoidable is the pain that is yet to come.

162 **अनाचार**

Anācāra : bad behaviour, devoid of customary observances, improper in behaviour.

163 **अनामय-प्रश्न**

Anāmaya-praśna : enquiring after health.

164 **अनामिका**

Anāmikā : the nameless ring-finger; name for the ring-finger. It is so called because the literary critics could not name a poet immediately next in eminence to Kālidāsa, who was counted on the little fingers. The story refers to an ancient custom of enumeration by counting on the fingers. Also known as *anāmā.* The finger which is used in the performance of religious acts or rituals. According to the *Purāṇas,* Śiva is said to have cut off the head of Brahmā with this finger. Despite the fact that this finger cut off Brahmā's head, it is even then considered as sacred.

165 **अनित्यता**

Anityatā : impermanence, transitoriness, the doctrine of impermanence or rather evanescence of phenomenal objects; momentariness (*kṣaṇikatva*) according to Buddha due to origin (*utpatti*), duration (*sthiti*) and decay (*vināśa*). The assumption that one biological form or species becomes changed into another over a long period of time.

166 **अनिमेष दृष्टि**

Animeṣa dṛṣṭi : gaze, staring. There are certain social pressures on individuals in conversation to comply to certain behavioural standards regarding amount of gaze, and length of glances, if they wish to make a favourable impression. Social variables affect the intimate patterning of gaze and speech in dialogue. *Animeṣa adṛṣṭi* occurs in social intercourse. *Animeṣam* means 'without closing the eyes'.

Animeṣa (unblinking) is a general epithet of all gods, whose eyes do not blink. There are various allusions to this in *Mbh* (*Ādi.* 33).

Although a high level of eye-contact from another person is usually interpreted as a sign of positive feelings on the part of the individual, there is one exception to this rule - staring which is known as *animeṣa dṛṣṭi.* When another individual gazes at us in a continuous manner, and maintains eye contact, regardless of any actions on our part, his or her behaviour may be interpreted as a sign of hostility rather than friendship. Research on animals suggests that stares are often used as a threatening gestures and frequently precede over attacks. One evidences many signs of tension and nervousness during the period of continuous gazing. Thus, *animeṣa dṛṣṭi* can communicate negative feelings.

167 **अनिरुद्ध-मुद्रा**

Aniruddha-mudrā : framing a style of *sūrpa* (willow) with curled fingers, when the full form is wrapped by thumbs from the bottom; it makes the gesture of *aniruddha (VD).*

"Aniruddha" means "un-obstructed and is one of the names of Viṣṇu and also one of the four *vyūhas* (aspects) of Vāsudeva.

168 **अनिर्वचनीय**

Anirvacanīya : inexplicable and indefinable. The term is often used to denote bliss derived for the carvaṇa of a literary piece of work suited to one's own sensitivity. In philosophy, the term is used to denote *māyā.*

169 **अनीक**

Anīka : face, front, point, army. The face conveys more information about the nature of an emotion (whether the person felt sad, angry, afraid, etc.), than about the intensity of the emotional state.

170 **अनुका**

Anukā : passionate woman

171 **अनुकूलक**

Anukūlaka : adaptors are specific behaviours that at some point in a particular individual's development served, a special function or purpose but are no longer part of the individual's behavioural repertoire. (a) For example, people under stress sometimes rub their eyes, as if to avoid viewing unpleasant sight. They may also cover or pick at their eyes, symbolically avoiding an unpleasant message. Adaptors occur largely outside people's conscious awareness, but they may be useful as cues indicating emotional states. (b) *anukūla* is one of the four varieties of hero, who is devoted to a single heroine and is ever faithful to her.

172 **अनुकृति**

Anukṛti : imitation, *(NS*, 1.57) clearly uses the term *anukṛti* (imitation) for drama in several places. He says *"loka-vṛttānukaraṇam nāṭyam etan mayākṛtam"*(NS, 1.112) 'I have created this *nāṭya* as the imitation of social lif ,and 'this *nāṭya* will be imitation of the seven continents: *sapta dvīpānukaraṇam nāṭyam etad bhaviśyati* (*NS*, 1.117). These references show that Bharata regarded the *nāṭya* as an imitation. Aristotle did the same. The speech, gestures, manners, appearance and dress of actors was the same as prevalent in the society of that time.

Imitation is the copying the actions of another intentionally.

173 **अनुचारिका**

Anucārikā : constant female attendants like a shadow, never leaving the king (*NS*, XXIV. 59-59).

174 **अनुनय**

Anunaya : form of speech and thought; also known as *anunīti* (*A*, 2.10.13; *NS*. 18.23); Supplication, request, courtesy. There are two types of requests: direct request and indirect request. The intention of the requesting partner can be made more explicit by a proximic shift towards the possessor, leaning towards the possessor, skin contact watching how somebody gets the alms, prolonged and lasting eye contact, and a begging expression on one's face. The intention of the requesting partner is made explicit by stretching to movements of the arm, touching the possessor, and pouting, in case nothing is given. Direct requests, which co-occur obligatorily with paralinguistic features, can be repeated, but indirect request is not repeated.

175 **अनुनासिक**

Anunāsika : a nasal sound. Comp. *mukhanāsikavacano nunāśikaḥ* (*Pāṇini*, 1.1.8).

176 **अनुपपत्ति**

Anupapatti : untenability, logical non-sequence, absence of validity, discord (a philosophical term), non-proof, no conclusive argument, a technical term in logic.

177 **अनुपबन्ध**

Anupabandha : (a) rising gradually and smoothly without breaking in speech. (b) In grammar it stands for a letter technically called "iti" (that which is added), belonging to *prakṛti, pratyaya, āgama* or *ādeśa.* (c) According to *Vedānta,* it stands for the four, *viz. viṣaya, prayojana, adhikārī* and *sambandha.*

178 **अनुपलब्धि**

Anupalabdhi : non-perception. It is the source, according to a school of *Mīmāmsā* of our immediate cognition of the non-existence of an object. For example, the non-existence of the jar is known by non-perception of it.

179 **अनुपातक**

Anupātaka : a class of sins comprising falsehood, theft, adultery, etc. (*Smṛti*). There are 35 kinds of *anupātaka,* which are described in the *Smṛti-* literature.

180 **अनुबन्ध**

Anubandha : indispensable elements in every *Śāstra.* These are *viṣaya* (the subject to be treated of), *prayojana* (the purpose of the subject), *sambandha* (the relation of the *Śāstra* to the *prayojana*) and *adhikārin* (the person entitled or competent to study). (b) In grammar, it stands for a letter intended to denote some peculiarity in inflection, accent, etc. (c) In the work of erotics, it stands for attendant gains. (d) In medicine it means the absence of excess in any of the three *doṣas.*

181 **अनुभव**

Anubhava : experience. It is of four kinds, namely, perception, inference, analogy and testimony. Knowledge gained through experience is called *anubhava* .Very often it is synonymous with *pramāṇa* (valid source of knowledge). Six valid sources of knowledge are known in philosophy. These are *pratyakṣa* (direct perception), *anumāna* (inference), *śabda* (testimony), *upamāna* (analogy), *arthāpatti* (implication) and *anupalabdhi* (non-perception). *Purāṇas* added two more sources of valid knowledge: *sambhava* (possible) and *aetihya* (tradition).

Thus *anubhava* is an event that has been lived through; it is the totality of personal consciousness. It is the knowledge or skill derived from practice or learning.

182 **अनुभाव**

Anubhāva : consequences, the total impact of acting, actions and gestures, physical manifestation of sentiments (NS, VII). The physical changes consequent on the rise of an emotion which are in real life are regarded as the effects of an emotion are called *anubhāva.* They are called *anubhāvas* because they follow the basic emotion and communicate it. These physical changes are of two kinds: (I) voluntary such as coquettish movements, etc, and (II) involuntary, e.g. tremors, choked voice, etc.' The involuntary are called the *sāttvika bhāvas.*

While explaining *rasa* and *bhāva,* Bharata has mentioned the representation of them by the *anubhāva,* as *anubhāra* are the outward expressions of mental states.

183 **अनुमान**

Anumāna : inference, knowledge through marks. It is the knowledge of objects not through perception but through the apprehension of some marks (*liṅga*) and is invariably related to the inferred objects. The invariable relation between the two is called *vyāpti.* In inference there are at least three propositions and atmost three terms - the *pakṣa* or minor term about which we infer something. The *sādhya* or major term which is the inferred object. The *liṅga* or *sādhana or hetu,* or middle term which is invariably related to the major and is present is the minor. Inference is *svārtha* and *parārtha* depending in whether it is meant for oneself or for others. Again the *pūrvavat, śeṣavat* and *smānyato dṛṣṭa* depending on whether it passes from cause to effect or *vice-versa* or whether it is based on observed points of similarity.

184 **अनुयोग**

Anuyoga : form of speech and thought (*Bṛhaddevatā,* 144-60); it is also called *codana* (*A,* 2.10.9); question, enquiry to clarify opponent's point of view, injunction.

185 **अनुराग**

Anurāga : love, attachment to god in which the object of love, eventhough realized and relished always, appears to have a fresh charm and be attractive every moment (*Ujjvalanīlamaṇi, sthāyī,* 102).

Anurāga is an emotional attraction or dependence between two persons.

186 **अनुलेप**

Anulepa : anointing, ointment. See *añjana, abhyaṅga.* The *anulepa* should have three ingredients, which are *karpūra* (camphor), *uśīra* (the root of the kuśa plant) and *candana* (sandal), or it should be made from sandal, *agaru* (aloe-wood), camphor, musk and suffron, which came to be five in number. This is called *pañcānulepana,* and is said to be dear to Viṣṇu; and it is said to accomplish all desires (*Agni P.* 267. 21-22).

187 **अनुवाक**

Anuvāka : repetition, saying after, a chapter of the *Veda.*

188 **अनुवाक्य**

Anuvākya : formula of invitation to gods (*darśana*), stanzas meant for inviting gods.

189 **अनुवाद**

Anuvāda : a text which contains something which has already been ascertained by other means; Comp. *tadanuvādiguṇaḥ kusumodgamaḥ* (*Raghu,* 9.30).

190 **अनुवादी**

Anuvādī : the note that makes *saṁvādī* note clearer. Literally it means the note that follows the note called *vādī.* In the works of music, all notes other than *saṁvādī* and *vivādī* are called *anuvādī.*

Note - 'vivādī' are the notes which are not used in a *rāga,* but sometimes they are used for the *rāga's* beautification.

191 **अनुव्रत**

Anuvrata : vows for laymen. The lesser vows meant for Jain-householders. They are abstinence from *himsā, asatya* (untruthfulness), *adattadāna* (stealing), *abrahmacarya* (sensualism), *parigraha* (attachment), *krodha* (anger), *māna* (egoism), *māyā* (hypocrisy), *lobha* (greed), *rāga* (personal attachement), *dveṣa* (hatred), *kleśa* (quarrelsomeness), *abhākhyāna* (scandals), *paiśunya* (gossiping), *paraparivāda* (telling ill of others), *rati-arati* (sexuality), *māyāmṛṣa* (sinful acts under the pretext of goodness) and *mithyādarśanaśalya* (ascribing reality to unreal).

192 **अनुवृत्त-दर्शन**

Anuvṛtta darśana : close look, a type of sight (*NS, VD*), engaged in closely observing any form.

193 **अनुवृत्ता दृष्टि**

Anuvṛttā dṛṣṭi : a type-of eyeball movement; looking an object carefully. In *Vikrama,* the *bhojapatra* has disappeared, and the *vidūṣaka* goes looking for it: he moves around the stage through *anuvṛtta* glance (*NS,* VIII. 108) as if to find something. It is the gesture of the glance by the special move of the eyeball; the glance with eyeballs in a searching style.

194 **अनुवृत्ति**

Anuvṛtti : continuity, repetition. When a particular aphorism or a part of it is necessary for completing the sense of a following aphorism, it is said that the former has *anuvṛtti.*The repitition is sometimes continuous when the word or words concerned are repeated in the immediately following rules. Sometimes the *anuvṛtti* applies not to the immediately following rules but to the remote ones (*Vyākaraṇa*).

195 **अनुशय**

Anuśaya : revocation, annulment (*Smṛti, Arthaśāstra*), inclination (Buddhism). According to Buddhism there are seven types of inclination: *kāmarāga* (attachment to worldly objects), *patigha* (enmity), *diṭṭhi* (wrong view), *vicikicchā* (doubt about the creed), *māna* (pride), *bhavarāga* (desire for existence) and *avijjhā* (ignorance). *Samyutta* V. 64-63. These are inherent tendencies leading to various kinds of evil inclinations.

196 **अनुषङ्ग**

Anuṣaṅga : a principle regarding sentences. It pertains to the extension of a word or clause from one sentence to another or other sentences provided all the sentences are of the same type or form.

197 **अनुस्तरणी**

Anustaraṇī : funeral cow. The cow that is offered as a gift in a funeral.

198 **अनुस्मृति**

Anusmṛti : the third stage of reflection (love) shown by the *NS* (XII). (a) In *Mālavikāgnimitra* (V), Mālavikā moves to the stage with certain changes in emotion of joy-*saharṣam*. (b) a new *aṅga* of *yoga* according to *Guhyasamāja* (163).

199 **अन्तःकरण**

Antaḥkaraṇa : mind heart, inner ego. According to *Sāṁkhya*-philosophy, it is designated with different names as *manas, buddhi* and *citta. Antaḥkaraṇa* is the condensed form of the senses as ice of water. It is controlled by pure consciousness. According to *Tantrāloka* (IX. 236) *antaḥkaraṇa* is the collective name for intellect (*buddhi*), egoity (*ahaṁkāra*) and mind (*manas*). The *Advaita* treats *antaḥkaraṇa* as being composed of four divisions, while the *Mīmāṁsā* treats it as composed of only one entity, namely, *manas*.

Antaḥkaraṇa is the conscious self and develops along with the person's development. It is the aspect of mind that is in touch with reality. It controls the instinctive desires - a firm control - a strong ego in psychological terminology.

200 **अन्तःपुर**

Antaḥpura : the royal residence, harem (*A*, 1.20.1; 1.21.23), female apartments, the *rāṇivāsa* of the queens. There was a certain area reserved for ladies in the palaces of the kings, where the king's wives and other ladies resided. In ancient India, besides *antaḥpura*, it was called *śuddhānta*, for it was considered a pious area. As this area was prohibited to outsiders, it was also called *avarodha*. It was protected by several guards and the chief security guard was invariably an old and respectable man, so that the security of *antaḥpura* was preserved. From the Sanskrit dramas, it appears that there used to be a garden, called *pramodavana*, where the king and his queens used to relax and enjoy.

201 **अन्तःस्थ**

Antaḥstha : interior, semi-vowels.

202 **अन्तकाल**

Antakāla : hour of death.

203 **अन्तर**

Antara : (a) inside, entrance, inner. (b) a technical term used in architecture, which means a moulding of the pedastal and base; literally the distance between any two objects, hence it implies a moulding which separates two other larger mouldings.

204 **अन्तरङ्ग**

Antaraṅga : intimate, akin. *Antaraṅgaṁ* means 'heart'. (a) a division of *Samprajñāta Samādhi*. (b) proximate to liberation in *Rājayoga*.

205 **अन्तरचक्र**

Antaracakra : name of an occult science for foretelling events (A, 1.12.1).

206 **अन्तराय**

Antarāya : obstacle, hindrance, hurdle.

207 **अन्तराय-संकेत**

Antarāya-saṁketa : barrier—signals: People feel safer behind some kind of physical barrier. If a social situation is in a way threatening, then there is an immediate urge to set up such a barricade. For a tiny child faced with a stranger, the problem is usually solved by hiding behind

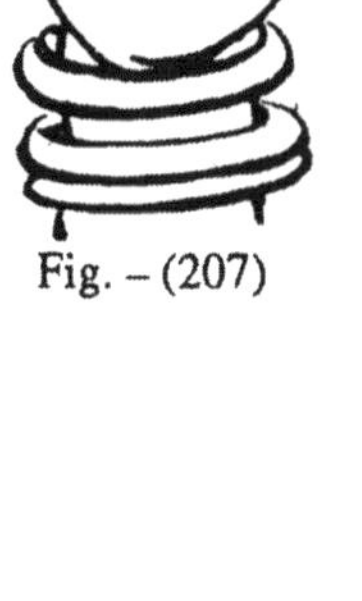

Fig. – (207)

its mother's body and peeping out at the intruder to see what he or she will do next. If the stranger insists on coming closer, then the peeping face must be hidden too. If the insensitive intruder continues to approach despite these obvious signals of fear, then there is nothing for it but to scream or flee.

Barrier signals may also check a person in participation in any action. In the Hill Maria society there is a taboo about women participating in the religious celebrations and ceremonies. No explanation is available in justification of this taboo except the remark that women are excluded because "who knows one of them may start her menstruation right at the shrine or during celebration, so why take the risk?" In same way women have to be completely secluded and even their faces should not be seen during menstruation. The husband of the woman is forced to sleep apart. Individuals are forbidden to start agricultural operations till the appropriate ceremony has been held and the whole village is able to get to work together. It is strictly a taboo for any woman to enter a granary or to sleep under one.

208 **अन्तराल**

Antarāla : intermediate compartment between the shrine and *maṇḍapa* - the intermediate porch.

209 **अन्तरिक्ष**

Antarikṣa : mid-region, sky, the atmosphere or firmament between heaven and earth, the sphere of the *Gandharvas, Apsarās,* and *Yakṣas.* Popularly it is known as sky. It is conceived as the finer aspect of the universe.

210 **अन्तरिक्ष-मुद्रा**

Antarikṣa-mudrā : gesture symbolizing the sky. *Muṣṭi* styled obliquely with the forefinger extended symbolize the sky (*VD*).

The intermediate region between the sky (*dyaus*) and the earth (*pṛthvī*), mid-plane, mid-region. *Antarikaṣa-loka* means the sphere of intermediary space where certain gods and souls reside. It is conceived as the finer aspect of universe.

211 **अन्तर्बाष्प**

Antarbāṣpa : suppressed tears, retaining tears.

212 **अन्तेवास**

Antevāsa : neighbour, companion.

213 **अन्तेवासी**

Antevāsī : 'pupil who dwells near his teacher' (*Ś.Br.*) The students had to serve the *Guru,* had to work under the Guru's sanctions, collect fire-sticks for the performance of *yajñas* and graze the cows.

214 **अन्त्य**

Antya : (a) being at the end, lowest, the lowest caste *Cāṇḍāla.* (b) the forest and mountainous region.

215 **अन्त्येष्टि**

Antyeṣṭi : funeral rites regarded as one of the sixteen or more *Saṁskāras* to be performed by the twice-born with Vedic *mantras* (*Manu,* II. 16). Funeral rites and rites after death vary in accordance with caste and religious position, nature of death, time and space factors, etc, connected with the deceased. The word *antyeṣṭi* is used in a wide sense which includes, apart from the disposal of the dead, all sorts of postmortem rites.

Accepting the death of someone we love is part of recovering from the trauma of loss. The need to deal with practical arrangements helps this process. The funeral and the ceremonies accompanying it have a considerable therapeutic value. We seem to have a deep need to mark major events in our lives with rituals that express the religious, social and psychological aspects of our own culture. A funeral gives those who mourn a way of making an important statement about their love of the deceased and the pain of bereavement. After the funeral ceremony relatives and friends may often gather to share a meal and to reminisce. This custom can be very supportive to the bereaved. It can also provide a stimulus for strengthening or renewing family relationships and even friendships. Funerals give the community the opportunity to honour both the dead person and the bereaved, and they give the bereaved an opportunity to find an outlet for their emotion. Frequently, this open expression of grief is echoed by other members of the community. This helps the bereaved to start working through their feelings and goes a considerable way toward coping with the strong and conflicting emotions they feel.

216 **अन्धविश्वास**

Andhaviśvāsa : superstition. A form of protective response unique to man is superstition. While he was busy improving the technology of realistic, down-to-earth body protection, from shields to bullet-proof vests and from suits of armour to fall-out shelters, he was also perpetually occupied with the business of inventing curious, magical acts of self-defence. These superstitious practices appear in every epoch of Indian culture. They are so numerous and so varied that whole encyclopedia may be compiled.

217 **अन्धवर्तकीय**

Andhavartakīya : a quail in a blind man's hand, accidental.

218 अन्न

Anna : food. Yaśodharā while commenting on *Kāmasūtra* (1.3.15) explains that food is of four kinds, *viz., bhakṣya, bhojya, lehya* and *peya*. The *bhakṣya* in real sense is *vyañjana*, which is a matter of culinary art. *Peya* or drink was of two kinds: boiled or otherwise. *Bhojya* includes sweets. *Lehya* could be a powder or liquid, tasting salty, sour and bitter and a little sweet.

In a famous story of *Daśakumāracarita* (2.6), Daṇḍin narrates how a young girl wins the heart of a suitor through her expertise in the preparation of food and drink. What she prepared and served was simple enough viz, rice with pulses, *ghee*, curd, vegetable and some appetizers, but she did it with great taste and skill. In Somadeva's *Yaśastilaka* we find a striking contrast between the food of the rich and that of poor. Śrīharṣa's *Naiṣadhīya* makes it clear that meat - eating was quite common at least among the princes.

The *NS* (1.121; III. 44-46) mentions *bhojya, bhakṣya* and *pāna* as the ingredients.

Certain types of food were specially noted for their colours. Thus white food (*śuklānna*) meant *pāyasa* (*khīr*); dark food (*nīlānna*) meant *kṛśara* (*khicṛī*); yellow food (*pītānna*) meant rice with clarified butter (*ghṛtaudana*); and red food (*raktānna*) meant rice with *guḍa* (*guḍaudana*) (*NS*, II. 39-40).

Again, different types of food were offered to different castes. Brāhmaṇs were offered *ghee* and *khīr* (*ghṛtapāyasa*) and Kṣatriyas were offered *madhuparka*, the traditional offering for honoured guests. Craftsmen were given *guḍaudana* (*NS*, II. 41-42). Again the Brāhmaṇs were given *sarpiṣ* (clarified butter) and *pāyasa;* TheKṣatriyas were given red food mentioned above. The Vaiśyas were given yellow food and Śūdras dark food. The most valued food was *madhuparka* which was to be offered to the chief priest and the ruler. Among the gods, Brahmā was offered *madhuparka*, Sarasvatī *pāyasa*, Śiva, Viṣṇu, Indra etc. *modakas;* Agni *ghṛtaudana*, Soma and Arka *guḍaudana;* Viśvedevāḥ, gandharvas and munis *madhupāyasa;* Yama and Mitra *apūpas* and *modakas;* pitṛs, piśācas and nāgas *sarpiḥ kṣīra* (NS, III. 37-45). Non-vegetarian food was offered to *bhūtasaṅghas, rākṣasas* and *dānavas*. Fish was offered to Varuṇa. Liquor was often served along with meat (*Ibid*). Meat juice was supposed to be invigorating and given as a part of military training and exercise (*Ibid.* X. 100).

The *Arthaśāstra* (2.15. 43-46) specifies the standard food for men of the upper (*āryāḥ*) and lower (*avarāḥ*) strata of society. For the *āryas*, rice with both oil or *ghee*, each equal to fourth part of rice, and salt equal to sixteenth part of *sūpa* is prescribed. For the *avaraṣ*, the quantity of *sūpa* was to be only one-sixth while oil was to be half.

219 अन्नप्राशन

Annaprāśana : rice-feeding ceremony. Feeding a child cooked food for the first time. Most *Smṛtis* prescribe the sixth month from birth as the time of this sacrement (*Mānava Gr.* 1.20-2).

220 अन्यापदेश

Anyāpadeśa : symbolism. The semiotic development of Sanskrit *rūpakas* finds its place in allegorical plays as well as in *uparūpakas*. It further developed in poetry and we have thousands of examples of *anyāpadeśa-śatakas*.

The *uparūpaka* varieties named *bhāṇa, preraṇa* and *bhāṇikā* adopt the *anyāpadeśa-* method of describing symbolically animals to suggest the intended idea and the dancer sings these with the gait of lion, elephant or other animals figuring in those songs. The animal semiotics for clever suggestion is employed in the *nāṭakas*. The animal symbolism is used to suggest the scenic situation also.

221 अन्योक्ति

Anyokti : saying something else; a figure of speech in which the real subject of comparison is suggested by explicit description of the object, where nevertheless, the two compared terms have no common property, but only a mode of action is common. *Anyokti* or *anyāpadeśa* is one of the popular devices of Sanskrit writers to convey their ideas and thoughts on human personalities, events etc. For example, a way -side tree rich with foliage but not giving any shadow to travellers will imply a rich but miserly patron.

222 अन्योन्य परिहरण

Anyonya-pariharaṇa : mutual avoidance: Certain rules of behaviour regulate the relations of kinsmen and affines. In the Hill Maria society, no man or woman should call his or her parents-in-law or younger sister-in-law by name. The Hill Marias evade the inconvenience which this rule sometimes causes by using nicknames which most men and women have.

A few strict relationship taboos separate some relatives from each other. There is no question of marriage or any other type of sexual relationship between them and even close contacts are meticulously avoided. The first set of such rules of mutual avoidance govern a woman and her husbands elder brother or brothers. The kinship terminology suggests that the elder brothers of the husband are like her own elder brothers. A woman should avoid all real and classificatory elder brothers of her husband. A man should similarly avoid the wives of his younger brothers. This taboo is strictly enforced among the Hill Marias. The relatives coming in these categories should not talk to each other as far as possible and should not have any direct communication with each other. The two should not be alone at any time. The woman should not mention her husband's elder brother by name. She may serve them food or water, if such an occasion ever arises, but should do this with an air of indifference.

A second set of taboos governs the relationship between a man and the elder sisters of his wife and a woman and the husbands of her younger sisters' husband. In this case the rules are not so rigid as those mentioned, but Hill Marias believe that the relatives in these categories should not joke among themselves. They should also not touch each other and should not be alone together.

The third set of rules of mutual avoidance govern a man and his daughter-in-law and *vice-versa* and a man and his mother-in-law and *vice-versa*. The former of these two holds more sensitive relationship, and eventhough a man can talk with his daughter-in-law and a woman with her son-in-law, they should not become intimate and such occasions between them should be few and far and should be avoided as far as possible. They should also not be alone together.

In Bihar region, each and every caste has certain relatives between whom restraints are widely called for. They are to avoid some relations for joking relationship. This is known as avoidance-relationship. Such a type of relations are more restricted between a man and his younger brother's wife. The woman so related does not sit, talk, or even gossip with anybody in his presence. She is veiled when her husband's elder brother is present in the house. She also covers her face (*ghūnghaṭ*) before her father-in-law, but unveiles before her mother-in-law. A woman should be respected with her husband's mother and father and is required to maintain a sort of disciplined behaviour. She can neither change her dress nor suckle her children near the avoidance relations. Such behaviour might have been intended to overcome the bitterness and to avoid family friends. This also shows a sense of respect and regard to elders.

223 **अन्योन्याभाव**

Anyonyābhāva : mutual non-existence. It is also called *bheda* (difference).

224 **अन्वयव्यतिरेक**

Anvayavyatireka : presence of one implies the presence of another, and absence of one implies the absence of another (*darśana*), connected with and excluded from a thing.

225 **अन्वाधेयक**

Anvādheyaka : a kind of *strīdhana* obtained by a woman after the marriage from her husband or parents (*Smṛti*).

226 **अन्वाभिधानवाद**

Anvābhidhānavāda : doctrine of a school of Mīmāṁṣakas. According to it, words have a power to denote not only things but also their purport or connection along with them. In other words, words do not express their sense generally but connectedly. They reject the view of the *abhihitānvayavādins*, and deny the necessity of postulating the function of *tātparya*.

227 **अपकर्षण**

Apakarṣaṇa : (a) drawing roughly the sentiment and feelings through the actions and functions of the appropriate gesture (*NS*, IX. 175). (b) it also means taking off garments.

228 **अपक्रान्त करण**

Apakrānta karaṇa : derived from the thigh position of the *cārī*, *i.e.* *valana* of thighs and then a *kuñcita* foot is raised (*NS*, IV. 139b-140a, X.31, IX. 255-6). After making the *valita* thigh *apakrāntā cārī* is performed with the hands moved in harmony.

229 **अपक्रान्ताचारी**

Apakrāntā cārī : the crossed feet with one foot in *kuñcita* position. When Śakuntalā is stopped by the pet doe of the *āśrama*, she turns back to see it in the *apakrāntā cārī* position. Thus from the *valana* of thighs, *kuñcita* foot is raised and then taken sideways; *valana* of *ūrū* is suggested. According to Bharata "from a *valana* of the thighs the *kuñcita* foot is taken and dropped in this *cārī*" (*NS*, XI.31), but Abhinava says that the *valana* of thighs indicates *baddhā cārī* (*NS*, *Ibid).*

230 **अपचरित**

Apacarita : rebellious (*A*, 7.3.13-14; 7.4.7; 7.5. 12-15).

231 **अपचार**

Apacāra : improper conduct, disobedience to Śiva's will, beginningless impurity.

232 **अपजिह्विका**

Apajihvikā : removal or destruction of the tongue (A, 14. 1.22).

233 **अपदृष्टि**

Apadṛṣṭi : looking with disrespect, not looking.

234 **अपदेश**

Apadeśa : (a) statement of the views of others (*A*). (b) pretext, aim.

235 **अपपात्र**

Apapātra : (a) *Caṇḍālas*, etc. with whom no social intercourse was possible. (b) *rajakas* etc. born in the reverse order of marriage. (c) one ostracised by kinsmen for the commission of some degrading sin. Literally, one not allowed to use vessels out of which members of other castes are to take food (*Smṛti*).

236 **अपमान-संकेत**

Apamāna-saṁketa : insult signals. The way in which one human being can insult another are many and varied. The range and diversity of our derogatory signals is enormous - and that is even before we have begun to open our mouths.

Almost any action can operate as an insult signal if it is performed out of its appropriate context - at the wrong time or in the wrong place. But the specialized insult signals we are concerned with here are slightly different. They are actions which are always insulting, no matter what the context is. They set out right from the start, to be rude, and mock, defy, threaten, tease, snub or humiliate. They vary in intensity from mild rebuffs to attempts at savage intimidation.

They also vary from locality to locality. It can also happen that visitors to a strange locality can unwittingly offend the locals by unintentionally making a rude gesture. A knowledge of the different insult signals is therefore useful. To understand how they operate it is helpful to arrange them into a number of basic categories, such as: (I) Disinterest signals (ignoring, laughing, attacking); (II) Boredom signals (mock-yawn, deep sighing, repeated examination of the wrist-watch); (III) Impatience signals (strumming with the fingers, tapping with the foot); (IV) Superiority signals; (V) Deformed - compliment signals (sarcastic insults); (VI) Mock-discomfort signals (the go away sign, the thumb jerk); (VII) Mockery signals (laughing at someone); (VIII) Symbolic insults (the hand taps against the top of the head, meaning 'I am fed up'; Punjabi 'snake-tongue sign, in which the insulter flickers an extended fore-finger back and forth like the tongue of a snake)' *Yājñavalkya Smṛti (vākpāruṣyaprakaraṇa)* enumerates four types of insulting gestures.

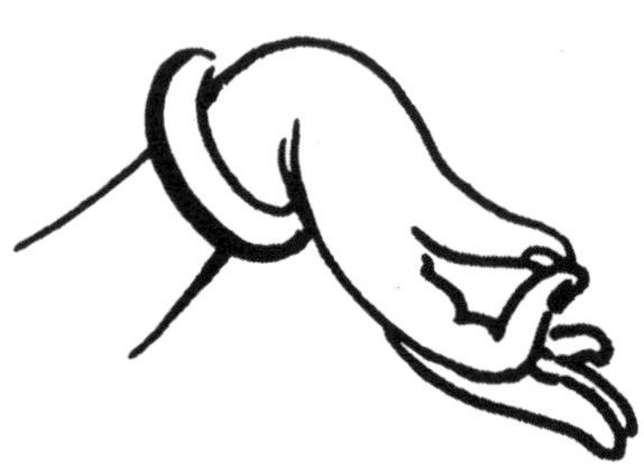

Fig. – (236)

Sometimes insulting gestures appear to have hurt the person no less than acts of physical assault. If the tribal society when the public is agitated, it treats the ruling class as *bhūt* (dead souls) fit only to be exorcised by the whiff of the winnowing fans and the noise of the drums. Far from being regarded as distinguished guests who brought prestige to a village by visiting it, they were unceremoniously rejected as pollutiing agents so that even the beds they had slept in had to be thrown away in a simulation of funerary rite. The tribes of Bastar cut the tree in which the elephant of the Diwan was tied during the Great Bhumkāl (Shukla, 1991). Far from being feared as the strong arm of the state Britishers were mocked and defied by the tribes flaunting their bows on them. In other words, what shocked de Brette was that these downtrodden and docile people had now audiciously lifted up their heads - a figure of speech signifying the very opposite of what bending and prostrating stood for. (Fig. 236)

237 **अपरा**

Aparā : material, mundane. *aparā-vidyā* is material knowledge. *Aparā śakti* is that aspect of *śakti* which confers a variety of material attainments upon the worshipper.

238 **अपरिग्रहा**

Aparigrahā : (a) a prostitute not attached to a particular individual. (b) *aparigrahā* is non-possession (*Yogasūtra*,II. 30-31).

239 **अपलाप**

Apalāpa : evasion, excuse, affection.

240 **अपवर्तित-त्रिका**

Apavartita-trikā : with their hips moving while women churning curd.

241 **अपवाद**

Apavāda : (a) special rule, exception (b) conflicting opinions. (c) false statement according to *Sāṁkhya*. (d) special injunction to bar out a false object according to the philosophers advocating the doctrine of *māyā*. (e) blame. (f) speaking ill of. (g) noise made by hunters.

242 **अपवारित**

Apavārita : secrecy, stage whisper. It is concealed speaking and is related to secrecy (*NŚ*, XXV. 89-90). It is indicated by a *tripatāka* hand - covering the speaker and the persons by whom it is not to be heard. In *apavāritam*, a secret is told to another by turning around. It is understood to be heard only by the person addressed. This is a talk in confidence (*Daśarūpaka* 1. 65-66). From the explanations given in the

NS, it seems that in *apavārita* the speech is concealed from all others on the stage, as it is connected with secrecy. According to Abhinava, the speech is concealed from all others as it is intended to be listened to by the particular character.

243 **अपवारितक**

Apavāritaka : it was revelation of a secret taking the spectators in confidence. It was conveyed by *tripatāka hasta* according to Bharata; but in later dramatic practice the convention was changed, perhaps for distinction, to the character turning his or her back to the stage, facing the audience, and delivering the line. The speech connected with secrecy falls under *citrābhinaya* (*NS*). The speech is concealed from all others as it is intended to be listened to by the particular character. Abhinava in *NS* III. 28): and *sarveṣām yannigūhyate eka eva śruṇuyāditi tadapavāritam* and *DR*(1.65) records: *rahasyaṃ kathyate anyasya* parāvṛtyāpavāritam. The *apavārita* makes a deliberate attempt to enlist the sympathy of the audience and becomes to that extent, a *kathana* (telling) of the *rahasya* (private opinion) to *anyasya* (another); and it differs from the *janāntika* because it makes a deliberate attempt to avoid over-hearing or conceal the talk from another on the stage and becomes, in that sense, a *rahasya kathana.*

244 **अपवार्य**

Apavārya : literally 'turning away (others)', this is a stage direction of frequent occurrence in Sanskrit dramas to indicate that a person is speaking 'apart, aside to another (opposed to *prakāśam* 'aloud') in such a manner as to be heard only by the person addressed. The technical gesture to indicate this is the *patāka* position of the hand. It is still prevalent in the Indian setting to stop some one to speak. When *apavārya* is used the character has actually to turn away and the speech is heard by one or more characters on the stage, excluding those to whom the "turning away" refers.

245 **अपविद्ध**

Apaviddha : rejected; one cast off by one's parents and accepted by another person as his son (*Smṛti*).

246 **अपविद्धक**

Apaviddhaka : churned up embrace; a type of embrace; piercing embrace where male is not involved: *Kṣepaṇam tu kevalam apaviddhakam nāma tadekatvādatraivāgatam* (*Jayamaṅgalā* commentary on *Kāmasūtra* 2.2.10).

247 **अपविद्ध-करण**

Apaviddha karaṇa : derived from *baddhā cārī;* a movement of the arms is also termed above; the hands mentioned in *Śukatuṇḍa* and *Kaṭakāmukha:* a crossing of the thighs in *baddhā cārī* is mentioned in the text (*NS*, IV. 64-65; IX. 60-62). The right hand in *Śukatuṇḍa* falling on the thigh and the left hand is held on the breast. It is used in gesticulation jealousy and anger.

248 **अपविद्ध-बाहु**

Apaviddha bāhu : the loose arm (*NS*, IX. 205-206).

249 **अपविद्ध-सूची**

Apaviddha sūcī : a type of hand-gesture. We find this position very often in the early Gupta period.

250 **अपविद्ध-हस्त**

Apaviddha hasta : circular arms. In *Śākuntalam* (IV), Sānumatī suggests a descent from the sky through the use of this arm - gesture and tossing of the ends of her clothes (*NS*, XII. 94 -95).

251 **अपवेष्टित-हस्तकरण**

Apaveṣṭita-hasta-karaṇa : The rounding up style of hand; also known as *āveṣṭita.* When fingers beginning from the fore-finger round up other fingers inside one by one, it is called *apaveṣṭita karaṇa* of a hand (*NS*, IX. 198-204).

252 **अपशकुन**

Apaśakuna : bad omen. Bad omens in ancient India might occur repeatedly during one single day: when a dove perched on the roof, it was certainly the harbinger of some misfortune. Bad luck was presaged also by the presence in the vicinity of the home of bees making honey or ants building their heeps (Hiraṇyakeśin, *Gṛhya Sūtra* 1.5, 17.5); and it was an unlucky sign when the right eyelid began to tremble nervously (*Raghu*, XIV. 49 - 50). The worst omen now a Hindu can possibly imagine is a cat crossing one's path. It pretends death and destruction. Even those Hindus who have discarded most of the religious beliefs of their community, are mortally frightened of a cat crossing their path while going on a journey; they would rather give up the journey or postpone it to some other date than continue after being forbidden by so terrible an omen.

253 **अपशब्द**

Apaśabda : slander, ungrammatical form.

254 **अपसृत-पार्श्व**

Apasṛta pārśva : the drawn away sides. In the *apasṛta* pose, both the sides of the waist should be placed in their original position, opposite to *vivartita.* It symbolizes returning (*NS*, X. 10-17) In it there is the revesion of *trika* from the *nivartita*

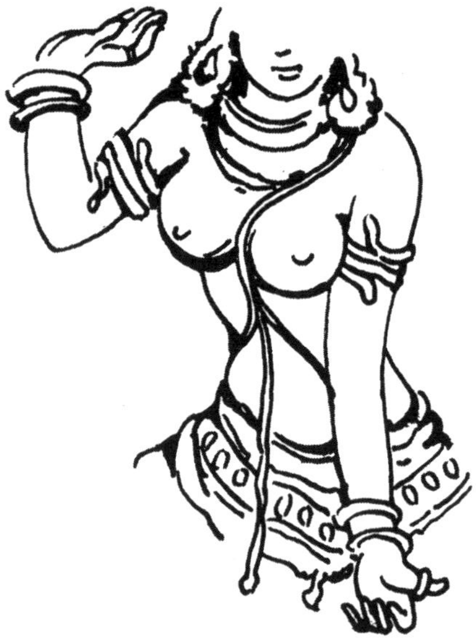

Fig. – (254)

position, *i.e.* turning around from the sideways position. (Fig. 254)

255 **अपस्मार**

Apasmāra : epilepsy. loss of recollection, loss of remembrance. One of the transitory states of mind. It is manifested by throbbing, sighing, trembling, running, falling down, perspiration, foaming in the mouth, motionlessness, licking lips with tongue and the like. *Apasmāra* (22 nd among the 33 *vyabhicārī bhāvas*) or epilepsy is a mental disease characterized by excess of suffering due to separation, or the excess of any other kind of fear or disgust, or caused by the evil influences of the planets.

In psychology, any group of nervous disorders characterized by either focal or generalized convulsions is known as epilepsy. The chief forms are *petit mal,* in which there may be only an extremely transitory loss of consciousness accompanied by blinking of the eyes or an automatic act.

Apasmāra-puruṣa is the demon-dwarf, who is the personification of epilepsy (*Suśruta*). Thus *apasmāra-puruṣa* (*i.e.* Śiva) is a symbol of spiritual darkness. The demon is symbolic of life's blindness, man's ignorance.

256 **अपस्यन्दिता-चारी**

Apasyanditā cārī : both feet in *samapāda* positions; reverse of the *spandita* posture; the other foot is put forward five *tālas* away from the first. This is explained by Abhinava as a reverse of *syanditā*(*NS*,X.26).

257 **अपहसित**

Apahasita : vulgar laughter, silly or unprovoked laughter. It shakes the whole body and causes tears to appear in the eyes. It is the laughter of the inferior class of people. It is one of the six *anubhāvas* of *hāsa.* It is the laughter on unsuitable occasions. It represents tears in the eyes, shoulders and head violently shaking.

Bharata in his *NS* has divided humour (*hāsya*) into three categories: *uttama* (excellent), *madhyama* (medium) and *adhama* (base). *Apahasita* is the first of the two types of the *adhama hāsya*, the second one being *atihasita* which transcends even *apahāsya* in its physical manifestations and crudeness. Indulged in by persons of low birth and culture, it shakes the whole body and causes tears to appear in the eyes. No attempt is made to restrain it (Garg, 1992. 542).

258 **अपहस्त**

Apahasta : the hand placed on the neck to drive out a person; also known as *galahasta.*

259 **अपहस्तित**

Apahastita : removed by hand, removed by force.

260 **अपहास**

Apahāsa : 'mocking laugh' (*Rāmāyaṇa*).

261 **अपह्नव**

Apahnava : denial; form of speech and thought (*Bṛhaddevatā* 144-60), irrelevant talk.

262 **अपाङ्क्तेय**

Apāṅkteya : non-diner. Those who are not fit to sit and eat in the same row as Brāhmaṇa diners; or those defiling a row of diners at *sraddha* on various grounds such as bodily and mentally defects, and disease, belonging to certain avocations, moral lapses, being guilty of crime, being followers of unorthodox systems, or being inhabitants of certain countries.

263 **अपाङ्ग**

Apāṅga : the outer corner of the angle of eye (*Mbh.*); God of love.

264 **अपाङ्गनेत्र**

Apāṅga-netra : having eyes with beautiful outer corners.

265 **अपाङ्गविक्षेप**

Apāṅga-vikṣepa : the phrase in *Kādambarī*(p. 257) denoting the eye-gesture.

266 **अपादान**

Apādāna : the limit of separation; ablative case (grammar).

267 **अपि च**

Api ca : these link-words between stanzas in lyrical passages of the drama are common enough (*Priyadarśikā*, 1.3; 3. 11-12). They were probably spoken in a different tone in the melodic recitative, and indicate generally a change in thought and metre. We can imagine that such pause must have been rather effective rhetorically. Similar to the use of *kiṃ ca* (and likewise) or again to indicate a contrast of *atha vā* (or rather, and yet). we can find its impact on the Hindi conversation: *aur kyā*. This type of utterance is very prominent in Hindi TV serial 'Musaddilāl 'where the heroine has the catch-word: *aur kyā*.

268 **अपोह**

Apoha : removal; excluding all things not coming under the category in point. *Nīlatva* (blueness) excludes all things that are not *nīla*.*Apoha* meant ability to work out the implications of what had been said (*Amarakośa*, 1.5. 70).

269 **अप्रमा**

Apramā : non-valid presentative knowledge. According to *Nyāya* it is divided into doubt *(saṁśaya)*, error (*bhrama* or *viparyaya*) and hypothetical argument (*tarka*).

270 **अप्राप्तफला**

Aprāptaphalā : the girl who has not attained puberity (*A*, 4.12.1).

271 **अभङ्ग**

Abhaṅga : It is that form of standing pose, in which the plumb line or the centre line, from the crown head to a point midways heels, passes slightly to the right of the navel. It indicates the slight shift of the weight to one side and the vertical is drawn from a different point. The distance of the two big toes ,nd the knees from the median (*madhyasūtra*) is also different. The emotional quality of the pose does not suggest complete concentration and poise but, instead, a slight deviation from it. The slightly dynamic, the erotic and delicately heroic figures are depicted in this pose. Gaurī or Kodaṇḍa Rāma be cited as examples. The deflection from the plumb line is relatively slight here; the weight is shifted to show the point of unrest but not of movement: here there is only a slight flexion of one knee. Although the plumb line (*sūtra*) passes from the crown of the head to a point midway between the heels, it presses through the right of the navel and not through the navel as in *samabhaṅga* pose. There is thus a shift of weight, which results in either a change in the position of hip or the placing of foot, or sometimes by the deviation of torso to one side. But the placing of the feet is far the most important method of depicting the *abhaṅga* pose in both dancing and sculpture: the *tryaśra* placing one foot (*NS*, XII. 163b-164b), without the knee bend or controlled *udvāhita* (*NS*, IX. 247-8) movement of the hips results in this stance: the sides move but slightly. The *āyata* and *avahittha sthānas* in dancing are the examples of the *abhaṅga* pose. The flowing figures of the verandahas of the Rāmeśvara cave in Elura are faithful representations of the *abhaṅga* pose, full of rhythm and yet suggestive of the unique pose.

272 **अभय-पताकहस्त**

Abhaya-patāka-hasta : we find the instance of this type of hand-gesture in Amarāvatī sculpture.

273 **अभयमुद्रा**

Abhaya mudrā : Many scenes from a ceiling of the Dilvārā temple Mount Ābū, present a variety of poses in *abhaya mudrā* with clear *patāka hasta*. It denotes blessing where left hand is open on the lap, right hand is raised infront of the chest with the fingers and thumb half-extended and with the palm facing forward.

Abhaya mudrā is a symbol of protection or shelter. (a) This is one of the *mudrās* or gestures. In this posture, the right hand is shown as slightly elevated and bent with palm turned outwards, the fingers being stretched out and raised. This

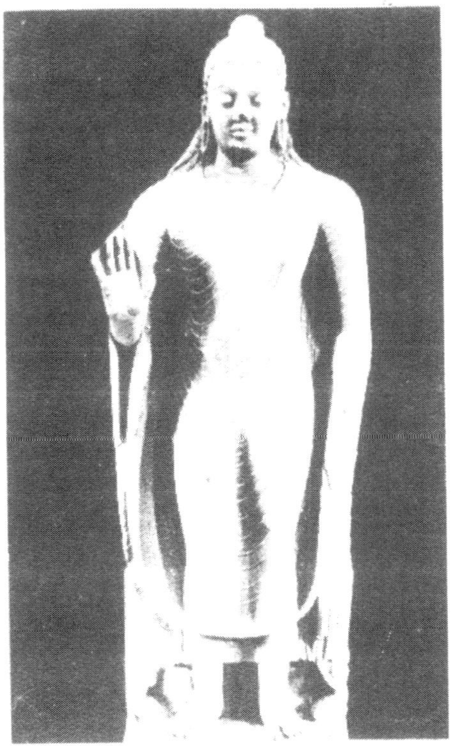

Fig. – (273)

mudrā can be compared with the expressions like *abhaya-hasta,* and *abhaya-śāsana.* In the former the palm is out stretched as in *abhaya-mudrā* and the latter is a gesture of assurance of protection, patronage, safety and security. The *abhaya mudrā* was employed in Buddhist iconography. It can be compared with other *mudrās* like the *varada* and *capeṭa-dāna,* from which it should be distinguished. In the *varada,* the palm or the hand is out-stretched downwards with fingers pointing down while, in the *capeṭa-dāna,* the palm is extended menacingly in the position of giving a slap. (b) in iconography it means hand-pose of the right hand indicating protection (no-fear). The entire palm with straightened fingers is held in front of the devotee, assuring him that he will be taken care of. Compare *varada-mudrā* and *abhaya-hasta.*

Abhaya-mudrā is an iconic *mudrā* depicting gesture of protection. The hand showing the *mudrā* should be slightly elevated and upturned, the palm facing outward, the fingers outstretched and raised. (Fig. 273)

274 **अभय-वरदहस्त**

Abhaya-varada-hasta : a type of hands gesture mentioned by *Bālarāmabharata.*

275 **अभय-शासनमुद्रा**

Abhaya-śāsana-mudrā : It is a gesture of assurance of protection, patronage, safety or security. (Fig. 275)

276 **अभय-हस्त**

Abhaya-hasta : the hand is invariably placed near the ear with the finger pointing upwards, near the chin or just below the chin. The other hand is extended down on its own side. The palm is out-stretched.

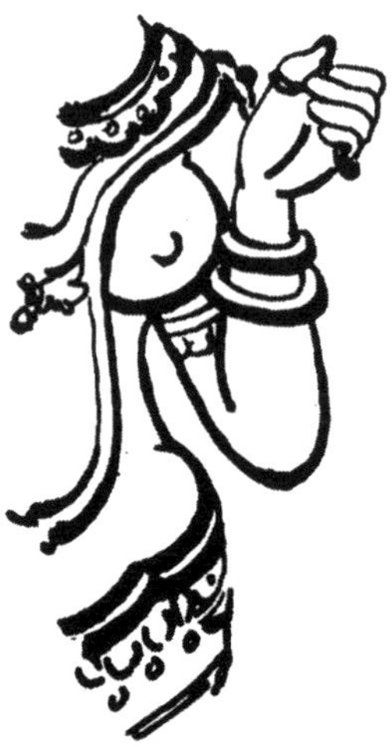

Fig. – (275)

277 **अभाव**

Abhāva : non-existence. It stands for all negative facts, and is of four kinds; *viz. prāgabhāva, dhvam§sābhāva, atyantābhāva* and *anyonyābhāva.* The first three together are called *saṁsargābhāva.* Non-existence is considered to be a negative category in the *Nyāya-vaiśeṣika.*

278 **अभिचार**

Abhicāra : sorcery. The magic spells or rites for malevolent purposes, *e.g.* killing an enemy (*Tantra, Smṛti*). *Abhicāra* is for the destruction of an enemy or the gain of prosperity. The *Agni Purāṇa* (262. 24-25) says that in sorcery the following may be used-oil, particles of corn, mustard, poison, blood and thorny faggots. Rites for performing black deeds and causing harm to others; for example *māraṇa* or killing, *vaśikaraṇa* or hypnotizing, *stambhana* or arresting, *uccāṭana* or driving away, *vidveṣaṇa* or creating bad blood and so on (*Śāradātilaka* XXIII. 123-25; *Śaktisaṁgama, kālī* VIII. 102-105).

279 **अभिज्ञान**

Abhijñāna : (a) a pass of recognition, an identity card (*A,* 2..21.2); sign, token (*Rāmāyaṇa).* (b) higher powers attained by the *arhats.* These are six in number: miraculous power (*ṛddhi*), heavenly ear (*dibbasotadhātu*), thought - reading (*paracittañāna*), knowledge of previous birth (*pubbenivasañāna),* heavenly eye (*dibbacakkhu*) and knowledge of extinction of one's own impurities (*āsavānam khayañāna*). (Fig. 279)

280 **अभितप्ता-दृष्टि**

Abhitaptā dṛṣṭi : a type of *sañcārī-bhāva-dṛṣṭi,* distressed glance; a glance with slowly moving eye-balls as per the movement of the eye-lids, indicating pain and distress. It suggests accidental hurt, distress, discourage and despondency.

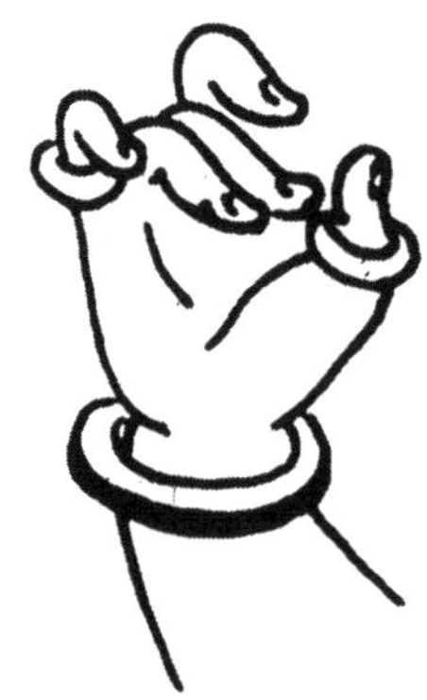

Fig. – (279)

281 **अभिधा**

Abhidhā : denotation; the function by which a word denotes its primary or conventional sense; literal meaning; word expressing the literal meaning. cf. *vācaka*. Primary meaning, literal sense. It is the inherent potency of a word to mean an object and a word possessing such meaning is also called *vācaka* or *śakta*. According to the *Nyāya*, the relation between a word and its meaning may be direct or indirect. The former is called *abhidhā* and the latter is known as lakṣaṇā.

Abhidhā is used in poetics to distinguish what is seen as the basic or central conceptual or referential meaning of words or signs, without the connotations or metamorphic meanings which they can acquire in particular contexts. In popular parlance we speak of a word's literal meaning.

282 **अभिधान**

Abhidhāna : designation.

283 **अभिधेय**

Abhidheya : designated; to be named; literal meaning to be expressed; also known as *vācya;* denotable thing. (Fig.283)

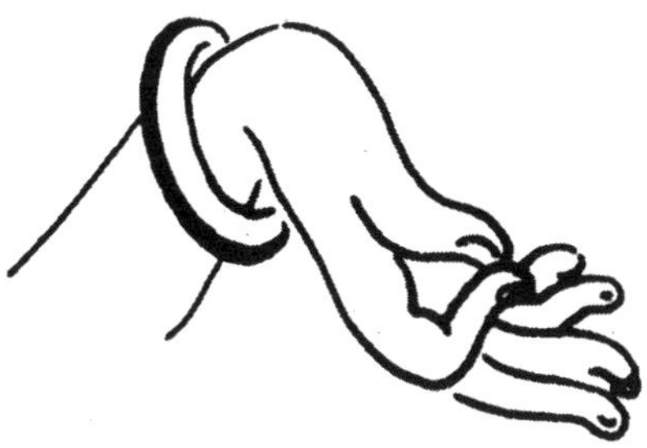

Fig. – (283)

284 **अभिनन्दन**

Abhinandana : methods of greeting. The method of greeting depends upon the social status of the persons meeting. When a man of very low position meets a person of very high rank, the former is expected to fall flat to the ground with hands folded in front. This custom of greeting is still in vogue in South India. The subjects who came with petitions to Zamindars and petty chieftains of the south were expected to greet their Highnesses in this manner. In Malabar such petitioners were not to wear upper garments, but appeared in loin cloths. The speech of the petitioner always was in terms of the meanest expressions when referring to himself and in the highest when referring to his patron. High officials of the state were allowed a little more freedom when visiting a Maharaja; they could come within a reasonable distance of His Highness, fold their hands at the chest and bow down to the ground. These methods of greeting were enforced only on the subjects of Maharaja. Others, for obvious reasons, were allowed to greet His Highness in any respectable manner prevalent among themselves. The Maharajas, however, are now an extinct race, and ministers have taken their place.

A son greets his father usually by bowing down and touching his feet, and raising the hand to his head. A young lady may also greet her parents in this way. In certain parts of India the father touches the feet of his daughters and daughters are not allowed to touch the feet of their fathers, while they usually touch the feet of their mothers. The same method of touching the feet is adopted by young men greeting their mothers, pupils, their teachers and laymen greeting venerable religious heads. Before the man touches the feet, the person greeted usually raises the supplicant by the hand, pretending that he is not so great a personage as to be greeted in this fashion.

Among equals, the usual method of greeting in North India or rather Hindustan proper is to repeat the name of Rāma twice thus: "Rām Rām". While uttering these words, the right hand is brought to the chest twice and the head slightly bowed. Among the Ārya-samājists the method of greeting is to fold the palms in front of the chest and say "Namaste" meaning "greeting to you". When done by ladies, this method of greeting looks much more graceful than the western method of shaking hand, and now it has become increasingly popular all over India. A variant form of it is *namaskār* which is used by the announcers of TV and radio also. Western method of shaking hands, was popular in the colonial period. Now it is popular among the elite class only. Among the better classes of people, educated in western style, wishing in English fashion and shaking hands are becoming common. But occasionally one comes across a highly educated Hindu lady who shows horror of touching the hand of a male. This is however an exception and Hindu ladies with modern education usually shake hands with men to whom they are introduced.

Brāhmaṇs greeting each other clasp the hands and in some parts of India say "*salām*". This method of greeting known as *namaskāra* (q.v.). The Brāhmaṇa is of course supreme in Hindu society. He never bows his head in salutation to any one who is not a Brāhmaṇa, and acknowledges with a benediction the greetings of all other classes. It is customary to greet a Brāhmaṇa on confrontation with folded hands touching the forehead and uttering *"praṇāma paṇḍitajī"*. This is to be maintained by all other castes in Bihar.

To a married Hindu woman her husband is like a god, and she should touch his feet before she starts for any good performance.

When two Gond friends or relatives meet, they clasp each other in their arms and lean against each shoulder in turn. A man will then touch the knees of an elder male relative with his fingers, carrying them afterwards to his own forehead. This is equivalent to falling at the other person's feet, and is a token of respect shown to all elder male relations and also to son-in-law, sister's husband, and a *samādhi*, that is the father of son or daughter-in-law. The term of salutation is *johār*, and they say it to each other.

Another method of greeting is that each should put his finger under the other's chin and then kiss it. Women also do this when they meet or a younger woman meeting an elder one will touch her feet and the elder will kiss her on the forehead and on each cheek. If they have not met for sometime they will weep. It is said that Baigas will kiss each other in the cheek when meeting, both men and women. A Gond will kiss and caress his wife after marriage, but as soon as she has a child he drops the habit and never does it again. When husband and wife meet after an absence of time, the wife touches her husband's feet with her hand and carries it to her forehead, but the husband makes no demonstration. The Gonds kiss their children. Among the Maria Gonds the wife is said not to sleep on a cot in her husband's house but on the ground; nor will a woman even sit on a cot in her own house, as if any male relative happened to be in the house, it would be disrespectful to him. A woman will not utter the name of her husband, his elder or young brothers, or his elder brother's sons. A man will take neither his wife's name nor that of her elder sister (Russell and Hiralal, pp. 131-32).

285 **अभिनय**

Abhinaya : acting bringing forth, dramatic performance, gesticulation. Acting is defined in Sanskrit dramaturgy as the imitation of a situation or action. It is treated under a four-fold division , *viz vācika* (vocal), *āṅgika* (physical, where the action is conveyed through bodily movement), *sāttvika* (emotive, in which the actor imitates the emotions warranted by the situation) and *āhārya* (communicative, which is communicated through medium of clothes, ornaments, etc).

A skilled professional actor acquires the capacity to use NV elements to portray character, emotion, attitudes - elements for which, for most of us, would not be under our control. A stage actor can, for example weep and laugh to order, make his voice crack with grief or roar with anger. Apart of social-skills training is concerned with helping us to become better actors, in the sense of being more aware of and more able to control behaviour which carries messages for others. Similarly, on receiving end, we can learn to be more aware of and to interpret behaviour of others. Thus, for example, when we are very close to a person we notice changes in facial expression or small movements that a stranger may not notice. Social - skills training is also concerned with teaching us to read others with greater accuracy, even if they are strangers.

The reason that people have less control over some bodily movements than other is simply that they are less accustomed to paying attention to them. For example we are relatively unaware of the movements of the feet or hands. Skilled actors, who are taught through direct study with feed back to monitor and control emotional expression in all parts of the body, show less "leakage" than ordinary people do.

Literally, *abhi* means towards and *ni* means to lead. *abhinaya* is that which leads or carries toward. As a technical term in dramaturgy it covers everything than an actor does and uses on stage in order to convey the meaning of the play to the spectators and evoke a joyful consciousness in them. The gesticulation is two-fold, which the *NS* treats under *dharmī - lokadharmī i.e.* the realistic practice and *nāṭya-dharmī* i.e. the theatrical or conventional practice.

The *abhinaya* has three aspects - *śākhā, aṅkura* and *nṛtta.*

Thus the *NS* has treated the *abhinaya* in detail. The *sāmānyābhinaya* and *citrābhinaya* are dealt with in *NS* after the four *abhinayas (Vācikābhinaya, āṅgikābhinaya, sāttvikābhinaya* and *āhāryābhinaya*) are described. It is clear that in course of time the conventions regarding the gestures were multiplied and these additions were also included duly. To illustrate, in the *āṅgikābhinaya* we have *śākhā, nṛtta* and *aṅkura* as the three aspects. But in the *sāmānyābhinaya* we have six aspects, e.g., *vākyābhinaya, sūcā, aṅkura, śākhā, nāṭyāyita* and *nivṛttyaṅkura.* Representation of the various ideas is treated in *citrābhinaya* in addition to the earlier treatment. The conventional *abhinaya* gained more prominence in the field of gesticulation. We find that in later works the uses of hand-gestures are much more in number. Whether every word is to be gesticulated or the purport of the sentence, depended on the nature of the character. Kallinātha (*SR*, ch. VII. p. 716) while describing the gesticulation of the *nāndī* verse in *Vikramorvaśīya,* in his commentary on *SR*, states the view that the gesticulation of the words as such only is enough, and by gesticulating the original word's termination is also gesticulated. It started from the imitation of the things and went on in a manner in which the likeness of the object became sometimes fainter. Such conventions came to be established which were based only on the interpretation of the expert. They included the gesticulation of abstract ideas as well.

The *NS* (XXII. 75-80) describes the dramatic representation as two-fold: *ābhyantara* (regular) and *bāhya* (not following the conventions). In the former the physical movements are not violent, hurried and complex. They are controlled by tempo, rhythm, and the measurements of *kalās*. It has the words clearly uttered, without any harshness. The latter is of opposite type, *i.e.* the movements etc. are according to one's free will, unaccompanied by instrumental and vocal music. Thus the *ābhyantara* follows the conventions laid down by *śāstra* and the *bāhya* does not follow them. Those who have not studied under a teacher and thus are ignorant of the *śāstra* perform *bāhyanāṭya*.

(b)—In iconography, three varieties of *abhinaya*, excluding 'vācika', are adapted. The disposition of the hands and fingers (like protection-giving *abhaya*, boon-bestowing *varada*, slap - administering *capeṭikā-dāna*, or warning *tarjanī-mudrā*), the flexions and movements - suggestions illustrate the first variety. The peculiar ornaments (like lotus for benevolent deities) illustrate the second variety. The *sāttvika* variety, however, is not often in evidence. The facial expressions of Indian icons are highly stylized and do not admit of readily recognizable mental states. The standard expression is tranquil or *śānta*. But we do find icons where smile (*smita*), bemusement (*vismaya*) or anger (*krodha*) are shown, mainly in the eyes and the lips.

286 **अभिनय-अङ्ग**

Abhinaya-aṅga : major limbs of gesticulation. Bharata has treated *abhinaya* under four-fold divisions: *vācika, āṅgika, sāttvika* and *āhārya*. Vipradāsa does not state the *āhārya abhinaya* separately. He refers to the three others as resulting from body, mind and speech. The style of action connected with mental states ultimately results in physical gestures. So the forms of gesticulation which remain chiefly are two: *āṅgika* (physical) and *vācika* (verbal). *Vācika* which is the means of understanding the meaning is not (fit to be) principal. Hence *āṅgika* remains only as the principal one which is adorned or perfected by *vācika*. This view of Vipradāsa (*Bharatakośa*, pp. 23-24) tells us how *āṅgikābhinaya* got prominence in the art of representation.

287 **अभिनयदर्पण**

Abhinaya-darpaṇa : is a famous work written by Nandikeśvara which completely deals with gestures. In addition to common examples of artistic gestures, as discussed in the *NS*, the *Abhinaya-darpaṇa* includes some special gestures, not referred to in *NS*, which circumscribes all the spheres of human behaviour.

288 **अभिनयदर्पणप्रकाश**

Abhinayadarpaṇa-prakāśa : written by Yadunātha Rājasiṁha of Orissa in the eighteenth century being the last work of Indian Gesturology.

289 **अभिनीति**

Abhinīti : expressive gesticulation; cf. *abhinaya*. (Fig. 289).

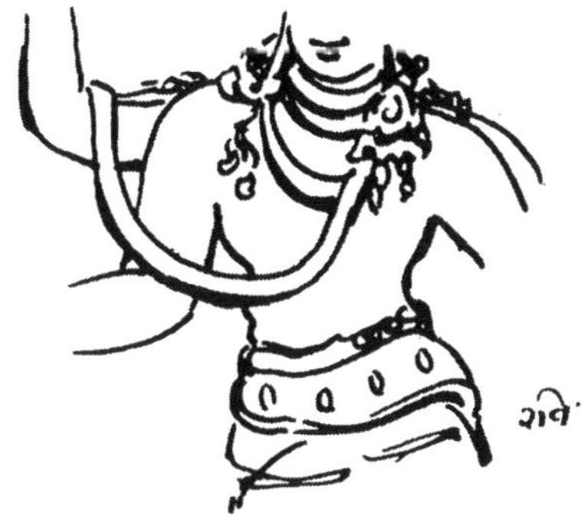

Fig. – (289)

290 **अभिमन्त्रण**

Abhimantraṇa : (a) invocation of secret *mantras*. (b) talks at love-sport.

291 **अभिमुखम्**

Abhimukham : in the presence of. When we say *abhimukham*, we talk about "face-to-face" communication. We use the face more than any other part of the body when we speak. For one thing, whenever possible, we "face" each other when conversing. The face is one part of the body that we do not usually cover up with clothing; its interesting, expressive changes are open and exposed. Cosmetics provide no adequate mask for one's facial expressions except the veils in some sections of Indian women.

292 **अभिरञ्जन-कला**

Abhirañjana-kalā : the art of entertainment (*Śukranītisāra*, 4. 308-11). It should be clear that if the purpose of the artists or the person was to entertain the public, the response they hoped to achieve was enjoyment—not laughter, necessarily, but amusement certainly. The kind of message was sent for fun, and the reaction desired was pure pleasure, or might be sometimes impure pleasure, but pleasure for sure.

Those were the four goals or purposes for which messages were produced according to *Śukranītisāra*.

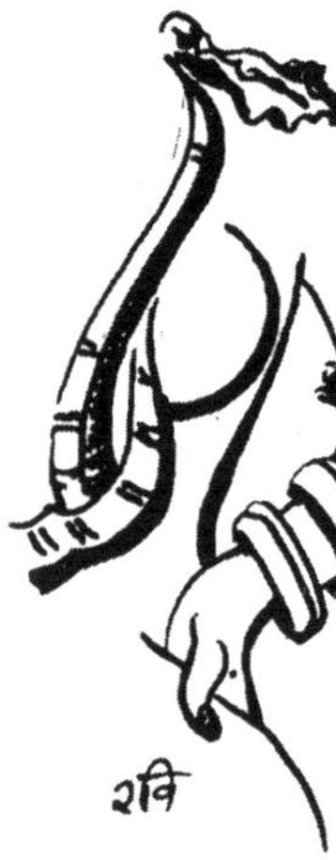

Fig. – (292)

293 **अभिलाष**

Abhilāṣa : longing, pining. The first stage in love-lorn condition. In *Śākuntalam* (I), the king looks at Śakuntalā longingly. It represents the initial stage in love-lorn condition. When physical love is aroused in a person at the very first sight or acquaintance, direct or indirect, it creates an acute longing for quick union. (Fig. 293)

294 **अभिवादन**

Abhivādana : salutation or bowing to a person. There are three kinds of salutations: *nitya* (obligatory every day), *naimittika* (to be done on certain occasions), and *kāmya* (to be done only if a person has certain rewards in view). A Brāhmaṇa should salute stretching forward his right arm on the level with his ears. But a Kṣatriya should do it by joining both the palms at the level with his chest, a Vaiṣya on level with his waist and a Śūdra on level with his feet. The salutation shall be by joining both the palms (*Ap. Dh,. S.* 1.2.5. 12-17).

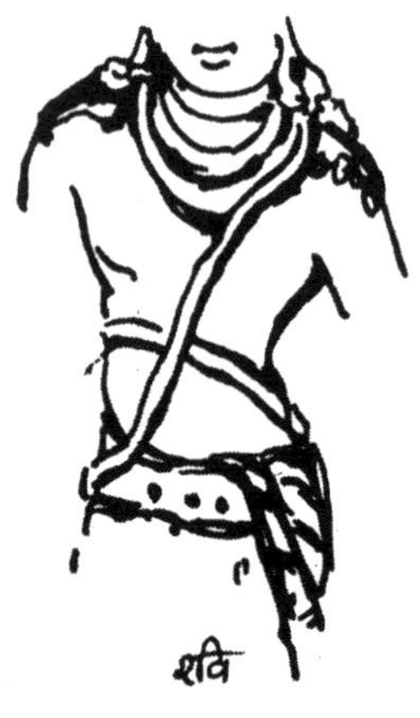

Fig. – (293)

A salutation display demonstrates that we wish someone well, or, at the very least, that we wish them no harm. It transmits signals of friendliness or the absence of hostility. It does this at peak moments - when someone is arriving on the scene, departing from it, or dramatically changing their social role. We salute their comings, their goings and their transformations, and we do it with rituals of greeting, farewell and celebration. (*Aṣṭādhyāyī,* 8.2.104).

The gestures of obeisance have figured prominently in the *Dharmaśāstra* as a key to a better life. Why, for instance, must a youth leave his seat and greet an older man ? 'For', says Manu, 'the vital airs of a young man mount upwards to leave his body when an elder person approaches; but by rising, prostrating and saluting he recovers them'(II. 120). There are many verses in that text devoted to the virtues of rising, prostrating, clasping of feet, etc. as indicative of subordinate status. And the authority of this language of body is derived not only from sacerdotal prescriptions but also from the power of state. Thus according to Abūl-Fazl (166-7), kings 'made regulations for the manner in which people are to show their obedience'. This was meant to promote 'true humility'. For instance, *korniś,* an approved mode of salutation at the Mughal court, signified that the saluter 'placed his head.... (the seat of the senses and the mind) into the hand of humility, giving it to the royal assembly as a present', and another, known as *taslīm,* that he was 'ready to give himself as an offering'.

The substitution of Mughal royalty by the British made little differnce to such feudal kinesics. They continued to operate as status markers in colonial India too. "When a Coorg meets an elder on a ritual occasion" wrote Srinivas, "he has to salute the latter by bending the upper half of his body and touching the elder's feet thrice with both hands. After each touch the younger man takes his hands to his forehead, where he folds them together." This, he remarked, was not very different from the form of salutation one adopted towards a deity (1952: 47,96). In fact, variations of 'bodily automatism' of this kind featured in all homologous relations - between father and son, husband and wife, landlord and tenant, high caste and low caste. In Madhya Pradesh, for instance, it was customary for the wife to demonstrate her fidelity by bending down before her husband at a distance and touching the earth with her fingers. A *Balāhī,* ranked as one of the lowliest in rural society in this region, would replicate this movement on meeting a Brāhmaṇa, bending forward to touch the ground and lifting his hands, palms folded to his forehead. Elsewhere, in Orissa, a Bauri untouchable had to adopt much the same self-debasing posture under similar circumstances. 'When we passed by higher-caste people', said Muli to the visiting anthropologist, 'we crouched so that one hand touched the ground, we walked by in that position, so that one hand touched the ground; we walked by in that position, so that our faces were toward the ground'. (Freeman, 85).

It was not the rise and fall of empires but the violence of the masses which alone interrupted from time to time this age-old avowal of subservience by gestures. Yet another index of the *adharottara*, this might have been the reversal feared by the dominant brahminical culture when among the many topsy-turvy features of the mythical *yugānta* (epoch's end) is counted Śūdras who were *jitākṣa* (controlled in the movement of their eyes), not unlike, presumably, their superiors in the *varṇa* hierarchy (Tararatna 1910, 58:59)

Ancient law-givers of India laid down specific norms and forms of salutation which vary from caste to caste. Superiority of the Brāhmạs and the inferiority of the Śūdras are clearly mirrored in the various modes of greetings and greeting responses prescribed for them in Sanskrit scriptures. The *Āpastamba Dharmasūtra* says, "a Brāhmaṇ shall salute by stretching forward his right hand on a level with his ear. A Kṣatriya holding it at level with his chest, a *Vaiśya* on a level with his waist. A Śūdra shall bend forward with the joined hand held low." According to an old Sanskrit text the Brāhmaṇa in salutation is to be addressed "*ehi*", the Kṣatriya as "*adrava*" and the Vaiśya "*agahi*". The Śūdra may be called by any loud sound (*ibid.* p. 208)". Manu ordains that while greeting, one should ask a Brāhmaṇa after his happiness, a Kṣatriya after his welfare, a Vaiśya after his prosperity, a Śūdra after his health. So rigid were the norms of greeting in those days that if a Brāhmaṇa unknowingly saluted a low caste man, he was required, according to *Atri-Smṛti,* to take bath immediately and get himself pure by taking *ghṛtam* (clarified butter).

The Indian custom of wishing or complementing has a distinct etiquette of its own. In the first place, while greeting or wishing, caste distinctions had to be observed with great care (*Bṛhaddharma Purāṇa, Uttara Khaṇḍa,* 1.35). For example, it was customary and imperative for the members of the lower caste to first extend their respect to a member of higher caste (*Ibid.* 1.34). Thus, a Brāhmaṇa was to be respected by the members of the lower castes who in return received his blessings. At the same time, it was not necessary for a Brāhmaṇa to give his blessings through words to a Śūdra (*Ibid,* 1.35). Then again, there were various ways of paying respects. Alberuni's statement that the Indians shook hands in different ways, obviously in a manner unlike Arabs, is worthy of notice (Sachau, vol. I, p. 182). But in India, there were several ways of expressing respect and greeting the elders. The most ordinary or common method of greeting was a *praṇāma* with folded hands, though other methods of greeting like *daṇḍavat-pranāma* or *sāṣṭāṅga-pranāma, abhivādana, namaste,* etc. were also in vogue (*History of Dharmaśāstra,* II, pt. I, p. 337) Generally, *namaskāra* was offered only to deities and spiritual leader (*Ibid,* 346), *daṇḍavat,* literally meaning to fall down like a staff, was a method of prostrating oneself before the *guru, purohita* or a teacher (*Ibid.* 342). The *sāṣṭāṅga* method of *praṇāma* involving touching the ground with the eight limbs of the body before an elder and was generally extended to the latter when he graciously obliged a person by a visit to his house. Touching the feet of the parents, both daily and on return from abroad, was a practice common to most of the *dvijas, i.e.* the Brāhmaṇa, Kṣatriyas and the Vaiṣyas (*Ibid,* II. I. 335).

Yet there were exceptions to some of these traditional ways of greeting. For example, a person paying a visit to his preceptor's house was expected to touch the feet of his *guru* and his wife. Yet, if the lady was young he was not to touch her feet but prostrate himself at a respectful distance or touch the dust some distance away from her feet (Kullukā, on *Manu,* II. 212, 216). Similarly, one was not expected to greet an elder brother with his mouth full of betel. Other restrictions are also worthy of notice. Meeting a lady, if she was the wife of one who is younger to him, the latter is not to take notice of her presence and avoid looking at her (*B.P.Uttara,* 1.4.3).

Similarly, younger brother's wife, son's wife is to be scrupulously avoided for being touched (*Ibid).* Another note-worthy feature is in regard to paying respect to the elders belonging to the lower castes. Even a *Śūdra,* if aged, is to be honoured by rising from the seat (*Hist. of Dharmaśsāstra,* II. I. 339). It is a matter of etiquette to prefix honourable words like *śrī, devī,* etc., before referring someone by name (*Ibid,* 344).

In Baiga society, the mode of greeting and salutation is regulated to some extent by kinship. When two *samadhī* meet, they catch each other's arms, pull them to and fro three times and say *Rām-Rām,* stooping slightly and touching each other's knees with the right hand. Two women, if they are *samdhin,* clasp each other's arms and touch each other's knees, but do not kiss each other. If they are drinking, they greet one another with *johār* instead of *Ram-Ram.*

When a husband meets his wife, he gives her no greetings and takes no notice of her if other people are around.

When a son meets his father he touches his feet, and the father raises him lightly under the chin, making a slight clucking noise with his tongue.

When two brothers meet, they clasp each other's arms, the younger touches the elder brother's feet and the elder one touches the younger brother's chin.

When a son-in-law meets his father-in-law, the greeting is the same, but he says: *Māmājī-Rām-Rām.*

When a girl comes home after a long journey, she falls at her mother's feet, the mother kisses her lightly on either side of the head, and they sit down opposite each other and both weep loudly for sometime (Elwin, 1937: 184)

In the village India, particularly in Gwalior region the mode of salutation is as follows; While passing by an old man, younger people first salute the older by saying, "Rām-Rām" or "Rāma-Rāma-Dādā", depending upon the classificatory relationship. No formal mode of salutation is practised among the close friends or among the younger boys.

Generally, the formal salutaion is much in vogue at the inter-caste-level. Low-caste-men are the first to say '*Rām-Rām*' to the *Ṭhākur*. However, young *Thākur* first salutes the old persons of other castes, who are in the classificatory relationship of *dādā*. This *Rām-Rām* salutation among the higher and lower castes on equal basis has started after the low-castes left their traditional affiliations with the *Thākur*. Before that, low-caste men used to pass stelthily in front of Thākur's house. If the *Thākur-sāheb* was seen, they used to say, "*Rām-Rām-huzūr*". But now, "*Rām-Rām*" is on equal level though low-castes are the first to greet the members of the high castes. Castes included in the same layer of caste-hierarchy (have been saluting each other on equal basis,). Age is also included on the same layer of social hierarchy as the first to salute being the younger in age (Mutatkar, 1978:122).

295 अभिविधि

Abhividhi : limit inclusive (in *Vyākaraṇa*). It is of two kinds; *viz. kālika* (relating to time) and *deśika* (relating to space. 'Winter lasts from *Kārtika* to *Caitra*' is the example of the former. 'It retained from Kāsī up to the region called Pātaliputra' is the example of the later. It is a technical term used in grammar (*Aṣṭādhyāyī*, 5.4.53).

296 अभिव्यक्ति

Abhivyakti : manifestation, intimation, revelation. According to NV communication, the face and facial expressions are focus of attention in sculptures as well as in body language. Most expressions are based on socially learned conventionalized cultural codes, which vary from culture to culture. The expression is meant to underwrite the appeal of an icon and arouse our emotions. Normally the expression of the "actor" will be positive, contended, purposeful, delighted, happy, gleeful, etc. There is a considerable empirical evidence to suggest that in our society women smile more than men, both in reality and dramatic scenes. Women are often depicted in a childlike state of expectation and pleasure.

297 अभिव्यक्तिवाद

Abhivyaktivāda : theory of revelation. Abhinavagupta's theory on revelation. According to this view *rasa is* revealed through *vyañjanā.*

298 अभिशाप

Abhiśāpa : form of speech and thought (*Nirukta* VII. 3; *Bṛhaddevatā* 144-60); also known as *śāpa* (*Bṛhaddevatā* 134-139).

299 अभिष्टव

Abhiṣṭava : form of speech and thought (*Bṛhaddevatā*, 134-139), eulogy.

300 अभिसार

Abhisāra : amorous visit (*Pratimā* III), rendezvous, attack.

301 अभिसारिका

Abhisārikā : It is the eighth variety of heroine based on the situation. She may be placed in. "She who lost her character at an early age, who has lost control over her mind, who goes to other's house secretly for sex-sport is called *abhisārikā*" (*Pañcasāyaka*, 5. 38). Such *abhisārikā* is referred to by many poets. Kālidāsa has described the *abhisārikās* as those who are going to their lovers house at night (*Megha*, 39). In Acts IV and V of *Mṛcchakaṭika*, Vasantasenā is depicted as an *abhisārikā*, who is brilliantly attired to meet Cārudatta (VI. 18). Her descriptions were surely preceded and followed by hand gestures: the expression of her face and gait must also have suited the occasion. It is also possible that some musical sounds suggesting thunder and rain were used, but these too, would be complemented by hand gestures and facial expressions.

NS instructs that (I) the courtesans should go to the lover with body beautifully decorated with various ornaments, walking slowly in the company of her attendants, with passion and joy, having delicate movements and intoxication. (II) The noble lady should go covering her face with a veil, walking timidly with limbs contracted, with face bent down looking back often. (III) A maid should walk to her lover with uneven steps and eyes beaming with amorous joy and talking disconnectedly in intoxication. After going in this manner, if the lover is sleeping, the noble lady should wake him with ornaments, and cool scents and her maid by fanning him with her cloth. The superior and middling types of women are not to gesticulate on the stage wearing garment, bath, applying unguents and collyrium, tying hair and using meagre dress or one garment only and dyeing of the lower lip. The inferior ones may do all this. But on certain occasions they too should not represent these.

The lying on bed should not be represented on the stage. The act should be ended by some meaningful speech. If due to some reason the lying down is to be represented, then kissing, embracing, tooth-bite, nail-cut, loosening the knot of the lower garment and pressing the bosom are not to be shown. Meals, watersport and whatever is shameful should not be enacted on the stage as the play is to be witnessed by the whole family together *i.e.* the father and the son, the daughter-in-law and the mother-in-law.

302 **अभिहास्य**

Abhihāsya : Joke, a matter for laughter (*A*, 5.4.14). Radcliffe - Brown (1952), in two classic studies on the topic of joking relationships, has outlined in the broadest of terms what may be called the socio-cultural parameters of "Joking" behaviour. His main point is that, for a variety of reasons specific to particular cultures, structural relations exist between groups that are manifested in particular kinds of verbal behaviour, either between individuals who are members of different structural groups or between people who differ on some other dimension than group membership but who nonetheless embody sets of roles that place them distinctly apart. Furthermore, these role relationships are not random: there appear to be certain dyads in which ritual joking relationships are never realized anywhere in the world for example, the father-son pair.

Joking occurs at a tension point in the social structure of a society, and it serves - as to many other kinds of social behaviour in Radcliffe - Brown's functional outlook - to maintain equilibrium between the conjuctive and disjunctive components of intrasocial relationships (1952: 95). Conjuctive component is based on friendship relations, while disjunctive component—antagonism forms the disjunctive component.

303 **अभिहित**

Abhihita : said, put.

304 **अभिहितान्वयवाद**

Abhihitānvayavāda :"When the meanings of words are connected in accordance with expectancy, compatibility and proximity, another sense arises called purport, which has a distinct form and which though not constituting the sense of the words is yet the sense of the sentence" (*Kāvyaprakāśa*, II. I). This view belongs to the *Mīmāmsaka* school of thought.

305 **अभिहितान्वयवादिन्**

Abhihitānvayavādin : one holding that the meaning of the sentence is the expressed meaning of the words themselves.

306 **अभ्यङ्ग**

Abhyaṅga : unguent, rubbing, anointing with oil. '*Abhyaṅgamardanam tailamupānacchatra-dhāraṇam* (*Manu.* 2.178). (b) a ceremonial on the wedding day when the bride and bridegroom are anointed with oil. In the ceremony when oil is applied to the crown of the head, and it trickles down and reaches all the limbs, it is called *abhyaṅga*. This ceremonial anointing is also attended to after sickness. It is a type of the marriage-ritual in the tribal society.

307 **अभ्यास**

Abhyāsa : reduplication, repetition, In grammar it stands for the earlier part of a reduplicated root. (b) cultivation of detachment (*vairāgya*) or freedom from passion in a systematic way (*Yogasūtra.* 1.12-14)

308 **अभ्युपपत्ति**

Abhyupapatti : form of speech and thought (*A*, 2.10.11); coming to the rescue, aid, acceptance, favour.

309 **अमर्ष**

Amarṣa : indignation, anger, impatience, wrath. It is the twenty-fifth *bhāva* among the thirty-three *vyabhicārī bhāvas,* as enumerated by Bharata. *Amarṣa* is the feeling of indignation, or anger, excited when one is censured, blamed or insulted by someone. Redness in the eyes, shaking of the head, knitting of the eyebrows, violent threatening, etc. are its external manifestations. It is represented by shaking the head, perspiration, thinking with downcast face, determination, looking for means and allies, etc.

Amarṣa is an emotion that creates grief. A great deal of understanding and forgiveness can be needed on both sides. It is difficult to predict how long this stage is likely to last as so much depends on how they resolve their feelings. If they fail to do this, they will probably sink into a despairing mood and become unable to cope with day-to-day activities.

310 **अमुक**

Amuka : 'such and such'—*Yājñavalkya.*

311 **अमृत-मुद्रा**

Amṛta-mudrā : gesture of the nectar. "Make the ring and the middle fingers interlocked between the two. Join tips of two middles and fore-fingers, then join the tips of the little fingers and make the two thumbs half-raised. It is *amṛta-mudrā*" (*VD*). *Amṛta* means immortality: the ultimate goal of life in the form of self realization. It is also conceived of in terms of nectar-essence which according to the *Tāntric* tradition, may be consumed from the body itself by yogic

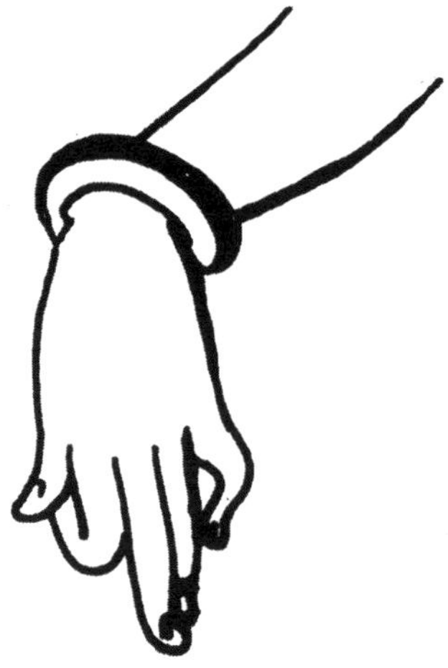

Fig. – (311)

processes, to revitalize the body. According to *Raseśvara* school, it may be prepared chemically. (Fig. 311)

312 **अम्बरीश-हस्त**

Ambarīśa-hasta : *kartarī-hasta* represents the mythical king *Ambarīśa* (Mirror of Gesture, p.47).

313 **अम्बुवाची**

Ambuvācī : earth's menstruation, ritual connected with fertility and vegetation symbolizing the period of earth's menstruation commencing between the seventh and eleventh day of month *āṣāḍha* (June-July). During this period widows must follow certain taboos since the act of procreation is forbidden to them. During the days of *ambuvācī* ploughing, sowing and other farm work is forbidden.

314 **अयत्नज-अलंकार**

Ayatnaja-alaṅkāra : involuntary graces of women are *śobhā* (beauty), *kānti* (charm), *dīpti* (radiance), *mādhuryam* (sweetness), *dhairyam* (self-control), *prāgalbhyam* (courage) and *audāryam* (nobility).

315 **अयि**

Ayi : used with vocative *ayi makarodyānam gacchāvaḥ* 'friend, let us go to the pleasure-garden'.

316 **अरण्यरुदित**

Araṇya-rudita : crying in the forest, vain lament.

317 **अराजकता**

Arājakatā : a state where there is no king and there is a complete anarchy. Vālmīki thinks that in a country where there is no king (in real sense) the farmers will not attend to the agricultural labours. Even the seed of food grains will not be sowed by them:

नाराजके जनपदे बीजमुष्टिः प्रकीर्यते

(*Ayo. Kan.* 67.10)

or there will be a tendency to disobey and undo things every-where:

नाराजके जनपदे पितुः पुत्रो भार्या वा वर्तते वशे

(Ibid)

There will be no prosperity:

नाराजके धनं चास्ति

(*Ibid.* II)

There will be difficulty in keeping the chastity of women

नास्ति भार्याप्यराजके

(Ibid).

There will be no developmental activities:

नाराजके जनपदे कारयन्ति शुभां नराः ।
उद्यानानि च रम्याणि हृष्टः पुण्यगृहाणि च ॥

(Ibid 12)

There will be both physical and mental starvation. There will be no festivities:

नाराजके जनपदे प्रभूतनटनर्त्तकाः ।
उत्सवाश्च समाजश्च वर्धन्ते राष्ट्रवर्धनात् ॥

(*Ibid.* 51)

There will be dearth of scholars:

नाराजके जनपदे जनाः शास्त्रविशारदाः

(*Ibid* 26)

There cannot be any happy man nicely dressed travelling in chariot and getting together being afraid of dacoits and culprits:

न वाहनैः शीघ्रगामिभिः नराः निर्यान्त्य-
रण्यानि नारीभिः सह कामिनः ।

(*Ibid.* 18)

No one can sleep without closing the doors:

न शेरते विवृतद्वाराः

(*Ibid.* 18)

Vālmīki thinks that even the army destined to safeguard the motherland from the attack of enemies may not fight for the sake of country:

न चाप्यराजके सेना शत्रून् विषहते युधि

(*Ibid* 24)

The whole system may be spoiled causing untold hardships and sufferings to the public leading to the ruin of the nation as a whole.

Kalhaṇa, the author of *Rājataraṅgiṇī* (VIII) writes that when the Kaśmirī king Sussala (1112-20 A.D.,) left his capital, Śrīnagar in 1120 A.D., the city experienced a state of *arājakatā*. When night fell, women, children and others were in terror. Some of the weak persons were slain, some were plundered and others were terrorised when their houses were burnt down by the enemy. This happened in a city which was without a king. This expression may be compared with a similar word *apuruddha,* which Kauṭilya mentions as transpiring when the law of punishment (*daṇḍa*) is kept in abeyance and it gives rise to such disorders like the *matsya nyāya,* when the strong swallowed the weak (*A.* 1.4.)

318 **अराल**

Arāla : cirly. crooked.

319 **अरालकटकामुख-नृत्तहस्त**

Arāla-kaṭakāmukha-nṛttahasta : a type of hand gesture in dancing; often occurs in sculpture. If the *alapallava* - style with palms upturned like a lotus-core (*padma-koṣa*), it is called *arāla-kaṭakāmukha* (*NS,* IX. 176-197).

320 **अरालकेशी**

Arāla-keśī : a woman having curly hair.

321 **अरालपक्ष्मनयन**

Arāla-pakṣma-nayana : of curved eye-lashes.

322 **अरालहस्त**

Arāla-hasta : bent hands. Hands raised from the sides; curve the fore-finger like a bow; make the thumb set in a curved order and the rest of fingers turned upward separately; it is called the *arāla-* gesture. This suggests physical and moral powers, persevarance, beauty, divinity, graveness, good omen and some other psychic thoughts, worth representing in dreams; repeatedly gathering and looking at lady's hairs, a complete description of one's own self. Making the *svastika* gesture with finger tips indicate the marriage fun, sexual love-play with the help of a circle and a respectful encircling by moving it like a cycle and a great congretion by the same way. It is also to be applied to show a thing fallen down on the ground. Moreover, it is used to indicate welcome, funeral, crushing, smelling, scent, etc. In addition, to them all other functions of the *tripatāka* - gesture may be employed in the *arāla* - gesture.

Touching the head would indicate greeting to invisible persons (*NS*, XXX. 72). The blessing is indicated by a pair of *arāla-hasta* (*NS*, IX. 47); In *Uttararāmacarita* (III), Sītā is invisible. Thus, while she can see Rāma, he can only hear her: she comes near him, lets him rest on her, but to him it is as he were seeing a vision: This is indicated through Rāma's holding the *arāla-hasta* over his head to show that he is addressing an invisible person (*NS*, XXII. 72). In Act IV of *Karpūramañjarī,* the marriage between the king and Karpūramañjarī is presented in pantomime. This is portrayed through a pair of *arāla-hasta* moving around each other. In *Uttararāmacarita* (VIII. 1), Madayantikā gesticulates perspiration and other emotions. This is enacted by wiping off the face with the *arāla-hastas* restlessly (*NS*, VII. 156). The palm is raised to face outwards. The second, third and little fingers are stretched straight, the finger crooked or curved and the thumb a little bent beside it and almost touching the tip of the finger. It is used to express nectar, drinking poison, benediction, dressing the hair, decorating the face, etc.

323 **अरिष्टलिङ्ग**

Ariṣṭaliṅga : sign of death. Certain signs observed in a patient on the threshold of death *(Suśruta-Saṁhitā* 1, p 284).

324 **अरूपवेला**

Arūpavelā : Time when the form of a person cannot be seen clearly (*A*, 5.6.3; 7.17.41).

325 **अरे**

Arē : an interjection ; calling to inferiors, hellow; cf. *Ātmā vā arē dṛṣṭavyaḥ. (Śat. Brāhmaṇa),* an example of paralanguage. It is even used in Hindi chiefly in addressing inferiors.

326 **अरेरे**

Arērē : interjection; calling out angrily; *arērē vācāṭa* (*Veṇīsaṁhāra,* 3).

327 **अर्कमुद्रा**

Arka-mudrā : gesture symbolizing the Sun. Two *vitastis,* joining finger-tips in a circular style symbolizes the Sun (*VD*).

328 **अर्गल**

Argala : bolt, bar.

329 **अर्गल-करण**

Argala-karaṇa : one leg is extended backward, feet are placed two and a half-*tālas* apart, the body is bent in a back convex curve, and both the hands are extended up and back\ to touch the ground (*NS,* 117 b - 118 a). The leg is stretched backward two *tālas* and a half apart from the other and the hand is moved in conformity with it in front. It is used in the movements of Aṅgada and others.

330 **अर्घ्य**

Arghya : respectful offering of water or water with unhusked rice-grains, flowers, etc. to gods or venerable persons. It is a present or gift indicating respect to a superior. A material of worship or respectful offering or oblation to gods or venerable men consisting of rice, *dūrvā* grass etc. with or without water:

āpaḥ kṣīram kuśāgram ca
dadhi - sarpiḥ sataṇḍulam I

yavaḥ siddhārthakaścaivā -
ṣṭāṅgorghyaḥ prakīrtitaḥ II

331 **अर्जुन-हस्त**

Arjuna-hasta : *tripatāka hasta* moved forward repeatedly represents Arjuna, the Pāṇḍava (*Mirror of Gesture*, p. 47).

A hero of *Mahābhārata* and one of the Pāṇḍava brothers, the third son of Kuntī, born as a result of her invoking Indra, Arjuna was a friend of Kṛṣṇa.

332 **अर्थ**

Artha : aim, purpose, cause, meaning, Yāska defines it as 'fruit or flower of speech'. (a) In certain cases it is the *puruṣārtha* meaning the ultimate aim of life. (b) that which is intended. (c) that which a given term or symbol stands for or designates. (d) the significance, often the emotional or motivational significance of something for an individual.

333 **अर्थतत्व**

Artha-tattva : the real nature of a thing; comp. '*yo arthatattvam avijñāya*' , the symbolic meaning.

334 **अर्थदर्शन**

Artha-darśana : judgement of a thing.

335 **अर्थपाक**

Arthapāka : maturity of sense.

336 **अर्थप्रकृति**

Arthaprakṛti : elements of the plot of a Sanskrit drama. There are five elements: *bīja, bindu, patākā, prakarī* and *kārya.*

337 **अर्थवर्जित**

Artha-varjita : meaningless.

338 **अर्थवाद**

Arthavāda : a statement of praise or censure in respect of a particular act in ritual (*S. Br.* 1.4.1.22). The *arthavādas* are of three kinds : (a) when an *arthavāda* text is in conflict with ordinary experience it is metaphorical (*guṇavāda*). (b) when something is definitely ascertained by other means of knowledge it is *anuvāda*; and when a text is not opposed to other *pramāṇas* or is not definitely ascertained otherwise it is called *bhūtārthavāda* (statement of an accomplished fact or of a past event).

339 **अर्थविद्**

Artha-vid : one knowing the meaning of a world; comp. *vivakṣitāmarthavidaḥ* (*Śiśu.* 2.15).

340 **अर्थापत्ति**

Arthāpatti : postulation; a means of valid knowledge according to *Mīmāmsā*, circumstantial inference; deduction of a matter from that which could not otherwise be. For example, a rat had eaten up the stick. So, by *arthāpatti* we may infer that the cake also, that was on the stick, was eaten up by it (*Darśana*). Knowledge by postulation arises where we have to postulate something as the only explanation of any apparent conflict. It is of two kinds: *dṛṣṭārthāpatti* and *śrutārthāpatti.* Sabara on *Jamini* (1.1.5.).

341 **अर्धचतुरस्रक**

Ardhacaturasraka : a type of posture mentioned in *Vikramorvaśīya* (III).

342 **अर्धचन्द्र-नखपद**

Ardhacandra-nakhapada : the curved marks with nails impressed on the neck and breasts, known as '*half moon nailprints*'. *Kāmasūtra* (2.4.14) records: *grīvāyām stanapṛṣṭhe vakro nakhapadaniveśo ardhacandrakaiḥ.* According to *Anaṅgarāga: grīvākuce vakranakha-prahāro datto ardha candrākhya udīrato asau.* Śrīharṣa in his *Naiṣadhīyacarita* (6,25, 6,66, 9,117, 11.122) has enormously used this type of scratch. Ratnākara (*Haravijaya* 4. 33, 7.7.) and Bilhaṇa (*Vikramāṅkadeva-carita*, 12.28) have used this sign in love-sport.

343 **अर्धचन्द्र-मुद्रा**

Ardhacandra-mudrā : The palm with curved fingers symbolizes the Vaiṣṇavite deity (*VD*).

344 **अर्धचन्द्र-हस्त**

Ardhacandra-hasta : half-moon hand; hand making gestures of the crescent moon; single hand gesture in which all the fingers bend to make a bow (*NS*, IX.43-45). When all the fingers are bent along with the thumb, it is called *ardhacandra* - gesture. This is used to indicate small trees, the crescent moon, the conch-shell, the pitcher (*Kalaśa*), the bangle, forcibly opening, exertion, thinking, etc. In addition to them, it indicates ornaments or a lady's buttock, waist and ornaments of the face, like ear-ring, named *tālapatra*, etc. in a dramatic performance.

In *Vikramorvaśīya*, the king enacts worshipping the Moon, addresses it in various ways, one of them being, "as one who is ever present on the crest of Śiva". This may be depicted through this gesture. Removal of armlets in *Mṛcchakaṭika* (I) is shown by this gesture; derived from the *patākā* by stretching the thumb. The palm faces upwards slightly. The four fingers are stretched together and the thumb is stretched to its fullest away from the rest of the fingers. It is used to express the Moon (on the eighth day), anxiety, prayer, greeting, meditation, bangle, wrist, mirror, ear of an elephant and a bow.

345 **अर्धनिकुञ्चित-स्थान**

Ardhaniṅkuñcita sthāna : crossed legged sitting posture.

346 **अर्धनिकुट्टक-करण**

Ardhanikuṭṭaka karaṇa : hand in *alapallava* style, legs do bend very much (*NS*, IV.70). One hand is moved near its shoulder having *alapallava* gesture, accompanied by the movement of the respective leg, with *udghaṭṭita* foot. It is employed in self-adulation.

347 **अर्धनिरीक्षित**

Ardha nirīkṣita : the side-long glance, a type of *Kaṭākṣa* (*Buddhacarita*, 8.40). It is a movement of the eyeball and the name for it in *NS* (VIII, 98b-100a) is *vivartana* : turning the eyeballs sideways; a movement used in expressing the erotic sentiment.

348 **अर्धपताक-हस्त**

Ardha-patāka hasta : half-flag hands. Two hands near one ear as we find in Bhuvaneśvara temples; single hand-gesture; the little finger of the *tripatākā* is bent. The hand is rested with the palm facing outwards. The thumb, first and second fingers are extended straight, the third and little fingers are bent into the palm. It is used to express two or both, knife, a horn, a tower, etc. It is only mentioned in *Abhinayadarpaṇa*. Bharata has not mentioned this gesture. If the little finger of the *tripatāka*-gesture is made curved, it is the *ardhapatāka*. The gesture is applied to indicate working with fruits, young leaves, both the banks of a river, a saw, a knife, a flat and two turrents of a gate (*AB*. verses 103-104).

349 **अर्धपर्यङ्कासन**

Ardha-paryaṅkāsana : an *āsana* or seated stance, described as 'half seated on the hams' is assumed by the kings in a relaxed mood (hence also sometimes called *mahārāja-līlā*) or by ascetics while practising meditation. Both the legs are on the same pedastal but one is bent with the knee raised up while the other is bent with the knee remaining horizontal. The term occurs in Buddhist iconography. The usual name for this *āsana* is *lalita* (graceful).

350 **अर्धमण्डली**

Ardhamaṇḍalī : a type of posture in south Indian sculpture. In this posture the feet are placed sideways, and the knees are also bent sideways.

351 **अर्धमत्तलि-करण**

Ardha-mattali karaṇa : a type of *karaṇa* (*NS*, IV. 88b-89a); derived from *mattali cārī*, but the crossing and extending of the feet is emphasized; *recita nṛtta hasta* extended and the left hand is placed on the hip. The feet are moved from *skhalita*, the left hand is in *recita* and the right placed on the waist. It is used in medium intoxication.

352 **अर्धमत्स्येन्द्रासन**

Ardhamatsyendrāsana : To perform this *āsana*, place the left heel near the *anus* and below the scrotum, touching the perineum space. Bend the right knee, place the right ankle at the root of the left thigh and rest the right foot on the ground, close to the left hip-joint. Place the left armpit over the top of the vertically bent right knee. Push the knee now a little to the back so that it touches the back part of the armpit. Catch hold of the left knee with the left palm; and then applying pressure at the left shoulder joint' slowly twist the spine and turn to the extreme right. Turn the face also to the right as much possible and bring it in line with the right shoulder. Swing round the right arm behind the back, catching hold of the left thigh with the right hand. Retain this pose for five to fifteen seconds keeping the vertebral column erect. Similarly, you can twist the spine to the left side. This will complete the spinal twist.

353 **अर्धमुकुला-दृष्टि**

Ardhamukulā dṛṣṭi : a type of glances with the *kuñcita* and *ekākāra* mentioned in *Mālatīmādhava* (I); half-burst bud-like glance; a type of *sañcārī-bhāva-dṛṣṭi* ; a glance with the lids half-shut in joy and the half-blown eyeballs slightly mobile, is called *ardhamukulā*. It gives vent to an air of joy in experiencing sweet smell, loving touch, etc. The eyelids are half-opened like bud in joy.

354 **अर्धयोगासन**

Ardha-yogāsana : variation of the posture of regal relaxation (*mahārāja-līlā*) where the right thigh is lifted up and the bent leg is secured by the chord of meditation (*yoga-paṭṭa*) which goes round the loins. The other leg is sometimes let down in a dangling stance.

355 **अर्धरेचित-करण**

Ardharecita karaṇa : *sūcīmukha hastas* make *recita*; the side is in *naṭa* position; the legs are in *nikuṭṭita* (*NS*, IV. 72-73; IX. 91, 239-40). The hand moving in *sūcīmukha* (touches the other), the foot is moved up and down and the side is bent. It is employed in ill-conceived movement.

356 **अर्धरेचित-नृत्तहस्त**

Ardharecita-nṛttahasta : a type of hand-gesture in dancing; the half-bent dancing hand; when the left hand is in *caturaśra*-style and right hand in *recita*, it is called *ardharecita* (*NS*, IX.176-197).

357 **अर्धविलोचन-संस्थान**

Ardhavilocana-saṁsthāna : the half-shut eye-pose. Half of an eye is visible on the face and covered to some extent under the eye-brow; but the other half is suggested. The pose of the fore-head is changeable proportionately. The cheek of the one side is half-diminished and partially visible. Only a peep of front neck-line is located. The chin is indicated with a *yava* (barley-like spot), From the breast to the half of the face is not visible. The lips are half-finished and other limbs are visible. If one of the two eyes is visible, it is called *chāyāgata*, or a shade-cast one, especially applicable in painting (*VD*, III. 39. 14-17).

358 **अर्धसम**

Ardhasama : a *vṛtta* (metre) in which the first and third feet and the second and fourth feet have the same metrical scheme.

359 **अर्धसम-स्थान**

Ardhasama sthāna : a class of postures according to *Viṣṇudharmottara*. It classifies all the postures into two general groups of *samasthānas* and *ardhasama sthānas*. Half-straight standing posture, name of a posture in iconograpy. In that posture one foot is firmly planted, while the other foot and leg indicate a movement.

360 **अर्धसूची-करण**

Ardhasūcī karaṇa : only the final position of the *sūcī cārī* is used when the right foot is in *kuñcita* and is placed on the side of the stationary foot (*NS*, IV. 137b-138a). The *alapadma* hand is held on the head and the right foot is in *sūcī*. (Fg. 360).

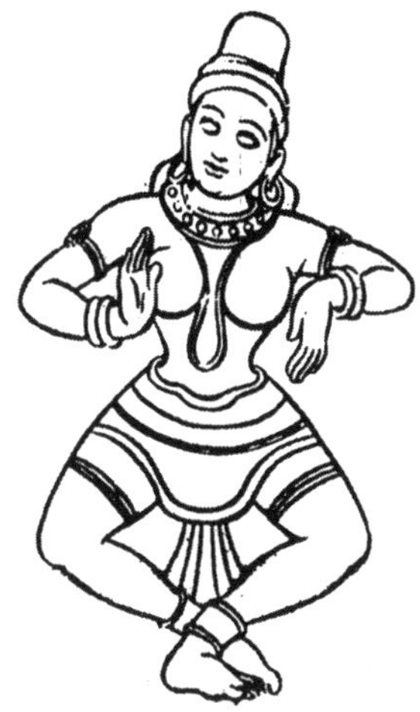

Fig. – (360)

361 **अर्धसूची-हस्त**

Ardhasūcī hasta : single hand gesture; half-needle hand. The palm is raised outwards. The second, third and the little fingers are bent into the palm. The first finger is extended and the thumb is held close to the edge of the palm, up to the first finger. It is used to express the idea of something coming up, sprouting a bird, a blade of grass, and a stalk of corn. If the fore-finger of the *kapittha hasta* style is raised upward, it is called *ardhasūcī* and is used to indicate a sprout, a tiny bird, a big insect etc. (*Abhinayadarpaṇa*, verses 167-168.) (Fig. 361).

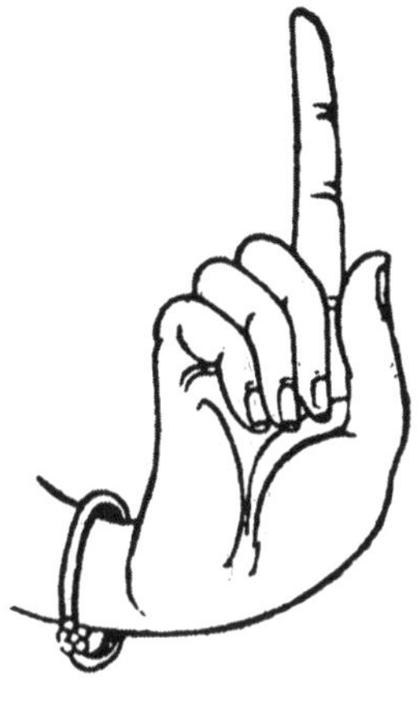

Fig. – (361)

362 **अर्धस्वस्तिक-करण**

Ardhasvastika-karaṇa : right hand in *karihasta* position; the left hand relaxed on chest; *svastika* of the feet (*NS*, IV 82-83). Legs are in *svastika*, the right hand in *karihasta* and the left on the breast. (Fig. 362).

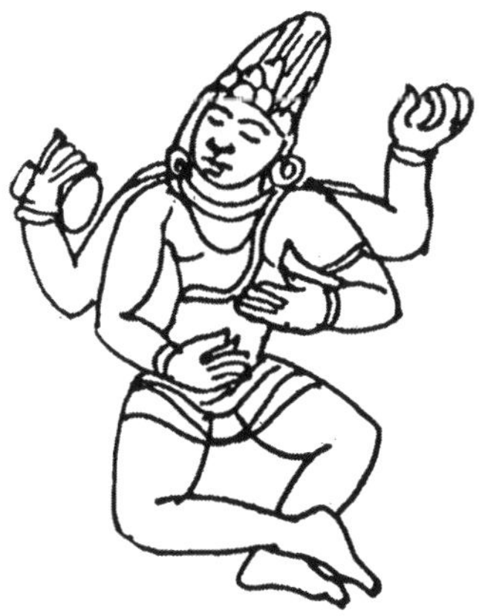

Fig. – (362)

363 **अर्धाक्षि**

Ardhākṣi : side-glance.

364 **अर्धार्ध-संस्थान**

Ardhārdha-saṁsthāna : The half-distributed pose (*VD*).

365 **अर्पण**

Arpaṇa : (a) literally offering or giving oneself out; an attractive and swaying delivery of speech which seems to fill the whole stage. (b) placing upon. *pādārpaṇānugraha-pūtapṛṣṭham* (*Raghu*, 2.35). (c) surrendering oneself to the will of God, or a deity.

366 **अलक**

Alaka : curly hair.

367 **अलक-चुम्बन**

Alaka-cumbana : kissing hair (*Naiṣadha* 18.41).

368 **अलक्तक**

Alaktaka : lac-dye to the feet used by ladies (*Śṛṅgārarasodaya-bhāṇa*, p.62). It is also known as *lākṣā*. It is known as *mahāvar* in Hindi and *lattuka* in Telugu. It is also called *altā* in Hindi region.

Alaktaka is a chemical colour, usually a red solution out of resin of certain trees. It is used by both the sexes to their feet for decoration or ritual purposes. Also, balls of cotton impregnated with a lac dye, a thin red stuff of cotton, like paper, consecrated to Durgā, with which Hindu women colour their feet, and is supposed to promote happiness and prevent distress.

Alaktaka dye was applied to the feet by young ladies (*HC*, I) The sky was suffused to red in the evening but Bāṇa fancies that the rosy colour was due to *alaktaka* as to look like new leaves (which are reddish) of trees. Kālidāsa (*Māl.3.*43; *Kum.* 5.78) has liking to this dye.

369 **अलग**

Alaga : One of the five types of *utplavanas* mentioned by Nandikeśvara.

370 **अलङ्कार**

Alaṅkāra : paralanguage, beautifier, decorator or embellishments; six in number; embellishment of the voice : loud, waxing (heated or excited), subdued, low, fast and slow. Loud voice is to be used in fright. Waxing is to be used in objecting, disputation, pride and crying. Subdued is used in situations of dependency. Low is used in natural speaking. Fast to be used in Jest. Slow is applicable for love.

Bharata and Dhanañjaya have discussed the twenty natural graces or *alaṅkāras* of women. (In their view these graces of a woman in her prime of youth are twenty.) Bharata elaborates (*NS*, XXII. 4-32) further that dramatic experts know the young women's graces support the sentiments in a drama and these consist of changes in respect of their faces and other limbs. Out of these changes, one is *aṅgaja* (*i.e.* caused by limbs) and next ten are *sāttvikas* (natural) grown up with the sentiments and psychological states are *ayatnajāḥ* (involuntary changes), *helā*, *hāva* and *bhāva* arising from one another, being different aspects of *sattva* are *aṅgaja* (physical).

The six *alaṅkāras* (embellishments of voice) according to Bharata are: *ucca, dīpta, mandra, nīca, druta* and *vilambita. Mandra* and *vilambita* intonations should be used in words containing pleasant sense and expressing state of happiness; *dīpta* and *ucca* in words expressing sharpness and roughness. The *vilambita* should be used in Erotic, the Comic and the Pathetic and *dipta* or *uccā* in the Heroic, the Furious and the Marvellous; *druta* and *nīca* in the Terrible and the Odious. Thus the intonation should be used to express the sentiments. The tempos resorted to in connection with the sentiments are three - *druta* (fast), *madhya* (medium) and *vilambita* (slow). The medium should be used in the Erotic and the Comic; - slow in the Pathetic and fast in the Furious, the Marvellous, the Odious and the Terrible.

(b) Decoration. One of the varieties of *āhāryābhinaya. Alaṅkāra* includes flower garlands, ornaments and drapery. (c) *Alaṅkāra* is one of the essential aspects of Indian iconography, and it extends to sculpture and architecture. The merit of an icon is said to consist in the beauty of the image as well as in the proper decorations. There is an elaborate lore concerning the ornaments for the different organs of the body and the decorative details thereof. The ornaments commonly found in the icons include those of the head, hair, ears, neck, chest, arms, hands, loin and legs. (see *ābhūṣaṇa/ābharaṇa*).

(d) *Alaṅkāra* is frequently mentioned as one of the daily ceremonies to be observed, and means then the putting of ornaments - decoration of body.

(e) The Sanskrit word *alṅkāra* is usually rendered by 'ornament' with reference either to rhetorical use of ornaments (figures of speech), or to jewellery or trappings. The Indian category of *Alaṅkāraśāstra*, 'the science of poetic ornament', corresponds, however, to the mediaeval category of rhetoric or art of oratory, in which eloquence is thought of not as an end in itself or art for art's sake, or to display the artist's skill, but as the art of effective communication.

371 **अलङ्कार्य**

Alaṅkārya : the beautified. To evoke emotions is one of the main purposes of our verbal communications without thereby bringing them nearer to poetry (Ānandavardhana, *Dhvanyāloka, Vṛtti* on II. 6).

372 **अलपद्म-हस्त**

Alapadma hasta : the blue-lotus. A type of hand-gesture, also known as *alapallava*, inward movement of the fingers (*Nāṭyaśāstra-Saṅgraha*); was used to show full moon as we find in *Śākuntalam* (Act III). It is also portrayed in Mathurā railings and Bhuvaneśvara temples, represents summer.

373 **अलपल्लव-नृत्तहस्त**

Alapallava nṛtta hasta : a type of hand-gesture in dancing (*NS*, IV.139); the lotus-leaf dancing hands; Two hands with the style of *udveṣṭita* in the fingers' tips, it is called the *alapallava* (*NS*, IX.176-197). A posture of the hand (*hasta-mudrā*), when the five fingers are separated and bent forward, making a hollow of the palm, resembling a flower in bloom. It is a gesture indicating offering of flowers. It is illustrated in the disposition of Nandikeśvara when he is attending on the dancing Śiva.

374 **अलपल्लव-हस्त**

Alapallava hasta : single hand gesture, same as *alapadma* in *NS*. According to *Nāṭyaśāstra-saṅgraha* it is a type of outward movement of the fingers. *Bālarāmabharata* derives it from *padmakośa* : slight difference in finger position; often used in iconography. The fingers are turned towards palm, beginning with little finger, standing on its side and separated from one another. It represents warding off "Whom do you belong to"? "It is not", unmeaningful words and woman's allusion to herself.

375 **अलमर्थ-वाक्**

Alamartha vāk : words denoting sufficiency during coition. Māgha (*Śiśupālavadha* 10,75) know these words:

> *Śītkṛtāni bhaṇitam kuruṇoktiḥ*
> *Snigdhamuktam alamartha vacānsi*
> *hāsabhūṣaṇaravaśca remaṇyaḥ*
> *Kāmasūtrapadatāmupajagmuḥ*

"Women made *sītkāras*, uttered pityful words and showed their love by expressing sufficiency. Their laughter and the sounds of their ornaments were as if the words stated in *Kāmasūtra*." Nayacandrasūri describes the behaviour of a young lady, who was a novice and who utters "oh, enough, no no" indistinctly:

> *ratikalām kalayatsu vallabhe*
> *kimapi kuñcimukhī sumukhā navā*
> *hā hā hā neti mameti vacomiṣān*
> *madanadīpanamantramivāsmarat*
> (*Hammīrakāvya*, 7.111)

He also pictures the courtship behaviour in another situation:

> *dadhre aṅgāni yathātikaṭhinānyeṣā navoḍhā rate*
> *śaṅke dhattā tathātikaṭhinam cetopi cittapriyaḥ*
> *mā mā mā mana muñca ha ha hetyullāpavatyām muhuḥ*
> *tasyā no kathamanyathāsya karuṇā taruṇyamāsādayat*
> (*ibid.* 7.116)

Some of the prohibitive utterances during coition have been mentioned by poets such as

(a) niḥsahāmi visṛja 'I can't tolerate, leave me", (*Jānakīharaṇa*, 8.31) and

(b) *mā mā māti māmalamit*' Now don't, do not commit any excess (*Kuṭṭini matam*, 158).

376 **अलसगमना**

Alasagamanā : lady who walks slowly (*Megha*, 84), a woman of indolent gait.

377 **अलसेक्षणा**

Alasekṣaṇā : whose eyes look tired.

378 **अलातक-करण**

Alātaka karaṇa : initial position of *alātā cārī*, final position of *ūrdhvajānu cārī* : a turn and the uplifted sideways movement of the knee are important points of the cadence; initial position of hands is at the level of the shoulders;

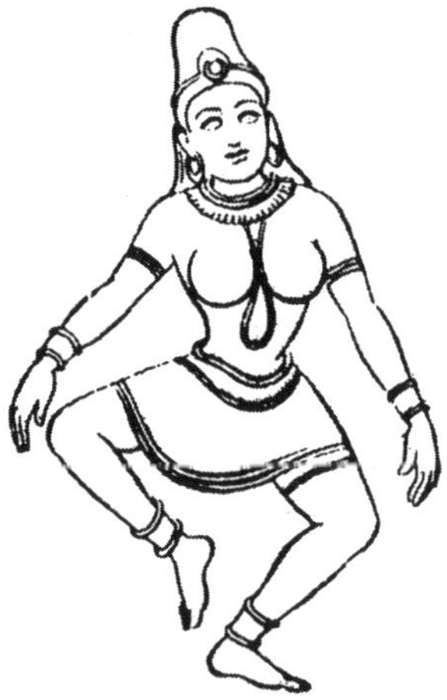

Fig. – (378)

in the final position they extend down (*NS*, IV.78b-79a, X.33,41). Making *alatā cārī*, the right hand is moved from the level of the shoulder and then *ūrdhvajānu cārī* is performed. This is used in graceful dance. (Fig. 378).

379 **अलाता-चारी**

Alātā cārī : foot is taken into back in *samapāda añcita* position, stretching of a leg with the *añcita* foot backwards; the foot is also lowered on its own side and the heels touch the floor first; *parivartita jaṅgā* ; *alātaka karaṇa* and *maṇḍala* and also *agrahāra* by the same name: the position seen in Sāñcī dryad is the best example. One foot stretched backward and then put up in by turning it and afterwards caused to fall on the heel. According to Bharata: "a foot is stretched backwards then it is turned round and its sole faces the other thigh and then its heel is brought down to the ground on its own side to make *alātā cārī* (*NS*, X.41).

380 **अलास्य**

Alāsya : a type of dance-movement in Amarāvatī sculpture; lit. not dancing.

381 **अलीक**

Alīka : untrue, false. False may be positive as well as negative.

382 **अलीक-निमीलन**

Alīka nimīlana : feigned closing of the eyes.

383 **अलीक-सुप्त**

Alīka supta : feigned sleep.

384 **अल्पप्राण**

Alpaprāṇa : unaspirates.

385 **अल्पविवर-घ्राणा**

Alpavivara ghrāṇā : lady whose nostrils are small, symbol of the Deer-lady (*Anaṅgaraṅga*, 3.20.21).

386 **अल्पाशना**

Alpāśanā : lady who eats little, quality of the Deer-lady (*Anaṅgaraṅga*, 3, 20, 21).

387 **अवकीर्णिन्**

Avakīrṇin : a *Brahmacārin* who has had sexual intercourse with a woman (*Manu*, XI. 118-21), having broken his vow of chastity.

388 **अवकुण्ठिता भ्रुकुटी**

Avakuṇṭhitā bhrukuṭī : a type of *bhrukuṭī* given by *Bālarāmabharata*.

389 **अवगुण्ठन**

Avaguṇṭhana : veil, wrapper. The ancient Indian garment worn by women. The purpose of this *purdah* system lay in the idea that was improper for married elite ladies to expose their faces to the gaze of strangers in daily intercourse. Within the advent of Islam, the higher caste Hindus adopted the Muslim custom *purdah* seclusion.

(a) In the north Indian village, newly married women do veil their faces when they go out for fetching water, or for other purposes. However, the older people complain about these 'girls of today' for not hiding their faces properly and for not wearing *sāris.*

(b) Name of a *mudrā.* Making a fist on the left hand, its forefinger is pointed downwards; then moving the forefinger forward and backwards in a controlled manner makes *avaguṇṭhana-mudrā* which is used in the rituals connected with the invocation of the deities.

390 **अवगुण्ठन-मुद्रा**

Avaguṇṭhana-mudrā : a hand pose formed by clasping all the fingers of the left hand with the thumb except the index finger which remains open and pendant. It is used in rituals with the invocation of the deities.

391 **अवतार**

Avatāra : literally meaning 'descent', 'coming down' incarnation, the myth of charisma. In ancient India myth of charisma was fabricated to establish the authority of the state. In ancient India the concept of *avatāra* was conceived to describe (*Mahābhārata* 12.24.27, 12.59-6-10) the achievements of extra-ordinary people. This concept can be compared to Weber's concept of charisma which is associated with certain personal attributes as virtue, courage and the like. It works successfully so long as the charismatic persons achieve spectacular victories in different fields. Now, it is true that charisma is attached to the concept of *avatāra* but it is more than mere charisma because it appeals to the traditional beliefs of the people and tries to rely *(āśramas)* on religious sanctions.

The expression refers to the divine appearance amidst mankind to extricate good folk from the misery caused by the wicked ones. The belief is that whenever virtue suffers and vice flourishes, god will manifest himself in some form to set things right (*Bhagavad - gītā*, 4.7-8).

392 **अवधूत**

Avadhūta : shaken away, struck down. (a) an *avadhūta* is one who has subdued the passions and estranged himself from the interests and emotions of mankind, abandoning religious observances and worldly restraints. According to the *Sannyāsopaniṣad* (XIII) they take food from persons belonging to all *varṇas*, except those who are charged with moral sins. They eat like an *ajagara i.e.* while lying down and opening only the mouth without any effort, and are solely absorbed in contemplation. *Avadhūtas* are divided into two classes—house-holders and recluses. In Bengal there are separate *akhāṛas* of these *Avadhūtas* and people of all castes join them. In Bengal, they are sometimes called *bāuls*, though *bāuls* are of a different order.

393 **अवधूत-शिरस्**

Avadhūta śiras : turning down of the head, head bent down once; a type of head movement. The head is first lowered down and then raised up. It is exhibited to communicate a message, to invoke a god, to open a conversation and beckoning to come in.

394 **अवनताङ्गी**

Avanatāṅgī : with stooping or symmetrical limbs.

395 **अवपात**

Avapāta : commotion, a type of *ārabhaṭī*. In Bharata's (*NS*, XX) view occurrence of fear, jubilation, panic, fall, puzzled behaviour, quick entrance and exit of characters should be known as *avapāta*. Abhinavagupta (*Abhinavabhāratī*, XX) states that *avapāta* occurs when there is quick entrance and exit of characters due to excess of fear and joy, and where there is tumult, running away caused by the words, falling down due to attack and the action is excited because of the flurried conduct of characters. It is called *avapāta* because the characters fall and run away in it.

396 **अवरोह**

Avaroha : the reverse order of *āroha* (music), descent.

397 **अवरोहण**

Avarohaṇa : descent of the *rāga* (notes) as defined by Mātaṅga.

398 **अवलगित**

Avalagita : linked opening. This is another sub-division of *vīthī* which is borrowed and used as *āmukha* device to suggest the opening of scene of a drama. As defined by Bharata, *avalagita* occurs when some other matter (pertinent to the drama) is included in the topic of dialogue and is thereby led to fulfilment (*NS*, XVIII.116-117). The classical example of *avalagita* as a form of *vīthī* is quoted from *Ratnāvali* (II) by Abhinavagupta. The *Vidūṣaka* is trying to divert Udayana's mind from his love-sick condition and is hoping that the portrait of Sāgarikā will please his eye. Udayana confesses his pleasure and also reveals his sincere love for Sāgarikā. This latter is unexpectedly included in the conversation about the portrait and thereby love (*sṛṅgāra)*, which is the principle theme of the play, is set before us: this is what is dramatically achieved. This unexpected connection or close-linking (*ava+lag*) of two matters is the feature of *avalagita.*

399 **अवलम्बितक**

Avalambitaka : (a) a type of nude and fixture position. In the Liṅgarāja temple of Bhuvaneśvara (11th century), the full-sized man in the standing position takes to his side a woman with thighs astride, her legs clasped round his waist, both being nude and "fixture" position (*Kāmasūtra*, II. 6.36). (b) suspended position. One of the postures of sexual union. In this posture the man supports himself against a wall, while the woman sitting on his hands throws her arms round his neck. The woman moves herself by her feet, which touch the wall (*Kandarpa-Cūḍāmaṇi*, 2.6.28-29).

400 **अवलोकन (दृष्टि)**

Avalokana (dṛṣṭi) : eyeballs drawn inside, given by *Bālarāmabharata.*

401 **अवलोकित दर्शन**

Avalokita darśana : looking downwards; a type of eye-gesture in which the movements of the eyelid and eyebrow along the vertical plane are on a upward movement, looking an object below but the pupils are hidden in eyelids, the glance with eye-balls fixed downwards (*NS*, VIII. 92-105).

'The lord who looks down' is knows as *avalokiteśvara* in Indian iconography. Here compassion is suggested. Compassion upon the suffering folk is the most popular and celebrated Bodhisattva.

402 **अवलोकित दृष्टि**

Avalokita dṛṣṭi : downcast eyes showing meditation. The eye-gesture of Citralekhā in *Vikramorvaśīya* (II), represents it.

403 **अवशीर्षक**

Avaśīrṣaka : 'having the head turned down' Suśr.

404 **अवस्था**

Avasthā : (a) Stage of development of dramatic action. There are five stages: *ārambha, yatna, prāptyāsā, niyatāpti* and *phalāgam.* (b) A technical term in *Yoga* which means age. Age is no bar for the practice of *yoga.* (c) State of experience. They are three: waking (*jāgrata*), dreaming (*svapna*) and deep sleep (*suṣupti*). (d) Women have been classified on the basis of their age as *bālā* (11-16 years), *taruṇī* (16-30 years), *prauḍhā* (30-55 years) and *vṛddhā* (beyond 55 years). (e) Condition.

405 **अवस्पन्दित**

Avaspandita : movement; a particular psychological state. Bharata defines it that in the matter arisen from auspicious or inauspicious, the other meaning is conveyed with cleverness, that is *avaspanditam* (*NS*, XVIII. 117-118). Abhinavagupta *(ibid)* interprets it that "*Śubhāśubha*" denotes fate. Therefore, when some inauspicious sense arises accidently, and with a desire to conceal that the answer is given having another sense with expertness. It conveys the inner sense like the throbbing of the eye. To explain it, he takes the example from *Veṇīsaṁhāra (*1.6), where the meaning accidentally arises that the sons of Dhṛtarāṣṭra are falling. There the answer is given, the calamity should be avoided and the swans are coming on the earth. (b) one of the constituents of *vīthī.* When auspicious or inauspicious meaning of the word is grasped, it is explained otherwise skillfully.

406 **अवहसित**

Avahasita : a broad laugh while ridiculing somebody. It is indulged in by the people of lesser culture and is accompanied by louder noise and shaking of the shoulders and head. It indicates queer actions, appearance or dress, etc., of a character on which account people are making fun of him.

407 **अवहास**

Avahāsa : making fun of (*A*,4.1.6). A particularly expressive aspect of NV communication is *avahāsa.* It involves a massive physiological reaction. The contractions of the facial muscles are the most noticeable. But, in addition, there are many contractions of the diaphragm and abdominal muscles so that the entire body shakes. As we reach full intensity, our blood vessels dilate and the production of tears increases until we may actually weep with laughter.

408 **अवहितपाणि**

Avahitapāṇi : holding anything in hand.

409 **अवहित्थ**

Avahittha : concealment of form or face.

410 **अवहित्थक-करण**

Avahitthaka karaṇa : derived from the *Janitā Cārī;* the hands are gradually lowered from a high position above the head towards the chest; the hands are also in *avahittha* (*NS*, IV. 155b-156a, IX,156, X.25). After performing *Janitā Cārī* the hands have fingers facing each other and dropped down slowly. It is used in secrecy.

411 **अवहित्थ-स्थान**

Avahittha sthāna : a type of *abhaṅga* pose prescribed for women (*NS*, XII. 163-164, 167-168), left foot in *samapāda* and right in *tyaśra* position, the reverse of the *āyata* pose, presiding deity Durgā. The standing posture for women. The left foot is in *sama*, the right foot placed obliquely at its side one *tāla* apart, hips slightly raised, one hand in *latā* and the other reaching the hips. It is used in natural conversation, determination, satisfaction, deliberation, conjecture, bashfulness, amorousness, sportiveness, grace, looking towards oneself, awaiting husband's arrival or towards the path of a lover and the erotic sentiment.

412 **अवहित्थ-हस्त**

Avahittha hasta : suppressed pride; both hands gesture from *Śukatuṇḍa hastas* (*NS*, IV.160). When two gestures in the *Śukatuṇḍa*-style are bent towards one's own breast and then are lowered down, it is called the *avahittha.* This is indicated for weakness, shyness to show and expose one's own body and anxiety (*NS*, IX,146-147). The *Bharata-Saṁhitā* accepts *avahittha* as a style of the joined hands. The *Abhinayadarpaṇa* edited by M.M. Ghose does not read it, but the *Mirror of Gesture* A. Coomaraswamy appreciates it. If two *alapadma* hands are placed on the chest, it is the *avahittha* style of the joined hands. It indicates the breast and to hold a play-ball. By another way, if the *Śukatuṇḍa* hands are held against the heart, it is the *avahittha.* It indicates debility, eagerness, thinness, wasting of the body etc. (*Mirror of Gesture,* p. 41).

413 **अवहित्था**

Avahitthā : concealment of emotions; a state of mind in which one makes a voluntary attempt to dissemble the expression of joy and similar feelings. A type of transitory state of mind. It is represented by speaking otherwise, looking downwards, breaking speech and pretended patience.

414 **अवाक्**

Avāk : having no speech, speechless (Ś.Br.).

415 **अवाच्**

Avāc : speechless (*AV*.X. 4.25).

416 **अवाचक**

Avācaka : imprecision. It is a poetic defect where the literal sense is inexpressive. It may occur in a word, in a part of word or in a sentence.

417 **अवाचिक**

Avācika : NV. It refers to a process in which others reveal their present feelings or emotional states through their facial expressions, the pattern of their eye-contact and the posture and the movement of their bodies.

NV communication is popularized in the Western Semiotics by the work of Argyle (1972) to distinguish language (verbal) from other semiotic systems of communication among human beings (NV).

NV communication can be subdivided into vocal and non-vocal and it very frequently used in the sense of non-vocal.

Obviously NV Communication is of prime importance in the discourse situation of face-to-face communication (Wales, 1990, 322-3).

Bharata in his *NS,* has coined the term *abhinaya* to denote NV language. He maintains that there are four different kinds of NV language. He suggested that a distinction should be made what he called *vācika* (sign language), *āṅgika* (action language), *sāttvika* (emotion language) and *āhārya* (object language). Ruesch and Kees (1956) pointed out in their early discussions three types of NV language: Sign language, action language and object language. Sign language, for him 'includes all those forms of codification in which words, numbers and punctuation signs have been supplanted by *gestures'.* Action language refers to the communicative consequences of ordinary actions. Object language comprises all intentional and non-intentional displays of material things. Ruesch goes on to point that not only do these different 'languages' differ from one another in mode of codification and in whether they comprise actions or the results of actions but they also differ in terms of the kinds of information they convey. He suggested, for example, that the kinds of messages which 'action language' conveys are different from the kinds of messages that are conveyed by the explicit use of gestures (or 'sign language', in his terms). Ekman and Friesen suggested that in considering any action (by implication from a comunicational perspective) one must see that it may differ in how it was acquired, the circumstances in which it may be employed, and in how it encodes whatever message it may convey. They further propose five types of NV behaviour: emblems, illustrators, affect displays, regulators and adopters.

Thus, *avācika* is most frequently used to refer to all of the ways in which communication is effected between persons when in each other's presence, by means other than words. It refers to the communicational functioning of bodily activities, gesture, facial expression and orientation, posture and spacing, touch and smell, and of those aspects of utterance that can be considered apart from the referential content of what is said. NV communication is usually concerned with aspects of behaviour which play an important role in establishing and maintaining interaction and interpersonal relationships.

418 **अवाच्य/ग्राम्य संकेत**

Avācya/grāmya saṁketa : obscene signals; not to be uttered *(Manu)*; Obscene signals are sexual actions which cause offence to those who witness them. Every culture has its sexual taboos and although these vary from place to place and time to time, it is generally true that the more 'advanced' a sexual action is considered to be, the more likely it is to be forbidden in public.

Obscenity can be observed in two distinct situations. The first is the 'vulgarly friendly' and the second is the 'deliberately malicious'. In the friendly situation, a man makes an advanced sexual gesture to a woman, or *vice versa,* and here the obscenity lies in the fact that their relationship has not reached the stage of intimacy where such a sign would be acceptable even in private. Since it is often done in public, it is even less acceptable and although no malice is intended, its message is nevertheless offensive. The classic example is the customer who makes an explicit sexual gesture towards the girl serving drinks in a bar. He feels free to make an open and direct comment, with his hands, concerning the shape of her breasts. This type of obscenity is quite different from the deliberate sexual insults aimed straight at a victim in a mood of insolent scorn and down right anger. Here the object is to use the 'dirtiest', taboo sign available as a symbolic form of attack.

The obscene gestures themselves are highly variable and are strongly influenced by the traditions of different subcultures in which they occur. They fall into five main categories: Male Phallic signs; Female Genital-aperture signs, copulatory signs, masturbatory signs and groping signs.

Some people may find even discussion of obscene gestures offensive. Although they may sometimes provoke retaliation, obscene gestures are essentially substitutes for aggression—miniature rituals that take the place of physical assault—and their social value in this respect has perhaps been underestimated in the past.

419 अविद्धवक्त्र-नृत्तहस्त

Aviddhavaktra-nṛttahasta : fixed bent-face-dancing hands. When two shoulders or elbows and palm-tips touch artistically and move in an opposite style (*parāṅmukha*), it is called *aviddhavaktra* (*NS*, IX. 176-197).

420 अविनाभाव-सम्बन्ध

Avinābhāva-sambandha : relation of non-duality, necessary connection of one thing with another.

421 अवियोग-व्रत

Aviyoga-vrata : a ceremonial in which food is to be distributed to helpless people.

422 अवीर

Avīra : (a) a woman having neither husband nor son. (b) a woman who is independent, but not gone astray (*Smṛti*). (c) Tāntric aspirants belonging to the probationary stages of *ārambha, taruṇa, yauvana* and *prauḍha (Paraśurāma-kalpasūtra*, X.58).

423 अव्याकरणिकता

Avyākaraṇikatā : a grammatism. ungrammatical speech. Each word is correctly formed and pronounced but the order is wrong, or there is an incorrect conjugation of verbs, declensions of nouns, and comparison of adjectives and adverbs. Parts of speech (say, a verb or preposition) may be omitted. If the message is present to a minor degree, it may be possible to decipher it. More severe cases speak nonsense often accompanied by preservation or stereotype. It may cause syntactic aphasia, incoherence and drivelling.

424 अव्याप्ति

Avyāpti : fallacy of inadequate extent (non-inclusion of a part of thing defined). For example, if we say that a student is one who reads in a school, the definition is too narrow because it excludes those who study in a college or other institutions.

425 अशौच

Aśauca : pollution, impurity. The clearest expression of ritual status is through the criterion of commensality in Indian villages. The commensal hierarchy is based on the theory that each caste has a certain quality of ritual purity which is lessened, or polluted, by certain commensal contacts with castes having an inferior quality. This is an application of what Stevenson (1954) has called the Hindu Pollution Concept, which lies at the root of ritual status. Commensal contacts include the cooking of food and its consumption. Drinking and smoking follow similar rules of exclusion.

Dharmaśāstras deal with two fundamental types of pollution. Linguistically they may be called *intransitive* and *transitive* pollutions. Each of these types of pollution is associated with distinctive paradigms: orderly variations on rules not unlike the declensions of grammar.

When a birth or death occurs in Ego's kin-group he is subjected to intransitive pollution. Defilement is believed to 'spread' through the kin-group, which is conceived. As in the grammatical instransitive, there is no object of action. The extent of intransitive pollution is proportionate to *varṇa* rank, *i.e.*, the higher the rank the less the pollution.

Transitive pollution is incurred through *interaction* with biological phenomena. It is subdivided into (a) internal pollution, in which Ego, acts upon objects and (b) external pollution in which the Ego is the object. External pollution is brought on if one contacts biological substance or process, for example by touching or eating dead matter or bodily secretions. The extent of transitive pollution is proportionate to *varṇa* rank. The extent of internal pollution is proportionate to the purity of the *varṇa* harmed. The extent of the external pollution is proportionate to the defilement of the *varṇa* contacted.

āśauca is another term for *aśauca*. The word *śauca* is formed from *śuci* (pure) with the negative prefix (Pāṇini, V.1.131; VII. 3.30). The *Mit.* on *Yāj.* (III.1) defines *āśauca* as an emergent attribute attaching to a person, which is removed by the lapse of time or bath and the like. It is of two kinds: *Janamāśauca* or *Sūtaka* (that rising on birth) and *mṛtakāśauca* or *śavāśauca* (that arising on death).

426 **अश्रान्तपदता**

Aśrāntapadatā : expressiveness of words (a) (*A*, 2.10.9).

427 **अश्रु**

Aśru : tears; flow of tears. (a) A sudden outburst of excessive wrath, grief or ecstasy causes a gushing outflow of tears from the eyes. (b) one of the temperamental states. It is manifested by wiping the eyes full of tears, shedding tear incessantly.

428 **अश्लील**

Aślīla : indecent, obscene, lewd.

429 **अश्व**

Aśva : (a) one of the five types of *utplavanas* mentioned by Nandikeśvara. (b) the horse. The horse was considered to be a sacred animal when it served as the king's mascot, and the god Viṣṇu incarnated himself in the form of a horse during the course of one of his incarnations (*avatāra*) into the world of men. Buddhism also had its divine horse in the person of *Bodhisattva Balāḥ* whose mission consisted in saving travellers in distress.

430 **अश्वक्रान्त**

Aśvakrānta : In certain *Tantras*, India has been divided into three regions one of which is called *aśvakrānta* or *gajakrānta*. According to *Śaktimaṇḍala Tantra*, the tract of land from the Vindhyan hill to the great ocean is called *aśvakrānta*.

431 **अश्वक्रान्त स्थान**

Aśvakrānta sthāna : *samapāda* and *sūcī*, also *agratala sañcara*; the second foot is lifted up, the knee is bent; used for catching hold of a branch of tree, plucking a cluster of flower (*NS*, XII.172b-173b). It occurs in *Mālavikāgnimitra* (Act III). The pose of *yakṣī* in Śāncī depicts this posture. One foot is in *sama* and the other bent on the forepart either ready for *sūcī* or not. It is employed in faltering, reeling, stumbling, taking a bunch of flowers and keeping it, fright, supporting the branch of a tree gracefully and holding the loosened garment, and in *lalita*.

432 **अश्व (नायक)**

Aśva (nāyaka) : the Horse-man. The man whose organ is twelve *aṅgulas* in length (*Kāmasūtra*, 2.1.1.). Vātsyāyana classifies men according to the size of their sexual organs. Such a man has a very long, but lean, face, ears, neck, lips and feet, fatty armpits, fleshy arms and strong, soft-course thick hair. According to *Angaṅgaraṅga* (3.18-19), while he walks he always keeps his feet in touch with the earth. He delights in big and robust woman. He rejoices very much in giving nail-cuts and tooth-cuts during sexual union.

433 **अश्व-मुद्रा**

Aśva-mudrā : the horse-like gesture. It can be formed by the *kṣurikā mudrā*.

434 **अश्वारोहण**

Aśvārohaṇa : horse-riding. The horse provides an interesting symbolicity in Indian culture. The open-legged posture of the rider and the rhythmic movements of the horse's body has a sexual undertone and this, combined with its size, strength and power, gives it a massive but unconscious appeal for girls approaching puberty.

The use of horses by low-born villagers was unacceptable to the Indian elite. No Balahi was permitted to ride on his horse past an upper-caste person or village, no Bania past a Bundela Rajput's house, no subordinate past his superior officer (Fuchs: 1950: 35; Russell and Hiralal II.453, III.293, IV.439).

Thus to ride on a horse was looked upon in the same light as the palanquins; and when a person of inferior consequence met a superior or a government officer while riding, he had to dismount from his horse as a mark of respect until the other had passed.

435 **अष्टकर्मन्**

Aṣṭa karman : eight-fold duties of a king.

436 **अष्टचोर**

Aṣṭacora : eight-fold thief: one who commits theft, one who incites another to stealing, one who gives food to a thief, one who lodges one, one who is on friendly terms with a thief and, one who gives hints to a thief, one who helps one, and one who hides a thief.

437 **अष्टताल**

Aṣṭatāla : a system of proportions; one of the basic units of the measurement of human form used in Indian sculpture. It is a type of height measurement. A textually permissible measure to be adopted for making human beings (*Bṛahat Saṁhitā* 68.7).

438 **अष्टदलपद्म**

Aṣṭadalapadma : eight-pettled lotus. Tāntric symbol in the composition of the *cakras* and without the human body and also in the diagram. The petals are said to contain the letters (*ka, ca, ṭa, ta, pa, ya, sa* and *la* (*Kāmakalāvilāsa*, 33).

439 **अष्टपाश**

Aṣṭapāśa : eight fetters leading to human bondage: *lajjā* (shame), *bhaya* (fear), *śaṅkā* (misgiving), *ghṛṇā* (hatred), *jugupsā* (upbraiding), *kula* (pedigree), *śīla* (manners) and *jāti* (birth or caste). *Paraśurāma-kalpasūtra* (X.70).

440 **अष्टमंगल**

Aṣṭamaṅgala : eight auspicious marks. The following eight things are said to be *aṣṭamaṅgala* : lion, bull, elephant, a fan, a jar, a banner, a drum and a lamp (*Agni*, 58.31): (Fig. 440).

मृगराजं वृषं नागं व्यजनं कलशं तथा ।
वेजयन्तीं तथा भेरीं दीपमित्यष्टमङ्गलम् ॥

441 **अष्टमैथुनाङ्ग**

Aṣṭamaithunāṅga : eight techniques required for sexual union. They are *smaraṇa* (evocative remembrance), *kīrtana* (uttering sweet words), *keli* (sport), *prekṣaṇa* (special look), *guhyabhāṣaṇa* (secret dialogue), *saṅkalpa* (determination), *adhyavasāya* (patience and perseverence) and *kriyāniṣpatti* (completion of sexual intercourse). *Dakṣa Saṁhitā* (VII. 31-32).

442 **अष्टाङ्ग**

Aṣṭāṅga : (a) eight limbs, denotes the right limbs of the human body, namely two hands, chest, forehead, two knees, and the feet. A salutation with all these limbs was known as the *aṣṭāṅga* or *sāṣṭāṅga namaskāra*.

Patañjali has developed the technique of *aṣṭāṅga-yoga* - the eight constituents of *yoga*, broadly divided into two categories, technically known as *bahiraṅga* (external) and *antaraṅga* (internal). The first category includes *yama* (abstinence); *niyama* (observance of conduct), *āsana* (posture) and *prāṇāyāma* (breathing technique). The second category enumerates *pratyāhāra* (withdrawal or control of senses), *dhāraṇā* (concentration), *dhyāna* (meditation) and *samādhi* (sublime equanimity). (b) *aṣṭāṅga pran∞āma* : a type of obeisance. Eight parts of the body (the two feet, two knees, two hands, the chest, and the head, hence called) are to touch the ground; The *Purāṇas* explain the *aṣṭāṅga praṇāma* as one where the eight units are feet, hands, knees, chest, head, eyes, speech and mind:

padbhyām karābhyām jānubhyām
urasā śirasā dṛśā
vacasā manasā ceti
praṇāmo aṣṭāṅga īritaḥ

(*Sk. P.* II. 9.29.28)

443 **अष्टाङ्गपातम्**

Aṣṭāṅgapātam : the salutation involving the touch of eight parts of the body (*hasta, pāda, jānu, vakṣa, mastaka, akṣi, grīvā, pṛṣṭhamadhyaga)* with the ground.

444 **असंयुत हस्त**

Asaṁyuta hasta : the single hand-gesture; the hands are of supreme importance in *abhinaya*. Their movements have been grouped under those of the single hand and those of combined (*saṁyuta*) hands. The single hand-gesture form a fairly complete alphabet for a language. According to *NS* (IX.82), the *asaṁyuta hasta* is employed to represent offering to a deity, carrying a casket, etc. It occurs in *Kumārasaṁbhava* (5.63) and elsewhere.

445 **असंस्तुत**

Asaṁstuta: not agreeing, obstinate. *Dhāvati paścādasaṁstutam cetaḥ* (*Śāk.* 1.31).

446 **असत्**

Asat : non-existence, bad, false.

447 **असत्कार्यवाद**

Asatkāryavāda : the philosophical doctrine according to which the effect is something new and does not preexist in the cause.

448 **असत्प्रलाप**

Asatpralāpa : incoherent chatter. The incoherent talk of persons who are just awakening, drunk, insane or childish. It is prattling about the matter not relevant in both the senses (*Daśarūpaka*, III; *NS*, XVIII.119). It is one of the thirteen constituents of *vīthī* in which the learned speaks what is beneficial in the company of fools, but it is not accepted as such.

449 **असम्भाषा**

Asaṁbhāṣā : prohibition to converse, absence of an opportunity to converse (*A*, 1.16.25.). In joint family system a father-in-law is forbidden to talk with his daugher-in-law. The elder brother can not talk to the wives of younger brothers directly, or address each other by name. All the familiarity between them is strictly forbidden in tribal as well as non-tribal society. An Indian couple is prohibited by convention to mention each other's name, even a pet-name. He will speak of her as the "mother of his child", the "one in the house", "the family". This rule is observed also by affines under the rule of avoidance.

Indian castes have some strict taboos on names and on conversation between the sexes. A man will only address

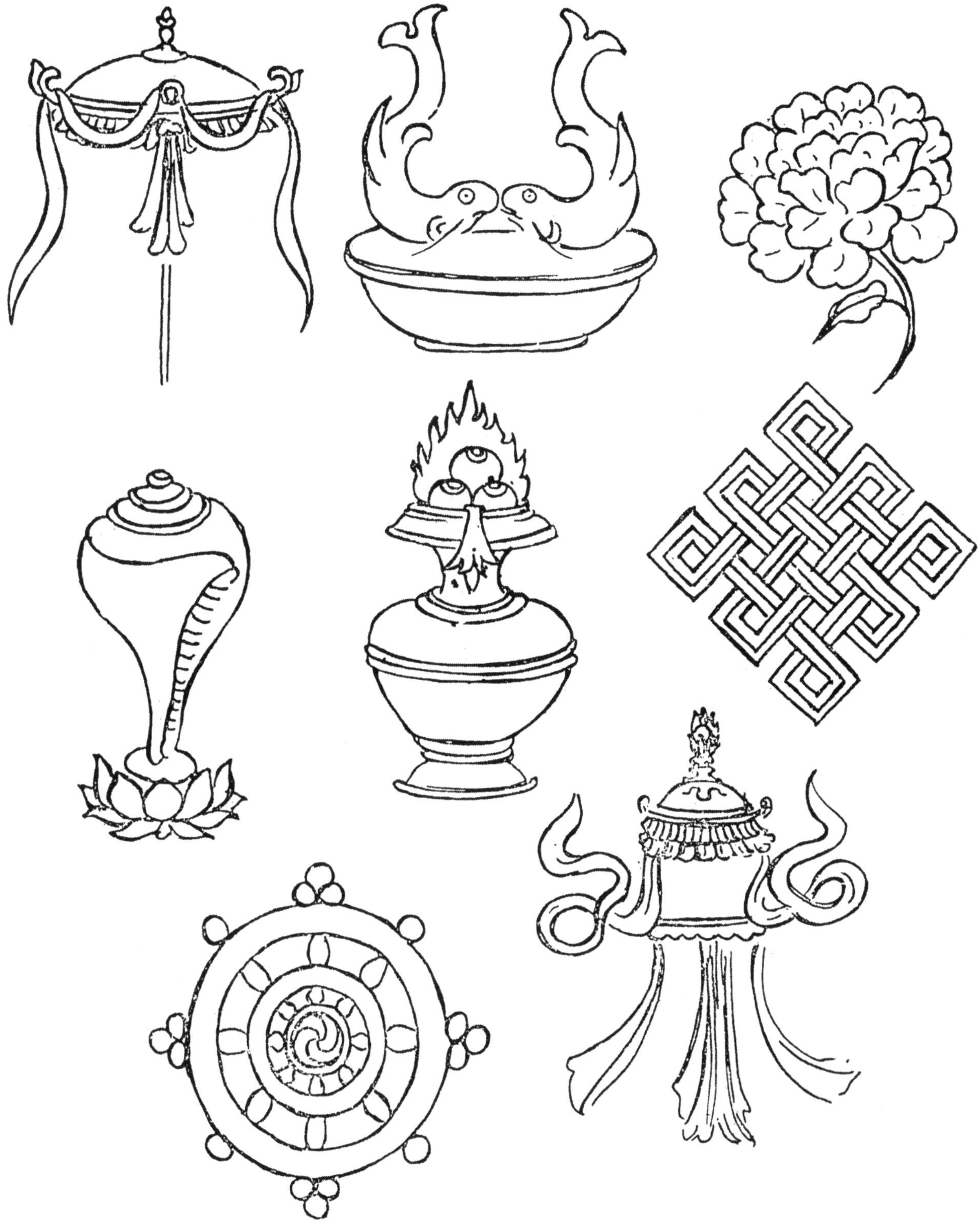

Fig. – (440)

his wife, sister, daughter, paternal aunt or niece directly. If he has occasion to speak some other women he will talk his daughter or other female relative with him and do his business through her. He will not speak even to his own son before a crowd. A woman will similarly only speak to her father, son or nephew. She will not speak to her elder-brother-in-law, and she will not address her husband in the presence of his father, elder brother, or any other relative whom he revers. A wife will never call her husband by his name, but always address him as father of her son, and, if she has no son, will sometimes speak to him through his younger brother. Neither the father nor the mother will call their eldest son by his name, but will use some other name. Similarly a daugher-in-law is given a fresh name on coming into the house, and on her arrival her mother-in-law looks at her for the first time through a guna or ring of baked gram-flour. A man meeting his father or elder brother will touch his feet silently. On meeting his sister's son or son-in-law will touch his feet and say "*Sāhib Salām* ." This custom is prevalent in the Baghelkhand region of Madhya Pradesh.

A woman should not talk to her father-in-law or husband's elder brother, neither these persons should talk to her. If this rule is violated, the woman and the family is considered to have lost the prestigious position. She is considered shameless and devoid of virtue.

In almost all the tribes and castes, the children would not speak before elders, but the Hill Marias of Bastar do not observe any such restriction. The boys may even reprimand the elders. Such an attitude on part of youngsters towards elders can not be observed in the neighbouring tribes like the Bison-horn Marias or Murias.

450 **असूया**

Asūyā : envy, jealousy. It is the state of intolerance for another's merits and prosperity, due to one's arrogance. Proclaiming another's faults, frowning, showing contempt, expressing anger through wrathful gestures, etc. are the external manifestations of this mental state. Some other gesticulations may also be enumerated such as decrying virtues of others, casting glances in jealousy, downcast face, knitting eyebrows, disregard and abuse in public.

451 **अस्त्र**

Astra : a weapon which is thrown, missile, sword, arrow, etc. Divine missile. *Astra* is contemplated in different initiations (*Agni,* 8.20-58).

452 **अस्त्र-मुद्रा**

Astra-mudrā : (a) If fingers of the *padma* gesture are collected, it is the *astra* (*VD*). (b) if the ring-finger dominates (likely acts as a substitute of the little one), it is the *astra* (*VD*). (c) gesture of the weapon. If a sound of the palm should be made with the forefingers of a fist, it is called the *astra-mudrā* (*VD*).

453 **अस्पर्श-योग**

Asparśa-yoga : doctrine of non-attachment, also known as *anāśakti-yoga* which strikes the balance between *pravṛtti* (desire) and *nivṛtti* (extinction of desire). It takes away the string or the binding from *karma* (*Manu,* 1.89). The *yoga* of no contact, free from all attchment. The *yoga* of transcendence whereby one realizes the supra-rational reality. The path to the realization of non-duality (*Māṇḍūkya-kārikā,* 39). The *Karmayoga* of *Gītā* is also one kind of *asparśa-yoga* as it lays down stress on desireless action.

454 **अस्मिता**

Asmitā : egotism. Sense of personality which consists in the seen (the self) being held as if identical with the instruments of seeing such as mind and sense-organs (*Yogasūtra,* 5-9). *dṛgdarśanaśaktyorekātmatevāsmitā (ibid.* 6). In the western psychoanalytic theory there are three mental structures. The infant is all *id.* The *id* is entirely unconscious and is the home of instincts of sex and aggression. Later in life, material that is unacceptable is repressed into the *id* by the ego. The ego is the conscious self and develops as the child develops. It is the aspect of the mind that is in touch with reality. The ego controls instinctive desires-a strong ego exerts a firm control. A weak ego is characteristic of someone who is impulsive and easily frustrated. The ego is largely conscious but there are unconscious ego processes- the defenses-At about the age of five the super ego appears. Its normal development depends on identification of the same-sex parent, and it represents our acceptance of parents' feelings of right and wrong, their morality.

In adult life there should be a balance between these three components and it is the aim of the *yoga* to achieve this balance. If the super ego is too strong, we feel guilty about all our pleasures. Where the *id* is too powerful then we see uncontrolled sexuality and aggression as in Rāvaṇa. In this account the self is the equilibrium of these three components.

455 **अहङ्कार**

Ahaṁkāra : self-consciousness, selfishness, self-conceit.

456 **अहंभद्र**

Ahaṁbhadra : dispute that I am superior, self-conceit.

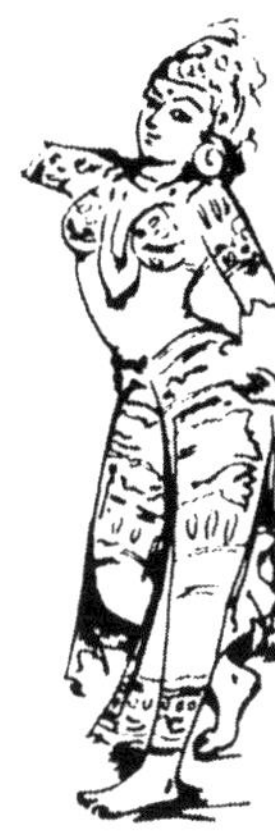

Fig – (456)

457 **अहह**

Ahaha : a particular interjection of sorrow or regret, alas, oh; *ahaha kaṣṭamapaṇḍitā vidheḥ* (*Bhāgavat*). It is prevalent in Hindi in the form of '*ae-hae*' ah, alas.

458 **अहह वाक्**

Ahaha vāk : groaning sound during coition made by the female partner (Dāmodaragupta *Kuṭṭinīmatam* 572).

459 **अहिंसा**

Ahiṁsā : non-voilence, non-injury. In his daily life and as a rule of conduct, what appeals most to the average Hindu is the philosophy of *ahiṁsā* or non-injury. Even those Hindus who eat meat will often shrink back in horror if asked to kill. In this matter, every Hindu is a Jain at heart. Thus, *ahiṁsā* is the Buddhist doctrine of non-violence. In a wide sense non-violence means that one should not harm others, avoid exploitation for furthering one's own interest, and behave with others as one would wish them to behave. In a narrow sense *ahiṁsā* emphasizes the non-killing of animals for religious purposes. The sentence *ahiṁsā paramo dharmaḥ* occurs frequently in *Mahābhārata* (VII. 182.38).

460 **अहे**

Ahe : a particle implying reproach, regret, separation.

461 **अहो**

Aho : particle showing joy, sorrow, surprise or wonder, often agreeable (*Ś-Br.*); *aho kāmī svatām paśyati (Rāmāyaṇa), aho bata mahatpāpam kartum vyavasitā vayam (Gītā). āhā* (Hindi) an exclamation of pleasure.

आ Ā

462 **आकम्पित शिर**

Ākampita śira : up and down movement of the head. It corresponds to *dīrgha kampita* mentioned by the *Mirror of Gesture*. Moved lightly: slowly up and down movement of the head and is used to give hint, to teach, to question, to address, to pass orders, to recognize, and calling by pointing out. The head is moved up and down slowly in *ākampita* while quickly and often in *kampita* (*NS*, VIII. 17-18).

463 **आकर्षण**

Ākarṣaṇa : attraction. We form impressions of other people's personalities, and much else about them, all the time usually without realizing that we are doing it. To understand how automatically you do this, try the following experiment: when sitting in a bus, look at a stranger for a few seconds, then close your eyes and reflect on what you have seen. You will find that in those few seconds you have formed impressions not only of sex, age and build, but also of ethnicity, profession and social class and of how warm, friendly, assertive neat and even of how trustworthy the person is. How do we form these impressions? How accurate are they?

First impressions are of crucial importance. Not only can they determine whether we decide to form a relationship with someone or not, but they can persist and colour our attitude to ward a person long after we have come to know them better. The first impression we form of someone depends on the first information we receive. This might be physical appearance, behaviour or a name. It might be person's social or professional role, their friends and family, or something someone has said about them. From what we observe we may make further assumptions that go far beyond what we can actually know and these can, sometimes be quite inaccurate.

As often as not, our first impression about someone is their appearance. We are likely to notice sex, height, build, facial expression, clothes, their general manner and who they are with. Vātsyāyana feels that attractive men are less intelligent than unattractive ones, but attractive women are more intelligent than the unattractive ones.

464 **आकर्षणी मुद्रा**

Ākarṣaṇī-mudrā : gesture of attraction. "From the gesture of *mahāmudrā*, keep the pair of fore-fingers in a bending style and exercise it with breathings of *prāṇa* and *apāṇa* as advised in *haṭhayoga*. This is called the *ākarṣaṇī mudrā* for those, who keep a close relation with the Paramount God." *(BT)*. 'This *mudrā* is said to be effacious in attracting the three worlds' (*Brahmāṇḍa P.*, II. 4.42.2). Thus in this *mudrā*, little and ring fingers along with the middle and forefingers are joined and made equal at the tips. Then making a hook of the middle finger, it is placed on the little and ring fingers, and the thumb is also joined with it.

465 **आकल्प**

Ākalpa : dress, ornament, adornment.

466 **आकल्प-विकल्प-तल्प-रचना**

Ākalpa-vikalpa-talpa-racanā : stretching the bed with the positive and negative thinking (Jayadeva: *Gītagovinda*, 6.3).

467 **आकांक्षा**

Ākāṅkṣā : *Nyāya-Vaiśeṣika* law of mutual expectancy. According to this law each word in a sentence must carry some meaning which is by itself incomplete and raises some expectation. See *āsakti*, *yogyatā* and *tātparya*. Words must be compatible in order to fulfil this condition, e.g. a mere string of words such as fire, man, water etc. does not produce a valid sentence. It needs mutual affinity between words. Thus, a sentence is a group of words which possesses expectancy, etc. Expectancy is the inability of a word to convey the meaning of a sentence on account of the absence of some other word. This expectancy is satisfied only when some other words are added to it.

468 **आकार**

Ākāra : the expression on the face (*A*, 1.15.7,19; 5.5.5-6), outward sign of emotion.

Ākāramauna is a related term. Here external form or feature shows silence but betrays feelings. Comp. *Kāṣṭhamauna*.

469 **आकाश**

Ākāśa : space. (a) a type of *bhramarī* mentioned by Nandikeśvara (*Abhinaya-darpaṇa*, 282-298). (b) sky, a free and open space (*ABr.* XIV.4). Space gives accommodation to all five substances (*ākāśasyāvagāhaḥ, tatvarthādhigama Sūtra*, V.18). It is eternal, pervasive and formless according to Jain philosophy. It includes our world (*loka*) and beyond (*aloka*). According to Jain philosophy, *ākāśa* affords room for the existence of all extended substances. It is infinite, eternal and imperceptible. It is divided into *lokākāśa* (organic) and *alokākāśa* (space beyond such world).

470 **आकाशभाषित**

Ākāśabhāṣita : The technique of speaking in the air. The actor adopts a variety of voices and must therefore be highly resourceful. It is specially seen in Bhāṇa, the monologue, which requires a special type of production. Bharata defines that addressing some on staying at a distance or not appearing in person or indirectly addressing some one who is not close by us called *ākāśabhāṣitam.* This mode of speaking will present the substance of a dialogue by means of replies related to various imaginary questions which may arise out of the play. Abhinavagupta agrees with Bharata *(NS,* XXV. 86-87; *Abhinava-Bhāratī,* p.280).

The related term *ākāśavāṇī* is *akāsbānī* in Halbi which means an oracle, an utterance not originating from a human source.

471 **आकाश-मण्डल**

Ākāśa-maṇḍala : the aerial *maṇḍala.* In the fights and movements of those moving in the air. They are to be employed also in fights, personal combats, and moving about on the stage with graceful and the sportive movements of the limbs and in accompaniment of instrumental music. They are described in detail in *NS* (Vol.II, 118-128). Aerial *maṇḍalas* are: *atikrānta, vicitra, lalita-sañcara, sūcīviddha, daṇḍapāda, vihṛta, alāta, vāmaviddha, lalita* and *krānta.*

472 **आकाशवचन**

Ākāśavacana : The technique of speaking in the air. It is the speech when the person addressed to is not on the stage. The dialogue is carried by uttering words in reply. A type of *citrābhinaya* (*NS*). Also known as *ākāśa bhāṣita.*

473 **अकाशिकी चारी**

Ākāśikī cārī : aerial, a type of *cārī (NS,* X). Those *cārīs* in which foot movements are performed more off the ground are *ākāśikī-cārīs.* These *ākāśikī cārīs* are sixteen in number: *atikrāntā, apakrāntā, pārśvakrāntā, ūrdhvajānu, sūcī, nūpurapādikā, dolāpādā, ākṣiptā, āviddhā, udvṛttā, vidyutbhrāntā, alātā, bhujaṅgatrāsitā, hariṇaplutā, daṇḍapādā* and *bhramarī.* These consist of the graceful movements of the limbs. They are to be used in the release of weapons like the arrow from a bow and thunderbolt, etc. The hands should precede, follow or accompany simultaneously the foot movements according to the importance of the hand gestures, the gaits or both. The hand should follow the foot movements, and the waist, the hand. After taking a step, gestures of the minor limbs should be used. When in a foot movement, the foot comes to rest on the ground, the corresponding hand should rest on the waist after its movement.

474 **आकाश्य**

Ākāśya : a stage-direction, looking at the sky. In Act III of *Śākuntalam,* the pupil enacts looking at the sky: the looking at the sky is a technical term here for addressing Priyaṁvadā who is at some distance. This mode of address according to Bharata is employed in addressing someone who is at a distance and who does not appear on the stage. According to *Daśarūpaka,* it belongs to *nāṭyadharmī* convention.

475 **आकुञ्चित मणिबन्ध**

Ākuñcita maṇibandha : opposite movement when the wrist is bent inwards; a reclining posture.

476 **आकुंञ्चित-शयन**

Ākuñcita-śayana : a posture of lying down. Limbs should be narrowed down and knees stuck to bed; it is to be used by persons afflicted with cold *(NS).*

477 **आकूत**

Ākūta : intention, purpose, gesture.

478 **आकूतपात**

Ākūtapāta : gesture indicating sentiment.

479 **आकृति**

Ākṛti : image, likeness, outward appearance. Excepting the hardy races of the Punjab, the Hindus are diminutive in appearance when compared with the peoples of Europe. The sole reason for this is often pointed out as the climate of the country. This is not quite correct. The climate has probably something to do with it, but the main cause of the poor physique of the Hindus is poverty of the lower classes and stupidity of the higher. The average Indian worker does not eat as much nourishing food in a month as an average European does in a week. Poor Hindus live on a starvation diet all the year round. Those who are worst off in this respect are the peoples of Southern states. The majority of the population of this area live on nothing more nourishing than rice gruel of poor quality and tarnished water.

The higher classes, on the otherhand, indulge in gluttony and avoid all work involving physical exertion. A Hindu who has enough money to maintain himself and his family thinks it demeaning to do any kind of manual work. Sports being considered childish, the tendency among the better classes of Hindus is to sit idle, sleep and gossip. The trading classes of cities are the worst sinners in this respect. The Bania usually starts work at about eight o'clock in the morning and leaves his shop at about nine in the evening. During the period he squats all along on a cushion or reclines on it and never leaves it except to answer calls of nature. He lunches and takes tea on the same cushion. Very naturally he develops a paunch and is unable to move about without the help of an automobile or cycle. For the hard-worked, famished Hindu labourer, the pot-bellied Bania is the embodiment of ease, comfort and material prosperity.

480 **आकेकरा**

Ākekarā : sight squinting slightly.

481 **आकेकरा दृष्टि**

Ākekarā dṛṣṭi : *Sañcārī bhāva dṛṣṭi* used in *sānta rasa* by moving the pupil (*tārā*) of the eye; half-shut glance (*NS*, VIII. 61-92). When in a glance the eyelids and eye-corners are winkled by halves and the eyeballs are turned up rapidly; it is called *ākekarā*. It is applicable to look at a distant object, separation and contraction.

482 **आक्रोश**

Ākrośa : form of speech and thought (*Bṛhaddevatā*, 144-60); to assail with angry words, speak aloud: उत्साहातिशयेन क्रियमाण: उच्चतमो ध्वनिराक्रोश:, for which cp. *TS.* VII. 2.1.4; also known as *ākranda* (*NS*, 18.16) reviling and abusing (*A*, 3.16.6; 3.18.12; 4.11.14).

483 **आक्षिप्त करण**

Ākṣipta karaṇa : derived from the *cārī* of the name but the final position of the *svastika* feet in *cārī* is not indicated in the *karaṇa*; hands and arms are also extended but no precise position indicated. The commentary adds that the hands are in *kaṭakāmukha* placed slightly on the side (*NS*, IV.115b-116a, X.37). The hand and the feet are thrown about swiftly. It is used in the gait of *Vidūṣaka*. (Fig. 483)

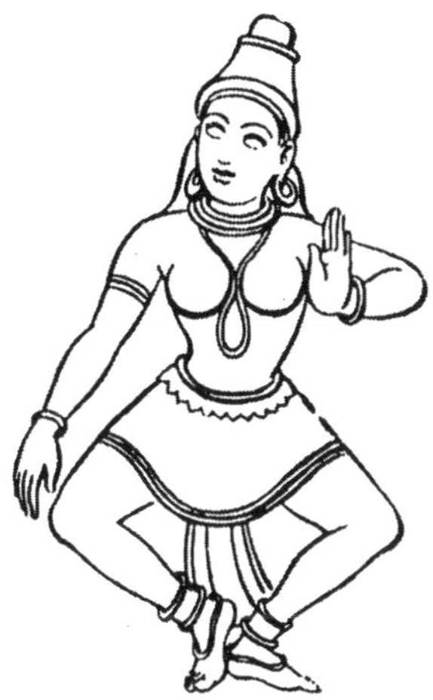

Fig. – (483)

484 **आक्षिप्त रेचित**

Akṣipta recita : The arm movement is circular, the hands are in *recita*; the knees are in spread out position (*NS*, IV. 80-81, IX. 220, X.262-63). The left hand is on the breast and the right in *recita* thrown up sideways and then the other in *recita* and *apaviddha*. It is employed in series of accepting and giving up things.

485 **आक्षिप्त शिर**

Ākṣipta śira : The face is turned up with a lifted head, given by *SR*.

486 **आक्षिप्ता चारी**

Ākṣiptā cārī : Feet in *samapāda kuñcita*; a *kuñcita* foot is lifted and then crosses the other leg and in the final position an *añcita* foot is placed three *tālas* apart; *kṣipta* knees associated with *ākṣipta recita karaṇas* and also an *aṅgahāra* by the same name. Lifting up a *kuñcita* foot and then taking it on the other side, and placing it on the ground with the heel crossing the shank of the other foot (*NS*, X.37).

487 **आक्षिप्तिका**

Ākṣiptikā : a type of movement of the head mentioned by *SR*, the face is turned up.

488 **आख्यान**

Ākhyāna : (a) form of speech and thought (*Bṛhaddevatā*, 144-60; *A*,2.10.4; *NS*, 18.18). (b) tale, story, legend. Legends relating to the events of hoary antiquity which were often recited by the Hotṛ in sacrifices before a select audience as a part of the ritual.

Ākhyāyikās (*HC*,II) were composed from very ancient times. The salient points are that it is in prose, has a high topic, is divided into sections called *ucchvāsa*, contains verses in the *vaktra* and *aparavaktra* metres which suggest coming events.

489 **आगम**

Āgama : (a) Valid mode of acquisition of property (*Smṛti*). (b) Augment, added to the primitive or basic word, during the process of formation of a complete word (*Vyākaraṇa*). (c) "Well-structured and traditionally communicated wisdom". The term *āgama* signifies the practice of worship rituals as well as the texts in Sanskrit which document, reflect and explain the rituals. The major divisions of the *āgama* are *Śaiva, Vaiṣṇava, Śākta, Jaina* and *Buddha*.

Sometimes, the *āgama* tradition is distinguished from the vedic tradition called *nigama*, which attaches little value to iconic worship and which lays great-stress on fire-rituals and sacrifices. *Āgama* is even projected as antagonistic to *nigama*. It may indeed have been so in the early stages of religious culture in the country, and now the Indian tribes alone follow the *nigama* tradition, while in the village India now *nigama* occurs almost as a subsidiary culture of *āgama*-cult.

490 **आग्नेय स्नान**

Āgneya-snāna : a kind of symbolic bath in which the body is smeared with holy ashes. It may be performed when one is either ill or unable to have a regular bath or when there is no time for one (*Parāśara*, XII.9.11).

491 **आघोष**

Āghoṣa : proclaiming, public announcement; also known as *āghoṣaṇa*. The echo of the tabors spread in all directions (*HC*,IV). Bāṇa fancies that it was the kettle-drum (*paṭaha*) that proclaimed immunity from danger to the whole world. Even now proclamations are made known to the people by beat of drum.

492 **आङ्गिक**

Āṅgika : kinesics. gestures or movements; one of the four types of *abhinaya*. According to Bharata's *NS*, it is divided into three types-namely, of the limbs (*śārīra*), of the face (*mukhaja*), and those relating to the movement of different parts of the entire body (*ceṣṭākṛta*). Gestures of the head are 13, the glances are 36, of the hand are 67, while there are others of the breasts, sides, stomach, waist, shanks, thighs and feet. (*NS*, VIII-X). These gestures are included in *abhinaya*.

The head, hands, chest, sides, hips and feet are the six parts (*aṅga*) of the body. Later texts speak of the six others — neck, arms, back, abdomen, thighs, shanks—as a further class, called *pratyaṅga*. Both of these are "limbs", or *śārīra*. The parts of the face (*upāṅga*) are the eyebrows, nostrils, lips, cheeks and chin. Actions involving the whole body, as in standing, sitting in different poses, or walking, are *ceṣṭā*. When the limbs are moved the action grows like the branches of a tree, one leading to another, and hence is called metaphorically, "branch" (*śākhā*). The action of parts of the face is called, following the same imagery, "sprout" (*aṅkura*), when with the spoken words imbedded within oneself like seeds, the actions show themselves above as sprouts on different parts of the face. Sometimes action precedes the word and indicates or paves the way for the coming words; in this case, the facial expression is called advance indication (*sūcā*).

493 **आङ्गिक भाषा**

Āṅgika bhāṣā : body language. Cues stemming from the position, posture and movement of another person's body which provide information regarding his or her emotional states and feelings.

The concept of body language is very old in India. This ancient Indian concept has only emerged in the Western communicative behaviour very recently. Both its written form and the scientific study of it have been labelled "kinesics". Body language and kinesics are based on the behavioural patterns of NV communication, but kinesics is still so new a science that its authorities can be counted on the fingers of one hand. Body language can include any non-reflexive or reflexive movement of a part, or all the body, used by a person to communicate an emotional message to the outside world. To understand this unspoken language, kinesics experts often have to take into consideration cultural differences and environmental differences. The average man, unschooled in cultural nuances of body language, often misinterprets what he sees. A study of body language is a study of the mixture of all body movements from the very deliberate to all the completely unconscious, from those that apply only in one culture to those that cut across all cultural barriers.

Most, but not all expressive behaviour is the expression of emotions and attitudes through body language—NV channels of communication. Each of the senses of a person is an open channel for receiving expressive messages. Some of the most important are visual, and they are sent mainly by face.

Bharata and Vātsyāyana estimate that the human face can make thousands of different expressions. My research pertaining to the tribal society shows that the tribes who never communicated with the elites have almost identical ways of expressing and interpreting six primary emotional expressions: happiness, sadness, surprise, fear, anger and disgust. Much more of a complicating factor is presented by facial display rules that vary from region to region, and even between the sexes.

494 **आङ्गिक व्यवहार**

Āṅgika-vyavahāra : kinesic behaviour. Human kinesic behaviour has been modified through history by changes in furniture style (the series of more relaxed postures and accompanying manners determined by new trend toward curved and softer sitting furniture), in clothes and hairdo (men's tight pants, jeans for both men and women, long or short hair in women, and long hair in men, all have produced conscious or unconscious gestures, manners and postures), etc., and just as actors must make an effort to more naturally in the clothes of the past, so the non-contemporary writer must make an effort to make his characters move in strange clothes.

495 **आङ्गिकाभिनय**

Āṅgikābhinaya : the physical gesticulation, gesture language, mime, gesture, movement of the body; further divided as follows: (i) *mukhaja* (facial) having *upāṅga* minor limbs such as eyebrows, eyelids, eyeballs, nose, lips, chin and mouth.

(ii) *Śārīra* (bodily): having *aṅga* - major limbs such as head, chest, waist, side, hips, thighs and feet.

(iii) *Ceṣṭākṛta* (resulting from the movements, residing in bodily movements) having three major parts (a) *śākhā* -

used frequently in dance. (b) *aṅkura* - used occasionally in dance. (c) *sūca* - not relevant for dance. The Act IV of *Śākuntalam* is full of *āṅgikābhinaya. Śākhā* is explained as the gesticulation relating to the limbs. The limbs are divided as major and minor.

496 **आचमन**

Ācamana : sipping water; see *ācāmodaka.* Before beginning religious ceremonics, before and after meals and before and after doing many other acts, it was enjoined that a man should sip water:

> *Snātvā pītvā kṣute supte bhuktvā rathyopasarpaṇe*
> *ācāntaḥ punarācāmedvāso viparidhāya ca*
> (*Yājna.* 1.196).

compare: *acavāin dīnhe pān* (*Mānasa,* 1.99).

497 **आचामोदक**

Ācāmodaka : water used for rinsing after meals (*A,* 3.8.8.); water meant for sipping; *ācamana:* to sip from the palm of the hand (*ch.up*); the act of sipping a little water from the palm of the hand by way of purification before means or religious ceremonies; known as *ācaman* in Hindi. *Vasiṣtha-Dharmasūtra* (III. 36. 31-34) records the social aspects of sipping: " A brāhmaṇa becomes pure by sipping water free from bubbles and foam, that reaches his heart. But a Kṣatriya by sipping water that reaches his throat. A Vaiṣya by sipping water that wets his palate. A woman and a Śūdra by merely touching water with the lips." *ācamana* is sipping of water which is one of the constituents of *Sandhyā* prayer. The ritual is to be performed in sitting posture facing north or east. The water should be sipped thrice from the right hand with which then the performer should touch his eyes, ears, nose, heart and head. The water is to be poured in the hollowed palm of the right hand which should be shaped in the form of a cow's ear (*Gobhila.* Gr.S. 1.2.5-6, Ap. *D.S.* 1.15.15-16, *Gaut.* 1.35-40, *Manu* 11. 58-62, *Yāj.* 1.18-21). In Tāntric tradition, *ācamana* is the symbolic purification of body by sipping water from the palm and sprinkling it on different parts of the body. It consists of the purification of the three forms of body, namely, gross, subtle and causal (*Mahānirvāṇa* V.39).

498 **आचार**

Ācāra : 'mode of action', (rites, norms and rules, observances, conduct, behaviour, customs and kindered characteristics pertaining to different stages of individual, family, communal, social and religious life. These are described in detail in *Smṛtis* and digests under different categories and specific terms. (1) For individuals, there are *ācāras* belonging to *śauca* category connected with cleanliness of the body. (b) the *saṁskāras* or sacraments connected with different stages of individual life form *ācāra* of a different category. (c) *vratas* or religious rites belong to another class which being effected make a particular thing or person fit for a specific purpose. (d) *Āhnika, tarpaṇa, mahāyajña, devayajña, vaiśvadeva, nṛyajña, dāna, pratiṣṭhā,* etc. also fall in the category of *ācāra,* a few of which are non-obligatory. (e) apart from the codified *ācāras,* there are customary ones connected with the harvest, seasonal changes, and so on. A few of them like Holi, Dīpāvalī, cart-festival etc., have assumed a national character. (f) in *Tantra ācāra* is the means of spiritual attainment which varies from person to person according to competence. They fall under two broad categories: *dakṣina* and *vāma.* It is generally held that those who participate in the rituals of pañca-makāra belong to the category of vāmācāra (Kaulamārgarahasya, II). According to a different tradition everyone is a follower of *Dakṣiṇācāra* by birth (*Prāṇatoṣaṇī,* VII. 7.532). In a few works we come across a two-fold division: *aghorācāra* and *yogācāra.*

Ācāra is a widely discussed concept in the normative science of India. Consideration of social behaviour shows an important fact about the concept of *ācāra,* namely that is not absolute, but relative. What is abnormal social behaviour to one group of people may be normal to another, and vice versa. Language as a part of social behaviour is similarly affected.

Ācāra, from the point of view of its meaning, may be either idiosyncratic (its meaning known only to one person) or shared. Behaviour which has shared meaning is said to be informative (*Manu.* 3.4), insofar as it conveys information to someone (*yasmindeśe)* other that the producer, but such behaviour will only also be communicative if the producer intended to send that information that was received. Bṛhaspati suggests that behaviour may be said to be interactive if, within the context of an interaction, it can be shown to influence the behaviour of other. Thus all behaviour (*ācāra)* is communication. Modern information theory also attests this hypothesis.

499 **आचिख्यासा**

Ācikhyāsā : narration, wanting to explain; here the intention of the speaker is neither praise nor blame; the speaker is rather unable to decide between the two. It is a form of speech and thought (*Nirukta* VII. 3; *Bṛhaddevatā,* 134-39).

500 **आच्छोट**

Acchoṭa : sound produced by fingers.

501 **आटविक**

Āṭavika : a forest chieftain (*A,* 1.10.3; 8.4. 41, 43).

502 **आटविकराज्य**

Āṭavika-rājya : those *āṭavika* kingdoms which were closely connected with Ḍāhala in Madhya Pradesh.

503 **आततायिन्**

Ātatāyin : murderer; designation of the following hostile persons: incendiary, poisoner, one armed with weapons, robber, one who wrests a field or carries away one's wife (*Smṛti*). Person who has his bow drawn, who endeavours to kill somebody, and in later texts anybody committing a serious crime. *Yogavāśiṣṭha* (1.4.46.9) records:

> *Udyatāsim viṣāgnim ca śāpodyatakaram tathā bhāryātikramaṇam caiva vidyāt saptātatāyinaḥ.*

504 **आताम्र**

Ātāmra : reddish.

505 **आताम्रस्फारितनेत्र**

Ātāmrasphāritanetra : eyes red and wide; quality of the Hare-man (*Ratirahasya,* 3.30.31).

506 **आतिथेयी**

Ātitheyī : hospitable. The Hill Marias are an extremely hospitable persons. Previously they used to welcome visitors outside the village and offer anything they could afford. The presentation might have been inmassive tuber or cucumber or any fruit or tuber. This practice, however, seems to have been given up, though girls and women still obstruct the way, more perhaps with an idea to get some money than for any sentimental or ceremonial purpose.

But ghoṭul is still the resting place for the stranger guest in the Hill areas. As soon as one reaches a village, the villages first look after the luggage carriers and give them ration and utensils so that one may cook, eat and return. They then bring rice in a leaf-cup, some chillies and salt. They normally do not have vegetables and they do not offer tubers. They instead bring a chicken. They readily and ungrudgingly bring water from the stream normally which is quite afar.

The hospitable character is also illustrated by the fact that the Hill Marias offer *salphī* to the stranger if he is passing by their *salphī* tree (*Caryota urens*). They never accept money in return of this hospitality. They say that it is their duty to entertain the guest.

507 **आतिथ्य**

Ātithya : hospitality.

508 **आत्मगत**

Ātmagata : soliloquy; interpersonal, alone-speak; the talk supposed not to be heard. When, overwhelmed with excessive joy, intoxication, fit of passion, fear, astonishment, anger and sorrow, etc.; one speaks in one's mind that type of talking is called *ātmagatam* (*NS,* XXV.88-89). This form of speech is indicated by the stage-direction *ātmagatam* or *svagatam.* Dhanañjaya (*Daśarūpaka,* 1.67) has mentioned that inaudible to all is regarded as *svagatam.* It falls under *citrābhinaya.*

Ātmagata is a well established dramatic practice found in Sanskrit dramas whereby a character, normally alone on stage, utters his thoughts and feelings, often directly to the audience like an extended ASIDE. Realistic in the sense that it reflects the practice of 'thinking aloud'. Soliloquy is an effective device for the sympathy of the audience: particularly so if the 'hero' is a villain. With the decline of poetic drama in India, however, the extreme use and extended utterances of soliloquy also declined.

Ātmagata : ātma *i.e. antas* means 'within' or 'inside' and '*gata*' means 'communication'. Can communication happen inside on human being? Can a person be both the sender and receiver of the message? - yes, our sages thought about it. As a matter of fact, when they thought, they were communicating themselves. They were sending messages themselves - not that they were talking or making noises, but they were sending and receiving messages. So the same human being was on the both ends of the communication process. They were *antaryāmī* and ātmasaṁvāda was a type of continuous dialogue coming into the brain from all over the body as well. Intra-personal communication is one of the five levels of modern communication theory. At this level communication takes place inside a human being.

509 **आत्मगुण**

Ātmaguṇa : the eight cardinal virtues. They are kindness to all creatures, forebearance, freedom from envy, purity, ease, right conduct, magnanimity and contentment (*Gaut. Dh. S.* VIII. 20-21).

510 **आत्मतुष्टि**

Ātmatuṣṭi : self-satisfaction, a type of the source of *dharma.*

511 **आत्मविक्रय**

Ātma-vikraya : selling oneself. Somadeva (*Nītivākyāmṛta*) opines: *na parecchānuvartanenātmavikrayaḥ* one should not sell oneself by living according to the will of another.

512 **आत्म-संस्कृति**

Ātma-saṁskṛti : self-esteem. means of the development of soul (*Sat.*XXVI.3), self-discovery. Probably, like most other people, the people during the Brāhmaṇa-age were aware of missing opportunities for greater self-fulfillment. They thought of trying to express their personality more effectively, made their relationships more satisfying, managed their emotions better, were more in control of the soul. Thus *ātma-saṁskṛti* was the expert knowledge of the inner soul. It was road to a better life. We need encouragement, not only from others but from ourselves, and if we allow ourselves to feel more cultured and more competent, other people are much more likely to form a favourable impression of us, and so reinforce our self-esteem. Thus it was a way of knowing one's personality stereotypes. These stereotypes are inevitable and indispensable. We cannot form impressions of people, not even of ourselves, without comparing and generalizing. Thus it was a greater insight into temperament - emotional makeup - as well as insight into dealing with social situations and problems. Through this they mapped their life, made their needs and expectations known.

Ātma-saṁśkṛti is the valuation we place on our own worth. It largely hinges on the extent to which we see ourselves as achieving the goal and standard that we feel are important, but the esteem of other people is also an important factor in conforming our worth.

513 **आत्मसम्पद्**

Ātmasampad : personal excellences (*A*, 6.1.6).

514 **आत्मस्तुति**

Ātmastuti : self-praise. a general rule of etiquette (*Manu* 1.4). The author said not to use first person in order that *ātmastuti* or *svapraśaṁśā* (self-praise) may be achieved. It is on considerations of objectivity that the avoidance of the first person is practised by literary men, say the commentators. These are general rules.

515 **आत्मानुशीलन**

Ātmānuśīlana : meta communicative content. In order to decide the message successfully, it is necessary to go beyond its absolute meaning. In the same way the encodes have to take into account the nature of social situation and the personal characteristics of the decoder, the decoder must consider the social space and time (*deśakāla*) and characteristics of the encoder or in order to understand what is being conveyed in the message.

516 **आत्रेयी**

Ātreyī : a woman who has bathed after her monthly impurity (*Smṛti*). *Ś.Br.* (1.4.1.13) records: ऋतुस्नाता आत्रेयी

Ātreyī-mudrā is a psychophysical technique for controlling the fire element. The technique is not disclosed.

517 **आदिकौशिक**

Ādikauśika : a person who goes about showing god's images in the time of *Arthaśāstra* (1.17.19).

518 **आदित्यदर्शन**

Ādityadarśana : also known as *niṣkramaṇa*, *upaniṣkramaṇa* or *nirṇayaṇa*. It is the rite of taking the child, when it is four months old, out of the house in open (*Manu* II. 34).

519 **आदेश**

Ādeśa : (a) substitute as contra-distinguished with *sthānin* (the origin). (b) Vedic injunctions आदेशस्योपव्याख्यानम् *Ch.Up.* तस्यैष आदेशः 'उपदेशः' *Kena.* (c) command.

520 **आधान**

Ādhāna : pledging or mortgaging (*Smṛti*).

521 **आधिवेदन**

Ādhivedana : marrying another woman when there is already the lawfully wedded wife (*Smṛti*).

522 **आधिवेदनिक**

Ādhivedanika : a kind of *strīdhana* presented to a woman by her husband on his marrying another woman (*Smṛti*).

523 **आधूत शिर**

Ādhūta-śira : head lifted obliquely upwards once, side bent of the head; raising once the head stantingly up. It is used to indicate pride, to look at one's own person, things by the sides and to suggest one's own self as a powerful one. *Sāraṅga-deva* (*SR*, IV., VII.55-56) counts it as one of fourteen Bharatan head-gestures, but the *NS* does not read it. (*NS*, VIII. 17-18).

524 **आनन्द**

Ānanda : bliss or rather pure bliss-consciousness in which the distinction of subject and object ceases. (a) It is the state of *mukti*, *mokṣa* or *nirvāṇa* in which the self becomes free from all fetters. It is a characteristic of *brahman*, others being *sat* (existence) and *cit* (consciousness). (b) pure joy, pure bliss of art, the state of aesthetic relishment. When beauty becomes the counter-part of *ānanda*, it tends to produce spiritual deeds and if it becomes the medium to experience *ānanda*, then it manifests itself into the fine arts.

525 **आनुनासिक्य**

Ānunāsikya : nasality.

526 **आपणक**

Āpaṇaka : shop. When a shop-keeper closes his shop in India, he says "increase the shop" (*dukān baḍhāo*) and when he opens the shop he says, "start the shop" (*dukān lagāo*). This is owing to the reason if he says to close the shop, it may indicate that the shop will be closed for good.

527 **आपद्धर्म**

Āpaddharma : safety-valve device, the law of calamity, duty when in distress. In the post-Mauryan period of troubles, many Brāhmaṇs were no doubt forced to take to many unpleasant jobs. Manu took the opportunity to regulate for all *jātis* what should be done by them in normal times and what in times of distress - the *āpad-dharma* doctrine. To reconcile this with duty lists and practices of earlier times, he introduced the theory of *kalivarjya*, practices which may have been permissible in earlier times, like widow-remarriage, exogamy, sharing meals with members of other classes, but which are to be avoided in dark *kali-yuga*, when men are no longer naturally righteous. Manu was terrified at the idea of *Varṇa-saṁskāra*, the confusion of caste, as it might upset the delicate social balance. But he introduced the flexible concept (*varṇa saṁskāra*) to assimilate numerous aboriginal tribes and foreigners, and give them a suitable place in the *varṇa-jāti* scheme, which could apparently also move up and down according to their strength and power, by suitable theoretic interpretation of the oral esoteric *Śāstriac* texts. This made the new castes beholden to the theocrats, and subservient to them.

Āpad is the period of distress or catastrophy when it is not possible to live in accordance with the norms prescribed by the *Śāstras. Manu* (X.116) enumerates ten means of maintaining oneself in *āpad* or distress which pertain especially to the Brāhmaṇs and Kaṣtriyas. This is based upon the idea that before a good life may be secured, life itself must be preserved.

529 **आपान**

Āpāna : act of drinking, a drinking party, a liquor-shop.

530 **आप्तालाप**

Āptālāpaḥ : kin terms of address are used by fellow - villagers unrelated by either real or ritual ties. This is in part an extension which enters into all social intercourse in India. A man meeting a total stranger in another village or town, will, call him brother (*bhāī*) or elder brother (*dādā*), and if he is of the succeeding generation, call him father's elder brother (*bāpū*). It would be considered a slight to call him by his name, even if he knew it. A story is told, for instance, of a shopkeeper who built up his trade from small beginnings. His son took over on his death; but he was haughty, and instead of calling people by their kin names, used their proper names. Within a few years his customers had left him, and he was penniless.

This wide use of kin terms is little more than a form of courtesy. It is different from the attitude of fellow-villagers towards each other, for these call each other 'village kinsmen' (*gānva kā ristā*) whether or not there is any mutual obligation between them.

This phrase *kundrū-karelā* is often used as a term of affection in the tribal region:

My fruit, my food

How good that you have come.

Terms of endearment current between Gond and Pardhān lovers are many and varied. For men there are such words as *Rājā* (kind), *baihā* (mad), *sāthī* (companion), *pyār* (darling), *chailā* and *rasiā* (flirt). For women there are *kalejā* (liver or heart), *prān* (life), *piāri* (darling), *mayā* (love\), *ciraiyā* (bird), *parewā* (dove), *koel* (cuckoo), *suā* (parrot), *balam* (playmate), *prem kī ciraiyā* (love-bird), *popsā* (lung), *gondāphūl* (marigold), *mere kalejā ke kuṭkā* (bit of my liver), *āmaral*, *kelāpān* (plantain-leaf), *rānī* (queen), *hīra* (diamond). Some of these can, of course, be used indifferently for both the sexes.

531 **आभङ्ग**

Ābhaṅga : slightly bent to one side. The plumb-line or the centre line, from the crown of the head to a point midway between the heels passed slightly to the right of the navel. In other words, the upper half of the figure is made to incline slightly towards its right side, without inclining anyway towards either of the attendant deities.

532 **आभरण**

Ābharaṇa : (a) ornaments. Bharata in *NS* has enumerated four types of ornaments: (I) *āvedhya* : to be pierced. The ear ornaments and the like, to be fixed by piercing the limbs. (II) *bandhanīya* : to be tied. girdle and arm band; (III) *Kṣepya* : to be put upon ankles and decorations of dress. (IV) *āropya* : to be put round the neck - golden neck - chain and various necklaces. (b) The expression refers to the stylized decorations on the icons in human form. Indian arts regard beauty (masculine or feminine) as in separable from ornamentation, and employs this detain invariably in the icons for display as well as for worship. Most of the forms and styles of ornaments in icons are adapted from the actual ornaments used by well-to-do Indian masses, especially on festive occasions and members of the royal house-hold; but some of them are of course derived from the artist's imagination and inventiveness.(Fig 532)

533 **आभरणकार**

Ābharaṇakāra : manufacturer of ornaments, one of the members of the dramatic troupe mentioned by Bharata (*NS*, XXXV, 21-28).

534 **आभाणक**

Ābhāṇaka : saying, proverb.

535 **आभासगत**

Ābhāsa-gata : objective experience; *viṣaya-rūpatā* (Vasubandhu, *Abhidarmakośa*, V.34). ***ābhāsavāda*** is the theory of appearance or creation in Kashmir Śaivism which holds that the universe consists of appearances which are all real in the sense that they are aspects of the ultimate

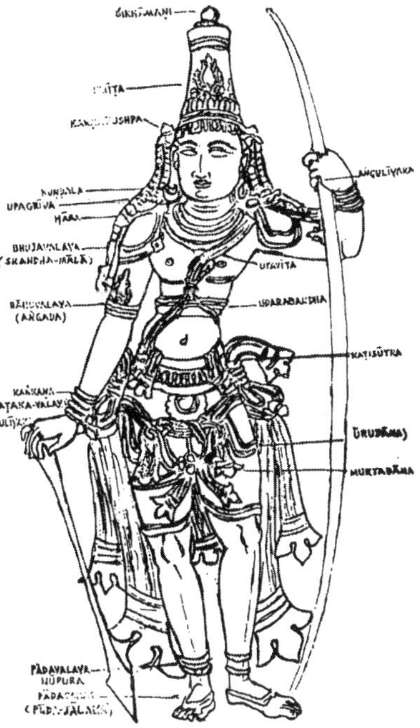

Fig. – (532), Female

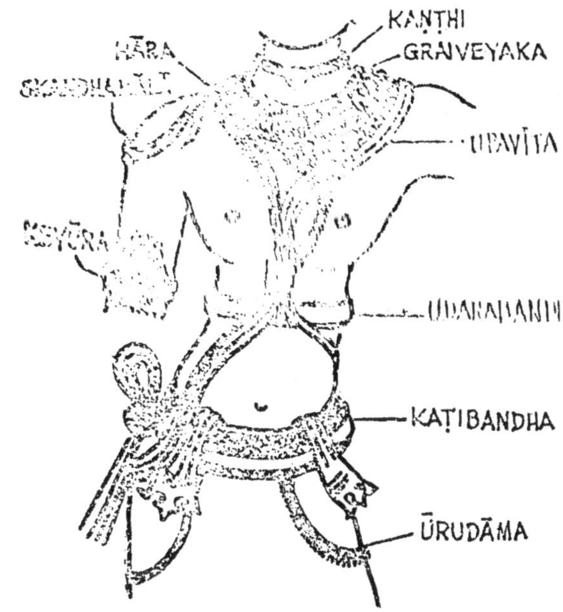

Fig. – (532), Male

reality (Abhinavagupta, *Paramārthasāra*, 12). (b) A theory in *Advaita* which posits the individual soul (*jīva*) in an illusory appearance of *Brahma*-intelligence. It is a variation of *Pratibimbavāda*.

536 **आभिजात्य**

Ābhijātya : nobility, dignity and grace. Dignity is a kind of rich elevation - neither too soft nor too harsh. It is charming on account of the profound skill manifested in the proper balance of softness and hardness. (Fig. 536)

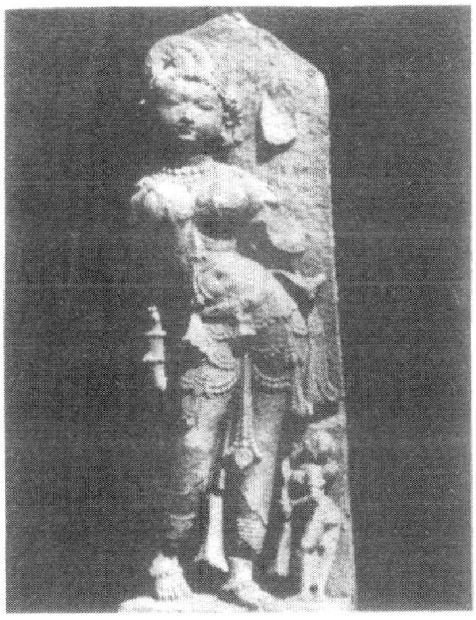

Fig. – (536)

537 **आभुग्न**

Ābhugna : a little curved or bent.

538 **आभुग्न ऊरु (वक्ष)**

Ābhugna ūru (*NS*, IX. 223) : relaxed chest with sunken shoulders, slightly bent chest; is the position where the torso and navel line is slightly bent forward: the position is however one of relaxation, looseness and not of tenseness; and thus it can express dispair, shyness, etc. there is only a slight curvation of the spine here and no change of weight takes place. The *ābhugna* style of the chest is used to indicate respect, pathos, fainting, grief, threat, sickness, heart-break, to touch, to rain, to be ashamed, as the sense may be.

539 **आभ्यन्तररति**

Ābhyantara rati : interior, inner coition. Sexual intercourse between a man and woman in which genitals of both come into close contact. There are twenty-seven types of such postures: nine types according to the length and depth of the genitals of man and woman, nine types according to the time taken in reaching the orgasm in both man and woman, and nine types according to the intensity of passion of men and women (*Ratiratna pradīpikā*, 4.1).

540 **आभ्यन्तरासन**

Ābhyantarāsana : seats in the royal courts;

The seats are two-fold (I) *bāhya* : for all people in general and (II) *ābhyantara:* relating to the king.

Simhāsana, the lion seat is for gods and kings; cane seat for family priest and ministers; the muṇḍa seat for the commander and the crowned prince; wooden seat for Brāhmaṇs; carpet seat for other princes - these are the seats in the royal courts.

In the case of the female characters there should be lion seat for the chief queen, muṇḍa seat for other queens, cane seat for the wives of the family priest and ministers; cloth, skin or carpet seat for concubines; wooden seats for wives of Brāhmaṇs and the female ascetics and the pillow for the courtesans. All other women should sit on the ground. This is the procedure in the royal court (*NS).*

541 **आमन्त्रण**

Āmantraṇa : (a) invitation, friendly persuasion, accentuation is involved, paralanguage feature (*Aṣṭādhyāyī* 8.1.33) rule of the accent. (b) courtship proposal. Hill Maria boy of Bastar who wants to "make" a girl offers her conventional drink and if she accepts, she passes the night with him. (c) This is the same as *nimantraṇa* according to *Manu* (III. 187, 191). But Pāṇini (III. 3.161) considers there to be a difference between the meanings of the two words. According to the *Mahābhāṣya, āmantraṇa* is an invitation which one is free to reject without incurring blame and that which is rejected without proper cause involves a fault or sin is called *nimantraṇa.*

542 **आमन्त्रण चिह्न**

Āmantraṇa-cihna : Calling signals, 'Come hither signs' in a woman. "A woman in love does not look at you straight in the eyes, but becomes confused after a moment and looks away. She manages on various pretext to let you see her body for a moment. She draws on the ground with her toes. She looks at you surreptitiously and smiles - either from time to time, or all the time. If a child is in her lap she kisses it and talks to it with conspicuous affection. If asked a question she looks down, says something unintellegible and confused, and smiles. On the one pretext or another she hangs about where her man is, talking loudly, in the hope that he will notice her; when she knows he is looking she carries on an animated conversation as cover. When he appears she smiles in his direction. She sits on a girl friend's lap and plays all manners of jokes. She strikes up acquaintance with her servants, plays games and chats with them - she then asks for news of him. She confides in her friends and talks to them about love. She will not let him see her unadorned - if a friend asks her to make her a garland she hands it over as if reluctantly. She sighs, looks sideways, beats her breasts with her hands, stifles when talking, taps her fingers, says ambiguous things and then is embarrassed, yawns, beats the man she loves with flowers, draws an elaborate brow-mark for her friend, touches her hips, opens her eyes wide, lets her hair down, visits the man's house on one pretext after another, sweats from her hands and feet, and wipes her brow with her arm - which does he like most among them? - so she questions her intimates privately with deep concern" (*Ratirahasya,* 13. 51-61).

543 **आमुक्तविवाहकौतुक**

Āmukta-vivāha-kautuka : with the nuptial thread tied round.

544 **आम्रेडित**

Āmreḍita : repetition is an aspect of human activity that deserves attention. In *Aṣṭādhyāyī* the rule *nityavīpsayoḥ* (8.1.14) is formulated which enjoins the repetition of the whole expression, when the sense of *nitya* (always) and *vīpsā* (each) is to be conveyed. This repetition rule has been formulated at levels of behaviour and through the developmental stages. Repeitition occurs in conversational behaviour to an astonishing degree in Sanskrit. Young people have remarkable tolerance to repetition due to *avyaktānukaraṇa.* In trauma, people are known to repeat a phrase on a particular movement (*Ibid.* 6.1.99). Some activities may be repetitious and helpful in their monotony, because, by following habits, the brain can be freed to other creative productivity. Thus, *jalpati jalpati* (he prattles interminably), *pacati pacati* (he cooks continuously), *bhojam bhojam vrajati* (each one, when he has taken his food, goes away) are some of the examples illustrative of this feature. But when the repetition activity is important, a person may balance novelty with repetition (*Ibid.* 6.1.98). Kālidāsa takes a different route to the literary creation to keep from being bored. This suprasegmental feature of Sanskrit is the most important. This prosodic component may be referred to as intonation., or the melody of Sanskrit language, or emotional expression. These intonational features can be correlated to movements in gestural communication.

545 **आम्-नहि-संकेत**

Ām-nahi-saṁketa : yes/no signals. Many people believe that there is only one way to signal yes and one way to signal No - the Head nod and the Head shake - and that these actions are global in their distribution. This is close to the truth, but it is not the whole truth. This process is reversed in Marathi-region.

546 **आयत**

Āyata : large, extended.

547 **आयत-दृष्टि**

Āyata dṛṣṭi : long-eyed; a type of glance according to *Bālarāmabharata* (pp. 137-139).

548 **आयत-भ्रुकुटी**

Āyata bhrukuṭī : a type of *bhrukuṭī* movement presented by *Bālarāmabharata.*

549 **आयत-मण्डल**

Āyata maṇḍala : a type of static movement.

550 **आयत-स्थान**

Āyata sthāna : standing posture for women (*NS*, XII. 163b-164a); *Samapāda* but second foot placed in *tyaśra*: no distance between the feet, right foot *samapāda*, left *tyśra, kaṭi* raised in *unnata;* the movement is really of the left side, hand in *latā*, used in dance often: frequently referred to in literature and seen in sculpture. *Āyata sthāna* is a type of *abhaṅga* pose; also known as *āyasta. Āyata* mentioned in the context of the holding of the spear etc. in the *VD;* is mentioned in the *NS* strictly in the context of the standing postures of women. the posture of Mālavikā in *Mālavikāgnimitra* (II.6) is one such example.

Thus the right foot is in *sama* and the other placed obliquely at the side one *tāla* apart, the face bright, the bosom raised, one hand in *latā* and the other reaching the hips. It is employed by women appearing first in the stage, offering handful of flowers, anger due to jealous love, twisting the first finger, prohibiting, pride, profundity, silence, recourse to resentment, looking to horizon, calling, dismissal, observing closely, anxiety and dissimulation. (Fig. 550)

551 **आयताधर**

Āyatādhara : a type of lip-movement mentioned in *SR*.

552 **आत्यतेक्षण**

Āyatekṣaṇa : long-eyed.

553 **आयुध**

Āyudha : weapons serving as attributes of different deities in their conceptual and iconic representation.

554 **आयुर्वेद**

Āyurveda : the Indian science of medicine; The *NS* describes that some portions of *nāṭyaveda* were adopted from the *upavedas* i.e. *āyurveda. Āyurveda* found place in the *NS* primarily in the treatment of *Vyabhicārī bhāvas.* Certain diseases and their symptoms were taken and applied as characteristic symptoms of certain mental moods on the lines of Caraka and Suśruta.

555 **आत्युष्मत्**

Āyuṣmat : long-lived, honouric term of address. (a) *āyuṣman :* O, long-lived one; a rathī (chariot-rider) should always be addressed as *āyuṣman* by the charioteer (*NS*, XVII. 65-94). *āyuṣmanta* 'O, long-lived' *AV.* honorific term of address *Ś.Br.* (b) *āyuṣmati* Lit. 'O! long-lived one' (*Priyadarśikā* III); a term of respect, address to women.

556 **आयुष्य**

Āyuṣya : a rite in the *jātakarma* consisting in muttering over the navel or in the right ear of the child a *mantra* to invoke the bestowal of long life (*Aśv. Gr.* 1.15)

(b) life, abundance of life.

557 **आरक्ताक्ष**

Āraktākṣa : pink-eyed.

558 **आरक्ताधरपाणिपादयुगला**

Āraktādhara-pāṇipāda-yugalā : lady whose lips, hands and legs are red; quality of the Deer-lady (*Anaṅgaraṅga*, 3.20.21).

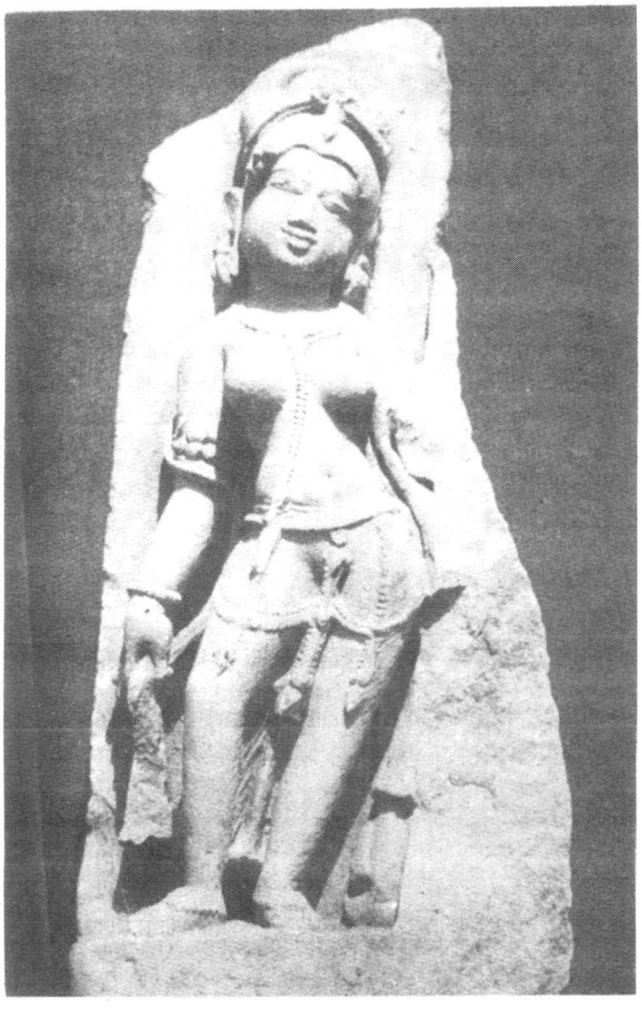

Fig. – (550)

559 **आरण्यक**

Āraṇyaka : (a) the tribe. Crossing jungles in ancient India was not without its dangers, because of the presence of the savage tribes, naked except for a string of leaves around the hips, men and women equally expert at shooting poisoned arrows from the thin, light bows; they were likely to attract strangers with the aim of securing a human victim to sacrifice to their gods. Some representations of the jungle dwellers are reproduced in K.N. Dixit, Excavations at Paharpur Bengal, in *Memoirs of the Archaeological Survey of India* (no. 55, pl XLIV); see also G. Yazdani, *Ajantā*, I, pl. XXX. A detailed description of a young *Śabara* (savage) chieftain of the Vindhya mountains is given by Bāṇa in his *Harṣacarita* (pp. 231-32).

Greater dangers for the caravans lurked rather in forests and wooded country, where organized bands of brigands were quite bold enough to confront such large groups for the sake of booty involved, and were experts at preparing careful ambushes.

The stories of the *Jātakas* deal extensively with this banditry, and there is hardly a tale concerning the itinerary of a caravan from one point to another which does not mention the organized bands avaiting it along its route.

(b) Primitives. The most so-called tribes in India are only people who have lost contact. The moment we get from haphazard notes to exhaustive, intensive study, and from isolated features to sets of relations between features, the empirical diversity recedes in the background, and on almost monotonous similarity springs forth. (c) one of the principal categories of *Vedic* texts. These texts were mostly composed by those sages who had gone into the forest after completing their lives as house holders.

The *Āraṇyaka* texts reveal a type of philosophical enquiry on the intricacies of life and the universe.

560 **आरण्यका/आरण्यिका**

Āraṇyakā/āraṇyikā : *a* forest-woman; the heroine of the play *Priyadarśikā* by Śrīharṣa (first part of the seventh century A.D). Her real name is Priyadarśikā, and she is daughter of King Dṛḍhavarman. She is carried off by Udayana's general, and is engaged as an attendant of Queen Vāsavadattā, under the pseudonym *āraṇyikā*. Priyadarśikā is eventually married by Udayana.

561 **आरण्यकोदनम्**

Āraṇyakodanam : Some inferior cerials as wild rice (*nīvāra, priyaṅgu,* and *śyāmaka*) were eaten by foresters in the *Sūtra-* period (800 BC - 300 BC); *Gaut,. Dh. Su.* XVII. 3; *Pāṇini,* III. 3.48; *Gobh. Gr. Su.* III. 7.22; *Baud. Gr. Śeṣa. Su.* 1.16.17.

562 **आरभटी**

Ārabhaṭī : the energetic style, the fierce mode; a particular style of theatrical presentation characterized by grand violent movements. Bharata (*NS.* XX. 63.7) defines *ārabhaṭī* as consisting of violent sentiments, which includes mostly the qualities of a bold person suited to an *ārabhaṭa,* and like an *ārabhaṭa*, it consists of my descriptions and desguises, is full of false pride and false words. Bharata mentions four varieties of *ārabhaṭī vṛtti: saṅkṣiptaka* (compression), *avapāta* (commotion), *vastūtthāpanam* (elevation of a plot) and *sampheṭa* (conflict). *Ārabhaṭī* is invariably attended with feats of jugglery and deeds of conjuration and conflicting situations. It is conspicuous in the form of bodily activities.

The *ārabhaṭī* is derived as *irayantīti arā arāśca te bhaṭāśca arabhaṭāsteṣāmiya-mārabhaṭī.* The dancers in *ārabhaṭī* style had their hair waving when they began to dance (*HC*, II).

563 **आरात्रिक शिरस्**

Ārātrika śiras : a type of head-movement given by *Abhinayadarpaṇa* and *SR* (IV. 7.76). the head, touching slightly both the shoulders, if moved, is *ārātrika.*. This is to be applied to salute others and to wonder.

564 **आरोपण**

Āropaṇa : attribution. The process through which we attempt to infer other's motives, characteristics, and intentions from the observation of their overt behaviour.

565 **आरोह**

Āroha : ascent of the notes in music.

566 **आरोहण**

Ārohaṇa : (a) ascent of the *rāga* (notes) as defined by Mātaṅga. (b) climbing. The images of climbing the hill and panting are sexual in the tribal region. The following folksong from the Maikal Hills suggests the same:

As you climb the hill
Even your lover's voice you cannot hear
You are panting so loudly
Some are breaking small branches
Some are plucking leaves
As you climb the hill.

567 **आर्तवादिन्**

Ārtavādin : speaking in distress (*A*, 12.2.33).

568 **आर्द्र**

Ārdra : wet, name of a *nakṣatra.*

569 **आर्द्राक्षतारोपण**

Ārdrākṣtāropaṇa: showering of wet unbroken rice. Matual showering of wet unbroken rice grains by the bride and bridegroom. It is the concluding part of the marriage rites (*RV.* X. 9).

570 **आर्य**

Ārya : an address form. (a) Brāhmaṇa should be addressed as *ārya* (*NS*, XVII. 65-94). The non-Brāhmaṇa's address the minister as *ārya.* The old-aged husband is addressed by all women as *ārya.* The younger brother should be addressed as *ārya.* (b) Āryan, noble, respectful, cultured.

571 **आर्यपुत्र**

Āryaputra : The husband in youth should be addressed by all women as *āryaputra* (*NS,* XVII. 65-94), son of an Āryan; also honorific designation of the son of person addressed, husband, sovereign.

572 **आर्यभाषा**

Āryabhāṣā : The language of the noble (*NS*, XVIII. 26-65); one of the four types of languages occurring in Sanskrit plays, *āryabhāṣā* belongs to the princely classes.

573 **आर्या**

Āryā : a wife is to be addressed as *āryā* or by referring to her father's or son's name (*NS*, XVII. 65-94); meaning 'respectable woman'.

574 **आर्ये**

Ārye : a Brāhmaṇī, a nun (*lingasthā*) or a female ascetic is to be addressed as *ārye* (*NS,* XVII. 65-94). The wives of priests and merchants are always to be addressed as *ārye.*

575 **आलस्य**

Ālasya : sloth, apathy, idleness, laziness, lethargy. It is the seventh *vyabhicārī bhāva* as enumerated by Bharata. *ālasya* is a state of mind in which one is averse to any kind of movement or activity due to weariness, pregnancy, and the like. Its external manifestations are yawning, sitting at the same place for long, as if one is tied down to it, aversion to any kind of work, lying down, drowsiness, sleep (*Sāhityadarpaṇa* III. 155), as if one is tied down to it and so on.

576 **आलाप**

Ālāpa : (a) name given to the practice of demonstrating or spreading out a *rāga* without any wording and *tāla.* (b) conversation (*Rāmāyaṇa*)

577 **आलाप-योजनम्**

Ālāpa-yojanam : discourse design (*Kāmasūtra,* 3.2.26). Vātsyāyana remarks that the stranger should first gesticulate to participate in conversation. A virgin girl never talks with a stranger (male), rather she throws an occasional glance to communicate her feelings: *Kaṭākṣaiḥ prekṣet iti ālāpayojanam.* When Duṣyanta meets for the first time with Śakuntalā, she does not speak and stands with her friend hug down: *Śakuntalā adhomukhī tiṣṭhati* (p.24). The opening of the topic before a virgin girl was against prevalent social behaviour. She stops *ativādinīm Priyamvadām.* In *Mālatīmādhavam* (p. 451), during the conversation, Mālatī keeps mum but with the attentive ear. Being disclosed, she looks at *avalokita* with objection: *Mālatī sāsūyamiva tam paśyati.* When Mādhava asks about it, she shakes her head: *Mālatī mūrdhānam cālayati* (*Ibid.* 451).

578 **आलिङ्गन**

Āliṅgana : embrace; Hugging at the moments of high emotions reinforces ties. Being hugged is a powerful childhood experience, and between adults it is reserved for intense emotional moments. Only the young lovers perform this dramatic tie - sign with any great frequency and they are in a more or less permanent condition of intense emotion whey they are together. For other adults, it is usually either a private sexual posture, or a 'break - and - remake' tie-sign. 'Break - and - remake' refers to farewells of daughters and their reunions with the mothers, these being the moments when the tie is being severed by physical separation or is reforming after it.

Exceptions to this rule include contact-dancing in the tribal areas, which is an area display incorporating a stylized version of the full-frontal body-contact in which the arms-enfolding element is curtailed. Watching a couple revolving on a dance floor (*racā*) is rather like seeing a couple grappling towards a Full Embrace, but failing through hand collision. The dancers enjoy the suggestion of the real thing without its full tie-sign implications.

Āliṅgana indicates the mutual love of man and woman in Sanskrit literature. Embrace between persons, who have not yet experienced a sexual union, is a favourite subject of Sanskrit poetry, but it does not find place in the Sanskrit dramas.

Āliṅganam : Embrace signals positive and intimate feelings. It is the first and essential part of coition. It indicates the mutual love of male and female. It has much importance in sexual act. It has been suggested (Vātsyāyana : *Kāmasūtra*,II) that *Nāgara* (higher-status people) initiate touching of lower status people and therefore for males it is a dominance signal rather than an affectionate one.

The *Kāmasūtra* (*ibid*) narrates twelve types of embrace, *viz. spṛṣṭakam* (touching), *viddhakam* (piercing), *uddhṛṣṭakam* (rubbing), *pīḍitikam* (pressing), *latāveṣṭitakam* (twinning), *vṛkṣādhirūḍhakam* (climbing a tree), *tilataṇḍulakam* (mixture of seasame and rice), *kṣīranīrakam* (mingling of water and milk), *ūrūpagūhanam* (embrace of thighs), *jaghanopagūhanam* (embraces of *jaghana*), *stanāliṅganam* (embrace of breasts), and *lalāṭika* (embrace of fore head). All these embraces are depicted by Kokkoka also. Kalyāṇamalla defines only eight types of embrace:

Vṛakṣādhirūdhamlilātaṇḍulākhyam
lalāṭikam jaghanaviddhake ca
ūrūpagūḍhāhvaya dugdhanīrē
tatrāṣṭamam vallarīveṣṭitam syāt

(*Anaṅgaraṅga* 9.2.)

Jyotirīśa accepts eight types of embrace which are described by Kalyāṇamalla:

vṛkṣādhirūḍha sañjakam prathamataḥ
tasmāllatāveṣṭitam
tasmājjaghanaviddhakāvapi
matavūrūpagūḍham punaḥ
Jñātavyam tilataṇḍulam rasavida-
māliṅganam yoṣitām
kṣīranīrapurassaram nigaditum
tasmācca lālāṭikam

(*Pañcasāyaka*, 4.32)

The *Nāgarasarvasva* agrees with the opinions of Kokkoka and Kalyāṇamalla but adds two more embraces, viz. *spṛṣṭakam* and *pīḍitam* which are stated by *Kāmasūtra*.

āliṅgana is known as *lipaṭnā* in colloquial Hindi.

Tulasīdasa in his *Mānasa* has used the word *bhenṭ*, cf, *bār-bār mili bhenṭi siy bidā kīnh sanmāni* (2.287), *Kahi pranāmu bhenṭi sab sāsū* (2.320.2), *ab bhari ank bhenṭu mohi bhāī* (6, 63.7), *bhenṭe hṛday lagāi* (*Mānasa*, 7.5), *kevaṭu bhenṭau Rām* (*Mānasa*, 2.241). (Fig. 578)

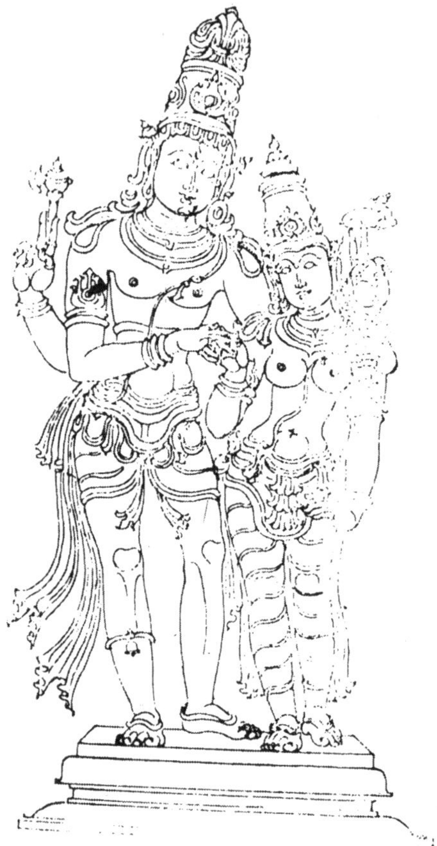

Fig. – (578)

579 आलिङ्गन-मूर्ति

Āliṅgana-mūrti : embracing posture, a form of Śiva iconically presented embracing Pārvatī, who is standing to his left. Śiva and Pārvatī are oriented towards each other. Śiva holds Pārvatī in embrace by placing one of his left hands on the left shoulder of Pārvatī or just above the waist. Pārvatī likewise holds Śiva in embrace by putting her right hand round him.

It is one of the placid forms of Śiva images depicting the god with his consort Umā, often in embracing posture. (Fig.579)

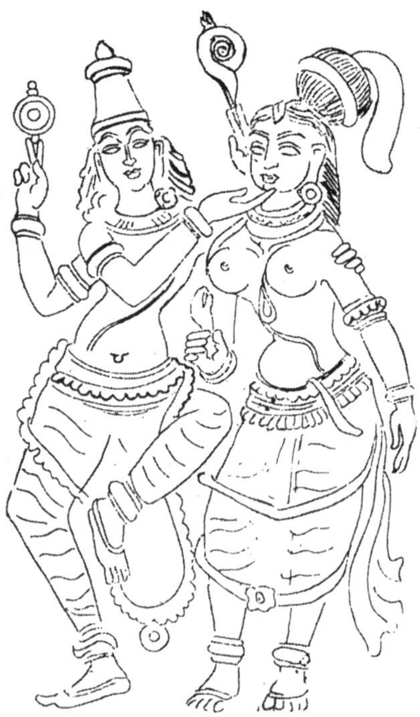

Fig. – (579)

580 आलीढ-पाद

Ālīḍha pāda : extended leg-position. The pose used for the representation of the shooting of the arrow (*NS*, X. 67-68). Bharata really prescribes two *sthānas* for the release of missiles, the *maṇḍala sthāna* and *ālīḍha*. The first relates to Indra. The feet are obliquely placed four *tālas* apart and is assumed in the use of weapons like the bow and thunderbolt. The ***ālīḍha*** is done by the right foot in the *maṇḍala sthāna* and the left pushed away five *talas* apart, an attitude common in Indian iconography, such as the Mahiṣāsuramardinī and other such figures: it is assumed in the release of missiles. In *Śākuntalam* (Act I), the king Duṣyanta enacts this pose while shooting the deer. Thus, *ālīḍha pāda* is a particular mode of standing in which the right knee is thrown to the front and the leg retracted. It is found is seated cult images. It resembles the attitude adopted in drawing the bow charged with an arrow: the right leg is outstretched while the left is slightly bent. When the position of the leg is reversed, it is called *pratyālīḍha*.

581 **आलीढ-स्थान**

Ālīḍha sthāna : a standing posture for men; *samapāda* feet in *tyaśra*, but one foot drawn five *tālas* apart *i.e.*, complete extension of one leg, the left knee slightly bent towards the side, *Rudra* presiding deity, to be used in *vīra* and *bhayānaka rasa*. The Vidyādhara from Rāṇigumphā Udayagiri caves may be seen in this posture. This pose can also be seen in Mathurā, Nāgārjunakoṇḍā and Amarāvatī sculptures. The pose Duṣyanta attained after the lively bit of acting was the *ālīḍha* (*NS*, X. 67-68). The right foot in the *maṇḍala* is extended 5 *tālas*. It symbolizes acts relating to Furious and the Heroic sentiments, the repartees in anger and intolerance, duel of wrestlers, looking at the enemies and attacking them and the release of weapons.

(b) The typical posture assumed by the tribes while on hunting procession is *ālīḍha*. The bow is held firmly with the right hand, and the arrow held in the left hand is harnessed to the bow.

582 **आलोकन**

Ālokana : a type of glance in which there is the bulging of the eyeballs, it also means the sudden opening of the eye.

583 **आलोकित-दर्शन**

Ālokita darśana : sudden look, a type of sight (*VD, NS*), suddenly seeing anything.

584 **आलोकिता दृष्टि**

Ālokitā dṛṣṭi : The relaxed position of eyeballs; the eye-gesture in which the movement of the eyeball is suggested; it also implies the sudden opening of the eyes, the glance of wide eye-balls in a sudden visitor-finding (*NS*, VIII. 92-105).

585 **आलोलित शिर**

Ālolita śira : trembling head; a type of head-movement known as *lolita* in *NS*.

586 **आवन्ती-प्रवृत्ति**

Āvantī-pravṛtti : western local usage. The people in the regions of western India like Avantī, Vidiśā, Saurāṣṭra, etc. have this *pravṛtti* which is characterised by *sāttvatī* and *kaiśikī* styles (*NS*).

587 **आवरण**

Āvaraṇa : the veil which keeps the soul away from freedom. In *Tāntric* tradition *āvaraṇa* sometimes means enclosure, nine of which form the *Śrīcakra*. It is known as *āvaraṇa-cakra* or *navacakra* (*Tantrarāja*, V. 9-11).

588 **आवर्त**

Āvarta : whirl, a circular mark on the body. The rightward *āvarta* on the hand (right) is auspicious; the same at the head of the vagina is indicative of queenship; a similar one on the navel, ears, breasts, to the right of the back bone is auspicious; but if it is on the waist, or the vagina proper , it is inauspicious (*Sk.P.* IV. 37.125). An *āvarta* on the back is not good; so is the case if one on head, forehead, and the chin (*Ibid.* 138). A woman having an *āvarta* on her back is expected to be unchaste (*Ibid.* 199.123).

589 **आवर्त-करण**

Āvarta-karaṇa : This is nearly derived from *Cāṣgati Cārī* even though *NS* (X.18) mentions that the feet are in *āvarta*. The Commentary adds that the hands move in *āveṣṭita* and *udveṣṭita* movement (*NS*, IV. 190b - 120 a; X. 118; IX. 216) After extending the *kuñcita* foot, it is moved again quickly and the hands are moved in conformity with the foot movement. It is employed in movements of heroes in moving forward.

590 **आवर्तित जङ्घा**

Āvartita jaṅghā : legs turned alternately. In the *āvartita* gesture the right leg goes to the left and the left to the *āvartita* gesture, to the right. It is also used to move round magnanimously (*NS*, X. 33-40). It takes place when the left foot is turned to right and the right to left. It is used in the moving about of Vidūṣaka. (*svastika* of shanks too is mentioned).

591 **आवर्तित-जानु**

Āvartita jānu : turned position of knees; here the toes of the feet face each other inwards: naturally such a position of the feet results in the knees also facing each other. This is used for jester's walking as this type of movement invariably produces a comic effect.

592 **आवाप**

Āvāpa : (a) the art and practice of love (*tantra*) to attract ladies (Yasodhara commentary on *Kāmasūtra*, II). (b) putting in, experimental insertion (*Darśana*).

593 **आवास**

Āvāsa : residence. The power of rural elite in all pre-industrial societies is perhaps most consipicuously displayed by the size and elegance of their residence. In periods of sharpening antagonism in the countryside this can provoke much hostility among the peasant masses. A Chhattisgarhi woman has bitterly contrasted it in her folksong: "I have five small children and only one little room, while so many *thakurs* have ten to twelve rooms". It is not to be wondered therefore that stately homes have often been the object of violence in many of the major peasant revolts in India.

All over the Indian continent difference in types of residence was - and still continues to be - a fairly accurate indication of difference in status. In colonial times this was true of distinctions between the rulers and the ruled as well as of those between the indigenous castes and classes themselves. As Anthony D. King has demonstrated so well by his researches, what he calls 'the bungalow- compound complex' functioned throughout this period as ' the basic residential unit of the colonial community' (Colonial Urban Development, London 1976: 32). Originating from a traditional house-type known in Bengal the bungalow was adapted to the urge of the governing elite to use residence as a space to demarcate itself politically and culturally from the natives without involving the actual loss of that direct physical contact so essential for purposes of administration. The result was of course that by the middle of the nineteenth century to bungalow, 'the most usual class of house occupied by Europeans in India', came to be regarded as a symbol of the authority of the whites and the Raj. In all hostile demonstrations against the government or its European associates, it featured almost inevitably as a target of popular wrath.

The size and character of the residence was also regarded as a clear indication of status differences among the Indians themselves. It was a integral enough to the culture of India show up in the regional language by way of a direct correspondence between caste names and hierarchically ordered names for caste dwellings. In general, a brick - built house was a decisive sign of affluence and high standing in the rural areas. This seems to have been the case in the Madhya Pradesh region too where by the end of the nineteenth century a *puccā* building had come to be recognized as evidence of the *mālguzārs'* prosperity and power raising them distinctively above the level of the mass of the tenantry: "They have almost without exception good *puccā* houses built with an elaborate main entrance (*darwāzā*) which is essentially distinguishable from the houses of the tenants, and around which cluster their cattle sheds and granaries". (Hoshangabad Settlement Report 1891-96). Fairly true to life, such structures testified to the disparity between the zamindars and the rest of the rural population both in terms of material sources and power.

The idealized description of landlord's houses, often seen as the earthly replica of Indra's celestial place in some of the traditional Indian songs reflects not only the admiration but also the envy for their occupants on the part of its talented by impoverished authors:

These symbols were attacked during the rebellious condition of the Indian folk. Thus by attacking the material symbols of governmental and landlord authority the insurgents tried to upset the established order.

594 **आवाह**

Āvāha : invitation, marrying. Interest in the choice of a marriage partner for a close relative is universal, and in our culture (rather in most of the cultures) marriages are arranged, enjoying a wedding treat. Our shared genes are more likely to be passed on successfully if the husbands of our female kin and the wives of our male kin are good matches.

595 **आवाह-विवाह**

Āvāha-vivāha : receiving and giving a girl in marriage, entertaing into marriage relations (*A*, 7. 15. 22; 9.6.70).

596 **आवाहन**

Āvāhana : calling or invoking (gods), particularly to *Agni* who sends for the gods to take part in the offerings. *Āvāhana* also means invitation to the means at the *Śrāddha.*

597 **आवाहनी-मुद्रा**

Āvāhanī mudrā : also called *trikhaṇḍa mudrā.* In this *mudrā,* palms are to be out turned, the thumbs joined under the *anāmikā*; invocatory gestures.

The invocatory songs along with gestures in the tribal society are almost reminiscent of the *Vedic* rituals invoking prosperity and plenty for the community. For the tribals the supernatural world, the world of *boṅgās,* of spirits and dead ancestors, is as real as the natural and social world he lives in. There is a benign or evil god in the neighbouring hill, the flowing stream at the outskirts of the village, the sacred grove and even the domestic kitchen. These gods take an intimate interest in human affairs and their blessings have to be invoked by appropriate propitiatory devices. Here ritual and gesture go hand in hand and serve and intimate and important social objective.

This gesture of welcoming is explained in *VD* as follows: "Extend both upturned hands with the thumbs curved and fixed on the mid-palms." In this *mudrā,* both hands are joined to form a cavity, and both thumbs are placed on the root-joints of the respective ring-fingers. This *mudrā* is used in the rituals connected with the invocation of the deities.

598 **आविद्ध बाहु**

Āviddha bāhu : arms closed tightly *(NS*, IX. 205-206).

599 **आविद्ध-वक्त्रकनृत्त-हस्त**

Āviddha vaktraka nṛtta hasta : a type of hand-gesture in dancing (*NS*). The two *patāka* hands are to have a graceful movement after touchig successively the opposite shoulder, elbow and the end of arm, with palms facing downwards.

600 **आविद्धा-चारी**

Āviddhā cāri : crossed-foot position (*NS*, X. 34, 38). A *kuñcita* foot extended where there is *svastika* (the shanks crossing and not touching each other) and bending it and then letting it fall on the ground with the heel. Abhinava (*NS*, X. 38) elaborates thus: "from *svastika* made without the shanks touching each other, *kuñcita* foot is stretched, brought to its own side and made to fall on its heels in the region of the other heel."

601 **आवृत-जङ्घा**

Āvṛta-jaṅghā *:* uplifted shanks (*NS*, IX. 257-8). When the left foot moves to the right, and right to the left, *svastika* of shanks too has been mentioned. Indicates jester's walk.

602 **आवेग**

Āvega : agitation. The sixteenth *vyabhicārī bhāva* (transient feeling) as enumerated by Bharata. It is a confused and agitated state of mind, accompanied by some quick reflex action, and resulting from the sudden and unexpected appearance of something desirable or undesirable. It manifests itself in contraction of body. When it is caused by some public calamity, it is manifested in relaxed limbs etc. (*Sāhityadarpaṇa* III. 143-4). The agitation of the king in *Mālavikāgnimitra* (Act V) is represented by rubbing the eyes, hurriedly moving from one place to another, and perhaps by weeping, too (*NS*, VII. 62). There are at least eight situations pertaining to the arousal of agitation:

(I) *due to portends*: looseness of all the limbs, distraction of the mind, loss of facial colour; sadness, surprise, etc.

(II) *due to violent winds*: veiling the face, rubbing the eyes, collecting the ends of the clothes worn, hurried going, etc.

(III) *due to heavy rains*: jumping together the limbs, running, looking for some cover or shelter, etc.

(IV) *due to fire* : eyes troubled with smoke , contracting all the limbs or shaking them, running with wide steps, fight, etc.

(V) *due to elephants* : hurried retreat, unsteady gait, fear, paralysis, tremor, looking back, etc.

(VI) *due to having something favourable* : getting up, embracing, giving away clothes and ornaments, tears, horripilation, etc.

(VII) *due to unfavourable news* : falling down on the ground, rolling about on a tough surface, running away, bewailing, weeping and the like.

(VIII) *due to calamity* : sudden retreat, taking up weapons and armour, mounting elephants, horses and chariots, striking, etc.

603 **आवेष्टित-हस्त-करण**

Āveṣṭita-hasta-karaṇa : If the fingers beginning with the fore-finger point inward gradually, the palm naturally faces inward. It is also known as *apaveṣṭita hasta karaṇa* (*NS*, IX. 198-204) *i.e.* The fingers, commencing with the forefinger and ending with the little finger, are gracefully turned towards the palm.

604 **आशिरः पाद**

Āśiraḥ pāda : from head to foot

605 **आशीर्वचन**

Āśīrvacana : (a) benediction, blessing, form of speech and thought (*Bṛhaddevatā* 134-139; *NS* XVIII. 25) (b) ex *āśīṣa* is a figure expressing a wish for prosperity, good fortune or reconciliation. (c) blessings are not to be accepted while on the bed or when one has not cleaned the mouth after food (*Skanda-Pūraṇa*, VI. 129.18). Also known as *āśīṣa*. A form of benediction, only bestowed by women and priests. *Vide* Tulasīdāsa: *nāu bārī bhāṭ asisahin* (*Mānasa*, 1. 319)

606 **आश्रम**

Āśrama : hermitage; Successive and essential stage during the course of life. Brāhmaṇism also propounded the theory that every man must during the course of his life, traverse four successive and essential stages (*āśrama*): first that of initiation, which marked the end of childhood. Until that moment (the age of initiation varied according to the caste) the child did not yet belong to the Āryan community, remaining outside society on its rural plane and having simply the potentially of being worthy of his ancestors. After the initiation which enabled him to enter into the life of ritual with the rank of student (*brahmacārin*), he attained through the sacrement of marriage, the state of householder (*gṛhastha*), thanks to which he in his turn possessed a domestic hearth, founded a family and brought it up following sacred traditions. The third stage saw him renounced his worldly goods and withdrew into a hermitage of which he became a member (*vānaprastha*). Finally, by an ultimate renunciation, he had to sever all relations with society and become an itinerant monk *(sanyāsin),* heedless *of* all contingency, concerned solely with achieving his *karma* and so ameliorating his future rebirths.

607 **आश्लेष**

Āśleṣa : embrace, contact.

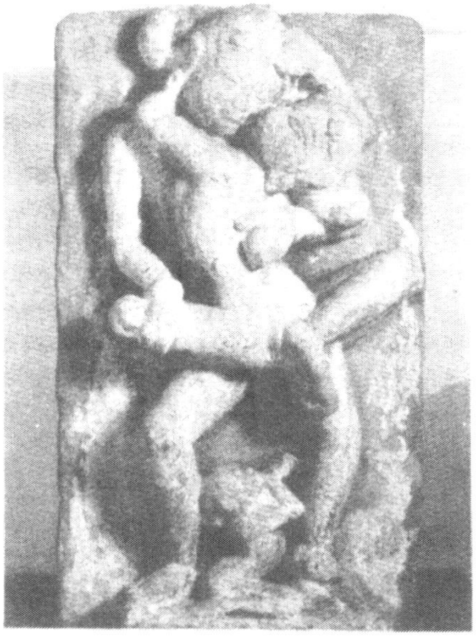

Fig. – (608)

608 **आश्लेष-सिद्धि**

Āśleṣa-siddhi : power accompanied by clasping, or embracing (*Yuktikalpa*, 164. 14-15). One of the six varieties of spiritual powers. By the loss of *hasta-siddhi* (power to touch by hand), the origination of progeny was made possible merely by the method of mutual embrace of the partners. (Fig.608)

609 **आसन**

Āsana : (a) the sitting posture, a beat, attitude, a type of stance position or pose in *nṛtta;* imaginary seat. It is understood to mean a seat or a mystic or any posture of sitting shown in the arrangement of lower limbs. Various kinds of such *āsanas* have been distinguished, namely *padmāsana* (the seat of lotus), *simhāsana* (the lion-throne or the seat of a lion), *sukhāsana* (an easy manner of sitting) and so on. When understood in a technical sense, the *āsana* was of various types such as *paryaṅka*, *vajraparyaṅka, lalita, bhadra, ālīḍha, pratyālīḍha* or *nāṭya* and a variety of *ardhaparyaṅka āsana.* Such modes of sitting were currnt among the Buddhists, who assigned spiritual significance to many of them. Thus the *vajraparyaṅka* implied deep contemplation and introspection, the *ardhaparyaṅka* indicated tranquility, the ālīḍha-valour, the *pratyālīḍha*-ruin and strong aversion, and the dancing in *ardhaparyaṅka* connoted anger and terror. Among the Jainas five types of these *āsanas* were specified, namely, the *paryaṅka, ardhaparyaṅka, vaira, khaḍga* and *vīra.* They were also known as *mokṣāsanas* as they were the postures assumed by a *jina* when he had or was on the way to attaining salvation (*mokṣa*). These were the *āsanas* generally adopted by Jain sages. The *paryaṅkāsana,* also known as the *padmāsana* or the *sampāryaṅkāsana* was a mode in which the Jain sage or devotee squats on a seat with his legs folded, the right one on the left thigh and the left leg on the right thigh, while the eyes are fixed on the tip of his nose, and the position of the arms varies. (b) a political expedient by which a king assumes an attitude of indifference to the activities of a belligerent power (*Smṛti*) (c) seat; the Hindus are very particular about keeping up social decorum, and the height of the seat one occupies is in direct ratio to the social position of the occupant. A man of lower caste cannot sit in the presence of a man of a higher caste. Men of the same caste, but having different social positions on account of difference in wealth or due to some prejudice, may sit in one another's presence, but the lesser man must be careful to occupy a lower seat than his superior. If seats of correct height are not available, the lesser man must stand. Social position being equal, age decides seniority. A person cannot sit on term of equality with his elder brother, father, uncle or any relative older than himself, but must stand in a respectable manner while talking to him. If the conversation is likely to last he is permitted to occupy a seat lower than the one on which his senior is seated. A woman shall not sit in the presence of an adult male of the same social position even if he is younger than she. In the case of old ladies, an exception is made of this rule.

(d) In *yōgic* practices *āsanas* are the postures which activate the latent centres in the body. Though said to be 84 in number, the principal *āsanas* are few: the backward bending postures like *bhujaṅga* (serpent pose), *śalabha* (locust posture), *dhanurāsana* (bow posture); the forward bending postures like *halāsana* (plough pose), *matsyāsana* (fish pose); twisting poses like *ardha matsyendrāsana* (half-posture of *yogi* Matsyendra); and central postures like *sarvaṅgāsana* (all limbs pose), *Śirṣāsana* (head pose), ect. Keep the spinal chord supple. According to *yoga* anatomy the principle nerve *suṣumnā* passes through the spinal column. The *āsanas* keep the spinal column supple and toned up to enable the seeker to release his stored up energy through the psychic passage within it.

(e) For eating or social conversation or resting, the tribes often sit with the buttock on the ground and the knees drawn up while sitting they search for a flat stone and then sit on it .

(f) In erotic practices, different postures of union have been suggested. Padmaśrī in his *Nāgarasarvasva* enumerated twenty-four types of postures of union (XXVII), seven types of postures of congress (XXVIII), two types of sitting postures of love-sport (XXIX), two types of back postures which are like animals (XXX), and seven types of standing postures (XXXI, XXXII).

(g) *āsana* : posture in copulation. Elwin (1947: 438) has enumerated four postures of copulation in the Muria region: (1) the girl prone on her back and the youth kneeling or squatting before her; (2) both sitting and facing one another; (3) the youth prone and fully extended above the girl who sometimes raises her legs and sometimes extends them; (4) and both standing, the girl supported against a tree or wall.

(h) seats in the court. In the Mughal court all the courtiers and the ambassadors were required to stand up in the places fixed for them according to their rank throughout the proceedings. The Rājput princes who were the Mughal *manasabdārs* had also to undergo the same treatment. They kept standing with their sub-vassals for hours together. The Mughal Emperor conferred the honour to sit in the court on a few privileged nobles or the princes of the royal blood (*Ain-i-Akbarī*, I. Blochman, 169)

In the Rājput-states the traditional customs about seating arrangements in the courts were sincerely adhered to. The nobles of the higher grade and those who were conferred the right of sitting in the court were allowed to sit in their respective places. The nobles of the lower grades and the remaining persons were kept standing throughout the proceedings of the court.

The seats were fixed on the right and the left of the ruler in rows. These were known as *jivani* and *davimisals i.e.* right and left flanks in the Mughal period. *Śukranīti* (I. 353-359) speaks of the arrangement of seats as follows:

"On the back side of the ruler sit his sons, brothers and nephew;

On the right side in a row sat the grandsons,

On the left side in a row sat the uncles and other persons of the royal blood;

In the front of the ruler were the *Senāpati* (commander-in-chief), ministers and other courtiers."

The Rājput courts mostly took their inspiration with regard to seating arrangement in the courts from the rules defined in the works of polity. However, no definite rules about the seating arrangements seem to have been in vogue in the earlier courts of India and it may be inferred that the one who come earlier to the court occupied the first seats without reservations of any kind. At such a time the classification and segragation among courtiers had not yet begun.

(i) There are different types of sitting postures for women in *NS*. (I) *sitting at case*: the feet should be gracefully kept apart (rested and bent) as in *vaiśākhasthāna* and the hips slightly raised, hands on the waist and thigh. (II) *Sitting in deliberation:* one foot should be stretched a little, the other resting on the seat and the head should be slightly bent to one side. (III) *Sitting in grief*: hands should be supporting the chin and the head resting on the shoulder with the sense and mind lost. (IV) *Sitting in fainting, intoxication, exertion, weariness and dejection:* The hands should be extended and the body loose, supporting on bow, etc. (V) *Sitting in offering libation of water to dead parents, muttering in- cantations, making ācamana,* etc: the waist should be raised up in which the hips and heels come together. (VI) Sitting in sickness, shame, sleep and meditation: all the limbs should be lumped together between legs and knee. (VII) *Sitting in pacifying the beloved and pouring ghee into the sacrificial fire*, etc. one of the stretched knees should be placed on the ground. (VIII) Sitting in worshipping a deity, pacifying the angry ones, bitterly crying, seeing the dead, fear of persons of low spirit, begging by the low persons, and attendance during the sacrificial work - the knees should be placed on the ground and the face should be downcast. Ascetics practising austerities should have this seat.

(j) The word *āsana* (derived from the root "*as*" to sit) has two meanings in the context of iconography: (1) posture of sitting, a manner of keeping hands and legs (*kara-caraṇādi-saṁsthāna-viśeṣa*) and (2) seat, on which one sits (*upaveśanādhāra*).

There are 108 *āsanas* prescribed in the *Haṭha-yoga* literature. *Nirukta Tantra,* as *tāntrika* book says that there are as many *āsanas* as there are living beings on earth, *viz,*. eighty-four lakhs.

(k) On the furniture of the house the *NS* gives detailed information about the different types of seats which were used for different classes of persons (*NS*, XII. 216). Thus for the crown-prince and commander-in-chief *muṇḍāsana* was prescribed. For the ruling queens *simhāsana* and for the princes in general *kuthāsana* which apparently refers to a rug-seat. A cane-seat or *vetrāsana* was prescribed for the wives of the royal priest and ministers. *Abhinavabhāratī* says that some regard *vetrāsana* to refer to a blanket seat. For the mistress of the king seats of cloth or leather were prescribed. For Brāhmaṇa women and women ascetics, *paṭṭāsana* was prescribed. For public women *masūraka* or a kind of pillow is mentioned. For other women the ground itself served as the seat. If *ati punītāsan baiṭhāre* (*Mānasa*, 1.45.5).

610 आसन-मूर्ति

Āsana-mūrti : a Viṣṇu image showing the god in a seated posture.

611 **आसन-युग्म**

Āsana yugma : adjacency pair. Many conversations are structured according to the first rule, in which the first speaker addresses a second one, and the second one answers. This type of sequence is known as an adjacency pair. It refers two sequential turns, the second of which is a reaction to the first. There are a number of types of adjacency pairs, including the question answer sequence (A:कियन्मात्रं नलं विप्र? B. जानुमात्रं नराधिप.), greeting-greeting sequence (A. नमस्करोमि B. नमोनम:), offer-acceptance/rejection sequence (A. पानीयं पातुमिच्छामि B. नोदास्यामि), complement-acceptance/rejection sequence (A. जयतु देव B. तथास्तु); and request-grant sequence (A. मिष्टा + नेच्छतवामि, B. नथास्तु लर्हि पानक मिंदानीम्).

612 **आसेक्य**

Āsekya : mouth-congress. one who gets another man to emit semen in his mouth.

613 **आस्फोटित**

Āsphoṭita : clapping the arms.

614 **आस्वाद**

Āsvāda : enjoying, taste, tasting aesthetics, one of the highest intellectual stales whose essence is to be *rasa*. Kālidāsa (*Megha* 43) records:

ज्ञातास्वादो विवृतजधनां को विहांतु समर्थ:
jnātāsvādo vivṛta-jaghanām ko vihātum samarthaḥ

615 **आस्वादन**

Āsvādana : Testing. One may get messages through tastes. We get messages as "I am concerned about you", or "I love you" from taste. When a child tastes a hearty meal prepared by the mother, he gets a message. What about a *devar* and *bhābhī* in Bendeli folklore? The *bhābhī* gave the *devar* (Hardaul) the tasty (?) *khīr*. one can send a message of love through a tasty dish.

616 **आहत-नाद**

Āhata nāda : audible sound.

617 **आहनस्या**

Āhanasyā : speech referring to lascivious character (*AV*); form of speech and thought (*Bṛhaddevatā*, 144-60), lascivious verses.

618 **आहार**

Āhāra : dinner. *Śukra* (III. 186) states that a person should not be too formal at the time of dinner and transactions:

āhāre vyavahāre ca tyaktalajjā sukhī bhavet.

Food habits were also semioticized in the feudal India. They are still different between strong and weak, between rich and poor, etc. A man capable of nothing, who can not be assigned any responsibility eats much. Strong persons prefer *roṭī*. General people take rice. Economically weak people are compelled to take stapple food or *sattū*.

In the Hindu society, a lot of thinking has been done on the purity and impurity of food. The food is of two types: *hita* (health-giving and good) and *ahita* (not conductive to health and harmful). According to *Bhagavad-Gītā* (17. 8-10), food is of three kinds: *Sāttvika* (superior), *rājasa* (middle) and *tāmasa* (inferior).

619 **आहार्य**

Āhārya : to be assumed, to be fetched, object language, external; relating to costume and make up; communicating objects; It is one of the four major parts of acting (*abhinaya*) defined in Sanskrit dramaturgy. It is the gesticulation with costume and make-up (*NS*, XXI. 192). That aspect of acting involving accessories such as hand and state properties, costumes, make-up, and decor.

Vipradāsa does not state the *āhārya abhinaya* separately. He refers to the three others as resulting from the body, mind and speech. According to him, the four styles of action are connected with them. He explains *kaiśikī* as derived from *keśa i.e..* hair and understands it as conductive to beauty and, *sāttvatī* from *sattva, i.e.* mind. The verbal gesticulation is well established in *bhāratī* and all the physical gestures are well established in the other three styles of action. The style of action connected with mental states ultimately results in physical gestures.

(b) Fetched - The domestic fire which is fetched (not produced by attrition) from a *Śrotriya's* house.

620 **आहार्य अभिनय**

Āhārya-abhinaya : object language; the extraneous representation. The characters of the various types when indicated first by dress and make-up, accomplish the representation easily by means of gestures and the like. The production of the play depends on *āhārya*. Abhinava says that it is like wall for with all the representation. Even though all the other histrionic representation is absent, the particular character is determined by the special dress and make-up. *Āhārya* indicates forms of gesticulation are connected with the actor's physique but the *āhārya* is something that is externally added.

It is four-fold: (I) *pusta* (the model work), (II) *alaṅkāra* (decoration), (III) *aṅgaracanā* (makeup or painting of the body) and (IV) *sajjīva* or *sajīva* (living creatures or different objects).

Āhārya is an 'object language' as known to modern western linguists. The way we decorate our bodies with clothing and surround ourselves with material goods can also communicate.

Take the simple matter of clothing. It's fine to say that the we a person dresses shouldn't affect our judgement of him. Perhaps it shouldn't. But research indicates that most of us place a lot of stock in a persons dress, particularly in the early stages of an association. A simple thing like eye-glasses can create a strong impression. In experiments, subjects frequently perceived this who wore glasses as more intelligent and industrious than those who didn't wear glasses.

Your home style and decorations, your choice and care of an automobile, also aid others in making judgements about you. You need only to look at advertisements for home furnishings or cars to see that admen know the symbolic value of the items they are "pushing".

621 **आहो**

Āho : particle implying question or doubt.

622 **आह्निक**

Āhnika : daily duties for an individual forming one aspect of *ācāra* (q.v). The principle matters of the *āhnika* are *śauca* (q.v) or rules relating to bodily purity, *saṅdhyā* (q.v.), *tarpaṇa* (q.v.), the five *mahāyajñās* (q.v), attending the fire, *bhojana* (q.v.), obtaining wealth, studying and teaching, gifts, going to bed, and performing sacrifices at certain stated times. *Manu* (IV. 52) enumerates the principal daily actions which must be performed in the morning: (a) answering the call of nature, (b) toilet, (c) bathing, (d) brushing the teeth, (e) applying collyrium to the eyes and (f) worship of the gods. The word *āhnika* is derived from *ahaḥ* which stands for the period from sunrise to sunrise including day and night.

623 **आह्वान**

Āhvāna : calling out relevant sentiments and feelings (*NS*, IX. 175); lit. call, invitation.

इ - I

624 **इक्षु**

Ikṣu : sugarcane (*AV*), *ūkh* (Bagheli), produced from the drop of nectar (*Brahmāṇḍa*, II.3.15.6, 7); *Ikṣuvikāra* means sugarcane juice (*Skanda* II. 2.39.16); sugarcane bits were distributed during the worship of Sarasvatī (*Brahmavaivarta*, 4.27).

625 **इक्षुदधि-हस्त**

Ikṣu-dadhi-hasta : The sugar ocean symbolism. The *alapadma* hand moved up and down symbolizes the sugar ocean (*Mirror of Gesture*, p. 48).

626 **इङ्गित**

Iṅgita : gesture; the gesture of motion of the various limbs indicating one's intentions; gestures suited to betray internal feelings; *ākāraiḥ iṅgitaiḥ gatyā gṛhyate antargatam manaḥ* (*Manusmṛti*, 8. 26); movement of the limbs (*A*, 1.15, 7,8; 5.5.5-6).

The most appropriate word for *iṅgita* in Hindi is *iśārā*. There are many sayings about the appropriateness of gesture:

(a) *aqlamand ko iśārā kāphī* (a hint is enough for the wise).

(b) *ek bār vo saudā beñce, do bār nain laaṛāve.*
saudā bece kare iśārā, kitne ko bilmāve.

(Now serves a customer
then ogles twice the time withal.
She sells her wares, disports her eyes
holds diverse men in thral)

627 **इङ्गित-विभावन**

Iṅgita-vibhavana : indication of gesture.

628 **इङ्गि·ताकार**

Iṅgitākāra : outward gestures and behaviour (*Kāmasūtra* 3.3.24) of a girl, who wants to show her love: (a) she never looks at the man in the face: *Sammukham vīkṣate.* (b) becomes abashed when she is looked at him: *tam tu vīkṣitā vrīḍām darśayati.* (c) under some pretext or another, she shows her limbs to him: *aṅgam apadeśaṇa prakāśayati.* Sanskrit literature is full of these examples. Śarmiṣṭhā diverts her glance and leaves the place due to bashfulness (*Yayāticarita*, p. 8). Malayavatī turns away her face (*Nāgānanda*, p.52). Mālavikā is abashed (*Mālavikāgnimitra*, p.68). Śakuntalā does not stand with her face turned towards Duṣyanta (*Śākuntalam*, 1.30). Mālatī shows gestures and exposes her limbs (*Kuṭṭinīmatam*, 692). She also exhibits her body. Certain women exhibit their hips, and breasts (*Kirātārjunīya*, 8.17). Padmāvatī looks at Śrīnivāsa with side-glances (*Śrīnivāsavilāsa campū*, *p.59*).

629 **इङ्गितादृष्टि**

Iṅgitā dṛṣṭi : moving glance, a type of glance (*Mirror of Gesture*, p. 41)

630 **इति**

Iti : thus, in this manner (at the end of speech, thought, enumeration). (b) going, motion, speed. Particle indicating end of direct speech or added to a predicative noun in statement.

631 **इतिवृत्त**

Itivṛtta : plot. Literally means an account of happenings, that is to say, the 'story' of events. It is the body rather than the soul of the drama (*NS*, XIX. 1): *'itivṛttam tu nāṭyasya śarīram prakīrtitam'* on which Abhinava comments: "*itivṛtta śabdavācyam tad vastu śarīram rasaḥ punarātmā*" (*AB*, vol. III, p.1). It is especially from the point of view of *itivṛtta* that the action - theoretical aspect of *Nāṭya* becomes explicitly manifest. There are three ways in which the *itivṛtta* is seen as constituting several stages or parts. The first of these is characterized as *avasthā*. The entire *itivṛtta* is treated as an action and is supposed to have five *avasthās* or stages: *ārambha, yatna, prāptisaṁbhava, niyataprāpti* and *phalāgama.*

632 **इतिहास**

Itihāsa : account of former events, legend, history. According to Kauṭilya (1.5), *itihāsa* included *Purāṇas, itivṛtta* (history), *ākhyāyikā* (story), *udāharaṇa* (illustrative stories), *Dharmaśāstra* (treatise dealing with legal matters) and *arthaśāstra* (political economics). These formed the subjects which a prince was expected to study during the afternoon, while he had to recite lessons, in military arts concerning elephants, horses, chariots and weapons in the forenoon.

633 **इतिहास-सम्वाद**

Itihāsa-samvāda : poetry of the great epics, composed by the great ascetic sages, which teaches universal morality, love of all human beings and renunciation of the world. It comes under the category of *nīti*, or the science of human norms, values and behaviour. (b) history is an unending dialogue between the present and past. Historical facts are in a state of constant change.

634 **इदन्ता**

Idantā : objective hood, (as opposed to *ahantā* or subjective hood (*Pratyabhijñā-hṛdaya*, 10).

635 **इदम्**

Idam : the know; the enjoyed; the object; the "itness" and so on. The opposite concept is *aham*, the knower or the enjoyer.

636 इन्द्रजाल

Indrajāla : Jugglery.

637 इन्द्रयोनि

Indrayoni : the teat-like flesh hanging at the root of palate.

638 इन्द्र-हस्त

Indra-hasta : a hand-pose, *tripatāka* and *svastika* in two hands indicate Indra (*AD*, 211-215). Indra, the chief of the gods and lord of the heavenly firmament, is the god of *Vedic* antiquity.

639 इन्द्राणिकम्

Indrāṇikam : the posture of the wife of Indra in coition prescribed for the Deer-lady (*Kāmasūtra*, 2.6.7). Wife of Indra, Śacī by name, is regarded more often as Indra's energy. She is represented with large breasts and thick thighs. (Fig. 639)

640 इन्द्रिय

Indriya : sense organs. The universe contains atoms and molecules which cause vibrations and radiation by means of regular movements, in so far as they affect the sense organs, they are called stimuli. The sense organs contain specifically reactive receptors in which stimuli evoke a potential which expands within receptor. If it exceeds a critical value, it brings about total depolarization and action potentials in the nerve fibre. By analogy with communications technology a stimulus may be conceived as information encoded by means of a frequency code and broadcast over the nerves. The quantity of information depends on the impulse frequency and *pañcendriyāṇi* (five sense organs), *viz.* the eye, the ear, the skin, taste and smell.

Bharata (*NS*) indicates that sense objects should be represented in the following manner:

(1) *Sound* should be represented by side-long glance, bending the head side-ways and putting the first finger near the ear.

(2) *Touch* should be indicated by the eyes slightly narrowed, eyebrows raised and touching the shoulder and the cheek.

(3) *Form* should be represented by holding the *patāka* hands on the head and moving the face slightly, looking intently with the eyes.

(4) *Taste* and (5) *Smell* should be indicated by eyes slightly contracted, nostrils expanded with exhaltation when they are favourable.

The favourable attitude of the mind should be represented by happy movements of limbs, horripilation and blooming of the face. When the unfavourable attitude is to be represented the head should be turned back, eyes and nostrils contracted and one should not look (towards the sense

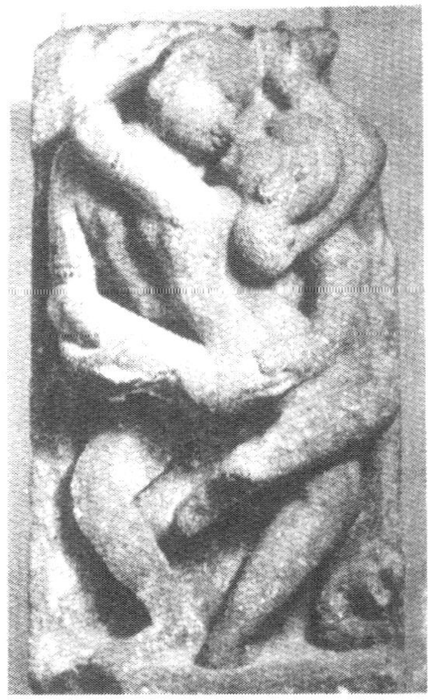

Fig. (639)

objects). The indifference should be shown by middle state, *i.e.*, not expressing either too much delight or too much abhorrence.

According to the Nyāya-vaiśeṣikas and Mīmāṃsakas *manas* or mind is also an *indriya*. The five external ones are of sound, sight, touch, taste and smell.

The *Praṣna Upaniṣad* (IV.2) enumerates ten *indriyas* —five sensory and five motor. These *indriyas* work under the control of the *manas*, the central organ whose chief functions are perception and action. Without mind the senses are useless (*Bṛhadāraṇyaka* 1.6.3). This is why the mind is called the chief of the senses. Without mind or *prajña*, speech does not make anything known.

641 इन्द्रिय-निग्रह

Indriya-nigraha : control of the ill-functioning of the sense-organs. In a restricted sense the term applies to absolute control of the sexual instinct.

642 इष्टापत्ति

Iṣṭāpatti : occurrence of what is desired; a statement by a debator which is favourable to his opponent: *iṣṭāpattau doṣāntaramāha.*

643 इष्टापूर्त

Iṣṭāpūrta : performing sacrifices and digging and doing other charitable works; sacrifices and pious works.

644 इष्टि

Iṣṭi : desire, impulse, desideratum (Patañjali's rules or explanations supplementing *vārtikas* of Kātyāyana) (b) sacrifice.

ई - Ī

645 **ईक्षण**

Īkṣaṇa : look, eye, view.

646 **ईक्षणिक**

Īkṣaṇika : a fortune-teller (*A*, 13.1.7); living on palmistry, palmist.

647 **ईति**

Īti : calamity: *ativṛṣṭiranāvṛṣṭir mūṣakāḥ śalabhāḥ khagāḥ (atyāsannāśca rājānaḥ ṣaḍete ītayaḥ smṛtāḥ)* = excessive rain, droughts, locusts, rats, parrots, and foreign invasions are mentioned as public calamities in *Mālavikāgnimitra* (V. Commentary).

648 **ईर्ष्या**

Īrṣyā : envy, jealousy.

649 **ईर्ष्यामान**

Īrṣyāmāna : annoyance caused by jealousy. It happens in the part of the women alone. This jealous pride could be overcome by consolation, meditation of a friend, disregard, change of topic or apologies.

When envy, or praise may be manifested by different paralinguistic features (*Aṣṭādhyāyī*, 8.2.10).

650 **ईशान**

Īśāna : lord Śiva, owning, ruling.

651 **ईशान-हस्त**

Īśāna-hasta : a type of hand-gesture mentioned by the *Nāṭyaśāstra-saṁgraha*. *Īśāna* is an aspect of Śiva. It is also the name of a *dikpāla*.

652 **ईशानी**

Īśānī : *Durgā*.

653 **ईशानी-मुद्रा**

Īśānī-mudrā : a type of hand-gesture. In the *kauverī* (q.v.) figure, if three fingers are stretched, it indicates *īśānī* (*VD*). *Īśānī*, the *Śakti* of *īśāna*, is one of the forms of Pārvatī. She is also called *Maheśvarī*.

654 **ईश्वर**

Īśvara : (a) capable of. (b) master, ruler, husband. (c) supreme being.

655 **ईश्वर-मुद्रा**

Īśvara-mudrā : a type of hand gesture. The pairs of the little-fingers and the ring-fingers are to be interlocked inside and to be joined together in interwals and the rest are extended. This makes *īśvara-mudrā*, that brings home all good omens (*VD*). *Īśvara* is the Supreme Being creating, maintaining and destroying the world and the only principle of the comprehension and attainment of grace (*prasāda*) through *bhakti* or devotion according to all theistic systems of India.

656 **ईश्वर-हस्त**

Īśvara-hasta : a type of hand-gesture. If *mṛgaśīrṣa* is in the left hand and *tripatāka* in the right, it is *īśvara*, the principle God (*A*, 205-210).

657 **ईषत्स्पृष्ट**

Īṣatspṛṣṭa : (a) slightly touched. (b) semi-vowels (*y*,r,l,v).

658 **ईहामृग**

Ihāmṛga : a type of *rūpaka*. It has the divine hero engaged in fight for divine lady. The plot is well-knit and convincing. It has mostly vehement males and has its constructions based on feminine anger. It should have commotion, excitement and angry conflict. The plot of love is to be based on causing discord among women and carrying them off and oppressing the enemies. When the killing of persons is about to take place, the battle should be avoided by some artifice.

उ - U

659 **उक्तप्रत्युक्त**

Uktapratyukta : speech and counter speech, one of the ten *lāsyāṅgas* enumerated in *NS*. It has a combination of speeches and counter speeches due to anger or pleasure, having words of censore, set to music. Here there is much dialogue expressing anger and conciliation. (*NS*, XXXI. 364-367).

660 **उक्ति**

Ukti : speech; an *arthaśleṣa* in which the second meaning is vulgar or risque (*Rudraṭa*, 10.1.4).

661 **उग्रता**

Ugratā : terribleness, fierce. Twenty seventh of the *vyabhicārī bhāvas.* It is manifested by killing, imprisoning, beating, and rebuking, etc.

662 **उच्च अलङ्कार**

Ucca-alaṅkāra : high voice embellishment. *Uccā* (high) proceeds from head and is of high pitch. It is used in speaking to anyone at a distance, in wonder, in rejoinder, in calling anyone from distance, in frightening anyone and in affliction, etc. (*NS).*

663 **उच्चाटन**

Uccāṭana : driving away. One of the *Ṣaṭkarmas* (six black acts) by which one can drive away one's rival from the land (*Śāradā*, XXIII. 125).

664 **उच्चार**

Uccāra : answering a call of nature (*A*, 4.9.21), excrement, evacuation.

665 **उच्चारपदेन प्रस्थित**

Uccārapadena prasthitaḥ : went out on a pretext of evacuation.

666 **उच्छिष्टम्**

Ucchiṣṭam : leavings, remainder. In *Sūtra*-period (800 B.C.–300 B.C), it was customary for a wife to eat food left in her husband's plate (*Ap. Dh. Su.* 1.5.17.11-13). It was considered improper to dine with one who gives his leavings to his pupils or gets up while others are eating (*ibid.* 1.5.16.33). Food left on a plate is never touched in India, except by certain "untouchables" (*bārī* in Baghelkhand) and very close relations, though here also custom is strictly regulated. A wife, for example, may eat the leavings of her husband, but not *vice versa.* The following *karmā* song from Mandla (English version) connotes the meaning:

You have got to go to the house of your father-in-law.
You'll get no meat or fish to eat:
You'll very soon tire of bones.
You may pick up the leavings of your mother-in-law
and eat them bit by bit;
But though she'll be flattered,
She'll continue to run you down.
O you'll have to go.
There is no escape.
You must go to your husband's house.

667 **उच्छूनक-रद**

Ucchūnaka rada : The swollen bite. Lower lips and cheeks are the places on which the swollen bite is made (*Kāmasūtra*, 2.5.7). *Kāmasūtra* (2.5.6) says, if the hidden bite is used forcibly, it is called the swollen bite: *tadevāpīḍanād ucchūnakam.* When the lovers create some pain in biting, it becomes swollen bite (*Śiśupālavadha*, 10.53); *Naiṣadha* 7.40, 18.94, 20.57, 18.129). Sometmes Kṛṣṇa's lips are bitten by an unknown Gopikā which pain Rādhā: *dasanapadam bhavadharagatam mama janayati cetasi khedam (Gita-Govinda*, 8.5). The lower lip of *Tārāpīḍa* was also bitten in amorous sports: *daṣṭadhara (Kādambarī*, p. 130).

Uñcha : gathering of abandoned corns one by one (*Smṛti).*

Utkaṭāsana : a type of sitting posture.

668 **उच्छेदवाद**

Ucchedavāda : nihilism. Seven groups of nihilists are mentioned in the Buddhist texts according to which the soul has no separate existence. It is same as the body itself and becomes extinct along with the body.

669 **उड्डियान-बन्ध**

Uḍḍiyāna-bandha : breathe out fully, contract and draw the stomach muscles in and take them upward above the navel portion. Retain and rest in this very posture. Literally *uḍḍiyāna* means 'to fly'. Allow the abdominal muscles to fly up in the cavity of the chest.

This flexion removes constipation and stimulates the digestive fire, removes intestinal disorders and worms, activates the liver and the kidney. It regulates the function of the adrenal glands and hypogastric plexus.

670 **उत्कटुकासन**

Utkaṭukāsana : sitting on the hams, squatting. उंकड़् बैठना

671 **उत्कण्ठ**

Utkaṇṭha : 'having the neck uplifted, longing for' Kālidāsa. In Act II of *Mṛcchakaṭika,* Vasantasenā enters in a love-lorn condition; the love-sickness is described as *Utkaṇṭhā2:*

this is equivalent to Bharata's *unmāda,* one of the stages of love in a woman, and would be represented by a fixed gaze, occasional deep sighs, absentmindedness (*NS*, XXII.177). Here *utkaṇṭhā* has been represented by a pair of *avahittha* hands (*NS*, IX.151). Vasantasenā is certainly absent-minded; she does not remember what she has said and knits her eyebrows (*bhrūkṣepa*) to answer her friend: this is the *utkṣepa* movement of the eyebrows of the *NS* (VIII. 123-124).

672 **उत्कण्ठिता**

Utkaṇṭhitā : eager. The maiden who decks all her limbs with various flowers, who is lovely, who is interested in sex, who has love towards her lover, who has fickle eyes, who waits for her lover for a longtime is *utkaṇṭhitā* (Kalyāṇamalla, *Anaṅgaraṅga,* 10.69):

> विविधकुसुममाला भूषिताङ्गी मनोज्ञा
> सुरतरसविलोला सानुरागा स्वकान्ते ।
> निवसति चटुलाक्षी वासगेहे चिरं सा
> वरकविभिरिहोक्ता सा किलोत्कष्ठितेति ॥
>
> Vividhakusumamālā bhūṣitāṅgī manojñā
> surata rasavilolā sānurāgā svakānte
> nivasati caṭulākṣī vāsagehe ciraṁ sā
> varakavibhirihoktā sā kilotkaṣṭhiteti

Jayadeva depicts Rādhā in the same manner.

673 **उत्कर्षण**

Utkarṣaṇa : elevation; drawing up relevant sentiment and feeling (*NS*, IX. 175).

674 **उत्कुटकासन**

Utkuṭakāsana : More frequently spelt '*utkuṭikāsana*' refers to a posture where one sits on the hams; with one of the legs folded and held upright and the other dangling down. Same as *utkaṭukāsana.*

675 **उत्क्षिप्त भ्रू**

Utkṣipta bhrū : raising the eyebrows (*Mirror of Gesture*)

676 **उत्क्षिप्त शिर**

Utkṣipta śira : head turned upwards; When the face is turned up with an *udvāhita* head; raising up the face, causing the same effect to the head. It indicates the use of divine weapons and lofty objects. It results when the face is raised up and is used in lofty objects and divine things.

677 **उत्क्षेप भ्रू**

Utkṣepa bhrū : raising the eyebrows, a type of eyebrow movement along the vertical plane, raising the eyebrows (*NS*, VIII.118-123). In *Mṛcchakaṭika* (II), Vasantasenā enters a love-lorn condition, the love-sickness here is described as *utkaṇṭhā.* Vasantasenā is certainly absent-minded. She does not remember what she has said and knits her eyebrows (*bhrūkṣepa*) to answer her friend: this is the *utkṣepa* movement of the eyebrows; upturned; a single eyebrow suggests passion, sportiveness, deliberation etc. and double eyebrows suggest joy, anger, violence, surprise, etc. (*NS*, VIII. 113-123). *Utkṣepa* is raising up of eye-brows singly or together — raising up of one eyebrow used in anger, deliberation, passion, sporting and in seeing and hearing naturally and the raising up of both used in wonder, joy and anger.

678 **उत्छृत स्कन्ध**

Utchṛta skandha : lifted up shoulders.

679 **उत्तमा प्रकृति**

Uttamā prakṛti : The superior nature is known for its self-control, wisdom, skill in diverse crafts, consideration, lofty objectives, reassuring those in fear, knowledge of different sciences (*śāstras*), depth and magnanimity and for the virtues of firmness and sacrifice (*NS*, XXIV. 2-3).

In the case of women, the superior type is noted for its gentleness, steadiness, smiling speech, compassion, service to elders, modesty, courtesy, natural qualities of beauty, noble descent and sweetness (*NS*, XXIV. 9-10).

680 **उत्तर**

Uttara : reply. (a) A figure of speech in which there are a number of questions and a number of respective answers which are all incomprehensible. (b) superior, upper. (c) defendant's reply in law-suit. *Uttaras* are broadly of four kinds, *viz. saṁpratipatti* (admission), *mithyā* (denial), *pratyavaskanda* (special plea) and *pūrva-nyāya* (plea of former trial. It occurs in *Smṛti* literature. (d) an indirect witness who learns from another witness who has seen or heard of a transaction, when the latter is going to a distant country or is on the point of death (*Smṛti).* (e) obsequial rites performed after *sapiṇḍīkaraṇa.*

681 **उत्तरकला**

Uttara-kalā : arts used after the coition, four in number (*Kāmasūtra,* 1.3.17-18).

682 **उत्तर-पक्ष**

Uttara-pakṣa : the superior party (*A*, 8.5.19).

683 **उत्तरपद**

Uttara-pada : reply with a note (*Manu*).

684 **उत्तर-भाषा**

Uttara-bhāṣā : vitiated reply in law-suit (*Smṛti*).

685 **उत्तरायण**

Uttarāyaṇa : the day from which the sun begins to go to the northern direction *i.e.*, when the apparent motion of the sun towards the north begins after *Makara-Saṁkrānti*, that is the last day of the month of *Pauṣa* (middle of January). It is regarded as very auspicious day.

686 **उत्तान**

Uttāna : stretched out, lying on the back.

687 **उत्तानवञ्चित-नृत्तहस्त**

Uttanavañcita-nṛttahasta : The two *tripatāka* hands are slightly bent obliquely and the shoulders and the elbows moved.

688 **उत्तानवञ्चितौ**

Uttāna-vañcitau : the flat-bent. When shoulders and elbows of hands are in the bending style and the *tripatāka* hands are styled obliquely, it is called *uttāna-vañcitau-uttānau* (flat) + *añcitau* (bent). *NS.* IX. 180.

689 **उत्तान-संस्थान**

Uttāna-saṁsthāna : the up-turned or upward stretched pose (*VD*).

690 **उत्तान-हस्त**

Uttāna-hasta : lifted up hands, the flat hand; one of the three movements of hands; the other two are: *pārśvagata* and *adhomukha* (*VD*, III.36). All these styles of hands are to be exhibited with the expressions of eyes, eye-brows and appearances of face.

691 **उत्तिष्ठन्ते**

Uttiṣṭhante : rise in revolt (*A*, 7.5. 30-32). Kauṭilya says that disaffected rise in revolt when there is an enemy attack. He further says that the subjects when impoverished become greedy, when greedy they become disaffected, when disaffected, they either go over to the enemy or themselves kill the master. (*A*, 7.5.27). Thus, disaffection is a step behind rebellion.

692 **उत्थान-द्वादशी**

Utthāna-dvādaśī : twelfth lunar day in the month of Kārtika (Oct.-Nov.) on which the recumbent (*śayana*) images are made seated (*āsīna*) symbolically.

693 **उत्पत्तिवाद**

Utpatti-vāda : theory of generation of *rasa* supported by various constituents-stimuli, consequents, accessories, etc.

694 **उत्पलपत्र**

Utpalapatra : (a) a nail scratch on the breast of a woman made by her lover, (b) a *tilaka* on the forehead.

695 **उत्पलपद्म-हस्त**

Utpalapadma-hasta : the blue-lotus hand; also known as *alapadma* and *alapallava*. "All the fingers turned to the palm standing independently and separately, make the gesture of *utpalapadma*." This is to suggest the sense of prevention, or quary like " of whom you belong to?", "It is not"; nonsense talk; self-assertive air of a lady (*NS*, IX. 85-86).

696 **उत्पात**

Utpāta : (a) an abnormal natural phenomenon foreboding a calamity. (b) portent (*Smṛti*); *Śubhāśubha-sūcaka-bhūta-vikāra*.

697 **उत्पाद**

Utpāda : 'having the legs stretched out', birth, production.

698 **उत्प्रास**

Utprāsa : Joke, loud laughter.

699 **उत्प्लावन**

Utplāvana : jumping movement. Five types have been suggested: *alaga, aśva, moṭita, kṛpālaga* and (Nandikeśvara).

700 **उत्प्लुत**

Utpluta : leap a type of *bhramarī* (*Abhinayadarpaṇa*, 282-292).

701 **उत्फुल्लकम्**

Utphullakam : the widely open posture in coition, practiced by the Deer-lady (*Kāmasūtra*, 2.6.7); (a) a variety of sexual intercourse with full open vagina. (b) full blown as flower.

702 **उत्फुल्लदृष्टि**

Utphulla dṛṣṭi : growing and bright look; suggests *utsāha*.

703 **उत्सङ्ग**

Utsaṅga : lap, embrace.

704 **उत्सङ्ग-हस्त**

Utsaṅga hasta : the lap-hands; both hand-gestures from *arāla-hastas*. When the *arāla*-style of gesture is stylized contrarily and been upturned, it makes the *utsaṅga*. It is used to indicate touch sensation, anger, indignation of women; but if it is in the style of pressing together, it suggests women, jealousy, etc (*NS*, IX. 132-4). In *Mṛcchakaṭika* (V.46), the embracing of Vasantasenā and Cārudatta is performed by a pair of *utsaṅga* hands (*NS*, IX. 139). In *Vikramorvaśiya*, the *usaṅga* hands represent the feeling of touch. Urvaśī touches the king by this gesture. In *Ratnāvalī* (III), the embracing is presented through *utsaṅga hastas* and the *nata grīvā*.

Thus in the *utsaṅga*, the *arāla* hands are placed in *svastika* position facing oneself and bent (right on the left shoulder and *vice versa*). It indicates touch (of the object beyond sight) and things done with great effort, acts of anger and indignation. To represent acts of jealousy by women it is pressed hard.

705 **उत्सर्ग**

Utsarga : a general rule opposed to a special rule or exception. For example, the general rule is that no creature should be killed. But an exception is that an animal may be killed in sacrifice (*Smṛti*). (b) dedication to the public. It is different from *dāna* or gift, because the latter is bestowed on an individual or a specific person. But when a male makes an *utsarga*, he gives up the thing for the benefit of all—*Sarvabhūtebhyaḥ utsargaḥ.*

706 **उत्सव**

Utsava : festival. Indian festivals are performed at well-delineated points in the annual productive cycle, and attest to the passage from scarcity to plenty (as at first fruits or harvest festivals) or from plenty to scarcity (as when the hardships of the winter are anticipated and magically warded against). The Indian villager recognizes them as a fixture in the annual schedule of public celebrations. Co-ordinated closely with the farm calender and the seasons they make up and established and irrevocable sequence. They are indeed almost as 'natural' to him, as, for instance, is the order of transplanting in monsoon and harvesting in winter to the rice-growing peasant of Chattisgarh. Religion helps to promote this 'natural' look of most folk-festivals and intercalate them with the seasonal routines of work on the land. It does so by, among other devices, inserting in their ritual procedure such markers as refer directly to agricultural products, many of them grown in the festival season. It is this mediation by religion of the natural conditions of the peasant's labour and its products which makes the villager look upon these festivals as pre-ordained as the coming of the rains and the hoar-frost and agricultural operations dependent on them.

707 **उत्सव-समाज**

Utsava-samāja : assemblage of people for sport.

708 **उत्सादन-कौशल**

Utsādana-kauśala : proficiency in cleaning; one of the 64 arts enumerated in *Kāmasūtra* (1.3.1.6); art of rubbing and kneading the body.

709 **उत्सारित-बाहु**

Utsārita-bāhu : slightly arched position of arms.

710 **उत्साह**

Utsāha : (a) enthusiasm and energy, fortitude, zest; the basic instinct underlying the types of the heroic sentiment (*Vīra rasa*). (b) effort, the spiritual energy exerted in aesthetic reproduction.

The heroic is to be gesticulated by firmness, steadiness, patience, heroism, charity, diplomacy, munificance, boldness of undertaking and the like.

The gaits in heroic should be represented as such according to Bharata. The actor should move with swift footsteps in various *cārīs*. In the excitement, the gait should be in proper *kalā* and *tāla* with *pārśvakrāntā*, *āviddhā* and *sūcī cārīs.*

711 **उत्साह-दृष्टि**

Utsāha-dṛṣṭi : a type of *bhāva-dṛṣṭi* enumerated by Bharata.

712 **उत्स्यन्दिता चारी**

Utsyanditā cārī : both feet in *samapāda* positions, moving sideways: in a criss-cross *recaka* movement (*NS*, X. 24-26; *SR*, VII. 934-5). The foot is moved gradually sideways in the manner of *recaka* movement. It is also known as *utspanditā-cārī* in which the foot moves slowly in the manner of the *recaka*. Abhinava (*NS*, X. 24) says that according to some the *recaka-nṛtta-hasta* is also used here.

713 **उत्स्वप्नायते**

Utsvapnāyate : 'talks in one's sleep' (*Mṛcch.*); gets up in sleep or from sleep and speaks incoherently. *Utsvāpagir* 'speech in sleep'.

714 **उदकस्पर्श**

Udaka-sparśa : touching parts of body with water preparatory to oath.

715 **उदकुम्भ**

Udakumbha : water-jar; jar filled with water. The practice of seeing a jar filled with water while going out was common (*Skanda*, II. 2.11.56) and is still prevelant. On the other hand, to have to witness an empty jar has been a sign of ill omen (*Brahmāṇḍa*, II. 3.38.32). Jars of various types are mentioned in rituals: *kumbha*, *ghaṭa*; *kamaṇḍalu*, *kalaśa* and *galantikā* etc.

Matsya-Purāṇa (22.43) symbolizes the jar with the ocean: कलशाः सप्तसागराः

One of the most important symbols that the jar represents is that of the womb; and with this concept it is used in fertility rite. चक्रतुः कलशे शुक्रं तपोपूर्णे मनोरमे *(Ibid).*

716 **उदर**

Udara : belly; the gestures of the belly are of three kinds. They are: (i) *kṣāma* (the slender), (ii) *khalva* (the depressed) and (iii) *pūrṇa* (the full). *NS*. X. 17-20. *VD*. (III. 1.63) reads *nimna* for *khalva* in the sense of sunken.

717 **उदरप्रदर्शनम्**

Udarapradarśanam : display of one's belly, it symbolizes one's hunger and begging of food. *pēṭ dikhānā* is a Hindi idiom which means to show one's belly, *i.e.* to beg for food.

718 **उदराकृतिविज्ञान**

Udarākṛti-vijñāna : sign of the stomach. Even, indicates enjoyments; pot-bellied persons are without any means; like serpent, poverty; of having lines, the person, has long life; if like a fish, wealth. (*Garuḍa*). If the stomach is uneven, that indicates lack of wealth, if it is thin, that is an indication of having many rivals and also of talkativeness (*Brahma*, 26.8.).

Stomach which is thin, emaciated and with three lines is supposed to be ideal beauty in Sanskrit literature. Words like *kṛśodarī* and *kṣāmodarī* testify it.

Bent a little due to the weight of the breasts, having three wrinkles, and marked with a delicate line of hair is said to be good. If it is shaped like a pumpkin or drum and has the hue of a barley-grain, it is said to indicate not only distress but even lack of character (*Sk.P.* IV. 37.51). A woman with a big stomach is said to be issueless. (Ibid)

719 **उदात्त**

Udātta : acute accent. It is produced from the higher places of articulation in mouth.

720 **उदान**

Udāna : one of the five kinds of breath. It is in the throat; speech and other activities belonging to the upper part of the body are attributed to it.

721 **उदाहरण**

Udāharaṇa : form of speech and thought (*NS*, 18.4; 18.7); illustration. A concrete instance guaranteeing the material validity of any argument.

722 **उद्गिरणम्**

Udgiraṇam : belching, known as *dakār* in Hindi. Belching is a type of overexposed signals. There are three basic types of belching; the ignorant, the deliberate and the accidental. A man who belches after a good meal because he comes from either a Brāhmaṇa-belcing culture or a public-belching class will shock a gathering.

723 **उद्गीथ**

Udgītha : lying down together with the woman for copulation (*Chāndogyopaniṣad*, 2.12. 1-2).

724 **उद्घट्टित करण**

Udghaṭṭita karaṇa : feet are in *udghaṭṭtita*, *i.e.* toe-heel movements, the hands are in *tala saṅghaṭṭa* derived from the *talamukha nṛtta hastas*. They are brought together and released (*NS*, IV. 163b-164b, IX. 186,286). The feet are in *udghaṭṭita* and hands ready for clapping and the side bent. It is used in excessive joy.

725 **उद्घट्टित पाद**

Udghaṭṭita pāda : when the *kuñcita* foot is followed by the *sama* or the *añcita*, *i.e.* when the toes touch the ground first and then the entire foot touches the ground with the heel striking the ground. It is used generally in *tāṇḍava* and sometimes to indicate high and medium speed (*NS*, X. 40-51). It takes place while standing on the fore-part of the foot and then touching the ground with the heel. It is used in *udghaṭṭita karaṇa*, once or more in the high or medium speed.

726 **उद्दीपन**

Uddīpana : inflaming, exciting, situation and environment, external objects of providing *bhāvas* to the maturity of *rasa*; any aggravating circumstance which lends poignancy to a feeling or passion.

727 **उद्धृष्टक**

Uddhṛṣṭaka : rubbing embrace. The *Kāmasūtra* (2.2.12) defines: "when two lovers are walking slowly together either in the dark or in a place of public resort or a lonely place and rus their bodies against each other, it is called the rubbing embrace". Dāmodaragupta says that only a fortunate will get that rubbing embrace incidently in a place of public resort:

> सहसा सङ्कटवर्त्मनि अवितर्कितं सम्मुखागतेन ।
> अभिलषितेनोद्धृष्टकं अनल्पशुभकर्मणा लभ्यम् ॥

Māgha (*Śiśu.* 7.15) has explained it indirectly. Rubbing type of embrace means that persons walking together at a procession or in the dark rub their bodies for a considerable time.

728 **उद्घ्यात्यक**

Uddhyātyaka : inquiry leading to dramatic opening, opening by inquiry, abrupt dialogue. It is one of the five limbs of *āmukha*. It is expected to draw attention to the play taken up for performance by naming it, or by suggesting its plots, characters and their qualities. There is no question of *pātra-praveśa* here. Following Abhinava's explanation, the word *uddhāta* is to be taken in the sense of a question, a querry. Thus it is a group of words which form an appropriate answer to the querry (*NS*, XVIII. 115-116; Abhinava comments). According to Bharata, when meaningful words, that is questions (whose answers may not be correctly known) put forward respectfully are joined with appropriate answers by others, that is clever people (*NS*, XXVIII. 115-116).

729 **उद्भूत-रूप**

Udbhūta-rūpa : manifest forms which are the indispensable conditions for perception.

730 **उद्यापन**

Udyāpana : Last rite in a *vrata* when undertaken only once. The concluding rite for observances which are to be continued for life is called *pāraṇa*.

731 **उद्वर्तन**

Udvartana : (a) rubbing perfumed substances on the body. (b) The act of ceremonial cleaning of icons, with materials that remove dirt and add brilliance. (c) twisting, smearing.

732 **उद्वर्तनोरु**

Udvartanoru : a raising and lifting of the things implying extension without the foot leaving ground; springing up thigh; a gesture of thighs by turning them very quickly and used in exercising limbs in a group dance (*NS*, X. 27-33). *Valana* and *apaviddha* movement of thigh (probably crossing of thigh, then uncrossing and motionless thigh).

733 **उद्वर्तित पुट**

Udvartita puṭa : upward movement of the eyelids. (*Bālarāmabharata*, pp. 142-143).

734 **उद्वर्तितोरू**

Udvartitoru : a type of thigh movement; a raising and lifting of the thighs implying extension without the foot leaving ground.

735 **उद्वाह**

Udvāha : the unique type of marriage the *Brahmāṇḍa-Purāṇa* (II. 15.4-5) mentions four unique types of marriages, in general, and calls them *udvāha*. The types of wives are here as follows: (1) *Kāla-krītā* :"purchased due to particular time" (or for a particular time); (2) *Kraya-krītā* "purchased out right"; (3) *Pitṛdattā* "given by the parents" and (4) *Svayaṁyutā* "united of her own accord.

कालक्रीता क्रयक्रीता पितृदत्ता स्वयंयुता ।
नारीपुरुषयोरे वमुद्वाहस्तु चतुर्विधः ॥

The first is the *veṣyā* (prostitute), the second is a *dāsikā* (slave), the third is termed *bhāryā* (wife), and the fourth is *yuktā* which is a love-marriage.

736 **उद्वाहितमुख**

Udvāhita mukha : turned up face; upturned face, a type of mouth gesture in *adbuta rasa*; turned up mouth (*NS*, VIII. 153-160);. It expresses pride, sportiveness, turning one out, disregard, nodding, pride of women, in saying 'go away' in disregard, and in saying 'so, indeed' and angry words. Also known as *udvāhi-mukha*.

737 **उद्वाहित-शयन**

Udvāhita-śayana : a type of posture for lying down. Head should be resting on the hand or shoulder and the elbow pressing the ground. It is used in the graceful reclining of the master (*SR*, VII. 1120).

738 **उद्वाहित शिर**

Udvāhita śira : a type of head movement, lifted up head (*NS*, VIII. 18-37); head-gesture used for looking up with appropriate movements of the eye (*NS*, XXV. 2-4); the head turned upside. It is used to indicate height, looking high up, self-estimation, etc.

739 **उद्वाहित स्थान**

Udvāhita sthāna : a reclining posture.

740 **उद्वाहिताकटि**

Udvāhitā kaṭi : upward movements of the hips (*NS*, XII. 247-248). When the hip is slightly raised and brought down; the carried up hips; to raise the both of the waist-sides slowly. It is used to indicate a movement of copulence in a man and amorous feeling (*NS*, X. 21-26) or graceful gait of women, when the hip is raised slowly from one side to the other. (Fig. 741)

741 **उद्वाहिता जङ्घा**

Udvāhitā jaṅghā : raised shank, the raised up legs; *udvāhita* is a gesture of legs, when it is raised high up and used in quick movement (*NS*, X. 33-40). It takes place when the shank is raised up. It is used in movements like going quickly. Actually Bharata mentions three movements—bending of knees, throwing of shanks outwards, and then raising them upwards. (Fig. 741)

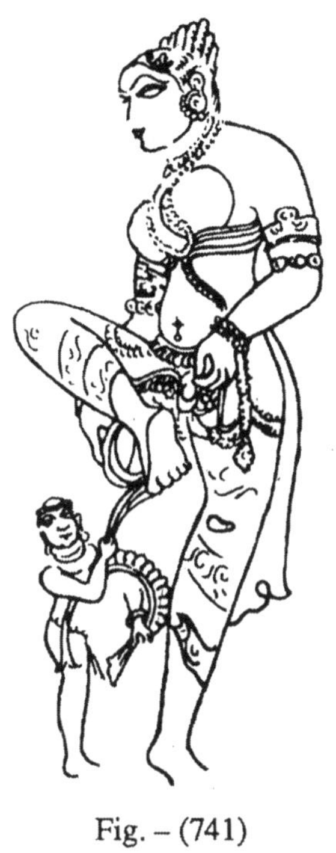

Fig. – (741)

742 **उद्वाहितोरु (उद्वाहित वक्ष)**

Udvāhitoru : torso thrown forward, upward movement of the chest; *udvāhita* movement of chest has to be considered as a position which results from the control of breath, rather than through a movement of the muscles: the deep breathing (*dīrgha niśvāsa*) which it can express is really the cause of this position for the chest is not bent down, and instead it is thrown forward, with a deep breath. The *udvāhita* is a style that indicates to raise up the chest. It is used to breath a heavy shy, to yawn (*NS*, X. 1-9), to look at lofty objects, etc.

743 **उद्वृत्त-अधर**

Udvṛtta-adhara : lip going upward; a type of lip-movement (*SR*); twisted lip.

744 **उद्वृत्त करण**

Udvṛtta karaṇa : the movement of the *karaṇa* is identical with the movements described in the *cārī* of that name:

745 **उद्वृत्त दर्शन**

Udvṛtta darśana : raising of the eyeballs (*Bālarāmabharata*, p.140), same as *samudvṛtta* of *NS*.

746 **उद्वृत्त-नृत्तहस्त**

Udvṛtta nṛtta-hasta : a type of hand-gesture in dancing (*NS*). If two hands in the *haṁsapakṣa* style and turned round like palm-leaf-fans, it is called *udvṛtta* or *tālavṛnta* (*NS*, IX. 176-197).

747 **उद्वृत्ता चारी**

Udvṛttā cārī : foot in *samapāda kuñcita*, derived from *āviddhā cārī*, its *kuñcita* foot is stretched and then touches the ground; a slight jump and turning round is suggested; *udvartita ūrū* and *udvāhita jaṅghā*; associated with *udvṛtta karaṇa*. The *kuñcita* foot of the *āviddhā cārī* taken round (*i.e.* the heel is brought near the region of the thigh of the other foot) and then letting it fall on the ground with a jump and moving round and then (the repetition of the same movement by) the other foot (*NS*, X. 40).

748 **उद्वेग**

Udvega : going swiftly; one of the 64 *sandhyaṅgas* according to Bharata (*NS*, XIX. 88) which includes the fear caused by the king and the robber.

749 **उद्वेष्टित बाहु**

Udveṣṭita-bāhu : loosened arms; suggesting the future fact or event with the meaningful wrist when, the arms are raised up, it is called *udveṣṭita* (*SR* IV. 7.323-345).

750 **उद्वेष्टित शिर**

Udveṣṭita śira : loosened head; a type of head-movement given by *Bālarāmabharata* which corresponds to *utkṣipta* of *NS*.

751 **उद्वेष्टित हस्त**

Udveṣṭita-hasta : loosened hand; single hand-gesture; only mentioned in *Bālarāmabharata*; variation *candrakalā* of *Abhinaya-darpaṇa*.

752 **उद्वेष्टित हस्त-करण**

Udveṣṭita-hasta-karaṇa : If the palm faces upward and the fingers beginning with forefingers move (open) outwards (away from the body), then it is *udveṣṭita karaṇa hasta* movement. When fingers rounded up by the fore-finger one after another from the out-side, it is called the *udveṣṭita karaṇa* of hand (*NS*, IX. 198-204) *i.e.* fingers beginning with the forefinger open outwards (*i.e.* away from the body), *i.e.* fingers bent in *āveṣṭita* are opened out in the same order.

753 **उन्नत जानु**

Unnatajānu : knee-position is the highest position which the *udvāhita* position of the shank (*jaṅghā*) can attain by raising the knee to the chest-level. The dance which Vikrama (*Vikramorvaśiya*, IV) does is one in which knees are more frequently used.

754 **उन्नत पार्श्व**

Unnata pārśva : a type of side-movement; the opposite position in sideways movement; the raised side. In the *unnata* pose of the side, the other side in comparision to the *nata* pose, should be raised up with the waist, the side, the arm and the shoulders. It is used to suggest going backwards (*NS*, X. 10.17) one side with the waist, the hand and the shoulders would be raised and the other side in the *nata*.

755 **उन्नताग्रीवा**

Unnatā grīvā : thrown up or raised up neck; upturned neck with face to see above (*NS*, VIII. 164-171), taking place when the face is upturned, used in looking up.

756 **उन्निद्र**

Unnidra : sleepless, blossomed, opened up.

757 **उन्निद्राम्बुजकोशतुल्य-मदनच्छत्रा**

Unnidrāmbuja-kośatulya-madanacchatrā : lady whose secret part is like a blossomed lotus-flower; quality of the lotus-lady (*Anaṅgaraṅga*, 1.11-12).

758 **उन्मत्तक करण**

Unmattaka karaṇa : The foot is in *añcita* and hands are in *recita*. It is used in pride due to extreme good luck.

759 **उन्मत्तप्रलपित**

Unmatta-pralapita : the words of a mad man.

760 **उन्मत्त रेचित**

Unmatta recita : the hands are in *recita* and the feet in *añcita* : there is a turn of entire body (*NS*, IV. 74-75; IX. 193,274-75; X.38).

761 **उन्माद**

Unmāda : hysteria, mania, insanity, an abnormal state of mind arising from ungratified persons or grief, or fear, or the like, and manifested in inopportunate laughter, or weeping, or singing in incoherent talking, or in similar other actions (*Sāhityadarpaṇa*, III. 160). One of the stages of love in a woman, and would be represented by a fixed gaze, occasional deep sighs, absentmindedness (*Abhinayadarpaṇa*, V. 155-7). In Act II of *Mṛcchakaṭika*, Vasantasenā enters in a love-lorn condition, of love-sickness here is described as *utkaṇṭhā* : this is equivalent to Bharata's *unmāda*, and would be represented by a fixed gaze, occasional deep sighs, absent mindedness. Other representations are as follows: laughing and weeping without any reason, crying, irrelevant talk, lying down, sitting and rising up running, dancing, singing, reciting, smearing the body with ashes and dust, taking grass and remains of flower-offering to deity, soiled clothes, rags, potshred, and earthen tray as decorations of the body many other senseless acts, imitation of others who are not present, etc.

Charka (*Nidāna sthāna*, 7.5) defines *unmāda* as the unsettled state of mind, intelligence, consciousness, perception, behaviour. There are different types of *unmāda*. In the *devonmāda* type there are symptoms of over-cleanliness, gentleness, purity, etc. The *guronmāda* type is obsessive and directive like the teachers. The *pitronmāda* is angry and authoritarian like the father. The *gandharvonmāda* type is erotic, musical fragrance-loving.

762 **उन्मादिनी-मुद्रा**

Unmādinī-mudrā : a type of hand-gesture. Palms to be touched each other in the form of a lotus petal, the index-fingers like the goad, the middle finger below the index fingers; the *anāmikās* straight, and the thumbs straight up like a staff (*Brahmāṇḍa*, II. 4.42.2).

763 **उन्मान**

Unmāna : (a) one of the six different sets of measurements of human-form; corresponding to the dimension of thickness. (b) the sixth stage in Tāntric spritual exercise.

764 **उन्मीलन**

Unmīlana : opening the eye. The act of 'opening', more specifically of the eyes of the icons *(netronmīlatal)*. This is a ritual, that is resorted to after the sculpting of the icon in stone is completed, and before the final installation. The sculptor would have left unfinished only the dilineation of the eye-balls and the vision (*dṛṣṭi*), which is done during this ritual. The icon is supposed to acquire 'life' and become worthy of worship only when this is done.

765 **उन्मेष-पुट**

Unmeṣa-puṭa : opening the eyelids ; a type of eye-lid movement, the movement of the eyelid along the vertical plane; opening the eyelids; opening eyelids in anger and allied emotions (*NS*, VIII. 106-113).

766 **उपक्षेप**

Upakṣepa : tone of speech, declaration (*Veṇīsaṁhāra*, Act IV). According to Bhaṭṭanārāyaṇa, it is not only words that communicate. Usually we are made inclined to listen to a speaker-if the voice sounds are pleasant or friendly. Actual voices create right impression. Some persons try to stimulate interest by using a bright and breezy or efficient sounding voice, others use a warm and cosy voice or seductive and intimate one. Some voices are insistant, pushing and aggressive.

Thus *upakṣepa* means a particular quality of sound associated with particular emotions or feelings.

767 **उपगूढम्**

Upagūḍham : embrace; *(Raghu* .13.16; *Kumāra* .4.17); *Sdyaḥ kaṇṭhacyutabhuja-latāgrantigāḍhopagūhanam (Megha* II.37).

768 **उपगूहन**

Upagūhana : embrace; see *āliṅgana* . Bhartṛhari (*Śṛṅgāraśataka* 2.22) has described the embracing behaviour of a girl at the first union:

अदर्शने दर्शनमात्रकामा
दृष्ट्वा परिष्वङ्गसुखैकलोला ।
आलिङ्गितायां पुनरायताक्ष्या-
माशस्महे विग्रहयोरभेदम् ॥

adarśane darśanamātrakāmā
dṛṣṭvā pariṣvaṅga sukhaikalolā ।
āliṅgitāyām punarāyatākṣyā-
māśasmahe vigrahayorabhedam ॥

769 **उपचार**

Upacāra : articles, metaphor, analogy, sequences in a session of worship, service offered to the deity. *Tantra-sāra* enumerates as many as sixty-four *upacāras* . In temple-worship usual number of *pacāras* offering are sixteen (*Ṣoḍaśopacāra*), (1) *pādya* (water for the feet) (2) *arghya* (water of adoration), (3) *ācāma* (water for sipping), (4) *snāna* (bath), (5) *vasana-bhūṣaṇa* (garments and ornaments), (6) *gandha* (sandal-paste), (7) *puṣpa* (flowers), (8) *dhūpa* (fragrant), (9) *dīpa* (light), (10) *naivedya* (food), (11) *punarācāmana* (water for washing the mouth), (12) *tāmbūla* (betel-nut and leaves), (13) *darpaṇa* (holding the mirror),

(14) *stotra* (laudatory verses and music), (15) *tarpaṇa* (water for satiation) and (16) *namaskriyā* (prostrations). For detailed description see *Tantrasāra* (51-52) and *Mahānirvāṇa* (VI. 78-79, XIII. 203).(b) formality of reception such as rising up, speaking words of welcome, making the customary vows etc. (*Śākuntalam* III. 16; *Raghu.* III. 11).

770 **उपचार-पद**

Upacāra-pada : more formality or flattery. In poetics *upacāra* refers to the way in which the tone of language will vary in appropriateness according to the social context: the situation and the relationship between addresser and addressee (s). All in all, factors such as public Vs. private occasion; side and status of audience; degree of acquaintance, etc., are important social constraints on formality; sometimes giving rise to code-or dialect switching. Terms of address are ready indicators of degrees of formality (Wales, 1989:186).

771 **उपचार-हस्त**

Upacāra-hasta : hands in salutation, a type of both hands gesture mentioned by *Bālarāmabharata;* also known as *praṇāmāñjali.*

772 **उपचाराञ्जलि**

Upacārāñjali : holding the hands in salutation; also known as *praṇāmāñjali.*

773 **उपचारिका**

Upacārikā : female servant.

774 **उपच्छदन**

Upacchadana : coaxing conciliation or inducement by sweet words.

775 **उपदेश/उपदिष्ट**

Upadeśa /upadiṣṭa : (a) form of speech and thought (*Bṛhaddevatā*, 144-60; *NS.* 18.19). (b) original enunciation, first and original precepts of teaching (*Vyākaraṇa*). (c) advice; sermon; gospel; discourse; teaching, training, According to the *Dharmasindhu* in the Kaliage there is non-*dikṣa* but only *upadeśa.*

776 **उपधा**

Upadhā: (a) a secret test of K loyalty and integrity (*Arthaśāstra*). (b) difference.

776 **उपनयन**

Upanayana : initiation into studenthood; it is regarded as the second birth. Shaved, bathed and dressed in new garments, wearing the sacrificial cord over the left shoulder and carring a staff in hand the candidate has to appear before the domestic fire where the preceptor touches him on the left shoulder with his left hand and draws the student's right hand towards himself with the *vyahṛtis* reciting the *Sāvitri* and an appropriate formula signifying the initiation. He next touches the pupil's heart region with a formula that proclaims the union of their hearts and recites a prayer imploring the different deities to endow the initiate with intelligence.The custom of the *upanayana* of girls prevailed down to the *Sūtra* period.

778 **उपनागरक**

Upanāgaraka : cultured (*Kāmasūtra*).

779 **उपनिषद्प्रयोग**

Upaniṣad-prayoga : a thing to be done in solitude, as administering poison to a king.

780 **उपन्यास**

Upanyāsa : one of the limbs of *sandhi.* Bharata defines it as a remark based on reason (*NS*, 19.78), while Dhanañjaya calls it stratagem. (b) novel.

781 **उपपातक**

Upapātaka : minor sin, a class of sins, lighter than *mahāpātakas* and comprising such sins as incest, giving up of Vedic study, allowing the time for initiation to Vedic study to pass, following the profession of dancing, singing, acting, cow-killing, fornication, etc. (*Smṛti*).

782 **उपप्रैष**

Upapraiṣa : form of speech and thought (*Bṛhaddevatā*, 144-60); invitation, summons.

783 **उपमा**

Upamā : Simile. It is a figure of speech whereby two concepts are imaginatively and descriptively compared.

784 **उपमान**

Upamāna : (a) one of the six different sets of measurement of human-form; position of different limbs in relation to each other, *e.g.*, the measurement of the inter-space between the two feet. (b) comparision, analogy as a means of valid knowledge (philosophy). (c) In grammar it stands for an object with which something is compared. For example when one's face is compared to Moon, the later is called *upamāna.*

785 **उपरिक्षिप्तोरु**

Uparikṣiptorū : a raising and lifting of the thighs (*Bālarāmabharata*).

786 **उपरीतक**

Uparītaka : a particular posture of sexual intercourse; also known as *viparītaka.*

787 **उपलक्षण**

Upalakṣaṇa : a mark, distinctive feature, something that has not been expressed: *asti nāsterupalakṣaṇam.*

788 **उपलिङ्गन**

Upaliṅgana : a sign, an indication (*A*, 3.12.51; 3.13.37). *Upaliṅgana* was the focus of study in Kauṭilya's semiotics, which analysed systems and meanings in different groups.

789 **उपवास**

Upavāsa : fasting. It is regarded as a means of purifying body and soul, of removing sins and of mental concentration.

> *cp. upāvṛttasya pāpebhyaḥ sahavāso guṇeṣu yaḥ;*
> *upavāsaḥ sa vijñeyo na śarīrasya śoṣaṇam.*
>
> (Cakrapāṇi on *Caraka* 1.7)

790 **उपविष्ट स्थानक**

Upaviṣṭa-sthānaka : a broad variety of posture.

791 **उपवीत**

Upavīta : sacred thread. The sacred cord in three strands that hangs down from the left shoulder across the chest and goes round the body from under the right arm.

792 **उपवेशन**

Upaveśana : sitting. For eating or social conversation or resting, the villagers along with the tribal folk, sit with the buttock on the ground and the knees drawn up. While sitting they search for a flat stone and then sit on it. In their houses they have one or two wooden blocks which they make themselves.

793 **उपवेष्टित-शिर**

Upaveṣṭita śira : wrapping up head, a type of head movement mentioned by *Bālarāmabharata.*

794 **उपशाय**

Upaśāya : rotation for sleeping (with the *moṭiyārīs* in Muria Ghotul).

795 **उपसंग्रहण**

Upasaṁgrahaṇa : clasping the feet and bowing; touching preceptor's feet in greeting or offering respect to bring under control (*Daśakumāracarita*, II. 2).

796 **उपसम्भाषा**

Upasambhāṣā : friendly persuation.

797 **उपसृत-करण**

Upasṛta-karaṇa : derived from the *ākṣiptācārī;* the commentary adds that the movement of the left hand is in *vyāvartita* and the right hand is held in *arāla* (*NS*, 152b—153 a, IX. 46, 217; X. 37). Also known as *upasṛtaka.* With one foot in *ākṣipta* and the hands in harmony, the body is bent. It is employed in approaching with modesty.

798 **उपस्थ**

Upastha : middle part, male and female generative organ.

799 **उपस्थकरण**

Upasthakaraṇa : to sit placing foot on right knee.

800 **उपस्पर्श**

Upasparśa : sipping water, bathing, touching, contact.

801 **उपहसित**

Upahasita : laughter of ridicule. It is the symbol of the middle class. It is one of the six *anubhāvas* of *hāsa.* In it the nose is expanded, eyes become squinting, and shoulder and head are bent.

802 **उपहास**

Upahāsa : ridicule; ridiculing form of insult. It is in one sense worse than an out-and-out threat. Ridicule displays hostility and belittles the victim at the same time. This is why open derision can so easily provoke the victim into an aggressive response. Several forms of contrived mockery are common. Ill concealed mirth, with the hand covering the mouth but deliberately not obliterating the suppressed laugh, but given in such a way that its usual concealement from the victim purposely fails.

803 **उपांशु**

Upāṁśu : in a low voice, in a whisper, secretly.

804 **उपांशु जप**

Upāṁśu japa : when the *mantra* is minutely audible to the ears of mutterer (alone), it is called *upāṁśu* (*Liṅga*, 1.85.21):

किञ्चित् कर्णान्तरं विद्याद् उपांशु स जय- स्मृतः

805 **उपाकरण**

Upākaraṇa : (a) bringing near. (b) a term signifying certain sentences called *praiṣa* with which one priest asks another to perform a sacrifice. (c) immolation. (d) commencement of studying the *Veda* after performing preparatory rites.

806 **उपाख्यान**

Upākhyāna : 'episode' (*Mahābhārata*).

807 **उपाङ्ग**

Upāṅga : supplement of supplement; minor limbs. It relates to face and is also known as *mukhaja.* Eyebrow, eyelids, eyeballs, nose, lips, chin and mouth constitute the *upāṅga* or minor limbs. (*NS*, VII.12-14). In *Daśakumāracarita* (*uttarapīṭhikā*, II) of Daṇḍin, Rāgamañjari dances with all her minor limbs (*upāṅgas*): her eyebrows are *recita* and her *dṛṣṭi* is *vibhrama*. With these movements she captures the hearts and eyes of spectators. These are different *viniyogas* (uses) of these minor limbs. Bharata uses the words *upāṅga* and *pratyaṅga* as synonymous.

It can be seen that minor limbs with the head as the major one are connected with the facial gestures. The six *upāṅgas* are eyes (*netra*), brows (*bhrū*), nose (*nāsā*), lips *(adhara)*, cheek (kapola) and chin (*cibuka*).

808 **उपादान-करण**

Upādāna-kāraṇa : material or inherent cause, like clay in the case of a jar. It is of two kinds: *vivartopādāna* (material of apparent or illusory transformation) and *pariṇāmopādāna* (material for real transformation). The followers of the *advaita* system believe in the concept of *apariṇāmī upādāna* or changeless stuff like *brahman* as opposed to *parināmī upādāna* (e.g. *māyā* or the mutable stuff of the world). The former is called *avikārī* and the latter *vikārī upādāna*.

809 **उपाधि**

Upādhi : a general property other than generic attribute *(jāti)*. (b) a limiting adjunct. (c) a vicious or mterial condition. (d) in *Advaita vedānta upādhi* is said to be a transformation of *māyā* which limits the true nature of *brahman*. (Śaṅkara on *Vedāntasūtra* 1.4.3).

810 **उपाध्याय**

Upādhyāya : one who teaches for livelihood a pupil a portion of the *Veda* or *Vedāṅgas*.The teacher should be addressed as *upādhyāya* according to Bharata (*NS*, XVII. 65-94).

811 **उपानह्**

Upānah : shoe sandal (*Mahābhārata*) with shoes on feet, one should not eat, salute or worship the god (*Gautam Dharmasūtra*, IX.45) Cf. *more saran rām kī panahī* (*Mānasa*, 2.234.2), *tehi ke pag kī pānhī, more tan kī cām* (*Dohāvalī*, 59).

812 **उपाय**

Upāya : expedient of royal policy. The four expedients are: *sāma, dāna, bheda* and *daṇḍa*. These terms mean respectively conciliation, gift, dissension and war.

813 **उपालम्भ**

Upālambha : form of speech and thought (*A*, 2.10.7), reproach, blame, objection (in reasoning), angry fault-finding (*Amarakośa*).

814 **उपासना**

Upāsanā : the act by which one can sit near god, worship (*Paraśurāma-kalpasūtra*, 1.1).

815 **उपेक्षा**

Upekṣā : neglect, indifference, it is one of the four *brahma-vihāra-bhāvanās* of Buddhism. In *yoga* the term has the same meaning: "to practise indifference towards the vicious". (*Yogasūtra*, 1.33).

816 **उरः पार्श्वमण्डल-नृत्त-हस्त**

Uraḥ-pārshvamaṇḍala-nṛtta-hasta : a type of hand-gesture in dancing (*NS*). The *alapallava* and *arāla* hands are moved by turns above the breast and on the sides.

817 **उरस्**

Uras : chest breast. The style of the chest are of five types: *ābhugna, nirbhugna, udvāhita, prakampita* and *sama* (*VD*, III. 1.62).

818 **उरसाकृतिविज्ञान**

Urasākṛti-vijñāna : sign of the chest. If even, fleshy and raised, kingship; if course, hairy and with protruding veins, a base person; a person with even chest is also wealthy; with round fat chest, prosperity to the person; uneven chest indicates poverty (*Brahma*, 26.14.15).

819 **उरुवेष्ट**

Uruveṣṭa : thigh-encirclement, as a kind of torture (*A*, 4.8.22).

820 **उरोजाकृतिविज्ञान**

Urojākṛtivijñāna : breast-signals.

Although the tribes do not analyse the parts of body or the face with the care given to this pleasant task by the more sophisticated Indian communities, they have a fully developed aesthetic tradition of the breast. This is natural in a people who but yesterday learnt to cover the upper part of their bodies with a cloth. Even now I have seen that the Hill Maria girls are without any upper cloth. When no strangers are about, tribal women discard as many clothes as possible. The breasts, so often seen, are always admired. A boy, asked the age of a girl, will answer by showing with his open hands the size of her breasts. 'She may have breasts as big as a coconut, or they may be small as a lemon, but they are beautiful and we love them', said a *chelik* at Masora. 'A girl's beauty is in her breasts'. But — and this is an interesting point— the breasts do not remain. After a child is born their loveliness departs. But always there are the shoulders; they never betray us'. In other words, sexual congress demands something to hold—'from holding comes joy-indescribable', in youth a *chelik* holds the breasts; later he holds the shoulders, and these never betray him, but go with him all his life.

There are many vivid similes for the breast, a whole vocabulary and system of classification, reminding us the

Kāmasūtra. As we might expect, several of the *chelik's* classifications are of small and immature breasts: the *parās dūdo* (like half-formed gourds); the *benjrī dūdo* (like small brinjals) at which the boys laugh saying, when will the brinjals in your garden be ripe?; The *bondo kuhk dūdo* (like little mushrooms); the *ṭhekā dūdo* (like small pots). The *kosādūdo* are compared to cocoons; they are the breasts of a girl only just matured; and the *urang kaskle dūdo* are also immature and 'flat as dog-fleas'.

Less admired are the *kurbin dudo*, small with long nipples, called 'monkey breasts' in mandla; the *toṛkā dudo*, another gourd breast but elongated and weaker which gives poor thin milk; the *chimnī dudo*, with long nipples 'like the funnel of a country lamp'; and the *chind ḍheṭi dudo*, the nipples of which are 'like the berries of the *chhind* shrub'. It is notable that in this group the breasts are classified according to the nipples.

The breasts of older women are the flat *kultā dudo*, the *herpunj dūdo*, long as country shoes and the *tiblo dūdo* which 'flop down like dripping water', a description which recalls the expression of Betul Gondi:*duduhk ḍing dong ātāng* ' her breasts are dangling like a blanket behind a cart'.

According to *Purāṇas*, one with spacious breast (*vistīrṇa*) is said to be of loose morals (*Sk.P.* IV. 37.44). One who has hair on this part is believed to give birth to a son; If the breasts are big like a pot of the water-wheel, the woman is of loose character (*Ibid.*58). Hence the breasts that are fleshy but not very high (*adūronnata*) are said to be good (*Bhav.P., Brāhma*, 35-36). If the breasts are like the hood of a cobra or are in colour like the tongue of a dog, the woman is sure to bring poverty (*Bhav.P., Ibid*) If they are curved the woman is prone to be cruel; if fleshless, she might become a widow; and if it is spacious she is of a quarrelsome nature (*Ibid.* 46-47).

821 **उरोमण्डल-करण**

Uromaṇḍala-karaṇa : derived from the *uromaṇḍala hastas; svastika* position to begin with; later arms open out; resembles the movement of the legs; *baddhā cārī* (*NS*, IV. 114-115; IX. 204, X. 15,21). Feet are drawn away from *svastika* and *aḍḍitā cārī* is performed. It is used in haughty movements. (Fig.821)

822 **उरोमण्डल-चारी**

Uromaṇḍala cārī : a type of movement where hands are raised to the chest.

823 **उरोमण्डल-बाहु**

Uromaṇḍala bāhu : a type of arm-movement.

824 **उरोमण्डल-हस्त**

Uromaṇḍala-hasta : a type of hand-gesture.

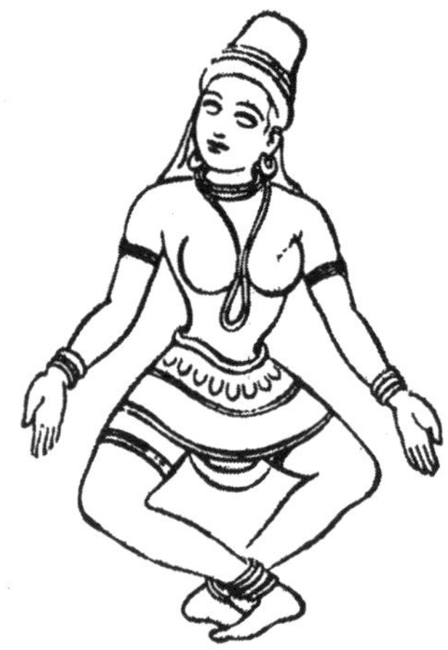

Fig. – (821)

825 **उरोमण्डलिन्-नृत्तहस्त**

Uromaṇḍalin-nṛttahasta : the breast-circling; a type of hand-gesture; after circling around one hand is held on top, and the other is hung down near the hips; one hand is held in *patāka* near the head and the other rests on the thigh. When two *haṁsapakṣa* hands are in the upper region of the body with a circling motion. It is called the *uromaṇḍalin* (*NS*, IX.176-197).

826 **उलूलु**

Ulūlu : meaningless words spoken to induce sleep in a child, crying aloud (*AV*).

827 **उल्बण-नृत्त-हस्त**

Ulbaṇa-nṛtta-hasta : a type of hand-gesture in dancing; the ups and downs. If two hands with the *āviddha* style are stretched up, it is called the *ulabaṇa* or *urvaṇa* (*NS*, IX. 176-197). The two *alapallava* hands in *udveṣṭita* are to be stretched up and waved.

828 **उल्बणम्**

Ulbaṇam : a type of weeping sound produced when a woman receives strokes (*āghāteṣu*) from the male partner during coition (Dāmodaragupta, *Kuṭṭanīmatam*, 155).

829 **उल्लेख्य**

Ullekhya : tatto (*NS*). Bharata thinks that the women of south used to *tatto* their bodies. The practice of tattoing is very common among the tribes. One of the Chhattisgarhi songs mentions its painful act: It is known as *godnā* in Hindi dialects. The following Halbi song is sung during marriage at the time of the worship of *kalaśa* which mentions *godnā*.

godnā gādālis jāle, godālis nonī
kon rājā le, kon rājā le
dongarāco gogin āyā duār buhārte rale āyā nī balle āyā
kitro kitro mol re nūnī
nito āgar dugāni vo āyā

The following Muria song refers to the tattooers:

aga bagādāṅg dumaki dāī
raigarḥ da dumking dāī
agā bagā bātang dāī
siṅgār koti bātaṅg dāī
daṇḍa molā kitāṅg dāī
huj tāsi punoṅg dāī
māt mol hevom dāī
māt koti hevāk dāī
māt siṅgār kotorom dāi.

i.e. Where do the tattoers came?
From Raigarh they came.
Why have they come here?
They have come to tattoo you.
They don't know how to tattoo.
What is their charge for tattoing the arm?
They don't know how to use needles.
If they let us know,
We tattoo ourselves.

A Gond woman from Balaghat says that life may take every other treasure from her, but she will carry her tatto marks even beyond the grave:

Yes, I will give you a pangle for your forehead,
But it will break very soon.
Let me tatto you instead,
And that treasure will instead,

Tatto marks are described in one of the riddles, as "A black dog that casts no shadow".

830 **उल्लेप-संस्थान**

Ullepa-saṁsthāna : the plastered up pose (*VD*).

831 **उल्लोकन-दृष्टि**

Ullokana-dṛṣṭi : a kind of glance enumerated by *Bālarāmabharata*; raising the eye-brows.

832 **उल्लोकित-दर्शन**

Ullokita-darśana : looking upwards; a type of the movement of the eyeballs in the up-down direction; the pupil is taken to the top; the movement of the eyelid along the vertical plane; taking the pupil up-looking at a high object; the glance with eyeballs turning upward (*NS*, VIII. 92-102).

833 **उल्लोकित दृष्टि**

Ullokita dṛṣṭi : same as above, but *NS* calls it *dṛṣṭi* instead of *darśana* ; taking the pupil up-looking at a high object. (Fig. 833)

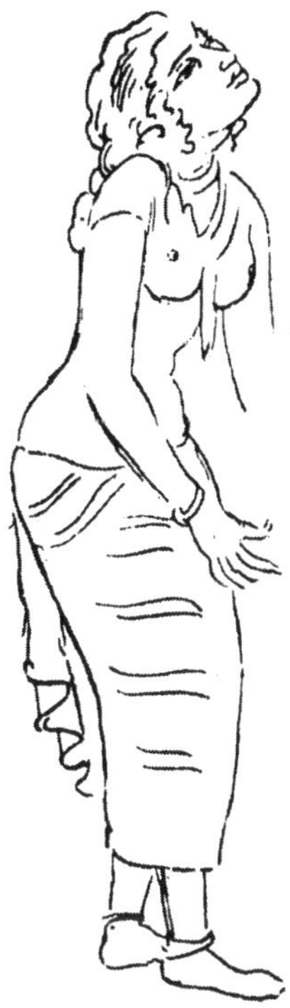

Fig. – (833)

834 **उष्ट्र-मुद्रा**

Uṣṭra mudrā : a type of hand gesture. The thumbs of the *añjali* (*Khaṇḍañjali*) are bent and moved up to indicate a camel (*Mirror of Gesture*, pp. 49-50).

835 **उष्णीष**

Uṣṇiṣa : turban, diadem, crown. (Fig. 835)

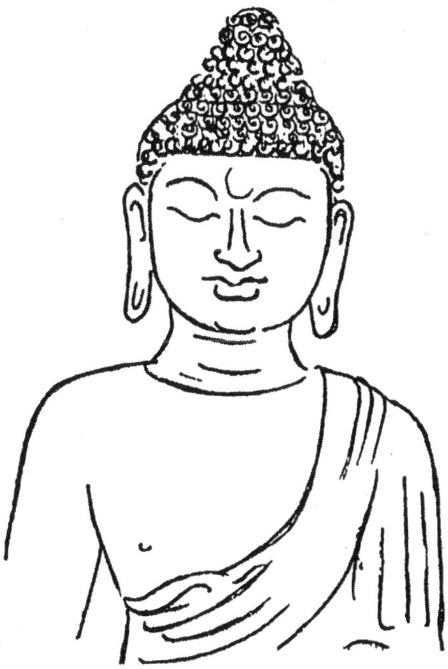

Fig. – (835)

ऊ – Ū

836 **ऊम्**

Ūm : expresses interrogation, anger, reproach, etc. Mostly occurs in the Hill Maria folksongs of Bastar.

837 **ऊरु**

Ūru : thigh. Five movements of thighs are listed in *NS* (IX. 250 b-256 b): *Kampana* (quivering), *valana* (turning), *stambhana* (stand-still), *udvartana* (springing up), *vivartana* (turning round) or *nivartana* (going through the pair of heels). Thighs like the trunk of an elephant or a plantain tree are appreciated in Sanskrit literature: *Karabhoru, rambhoru.* The thighs of women should be like the trunk of an elephant, or the stalk of the plantain tree. It they are so they give sexual enjoyment; if they are clotty, they indicate misfortune; if hairy and thin it is indication of death (*Bhav.P. Brāhma,* 5. 27 - 28).

838 **ऊरुभङ्ग**

Ūrubhaṅga : (a) fracturing of the thigh. (b) name of one of the 13 dramas attributed to Bhāsa.

839 **ऊरुभिन्नी**

Ūrubhinnī : having legs wider apart; contrasted with *saṁhitorūḥ, śaphorūḥ*

840 **ऊरूद्वृत्त करण**

Ūrūdvṛtta karaṇa : derived from the *cārī* of that name: the knees are bent in *nata* and the thighs are in *vivarta;* hands move in *vyāvartita* and then rest on hips in the final positions (*NS*, IV. 158b-159a, IX. 256b-257a, X.22). The hand is in *vyāvartita* and then bent and placed on the back of the thigh, the shanks in *añcita* and *udvṛtta.* It is used in amorous anger, jealousy, request etc.

841 **ऊरूद्वृत्ता चारी**

Ūrūdvṛttā cārī : feet in *samapāda agratala saṁcāra; agratala saṁcāra* foot pointing sideways at a little distance from the other foot; *udvartana*-rising up, tense position but no lack of contact with ground; *ūrūdvṛtta karaṇa* is also suggested; the stopping of Śakuntalā by the pet doe of *Aśrama* (*Śāk.*IV) is portrayed. Thus, the heel of a *talasañcāra* foot is moved outward (*i.e.* towards the back of the other), the shank bent and raised as it is turned towards the shank of the other. The thigh is turned up. Bharata describes it thus: "*agratalasañcāra* foot-heel facing outwards, thigh *añcita* and *udvṛtta*" (*NS*, X. 22). Abhinava (*Ibid*) explains thus: "The heel of one foot in *agratalasañcāra* is placed facing the back of the other foot. One of the shanks with the knee bent and turned inward faces the other shank. Then it is called *ūrūdvṛtta cārī.* It is employed to indicate shyness, jealousy, etc."

842 **ऊरूपगूहन**

Ūrūpagūhana : embrace of the thighs (*Kāmasūtra* 2.2.24) explains this in the following manner: *tatra ūrūsaṅdaṁśenaikamūrūmūrūdvayam vā sarvaprāṇam pīḍayedityūrūpagūhaṇam.* Embracing the beloved with stout thighs so as to press her firmly, with the male thighs and arms. When the lover tightly claps the thighs of his aroused beloved between his own thighs.

843 **ऊरूस्तम्भम् चुम्बनम्**

Ūrūstambham cumbanam : kissing thighs (*Caṁpūbhārata,* 3. p. 100).

844 **ऊर्णनाभ**

Ūrṇanābha : spider.

845 **ऊर्णनाभ-हस्त**

Ūrṇanābha-hasta : the fingers of *padmakośa* are bent. Spider-hand-gesture; Single hand-gesture; occurs in iconography where round objects like the ball, etc. are held. The palm is raised facing down wards and hollowed. All the fingers are spread out and bent and the thumb is bent also. It is used to express scratching the head, head of lion, tortoise, desperation and spider. When the fingers of the *padmakośa* hand are made curved, it is called the *ūrṇanābha.* This is used to hold one by hairs, to scratch one's own head, to indicate leprosy, to enact a lion, a tiger, etc. to take a piece of stone, etc. (*NS*, IX.114-115).

846 **ऊर्ध्वगत बाहु**

Ūrdhvagata bāhu : the up-going arm (*NS*, IX. 204-205).

847 **ऊर्ध्वग-हस्त**

Ūrdhvaga hasta : Upward movement of the hands, going upward, indicates the upward movement at the level of hand.

848 **ऊर्ध्वजानु करण**

Ūrdhvajānu karaṇa : the leg-positions are exactly the same as the *cārī* of that name (*NS*, IV. 85-86, X.33). Throwing up a *kuñcita* foot, the knee is held up to the level with the breast and the hands are moved in harmony. (Fig. 848)

849 **ऊर्ध्वजानु चारी**

Ūrdhvajānu-cārī : the movement where a *kuñcita* foot is lifted upwards to the breast level, and the other foot is motionless and *samapāda* (*NS*, X.33). Lifting up a *kuñcita* foot so that the knee would be on the level of breast and the second foot steady in turn. According to Bharata (*NS*, *Ibid*) "the *kuñcita* foot is raised, the knee level is with the breast, the other leg is motionless. This movement is repeated by both the feet."

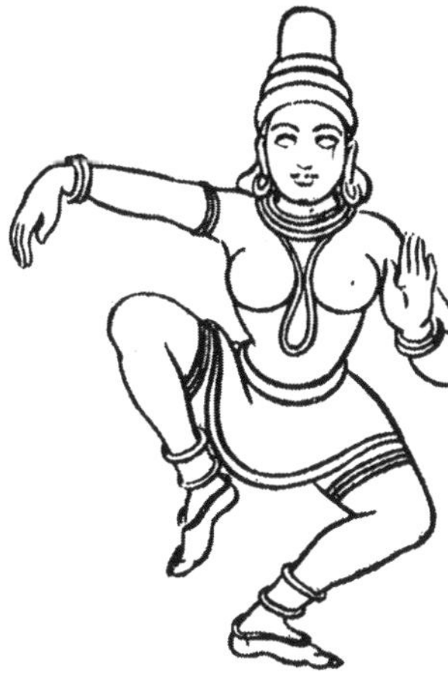

Fig. – (848)

850 **ऊर्ध्व-दृष्टि**

Ūrdhva dṛṣṭi : having an upward gaze, looking upwards. It is natural for one in a pensive mood to be gazing blankly at the sky (*Mbh.*) (b) one of the attitudes of the face, where the eye-balls are rolled up, with the gaze on an object above. It is usual for the ascetics (*yoginīs*) to be represented thus.

851 **ऊर्ध्वपुण्ड्र**

Ūrdhvapuṇḍra : mark on forehead made with different articles for sectarian identification, vertical line marked with sandal on the forehead (a sectarian mark)

852 **ऊर्ध्वबाहु**

Ūrdhvabāhu : 'with uplifted arms' (*Taittirīya Saṁhitā*), having the arms lifted up.

853 **ऊर्ध्वमण्डल-हस्त**

Ūrdhvamaṇḍala-hasta : a type of hand-gesture.

854 **ऊर्ध्वमण्डलिन् नृत हस्त**

Ūrdhvamaṇḍalin-nṛtta-hasta : a type of hand-gesture in dancing. The two hands have circling movements near the upper part of the body.

855 **ऊर्ध्वमुख**

Ūrdhvamukha : 'having the mouth turned up' Kālidāsa.

856 **ऊर्ध्वमुखहस्त**

Ūrdhvamukha hasta : a type of hand-gesture where fingers point upwards.

857 **ऊर्ध्वलतापाद**

Ūrdhvalatāpāda : arch of the extended leg takes the foot to the high head-region.

858 **ऊलूकी (ऊलूकिनी) मुद्रा**

Ūlūkī (ūlūkinī) mudrā: "get the two eyeballs inside the eye-pits and the face too grave. Then make a gesture of the bud by the right hand with four bent fingers. Keep the thumb underneath the bud. This is *ūlūkinī mudrā* that makes the world static and dynamic, visible clearly" (*BT*).

859 **ऊह**

Ūha : (a) ability to think out what had not been explicitly said, imagining ; for example, in the sentences, *agnaye juṣṭam nirvapāmi* the word *sūryāya* is to be imagined for *agnaye* as occasion arises. (b) change, modification. (c) logical consequence or connection. (d) substitution of another word or words in part of a *mantra.* Certain alternations and adaptations are necessary in the matter of *mantras, sāmans* and *saṁskāras* according to the *mīmāṁsakas.* (e) The word ordinarily means *tarka* or *reasoning: adhyāharastarka ūhaḥ* (*Amarakośa,* 1.5.70). (f) It also means conjecture. This is a case of doubtful knowledge where one alternative look more probable. This is also a case of *anavadhāraṇam jñānam,* indefinite cognition, conjecture defers from doubt *(saṁśaya)* in that it definitely learns one of the two alternatives.

ऋ - Ṛ

860 ऋक्षमुद्रा

Ṛkṣa-mudrā : Symbolizes a bear; *padmakośa* facing down by the right hand and *patāka* placed on the back of the left indicate the bear (*Mirror of Gesture,* pp. 49-50)

861 ऋग्वेद-मुद्रा

Ṛgveda-mudrā : gesture symbolizing *Ṛgveda.* Extend the little-finger and curve the thumb at the roots (*VD*).

862 ऋजु-संस्थान

Ṛju-saṁsthāna : the straight-looking position. The face should be made handsome. From breast to belly and again from shoulders, hip and thighs; the figure will go on diminishing. The forth part of the nostril and lips would have an intelligent look. The three-fourth parts of other limbs will diminish proportionately. Other parts of the figure would look beautiful with due diminutions. They should represent various poses as indicated in the *Karaṇa* chapter of *NS* (*VD* III. 39.7-9).

863 ऋज्वगत

Ṛjvagata : physical gestures in iconography.

864 ऋत

Ṛta : law Vedic term for the lows by which the world is governed. It includes natural, social and moral laws and as well. It is an expression of the unchanging, regular cyclic rhythm in nature. the Devas are said to be born in *ṛta* and governed by it. It also stands for the concepts of 'truth' or 'right' as also for 'the order'.

865 ऋतु

Ṛtu : (a) season. (b) mensis.

866 ऋतुकाल

Ṛtukāla : mensis, time favourable for conception, *i.e.* 16 nights from menstrual discharge.

867 ऋतुस्नाता

Ṛtusnātā : a woman who has bathed after menstruation and who is, therefore, fit for intercourse.

868 ऋभु

Ṛbhu : an expert artist. (b) three divine artisans mentioned in the *Vedic* texts.

869 ऋषि

Ṛsi : seer, sages or saints who acted as spiritual advisers of people and performed rituals for their welfare. They lived in seclusion in the forests. In the fourfold *āśrama*-scheme they had reached the *vānaprasthīya.* They also acted as teachers and students and used to live in their hermitages. The institution was known as *ṛṣi-kula.*

ए - E

870 **एक दृष्टि**

Eka-dṛṣṭi : (a) fixed gaze. (b) of fixed gaze. cf. *ekṭak rahe nayan paṭ rokī* (*Mānasa*, 1.1.48).

871 **एक पत्नी**

Eka-patnī : faithful wife.

872 **एकपद**

Ekapada : a particular posture in sexual intercourse. (Fig. 872)

873 **एकपरिग्रहा**

Ekaparigrahā : a prostitute attached to one person (*A*).

874 **एकपात्र**

Ekapātra : inter-dining between high and low (*A*, 11.1.10).

875 **एकपाद-स्थानक**

Ekapāda-sthānaka : a type of posture, standing on one leg. A man wishing to aks favour in a humble manner stands on one leg and folds his cloth round his neck to show that his head is at his benefctor's disposal; and he takes a piece of grass in his mouth by which he means to say, "I am your cow". This type appears to be based on the *Vedic Aja Ekapāda.*

876 **एकपार्श्वगतस्थानक**

Ekapārśvagata sthānaka : a type of posture.

877 **एकभक्त**

Ekabhakta : 'eating only one meal' (*Kauśika sūtra*); a

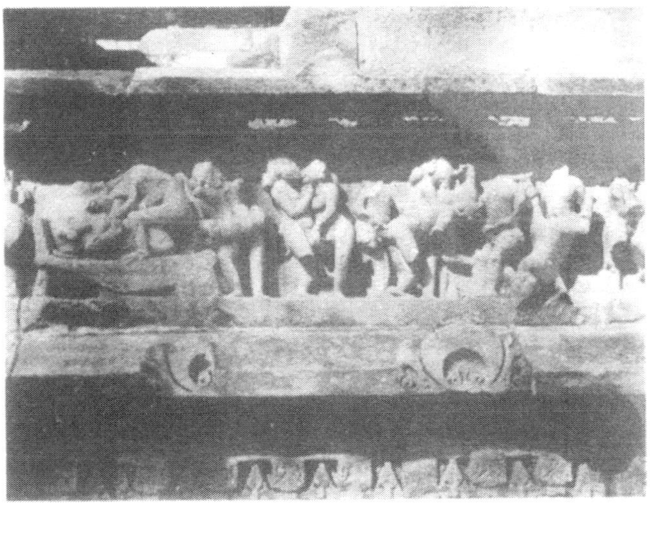

Fig. – (872)

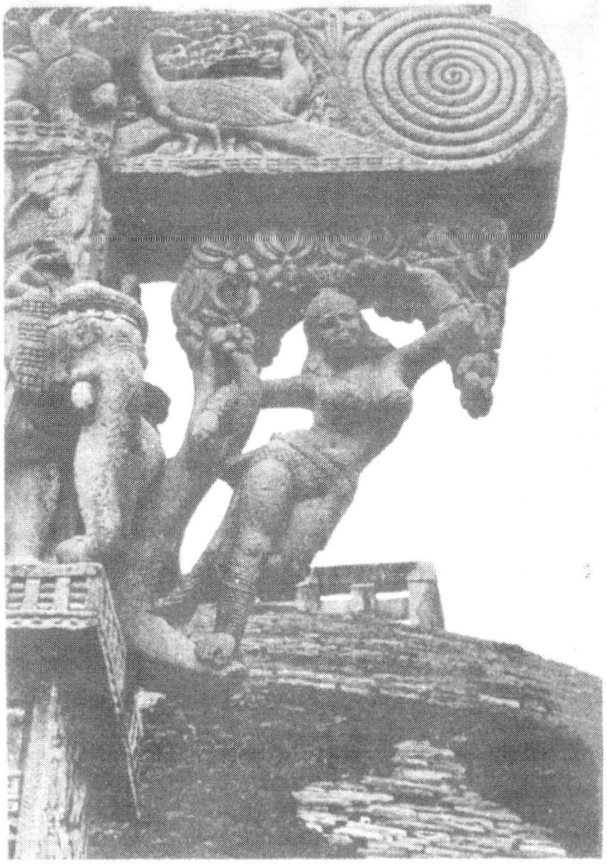

(Fig. 875)

penance for the expiation of minor sins. It consists of taking only one meal a day for a month.

878 **एकलिङ्ग-मुद्रा**

Ekaliṅga-mudrā : a type of hand-gesture. "With the thumb of the little fist, entered inside the right; the thumb is to be held by the right and with the rest of the fingers, the root or the base of the *liṅga* should be made". (*BT*).

879 **एकवाक्यता**

Ekavākyatā : rules for reconcilling differences in conflicting texts. When several sentences, conveying its own sense, are brought together, one is principal and the other is auxiliary, they form one syntactical whole, called *mahāvākya* (*Vedānta-sūtra*, III. 4.24).

880 **एकव्रत**

Ekavrata : eating only once a day.

881 **एकाक्षर**

Ekākṣara : (a) monosyllabic. (b) one letter.

882 **एकाग्रता**

Ekāgratā: singularity of mind according to *Yogasūtra* (III. 11.12), one-pointedness of mind, attention. It implies the focusing of the mind on one object to the exclusion of all other objects. As the *Gītā* (VI.12) puts it, "making his mind one-pointed, controlling his thought and sense, let him practise *yoga*."

883 **एकान्तसिद्धि**

Ekāntasiddhi : absolute success (*A*, 7.3.5), in which success is certain (*A*, 7.7, 11, 22).

884 **एकोच्च स्कन्ध**

Ekocca skandha : a type of gesture when the shoulder is pushed back with tension.

885 **एकोदक**

Ekodaka : a relative connected by the offering of funeral libations of water to the same deceased ancestor.

886 **एडकाक्रीडित-करण**

Eḍakākrīḍita karaṇa : derived from the *cārī* of that name: jumping with *talasañcāra* feet; the torso is slightly bent and twisted (*NS*, IV.157b-158a, X.20). Jumping with *talasañcāra* feet the dancer comes to the ground with body bent and turned. It is used in the gait of inferiors.

887 **एडकाक्रीडित चारी**

Eḍakākrīḍita cārī : both feet in *agratalasañcāra* positions; *utplava*. Jumping of toes; *eḍakākrīḍita karaṇa* and *maṇḍala;* also known as *eḍakākrīḍitā*. Jumping up and down with *talasañcāra* foot in turn, constitutes this *cārī* (*NS*, X.20). Abhinava says that since this is like the movement of a goat, it is termed thus, for *elaka* means goat (*AB* on *N*, X.20).

888 **एदिधिषुः पतिः**

Edidhiṣuḥ patiḥ : husband of a younger sister, whose elder sister has not yet been married.

ऐ - Ai

889 ऐ

Ai: an interjection to attract attention; *ai, vācam dehi* (*Bhaṭṭikāvya*, 6.18).

890 **ऐतिहासिक**

Aitihāsika : (a) historical. (b)historian. *Purāṇas* record that history is a continuous process of interaction between the historian and his facts, and ending dialogue between the present and past. *See itihāsa-saṁvāda* the historians work is a kind of synthesis of the empirical and theoretical approaches to the subject of study. History is a continuously developing science, and what was yesterday a "non-fact" may tomorrow prove to be a well-established and generally recognized fact. It is wrong to declare an undiscovered fact to be non-existent, non-historical. The *purāṇakāra* is continually searching for knowledge, and he has practically unlimited possibilities for augmenting the stock of his scientific instruments. It would be unjustifiable to restrict his scope of vision to the mythical approach only. His choice of subject was conditioned by the environment and the times in which he lived, his views of life in all its aspects and problems - political, economic, social, religious, and moral. Indeed, the *paurāṇic* choice is ultimately determined by his socio-political position.

891 **ऐन्द्रजालिक**

Aindrajālika : magic, jugglcry (*A*, 2.18.19).

892 **ऐन्द्र स्थानक**

Aindra sthānaka : a type of posture.

893 **ऐश्वर्य**

Aiśvarya : power, prosperity, sovereignty, supremacy.

894 **ऐश्वर्य मुद्रा**

Aiśvarya mudrā : gesture symbolizing faculty. When the back of one palm is placed on the other and the little finger of one should touch the other, it indicates *aiśvarya* (*VD*).

ओ - O

895 **ओ**

O : an interjection of calling, hello, ho.

896 **ओजस्**

Ojas : (a) one of the excellence of poetry, creates the mental state of *ātma-vikāsa,* it exists in *vīra, bībhatsa* and *raudra.* (b) *ojas* also means strength, vigour, energy, power, ability, etc.

897 **ओड्रमागधी-प्रवृत्ति**

Oḍhramāgadhī-pravṛtti : Eastern local usage. People in the eastern India like *aṅga, vaṅga, kaliṅga,* etc. have this *pravṛtti.*

898 **ओतप्रोत**

Otaprota : mixed like the woof, crosswise and lengthwise.

899 **ओदन**

Odana : grain mashed and cooked with milk, porridge, boiled rice or any pap or pulpy substance used as sacrificial oblations. *Odanapacana* is the name of the fire on the South alter. *Odana-pāṇinīya* means one who studies Pāṇini for the sake of getting boiled rice (*Kāśikā* on Pāṇini VI. 2.29, Patañjali on Pāṇini 1.1.73). (b) boiled rice.

900 **ओम**

Om : a sacred syllable "Om" is believed to be the mystic word that is the receptacle of various gods; and from it all aspects of speech are believed to have come forth. The word "Om" (actually a-u-m) is said to have been the first expression from the mouth of the supreme deity - Śiva is believed to have said that 'Om' was first produced from his mouth and indicated Śivà himself. (b) *Om* is the most prominent among the symbol (*pratīka*) under which the *upāsanā* of the supra-sensible *brahman* is possible (*ch. op* 1.1.1). (c) *Om* expresses affirmation or assent, yes, so be it. (d) uttered as a holy exclamation at the beginning and end of the *Vedas* or commencement of prayer or *yogic* practice. (e) The curved fore-finger on the extended left thumb indicates *Om* (*VD*).

901 **ओवा**

Ovā : a particular exclamation at sacrifices *(Lāt. Sr.* VII).

902 **ओष्ठ**

Oṣṭha : lit. hot in kissing (*uṣ*=hot); the lower lip; lip.

903 **ओष्ठ्य**

Oṣṭhya : labials.

औ - Au

904 **औचिती**

Aucitī : appropriateness, congruity as one of the several circumstances which determine the exact meaning of a word in a sentence; the soul of good poetry propounded by Kṣemendra in his *Aucitya-vicāra-carcā.*

905 **औचित्य**

Aucitya : propriety. What befits a particular thing is proper, and the state of being proper is propriety or *aucitya.*Kuntaka accepts it as an essential quality. *Rasa* exists only in the observing the rule of appropriateness. According to *Śukranīti* (4.25.26) the concept of propriety is the soul of poetry or any art forms.

Generally meaning 'suitability', *aucitya* has been a pervasive concept in stylistic theory since classical times, and has recently been extended into socio linguistics, and functional approaches to the study of language. *Aucitya* to subject matter was regarded as a virtue in rhetoric from *kuntaka* onwards. Its most important realization is the concept of *rasa.*

906 **औत्सुक्य**

Autsukya : impatience. The twentieth among the thirty-three *vyabhicārī bhāvas.* It is manifested by sighs, thinking with downcast face, sleep, drowsiness, desire for lying down. *Autsukya* is the feeling of impatience in respect of attaining the desired gain or advantage without the slightest loss of time. It is occasioned by the absence of what is desired: flurry, anxiety, etc, are its external manifestations.

907 **औदकस्नान**

Audakasnāna : bathing in a river. It is also known as *varuṇa-snāna.*

908 **औदार्य**

Audārya : courtesy, generosity, magnanimity. It consists in polite and courteous behaviour at all times (*Daśarūpaka,* 11.36). It is courteous behaviour in all situations. Abhinava (*NS*, III, 163) explains it as not speaking harsh words even in intolerance, jealousy, anger, etc (*NS*). Making gifts, bestowing favours and speaking sweet words to enemies as well as to one's own people constitute *audārya* (*NS*). The concept of *audārya* is well presented in the following poem:

> *dānamabhyavapattiśca tathāca pratibhāṣaṇam.*
> *svajane vā pare vāpi tadaudāryam prakīrtitam.*

909 **औपरिष्टक**

Aupariṣṭaka : felletio, mouth-congress, or oral sex. The ninth *adhyāya* of the second *adhikaraṇa of Kāmasūtra* (2.9.1) deals with mouth congress or fellatio. Vātsyāyana says that it was done by the eunuchs, who were of two types: *strīrūpiṇī* (disguised as females) and *puruṣarūpiṇī* (disguised as males)

Yājñavalkya (*ācārādhyāya*) has called such person *mukhebhagaḥ i.e. yaḥ paramukha eva bhagakāryam karoti* "one who uses other's mouth as vagina".

Aupariṣṭaka is usually performed with enunchs, who drive their imaginative pleasure in mouth-congress. It is the source of their livelihood as the enunchs lead the life of courtesans.

Works on erotics prescribe eight stages of such a congress. Gangaram Garg (*Encyclopaedia of Hindu World,* 1992: 806-7) has described them as following.

(a) *Nimittaka* or the nominal congress. When the enunch holds the male organ with his hand and placing it between his lips moves his mouth about.

(b) *Pārśvatodaṣṭa* or biting the sides. When covering the end of the penis with his fingers collected together like the bud of a plant or flower, the enunch presses the sides of it with his lips, also using his teeth.

(c) *Bahiḥ-sandaṁśa* or pressing outside. In this the eunuch presses the end of the penis with his lips closed together, and kisses it as if he were drawing it out.

(d) *Antaḥ-sandaṁśa* or pressing inside. In this posture the eunuch puts the penis further into his mouth and presses it with his lips and then pulls it out.

(e) *Cumbitaka* or kissing. When holding the penis in is hand, the eunuch kisses it as he were kissing the lower lip.

(f) *Parimṛṣṭaka* or rubbing. When after kissing it, the eunuch touches the penis with his tongue everywhere, and passes the tongue over the end of it.

(g) *Āmra-cūṣitaka* or sucking as a mango fruit. When the eunuch puts half of the penis into his mouth and forcibly kisses and sucks it.

(h) *Saṅgara* or swallowing up. The last stage, when the consent of the man the eunuch puts the whole penis into his mouth and presses it to the very end as if he were going to swallow it up.

The *aupariṣṭaka* is practised also by the unchaste and wonton women, female attendants, and serving maids, that is those who are not married to anybody, but who live by shampooing.

The ancient authors are of the opinion that this type of sexual union is a low practice and is opposed to the injunctions of the *Dharmaśāstra.*

There is a more pervert form of *aupariṣṭaka* in which men, instead of getting their penis sucked by women or eunuchs, suck and perform other acts in the vagina with their tongue.

This is also of eight types as follows:

(a) *Adhara-spurita.* In this the man pulls the *labia majoria* of the vagina with his tongue and lips and kisses them.

(b) *Jihvā-bhrāmaṇaka.* In this the man touches the vagina with his nose and then inserting his tongue moves it inside the vagina.

(c) *Jihvā-mardita.* In the first instance, the man kisses the vagina with his nose and lips, then agitates the opening of the vagina with his tongue, and finally vigorously penetrates in the vagina and agitates it.

(d) *Cūṣita.* In this form, the man sucks the vaginal fluid secreting as a result of the *jihvā-mardita,* as above.

(e) *Ucchūṣita.* In this form the man with both the hands raises the thighs of the woman, kisses her navel and vagina, and then inserting his tongue inside her vagina, moves it all-around and finally sucks the vaginal discharge.

(f) *Kṣobhaka.* In this form, the man, catching hold of the thighs of a woman brings her vagina near his chest, supports his head on the hands of the woman, then penetrating his tongue in the vagina, performs intercourse with it, and finally sucks all the vaginal fluid which may discharge during the process.

(g) *Bāhu-cūṣita.* In this form the man in sitting or standing position catches hold of the waist of a woman who may be lying in a bed and putting the waist on his shoulders (feet of the woman stretched on the shoulders so that the neck of the man is in the centre), penetrates his tongue in the vagina, performs intercourse with it and then finally sucks up all the vaginal fluid which may have discharged in the process.

(h) *Kākila.* It means like a crow. When a man and a woman lie down in an inverted order, with the head of the one towards the feet of the other, and carry on congress wherein the man with his mouth sucks the woman's vagina and the woman with her mouth sucks the mans penis (*Ratirahasya,* 10.66; *Kandarpa-cūḍāmaṇi* 2.9.1-39; *Smaradīpikā* 114-25, *Bābhravya-Kārikā* 2.42-50, *Rati-ratna-pradīpikī* 6.21.53).

910 **औरस**

Aurasa : legitimate son (*Smṛti*).

क - Ka

911 **कक्ष**

Kakṣa : armpit. The arm-pit is defined as the base of the arm *bāhumūla).* Varāhamihira *(Bṛhat Smhitā,* LXVIII) has presented some of the characteristics of arm-pits of men as such : men whose arm-pits do not perspire, and are plump (fleshy), raised, having good smell, ever and hairy are to be understood as wealthy; otherwise (if they perspire, are without flesh, sunken, foul-smelling and bereft of hair), as penniless'. vide the following :

निःस्वेदमांसलाः कक्षाः सुगन्धा रोमसङ्कुलाः।
धनिनां तु विजानीयान्निर्धनानामतोऽन्यथा ॥

912 **कक्षसूत्र**

Kakṣasūtra : one of the five *sūtras* (vertical axes) enumerated by *Śilpaśāstra* texts. It is drawn from the armpit, by the side of the hip and calf, and terminates on the fifth toe of the feet. The other four *sūtras* are the *Brahma-sūtra* (axis), *Madhya-sūtra* (medial plump-line), *Pārśva-sūtra* (the side plumb-line) and the *Bāhu-sūtra* (the shoulder plumb-line).

913 **कङ्कण-बन्धन**

Kaṅkaṇa-bandhana: The part of marriage ritual in which the couple garland each other and tie a thread with a turmeric piece on each other's hand. *Kaṅkaṇa* is bracelet chaplet, a band or ribbon put round the wrist of a bride.

Kaṅkaṇa is also called *valaya* or *kaṭaka.* It is an ornament indicating auspiciousness worn on the hand, especially on the wrist. Several of them are worn on each hand. The bracelet is in the circular shape (hence called *'valaya'*), made of metal (usually gold, *suvarṇa-kaṅkaṇa*) or conch shell (*śankha-valaya*), studded with pearls (*maṇi-kaṅkaṇa*) or shaped like a lotus-stem (*mṛṇāta-valaya).* The word *kaṅkaṇa* is explained as "that which expresses auspiciousness"- *kam śubham kaṇa śabde.*

The striking thing about the holy places in India (*tīrtha*) is that one is ordained to throw a golden bracelet,according to a ritual. The bracelet may be of any size and weight, depending upon the status and monetary position of a person:

स्नात्वाग्नितीर्थे विधिवत् कङ्कणं प्राक्षिपेत्ततः ।
सुवर्णस्य महादेवि यथा वित्तानुसारतः ॥
(*Skanda Purāṇa,* VII.1.35.115)

914 **कङ्कत/कङ्कतिका**

Kaṅkata (kaṅkatikā) : comb. It is said that, it is the greatest pleasure for a woman when her husband combs her hair. Even Kṛṣṇa is said to comb and arrange the hair of Rādhā (*Brahmavaivarta,* 57.17-24). The Muria girl combs the hair of her mate in the Ghotul.It is the second stage of courtship.

The gift of a comb is regarded as a sign in the Muria region that lovers intentions are really serious ; in some Ghotul it may not be given directly, but must pass through the Kotwar's hands so that he may keep a check on Ghotul romance (Elwin,1947:434).

Jāhnavī advises Śaṅkara to comb the hair of Pārvatī with a golden comb in *Brahmavaivarta* (*Śrīkṛṣṇa,* 45.16):

स्वर्णकङ्कतिकां धृत्वा केशान्मार्जय योषितः ।
कामिन्याः स्वामिसौभाग्यं सुखं नातः परं भवेत् ॥

Cf. *Meghadūta* (II,22.39) which indicates the arranging of the hair of the beloved to be a privilege of the lover.

915 **कच**

Kaca : hair. Hair on the head is a focus of creativity and expression, providing stronger gender signals. Styles for men's and women's differ according to subcultures. These signals are arbitrary, reflecting cultural stereo types of our sex roles.

The best way to study body adornment is to start with the hair. There are obviously enormous possibilities for decorative modification of hair but always of temporary kind, since whatever is done is soon undone by the withering of old hairs and growth of new ones.

The curious thing about human head hair is that it is so long. If left to itself it would grow to great and cumbersome lengths in both males and females, and it seems likely that some sort of attention must have been paid to it even by our earliest ancestors.

Whatever its original value, the head hair of mankind has for centuries been a vital decoratives organ, often being employed as an additional gender signal by dressing it differently on males and females. It has also been worn in a hundred different styles as a badge of age or status; Today the artificial hair can easily take the lion's share of available space.

916 **कचग्रहणम्**

Kacagrahaṇam : Holding of hair indicates control, as is seen from the account of Kātyāyanī's fight against the demon Mahiṣa. Kātyāyanī did not kill him but held his hair to subdue him for good (*Skanda,* VI.121.71):

एनं कचग्रहं कृत्वा धारयिष्यामि सर्वदा ॥

It is difficult to say if the idea is taken from initiatory rites related to the Śākta-cult; for holding hair in a cutting position and sexual union at the same time, with the initiate in a sitting posture.

917 **कच्छप-मुद्रा**

Kacchapa-mudrā : The gesture of a tortoise. Making the left palm up-turned, place the right on it; draw middle fingers by the two fore-fingers; extend the thumbs forward and make the rest fingers like the feet of a tortoise. Then move the thumb in the way of going-in and coming-out position. This makes a *Kacchapa-mudrā*. This *mudrā* is favourite of all gods, leads slaves and servants to flee and brings quick success in the *melāpa* (union). Possible it suggests a congregation of *Tāntric* devouts; or *cakra*; or a union of *Jīva* and *Śiva* (*BT*).

918 **कञ्चुकी**

Kañcukī : designation of a character in Sanskrit drama. He is a Brahmaṇa endowed with various good qualities, moving about in the harem and expert in all kinds of work.

The entry to the court was regulated by the *kañcukī (chamberlain)* which was known in Hindi as *ḍorhīdār* and who resembled the *daṇḍadhārī* of Sanskrit dramas. If the visitor was a ruler or a courtier, *ḍorhīdār* checked his dress and if some discrepancy in the prescribed court-dress was noticed, it was got corrected before entry. The *ḍorhīdār* then informed the ruler or the office-in-charge of reception in the court and with his permission the visitor was allowed to enter the court . The *Cobadār* or *ḍorhīdār* announced the name, the rank and the *viruda* (titles) of the visitor or courtier and the ruler thus being informed of his privilege accorded him due honours.

919 **कटक**

Kaṭaka : (a) army (b) golden bracelet (*Hc*, I) placed on the left forearms; even now rich men wear golden bracelets on their left fore-arms. (c) bracelet or bangle, decorating the hand, especially the wrist. It is also a posture of the hand, where the thumb is joined to the forefinger and middle finger, and other two fingers are stretched out. The posture is also called the *siṁhakarṇa - mudrā*, because it resembles the ears of a lion. If both the hands are in this posture, and they are crossed to assume the shape of a *svastika*, the resulting posture is known as *Kaṭaka - vardhana* (or *Kaṭakāvarta*), a family dance posture in iconography.

920 **कटकवर्धमानक-हस्त**

Kaṭaka-vardhamānaka-hasta : a type of two hands gesture, an embrace is suggested (*NS*, IX.139). This gesture can be seen in *Mṛcchakaṭika* (Act IV).

921 **कटक-हस्त**

Kaṭaka hasta : a type of *hasta-mudrā* (hand gesture) in iconography. It is mentioned in *Hastalakṣaṇadīpikā*, but the position of the thumb and forefinger varies. The ring finger and the little finger are the same. If the middle and the ring-fingers are placed joined over the *Saṁdaṁśa* - hand, it is called the *Kaṭaka-hasta*. It is used to call some one out and to walk suggesting a motive (*Abhinayadarpaṇa*, verses 160 - 169).

922 **कटकामुख-हस्त**

Kaṭakāmukha-hasta : a type of hand-gesture; *kaṭakāmukha* means the mouth of an army base. When the ring-finger and the little finger of this gesture are bent and raised, it is called the *kaṭakāmukha*. The palm is raised outwards. The third and little fingers are extended and bent very slightly, the first finger and thumb curved forward to touch at the tips, and the second finger bent to touch the base of the thumb. It is used to indicate a sacrifice, an oblation, an umbrella, drawing up reins, holding a mirror, powdering, holding a garland, gathering cloth ends, churning, drawing a bow slowly, plucking flowers, wielding long whip, drawing out a goad, and a rope, representing a lady, holding a pearl necklace, given betel leaves, applying scent, breaking a twig and holding a fan, etc. (*NS*, XI. 60 - 63).

A pair of *kaṭakāmukha* hands crossed at the wrist released or taut in *Śākuntalam* (I) indicates speed or slow motion of the chariot. It has also been used for painting (*Ibid*, Act IV). The plucking of blossoms from a tree is also done through gesture (*Mālavikāgnimitra*, III). The garland is represented through a pair of *kaṭakāmukha hastas* held near the head in *Vikramorvaśīya* (I).

It is also known as *khaṭakāmukha*.

923 **कटकावर्त-हस्त**

Kaṭakāvarta hasta : both hands gesture (*Bālarāmabharata*)

If both the hands are in thumb — Joined to the fore-finger and middle finger, and the other two fingers are stretched out, crossing to assume a shape of *svastika*, the resulting posture is known as *kaṭakāvarta*.

924 **कटकावर्धमानक-हस्त**

Kaṭakāvardhamānaka hasta : a type of hand - gesture bowing to an object; also known as *Kaṭaka - Vardhamānaka*. If a *Kaṭaka (Mukha)* gesture is framed on the wrist-point of another *Kaṭaka (Mukha)*, it is known as *Kaṭaka- Vardhamānaka*. It is applicable in amorous suggestion and expressing deep regards, like bowing down to a revered one (*NS*. IX. 131). (Fig., 924)

925 **कटाक्ष**

Kaṭākṣa : a killing look, an amorous glance, side glances. The eyebrows are contracted and there is a sideways movement (*vivartana*) of the eye-balls (*NS*, VIII. 47). In

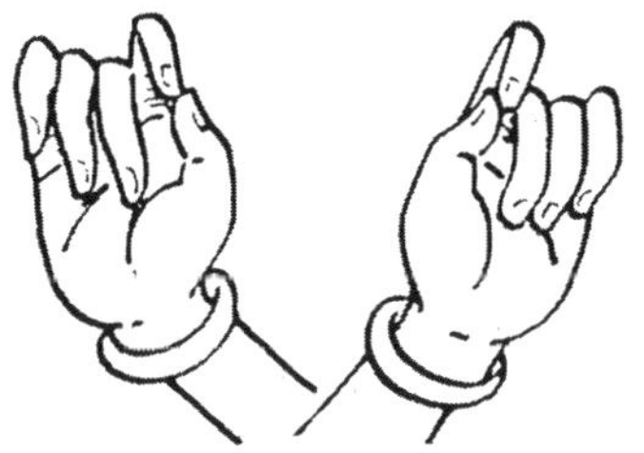

Fig. – 924)

Mālatimādhava (I.28), the verse lists a number of eye-movements. Bhavabhūti has listed here various types of side-glances such as, *viṣādinī*, *lalitā* and *snigdhā.*

Kaṭākṣa is the *darśana* (look) instead of the *dṛṣṭi* (glance). It is also known as *vivartana.* The *kaṭākṣa,* so frequently mentioned in Sanskrit literature, is in reality a movement of the eye-ball and the name for it in the *NS* is *vivartana,* turning the eyeballs sideways, a movement used in expressing the erotic sentiment (*NS,* VIII. 98 b–100 a).

The *kaṭākṣa* with which the women of Ujjain will look at the cloud in *Meghadūta (*40) is the *vivartana* (side-long) movement of the eye-ball. *Snigdhāḥ kaṭākṣāḥ* are mentioned in *Priyadarśikā* (1.5). Sidelong glance of love are frequent in Sanskrit literature. In Bhāsa's *Bālacarita* (Act I) Vasantasēnā's eyes are frightened and her eyeballs move around in *kaṭākṣa.*

The 'oblique' look or 'side - glance' is associated both in poetry and *Tantras* with "goddess compassionate look". It is pity that in the Hindi usage this word has acquired the opposite connotation of a "critical look". The 'side-glance', in relation to beauty,is both sophisticated and shy; and it is such shy sophistications that are "the green fuse" that has driven our aesthetic life forward.

In Hindi, *kanakhī* means the corners of eye, *i.e.* sidelong looks or glances.

926 **कटाक्षावस्था**

Kaṭākṣāvasthā : situations of side-glances.

927 **कटि**

Kaṭi: waist, buttocks, hips.NS has enumerated five movements of *kaṭi,* while *Bālarāmabharata* lists nine movements of the hips. Some of these movements are the *udvāhitā* (when the hip is slightly raised and brought down), *prakampitā or kampitā, recitā* (a circular movement), *chhinnā* (turning from the point of *bhāra-sūtra*), *nivṛttā* or *vivṛttā (*turning to the back), etc, *NS.* IX. 246.

The rhetoricians consider the use of *kaṭi* as vulgar and colloquial. In "*kaṭiste harate manaḥ*", the word *kaṭi* is said to be vulgar (*grāmya*).

928 **कटिकरण**

Kaṭi-karaṇa : derives its name from the position of *kaṭi,* movement of the thigh.

929 **कटिच्छिन्न-करण**

Kaṭicchinna karaṇa : movement of the broken thighs. The *kaṭi* is in the *chhinna* position and hands are in *pallava* (*NS*, IV. 716 - 72 a, IX.254). The waist is turned alternately and both hands in *pallava* are held on shoulders repeatedly. This is used in wonder. (Fig. 929)

930 **कटिदेशलक्षण**

Kaṭideśa lakṣaṇa : waist-signals. If the waist is thin, it indicates royalty; if like a monkey, it indicates poverty. The enlarged rounded buttocks appear to be an ancient sexual signal, the human equivalent of the sexual swellings of other primate species. In monkeys and apes these swellings increase and decrease in size with the monthly cycle of the females, rising to their maximum dimensions at the time of ovulation. In the human female there is no such change, the buttocks remaining 'swollen' throughout the adult breeding life-span and the females being sexually responsive at all times.

The rounded hemisphere of the female buttocks are echoed by the rounded hemispheres of the breasts and, to a less obvious extent, by the roundedness of the shoulders and knees. It is almost as if 'smooth hemisphere of flesh' are the key female gender signal for the human species, and

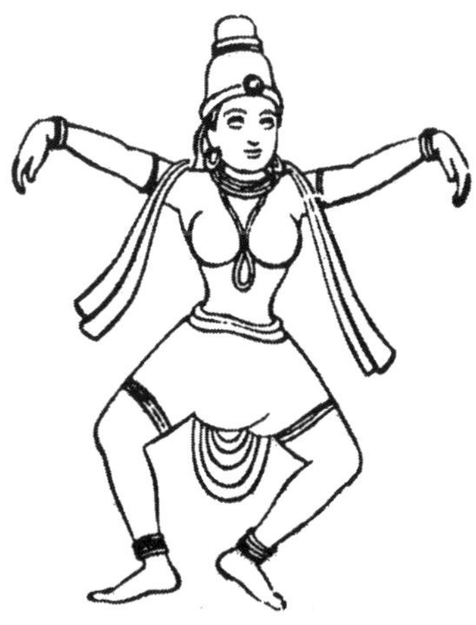

Fig. – (929)

there is every region to believe that the male response to the basic shape has become an inborn reaction. There is no way of proving this, of course, but it would be rather careless of our species to have given up a genically controlled Life Insurance Policy of this kind.

In Sanskrit literature the buttock signal is taken to much greater extremes than we are used to in modern times. The buttocks are described as enormous and fatty protrusions. It seems probable that for Sanskrit writers steatopygia was rather the normal than the rare condition, and that the present day Andamani women are merely the last remnants of the original shape of woman kind as she was seen thousands of years ago. Perhaps the modern male response to female 'hemisphere' owes its strength to this ancient condition, when the female must have been transmitting such powerful gender signals from her buttock region.

Male buttocks :According to Varāhamihira (*Bṛhat - Saṁhitā*, LXVIII), a man with very stout buttocks becomes penurious; with fleshy or muscular ones, happy; with an extra half-buttock one each side, a killer of tigers, and with frog-like ones, a king.

A man with a waist similar to the lions becomes a king; with one like that of a monkey or camel, penniless :

सिंहतुल्या कटिर्यस्य स नरेन्द्रो न संशयः।
श्वशृगालखरोष्ट्राणां तुल्या यस्य स निर्धनः ॥
समोदरा भोगयुता विषमा निर्धनाः स्मृताः॥

931 कटिभ्रान्तकरण

Kaṭibhrānta karaṇa : There is a *recita* movement of *kaṭi;* the feet are in *sūcī cārī,* the arms have a circular movement in *apaviddha* (*NS*, IX. 246-47, 220; X.34). After performing *sūcī cārī* the right foot is placed at the side and the waist moved round. It is used in gaits.

932 कटिरेचक

Kaṭi-recaka : the movement of the waist (*NS*, IX. 244 b-248 a), hip movement (*NS*,IV. 252-256). In it *trika* is lifted up and the waist is turned as well as drawn back. It is one of the four *recakas.*

933 कटि-सम-करण

Kaṭi-sama-karaṇa : The *kaṭi* is in the *sama* position; feet are to be separated from *svastika* position without moving the hips: the chest often *udvāhita* from the *pārśva nata* position; hands are held on the navel in *kaṭakāmukha* (*NS*, IV. 80 b-81 a, IX.52-53, 231). After *svastika,* foot is separated, the two hands are on the navel and the waist respectively and the side in *udvāhita.* It is used by *sūtradhāra* at the incantation of the *jarjara.*

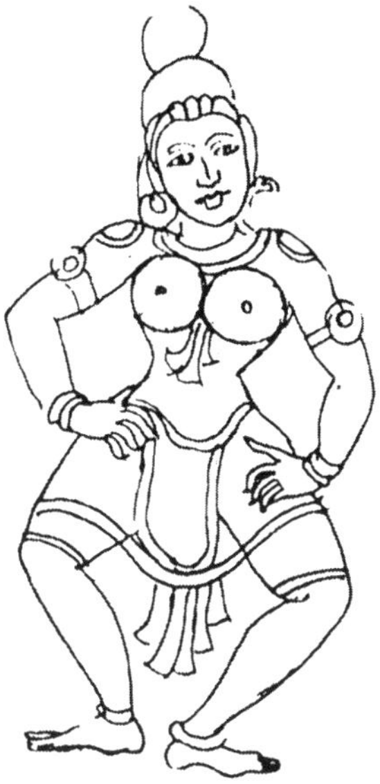

Fig. – (933)

Kaṭisama is a bodily posture where the legs are removed from each other in a *svastika* form, and both hands are placed on the waist at the level of the navel: *svastika-prasṛtaḥ pādaḥ karau nābhi-kaṭisthitau.* (Fig. 933)

934 कटिसूत्र

Kaṭisūtra : (a) hip-line. one of the three horizontal axes which passes through the hip and the girdle in *Śilpaśāsta.* The *Kaṭisūtra* is utilized to the full as the centre of the movements of the hips, thighs and feet. (b) it is a type of girdle of the waist. It is a plain thread that goes round the loins, and thus called *kaṭi-sūtra.* If the girdle is a strip of cloth, it is called *kaṭi-vāsa.* If it is a band, shaped like a chain and fitted with small jingling bells, it is called *kaṭi-śṛṅkhalā (Sankarī* in dialects). All these are the varieties of *kaṭi-bandha.*

935 कटिहस्त

Kaṭi hasta : a type of hand-gesture in iconography, not mentioned in *NS.*

936 कट्यवलम्बित-हस्त

Kaṭyavalambitahasta : a type of *hasta-mudrā* in *Śilpaśāstra.* It is a posture of the hand, placed on, or near the waist, while standing. There are many variations in this posture. It is usual for the lift of normal hand to assume this posture. The arm is brought down straight and the hand is turned upwards with palms on the thighs or the arm itself slightly bent to bring the hand to the level of the loins. The position of the fingers in this posture also shows great variation. The hand is sometimes made to hold the girdle or the ends of the loin-cloth, or to hold a weapon like the bow (in

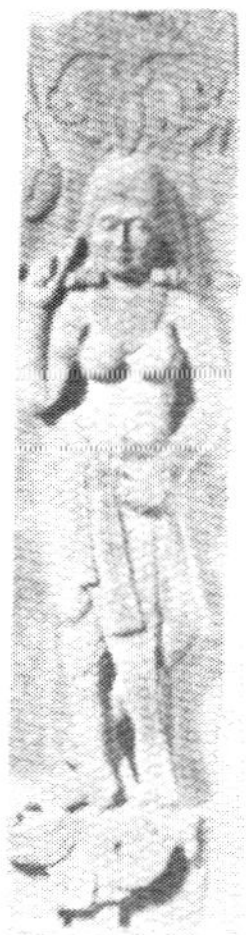

Fig. – (936)

icons of Rāma) or mace (in icons of Viṣṇu) more usually, however, it is a free hand indicationg dignity of bearing.

937 कट्याभरण

Kaṭyābharaṇa: ornaments of hips (*NS*). (a) the *talaka* (below the novel) and *sūtraka* (still lower) are meant for men. (b) females: *talaka* (set with network of pearls), *mekhalā* (girdle with 8 strings), *kāñcī* (girdle with one string), *raśanā* (girdle with 16 strings) and *kalāpa* (with 25 strings).

938 कठिनगुरु कुचा

Kaṭhina-guru-kucā : lady whose breasts are big and hard, quality of the Elephant-lady (*Pañcaśāyaka,* 2.14)

939 कणका-मुद्रा

Kaṇakā-mudrā: a type of hand-gesture. "Join the two hands and keep wrists in the opposite position with the special style and previous strength. This is the gesture known by the name of *kaṇakā* applicable for all sorts of functions" (*BT*).

940 कण्ठ

Kaṇṭha : neck, throat; *kaṇṭhāśleṣa* (neck-embrace).

941 कण्ठग्रह

Kaṇṭhagraha : embracing, cutting of the neck.

942 कंठध्वनि :

Kaṇṭhadhvaniḥ: voice. It is mentioned variously as - swan-like, thunder-like, heron-like, jar-like and drum-like, all indicating royalty and fortune. Dry harsh voice indicates cruelty; weak cracked voice is indicative of low birth (*Brahma,* 26. 6264).

943 कण्ठभङ्ग

Kaṇṭhabhaṅga : stammering.

944 कण्ठलग्न

Kaṇṭhalagna: throwing the arms round the neck (in embrace); *gale lagānā* is the Hindi translation of *kaṇṭhalagna* which means 'embrace'. The following Hindi verse confirms the same:

नदी किनारे सारस बोले, मैं जानूं पिया मोर रे ।
आ पिहरबा गले लगा लूँ, जग में जीना छोड़ रे ॥

nadī kināre sāras bole, main jānū piyā mor re ā piharbā gale lagā lūn, jag men jīnā choṛ re ."A crane screamed on a bank. It was my love, I thought. Let me embrace you, love! We've got short time to live."

945 कण्ठसूत्र

Kaṇṭhasūtra : a kind of close embrace, thus defined: *yatkurvate vakṣasi vallabhasya stanābhighātaṃ nibiḍōpagūhāt pariśramārtham śanakairvidagdhāstatkaṇṭhasūtram pravidanti santaḥ.*

Comparare : *kaṇṭhasūtramapadiśya yoṣitaḥ* (*Raghu* 19.32).

946 कण्ठाकृति

Kaṇṭākṛti : display of the neck. Neck like a conch is an ideal beauty in Sanskrit literature : *kambukaṇṭhī.*

947 कण्ठाभरण

Kaṇṭhābharaṇa: Ornaments of the neck. (a) divine and royal males: *muktāvalī* (pear necklace), *harṣaka* (having the shape of a snake, etc.) and *sūtraka* (golden neck-chain). (b) females: *muktāvalī* (pearl necklace), *vyālapaṅkti* (ornament with snake motif), *mañjarī, ratnamālikā* (jewelled necklace), *ratnāvalī* (bigger jewelled necklace), *sūtraka* (the necklace with 2, 3, or 4 strings) as well as golden chain (*NS*).

948 कथना

Katthanā : form of speech and thought (*Bṛhaddevatā,*144-60), boasting.

949 कत्थक

Kathaka : narrator. In a base-relief from Sāñcī, there is a representation of a group of *kathakas* with their recitations accompanied by music in some degree, the *kathakas* danced and indicated by gestures the sentiments of the characters they represented.

950 **कथा**

Kathā : (a) story telling sessions provide both practice and pleasure in the tribal areas. These range from the recounting of events which may have occurred in their home village, through explanatory and cautionary tales. (b) debate according to *Nyāya sūtra*. The metaphysical truths, such as : *brahman* or supreme soul, *saṁsāra* or transmigration etc. are almost impossible to enquire. But Indian scholars explored many ways for such inquiries. One way was to organize debates. The debates have been exhaustively dealt in the *Nyāyasūtra* of *nyāya* philosophy. According to them, debate is called *kathā*. The *kathā* or debate is of three kinds: *Vāda*, *Jalpa* and *Vitaṇḍā*.In *Jalpa* and *Vitaṇḍā* the principle aim was to achieve effect and victory, therefore, the learned, impartial and unbiased interrogators were made compulsory to attend such debates with the right to cross - question both the parties and give the right judgement.

Jainas classified debate into two types: (a) *vītarāga-kathā* and *vijigīṣu-kathā*. *Vāda* of *nyāya is* considered here to be *vijigīṣu-kathā*.

951 **कथाप्रसंग**

Kathāprasaṅga : conversation. When we make conversation, we learn from our listener's postures and facial expressions whether we are boring or interesting. We feel attractive or unattractive depending on whether we do or do not attract others. One way of finding about a conversational style is by listening to see how often one uses the words "I" and "my" in conversation. It can be surprising to discover in Sanskrit dramas how frequently these occur, not only as opening gammits but also as interjections when the characters are talking. Whatever the subject, there are always plenty of people waiting for an opening to talk about themselves or about someone or something closer to their own interests. Those who can and do listen attentively, ask questions and show a genuine interest in person to whom they are talking, are more than halfway to becoming highly regarded and valued companions. The process of self disclosure proceeds by turn-taking (*kathāprasaṅga*) stages.

952 **कथावतार**

Kathāvatāra : beginning of a story, introduction to a *kathā*.

953 **कथिनी**

Kathinī : female story-teller (*NS*, XVII.53-57)

954 **कथोद्घात**

Kathoddhāta : abrupt opening of the story. A variety of *uddhātyaka* (c.f.), opener of the story. It uses equivocation of double meaning which facilitates the second meaning relevant to the dramatic story (*kathā*), suggesting its opening. The meaning of *kathoddhāta* may be cited from the opening of *Mudrārākṣasa* where the *sutrādhāra's* statement refers to the eclipse of *Candra* (moon) by Rāhu and Kauṭilya, behind the curtain, understands to mean the over-powering of Candragupta. This is a case where *sūtradhāra's* words or the sense of his statement is misinterpreted and taken as different. Really it is not *uddhātyaka as Sāhityadarpaṇa.* (VI.34) maintains. It is an example of *kathoddhāta.*

Bharata defines *kathoddhāta* as "that dramatic opening where a character enters the stage taking the cue from the words of *sutrādhāra* or from the sense his words convey to his own understanding" (*NS*,XX.35). The cue may be either *vākya* 'sentence' (as in *Ratnāvalī.* I.6) or *vākyārtha* 'sense' (as in *Pratimāniruddha* quoted by Abhinavagupta).

In this opening the emphasis is on *pātra-praveśa.* But the words or their sense by equivocation; and the challenge thrown out by the character relates to the dramatic story and its major event.

955 **कदलीसंकेत**

Kadalī-saṁketa: banana-signal. Banana is a signal in different manifestations. Banana-leaves are used to decorate the pitcher on auspicious occasions. Twin banana should not be taken by any one, except old men and women. It is believed that one who takes, may give birth to twin children. Banana is a metaphor for sexual intercourse and to ask a Hindu girl to take her banana means catch hold of the male organ.

956 **कनिष्ठा**

Kaniṣṭhā : 'little finger' *Yājn.*: also *kanyasā.*

957 **कन्दर्प-गेहम्**

Kandarpa-geham : vagina (*Pañcaśāyaka*, 2.12)

958 **कन्धर**

Kandhara : neck.

959 **कन्धरांश शिर**

Kandharāṁsa śira : a type of head-gesture.

960 **कन्यादान**

Kanyādāna : The gift of the bride. In this rite the father of the girl asks the bridegroom not to prove false to the bride in *dharma, artha* and *kāma,* and he responds with the words, "I shall not do so" *(nāti carāmi).* This is done even now *(Pār Gr.* 1.4, *Mānava Gr.* 1.8.6-9)

961 **कन्या-शुल्क**

Kanyā śulka : bridegroom price; bride price; dowry.The *Skanda Purāṇa* (VI.241. 35-36) states that nothing should be taken for the girl in return and states that even the *ārṣa* type wherein a pair of cow and bull is accepted for the girl is equal to "selling of the girl": शुल्कं अण्वपि कन्यायाः कन्याविक्रयपापकृत्।

962 **कपटमुखम्**

Kapaṭamukham : masks. There are many methods with which Indians defend their personal zones of space, and one of them is masking. The face we present to the outer world is rarely our real face. It is considered exceptional, almost peculiar behaviour to show what we really feel in our facial expressions or in our actions.

Day after day we cover up this bare human being. We hold ourselves in careful control lest our bodies cry out messages. Our minds are too careless to hide. We smile constantly, for smile is a sign not only of humour or pleasure but it is also an apology, a sign of defence or even an excuse. These smiles are simply the masks we wear.

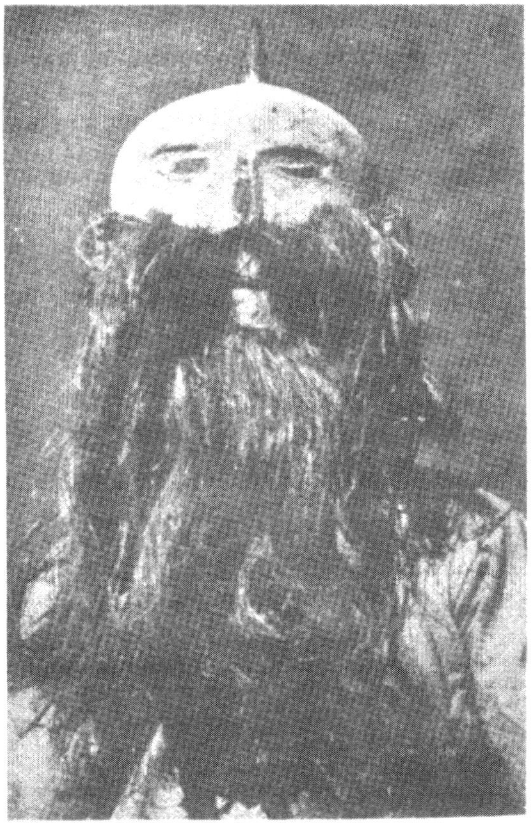

Fig. – (962)

The masking process goes beyond the facial muscles. We mask with our entire body. Women learn to sit in a certain way to conceal their sexuality, especially when their skirts are short. Men wear loin cloth or underwear that often binds their sexual organs. Women wear brassieres to keep their breasts and mask too much sexuality. Tribal women don't do this.

Again, there are certain situations in which the mask drops. The dropping of the mask tell us a great deal about the need to wear the mask. In mental situations the mask is often dropped. Masking cannot cover involuntary reactions.

The need to mask is often so deep that the process becomes self-perpetuating, and the mask cannot be taken off or let down. There are certain situations, such as sexual intercourse, where the masking should be stopped in order to enjoy love-making to its fullest, and yet many of Indians are only able to unmask in complete darkness. We are so afraid of what we may tell our partners by body language, or of what we may reveal with our faces, that we attempt to cut off the visual end of sex completely and we raise moral bulwarks to help us do this. "It's not decent to look", "The sexual organs are ugly". "A nice girl doesn't do that by day light". And so on.

The key to most masking in our society is often contained in books of etiquette. These will dictate what is proper and what isn't in terms of body language. Bhartṛhari even describes how to ignore women: "Oh friend! you should carefully avoid from a distance the contact of a woman-serpent that is deadly poisonous from its very nature, commanding the fiery arrows of side glances and wearing the hood of graceful and amorous sports; for, those who are bitten by ordinary snakes are liable to cure by use of medicines, but persons bitten by serpentine ogles of cleaver women are entirely incurable even through the skill of renowned charmer."

Part of our knowledge is thus learned or absorbed from our culture, and part is taught specifically. But the technique of masking, though it is universal among mankind, varies from culture to culture.

In any culture there are permissible moments when the mask may slip. Beggars in India are well aware of the "hate stare" that a city-dweller can give to them. Here the city-dweller sees the beggar as a non-person, an object not worth concerning himself about. Children, in our society, are treated as non-persons quite often and so are servants. We feel, perhaps consciously, perhaps unconsciously, that before these non-persons no mask is necessary. We cannot worry about hurting the feelings of a non-person. How can we have feelings to heart? (Fig. 962)

This attitude is usually seen as a class-oriented thing. A class in society will apply it to the class beneath; higher-status people will apply it to lower-status people. The boss may not bother to mask in front of his employee.

In India the masking procedure may be a physical one. The custom of women wearing veils is primarily to allow them to conceal their true emotions and also protect them from any male aggression. Here body language is so much recognized that it becomes an accepted fact that a man, with the slightest encouragement will try to force sexual intercourse with a woman. The veil allows the woman to hide her lower face and any unintentionally encouraging gesture.

Along with the constant need to guard our body language, to keep a tight reign on the signals we send out. There is also a paradoxical need to transmit wildly and freely, to tell the world who we are and what we want, to cry out in the wilderness and be answered, to drop the mask and see if the hidden person is being in his own right, in short, to free ourselves and to communicate.

The tribe does. He is scantly clothed. The private parts of men are hardly concealed under the very scanty loin-cloth and the upper part of the women is unmasked. They bathe naked and even play with the sexual organs, throbbing of which amuses them.

963 **कपाल**

Kapāla: (a) skull. *Gautama* (IX.8.21) opines that in speaking of a skull one should use the word *bhagāla* instead of *kapāla*. *Kam mastakam pālayati iti kapālaḥ*. (b) symbol of the womb (*Vāmana* 31.14-17).

964 **कपाल-मुद्रा**

Kapāla-mudrā : the skull-gesture. "Now for the purpose of extracting nectar, dripping down from the *sahasrāra* lotus situated in the cerebrum, make the left palm flat and the long extended fingers curved. Adjust them up to the tips of lips, as the spiritual strength, accumulated previously, does allow. Then get the cerebral lotus, the sixteenth nectarial part of Divinity, extracted. With the nectar drops, dripping down from the above lotus centre and mediating the *gaṇayantra* or *janayantra*, the devout may make the three-fold world. The devout, who is well-up in making and applying this *mudrā* or *yantra* may be the hero of *Khecarī-cakra*." (*BT*).

965 **कपालिका-मुद्रा**

Kapālikā-mudrā : gesture of *kapālikā* "frame the *khaṭvāṅga-mudrā* with the right hand; and place it on the left palm. Then make a fist by the left; keeping the forefinger in the pose of a goad (*aṅkuśa*) and surround it with three right-fingers and thumb. Thus framing a gesture of a goad with the left hand, is *kapālikā mudrā* (*BT*). It is the *ramyā-śakti*..It is the personification of that aspect of *śakti* which becomes sexually passionate on seeing the performance of her rites (*Niruttara-Tantra*,XV).

966 **कपालिनी-मुद्रा**

Kapālinī mudrā : gesture of *kapālinī*. (a) "one should first tie the *kapālinī mudrā* on his right hand. Put the right hand upward, make the fingers up-tipped and extend the thumb straight." (*Brahmyāmala-Tantra*, 6.4). (b) "of the thumb is made a little extended, this may also be called *kapālinī*, a favourite gesture of Mother Gods" (*Ibid*). (c) "welcome the left elbow, extend the little finger of the fist, place it from the mouth to the joint of two lips-the upper and the lower; make the eyeballs stern-looking and then open widely the mouth, this will make the *kapālinī-mudrā* - a very favourite one of Mother Gods" (*Ibid*).

Kapālinī is also called *bhīma-rūpā*.They did not believe in the *Vedas*. They used to drink wine in human skulls.

967 **कपित्थ हस्त**

Kapittha hasta : elephant apple; a type of hand-gesture like *patāka* except for the thumb-position (*Hastalakṣaṇadīpikā*). On *Bālarāmabharata* it's a variation of *triliṅga hasta;* occurs in iconography but as a variant of *muṣṭi*. The palm is raised outwards. The second, third and the little fingers are bent into the palm and the first finger is bent forward; the thumb is bent to touch the tip of the first finger. It is used to express the holding of cymbals, holding flower, holding a rope, offering lights, milk, showing a dance, pounding seed and winding, holding weapons like sword, bow, spear etc. When the thumb is pressed on the fist of the *Śikhara—hasta* and the fore-finger is curved it makes a *kapittha hasta* (*NS*,IX, 52-53). It presents true and wholesome deeds. (Fig. 967)

968 **कपिल-कच-कलाप**

Kapila kacakalāpa: lady whose hair are red in colour, quality of the Conch-lady (*Ratirahasya*, 1.18.19).

969 **कपिल-मुद्रा**

Kapila-mudrā : gesture symbolizing the sage Kapila. Put the right thumb on the extended fingers and the left thumb on the right. This symbolizes *kapila* (*VD*).

970 **कपोत-मुद्रा**

Kapota-mudrā : the gesture of a dove. The *kapotaka* hand fluttered indicated a dove (*Mirror of Gesture*, pp. 50-51d). In *Atharva Veda* (VI.27.1), a dove was regarded as an ill-omened bird and the messenger of Death.

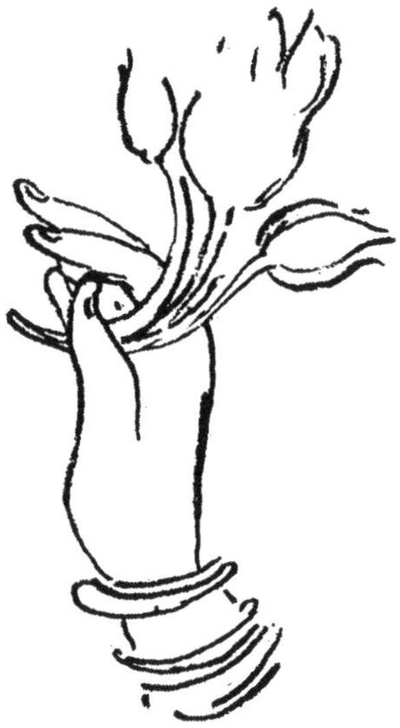

Fig. – (967)

971 **कपोत-हस्त**

Kapota hasta : the pigeon-hands; both hands gesture in all the texts. The agitation and fear of the two friends caused by the sudden appearance of a monkey in *Ratnāvalī* (Act II) is suggested by using a pair of *kapota-hastas* (*NS*, IX. 132 (a). This type of gesture also occurs in *Kumārasaṁbhava* (5.63). In it the two hands are joined at their bases, tips and sides. When two hands with the *patāka*-style are joined together side by side; it is the *kapota-hasta.* This is used to present or offer something in a hostile sense, to blow down, to invite respected persons, etc. When placed on the breasts, it suggests cold, terror, etc. To suggest an uncanny talk; or reference; as 'it is this'; fingers of this style should be first rubbed together and then separated. It also indicates "this much to be done now" and "this is not fair for time-being"; etc.

Both the *añjali*- hands meet their side to form the *kapota-hasta.* To indicate approach with modesty, salutation and talk with venerable persons, it is held on the breast. Women should represent cold and fear with this hand placed on the bosom and shaking. This hand released after the meeting of fingers indicates anxious words, "this much" and "not to be done now."

972 **कपोल-चुम्बनम्**

Kapola-cumbanam : Kissing cheeks *(Campū Bhārata,* 3.74; *Naiṣadha,* 18.41).

973 **कपोतहस्तक**

Kapotahastaka : a mode of folding hands in supplication.

974 **कपोल**

Kapola : cheeks. There are six types of cheeks gestures (VIII.137): *kṣāma* (sunken cheeks), *phulla* (full blown cheeks), *pūrṇa* (raised) *kampita* (throbbing) and *sama* (natural). In technical terminology *kapola* is termed as *gaṇḍa* (q.v.)

975 **कपोलचुम्बनम्**

Kapola-cumbanam : kissing of the cheeks. It is said that Baigās will kiss each other on the cheek when meeting, both men and women. A Gond will kiss and caress his wife after marriage, but as soon as she has a child he drops the habit and never does it again.

976 **कपोल-ताडनम्**

Kapola-tāḍanam : striking the cheeks in confession of fault.

977 **कपोलमुखलेखनम्**

Kapola-mukha-lekhanam : nail-prints on the cheeks. A term used in *Yayāticaritam* (5.7) to refer to the scratching of the cheeks which are involved in arousing the sex. Māgha (*Śiśupālavadha,* 10.78) in *nakhalakṣma kapolaiḥ*) and Ratnākara (*Haravijaya,* 2.47) in *nakhakṣatapadāni kapolabhittibhāgeṣu* have communicated the same idea. Māgha explains that 'the nail-marks scratched on navel and the wounds done by teeth are telling about the amorous acts enjoyed by the lovers in secret, though they have no mouth *(Śiśu.* 11.29).

978 **कपोलराग**

Kapola-rāga : flush in the cheek.

979 **कबन्ध**

Kabandha : trunk; Within the trunk area, Indian gesture distinguish the chest, stomach and breast. The hand lays on the chest in 'servant' and 'warry', on the stomach in 'full', 'hungry' and 'stomach-ache' and on the breast for 'woman'.

980 **कबन्धी-मुद्रा**

Kabandhi-mudrā : gesture of *kabandhī.* "If the extended fingers of a hand are tied with opposite fingers of the other hand and the figure so made is moved by the left hand, it is called *kabandhī*" (*BT*).

981 **कमण्डलु**

Kamaṇḍalu : water-pot (of ascetics)

982 **कमलमृदुपाणि**

Kamalamṛdupāṇi : lady whose hands are soft like lotus, quality of the Mare-lady *(Ratirahasya,* 3.22-26).

983 **कम्प**

Kampa : quiver, shiver. One of the temperamental states. It is manifested by quivering, throbbing and shivering.

984 **कम्पन (अधर)**

Kampana-adhara : throbbing lips; the trembling of lips in *bhayānaka* and *raudra rasa.* In *Mālavikāgnimitra* (Act V),

Mālavikā enacts fear through trembling of lips (*NS*, VIII. 142-43); quivering of lips; indicates trembling, cold, fever, anger, and victory, pain, fear, and swiftness, etc.

985 **कम्पनी-मुद्रा**

Kampanī-mudrā : winnowing-gesture. "The ends of both the palms should be made extended and to be taken as if new grown reddish leaves of a tree. When they are thus winnowed like fans — it is called the gesture of *kampanī*" (*BT*).

986 **कम्पनोरू**

Kampanorū : trembling thighs, repeated toe-heel movement. An up and down movement as a result of a repetitive toe-heel movement of the feet; same as *kampitorū*. It is the gesture of *kampana* of the thigh, when two heels are repeatedly made up and down. It is used in the frightened movements of persons (*NS*, X.27-33). It also indicates the gait of low-class people.

987 **कम्पित कटि**

Kampita kaṭi : trembling hips; hips moving up and down, quick movement of hip from side to side. It is used to walk of a hunch-back, a dwarf and to indicate the way of inferior people (*NS*, X.21-26); see *prakampita kaṭi*.

988 **कम्पित गण्ड**

Kampita gaṇḍa : trembling cheeks, throbbing cheeks; a type of facial expression in *bhayānaka rasa;* quivering cheeks; this indicates anger, pleasure in the mind of a person (*NS*, VIII, 129-134); also used in anger and joy.

989 **कम्पित तारा**

Kampita tārā : trembling of the pupil; an eye-gesture in *bhayānaka rasa.*

990 **कम्पित शिर**

Kampita śira : trembling head; a quick movement of the head in a fast tempo, quick and copious use of ākampita (q.v.); it indicates anger, argument, understanding, assertion, threatening, sickness, intolerance, and speeches with excessive questioning. (*NS*, VIII.17-18).

991 **कम्पितोरू**

Kampitorū : trembling thighs; see *kampanorū*. It results when the heels are raised and lowered repeatedly. It is used in the gaits of low type characters and in fear.

992 **कम्बु-कण्ठी**

Kambu-kaṇṭhī : lady whose neck is like a conch, quality of the Deer-lady (*Pañcasāyaka*, 2.12).

993 **कम्बुग्रीवा**

Kambu-grīvā : having shell-like neck, having neck marked with three lines.

994 **कर-ग्रहणम्**

Kara-grahaṇam : taking the hand in marriage.

995 **करग्राह**

Karagrāha : a husband (who takes the hand).

996 **करङ्किणी-मुद्रा**

Karaṅkiṇī-mudrā : a type of *mudrā.* Make your face down-looking and have repeated loud laugh, it is called *karaṅkiṇī.* This is very favourite to divine Mothers and Gods" (*Brahma-yāmala-tantra*).

997 **करण**

Karaṇa : (a) gait, a cadence of movement made up of an initial static position, a movement in the space and a final pose; *Cāl* in Hindi. Movement of both the feet produces a *karaṇa. Karaṇa* is the primary movement of the body. It is the final pose. The *karaṇa* is a unit of movement, is perhaps the most important subject discussed in *NS* in the *nṛtta* technique of dance. It is indeed a cadence culminating a pose. Since this unit of movement is built up by successive positions of the different limbs, it is important to take into consideration the movements of the different limbs (*NS*, VII, IX, X, XII). In analysing the *karaṇa* as a unit of movement, the cadence has to be broken up into its constituents of movement of the *aṅga* (the major limbs) and the *upāṅga* (minor limbs). Most of the names of the *karaṇas* are also derived from particular movement of the major and minor limbs. There are 108 *karaṇas* enumerated.

(b) That which is the most helpful in the accomplishment of an action (in grammar), means and purpose—*sādhakatamam.*

(c) *Karaṇas* (*tāṇḍavas*) are not to be danced isolately. They are always to be accompanied with the artistic styles of the face, the eye-brows, the eyes etc. In a word, no gesture is styled alone in a dance-drama. The demonstration of any gesture of the hand, the face, the neck, the cheek, the arm, the breast, the sides, the waist, the hip, the thigh, the leg, the feet etc. along with other limbs should respond respectively.

998 **करण गङ्गावतरण**

Karaṇa gaṅgāvataraṇa : an acrobatic gait, as in the sculptures at Cidambaram temples.

999 **करण-निवेश**

Karaṇa niveśa : a type of *karaṇa* found in Mauliśvara temples of Aihole.

1000 **करण-मत्तलि**

Karaṇa mattali : a type of *karaṇa.*

1001 **करण-मुद्रा**

Karaṇa-mudrā : a hand pose.It shows the hand held palm facing outward with the index and little fingers erect, while the two middle fingers are pressed towards the palm of the hand by the thumb.

1002 **करण-ललाटतिलक**

Karaṇa lalāṭatilaka : one foot is raised to touch the ground, a type of *karaṇa.*

1003 **करण-ललित**

Karaṇa lalita : a type of *karaṇa* where *karihasta* is used.

1004 **करण-शकटास्य**

Karaṇa śakaṭāsya : a type of *karaṇa* where both the legs are raised and extended up with the torso touching the ground.

1005 **करतल**

Karatala : palm of the hand. To itch the palm is a superstition in India that some money will come to his hand.

About the general divination from the palm, it is said that it should be soft in the middle, elevated at sides, reddish, and there should be no cavities when the palms are joined. A palm with only a few prominent lines is excellent. In the case of girls, if the palm has many lines, it is said to be an indication of being a widow, and if there are no lines it is a sign of poverty and misery. If the veins are prominent on the palm, she is sure to be a beggar (*Sk.P.* IV.37. 70-71):

Vidhavā bahurekheṇa virekheṇa daridriṇī
bhikṣukī suśirāḍhyena nārī karatalena vai

The following signs on the palm are auspicious: fish, *svastika,* lotus, a circle from the right, conch, umbrella, and a tortoise. With these signs she is believed to give birth to a prince. If there is the sign of a balance, the woman is likely to be the wife of a merchant; if she has lines forming the figure of a horse, elephant or a bull, she is likely to give birth to a son who would be a *tīrtīthaṅkara* (Jain ascetic). If at the root of her hand the lines indicate two bracelets, she would be the wife of a farmer. If there are the signs of *cāmara, aṅkuśa* (goad) or *kodaṇḍa* (bow) she is likely to be the wife of the king. If a line starts from the root of the thumb and goes to the little finger, the girl (or woman) is a killer of her husband (*Ibid.* 79.79). With the signs resembling crow, fox, frog, jackal, scorpion, donkey, camel and cat on the palm, the girl or the woman is sure to bring grief to her family. If there is an unhindered line from the base of the index finger to that of the little finger, it shows long life (*Ibid.* IV. 11.66). With short reddish lines a person is always happy (*Ibid.* 68).

Varāhamihira (*Bṛhat-Saṁhitā,* LXVIII) has presented the following signs of palms - pertaining to men - 'Men with sunken palms are without patrimony; with the palms having round depressions, wealthy; with raised ones, philanthropists; with rugged ones, cruel and poor; with those red like lac very opulent; with yellowish ones, addicted to forbidden women; and with rough and dry ones, penniless. Vide Prahlāda:

पाणिपादतले रक्ते नेत्रान्ते च नखस्तथा ।
तालुजिह्वाधरोष्ठं च सप्तरक्तः श्रियः पदम् ।
यस्य हस्ततलं सम्यक् कठिनं स हि कर्मकृत् ॥

1006 **करतलामलक**

Karatalāmalaka : an *āmalaka* in the hand, expresses ease and clarity of perception.

1007 **कर-ताडनम्**

Kara-tāḍanam : striking. (*Anaṅgaraṅga,* 10.50)

1008 **करताडनविधम्**

Karatāḍanavidham : types of striking. *Kāmasūtra* (2.7.2) classifies it into four types: *taccaturvidham arahastakam prasṛtakam muṣṭiḥ samatalakamiti. Pañcasāyaka* (5.27.28) designates it differently: *Santāḍita, patākam, kuṇḍala* and *bindumālā.* Kalyāṇamalla (*Anaṅgaraṅga,* 10.51) also divides strokes into four classes.

1009 **करताल**

Karatāla : clapping the hand; *sā jahāsa dattakaratāla-muccakaiḥ (Śiśu.* 15.39) (Fig. 1009)

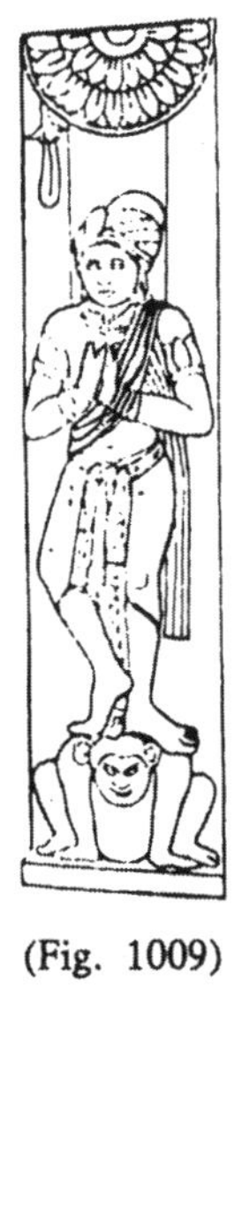

(Fig. 1009)

1010 **करताली**

Karatālī : clapping the hands.

1011 **करन्धय**

Karandhaya : kissing the hand. *hāth cūmnā* in Hindi means to kiss one's hands in reverence. This is the common practise among the Muslims of India.

1012 **करन्यास**

Karanyāsa : feeling the deity in the palms. The fingers and the back of the hand are used to invoke deities in the forms of letters (*Tantrasāra,* 88).

1013 **करपीडन**

Karapiḍana : marriage; *pāṇipiḍanam* (marriage).

1014 **करभोरू**

Karabhorū : a woman whose thighs resemble the trunk of an elephant (Symmetrical).

1015 **करमाला**

Kara-mālā : finger-count.The word denotes a method of performing *'Japa'*, keeping the count on the finger-joints of one's own right hand, instead of on beads of rosary (see *akṣa-mālā*). In this method the middle digit of the ring finger marks the beginning of counting, and moving in the right direction *(pradakṣiṇā),* till the bottom-most digit of the fore- finger is reached, thus giving a count of ten. The word also, infrequently, however, refers to the rosary (*mālā*) carried in the hand (*kara*).

1016 **करस्फोट**

Karasphoṭa : slapping the hands together.

1017 **करस्वन**

Karasvana : clapping the hands.

1018 **कराग्र**

Karāgra : forefront of the hand; *karāgre vasate Lakṣmīḥ.*

1019 **कराघात**

Karāghāta : a stroke or blow with the hand.

1020 **करालम्ब**

Karālamba : helping hands.

1021 **करिहस्त**

Karihasta : a type of hand-gesture.One arm is thrown across the body. The extended arm moves in line with the shoulder level, whereas according to *NS* and contemporary practice, it should be slightly obliquely curved or flexed, with the forearm on a lower level than the upper arm.

1022 **करिहस्त करण**

Karihasta karaṇa : feet in *añcita* position (*NS*,IX.199). One hand is on the breast and the palm of the other in *udveṣṭita* and the foot in *añcita.* (Fig. 1022)

1023 **करिहस्त-नृत्तहस्त**

Karihasta-nṛtta-hasta : an elephant trunk dancing hand.If the *latā*-hands in the same style are held up and swung to and fro and the *tripatāka* - hand is placed by the ear, it is called the *karihasta* (*NS*, IX. 176-197).

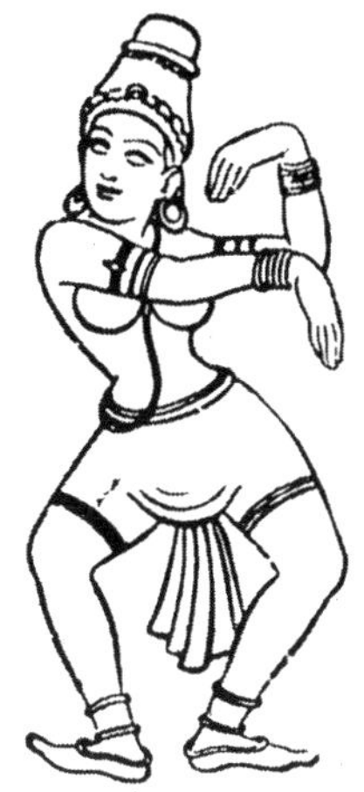

Fig.–(1022)

1023 **करुण**

Karuṇa : pathetic sentiment. What-so-ever form, action, nature and behaviour are suggestive of separation, banishment, distress, pathos or any kind of untowards, etc. is the characteristic feature of the pathetic. It should positively revive compassion, pity, sympathy, grief, etc. in the heart of a relisher (*VD.* III. 43.4).

Bharata (*NS*, VI) states that the pathetic sentiment proceeds from the permanent mental state of sorrow (*śoka*). It should be represented on the stage by means of consequents such as shedding tears, lamentation, dryness of the mouth, change of colour, drooping limbs, being out of breath, loss of memory and the like.

Sentiment of compassion, idea of pain as Buddhistic primal compassion *(karuṇā).* Seeing the beauty of the creation of great creator, artist becomes unhappy with the feeling of inferiority for himself. Inferiority can be born either by seeing something greater than oneself or realizing the imperfectness of oneself. In both the ways *karuṇa* plays a great role in artist's mind.

1025 **करुणा**

Karuṇā : term used basically to denote compassion of Buddha. *Karuṇā* is symbolised in the form of Avalokiteśvara, the great compassionate Bodhisattva. Buddha adopted the idea of *ahiṁsā,* non-violence, turning it into the first ethic of compassion in religious history. The Buddha objected to violence, not because it was polluting, as in Jainism, but because it was cruel, the active agent of suffering. Secondly, the Buddha made his ethical disposition the means to achieve salvation, *nirvāṇa*, or liberation. For Buddha, a pure mind and a compassionate heart lead to release from suffering. Inward detachment from the world should be outwardly expressed in ethical conduct. In the Bodhisattva the Buddha's ethic of compassion comes to flower.

1026 **करुणारसदृष्टि**

Karuṇārasadṛṣṭi : a type of eye-gesture where the upper eyelid is lowered.The eyeball is at the rest. The gaze is fixed on the tip of the nose, and a tear is held in the eye (*NS*, VIII. 49).

In *Vikramorvaśīya* (Act V), there is the depiction of *bhāva karuṇā*.To depict this *bhāva*, the above glance is used. If the upper eyelid of a glance comes down, the eyeball is in a resting mood to express one's mental agony and the vision is fixed at the tip of the nose with tear-shedding eyes; it suggests the pathetic.

1027 **करैत**

Karaita : The name of a variety of snake in *Atharva Veda* (V.13.5) meaning "found among the *kirātas*, one of the barbarous tribes who inhabit woods and mountains and live by hunting. The *karaita* is one of the most deadly of Indian Thanatophidia. It occurs in the tribal legends of Bastar. It is an echo of the following *Atharvan* hymn:

Listen to me, black snakes and hateful creatures, Lurker-in-Grass, Karaita and Brown, and Spotly, Approach not near the house my friend in habits; give warning, and rest quiet with your poison.

(Griffith, *Hymns of the Atharvaveda*, Varanasi, 1968, vol.I, p.208)

1028 **करोटि-मुद्रा**

Karoṭi-mudrā : the skull-bowl gesture. Place the two palms of both the hands in an opposite order and mat fingers of them among themselves. Covering them thus on the palms, press the outer fingers, as required to make a *karoṭi-mudrā* (*BT*).

1029 **कर्कट-मुद्रा**

Karkaṭa-mudrā : a type of hand-pose. (a) the *karkaṭa*-hand directed downwards indicates a scorpion (*Mirror of Gesture*, pp.49-50) (b) the *līna-karkaṭa* hand indicates a crab. The *karkaṭa* with the right hand directed upwards and placed on the left hand. Fingers are to be made interlocked (*Mirror of Gesture*, p. 51).

1030 **कर्कट-हस्त**

Karkaṭa hasta : the crab-hands. Both hands gesture. Interlocking the hands; hand held at the back of the neck, fingers of both the hands interlocked. (*NS*, IX. 133 b-134 a). Buddha images are depicted in this gesture. If fingers in the folded *patāka* come out through their alternate gaps, it is called the *karkaṭa*. It is used to massage a body pleasantly, to yawn after break of sleep, to indicate a big body, to support the chin and to hold a conch-shell.

1031 **कर्ण**

Karṇa : ear. There are many gestures related with the ear: (a) *kān umeṭhnā* to pull or twist one's ears, to chastise. The following proverb has the same sense:

कुम्हार पर बस न चले, गधे का कान अमेठे

"He can not hurt the potter, so he pulls his donkey's ear". (b) *kān pakaḍ ke uthnā baiṭhnā* to make one rise and sit alternately with his hand on his ears; a punishment still prevalent in schools. (c) Varāhamihira (LXVIII) has depicted the personality on the basis of the shape of the ears.

1032 **कर्णं ददाति**

Karṇam dadāti : attentive ears (to speech). Śakuntalā, being the virgin lady, at first meeting with Duṣyanta does not talk, but lends attentive ear to his speech:

> vācam na miśrayati yadyapi madvacobhiḥ
> karṇam dadātyabhimukham mayi bhāṣamāṇe
> (*Abhijñāna Śākuntalam*, 1.30)

1033 **कर्णपरम्परा**

Karṇa-paramparā : from ear to ear, hearsay.

1034 **कर्णमर्द**

Karṇamarda : 'touching the ears as a sign of disgrace or repentance.

1035 **कर्णलग्न स्कन्ध**

Karṇalagna skandha : shoulder pushed in front.

1036 **कर्णवेध**

Karṇavedha : a *saṃskāra* or rite, 'ceremony of piercing the ears'. Piercing the lobes of the ears of the child. This rite is omitted in almost all ancient *Smṛtis*. It is mentioned in *Vedavyāsa-Smṛti* (1.19). Also known as *karṇabheda* (*Skanda*, IV.II,41).

1037 **कर्णाकर्णि**

Karṇākarṇi : from ear to ear.

1038 **कर्णाकृतिविज्ञान**

Karṇākṛti-vijñāna : sign of ears. If flat and fleshless, the person is given to enjoyment; a short-eared person is a miser; if the ears are like an arrow (*śaṅkukarṇa*), the person is to be a king; if there are hairs (*romakarṇa*), he has short life; a broad-eared (*bṛhatkarṇa*) person is wealthy; a king; if dangling and fleshy, he is a king (Garuḍa). If ears are flesh-less, it is an indication of defeat in war; if flat, enjoyment; if short, he is miserly; if hairy, the person has long life; if they are inclined or sticking to the head, they indicate cruelty. Various types are mentioned such as pearl-ears, conch-ears, long-ears, and spacious ears, all indicative of goodness, including wealth, long life (*Brahma*,26, 74-75). 'With ears devoid of flesh men meet with tragic ends; with flat ones, become enjoyer of many pleasures; with short ones, miserly; with conical ones, commanders of armies; with hairy ones, long-lived ones; with broad ones, wealthy; with those filled with veins, cruel; with hanging and fleshy ones, happy.

ह्रस्वकर्णा महाभोगा महाकर्णाश्च ये नराः ।
आवर्तकर्णा धनिनः स्निग्धकर्णास्तथैव च ॥
दीर्घायुषः शङ्कुकर्णाः स्फुटकर्णा महाधनाः ।
सुखान्विता दीर्घकर्णा लम्बकर्णास्तपस्विनः ॥

1039 **कर्णाभरण**

Karṇābharaṇa : ornaments of the ear. (a) ornaments of the divine and royal males. *Kuṇḍala* (ear-ring) to be worn in the lower lobe of the ear. *Mocaka* (ear pendant) in the central part of the ear and *kīlā*, at the top of the ear (*NS*). (b) ornaments of the females. *Kuṇḍala, karṇikā, karṇavalaya, patrakarṇikā, karṇamudrā, (*entwining the ear), *karṇotkīlaka* (ear-top), *śikhipatra* (ear ornament studded with multi-coloured jewels, in the shape of peacock feather) various kinds of *dantrapatras* (of ivory) set with jewels and *karṇapūra* (*NS*).

1040 **कर्णे कथयति**

Karṇe kathayati : observe this aurmatic device in *Priyadarśikā* (Act. III) employed to avoid anticipating the discourse of the plan which is later set forth by the king himself. *Kān meṅ kahnā* is a Hindi idiom which symbolizes whispering in one's ear. It is also known as *kānāphūsī, khusurphusur* and *kānābātī* (speaking in a low tone).

1041 **कर्णे जपः**

Karṇejapaḥ : back-biter, informer, *karṇejapaḥ sūcakaḥ (Mahābhārata,* III. 213).

1042 **कर्णोपकर्णिका**

Karṇopakarṇikā : rumour.

1043 **कर्तरी-उत्प्लवन**

Kartarī utplavana : a type of jumping posture mentioned by Nandikeśvara. *Kartarī* or *karttari* is a small knife which serves as a weapon of god. *Kartarī* is also a form of *mantra* containing two letters (*Tantrarāja,* XXXV. 28-29).

1044 **कर्तरीमुख-हस्त**

Kartarīmukha hasta : Face of the arrow shaft. Single hand gesture.When in the *tripatāka*-gesture (q.v.), the fore-finger is bent, it is *kartarīmukha.* If pointed downwards, it indicates the foot-steps of travellers, decorating feet with appropriate colours. With fingers raised up, it indicates things to be observed, or blowing horns and writing letters. By the pair of finger of the gesture, bent back-ward, it indicates falling down, death, transmission, reversion, cogitation and placing a thing in trust with the process of joining and disjoining alternately two hands of the *kartarīmukha;* it may indicate a stag (*ruru*), an yak (cāmaraḥ), a buffalo, an axe, a heavenly elephant, a palace-gate, and the peak of a hill (*NS,* IX. 32-35). In *Mṛcchakaṭika* (Act II), gopuram of the temple is shown by the two *kartarīmukha hastas.* The enactment of the decorating Mālavikā's feet for the *aśokadohada* is represented in *Mālavikāgnimitra* (Act III) through the above hand gestures (*NS,* IX. 39-41). The hand is raised with the palm facing outwards. The first and second fingers are extended straight up, the third finger is bent into the palm and the thumb is placed to touch the tip of the finger. It is used to express opposition, disagreement, falling separation (of lovers), a creeper, yearning, buffalo, deer, fly, hill-top and elephant.

1045 **कर्तरी-मुद्रा**

Kartarī-mudrā : a type of hand-pose. "In a hand, with fingers kept separately and positioned all round. The hand, expressing the sense to squeeze, to press and to kill etc., the *mudrā* is called *kartarī.*" (*BT*)

1046 **कर्तरी-स्वस्तिक-हस्त**

Kartarī svastika hasta : both hands gesture (*Abhinayadarpaṇa*) not mentioned in *NS.* If the *svastika* gesture is made by framing two *kartarī* styles, it is *kartarī svastika.* It is used to indicate hill-tops, trees and branches.

1047 **कर्तरी-हस्त**

Kartarīhasta : a type of *hastamudrā. Kartarī* is any cutting instrument (from *'kṛti' chedane*) but often refers to scissors or short sword. There is a hand-pose (*mudrā*) known as *kartarī-hasta* , where the fore-finger and the middle finger are crossed to resemble the scissors.

1048 **कर्म**

Karma : (a) motion. Praśastapāda (c.5th century A.D.), Commentator of *Vaiśeṣika-sūtra* is perhaps, the first writer to deal with motion. Motion or *karma* is distinguished from momentum or *vega* in that while the former is instantaneous (*kṣaṇika*) the latter has a persistent tendency and implies a series of motions. Motion may or may not be caused by contact with matter. Motion, not caused by contact, may be caused by volition (*prayatna*), gravity (*gurutva*), fluidity (*dravatva*) or by the universal final cause, *adṛṣta* (the unknown cause), the first motion in atoms in the beginning of creation. Motion, caused by contact, may be due to direct contact with a body exerting continued pressure (*nodana*) or to direct contact for an instant with a body that produces an impact (*abhighāta*) or to direct contact with an elastic body which exercises a moving force by means of its elasticity (*sthiti-sthāpaka*) or to contact with a body which itself is in contact with another possessing *vega* or momentum. The motion of fluids may be current (*syandana*), upward (*ārohṇa*), capillary (*abhisarpaṇa*). Vertical motion (*sammūrchana*) and mere-motion may also be noticed.

(b) the act. *Karma* is conceived as the effect of former deeds on one's present and future condition; it attaches to the soul and provokes joy and sufferings in it, leading it towards reward or punishment. A meritorious deed diminishes the total of rebirths to come; a bad deed increases that total. This principle has been accepted by all philosophical systems of India and expounded unceasingly ever since.

(c)physical movement. According to the *vaiśeṣika* system it is one of the seven categories of reality. There are five kinds of *karma: Utkṣepaṇa* (throwing upward), *ākuñcana* (contraction), *prasāraṇa* (expansion) and *gamana* (locomotion). (d) *Karma* is action more particularly, the law of redistribution by which one's past action, good or bad, determines one's future fate.

(e) conduct; code of conduct. Conduct implies action, or *karma. Karma* is divided as (1) *pravṛtta* (continued with effort) and (II) *nivṛtta* (ceased or without desire). On the plane of daily duty *karma* is eight fold: (1) *śauca* (purity), (2) *ācamana* (sipping of water), (3) *virecana* (purging), (4) *bhāvanā* (feeling), (5) *pāka* (accomplishment), (6) *bodhana* (feeling), (7) *dhūpana* (fumigating) and (8) *vāsana* (dwelling). In the context of ritual *karma* is said to be three-fold: (i) *sañcita* (accrued from previous birth), (ii) *kriyamāṇa* (being done at present) and (iii) *prārabdha* (what has started and will be enjoyed in the next birth; *Śiva*,IV.23. 42-44).

(f) the doctrine according to which all actions, good or bad, produce their proper consequences in the life of individual who acts. In its original sense *karma* had no ethical connotation, it was simply a biological law of causalty linked with that of *saṁsāra*, rebirth. Both concepts are the product of the synchronic and fundamental sense of tribal solidarity.

1049 **कर्मकाण्ड**

Karmakāṇḍa : A theoretical division of *Vedic* texts. It pertains to those portions which apply to some ritual or sacrifice.

1050 **कर्ममार्ग**

Karmamārga : (a) the so-called external means for achieving the highest object of life: the performance of ritual and ceremonies. (b) the cycles of activity and quiescence play an important part in *Tantric* philosophy: 'one attempt to make the universe intelligible regards it as an eternal rhythm playing and pulsing outwards from spirit to matter (*pravṛtti*) and then backward and inwards from matter to spirit (*nivṛtti*)... The *Tāntras* recognize and consecrate both movements, the outward throbbing stream of energy and enjoyment (*bhukti*) and the calm returning flow of liberation and peace. Both are happiness, but the wise understand that the active outward movement is right and happy only up to a certain point under certain restrictions' (Elliot LXXXI). During the *Tāntric* rite, the devotee exhausts the forces of activity, the outgoing path, and begins to cultivate quiescence (*Tantra-rahasya*, 150).

1051 **कर्मयुग**

Karma-yuga : Kali age.

1052 **कर्मयोग**

Karmayoga : action without any desire of the fruit thereof. Each act is prompted by a particular motive and it is the motive that governs its nature. Because an act is undertaken for the definite purpose of enjoying its result, the result affects the soul. But if action could be performed without a desire for the personal enjoyment of the result, then it would be devoid of its stings. *Karma* thus becomes *karmayoga* in which the soul remains unaffected. This doctrine is set forth in the *Bhagavadgītā* in great detail. According to this doctrine there is no such thing here as progress; value lies in the sameness, in the repeated pattern of the known, not in novelty. What is good in life is exact identity with all past experience, and all mythical experience. *Karmayoga*, the spiritual path of action, as distinct from the spiritual path of contemplation *(jñānayoga)*, is the antithesis of the Protestant work — ethic: no job, no labour, no drudgery should be performed for a reward outside the act. All work contains its own satisfaction. The present should not be regarded as a means to future satisfaction; the present is not evaluated in terms of its place within a course of action leading upward to a worthy end.

1053 **कर्मविपाक**

Karmavipāka : the fruition of evil deeds, the consequences of one's own action. The *Smṛtis* hold that if a sinner does not undergo proper penance he has to suffer torments in hell.

1054 **कर्मसन्यास**

Karmasanyāsa : renunciation of works for worldly gains. This doctrine presupposes a belief that ultimately finite beings are tools for the implementation of divine plans.

1055 **कर्माश्रय-कला**

Karmāśraya kalā : erotic arts depending on action. 24 in number *(Kāmasūtra*, 1.3. 17-18).

1056 **कर्मेन्द्रिय**

Karmendriya : the five organs of action, according to the *Sāṅkhya*.They are located in the mouth, hands, feet, anus, and the sex-organs performing the function of speech, prevension, movement, excretion and reproduction respectively (*Sān.kār* 26.28).

1057 **कलश-मुद्रा**

Kalaśa-mudrā : the gesture of a pitcher. "Branches (fingers) of both the hands should be extended, dividing it by the face and the middle. This is *kalaśa-mudrā* which is over brimmed with the nectar-deposit and applied in success of *mantra* and welcome." (*BT*)

Kalaśa is an important part of the physical apparatus of many different types of rituals in India, and is regarded as a physical locus of divinity on the alter while the ritual in progress. It is good augury to meet with an earthen pitcher of water or a *dhobi* while going out early in the morning. *Kalaśā* is different from *kamaṇḍalu* or *kuṇḍika*, which is smaller in size and is provided with a projecting pipe for discharging water. *Kalaśa* or jar is used on auspicious occasions like marriage, coronation, etc. *Kalaśa* also symbolizes an ocean: कलशाः सप्तसागराः (*Matsya*. 22.43).

1058 **कलश-हस्त**

Kalaśa hasta : both hands gesture.

1059 **कलह-हस्त**

Kalaha-hasta : quarrelsome hand, a type of both hands gesture mentioned by *Bālarāmabharata*.

1060 **कलहान्तरिता**

Kalahāntaritā : lady separated by quarrel; a variety of the heroine who is separated from her lover consequent upon a quarrel with him. *Kalahāntaritā* is one who, having repulsed out of indignation her guilty lover, who had tried his best to appease her is filled with remorse after the latter has already left ill (*Sāhityadarpaṇa*, III.82). She goes away from her lover who bows down to her. She discards him with harsh words. After her departure, she suffers due to separation (*Pañcasāyaka*, 5.35).

Kalahāntaritā is a heroine whose lover does not turn up having left her due to jealousy or quarrel and hence she becomes intolerant (*NS*).

1061 **कला**

Kalā : art, sciences dealing with the traditional sixty-four branches which some authorities reckon as 528 (*JRAS*, 1924, pp. 355-367); any art or accomplishment depending on skill art as avocation: the *bāhya-kalās* (external art or practical arts) are usually listed as sixty-four in number, some being identical with vocational *śilpas;* there are 64 ***kāma-kalā*** or *abhyantara*-art of love. (b) the term is also used to denote 'parts' or 'portions' of the various arts. (c) in *Tantra* it means letter or *varṇa*, which reflects symbolically an aspect of the Great Mother. (d) Yaśodhara in his commentary on the *Kāmasūtra* (1.3,15) lists the 64 *kalās:*These including (1) singing, (2) dancing, (3) instrumental music, (4) knowledge of scripts, (5) eloquence, (6) painting, (7) modelling, (8) leaf-cutting, (9) garland-making, (10) tasting, (11) examination of gems, (12) serving, (13) stage-craft, (14) instrumentation (*upakaraṇa-kriyā*), (15) weights and measures, (16) science of livelihood, (17) veterinary sciences (*tiryagyoni cikitsitam*), (18) hypocritical knowledge of heterodox sects, (19) skill in games, (20) *vaicakṣaṇya* (speech competence), (21) massage, (22) bodily decoration, (23) knowledge of heterodox sects and (24) *viśeṣakuśalam* and twenty arts connected with erotic enterprise. The list in *Kāmasūtra* is similar in many respects. It adds perfumes, jugglery, sleight of hands, preparation of strange dishes, mixing of drinks, riddles, reading of books, theatrical and literary arts, textiles, carpentry, architecture, examination of coins, metallurgy, knowledge of precious stones, science of health of trees, fighting of rams, cocks, etc., training birds to sing, knowledge of dialects, of omens, mechanics, metrics and athletics. These lists include industrial and fine arts with minor decorative arts, games and erotic arts. The last ones include the arts of professional heritage for their royal and bourgeois patrons.

The Sanskrit names for the above arts are as follows: (1) *gāna* (music), (2) *vādya* (instrumental music), (4) *naṭana* (dance), (5) *nāṭya* (acting), (6) *ālekhya* (painting), (7) *bahurūpadhāritva* (assuming various forms), (8) *taṇḍula-prasūna-bali-vikārakriyā* (to prepare squares etc. in the temples with rice and flowers), (9) *dantavastrāṅgarāgādi-nirmāṇa* (making dental preparations, clothes and unguents), (10) *maṇibhūmyādinirmāṇa* (laying out floors, etc.), (11) *śayyāvidhāna* (preparation of bed), (12) *jalavādya* (playing upon *jalataraṅga),* (13) *udaka-krīḍā* (aquatic sports), (14) *vicitra-vidhāna* (turning a boy into old and *vice versa),* (15) *mālāgranthana* (preparing a garland), (16) *śekharāpīḍayojana* (adornment with chaplets etc), (17) *nepathya-racanā* (knowledge of the costumes of an actor), (18) *karṇapatra-bhaṅganirmāṇa* (drawing lines or figures for ornamentation), (19) *sugandha-yojana* (use of perfumes), (20) *bhūṣaṇa-yojana* (use of ornaments), (21) *aendrajāla* (jugglery), (22) *rūpanirmāṇakauśala* (turning an ugly person into a handsome one), (23) *hastalāghava* (dexterity), (24) *bhojyavikāra* (cookery), (25) *pānaka-rasa-rāgāsava-yojana* (preparing various drinks, drugs and wines), (26) *sūcībāṇakarma* (needle work and archery), (27) *sūtrakrīḍā* (knowledge of the various entertainments in which thread is used), (28) *prahelikā* (riddles), (29) *pratimālā* (reciting *ślokas* beginning with the letter with which one recited by one's adversary ends), (30) ***durvañcaka-yoga*** (knowing with cheats and rogues), (31) *pustaka - vācana* (seeing plays), (33) *kāvya-samasyāpūrti* (completing a *śloka* whose one part has been supplied), (34) *paṭṭakā-vetra-bāṇa-vikalpa* (skill in the use of cane, cord and *nīvāra* etc.), (35) *tarkakarma* (disputation), (36) *takṣaṇa* (carpentry), (37) *vāstuvidyā* (architecture), (38) *ratna-parīkṣā* (testing gold and gems), (39) *dhātuvāda* (science of chemistry), (40) *maṇirāgākarajñāna* (science of jewellery), (41) *vṛkṣāyurveda-yoga* (botany and the science of healing), (42) *meṣakukkuṭa-lāvādi-yuddhavidhi* (science of cock-fighting, etc.), (43) *śuka-sārikā-pralāpana* (speech training of parrots, etc), (44) *utsādana* (rooting out enemies), (45) *mlecchita-vikalpa* (study of things pertaining to non-Aryans), (46) *deśabhāṣājñāna* (knowledge of dialects), (47) *puṣpa-śakaṭikā* (preparing flower-carts), (48) *nimitta-jñāna* (knowledge of causes or signs = omen reading), (49) *yantra-mālikā* (charms and armlets), (50) *dhāraṇa-mātṛakā* (cultivation of retentive memory or knowledge of the art of changing oneself by mere wearing something), (51) *samarācya-samapāṭhya* (to repeat what has been recited or read by another person, though one does not know the language in which the recitation has been made), (52) *mānasī-kāvyakriyā* (versification in mind), (53) *abhidhānakośa* (knowing the names of various things), (54) *chandojñāna* (knowledge of metres), (55) *kriyāvikalpa* (to achieve one's objective by diverse acts or efforts), (56) *chalita-yoga* (using all means good or bad including deceit), (57) *vastra-gopana* (preservation of clothes), (58) *dyūta-viśeṣa* (efficiency in the art of gambling), (59) *ākarṣa-krīḍanam* (excellence of dice), (60) *bālaka-krīḍanaka* (efficiency at making toys), (61) *vainayikī-jñāna* (knowledge of submission and flattery through which king's favour is obtained), (62) *vaijayikī-jñāna* (knowledge of the means of conquest), (63,64) *vaiyāsakī-vyāyāmakī-vidyā-jñāna* (knowledge of legends and exercises).

Though Indian classics have vivid references of different primitive arts, yet the tribal or preliterate art along with classical art-forms is fast decaying; it is being substituted by other forms of art acquired from the surrounding cultures. Throughout all these types of art we can see in the tribal man an artist whose worth, given the same opportunities, is on a par with that of his neighbours.

But in spite of the changed atmosphere, a number of traces of tribal art still remain. One of the most colourful pieces of attire occasionally worn by the hill tribe people is the head-dress of finely polished bison horns or, in their absence, of buffalo or bullock horns or other substitutes. These are conspicuous among the Bison-horn Māriās of Bastar, who owe their name to them and are only born on solemn occasions, especially marriage. Unfortunately these practices are also in decay. In the Saora pictographs, stamp of tribal art is vigorous.

But where preliterate art seems to remain most pure is in the use of their combs. Few are the tribes which try to make them sharply or decorative. It is among the Māriās where their shape is more artistic and their role more meaningful. It is all in one, a head apparel, an object of art, and a token of affection. In some tribes the presentation of a comb by the bridegroom to the bride is essential for marriage.

Tribes of Bastar decorate their tobacco chewers or tobacco containers, some of which show considerable artistic value. Besides tribal dances with their freshness and variety, the use of ceremonial masks like the Gonds and Baigās, and of certain artistic motives, as the peacock and elephant, have profusely enriched tribal imitation art as it is practiced now.

But where the aboriginality of art is seen at its best is in the representation whether magical or natural of hunting scenes. As Verrier Elwin puts it, 'For the preliterate the hunt is a surrogate for cinema, detective thriller and religious adventure. For besides giving food and excitement, the hunt is an important exercise in magic and religion; on its success before sowing the seed depends the harvest'. It must not be forgotten that the Indian tribesman no matter what his actual occupation is, is at heart a hunter. Hence the freshness, expressiveness, realism and variety in the portrayal of hunting scenes, which link his art with the hunting art of other cultures some of which are prehistorical.

1062 **कलापक**

Kalāpaka : three *karaṇas* constitute a *kalāpaka*, a tuft of braided hair, a sectarian mark on the forehead of an image. (*Mānasasāra*, 1.16).

1063 **कलायन**

Kalāyana : acrobat. Acrobats showed off their extraordinary talents to the accompaniment of an orchestra whose big drums slung from cross-straps, sharped-toned flutes and piercing clarinets added their clamour to the cries of the mountain banks trying to attract a crowd. These acrobats built huge pyramids by climbing on each other's shoulders. A bas-relief from Bharhut, dating from the second century B.C. and now in the collection of Allahabad museum, represents a team of fourteen people, seven of them, with their hands raised above their heads, are gripping in their hands the ankles of two men, who are supporting a young boy in similar fashion. From the summit of this living pyramid he acknowledges the cheers of the crowd by raising his arms and waving the scarf which is the sign of his profession.

1064 **कलिकलह**

Kalikalaha : oral and bodily quarrel.

1065 **कल्कि-हस्त**

Kalki-hasta : a type of *hasta-mudrā.* hold the *patāka* with the right hand and the *tripatāka* with the left. This style denotes *kalkin* (*Ad*, 216-225.). *Kalki* is the tenth incarnation of Viṣṇu on earth to uphold *dharma* and eliminate evil.

1066 **कल्प-मुद्रा**

Kalpa-mudrā : gesture symbolizing the *kalpa.* If the hand of *sāmaveda* (q.v) is directed towards the south, it is *kalpa* of the *Vaiṣṇavite* cult (*VD.*). *Kalpa* is a branch of the *Vedāṅga.* In the Vedic tradition *kalpa* refers to ritual texts which is divided into *Śrauta-Sūtras, Gṛhya-Sūtras* and *Dharma-Sūtras,* dealing respectively with sacrificial rites, domestic rituals and social rules.

1067 **कल्याणी वाक्**

Kalyāṇī-vāk : benign speech, meritorious tongue. Sophistication can well be understood by listening one talking, since the way of talk and the use of language reveal the hidden personality of an individual. One word well understood and properly pronounced leads one to permanent bliss, so says Patañjali, the greatest authority among the *munitraya* of Sanskrit grammar *viz.* एकश्शब्दः सम्यक् ज्ञातः सुष्ठु प्रयुक्तः स्वर्गे लोके कामधुग् भवति. If the word is not used properly, Patañjali warns the people about the dangers that may occur: सो वाग्वज्रो यजमानं हिनस्ति the misused words will kill the very person who uttered them. For a proper apprehension and correct use of language, a correct knowledge of the science of grammar is inevitable. Even in the remote past parents paid much attention to the proper study of grammar for the said reason and the same is evident even in a current saying prevalent in the society: *viz.*

यद्यपि बहुनाधीषे तथापि पठ पुत्र व्याकरणम् ।
स्वजनः श्वजनो माभूत शकलं सकलं सकृत् शकृत् ॥

"Even if not mastering much, dear son! learn grammar, so that the word *śvajana* (kinsmen) may not be uttered as *svajana* (dogs), *śakalam* (little) as *sakalam* (the whole) and *sakṛt* (once) as *śakṛt* (dung)".

The words of Patañjali and the popular saying afford enough proof to the deep-rooted traditional belief in the meritorious use of tongue, Vālmīki too had noted this meritorious aspect of speech in *Rāmāyaṇa.* Hanūmat was very clever to use the words blended sweetly in a self confident manner cherishing great love: वाक्यज्ञं मधुरैर्वाक्यैः स्नेहयुक्तमरिन्दमः (*Kiśk. Kān.* 3.28).

The poet notes keenly all the nobilities enriched in his talk. He observes: even in the long descriptive talk made by Hanūmat, no mistake was found. It was free from solicism, devoid of mistakes and free from gesticulation. Gestures in talk are a natural phenomenon. Words uttered accompanied by gestures, convey the idea easily. But too much gestures may mar the beauty of the talk and it may not impress the hearer even if the content of the talk is great. So, as far as possible, one may avoid gestures in a talk which may mar the beauty of the speech. Rāma watched closely Hanūmat and to his astonishment he could see no unnecessary gestures on him while talking. Neither in face, eyes, forehead, eyebrows nor in any limb the vulgarity of the speech is seen:

न मुखे नेत्रयोर्वापि ललाटे च भ्रुवोस्तथा ।
अन्येष्वापि च गात्रेषु दोषाः संविदितः क्वचित् ॥

(*Kiśk.Kān.* 3.31)

There is a midway in the talk according to Vālmīki. The sound pronounced in high pitch and low pitch is not appreciable when narrating things to somebody especially to great people. A gentleman should adopt a midway sound on such occasions according to the poet. The mild sound in medium pitch is a symbol of impartiality and it is dependable also. The speech delivered by Hanūmat, Vālmīki could see, was with necessary brevity and in medium voice. It was dependable, not slow not fast and at the sametime courageous:

अविस्तरमसन्दिग्धमविलम्बितमव्यथम् ।
उरस्थं कण्ठकं वाक्यं उवाच मध्यमे स्वरे ॥

(*Ibid.* 32)

In the present context Rāma could observe Hanūmat presenting clearly with uninterrupted flow of words in the right legitimate sequence and thus the whole narration has become praiseworthy and attractive:

संस्कारक्रमसम्पन्नामद्रुतामविलम्बिताम् ।
उच्चारयति कल्याणीं वाचं हृदयहासिनीम् ॥

(*Ibid.* 33)

The poet is noting the magic influence that a noble talk can bring on the hearer. An ardent enemy can be defeated by the power of talk. The wonderfully attractive speech of Hanūmat that emanates from the root cause of speech *viz. paśyantī, madhyamā, vaikharī* is capable of melting the heart of an enemy with the raised sword:

अनया चित्रया वाचा त्रिस्थानव्यंजनस्थया ।
कस्य नाराध्यते चित्तमुद्यतसेररेरपि ॥

(*Ibid.*34)

This absolute faith in the uttered word, repeatedly re-affirmed in successive periods, is the first important stand of unity in the tradition. As *vāk* was *kalyāṇī-vāk,* so the poet or *kavi* was the human counterpart of the creator, autonomous, comprehending, all-encompassing. Language and illumination were identical.

1068 **कवच**

Kavaca : (a) protective symbols, (b) armour, a device associated with an incarnation (*mantra*); could be tied on the right arm or round the neck; never to be given to anybody. Among the magical *mantras* an important devices is the *kavaca* (the protective device). This device includes the writing of a *mantra*, along with the mystic letters, and tying it on the right arm, or in the neck with the help of a thread. It is said that such a *kavaca* should never be given away even in the worst calamities (*Brahmāṇḍa*, II. 3,33.39):

एतत्तु कवचं वत्स न देयं संकटेऽपि च ।

A *kavaca* of a *mantra* may be a letter in the *mantra*. Thus it is said that in the five lettered *mantra* —*namaḥ śivāya*, *the kavaca* is *Śi* in *śivāya* (*Śiva*, VII. 2. 13.52), (c) *kavaca* is a sacred *mantra* in *tāntric* practices. It has a *ṛṣi* (seer - composer); and the *mantra* is to be considered in a tiny box and worn round the right arm or round the neck as a talisman. (d) the *kavaca* of Sarasvatī may be read on golden bead:

कृत्वा सुवर्णगुटिकां गन्धचन्दनचर्चिताम् ।
कवचं ते ग्रहीष्यन्ति कण्ठे वा दक्षिणे भुजे ॥

(*Brahmavaivarta, Prakṛti*, 4.27)

1069 **कवच-मुद्रा**

Kavaca-mudrā : a type of fists gesture. when two fists are joined at the ends of fore-fingers, it is called the gesture of *kavaca* (*VD*). *Kavaca* is armour made of metal, wood or hide. Apart from the material armour which protects the body, there is occult armour consisting of *mantras* for the guard of the spirit of the devotee. *Kavacas* are connected with the names of different *Tāntric* deities and they are supposed to be more efficacious than worship, meditation, etc. (*Śyāmārahasya*, IV).

1070 **काक**

Kāka : the crow. The crow, garrulous, inquisitive and greedy, was made responsible for transmitting love-messages and also for delivering oracles in ancient India. If one happens to see a mating of crows, it is good omen and he is very fortunate in Mithilā-region. The cry of the crow is an evil omen (*Bṛhat Saṁhitā*, 95.19).

Varāhamihira has written a separate chapter titled *Vāyasavirutam* in his *Bṛhat-Saṁhitā* (XCV) where he analyses the effects of cries of crows on human beings. If crows caw while deciding something, it is a sign of bad omen, according to Bhil belief:

The crows were cawing
when we made your marriage arrangements, my son
Do not go to your father-in-law's house.

(Bhili-folksong)

(b) Gonds seek help from the crow whether rains will be normal and adequate. If a crow in carrying a straw to build its nest holds it in the middle, they think that the rains will be normal and adequate; but if the straw is held towards one end, that the rains will be excessive and deficient (*Russell and Hiralal*, II.107).

1071 **काकतालीय**

Kākatālīya : accidental.

1072 **काकपक्षक**

Kākapakṣaka : side locks of hair on the temples of the boys. *Kākapakṣa* was a special hair-do for the young boys according to Kālidāsa (*Raghu.* 3.43).

1073 **काकम्**

Kākam : a particular posture in coitus.

1074 **काक-मुद्रा**

Kāka-mudrā : gesture of a crow. The *sandaṁśa* and *mukula* hands indicate a crow (*Mirror of Gesture*, pp. 50-51).

1075 **काकलि**

Kākali : low sweet tone (at the beginning of music).

1076 **काकि-मुद्रा**

Kāki-mudrā : a type of mouth-pose. Shape your mouth like a crow beak and drink in air slowly and gradually. The *kāki-mudrā* is an eliminator of many diseases.

1077 **काकु**

Kāku : intonation; a paralinguistic feature, change of the voice under different emotions: *kākuḥ striyāṁ vikāro yaḥ śokābhītyadibhirdhvaneḥ (Amarakośa). bhinnakaṇṭhandvanirdhīraiḥ kākurityabhidhīyateḥ (Sāhityadarpaṇa) alīkakākukaraṇa-kuśalatāṁ* (*Kādambarī*, p. 222), *kāme kānte sārasikā kākurutena* (*Śiśu*, 6.76) Hence a word negation used in such manner that applies the contray (affirmative), as in questions of appeal. *Kāku* is also a type of *vakrokti* in which the rejoinder is not stated, but is conveyed through an ironic inflection of the voice (Rudraṭa, *Kāvyālaṅkāra*, 2.16; *Kāvyaprakāśa*, 103).

Kāku is intonation according to the nature of the sentence. Sentences whose meaning is to be deduced from the context, and those that are straight forward, require different means of voice manipulation.

There are two ways of intonation according to Bharata *sākāṅkṣa* (with expectancy) as the sense of the sentence is not completely expressed and *nirākāṅkṣa* (without expectancy) as the sentence is completely expressed. The former has notes from the throat and the breast and begins with high pitch and ends in a low pitch and its *varṇa* and *alaṅkāra* are not complete; the latter has notes from the head beginning with a low pitch and ending in high pitch and its *varṇa* and *alaṅkāra* are complete.

It is not surprising that when we try to read another person's feelings we concentrate on their face. However, the quality of their voice also carries an important part of the message - 38 per cent of it, if attempts to qualify so precisely can be taken seriously. It is not just the look of pleasure in another's face that tells us they are glad to see us but the warmth and enthusiasm in their voice. We judge people's confidence by how steady and resonant their voices are. Talking on the telephone, we can see the other person's sad face vividly in our minds when we hear their sad tone.

In western phonetics intonation describes the distinctive prosodic patterns or contours of rose and fall in pitch or tone in speech utterances.

Kāku is a type of Kinetic tone in Indian linguistics and Vātsyāyana has researched potential differences in intonation patterns between the sexes.

1078 **काङ्‌गुल-हस्त**

Kāṅgula-hasta : single hand-gesture *(NS). Abhinaya-darpaṇa* derives it from the *padmakośa.*It is known as *gāṅgula* in *Bālarāmabharata.* Rarely used in iconography. The middle-finger, the fore-finger and the thumb are directed to three separate directions. The ring-finger bent and the little finger raised. All these make the *kāṅgula*-gesture. This indicates green fruits, all sorts of light work. By flinging fingers of the gesture, one may indicate such works which are done under the force of words of anger, castes and women. This also indicates emerald, red gems and other jewels. Sometime it points out foot-prints of cats (*NS*, IX. 82-84), raw fruits and small ones, angry words of women; it is to be employed by turning out the thumb, first and middle finger.

1079 **कानीन**

Kānīna : son of an unmarried woman *(Smṛti).*

1080 **कान्ता**

Kāntā : beloved, mistress, wife, beautiful woman.

1081 **कान्ता-दृष्टि**

Kāntā dṛṣṭi : amorous glance: a type of glance used in *sṛṅgāra, a rasa dṛṣṭi. In Mālatīmādhavam* (1.27), it is used for pleasure *(harṣa);* contraction of eye-brows and casting of side-glances in love, resulting to the erotic. With a feeling of love a sidelong look is cast with the eye-brows contracted. It has its origin in joy and good temper — it is used in the erotic sentiment:

harṣaprasāda-janitā kāntātyantam samanmathā
sabhrūkṣepakaṭākṣā ca dṛṣṭiḥ śṛṅgāriṇī matā

1082 **कान्ति**

Kānti : charm

(a) loveliness of the subject, especially in a portrait. (b) *śobhā* which is full of the passion of love is *kānti:*
sā śobhā rūpabhūṣādyairyatsyādaṅga vibhūṣaṇam
śobhaiva kāntirākhyātā manmathā pyāyanojjvatā

1083 **कापटिक**

Kāpaṭika : a student acting as a spy *(Smṛti),* deceitful, disguised.

1084 **कापालिक**

Kāpālika : follower of a particular *Śaiva* sect characterized by carrying skulls in the form of garlands and eating and drinking from them. The *kāpālikas* who mainly worshipped the *kapālin* form of Śiva, seem to be an obscure sub-sect of the *Paśupata*-system of the *Śaivas.* It is in the *Bṛhat Saṁhitā* (LXXXVI. 22) that they are usually adorned with garlands of human bones, take their food from human skulls, drink wine from the skull of a Brāhman and offer oblations of human flesh. One of the earliest literary references to the *kāpālikas* occurs in the *Maitrī-Upaniṣad* (VII.9), wherein they are known as "thieves". The *Upaniṣad* also ordains that 'one should not reside with them'. An exhaustive account of this form is to be found in *Mālatimādhavam* of Bhavabhūti. It is stated that they had matted hair tied upward in a knot. They always kept with them an internal weapon (*khaṭvāṅga*) and fastened bells to it. The work informs us that a *kāpālina*, Aghoraghaṇṭa by name, wanted to sacrifice to Cāmuṇḍā the holy lady, Mālatī, who had been procured for the purpose by his terrible female disciple Kapālakuṇḍalā. Their practices probably show the influence of *Tāntric* practices on Śaivism. The *kāpālikas* are generally depicted as ascetics falling from grace through the lure of beautiful women or other worldly desires. *Kāpālikas* are lost sight of in the later period, and their sect is replaced by that of *Aghorīs.*

1085 **काम**

Kāma : love, desire, particularly sexual desire. (a) One of the three aims of human existence, desire, sex, the pleasure of senses, love-sport, one of the four *puruṣārthas* in Indian culture. Dāmodaragupta opines that it resides in the side-glances of women-in-love; *lalalānayanānta-vilokanam vasatiḥ (Kuṭṭinīmatam* 1). The conception of sexual dualism as a cosmogonic principle of the creative process in terms of procreative process has given much importance to the *kāma*-doctrine. In the *Kāmasūtra* of Vātsyāyana it is categorically stated that without *kāma* or desire (and the sexual urge) *artha* or material prosperity is not possible, and without *artha* it is impossible to follow the way of *dharma.* (b) desire, according to Bhīma of *Mbh.*, is the supreme motive of all action; he quotes the *Vedic* creation-myth to support his claim, for it is through desire that the primordial man (*puruṣa*) creates the world. Liberation, too, is the fruit of desire. (c) *kāma* is the characteristic distinction between male and female, or between the organism that produces the egg and produces the sperm cells. It is the process of reproduction. It is also the organic pleasure or satisfaction associated with stimulation of the genital organs.

1086 **कामकटिबन्ध**

Kāmakaṭibandha : breast, thigh and buttocks of a woman.

1087 **काम-कला**

Kāma-kalā : The sexual art. In the metaphysical doctrine of *saṁbhava-darśana,* Śiva and Śakti in the form of *prakāśa* and *vimarśa* (light and feeling or appearance) unite and there Śiva assumes the form of *bindu* (drop) and Śakti as *nāda* (sound). The *bindu* and *nāda* become united, form one compound *bindu* and that substance represents the intense unity of affinity between the female and male energies and is called *kāma-kalā.* (b) a *tāntric* ideology of representing the mother-goddess in terms of three dots (*bindu*) arranged in a triang. The dot at the apex is said to be the face of the deity, and the two dots below the breasts. The three dots separately delineated indicate the triad of powers (*kriyā, icchā* and *jñāna*). With their corresponding *guṇas (tamas, rajas* and *sattva*). *Kāmakalā* may also be represented graphically as a triangle. The conception is highly esoteric and mystical.

1088 **कामकेलि**

Kāmakeli : amorous sport, dalliance, coitus.

1089 **कामतत्त्व**

Kāmatattva : theoretical interpretation of sex symbolism. According to *Tantrāloka* (III-150) the effect of sexual intercourse brings a mental detachment which is conducive to obtaining pure knowledge. The following Bhili song is full of sexual images of *Tantrāloka:*

The well is too deep and narrow for me
To fill water from.
If I fill the water-pots,
I cannot grind the maize,
If I grind the maize,
I can not make the bread.
If I make the bread,
I cannot make the curry.

1090 **कामदशा**

Kāmadaśā : lover on condition. It is of ten kinds and phases: *abhilāṣā* (longing), *cintā* (anxiety), *smṛti* (recollection), *guṇakathanam* (describing virtue), *udvega* (dejection), *unmāda* (hysteria), *vyādhi* (illness), *jaḍatā* (unconsciousness), *mṛti* (death).

1091 **कामदेव**

Kāmadeva : god of love, cupid.

1092 **कामदेव-हस्त**

Kāmadeva-hasta : a type of hand-gesture. *Śikhara* with left and *kaṭakāmukha* with the right makes Kāmadeva (*Ad,* 205-210).

1093 **कामरुहा-मुद्रा**

Kāmaruhā mudrā : a type of *mudrā.* "Make your face smiling and happy, cover from the inside the top of the rectum and have a mild laugh. This will make your gesture of *kāmaruhā" (BT).*

1094 **कामरूपिणी-मुद्रा**

Kāmarūpiṇī-mudrā : a type of *mudrā.* "In making each circle stop down from the navel-point by the left in an opposite direction, or in each round bow down by the left from an opposite direction, when these rounds are to be also made with a happy look the gesture should have the name *kāmarūpiṇī" (BT).*

1095 **कामशास्त्र**

Kāmaśāstra : (a) science of erotics, sexology. Kokkoka states the uses of this science: gaining easily a lady who is difficult to gain, pleasing who is gained, and uniting with one who is pleased, are thus uses of studying the erotic science:

asādhyāḥ sukam siddhiḥ siddhānām cānurañjanam
raktāyāśca ratissamyak kāmaśāstra prayojanam

(*Ratirahasya,* 1.7)

(b) science of love-making, a treatise written by Vātsyāyana on love-making, titled *Kāmasūtra.* It is the text-book of erotic science.

1096 **काम-सांकेतिकी**

Kāma-sāṅketikī : Sexual symbolism. The representation by any object or event of the sex organs or sexual behaviour. Thus in psychoanalytic dream interpretation, narrow, pointed objects, such as knives, keys, chimneys, and snakes, are often taken as phallic symbols, while soft, round and indented objects such as hats and vases, are treated as female symbols.

Intercourse is said to be represented by many activities, such as climbing trees and riding horses. According to Freudian theory, this kind of symbolism has the function of disguising the sexual meaning from the conscious mind where it would otherwise be unacceptable.

The following Muṇḍā poem makes an interesting use of sexual symbolism:

Red *altā* on your feet
yellow turmeric on the palms
which *altā* field did you enter
whose turmeric field did you go to?
Tell me truly, dear,
Did you enter a house of turmeric?

In tribal societies red is often a symbol for life, energy and sex. The *sindūr* or vermillion mark on the forehead and in the parting of the hair is a symbol of married life. Red also stands for blood. Similarly, turmeric has associations with marriage and loss of virginity. Entering an *altā* field or a house of turmeric, therefore, suggests loss of virginity or sexual intercourse.

In the Muṇḍā poem the "well" is a symbol for vagina;

There is a well at the end of the village
Its brick walls shine and glitter
....
The bucket went down and down
The poor girl how she wept
And wept.

The well in tribal society is very much of a social institution. It is the club of the village women where they come to fetch water and exchange the gossip of the day. The well is trysting place for covers. But it also is used as a symbol of the female sex as in the earlier example. A Gondi song upbraids a girl:

O little well, you give no water
your youth is past
Think well, your youth is ended.

While a Dhanwar song says a girl who has come of age:

She still
Looks like a parrot
But the well
Is full of water now.

In most modern symbolism a symbol may indeed embody much that is important to what it symbolizes, but tribal symbolism asserts a real identity.

(b) sexual riddles are interesting as showing how direct and forthright are Muria's references to the genitals. Games may also embody sexual symbolism. In one of the Muria games, the girls bend forward, each holding a stick in her hand to represent a penis, and dance with jerky movements of the buttocks that closely stimulate the sexual process. As they dance they sing:

nānnān cingro	Little little prawn hairs
bare lām kāṇṭā	very long thorn,
kahān gai ho	where has he gone,
Nanda purihā Rājā	the Raja of Nandapur.

The 'little prawn hairs' are the public hairs and the long thorn is the penis of the boy.

There is a taunt song from Muria which is symbolically loaded:

Here's a twig of the ebony tree,
Here's the twig you were telling me of
No one can use it at either end.
I have offered water in a brass pot,
I have offered gruel in a leaf-cup,
I have served him rice in a dish,
I have given him curry in a leaf-cup.
But he does not speak to me.
He doesn't know what to do.
I cannot live just looking at his house,
I cannot live just to fill my belly.
I can only live if my heart is filled.
I will go away to my father's house.
How can I live so long
Without my proper work.

The symbols in this song are sexual. The brass pot, the leaf-cup, the dish, and the twig are symbols of the female and male genitalia. In the concluding line the girl declares that life is something more than just looking after a house or filling one's stomach with food. The word in the eighth line means 'he does not speak to me' *i.e.* 'he does not have intercourse with me', and thus gives the key to the whole song.

Ratirahasya prefers to call *kāmeṅgitam* instead of *kāma-sāṅketikī*. It makes the following observation;

प्रच्छन्नौ व्रजतः स्तनौ प्रकटतां श्रोणीतटं दृश्यते ।
नीवी च स्खलति स्थितापि सुदृढं कामेङ्गितं योषिताम् ॥

'The breasts heaving under concealment, the line of the abdomen exposed, the fastening at the navel slipping loose although in place, must be interpreted as invitations to love from women'. There can be no measure of restraint in an orgy:

रतिचक्रे प्रवृत्ते तु नैव शास्त्रं न च क्रमः

1097 **कामसूत्र**

Kamasūtra : It was written by Vātsyāyana during the first century A.D. and belongs to a tradition of courtly love which still has the traces of tribal lore. For Vātsyāyana, each type of lover has a separate point of view, and he asserts the usual Indian principle of an ethic for each according to his own nature. He then proceeds to number and classify in hierarchical order each type with systematic body language and haptics. But his broad-minded situational approach is more enlightened than theories of modern communication scientists. Vātsyāyana, then, is an interesting example of the intellectual who adopted a liberal outlook within the pluralist frame of Indian social hierarchy.

1098 **कामाग्नि**

Kāmāgni : heat of sex. In India, ritual impurity is a function of sexual maturity. A boy up to the age of ten or twelve and a girl before her first menstruation are not open to contagion and cannot by *chuā*. The clothes of a child can become *chuā* but not his person. Suppose a woman is preparing breakfast in the fire room in the early morning and wants something from the kitchen she cannot go into the kitchen herself without bathing, but she may ask a young child to take off his clothes and fetch what she wants. From her first menstruation till her marriage a girl is considered to be impure and cannot enter the kitchen or fetch water for cooking rice.

Sex is associated with heat. The blood of young men and nubile girls is described as "hot" and the blood of old people as "cold". Sexual intercourse is believed to make the blood very hot. Before the advent of sexual heat the bodies of children are impervious to impurity: they do not share in the ritual impurity consequent upon a birth or death in the family, they can enter the kitchen without bathing, they can even cook for *Bhaktas*. It seems that sexual heat 'cooks' the body internally and opens it to impurities in the same way as the heat of fire makes cooked food pervious.

In the tribal setting, sex is good thing. It is never concealed. It is healthy, beautiful, interesting, the crown and climax of love. Love indeed is meaningless, inconceivable without sex. Such is the simple tribal philosophy.

Agni was called *kāma* in *Atharva Veda* (III. 21.4). A hymn invokes Agni to madden a man with love (*ibid.* VI. 130.4), another text states, 'Agni is the cause of sexual union. When a man and woman become heated, the seed flows, and birth takes place' (*Śatapatha Brāhmaṇa* 3.4.3. 4-5). When Kāma pursues Śiva, he wounds him with the arrow called *santāpa* (the Heater) and thus wounded, Śiva heats the whole universe (*Vāmana*, 6.44). This is the myth of Kāma and Śiva.

Several interesting manifestation of the sexual symbolism of fire may be seen among the Agaria tribe, whose religion centres around fire (Elwin, 1942: 115,118). Verrier Elwin notes the natural analogy between the action of the fire-stick and fire-drill and the sexual act (see *prakarman*), an analogy which is supported by Vedic ritual symbolism. Two Agaria myths illustrate this symbolic link: "A sage performed asceticism for twelve years without food and water, meditation upon fire although he had no fire and had never seen any fire but the fires in the sky. At last fire in the form of a virgin stood before him and said, 'I am very cold. Make a fire for me', she showed him how and he made a fire, but when he saw the fire, the sage's nature changed, and he gave up his asceticism and went to the nearest village... The dry bamboos there rubbed against one another in the wind and caught fire, and so fire began in the world." Here, the culture-hero is superimposed upon the motif of the ascetic seduced and led from the wilderness to civilization (the nearest village). The bamboo reed, associated with the seed of fire in Śaiva mythology, plays a new role here as the source rather than the receptacle of the blazing seed. Another Agaria myth bears a more striking resemblance to the episode of Agni and Sudarśanā: "The Sun sought the beautiful daughter of a king, but the king put out one of the sun's eyes. The sun then took his full fiery shape and destroyed the kingdom. The princess, pregnant, ran away and jumped into a pot of butter-milk, later she gave birth to a son called Jwālā Mukhī (Fire mouth). When he grew up and the other boys teased him for having no father, his mother told him the story of his birth. He sought the sun across the ocean, and captured him, and Jwālā Mukhī cursed the sun to go to his wife (the Moon) only during her (fertile) period. The sun then cursed Jwālā Mukhī that he would disappear like ashes. When the sun saw an Agaria with his wife, he kicked them and knocked them over. The Agaria cursed the sun: if you ever go to your wife, you will die".

Several Śaiva motifs occur here in curious transformations. These motifs are all associated with Śiva (through his connection with fire and the sun) and with the Agaria Sun god for the same season: the sexual symbolism of fire in Indian tradition.

1099 **काय**

Kāya : the body. It is regarded in Tāntrism as the microcosm of the universe. *Kāyasādhanā* is the disciplining of body in *Tantra.*

1100 **कारणशरीर**

Kāraṇa-śarīra : the inner rudiment of the body, subtle body that clings to the soul after death.

1101 **कारुक**

Kāruka : artisan. He was the member of the dramatic troupe and fashioned objects by means of lac, stones, iron and wood (*NS*).

1102 **कार्तवीर्य-हस्त**

Kārtavīrya-hasta : a type of hand-gesture. two *patāka-hastas* near shoulders represent the mythical king Kārtavīrya (*Mirror of Gesture*, p. 47). Kārtavīrya originally a king of Haihaya dynasty, Arjuna by name, ruling over Māhismatī, and son of Kṛtavīrya, was a folk hero, later deified.

1103 **कार्त्तिकेय-हस्त**

Kārttikeya-hasta : a type of hand-gesture. *Triśūla* with the left and *śikhara* with the right; indicate Kārttikeya (*AD*, 205-210). Kārtikeya is one of the names of Skanda, who was once worshipped extensively all over the country but now mainly in the Southern states of Tamil Nadu and Karṇāṭaka.

1104 **काल**

Kāla : meaning both time and death. According to Indian temporal scheme; the 'prestige of beginning' is most clearly asserted in the cyclic theory of creation of the world, its differentiation through the four successive '*yugas*', till its destruction and re-examination. Indian society was probably aware that the time sense of surrounding tribal societies was even more consistently non-linear than their own. In the *Nyāya-vaiśeṣika* system, a solar day of twenty-four hours is stated to contain 30x30x30x18x2x2 units *(kṣaṇas)* of time. The *Nyāya* unit of time, therefore, measures 2/45 of a second. The smallest measure of time, according to astronomers, is *truṭi* or 1/33750 of a second.

The concept of time is somewhat different in the tribal areas. According to Jain philosophy time is a substance characterized by *vartanā* (continuity), being an accessory cause of change. The moments of time are individually separate like jewels in a heap of jewels *(Paramātma-Prakāśa*, 2.21).

The tribal concept of time is somewhat different. The Hill Māriās of Bastar entirely live in the present. He does not look before and after and does not at all pine for what is not. Perhaps this is the reason why he keeps himself so happy and gay when the past is not remembered and the future is not worried for; the present is bound to be a lovely time. It is not clear as to why the Hill Maria do not remember the past, but one reason appears to be their poor memory. In 1965 when the writer visited village Karaṅgāl, he noticed a fresh grave which was found to be the grave of the village Paṭel. The Paṭel had died only about ten days back, but on asking what the name of the Paṭel was, the Karaṅgāl Marias took quite sometime to remember it. In fact, they could tell the name only after the villagers from other hamlet also assembled and they talked amongst themselves.

The attitude and character of the Hill Maria to live entirely in the present and not remember the yesterday or worry for the morrow is born of his environment, his habitat and his way of life. There is nothing permanent in his life; everything is transient, everything is shifting in nature. The *penda* sites are changed and so do the village sites. With every change the house changes and a new one is constructed, the old grave-yards are abandoned, the pools of drinking water are given up, the beautiful building is left to be eaten up by white ants.

So there is no permanency and when there is no permanency there is no attachment. The non-attachment makes him live wholly in the present. For, as Veḍtā Eḍmā of Kutul said, who knows if the wife who has gone to pluck *siyārī* - leaves for the eating cups and leaves will return home: she may be eaten up by the tiger as happened in 1967-68, So, his argument was when there is no certainty about the next moment and when one cannot do anything about it and again when everything is shifting, everything is fleeting, why look back and be sorry about it or look ahead and hope?

Time is included in *anastikāya-dravya* in Jain-philosophy, because it does not extend in space. Like space it is infinite and imperceptible. For practical purposes time is divided into limited periods, such as minutes, hours, days, months and *yugas*. This is conventional division of empirical *(Vyāvahārika)* time limited by beginning and end. But the transcendental *(pāramārthika)* time is infinite, one and indivisible.

1105 **कालकर्णी-मुद्रा**

Kālakarṇī-mudrā : a type of *mudrā*. "keeping two fore-fingers a little auspiciously bent make your two palms joined together and opened. They are to be joined to the mouth with the position of loose-fingered palms. This is the *kālakarṇī mudrā*, a very good gesture that may control the entire cosmic world." (*BT*).

1106 **कालचक्र**

Kālacakra : the wheel of time. (a) The Indian cyclical concept of continuous change is associated with the wheel or *cakra* - the perfect shape with the focal point of the universe situated at its centre in the mysterious stillness. This direct association of cyclical time with man's efforts to preserve the ecology in a state of balanced equilibrium is most important. The prolonged period during which India's economy was linked with the system of non-commodity producing village communities, low productivity, restrictive social organization, conformist religious thought, and immediate sensory experience of simultaneous, non-sequential relations, certainly contributed to the endurance of this concept of cyclical time even in modern times. (b) a minor nerve-cycle. It is also known as *lalanā-cakra*. *Kālacakra* denoting the wheel of time is the principal god of the Tāntric Buddhist *kālacakrayāna*.

1107 **कालनिर्णयविज्ञान**

Kālanirṇaya-vijñāna chronemics: Chronemics is an area of study that deals with our conceptualization and handling of time as a biopsychological and cultural element lending specific characteristics to social relationships and to the many events linked with the communicative continuum, from linguistic syllables and flitting gestures to meaningful glances and silence. Since chronemic behaviour identifies situational contexts, cultural backgrounds and personality and biological configurations, one could look for these in narrative literature, as complementary to other communicative activities; not only 'social time' (time as handled in social relations within a culture as well as cross - culturally.), but 'interactive time' (time used in the various forms of interactiive) encounters, and in the production of different community activities themselves (F. Poyatos).

In Indian setting, time is not merely a sequence of seasons; or cycle of activities; it is also life and death, pain and pleasure, as depicted in the following *Khond* poem:

Āsāḍh comes
And how she goes
And where?
Where does Time go?
It comes - only to go?

And time is also Death, it ceaseless on life to be captured:

At your back
Death watches you
From dawn to dusk
He keeps a watch on you.

The *Khond* poem refers to the world as a dance-hall of persons; a *"dhobīghāt" i.e.* a place where washermen wash soiled clothes.

There is yet another class of chronemic signs which represents social rank and grade in terms of distances. Thus temporal distances indicating degrees authority were often expressed as rights of precedence. In nineteenth century Calcutta clan leaders used to fight over precedence during the ceremonial distribution of sandal paste and flowers at sacred recitals and funeral banquets (Bandopadhyaya, 28). Again in Mālwā, according to Mayer, a wife's standing in her husband's family varied according to whether she was allowed to have her meal at the same time as the other women of the household or afterwards (Mayer: 220). Among the Coorgs the headman was traditionally called the *mūya payanda*, which means having precedence and is synonymous to *agre agre viprāṇām* (Brāhmaṇs first). Srinivas (1952: 63,205) observes,'the sense of precedence is ubiquitous'. It was the headman who took the first shot at target—shooting contests on ritual occasions, it was he who led the village dance at harvest festivals, and it was his pack-bullocks which had the right to lead a caravan. Precedence such as this governed relations between castes as well. In Nimar district a high - caste villager's bullock-cart had the right of way over a Balahi's, and in agricultural operations high - caste farmers had the right to help themselves first to the local supplies of labour: only after they are satisfied will field servants go to work on the fields of their Balahi creditors (Fuchs, 81,93).

1108 **काल-पुरुष**

Kāla-puruṣa : time which is responsible for all phenomenal changes, is imagined as a person. The body of this personalized Time comprehends the twelve zodiacs as limbs: head (*meṣa*), mouth (*vṛṣabha*), arms (*mithuna*), chest (*karkaṭaka*), belly (*simha*), loins (*kanyā*), below the navel (*tulā*), public region (*vṛścika*), thighs (*dhanus*), knees (*makara*), legs (kumbha) and feet (*mīna*) cf. *Bṛhatjātaka*.

Skanda-Purāṇa (VII. 237.24) has anthropomorphised time. Kāla is described as being terrible in appearance, with a clean shaven head, and black and tawney in appearance. He has a broom-stick, a great banner and the Japā flower as his insignia. He rides an ichneumon and has the ear-rings prepared from *rattikā*.

करालो विकटो मुण्डः पुरुषः कृष्णपिङ्गलः ।
सम्मार्जनीमहाकेतुर्जपापुष्पावतंसकः ॥
कृकलासवाहनश्च रत्तिकाकर्णभूषणः ।

1109 **कावेरी-हस्त**

Kāverī-hasta : a type of hand-gesture. The river Kāverī. The *catura*-hand moving upward and downward denotes river *Kāverī* (*Mirror of Gesture*, p.48). The South Indian river which flows in Karṇāṭaka and Tamil Nādu.

1110 **काव्य**

Kāvya : poem characterized by the *guṇas* and *alaṅkāras* but free from defects; sentence laden with sentiment.

1111 **काव्यसंहार**

Kāvyasamhāra : one of the 64 *sandhyaṅgas* in dramaturgy (*NS*, 19.103). Bharata includes giving and receiving boon in it, while Dhanañjaya includes the receiving of the boon only.

1112 **काव्यसमस्यापूरणम्**

Kāvya-samasyā-pūraṇam : filling up missing words, phrases sentences, etc. in a verse. One of the 64 arts given by *Kāmasūtra.*

1113 **काष्ठमौनव्रत**

Kāṣṭhamaunavrata : not to communicate even by signs or movements of limbs.

1114 **किंवदन्ती**

Kiṃvadantī : rumour.

1115 **किटकिटायते**

Kiṭakiṭāyate : 'grates the teeth', *Suśr.*

1116 **किलकिञ्चित**

Kilakiñcita : hysterical mood. It consists of frequent combinations of smiling, weeping, laughter, fear, sickness, fainting, sorrow and fatigue due to joy (*NS*).

1117 **किलाकलायते**

Kilakilāyate : 'cries expressing joy', *Divyāvadāna.*

1118 **कीर्तन**

Kīrtana : Ordinarily the laudatory recital, verbal and literary of the name and qualities of a person. Its technical meaning consists in the repeated utterance of the name and description of the qualities of God or the devotional object, of the nine modes of *bhakti* or devotion, *kīrtana* is the second.

1119 **कीलक-हस्त**

Kīlaka hasta : both hands gesture *(Abhinayadarpaṇa)*, not mentioned by *NS.* (a) If the little fingers of the *mṛgaśīrṣa*-style are bent inward close to each other, it is the *kīlaka* hand, used to denote the tender love and the loose talk. (b) *Kīlaka* also means a Tāntric *Nyāsa.*

1120 **कुक्कुट**

Kukkuṭa : cock.

1121 **कुक्कुट-हस्त**

Kukkuṭa-hasta : gesture of a cock. The *bhramara* hand indicates a cock (*Mirror of Gesture*, pp. 50-51). The wild cock with a flaming crest, symbolizing a fire-brand or flames of fire, is the emblem of Kārtikeya.

1122 **कुक्षि**

Kukṣi : stomach, belly. A woman with a spacious one is apt to be more productive; one with a belly like that of a female frog is believed to give birth to a son who would become a king *(Bhav.P; Sk.P.).*

1123 **कुच**

Kuca : female breast (subject to the nail-scratches: *kuc vilekhane karṣaṇe kucaḥ*), teat.

1124 **कुचकुड्मल**

Kuca-kuḍmala: budding female breast, teat, bud-like teat.

1125 **कुच-चुम्बनम्**

Kuca-cumbanam : kissing breasts. *cumbanāya kalitapriyākucam (Naiṣadha,* 18.105).

1126 **कुञ्चित**

Kuñcita : curved, crooked.

1127 **कुञ्चित-ऊर्ध्व-लतापाद**

Kuñcita-ūrdhva latāpāda : one of the legs backward-upward contracted.

1128 **कुञ्चित-करण**

Kuñcita karaṇa : half-kneeling position. The leg bent at the back has the knee in contact with the ground and the calf-raised. The other leg is bent in front with a *samapāda* foot on the ground. The right hand in a slightly raised position is in *alapallava* on the left side (*NS,* IV.112 b-113 a). The foot is in *añcita* and the left hand in *kuñcita* held at the left side with palm upwards. It is used to indicate greatly delighted deities. (Fig. 1128)

1129 **कुञ्चित गण्ड**

Kuñcita gaṇḍa : contracted cheeks. This gesture has been suggested in *bībhatsa rasa;* shrunk cheeks; suggests hair-startling, touch, cold, fear, fever, (*NS,* VIII. 129-134) and horripilation

1130 **कुञ्चित जानु**

Kuñcita jānu : contracted knee. Indicates the final position in which the knee touches the ground as the sitting *āsana* positions.

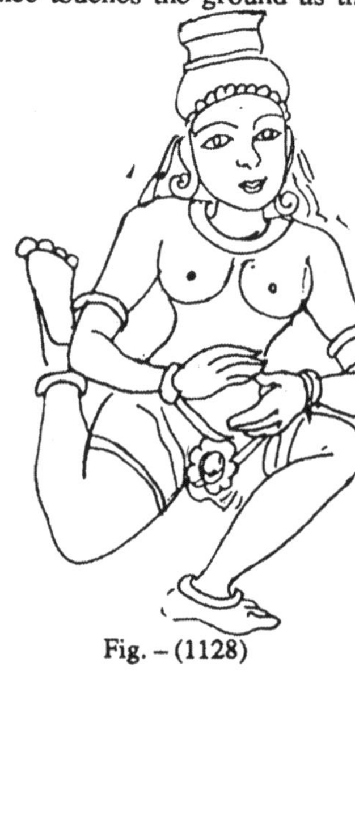

Fig. – (1128)

1131 **कुञ्चित पाद**

Kuñcita pāda : The position where the toe and the ball of the foot touch the ground; heels raised up and toes and hind foot bent; *kuñcita* is to express aristocratic gaits and turning round from the right to the left and from the left to the right (*NS*, X. 40-51), and the *atikrāntā* steps. "Toes bent, heel raised, arch bent *i.e.* the toes and the ball of the foot touch the ground and the heel is raised." (Fig.1131)

1132 **कुञ्चित पुट**

Kuñcita puṭa : contracting the eyelids; contracted eyelid, a type of eye-gesture suggested in *jugupsā;* contraction of eyelids to express a sense of seeing an undesirable thing, smelling such as a scent and feeling a similar touch (*NS*, VIII. 106-113).

1133 **कुञ्चित बाहु**

Kuñcita bāhu : the recoiled arm, contracted arm; relates to the position of the extended and fixed forearm when the hands extend out at the level of the chest and return to the area of chest. (*NS*, IX. 205-206).

1134 **कुञ्चिताग्रीवा**

Kuñcitā grīvā : slightly bent, contracted neck; taking place when the head is bent down; neck is slightly bent. Cf. *Avadhūta* (*NS*, VII); turned back neck with head. It is to indicate protection of the head and neck; used in pressure of weight and in protecting the neck.

1135 **कुञ्चितादृष्टि**

Kuñcitā dṛṣṭi : contracted glance. Eyelashes and eyelids are both contracted and so are the eyeballs (*NS*, VIII. 71). The ends of eye lashes are bent slightly. This glance is referred to in *Mālatīmādhavam* (1.27); contracted glance, a type of *sañcāribhāva dṛṣṭi*. In the glance of *kuñcita*, ends of eyelashes bend due to contraction of eyelids and eyeballs. This suggests envy, hatred, undesirability, objects visible with difficulty and pain in the eye.

1136 **कुञ्चिता भ्रू**

Kuñcitā bhrū : contracted eyebrow, contracting the brows. A type of eye gesture in *hāsya*. In *Kumārasaṁbhava* (V), the eyebrows of Pārvatī become arched in *kuñcita*. Kālidāsa talks of *kuñcita bhrū* rather than the *kuñcita* eyelid (*NS*, VIII. 114 b- 118 b, VIII. 123 b-126). *Kuñcita* eyebrow-movement is also used for manifestation of affection; curving one or both the eyebrows slightly to suggest affection, and hysterical mood. *Kuñcita* eyebrows movement is used for affection, while the *kuñcita* eyelid movement is prescribed when the object seen (disgusted Śiva in *Kumārasaṁbhava*) is unwanted or unwelcome.

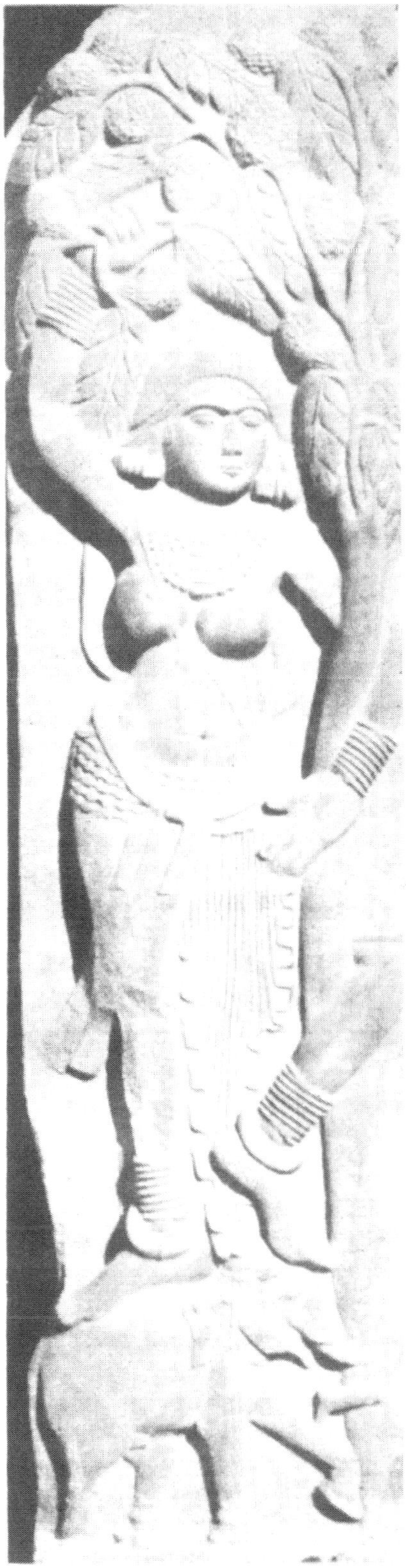

Fig. - (1131)

Kuñcita means slightly bending the eyebrows singly or together, used in manifestation of affection, pretended and hysterical mood.

1137 **कुञ्चितासन**

Kuñcitāsana : crossed-leg sitting posture.

1138 **कुटिल-केशी**

Kuṭila-keśī : lady whose hair are curly *(Kumārasaṁbhava,* 8.45).

1139 **कुटिल-हस्त**

Kuṭila-hasta : single hand gesture. Only mentioned in *Bālarāmabharata;* derived from the *kapittha.*

1140 **कुटिलाङ्गुलचरणा**

Kuṭilāṅgulacaraṇā : lady whose legs have crooked fingers; quality of the conch-lady (*Anaṅgaraṅga,* 1.17).

1141 **कुटिलेक्षणा**

Kuṭilekṣaṇā : lady whose glance is unsteady, the quality of the conch-lady *(Anaṅgaraṅga,* 1.15-16).

1142 **कुट्टन-चिबुक**

Kuṭṭana cibuka : rubbing teeth, chattering of teeth; a type of facial expression. Chin-gesture in *bībhatsa and bhayānaka rasa;* rattling of upper teeth with the lower; It is indicative of fear, cold, fever, old age and sickness (*NS*, VIII. 141-146).

1143 **कुट्टनाधर**

Kuṭṭanādhara : tremulous movements of the lips (*NS,* VIII. 144-46); used for pain, cold, fear, etc., occurs in *Śākuntalam* (1.19).

1144 **कुट्टनी**

Kuṭṭanī : procures, bawd, go-between.

1145 **कुट्टनीमतम्**

Kuṭṭanīmatam : a poem written by Dāmodaragupta (eighth century A.D.) on performance of dance and drama. The essentials of performance are emphasized: the soft and vigorous tempo and styles, the delivery of speeches in Sanskrit, and Prākṛit with appropriate pitch, intonation and clarity, emotional state of characters, their make up, their acting. A practical realization of the *NS* is to be seen here.

1146 **कुट्टमित**

Kuṭṭamita : pretended anger; gesture of sweet reluctance. In Act II of *Śākuntalam,* Śakuntalā enacts grace of sweet reluctance. It is pretended distress even though actual joy is experienced. It is produced through joy and confusion with the hair, bosom or lower lip, etc. are touched by the lover (*NS*).

1147 **कुट्टार**

Kuṭṭāra : sexual intercourse.

1148 **कुण्डलिनी**

Kuṇḍalinī : name of the dormant spiritual energy in the human body. It is fancied to encircle, like a serpent, the *mūlādhāra.* Besides the individual *kuṇḍalinī,* the *Tantras* conceive also *mahākuṇḍalinī* at the root of universe. (Fig. 1148)

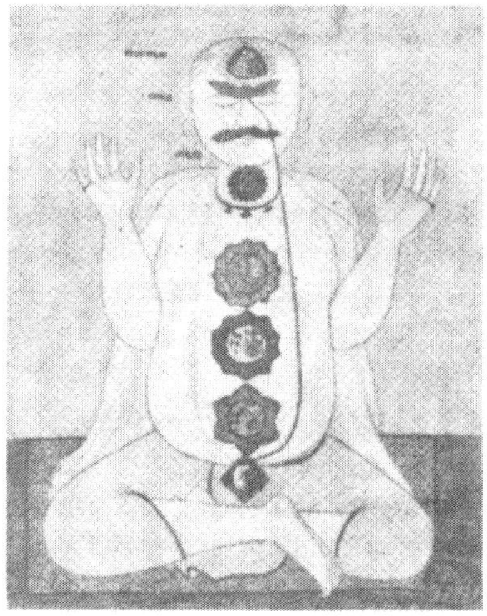

Fig. – (1148)

1149 **कुतकूतयति**

Kutakūtayati : tickle; The use of comb to titillate the skin is a haptic behaviour. Muria boys and girls are susceptible to tickling, which has been described as the most intellectual mode of touch sensation and that with the closest connection with the sexual sphere. As the *motiari* dresses *chelik's* hair and with her comb gently tickles and stimulates his back and arms, he responds by fondling her breast, by stroking her legs (which are usually placed round his body): as she massages the girl often grips the boy's waist between her knees) or by boldly tickling her,

Tickling is a type of physiological stimuli. Anyone who has played with young children knows how easy it is to make them laugh by tickling. But laughter requires more than a physiological stimuli. For example, if you try tickling yourself, virtually nothing happens. And you can imagine what would happen if you tried to tickle a complete stranger in the street. For tickling to produce laughter you need first a partner, and second a special relationship with them. Motiari laugh when tickled by their partners. But they will not laugh, and may even cry, when this is done by strangers.

In a creation myth from Orissa it is told that "Mahādeo invented tickling, and as the primeval brother and sister tickled each other, lust came into them" (Elwin, 1954: 422-23).

(b) *Kutakūta* (Bagheli *kutukī*) is a complex cutaneous quality elicited by striking the skin lightly, especially in sensitive regions. Tickling involves a strong feeling tone, attempts to escape the source of stimulation, and uncontrollable laughter.

1150 **कुतूहल**

Kutūhala : eagerness, curiosity. To be impatient to see a thing of beauty is *Kutūhala (Sāhityadarpaṇa,* III. 109). *kutūhala* is the tendency to explore, to investigate, to seek knowledge. It is one of the the primary drives, along with sex, hunger, thirst, etc.

1151 **कुतूहलशाला**

Kutūhala śālā : place where wandering ascetics and also teachers and philosophers congregated for religious, philosophical and other discussions (*Dīghanikāya* 1.179).

1152 **कुदृष्टि**

Kudṛṣṭi : the evil eye. Attitudes about family competition is expressed in the widespread beliefs about the evil eye and precautions taken against it. An envious glance is conceived of as destructive and there has developed an elaborate set of techniques for diverting and absorbing such glances into visual decoys so as to avert their destructive effect. The placements of house-entrances and the alignment of village streets are all consciously planned with these principles in mind.

The object of the evil eye are typically areas in which people are perceived to excel in wealth, success, or beauty. It is not surprising that young children are a focus of an evil eye concerns since they represent the potential prosperity and competitive advantage of one family over another. One rather anti-social method by which families exercise their children's illness is indicative of the underlying competitive attitude focused on children's well-being. Exorcistic substances are placed on well-travelled public lanes at night. When these substances, usually a recognizable pattern of a row of three white dots, are accidently touched by passersby, the illness and the evil eye are to be transferred to their families.

In *Vedic* period, a salve *(añjana)* amulet was employed against the dread Evil Eye *(Atharvaveda,* 44.5). To ensure that a child shall be long lived, the friendly god Mitra was invoked to protect it. Mitra never injures the animate or inanimate (*Ś.Br.* V.3.2.6-7), and hence to gaze steadfastly at an object, 'with the eye of Mitra' will annihilate any evil influences adhering to it; a steadfast gaze is a ritual technique to appease a particular object (see.J. Gonda, *Eye and Gaze in the Veda,* Amsterdam, 1969, p. 43).

Gonda (*ibid* 19) points out that the 'effect of a destructive action in the ritual sphere is enhanced when it is accompanied by a look directed towards the object (or person)... a look was consciously regarded as a form of contact". Here there is suggestion of the Mitra's eye.

A more immediate link between illness, death, and sin is found in the area of *najar,* the evil 'eye' in village India. The sin which is believed to activate *najar* is jealousy (*īrṣyā* or *āha*) which is considered a powerful destructive emotion. Tulasīdāsa's dictum that 'even gold can not bear the jealousy of a poor man' is sometimes heard all over Madhya Pradesh.

The belief in the 'evil eye' is nearly universal in tribal India, and also quite common among the Kōrkūs. It is called *nanjar.* Strangers, persons with piercing eyes, squinters, even sufferers from contract may easily be suspected of having the Evil Eye. The Evil Eye is cast either unwillingly or deliberately on living objects, while on inanimate objects it has no effect. An intense feeling of desire, envy or hatred has its evil effect; it makes plants, animals and even human beings lose their vitality, sticken and die slowly. Thus barren women may cast an Evil Eye on healthy children who soon fall sick and die; an envious neighbour casts a spell on a fellow farmer's splendid crop and it begins to wither and shrivel up. Somebody takes a fancy to a bullock or any other animal which its owner is unwilling to sell. He might as well sell it, for, so the Kōrkūs believe, through frustrated desire of the would-be buyer it would soon sicken and die. But especially vulnerable are babies, pregnant women, a bridal pair, persons starting on a journey or an important enterprise.

Special precautions have to be taken to ward off the Evil Eye. Vows are taken or the *parihār* is requested, against a fat face, to recite incantations or to tie amulets around the neck of the person or animal threatened by the Evil Eye. Defences against the 'evil eye' include the placing of 'clampblack' around children's eyes, the wearing by children of black threads around their waists and wrists, the marking of domestic territorial boundaries during a family's yearly worship of its family god, and so on. Babies, the most vulnerable to attack by *najar,* are given regular doses of calf urine, which is held to be one of the purest substances imaginable.

The evil eye is as much dreaded to Hindus as the ill omen. Crops are protected in Indian villages by putting up scare crows which may divert the attention of evil-eyed individuals. It is the first look that is deadly and if the scare crow manages to catch it, the crop is saved. Good crops, good looking children, beautiful young men and women, are all believed to be particularly amenable to the influence of the evil eye. While crops are usually protected by scare crows, living beings are protected by lockets and charms specially prepared to ward off the evil eye. Cattle, dogs, in fact any desirable or beautiful thing is apt to be destroyed by the evil eye. But every weapon his its counter weapon and the Hindus have many preventives against the evil eye. The astrologer or the necromancer is always ready to perform, on payment of a small fee, certain magic rites to prevent the influence of the evil-eye or to remedy its ill effect when affected.

The basis of the belief in the evil eye is that certain people have a glance that can bring bad luck. As a protection against this, one must either avoid their stare or, alternatively, make their stare avoid you. If you can stop them looking into your eyes you are safe, and so gestures are worn as amulets which are so audacious that they will catch the eye of the evil one.

The sight of the following is believed to be evil and destructive to the cause according to the *Purāṇas*: black grain, cotton, dried grass, a tonsured mendicant (*muṇḍa*), a person smeared with oil, a Buddhist or Jain mendicant *(nagnaka)*, iron, mud, a eunuch, chatt (*Agni.* P. 230. 2-8). Other ill omens include seeing one's own reflection or shadow without the head, not seeing the star called Arundhatī, seeing a naked dark woman, with hair scattered and with a sword in her hand (*Skanda P.* VI. 79. 19-22). *Brahmavaivarta Purāṇa* (35. 26-28) adds that the sight of a pot - maker, oil - presser, hunter and that of a person living by serpent-play is also inauspicious. A corpse is an auspicious sight, but one being burnt on the pyre is evil (*Ibid.* 29), a broken pot or an empty pot, salt, a tortoise etc. are inauspicious; also mentioned as evil sight are the priest who sacrifice for a Śūdra (*Ibid.* 31, *Śūdrayājaka)*, a village priest, one who lives by a temple or a deity and also a medicine man (*vaidya, Ibid.* 45) and medicine. For similar ill omens see also *Matsya Purāṇa* (158-31; 162.36; 236.2; 237.1, 242-3), *Śiva Purāṇa* (II. 15. 5) and *Brahmāṇḍa Purāṇa* (II. 3.38. 30, 4. 21. 5).

1153 **कुपित**

Kupita : rebellious, risen in revolt (*A*, 1.13.15; 5.1.21).

1154 **कुपुरुष**

Kupuruṣa : evil person. Some individuals often get a notoriety in the localities they live for bringing bad luck to people. Every enterprise they engage in is believed to end in failure. Their very sight is obnoxious and portends evil. The fear of unlucky persons is common to all Indian villages. Such persons are shunned by the villagers and their presence at a social gathering is resented. These persons may be of respectable families but they are not less obnoxious on that account.

1155 **कुमारी-माता**

Kumārī-mātā : virgin mother. The ideals of Hindu womanhood are those of virgin and mother, but nowhere in their ritual system is there any acknowledgement of the fact that in order for a virgin to become a mother is it necessary that she should have sexual intercourse and become impregnated. It is, therefore, not without significance that the female deity *mātā*, although both named and worshipped "mother" is depicted as a virgin having neither husband nor child. She is, indeed, both virgin and mother, and through the paradoxical nature of her sexual status, has the power to bestow male children upon those who worship her.

As an unmarried girl, a woman is worshipped as a virgin, and as a mother she has the opportunity to gain status and authority; but as a wife, a woman has very little status at all. The special sexual attributes of wives are much feared by men and scrupulously avoided as dangerous and ritually unclean. Thus virginity and motherhood are highly esteemed states in Hindu society but wifehood and sexuality are those aspects which devalue a woman and make her the inferior of a man. These contradictory values are resolved through two dominant ritual symbols both anomalous in character: "the mother goddess who is also a virgin" and "Mother Cow". In both of these the values of female fertility and motherhood are emphasized while those of impurity of birth and sexuality are denied. (b) The form of the Mother-goddess as a young girl.

1156 **कुम्भक**

Kumbhaka : closing the nostrils and mouth so as to suspend breathing.

1157 **कुम्भ-दासी**

Kumbha-dāsī : a woman in keeping, bawd *(Kāmasūtra).*

1158 **कुम्भ-विवाह**

Kumbha-vivāha : a ceremony for girls to avoid widowhood. The day before the marriage several gods are invoked in a jar of water. The water is then sprinkled over the girl.

1159 **कुम्भीक**

Kumbhīka : an impotent who gets copulated in his anus or who copulates in the anus.

1160 **कुम्भीर-मुद्रा**

Kumbhīra-mudrā ': gesture indicating a crocodile. The *patāka* hands are crossed and held apart to indicate a crocodile (*Mirror of Gesture*, p. 51).

1161 **कुल**

Kula : clan or family. The term is also used in the sense of spiritual lineage. This lineage is equated with *gotra* in *Kulārṇava* (XVII). *Kaulamārga* or *kaulācāra* is thus a way of *sādhanā* restricted within the spiritual lineage of a particular group of *Tāntric* teachers.

1162 **कुलटा**

Kulaṭā : an adultress, an unchaste woman. An adultress is regarded as a fallen woman, slur on the family and is never to be associated with the main sentiment.

1163 **कुल-संकेत**

Kula-Saṅketa : technical mysteries of *Kaulamārga*. These relate to the practices in connection with *karma* (initiation), *pūjā* (worship), *mantra* (spell), *tantra* (way), *mantra-yantra-likhana* (drawing of diagrams), and so on (*Kulārṇava*, II).

1164 **कुवाक्य**

Kuvākya : 'censorious speech' *Pañcat.*

1165 **कुवाच्**

Kuvāc : bad tongue the black tongue; Known as *kuvāc* in Bagheli-Hindi. The black-tongue generally goes with the *kudṛṣti* (evil-eye). The word of the man with the black tongue is believed to be more deadly than the sword. If a person afflicted with this malady remarks, on seeing a child, that it looks sweet or healthy, the child is feared to fall ill and die. If he casually mentions, on seeing a mango tree in blossom, that the flowers appear to promise a good crop, the tree is feared to wither away in a couple of days' time. The words of the evil-tongued person should be unintentional to have the deadly effect. There is the story of such a person in South India who was cleverly engaged by a farmer to get his field rid of the weeds that were growing thick with the seedlings. The evil-tongued person was invited by the farmer to his house and treated to a sumptuous repast; after which he took his guest for a walk in the fields. The farmer expected that the guest would notice the weeds and pass some remarks about their thick growth, but unfortunately the evil-tongued person appeared to interest himself in everything except the weeds. After many unsuccessful attempts to attract his guests attention to the weeds, the farmer as a last resort casually pointed out to him how thick the weeds were growing in his fields. Upon this the evil-tongued person observed that though the weeds were growing thick, the few seedlings appeared extraordinary strong. The result was, the next morning the seedlings were found withering away and the weeds flourishing; so at any rate the story goes.

Because of this universal fear of the evil tongue among the Hindus, it is bad manners for a stranger who happens to visit a house to speak well of anything. If, for instance, a visitor to a Hindu household were to remark of the guest's baby "how sweet", it will be an unpardonable insult to him. If a good meal is praised it will be no compliment to the cook. A good piece of furniture should not be spoken of with admiration, a promising young lad should not be mentioned as such. In all these matters, as well as in everything else, it is best not to express one's admiration at all. Nor should they be condemned. When visiting a Hindu, the golden rule is to observe all but speak little.

1166 **कुबेर-मुद्रा**

Kuvera-mudrā : a type of hand-gesture. *Padma* with the right and *gadā* with the left hand, denote *kuvera* (*AV*, 211-215.).

1167 **कुशलप्रश्न**

Kuśalapraśna: greeting. Manu ordains that when greeting, one should ask a Brāhmaṇa after his happiness, a Kṣatriya after his welfare, a Vaiṣya after his prosperity, a Śūdra after his health. So rigid were the norms of greeting in those days that if a Brāhmaṇa unknowingly saluted a low caste man he was required, according to *Atri Smṛti*, to take a bath immediately and get purified by taking *ghee* (clarified butter).

Thus, vocabulary, too, served for caste markers in ancient India. Among acquaintances, phatic statements about each other's health had to include the word *kuśala* if addressed to a Brāhmaṇa, *anāmaya* to a Kṣatriya, *kṣema* to a Vaiśya and *anārogya* to a Śūdra (*Manu*, II. 127).

(a) This tradition of using language as a register of caste status was very much in vogue in ancient India. (b) when two Gond friends relatives meet, they clasp each other in their arms and lean against each shoulder in turn. A man will then touch the knees of an elder male relative with his fingers, carrying them afterwards to his own forehead. This is equivalent to falling at the other's feet, and is a token of respect shown to all elder male relatives and also to a son-in-law, sister's husband, and *samadhī*, that is the father of a son or daughter-in-law. Their term of salutation is 'Johār', and they say it to each other. Another method of greeting is that each should put his fingers under the other's chin and kiss them himself. Women also do this.

1168 **कुशीलव**

Kuśīlava : a professional dancer *(Smṛti)*; a bard (*A*. 1.12.9); a singer (*A*, 1.12.13); a mime, an actor (*A*, 1.18.12, 12.21.16, 3.13.30, 3.18.9, 4.1.58, 4.4.3). The term *kuśīlava* which sometimes denotes an actor is derived from Kuśa and Lava of *Rāmāyaṇa*, who sang Rāma's deeds before Rāma. When the actor in general lost his status in society due to loose morals, the word *kuśīlava* got the interpretation of "One having bad character". He arranged the various musical instruments properly and was an expert player of musical instruments (*NS*).

1169 **कुसुम**

Kusuma : flower of menstrual blood, menstruation, blossom.

1170 **कुसुमतण्डुलवलिविकल्पकला**

Kusuma-taṇḍula-vali-vikalpakalā : greeting and entertaining guests with betels and decoration of houses with colours and flowers. One of the 64 arts enumerated by Vātsyāyana.

1171 **कुसुमाञ्जलि**

Kusumāñjali : handful of flowers.

1172 **कुहक**

Kuhaka : a magician, a juggler or a puppet-player (*A*, 1.20.18, 4.1.65), hypocritical, deceit.

1173 **कुहरित**

Kuharita : sound, cry of cuckoo, sound created in copulation.

1174 **कूक्ति**

Kūkti : a bad expression.

1175 **कूजित-विरुत**

Kūjita viruta : cooing. The sound of cooing made by the female partner in coition (*Kāmasūtra*, 2.7.6). Jayadeva mentions this cooing sound in his *Gīta-Govinda* (7.5) through the mouth of Rādhā:

dayita-vilokita-lajjita-hasitā
bahuvidhakūjita-ratirasa-rasitā

Bilhaṇa's hero remembers her beloved, who being exhausted by the exertions of the sex-act, spoke many sweet coaxing words, the right meaning of which was made difficult owing to the syllables coming out in broken order in a trembling indistinct voice:

adyāpi cāṭuśatadurlalita citārtham
tasyāḥ smarāmi surataklamavihvalāyāḥ
avyakta niḥsvanita kātara kathyamānā
saṅkīrṇa varṇaruciram vacanam priyāyāḥ

(*Caurpañcāśikā* 21)

Here the poet has mentioned the muttering sound of his beloved.

1176 **कूटनाम**

Kūṭanāma : teknonymy. Generally, among all cases in Indian culture or areas a person is referred as "father" or "mother" of his or her child or called the house-wives who have no children as *barkī, majhlī,* or *choṭkī* or *bahū* of such and such village, *i.e.* associating the name of the village to which she belongs. This is called 'teknonymy'. Those who have avoidance relation, cannot utter the name of their superior, they use teknonymy. According to Murdock (G.P. Murdock, *Social Structure,* New York, 1948) "teknonymy means a typical form of calling a person who has had a child, such as 'father of so and so, or mother of so and so. Thus parental name is associated with children's name". This type of teknonymy is used generally by women. The wife who never calls the name of husband or husband's elder brother, 'calls bābū's father' for her husband, etc. She interprets in indirect way. This custom is observed by the younger group of women. This system is not restricted to family, but outside also.

Kūṭa is collection or collective entity. The term is applied as a prefix to denote secrecy.

1177 **कूटपाश**

Kūṭapāśa : a trap. (Fig. 1177)

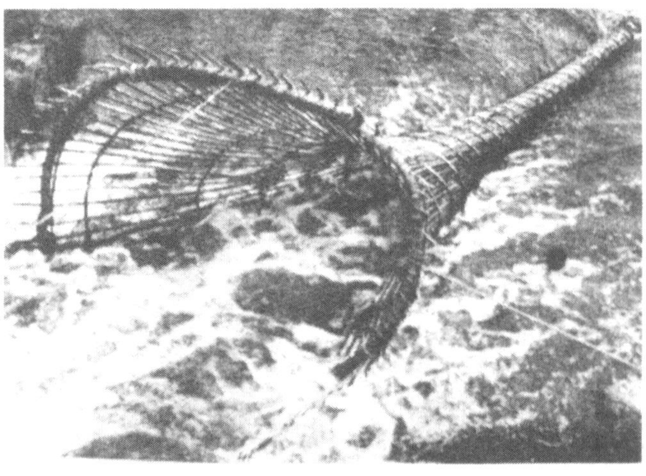

Fig. - (1177)

1178 **कूटवागुरा**
Kūṭa-vāgurā : snáre of fraud and deceit.

1179 **कूपमण्डूक**
Kūpamaṇḍūka : one who has had no experience of the world at large.

1180 **कूर्च**
Kūrca : (a) beard and moustache. The application of beard, according to Bharata's *NS*, should be according to region, condition and age. It is of four kinds: (1) *Śuddha*: shaven. The shaven beard should be in the case of religious mendicants, ministers and priests, those indifferent to sexual pleasure and those initiated for some vow. (II) *Vicitra* : The smartly done beard should be in the case of divine males, the king's, princes, kings officers, amorous persons and proud young persons. (III) *Śyāma*: the dark beard should be employed in the case of those who are unhappy, struck by calamity and those that have not fulfilled their promise. (IV) *Lomaśa:* the hairy beard should be in the case of sages, ascetics, men observing long lasting vows and those wearing tattered garments (*NS*).

Thus from the above classification it emerges that Brahmacārins, mendicants, *amātyas,* and priests shaved their beard completely, while kings, princes and those dependent on the kings trimmed their beard in diverse ways. Those in trouble or engaged in austerities let the beard grow even though it had been shaved earlier. Sages and ascetics engaged in long vow kept long beards (*NS*, XXI. 115-120).

(b) mid-point between the eyebrows (*bhruvormadhya).*

1181 **कूर्चाकृतिविज्ञान**
Kūrcākṛti-vijñāna : sign of the beard. If the beard is red, the person is indicated to be a thief (*Garuḍa*). If it is smooth and without showing stubs, it indicates royalty; if reddish, short and course, it indicates the person to be a thief (*Brahma*, 25.48-49).

1182 **कूर्म-मुद्रा**
Kūrma-mudrā : (a) type of *tāntric*-gesture mentioned in *BT* but not defined. (b) gesture symbolizing Kūrma of the Vaiṣṇavite cult. The down-turned curved *patāka* indicates the God Kūrma (*VD*). Kūrma means tortoise, Connected with the sun, and symbolizes the life-sap of the universe.

1183 **कूर्म-हस्त**
Kūrma hasta : both hands gesture *(Abhinayadarpaṇa)*, not mentioned in *NS*. If tips and little fingers of the *cakra* style are bent; it is the Kūrma that denotes a creature of the same name.

1184 **कूर्मासन**
Kūrmāsana : a type of posture. A *yogic āsana* in which the heels are placed crosswise under the gluteals.

1185 **कूर्मोदर**
Kūrmodara : stomach like the shape of a tortoise, quality of a Bull-man *(Ratirahasya,* 3.32-33).

1186 **कृतज्ञता**
Kṛtajñatā : gratitude. The fulfilling of promises given to somebody is considered the symbol of gratitude. In ancient India oral promises had as much value as that of a written document of the present society. So the word was a bond. Break of oral promises was considered a crime. People showing ingratitude were not respected. The sin due to intoxication can be forgiven and also the theft and breakers of *vṛtas,* but to ingratitude there was no relief according to Vālmiki:

> ब्रह्मघ्ने च सुरापे च चोरे भग्नव्रते तथा ।
> निष्कृतिर्विहिता सद्भिः कृतघ्ने नास्ति निष्कृतिः ॥

(*Kiṣkāṇ* 34.12)

Maximum severe punishment is ordered to them. He is to be mercilessly killed by all. If the gratitude to a friend is not shown in time, it may not serve the purpose:

> यस्तु कालव्यतीतेषु मित्रकार्येषु वर्तते ।
> स कृत्वा महतोप्यर्थान् न मित्रार्थेन युज्यते ॥

(Ibid. 14)

Vālmiki had utmost contempt for the ungrateful people: He is so hard on them that he goes to the extent of saying that even the corpse, if laid out, will not be touched by the flesh eating animals like fox or dog:

> कृतार्थह्यकृतार्थानां मित्राणां न भवन्ति ये ॥
> तान् मृतानपि क्रव्यादाः कृतघ्नान् नोपभुञ्जते ॥

(Ibid, 73)

1187 **कृत-प्रवेश**
Kṛta-praveśa : who is permitted to enter (*A*, 2.28.19, 4.10.7).

1188 **कृताञ्जलि**
Kṛtāñjali : folding the hands, respectfully.

1189 **कृते प्रति कृतं कुर्यात्**
Kṛte prati kṛtam kuryāt : tit-for-tat-theory. A theory of relationship between the male and female partner in courtship-behaviour expounded by Vātsyāyana. 'Whatever things may be done by one of the lovers to other, the same should be returned by the other;

kṛite prati kṛtam kuryāt tāḍite prati tāḍitam
karaṇena ca tenaiva cumbite prati cumbitam

(*Kāmasūtra.*, 2.3.34)

The explanation of this approach is well documented in the courtship-behaviour of Rādhā and Kṛṣṇa. Rādhā hugs him with her arms; she pierces him with her breasts, she pains him by nail-prints; she bites his lips; she beats him with her hips:

dorbhyām saṁyamitaḥ payodharabhare oṇāpīḍitaḥ pāṇijaiḥ
āviddho daśanaiḥ kṣatādharapuṭaḥ śroṇitaṭenāhataiḥ

(Jayadeva, *Gita-Govinda,* (12.3).

कृते प्रति कृतं कुर्यात् is well-known maxim of Sanskrit. It means "Do what everyone else is doing", or "Always try and beat the other person". This rule called "tit for tat" was very important. Its strategy was: cooperate on the first interaction, and then do whatever your partner does. The three principles summarize this strategy: (I) begin by cooperating, (II) stop cooperating only if your partner does so, (III) be forgiving. It also suggests that its very simplicity may be virtue. Further more, this form of reciprocal *paramārtha* is not blind. The tit-for-tat strategy responds quickly to a lack of cooperation by the withdrawal of its own. Although this may seem like primitive justice, it is at least consistent.

1190 **कृत्या**

Kṛtyā : magic, action, sorceress, witchcraft (*AV.* IV. 9.5), also, a beautiful female form created for malevolent practices.

1191 **कृष्णमुद्रा**

Kṛṣṇa-mudrā : a type of hand-gesture. Gesture symbolizing Lord Kṛṣṇa, *patāka*-hand symbolizes Lord Kṛṣṇa (*VD*).

1192 **कृष्णसारमृगमुद्रा**

Kṛṣṇasāra-mṛga-mudrā : a type of hand-gesture, indication of the black deer. The thumb and the little-finger of the *muṣṭi*-hand are extended (*Mirror of Gesture,* pp. 49-50).

1193 **कृष्णहस्त**

Kṛṣṇa-hasta : a type of hand gesture. The gesture of the *mṛgaśirṣa* with the two hands and placed them corresponding each other; indicates Kṛṣṇa (*AD*, 216-25.)

1194 **कृष्णाहस्त**

Kṛṣṇā hasta : a type of hand-gesture. The Kṛṣṇā river. The *siṁhamukha* hand moving upward and downward indicates river Kṛṣṇā (*Mirror of Gesture,* p. 48).

1195 **केतुमुद्रा**

Ketu-mudrā : a type of hand-gesture; gesture of Saturn II. The thumb at the root of the moving forefinger (*VD*). Ketu is 'one of the nine planets.

1196 **केतुहस्त**

Ketu-hasta : a type of hand-gesture. *Sūcī* with the left-hand and *patāka* with the right, make the symbol of Ketu, the planet god (*AD*, 250-258).

1197 **केलि**

Keli : amorous sport. Amorous sports of the heroine with the hero is *keli* (*Sāhityadarpaṇa,* III. 110).

1198 **केलिकला**

Kelikalā : art of love-sport *(Anaṅgaraṅga,* 10.68).

1199 **केलि-कुञ्चिका**

Keli-kuñcikā : wife's younger sister.

1200 **केलिषु निषेधवाक्यम्**

Keliṣu niṣedha-vākyam : prohibitive sentences of ladies uttered in coition (Ratnākara, *Haravijaya,* 27.35).

1201 **केश**

Keśa : hair. "The head of the goblins, mad men and ascetics represents long hair. The heads are shaved in the case of Śākya, Śrotriya, Nirgrantha, Parivrājaka and those initiated for vows or sacrifice. For other sects the head should be shaven or should have long or short hair according to their vows. The amorous people, rouges and king's officers should have curly hair. The boys should have three tufts of hair. The sages should have matted hair. The *ceṭa* (menial) should have *triśikhā* (having three locks of hair on the head) or shaven head. Vidūṣaka's head should be bald or should have *kākapada* (a hair-cut resembling crow's foot in shape.)

The world of hair in women is very much charming, though *NS* has not paid any attention to this aspect. Due to its sexual appeal, perhaps it was the subject of *Kāmasūtra.*

Black, long and curly hairs are the symbols of ideal beauty in Sanskrit literature; such as *asitakeśī, dīrghakeśī, kuṭilakeśī.*

The primary (or somewhere secondary) sexual character as important as the breasts is the hair in the aboriginal tribes. Hair has a very strong erotic attraction for the Baiga, the men especially pay a lot of attention to dressing it in the most becoming fashion. In women it is the loosened back and fastened in a bun with a bright colour *phundrā* that alternately excites delighted attention. The Baiga says "a girl whose hair falls to the waist! when she is combing it, with a gleamer ḍhār in her ears, and a bright *phundrā* in her hand , how lovely she looks:

The girl whose beauty captures the mind stands beneath the tree.
Her hair is all about her shoulders, She glances down the forest-path to see who comes.
And again:
Her long hair is all scattered on the ground,
I am going to pluck the flowers.
At sunset her hair is all scattered on the ground,
I am going to pick the flowers.
At bed-time her hair is all scattered on the ground,
I have picked a leafy flower.
Long hair is also attractive in men:
That boy with his small mouth and long hair,
Looks very handsome.
I will run away with him.
Men also tie their hair into a bun with a gay-coloured wool.
The ornaments in the hair ary very important:
In her hair are tied two Jhopā
Her lover too has tied a Jhopā
in his hair.
Flowers are also tied in the hair, and a *karmā* from Shahpura (Mandla) illustrates this custom very charmingly:

I went to the hill to pluck leaves from the forest, mother.
I looked here and there and I picked good leaves, mother.
Then I saw a flower of seven colours, mother.
I picked it and hid it in the fold of my dress, mother.
I stuck it in my hair for my adoring, mother.

(b) Varāhamihira (LXVIII) has certain predictions of men on the basis of hair-do. "one becomes king, if the hairs of head are single in each pore. One becomes penniless with the hair being many in a pore. vide the following:

एकैकसम्भवा स्निग्धाः कृष्णा नातिघनाः कचाः ।
पूजिता विपरीताश्चा निर्धनानां प्रकीर्तिताः ।।

1202 **केशग्रहणम्**

Keśagrahaṇam : dragging the hair is conferring benefits during intense love: *keśagrahaṇam anugraham* (Damodaragupta, *Kuṭṭanīmatam,* 377).

1203 **केशबन्ध**

Keśabandha : hair-dressing, in general , and different styles of tying up into ornamental knots *(bandha)* the strands or braids of hair in particular, have been of considerable interest among the Indian population since very early times; and naturally our sculptors and painters have interested themselves in portraying the different styles, which are artistic and elegant, among both men and women. There are different types of knots such as *kurīra* (crest), *śikhaṇḍa* or *kākapakṣa* (side locks), embellished with flowers (*puṣpa*), peacock-feathers (*barhi*) or jewelled bands (*ratna-paṭṭa*). These are applicable to the males. In females *alaka* (curled locks), *cūrṇa-kuntala* (curly ringlets) and tiny curls arranged on the forehead (*bhramaraka*), *dhammila* (hair rolled into a round bun), *eka-veṇī* (single but elaborate plait), *kurīra* or *mauli* (hair tied into a crest on top of the head), *alaka-cūḍaka* (curled hair parted in the middle and arranged in locks falling at the sides) and dome-like knots on one side of the head.

1204 **केशबन्ध-नृत्तहस्त**

Keśabandha-nṛttahasta : hands gesture. The two hands move out from the nape of the neck (*NS*, IX.197); binding up hairs; of two hands with the *patāka* gesture come down from the root of hairs to the two sides (of the waist), it is the *keśabandha.* The two hands are moved out from the hair knot and held on the sides.

1205 **केशमर्दनकौशतुकलम्**

Keśamardana-kauśalam : proficiency in braiding. One of the 64 arts enumerated in *Kāmasūtra (*1.3.18).

1206 **केशाकेशि**

Keśākeśi : hair to hair, head to head fight.

1207 **केशान्त**

Keśānta : the rite of shaving the hairs on the head and other parts of the body. Same as *godāna.* This sacrament is no longer in vogue (*Manu,* 11.65).

1208 **कैरिणी-मुद्रा**

Kairiṇi-mudrā : a type of hand-gesture. pertaining the summary. Extend two arms with their forehands curved. The front parts of the fore-hand with their half-curved position may appear as if a joined palm. Then place the curved fore-fingers on each thumbs and entangle both the arms with a curvature one after another. All these make the gesture of *kairiṇī.* This belongs to a semi-God (*VD*).

1209 **कैशिक न्याय**

Kaiśika-nyāya : striking in the head. It is similar to *Bharata-nyāya;* but the weapon should be flourished over the head and made to strike it (*Śāraṅgadhara paddhati,* 80. 75-82).

1210 **कैशिकी वृत्ति**

Kaiśikī vṛtti : the graceful style. It is the most delicate style and is suited to *sṛṅgāra rasa.* Bharata (*NS*, XX.53,56) defines *kaiśikī* as the style which is specially interesting on account of the charming costumes worn by dramatic personal mostly women and in which many kinds of dancing and singing are included and the themes acted are the practices of love and are connected with its enjoyment. Bharata mentions its four varieties: *narma* (pleasantry), *narmasphiñja* (beginning of pleasure), *narmasphoṭa* (unfoldment of pleasure) and *narmagarbha* (covert pleasure).

1211 **कोकिल**

Kokila : the cuckoo awoke amorous desires with its langurous cries in ancient India. Female cuckoo is supposed to bestow fortune, wealth and sons:

सौभाग्यं द्रव्यपुत्रांश्च देहि मे कोकिले नमः ।

(*Bhaviṣya*, Uttara, 11.14)

In the Bhili culture cuckoo is the symbol of a newly married woman. Following Bhili folk-song conveys the same sense:

O Cuckoo bird?
There is a plantain tree with long leaves in the field.
Cuckoo bird, you go to the market first.
There you will find your brother
He will come to take you back home.

1212 **कोकिल-मुद्रा**

Kokila-mudrā : gesture of a cuckoo. The *arāla* hand fluttered indicates a cuckoo (*Mirror of Gesture*, pp. 50-51).

1213 **कोप**

Kopa : an insurrection, a revolt (*A*, 1.13.20; 1.16.29) Kauṭilya defines *kopa* as a revolt or anger of the people. The *kopa* can be of two types (I) *ābhyantara kopa:* revolt in the interior areas and (II) *bāhya kopa:* revolt in the outer regions. The revolt or rebellion is essentially anger of the people or *prakṛti kopa.* He says, "Immoderation, such as passion and shame, rouses one's own constituents, wrong policy, rouses foreign constituents. Both these amount to demoniacal conduct. a change in one's own people is revolt (9.71.3)". This means that when the people change their opinion about their king, they revolt or rise against him. There are many causes of revolt but basically revolts occur because of change in attitudes of the people. They change their opinion because of the wrong policies of the king which he pursues due to lack of self-control (*A*, 1.6.11).

It seems that Kauṭilya divides revolts in two types: (1) *prakṛti-kopa:* people revolt against the king because of disaffection and anger - it is a rebellion carried out by the people due to unjust policies of the king. (2) *bāhya kopa:* the second type of rebellion is caused by external instigation and it is supported by treasonable elements and disgruntled officers of the state. This type of rebellion may occur in the interior or outer regions of the state. It can be safely argued that the first type of revolt is some sort of popular uprising and he concedes a fact that it might be supported by a large number of people. The second type of rebellion is a type of inter-state rebellion.

1214 **कोपक**

Kopaka : inciting to rebellion, stirring to revolt (*A*, 1.18.1, 4.11.11, 5.6.32, 7.6.10), enraged, leading to revolt (*A*.9.4.12). Kauṭilya says that the enraged means "one who is cheated after being promised certain things of two persons equally skilled in some art or useful service, the one who is humiliated, one who is in disfavour because of the favourite of the king, one who is defeated, after being challenged to a contest, one who is distressed by banishment, one who has not achieved his object after incurring expenditure, one who is hindered from doing his duty or receiving his inheritance, one deprived of honour or office, one held back by members of the family, one whose women-folk are molested by force, one who is put in prison, one who is fixed after losing his suit in court, one prevented from indulging in wrong conduct, one whose entire property is confiscated, one tormented in confinement, one whose kinsmen are exiled or killed. Due to above reasons these people are enraged and they are willing to rise in revolt against the king" (*A*, 1.14.2).

1215 **कोपं नाटयति**

Kopam nāṭayati : enactment of anger. In *Vikramorvaśīya* (Act. II), the queen is in a rage and has a heated argument with the king. She leaves in great anger: she manifests here the jealous anger through tearful eyes, touching the chin and lips, shaking of the head, knitting of the eyebrows, curling of fingers and assuming the *āyatasthāna* posture.

The persistence of beliefs and judgements help to explain why expressed emotions have a way of flooding back. The queen perceives that she has been offended in way that matters. She does not have convincing reasons for revising her judgement, her frustrated emotional expression builds up to the point where the king becomes the victim of her anger. The evoking stimuli of offendedness which elicited an effect here may well differ from one culture to another.

1216 **कोमल कुन्तल**

Komala kuntala : soft hair. quality of the Hare-man (*Anaṅgaraṅga*, 3.16).

1217 **कोमलपल्लव-लघुभुज**

Komalapallava-laghubhuja : whose shoulders are long and soft like sprout, quality of the Deer-lady (*Anaṅgaraṅga*, 3.20.21).

1218 **कोयष्टिक मुद्रा**

Koyaṣṭika-mudrā : gesture of a paddy-bird. The *arāla*-hand with the right hand, the *patāka* hand with the left and the hands touch each other to indicate this bird (*Mirror of Gesture*, pp. 50-51).

1219 **कोश**

Kośa : sheaths. (a) According to *tantras*, the human body consists of five *kośas* or sheaths, *viz. annamaya-kośa, prāṇamaya-kośa, manomaya-kośa, vijñānamaya-kośa* and *ānandamaya-kośa.* (b) In works dealing with politics, it means treasury, exchequer, one of the seven constituents *(aṅga)* of the state. (c) the relative position of the individual soul and the pure blissful soul is explained in the *Upaniṣads* by the concepts of five sheaths or *kośas.*

1220 **कौतुक**

Kautuka : curiosity. Indians in general are very curious to know. Perhaps because of the isolated life they lived for centuries, the castes and tribes are extremely curious about the outside world. This tendency is more observed in the village or forest life in comparison to the urban life. (Fig. 1220)

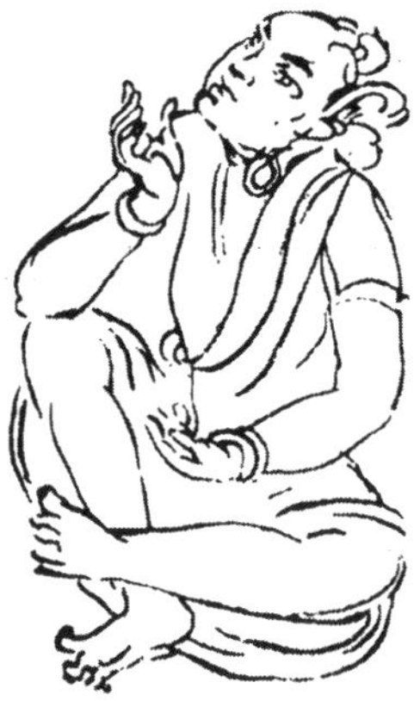

Fig. – (1220)

1221 **कौपीन**

Kaupīna : recluse. (a) private part of the body nakedness (c) angly cover (*A* 8.3.61), (d) a strap that passes in between the legs and covers privy parts. About the wearing of a recluse (Skanda, VII. 1.206. 9-10), it is said the *sannyāsī* should wear a *kaupīna* which is a strip of cloth just to cover the private parts; a garment coloured with a red dye. A *kaupīna* is mentioned as a gift to an ascetic (*Ibid.* VII. 1.9.142).

1222 **कौवेरी-मुद्रा**

Kauverī-mudrā : a type of hand-gesture. When all the fingers in the gesture are contracted, it is the gesture of *kuvera* (*VD*).

1223 **कौस्तुभ-मुद्रा**

Kaustubha-mudrā : a type of hand-gesture. Gesture symbolizing the *kaustubha-maṇi* of the Vaiṣṇavites. (a) The *mukula*-hand with the curved little finger symbolizes the *kaustubha* of Vaiṣṇavites (*VD*). (b) Place both the hands, facing each other, with their fingers interlocked together and indicated by the thumb. (*VD*).

1224 **क्रन्दसी-रोदसी**

Krandasī-rodasī : heaven and earth. The *Ṛgveda* (X. 121.6) mentions two worlds which are conceptually related to each other, but rarely come together. They are *krandasī* and *rodasī.* The concept of crying is inherent in both etymologically; Sāyaṇa actually connects them at two places while commenting on the word *krandasī*, rendering as *rodasī* (11.12.8 *krandasī-rodasī śabdam kurvāṇe*) at one place and giving the general meaning of the word *rodasī*, which is Heaven-and Earth at another, explaining that the heaven and earth are called *rodasī* as they are associated with crying (weeping) of *prajāpati* when he found himself alone in the primeval waters (*RV*, X. 126.6). The exploit of separating the Heaven and the Earth has to be understood together with the fear of the primordial parents (Cf. II 12.1. *yasya śuṣmad rodasī abhyaṣetām*) and their resultant cry of despair at being away from each other. This cry is hinted in the word *krandasī.* The concept is that the two worlds joined up in a unit, in a close clasp; and when, at the beginning of creation, they sought to be separated, as the first ever signal of creation, they are believed to groan or grumble, and invoke Indra, being disturbed in their clasp. The clasp of the world is mentioned in other places also (*Jain. Br.* III. 72 *ime vai lokāḥ saha āsan*) where the three worlds are indicated, including the mid-region). The *Ś.Br.* (1.4.1.22) states that all the three worlds were close together, mentions that the heaven was so near that it could be, touched (*unmṛśyā haiva dyaur āsa*). Both indicate the primordial couple in one mass without distinction or clarity of form. It is the separation that gives them distinct form. It is to be noted that the separation motif is not unique to the *Vedic* mythology. It obtains in tribal Bastar and the rustic Indian villages. According to the tribal myth, formerly the sky was very close to the earth; and it actually touched the roof of the hut of the primeval old woman (who, like Indra or the prime Hero must always precede the cosmic air of creation). Once she got angry that she could not have sufficient room for her movements, and hit the sky with her broom-stick. Instantly the sky went up and stands there permanently. In conceptual development it appears the separation of *krandasī* or *rodasī* is only a forerunner of the cosmic egg which is said to break into two, the upper part becoming the sky and the lower one earth. The myth of *krandasī* has to be taken as the first step in the protophilosophical myths of creation.

1225 **क्रम**

Krama : a mode of reciting *Veda.*

1226 **क्रान्तक-करण**

Krāntaka karaṇa : derived from the *atikrāntā cārī* where one *kuñcita* foot is lifted, put forward and extended. The hands are described as *ākṣipta* in the text, but commentary adds that in initial position, the hands move in the *vyāvarta* movement; in the intermediary position they are in *parivartita.* They are finally held in *kaṭakāmukha* in the chest-region (*NS*, IV. 111 b-112a, IX, 60-63, 218; X. 217). The *kuñcita* leg is bent behind the back and *atikrāntā cārī* is performed and the two hands are thrown. It is employed in haughty movements.

1227 **क्रान्तासन**

Krāntāsana : a type of sitting posture.

1228 **क्रिया**

Kriyā : communication, non-deceitful communication. *Apratārakaḥ lekhakaḥ* (Viśvarūpa on *Yaj.* II, 92); proof in law-suit. The Cākyārs employ the *kriyās* in the representation, *e.g.* when the stage direction is '*sagarvam*', the actor expresses the pride by his movements suggestive of the speech and then the actual speech is recited in which meaning of the speech is expressed more effectively by the help of physical gestures. (b) doing, verb, movement, *kriyā* in this sense can refer to physical acts or activities, speeches and thoughts. Dramatic action therefore does not necessarily imply dynamic movement. *Vāk-kriyā* in dialogue serve economically to verbalize actions (*e.g.* love-making, quarrelling, etc.).

1229 **क्रियाकल्पकला**

Kriyākalpakalā : activity as a communication tool, art of commenting on poems, one of the 64 arts given in *Kāmasūtra* (1.3.16). Body gestures, movement and posture can be related to what the actor is doing. (1) Touch : the finger brought to the mouth or face can signify thoughtfulness but of a dissociated kind; women and children are often shown with the tips of their fingers in the mouth. Finger to finger touching similarly implies dissociation. Women more than men are pictured touching, or delicately fingering objects, tracing their outline, caressing their surfaces. This ritualistic touching is different from functional touching like grasping or holding. Self-touching is again something that women do more than men; it conveys the impression of narcissism, admiring one's own body and displaying it to others, so that everyone can share the admiration of this delicate and precious thing. Sometimes the act of touching is displayed onto things - sun, wind, or water on the naked body when swimming etc. The feel of clothes against skin - satins, silks, furs - is conveyed as a pleasurable thing. (2) Body-Movement : This might be quite functional, *i.e.* simply related to what the actor is doing. These movements may be exaggerated, ridiculous or child-like, calling into question the competence of the performer. (3) Positional communication : The relationship between hero and heroine, hero and subjects are extremely significant, and are shown by their position within the frame of picture. Superiority, inferiority, equality, intimacy and rank can be signified by people's position, size, activity and their relationship to the space around them, the furniture and to the viewer. Close-up shots, for instance, are meant to signify more intimacy and identification than long-shots.

1230 **क्रियापद**

Kriyāpada : the stage of action. This consists of the examination of witness of both sides, production and inspection of material things and inspection of locale (*Manu Smṛti,* 18.40).

1231 **क्रुद्धाभावदृष्टि**

Kruddhābhāva-dṛṣṭi : a type of glance used in *raudrarasa.* It is an angry look suggesting ferocity with motionless and drawn up eye-lid, eye-balls turned up and the eye-brows of frawningly joined together. This suggests the furious (*NS*, VIII. 52-53).

1232 **क्रूरचेष्टा**

Krūraceṣṭā : lady whose gestures are crooked, quality of the Elephant-lady (*Ratirahasya*, 1.18.19).

1233 **क्रोध**

Krodha : wrath, anger, enragement, *krodha* is the basic instinct underlying the *Raudra Rasa*, the sentiment of furiousness or the ferocious. It is predominant in *Veṇīsaṁhāra. Krodha* is aggressive reaction to being wronged or not respected, with acts of auto-aggression (hitting, shaking, destroying, wounding and killing). Lips quiver in anger (*Kumārasaṁbhava*). Eyes grow red in anger (*Ibid*). In anger eyebrows become arched in *kuñcita* as in the case of Pārvatī at the approach of disguised Śiva. The furious is to be represented by (the *anubhāvas* like) red eyes, unturned eyes, knitting of the eyebrows, fierce look, bitten lips, throbbing cheeks, pressing one hand over the other hand and the like. It may have five counterparts : (I) Against enemies : knitting of the eyebrows, fierce look, bitten lips, hands clasping each other, touching one's shoulder and breast. (II) When controlled by superiors : slightly down cast eyes, wiping off slight perspiration and not expressing any violent movement. (III) Against beloved woman : very slight movement of the body, shedding tears, knitting eyebrows, sidelong glances and throbbing lips. (IV) Against one's servants : threat, rebuke, dilating eyes, and casting contemptuous looks of various kinds. (V) Artificial : betraying signs of effort.

The gaits of furious sentiment are also defined by Bharata. The gait of *Daityas, Rākṣasas,* and Bhīmasena and such others; the actor should stand 4 *tālas* apart and move with 4 *tālas* wide.

Anger may sometimes signal a loss of control but it can be equally a signal of determination to oppose what you do not accept and make your influence felt. A jabbing finger helps the man to communicate how much the point he is making matters to him. He leans forward, using his posture to make it clear that he is not simply mentioning by asserting what he says. Anger galvanizes us for action in a fight or an argument. However, it may also concentrate attention in ways that interfere with communication. When angry, we do not listen effectively. Anger is catching - thus angry words may fail to win us a sympathetic ear.

Wild expression on the face, a thumping heart, trembling limbs, breaking out into a cold sweat, a sudden release of extra adrenaline in the blood stream and a sharp rise in the blood pressure... these go into the set of symptoms that a person manifests either when he is on the verge of a coronary attack, or when he is in the throes of intense, uncontrollable rage. This fact makes the connection existing between the two states amply evident. Blood pressure and anger are also said to be interdependent.

Perhaps that is why Indian seers regarded it as one of the six great foes of the human mind that a man had to conquer before he could aspire to be a man of God.

But somewhere along the way, values turned topsy-turvy. Today we have reached what can aptly be called an "angry age". Not only is everybody angry with everything, but anger is actually being glorified in fiction, films and even in real life. The "angry young man" has become the hero to be admired and emulated.

1234 **क्रोध-दृष्टि**

Krodha-dṛṣṭi : a type of *bhāva-dṛṣṭi* enumerated by Bharata.

1235 **क्रोध-मुद्रा**

Krodha-mudrā : gesture of anger. The *sikhara* framed with the left hand (*VD*).

1236 **क्रोधिनी-मुद्रा**

Krodhinī-mudrā : enraging. The gesture is to be so made as if something is being taken out of the palm and the midpalm is striken by the middle finger and then joined with it. This is the gesture of *krodhinī* (*VD*).

1237 **क्रौञ्च-मुद्रा**

Krauñca-mudrā : gesture of an osprey. The *sūcī* hand relaxed indicates an osprey (*Mirror of Gesture,* pp. 50-51).

1238 **क्रौष्टिकी-मुद्रा**

Krauṣṭikī-mudrā : a type of *mudrā*. "Eyes should be made wide and the mouth should be placed on the left hand. Put the right arm above the left a little curved by the left side. This is called the *krauṣṭikī-mudrā*, which may be used for the purpose of *melāpaka* " (*BT*).

1239 **क्लान्त विलोचन**

Klānta vilocana : a type of eye-gesture for weariness, sickness, etc. In Bhāravi's *Kirātārjunīya*, we find the evidence of this gesture. Mallinātha's commentary interprets *klānta vilocana* as *glāni dṛṣṭi* (*NS*, VIII. 67 and 88). It is one of the thirty six glances of *NS* (VIII. 67 and VIII. 88). It is used for weariness, sickness, etc.

1240 **क्लीब**

Klība : impotent, unmanly, neuter gender, the inability of the male to perform the sex act, a feeling of inability to control events.

1241 **क्षत**

Kṣata : biting of the woman at the time of sexual union (*Kāmasūtra*, 2.1..13). It is known as *nocnā* in Hindi.

1242 **क्षतनखपयोधर**

Kṣatanakhapayodhara : nail-prints on the breasts. Nail-prints pertaining to breasts occur in *Sanskrit* poetry. *Kāminī kucataṭeṣu padāni akriyanta* (*Śiśu.* 10.57); *kṣatanakhapayodhara* (*Ibid.* 5.23); *kucau nakhakiṁśukārchanam* (*Naiṣadha*, 18.101); *dayitanakhakṣatam stanāgre* (*Haravijaya*, 17.12); *Kucakalaśataṭeṣu kāminīnām dayitanakhakṣata* (*Ibid*, 27.54); *nakhavraṇam* (*Madhurāvijaya*, 5.61); *nakhalipi* (*Vikramāṅkadevacarita*, 6.16); *nakhapadam stanamaṇḍale* (*Caurapañcāśikā*, 35); *nakhalipighanastanabhāram* (*Gita-Govinda*, 2.6); *tasyāḥ pāṭalapāṇijāṅkitamuro (Ibid. 12.5).*

1243 **क्षत्रिय-हस्त**

Kṣatraiya-hasta : a type of hand-gesture. Hold the *śikhara* gesture with the slanting style and the *patāka* with the other hand; this indicates a *kṣatriya*, the warrior class (*AD*, 226-231).

1244 **क्षाम गण्ड**

Kṣāma-gaṇḍa : fallen of sunken cheeks; a type of gesture pertaining to cheeks commonly seen in *karuṇa rasa*; "weak down and depressed" is a static gesture of the cheek to suggest and exposure of sorrow and pathos (*NS*, VIII. 129-134).

1245 **क्षामोदर**

Kṣāmodara : the slender belly. The slender pose of the belly is indicative of laughing, weeping, breathing, deep shy and yawning (*NS*, X. 17-20).

1246 **क्षामोदरी**

Kṣāmodarī : lady who has a small belly, quality of the Art-lady (*Pañcaśāyaka*, 1.7).

1247 **क्षिप्त जङ्घा**

Kṣipta jaṅghā : the thrown out legs; throwing the shanks outwards; spread out shanks sculptured in Rājasthān temples. Amarāvatī presents this position in sculptures. *Kṣipta* is also a feat of the leg in which legs are flung. It is used to show the physical feats, the *tāṇḍava*-dance and *yoga* (*NS*, X. 33-40).

1248 **क्षिप्त जानु**

Kṣipta jānu : spread out knees indicating the outward sideways position. Here the legs are bent and the knees are turned outward. This is the position of the knees which we find in basic stance of Bharatanāṭyam today. The shanks form an acute angle with the thighs. It is akin to the demi-plie of the classical western ballot.

1249 **क्षीर-जलकमालिङ्गनम्**

Kṣīra-jalakam-āliṅganam : mingling of water and milk-type of embrace. The *Kāmasūtra* (2.2.20) describes the 'embrace of milk and water' thus : "when a man and woman are very much in love with each other and not thinking of any pain or hurt embrace each other as if they were entering into each other's body either while the woman is sitting on the lap of the man or in front of him or in bed." Māgha (*Śiśu*. 7.19, 10.48) illustrates it in different verses. Bhāravi (*Kirāta*. 9.48) describes this embrace as external cohabitation. Ratnākara (*Haravijaya*, 27.41) has also depicted.

It is also known as *kṣīra-nīraka* or 'the milk - and - water embrace' when the woman lies in her lover's lap or on the bed, with her face turned to him, giving him sweet and close embraces; and both press body to body heedlessly in a storm of passion.

1250 **क्षुरिका-मुद्रा**

Kṣurikā-mudrā : a type of hand-gesture. "The little, the fore-finger and the thumb should be joined together in a round form. The middle finger and the ring finger, should remain straight and parallel. This figure should be attached to the lower part of the hand. The complete gesture is called *kṣurikā-mudrā;* which may kill anybody's life immediately. This gesture is further applicable to enter into the body of any other man; whenever he likes in the process of removing all sorts of bad omens and drawing near anybody else, whom he likes to subjugate" (*BT*).

1251 **क्षेप**

Kṣepa : form of speech and thought, speech with omissions. (*Bṛhaddevatā* 144-60)

1252 **क्षेपण-मुद्रा**

Kṣepaṇa-mudrā : throwing hand gesture. One of the hand-postures, rarely seen in icons other than those belonging to the Vajrayāna ideology, indicating the sprinkling (*kṣepaṇa*) of nectar (*amṛta*) by the right hand from the vessel held in the left hand. The *mudrā* of sprinkling exhibited by the Buddhist Nāmasaṅgati. The two hands are joined, palm to palm, with fingers extended and pointed downwards to enter a vessel containing nectar.

1253 **क्षौरकर्म**

Kṣaura-karma : cutting of hair. Though hair figures varies in many accounts, tonsure, or cutting of hair at holy places has been enjoined. The tonsure of widows was a common practice (*Skanda*, III. 2.37.26).

1254 **क्ष्वेडा**

Kṣveḍā : indistinct sound (of teeth).

ख – Kha

1255 **खड्‌गन रत**

Khaṅgana-rata : cohabitation of saints. *Khaṅga* is sword in Sanskrit. The carriers of swords were known as *Khaṅgana*. Varāhamihira in his *Bṛhat-Saṁhitā* has depicted the signs of swords- *Khaṅga Lakṣaṇam (L)*.

1256 **खटक**

Khaṭaka : One who arranges marriage, marriage - broker.

1257 **खटकावर्धमानक हस्त**

Khaṭakāvardhamānaka hasta : a type of hand-gesture. One *kaṭakāmukha* (q.v.) hand is placed on the wrist of the other *kaṭakāmukha* hand either in *svastika* position or facing each other. It symbolizes love-making and salutation.

It is also called *kaṭakāvardhamānaka hasta* (q.v.).

1258 **खटिक**

Khaṭika : half-closed hand.

1259 **खट्वा**

Khaṭvā : cot, bed-stead.

1260 **खट्वाङ्ग**

Khaṭvāṅga : banner on the shoulder of those who observe religious rites.

1261 **खट्वाङ्ग-मुद्रा**

Khaṭvāṅga-mudrā : a type of hand-gesture. "Raise the left hand up, keep the forefinger standing and affix other fingers with the fist. This will make a *khaṭvāṅga mudrā" (Brahma-Purāṇa). Khaṭvāṅga* is a magic wand. The stick is generally surmounted either by *Vajra*, the *Kapāla*, the *Triśūla*, a banner, or all of them.

1262 **खट्वारूढ**

Khaṭvārūḍha : addicted to lying on a bed : *khaṭvārūḍho jālmaḥ*, one doing what is prohibited.

1263 **खट्वारोहण**

Khaṭvārohaṇam : ascending on the cot, a part of marriage ceremony in some parts of India. Among the Maria Gonds of Bastar the wife is said not to sleep on a cot in her husband's house, which would be thought disrespectful to him, but on the ground. Nor will a woman even sit on a cot in her own house, and if any male relative happened to be in the house, it would be disrespectful to him. If lying on the cot, persons at once get up and sit if an elderly man approaches. Manner of sitting on the cot was also decided by social custom in feudal India. In the Gwalior region, the *Thākur* could share the cot only with the *Baniā* and *Gosāī*. The Brāhmaṇa was shown respect by giving him a separate cot to sit. *Nāī* (barber) could sit on the cot while massaging the body, all others sat on the ground in the presence of the *Thākur*. The Chamār and the Korī could not sit on the cot with caste people of middle layer in caste-hierarchy. These practices continue as yet. But now, thc low caste persons do not stand up to respect the *Thākur* if they happen to visit their localities. For some *Thākurs*, some Camār or Korī may stand up, but it is not followed as a general pattern (Mutatkar, 1978: 123).

The above type of class-consciousness may not be seen in the tribal regions. The Hill Maria is further an exception, where there is no trace of class-society. No tribe and no people would display the boldness and audacity to sit on the cot by the side of the visiting official in India, leave alone sleeping on the cot, during meetings and enquiries. But among the Hill Marias it is a common sight. If a spare cot is available they will not hesitate to occupy it and will even sleep on it while the enquiries are going on.

At Kutul and Dhobe they even sat on the very cot on which the present writer was sitting and that too just by his side. Bison-horn Marias, Kamār, Bhunjia, Baiga or no other tribe would think of taking his liberty with the outsiders, and particularly with the visiting officials. While the enquiries were going on at Kutul, two boys lay down on the cot.

1264 **खट्वा हस्त**

Khaṭvā-hasta : a type of hand-gesture (*Abhinayadarpaṇa*). When thumbs and forefingers of two *catura* hands are released free; it is the *khaṭvā*. It indicates a bed and a palanquin.

1265 **खड्‌ग-मुद्रा**

Khaḍga-mudrā : the sword gesture. (a) "Make the right hand up along with three fingers not clung to each other; it is called the gesture of *khaḍga" (Brahmayāmalatantra*). (b) "Three fingers pressed by the thumb and the little finger are to be positioned up-lifted. With this feat, turning the hand up, brandish it repeatedly. This is called the *khaḍga-mudrā* (the gesture of the sword). This too destroys the waves of bad omen in a devout and does not allow to leak out the sacred care" *(Ibid)*. (c) One finger of the *kapittha* touches the palm back to form a gesture which symbolizes the Vaiṣṇavite deity *(VD)*. (d) Thumbs of both the hands are placed inside the curved pairs, the ring and the little-fingers. The rest four fingers of both the hands are extended jointly forward. This makes a *khaḍga*-the sword *(VD)*. The sword is the symbol of wisdom which is believed to destroy the darkness of ignorance by the luminous rays issuing out of it.

1266 **खड्गहस्त**

Khaḍga-hasta : having sword in hand. The bridegroom of the lower castes holds sword in his hand during marriage ceremony. Holding of the sword in hand by the bridegroom is an emblem of Rāma. This emblem occurs in the *Brahmavaivarta-Purāṇa* (Śrīkṛṣṇakhaṇḍa. 107.35) during the marriage ritual of Kṛṣṇa and Rukmiṇī, where Kṛṣṇa holds a sword in the hand as an emblem of Rāma : Rāma also says :

खड्गं शुभं तदा धार्यम् मम चिह्नं करे स्थितम्

(*Skanda.* III 2.33.34).

(b) For killing a Brāhmaṇa, *Kūrma Purāṇa* (II. 30.16) records that for the expiation the sinner should roam for twelve years with a sword in one hand and in the other a skull.

1267 **खण्ड**

Khaṇḍa : Three *karaṇas* in combination form a *khaṇḍa* and three or four *khaṇḍas* constitute a *maṇḍala* (*NS*, X. 3-4).

1268 **खण्डखट्वारोपितवृद्धदासीविवाह**

Khaṇḍa-khaṭvāropita-vṛddha-dāsī-vivāha : *Kādambarī* (Kale, p.26) mentions a special type of marriage ceremony in reference to spring-festival. In it, on a high bedstead it was represented as if a man marrying an old maid-servant. *Khaṭvāropita*-ceremony is still prevalent in Baghelkhanda of Madhya Pradesh.

1269 **खण्डन-चिबुक**

Khaṇḍana cibuka : teeth repeatedly coming together; frequent touching and separating of teeth a type of facial expression where gesture of the chin suggests *śṛṅgāra rasa;* joining repeatedly two lips with teeth. It suggests to utter *mantras*, study texts, speaking, eating and doing the like (*NS*, VIII. 141-146).

1270 **खण्डसूचिस्थानक**

Khaṇḍa sūcī sthānaka : a type of posture.

1271 **खण्डाभ्र**

Khaṇḍābhra : the broken-cloud-bite. Breasts are the suitable place for this type of bite (*Kāmasūtra*, 2.5. 16-17), lit. bit of cloud, amorous bite.

1272 **खण्डिता**

Khaṇḍitā : woman enraged with jealousy. A betrayed woman whose husband or lover has been guilty of infidelity and who is, therefore, angry with him. *Khaṇḍitā* is one who is filled with jealousy, seeing that her beloved, who has just approached her, bears on his person the marks of his union with another lady (*Sāhityadarpaṇa*, III. 75). "That woman, whose husband's eyes are red and lazy due to having no sleep and whose limbs are marked by all the signs of sexual sport due to the co-wife and who having arrived in the morning speaks sweet words with fear, is called *khaṇḍitā* (*Anaṅgaraṅga*, 10.52). This type of heroine is described in most of the *kāvyas* (*Mēgha*, 39; *Śrīnivāsavilāsacampū*, p. 124).

According to *NS*, *Khaṇḍitā* is a heroine whose lover does not turn up when the conjugal union is due, owing to his attachment for other woman and thus she is distressed by his not coming.

1273 **ख-पुष्प**

Kha-puṣpa : menstrual blood required in *Tāntric* worship. (a) The blood of a virgin is known as *raktacandana*, that of a married woman is known as *kuṇḍodbhava* and that of widow is known as *golodbhava.* (b) flower in the sky, *chimera.* It is an emblem of what is absolutely non-existent. Such emblems are summarized in the following verse :

एष वन्ध्यासुतो याति खपुष्पकृतशेखरः ।
मृगतृष्णाम्भसि स्नातः शशश्रृङ्गधनुर्धरः ॥

1274 **खर-मुद्रा**

Khara-mudrā : a type of hand-gesture, indication of a mule. The *nāgabandha* hands directed upward indicate a mule (*Mirror of Gesture,* pp. 49-50).

1275 **खल्वाटता**

Khalvāṭatā : baldness. Baldness transmits a double-signal : maleness and advancing stage.

1276 **खल्वोदर**

Khalvodara : The depressed belly. The depressed or empty belly suggests disease, austerity, fatigue, penance and hungry mood (*NS*, X. 17-20).

1277 **खसूचि**

Khasūci : one who stares at; expression of reproach: *Vaiyākaraṇa-khasūciḥ.*

1278 **खुरक**

Khuraka : a kind of dance with a *rāga* sung in fast and medium tempo *(Bhāvaprakāśa)* : paralanguage feature predominant.

1279 **खेचरी-मुद्रा**

Khecarī-mudrā : posture of sky-wanderers "When mind is completely concentrated with no end, the wind is still without the *kumbhaka* process and the same is *automatically fixed*, it is called the *khecarī-mudrā*. It is a *mudrā*, but there is no movement" *(Jñānasảnkalinī-Tantra)*. This *mudrā* is meant generally for *yoginīs*. The right hand to the left side, and the left to the right side; the hands turned; the little finger and the *anāmikā* of both touching each other and crossed over the index finger (*Brahmāṇḍa-Purāṇa*, II. 42.2).

Massage the tongue daily like the process of milking with the help of butter. Also pull it daily with an iron tong or the fingers. Practise it daily for a long time till the tongue is elongated to such an extent that it touches the middle of the eyebrows and becomes fit for *khecarī*. Then up-turn the tongue and make it pass through the upper cavity of the palate slowly. Now gaze at the middle of the eyebrows. This is *khecarī mudrā*.

This practice needs patience and perseverance. One who practises *khecarī* does not suffer from hunger, thirst, tiredness, or langour. Neither illness nor decay comes near him and his body becomes pure.

Thus, *khecarī-mudrā* is that type of *yogic* posture which bestows spiritual attainment and enables one to overcome disease and death (*Haṭha-yoga Pradīpikā*, III.67).

1280 **खेद**

Kheda : one of the 64 *sandhyaṅgas* (*NS*, 19.94). It is the fatigue arising from mental fatigue and physical exhaustion. (b) behaviourally, the diceased ability to do work, a subjective feeling of tiredness after a prolonged work or nervous tension, impaired sensory or nervous activity following prolonged stimulation, such as occurs in retinal or auditory fatigue.

1281 **खोर**

Khora : lame, limping (*Kśs*, XXII. 3.19), crippled.

ग – Ga

1282 **गगनकुसुम**

Gagana-kusuma : sky - blossom, unreal thing.

1283 **गङ्गावतरण-करण**

Gaṅgāvataraṇa : a type of gait to show the Gaṅgā flowing. It is rendered in many ways. It may be done by curling of the leg behind like a scorpion's sting and hands hold down, breast erect and the head lowered. The other way was the *Viṣṇukrāntā karaṇa* and *tripatāka hastas* held over the uplifted foot to show the Gaṅgā flowing. The third way is the acrobatic as in the sculptures of Cidambaram. Any of these movements might have been attempted in *Abhijñāna Śākuntalam* (Act VI) for showing Sānumatī descending from the celestial chariot (*NS*, p. 188). According to Bharata, these *karaṇas* or gait might represent the riding of a celestial chariot and the descending from the sky: simple steps are used for this, beginning with *samapāda sthāna* and when mounting these vehicles, the body is to be held up and when alighting, the body is to be held down (*NS*, XII. 88-92). In this particular case, Sānumatī suggests a descent from the sky through the use of the *apaviddha* arms and tossing of the ends of her clothes (*Ibid*, XII. 94-95). Commonly it is a acrobatic *karaṇa* rarely seen in dancing; hands are *tripatāka*, the feet and the heels are lifted up and weight of the body rests on the hands (*Ibid.* IV 168 b-169 a). It is employed in the descent of the Gaṅgā on earth.

1284 **गङ्गाहस्त**

Gaṅgā-hasta: : a type of hand - gesture. The River Gaṅgā. The *tāmracūḍa* moving upward and downward indicates river Gaṅgā (*Mirror of Gesture*, p. 46)

1285 **गज**

Gaja: : the elephant was perhaps the noblest of all animals, for it was claimed that a cloud gave birth to it. Symbolizing strength and wisdom, stability and prudence, it had an illustrious representative in the brāhmanic patheon in the person of Gaṇeśa, son of Śiva, elephant-headed and patron of intellectuals.

1286 **गजक्रीडितक करण**

Gajakrīḍitaka karaṇa : name derived from *gajadanta hasta*, but the movement of the hands here has nothing in common with the *hasta*; instead it resembles the *karihasta* except for the crossing of extended arm. Left hand is near the ear and right arm is extended to its own side. The leg position is of *dolāpāda cārī* (*NS*, IV. 128-129, IX. 154, 198, 199). The left hand is bent and brought near the ear, the right hand in *latā* and the *dolāpāda cārī* is performed.

1287 **गजगति**

Gajagati : (a) lady whose gait is like an elephant, quality of the deer-lady *(Anaṅgaraṅga*, 3.20.21), (b) stately or majestic gait.

1288 **गजगामिनी**

Gajagāminī : a woman of stately gait.

1289 **गजदन्त-हस्त**

Gajadanta hasta : a type of hand-gesture, the elephants' tusks, both hands gesture formed from *sarpaśiraḥ* *(NS)*. When two gestures of the *sarpaśiraḥ* touch opposite arms by the elbows in a cross-way style, it is called the *gajadanta*-gesture. This is used to indicate the marriage ceremony of a pair of bride and a bridegroom, to uplift a piece of heavy stone, to clash against a pillar and to uproot a tree (*NS*, *IX*. 144-145).

1290 **गजनिमीलित**

Gaja-nimīlita: : shutting the eyes (at anything) as an elephant does.

1291 **गजहस्त**

Gajahasta : one of the common hand gestures mentioned in Indian iconography. The posture of holding one of the arms dangling down by the side, or holding it across the chest, like the trunk of an elephant . The left arm of the Devī illustrates the former instance, while the left normal arm of Naṭarāja *Gajāsura - saṁhāra - mūrti*.

1292 **गड्डलिका-प्रवाह**

Gaḍḍalikā - pravāha : a stream of sheep, used to signify blindly following other people as sheep do.

1293 **गण**

Gaṇa : (a) an association of merchants. (b) an association of men living in a village, etc. (c) a tribal community. (d) in metrics it is a metrical unit consisting of three syllables, represented by a letter. There are eight *gaṇas* representing the various permutations and combinations of the long and short syllables. (e) an attendant of Śiva. The motive is that sincere worship of Śiva with faithful austerity leads one to the favour of Śiva, and the highest favour is the position of *gaṇa*. The most famous of the *gaṇas* is Gaṇapati or Gaṇeśa the leader of the *gaṇas*). Another famous *gaṇa* is Puṣpadanta (*Skanda*, VII. 1. 180. 1-3).

1294 **गणक**

Gaṇaka: astrologer (*VS*, XXX. 20, *TBR*. 111.4.15), reckoner.

1295 **गणचक्रक**

Gaṇacakraka : dinner party of cultured men.

1296 **गणदीक्षा**

Gaṇadīkṣā : initiátion of a number on class.

1297 **गणपाठ**

Gaṇapāṭha : a collection of series of words falling under the same grammatical rule.

1298 **गणाचार**

Gaṇācara : one of the *pañcācāras* or five Vīra-Śaiva codes of conduct. It represents the spirit of vindication. The Vīra-Śaivas should not tolerate adverse remarks. As a member of the community one has to strive for its upliftment. This attitude is known as *gaṇācāra.*

1299 **गणेश-हस्त**

Gaṇeśa-hasta : a type of hand gesture. *Kapittha* hands, placed on thighs, suggest Gaṇeśa (*AD*, 205-210).

1300 **गण्ड**

Gaṇḍa : (a) cheeks. The gestures of the cheeks according to the *rasas* are six as follows : *phulla* (blown) or *sama (śṛngāra) ; kampita* or *kuñcita (bhayānaka), pūrṇa* or *phulla (hāsya); kṣama* (depressed) in *karuṇa rasa ; sama (adbhuta); pūrṇa* (fully expanded) or *kampita (raudra); pūrṇa (vīra); kuñcita (bībhatsa).* Cheek-movements fall under facial expression. These occur according to the muscular possibilities of these parts of the face. (b) one of the thirteen *aṅgas* of *vīthī* in the view of Bharata. Gaṇḍa occurs due to excitement, confusion, quarrel, reviling and many people's abusive talk (*NS*, *18*.125-126). In the words of Abhinavagupta *gaṇḍa* is like *gaṇḍa* as it contains the matter to happen. It is a sentence, little incomplete. Abhinava cites for example the speech of Kañcukin and Duryodhana in the second Act of *Veṇīsaṁhāra* about the breaking of the banner. Dhanañjaya (*Daśarūpaka*, III. 18) opines that *gaṇḍa* is related with the matter in hand, is uttered suddenly and in incomplete sentences. In constellation, *gaṇḍānta* indicates calamity (*Skanda*, VII. 2.17. 133-134).

1301 **गण्डपरावृत संस्थान**

Gaṇḍaparāvṛtta saṁsthāna : The turned-cheek position. The extent of the neck should be waned by one *kalā*. A *kalā* indicates here a width of one finger of an artist. The width of the whole neck-part is ordinarily four fingers. The arm, the cheek, the fore-head, the breast, the hip, the buttock are to be diminished by two *kalās* proportionately and the position, not very much waned by a side-glance, is called the turned-cheek pose (*VD*. III. 39.21-23).

1302 **गण्डभेदक**

Gaṇḍa-bhedaka : pick-pocket, thief.

1303 **गण्डभेरुण्ड-मुद्रा**

Gaṇḍabheruṇḍa-mudrā : a type of hand-gesture. *ardhacandra*-hands faced downward touching at the wrists with fingers stretched indicate at *gaṇḍabheruṇḍa.*

1304 **गण्डसूचीकरण**

Gaṇḍa sūcī karaṇa : one foot is in *sūcīpāda,* the other in *samapāda* position, the side is bent in *nata.* Hands are in *kuñcita* and *sūcīmukha. Nṛtta hastas* during the movement in the final position one rests on the chest and the other is a *sūcī asaṁyuta hasta* on the cheek (*NS*, IV, 131b-132 a, IX. 67-74, 191, 239). The foot is in *sūcī* position, the side bent, one and placed on bosom and the other bend touching the cheek. It is used in decoration of the cheek.

1305 **गण्डाकृतिविज्ञान**

Gaṇḍākṛti-vijñāna : signs on the cheeks. If they are *nimna gaṇḍa* (low), the person is given to enjoyment; if he is *sàṁpūrṇa-gaṇḍaka* (full-round-cheeked) he is a minister (*Brahma*, 26. 41-43). Varāhamihira (LXVIII) seems to be the source of the above statement :

1306 **गण्डूष**

Gaṇḍūṣa : mouthful of water for rinsing.

1307 **गतागत**

Gatāgata : going and coming.

1308 **गतागत-स्थान**

Gatāgata sthāna : a *sthāna* (posture for women). In it the female dancer, about to move forward, hesitates with one foot raised. (Fig. 1308)

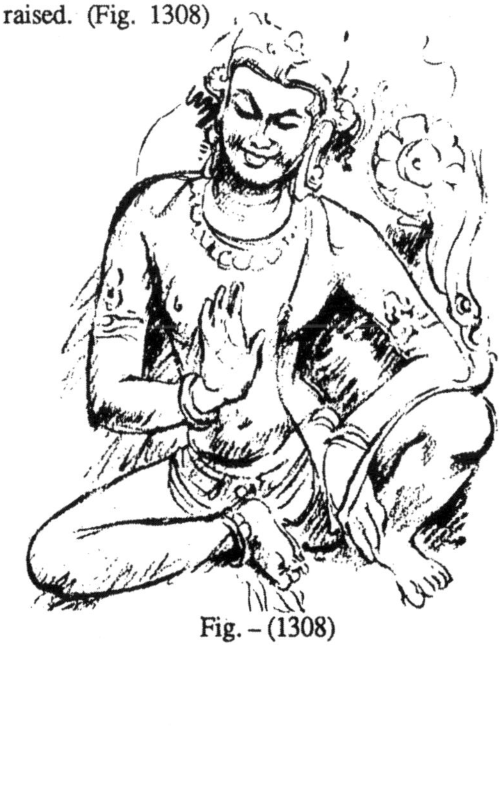

Fig. – (1308)

1309 **गतानुगतिक**

Gatānugatika : addicted to follow old ruts.

1310 **गति**

Gati : class of movements, walking. The gait or style of walking should be in accord with the level and status of the character : firm, medium, and fast, corresponding to high middle and low characters. But in all cases, the gait will be governed by the context and the emotional condition. The gait with which an actor enters reveals him, his character, and state of feeling; indeed his whole being.

The steps of gods, *Dānavas*, *Yakṣa*, Kings, *Pannagas* and *Rākṣasas* should be four *tālas* wide. The gait in the *atikrāntā cārī* , with steps 2 *tālas* wide, the left hand in upturned *arāla* near the bosom. The limbs should not be drooping nor motionless nor excessively moving. Ascetics, permanent celibates, observes of vows, etc. should move steady eyes looking at a distance of 4 hands in front, with presence of memory, with body and mind steady, with the proper sectarian mark and the modest clothes dyed in red. The bulky person's gait would have feet raised slowly, dragging the body with great effort. A lunatic moves with irregular steps. The dwarf may not have wide and quick steps. The menials walk bending one side, head, hand, and foot with the eyes contemplating on the purpose. The persons of inferior caste move looking about, avoiding the contact of other people (*NS*, Vol. II, 138).

1311 **गतिभंग**

Gati-bhaṅga : unsteady gait.

1312 **गतिशिक्षाकला**

Gati-śikṣā-kalā : art of training of speed and motion. It is also called *sūta-vidyā* or the science of driving carts, chariots and other vehicles (*Śukra-nītisāra*, 4. 320-22).

The gait of persons was socially conditioned in India. The superior and middling persons should have *Vaiṣṇava sthāna*. The breast should be raised even and *caturasra* (symmetrical). The neck should not be raised very much and should be steady and 8 *aṅgulas* apart from the ears. The neck should balance the head gracefully like a peacock and the chin should be 4 *aṅgulas* apart from the left at the waist. The distance between the feet should be 2 *tālas*. The steps should be according to the measure of his own hand. The steps should be 4 *tālas* wide in the case of gods and kings, two in the case of middling types and one in the case of women and low characters respectively with 4 *kalās*, 2 *kalās* and 1 *kalā* time measures. The tempo should be slow in the case of superior persons, medium in the case of middle class people and fast in the case of inferior characters according to their nature and the mood. In the natural gait, the superior character is to raise his knee up to the waist and in the case of *cārīs* used in fight, up to the breast. When the person in walking with his equals, the tempo would be according to his rank, *i.e.* 4,2 or 1 *kalā*. If the superior character is walking with the middling one and the low type characters, for one step of his the middling one would have two steps and the low ones would have four.

1313 **गत्याकृतिविज्ञान**

Gatyākṛti-vijñāna : the sign of gait. It is said that if a person's gait is like that of a swan or a parrot, he would become a king; if like a bull, lion or an elephant, it is indicative of enjoyment, it is like the ripples in the water, it is indication of poverty, if like that of a crow or an owl, that portends sorrow, and if it is like that of a dog, camel, buffalo, donkey or a pig, that is indicative of loss of fortune *(Bhaviṣya*, 39-42). Varāhamihira (*BS*, LXVIII) symbolizes *gati* as follows. Men become kings, if their gait resembles that of lions, swans, intoxicated elephants, bulls or peacocks; rich, if their gait is slow and without any sound and indigent, if their's is brisk and leaping.

शार्दूलहंस समदद्विगोयतीनां
तुल्यो भवन्ति गतिभिः शिखिनां च भूपाः।
येषां च शब्दरहितं स्तिमितं च यानं
तेऽपीश्वरा द्रुतपरिप्लुतगा दरिद्राः।।

1314 **गदा-मुद्रा**

Gadā-mudrā : mace-gesture; (a) gesture symbolizing the club of Viṣṇu. If two *kapittha* hands placed one after another near the chin, it is the *gadā-mudrā (VD)*. (b) gesture of the club. Curve four fingers and extend the thumb. This makes the gesture of a *gadā (VD)*. (c) if the fist is placed on the waist, it is *gadā - mudrā*, that removes all bad omens *(VD)*. (d) make fists by the two hands and join fingers of both the hands (*VD)*.

1315 **गद्गद**

Gadgada : choked, flattering, unable to speak. (b) sound produced in the throat (a little distinct), stammering, indistinct utterance.

1316 **गद्गदस्वर**

Gadgada-svara : of flattering speech. (b) faltering speech.

1317 **गद्गदोक्ति**

Gadgadokti : flattering speech (*Ratirahasya*, 1.18.19), lady who flatters in speech, quality of the conch-lady. It is known as *laṛbaṛānā* in colloquial Hindi.

1318 **गद्गद्मधुरोक्ति**

Gadgadmadhurokti : lady whose voice is sweet, quality of the Mare-lady *(Ratirahasya*, 3.22-23).

1319 **गद्गद्वाक्**

Gadgadvāk : it is heard when women are in coition (Bhāravi, *Kirāta* 9.50).

1320 **गन्धपुष्पविभागज्ञा**

Gandha-puṣpa-vibhāgajñā : the women skilled in the art of perfumes and flowers *(NS*, XXIV. 30).

1321 **गन्ध-मुद्रा**

Gandha-mudrā : a type of hand-gesture. Make the left hand upturned and the right hand down-faced, the middle and ring-fingers of both the hands should rest in a curved style on the thumbs and fore-fingers and the little fingers should be preserved by middle fingers. This is *gandha-mudrā* and is also considered another form of the *dravya-mudrā (VD).*

1322 **गन्धयुक्तिकला**

Gandhayuktikalā : preparation of various scents and their compounds. One of the 64 arts given by *Kāmasūtra.* The *Agni Purāṇa* (224.20.24) lays down the following processes of preparation of perfumes: (1) *śauca* (purification), *ācamana* (washing), *virecana* (purgation, evacuation of unnecessary matter), bhāvana (steeping, infusion, saturating a dry powder with fluid, scenting), *pāka* (heating, boiling, cooking), *bodhana* (burning incense), *dhūpana* (fumigating) and *vāsana* (perfuming). According to *Agni-Purāṇa* (224.33), the process of preparing scented oil is this.

1323 **गन्धशास्त्र**

Gandha-śāstra : science of smell, name of work written by Gaṅgādhara (1200 A.D.).*Gandhaśāstra* was a special art which was useful in both secular and religious art-forms of antiquity as yet it has been prevalent in India, in the temples, god-houses, in the household which are incensed with sandal, rose and variety of smells of different flowers. According to Gaṅgādhara perfume pleases gods, contributes to the comfort of men and delights the hearts of kings, and accomplishes ladies, beside making its devotees prosperous.

Gandha means smell. It has broad varieties. (a) *parimala* is the fragrance that arises on crushing (as of some kinds of leaves); while (b) *āmoda* is fragrance that is pervasive as of jasmine, or pārījāta. (c) *surabhi* is used of pleasing scent as of *Campaka.* This is illustrated thus :

कस्तूरिकायाः आमोदः
कर्पूरे मुखवासनः ।
बकुले स्यात् परिमलः
चम्पके सुरभिस्तथा ॥

Another type of classifications is known as (a) *nirhāra* in which fragrance attracts from a far, while (b) anything of pleasing smell is *sugandhi.*

1324 **गन्धाष्टक**

Gandhāṣṭaka : eight fragrance substances: *candana, agaru, karpūra cora, kumkuma, gorocanā, jaṭāmāmsī* and *kāpi* - combined together and used as a substitute for wine. (*Śāradātilaka*, IV. 79-80).

Those eight fragrances, acting through our sense of smell have an effect on our nerves and moods was known to *Śāradātilaka.* Our ancient scholars intutively arrived at the effect different fragrances have on our nerves, but they were unable to explain the mechanism.

Now modern science has stepped in to show how fragrances act through our olfactory nerves, which, in their turn, transmit certain impulses to our brain and thereby affect own nerves and moods. Though it is yet to be established why different fragrances send different impulses to the brain and produce different moods, research is being done on this.

The mechanism is not fully explained but observation and study have shown how we can make use of certain fragrances to reduce the stress and strain of the day-to-day modern life.

It is not known that certain atoms or fragrances soothe and calm our frayed nerves and help to relax, while others are invigorating and perk us up. While the fragrances of lavender, *khaśa and* jasmine soothe us, the scents to lime, mint and pine perk us up.

The fragrance of *candana* (sandalwood) is, however, soothing and at the same time uplifting. Our ancestors realised this. That is why sandalwood paste is used in all our religious functions. So was the fragrance of incense or *dhūpa.*

Our mothers used to burn powdered *dhūpa* not just for religious worship; it was burnt every evening in the rest of the house too. The fragrant , light smoke drove away mosquitoes and other insects and induced a calm mood.

While talking of Indian perfumes or fragrances, one must mention *itra.* This is made mainly from the rose, but also from *khasa.* The former is, however, more popular than the *khasa* in India. *Itra* is a concentrated scent and hence not to be applied liberally.

A mild dab of rose *itra* gives a nice feeling but still it is sensual. *Khasa,* on the other hand, has a cooling effect, especially during summer.

Perfumes and fragrance are basically of four types, namely:

(a) Soothing and relaxing,

(b) Invigorating,
(c) Inducing religious feeling (not in the narrow sense, of course), and
(d) Sensual and romantic.

Considerable research was done in this country in the period of Vātsyāyana on this subject. While modern misses use a hair-dryer after a shampoo, in the olden days, ladies would have an oil bath and then sit near some burning *dhūpa*. The mild heat of the smoke would not only dry the wet hair without any damage to it, it would also make it fragrant. Maybe, once in a way, when time permits, this method of drying washed hair could be tried.

Indians have a fondness for strong scents, though most of the foreign perfumes, especially the French ones, are mild. A perfume could be mild and yet sensual and sometimes heady, creating a romantic mood.

Thus, with the judicious use of light aromas and fragrances, ancient Indians influenced their moods. India was rich in its herbs and roots and these produced many fragrances which influenced their varying moods and tattered nerves.

1325 **गमनाभिनय**

Gamanābhinaya : the gesture of walking (*Mālatīmādhavam*, IX.4).

1326 **गम्भीररुक्षस्वरा**

Gambhīra-rukṣasvarā : lady whose tone is deep but rough, quality of the Elephant-lady (*Anaṅgaraṅga*, 3.24-25).

1327 **गरुड**

Garuḍa : a type of *bhramarī* mentioned by Nandikeśwara (*Abhinayadarpaṇa*, pp.282-298)

1328 **गरुड-पक्षक-नृत्तहस्त**

Garuḍa-pakṣaka-nṛtta-hasta : a type of hand-gesture; Garuḍa's wings. If the hands are stylized with down-turned palms with fingers-joined, it is the *garuḍa-pakṣa* (*NS*. IX. 176-197). The two *patāka* hands pointing downwards placed near the region of the hips are moved up quickly, turning the palms.

1329 **गरुडप्लुतक करण**

Garuḍaplutaka-karṇa : one leg is stretched back and the feet is in *añcita*. This *karaṇa* really belongs to the *vṛścika* variety with a difference: the uplifted leg has an unfolded knee and not an arched one as in the *vṛścika karaṇas*. The side is *unnata:* the hands and arms move in *latā recita* (*NS*, IV. 130b-131a, IX.236-237). The leg is extended at the back, one hand is in *latā* and the other in *recita* and the breast is raised up. It is used in the fight of eagle.

1330 **गरुड-मुद्रा**

Garuḍa-mudrā : gesture symbolizing the Garuḍa. If the middle finger is extended on the *akāra* hand, it symbolizes Garuḍa, the carrier bird of Viṣṇu. *(VD).*

1331 **गरुडवाहन-मुद्रा**

Garuḍavāhana-mudrā : a type of hand-gesture, symbolizing Viṣṇu carried by Garuḍa . If the middle finger touches the tip of the thumb then it symbolizes (*VD).*

1332 **गरुड-स्थानक**

Garuḍa-sthānaka : a type of posture.

1333 **गरुड-हस्त**

Garuḍa hasta : both hands gestures (*Abhinayadarpaṇa),* not mentioned in *NS*. Two *ardhacandra* hands, when held with palms and thumbs are tied together; it is the Garuḍa that indicates the carrier of Viṣṇu.

1334 **गर्दभ-मुद्रा**

Gardabha-mudrā : gesture of an ass. The *bhinnāṅguli* hand represents an ass. Fore-fingers of the *khaṇḍāṅguli* hand are bent and contracted to indicate an ass (*Mirror of Gesture*, pp. 49-50). The ass has been a symbol of the lusty tendency in Indian tradition. He is termed *dviretas,* as he places his semen in the female ass and also in a mare (*Taitt. Saṁ*. V.1.5.5; VII.1.1.2.; *Śat. Br*. VI.3.1.23;) For the belief that if a pregnant woman sees the coitus of asses her would-be child will become strong, see *Bhāratīya Sanskriti Kośa* (Vol . II).

1335 **गर्भ-दोहद**

Garbha-dohada : longing of a pregnant woman.

1336 **गर्भमन्थरा**

Garbha-mantharā : slow due to pregnancy.

1337 **गर्भाधान**

Garbhādhāna : impregnation. (a) The rite for causing pregnancy which requires sexual intercourse on an appointed day with *mantras* and purificatory observances (*Gaut*. VIII.14, *Yāj*. 1.11). It is one of the main *Saṁskāras* (consecrations). It elaborates that *garbhādhāna* (conception) should be performed after marriage, by having union with the wife for the first time on even days after her menstruation if he desires a son, leaving the first three days of the period of sixteen nights (*Agni*, 32.1-3).

(b) There are some taboo related with the pregnant woman in the Gond. A pregnant woman must not go near a horse or elephant, as they think that either of these animals would be excited by her condition and would assault her. In case where labour is prolonged they give the woman water to drink from a swiftly stream, or they take pieces of wood from a tree struck by lightning by a thunder-bolt, and make a necklace of them and hang it round her neck. In these instances the swiftness of the running water, or the lightning or thunder-bolt, is held to be communicated to the woman, and thus she will obtain a quick delivery or else they ask the Guniā or sorcerer to discover what ancestor will be reborn in the child, and when he has done this he calls on the ancestor to come and be born quickly (Russell and Hiralal, III, 83-84)

1338 **गर्व**

Garva : a type of *vyabhicārī bhāva* meaning the feeling of pride (*Sāhityadarpaṇa,* III. 154). It is manifested by disrespect for others, harassing, not giving reply, not greeting others, looking to oneself, roaming, contemptuous laughter, harsh words, transgressing commands of the superiors, insulting others, etc. In the case of persons of the inferior type, (boastful) movement of the eyes and the limbs is to be employed. (b) Vijjikā, the Sanskrit poetess has her own pride :

Daṇḍin lied when he said

The Goddess of poetry was wholly white, Vijjikā, he hadn't met me, dark as a blue lotus petal.

(Eng. rend. Vātsyāyana and Mishra)

1339 **गल**

Gala : throat, neck. The name Gālava is explained as such in *Brahma Purāṇa* (7.106-7): his mother sold him tying by the neck so he was called Gālava.

1340 **गलग्रहणम्**

Galagrahaṇam : seizing the throat.

1341 **गलदक्षर**

Galadakṣara : with choked throat.

1342 **गलहस्त**

Galahasta : seizing of the throat *(Kathās'),* to seize by placing a hand on the throat.

1343 **गलहस्तिका**

Galahastikā : seizing by the neck, collaring.

1344 **गलितग्रीवा**

Galitagrīvā : dropped neck, a type of neck-movement (*SR,* VII. 329-334).

1345 **गलेचोपक**

Galecopaka : moving the neck.

1346 **गल्पगोष्ठी**

Galpagoṣṭhī : gossiping seminar. One of the seminars mentioned by Bāna in *Harśacarita.*

1347 **गवीनी**

Gavinī : the two mounds of the *yoni* (vagina) (*TS,* iii. 3.10.1)

1348 **गाङ्गुलहस्त**

Gāṅgula hasta : single hand gesture.

1349 **गात्रलक्षण**

Gātra lakṣaṇa : signs of the limbs. "Whenever limb of the body is rough, without flesh, and full of veins, it is considered to be inauspicious; and the opposite of these is beneficial. One becomes a monarch if one is broad in three limbs, deep in three, raised in six, short in four, red in seven, long in five and slender in five. The five long limbs are (1) the space between the paps or nipples, (2) arms, (3) eyes, (4) nose and (5) jaws. The four short ones are, neck, top of the thighs, root of the back, and shanks. The five slender ones are-finger-joints, hair, teeth, nails and skin. The six raised ones are arm-pits, belly, chest, nose, shoulders and forehead. The seven red ones are-the palms, soles, corners of the eyes, nails, palate, tongue and the lower lip. The three deep ones are-voice, courage and navel. Lastly the three broad ones are-the chest, face and forehead' (*Bṛhat-Saṁhitā,* L XVIII). Govindarāja quotes a number of authorities by name and otherwise. Some of the authors and works mentioned by him are: Vararuci, Nandī, Kātyāyana, Garga, Mihira, Nārada, Brahmā, Brahmapurāṇa, Brahmāṇḍa, Sāmudrika etc.

It is auspicious for men to have (a) the three *viz.* navel, voice and courage, deep; (b) the three *viz.* breast, fore head and mouth, broad; (c) the six *viz.* chest, arm-pits, nails, nose, face and the nape of the neck, raised; (d) the four *viz.* the genital organ, back, neck, and shanks, short; men become happy with the following seven-corners of eyes, feet, hands, palate, lower lip, tongue and nails, red; (f) very happy with the following five, *viz.* teeth, finger, knuckles, hair, skin and fingers, thin and (g) monarch without doubt with the five *viz.* jaws, eyes, arms, nose and the space between the paps, long.

(2) *gātramoṭana* yawning.

1350 **गाथा**

Gāthā : song, music : सुभाषित्वेन गीयते इति (*TS,* V.1.8.2); गाथा नाराशंसी *gāthā-nārāśaṁsī* : epic songs and those in praise of heroes अग्निचयनप्रकरणे यमगाताभिः परिगायतीति विहिता मन्त्रविशेषा गाथाः। मनुष्यवृतान्त प्रतिपादिका ऋचो नाराशस्या।। (*Ś.Br.* XI.5.6.8). The *gāthās* which are mentioned in the *Vedic* literature, may be regarded as the oldest representatives of folk-ballads. The word *gāthin* meaning a singer is found in many hymns of *Ṛgveda*. In this work, the word *gāthā* is used in a special sense and it has been differentiated from *raivī* and *nārāśaṁsī*. The *gāthās* were regarded as human whereas *ṛks* were divine. The man played an important part in the composition of *gāthās* and they were never used as *mantras*. The laudatory hymns sung in the praise of a particular king or hero in ancient India were known as *gāthās*. We may find some fine specimens of *Vedic gāthās* in *Śatapatha* and *Aitareya Brāhmaṇas*. The *Aitareya Brāhmaṇa gāthās* have been termed as *yajña gāthā* (sacrificial hymns) and also known as *ślokas*. The historical tradition of these *gāthās* may be traced in *sūtras* up to the *Mahābhārata*.

Songs in praise of variant persons are known as *gāthā nārāśaṁsī*. They gradually developed into lengthy ballads and various song-cycles with intricate plots.

The word *gāthā* in the sense of song or *mantra* is many times referred to in *RV* and other works. Its origin is traceable to an oral tradition prevalent among the people of ancient India. *Par.Gr.S.* (1.8.11-13) while describing the marriage-ritual says that in matters relating to marriage and funeral rites the custom as prevalent in the villages concerned is the supreme authority.

1351 **गाम्भीर्यं**

Gāmbhīrya : gravity, one of the temperamental aspects in the case of males when the outward changes in cases of anger, joy and fear are not noticed, it is *gāmbhīrya (NS)*.

1352 **गायत्रीमुद्रा**

Gāyatrī-mudrā : a type of hand-gesture; (a) when all fingers are turned in the middle of a palm, it is *Gāyatrī*, *a* symbolic gesture *(VD)*; (b) make two hands flat, place one on the other and keep their nails in an equal position. This is the gesture of *Gāyatrī (VD)*. *Gāyatrī* is the celebrated *Vedic* meter *(chandas)* of twenty four letters in three lines, it came especially to signify a hymn in that meter addressed to the Sun-god, Savitṛ. (*RV.* 3.62.10).

1353 **गारुड**

Gāruḍa : charms and magical formulas, did, in fact, cover the smallest contingencies of daily life. With the onset of a headache, the sufferer hastily transferred the pain to the hills and forests. A yawn or sneeze called for a wish to be quickly pronounced: "May steadfastness and wisdom inhabit me" (Hiraṇyakeśin, *Gṛhyasūtra* 1,5,16,2) or "Long life to such-and-such person (Cullavagga V.33.3) although such exclamations were perhaps a bereft of real meaning as when we say 'God bless you': or 'The best of health': When a drop of rain fell on one, it was a sign of good-luck (Hiraṇyakeśin, *loc.cit.*, I, 5.16.6); if it was a bird-dropping, it presaged happiness, but it was necessary to remove it without touching it with one's hand and then wash oneself with water (*Ibid*, 1,5,17,5). (b) serpent-charmer was known as *gāruḍi*. He was also the magician (*Garuḍa*, 1.197.1-54).

1354 **गालिदानम्**

Gāli-dānam : abusive language, reproach. There is a phrase *gālidānam* in verse 38 of chapter second of *Mānasollāsa* written by Someśvara (early twelfth century). One can easily suspect it as a colloquial Hindi term for reproach or abusive language. The word is not unknown in other colloquial modern Indo-Aryan languages. This word also occurs in *Rājataraṅgiṇī* (VI.157), *Bhartṛhari* (III. 133) and *Bodhasaralayoga* (14). An interesting detail of marriage of Śiva and Pārvatī is mentioned the teasing (abuse) by the smiling and joking women of city, pointing at the couple and others, after the marriage (*Śivapurāṇa*, II 53.18) :

तदानीं पुरनार्यश्च गालीदानं व्यधुर्मुदा। मृदवाण्या हसन्त्यो यत्नश्चतान्।।

The abuse appears to be erotic, with an idea of promoting fecundity. It is still a common practice in Indian villages and tribal folk.

The use of the abusive language on the occasion of wedding is a custom we come across in most tribal societies in India as well as in rural Hindu communities. Songs known as *gāli* or *gāri* (abuse) have become a well-known part of Hindi folk-songs. This is done as a measure of safety-valve. The inferior is free to abuse the superior.

Abuses are structured on different aspects. (a) Fucking is one of them. It was also prevalent during the time of Yajñavalkya:

abhigantāsmi bhaginīm mātaram vā taveti ha *(Yajña, vyavahārādhyāya)*. I will fuck your sister/mother; and it was classified under the *Vākpāruṣya* and the person uttering these abuses was liable to be punished by 25 *paṇas*. These two abuses are still very much common in Indian society uttered as *bahincod* (sister fucked) and *madar-cod* (mother-fucked). (b) Most of the wedding songs of rural and tribal India, especially the ones to taunt the opposite clans or parties (bride-grooms party), are very obscene, employing a language which has a sexual impact. There is too much repetition of this theme and the tunes of marriage songs. The use of sexual symbolism is common both in tribal songs and their poetry. The commonest symbols they use are the following: hill, husking, pestle, horse, coconuts, well, pond, etc.

1355 **गिरिक-मुद्रा**

Girika-mudrā : a type of hand-gesture. The fore-finger of the *mukula*-hand is bent and moved to and fro to indicate a mule (*Mirror of Gesture*, pp.49-50).

1356 **गीतिमुद्रा**

Gīti-mudrā: the song-gesture. "Making the two eyes glowing, the mid-point should flutter delightfully, beautifully and flapping, the two eyebrows equally in them. Then laugh a little, as the previously accumulated spirit pursuits. By the left, making the fingers down-faced, join three of them. This is called *gīti-mudrā*. Making the *mudrā* with due care, one may sing either *caryā*-song, or the hymns of *sāman*". *(BT)*

1357 **गुण**

Guṇa : (a) quality, any specific merit in a work of art, also factor, qualification in the phenomenal universe *(guṇatraya)*, purity *(sattva guṇa)* action *(rajas)* expansion, continuation and (inertia) *tamas*. (b) a political expedient. These are six: *sandhi*, *vigraha*, *yāna*, *āsana*, *dvaidhbhāva* and *saṃśraya*. (c) according to *Nyāya-vaiśeṣika*, there are 24 kinds of qualities. *rūpa* (colour), *rasa* (taste), *gandha* (smell), *sparśa* (touch), *śabda* (sound), *saṅkhyā* (number), *pariṇāma* (magnitude), *pṛthakatva* (distinctness), *saṁyoga* (conjunction), *vibhāga* (disjunction), *paratva* (remoteness), *aparatva* (nearness), *buddhi* (cognition), *sukha* (pleasure), *icchā* (desire), *dveṣa* (aversion), *duḥkha* (pain), *prayatna* (effort), *gurutva* (heaviness), *dravatā* (fluidity), *sneha* (viscidity), *saṁskāra* (tendency), *dharma* (merit) and *adharma* (demerit; (*Vaiś. Sūt.* 1.1.16). (d) commonly *guṇa* is understood to mean some unchanging characters of a substance. They adhere to specific substances and cannot exist by themselves.

Guṇadharma means certain duties, such as the protection of subjects in the case of a king. *Guṇa-karma* means quality and action ; the nature of the work one performs; the basis of the *varṇa*-system; according to *Bhagavadgītā*. *Guṇasthānas* are fourteen steps to liberation from *karma* according to the Jain-conception. *Guṇa-vāda* is one of the three kinds of *arthavāda*.

(e) Attribution. The consequences of attributing the causes of behaviour to the actor's attentions and dispositions, and thus from these attributions to further inferences about the person's characteristics, can have profound effects on our relationships with that person.

1358 **गुलिकानादसंकेत**

Gulikānādasaṁketa : gun-salute. Salutes ranging from nine to twenty one guns were assigned to different princes in India during British period; a prince with a salute of eleven guns or more was addressed as "His Highness". Such honours could be used to bring pressure to bear upon individual princes. In 1865, the Raja of Jhābuā was deprived of his salute, and also fined ten thousand rupees, when the British government learnt that he had allowed a rebel to his own protection (Kenneth Ballhaf Chet, *Race Sex and Class under the Raj*, Delhi 1979,7).

1359 **गुल्फ**

Gulpha : ankles. The movement of the ankles does not find place in *NS* which is done by other texts. Many characteristics of ankles of the women have been depicted in the *Purāṇas*. They should be fleshy, without showing the veins and reddish (*Sk.P.* IV. 37.12.17).

1360 **गुह्य**

Guhya : vagina (*Ratirahasya*, 3.22.26); *guhyadeśam* (*Pañcaśāyaka*, 2.14). (a) There were *guhya-liṅgas* (secret *liṅgas* of Śiva). *Guhya-sādhanā* meant the secret ritual in *Tāntric* Buddhism based on vagina and the *guhya-samāja* was the secret society which performed it. (b) the genital organ that is broad and of the shape of the *Aśvattha (Ficus religiosa)* leaf was a sign of beauty according to *Bṛhat-Saṁhitā* (LXX).

अश्वत्थपत्र सदृशं विपुलं च गुह्यम्

1361 **गूढक**

Gūḍhaka : the hidden bite. Lower lip is the place on which hidden bite is made (*Kāmasūtra*, 2.57).

1362 **गूढोक्ति**

Gūḍhokti : veiled reference in the presence of person really referred to (*Kuvalayānanda*, 87.1).

1363 **गृध्रावलीनक-करण**

Gṛdhrāvalīnaka karaṇa : the feet are in slight *añcita* and the knee is bent in the initial position. During the movement the leg moves front and back. The hands and arms are stretched in *latā*. The side is stretched and extended in *prasārita* (*NS*, IV. 134b-135a, X.235-256). One foot is extended backwards with the knee slightly bent and the hands are out-stretched. It is used in gesticulation of birds.

1364 **गृह**

Gṛha : the house. The construction of house (especially in the village) is in keeping with the social and domestic notions of the Hindus. In front of the house there is usually a spacious courtyard where untouchables and other low-born visitors may stand and speak to the male members of the family who occupy the verandah of the house for the purpose. At the foot of the verandah there is a low platform for the accommodation of "touchable" visitors of low social status who cannot be admitted into the verandah which is open only to the men of equal status. These may sit with the male members of the family on terms of equality and transact business, the visitor and the host usually squatting on the same mat, when they are of equal age, and chewing betel leaves. A door leads from the verandah into the house proper. The entrance usually is into a hall which opens into an inner courtyard on the sides of which are built the rooms in which the members of the family live. The male members occupy the more spacious and airy rooms and the hall nearest to the front verandah, and the ladies occupy the darker and smaller rooms, away from the verandah and near the kitchen. Only very intimate male relatives are allowed to cross the verandah into the house proper.

The doors of a house should be kept open in early evening. It is believed that the goddess of wealth enters into the house during this period.One should not sit on a *caukhaṭ* in the evening time. It brings misfortune in the family.

The housing conditions depend on the economic stability and accordingly it varies with *pakkā*, *kaccā* and thatch roof, the house-structures vary in relation to Muslim and tribal communities.

Still about 80 per cent of the rural houses in India have walls made of inferior materials like grass, leaves, bamboo and mud. The grass or leaves-made walls houses are characteristics of tribal groups and by the people of lower rung of the Indian society. A large bulk of houses do not have any benefit of windows. In most cases, apart from the main door, if at all there is any inlet for air and light it is provided by few elongated holes made into the walls. The luxury of a separate kitchen being rare in the villages, the walls and the roofs get a thick coating of soot coming out of the ovens located in the house. In such housing conditions, people are living generation after generation. Besides, there is unhealthy congestion too, 26 per cent of the population of India belong to one room household where on an average, 5 persons share one room.

And yet it is only the more fortunate ones who have the benefit of firm walls and protection roofs. Bulk of the poor people both in the rural and urban areas do not even have such a privilege. The roofs on their houses very often have no protection against rain, as they are hardly able to replace the upper covering of the grass or straw at the desired interval. These materials have to be bought and they have no resources. The feeble grass and reed walls of their houses have many chinks and cracks through which the strong winds of a storm have unhindered entry. And the people go on living in them, sometimes supporting the walls and roofs during heavy rains and fearful storm, some other time consoling the children who are yet unused to the onslaught of water right in their houses. And still at other times nursing the sick who do not have the benefit of pure air and clean light.

The house is a critical focus of life of any individual since he is forced to return to it for periodic protection. The house then becomes a universal feature of the regions permanently occupied by human beings is one of the most fundamental demands of cultural geography. The rural house in India is both geographical and economic index. The building materials, ground and vertical dimensions, nature of roofs, aspects of plan and form are all related to geographical environment.

The average house is a quadrangular structure built of mud-walls, and sloping tiled roofs. The typical house consists of a central courtyard (*āngan*) and surrounding rooms. Tiled verandah in front of the house is not uncommon. Sometimes verandah may occur inside the house also on one or more sides of the *āngan*. Such house may be 11 to 14 yards. The rooms are 7 to 10 feet wide and length varies according to the function of the rooms generally 8 to 12 feet. Each room has generally one door, about 3x5 feet, which is smaller than the main entrance of the house. Main entrance of the house leads from verandah into one of its rooms which opens direct into the courtyard or through an outer verandah. This is the description of the typical rural house in India. (b) The Gond does not like to live in a street. He like a large *bāṛī* or fenced enclosure, about an acre in size, besides his house. In this he will grow mustard for sale, or his own annual supply of tobacco or vegetables. He arranges that the village cattle shall come and stand in the *bāṛī* on their way to and from pasture, and that the cows shall be milked there for some time. His family also performs natural functions in it, which the Hindus will not do in their fields. Thus the *bāṛī* get well manured and will easily give two crops in the year, and the Gond sets great store by this fields. (Russell and Hiralal, II. 119).

1365 **गृहप्रवेश**

Gṛhapraveśa : a rite entering the new house. A new house can be used only after the performance of *gṛhapraveśa* which enables it worth living for Lakṣmī - the goddess of wealth.

1366 **गृहाचार**

Gṛhācāra : house-customs, the duties of a householder or his wife to a guest.

1367 **गृहालिका**

Gṛhālikā : The lizard. The wall lizard is a prophet among the Hindus. The noise it makes, its position on the wall or ceiling, its fall from the wall by accident, are all capable of revealing the future. If a lizard falls on one's head, the happening is indicative of death. If it falls on the right part of a person's body, it brings him luck, if on the left, mishaps. There is an elaborate literature on wall lizards, and many Hindus carefully study it and daily consult the omens. The classical literature on the subject is known as *Godhā-śāstra* or *Gowli śāstra* or the science of the wall lizard.

Even today it is thought in the village India the lizard falling on the body is inauspicious.

1368 **गृहोपस्करः**

Gṛhopaskaraḥ : furnishing the home. The home and its furnishings vary tremendously in size and scale, according to whether their prospective owner in ancient India was rich or of modest means, townsman or villager. The village house was by far the most common type of dwelling. It consisted of one single ground floor, only, the floor of beaten earth, mud walls, a single door, and rarely more than one window; the latter being narrow and covered with a wooden lattice. The roof was made of palm-leaves, reeds or matting, hemispherical in shape if the walls were round, or, if the walls were square, either semi-cylindrical or pointed and two-sided. Its bamboo framework, struts and wooden. cross-pieces, and the dividing mats hanging from it were all particularly vulnerable to the fires which often ravaged the villages, under conditions where no effective counter-measures could be undertaken. The damage caused periodically by the rainy season to the roofs and walls necessitated extensive repairs as soon as dry weather returned. The plan was simple, and consisted mainly of the bedroom, facing north, the pantry, and the room in which the master received his guests.

The furniture was extremely sparse, and there were no seats of any kind, since everyone sat on the ground. The chief piece of furniture was a bed with a wooden or bamboo frame, set on four shaped legs, and a framework of diagonally crossed cords; this base was sometimes covered with matting or a piece of material. Rattan stands shaped like sand-glasses, on which a tray was placed, took the place of tables and sideboards. It was called *bhojanaphalaka* or *pattankaṇḍolikā* in Pāli. These supports are still in use today, either as an article of furniture, or by street traders who use them as the base for a tray displaying their wares.

While the common people lived in simple, even impoverished, domestic surroundings, city dwellers and families in easy circumstances possessed more extensive and better built houses.Such houses were usually several storeys high, with two white-washed facades, one opening on to a street or avenue by an entrance door furnished with a stone threshold and framed by two stone benches, while the other looked over a private garden containing various supplementary buildings. Such a house was, in fact a villa in the Roman sense of the word. In these more luxurious homes, the furniture was more elegant and more varied than to be found in rural houses. The bedroom of the master of the house contained a soft bed covered by a white bedspread, furnished with two pillows, one for the head and one for the feet, and surmounted by an elaborately decorated canopy. His room was large enough to contain, in addition, a *dīvān* and a small table on which were ranged unguents and cosmetics; on one side was a basket containing the garlands of flowers with which he bedecked himself each day; there were also containers of the betel leaves and jars of perfumes. These all had a part in his daily toilet. Near the *dīvān* a cuspidor on the floor stood ready to receive the red expectoration caused by betel chewing. There was also another table for painting purpose. A chessboard was in position near the bed, and a viṇā hung on the wall.

1369 **गृह्यसूत्र**

Gṛhya-sūtra : manuals giving the rules for the numerous ceremonies applicable to the domestic life of a man and his family from birth to grave. Domestic rituals date from very ancient times, and had thrived on folk tradition, which was, in many cases, unrecorded.

1370 **गेयपद**

Geyapada : the *geyapada* comprises mainly a song in the form of dialogue between a male and female. The song is actually a form of *maṅgala* and comprises primarily *Parameśvara śṛṅgāra* (*NS,* XXI.332-38).

1371 **गोत्र**

Gotra : clan. "All persons who trace descent in an unbroken male line from a common male ancestor (Kane). *Gotra* or ancestry was quite an important as caste, perhaps even more so, and the concept had some affinity with that of the clan, evoking perhaps the distant age when the Aryans had not yet totally lost their tribal character. The *gotra* claimed authentic or, more often, mythical ancestors, whose names were recited each day in the domestic ritual. To belong to a *gotra* was, to all intents and purposes, the prerogative of brāhmaṇs alone, and they believed firmly that they were the descendants of the saintly personages of *Vedic* times. The kṣatriyas and vaiṣyas could hardly have the same pretensions; nevertheless, certain members of these castes did dare to assert an exalted lineage, braving the ironic amusement of blue-blooded brāhmaṇs. As far as the low castes, they had no right whatsoever to any ascending line of this sort.

The significant instance where tribal society has had a direct influence on caste society includes the derivation of the

Aryan and Brāhmaṇa exogamous clan, or gotra, from th virtually universal clan organization of the tribes. The endogamous caste is subdivided into exogamous gotras - the word is Sanskrit for cow-pen (each gotra had its own branding mark for cattle held in common). This idea may have been assimilated by peripatetic Brāhmaṇas who inter married, as ancient texts record, with tribal women ; it was subsequently imitated by the kṣatriyas and eater by the lower castes who wished to raise their status. The idea has recently turned full circle : Hinduized tribes anxious to conceal their totemic names have borrowed the names of Brāhmaṇic gotras.

"A clan is sub grouping hose membership claims descent from a common ancestor, without actually being able to trace genealogical links in all cases. Since descent is traced through either the male or the female maternal - patriclans or matriclans. A clan is exogamous, and bears a name whereby members identify themselves. Further, a clan is not ordinarily a localized group.

1372 **गोत्रस्खलनम्**

Gotraskhalanam : blunder regarding name, speech error. an example of paralanguage. Cupid addressed Rati with a wrong name in *Kumārasaṁbhava* (4.8). Agnivarṇa utters the names of others ladies in dream (*Raghu*, 19.22). Bhāravi pictures the same situation (*Kirāta*). In *Setubandha*, the love-lorn Rāvaṇa could not hide the name of Sītā before his wife (11.9). *Yudhiṣṭhiravijaya* (2.74), *Amarukaśataka* (23), *Priyadarśikā* (4.3), *Mālavikāgnimitra* (3.22) and *Ratnāvalī* (3.14) are full of such errors. In *Vikramorvaśīya* (Act III), from the conversation of the pupils of Bharata, Gālava and Pallava, we learn how the audience reacted to this play, called the *Lakṣmī - Svayambara* (a play within play). The lyrics for this play were composed by Sarasvatī herself and the audience was completely absorbed in the portrayal of different *rasas*. Urvaśī, in the part of Lakṣmī, gave herself away by the fatal mistake of saying "Pururavā" instead of "Puruṣottama" - an unforgivable lapse for the actress who must completely annihilate herself and rise above personal emotion. The celestial dancer's fault brings upon wrath of the god; to expiate she must descend to earth and bear a child to the king, love for whom caused her to speech error.

1373 **गोदान**

Godāna : a sacrament which consists in shaving the head and also the hair on the other parts of the body. Also called *Keśānta*. It is observed during initiation and other turning points of life (*śat. Br.* III. 1.2.4; *Baud Dh.S.* 1.2.7; *Manu* II. 65; Yāj. 1.36).

1374 **गोमती-विद्या**

Gomatī-vidyā : laudation of cows so that abundant benefits may be obtained from them. Varāhamihira in his *Bṛhat-Saṁhitā* (LXI) has given the feature (*golakṣaṇaṁ*) of cow *bestowing* good and bad luck :

Cows with dirty and dry eyes, shedding tears, and resembling those of rats are not auspicious; nor are those that have flat, shaking horns, that are black and red in colour or have the colour of assess. So also are those that have ten, seven or four teeth, drooping hornless head depressed back, short and thick neck, middle resembling barley corn, broken hoofs, very long and blackish tongue, very small or very big ankle-joints, big hump, weak body and fewer or more limbs.

साम्राविलरूक्षाख्यो मूषक नयनाश्च न शुभदा गायः।
प्रचलच्चिपिटविषाणाः करटाः रवरसहशवर्णाश्च॥
दशसप्तचतुर्दनत्यः प्रलम्बमुण्डानना विनतपृष्ठचः।
ह्रस्वस्थूल ग्रीवा यवमध्या दारितखुराश्च॥
श्यावाति दीर्घजिह्वा गुल्फै रतितनुभिरनि बृहद्भिर्वा।
अजतककुदाः कृशदेहा नेष्टाहीनाधिकाङ्ग्यश्च॥

1375 **गोमूत्रिका**

Gomūtrikā : going zigzag as the urine of a cow.

1376 **गोष्ठी**

Goṣṭhī : (a) a type of *uparūpaka* which has nine or ten Prākṛta heroes and five or six beautiful heroines. Bhoja gives it as the representation of sports of Kṛṣṇa in Gokula and the killing of the *Asuras* by Kṛṣṇa.

1377 **गौ**

Gau : the cow. Among ancient Indians, the cow was surrounded by great respect, though not yet the object of the cult which was later devoted to it; it was granted an important place in the semi-divine hierarchy because all its products had a part in ritual. The bull Nandi, the God Śiva's mount, was one of the most august of all bovines and held divine status.

1378 **गौडी**

Gauḍī : (a) name of a *rīti* or a particular mode of arrangement of words in a literary composition. (b) wine distilled from molasses.

1379 **गौमुद्रा**

Gau-mudrā : the gesture of a cow. The *saṅkīrṇa-mudrā* represents this. The middle-finger is bent and all other fingers extended to indicate a cow (*Mirror of Gesture*, pp. 49-50).

1380 **गौर**

Gaura : (a) white, shining, beautiful. (b) a kind of buffalo, Bos gaurus (*TS*, 1. 16.5) गौरो न तृषितः पिब गौरमृग इव so on. (*Ś. Br.* 1.2.2.3) गौरी महिषी the cow of Bos gaurus

1381 **गौरी-पूजा**

Gaurī-pūjā : a special ritual during marriage ceremony (Skanda, VI.113). In the *Gaurī-pūjā*, the muttering of five syllables (namaḥ Śivāya) a certain number of times is enjoined prior to taking even water. Gaurī is the name of Pārvatī, She is visualized as a girl of ten or eight years. Gaurī means a girl prior to menses, one who has yet to attain menstruation. According to *Skanda Purāṇa* (VII.1.205.82,84) a Gaurī is said to be the best. Rohiṇī (nine years) is the middle quality, Kanyā (ten years) is the lower-middle and Rajasvalā (menstruvating) is the lower. A girl should be married before she becomes *rajasvalā*.

1382 **गौरी (महायोगेश्वरी) मुद्रा**

Gaurī (Mahāyogeśvarī) mudrā : a type of hand-gesture. "Join eight fingers of both the palms with their middle knots coming out and the two thumbs are well joined together; making the joined hands like the belly (midpart) of a pitcher. It is called the *mahāyogeśvarī mudrā* and is honoured as to be the best among all the *mudrās*." (*BT*).

1383 **ग्रथन-ग्रन्थन-कला**

Grathana-granthana-kalā : the art of garlanding, selecting, and compiling beautiful and precious things and thoughts (*Śukranītisāra*, 4. 308-11).

1384 **ग्रथितं बध्नाति**

Grathitam badhnāti : this is a custom (*Priyadarśikā*, Act. III) still prevailing in India when one wishes to remind oneself of a purpose definitely undertaken. *gāṁtha-bāndhnā* in Hindi.

1385 **ग्रन्थिबन्धन**

Grantibandhana : marriage in which the garments of the bride and bridegroom are tied.

1386 **ग्रन्थिभेद**

Granthibheda : cut-purse, pick-pocket.

1387 **ग्रसन-मुद्रा**

Grasana-mudrā : a type of pose; occurs in *BT* but not defined.

1388 **ग्रामचर्या**

Grāma-caryā : village-ways, sexual enjoyment.

1389 **ग्रामसीमा**

Grāmasīmā : the village boundary. In many parts of India village boundary is a particularly sacred mark of territoriality. A host of godlings and rituals are its ubiquitous symbols. Srinivas mentions a 'familiar deity in Telugu and Tamil villages' whose name, Ellammā, literarlly means "boundary mother" (1952 : 57). He also describes the worship of the boundary stone, *allai-kal*, which is very commonly regarded as a habitation of a local deity, and might be called a shrine or symbol with equal propriety. The central Indian village studied by Mayer, too, had a number of shrines of this kind.

1390 **ग्रामागारम्**

Grāmāgāram : village houses in ancient India were lower and more modest than town ones; their outer walls were covered with a mixture of lime, earth and cow-dung, the last being considered as a purificative agent (Hsüng-Ch'uang : Beal, *op. cit.*I, p.74). The shops were more like street-stalls, and the crowd that passed by their displays were of more humble-stock: farmers returning from the fields, pushing ahead of them a small flock of skinny sheep; ragged foragers, grey with *chatt*, a sickle stick through their belt, carrying home trusses of hay tied around their hips (*Harṣacarita*, p. 239); women balancing on their heads large bundles of forage rolled inside a mat, to be used as animal fodder (depicted in the Kṛṣṇa cavern of Mahābalīpuram); parters trotting along, laden with baskets suspended from each end of a pole carried across the shoulders. Then there were artisans in the process of delivering their merchandise, pedlars transporting their gim crackery in a bag, strolling players looking for a suitable place to present their turns. Cattle mingled freely with the human throng. Heavy wagons drawn by bullocks (*grāmaśakṭa*) rolled among the main streets; there were, as they still are today, massive wooden constructions built by the village carpenter (who was called *tvaṣṭṛ* in the *Vedas* and a *rathakāra* in the *jātakas*), who followed time-honoured traditions in the matter of design. These vehicles were surmounted by hooped ribs covered by matting, and were used particularly for transporting grain at harvest time, the peasants entire family, out in the fields, sought respite from the hot sun by sitting under its awning.

1391 **ग्राम्यधर्म**

Grāmyadharma : village-habit, country-act, sexual intercourse. The *Brahma-vaivarta-Purāṇa* (1.58.75) calls day-time-sex as *grāmya-dharma* (unsophisticated act) and says that it is sinful.

1392 **ग्राम्यम्**

Grāmyam : uncultured. absence of clusters and predominance of simplicity.

1393 **ग्राम्यसुख**

Grāmya-sukha : a vulgar pleasure (*A*, 1.17.20), sleep, sexual intercourse (study its implications on Indian culture in villages).

1394 **ग्राम्या**

Grāmyā : improper speech (defect). (b) the country girl, who charms an anonymous Sanskrit author and accepts :

I grew up in a village,
live in a village,
and can't even imagine
the look of a town,
But I can take
The townsmen from their wives.
I am - what I am.

1395 **ग्रास-वक्त्रा-मुद्रा**

Grāsa-vaktrā mudrā : a type of mouth-gesture; "open mouth as much as you can and thus show all your teeth. This is *grāsavaktrā*" (*BT*).

1396 **ग्रीवा**

Grīvā : neck-movement. It can farm *recaka* also. The gesture of the neck had much psychic and aesthetic value. They are nine; responsible to bring success to other gestures, related to the head, or the face part. They are : *Sama* (natural), *nata* (bent), *unnata* (raised up), *trasra* (broken = slant to side), *recita (moved an shaken), kuñcta(turned backneck with head), añcita* (a neck with the turned back head), vāhita (a neck turned sideways with the face), *nivṛtta* (a neck with the face-front). *VD* (Pt. III. Vol. I, p. 61) appreciates only seven gestures of the neck; as *añcita, recita, mukta, vivṛtta, catura*, prasārita and *stabdha*; of which *añcita* and *recita* are common.

1397 **ग्रीवाकृतिविज्ञान**

Grīvākṛti-vijñāna : sign of the neck If flat, indicates poverty; if veiny and like a parrot, happiness; if like a buffalo's, bravery; if like that of a deer, well-versed in sciences; like a conch, kingship; long-necked voracious eater (*Brahma*, 26.9). The female neck should have three lines covering about four fingers; this is indicative of getting decorations. If the neck is slender, it is indicative of poverty; if long the woman would be unchaste, If the neck is short, her issues will die (*Bhav. P.*). Varāhamihira (*BS*, LXVIII) presents the following features of the neck; one is penniless with a neck that is flat, dry and full of veins; heroic with one like that of a buffalo; meets with one's end by weapons with a neck similar to a bull's; a king with one having three lines or folds (conch-like); and a glutton with a hanging (or long one). Men become wealthy, if their back is neither split or filled with hair; and miserable if it is otherwise. A conch-like neck is thus described:

वालित्रयचितग्रीवः कम्बुग्रीवोऽभिधीयते ॥

vide the following lines written by Utpala :

ग्रीवा च वर्तुला यस्य स नरो धनवान् स्मृतः ।
कम्बुग्रीवा नरा ये तु राजानस्ते न संशयः ॥
दीर्घग्रीवा नरा ये तु तेऽपि दुःखस्य भागिनः ।
वक्रग्रीवा नरा ये ते दाम्भिकाः पिशुनास्तथा ॥
निःस्वस्तु चिपिटग्रीवः शुष्कग्रीवस्तथैव च ।
शूरस्तु महिषग्रीवः शस्त्रान्तो वृषकन्धरः ॥
सुस्निग्धं मांसलं पृष्ठमभग्नं चाप्यरोमशम् ।
सघनानां विपर्यस्तं निर्धनानां प्रकीर्तितम् ॥

See Prahlāda

ग्रीवा च जघनं पृष्ठमूलं जङ्घे तथैव च ।
ह्रस्वानि यस्य चत्वारि पूजामाप्नोति मानवः ॥

A woman whose neck is too short becomes utterly penniless; too long, cause of the extinction of the family; and too broad and flat, cruel;

ह्स्वयातिनिःस्वता दीर्घया कुलक्षयः ।
ग्रीवया पृथूत्थया योषितः प्रचण्डता ॥

(*Bṛhat-Saṁhitā*, LXX.18)

1398 **ग्रीवाभङ्ग**

Grīvābhaṅga : movement of the neck (Kālidāsa, Abhijñāna Śākuntalam, 1,6). A neck functions emically distinct. For example, in 'choke' the open hand grasps the throat but in 'stomach-ache' it presses the stomach.

1399 **ग्रीवा रेचक**

Grīvā recaka : one of the four types of *recaka* where movement of the neck is suggested (*NS*, VIII. 171-175). It is the raising up, lowering and bending sideways and moving round the neck.

1400 **ग्लाना दृष्टि**

Glānā dṛṣṭi : dull glance, a type of *sañcārī-bhāva-dṛṣṭi*. A look with eye-brows and eye-lashes moving lazily and the eyeballs almost shut under eye-lids due to excessive tiredness. It suggests illness, epilepsy, weakness, and dullness (*NS*, VIII. 61-92). The glance is loose, the eyebrows, eyelids and eyelashes are languid moving slowly and the pupils sinking.

1401 **ग्लानि**

Glāni : aversion. one of the transitory states of mind. It is represented by weak voice, lustreless eyes, pale face, slow gait, want of energy, loss of colour of the body, change of voice and others. It is a turning away from something in disgust or dislike; it is also a negative reaction to a specific thing.

घ – Gha

1402 **घट**

Ghaṭa : jar, pitcher; (a) a pot full of water which is used either by itself or in addition to other forms to represent the deity or the formless all pervading spirit. (b) the word *ghaṭa* or vessel is also used to designate the human body, and the space within it (*ghaṭākāśa*) designates the soul. It is held that as there is no difference between the space inside the *ghaṭa* and that outside it, so also there is no difference between the individual and universal soul. Also known as *kumbha* and *pūrṇakumbha*.

1403 **घटक**

Ghaṭaka : one who arranges matrimonial alliances, agent, geneologist.

1404 **घटमान**

Ghaṭamāna : a poet composing miscellaneous verses but not a sustained poem.

1405 **घटाटोप-वाक्याडम्बर**

Ghaṭāṭopa-vākyāḍambara : bombastic use of words, the generality of the *Oḍra-māgadhī pravṛtti* (*Abhinavabhāratī*, I.C.).

1406 **घटिका**

Ghaṭikā: an ancient device to indicate one-hour time. During marriage ceremony, the priest used to enter the chamber where in the *ghaṭikā* (Jar) was kept. It was usually a small vessel with a hole that would let in water; when the *ghaṭikā* sinks it indicates about an hour. Till the time the *ghaṭikā* remained to be sunk, the chanting of *Om* went on (*Śiva*, II 46.3).

1407 **घट्टित-पाद**

Ghaṭṭita pāda : the pose when heel touches the ground. Striking the floor with the heel-part of the foot and is used in rapid dance. Also known as *ghaṭṭita caraṇa* (*SR*, IV. 7.323).

1408 **घट्टितोत्सेध-पाद**

Ghaṭṭitotsedha-pāda : heel-toe movement is indicated. Striking the floor with the heel and the fore-foot. This is used in rapid dance. Also known as *ghaṭitotsedha-caraṇa* (*SR*, IV. 7.323).

1409 **घण्टापथ**

Ghaṇṭāpatha : royal road, highway.

1410 **घण्टारव**

Ghaṇṭā rava : sound of bell. The sounding of the *ghaṇṭā* is mentioned in the *Purāṇas* at typical and specific periods at the time of worship, at the sleep of the god, at incense, at waving the lamp round the god's image, at the bath of the god's image, and at anointing it. The *ghaṇṭā* is the emblem of the goddess Ekānaṁśā, who was three eyed and was created from the body of Pārvatī (*Skanda*, 1.3.19.45) : घण्टाहस्ता त्रिलोचना

Ritual bell made of bronze, employed during worship of deities, especially in some sequences like administering bath (*snāpana*), offering incense (*dhūpa*), waving lights (*nīrājana*), and presentation of food (*naivedya*). The sound of bell is said to be dear to the gods and also to dissolve all demerits (*sarve doṣāh pratīyante*). The bell, when sounded, beckons the gods to come, and drives away evil spirits that abound in that atmosphere :

āgamārtham tu devānām gamanārtham tu rākṣasām

kurvetghaṇṭāravam tatra devatāhvāna lāñchanam

1411 **घनोरू**

Ghanorū : having thick and well-set thighs.

1412 **घर्घररवा**

Ghargharaavā : lady whose voice is rough, the conch-lady (*Pañcaśāyaka*, 1.8).

1413 **घात**

Ghāta : blemishes, a stroke that kills the communicative competence, impediments, defects (*NS*, XXVII.19). (a) The *ghātas* or blemishes are of four kinds : (a) engendered by Fate. (b) occasioned by one's own defective performance. (c) by the malicious action of the rivals and (d) as a result from an unforeseen - accident. Among the *ghātas* which are self-made, Bharata lists the following : an actor forgetting his lines, reciting speeches which are not in the script, losing nerve on the stage, exaggerated display of emotional states, improper movements, slipping or ornaments or head-dress, and the selection of an actor unsuitable to the dramatic role (*NS*, XXVII. 19-37). *Vikramorvaśīya* records how Urvaśī's error spoiled the dramatic performance. At a certain part in the dialogue when she was to confess her love for Viṣṇu (Urvaśī was playing the role of Lakṣmī), with her mind obsessed by her own private love for Pururavā, said the king's name instead of Viṣṇu. Bharatamuni was so enraged at this error and deviation from the text that he cursed Urvaśī and banished her from the Heaven. In the words of the *NS*, this is a *ghāta* which is self made, perpetrated by the actor; and it proves how suicidal a mistake on the part of an actor can be in ruining a performance and his or her own standing as an artiste.

1414 **घुटिका**

Ghuṭikā : knee.

1415 **घुटिकाभरण**

Ghuṭikābharaṇa : ornaments of the ankles were meant for the women only (*NS*). Bharata enumerates them as such: *nūpura* (to be worn below the knee), *kiṅkiṇī* (with small bells), *ghanṭikā*, *ratnajālaka* and gingling *kaṭakas.*

1416 **घूर्ण गण्ड**

Ghūrṇa-gaṇḍa : expanded cheeks, a type of cheek-gesture; it is used in energy and pride.

1417 **घूर्णितकरण**

Ghūrṇita-karaṇa : *valita* of one hand and *dolā* of the other. Feet in *svastika* position and then the legs are extended (*NS*, IV. 92-93, IX. 148). The right hand is moved round in *vartita* and the left in *dolā* and the foot is moved from *svastika.*

1418 **घृत-प्रतीक**

Ghṛta-pratīka : one whose face is glistening with ghee (*AV*, III. 1.18).

1419 **घृत-मुद्रा**

Ghṛta-mudrā : a type of hand-gesture. Place two curved fore-fingers on middle ones and both the thumbs on little ones. This makes the gesture of *ghṛta*-ghee (*VD*).

1420 **घोरचक्षुस्**

Ghoracakṣus : of frightful appearance, having fearful eyes (*TS*, VII. 28.2), having terrible eyes.

1421 **घोरवर्पस्**

Ghoravarpas : a frightful appearance (*TS*, 1. 64.2).

1422 **घोरसंस्पर्श**

Ghorasaṁsparśa : being too hot for touching (*AV*, 1. 64.2).

1423 **घोष**

Ghoṣa : indistinct sound, battle-cry (*TS*, iii 30.16) सं घोषः शृण्वे घुष्यमाणः; घोषा *Ghoṣā* : name of a woman (*TS*, i 122.5); एतन्नामिका ब्रह्मवादिनी noise, proclamation, report, rumour, fame, hut, cow-herd, herdsmen's station : गङ्गायां घोषः (b) the various aspects of sounds are also said to be efficacious in sorcery. Thus, the *ghoṣa* is said to be for cleaning oneself (*Śiva*, V. 26, 44-46).

1424 **घोषक**

Ghoṣaka : ranchers (NS, XVII. 53-57), one who proclaims, crier, bell-man.

1425 **घोषणा**

Ghoṣaṇā : resounding, resonant, sonant (in Grammar).

1426 **घ्राणम्**

Ghrāṇam : nose, odour, smelling. We get interesting messages through smell. We can smell the persons and recognize them. We may not need to taste some food to get a message that it is spoiled, smelling the stuff may be enough for us.

After touch smell is a powerful stimulant. Charming is the freshness of the open hill and forest (in tribal situation), but more charming still, say the Muria youth, is the smell of perspiration, oil, wet earth, a suggestion of urine, all tempered by the bitter-sweet wood-smoke, which is regarded as the peculiar aroma of the *ghotul*. The Oraon *dhumkuria* have a quite different smell in which the odour of urine is much more prominent. The Bison-horn Maria again have a strong, and rather attractive smell not unlike the Savara but quite distinct from the Muria. The *ghotul* smell is unforgettable; it is not unpleasant even to a stranger's nostrils; and boys have told me that they have found it a strong sexual stimulant. 'The smell of the wood-smoke in a girl's hair, how exciting it is' exclaimed a *Chelik* at Markabera. So is the smell of cow-shed clinging to boy or girl, a clean healthy smell with good associations. At Temrugaon the boys loved the scent of marigolds that the *motiari* put in their hair and declared them to be their favourite flower.

No artificial scents are used, and this means that both boys and girls have to be very careful about bodily cleanliness; an unpleasant vaginal odour is mentioned as specially inhibiting to desire; there is a saying *munh sundarī gāṇḍ gandarī*- however beautiful the face, if a girl has a dirty body, she will not be admired.

The smelling symbols of a dog have been well-defined by Varāhamihira (LXXXIX). If a dog smells the left knee, get money, if the right knee he will have quarrels with women; if the left thigh, enjoyment of sexual pleasures; if the right thigh, dissensions with very dear friends.

वामं जिघ्रेज्ज्ञानु ब्रित्तागामाय
स्त्रीभिः साकं विग्रहो दक्षिणं चेत् ।
ऊरुं वामं चेन्द्रियार्थोपभोगः
सव्यं गिघ्रेदिष्ट मित्रैर्विरोधः ॥

1427 **घ्रोणिक हस्त**

Ghroṇika-hasta : smelling hand; single hand-gesture in *Hastamuktāvalī;* does not occur in *NS.*

च Ca

1428 **चकित**

***Cakita*:** confused. To be afraid or confused, for one reason or the other, in the presence of the hero (*Sāhityadarpaṇa*, 3.130). It is the disturbed, emotional and unclear thinking.

1429 **चकित नेत्र**

***Cakita netra*:** large eyes. The women of Ujjain have large eyes and through graceful movements they allure the cloud-messenger (*Pūrva Megha*, 29), *Cakita-hariṇī-prekṣaṇā* (*Megha*, 84).

1430 **चकोर**

***Cakora*:** The partridge had the reputation of feeding on the rays of moon in ancient India, said to subsist on moon-beams.

1431 **चक्र**

***Cakra*:** (a) one of the subtle centres of the body (*SR* 1.3.23). (b) one of the seven types of *bhramarī*. (c) a magic circle to protect a person away from miseries. Lakṣmaṇa draws such a circle to keep Sītā safe when she urges him to go after the golden deer. (d) a mystical circle according to *Tantras*. The human body is supposed to have the following cakras: *mūlādhāra, svādhiṣṭhāna, maṇipūra, anāhata, viśuddha* and *ājñā*. (e) wheel. The antiquity of the wheel and its symbolism goes back to the Vedic period. The wheel is symbolic of life, ever-renewing itself in a cycle (*bhava-cakra*) of time as producer and consumer of everything (*kāla-cakra*) of invariable law governing matter and energy in the nerve-channels (*nāḍi-cakra*), of the cyclical progression of zodiacs (*rāśī-cakra*), and of the fortunes of human beings (*bhāgya-cakra*). (f) used in a variety of senses, symbolising the endless rotation of Śakti. In *Tāntric* rituals there are different *cakrasthānas* in which male and female aspirants assemble and perform the rites of *pañcamakāra*. (g) the term *cakra* is also used to denote *yantras* (various mystical diagrams) which are variously known as *trikoṇa, aṣṭakoṇa* and so forth. (h) the term is also used to denote nerve-plexuses within the body. (i) the *cakra*, literally 'wheel', has various meanings; the universal law, it's reflection in the moral law of man; the universal power, and the focus of spiritual power in human consciousness ; the universal sun, and the inner light of illumination. The rim of *cakra* symbolizes the world in its entirety, infinite movement, the unending cycle of life, death and rebirth. The spokes represent the different paths which led from the rim to the hub, from movement to peace, from sorrow to *nirvāṇa*, truth, realization. Thus the wheel represents tolerance, law, sovereignty, the universal and the individual, stability and movement. It also stands for the spiritual faculties of man, there are seven inner *cakras* of psychic power. When these hidden forces of mind and body are released the individual becomes a *cakravartin*. (Fig. 1431)

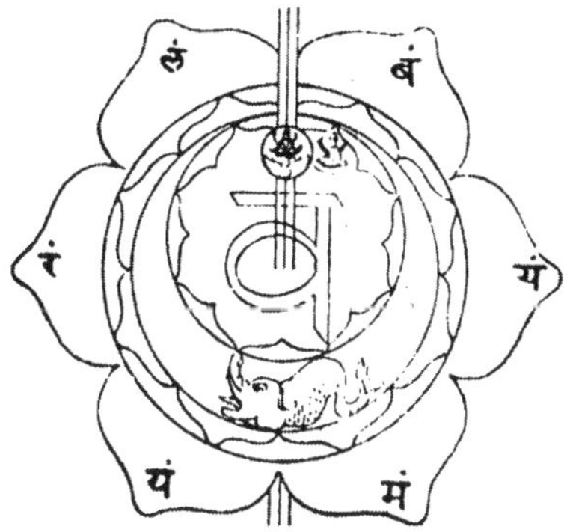

Fig. – (1431)

1432 **चक्रगति**

***Cakragati*:** rotation, revolution.

1433 **चक्रमण्डलकरण**

***Cakramaṇḍala karaṇa*:** derived from the *aḍḍitā cārī*, but the definition seems incomplete. The hands are in *uromaṇḍala*. The name *cakramaṇḍala* really gives a clue to the *karaṇa*; for this is an acrobatic position in which the arms pass between the thighs to touch the ground (*NS*, IV. 113b-114a), IX. 204, X. 23). *Aḍḍitā cārī* is performed with the arms hanging and the body bent. It is used in haughty movements.

1434 **चक्रमुद्रा**

***Cakra-mudrā*:** "turn round the pair of hands with two extended fingers, tied together with alternate palms, placed in an appropriate position. This is called the *cakra-mudrā*. It is a very favourite gesture of mine, as well as my attendants" (*BT*). (b) "Make two wrists well-connected and two hands going in two opposite directions in the position of clenchen fists. When they are thus moved repeatedly in an extending style; it is called *cakra mudrā*, applicable to wipe out storm, the thunder, clouds, etc. This is also a symbol suggesting a high class *tāntrika* assembly." (*BT*). (c) Join tips of the thumb and the middle on symbolized *cakra*, the wheel of Viṣṇu (*VD*). (d) Extending all the fingers, join them, back on the palm. This is a *cakra* (*VD*).

1435 **चक्रवाक**

***Cakravāka*:** crane, ruddy goose. The couple of these birds are referred to as model of conjugal love in post-*Vedic* literature. A love-bird that becomes separated from its mate at night. The particular bird used in the love-episode is the cakravāka the most appropriate, for according to Indian folk-lore the cakravāka is a lovebird who becomes separated from his mate every night and cries mournfully for her until dawn, thus symbolizing erotic love in separation. The burning of the Kāma/Agni bird by an ascetic's glance appears in a myth as well : "A forest-dweller of great *tapas* was resting under the branches of a tree when a female crane released her droppings on him. The sage became enraged and burnt the bird to ashes with a glance" (*Kathāsaritsāgara,* 56. 170-2). This relates to the Śiva's myth burning the Kāma.

1436 **चक्रवाक-मुद्रा**

Cakravāka-mudrā : gesture indicating a kind of pelican. *alapadma*-hands fluttered indicates the pelican bird (*Mirror of Gesture*, pp. 50-51).

1437 **चक्रहस्त**

Cakra hasta : both hands gesture (*Abhinayadarpaṇa*) not mentioned by *NS.* The palms of *ardhacandra hasta* are put across each other, they make the gesture of *cakra.* It indicates the *cakra* of Viṣṇu. *Cakra* is a wheel, disc or circle. Usually the Sun wheel, the characteristic symbol of Viṣṇu. It is also a Buddhist symbol suggestive of the *Dharmacakra-pravartana* or setting the wheel of law in motion.

1438 **चक्राह्व-परिष्वजनम्**

Cakrāhva pariṣvajanam : Dāmodaragupta (*Kuṭṭanīmatam* 581) has introduced this *cakravāka* type of embrace experienced by a slender lady.

1439 **चक्षु**

Cakṣu : sight, eye. (a) sight is an apprehension, it is seized by *rūpa* (aspect as an over-apprehender, as indeed by the eye (*cakṣu*) one sees things (*rūpāṇi*). (*Bṛhd. Upaniṣad,* III. 2.3. and 5.). (b) the receptor of vision.

1440 **चक्षुर्मन्त्र**

Cakṣurmantra : (a) bewitching with eyes, (b) magic of the eye. (Fig. 1440)

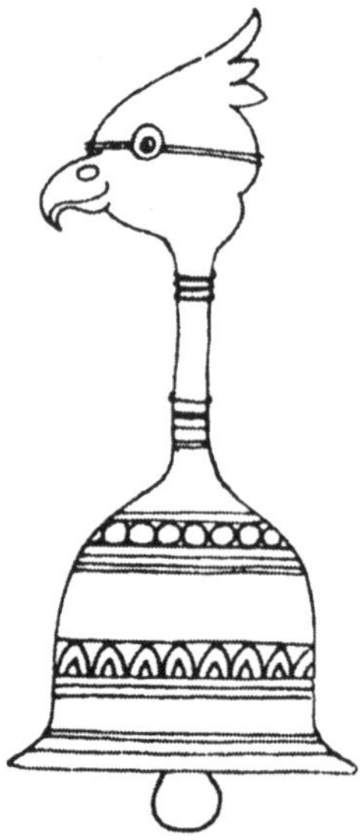

Fig. – (1440)

1441 **चक्षुर्विषय**

Cakṣurviṣaya : object of eye. *Yasminneva muhūrte cakṣurviṣayam gatosi me sakhyāḥ* (*Kuṭṭanīmatam,* 288). The most fundamental primary mode of interpersonal encounter is the interaction between two pairs of eyes and what is mediated by this interaction. For it is mainly here, throughout the wide ranges of social encounter, that people actually meet.

1442 **चक्षु-विज्ञान**

Cakṣu-vijñāna : The science of perception (Buddhist belief). In the *Kathāvatthu* (XVIII. 9) the Mahāsaṅghikas are said to have held the opinion that the organs of sense perceive directly and not by their perceptive faculty (*Vijñāna*). Thus also the view of Vaibhāṣikas. The *Śaila*-schools and the Theravādins hold the opposite view.

1443 **चक्षुर्व्यापार**

Cakṣuvyāpāra : action of the eye is manifold in Bharata as depicted in this treatise : such as

a) *apāṅga* (side-glance) कनखियाँ
b) *ākekarā* (half-closed) तिरछीनजर
c) *udabhrū* (with eyelashes upturned) ऊपर को पलक
d) *unmukha* (raised upwards)
e) *kuñcita* : सिकुडी
f) *sāsra* उत्कण्ठा एवं व्यारसने आंसुषोवाली

Varāhamihira (LXVIII) has counted the *spandana* (throbbing) of the eyes and has predicted certain personalities :

द्विमात्रस्पन्दिनो ये तु धनिनस्ते प्रकीर्तिताः ।
त्रिमात्रस्पन्दिनो ज्ञेयाः पुरुषाः सुखजीविनः ॥
चतुर्मात्रनिमेषश्च धनवान् परिकीर्तितः ।
दीर्घायुषो धर्मरताः पञ्चमात्रनिमेषिणः ॥

1444 **चक्षूराग**

Cakṣūrāga : eye-love, love at first sight, love as manifested by the exchange of glances (*HC,* VI). *Uttararāmacarita* (V) defines the term : *bhūyasā jīvidharma yadrasamayī kasyacit kvacit prītiḥ; yatra laukikānām upacārastārā maitrakam cakṣūrāga iti.*

1445 **चटु**

Caṭu : flattering words (Daṇḍī, 2.35), agreeable speech, amorous chattering.

1446 **चटुल नेत्र**

Caṭula netra : vivacious eyebrow (*Uttararāmacarita,* 3.19). A circular movement of the eyes in which the eyeball makes a complete circle. Unsteady eyes.

1447 **चण्ड-सम्भोग-रत**

Caṇḍa-saṁbhoga-rata : intense carnal desire, quality of the Horse-man (*Pañcasāyaka*, 2.11).

1448 **चण्डाल**

Caṇḍāla : (a) name of the caste sprung from the union of śūdra male and a Brāhmaṇa female. (b) offspring of an unmarried woman. (c) one born as a result of a man's union with a *sagotra* girl. (d) son of one who, after becoming an ascetic, comes back to the householder's life (*Smṛti*). (e) *caṇḍālī* is the female energy having the force of fire which resides in *nirmāṇa* according to *Tāntric* Buddhism. It kindles the *Saṁbhoga-cakras*.

1449 **चण्डेश-मुद्रा**

Caṇḍeśa-mudrā : if the fore-fingers are bent in the *añjali*, it is *caṇḍeśa* (*VD*). *Caṇḍeśa* is the name of Śiva and is found in iconic form. He is the chief of the host of *gaṇas*.

1450 **चतुर करण**

Catura karaṇa : left hand in *alapallava* and right hand in *catura*, feet movement is *udghaṭṭita*, the right shank is bent in *nikuṭṭita* or *kuñcita* (*NS*, IV. 99-100, IX. 91, 93, 266). The left hand is in *añcita* (*i.e. alapallava*), the right hand in *catura* and the right foot in *kuṭṭita*. It is used in the *sūcī* gesticulation of Vidūṣaka indicating wonder. (Fig. 1450)

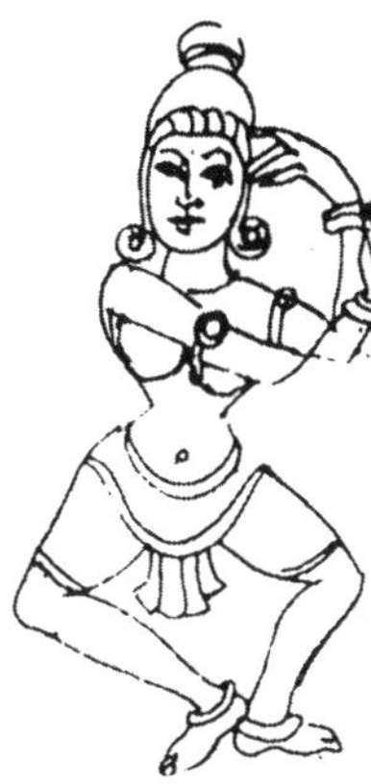

Fig. – (1450)

1451 **चतुर ग्रीवा**

Catura grīvā : sweet and placid movement of the neck indicates placidity and satisfaction (*VD*, III. 1.61).

1452 **चतुर (भ्रू)**

Catura : the widening of the eyebrows; extending the brows in a charming fashion. The movement of the eyebrow along the horizontal plane (side to side). Eyebrows are pleasantly extended; to move and expand eyebrows slightly in a pleasing way. It suggests love, sportiveness, gentle objects, awakening and pleasing touch (*NS*, VIII. 113-123).

1453 **चतुरस्र**

Caturasra : a place within four lines, astrological term, four-cornered, symmetrical, proportionate, handsome.

1454 **चतुरस्रक स्थान**

Caturasraka sthāna : a type of posture mentioned in *Vikramorvaśīya*.

1455 **चतुरस्र-नृत्त-हस्त**

Caturasra nṛtta-hasta : a type of hand gesture in dancing, found in dance poses of sculpture (*NS*). When two hands in the *Kaṭakāmukha* style are held before the breast at a distance of eight fingers in a parallel position of the shoulders and the elbows of both the hands, it is called the *caturasra* (*NS*, IX. 176-197).

1456 **चतुर हस्त**

Catura hasta : the clever hand, semi-circle hand. The palm is faced outwards and hollowed. The first, second and third fingers and thumb are bent like a hooded snake, and the little finger is extended straight. It is used to express the sense of sorrow, policy, discipline, penance, moving conjecture, truth, playful, converse, copper, sweetness, face, breaking, etc. Three-fingers are extended, the little-finger is up and the thumb is at the root of the middle-finger. All these make the gesture *catura-hasta*. This suggests the sense of eyes, efficient, impartial, very clever, young boys and girls, cleverness, reviewing, appropriate words and diet, truth and priority. By one, or two, or a little cycling hand or hands, reserved and practical for the character, rejected behaviour and shame, smile of eyes, stretching of a lotus petal, or a leaf and the ears of a deer may be indicated. All these are to be demonstrated with the half of the *catura-hasta*. In addition to them, it suggests devices (*līlā*), interest, love, recollection, intellect, thoughtfulness, mercy, growth, epithet, desire, love-making, judgement, propriety, piety, cleverness, sweetness, generosity tenderness, happiness, conduct, cessation, news, reason, dress, green grass, a little property, and poverty, sexual intercourses, fault and quality, young age, houses, wife and various colours are to be suggested by the gesture *catura* (*NS*, IX. 87-94). By raising the *catura* gesture up, it indicates white; making a circle, it indicates red and yellow and by rubbing it with another, it indicates blue or black.

Single hand gesture. In *NS* (IX. 184) it has two variants : one is the *catura*, the other is derived from the *sarpaśiras hasta*. *Bālarāmabharata* derives it from the *mṛgaśīrṣa hasta*. The lotus petals in *Ratnāvalī* (II) are shown by this gesture.

Here three fingers are stretched, little finger raised up and the thumb in the midst of them.

1457 **चतुरुन्नत हस्त**

Caturunnata hasta : single hand gesture derived from the *patāka*, only mentioned in *Bālarāmabharata*.

1458 **चतुर्दश लोक मुद्रा**

Caturdaśa-loka mudrā: Fourteen cosmic spheres, seven upper spheres and seven lower spheres. Seven upper *lokas* (spheres) are : *bhuḥ, bhuvaḥ, svar, maha, jana, tapas,* and *satya*. To include them use the *patāka* hands twisted upward as per the seven scales in order as mentioned here. Similarly, there are seven lower spheres of worlds as : *atala, vitala, sutala, talatala, mahātala, rasātala, pātala*. To indicate them also exercise the twisted styles of the *patāka* hand moving downwards in order of the seven scales as mentioned above (*Mirror of Gesture*, p. 48).

1459 **चतुष्पथ**

Catuṣpatha : cross-road. The cross-road is one where four roads meet. The worship of a *catuṣpatha* (or a *catvara*) has been enjoined for prosperity and freedom from evils (*Matsya P.* 204. 25-27).

Like the cross-roads, the place where three roads meet (*trika*) is said to be special. At these places, female powers, both good and evil, are supposed to reside (*Sk. P.* 1.2.47. 79-80). It is said that the women who weep at the *catvara* or a *trika* fall a victim to evil powers; and if the women are pregnant, the foetus is taken away and eaten by these evil powers (*Sk. P.* VI. 88. 44-53). The belief in *catvara* or *trika* can still be noted among the tribes.

1460 **चन्द्रकला-हस्त**

Candrakalā hasta : single hand gesture (*Abhinayadarpaṇa*), not occurs in *NS*. If the thumb is separated from the *sūcīmukha*, it makes the *candrakalā*. It is used to indicate the Moon, the mouth, the measurement of a *pradeśa* (the length from the thumb tip to the fore-finger's tip) and a thing of that length, the crown of Śiva, the river Gaṅgā and a club (*Abhinayadarpaṇa*, verse 132-133). *Candrakalā* is the symbol of crescent moon which exists on the crown of most *Tāntric* goddesses as the source of ever-flowing nectar. It is also found on the matted locks of Śiva (*Mahānirvāṇa*, XIII. 7).

1461 **चन्द्रभागा-हस्त**

Candrabhāgā hasta : name of the river Cenāb. The hand moving upward and downward denotes this river (*Mirror of Gesture*, p. 48).

1462 **चन्द्र-मुद्रा**

Candra mudrā : gesture symbolizing the Moon. The ring-finger curved half symbolizes the Moon (*VD*).

1463 **चन्द्रलेखा**

Candralekhā : (a) digit of the moon. (b) particular nailscratch in the coitus: *grīvāyām stanapṛṣṭhe ca nakhapadasanniveśo ardhacandrākaḥ sarvasthāneṣu nātidīrghā lekhā* (*Kāmasūtra*).

1464 **चन्द्र-हस्त**

Candra-hasta : If an *alapadma* is in the left and *patāka* is in the right, it is the Moon (*AD*, 216-225).

1465 **चपलता**

Capalatā : fickle - mindedness. one of the transitory states. It is manifested by harsh words, rebuke, beating, killing, taking prisoner, goading, etc.

1466 **चपेट**

Capeṭa : a blow with the palm of hand.

1467 **चपेट-मुद्रा**

Capeṭa-mudrā : a symbol of beating. The palm is extended menacingly in the position of giving a slap.

1468 **चपेटाघात**

Capeṭā ghāta : the palm. Pronation and supination refer to the direction of the palm as a result of wrist - rotation. If the hands are positioned horizontally, pronation refers to downward (and inward) direction of the palms, and supination refers to upward (and outward) direction. As for the wrist itself, pronate wrist appears as a point of reference in 'what time is it' and contrasts with the whole wrist in 'bracelet'. This constitutes only an analogous contrast, however, and no gesture involving contact with the 'palm side' of the wrist (supinate wrist)appears in my collection.

(b) *capeṭadāna* is also a *mudrā* or hand-pose found in certain Buddhist icons which show the right hand menacingly extended upwards, just as though it is ready to slap someone.

1469 **चमत्कार**

Camatkāra : when five limiting conditions of the individual subject are removed, one experiences *camatkāra* literary delight. The supernatural and unexplicable joy produced by a literary composition. It is the essence of *rasa*. (b) surprise, charm.

1470 **चरकाचार्य**

Carakācārya : One who instructs how to dance on the tip of a bamboo (*T Br.* III. 4.16). *Carakas* were travelling scholars mentioned in the Pāṇini's *Aṣṭādhyāyī* who after completing their education used to wander in different countries to gain experience. In the Pāli texts *carakas* are replaced by *parivrājakas.*

1471 **चरण**

Caraṇa : (a) steps. (*A D*). (b) various schools of the *Veda.* (c) a body of people who, though pledged to the reading and study of a particular *śākhā* or branch, have a wider curriculum which may include other texts. (d) features of feet *caraṇalakṣaṇam.* Varāhamihira gives the following characteristics of a king's feet:

अस्वेदनौ मृदुतलौ कमलोदराभौ
श्लिष्टाङ्गुली रुचिरताम्रनखौ सुपार्ष्णी ।
उष्णौ शिराविरहितौ सुनिगूढगुल्फौ
कूर्मोन्नतौ च चरणौ मनुजेश्वरस्य ॥

The following verses occur in the *Prahlāda-Sāmudrika* relating to the feet:

आरक्तमृदुनीरन्ध्र ऋज्वङ्गुलिकरांघ्रिकः ।
न स्विन्नपाणिपादश्च भाग्यवान् भवति ध्रुवम् ॥
कूर्मपृष्ठाग्रपदवान् किंचिदुष्णांघ्रिरेव च ।
सद्बुद्धिस्सुन्दरो याश्च स भवेज्जनवन्दितः ॥

Varāhamihira further comments : "Poverty and grief are produced by feet that have the shape of winnowing baskets, that are very rough, that have white nails, that are crooked or long, that are full of veins, that are very dry and have far - removed toes. Travelling is the effect of having the feet that are raised in the middle; destruction of the family is the result of tawny feet; and cohabitation with forbidden women, of those that are yellow."

1472 **चरणन्यास**

Caraṇa-nyasa : footsteps.

1473 **चरणभेदः**

Caraṇabhedaḥ : various styles of feet. The *NS* devised the functions, of the complete leg-part into three parts: the *ūru* (thigh), the *jaṅghā* (foreleg) and the *pāda* (feet); but *SR* (IV. 7. 92-95) included them into one *i.e. caraṇabhedaḥ* as *sama, añcita, kuñcita, sūcī, agratala sañcara, udghaṭṭita, tāḍita, ghaṭitotsedha, ghaṭṭita, mardita, agraga, pārṣṇiga and pārśvaga.* The first five styles of feet excluding the *sūcī* are the same with the *NS* and the rest eight are the special contributions of the *SR.*

1474 **चरणस्पर्श**

Caraṇasparśa : Touching the feet, a common method of greeting in the village and tribal regions. A younger woman meeting an elder will touch her feet, and the elder will then kiss her on the forehead and on each cheek. If they have not met for some time they will weep. When husband and wife meet after an absence the wife touches her husband's feet with her hand and carries it to her forehead, but the husband makes no demonstration. Indians kiss their children.

In the Halba Society, the bridegroom's father visits the bride and washes her big toes first with milk and then with water. After this the mother and father of the bride come and wash the feet of the couple with milk and water.

Daily social relations in the village are marked by other numerous gestures of deference. Some of these gestures mark men as higher than women; others mark parents as higher than children. I am told that when married couples arise in the morning, the wife symbolically takes the dust from her husband's feet. When a son departs from the village, he takes the dust from the feet of both parents.

The offender may also spring forward and with his right hand symbolically takes the dust from the headman's feet (in *pañcāyata* situation) and licks it from his fingers.

Touching someone's feet symbolises respect. It is an emotional act. It is a gesture of love, not obeisance only. Of course, with the spread of western culture this tradition will not survive long.

1475 **चरणामृत**

Caraṇāmṛta : water with which either an image has been washed or the feet of a Brāhmaṇa.

1476 **चरित्र-बन्धक**

Caritra-bandhaka : a mortgage. In it the creditor relying on the honesty of the debtor, lends a big amount against the mortgage of a small property. Or, the debtor, relying on the honesty of the creditor, borrows a small sum by mortgaging a big property (*A*).

1477 **चरैवेति**

Caraiveti : march on, conquering and to conquer; the capacity of man to move out of his frontiers in order to live abroad. This indeed constitutes the celebration of *Aitareya Brāhmaṇa* (VII, 15). Cult of "march on". During the five thousand years or so exhibited here the Indian peoples seemed all the time to carry out in life. This ideal of "go on" and to function, so to say, as the living embodiments of "social mobility", both horizontal and vertical. All these movements from region to region and family to family could not but set in motion strong demographic convention-currents, leading very often to metabolistic re-arrangements. The fall of the high and the elevation of the low. Hinduism has always proved to be a proselytilizing religion and culture embodying the spirit of "March on". It has always been on the go, "conquering and to conquer", fresh regions and races. From the seventh to thirteenth century Hindu culture was making converts not only within the still un-Hindu nooks and corners of continental India but also among the most heterogenous peoples of Greater India. In the thirteenth and fourteenth centuries the *caraiveti* or expansion of Hindu culture was like-wise in evidence in the new or modern Indian literatures. The message of Rāmdās is thus ideologically akin to and sociologically identical with, the *Aitareya Brāhmaṇa* (VII. 15) cult of *caraiveti* for Hindu culture, of which thousand and one expressions have been encouraged in the diverse regions of Indian all through the ages.

Spatial mobility - so highly developed among nomadic foodgatherers - serves thus as a means to neutralize the causes of social friction. The person at variance with a kinsman or fellow tribesman experiences no difficulty in moving to another group, and tensions lesser or disappear when face-to-face contact is broken off.

1478 **चर्चरी**

Carcarī : (a) both song and dance in a high-pitched voice (*Karpūramañjari*). (b) striking of the palms. (c) joyful and playful speech.

1479 **चर्पट**

Carpaṭa : open palm of the hand with fingers extended.

1480 **चर्पटिका**

Carpaṭikā : the *capātī* signal: The *capātī* - signal was more widespread. It was the flat unleavened bread made of wheat, maize or barley flour, which constitutes a staple of the popular diet in many regions of the subcontinent. Its circulation during the winter of 1856-57, in what was then the north-western provinces, the scene of the great disturbances of the next two years, has been publicized more than any other sign of an Indian rebellion for reasons not only of its intrinsic importance but also of a historic miscognition. A symptom of collective anxiety and uneasiness in an agrarian society poised on the brink of a violent upheavel, it was regarded by some as the index of a conspiracy behind the mutiny. This error has however had its uses: by mistaking the sign of a spreading unrest among the peasantry for that of a sepoy rebellion it has helped to underline the ambiguity generated by their overlap.

Clearly we have an instance here of a visual sign acquiring a new meaning in much the same way as 'shifts in application' of words and figurative usage tend to generate polygemy in natural languages. The power of analogy seems to have helped to shift the sense of circulating *capātī* from pathology to politics: a carrier of one kind of catastrophe it came now to symbolize, by semantic slide, a catastrophe of an altogether different kind and the calamity that had overtaken the Marāṭhā empire was believed to be about to visit to the British too. The sign was thus assigned a predictive function - the function of an omen exuding evil forebodings.

1481 **चर्वणा**

Carvaṇā : synonymous of *abhivyakti* means *vītavighnapratīti* cognition rendered from obstacles, the *vibhāvas* which are designated as *vighnaprasāraka*. Gradually, as obstacles disappear, the state of gradual deployment manifests like a rumination of grass by the cow.

1482 **चलन-दृष्टि**

Calana dṛṣṭi : trembling glance; a type of eye-gesture in which movement of the pupil is suggested, occurs in bhayānaka rasa. In calana, eyeball-movement is used to express states and sentiments. The eyelids are drawn up and the eyeballs are trembling.

1483 **चलन्मणिबन्ध**

Calanmaṇibandha : the combination of the outward and inward movement.

1484 **चलन्मधुकर-हस्त**

Calanmadhukara—hasta : single hand gesture (*Hastamuktāvali*) same as *bhramarī* of *NS.*

1485 **चलित-भ्रुकुटि**

Calita bhrukuṭi : tremulous eyebrows; a type of *bhrukuṭi*-movement.

1486 **चलित शिरस्**

Calita śiras : tremulous head, movement of the head.

1487 **चलित संस्थान**

Calita saṁsthāna : the moving crooked moving pose (*VD*).

1488 **चलितासन**

Calitāsana : a type of tremulous posture.

1489 **चलितोरु**

Calitoru : movement of the chest has been recorded by *Bālarāmabharata*. *Calita* is a slight movement of the chest which can be used by excitement (*romāñca*) etc.

1490 **चलु**

Calu : mouthful of water, *cullū* in Hindi.

1491 **चाक्षुष-व्यवहार**

Cākṣuṣa-vyavahāra : visual behaviour:

An icy glance, a seductive or a pleading stare, and inquisitive look, shifty eyes - are all inferences made from observations of another's visual behaviour. Whether intended for effect or the result of observer's attributions, these are impressions often conveyed by "that certain look". The significance of the eyes is noted by Heron (1970:244) in his philosophical essay on the gaze: "The most fundamental primary mode of interpersonal encounter is the interaction between two pairs of eyes and what is mediated by this interaction. For it is mainly here, throughout the wide ranges of social encounter, that people actually meet".

1492 **चाक्षुषशास्त्र**

Cākṣuṣa śāstra : the science of seeing, Ophthalmology. A *Gāndharvic* science first communicated by Manu to Soma who passed it on to Citraratha, who in turn revealed it to Arjuna, who secured it without any rigid vow or penance. Citraratha acquired it after sever austerities. By means of this power one enabled to see whatever one wished to see.

1493 **चाक्षुषी-दीक्षा**

Cākṣuṣī-dīkṣā : glance-initiation. A form of initiation in which the *guru* or preceptor having concentrated his mind on the supreme being converts the disciple with only one glance. It is otherwise called *dṛk-dīkṣā* (*Kulārṇava,* XIV., *Śāradātilaka* V. 127-140).

1494 **चाटु**

Cāṭu : pretty speech, flattery, coaxing; Cāṭukāra 'flatterer'.

1495 **चातक**

Cātaka : the cātaka bird is known to drink only the drops of rain in svāti *nakṣatra.*

1496 **चातक-मुद्रा**

Cātaka-mudrā : the *lāṅgula* or *kāṅgula*-hand fluttered indicates a cātaka, a kind of sparrow, *(Mirror of Gesture,* pp.50-51).

1497 **चातुरी**

Cāturī : subtlety. It is true that subtlety is a Hindu characteristic. During the Muslim and British domination the Hindus, a subject race, had to strain their wits to the utmost to be able to live in peace with their rulers. Hence they had developed a characteristic evasiveness towards all strangers. Among themselves, however, they are more outspoken and straight-forward. Hindu mercantile communities, it is true, do not always believe that honesty is the best policy; but the merchants all over the world are subtle, secretive, and evasive, though courteous and polite.

1498 **चामर-मुद्रा**

Cāmara-mudrā : "Press hard the right hand taking it by the left. From the hand with its fingers extended, make an alternation by a half-finger. When this is moved again and again, it is called the *cāmara-mudrā" (BT).* (b) if the middle finger drops from the *kapiṭṭha* hand, it is the *cāmara-mudrā* (gesture of the tail of *cāmarī*) which symbolizes a Vaiṣṇavite deity (VD). *Cāmara* or the fly-whisk consisting of the tail of the *yāk.* It is used during the performance of any worship (*Agni,* 245. 1-2).

1499 **चारिका**

Cārikā : women attendants in the royal palace were divided into three classes, *viz. anucārikā, paricārikā* and *saṁcārikā* (*NS,* XXIII. 53-58).

1500 **चारित्र**

Cāritra : certain rules of moral behaviour recorded in Hemacandra's *Yogaśāstra* in which we have an interpretation of the five Jain vows. Certain external rules of conduct are also included in this category, *e.g. īryyā* (precaution while walking to prevent oneself from treading on insects, etc.), *bhāṣā* (to talk pleasantly), *iṣaṇa* (to beg alms in proper monastic manners), *dānasamiti* (inspection of seats to avoid transgression), *utsargasamiti* (careful movement of the body), *manogupti* (to remove all false thoughts), *vāggupti* (absolute silence), *kāyagupti* (steadiness of the body), etc.

1501 **चारी**

Cārī : the movement of the lower limbs. The word *cārī,* derived from root *car* (to move) denotes the aggregate of various graceful movements of the feet, shanks, thighs and hips performed simultaneously. It is the unit of movement of the human body. Bharata devotes one chapter to this and says that "whatever has been prescribed as *nāṭya* is included in the *cārī* and no part of it can take place without the same" (*NS,* X.5). Since *cārī* is also a part of a system of exercise, its various forms are related to one another and cannot be considered in isolation. The *cārī* results from movement with one foot, movement of both feet produce a *karaṇa.* Thus, *cārī* is a link between the static positions indicated by the term *sthānaka* and cadences of movement denoted by the term *karaṇa. Abhinayadarpaṇa* mentions eight types of *cārī. Cārīs* may be *mārga* (classical or standard) and deśī(regional). The latter is divided into two classes, *viz. bhaumī* (terrestrial) and *ākāśī* (aerial). A kind of *bhaumī cārī* is *samapāda.* In it one has to stand with the feet close together, the toe-nails on a level. A kind of *ākāśī cārī* is *alāta.* In it one foot is stretched backward with its sole facing the other thigh. Then its heel is brought down to the ground on its side.

The *cārī* is basically an aesthetic device of the artistic representation of the dance-culture; but its direct aim is to find out an interesting way for body-building. No *cārī* is complete, if it is not inspired with different exhibitions of *mudrās*; a *tāṇḍava*, or a *karaṇa.* It is never appreciated, if it is not performed according to the rule of the *cārī-maṇḍala.* Technically the movement of a foot in a dance are called the *cārī;* it is a *karaṇa*, which is exhibited by two feet. A series of a dance with some *karaṇas*, is called a *khaṇḍa* and by three or four *khaṇḍas* a *cārī-maṇḍala* (a cycle of *cārī*-dance) is completed. There is no action in a dance-drama, which does not come within the purview of a *cārī.* All the actions of dances in Indian dramaturgy are devised in accordance with the rules of the *cārī* (*NS*, X.51-54).

Cārī is the movement of the limbs below the hip. In *cārī* the movement of the foot is prominent, which is accompanied by the movements of shank, thigh, and also waist. Such movement of one foot is called *cārī.* Both the feet movement together would be a *karaṇa.* The single *cārī* movement related to each other constitute *vyāyāma* (exercise).

The importance of *cārī* is summed up in *NS* (X.6):

yadetat prastutam nāṭyam taccārīśveva saṁjñitam
nahi caryā vinā kiñcinnāṭye aṅgam sampravartate

1502 **चारु दर्शना**

Cāru-darśanā : a good-looking woman. (Fig. 1502)

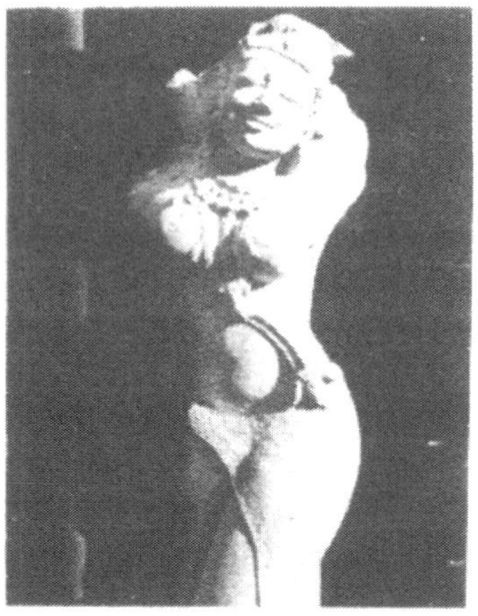

Fig. – (1502)

1503 **चारु हासिनी**

Cāru hāsini : sweetly smiling, name of a metre also.

1504 **चालक**

Cālaka : when employed with *recakas* (*NS.* V.) without loss of grace, *vartanās* (q. v.) are called *cālakas.* Kallīnātha following Kohala describes fifty *cālakas.*

1505 **चालक-बाहु**

Cālaka bāhu : the swinging of the arms.

1506 **चालन दृष्टि**

Cālana : a type of glance by the movement of the eyeball, movement of the eyeballs in fear or joy (*NS*, VIII. 92-105).

1507 **चाष्**

Cāṣ : blue jay (bird). The flight of the cāṣa bird to the right of a person or the sight of the cāṣa when a man starts on a journey was an omen indicating prosperity (*HC*, VII).

1508 **चाषगति चारी**

Cāṣagati cārī : Foot in *samapāda* position. A light jump: first right foot move front and back and then left foot back and front. One *tāla* distance movement, *cāṣagati maṇḍala.* The right foot is put forward one *tāla* and then drawn back two *tālas* and then the left foot drawn back with a slight jump to meet the right. Bharata (*NS*, 10.18) defines it thus: "The right foot is put forward and then taken back and front similarly". But since this is not too clear *Abhinava* (*Ibid.*) explains thus: "The right foot is put forward by a span (*tāla*) and drawn by two spans, then simultaneously with jumping movements both the feet approach each other a little and separate, (or) separate and approach each other. This is termed *cāṣagati* and is used in frightened movements etc. *Cāṣ* is the Sanskrit version of bluejay (bird).

1509 **चित्त-वृत्ति**

Citta-vṛtti : fugitive emotions and creature-images, fluctuations of the mind, mind and mental discipline.

1510 **चित्तविक्षेपक्रिया**

Cittavikṣepakriyā : acts of mental derailment have been discussed by Pāṇini through the rule (*Aṣṭādhyāyī*, 8.2.97) governing a particular accent for a particular period.

1511 **चित्तवृत्ति**

Cittavṛtti : disposition of mind, inclination.

1512 **चित्तासङ्‌ग**

Cittāsaṅga : attachment of the mind; also *manaḥ saṅga.*

1513 **चित्तोद्रेक**

Cittodreka : pride, arrogance.

1514 **चित्र**

Citra : painting. It is known as manifestation of whole body together with its curves and tapering limbs in the idol.

1515 **चित्रक**

Citraka : painting on the forehead. It is a kind of painting put on the forehead by ladies (*Sarvasvakavikulānanda-bhāṇa*, p. 51). It is different from *tilaka* applied by ladies on their foreheads. It is prepared with musk and other spicy articles.

1516 **चित्रकथा**

Citrakathā : charming or entertaining story.

1517 **चित्रकला**

Citra-kalā : the art of painting (*Śukranītisāra*, 4.320-22).

1518 **चित्रगत**

Citra-gata : represented (in a work of art) in a painting or picture.

1519 **चित्ररतासन**

Citraratāsana : *The Kāmasūtra* (2.6.35-46) describes many types of congress which are popularly known as *citrarata: sthitarata, avalambitaka, dhainukamāsana, aiṇey—am, chāgalam, darbhākrāntam, mārjaralalitakam, vyāghravaskhandham, gajopamarditam, varāhadhṛṣṭakam, turagādhirūḍhakam, saṁghāṭakam, gauyūthikam, adhoratam.* All erotic writers accept these and expand the number of postures.

1520 **चित्राभास**

Chitrābhāsa : under *citrābhāsa* comes those idols which are formed inside the wall and cloth and paint therein.

1521 **चित्राभिनय**

Citrābhinaya : representation through pictures (*NS*, XXV), special representation of particular objects and ideas. The peculiarity required at times of the representation through pictures, etc. which was not mentioned before is described under *citrābhinaya.*

To indicate morning and evening, day and night, sky, seasons, clouds, large lakes, interiors of forests, directions, planets, and the stars and anything that is slightly fixed (in the sky), both the hands are raised in *patāka* and *svastika* position and the head is upturned, using various glances. The objects on the ground to be indicated with the same gestures of hands and the head, by looking downwards. The moonlight, happiness, wind, flavour and smell should be gesticulated by gestures representing touch-and horripilation. To indicate the sun, dust, smoke and wind, one is to cover one's face with clothes. Heat of the ground and of any other kind should be indicated by looking up with half closed eyes and the rising and setting of the sun by representing the sense of wonder. To indicate objects pleasant and happy, one should touch limbs, having horripilation and those of sharp nature one should not touch the limbs and show uneasiness and show narrowing of the mouth. The objects or the ideas which are grave and noble should be gesticulated with limbs having *sauṣthava* and with pride and conceit. The *arāla* hands kept on the place where sacred thread is held and then separated from *svastika* position would indicate objects like necklace and garlands. The idea of entirety should be shown by moving the first finger, looking round and pressing the *alapadma* hand. To indicate anything audible or visible whether it relates to the person speaking or spoken to or anyone else, one should point to the ears and eyes respectively. Lightening, shooting stars, thunder and sparks of fire should be represented by frightened limbs and twinkling of eyes. To indicate anything undesired, hands should be in *udveṣṭita* and *parāvṛtta*, head bent, looking obliquely and avoiding contact (*NS*, III. 268). Hot wind, darkness and lustre are to be gesticulated by covering the face and dust, rains, insects and bees are to be warded off by covering the face; lions, bears, monkeys, tigers and other beasts of prey are to be indicated by *padmakośa* hands pointing downwards in *svastika* position; in saluting the elders the *tripatāka* hand should be in *svastika;* and in holding up whip the hand should be in *kaṭaka* and *svastika.* The numbers up to ten should be indicated by fingers and multiples of ten, hundred and thousand by two *patāka* hands. The umbrellas, banners, banner-staffs and various weapons should be shown by holding a staff; memory and meditation by fixed attention, downcast eyes, head slightly bent and the left hand in *sandaṁśa.* The representation of offspring should be by head in *udvāhita* and hands in *haṁsapakṣa* held on the right side. The past, completion, destruction and words uttered in weariness should be indicated by taking left hand in *arāla* to the head. Each season should be indicated by the characteristic, costume, activity or the scenery which is proper to it.

In the representation of their own nature men should assume Vaiṣṇava posture and women, *āyata* or *avahittha.* But due to special occasion the other postures may be used in the representation of the various states in different types of plays. The movements of men should be characterized by sportive and patient physical actions and of women by delicate and sportive *aṅgahāras.*

The parrots, *sārikās* and small birds should be indicated by the fingers of the *tripatāka* hand moving and big ones like peacocks, cranes, swans, etc. by appropriate *recakas* and *aṅgahāras.* A swing should be indicated by swinging movements, agitation of limbs and holding the string.

The recitation in sleep should be with slow voice, the words, sometimes distinct and sometimes indistinct and the meaning of the word repeated twice depending on the recollection of the past. The recitation of the old people should be with faltering voice with some syllables dropped, that of children should have incomplete syllables and sweet voice.

Secret words are to be whispered in the ear; when some past incident is to be repeated due to necessity, it should also be spoken in the ear to avoid repetition.

1522 **चित्रार्ध**

Citrardha : in the category of *citrārdha,* only half upper-portion of the body (up to the bustline) is shown in the idol.

1523 **चित्रिणी**

Citriṇī : the Art-lady. "She is an Art-lady whose gait is beautiful. Who is neither too tall nor too short. Whose limbs are thin. Whose hips and breasts are broad. Whose legs are equal like the legs of crow. Whose mucus odour is like that of honey. Whose neck is like conch. Whose voice is like of cakora. who knows dancing, singing, etc, whose secret part is round swollen and contains much mucus and few public hairs. Whole glances are naturally unsteady. Who has interest in external coition. Who likes little sweet food and who likes various arts", (Kokkoka, *Ratirahasya,* 1. 14. 15).

1524 **चिनमुद्रा**

Cinamudrā : The hand gesture known to Indian iconography in the context of meditation and exposition.

1525 **चिन्ता**

Cintā : anxiety. Thinking is enacted in *Śākuntalam* (2.7) by sighing, deep breathing and in expression of absent-mindedness (*NS*, VII. 77-78). In *Mālavikāgnimitra* (Act II), Mālavikā enters a state of anxiety (*cintā*) and shows this with half-closed eyes, touching the *valaya* (bangles), the *nīvī* (navel) and thighs. In *Veṇīsaṁhāra* (2.2), there is the enaction of anxiety.Thus *cintā* is enacted by deep breathing, sighing, agony, meditation, thinking with a downcast face, thinness of the body etc.

People may experience anxiety in all kinds of situations, including about task-achievement, as in examination, anxiety about asserting oneself in company, about one's response to potentially painful interventions, Extreme anxiety can become phobic, and this is found with respect to, for example, closed spaces, open spaces, and creatures like snakes and spiders. Whatever the anxiety-evoking situation, the experience of anxiety has certain invariable components. One component is physiological - sweating palms, butterfly stomach, increased heart rate, tremors and dry mouth. Another component is attentional, that is being unable to concentrate on the elements of the task, or behaviour in hand, and concentrating only on fearful thoughts about the situation. This is particularly obvious in situations like examinations or social occasions where one attends not to the actual performance but to the consequences of not performing well, or one experiences attention - moving from one irrelevant stimulus to another. Another is simply the unpleasant thoughts and predictions surrounding the frightening situation. Anxiety also produces failure of memory, both in retrieving and in storing new material. And it leads to poorer performance and rigid, inflexible approaches to problem. (b) thus *cintā* is the feeling of mingled dread and apprehension about the future without specific cause for fear; a chronic fear of mild degree; a secondary drive involving an acquired avoidance response; In the presence of the conditional stimulus the animal subject displays behaviour interpreted as evidence of anxiety, including urination, defecation etc.

1526 **चिबुक**

Cibuka : the chin. Under facial expression, the chin plays an important role to produce different types of sentiments. According to different *rasas,* it is classified as follows: *Sama* or *khaṇḍita* (*Śṛṅgāra*), *kuṭṭana* or *chinna* (*bhayānaka*), *lehana* or *cukkita* (*hāsya*), *sama* or *chinna* (*karuṇa*), *daṣṭa* (*raudra*), *sama* (*vīra*), *chinna* or *kuṭṭana* (*bībhatsa*). There are also other two movements of the chin: *grahaṇa* and *niṣkarṣaṇa.* Though these are called the gestures of the chin (seven in total), yet tooth, the tongue, and the upper lip act there (*NS*, VIII. 141-146).

The lower face or chin tabula appears in Indian 'pleading' where the hand grasps the chin or beard. This may contrast with 'bad smell' in which the hand graps the nose.

SR has treated the movement of chin due to movements of teeth - *dantakarmāṇi* (*SR*, VII. 500 - 506), but movement of the lips and tongue is also involved there. In fact, the chin or its various types are indicated by actions of tongue, teeth and lips. Hence Bharata (*Ibid.*) describes actions or types of actions of teeth. Śāraṅgadeva has mentioned eight (while Bharata only seven). Of these *grahaṇa* is mentioned instead of *lehana* and *niṣkramaṇa* is not additional one mentioned by him (*SR*, IV. 496 - 97).

1527 **चिबुक लक्षण**

Cibuka-lakṣana : sign of the chin. Long uneven chin indicates lack of wealth; fleshy one indicates wealth (*Bhaviṣya*, 26.12.17).

In the Gond society the method of greeting is that each should put his fingers under the other's chin and then kiss them himself. Women also do this when they meet.

In *Bṛhat-Saṁhitā* (LXVIII) various signs of the chin suggest different meanings. 'Very lean and long chins suggest poverty; while fleshy ones, wealth; straight (not crooked) lower lips resembling the ripe *bimba* (*Coccina indica*) fruit make men kings; while lean (without flesh) ones, indigent. The upper lips being split, cut, colourless and dry make men penurious. The teeth being clean, equal and close-knit and the canine ones very sharp and equal are auspicious.

Prahlāda opines :

चिबुके यस्य रोमाणि न वक्षसि न गण्डयोः ।
कुटिलं तं विजानीयात्समर्थं च खलं नरम् ॥

Cf the following :

रक्ताधरो नरपतिर्धनवान् कमलाधरः ।
स्थूलोष्ठा बहुलोमाश्च शुष्कैः क्षीणैश्च दुःखिताः ॥

1528 **चिह्न**

Cihna : mark, sign, symbol, symptom.

1529 **चुक्कित चिबुक**

Cukkita cibuka : keeping the two rows of teeth wide apart, a type of facial expression in *hāsya rasa* when the chin is in *cukkita* position (*NS*, VIII. 148).

1530 **चुक्षित चिबुक**

Cukṣita cibuka : lips separated widely apart; a type of facial expression with the movement of the chin full extended; orderly separated two jaws. It is used in yawing (*NS*, VIII. 141-146). Same as *cukkita*.

1531 **चुचुक**

Cucuka : nipples of breast, meant for pressing. *stanavṛnta*.

1532 **चुड्की**

Cuḍki : name of a goddess. This goddess has no idol or symbol. She is believed to stay in the sound made by the thumb and the middle finger; and it is said that this sound is to be made before her (*Skanda Purāṇa*, 2.8.8. 30-32):

अग्रे तस्याः सदा कार्यो
नृभिरंगुष्ठतो ध्वनिः ।

Cuḍkī is *cuṭkī* in Hindi and means the sound produced as above.

1533 **चुम्बन**

Cumbana : kiss, kissing, Vātsyāyana (2.3) has done a detailed analysis of the couples who were engaged in kissing one another. It is worth noting here that still today there is hardly any literature on the behaviour of human courtship. So, Vātsyāyana is the sole authority in this field.

Vātsyāyana has mentioned that kissing is the key of love. To him, kissing implies a bond between the couple. He says: "Kissing and other things like embrace and pressing, etc. (*i.e.* tactile behaviour) should be done moderately (which carries sexual meaning); they should not be continued for a long time (it can be frightening and arise anxiety as well) and should be done alternately: on subsequent occasions, however, the reverse of all this may take place and moderation will not be necessary. They may continue for a long time and for the purpose of kindling love, they may be all done at the same time: *tāni prathamarate nāti vyaktāni viṣrabdhikāyām vikalpena ca prayumjita tathābhūtatvādrāgasya tataḥ paramatitvararyā viśeṣavat sumuccayena rāgasandhukṣaṇam* (*Kāmasūtra*, 2.3. 4-5). An important feature of the behaviour of courtship, indeed, appears to be that it should create some degree of sexual arousal in the partners. It seems that the 'kissing round' of the sort we find in *Kāmasūtra*, which is obviously so characteristic of a certain stage of courtship, has this function.

Touching a companion with the lips is not a simple tie-sign, but a whole set of signs, according to the area of the body kissed. The most intimate form of kissing is the mouth-to-mouth kiss it is the mutual cheek kiss, which occurs as a low intensity form of it. Other kisses can be scaled according to how high or low they are on the body, as Vātsyāyana has tried. They are the forehead kiss performed by Muslims reflect an appropriately lower status. It is the kiss of reverence or formal deference.

It is curious to note that all the courtship behaviour such as massaging and tickling, the kiss as a means of sensory excitement is but little used in tribal societies except the Muria. In some parts it may by seen with lips upon the skin. Kiss does not appear to be on the lips, nor does the tongue play any part. For the Muria, the kiss is a highly concentrated form of massage with lips upon the skin. Boys kiss the face and breasts.

The kiss, both among Baiga and their neighbours the Gond, plays a very small part in love-making, though it is more commonly practised by the Pankā and Pardhān. It seems that the mouth has lost much of its erogenous character in the tribal region. Psychologists may trace the connection between the long period of suckling, devotion to the breast and indifference to kiss in tribes.

Nor do the Baiga have any tactile substitute for kiss, they do not louse, or scratch or bite, or nip the eyebrows: *fellatio* is unknown, and *penilinetus* very rare. Even an erotic expert like Lakhat assured Elwin (1937:264) that he had never kissed a girl in his life: "Our bodies kiss", he said, "so why should we use our mouths"?

The position adopted during intercourse does not favour kissing. Dhansingh has kissed, but very seldom. Mahtu once saw an English woman kiss her husband, a forest officer, and thought it disgusting. In Kawardhā, however, Elwin (*Ibid.*) was told that young people do kiss, though they stop the practice after the birth of a child. They bite the cheeks with their teeth. While the girl is lying before him, he lifts her up, he kisses her, he puts her down again. They even kiss on the lips, but it is not a long protracted kiss, and the tongue plays no part in it.

A practical reason for the low value system of kissing may be the filthy mouths and foul breath of the Indians. I remember once discussing this point with a group of Muria and suggesting that a man whose mouth stank of stale tobacco could hardly expect to be a successful lover. The next morning, three of the company declared that they had abandoned smoking for ever.

(b) kissing is a ritual in the plantation of trees which promotes their growth. Accordingly performer kisses his wife with a *mantra:* चुम्बयेन्मंत्रयेत्तत: (*Bhaviṣya*, 1.10.28).

1534 **चुम्बन-विधम्**

Cumbana-vidham : types of kissing. Padmaśrī (*Nāgarasarvasva*, 4.3) enumerates seven types of kiss with marking sound and seven types of kiss with non-marking sound (soundless kiss). The *Ratirahasya* (6.2.9) divides the kiss into 14 types: *nimitikam, sphuritikam, ghaṭṭitakam, tiryak, pīḍitam, vighaṭitam, aradam, uttaram, saṁpuṭam, anuvadanam, anvardham, pratibodhakam, chāyā, saṁkrāntam.* Only six types of kisses are referred to by the *Pañcasāyaka* (4.43.48): *nimitikam, sphuritam, dṛṣṭam, pīḍitam, saṁpuṭam, samauṣṭham.* Padmaśri has divided kiss mainly into two divisions: *niḥśabda* and *saśabda.* All these classifications are based on the data given by *Kāmasūtra* (2.3. 9-30) which classifies kissing into 19 types: *nimitikam, sphuritikam, ghaṭṭitakam, samam, tiryak, udbhrāntam, avapīḍitikam, uttara-cumbitam, saṁpuṭakam, jiḥvāyuddham, pīḍitam, añcitam mṛdu, rāgadīpanam, calitakam, pratibodhakam, chāyā, saṁkrānta.*

1535 **चुम्बन-स्थान**

Cumbana-sthāna : places of kissing, kissing round. The detailed study of kissing round in *Kāmasūtra* draws certain places which are supposed to be the places of arousal. The *Kāmasūtra* (2.3.6) states that the following places are meant for kissing; the forehead, the hair, the cheeks, the eyes, the breasts, the lips and the interior of mouth: *lalāṭāla kapolanayanavakṣastatoṣṭhāntara mukeṣu cumbanam.* Kokkoka (*Ratirahasya*, 7.1) agrees with all these places but adds one more place, *i.e.* throat. Kalyāṇamalla has enumerated various kissing rounds:

Adharākṣi-kapola-mastakam vadanāntaḥ stanayugma kandhare'
Vihitāni padāni paṇḍitaiḥ parirambhādanu cumbanasya hi

(*Anaṅgaraṅga*, 9.11).

"Lips, the eyes, the cheeks, the head, the inner part of the mouth, the breasts and the neck are the places for kissing".

There are certain regional variations in kissing round. Vātsyāyana has mentioned that the people of Lāṭa-region kiss on the following places: the joints of the thighs, the arms and the navel: *ūrūsandhi-bāhunābhimūleṣu lāṭānām* (*Kāmasūtra*, 2.3.7). Kokkoka has also narrated the kissing behaviour of the Lāṭa-people:

nayanagala kapolam dantavāso mukhāntaḥ
stanayugalalalāṭam cumbanasthānamāhuḥ
dadhati jaghanābhimūlakakṣāsu cumbana-
vyatikarasukhamuccaiḥ desasātmena lāṭaḥ.

1536 **चुम्बिते प्रति चुम्बितम्**

Cumbite prati cumbitam : kiss for kiss, a case of active partners in sexual arousal (Vātsyāyana, *Kāmasūtra*, 2.3.44). Jayadeva (*Gita-Govinda*, 12.3) has presented Rādhā as a woman who knows this action-reaction-theory."

1537 **चुलु**

Culu : 'handful of water' *Bālabodhanī, calu* 'mouthful of water' Pañcat.

1538 **चूडाकरण**

Cūḍakaraṇa : tonsure; it is the eighth Hindu *Saṁskāra.* The distinguishing feature of this sacrament is the arrangement of the hair tuft (*Sikhā* or *cūḍā*) as the name of the *Saṁskāra* suggests (Suśruta, *Śārīra* VI. 83; *Laghu-Hārīta* IV; *Vīramitrodaya* 1.296).

1539 **चूडाभरण**

Cūḍābharaṇa : ornaments of head *(NS)*. *Cūḍāmaṇi* (crest-jewel) is to be worn on the top of the head by divine and royal males and *mukuṭa* (the crown) above the head. Head ornaments for females were also prescribed by Bharata. *Śikhāpāśa, śikhāvyāla, piṇḍīpatra, cūḍāmaṇi, makarikā and muktājāla* Abhinava explains *śikhāvyāla* as that in which the image of serpent was formed like the pericarp of the flower at the centre and round it the *piṇḍīpatra* was formed by circular leaves like petals. *Cūḍāmaṇi* was to be worn at the centre of the head, then *makarapatra* and then pearlnet reaching the forehead. *Veṇīguccha* appears to be an ornament to be tied to the braided hair.

1540 **चुत**

Cūta : (a) mango. (b) female generative organ.

(c) mango-leaves were used for preparing wreaths at welcome. When Pārvatī started the holy vow, wreaths of mango-leaves were seen on the royal path (*Brahmavaivarta*, Gaṇapati-khaṇḍa, 6.30.31). It was supposed that the offerings of mango-leaves results in destruction of fever (*Agni*, 81. 50-52).

1541 **चूर्णपाद**

Cūrṇa pāda : simple steps (*NS*, XII. 88-92). In *Śākuntalam* (Act I), the king enters with simple steps.

1542 **चूषण**

Cūṣaṇa : sucking, sucking of the nipples by children, sucking of the nipples of a girl by a man; four types of sucking has been enumerated by Padmaśrī in his *Nāgara-sarvasva* (XXVI).

1543 **चेलक**

Celaka : clothes, garment. (a) Celika in Halbi means the young unmarried youth (bearing the clothes). (b) It may be particularly noted that a blue or black (*nīla*) garment was taboo normally in ancient Indian society as with the modern tribes, but a wick prepared from a *nīla* cloth was especially enjoined at the worship of Kāma (the love-god). The day for Kāma is said to be the Full - Moon - day of Caitra (*Skanda*, VI. 245. 33).

1544 **चेष्टा**

Ceṣṭā : gesture, that which is produced by the movements of limbs. A gesture is usually deemed to be an action or effort by which a thought, feeling, or intention is given conventional and voluntary expressions. By gesture I understand a conscious or unconscious body movement made mainly with the head, the face alone, or the limbs, learned or somatogenic, and serving as a primary communicative tool, dependent or independent from verbal language; either simultaneous or alternating with it, and modified by the conditioning background (smiles, eye movements, a tic etc.)

In poetics gesture has been synonymed such as:

ākūta-vyañjitāśceṣṭā iṅgitam buddhikāritāḥ
ākāraḥ punarāmnātastā evābuddhikāritāḥ

Varāhamihira (505 A.D.) in his *Bṛhat Saṁhitā* (LI) has opined that through gestures and utterances one can depict the personality of a person: चेष्टाव्याहृतिभिः शुभाशुभफलम्

Parāśara has the same concept:

तत्र देशे दिशः कालं व्याहारं द्रव्यदर्शनम् ।
अङ्गप्रत्यङ्गसंस्पर्शं समीक्ष्य फलमादिदेश ॥

(b) movement of a bodily part for the purpose of communication.

1545 **चेष्टाकृत**

Ceṣṭākṛta : the physical gesticulation. One of the three types of *āṅgikābhinaya*; residing in bodily movements (*NS*). The entire movements of the body as in *aṅgahāra, nyāya, maṇḍala, cārīs*, etc. would come under *ceṣṭākṛta*. The *ceṣṭākṛta* is described as six-fold: (a) *vākyābhinaya* (gesticulation of words), (b) *sūcā* (index), (c) *aṅkura*, (d) *śākhā*, (e) *nāṭyāyita* and (f) *nivṛttyāṅkura*.

1546 **चेष्टित**

Ceṣṭita : gesture, manner of life activity, effort.; also known as *iṅgita* which is *manovyāpāra*. Movement or behaviour on the part of an organism. (b) any mental or physical process. (Fig. 1546)

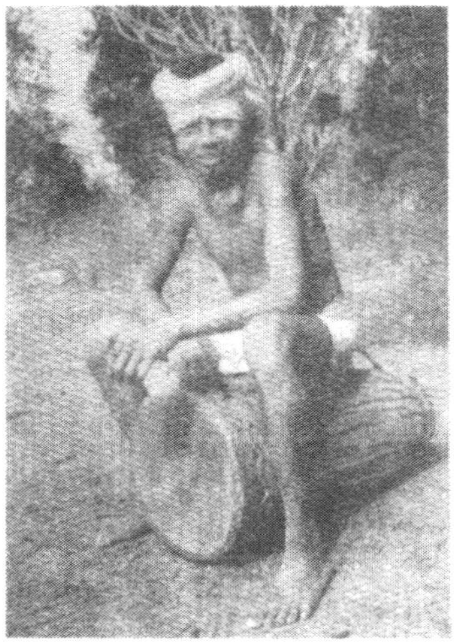

Fig. – (1546)

1547 **चेष्टितयुक्ति**

Ceṣṭitayukti : verbs signifying motion.

1548 **चौर्यरत**

Cauryarata : secret sexual enjoyment; also known as cauryasuratam.

1549 **च्युतसंस्कृति**

Cyuta-saṁskṛti : lacking correctness, grammatically wrong.

छ Ch

1550 **छत्र**

Chatra : the umbrella or parasol stuck on the aureola (*prabhāvalī*) of the deity as a mark of royal dignity. It is probable that the practice began with a single or triple *chatra* placed over the *stūpa* in the early Aśokan period. The *chatra* was held above the king when he sat at court or went out in a procession, with other emblems like fly. -whisk (*cāmara*), solar disc (*sūryapāna*), lunar disc (*candra-pāna*) and banner (*dhvaja*) which accompanied him.

The *chatra* is also one of the equipments of a sage or student, others being the sacred water-pot (*kamaṇḍalu*), sandals (*pādukā*) head-gear (*uṣṇīśa*) and staff (*daṇḍa*). One of the *avatāras* of Viṣṇu, Vāmana, is shown holding the *chatra* in the right hand and water-pot in the left.

1551 **छत्रधारणसंकेत**

Chatra-dhāraṇa-saṁketa : umbrella-insignia. Umbrella was one of the guarded symbols in feudal India. A part of the insignia of feudal monarchies the umbrella retained some of its importance as an exclusive 'sign of noble rank... not permitted to the commonality', even after it had ceased to be an appanage of kings (Russell and Hiralal, II. 451; Abūl - Faz: 52 mentions the *chatra* and the *Saya-ban* among the 'ensigns of royalty'). Throughout the colonial period it continued to operate as a general index of dominance and subordination, sorting out, especially in the rural areas, the rulers and the ruled, high caste and low caste, and so on: in Champāran no Indian 'whatever his status' could hold an umbrella on his head in the presence of a white planter, nor could a Bania do so while passing by a Bundela Rajput's house in Sagar (Kripalani, J.B. *Gandhi*, New Delhi: 1970: 453).

1552 **छत्र-मुद्रा**

Chatra-mudrā : the gesture of an umbrella. "style the left palm in the first, raise up the fore-finger and place the right-palm over it as an umbrella in a torrential rain-fall. This makes the *Chatra-mudrā* " (*BT*).

1553 **छन्दस्**

Chandas : rhythm, metrical structure, delight, desire, song, prosody.

1554 **छन्दो-विचिति-मुद्रा**

Chando-viciti-mudrā : gesture symbolizing *chando viciti*, a part of *Vedāṅga*, down-turn two *kaṭakāmukhas* to form this gesture (*VD*). *Chando-viciti* is the treatise leading to the knowledge of metres.

1555 **छल**

Chala : deceptive speech. In the words of Bharata, the speech having another sense, causes, deception, laughter and anger; is called *chala* (*NS*, XVIII. 123). According to Dhanañjaya (*Daśarūpaka*, 3.18) it arises from deceit that misleads by means of unfriendly words that seem friendly. Visvanātha (*Sāhityadarpaṇa*, VI. 258-259) taxes it in the sense of deceiving the other by means of words through unfriendly yet having the semblance of friendliness.

It is one of the thirteen constituents of *vīthī* in which the words having different meanings create anger and laughter.

(b) *chala* is a kind of unfair reply. In using *chala* an attempt is made to contradict a statement by taking it in a sense other than the intended one. It is one of the sixteen philosophical topics of the *nyāya*.

(c) deception, fraud (*Daśa*. III. 18), casuistry; three kinds: *Vākchala* (verbal casuistry), *sāmānyachala* (generalising casuistry), and *upacāracchala* (figurative casuistry). The immediacy toward an addressee is greater when one is truthful than deceitful.

1556 **छलितकयोगकला**

Chalitaka-yoga-kalā : tricky and critical composition to delude other, art of deception. One of the 64 arts given by *Kāmasūtra*. Unlike other species, humans have a capacity for self-monitoring and, as Vātsyāyana has presented, have the capacity to minimize the spontaneous expression of feeling to a great extent. This capacity also provides the potential for deception and found in other species. The latter implies that when we are trying to detect emotional states in others, we may have to rely on those cues over which they have less control. It is a type of "leakage" which is a source of information for the deceitful (*Kapaṭapūrṇa*) persons. Skilled actors, according to Bharata, who are taught through direct study with feedback to monitor and control emotional expression in all parts of the body, show less "leakage" than ordinary people do.

The *Chalitayoga* brings into focus another interesting point about the expression of feeling through non-verbal channels. If one can control feelings, one can, presumably, feign them too. To feign emotions via those expressive movements which are generally believed to be spontaneous and uncontrollable makes one immune to responsibility for them. One can use such a channel for conveying a message about one's feelings while disclaiming the message. This possibility equips the NV channels with a subtlety and flexibility which language, intentional and therefore committing as it is, often lacks, Expression of emotion is important not only for detecting the internal states of others during interaction, it is important also for people's experience of it, that is the physical expression of emotion is closely linked to the experience of it.

1557 **छवि**

Chavi : beauty, image. In the eyes and on the lips of a villager or city-dweller, a tribe is rather a coarse fellow who does not always know his place, and who is simple-minded and jungly. The tribes look upon these people as primarily traders (*haṭeyā*), lacking in the martial values, ready to cheat and ready to trick, and successful only through deceit. The symbols of difference are categorical imperative: Gonds never trade; Gonds abhor milk; Gonds (used to) eat beef. Hindus trade, reverence milk as the product of cow, and have few greater sins than to eat beef. But these differences are overly presented. Both have lived side by side for many centuries, sometimes fighting, sometimes keeping their distance, exchanging goods. Consequently some of the covert characteristics are the same.

In *chavi* - type of popular usage and media studies image has acquired connotations of falseness. What Leech(1974) calls image- building depends on the suppression of undesirable associations and the promotion of desirable ones in both visual and verbal terms.

1558 **छाग-मुद्रा**

Chāga-mudrā : gesture of a goat. The *śikhara* hands in contact of face to face indicate a goat (*Mirror of Gesture*, pp.49-50).

1559 **छात्र**

Chātra : pupil, one who increases the strength of his teacher (not *chādayati doṣān* etc.).

1560 **छादनम्**

Chādanam : covering; One of the 64 *sandhyaṅgas (NS*, 19.94); words caused by insult for some purpose. Abhinava says it is termed as *Chādanam* because it ends the blot of insult; disrespect.

1561 **छाया**

Chāyā : shadow, clever imitation of other styles or dialects (*Agnipurāṇa*, 342.21.25). Four styles are enumerated: *lokokti* (the vernacular), *chekokti* (the scholarly jargon), arabhokti (the children's speech) and *mattokti* (the talk of drunks). (b) A taboo regarding taking shelter in the shadow of the Vibhītaka tree, Arka tree, Karañja tree obtains, likewise one is forbidden to take shelter in the shadow of a pole, a lamp or a man and other creatures (*Liṅga*. 1.85.47).

1562 **छाया-चुम्बनम्**

Chāyā—cumbanam : reflexive kiss. *Kāmasūtra* (2.3.30) defines: "A kiss showing the intention in which a person kisses the reflection of his beloved in a mirror, in water or on a well: *ādarśe kuḍy salile vā prayojyas-chāyācumbanam ākarapradarśanārthameva kāryam.* There is a detailed description of this type of kiss in *Naiṣadha* (16.65; 20.25).

1563 **छायानाटक**

Chāyā-nāṭaka : shadow-play. It denotes a drama in the state of a shadow. The oldest of these species is the *Dūtāṅgada* of Subhaṭa (13th century A.D.).

The word *leṇaśobhikā* in one of the Mathura inscriptions is taken by Jacob to mean a woman who operates a shadow play. The Sītābeṅgā cave is thought to have served as a shadow theatre. Luders means that the word stands for "cave-actress".

1564 **छिक्का**

Chikkā : sneeze, sneezing. Varāhamihira (*BS*, LXVIII) prefers *kṣut* instead of *chikkā*. He has presented some signs related with sneezing. According to him "The sneezing of the wealthy is either only once, or twice or thrice and high-pitched and resonant; while that of long-lived, prolonged and of the same pitch throughout." Bhaṭṭotpala refers to other commentators who interpret the *Bṛhat-Saṁhitā* verse thus:" The rich sneeze but once; while the long-lived twice or thrice in succession making it high-pitched, resonant, prolonged and of the same pitch throughout. He prefers the second interpretation in view of Parāśara's statement:

सकृत् क्षुतं भोगवतां द्विर्धनाय चिरायुषे ।
चतुः स्याद्रोगनाशाय परमस्मात् तदीशजाः ।।

Sneezing of cows is inauspicious according to *Bṛhat-Saṁhitā*. If one sneezes, one should perform *ācamana* (water-sipping) or look at the sun (*Brahma*. 221.68). According to *Garuḍa Purāṇa* (1.97. 9-10) at a sneeze one should not sip water, but should touch one's right ear. It is a censurable act to sneeze at the twilight (*sandhyākāle*), that is infested with evil powers (*Brahma*. 3.110.21). If a man sneezes during or at the end of sexual intercourse, he may die in the fifth month (*Skanda*. IV, 42. 2-23).

1565 **छिन्न करण**

Chinna karaṇa : the *kaṭi* is bent in *chinna*. The *alapadma hastas* are held on the hip. The feet are in *Vaiśākha sthāna*. (*NS*, 105b-106a, IX. 91, 245; X.61). The *alapadma* hand is placed at the waist, which is *chinna* by turn and the posture in *Vṛścika*. It is employed in movements of the limbs and breaking of the *tāla*.

1566 **छिन्न चिबुक**

Chinna cibuka : teeth closely meeting; tight interlocking of teeth; a type of chin-movement when the chin is in position of closing the jaws. This facial expression is suggested in *bhayānaka, bībhatsa* and *karuṇa rasas*; close contact; It is used to indicate fear, disease, cold, crying, angry mood, madness, physical exercise etc. (*NS*, VIII. 141-146).

1567 **छिन्नाकटि**

Chinnā kaṭi : turned aside, a twist of the waist as if cut off; hips turning from the point of *bhadra-sūtra*. It is an artistic twist of the waist used indicating hurry in actions and looking things all around a man (*NS*,X.21-26). *Valana* of the middle *i.e.* turning of the middle (of the body) obliquely on the sides.

1568 **छेकालाप**

Chekālāpa : clever conversation.

1569 **छेकोक्ति**

Chekokti : indirect speech, double entendre.

1570 **छेदन**

Chedana : cutting up relevant sentiment and feelings through appropriate gesture (*NS*,IX.175).

1571 **छोटिका**

Choṭikā : (a) snapping the thumb and fingers together. (b) piece of cloth put between the legs to cover privities.

ज Ja

1572 **जगदेकचक्षुस्**

Jagadekacakṣus : sun. Daily homage to the sun, at its rise is extolled. The most popular method of paying homage is by offering seven handfuls of water:

क्षिपेज्जलांजलीन्सप्त मनोदुःखविनाशनम्

(*Agni.* 252.17)

The sun is said to be invoked to bestow good health (*Skanda.* V. 3.155. 115). The student is ordained not to see the rising sun: न पश्येच्चार्क उद्यन्तम् (*Agni* 155.15). This is well-known rule in the *Smṛtis*; and it is the general instruction for all that the rising and the setting sun is not to be seen: उद्यन्तं अस्तं यन्तं च वर्जयेद् दर्शने रविम् (*Brahmāṇḍa.* 1.2.10.23).

1573 **जघन**

Jaghana : hips. Hips which are fleshy, big and broad are appreciated in Sanskrit literature with terms like *pīnajaghanā, gurujaghanā,* and *viśālajaghanā. Jaghana* is the front portion of a woman's hips (hinderpart = *nitamba*), pundendum. *Jaghaninī* means having broad hips *i.e. pṛthula-jaghanā.*

1574 **जघनकूपक**

Jaghana-kūpaka : hollows in the middle of each buttock - a sign of beauty.

1575 **जघनगौरव**

Jaghana-gaurava : weight of the hips.

1576 **जघनचपला**

Jaghana-capalā : moving hips, libidinous woman.

1577 **जघनरन्ध्र**

Jaghana-randhra : vagina (*Ratirahasya,* 1.18-19). The following Chhattisgarhi Dadariyā also places the vagina between the two thighs:

Candā ke uge sūraj cal dey.
dono jaṅghiyā ke bīc marad ras ley

1578 **जघनोपगूहन**

Jaghanopagūhana : embrace of the hips (*Anaṅgaraṅga,* 2.1.3).

1579 **जघन्यम्**

Jaghanyam : penis, coitus, mean act.

1580 **जङ्घा**

Jaṅghā : shanks, leg, above shin, the part of the leg in between the knee and the ankle-shank; leg; Movements of the shanks. The *NS* (IX. 257-8) lists five positions of the shanks, which arise out of the extension and flexion of the leg, the manipulation of the knee and ankle-joint and the placing of the feet. We have thus *āvartita* (turned), *nata* (bent), *kṣipta* (throwing out), *udvāhita* (raised), and *parivartita* or *parivṛtta* (turned back). The *SR* and *Nāṭyaśāstra Saṁgraha* list these but also mention five additional movements. The five additional movements are: *niḥṣṭra* (the leg is extended forward high), *parāvṛtta* (variation of *parivartita*), *tiraścina* (knees with an outward sideways bend touches the ground), *saṁhata* (perfect equilibrium) and *vivṛta* (both knees turned outwards and the feet well apart). (b) the middle portion of the temple which is above the basement and below the *śikhara.*

1581 **जङ्घाकरिक**

Jaṅghākarika : active with legs, runner; also *jaṅghākārika.*

1582 **जङ्घालक्षणम्**

Jaṅghā lakṣaṇam : signs of the shanks, If covered with less hair and like the elephant's trunk it is good; if on this part in one pore there is only one hair it is indicative of royalty; if there are two in one pore, it indicates wisdom, and the person is bound to be a wise man and a *śrotriya;* but if there are three in one pore, it is sign of poverty and also of disease; surely so if also the knees are fleshless (*Garuḍa,* 1.63.4). The shanks of the women symbolizes:

If it is not showing veins and be, in complexion like the cane used for an arrow in hue, it indicates fortune. If round and having scanty hair, it is the indication of riding on elephants or horses. Hairy shanks indicate distress; if they show muscles like a ball, or if curved like the shank of a crow, the indication is the lass of husband (*Bhav. P. Brahma,* 5.12; *Garuḍa P. Ibid; Sk.P.* IV. 37, 15-16).

Varāhamihira (LXVIII) enumerates the following features of male shanks. "If the shanks are round with sparse and thin hair, the thighs, beautiful, resembling the elephant's trunk, and knees, well-developed *i.e.* fleshy, and even, the person concerned becomes a monarch; while shanks re-sembling those of jackal or dog conduce to pennilessness.

1583 **जङ्घाभरण**

Jaṅghābharaṇa : ornament of shanks meant to women only. It was *pādapatra.*

1584 **जटा**

Jaṭā : matted hair worn in different ways by ascetics under a vow and by yogis engaged in penance. In order to free themselves from the necessity of frequent care of the hair, they used to apply to the hair milky exudation of some tree like the banyan, and twist the hair into convenient strands and coils. This would prevent dirt and lice from setting on the head, and also keep the hair-strands always in order. In iconography, we find matted hair associated with Śiva, some forms of Devi, some forms of Kārtikeya and Śāstā, and sages in general.

There were several styles of wearing matted hair which are proved from the iconic evidences. (a) one of the most frequent seen is the strands of matted hair being twisted and coiled up in the shape of a tall crown. This is known as *jaṭā-mukuṭa.* All forms of Devi and Viṣṇu are shown with this kind of hair arrangement. (b) *jaṭābandha* (also called *jaṭā-kalāpa*) is the strands of matted hair being wound round the head with a top-knot. This can be seen in the images of sages. (c) another type of *jaṭā* is where the strands of matted hair are arranged as a circular halo round the head. This is known as *jaṭā-maṇḍala,* and this may be seen in most of the eight forms of Bhairava. (d) the long tresses of matted hair are allowed to fly about when representing some forms of Naṭarāja. This is sometimes known as *jaṭā-kalāpa,* incidental to vigorous movement of the bodys. (e) the masses of matted hair may be arranged to be tied in sections gracefully on both sides of the head. This is known as *jaṭā-bhāra,* and is seen in many of the variant forms of Śiva. (f) one of the various modes of repeating the *Veda.*

1585 **जटामुकुट**

Jaṭāmukuṭa : mass of twisted hair, the crown of matted hair. The hair is tied up above the head in such a way as to resemble a crown or a tiara. Other related terms are *jaṭākalāpa, jaṭājāla, jaṭābandha, jaṭāmāraḥ* and *jaṭāmaṇḍalam.*

1586 **जटा-मुद्रा**

Jaṭā-mudrā : the clotted hairs gesture. If the fore-finger is extended, three fingers are curved and placed on the thumb of the said hand. Then it is *jaṭā* (*VD*). The *jaṭā-mudrā* indicates combing of hairs, after taking the respective badges, like *tripuṇḍa, triśūla, padma, cakra,* etc. as indicated for the respective sect.

1587 **जड**

Jaḍa : matter. (a) the non-conscious which by itself inert, devoid of sentiency and is mutable. (b) cold, stiff, dull. (c) winter. (d) *jaḍam* = water. According to the gradation into which the Indian classifies phenomena, the one is the apex of the pyramid, the many are its base; union is hierarchically superior to division, the undifferentiated to the differentiated. *Avidyā,* ignorance, sees everything as separate differentiated; *Vidyā,* true knowledge, unitary knowledge, is the synoptic vision of the whole. Here we touch on the theme of inclusiveness and holism. It must be contrasted with a contrary trend towards a dualistic, rigorous, ascetic outlook as through in its application as in the history of thought, If, for the sake of clarity, a comparison may be made with western concepts, this refers to the relation of matter and mind; that is, man and Brahman, or empirical reality and transcendental reality.

1588 **जड़ता**

Jaḍatā : stupor, incapacity for action; regarded as one of the thirty-three subordinate feelings. It is a static state of mind. It is caused by seeing or hearing something agreeable or disagreeable. Gazing with unwinking eyes, remaining silent not uttering any word, speaking indistinctly, aversion to all work, dependence on others, etc. (*Daśarūpaka,* IV. 13) are the external manifestations.

(b) in philosophy, *jaḍa* means matter, the non-conscious which by itself inert, devoid of sentiency and is mutable. (c) in psychology, *Jaḍatā* means a severely retarded condition in which the individual is inaccessible to stimuli, shows loss of orientation, and makes few or no motor responses.

1589 **जडशक्ति**

Jaḍaśakti : the material cause of creation.

1590 **जनन**

Janana : procreation. The term is also used in the sense of processing a *mantra,* its gradual recovery from the *mātṛkā-yantra* (*Tantrasāra,* 54). (b) begetting, causing, birth, family, offspring.

1591 **जननेन्द्रिय**

Jananendriya : genitalia, sexual organs. The anatomical knowledge of the genitalia of the tribes is slight, but they compensate for it by an extensive mythology of sex, which is, more elaborate in Muria in comparison to other tribes.

It is remarkable that the Muria seem to regard the sexual organs, whether male or female, as living things with an independent life of their own. For example, one of the reasons given for forbidding urination inside the ghotul is that the girls' urine would smell abominably because her *labia majora* are always chewing her urine as she walks about - just as a goat chews its food, and therefore a girl's urine smells as strongly as a goat's.

There are several stories about the vagina, though the Vagina Dentala legend, known throughout central provinces and Orissa, is comparatively rare. Elwin (1947: 423-4) records the following story from Masora (I) Long ago the Vagina had the power of leaving its body at night and going out to feed in the fields. It had teeth with which it could eat; it would stay out all night grazing in the fields and return satisfied in the morning.

By and by the village people began to say, 'what is this thing that comes at night and eats up our crops? Let us set traps and catch it'. So they set traps in their fields, and that night when the Vagina came to feed they were caught and the villagers collected them and took them to Gaita's house in a big basket. They shut them up in an inner room and went to report the matter to the Raja. The Raja sentenced the vaginae to be hanged.

When they heard this, the villagers were frightened, for they said, 'How are we to live with our wives if their organs are destroyed?' So they went to the Raja asking him to forgive them and promising to repay the owners of the fields for whatever damage had been done.

The Raja said, 'First of all the teeth must be broken and removed from the Vaginae. Whoever can do this will be rewarded'. No one knew how to do it until at least a one-eyed police man, who himself had a knife growing from his penis, declared that he would deal with the matter. With his knife he removed the teeth and then with hammer and nails fixed every Vagina back in its place. The nail he used is the clitoris which stands above the Vagina to hold it steady. The vaginae then cursed the man who had done them this injury and turned him into a pig. Even today the pigs' penis is shaped like a knife.

Similar stories among the Bison-horn Maria relate how a man once caught a vagina eating his gram and knocked its teeth out with a pestle ; in another tale, from Kameli, people used to feed the wandering vagina out of charity. When it was satisfied it would pen its mouth and do men no harm. Even now the vagina has not forgotten its old habit of eating gur and gram and still tries to 'bite' the male member by its muscular contractions.

A rather similar tale from Palari (Kondagaon tahsil) connects the incident with Bhimul and his wife:

The Vagina used to creep out of the body where it lived and go in search of maize and cucumbers. It would nibble its way through a fence and steal from the field. The farmers made fences of iron and now when the Vagina tried to get through, its teeth were knocked out by iron. A small bit of iron stuck in the Vagina's mouth and became clitoris. When the teeth came out, blood flowed from the mouth and the Vagina went to Bhimul for help.

Now the penis of Bhimul was five hands long and he cut it into several pieces, each four fingers long. He put one piece into the Vagina's mouth and said, "Don't eat cucumbers or maize any more; from today this will be your food'. But the bleeding did not stop, and Bhimul said, 'It will stop soon and then after a month it will bleed again'. Such was the beginning of women's menstruation.

There was blood at the end of Bhimul's penis where he had cut it. It went into the belly of the woman to whom the vagina belonged and she conceived. This is how the birth of children began.

In those days men had no genitals. One day they went to Bhimul to complain about this. He fixed a bit of his own penis with wax between the thighs of a man. Such was the beginning. But the penis fell off as the wax melted. They went to Goroṇḍi Doari (Bhimul's wife) and she put two small chickens under the penis to support it. Such is the origin of the testes.

Elsewhere the Muria said, 'the tests are the children of the penis and have sapped their father's strength. Only when the children restore the strength can their father work.

Another Vagina Dentala story comes from Keolari:

There was a Rākśasa's daughter with teeth in her vagina. She used to live mostly as a tigress and kept ten or twelve tigers always with her. When she saw a man, she would turn into a pretty girl, seduce him, cut off his penis, eat it herself and give the rest of his body to her tigress.

One day she met seven brothers in the jungle and married the eldest so that she could sleep with them all. After some time she took the eldest boy to where her tigers lived, made him lie with her, cut off his penis, ate it and gave his body to the tigers. In the same way she killed six of the brothers till only the youngest was left.

When his turn came, the god who helped him appeared in a dream saying, 'If you go with this girl, make an iron tube, put it into her vagina and break her teeth! The boy acted according to his dream, and when the tigers came for his body, he climbed on a mango tree and made himself very small. The tigers chased him and the girl too became very angry. He cursed her, 'Let nothing but your face remain'. And so it was; she became a bat which eats, excretes, urinates and copulates through one and the same hole. One of the mangoes opened and the boy crept inside. A parrot carried off the mango to the Raja's palace.

The parrot dropped the fruit, it broke open, out came the boy and after various adventures married the Raja's daughter.

Sometimes it is said that originally the vagina was situated below the knee of the left leg. One day a chicken pecked at it, and it jumped up to a place of safety between the thighs where it has remained ever since. But it was wounded and blood still flows from it every month. From Bara Dongar comes the tale of the vagina which died: (4) one day a vagina died and its companions were wondering what to do with it. "Shall we cremate it or bury it? " said some, but others said, 'Let us divide it among us'. They cut it up and each stuck a portion on itself. This is the origin of the lips (*labia majora*). The woman whose vagina died was the first hermaphrodite.

In the same style is a story of Alor, which has a competition-motif: (5) the breasts and the vagina had a quarrel. 'I am the greater', said the vagina. 'It is for my sake that men go mad and die?

'No', said the breasts. "We are greater. It is our beauty that men come to see. If there were no breasts, Who would come to you'.

'If there was no vagina, who would bother about you? Do men chase a flower or a lovely stream?'

'Men see us from afar and excited by our beauty draw near. It is only then that they notice you; first they touch us, then you'.

'But no one gets pleasure from touching you'.

'But if they didn't see and touch us, how would they be excited?' 'you would be neglected entirely.'

So quarrelling the vagina and the breasts parted and went their ways. As they went along, the breasts met a man and he took them aside and began to fondle them. But when he looked dowe and saw nothing there, he was disappointed away.

Then the breasts went to the vagina and said, " come, sister, you have won the battle; you are the greatest of all".

Elwin has presented a large number of similar legends recorded from the Gond, Pradhan, the Bison horn Maria, the Juang, and the Gadba in his book *Myths of Middle India.*

The results show that both sexes agreed that touches to the genital area, regardless of kind, convey sexual meaning.

There are also legends about the penis. Originally it was of gigantic size: (1) Once the penis was so long that a man lay in bed it could get out of the house and penetrate a woman hundred yards away. When he went abroad, a man would wind it round his waist and tuck in the end.

One day a penis broke through the wall of the house, entered a woman, came out of her mouth, dipped its head into a cooking pot and ate all the supper, and in with -drawing killed the woman. Then all the women came to cut it off. The man grasped his penis with his hand, but that was all he could save. The women cut it off and it is now only a hands-breadth long.

The Bison-horn Maria attribute this incident to a man named Baikesa and say that he himself cut off his long penis through shame when it touched a woman not his wife by mistake. Another version of the tale, however, connects the disappearance of the long penis with the Vagina Dentala legend. (2) In the old days there were teeth far back in the vagina. One day when the long penis went in, the teeth cut it and all that remained was a stamp of its present length. Angry at this, the man brought a rice husker and broke off the teeth. In those days the penis itself was covered with thorns, it stood up like a semur tree. But there were no thorns at the root. The thorny part was cut off, and the smooth part remains to this day.

In this mythical past it was man, not woman, who was subject to a menstrual period: Formerly men had to live outside their homes every month. They used to tie hollow bamboos over the penis to catch the blood. One day a girl saw this and laughed at the man. He pulled the bamboo off and threw it at her. Since then women have suffered this flowing of the blood instead of men.

1592 **जनप्रवाद**

Janapravāda : rumour, report; also *janāpavāda.*

1593 **जनमर्यादा**

Jana-maryādā : established usage.

1594 **जनश्रुति**

Janaśruti : rumour, news, censure; anonymous speech signal. This was of course by no means a uniquely classical experience when Rāma had to part with Sītā due to rumour. It was the carrier of insurgency in the pre-literate society. In India, governmental anxiety about rumours can be traced as far back as the Kauṭilyan State. "Spies shall also know the rumours prevalent in the state", prescribes the *Arthaśāstra* (23) Rumour was of course an ideal instrument for making the sacerdotal function of the mediators known to the masses.

1595 **जनान्तिक**

Janāntika : personal address, whispering aside to another on stage; The stage-direction- *Janāntikam* occurs often and we know from Bharata and other authorities such as the authors of *Daśarūpakam* and *Saṅgītaratnākara* that it is depicted through the *tripatāka hasta.* Bharata does not say specially that the *tripatāka hasta* is used for an aside; but one of the uses is to place it near the mouth and the ears; and the convention emerged out of this. Bharata talks of *Janāntika* on his chapter on special representation and does not mean the use of the *tripatāka hasta;* he also does not say how it is to be represented on the stage.

The last evidence coming from the texts themselves is that of the aside (*Janāntikam*), in which one speaks to someone on the stage, but leaves others out of hearing. This aside is to be spoken with the actor placing his hand in the *tripatāka* pose in the direction of those to be avoided and turning this face in the opposite direction toward those who are to hear his words.

Thus, *janāntika* is a private conversation between two dramatic characters which intends to exclude all other characters present on the stage. Such a speech was delivered by a character making the *tripatāka* hand-gesture: second finger near the small finger and the thumb bent, the other three fingers held erect, and the hand held up over the shoulder.

The form of the speech in which persons standing close by are not supposed to listen to the words spoken to some one else due to the need of the play falls under *citrābhinaya.* Abhinava explains that it is concealed from the particular character only: It is "aside" made to avoid a single character on the stage:

जनान्तिकम् एकान्तिकत्वं चैकस्यैव निगूह्यत इति विशेषः *CNS*, Vol. III, 28); अन्योन्यामन्त्रणं यत्स्याज्ञनान्ते तज्जनान्तिकम् (Dr.I. 65). In *janāntika,* the persons on the stage are excluded by the raising of the hand with the three fingers stretched';the speech must be by way of interpreting the matter in hand and it must be addressed to a particular person by name and the speech must be replied to by the person addressed who also has to address the first by name. In *Janāntika* two speeches are involved. The idea in *Janāntika* becomes complete only when the second speech is uttered.

1596 **जनित-करण**

Janita karaṇa : derived from *janitācārī,* where one foot is in *agratalasañcara.* One hand is in *muṣṭi* near the chest and the other is hung in *latāhasta* (*NS*, IV. 154b-155a, IX. 274-275, X.25). With one hand on breast and the other hanging loosely, the foot is moved in *janitā cārī.*

1597 **जनिताचारी**

Janitā cārī : both feet in *agratalasañcara,* feet two *tālas* apart, *Janitā karaṇa.* The foot is in *talasañcara, muṣṭi* hand held on breast and the other hand moved befittingly. In other words, one foot is in *agratalasañcara;* one hand is kept in the *muṣṭi* pose on the chest and other extended out (*NS*, X.25). Abhinava (*NS,Ibid.*) says that *agratalasañcara* movement is important here. The other movements are only secondary. In fact he goes so far as to say that this is the basis of all the *cārīs.* Hence the name *janitā.*

1598 **जप**

Japa : muttering. In the context of muttering, it is said that a thread with a knot or the central bead or without it is to be used; the muttering is done in mind; if the muttering is done loudly, the *anāmikā* and the thumb are to be used. When the *tarjanī* and the thumb are used, the *meru* is not to be crossed. (*Skanda*). (b) to internalize and mutter the syllables relating to the identity of *guru, mantra* and *devatā* - the personal or sectarian god - by the worshipper. It is conceived as the easiest process of spiritual attainment. There are three kinds of *Japa: vyakta* (manifested), *avyakta* (unmanifested) and *sūkṣma* (subtle), also called *vācika, upāmsu* and *mānasa* respectively. The first is loud utterance heard by everyone, the second is whispered and to be heard only by the practitioner himself, and the third is mental and is heard by none. There are other three categories of *Japa: nitya* (to be done everyday), *naimittika* (to be done occasionally) and *kāmya* (to be done by some special purpose; *Yōgasūtra* 1.28; *Kulārṇava* XV; *Śāradātilaka*, IV. 55-56). The *Smṛtis* prescribe *japa* as part of *saṁdhyā* adoration (*Yāj.* 1.99, *Manu*, II 85). *Japa* is supposed to remove sin. It should be performed while seated on *kuśa* grass either in the house or on a river bank or some other sacred place. The repetition of the *mantra* should be counted on one's fingers, or by drawing lines, or telling the beads of a rosary (*Raghu*, XI. 66; *Kādambarī* 37). *Japa* is regarded as the best way of prayer for Śudras and women.

1599 **जपमाला**

Japamāla : rosary, garland of beads used at the time of muttering the divine name (*Sk.P.* II. 5.10-6-7). The most important of the rosaries is said to be the one prepared from the *rudrākṣa* (*Agni P*, 309.16). If a rosary is to be made, it could be with *meru* (the big bead) or without the *meru,* whence starts the *japa* (muttering). When one circle of the muttering is completed the *meru* is to be crossed over. The *japa* is to be made with the beads counted with the thumb and the forefinger, but when the *meru* is to be crossed over, it should be so crossed over with the *anāmikā* and the thumb, and never with the fore-finger. If the rosary falls down from the hand, a *Japa* is to be performed three hundred times (*Ibid.* 4.5):

Pramādātpatite sūtre japtavyam tu śatatrayam.

Japamāla is the means of mental concentration (*Japayoga*) the means of *japa.* The last feature of *japa* ritual is known as *japa-samarpaṇa.* After the *japa* is complete it is used to be surrendered to the deity (*Śyāmārahasya,* III).

1600 **जम्बु**

Jambu : the rose-apple tree, *Eugenia jambolana. Kauśikasūtra* has indicated its significance; known as *jāmun* in Hindi. *Jāmun* branch and piece of meat left on door - step at night symbolizes in the Hill Maria that the man from the house was killed in hunt.

1601 **जयघोष**

Jayaghoṣa : shout of victory; also *Jayaghoṣaṇā, Jayaghoṣaṇam.*

1602 **जयस्तम्भ**

Jayastamgha : column of victory.

1603 **जरत्कर्पट**

Jaratkarpaṭa : wearing torn clothes.

1604 **जलनिधि-हस्त**

Jalanidhi hasta : water-ocean. The *patāka* hands moved up and down denote the water-ocean (*Mirror of Gesture*, p. 48).

1605 **जलाञ्जलि**

Jalāñjali : handful of water offered to the ancestors. *Nivāpāna* and *nivāpāñjali* are also used in the same sense (Kālidāsa, *Raghu.* 8.123).

1606 **जलौका-मुद्रा**

Jalaukā-mudrā : gesture indicating a leech. The *sūcī* hands moved along indicates a leech (*Mirror of Gesture*, p. 51).

1607 **जल्प**

Jalpa : wranging, gossip, a mode of argumentation in which a man carries on while knowing himself to be wrong or unable to defend himself properly against his opponents except by trickery and other unfair means of arguments. In it the main object is to overthrow the opponent rightly or wrongly (*Darśana*); that form of discussion in which one argues in favour of one's own proposition and contradicts the opponent is called *jalpa.* (b) gossip. Falsehood often falls into the realm of gossip, and here the result can be just as effective as though facts had been reiterated - again showing how futile is the concept of truth/untruth. Gossip itself manipulates, whether or not it is true. When gossiping, the participant may articulate the lie with paralinguistic effects - a lowered voice or a whisper. Gossip can also be useful in passing information. (c) *Jalpa* is a part of debate (*kathā).* A debate organized between the representatives of rival schools, to discuss the controversies for effect and victory, is called *jalpa* (wrangling). In this contestants depend upon the false means like: *chala* (quibble), *jāti* (futile objection), and *nigraha - sthāna* (points of defeat), other than the evidence and logic: *Yathoktopannas - chala - jāti - nigrahasthāna - dohanosapālambho jalpaḥ* (*Ibid*, 1.2.2). The discussion between Yājñavalkya and other scholars, which took place in the court of Janakarāja, is described in *Bṛhadāraṇyakopaniṣad* as *jalpa.*

Later, Jain and Buddhist philosophers also came forward with their new concepts of debate. Buddhists refuted the *Nyāya* - theory of using *chala, jāti* and *nigraha-sthāna* in debates. Simultaneously, they themselves introduced two *nigraha - sthānas i.e. asādhanāṅga* - vacana and *adoṣodbhāvana.* But Jains refuted the whole concept of *Nyāya* and Buddhist philosophers. According to them proving one's dogma and tenets honestly is the right concept of *vāda,* not through *chala, jāti* and *nigraha-sthānas* (Akalaṅkadeva, *Siddhi-Viniścaya-ṭīkā,* pp.315-17; Vidyānanda, *Aṣṭahasrī,* p 87; Prabhācandra, *Prameya - Kamala mārtaṇḍa,* p. 640).

In summary, *jalpa* is the wrangling or arguing by which the parties aim to achieve victory by proving their points. It is one of the philosophical topics of *Nyāya.* Such wranglings are common in ordinary life in which invalid reasons and arguments predominate. In *Ṛgveda jalpi* means a maze of speculation (VIII. 48.14).

Speculation or falsehood often falls into the realm of gossip, and here the result can be just as effective as though facts had been reiterated again showing how futile is the concept of truth/untruth.

1608 **जवनिका**

Javanikā : curtain (in drama)= *yavanikā.*

1609 **जवनिकान्तर**

Javanikāntara : (a) the retiring room. (b) an act of *saṭṭaka.*

1610 **जहि-जोड**

Jahi-Joḍa : in the habit of hitting one's chin. The men keeping beards are seen touching the hair of the beard.

1611 **जागर**

Jāgara : keeping awake, the vow of remaining sleepless throughout the night, Keeping awake during night on the days of vows, or on the days when idols of gods are established, or on festive days is an old age tradition attested even in *Ṛgveda* (V. 44.14; 15; VIII. 89.1). Keeping awake before the idol is associated with songs and dances: गीतं वाद्यं तथां नृत्यं पुराणपठनं तथा (*Padma, Uttarakhaṇḍa,* 39.7-10). It is known as *Jagār* in Bastar. This relates to Pārvatī and Lakṣmī. On these days Pārvatī and Lakṣmī are said to get up after four months of sleep. In Hindu tradition, Viṣṇu sleeps on *ekādaśī* that falls in the month of Āṣāḍha, which is called *'śayanī'* sleeping. The *prabodhinī* comes in Kārtika (*Ibid,* 97. 10-13).

Jāgratā is the waking state. *Jāgarotsava* is a festival celebrated with vigile in Bastar, particularly observed by the tribes speaking Āryan dialects.

1612 **जातकम्**

Jātakam : (a) ceremony performed after the birth of a child, (b) astrological calculation of nativity. (c) former births of Buddha and their history, aggregate of such books. (d) known as *puruḍ* in Gondi. On the fifth or sixth day of the birth of child, the naval chord is cut off with the ceremonial occasion.

1613 **जाति**

Jāti : caste, relatives. The most dangerous of all fears is from the relatives: (*Bṛhaspatisūtra,* III, 12). Bṛhaspati has given us a bit of his mind in the following *sūtras:* (a) people are happy when relatives are in trouble (*Ibid*), (b) relatives, Cruel in their hidden hearts, cause troubles (*Ibid,* 11). (c) friendship is like a drop of water on a leaf (*Ibid,* 14).

The conception of such a reality in human relations is not peculiar to Bṛhaspati. This approach has implications for general epistemology. L.Dumont, *"Religion, Politics and History in India,* The Hague: Mouton, 1970.104-6) summarizes..." in short, the caste system should be seen as less "exploitive" than democratic society. If modern man does not see it this way, it is because he no longer conceives justice other than as equality." (d) *Jāti* is an unfair reply based on false analogy; for example 'sound must be eternal because it is incorporeal like the sky'. It is one of the sixteen philosophical topics of the *Nyāya.* (e) In Buddhism the term means birth for worldly existence. (f) The term is also equated with *varṇa* or caste. The expression *jātidharma* (rules of caste) occurs in *Gautama* (XXI.20). There was a class of sins effecting loss of caste (*Jātibharṁśakara*) (g) *jāti* was one of the social variables in *NS.* The problem of adjusting diverse social and ethnic groups within the scheme of the four *varṇas* had been solved by the *sūtras* and the *smṛtis* by elaborating the concept of *jāti* and misceganation. The *Manusmṛti* (Ch.X) gives it a systematic and elaborate exposition. In the *NS,* hardly any reference is to be found to this mixed *jātis,* from which it may be concluded that they did not constitute any distinct and prominent element of the social spectacle. Apparently, their dress, appearance, speech and manners approximated to those of the primary *varṇas,* on the other hand the *NS,* does mention a number of these ethnic groups as *jātis* which included frontier or immigrant peoples or refer to specific *Janapadas.* Thus, we have mention of the Kirātas, Barbaras, Āndhras, Draviḍas, Kāśī-kośalas and Pulindas who were all to be represented as dark in complexion (*NS,* XXI. 108-109). Again, there is mention of Śakas, Yavanas, Pahlavas and Bāhlīkas who were to be represented as fair (*Ibid,* XXI. 110).

1614 **जातिभाषा**

Jātibhāṣā : common language (*NS,* XVIII. 26-60). One of the four languages occurring in Sanskrit dramas. *Jātibhāṣā* is two fold or it has various forms as prescribed for the use on the stage. In *Jātibhāṣā* some works even from *mleccha* vocabulary do occasionally creep in as are spoken in Bhāratavarṣa. The language most commonly spoken in dramatic literature is *Jātibhāṣā.* Bharata states that *pāṭhya* in *Jātibhāṣā* is of two kinds. Prākṛta and Saṁskṛta and which relates to the four castes. In the case of *dhīroddhata, dhīralalita, dhīrodātta* and *dhīrapraśānta* type, the *pāṭhya* should be in Sanskrit. Heroes of all these classes are to use *Prākṛit* when the occasion demands that; as for example Arjuna disguised as Bṛhannalā uses Prākṛit. In the case of even a superior person (in caste) not educated or poor or due to other causes and intoxicated with kingship or wealth, etc. Sanskrit should not be used. To persons in disguise, *i.e.* a person in disguise of different kinds of professional and religious mendicants, śramaṇas, and ascetics, jugglers, should be assigned the Prākṛta *pāṭhya.* Prākṛit should also be assigned to *Bhāgavatas, tāpasas,* children, persons possessed of spirits, of the lower order, women, persons of low birth, lunatics and eunuchs. But to itinerent recluses, sages, Buddhists, pure *śrotriyas* and others who have received instruction in the *Vedas* and wear costumes suitable to their position, should be assigned Saṁskṛta pāṭhya, Sanskṛta *pāṭhya* is also to be assigned to the queens, courtesans, female artists to suit special times and situations in which they may speak. In the production of a play their native language should not be assigned to tribes such as Barbara, Kirāta, Āndhras and Dramila. To pure tribes of these name should be assigned dialects current in *Śauraseni.* The producers of plays, may, however, at their option use local dialects, for the plays may be written in different regions. Bharata mentions seven dialects assigned to different people which are: *Māgadhī, Avantijā, Prācya, Śauraseni, Ardhamāgadhī, Bāhlīka,* and *Dākṣiṇātya.*

1615 **जात्यपकर्ष**

Jātyapakarṣa : a lower caste; a fall in caste status which is caused by an advantageous marriage or by following a higher ranking occupation through successive generations.

1616 **जात्युत्कर्ष**

Jātyutkarṣa : a higher caste; a rise in the caste status which is caused by an advantageous marriage or by following a higher ranking occupation through successive generations.

1617 **जानु**

Jānu : knees. Knees are most important in the *nṛtta* technique of Indian dancing. The useful and detailed study of the foot and their contact with ground, the meticulous perfection of the basic and secondary positions attained by the knees as a consequence give each classical Indian dance style its particular character. The dance which Vikrama does in the fourth act of *Vikramorvaśīya* is one in which knees are most frequently used.

Bālarāmabharata treats the knee and shank movements from different angles: it divides knee-movements into six classes by virtue of the formation. They result in, and their use in different types of sitting and standing and reclining postures. According to their uses (*viniyoga*), the *jānu*-movements have been classified as those for the (a) *sthānas* (b) *karaṇas*, (c) *āsanas*, (d) *gati*, (e) *maṇḍala* and (f) *śayana*. In terms of the movements of the shank possible from the knee-joint, two broad categories are made: the first relates to the flexed position of the knee, when it is bent in various directions and at different levels; *i.e.* front, low, up and sideways; the second relates to the stretched and extended positions of the lower leg: here the thigh and the shank are considered to be one unit.

In the first category termed as the *sthānāṅga-jānu-bheda*, we have the following positions: *samadīrgha*, *samanata*, *ekajānunata*, *kuñcita*, *kuñcitocca*, *kuñcitoccatara* and *kuñcitoccatam*. The second and third movements denote a front bend of the leg: the fourth is the slight raising of the knee, which is used to denote climbing stairs etc. The last three are the sideways movements of the knee-joint, which result in the flexed position of the shank. These indicate the relative position of the raising shank from the ground and are comparable to the *kṣipta* and *udvāhita* positions of the *NS*, and the *bahirgata* position of the *SR*. These positions are akin to the seven movements of the knee-joint described in *SR* and *Nāṭyaśāstra-saṁgraha*, but are not identical. In the second category, the extended positions of the shank and the thigh are enumerated by Bālarāma; thus the front extension and elevation, the sideways extension, the back extension and the sideways extended elevation from the ground are all classified, such as the *daṇḍapāda*, *kṣipta*, *puraḥ*, *paścāt*, *pārśvataḥ*, *dīrghaprasāraṇa* and *sama*, etc. (*Bālarāma-bharata*, p. 261). Each extension is further subdivided but it is not necessary to go into the details of these classifications here.

The movement of the shanks (*jaṅghā*) and the movements and positions of the knee-joint (*jānu*) enumerated in *SR* (VII. 362-368, 372-376) and *Nāṭyaśāstra-Saṁgraha* (pp. 456-465; 471-477) have to be studied together, as one supplement to the other. The ten movements of the *jaṅghā* (shanks) and the seven movements of the knee-joint (*jānu*) may be classified.

1618 **जानुचलनम्**

Jānucalanam : balancing on knees.

1619 **जानुलक्षणम्**

Jānu lakṣaṇam : "signs of the knee. If the knees are not fleshy, that is the indication of death in journey (*Bhaviṣya*, 37.38); if small and course it indicates poverty; if fleshy that is the indication of royalty.

A Gond touches the knees of an elder male relative with his fingers, carrying them afterwards to his own forehead. This is equivalent at the other's feet, and is a token of respect shown to all elder male relatives and also to a son-in-law, sister's husband, and a *samdhī*.

Signs of the knees of women are depicted in the *Purāṇas* with knees like those of a lion or a cat, glory and fortune is indicated; with those of the shape of a jar the woman is a road-wanderer; with protruding veins she is an injurious nature, if fleshless, the woman is wanton (*Bhav. P. Brāhmakhaṇḍa* 5, 23-24). Normally good knees should be rounded and fleshy.

"A man with bony knees dies abroad; one with small knees becomes attractive; one with large and rugged ones, indigent; one with sunken ones, vanquished by women; one with fleshy ones, a king; and one with very thick ones, long-lived. (*Bṛhat-Saṁhitā*, LXVIII).

1620 **जार**

Jāra : lover, paramour of a married woman.

1621 **जारासक्ति**

Jārāsakti : adultery. For women who committed adultery in *Purāṇic* period, the punishment after death was to insert a heated iron cylinder in the *smaramandira* (vagina). The punishment to an adultress was that her head was shorn of hair, her nose and ears were cut, and she was driven out of the locality; she also lost her *gotra* (*Skanda*. III. 3.19.51). Tribal clan traditions also demand the punishment for unfaithful wives. A Maria Gond murders his wife for infidelity. Among the most Gonds there is a fear that adultery will bring upon them wrath of the *hānāl* (ancestor). But if an unmarried girl becomes pregnant and becomes a man's wife by living in his house (*paiṭhū*), a feat is given to the clan members and the man pays the usual bride-price. Elvin (Muria and their ghotuls 638) that "adultery is not only socially condemned, it is very dangerous; it castes a light on the village, it ruins the ritual hut, it diverts the fisherman from his catch; it brings wild beasts upon the cattle, and it causes the offenders to swell all over, and perhaps even dies".

1622 **जिज्ञासा**

Jijñāsā : desire tó know; the intensive exercise of mind, an investigation, according to *vārttika* on Pāṇini (III. 1.6). In the *Brāhmaṇas* it implies a discussion about some ritual practice and in the *Upaniṣads* it is used in reference to spiritual concept. In Indian philosophical terminology *Jijñāsā* is the process of finding both *pramāṇa* (source of knowledge) and *prameya* (the object of knowledge).

1623 **जिह्मा दृष्टि**

Jihmā dṛṣṭi : a type of glance, mentioned in *Mālatīmādhavam* (4.1.2); a type of *sañcārī bhāvadṛṣṭi*; a crooked glance, a glance with eyelids hanging down and a little contracted eyeballs, cast itself out cunningly and crookedly; is called *jihmā*, It suggests envy, stupor and indolence.

The following *suāgīt* from Chhattisgarh presents the *Jihmā* glance:

सुन्दर मनमोहना तिरछी नजर मारय ।
रे सुवना ! आँखी म मारे है कुलेल ।।

sundar manamohanā tirchī najar māray
re Suvanā! ānkhī ma māre hai kulel

1624 **जिह्वा**

Jivhā : the tongue. Tongue-showing enlarges the appearance of the mouth area by making the tongue visible between the lips. The use of tongue-showing may be seen during an involving activity. Some tasks require concentration because they are difficult (e.g. threading a needle) or risky or both. The tongue-showing may be experienced during the social interaction itself. Children often show tongue while being reprimanded for having engaged in some forbidden activity. Some tongue-showing appears to result simply from encounters with persons known to be critical frequently. Sometimes tongue showing involves physical weakness or inability to perform a task. Adults sometimes tongue-show when singled out for attention. Individuals sometimes tongue-show at the instant of being surprised. The children sometimes tongue-show while trying to avoid and encounter. A further tongue-showing may be seen at the initiation of a conversation which might become an undesired interaction. It may be observed in mocking and teasing.

Thus, among the facial expressions with which one communicates are a number of ways of making the tongue visible. Most commonly, the tongue is inserted between the lips but not protruded for; it may however, be further extended and rolled downward on variously pointed.

The Hindu-goddess Kālī is an example of tongue-show which implies the aversive communication.

The three forms of tongue-protrusion may be seen in Indian setting: the concentration tongue, the rude tongue (as of Kālī) and the sexy tongue.

1625 **जिह्वाकृतिविज्ञान**

Jihvākṛti-vijñāna : sign of the tongue. If it is darkish and spotted, the person is dear to all; if it is thick and dry, that is an indication of constant anger; if white, the person is given to clean habits; if it is like a lotus petal and thin, long and beautiful, the person has chances of being a leader of men; if moist, with red tip, the person is a knower of various lores (*Brahma*, 26.57-59).

Piercing of the tongue is a common practice in the *javārā* rite of the goddess Kālī.

Varāhamihira (*BS*, LXIII) has presented *Jihvālakṣaṇa* which is a clue to understand men on the basis of the shape of the tongue. 'Men who enjoy the pleasures of life have tongues that are reddish, long, tender and quite even, while the poor have them white or dark and rough. The same rules hold good in the case of the palate too.' cf. the following:

कृष्णजिह्वा भवेद्यस्य समला यदि वा भवेत् ।
स पापवान् भवेन्मर्त्यः कुक्षा स्थूला तथा भवेत् ।।
श्वेतजिह्वा नरा ज्ञेयाः शौचाचारविवर्जिताः ।
पद्मपत्रसमा जिह्वा सूक्ष्मा दीर्घा सुशोभना ।।
न स्थूला नातिविस्तीर्णा येषां ते मनुजाधिपाः ।
निम्ना दीर्घा च ह्स्वा च रक्ताग्रा रसना यदि ।।
सर्वविद्याप्रवक्ता ऽसौ भवेन्नास्त्यत्र संशयः ।
कृष्णतालुर्नरो यस्तु स भवेत् कुलनाशनः ।।
विकृतं स्फुटितं यस्य तालुः तस्य न शोभनम् ।

1626 **जिह्वायुद्धं चुम्बनम्**

Jihvāyuddham cumbanam : fighting of the tongue kiss. On occasion of 'clasping kiss' if one of them touches the teeth, the tongue and the palate of the other with his/her tongue, it is called 'fighting of the tongue: *tasminnitaropi jivhāya asyāḥ daśanāni ghaṭṭayettālujivhām ceti jivhāyuddham* (*Kāmasūtra*, 2.3.23). Dāmodaragupta has depicted this type of kiss:

Vigallolam cumbanan avayavaniṣpeṣaniḥspṛhomardaḥ!
antaḥ praveśaneccham nirbharaparirambhaṇam yasmin

(*Kuṭṭanīmatam*, 378)

Nala often drank the tongue of Damayanti, when he was not satisfied with kissing lips:

prasmṛtam na tvayā tāvadyan. mohana vimohitaḥ!
atṛpto adharapāneṣu rasanāmapibam tava

(*Naiṣadha*, 20.78).

Three types of tongue-battle has been enumerated by Padmaśrī in *Nāgarasarvasva* (chapter XXV).

1627 **जीर्ण-मुद्रा**

Jīrṇa-mudrā : if two tips are rubbed by *sandaṁsa* gesture, it is the *jīrṇamudrā* representing the self (*VD*).

1628 **जुगुप्सा**

Jugupsā : abhorrence, disgust, hatred. It is the basic instinct underlying the *bībhatsa rasa*, the sentiment of disgust, the nauseous or hideous. The disgust is to be gesticulated by (the *anubhāvas* such as) contraction of all the limbs, narrowing down of the, mouth and eyes, vomitting, spitting and disgust, heartache and the like.

The gaits in disgust also vary according to *NS*. The actor should move in steps with *eḍakākrīḍitācārī* on the cremation ground or battle field, odious to look at. The steps should be in quick succession, sometimes falling near and sometimes far; the hand should follow the feet.

1629 **जुगुप्सा-दृष्टि**

Jugupsā-dṛṣṭi : censured glance; a type of *bhāvadṛṣṭi* enumerated by Bharata.

1630 **जुगुप्सा-रस-दृष्टि**

Jugupsārasa-dṛṣṭi : a type of glance, used in *bībhatsa rasa*.

1631 **जुगुप्सा-संकेत**

Jugupsā-saṁketa : hatred signals. The Bison-horn Maria has various symbolic methods of expressing their hatred. One of these is to remove three handfuls of straw from an enemy's roof. Another symbol is to pull out a few of the public hairs and to whistle loudly with one finger in the mouth.

In Hindi *āxthū* is an imitative hatred signal for the sound of hawking and spitting; tush, pooh, fie. It is also a proverbial saying:

āxthū terī gāṇḍ me
ṭakā tere hāth me

1632 **जुगुप्सिता भावदृष्टि**

Jugupsitā bhāvadṛṣṭi : It is a hateful look with eye-lids not joined together, but contracted. The vision is so acute, as if the object is before the eyes. It suggests the sentiment of the disgustful (*NS*, VIII. 52-53). The glance is soiled in which the eyelashes are contracted, the pupils covered and turning away from the object coming in view.

1633 **जृम्भा**

Jṛmbhā : yawn.

1634 **जोष-वाक्**

Joṣa-vāk : agreeable speech (*TS*,VI. 59.4); *joṣam* means silently.

1635 **ज्योतिरिङ्गण-मुद्रा**

Jyotiriṅgaṇa-mudrā : a firefly gesture. The *haṁsamukha* hand denotes it. The thumb is joined to the topmost joint of the middle finger and the hand is relaxed to indicate a firefly (*Mirror of Gesture*, pp. 50-51).

1636 **ज्योतिष**

Jyotiṣa : astrology. The folk of India, like their brethren all over the world, are superstitious, No people of modern world have such firm a belief in astrology as the Indians. Astronomy and astrology are indistinguishable in India. The astronomer is often the astrologer too. On the birth of a child its horoscope has to be cast. Every king had his official astrologer and without this gentleman's advice, His Highness never embarked upon any serious enterprise. The time for any important ceremony, religious or otherwise, was fixed by an astrologer. This applies even today to the Indian politicians and the rich. Every village has its astrologer and he fixes the time for every undertaking, whether of the individual or of the community. In the villages, when anybody falls sick, the first person consulted is the astrologer as the malignant influences of evil planets are believed to be the primary cause of diseases. The village astrologer is a powerful dignitary; but he is often ignorant and malicious and may not have even an elementary knowledge of the ancient Sanskrit authorities on astrology. These hoary sages, by the way, do not appear to have been infallible in their predictions.

1637 **ज्योतिष-मुद्रा**

Jyotiṣa-mudrā : gesture symbolizing *jyotiṣa*, a part of *Vedaṅga*. Make two *kaṭakāmukhas* to symbolize *jyotiṣa* (VD).

1638 **ज्वालिनी-मुद्रा**

Jvālinī-mudrā : burning gesture. "Place both thumbs on the back of both the palms. Next join two curved fingers, joined each other. When this is in a little quivering state, it is called the *jvālinī*, which makes all the created beings submissive. (*BT*).

झ Jha

1639 झङ्कृति

Jhaṅkṛti : Jingling sound. An anonymous Sanskrit author symbolizes the jingling sound in the following verse (translated):
Clumsy! pick up what's on the ground;
don't shake the *Śephālī* branches.
That jingle of your armlets
irritates your father-in-law.

1640 झञ्झा

Jhañjhā : raining - noise.

ज्ञ Jñ

1641 ज्ञान

Jñāna : knowledge or cognition. It is divided into *anubhava* or presentive and *smṛti* or representative. According to the *Nyāya*-system, each of the two may be valid *(yathārtha)* or non-valid (*ayathārtha*). From the religious point of view it is that which eliminates suffering which arises from *avidyā* or false notions. It is basically of two kinds: *baudha* (intellectual) and *pauruṣa* (intuitive)-. By meritorious practices the latter is developed within the human being and is conductive to *mokṣa* or liberation. It should, however, be supplemented by some sort of intellectual attainment. This is possible through the study of the scriptures, deep meditation and so on (*Tantrāloka*, 1.41). *Tāntric* cult recognises the seven stages of knowledge (seven *ācāras*) which is known as *jnānabhūmikā*. The four means of *tāntric* knowledge are: *anupāya, sāmbhavopāya, śāktopāya* and *ānavopāya* are termed as *jñānacatuṣka*. A particular form of Śiva is known as *jñāna-dakṣiṇā mūrti*. The portion of the Vedic texts which deals with the supreme knowledge is *jñāna-kāṇḍa*.

1642 ज्ञान-मुद्रा

Jñāna-mudrā : (a) a type of *hasta-mudrā* known in Indian iconography. (b) gesture symbolizing the deity of knowledge. The *dharma mudrā* (*q.v.*) styled in the reverse way, is *jñāna-mudrā* (*VD*). The posture of the right hand, which denotes the possession and communication of the highest wisdom (gnosis) that liberates the beings from phenomenal bondage. The top of the fore-finger (representing the individual or *jīva*) is made to rest on the top of the thumb (representing the cosmic spirit, God or *īśvara*), suggesting union or absorption (*sāyujya*) or awareness on the part of the individual of belonging to Godhead entirely (*seṣa-bhāva*).

1643 ज्ञानविज्ञान

Jñāna-vijñāna : sacred and miscellaneous knowledge. According to *Gitā Jñāna* means 'I am in all things (=Brahman)' and Vijñāna stands for 'all things are in me (=Brahman)'. Knowledge of spiritual matters is *Jñāna*, while that of material things is *Vijñāna*.

1644 ज्ञानशक्ति

Jañāna-śakti : the 'power of knowledge' which according to the *Vīra-Śaivas* is associated with *guru-liṅga* symbolizing the preceptive modification of the supreme being.

1645 ज्ञानाभियोग

Jñānābhiyoga : application of learning (*Caraka Saṁhitā, Vimāna*, 8.14)

1646 ज्ञानेन्द्रिय

Jñānendriya : organs of knowledge. There are five external organs and one internal. The former correspond to the five external senses and are the organs of smell (*ghrāṇa*), taste (*rasanā*), sight (*cakṣu*), touch (*tvak*) and hearing (*śrota*). They are physical in nature and each of them is constituted by that very same physical element whose qualities are sensed by it. Mind (*manas*) is the internal organ which perceives such qualities of the soul as desire (*icchā*), aversion (*dveṣa*), striving (*prayatna*), pleasure (*sukha*), pain (*duḥkha*) and cognition.

ट Ṭa

1647 टक्करा

Ṭakkarā : collision (blow on the head).

1648 टगर

Ṭagara : squint-eyed.

1649 टङ्कार

Ṭaṅkāra : twang, clang.

1650 टङ्गा

Ṭaṅgā : leg; *tāṅg* in Hindi.

1651 टिप्पण (क)

Ṭippaṇa (ka) : commentary, gloss.

1652 टीका

Ṭīkā : commentary.

1653 टेर

Ṭera : squint-eyed.

ठ Ṭha

1654 ठक्कुर

Ṭhakkura : (a) title of respect. (b) idol, deity.

ड Ḍa

1655 **डमर**

Ḍamara : a riot, a revolt (*A*, 2.6.20), plundering, robbing.

1656 **डमरु**

Ḍamaru : drum. A folk or tribal musical instrument belonging to the percussion family used extensively in the countryside by acrobats, street-dancers, priests and *shamans*, especially of *tāntric* persuasion. It is a short of kettledrum, but very diminutive in size, and held in the hand. It is made of two inverted bows (*guṭikā dvaya*) of wood or clay, joined at the bottom and the open ends being covered with parchment of membrane. Strings with beads at their ends are attached to the slender middle portion (*kṣīṇamadhya* where the two inverted bowls are joined). When the drum is turned on the head, a rattling sound is produced in rhythmic patterns, as the beads strike the membrane on the open ends alternately.

It is usually held in the right upper hand of the dancing Naṭarāja, and a variation of the instrument can be seen in the hand of *bhikṣāṭana* form of Śiva.

1657 **डामरिक**

Ḍāmarika : a rioter (*A*.4.9.24), tumultuous, fearful, dreadful.

1658 **डिक्करी**

Ḍikkarī : young woman; *dhāṅgṛī* in Halbī

1659 **डिम्ब**

Ḍimba : an affray, a riot (*Arthaśāstra*, 1.17.42). (b) egg, ball, simpleton, body.

1660 **डीन**

Ḍīna : flight of a bird. Note *Nīla* on *Mahābhārata* (VIII. 41):

उड्डीनमूर्ध्वगमनमवडीनमधोगतिः ।
प्रडीनं सर्वतोयानं डीनं गमनमात्रकम् ॥
निडीनं शनकैर्यानं संडीन ललितं गतम् ॥
तिर्यग्डीनगतं प्राहुस्तिरः प्रचरणं बुधाः ।
तान्याशाभेदभिन्नानि चत्त्वारि प्रतिजानते ॥
विडम्बितं विडीनं स्यात् परिडीनं तु सर्वतः ।
पश्चाद्गतिः पराडीनं स्वर्गगं सुडीनकम् ॥
आभिमुख्येन गमनमभिडीनं प्रचक्षते ।
यानं तु महाडीनमाहुः पवित्रामूर्जिता गतिम् ॥
निडीनं निश्चलं यानं प्रचण्डमतिडीनकम् ।
अवरोहोऽवडीनं स्यात् प्रडीनं चित्रमुच्यते ॥
गत्या ललितया पूर्वमुपक्रम्य समन्ततः ।
परिक्रम्य प्रपतनं संडीनं डीनडीनकम् ॥
संडीनोड्डीनडीनं स्यात् तदेवोर्ध्वप्रकम्पनात् ।
गतौ गत्यन्तरोद्भेदो भवेड्डीनविडीनकम् ॥
क्षणात् संगत्य निक्रम्य पक्षसम्पातमुच्यते ।
ऊर्ध्वाधोगतिसंभेदः समुदीषं प्रचक्षते ॥
संकल्य पक्षगमनमुच्यते व्यतिरिक्तकम् ।
षड्विंशतिरमी भेदाः पातानामिह दर्शिताः ॥

1661 **डुण्डुप-मुद्रा**

Ḍuṇḍupa-mudrā : gesture of a kind of snake. The *kartarī* hands faced upwards, placed on the other fore-arm and the *kartarīmukha* with the left hand (*Mirror of Gesture*, p. 51).

1662 **ढक्का**

Ḍhakkā : kind of drum.

1663 **ढोल-संकेतन**

Ḍhola-saṁketana : drum-signalling. I have noted in my book *Ādivāsī-saṅgīta* (Bhopal, 1986: 155-158) that the Hill Marias of Bastar have drum codes; and they send message by the beat of drum. This sending message by beating of drums is perhaps a feature strictly confined to the Hill Marias. (b) drumming in Māndrī dances are sexual signals. It is said that the best lovers are those who use home-made wooden drums and not earthenware drums brought in the bazar. It is considered that only a very ardent lover would go to the trouble of making a drum out of wood. 'Such men are strong and can break the horns of a deer'. Any girl will go to them rather than to those who are content with mere bazar products. A *chelik* who can beat a wooden drum knows well how to beat a girl in love. (c) among the Maria Gonds a drum is beaten to announce a death, and the news is sent to relatives and friends in other villages (Russell and Hiralal, III. 89).

त Ta

1664 **तङ्गल्व**

Taṅgalva : addicted to a woman's thighs (*AV*, VIII. 6.21), also known as *ṭaṅgalva* which has its impact on Hindi *ṭāṅg*.

1665 **तटस्थ-लक्षण**

Taṭastha-lakṣaṇa : accidental quality as opposed to *svarūpa lakṣaṇa* or natural attribute.

1666 **तत्त्व**

Tattva : evolutes. (a) The word (literally 'that-sess', suchness') means truth, reality, principle of existence and metaphysical categories. (b) The science of the Cosmic principles. (c) In *Tantra* the term denotes critical values and positions one has to pass through successively. To experience a *tattva* is to become it, for each represents a stage of actual realisation. (d) It is also used for substance and essence. For example, *pañca-tattva* means not the ritual with five articles but the offering of the *tattvas* or principles they represent. (e) In regard to the science of cosmic principles *tattvas* mark different stages of evolution. According to the Śaivas there are thirty six *tattvas*, to the Vaiṣṇavas thirty-two, and to the Sāṅkhya twenty. (f) The *tattvas* or evolutes of *prakṛti* are ten in number. (g) *Tattva* also means transcendental truth : *pāramārthika satya.*

1667 **तत्वाख्यान**

Tattvākhyāna : literal description, a type of hyperbolic exaggeration. It is next step to *caṭu;* e.g., *na padmam mukhamevedam na bṛṅgau caksuṣī ime,* that is no lotus, that is a face, those are not bees, they are eyes.

1668 **तत्र भवत् (भवान्-भवती)**

Tatra bhavat (bhavān-bhavatī) : your honour, venerable.

1669 **तथता**

Tathatā : 'suchness', or 'thatness' which is immutable, unchangeable, beyond concept and distinction : *tathatāvikāra* nirvikāravikalpā nirvikalpā. Same as *Śūnyatā. Tathatā* is neither anywhere nor arises from anywhere, nor belongs to anything. Hence, it is non-dual and one. *Tathatā* has two aspects, conditioned and unconditioned, the former being manifested in the empirical sphere and the latter in the transcendental (*Aṣṭasāhasrikā - prajñā - pāramitā,* 307).

1670 **तनुदान**

Tanudāna : offering the body (for sexual intercourse).

1671 **तनुसञ्चारिणी**

Tanu-sañcāriṇī : moving the body delicately, a girl.

1672 **तन्त्र**

Tantra : (a) the art and practice of love (*Kāmasūtra*, II, *Yaśodhara* commentary), (b) loom, warp (*tantu-vāya*), (c) doctrine (*śāstra*), (d) system (*siddhānta*). (e) book (*grantha*), (f) prescriptions (*iti kartavyatā*), (g) rules (*niyamādi*). (h) The *tantra* is primarily a collective expression for practical discipline, derived originally from numerous folk practices and tribal cults, and therefore its philosophy was never crystalized or systematized. Indeed the need was never felt, for the instructions were oral and their relevance situational, they also vary according to the attitudes, needs, inclinations and abilities of the practioners, The practical aspect of *Tantra* teaching was adapted to Śaiva, Vaiṣṇava, Śākta, Buddhist and Jain ideological frameworks. Thus, we now have *tāntric* traditions which are regional and sectarian.

But some basic ideas appear to prevail alike in all these traditions : the idea of energy (*śakti*) : correspondence between the structure of the universe and that of individual (*brahmāṇḍa-piṇḍāṇḍa-sāmarasya*), the tripartite division of volition (*icchā*), cognition (*jñāna*) and action (*kriyā*) in spiritual practice; the serpentine form of human energy dynamics (*kuṇḍalinī*), the role of several psychic complexes (*cakra*), the dichotomy and integration of male and female aspects (*Śiva-Śakti, puruṣa-prakṛti, yab-yam, yuganaddha*); the supreme importance of the master (*guru*) who provides initiation (*dīkṣā*) and guidance; the role of mind control (*yoga*) and attainment of supernatural power (*siddhi*); the value of mystical formulae (*mantra*); mystical diagrams (*yantra*); esoteric postures (*āsana*) and gestures (*mudrā*); the visualization of divinities (*devatā*); the classification of practioners into *sāttvika, rājasa* and *tāmasa* types; and collective worship (*maṇḍala-pūjā*). The employment of sex imagery with mystical overtones is also common, as also the use of an enigmatic language (*Sandhā-bhāṣā* 'mystery language' or 'hidden saying'.

Thus though *tantra* is a general term for any system serving as the guiding principle of work, yet in religious sense *Tantra* first came to mean 'the scripture by which knowledge is spread'. In the next stage it was defined as a class of texts which promulgates profound matters concerning *tattva* and *mantra* and which is therefore looked upon as a technical branch of pure knowledge.

(i) religious works, medieval, involving the use of ritual sexuality. *Tantra,* derived from the Sanskrit root *tan,* to expand, means a system of languages designed to achieve expansion of knowledge. Among these languages are erotic, ritual, poetry, speculative texts, painting and scripture, which constitute a special semantic-verbal, pictorial, corporeal. The idea that the human body is microcosm is essential to *Tāntric* art, and it is expressed ritualistically in a number of ways. Both *Tāntric* sexual rites metaphors for the fire sacrifice, while the body of the woman is a homology of the *Vedic* alter. The ritual partner becomes a mystical terrain to be explored like the streets and sanctuaries of a holy city by a pilgrim. The *Tāntric* poet Sahāra even discovers a sacred geography in his own body:

I have walked with pilgrims, wandered round holy places. Nothing seems more sacred than my own body. Here flow the sacred Jamunā and the mother Ganges, Here are Prayāga and Benaras, here the Sun and Moon. Based on a magical physiology and an erotic alchemy, *Tantra* aims at the restoration of unity by the conjunction of opposites. The root conjunction is the primordial mystery of the androgyne-*puruṣa,* or cosmic archetype of the human species-before differentiation into male and female, pure and impure castes, good and evil. The *tāntric* anatomy of the human body is conceived on the analogy of the earth and sky, its members associated with sun and moon, stars and planets, changing conjunctions. Thus under the sign of sun in this magical physiology, the right axial vein symbolizes the masculine aspect and is associated with the tongue, subtle breath (*prāṇa*), the consonants of the alphabet, and the river Jamunā. The left vein, under the sign of the moon, which symbolizes the feminine aspect, is associated with exhalation, the vowels, and the river Ganges. The central vein, which unites the right and left veins is a king of double helix, marks the point of intersection and metamorphosis of masculine and feminine.

1673 **तन्त्रता**

Tantratā : the principle by which a sinner becomes free from several similar sins by performing only once the penance prescribed for the perpetrator of such a sin *(Smṛti).*

1674 **तन्त्रयुक्ति**

Tantrayukti : (a) a group of forms of speech. *NS* (1.1.23-24) reads it also as a *lakṣaṇa* and enumerates terms like: *saṁśaya, prayojana, dṛṣṭānta, siddhānta, pratijñā, hetu, udāharaṇa, upanaya, viparīta, nigamana, avayava, tarka* or *ūhā and nirṇaya.* Here the forms of thought have been distilled from the earlier mixture, just like the theoreticians of *alaṁkāra* drew from it the forms of poetic speech. (b) method of treatment of a subject (*A,* 15.1.17). (c) main canons or principles of exposition of a *śāstra.*

1675 **तन्त्री**

Tantrī : string, cord, lute, vein.

1676 **तन्त्रीमुख-हस्त**

Tantrīmukha hasta : single hand gesture mentioned in *Hastamuktāvalī,* not occurs in *NS.*

1677 **तन्मात्रा**

Tanmātrā : five potential elements of sound, touch, colour, taste and smell, giving rise to the *mahābhūtas* (gross elements) according to *Sāṅkhya.* From the essence of sound is produced *ākāśa,* from that of touch air, from that of colour light or fire, from that of taste water, and from that of smell earth.

1678 **तन्वी**

Tanvī : delicate body, quality of the Deer-lady (*Pañcaśāyaka,* 2.12), slender woman.

1679 **तपस्**

Tapas : austerities, self-mortification, the heat of asceticism. The term occurs in post *Ṛgvedic* literature in the sense of fervour (*Śat. Br.* X. 5.3.1), *tapas* also means heat. It was held in India from Vedic times onwards that *tapas* (originally 'burning glow', but afterwards used of fasting and other forms of self-mortification) worked out its effects by itself, without the intervention of any deity. This is only the more remarkable since it is almost certain that in India, as elsewhere, the ecstatic state of mind which rendered such austerity possible was originally often regarded as due to the inspiration of spirit. But it is, so far as I know, never mentioned that the supernormal effects of the austerity were due to the spirit from whom the inspiration came. The effects were due to the austerity itself. Very often indeed there was no question of any deity's help in the determination to carry out the self-torture-just as in the case of the *pujārī's* at the *ghāṭs* in modern India.

Tapas is said to be the key for many things. The word *tapas* actually indicates heating the body by means of austerities, including going without food and water. There were different types of penances in ancient India, such as stay continuously in water for a period, remain standing with hands raised up, being naked and keeping silence, sitting in the midst of fires, remaining in water in the winter season and in the open space in the rainy season, eating dry leaves, taking mainly seed up, etc. (*Skanda* . VII. 3.37.13).

1680 **तप्तमुद्रा-धारण**

Taptamudrā-dhāraṇa : tatooing method. making marks of conch, discuss, etc. (weapon of Viṣṇu) on limbs or other parts of the body with heated copper or the like. It is a custom followed by the Madhvas. In Chhattisgarh, the whole body of a sect is tattood with the name of Rāma.

1681 **तमस्**

Tamas : ignorance, darkness; the constituent of *prakṛti* which is of the nature of indifference and is heavy (*guru)* and enveloping (*varṇaka*). It gives rise to drowsiness, sloth, stupidity, ignorance and carelessness.

1682 **तमाखु**

Tamākhu : tobacco. The Halbī dialect of Bastar presents a riddle on the tobacco: *Khāyale hotī man pirītī,* which means 'something which arouses passion while one intakes it'. (b) according to a tribal tradition, when Gaurā (Pārvatī) married Mahādeó she sent her parrot to spy on him when he drank opium and smoked bhang. The parrot, sent on an anti-ascetic errand, here assumes the role of kāma and serves Pārvatī. Another tribal myth uses the smoking of tobacco to resolve the conflict between the ascetic and his wife as well as the confusion between hunger and sexual appetite: "From the day of his birth, Father Mahādeo was a little mad. One day he came hungry and kept asking Pārvatī for food. She was young and thought that Mahādeo desired to take his pleasure with her. She kept smiling at him instead of preparing his food, and after ten years had passed, Gaṇeśa was born. Still Śiva continued to ask food, and Pārvatī, becoming weary of him and of the child, went to the forest and said to the forest deity 'make my husband love me'. The deity gave her tobacco, which she brought home to Śiva He smoked happily and stopped asking for food' (Elwin 1949.481; Thomas 1954.177-8); (Thomas 1959.118). Here, Śiva's addiction to tobacco solves only one of the problems-his request to be fed. (c) no kind of sanctity attaches to tobacco, and certain classes of Brāhmaṇa are forbidden to smoke though they may chew the leaves. Tobacco prohibited by the Sikhs, the satnāmīs, and some other Vaiṣṇavite sects. Tobacco was first introduced into India by the Portuguese in the fifteenth century. In this case as a new and foreign product it could have no sacred character in Hindu scriptures.

1683 **तर्क**

Tarka : conjecture; argument justifying a certain conclusion. It is an important aid to the attainment of valid knowledge and is one of the sixteen philosophical topics of *Nyāya*.

1684 **तर्कमुद्रा**

Tarka-mudrā : right hand raised to chest and slightly constricted. (Fig. 1684)

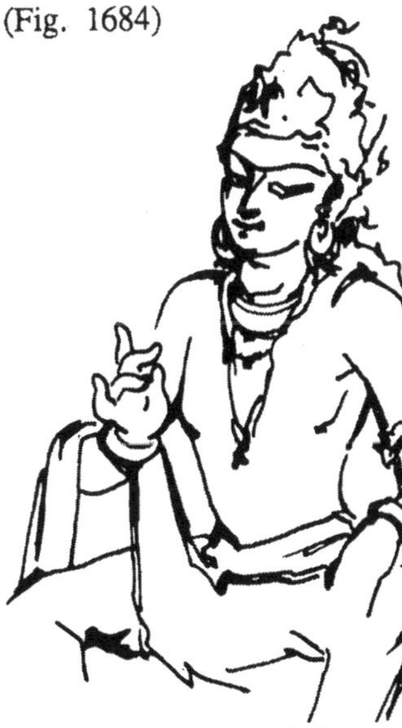

Fig. – (1684)

1685 **तर्जन-हस्त**

Tarjana-hasta : threatening hand; a type of hand gesture in Indian iconography.

1686 **तर्जनी**

Tarjanī : forefinger. On the plane of the *adhomukha hasta*, the showing of the forefinger by Śakuntalā means asking her friend to keep quiet.

Tarjanī is a *mudrā* in which the forefinger is raised upright to indicate a threat or admonition (*tarj bhartsane*); the other fingers are folded over the palm. This is usually a posture of the right hand in the representation of some gods or goddesses in their ferocious aspect (like Durgā and Śiva). The posture of the hand can also be seen in the images of door-guardians (*dvāra-pālakas*) and Nandī (the attendant of Śiva).

1687 **तर्जनी-तोलन**

Tarjanī-tolana : showing the finger : *vastra-vikrayādau tarjani-tolanam* (showing the finger in the sales of clothes, etc).

1688 **तर्जनी-मुद्रा**

Tarjanī-mudrā: is a hand pose in which the index finger is raised in a menacing attitude while the other fingers are clenched in the fist. If a *pāśa* (noose) appears round the index finger it is called *tarjanī-pāśa*. This *mudrā* is characteristic of certain Buddhist icons.

1689 **तर्जनीहस्त**

Tarjanī-hasta : single hand gesture, same as above; fore-finger-hand; The Indian sign for something perfect is derived from the hand posture for precision. If we want to say that something is precise or exact, we make the movement of holding something very small between the tips of our thumb and forefinger. People all over the world do this unconsciously when speaking about some fine point. The object they hold is imaginary—they merely go through the motions of holding it, and in this way they automatically form a ring or circle with the thumb and forefinger. When the foreginger of the right hand is shown piercing into this ring, it means calling a woman for copulation. Here the thumb+forefinger forming the ring stands for vagina and the forefinger of the right hand symbolizes penis

1690 **तर्पण**

Tarpaṇa : (a) presenting libation of water to the deceased; remembrance of deities, sages and fathers after the recital of *Gāyatri* hymn during worship. It is an offering of water and a constituent part of *snāna* or bathing which is to be done while standing in the water (*Manu*, II.176; *Parāśara* XX. 12-13). (b) *Tarpaṇa* is also a term for processing *mantras* (*Tantrasāra*, p. 54).

1691 **तलपुष्पपुट**

Talapuṣpapuṭa : a particular position of hand in dancing.

1692 **तलपुष्पपुट-करण**

Talapuṣpapuṭa-karaṇa : feet in *agratalasañcara,* side in *sannata,* limbs in *sauṣṭhava;* also known as *puṣpapuṭahasta-karaṇa* (*NS.* IV.61,IX.150,X.89). The hand in *puṣpapuṭa* is held on the left side and the foot is in *agratalsañcara* and the side *nata.* This is used by *Sūtradhāra* in scattering flowers on the stage.

1693 **तलमुख-नृत्तहस्त**

Talamukha-nṛtta-hasta : a type of hand-gesture in *NS;* slanting square. If two hands of the *caturaśra* gesture are held obliquely facing each other, it is called the *talamukha* (*NS,* IX.176-197).

1694 **तलमुद्रा**

Talamudrā : gesture symbolizing a Vaiṣṇavite deity. The *patāka*-hand with the curved fore-palm (*VD*).

1695 **तलयुद्ध**

Talayuddha : palm-fight.

1696 **तलविलसित-करण**

Talavilasita-karaṇa : One leg is extended. The feet position resembles the *añcita* feet, for the toes are turned up and the soles of the feet are visible. Hands are in *patāka* which separate and meet as they move from a high position to a low one. Palms face down (*NS,* IV.116b-117a). The foot with the toe and the sole turned upwards is extended high on the side and the palms of the hands are bent. It is used in the movement of *Sūtradhāra.*

1697 **तलसङ्घट्टित-करण**

Talasaṅghaṭṭita-karaṇa : derived from the *dolāpādācārī* : the distance between the two feet in the final position is two *tālas.* The hands come together and clap and are released in *recita* movement (*NS,* IV. 135b-154a, X.36). After *dolāpādā cārī* the hands have the palms clashing each other and then the left hand is in *recita.* It is used in compassion.

1698 **तलसम्फोटित-करण**

Talasaṁphoṭita karaṇa (hasta) : *talamukha* hands clasped and clapped. Feet and leg in *atikrāntā cārī.* Knees are spread in *kṣipta (NS,* IX.168). Also known as *talasaṁsphoṭita.* The leg is lifted up quickly in *atikrāntā* or *daṇḍapādā cārī* and then made to fall in front, with the hands in *talasaṁsphoṭita* *i.e.* the hands with palms striking each other as in clapping (*SR,* III, 701). (Fig. 1698)

1699 **तलात्रय**

Talātraya : a measure which the worshipper adopts to protect himself from malefic influences. It consists of three 'taps' with the fingers of the right hand on the left palm, in a vertical plane one above the other, as if erecting an imaginary pillar in the front of worshipper.

1700 **ताडन**

Tāḍana : beating, appropriate to suggest relevant sentiment and feelings (*NS,* IX.175). A Baiga who allows himself to be beaten by a woman or by a member of another tribe of caste will be excommunicated. A Baiga being beaten by a person of a status lower than his own has thereby lost his own normal stature. He is 'polluted' and automatically passes on this pollution to anyone with whom he has social contact. By excommunicating him the society protects itself against such contact without necessarily passing moral judgement. (b) processing of *mantras.* Each letter of the *mantra* concerned should be recited either ten times or a hundred times. *Tāḍana* is also done by writing the letters and sprinkling sandalwood water on them (*Tantrasāra,* p.54).

1701 **ताडन-पताका**

Tāḍana-patāka : both hands gestures mentioned only by *Bālarāmabharata.* Comes nearer to the *niṣadha* of *NS.*

1702 **ताडनम्**

Tāḍanam : striking (*Kalyāṇamalla, Anaṅgaraṅga,* 10.51). According to the congruence of hypothesis, intimate tactile behaviour should be rated negatively when the inter-personal relationship does not warrant it. The kind of touch that

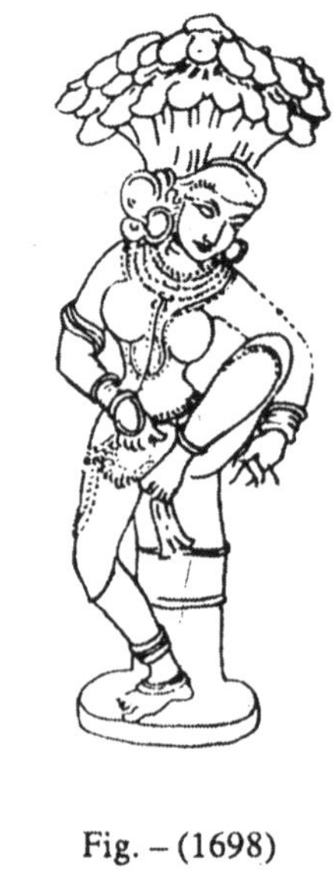

Fig. – (1698)

should be most sensitive to relational congruence is the stroke. Since Damodaragupta has shown it to be the most favourite form : *upakāraḥ tāḍanam (Kuṭṭanīmatam,* 377). The stroke which has connotations of love and sex is viewed as significantly less invasive of privacy when coming from a stranger. The finding is consistent with our hypothesis that psychological comfort, discomfort is dependent upon the congruence between tactile intimacy and inter-personal intimacy. Bhartṛhari has described the striking behaviour of a girl at the first union:

मधु तिष्ठति वाचि योषितां हृदि हालाहलमेव केवलम् ।
अतैव निपीयते ऽधरो हृदयं मुष्टिभिरेव ताड्यते ॥

madhu tiṣṭhati vāci yoṣitām
hṛdi hālāhalameva kevalam
ataiva nipīyate adharo
hṛdayam muṣṭibhireva tāḍyate

(*Śṛṅgāraśataka*, 2.51)

1703 **ताडित पाद**

Tāḍita pāda : It is the variation of the *sama,* when the floor is hit hard by the forepart of the toe after the heel has been in contact with the ground. Stepping on by the heel and striking the floor by the fore-part of the foot. It is used to express anger and pride. Also known as *tāḍita caraṇa* (*SR*, IV. 7.322).

1704 **ताडिते प्रति ताडितम्**

Tāḍite prati tāḍitam : blow for low. Vātsyāyana means that if the woman strikes a person, he should also strike in return. Stroke for stroke tells the level of intensity in sexual arousal (*Kāmasūtra*, 2.3.34). We find this reference in *Kuṭṭanimatam* (685) where both the lovers strike in the swimming pond by the streams of water.

1705 **ताण्डव**

Tāṇḍava : vigorous and masculine dance performed by Śiva, and taught by his attendant Taṇḍu to the progenitor of art in India, Bharata (and hence called *tāṇḍava*). This is distinguished from *lāsya,* which is essentially a feminine and delicate dance-form, and which is said to have been first performed by Pārvatī (*Tāṇḍavam Nīla-Kaṇṭhaḥ, Śarvāṇī lāsyam*). Pārvatī taught lāsya to her devotee Uṣā, daughter of *asura* Bāṇa (*AD*). There are many varieties of *tāṇḍava*. Agastya's *Bharata-sūtra* enumerates as many as 108 varieties. (b) *Tāṇḍava* symbolizes the dance of death. (Fig.1705)

1706 **तात**

Tāta : the old men should be addressed as tāta according to Bharata (*NS*, XVII, 65-94); a disciple or a son is to be addressed by the *guru* (teacher) or the father as tāta.: my dear.

1707 **तात्पर्य**

Tātparya : intended meaning of a whole sentence; understanding of the context (*prakaraṇa*) or the intention of the speaker. *Tātparya* (intentionality) plays a prominent role in speech Act theory, especially in the work of Mammaṭa. Here interest is centred on the communicative intention of the speaker in performing an elocutionary act successfully, and the hearer's recognition of this intention. In understanding speech acts in written texts it is the reader's interpretation which is the determining factor, albeit based on the assumption of a recognition of the writer's *'tātparya'*.

1708 **तात्पर्यार्थ**

Tātparya-artha : import meaning or significance of the whole phrase or work of art, as distinct from that of its separate parts or elements; suggested meaning.

1709 **तामस**

Tāmasa: A classification of human form based on the assumed temperament and functions they represent it. The form (icon) is shown as fierce, angry and violent, carrying weapons of destruction, then the form is *tāmasa*. The posture of *tāmasa* icon may be *atibhaṅga* or *ālīḍha* or *yānaka*. All *ugra* and *Saṁhāra mūrtis* belong to the *tāmasa* type. The *ābhicāra mūrti* also is *tāmasa*, while *Vīra* and *bhoga-mūrtis* are *rājasa;* and *yoga-mūrti* is *sāttvika*. In the classification of icons into *uttama, madhyama* and *adhama*, the *uttama* images are *sāttvika*, the *madhyama* ones are *rājasa* and the *adhama* are *tāmasa*.

1710 **ताम्बूल**

Tāmbūla : betel. The betel was a symbol of honour in ancient India. Bāṇabhaṭṭa knows about the *tāmbūla karaṇakavāhinī* (the betel-box-bearer) who used to supply

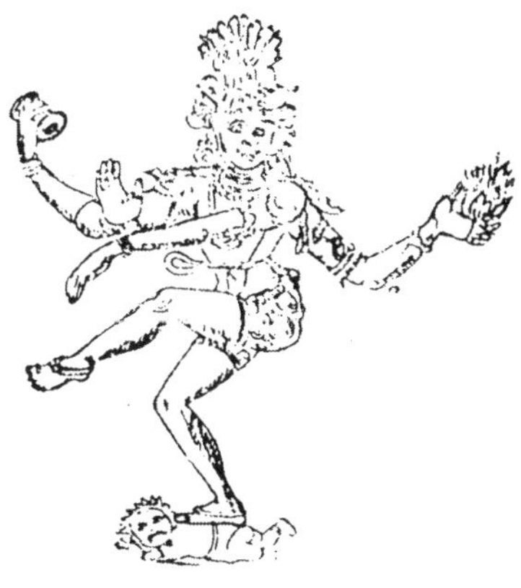

Fig. – (1705)

betel-nuts in the court. When any host used to visit the palace or the house of the *nāgaraka,* he was offered betel covered with silver and golden leaves. When it was time to declare the proceedings of the court as closed, the Māharājā distributed betel leaves to his nobles. The nobles of higher grades received the betels from the hands of the ruler himself, while others received it from the superintendent of the department of betels and scents (*Tod,* I.377).

Tāmbūla or *pān* has a significant role to play in the day today life of the people. *Pān* prepared with various spicy articles is regularly consumed by many (*Śṛṅgāmañjarībhāṇa,* p.109).

The offering of *pān* as a token of love has a significance. *Pān* is given and taken in non-tribal India by persons as a token of friendship and affection. In tribal India tobacco has the same function.

Courtesans engaged by rich clients demand among other things hundreds of costly *pān* a day. *Pān* is also offered to guests who visit the houses of courtesans.

Varāhamihira in his *Bṛhat-Saṁhitā* (LXXVII) has symbolized the use of the betel. "Betel stimulates love, reveals physical charm, enhances personal magnetism (*i.e.* makes one attractive) gives good smell to the mouth, strengthens the body, and dispels diseases arising from the vitiation of phlegm. It also bestows many other advantages.

> कामं प्रदीपयति रूपमभिव्यनक्ति
> सौभाग्यभावहति वक्त्रसुगन्धिताञ्च ।
> उर्जं करोति कफजांश्च निहन्ति रोगाँ-
> स्ताम्बूलमेवमपरांश्च गुणान् करोति ॥

Kṣīrasvāmin, the commentator adds that the other benefits are cleaning the throat, clearing the urins and removing toxins. According to Varāhamihira, betel leaves used with a moderate dose of lime imparts red-colour (love); an extra quantity of betel-nut spoils colour (or passion); excessive lime produces bad smell in the mouth; while an extra quantity of betel-leaf gives pleasant smell:

> युक्तेन चूर्णेन करोति रागं
> रागक्षयं पूगफलातिरिक्तम् ।
> चूर्णाधिकं वक्त्रविगन्धकारि
> पत्राधिकं साधु करोति गन्धम् ॥

In the next verse the author advises people when they should use more of leaves and when more of the betel-nut:

> पत्राधिकं निशि हितं सफलं दिवा च
> प्रोक्तान्यथाकरणमस्य विडम्बनैव ।
> कक्कोलपूगलवलीफलपारिजातै
> रामोदितं मदमुदा मुदितं करोति ॥

'At night it is beneficial to have an over-dose of betel leaf, while by day, of arica-nut. To change this order is a mere farce of betel-chewing. When betel-leaf is made fragrant by means of kakkola (Lutta echinata) arica-nut the fruit of Lavalī (*cicca acida*) and *jātiphala (myristica fragrans*), it makes one happy with the joy of amorous ardour.

The author here gives a good tip to those who chew *pān* or *tāmbūla.* Tobacco, no doubt, was not known in India at that time (505 A.D.). Betel leaves were chewed with lime and betel nut and swallowed. It helps digestion too. Caraka praises this habit.

1711 **ताम्रचूड-हस्त**

Tāmracūḍa-hasta : cock-like gesture; Single hand gesture. It has two variations in *NS:* first a variation of *bhramara,* the second derived from *muṣṭi. Mirror of Gesture* derives it from *mukula:* with no definite thumb-position given. Occurs also as bāṇa with slight variation. *Hastamuktāvalī* derives it from the *muṣṭi:* the finger-positions differ. Also occurs as *aṅkuśa.* Rarely found in iconography. The palm is raised facing outwards. The third and little fingers are bent into the palm. The first finger is bent and touches its own base, the second finger is bent forward, and the thumb goes to touch it at the first joint. It is used to express a cock, writing or drawing, camel, calf, the number three, *Vedas,* a leaf, etc. *Tāmracūḍa* means 'the copper-topped cock' or a snake of the same name. In a *tāmracūḍa* gesture, make a princers with thumb and the middle-finger. The fore—finger is curved and the rest fingers should touch the mid-palm, or, in a *tāmracūḍa* hand all the fingers should remain curved with the little-finger stretched and the thumb presses the other fingers from above. The first style is used to indicate scolding by a loud separating sounds of hands. It further suggests marking times (*tāla*), to bring into confidence, to hurry up and point out, to indicate differentiation of time, like *kalā, kāṣṭha, nimeṣa, kṣaṇa* etc. and to welcome the young sunshine. The second style of the same by a single hand indicates numbers like hundred, thousand and lac. The quick presentation of this style suggests sparks of fire and drops of water (*NS,* IX, 116-120).

1712 **तारस्वर**

Tārasvara : the high pitch crescendo (Bhāsa, *Bālacarita* III).

1713 **तारा**

Tārā : eyeball. The movement of the eyeball is analysed according to sentiments (*rasa*), dominant states (*sthāyī bhāva*) and transitory states (*vyabhicārī bhāva*); wherever it is not done by explicit statement, it is done by implication when Bharata prescribes uses (*viniyoga*) of these movements. Bharata has enumerated the following eyeball-movements:

vivartana, prākṛta, samudvṛtta, kampita, niṣkrama, calana, praveśana, pāta, bhramaṇa, samudvṛtta bhramaṇa, valana, sama and *ākekarā,* In *Mṛcchakaṭika* (Act I), the eyes of Vasantasenā are frightened and her eyeballs move around in *kaṭākṣa.*

Pupils are affected both by the light and emotional changes. If we see something that excites us, whether with pleasurable anticipation or with fear, our pupils expand more than usual for the existing light conditions. If we see something mildly distasteful they contract more than they should in the existing light conditions. These changes normally occur without our knowledge and, since they are also largely beyond our control, they form a valuable guide to our true feelings.

Women as well as men find naked bodies very much more exciting than clothed ones and their pupils enlarge. Pupil signals are in fact detected by onlookers in ordinary day-to-day social contacts using nothing but their own eyes, and that those emotional pupil changes are being used as a social communication device.

1714 **तार्क्ष्य-मुद्रा**

Tārkṣya-mudrā : gesture denoting a Vaiṣṇavite deity. The fore-finger of one hand joined with the same of the other and the thumb with the thumb in the same way (*VD*).

1715 **ताल**

Tāla : division of human form. (1) The unit in architecture, measurement rules of proportion in architecture. (2) striking hands on thighs to challenge some one for wrestling (*AV*, V.29.15) still prevalent in Hindi. (3) *tāla* is the distance between the tip of the thumb and that of middle finger, when they are fully extended. It comes to about nine inches.

1716 **तालवञ्चर**

Tālavañcara : musicians who keep time (*Rāmāyaṇa)*; also known as *tālāvacara* 'one who sings and dances striking palms.

1717 **तालवृन्त-नृत्तहस्त**

Tāla-vṛnta-nṛtta-hasta : palm-leaf-fan-dancing hands. If two hands in the *haṁsapakṣa* style are turned round like palm-leaf-fans, it is called *tālavṛnta (NS*, IX.176-97); see also *udvṛtta nṛtta-hasta.*

1718 **तालावचर**

Tālāvacara : a dancer (*A*, 2.4.11, 2.27.29, 3.4.22), one who sings and dances striking palms. (Fig. 1718)

1719 **तालु**

Tālu : palate.

1720 **तालवाकृतिविज्ञान**

Tālvākṛti-vijñāna : sign of the palate. With a dark one, the person is a destroyer of his family; with a yellowish one, he shares sorrow and joys equally in life. Various types such as lion-palate, elephant-palate and lotus-palate are mentioned: in all these cases the person is said to be rich, royal and of good temperament (*Brahma,* 26.60.61).

1721 **तिरश्चीनग्रीवा**

Tiraścīna grīvā : oblique neck: a type of neck-movement, a gliding movement to the side (mentioned in *Abhinayadarpaṇa* but not mentioned in *NS). Tiraścīna* is a style of the neck; what is directed to both the sides and to the upside direction. It is used to indicate an exercise with a sword and style of snake-like movement.

1722 **तिरश्चीन-जङ्घा**

Tiraścīna jaṅghā : It is one of the positions which the *kṣipti* movement of the shank can attain. Here the knee with an outward sideways bend touches the ground. Such an outstretched sitting position is frequently seen in *Bharatanāṭyam.* Here movement is in intermediate position where the knee is in contact with the ground but the thigh is lifted up.

1723 **तिरश्चीनशिरस्**

Tiraścīna śiras : a type of head movement, a gliding movement to the side.

1724 **तिर्यग्गतबाहु**

Tiryaggata-bāhu : the middle level and the range is from side to side, the slanting arm (*NS*, IX.205-206).

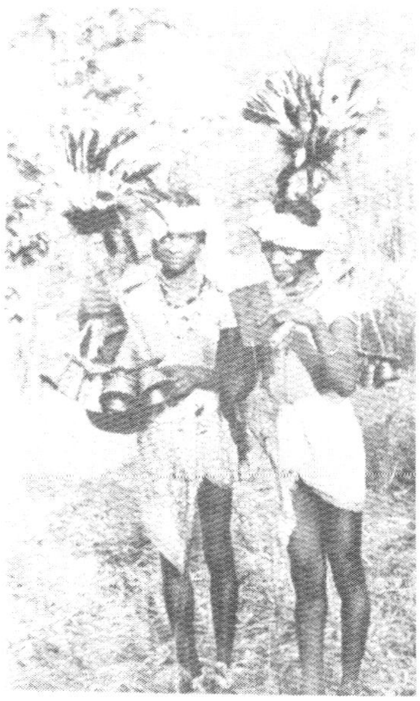

Fig. – (1718)

1725 **तिर्यन्नतोन्नत-शिर**

Tiryannatonnata śira : a type of head-movement given by *Abhinayadarpaṇa* and *SR* (4.7.74). The head in the position of up and down, slantingly, indicates delicate pose of a beautiful girl.

1726 **तिलक**

Tilaka : mark on the forehead usually made with sandalwood paste. An auspicious mark pointed in vermilion on the forehead.

1727 **तिलतण्डुलक**

Tilataṇḍulaka : mixture of *tila* and rice-like embrace. "When lovers lie on bed and embrace each other so clearly that the arms and the thighs of one are encircled by the arms and thighs of the other and are as if were rubbing up, it is called *tilataṇḍula: Śayanagatāvevorūvyatyāsam bhuyavyatyāsam ca sasaṅgharṣamiva ghanam saṁsvajete tattilataṇḍulakam (Kāmasūtra,* 2.2.19). Śriharṣa (*Naiṣadha,* 18-96) describes this embrace when he gives a detailed picture of the sex-sport of Nala and Damayantī. Close embrace in which the two are so united as sesamum seeds and rice.

1728 **तुङ्गभद्रा-हस्त**

Tuṅgabhadrā-hasta : the river Tuṅgabhadrā. *Haṁsāsya* hand moving upward and downward indicates river Tuṅgabhadrā (*Mirror of Gesture,* p.48).

1729 **तुङ्गवक्षोजभार**

Tuṅgavakṣoja-bhāra : lady whose breasts are high and weighty, quality of the mare-lady (*Pañcasāyaka,* 2.13)

1730 **तुच्योदरी**

Tuccodarī : lady who has thin stomach, quality of the Deer-lady (*Anaṅgaraṅga,* 3.20.21).

1731 **तुलसी**

Tulasī : *basil,* sacred to the Vaiṣṇava cults. Clay taken from the root of the plant is used to make the mark on the forehead after bath.

1732 **तुल्यपान**

Tulyapāna : drinking together.

1733 **तूष्णीक**

Tūṣṇika : silent (*Śat.* i.I) (2) **मंत्रवर्जित** without the application of verse (*Śat.* 3); *tūṣṇīm* : silently.

1734 **तूष्णीका**

Tūṣṇikā : silence. Silence is often communicative and its appropriate uses must be learned. Among other things it can communicate respect, comfort, support (*maunam śvīkṛtilakṣaṇam*), disagreement, or uncertainty. In many societies people do not talk unless they have something important to say. As Gardner (1966) has observed the Puliyānese of South India are neither particularly cooperative nor competitive, and individuals tend to do their own things. They do not find much to talk about, and by the time they are 40 or so they hardly seem to talk at all.

1735 **तृणोदक**

Tṛṇodaka : grass and water (*Ś.Br.* XIV).

1736 **तेजस्**

Tejas : spiritedness. (a) One of the temperamental aspects in the case of males. Not tolerating the insult or reproach at the hands of the enemies, even at the cost of life, is *tejas (NS).* (b) fiery splendour, glory, fiery destructive power, energy. It is the fiery energy, potentially destructive unless transferred or controlled.

1737 **तैजस अहंकार**

Taijasa ahaṁkāra : egoity arising from heat which is the cause of the ten sense organs and mind (*Śāradātilaka,* 1.19).

1738 **तैजस वर्ण**

Taijasa-varṇa : same as *āgneya-varṇa* i.e.*i, ai, kha, cha, tha, ṭha, pha, ra* and *kṣa,* said to have sprung from heat or *tejas (Prapañcasāra* III. 70-72).

1739 **तोमर-मुद्रा**

Tomara-mudrā : the javelin-gesture. "Pose the left hand like a bud and keep it in a bending style. Thus, holding the right arm, make *tomara-mudrā.* This is a best gesture to win a *vetāla* (a ghost) and it helps to accomplish all the desired works. It is sometimes observed to win success in such rituals which are indicated to be done at the cremation ground". (*BT*).

Tomara is an iron-club which cuts and severes (*tumpati hinasti*). It has the body made of wood, with an iron head; it has a tail-like appendage. The head is shaped like the serpents hood. It is three cubits long, each cubit equal to 24 *aṅgulas.* It is seen held by multi-armed divinities.

1740 **तोयस्-मुद्रा**

Toyas-mudrā : gesture symbolizing water of the Vaiṣṇavite cult. The *patāka*-hand curved with the thumb extended symbolizes water (*VD*).

1741 **तोरण**

Toraṇa : arched door-way, canopy. The custom of erecting a ritual-canopy obtains at various places, the belief being that thereby the advance would be successful and the future events rewarding (*Skanda,* II.2.11.56). This practice is seen even today at such festivals as the marriage, *polā* etc. During *polā*-festival cattle are taken under the canopy (*Agni,* 268.62).

1742 **तौरिक**

Taurika : he was 'expert in playing on all the musical instruments. (*tūra* : a musical instrument). (Fig. 1742)

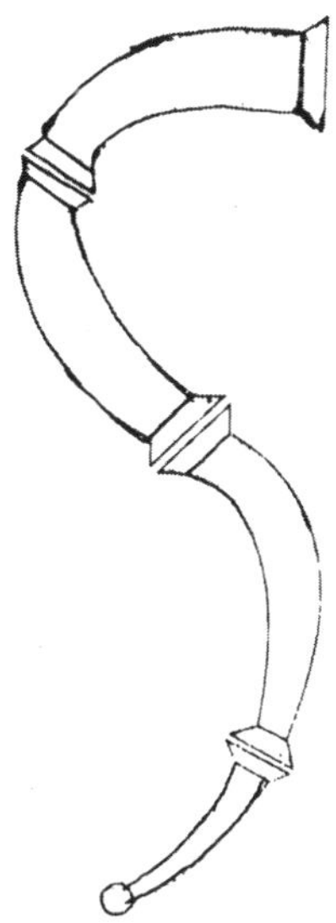

Fig. – (1742)

1743 **त्यक्तलज्ञः**

Tyakta-lajjaḥ : informal (*Śukra* III. 186) *āhāre vyavahāre ca tyakta lajjaḥ sukhī bhavet.*

1744 **त्रपा**

Trapā : shame, bashfulness; *trapāraṇḍā* 'harlot'.

1745 **त्रस**

Trasa : animated beings classified into those (a) with five-senses (*e.g.* men); (b) four-senses (*e.g.* bees); (c) three-senses (*e.g.* ants); (d) two-senses (*e.g.* worms); One-sense (*e.g.* plants) according to Jain conception.

Ekendriya (one-sensed *jīvas*) possess only the sense of touch; *Dvindriya* (two-sensed) taste and touch; *Trindriya* (three-sensed) touch, taste and smell; (*Caturindriya* (four-sensed), sight in addition; and *Pañcendriya* (five-sensed) in addition, hearing (*Uttara* XXXVI.171).

1746 **त्रस्तादृष्टि**

Trastā dṛiṣṭi : frightened glance. The eye-gesture suggesting fear. Here the eyelids are drawn up and eyeballs are trembling and the middle of the eye is full brown. Frightened glance, a type of *sañcārī-bhāva-dṛṣṭi* (*NS*, VIII. 61-92). A glance with the fear-striken eyelids, the trembling eyeballs and the panicy air is called *trastā.* It suggests fear, consternation, etc. The eyelids are turned up in fear, the pupils throbbing, the middle of the eye full blown due to panic.

1747 **त्रस्ता विभ्रान्तदृष्टि**

Trastā vibhrānta dṛṣṭi : the glance frequently used to represent the *sthāyī bhāva.*

1748 **त्राटक**

Trāṭaka : unwinkling gaze at the luminated object. (b) a form of yogic *ṣaṭkarma.* The aspirant has to focus his eyes on a point until they begin to water. It makes possible the attainment of *Śāmbhavī-śakti.* It is supposed to cure eye-diseases and give divine insight (*Gheraṇḍa*, 1.54-55).

1749 **त्रास**

Trāsa : fear. The penultimate among the thirty three *vyabhicārī bhāvas,* as enumerated by Bharata. *Trāsa* is a disturbed state of mind occasioned by thunder, lightning, meteors, etc. It is externally manifested in trembling, etc. (*Sāhityadarpaṇa* III,164). It is transient feeling of *bhaya* (terror). Other representations are as follows: contraction of limbs, shaking, tremor of the body, paralysis, horripilation speaking with choked voice, etc.

1750 **त्रिक**

Trika : a type of *bhramarī,* the sub-unit of the movement. In *Vikramorvaśīya* (Act IV), there is the turning round the *trika* gracefully (*NS*, XII. 128-130). (b) lower portion of the backbone, loins, hips. (c) a place where three roads meet, a triad a group of three. At this tri-path female powers, both good and evil, are supposed to reside. Hence it is said, that in the *navarātra* period in the month of Āśvina, at this place food-offerings are to be placed, and incense is to be burnt (*Skanda.* 1.2.47. 79-90). It is said that the woman who weeps at the *trika* fall a victim to evil powers, and if the women are pregnant, the foetus is taken away and eaten by these evil powers (*Ibid.* VI.88.44-53).

1751 **त्रिकालज्ञ**

Trikālajña : knower of past, present and future events.

1752 **त्रिकोण**

Trikoṇa : triangle, also known as *yoni* and symbolizes vagina. It is said to be due to the elevation of *vindu* (*Kāmakalāvilāsa,* XXII).

1753 **त्रिगत**

Trigata : a conversation of a triad of actors, guesses made at the cause of a sound which is ambiguous. According to Bharata (*NS*, 18.123) in which several meanings are attached with devices because of similarity of sound, and which may be comic or not comic, should be known as *trigatam.* According to Abhinava (*Ibid*) "*śrutisārupyād*" means because of similarity of words, and the word *'bhāvaḥ'* implies in question-answer form; words can be used through various devices like *kāku* etc. *"tri"* is used to denote many, *i.e.* more than one. Abhinava also adds that in a sentence the main answer applies to many common questions.

1754 **त्रिनेत्र**

Trinetra : the third eye. The third eye is a natural symbol for extraordinary or magical vision, and such it appears throughout world folk-lore. In India, it is the attribute of the great Indian magician, the *yogi.* This is its primary connotation as an attribute of Śiva, an ascetic and anti-erotic force which is used to burn *kāma.* The normal eyes symbolize sun and moon, while the extra eye represents fire (*agni*).

1755 **त्रिपताक-हस्त**

Tripatāka hasta : three parts of the flag. With the *patāka*-gesture, while the ring-finger is curved, it is called *tripatāka.* It is used to welcome, to come down, to bid fare-well, to check, to enter, to lift up, to bow down, to give or to set examples, to start various talks, to touch auspicious things by head and affix them, to wear a turban and a crown and to cover the face, the nose and the eye. By the two fingers this gesture, static and moving, also indicates fight of small birds, streams, snakes, bees and the like. With the help of the ring-finger of the *tripatāka* gesture, we may enact dramatically wiping tears, making *tilaka* (*patralekha,* etc.), rubbing of eyes and showing the curled hairs on the fore-head (*NS,* IX. 27-31). We follow here the *Kāśī*-recension. The other recensions add something more as "two *tripatāka*-hands, held like a *svastika,* represent adoration to the feet of venerable person (*guru*). Two such hands, when meet each other's end, represent a marriage".

Separated and moved to the fore-head, they indicate a king when obliquely forming a *svastika,* they represent planets. To indicate an ascetic, they are to be raised with palms turned forward. To represent a door, they are to face each other. Submarine fire, battle and sea-monsters are to be indicated by two *tripatāka* hands, first raised near one's face, and then moved with the fingers pointing downwards. With these very hands it should be indicated jumping of monkeys, waves, winds and women. To show the crescent moon, one should put forward its thumb, and to indicate a king's march (against his enemy) this hand should turn itself towards the back (*NS,* IX.32-37). In Act II of *Karpūramañjarī,* Sāgarikā wipes her tears with the *tripatāka hasta,* when her friend notices that she has been weeping in the course of painting a picture. The palm faces outwards. The thumb and first, second and little fingers are kept straight. The third finger is bent into the palm. It is used to express the holding of a trident, turning round, crown, tree, flower light, arrow, invocation, book, stroking the hair, lamp, etc.

1756 **त्रिपुण्ड्र**

Tri-puṇḍra : three horizontal lines on the forehead, marked by sacred ash or sandal paste, to indicate devotion to Śiva. Triple mark of ashes which the *yogis* bear on their foreheads. It is highly extolled by the *Pāśupatas (Kādambarī).*

1757 **त्रिपुरसुन्दरी**

Tripura-sundarī : Śiva is symbolically identified with the letter a̲ and śakti with h̲. The h̲ and a̲ are symbolic representation of *kāma-kalā, tripura-sundarī* who stands for *ahaṁ* (ego) hence, it is that all her developments (*i.e.* the whole creation) have egoism and individuality and all her souls are but forms of *tripura-sundarī,* 'a̲' and 'h̲' being the first and last letter of Devanāgari alphabets contain between them all letters and through them all words that is whole speech, and just all things are produced from *tripura sundarī,* so are all words which express the things. She is called thus *parā,* the first of the four kinds of speech.

1758 **त्रिबलि**

Tribali : three folds of skin above the navel of a woman, a mark of beauty.

1759 **त्रिभङ्ग (स्थान)**

Tribhaṅga (sthāna) : a type of pose standing with three bends. Denotes greater deflection from the plump line and is used to depict the heroic mood. The *tribhaṅga* indicates a complete shift of weight from one leg to other; for here one leg is in contact with the ground, the other can be lifted up and drawn away and in doing so the balance has invariably to be maintained by shifting the torso to the opposite direction. There are, therefore, three distinct divisions of the head, torso, and the legs from the vertical median; the central plumb line (*sūtra*) passes through the left or right pupil, the middle of the chest, the left or right of the navel down to the heels. The human figure is divided along the three horizontal *sūtras* (namely the *hikkā,* the *bhadra* and *kaṭi*) and each unit moves in an opposite direction to the first: thus if the head and hips deflect to the right, the torso deviates to the left. This is one of the significant similarities of technique between Indian sculpture and Indian dancing. The conception of *tribhaṅga* indicates clearly the basic laws which are followed in the depiction of human movement: the human form is broken up into the units of the head, the torso (above the navel line) and the lower limbs below the *kaṭi sūtra* (hip-line) and the manipulation of these in different ways. Most of the sculptural representation of Indian dancing can be classified as the *tribhaṅga* pose and the finest example of Indian sculpture, such as images of Śiva and Naṭarāja and the *nṛttamūrtis* of Sarasvatī, Kṛṣṇa and Durgā, are all in *tribhaṅga* pose. The *cārī*, or *karaṇa* or *maṇḍala* of the *NS*, when analysed in terms of the static posture they finally attain, can also be analysed either in terms of *tribhaṅga* or the *atibhaṅga* pose.

The posture that the tribes often adopt while standing is the same as can be commonly observed among the village folk. Again the standing attitude can more commonly be seen in young boys and men rather than girls and women. They stand, so to say, on foot the other knee bent so that the sole of the foot may rest against the outer side of the standing leg, the arm on the same side as the bent knee catching hold of a bough or something for steadyness. When not standing in this position, the most common posture is to put weight on one foot and keep the other foot relaxed with the knee slightly bent. The feet are changed alternatively.

The *tribhaṅga* pose of the tribes has its head and hips disposed about one *aṁśa* to the right or left of the centre line.

1760 **त्रिभद्र**

Tribhadra : sexual union.

1761 **त्रिलिङ्ग-हस्त**

Triliṅga hasta : single hand gesture. *Triliṅga* is the region called Telaṅgāṇā. It may be three genders also.

1762 **त्रिवलिका**

Trivalikā: 'having three folds on belly or neck' *Rāmāyaṇa*.

1763 **त्रिविक्रम-मुद्रा**

Trivikrama-mudrā : gesture symbolizing the Vaiṣṇavite deity Trivikrama. The length from the thumb-tip to the little-finger-tip indicates *Trivikrama* (*VD*). Associated with Vāmana incarnation of Viṣṇu. In popular imagination, *trivikrama* is the dwarfish Vāmana transformed into a mighty and marvellous form filling the three realms, the earth, the mid-region and the high heavens.

1764 **त्रिशूल**

Triśūla : trident. Also called *tri-śikhā* (triple-flame) and *tri-śīrṣaka* (three pronged) is held in the hand of Śiva and some forms of Devi. *Viṣvakarmā*, the celestial artisan is said to have fashioned it for Śiva out of the effulgence known as *Vaiṣṇava-tejas* got by churning the solar disc (*Viṣṇu Purāṇa* 3.2). It is used by the Śaivite *sādhus*.

Triśūla is known as *sele* in Gondi and it is the emblem of *Persā Pen* or great god of a clan (c. Von Haimendorf, *Raj-Gonds of Adilabad*, p. 165). Once upon a time Gond hunters used only a sharpened stave as a spear. Two beliefs are involved in the sacred *sele* (*triśūla*). After release from captivity, the Gond brothers went to Dhanegaon whey they dispersed from Dhanegaon, each of the four groups of Gond gods is said to have carried a *sele* with them to be taken to their new homes. Another belief is that some of the human ancestors of the Gonds turned into god and took the form of *sele*. The *sele* were made on the instruction of God Śambhu by Revā guru who lived in Revā on the bank of the Narmadā river (*Ibid.* 119).

The four original *seles* were later divided into pieces so that one *sele* could be given to each clan. The *sele* as well as the other emblems of Gond clans could have led to the emergence of temples where they could be kept.

1765 **त्रिशूल-हस्त**

Triśūla hasta : trident hand; single hand gesture (*Abhinayadarpaṇa*). The palm is raised facing outwards. The first, second and third fingers are extended straight, and the little finger is bent into the palm, with the thumb folded into the edge of the palm, and straight against the first finger. It is used to express the trident, three-together, wood-apple,a leaf, etc. If the thumb and the little -fingers are curbed, it is the *triśūla*. It is used to indicate a leaf on a wood-apple, trinity, etc.

Triśūla (trident) is a symbol often associated with Śiva and his consort Durgā or Kālī.

1766 **त्र्यङ्गुलं चुम्बनम्**

Tryaṅgulam cumbanam : the fingertips kiss. The man kisses his fingertips and then fans them out, flinging them towards the girl. This action of throwing a kiss could, of course, be done as a salutation or a direct act of praise, but is also seen as a signal performed for the benefit of his male companion, when the girl is not watching. The gesture is aimed at a girl,but the message is directed at his friend. This gesture is also common in France.

1767 **त्र्यस्र-पाद**

Tryasra-pāda : obliquely placed foot. The foot is kept on the ground as *sama* but the heel points inward and the toes sideways *i.e. sama* foot with the toes kept obliquely (*NS*, IX. 266-80).

1768 **त्र्यस्रा ग्रीवा**

Tryasrā grīvā : bent obliquely; resulting when the face is turned sideways; neck bent with face turned sideways (*NS*. VII. 171-175) broken or slant to side; It indicates to carry a heavy load and to feel sorrow.

1769 **त्र्यह-स्पर्श**

Tryaha-sparśa : in *Jyotiṣa*, it takes place if, from one sunrise to another, two lunar mansions end and a third begins.

1770 **त्वगिन्द्रिय**

Tvagindriya : touch as an *Indriya. tvak* skin.

1771 **त्वंकारं च गरीयसः**

Tvaṁkāram ca garīyasaḥ : To address one's superior by *tvam* (intimate hence derogatory) pronoun is an offence (*Manu*, XI. 205). see *Samīpārthaka* for detailed description.

To address one's superior by T was an offence according to Manu and required a penitential bath, fasting and a conciliatory bow before the offended person as a corrective.

When the feudal authority structure of a society like that presumed by Manu is overturned, the conventional use of T-V as a particularly sensitive register of existing power relations comes under attack at the same time. It is a sign of peasant's subalternity that the powerful person addresses them in terms of T while they respond by V. Manu thought of their reversals and tried to ritualize it as a safety measure. *Tvaṁkāra* was a symbol of insult to the superiors.

Yājñavalkya (III. 292) says: "One who addresses his superiors by 'thou' shall bathe, fast for remaining period of the day and appease the offended persons by submission and salutation".

थ – Tha

1772 **थूत्कार**

Thūtkāra : sound made in spitting.

द – Da

1773 **दंश**

Daṁśa : biting is showing delight according to Dāmodaragupta : *mude daṁśaḥ (Kuṭṭinīmatam,* 377).

1774 **दंष्ट्रा**

Daṁṣṭrā *:* jaw, large tooth.

1775 **दंष्ट्रिणी-मुद्रा**

Daṁṣṭriṇī-mudrā : jaw-gesture. "Expand your leg and contract the right. Lead your eyeballs inside the eyepits. Then have fickle moves of your eyebrows, other fingers are to be so styled as if they are holding a willow. Engage your two fingers to expand the mouth with two fingers at two jaws from two sides. Bring in and out your tongue with force. Raise a loud roar of consternation and laugh a loud and terrible laugh. These eight symbolic gestures represent Bhairava himself. This is the *daṁṣṭriṇī-mudrā,* which has an identity with the rise of *raśmi-cakra* the circle of all colourful brilliance." (*BT*).

1776 **दक्षिण**

Dakṣiṇa 'right (hand)' *RV.* Things auspicious to the right are a blazing fire, a brāhmaṇa, a prostitute, a garland of flowers, curds, flag, *pāyasa* (soup - like milk - product), a gem, gold, silver, pearl, wine, flesh, sandal, honey, clarified buffer, fruits, parched grains, prepared food, a mirror, an idol of a divinity, a white garment, a mountain, a cloud, a jar filled with water, *dūrvā* grass, wet cow-dung, weapons, a conch, an arrow (*Brahmav. Purāṇa.* 28 - 29, *Agni P.* 230.9, *Matsya P.* 242.15). The texts also mention a corpse to the right as an auspicious omen. The beasts mentioned as being auspicious to the right are a cow with a calf, elephant and a white horse (*Agni P.* 294.38; *Bhāg. P.* 1.11.18). Also mentioned as auspicious to the right are a deer, monkey, cat, dog, a pig, birds, mice and the ichheumon (*Garuḍa P.* 1.60.12). A Swan (*Brahmavai. P.* 70.25), a cāṣaka bird (*Ibid.* 23) and the *hārita,* or birds in general, to the right side are good omens (*Ibid*); also a peacock and a parrot (*Ibid.* 28-29).

1777 **दक्षिणपार्श्व**

Dakṣiṇa-pārśva : the right side. Among the males of Hindus, the right side is considered more lucky than the left. While entering a house, a conscientious Hindu puts his right foot first. No gift is received or given with the left hand. If the gift is too big to be held by one hand alone, both the hands may be used, but never the left hand alone. A gift accidently dropped while giving, is believed to have been given grudgingly, and considered unlucky to the receiver. The left hand is not only unlucky, but unclean. This is mainly because the Hindus use the left hand for washing after attending the calls of nature. It is probably this sense of ceremonial uncleanliness that led to its being considered unlucky. No orthodox Hindu will eat anything with the fingers of his left hand.

1778 **दक्षिणा**

Dakṣiṇā : 'fee to priest' (*RV*), 'gift' (*Manu*); sacrificial fee and also the fee for making a gift. It should consist mostly of gold, but if the gift itself is the gold then *dakṣiṇā* as fee of making the gift, also to be received by the donee, may be silver. (*Gautama Dh. S.*, 16-17, *Agnipurāṇa,* CCXI. 31). Among other articles which can be offered as a sacrificial fee the best is a cow. The sacrificer may also give goats, sheep, horses, elephants, clothes, chariots, slaves, corns, etc. (*Ap. Sr.* XIII. 5-7, *Śat. Br.* IV. 3.4)

The above selection from Sanskrit literature depicts *dakṣiṇā* form both a social and economic point of view. First, it emphasizes the idea that dakṣiṇā is a behavioural recognition, validation, and means for perpetuation existing social relations. Second, it points out that *dakṣiṇā* is not a disinterested voluntary, free presentating of goods, but a part of very complex network of distribution which is deliberate, interested, and compulsory. Three obligations are involved in *dakṣiṇā* as part of this total network and are partially responsible for its perpetuation : the obligation to give, the obligation to receive, and the obligation to repay (in spiritual sense). These obligations are a result of existing relationships and their perpetuation.

1779 **दक्षिणाचार**

Dakṣiṇācāra : well behaved, noble.

1780 **दक्षिणाभिमुख**

Dakṣiṇābhimukha : facing south.

1781 **दक्षिणामूर्ति**

Dakṣiṇāmūrti : Śiva seated facing the south when instructing the sages.

1782 **दक्षिणावर्त**

Dakṣiṇāvarta : turning from left to right.

1783 **दक्षिणेक्षण-स्फुरण**

Dakṣiṇekṣaṇa-sphuraṇa : The throbbing of the right eye. This indicates some calamity in the case of women (*Kādambarī,* p. 80).

1784 **दक्षिणेतर**

Dakṣiṇetara : left, other than right.

1785 **दग्धकाक**

Dagdha-kāka : inauspicious crow, a raven.

1786 **दण्ड**

Daṇḍa : (a) staff, especially that held by one at the time of *upanayana.* (b) sceptre or rod as a symbol of royal power or judicial authority. (c) a political expedient by which a king invades an enemy's country. (d) the army, military power and sovereignty. (e) punishment, sometimes personified. (f) fine. (g) 1/30 part of a day or night. (h) 1/60 part of 24 hours, equivalent to 24 minutes (*jyotiṣa*). (i) the end of the purpose of the state according to Kauṭilya was maintenance of law and order in the society because he held a view that if there was no *daṇḍa* or political power in the world, the logic of fishes would prevail, hence he said," if *daṇḍa* used unjustly, it enrages even forest authorities how much more than the house holders if not used at all. It gives rise to law of fishes. For the stronger swallows the weak in the absence of *daṇḍa* (*A*.1.4.11). "The long staff, cudgel or stick, unornamented and plain, held in the hand and lifted up (*ūrdhvasthiti*) in order to punish the evil-doers. While its employment is to beat the miscreant and subdue him, it symbolizes authority to punish. Hence, *daṇḍadhara* (bearer of the staff) refers to a person who is empowered to punish. In this sense *daṇḍa* is a powerful weapon.

(j) punishment. Literally *daṇḍa* means rod of punishment or the sceptre of chastisement. U.N. Ghoshal explains the meaning of *daṇḍa* as follows : "*daṇḍa* is declared to be the surest and the most universal means of ensuring public security and as such to be the foremost ruling and active principle" (*A History of Indian Political Ideas,* 86). It is realised that *daṇḍa* or coercion is necessary to keep people down and to make them obedient. In Chapter 15 of the Śāntiparva (*Mahābhārata*) Arjun explains the importance of *daṇḍa,* declaring that it protects the lives and properties of people when all else are asleep. *Daṇḍa* protects *dharma;* so wise people say that *daṇḍa* is *dharma* itself.

Manu's ancient fear of consequences are well known to us. For if the king did not exercise his power of punishment (*daṇḍa*) relentlessly enough, 'the crow would eat the sacrificial cake, the dog licks up the food put out for ritual oblation and no right of ownership (*svāmyam*) would be there for anyone to retain' - in short, we are warned, ' the lower would become the higher *pravarteta adharottaram* (7. 20-21).

Many of the offences prescribed for punishment (*daṇḍa*) in the *Smṛti*-texts constituted crime in so far as they were reversals of the existing codes of deference.

This helped the elite class to exercise with impunity their traditional right to discipline members of the lower classes and castes for using the language, dress, transport and other status symbols of their social superiors. For a chamār to speak like a Rājput, for a Bareia to sport a turban like Patidar, for a Balahi to ride a horse through a Bundela village, for a peasant not to leave his cot and stand up at the sight of his landlord—were all regarded as acts of inversion and severely punished.

1787 **दण्डकपालिन्**

Daṇḍakapālin : carrying a staff and skull.

1788 **दण्डकासन**

Daṇḍakāsana : a particular pose of sitting like a rod.

1789 **दण्डकरेचित-करण**

Daṇḍakarecita karaṇa : derived for the second or final position of the *daṇḍapāda cārī.* One knee is in *kṣipta* and the other leg is stretched out like a staff. The arms and hands are in *daṇḍapakṣa* and are moved in *recita* (*NS,* IV. 101b - 102a, X. 44). The hands and feet are thrown freely on all sides like a staff and are moved in *recita.* It is used in the case of haughty persons or great joy.

1790 **दण्डग्राह**

Daṇḍagrāha : staff-bearer.

1791 **दण्डधारणसंकेत**

Daṇḍa-dhāraṇa-saṁketa : signal of the holding of the staff particularly at the time of *Upanayana.* The holding of the staff is also symbolic to different castes in India. According to *Vasiṣtha - Dharmasūtra* (XI. 52-57) "The staff of a brāhmaṇa may be made of *palāśa* wood. That of a kṣatriya of the wood of the banyan tree. That of a vaiṣya of *udumbara* wood. The staff of a brāhmaṇa shall be of such a length as to reach the hair. That of a kṣatriya the forehead. That of a vaiṣya the tip of the rose".

1792 **दण्डनीति**

Daṇḍanīti : (a) application of rod. (b) administration of Justice. (c) the system of civil and military administration taught by Cāṇakya.

1793 **दण्डपक्ष**

Daṇḍapakṣa : a type of body movement (*NS,* IV. 95,8. *SR,* VII. 642).

1794 **दण्डपक्षक-नृत्तहस्त**

Daṇḍa-pakṣaka-nṛtta-hasta : standing swan's wings. If two hands in the *haṁsapakṣaka*-style moving alternately stand like a staff, it is called the *daṇḍapakṣaka* (*NS,* IX. 176-197).

1795 **दण्डपक्षकरण**

Daṇḍapakṣa-karaṇa : the *karaṇa* is derived from the *ūrdhvajānu cārī.* The hand position is that of the *daṇḍapakṣa nṛtta hastas.*

The feet and hands together give the impression of a staff : the arms are *latā hastas* here (*NS.* IX. 198, 202). Performing *ūrdhvajānu cārī*, the hand in *latā* is placed on the knee.

1796 **दण्डपक्षनृत्तहस्त**

Daṇḍapakṣa nṛtta hasta : a type of hand gesture in dancing (*NS*). The two *haṁsapakṣa* hands are moved alternately and then held out like a staff.

1797 **दण्डपक्षहस्त**

Daṇḍapakṣa hasta : two *haṁsapakṣa* hands are more alternately and then held out like a staff, *i.e.* in diagonal position.

1798 **दण्डपाद**

Daṇḍapāda : a foot-gesture (*SR*, VII. 711, 965, 1015, 1186), particular type of striking with foot.

1799 **दण्डपादकरण**

Daṇḍapāda karaṇa : a type of movement (*NS*, IV. 143). Initial position of the *nūpura-cārī* (*i.e.* crossed position of feet) : in the final position one leg is extended to its own side so as to make a staff. The *karaṇa* ends in the *daṇḍapāda cārī*. The arm-movement is in *āviddha* where the hand is moved from an outer position (*NS*, IV. 142b-143a, IX. 220, X.35,44). After performing *nūpurapādikā cārī daṇḍapāda* should follow and the hands should be in *āviddhavaktraka* quickly. It is used in moving about in pride.

1800 **दण्डपादा चारी**

Daṇḍapādā cārī : staff-like movement. Feet in *samapāda añcita* positions. Initial position of the *nūpura-pāda-cārī*. The leg is then stretched and the foot is brought down. *Kṣipta* and *udvāhita* knees and thighs *daṇḍapāda, daṇḍapakṣa, daṇḍaka-recita-karaṇa* and *daṇḍapāda maṇḍala*. The foot in the *nūpurapādikā* to be extended forward quickly with the *āviddha* (*i.e.*, the tip of the knee facing one's own body). According to Bharata (*NS*, Vol. II. p. 105) " a *kuñcita* foot as in *nūpura-pāda* is extended forward. Thigh, knee and shank are straight as a staff.

1801 **दण्डप्रणाम**

Daṇḍapraṇāma : prostration of the body at full length.

1802 **दण्ड-मुद्रा**

Daṇḍa-mudrā : gesture of the rod. Two hands and arms are extended (*VD*). It is known as *daṇḍavat* in Hindi, It is a type of prostration, lying with one's face on the ground. It is a reverential mode of salutation still practised by the Hindus in their temples and before men of high caste and position.

1803 **दण्डरेचित**

Daṇḍa-recita : a type of movement (*NS*, IV. 102, *SR*, VII. 651).

1804 **दण्ड (वज्रदंष्ट्र) मुद्रा**

Daṇḍa (vajradaṁṣṭra) mudrā : "when these two hands are tightly jointed together, just as the previous style; it is called either the *daṇḍamudrā*, or the *vajradaṁṣṭra mudrā*. The only difference between two is that hands are tightly closed here from the elbow to the wrist" (*BT*).

1805 **दण्डवत् प्रणाम**

Daṇḍavat praṇāma : a type of obeisance, falling down before a deity or a dignitory like a staff. In this type a person has to fall down on the ground, slightly to the southern (or right) quarter of the deity, with face down (*Sk.P.*II. 9.29.26.).

1806 **दण्डहस्त**

Daṇḍa-hasta : a type of hand-gesture in iconography.

1807 **दण्डिन्**

Daṇḍin : (a) carrying a stick. (b) a Sȧnyāsin, name of an order of ascetics founded by Śankara. (c) door-keeper, police-man.

1808 **दत्तकर्ण**

Dattakarṇa : listening to, giving ears to.

1809 **दत्तदृष्टि**

Dattadṛṣṭi : looking on, directing eyes towards; cp. *baddhadṛṣṭi, dattākṣa.*

1810 **दत्तनृत्योपहार**

Dattanṛttopahāra : presented with compliment of dance.

1811 **दत्तात्रेय-मुद्रा**

Dattātreya-mudrā : gesture symbolizing Dattātreya of the Vaiṣṇavite cult. The *patāka*-hand curved in the middle of the hand symbolizes God Dattātreya (*VD*).

Dattātreya is regarded as a minor incarnation of Viṣṇu (Datta means of son of Atri). He is unity of Brahmā, Viṣṇu and Śiva.

1812 **दधिसागरहस्त**

Dadhi-sāgara hasta : the curd-ocean. The *tripatāka* hands moved up and down denotes the curd-ocean (*Mirror of Gesture,* p. 48).

1813 **दन्त**

Danta : gestures of teeth; are five in number : *kuṭṭana, khaṇḍana, chinna, cukkita* and *samatā* (*VD*, III. 1.25/41-47). The *NS* reads six in the place of five; as *kuṭṭana, khaṇḍana, chinna, cukṣita, lehana* and *sama.* There is no difference among five excluding *lehana.* The fourth one *cukṣita* and *cukkita* are nearly the same with a slight change in wording.

Cukkita is likely the *Prākṛta* conversion of *cukṣita* with no difference in sense and application.

Some of the Hindi idioms symbolized different gestures of teeth : (a) *dānt bajnā* 'to chatter'. (b) *dānt pīṣā* 'to gnash one's teeth, to be in great rage'. (c) *dānton tale aṅgulī* 'to put or press one's forefinger between one's teeth, as one does when he is struck with astonishment, to express surprise, to be amazed'.

1814 **दन्तकूर्चक**

Danta-kūrcaka : the tooth-brush, the tooth-stick. "The stick which a Brāhmaṇa rinses his teeth is to be twelve inches long, that of a Kṣatriya is to be eleven, that of a Vaiśya ten; and that of a Śūdra nine" (*Manu*).

1815 **दन्तक्षत**

Dantakṣata : biting, cheeks are prominent place of biting in amorous sport. Hence Māgha (*Śiśu.* 10.86)

says : *yasyaiva vraṇastasyaiva vedanā*
bhaṇati tajjano alīkam
dantakṣatam kapole vadhvāḥ
vedanā sapatnīnām

Padmaśrī (*Nāgarasarvasva,* XXIII) has enumerated eight types of tooth prints.

1816 **दन्तदर्शन**

Dantadarśana : showing teeth, display of teeth (said of a dog or a jackal).

1817 **दन्तधावन**

Dantadhāvana : brushing the teeth, cleaning of teeth. According to *Skanda Purāṇa* (II. 4.5.11) on the day of a fast, on the ninth day in a month, on the 6th day, on the day of a *śrāddha,* at the solar eclipse or on the full-moon and the new-moon day one should not brush teeth. *Dantadhāvana* is recommended for physical purification and has to be done in the morning and after meals. The texts describe the length and breadth of the twig, trees from which the twigs and the *mantras* to be recited when using a twig as a brush (*Yaj.* 1.98; *Dakṣa* II. 6; *Viṣṇu Dh. S.* LXI. 16). The *Tait. Saṁ* (II. 5.1.7) says that brushing of teeth is forbidden to women during their monthly periods.

1818 **दन्तलक्षण**

Danta lakṣaṇa : sign of the teeth. Teeth like the buds of the *Kunda* flowers, and shining, indicate royalty; those having teeth like those of a bear or a monkey are always hungry teeth like those of a lion or those of a donkey are endowed with good qualities; crooked and parted teeth indicate sorrow in life. Full thirty-two teeth indicate the person to be a king; if thirty one, the person get enjoyment; if thirty he has equal share of joy and sorrow in life; but if only twenty nine, he gets only sorrow (*Bhaviṣya,* II.26.56).

1819 **दन्तुर**

Dantura : having projected teeth, having bristling or uneven teeth.

1820 **दम्पति-हस्त**

Dampati-hasta : the gesture indicating a couple, holding the *Śikhara* gesture with the left hand and *mṛgaśīrṣaka* with right, if a couple stands taking hands each other; it indicates a couple (*AD,* 231-244).

Dampati means the couple. It is general complaint of the older people in India that younger generation does not pay them respect. "The times have changed" they say, changes do seem to come in the inter-personal relations among the members of the family, lineage and caste. The changes are prominent at the inter-cast level.

There is little change in husband-wife relations in any cast in the village. Newly married couples do not talk face to face on village streets, while the older ones do not mind, even quarrelling publicly. It is a fact that there has always been relative female dominance among the *Korī* and the *Camār,* which is still observed. Verbal wars are frequently heard in their localities. The informants report that it is due to the earning capacity of women. They hold the same ideas about earning urban women.

1821 **दर्पण**

Darpaṇa : hand-mirror, held in one of the hands of feminine deities, is also regarded as one of the eight auspicious objects (*aṣṭamaṅgala). Nāradīya - Saṁhitā* (27.55) gives an elaborate description. Literally *darpaṇa* means 'causing vanity'. (b) There are a number of rituals mentioned in the *Gṛhyasūtras* wherein a mirror is employed. There is no doubt, that the holding of the mirror, like many such acts in ritual - context, is symbolic.

1822 **दर्पणदर्शन**

Darpaṇa darśana : seeing in the mirror. It was a common practice during the *Purāṇic* period to see the bridegroom reflected in the mirror (*Skanda,* I. 2.26.22) when he started for the bride's father's house.

1823 **दर्शन**

Darśana : (a) additional looks. There are eight additional looks excluding thirty-six different types of glances (*dṛṣṭi*) described in the context of the muscular movements of the eyeballs. These looks may be enumerated on the basis of different *rasas: kaṭākṣa (śṛṅgāra) niṣkrāntā* 'a terrified still glance' *(bhayānaka), madhya* 'gaze at the tip of the nose and very slow movement of the pupil' (*karuṇa*), *vilokita* *(adbhuta), vismita* 'eyes are flushed' *(raudra)*, glowing and bright look *(vīra), utphulla (utsāha), milita* 'closing and turning away from the object' *(bībhatsa). Ullokita darśana* has a downward accent, while *parlokita darśana* has an upward accent. In the later texts *dṛṣtis* are termed *darśana*. Thus, there is synonymity between *darśana* and *dṛṣṭi*. Some of the major types of *darśanas* are : *ullokita, avalokita, sācī* and *sama, anuvṛtta, ālokita, vilokita, lokita (VD)*. (b) The Hindus bclicvc that it is lucky to havc a look at kings, saints, heroes and other well-known persons. Seeing such persons is known as *darśana. Darśana* is supposed to bring good luck in the spiritual as well as the material sphere. When any important personage visits a city or town, the crowds that gather to have *darśana* are enormous. The nearer a person approaches the great man the better is the effect of the *darśana*. Hence the efforts people make to get near him are such that with the best police precaution the crowds in India often get out of control and lead to utmost confusion. It may, however, be mentioned that the eagerness to have a close view of a great man is universal among the mankind and the Hindu idea of *darśana* is but an exaggeration of it. (c) the third sensory organ, seeing. We get messages from three kinds of things that we see : (1) object, (2) action, (3) space. We view the person as an object, a thing, a physical or material entity. We see the person's features, physique, clothing and jewellery. We not only get messages from objects we see; we also get messages from actions we see. We do receive messages from space — from amounts of space, from arrangements in space, and from distances through space. (d) the sight of certain objects has been said to be commendable, while of others to be not good. Even a marriage procession has been said to be an auspicious thing to be seen : *vivāhadarśane koṭisvarṇaphalam labhet.* (e) The vision and realisation of truth by which a man becomes free from all fetters and attains liberation (*Manu* VI. 74). It also means both perception as well as a philosophic point of view.

1824 **दर्शनपथ**

Darśana-patha *:* the range of sight; also known as *darśanagocara, darśanabhūmi, dṛṣṭi viṣaya (Mālavikāgnimitra).*

1825 **दलित**

Dalita *:* broken, torn asunder, crushed.

1826 **दशन**

Daśana : tooth; *daśanacchada* 'lip' (covering teeth).

1827 **दशन-गुण**

Daśanaguṇa : quality of good teeth. Vātsyāyana has the liking to the good quality of the teeth when he records : *samāḥ snigdhacchāyā rāgagrāhiṇo yuktapramāṇāḥ nischidrāstīkṣṇā iti daśanaguṇāḥ (Kāmasūtra,* 2.5.2) "They should be equal, possessed of brightness, capable of being coloured, of proper proportions, unbroken and with sharp ends."

1828 **दशनच्छेदनविकल्प**

Daśanacchedana-vikalpa : types of biting. Vātsyāyana (*Kāmasūtra* 2.5.4) has classified biting into eight types, *viz. gūḍhakam* (the hidden bite), *ucchūnakam* (the swollen bite), *bindu* (the point), *bindumālā* (the line of points), *pravālamaṇi* (the line of coral), *maṇimālā* (the line of jewels), *khaṇḍābhrakam* (the broken cloud) and *varāhacarvitakam* (the biting of the boar).

1829 **दशनरदनस्थान**

Daśanaradana-sthāna : places of biting. Vātsyāyana says that all the places that can be kissed and pressed with nails are also the places that can be bitten except the upper lip, the interior of the mouth and the eyes : *uttaroṣṭamantaramukhama nayanamiti muktvā cumbanavaddasanaradana sthānāni (Kāmasūtra* 2.51; *Ratirahasya* 9.1 : *Anaṅgaraṅga,* 9.30).

1830 **दशनवसनाङ्गरागकला**

Daśana-vasanāṅgarāga kalā : sexuality can be a major ingredient in certain kind of body art. In the *Kāmasūtra* it is one of the sixty-four arts pertaining to the colouring of the teeth, garments and body. Vātsyāyana (*Kāmasūtra* 1.3.16) tells us that women should be skilled in the sixty four cosmetic arts, including the colouring of teeth, nails and bodies and tattooing.

In Ancient India a people might be both painted and tattooed, and the motive for this might be simultaneously sexual, social and women who painted their faces with sandalwood paste and musk and covered their bodies with designs of the most erotic nature. Yet in Indian religious thought a sense of bodily aesthetics was linked to and inner harmony of the soul which the pragmatic and hypocritical Englishmen could hardly grasp.

The irony is that having effectively killed Indian body painting, we are ourselves becoming more interested in our bodies. Paint and pattern do not celebrate in symbol the Indian body; they celebrate the conformity of fashion. The ideal western body is an artificial construct based on the whim of fashion. Before the colonial period, an Indian woman was a mature women, with an emphasis was on breasts and buttocks. After that she became a wraith. The emphasis is now on youth, slim thighs and buttocks in tight Jeans.

In the ancient society, the decoration of body changed according to occasion or status. Without elaborate clothing and other devices, Vātsyāyana developed a whole language of body art in which feelings, aesthetic sense and cultural attitudes were expressed by colourful designs, intricate tattooing, oils, fragrances and hair styles.

This Indian body is still symbolic in which the decoration transmits messages about groups or individuals. By transforming the natural body into a cultural body the individual subordinates himself to the common social values of his group. The Indian body has become a kind of model of Society, which aesthetically communicates customs and role relationships from individual to individual. Some of the main aspects of body decoration in India are as follows : the painted body, the tattooed body, the sacred body, the mutilated body, the plastic body, the symbolic body, the sexual body, the animal body, the social body and the religious body. Here are some of the descriptions in short.

The Andamanese ornament their bodies with clay and pigments, and the elaborate designs painted on both men and women would seem to have primarily aesthetic origin. The painting is done by the women, who decorate each other, their husbands and their male relatives, competing with each other in the designs, which are not ritually or rigidly prescribed by custom. Andamanese women paint special patterns for special occasions : feasts, dances and ceremonies. Even a corpse may be painted brightly before it is buried.

The Hindu ascetic keeps his head shaven to symbolize his total rejection of all bodily and worldly pollution. However, in Hindu society, as well as the shaven - headed ascetic, there is another type of holy man who leaves his uncombed, uncut hair in a long matted mess as a manifestation of the sacred. In fact all high-caste Hindus go through a period in their lives when their hair is left matted : from birth a Hindu boy's hair is never cut until the day of tonsure, when it is cut and given as an offering at the shrine of a God. So there are two basically opposed ways of achieving a state of sacredness, either by shaving the head and rejecting the world (as in the case of most monastic orders) or, like the prophets, leaving the hair uncut and becoming subject to ecstasy and divine possession.

Hair my be a symbol of sexuality and pollution Hair, like bodily secretions such as sweat, blood and urine, is a magical substance in thought of all the Indians.

Body decoration is in some way a kind mimicry of nature. The primitive people have attributed both painting to an attempt by humans to resemble the animals among which they live. Bison-horn Maria of Bastar demonstrates by his headdress his society's symbolic relationship with them.

But man wants to display his 'cultural' human qualities, not his 'natural' beastly attributes. Body hair is an example. Many Hindus prefer to remove hair on the body to distinguish themselves from brute creation. They believe they are more desirable without body hair. Even the tribes consider that a handsome man is a man with no body hair except on the head, and spend hours in plucking and shaving superfluous hair. The facts seem odd : we go to extremes to remove natural hair, yet public hair and armpit and body hair are natural sexual stimulants and grow in areas where the skin contains scent glands. Public hair is a scented recognition signal and a stimulant to sexual excitement (particularly in *Vedic* Age) - yet we shave it off. The reason is clear : a hair body is an animal body. Body hair is now supposed beastly and has to go in the interest of humanity.

Related with the social body, tattoos, scarification and painting may all provide signs of group belonging. In Hindu society, each Brāhmaṇa sub-caste had its own particular style of body-painting, usually an arrangement of lines, dashes or circles on the forehead, cheeks and chest; the followers of 'Śiva and Viṣṇu had special signs. The primitive tribes in the same way have tattoo signs.

Among Hindus, the painted body (and even rules of hygiene) are closely connected with religious beliefs. Śiva worshippers, for example, cover the forehead and various parts of the body with *bhasma* (cowdung ashes) or with ashes taken from the place where the dead bodies are burnt; Some smear the body from head to foot, others paint broad bars across the arms, chest and belly in memory of the long penance of Śiva. The Nāgās of East Assam think of the *tilaka* or caste mark on the forehead as a diminutive human shape and guard it from the infectious influence of strangers with an attached wormwood leaf, an effective disinfectant against the evil spirits. Generally in Hindu thought the *tilaka* is a sign of the seat of the soul and it is painted on the forehead as part of a general Hindu code. A bare forehead is a sign of mourning and fasting; but the presence of the *tilaka* also indicates that the daily ritual ablutions have been performed; before these ablutions, with the forehead bare, the person is in a state of impurity.

Thus, body painting, tattooing, even hairstyles, are concerned with the perennial questions all human beings have asked : "who am I? who are we? As long as there is an attempt to find an answer, people will continue to make up.

However, the purpose of Vātsyāyana was much more than putting on a mask. In colouring the skin he aimed to imprint on the mind all traditions and philosophy of Hinduism; the body was used to convey messages about Indian values. Body art was basic to Vātsyāyana's social and aesthetic outlook.

Even then, tattooing, scarification and painting as art forms seem to belong to the lost world of the primitive. It seems that, after all, our own world is condemned to mass-produced cosmetics, wigs and other beauty aids, and that our body decoration will never again be dictated to by social needs, aesthetic ideals or religious beliefs, but by fashion.

Bharata in his *NS* has dealt with this art. on the forehead *tilaka* mark with many artistic touches should be painted and the design above the eye-brows should have semblance of flowers. On the cheeks *tilaka* and *patralekhā* (drawing of decorative designs with scented pigments) should be there, collyrium should be applied to the eyes and lips dyed red. The fore-front teeth should be white or dyed variously for when they are coloured, their beauty is enhanced. They should be coloured like pearls in the case of young girls or red like lotus leaves. When dyed in emerald colour the beauty of tender leaves is obtained by the lower lip.

The women whose lovers have gone abroad and those that are afflicted with calamity should have one braid of hair and the dress soiled. Those who are separated from lovers should have white dress, a few ornaments and disregard for cleanliness. Women's dress should be white in religious activity.

1831 **दशनोच्छिष्ट**

Daśanocchiṣṭa : kiss.

1832 **दशरथ-मुद्रा**

Daśaratha-mudrā : *ardha patāka* hands demonstrated crosswise denote Daśaratha, the mythical ruler (*Mirror of Gesture*, p.47).

1833 **दशरूपक**

Daśarūpaka : Dhanañjaya's work describing the ten forms of drama.

1834 **दशहरा**

Daśaharā : taking away the ten sins; a festival in honour of Durgā (held in Bastar) on the tenth day of Āśvina.

1835 **दशाङ्गधर्म**

Daśāṅgadharma : ten-fold duty. *Vāmana Purāṇa* (14.1) mentions 'ten-fold duty' which comprises non-injury, truth, non-theft, giving gifts, pardon, control, pacification, benevolence, purity and penance.

1836 **दष्ट चिबुक**

Daṣṭa cibuka : biting of lower lip with teeth, lips between the teeth; lower lip is bitten by teeth. The movement of the chin in *raudra rasa;* cutting lower lip by teeth. It expresses anger or some furious actions (*NS*, VIII. 141-146).

1837 **दष्टाधर**

Daṣṭādhara : bitten lower lip; also termed *gāḍha-dantapada-tāḍitādharam.* Lower lip is injured owing to the deep tooth-mark. Śiva injured the lower lip of Pārvatī in the amorous sport (*Kumārasambhava*, 8.88) *daṣṭamuktamadharoṣṭham-ambikā* (*ibid*, 8.18) the lower lip of Pārvatī was bitten by Śiva.

1838 **दाक्षिणात्या-प्रवृत्ति**

Dākṣiṇātyā-pravṛtti : Southern local usage. The southerners have abundance of *Kaiśikī.* They prefer music and dance and their gestures are clever and graceful. The people in the region that lies between southern ocean and the Vindhya mountain are to have this *pravṛtti* (*NS*).

1839 **दान**

Dāna : (a) a liquid substance exuding from elephant's body (*Gajaśāstra*), (b) gift : one of the four means (*upāya*) of influencing one's enemy in one's favour (*Smṛti*). (c) a variety of gifts given at important occasions. Most of the gifts are enjoined to be given on the occasion of the completion of a certain *vrata* (*vow*), or at funeral rites or on auspicious constellations (*Varāha Purāṇa*, 54-65). (d) There are six *aṅgas* or constituents of *dāna* : the donor, the donee, charitable attitude (*śraddhā*), the subject of the gift, proper time and proper place (*Manu*, IV.226-27). *Dānas* are divided into *nitya* (whatever is given everyday such as food etc.) and *naimittaka* (what is given at specified times) and *kāmya* (what is given motivated by desire to secure progeny, victory, prosperity, heaven, wife, etc.). There are proper times for making gifts, specially recommended is the time of eclipse, the end of the lunar months and on holy days.

(e) The religious nature of all social activity is revealed in the gift to Brāhmaṇ; material good in exchange for a spiritual good. Thus material goods are transformed into values. Since the Brāhmaṇa represents the apex of religious status all exchange of services gravitates round his pivotal role. The king is guardian of all material wealth, or if one likes, its agent. The Brāhmaṇa priest is the microcosm of the microcosmic Brahman, or Divine substratum, the point where the sacred in man meets the universal sacred priest as repository of universal Brahman. Through the sacrifice the priest mediator transmits the sacred to the king, and through the king it flows into the body of society. The circle is completed by the substance of the sacrifice itself, the gift of sacrificial animals which the society itself offers. While we are still some distance from explaining caste gradation, we have arrived at the unitary hierarchical order which encircles it. The religious and economic unity of the society is inseparably linked with the cosmic order. 'Hierarchy integrates the society by reference to its values' (Dumont).

In the *jajmāni*-system the village is the locus within which there exists and exchange of services and gifts between patron and client, and payment in kind is the general practice.

This system ensures the services of specialists and their subsistence; in exchange they receive annual gifts of products from the soil - a fixed portion of the crop. The decadence of the *jajmāni* system in modern times originates precisely where we would expect it - in moneterization. Once the profit motive was introduced into economic relations between villagers the ideals of sacrifice, service and reciprocity were dealt with a severe blow. (Fig. 1839)

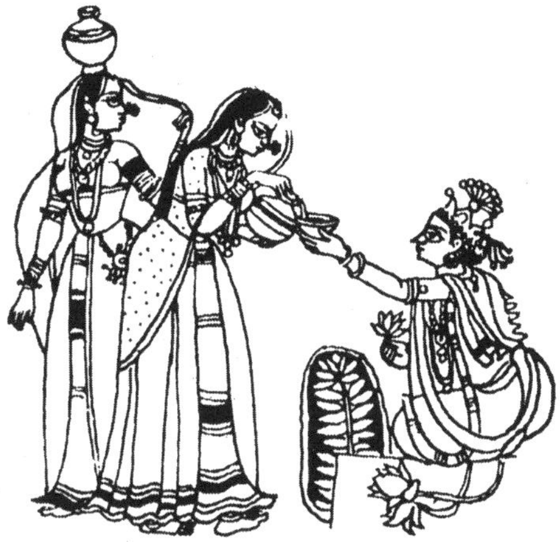

Fig. – (1839)

1840 **दानमादानम्**

Dānamādānam : giving-and-taking behaviour. The value of rules regulating giving-and-taking behaviour is evident in Indian society. To be dependent upon one another provides security; having obliged others through gifts ties a net strong enough to protect an individual hit by bad luck of disaster. Besides constituting a safety device, sharing and receiving is an important factor in the binding process, on the psychological level. It appears, mediates, diminishes tension, or just simply helps to make friends.

Eyebrow flash and proximic shift towards a potential giver are prerequisites for any contact. Offering a gift is mostly accompanied by continued eye contact, stretching out the palms and touching the addresses. The refusal to give can be stated by breaking skin contact with the requesting partner, making a proxemic shift away from him, drawing back the object, covering it with hands, turning off movements of rump and head, continuing, or starting a dyad with a third partner. It may be accompanied by an embarrassed smile and/or avoidance of eye contact.

While simply taking an object is an aggressive act, giving has the general function and meaning of appeasement and tension relieving.

1841 **दारुगर्भा**

Dārugarbhā : wooden doll.

1842 **दास**

Dāsa : slave, Śūdra, servant.

1843 **दासी**

Dāsī : slave - girls. Among gifts slaves and slave-girls are mentioned in the *Skanda - Purāṇa* (V. 1.53.23). The slave - girls are divided into four types - *devadāsi* (temple - girls), *brahmadāsī* (a girl with a brāhmaṇa), *svatantrā* (free-lancing) and *Śūdra-dāsi* (a girl with a Śūdra). The first two are said to have the status of a kṣatriya woman, the other two are said to be on par with prostitutes (*Brahmāṇḍa P.*, II. 4.8. 11-12). The temple - girls are termed *kāmadā*, which would indicate their sexual purpose, and also *bhoga - sutā*, which supports the same idea.

1844 **दासीपुत्र**

Dāsīputra : son of a female slave : expresses contempt.

1845 **दासीब्राह्मण**

Dāsībrāhmaṇa : a brāhmaṇa who is going after a *dāsi.*

1846 **दिक्-कन्या**

Dik-kanyā : a quarter of the sky as a virgin; also known as *dikkāntā, dikkāminī, dik - sundarī, digaṅganā.*

1847 **दिक्-कर**

Dik-kara : a youth; *dikkar* Halbi; *dik-karī*, 'a young woman' in Halbi *dikkarī.*

1848 **दिक्काल**

Dikkāla : time and space : The perceiving of space and time is dependent on the organization of the organism. The interaction of time and space effect on human behaviour. The comparison between cultures of the use of time and space provides some insight. It is curious that in dreams one encounters the anachronism of scenes where persons from different periods of one's life are interacting.

The consideration of time calls for communicating the concept of 'yesterday' and 'tomorrow'. Varāhamihira (505 A.D) under the chapter digdāhalakṣaṇa (*Bṛhat-Saṁhitā* XXXI. 1-5) has presented signs of glow at the horizon. He says "A calm sky, glossy and bright stars, breeze blowing in a clock-wise direction, and the blaze in the horizon with the colour of gold, are for the prosperity of mankind and kings :

नभः प्रसन्नं विमलानि भानि प्रदक्षिणं भाति सदागतिश्च ।
दिशा च दाहः कनकावदातो हिताय लोकस्य सपार्थिवस्य ॥

1849 **दिक्शूल**

Dikśūla : particular days on which travel is not allowed in certain directions. The East is generally favourite direction for the castes and tribes both. In his field the Gond will draw his first furrow facing the East and he will commence reaping. He thinks by doing so he will get bumper crop. When marriages are performed the bridegroom and bride are made to stand facing the East for the purpose of pouring water over their heads. Act begins facing the East. Similarly *ānālkuṇḍa* (*Pitar*) is kept inside the house to the East. Around Jagdalpur a dead body is burnt on the pyre with its head to the north and its feet to the south. In Bhopalpatanam it is burnt with its head pointing to the East and its feet to the West.

1850 **दिक्स्वस्तिक-करण**

Diksvastika karaṇa : describes the sideways movement. Hand and feet in *svastika.* One continuous movement and sideways of crossed feet and hands (*NS,* IV. 77-78). With *svastika* of hands and feet, the dancer turns in all the four directions. It is employed in the movement of the body while singing.

1851 **दिगन्तरम्**

Digantaram : distances in space. Distances in space both laterally and vertically were used as status markers. 'The regulation of the difference among men in rank' at Akbar's court was quite clearly a matter of seating and standing arrangements : the nearer a royal prince or noble was to the throne; the more important he was supposed to be (Abul-Fazl : 168 - 9).

Distance was still very much in evidence as an index of seniority in age and caste in rural society. It was a part of Coorg etiquette that a youth did not walk with and elder side by side but a few respectful paces behind him (Srinivas : 1952 : 48). In formal gatherings around a cot in a UP village often conformed to the same pattern." If all are members of one caste, the oldest person sits at the head of the cot.... others sit next in order of prestige ranking. If a Brāhmaṇa is present he will be offered the head seat. Lower caste persons and sometimes also poor Rajputs will sit on the floor and untouchables at a slight distance from the group (Gumperz : 159). Notice how the inferiority of the poorer Rajputs and untouchables is indicated by the fact of their having to squat on the floor while the Brāhmaṇa has his seat on the cot. This constitutes yet another aspect of proxemics, that is, the expression of hierarchical differences in terms of levels of seating. The subordinate must not be seated above the superordinate. A unmistakably feudal notion, this too has an ancestry stretching back to the *Smṛtis.*

Manu (II. 1 98) says : "When his teacher is high, a pupil must let his bed or seat be low." The principle worked with the followers of Islam as well. When the Pir Pagaro was taken out in a ceremonial procession, a devout Hur, we are told, left her perch of the roof of a nearby house so that she would not be situated higher than her spiritual leader when the latter passed along the road (Lambrick, H.T. *The Terrorist,* London, 1972 :31). Secular authorities also operated by the same sign. Beals observed that in Gopalpur even the more important men of the village would, when they called on the landlord sit on the ground beneath the platform occupied by the latter (Beals, Alan R. *Gopalpur,* New York, 1962 : 61).

Distance thus was a measure of prestige. No wonder that the followers of Birsa remembered this when explaining to their people how they 'had lost their honour and were biting dust' they mentioned that the Mundas were, among other humiliations, barred by the Raja and the Zamindars from using chairs and high seats (Singh, Suresh. *Dust storm and Hanging Mist,* Calcutta, 1966: 77). Indeed their revolt, like all others of its kinds, was made up of the peasant's wage to recover his self - respect by eliminating or turning against his oppressors the apparently innocuous, because traditionally tolerated, signs of subalternity, such as those of prescribed distances, which had been imposed on them. Inversions of this order occur frequently and on a large scale in the course of all such massive explosions of violence. The rule of differential heights is broken whenever the peasants ride past a landlord's or an upper-caste man's house on horseback during a riot in defiance of customary prohibitions. The calculated and otherwise inviolable margins of avoidance in a caste - ridden society sensitive to pollution are necessarily infringed when-ever they raid a Zamindar's or a bania's residence, or lay their hands on the person of anyone in authority.

Anthropological literature is packed with details of prohibitions imposed on low-caste villagers with regard to riding, access to upper-caste houses, etc. Thus, in Nimar district of Madhya Pradesh, 'a Balahi riding a horse must dismount when he meets a high-caste man or when he passes through a village. Rajputs often force a Balahi rider to dismount if he forgets to do so. (Fuchs : 81). Again, in Malabar a high-caste Hindu's main house used to be located, according to Logan, at the very centre of a rectangular residential space surrounded by garden. The reason for the selection of this spot is explained to be that a Malayali tries to be as far as possible away from the polluting caste people who may approach the house as far as the fence, but may not enter the garden (Logan, *Malabar,* Vol. I, Madras, 1951 : 84).

Such symbols constitute the staple of peasant grievances. The rural masses everywhere use these both as a measure of their own deprivation and as objectives worth fighting for when roused to do so. These figures therefore conspicuously in all rebel discourse in that ancestral voice of insurgency, in the Birsaite propaganda on the one of the ulgulan. A Chhattisgarhi folk song says : "They are clad in velvet, while we go dressed in course cloth. They have the good bread, we have husks and straw, they have shelter and each in their fine manors, and we have hardship and toil, the wind and the rain in the fields. And from us must come, from our labour, the things which keep them in luxury :-

Dress, food, Mansions - these and other things which keep them in luxury, crowd into all *cahiers de dolences* whereever they originate. *Annadācaraṇa Tarkacūrāmaṇi,* a modern *Sanskrit* poet has also lamented on this type of social distance :

Adopted to the tribal conditions, the same sort of contrast is implied in the Muṇḍā *pracārakas'* enumeration of the wrongs suffered by their tribe : "The Raja and Zamindars exploited them and reduced them to a position of carriers (forced and unpaid labourers) and dependents, deprived them of their clothes, their *dhoti* and garments, turban and footwear; they could not use even an umbrella. They were not allowed to sit on chairs and high seat, to enter a temple or to eat from golden or silver or brass plates" (Singh : 77).

The list ofcourse could be longer. For the authority the elite had over the peasantry was nearly all-pervasive and symbolised by many objects and attitudes. Indeed the struggle for any significant change in existing power relations in the countryside often appears as a contest between those who are determined to retain their tradition monopoly of such status symbols and others who are keen on appropriating them that is- as a cultural conflict. This is why all dominant cultures are particularly sensitive to anything which even remotely looks like usurpation and quick to discipline offenders.

1852 **दिगम्बर**

Digambara : skyclad. The term is applied to deities who are represented as devoid of clothes (*viz.* nude). Some forms of Śiva answer to this description (e.g. *Bhikṣāṭana - mūrti, Kaṅkāla - mūrti;* the Bhairava is generally represented as naked. All the *tīrthaṅkaras* are prescribed to be shown without garments (*vivastra*). Images of Bāla - Kṛṣṇa are also shown naked.

Nakedness is an erotic symbol. The sexual aspect of Śiva's nakedness is particularly apparent in the Pine forest. He is naked in the earliest *Mahābhārata* (XIII. 14. 101-2) reference to his love-play with the wives and daughters of the sages, and the commentator uses the epithet *digambara* for this purpose.

1853 **दिगम्बरी**

Digambarī : the feminine version of *digambara.* The name refers to the goddesses (usually forms of Pārvatī) that are represented as nude. Especially, Hingulā -devi is known as *digambarī. Kulārṇava - Tantra* describes Durgā as '*digambarī*', and *dhyāna - śloka* of Kālī describes that the goddess is "dark like the rain - bearing cloud and utterly nude" : *mahāmegha - prabhām caiva digambarīm.*

1854 **दिग्धहस्त**

Digdhahasta : having a poisonous arrow in hand.

1855 **दिधिषू**

Didhiṣū : the girl whose younger sister is married before her own marriage. (b) suitor. (c) In *Skanda Purāṇa* (VII. 1. 207.49) the word indicates a freshly married woman. Husband's younger brother was called *didhiṣū-pati* in the event of the death of the husband and marring the elder-brother's wife.

1856 **दिधिषू-हस्त**

Didhiṣū-hasta : a sister of the husband hand; If at the end of the *devara-hasta* (q.v.), the hand of a woman is held by the right hand; it indicates the hand of a sister of the husband (*AD*, 231-244).

1857 **दिनचर्या**

Dinacaryā : daily work.

1858 **दिलीप-हस्त**

Dilīpa-hasta : *patāka-hasta* represents the mythical king Dilīpa (*Mirror of Gesture,* p. 47).

1859 **दिवसमुद्रा**

Divasa-mudrā : day's wages; *dihāṛī* in Hindi of Bombay region.

1860 **दिव्या मुद्रा (कान्ता मुद्रा)**

Divyā mudrā (Kāntā mudrā) : "the first circle of dance should be performed with encircling hands in the position of the *daṇḍakāsana* and keeping the neck and the head erect. The arm and elbow of the hand should be kept parallel and equal to the knee-joint. One of fore-fingers of a clenched fist is to be made straight and extended and the other is to be placed on the cheek, according to the rule, in a bending style. The fore-finger joining the thumb is to be curved for the purpose referred to above. The rest of fingers are to be extended in a style of stair-case. The countenance should be made happy and peaceful. This is the greatest gesture called *kāntā* which increases one's own knowledge (*BT*).

1861 **दीक्षा-मुद्रा**

Dīkṣā-mudrā : gesture of initiation. If the thumb is placed between the *kaniṣṭhā* (the little finger) and the ring-finger, it is *dīkṣā (VD).*

1862 **दीनाभाव-दृष्टि**

Dīnābhāva-dṛṣṭi : gaze at the tip of the nose. A type of glance in *karuṇarasa.* It is a distressing glance with the eye-lid a little lowered down and eye-balls swollen slightly and moving lazily. It suggests pathos (*NS*, VIII. 52-53).

1863 **दीपन**

Dīpana : over three octaves in speaking, invigorating, kindling.

1864 **दीप-मुद्रा**

Dīpa-mudrā : gesture of a lamp. One fore-finger is joined to another and the little finger is similarly joined to another. Rest fore-fingers (two middle and ring-fingers) are raised touching their respective backs. Thumbs are raised up. This makes the gesture for a lamp-*dīpa-mudrā (VD). dīpa* is the sacred lamp fed with *ghee* or clarified butter.

1865 **दीप्त अलङ्कार**

Dīpta-alaṅkāra : excited voice-embellishment. *dīpta* proceeds from head and is of higher pitch. It is used in reproach, quarrel, debate, indignation, yelling (abusive speech), defiance, anger, valour, pride, sharp and harsh words, lamentation, etc. *(NS).*

Alaṅkāra of Bharata is the pitch in modern linguistics. Pitch can be varied or charged from low to high. The pitch patterns are based on relationships between pitches rather than on absolute pitch values. Some people speak in a too high key all the time, and others speak in too low a key all the time.

1866 **दीप्ताग्निप्रमदारतः**

Dīptāgni-pramadā-rataḥ : cohabitation with intensely passionate woman, quality of the Horse-man (*Ratirahasya,* 3. 34-35).

1867 **दीप्ति**

Dīpti : radiance. It is high degree of charm, one of the natural graces of women.

1868 **दीर्घकचा**

Dīrghakacā : lady whose hair are long, quality of the conch-lady (*Pañcasāyaka,* 1.8).

1869 **दीर्घनिद्रा**

Dīrghanidrā : death, long sleep.

1870 **दीर्घनेत्रा**

Dīrghanetrā : woman of long eyes, quality of the Deer-lady (*Pañcasāyaka,* 2.12).

1871 **दीर्घप्रोन्नतकाक्षलम्बितभुज**

Dīrghapronnatakākṣalambitabhuja : the man whose shoulders are high and long, quality of the Bull-man (*Ratirahasya,* 3.32-33).

1872 **दीर्घबाहु**

Dīrghabāhu : woman having long shoulders, quality of the Deer-lady (*Pañcasāyaka,* 2.12).

1873 **दीर्घरत**

Dīrgha-rata : dog, copulating for long time. Cp. *ratikīla.* Good and bad omens are associated with dogs. A dog seen at the left of the army-camp is indicative of death. If a dog barks at the royal palace, of king, and in the inner apartment of a house-holder, it portends to death (*Agni* 232-14). But if a dog smells the left part of the body of a person, it is conducive to success in endeavour; if the dog smells the right part, it brings fear; the same is the case if he smells the left arm (*Ibid.* 15). If a dog comes facing at the time of departure or journey, then it ruins the journey being an evil spirit (*Ibid.* 16). If he sits or stands in the way (*mārgāvarodhakaḥ*) it indicates thieves. If he faces with a bone in his mouth, it portends loss of gain, and if he has a string or a strap of cloth in his mouth, he portends sin (*Ibid.* 17) if he has a shoe or sandal in his mouth, or flesh in mouth, he is conducive to wealth (*dhānyaḥ*); but if he has any inauspicious thing or a hair in mouth, it is a sign of misfortune (*Ibid.* 18). If he comes ahead after passing urine, it portends fear for the man who sees him; but after passing urine if he goes away to an auspicious place or tree, it portends auspicious for the person who sees him thus (*Ibid.* 19-20). The mouth of a dog is said to be pure (*Agni* 156.10).

There is the mention of *kurkurī-tīrtha* on the *Narmadā,* which tells the auspiciousness of the dog (*Skanda,* V.3.205.2)

1874 **दीर्घस्फारितविलोललोचन**

Dīrgha-sphārita-vilola-locana : wide and unsteady eyes, quality of the Horse-man (*Ratirahasya,* 3.34.35).

1875 **दीर्घाङ्गुलि**

Dīrghāṅguli : long-finger, quality of the Horse-man (*Ratirahasya,* 3.34-35).

1876 **दुग्धजलक**

Dugdhajalaka : embrace like that of milk and water.

1877 **दुग्धसागरहस्त**

Dugdha-sāgara hasta : the milk-ocean. The *sarpaśiraḥ* hands moved up and down denote the milk-ocean (*Mirror of Gesture*, p. 48).

1878 **दुरक्षर**

Durakṣara : an evil word.

1879 **दुरवेक्षित**

Duravekṣita : evil look, improper look.

1880 **दुरालाप**

Durālāpa : abuse.

1881 **दुरालोक**

Durāloka : unpleasant look, dazzling (*Veṇīsaṁhāra*, Act II), difficult to be perceived; *durālakṣya.*

1882 **दुर्गसन्तारिणी (नाव) मुद्रा**

Durgasantāriṇī (nāva) mudrā : "When fingers of both the hands are interlocked with the pair of little fingers and thumbs up, it is called the gesture *nāva* or *durgasantāriṇī* by name which removes all bad omens and grants everything what a man can desire" (*BT*).

1883 **दुर्निमित्त**

Durnimitta : evil omen, inauspicious signs. In *Śākuntalam* (5.12). Śakuntalā gestures the evil omen: *durnimittamabhinīya.*

Some of the evil omens of north Indian villages are as follows: (a) early in the morning or while going out with a motive, one should not be confronted with one eyed man, a *telī*, a *barhaī* and a widow. These persons indicate bad omen which comes in the way of success as hindrance. The whoie day may be worst attracted:

(b) while going out one should not be called back. And if someone sneezes while a man is making a start, he has to sit for a while and is to make a new start. This indicates the failure in success.

(c) a *halvāī* does not sell *batāsā* for the first time in the morning at any cost, because this is regarded as a bad start. If this custom is violated, the sale of whole day many run stock.

Among general ill omens are mentioned the following in the *Purāṇas* : when suddenly there is a sound like that of a drum, etc. in the sky, there is indication of danger; sudden arrival of wild beasts and wild birds into the locality and the departure of domesticated beasts into the forest; roaming of female jackals near the royal gates; carrying of the cock in the evening and of the jackals in the morning; entry of the pigeon into the house; the mating of crows being seen, bees making a hive in the house; sudden fall of the canopy, sudden non-blazing of the fire and oozing of waters from the jars (*Agni. P.* 263. 26-32); appearance of a *Gandharva - nāgara*) (City of the Gandharvas) in the sky, uncommon and crooked raid (*Ibid.* 263.13). The *Purāṇic* ill omens confirm with the *Bṛhat - Saṁhitā* of Varāhamihira (505 A.D.).

1884 **दुर्भगा**

Durbhagā :a wife disliked by the husband (*A*, 13.1.16), unfortunate woman, personified old age, of evil effort.

1885 **दुर्मल्लिका**

Durmallikā : a variety of the *uparūpakas*. It has four acts and its heroine is grown-up and town-bred. The secret enjoyment etc. are described in private by a female messenger in vulgar manner.

1886 **दुर्वाचकयोग**

Durvācakayoga : speaking in such a manner that it should not be understood easily, one of the 64 arts mentioned in *Kāmasūtra* (1.3.16). Composition of verses with difficult verses and senses.

1887 **दुष्टे दुष्टमाचरेत्**

Duṣṭe duṣṭamācaret : tit-for-tat conduct. About the general code of conduct the following is said : "one should return what is done to him; for an injury a return-injury should be made; there is no fault if to the vile, one behaves in a vile way" (*Skanda*, VI.162.19).

1888 **दूती**

Dūti : go-between female messenger, female partner of the aspirant (*Tantra*), go-between. (b) Buddhist nuns, female ascetics, hand maids, nurses, virgins, washer-women, flower-sellers, corrupt women, female companions and barbers' wives served as go-betweens. As these were the causes of the ruin of respectable families, people were aware of them :

भिक्षुणिका प्रव्रजिता दासी धात्री कुमारिका रजिका ।
मालाकारी दुष्टाङ्गना सखी नापिती दूत्यः ॥

It is well known that during the period of Varāhamihira (505 A.D.) Buddhism was very popular in India, and so were their nuns, In the *Alaṅkāraśāstra* the following *dūtīs* are mentioned :

दूत्यः सखी नटी दासी धात्रेयी प्रतिवेशिनी ।
बाला प्रव्रजिता कारूः शिल्पिन्याद्याः स्वयं तथा ॥

In this connection we can remind ourselves of what Arjuna says on *Kulajana-vināśa* (*Gītā* 1.41-42) :

अधर्माभिभवात्कृष्ण प्रदुष्यन्ति कुलस्त्रियः ।
स्त्रीषु दुष्टासु वार्ष्णेय जायते वर्णसङ्करः ॥
सङ्करो नरकायैव कुलघ्नानां कुलस्य च ।
पतन्ति पितरो ह्येषां लुप्तपिण्डोदकक्रियाः ॥

1889 **दूतीयाग**

Dūtīyāga: ritual union with *dūtī* is known as *dūtīyāga*. Her organ is conceived of as the sacrificial fire and the semen of the aspirant as the clarified butter which is to be offered in the fire (*Paraśurāmakalpasūtra*, X. 63).

1890 **दूरात् हूत**

Dūrāt-hūta : calling a person from a distance. There is a rule as regards to calling formulated by Pāṇini : *dūrāt-hūte-ca (Aṣṭādhyāyī*, 18.2.84). It is a paralinguistic formula. It is also the colloquial aspect of Sanskrit.

In the act of calling a person from a distance, there is the raising of voice pitch in a quasi-interrogative fashion. When the addressee who is so called is inferior to the speaker, the address form generally includes some intersectional particles. Such particles are never used for addressing or even calling seniors unless of course the speaker intends to insult him and invite his wrath and displeasure. While calling, hand waving is an important gesture.

1891 **दूरदर्शन**

Dūradarśana : vulture; *dūradarśanam* 'far-sightedness'.

1892 **दूरबन्धु**

Dūrabandhu : banished from wife and kindred.

1893 **दूर-वस्त्रक**

Dūra-vastraka : naked.

1894 **दृक्-दीक्षा**

Dṛk-dīkṣā : see under *cākṣuṣī-dīkṣā*.

1895 **दृग्गोचर**

Dṛggocara: visible, range of sight.

1896 **दृप्ता भावदृष्टि**

Dṛptā bhāvadṛṣṭi : it is an energy-striking look with motionless eyeballs expressing haughty temper and indomitable courage. It suggests prowess. (*NS*, VIII. 52-53). It is used in energy. The glance is steady and widened in which eyeballs are motionless.

1897 **दृशालिङ्गनम्**

Dṛśāliṅganam : embrace through eyes. Anantabhaṭṭa (*Campū Bhārata*, 3.89) imagines that in summer the lovers who are tortured by heat and who are unable to hug each other due to sweating embrace through glances.

1898 **दृशि**

Dṛśi: power of seeing (*Vedānta*).

1899 **दृश्य**

Dṛśya : visible (*RV*), the phenomenal universe, visual presentation. It also refers to those devices which modify or affect a viewer's conceptions and attitudes towards a visual presentation. *dṛśyetaram* is invisible.

1900 **दृष्टान्त**

Dṛṣṭānta : (*NS*, 18.22) : form of speech and thought. (b) an example which illustrates a general rule. It is one of the sixteen philosophical topics of the *Nyāya*. (c) a figure of speech in which a statement is illustrated with an example (*Kāvyaprakāśa*, X. 102).

1901 **दृष्टि**

Dṛṣṭi : glances. The treatment of the eye-gesture comes under the *mukhaja-abhinaya* (facial expression) according to *NS*. The *NS* describes thirty-six types of glances excluding the eight additions looks (*darśana*) described in the context of the muscular movements of the eyeballs. Of these thirty-six, eight refer to *rasa* (sentiments), another eight to the *sthāyī bhāva* (the dominant states); the names of the first sixteen can practically be identified with the names of the *rasa*, and the *sthāyī bhāva;* the name of the *vyabhicārī dṛṣṭi* correspond closely to the name of the *vyabhicārī bhāva* and are sometimes identical.

The first sixteen glances are described in great detail in terms of the muscular movements of the eyeballs, eyelids and the eyebrows and, occasionally the colour of the eyes. Whatever the movements of the eyeballs, eyelids and the eyebrows have not been mentioned in technical terms, the descriptions indicate the precise movement. The twenty glances of the *vyabhīcari bhāvas* (transitory states) are more difficult to analyse in terms of the movements of the eyebrows, eyelids and eyeballs.

The *SR* (VII. 377-429), the *Naṭyasāstra-saṅgraha* (pp. 482-524), the *Bālarāmabharata* (pp. 118-120), and the *Saṅgītamakaranda* (pp. 110-112) all follow closely the classification of *dṛṣṭis* of *NS*. The text used by Coomaraswamy in the *Mirror of Gesture* (p.40) enumerates forty-four glances of which some like the *sācī dṛṣṭi* are ascribed by Bharata; the others are more or less in accordance with the *vyabhicarī dṛṣtis* of the *NS* with a few omissions and a few additions, such as the *iṅgita, dūra*, etc. *(NS*, VIII. 41 and 63; VIII. 55). The twenty glances belonging to the *vyabhicārī bhāva* can be grouped according to their respective *sthāyi bhāva*, but since they are used to represent subtle shades of emotion and sentiment, it is best not to regroup them in terms of the *sthāyi bhāva*. Very often in the description of the *dṛṣtis* of the *rasa* and *sthāyi bhāva* the names of the *vyabhicārī dṛṣtis* are frequently used by Bharata. Thus *ākekarā* and *trastā vibhrāntā* are frequently used to represent *sthāyi bhāva*.

The *dṛṣtis* inclusive of the movement of the eyeballs the iris and the pupil of the eye, eyelids, and the eyebrows form an important part of the *abhinaya*-technique of Indian dance and drama, and in fact the *āṅgikābhinaya* in dancing (where speech is not used) uses for its expression most effectively the muscles of the eye and different parts of the face. The *mukhajābhinaya* (facial expression) has been given a very significant role in Indian dance and drama.

In short, there are eight kinds of eye movements corresponding to the same number of permanent emotions (*sthāyi bhāva*), an equal number corresponding to the various *rasa*, and others for the thirty-three or thirty-six transitory emotions (*saṁcārī bhāva*). The actions of the eye go with others of the pupil of the eye, the eyelids, and the brows. Over and above the specific movements of the eye and its related parts, and a similar number of specific movements each for the nose, cheeks, lips and chin, the overall emotional state expressed through the face (*mukharāga*) may be : natural or neutral, clear or pleasing, passionate or flushed, or dismal. These are very important, and it is the appropriate overall facial expression which is the base for specific movements of the various parts of the face.

1902 **दृष्टिपथ**

Dṛṣṭipatha : range of the eye.

1903 **दृष्टिपूत**

Dṛṣṭipūta : having carefully observed.

1904 **दृष्टिभिः आह्वयन्ति**

Dṛṣṭibhiḥ āhvayanti : inviting gesture; ladies invite by their gestures (*Mṛcchakaṭika*, 4.16). This shows the flirting nature of a sexy person.

1905 **दृष्टिविभ्रम**

Dṛṣṭivibhrama : amorous play of the eyes.

1906 **दृष्टिविष**

Dṛṣṭiviṣa : having poison in the eyes, poisoning by the mere look, sort of snake. Snakes represent death and the underworld, but also rebirth (for they slough their skins and are reborn). They are also connected with the *yogic* aspect of Śiva and his phallic emblem. In spite of this ambiguity in the symbolism of snakes, birds and snakes as natural enemies symbolise opposition in Indian thought. Both animals are used as disguises in the interruption of episodes, as is their mediating form, wind, which plays a creative role in the cosmogony and a destructive role at doomsday, where it further mediates between the conflagration and the flood.

1907 **दृष्टिसिद्धि**

Dṛṣṭi-siddhi : power of vision (*Yukti-dīpikā*, 164. 14-15) one of the six varieties of spiritual powers. In the next stage an offspring was produced by mere wishful amorous glances of parents (See *Mahābhārata*, XV.30.22).

1908 **दृषिका**

Dṛṣikā : 'appearance' *RV.*

1909 **देव**

Deva : the king is to be addressed by his servants as well as subjects as *deva*, but when he is an overlord king (*sārvabhauma*) then always *bhaṭṭa* by his servants (*NS*, XVII. 65-94).

1910 **देवजनविद्या**

Devajanavidyā : science of the ghosts and spirits.

1911 **देवतोषणकला**

Deva-toṣaṇa-kalā : the art of pleasing gods, worship. It is related to *Atharvaveda* and explained in *tāntrika* culture (*Śukranītisāra*, 4. 320-22).

1912 **देवदासी**

Devadāsi : a girl engaged for dancing in temple, dancing girl attached to a temple. She is also known by the term *bhāvinī*. The institution is referred to in *Rājataranginī* (IV.269).

1913 **देवपादाः**

Devapādāḥ : the royal feet or presence, a respectful address.

1914 **देवयोनि**

Devayoni : divine origin, demi-divine; gods and guardian spirits. Once the reality of the supernatural world had been admitted, the ancient Indians highly developed talent for classification set to work dividing the gods and guardian spirits, into various categories. There were *yakṣas*, who preferred to live in big trees, and the *nāgas*, who lived in caverns and subterranean waters; they are dealt with more fully in Sanskrit literature. There were also the *vidyādharas*, who had human form, were expert magicians and were specially adept at marrying an young woman when they found her sufficiently seductive. The *gandharvas* were celestial singers and musicians living in splendid cities, who wooed women and minds of men urging them to indulge in wine, gambling, and love-making. Their wives and lovers, called *apsarasas*, were water nymphs whose beauty, created for the sensual delight of the gods, inspired passion in the hearts of all men who saw them, including ascetics, though they themselves preferred to choose their husbands from among warriors killed on the field of battle. It seems, though, that these nymphs were at the mercy of any man who was lucky enough to surprise one of them bathing in a river and succeeded in stealing her clothes. Although each of these semi-divine categories possessed its own characteristics, these fanciful beings shared some common features; they had a very long life-span, but they were, nevertheless, mortal, vulnerable to certain wounds, and might even be captured by men through trickery. They were able to make themselves invisible or to assume human shape, and they understood the language of the animals as well as all mankind's dialects. However, they were endowed with only relatively limited magical powers, and most of them, for instance, were unable to divine the thoughts or plans of human beings unless these were spoken aloud in their presence. They were organised in a fashion similar to human society, forming distinct peoples, possessing chieftains or even kinds, living in towns and palaces, making war and serving often as emissaries on behalf of their rulers both in celestial and human worlds.

1915 **देवर**

Devara : younger brother of husband.

1916 **देवरहस्त**

Devara-hasta : a brother of the husband gesture. If the *śikhara* gesture is with the left hand and the *kartarīmukha* with the right held on the both sides, it indicates a brother of the husband (*AD*, 231-244).

1917 **देवरात्रि**

Devarātri : a night-long festival in honour of a deity (*A*, 4.3.15), very akin to *jātrā* in Bastar.

1918 **देवल**

Devala : one who shows images and begs, show-man of images.

1919 **देववाणी**

Devavāṇī : Sanskrit language. That the speech act was clearly a rebirth of man was an idea reflected in the name of the language itself. The name 'Sanskrit' does not have any racial, geographical or historical connotation. Etymologically the word 'Sanskrit' is composed of two segments, *sam* and *kṛta; sam* meaning 'well', 'properly', 'fully' and *kṛta* 'done', 'fashioned', 'made'. The infixed sibilant between the two segments denotes, according to Pāṇini, a definite purpose, *viz,* to be purified of taint and to be imbued with power. Sanskrit was not merely a language artificially created for use by the elite as often wrongly assumed; it was a language developed by a cumulative mind intent upon resurrecting its powers to achieve good. Language was continuously winnowed and sifted; it was through such a process that the Goddess of Speech was being perpetually rediscovered. In turn she reinvested words with power.

1920 **देवहस्त**

Devahasta : Each mood of a god has a prescribed hand-gesture in *śilpaśāstra* and seldom do we find the sculpture erring against this. The *devahastas* described by the *Abhinayadarpaṇa* can be applied fairly accurately to the *hastas* of different gods and goddesses seen in Indian iconography. The *śilpaśāstras* mention only a few *hastas* and many of them repeat the *hastas* of the *NS* and other texts of dramaturgy. The most common *hastas* are the *varada*, the *abhaya*, the *kaṭaka*, the *sācī*, the *tarjana*, the *kaṭyavalambita*, the *daṇḍahasta*, the *vismaya hasta* and the *añjali hasta*. The South Indian texts also mention the *nidrita hasta*. The *gaja hasta*, the *siṁhakarṇa hasta* and *kartarī hasta*.

1921 **देवाक्रीड**

Devākrīḍa : playground of the gods.

1922 **देवानां प्रिय**

Devānām priya : a fool, dear to the gods, *i.e.* a fool or a simple person.

1923 **देवालय**

Devālaya : the temple (as a centre of social life). To the Hindu, the temple is not only a place of worship but the centre of social life. In fact, it is quite impossible among Hindus to distinguish between social and religious institutions. The higher castes, especially in the village have very little social life except in the temple. The temple tank is the public bath of the Hindu, and is a centre of immense activity because of the religious needs for bathing in the morning and evening, and for performing ablutions. The foot of the inevitable Banyan tree that stands at the gateway of every important Hindu temple is the resort of all gossip-mongers, and even the elders of the village who wish to hear the news of the day repair to this rendezvous of public gossip, and air their opinions on politics and philosophy. Young men on the look out for brides often loiter about the gates and compound of the temple, keeping a watchful eye on the figure and poise of the pious young ladies who throng to the temple in the mornings and evenings with offering of flowers, scents and grain for the gods.

Public entertainments are usually held in the temple or in a place near about. As we know that the public entertainments of the Hindus are religious in character and their dances, pantomimes and plays always take place in the premises of the temple, and are attended by almost all the men and women of the locality. Every temple celebrates at least one major feast of the tutelary deity in a year, in which not only the village in which the temple is situated but even neighbouring villages and men and women from distant places take part

The temple was/is the symbol of Hindu religion. In India the temple was an outstanding symbol of Hindu religion and often of the prestige of a local Hindu landlord if it happened to be patronized by his family or situated within his residential precincts. As such it often figured as a focus of conflict between Hindu landlords and peasantry. Being denied the right to enter a temple was among the grievances. Guru Ghāsīdasite *pracārak* and much of it in their propaganda against zamindars. Attacks on the temples acquired a very special significance when the peasantry concerned happened to be Muslims. We have a number of cases in Indian history where it is said that Muslims polluted the temples. In such cases desecration was used by both the parties to undermine each other's prestige.

The ideology that the deity is to be treated even as a human king is treated was in the background of its non-accessibility. Not all the devotees can enter all parts of the temple, as everyone can not enter the interior part of a palace. Distinctions of class, official and social status, caste privileges, cleanliness, convention and other factors determine the accessibility to the temple.

1924 **देवी**

Devī : In a play king's wives are to be addressed by servants and attendants as *devī, svāminī, bhaṭṭinī* (*NS*, XVII. 65-94). The chief queen is to be addressed *devī* by the king, but other queens are addressed *bhoginī.*

1925 **देवीमुद्रा**

Devī-mudrā : gesture symbolizing the Supreme Energy. Make the two hands upturned with the curved thumb and other finger; put them inside the palm-pit in such a way, that the nails should remain hidden. Then join the backside of one palm on the back of the other. The two thumbs are to be placed on an equal position and make the complete figure like a garland. This symbolizes the Paramount Energy or *Devī (VD*).

1926 **देशजधर्म**

Deśaja-dharma : social behaviour. Kokkoka in his *Ratirahasya* (1.8) stresses the need that a man should know the types, natures, qualities and behaviours of others according to the country, gestures, conditions and intention : *Jāti-svabhāva-guṇa-deśajadharma- ceṣṭā, bhāveṅgiteṣu ca.*

1927 **देशत्व**

Deśatva : territoriality, individual's preference for areas and objects; Privacy is a state in which one has control over other people's access to one's person or information about one's person. Most people have two potentially opposite needs : one is to be available to others for social contact; the other is to have privacy. Some people need more privacy, others more social contact. If we think about the environment, whether on the level of public spaces or domestic spaces, we can see features which reflect these two needs. In the elite society of India the door is a ubiquitous architectural feature, and curtains are almost obligatory parts of their domestic props. The possibility of closing or opening doors and curtains is a device for signalling availability. Vātsyāyana (*Kāmasūtra*, 6.47) has drawn attention to the prevalence of back (private)regions and front (public) regions both in domestic settings and public settings. Back-regions, which in houses include bedrooms and bathrooms sometimes kitchens are regions in which only intimates may penetrate without invitation. Front regions are open to public.

Vātsyāyana has pointed out the widespread relationship between power and rank on the one hand, and the size both of buffer zones and territory. The more important a person (in a social sense) the less others are permitted to approach him closely, speak of him within earshot, and the greater the size and number of areas which he is permitted to control. Probably one of the most trying features of poverty is the lack of privacy that typical of the living conditions of the poor and the public institutions allocated to him.

1928 **देशदेवता**

Deśadevatā : tutelary deity of the region (*A.* 13.5.8).

1929 **देशधर्म**

Deśa-dharma : the traditional practices and usages prevalent in a region.

1930 **देशभाषा**

Deṣabhāṣā : dialect.

1931 **देशभाषाविज्ञान**

Deṣabhāṣā-vijñāna : science of vernacular dialects, knowledge of vernacular dialects, dialectology. one of the 64 arts enumerated in *Kāmasūtra* (1.3.16). Learning of all major and allied languages current in the continent.

1932 **देशाचार**

Deśācāra : usages of country, public behaviour. *Yasmin deśe yathaiva ācāraḥ tathaiva grāhyaḥ.* Bharata while analysing the costumes records that women on earth should be dressed according to their countries. *Āvantī* ladies should have curly hair; *Gauḍī*, mostly curls having *śikhāpāśa* and braid of hair; *Ābhīra* women, two braids of hair and deep blue garment; women of northeast, *Śikhaṇḍa* held up and hair covered by garment; women of south, *ullekhya, kumbhi-bandhaka* (tying of hair in a small-jar-like shape) and*āvartalalāṭika* (forehead ornament).

Bharata in his discussion of body painting says that the concept of colour is regionally understood. The colour should be used according to the need of the situation, country and birth. *Kirāta, Barbara, Āndhra, Draviḍa, Kāśi, Kośala, Pulinda* and *Dākṣiṇātya* should be generally northern region should be generally black. *Śaka, Yawana Pallavā, Bāhlika* and those in the northern region should he *gaura* (white); *Pāñcāla, Śaurasena, Māhiṣa, Oḍramāgadha, Aṅga, Vaṅga* and *Kaliṅga* should be dark blue. Brāhmaṇas and Kṣatriyas should be *gaura;* Vaiśya and Śūdra, *śyāma.*

The application of beards should be according to the region, condition and age. It is of four kinds - *śuddha (*shaven), *śyāma* (dark), *vicitra* (smartly done) and *lomaśa* (hairy). The first should be in the case of religious mendicants, ministers and priests; those indifferent to sexual pleasure and those initiated for some vow. *Vicitra* should be in the case of divines males, the kings, princes, king's officers, amorous persons and proud young persons. *Śyāma* should be employed in the case of those who are unhappy, struck by calamity and those who have not fulfilled their promises. *Lomaśa* should be in the case of sages, ascetics, men observing long lasting vows and those wearing tattered garments.

1933 देशान्तरवासेन जितक्लेषो भवति

Deśāntaravāsena jitakleṣo bhavati : one becomes superior to weakness by residing in other regions or countries (*Bṛhaspati-Sūtra* III.2). *Bṛhaspati* means that it is by the overpowering those unfavourable or unpleasant conditions that the person acquires the mental and moral attributes of *pauruṣa* (q.v.).

1934 देशी स्थानक

Deśī-sthānaka : a broad variety of postures; regional postures.

1935 देशोपदेश

Deśopadeśa : a satirical sketch of the daily life of Bengali students in Kashmir during 11th century A.D. presented by Kṣemendra. In the 6th Chapter of *Deśopadeśa* he describes astutely the vicious activities of a student from Bengal. The aim of Kṣemendra through this work is to uphold morality :

ये दम्भमायामयदोषलेश -
लिप्ता न मे तान्प्रति कोऽपि यत्नः ।
किन्त्वेष हासव्यपदेशयुक्त्या
देशोपदेशः क्रियते मयाद्य ॥ ३ ॥

Kṣemendra has used well this sacred weapon of satire to strike his blows on hypocrisy and corruption which had polluted the society of Kashmir in his days.

In the 6th Chapter of *Deśopadeśa,* he pays ironical homage to a student who like Śiva is the usurper of the pleasing half at the free-feeding house (सत्रे वामार्धहारिणे), is terrible (उग्र) addict (विषभक्ष), and armed with spear at night : as if a true picture of the student in the modern age. With bright - coloured dress and with body decorations, he is ashamed of holding in his hand the first page of a book (VI. 5). He is proud of his new shoes producing a hard cracking noise and walks slowly looking at his waist girt with a red belt for keeping the knife :

उपानत्कुत्सिता रावगर्वितः स शनैर्व्रजन् ।
लोहितक्षुरिकापट्टवेष्टितां वीक्षते कटीम् ॥ (VI. 12)

Highly fraudulent, the Gauḍa student pretends to be very pure. While walking he avoids the touch of any body and tucks up his upper cloth in his armpit :

स्पर्शं परिहरन् याति गौडः कक्षाकृताञ्चलः ।
कुञ्चितेनैव पार्श्वेन दम्भभारभरादिव ॥ (VI. 9)

If he excels the sages in do-not-touchism, he competes them in five penances also. His five penances are indulgence in prostitutes, gambling, spying, hunger strike and stabbing others :

वेश्यासक्तो द्यूतकरश्चाक्रिकः प्रायकृत् सदा ।
कुक्षिभेदी मठवने छात्रः पञ्चतपा मुनिः ॥ (VI. 31)

He poses to be very innocent in the presence of ladies but in his heart of hearts he is in search of lady killing :

हसन्ति किं भणन्तीति मुग्धोक्त्या परयोषितः ।
विश्वास्य सेवते धूर्तः सत्रभोजनवर्णनैः ॥ (VI. 12)

As regards family, he announces himself to be a *thakkura* :

गौडो गर्वोन्नतग्रीवष्ठक्कुरो ऽस्मीति भाषते (VI. 36)

But Kṣemendra feels that in his own region the chap must have been a barber or shoe maker or fisherman or butcher because he does not know even *saṁdhyā* :

नापितश्चर्मकारो वा धीवरः सौनिको ऽपि वा ।
स्वदेशे देशिको नूनं सन्ध्यापाठं न वेत्ति यत् ॥ (VI.12)

He is not acquainted well even with alphabets but is still arrogant about his scholarship. Not to speak of *svastipāṭha,* he hardly knows *oṁkāra,* but is bent upon defeating the old Kashmiri scholar :

छात्रः प्रवृत्तः पाण्डित्ये वृद्धकीरजिगीषया ।
कष्टेन जानात्योङ्कारं स्वस्तिज्ञाने कथैव का ॥ (VI. 7)

With no background at all, he commences *Tarkaśāstra* the study of Patañjali's *Mahābhāṣya,* and *Mīmaṁsāśāstra* :

अलिपिज्ञो ऽ व्यहंकारस्तब्धो विप्रतिपत्तये ।
गौडः करोति प्रारम्भं भाष्ये तर्के प्रभाकरे ॥ (VI. 8)

Most ill - mannered, he treats all discourteously. He scolds everybody without any reason for provocation (VI. 42). No one dare oppose him whose belly is already marked with injuries made with knife and who would not shrink from using it against his fellow boarders :

अनेकक्षुरिकाघातक्षुण्णकुक्षेः क्षयैषिणः ।
को नाम गौडयक्षस्य सत्रे याति विपक्षताम् ॥ (VI. 2)

Under slightest provocation, he beats and throws out the servants of the hostel and tolerates only that servant whose wife is young :

क्रुद्धः कर्मकरान् सर्वान् निरस्य लगुडाहतान् ।
तमेव सहते दासं तरुणी यस्य गेहिनी ॥ (VI. 11)

With a cloth around his belly, with his hair arranged in a knot and with a rod in his hand he seems to be bent upon the extinction of the institution :

उदराबद्धवस्त्रेण ग्रान्थिजूटेन नादिता ।
लगुडोद्धतहस्तेन छात्रेणोन्मूल्यते मठः ॥ (VI. 25)

Just as the bigger fish eats the smaller, so he snatches away things from the weak boys :

मत्स्या मत्स्यमिवाश्नन्ति भागीकृत्यातुरं क्षणात् ।
छात्राश्छत्रकरण्डादिपटशाटककम्बलैः ॥ (VI. 39)

Hunger strike is a weapon misused by him. With such students residing in it, the institution is no more a institution; it has become an abode of rogues and appears to be a cave in the wooden mountain full of old demons :

नायं मठः शठमठः प्रांशुर्हठमठोऽपि वा ।
वृद्धराक्षसपूर्णेयं घोरा दारुगिरेर्गुहा ॥ (VI. 41)

With this pungent picture of an indisciplined student drawn with piquant skill, Kṣemendra has detected and brought to light the loopholes in the educational institutions of his day. (Ghai, 1968).

1936 **देहधर्म**

Dehadharma : activity of the body; one of the two types of *dharma,* the other is *dravya-dharma. Dehadharma* includes washing, स्नानादि देहिकम् : (*Matsya,* 251.4).

1937 **देहदीप**

Dehadīpa : eye - the lamp in the body.

1938 **देहनिपीडन**

Deha-nipīḍana : embracing tightly is exaltation according to Dāmodaragupta (*Kuṭṭanimatam,* 377).

1939 **देह-साधना**

Deha-sādhanā : see *kāya - sādhanā.*

1940 **देहसुख**

Dehasukha 'agreeable to the body' (*Bṛhat Saṁhitā*).

1941 **देहात्म्यवाद**

Dehātmyavāda : one of the five basic principles of the Cārvāka philosophy. It means that the concept of soul apart from the body is baseless.

1942 **देहि मे तमाखुचूर्णम्**

Dehi me tamākhu cūrṇam : give me a little tobacco : *uccuṭu poga īmu* (Bison-horn Maria). Tobacco is a metaphor for sexual intercourse and has other, more diffuse implications in Bison - horn Maria culture as well. As far as I can determine, the *Vedic* people used public hair as a metaphor in this way. But asking for tobacco is specifically the definition of Gond culture.

Elwin (1947) has reported the use of this metaphor in several related contexts by the Maria Gonds. The metaphor appears especially in songs and ceremonies. A song sung while the marriage booth is being built has the lines :

That girl is beautiful
give her some tobacco
Take her, press her.

A song used in a game in which girls touch parts of their bodies successively at each line- *i.e.,* ankles - waist - breasts - shoulders - hands over head - goes :

Brother has gone to his village
In his purse is sweet tobacco
Will he eat the sweet tobacco?
(Elwin, 1947 :578)

Also, tobacco is used as a love-charm, and tobacco leaves are used in village sacrifices on the return to the native village of young men who have been visiting neighbouring villages. These visits are often for the express purpose of finding suitable mate. The tobacco is tied in front of a sacred tree when the boys return home the tobacco is taken down ceremonially and smoked (Elwin 1947:442).

Note particularly the contexts in which the metaphor is used. They are either overtly sexual or, as in the marriage preparations and ceremony, indirectly but obviously related to sexuality : "Let me copulate".

The young Maria man may use this metaphor when he is sexually aroused. Likewise women also use it. The females answer may be an emphatic denial, in which she recognizes the metaphor by refusing to acknowledge it :

poga ille
"I don't have any tobacco".
The male may again insist :
poga uccuṭu īmu īmu
'Give me a little tobacco, please.'
The female may utter :
ille
"no"

The whole conversation may be persuading. The intonation pattern will be very polite and flattering.

Ultimately the girl agrees saying "I have no tobacco, I will not come." The nice girl says "no" to mean "yes".

1943 **दैन्य**

Dainya : wretchedness, miserable condition; a type of *vyabhicārī bhāva,* which indicates miserable condition. Want of self-control, headache, dullness of the body, absent - mindedness, giving up of cleansing of the body, etc. are its transitory states.

1944 **दैव**

Daiva : fate or destiny which is believed to be the collective force of one's actions in past lives (*pūrvajanma kṛtam karma*). Among the conditions responsible for success of any work the *Bhagavadgītā* (XVIII. 14) mentions both *ceṣṭā* (effort) and *daiva.* (*Yāj* 1.351) says that just a chariot cannot move on one wheel, so fate (*daiva*) without personal endeavour (*puruṣakāra*) cannot lead to success. *Kādambarī* records that deeds done in the past result in something which is known as *daiva* : *Janmāntarakṛtam karma taddaivamiti kathyate.* The faith in destiny is a common phenomenon in Indian society. The following Chhatisgarhi proverb depicts the same : *tiriyā mirtinī bānjhil, dhanī lagāvā dose; ye to likhnā Bramhā kā, bālak kahān se hoy* (The wife is childless, barren; the husband thinks that the fault is with her, but this is decreed of Brahmā, whence then can she have a child?). The traditional Indian society as such obviously favours the game of chance over the game of competition. Implicit in the social order is submission to destiny. Even a righteous king like Yudhiṣṭhira of Mahābhārata is steeped in the aristocratic ideal of remaining impassive in the face of *daivam*, regal destiny he declares that Fate alone controls all men, and Fate is stronger than all three motives combined. Not by any action of his own can a man attain a goal that is intrinsically beyond his reach. Thus the one man who is the very embodiment of truth submits to his fate.

1945 **देलापाद-करण**

Dolāpāda karaṇa : derived from the *cārī* of that name. One *kuñcita* foot swings from side to side ending in an *añcita* foot. Weight of the body is on *samapāda* foot. Hands accord with the feet and are also in *dolā* (*NS*, IV. 120b-121a, IX.148, X.36) Throwing up the *kuñcita* foot, it is moved in the swinging manner from side to side. The hands are moved in conformity with the foot movement.

1946 **दोलापाद-चारी**

Dolāpāda cārī : both feet in *samapāda kuñcita. Kuñcita* feet lifted to its own side, moved and then touching the ground as an *añcita* foot : two *tālas* difference approximately. *Udvāhita* or *kṣipta* knees and thighs.

Associated with the *karaṇa* of the same name. Lifting up a *kuñcita* foot and moving it from side to side and then causing it to fall on the ground in the *añcita* posture (*NS*, X.36).

1947 **दोलाहस्त**

Dolāhasta : the swinging hand, both hands gesture. Extended arms move downwards. Hands stretched down. A most appropriate rendering of love-distraction or enacting of fainting in *Vikramorvaśīya* (Act III). The *dolāhasta* may be seen in the figures of Mathura. When the *patāka* gestures in both the hands are free, loose and hanging, it is called the *dolā-hasta.* It is used to suggest hurry, sadness, fainting, pride, emotion, disease and wounded by enemy (*NS*, IX. 138-139).

One of the *karaṇas* (hand postures) is classical dance known as *bhujaṅga-trasita* (frightened by the sudden discovery of a snake right near the foot), characterised by the swing (*dolā*) of one of the arms, either across the chest or on one side. The hand in this *karaṇa* is seen in the forms of Naṭarāja. The texts like the *Nāṭyaveda-vivṛti* prescribe that when one arm is in the *dolā-hasta,* the other must be in the *kaṭaka*-posture (*Krameṇaiko dolāhastaḥ param kaṭaka iti karaṇam*); and also that the arm that is in the *dolāhasta* posture have that shoulder slightly drooping; and further that the hand in the *patāka* posture must be stretched forward (*patākau tu pralambitau*).

1948 **दोष**

Doṣa : faults, blame, defects, demerit. These are five according to *Mahābhārata* (XII. 232. 4-7) : *kāma* (lust), *krodha* (anger), *lobha* (covetousness), *bhaya* (fear) and *svapna* (sleep). These are disturbances in the path of *Yoga.* (b) In *tāntric* belief *doṣa* means defects in regard to *mantras.* Defective *mantras* like *chinna, ruddha,* etc. do not produce any results (*Śāradātilaka,* II. 64-108). (c) *Kāvyaprakāśa* (VII. 49) and *SD* (VII.1) have enumerated *doṣas* (defects) in pronunciation which repress the primary meaning. They are as follows : (i) *grasta* (pronouncing at the root of the tongue), (ii) *nirasta* (pronounced with undue force), (iii) *avalambita* (pronounced in proximity with other vowels), (iv) *nirhata* (dry), (v). *ambūkṛta* (pronounced in mouth, indistinct), (vi) *dhmāta* (though short yet pronounced like a long vowel), (vii) *vikampita* pronounced with tremulation), (viii) *sandaṣṭa* (as if bitten), (ix) *eṇīkṛta* (of doubtful or indistinct form), (x) *ardhaka* (half, though long yet pronounced as short), (xi) *druta* (quickly pronounced), (xii) *vikīrṇa* (extended into another vowel), (xiii) *kalā* (pronounced in a different place).

1949 **दोषाक्षर**

Doṣākṣara : words of blame.

1950 **दोषारोपण**

Doṣāropaṇa : blaming. When envy, praise, anger or blame is expressed, there is a change in the accent of the user, which has been represented by Pāṇini (*Aṣṭādhyāyī,* 8.2.103) through a rule.

1951 **दोहद**

Dohada : cravings of pregnancy. The cravings of pregnancy are believed to be due to the erratic and uncertain desires of the child in the womb, but where as there is usually a belief that it is essential to gratify these cravings (*dohadapūrti*), I found some Bison-horn Marias of opinion that to do so was dangerous. 'If she eats earth, she will die. if she craves for fish and gets it, she will die.' But at Guḍrā they took the conventional view and held it was more dangerous to deny the cravings than to fulfil them. Long ago, I was told, a woman wanted a plantain and could not get it; the child was born with a plantain in his hand. Another woman demanded butter milk and when her request was denied, her hands and feet swelled. (b) the element that produces flowers in plants (*śabdārṇava*); desire of plants at budding time (as of Aśoka to be kicked by a young lady).

1952 **द्युति**

Dyuti : one of the 64 *sandhyaṅgas*. According to Bharata (*NS*, 19.91), it is known as the words spoken in contempt. Dhanañjaya defines it as reprimanding and inciting the feelings.

1953 **द्रव्य-मुद्रा**

Dravya-mudrā : extend two hands with the *svastika* position, two middle and two little fingers are also to be used with their extended ends and then place both the curved fore-fingers on backs of their respective middle fingers. This is the *dravya-mudrā*, that indicates one's own self or soul (*VD*). *Dravya* is a common term in Indian philosophical tradition which is generally understood substance, the which is capable of becoming this or that.

1954 **द्रुत-अलङ्कार**

Druta-alaṅkāra : fast voice-embellishment. *Druta* proceeds from the throat and is fast. It is used by women soothing children and in fear, cold, fever, panicky condition and communicating urgent business (*NS*).

1955 **द्रुतगति**

Drutagati : quick walk. (a) quality of the horse-man (*Ratirahasya*, 3.34-35). (b) quality of the conch-lady (*Anaṅgaraṅga*, 1.15-16).

1956 **द्वन्द्व-समास**

Dvandva-samāsa : compound of noun-phrase formed according to some rules of Sanskrit grammar.

1957 **द्वन्द्व-सिद्धि**

Dvandva-siddhi : power of mutual friction (*Yukti-dīpikā*, 164.14-15). By and by, when the power of embracing had also lost then progeny was made possible by the gross sexual intercourse (*dvandva-siddhi*). In this *siddhi* was prevailed the egoistic notion of 'this is mine,_'this is mine' which resulted in the migration of *puruṣ* from one body to another and this state is continued until he is released (*Yuktidīpikā*, p. 143, 144).

1958 **द्विपदिका**

Dvipadikā : a few steps; *dvipadikayā parikramya* (*Vikrama*. IV. 14).

1959 **द्विप्रवाजिनी**

Dvipravājinī : going after two men, unchaste woman.

1960 **द्वि-भङ्ग**

Dvi-bhaṅga : The body stance in the standing posture with the two bends, the loins (*kaṭi*) being the meeting place of the bends (see *bhaṅga*). The images of standing Durgā are prescribed to be either in this stance or in the stance of equipose (*samabhaṅga*). In the Devī accompanying a God, it is usual for the part of the body above the loins to bend towards the God.

1961 **द्विरागमन**

Dvirāgamana : second entry of a bride.

1962 **द्वैत**

Dvaita : duality.

1963 **द्वैध**

Dvaidha : duality, difference, conflict, dispute, diversity. (b) two-fold knowledge, doubt. Hindus were faced with what almost amounted to an existential choice between the life of the spirit and the life of the body. The poet Bhartṛhari praises the both ways :

> In this vain fleeting universe, a man
> of wisdom has two courses, first he can
> Direct his time to pray, to save his soul,
> And wallow in religion's nectar bowl.
> But, if he cannot, it is surely best
> To touch and hold a lovely woman's breast,
> And to caress her warm round lips, and thighs,
> and to possess that which between them lies.
> (Brough, No.167)—

Scripture could be cited to support either preference. Bhartṛhari himself experienced this dilemma - that none of life's possibilities are what they seem to be.

1964 **द्वैधीभाव(द्वैध)**

Dvaidhībhāva (dvaidha) : indecision, disunity, division. One of the six kinds of royal policy (*guṇa*).According to some, it means double dealing, keeping apparently friendly relations with the enemy. According to others, it means making peace with one and carrying of war with another (*Arthaśāstra*).

1965 **द्यामुष्याण**

Dvyāmuṣyāṇa : one belonging to two fathers (*Matsya*, 49.33); adoption. A brāhmaṇa could be adopted by a kṣatriya. Bharadvāja was a brāhmaṇa; and he was adopted as a son by Bharata, a kṣatriya. Son born of *niyoga* : descendant of two fathers.

ध – Dha

1966 **धन**

Dhana ; wealth, *Bṛhaspati Sītra* (VI. 10-12) announces that "the world has its roots in wealth" ; धनमूलं जगत् and everything is to be found there सर्वाणि तत्र सन्ति. Further we are told that the man without wealth is as if he were dead. In these messages an Indologist might be tempted to suspect the germ of Marxist economic interpretations of history". But Bṛhaspati is not a monist. He makes his position clear in the very next *sūtra* (13) which says that "in the same manner (*evam*), one should acquire learning which is the root of *dharma* : धर्ममूलं च विद्यामर्जयेत् He emphasizes that the world has its roots in *vidyā* : (*Bṛhaspati sūtra,* VI.14) and the knowledge again is all विद्या पुनः सर्वम् (*Ibid.*15).

1967 **धनुकासन**

Dhanukāsana : a type of posture. The man is standing bending a little, and in this position, has coitus-position. How could the woman be? Not lying on her back. She has to be raised in such a way that her *madhyā* comes up to the organ of the man and she has to look like a winnowing basket throwing grain out. This could not be, unless, she stands with back up with her buttocks to the man who hold the part, and supports her body with her hands and feet, all on the ground.

1968 **धनुरासन**

Dhanurāsana : bow-posture. This is a combination of *bhujaṅga* and *śalabha āsanas,* with the addition of catching the ankles with the hands. These three form one set of *āsanas.* As in *bhujaṅga* and *śalabha āsanas,* lie flat on the ground, face downwards, and relax all muscles. catch hold of the ankles with the hands and raise your chest and head, expanding the chest and keeping the arms and forelegs straight and still. Retain this pose as long as it can be kept comfortably. The whole body rests on the abdomen and gives it a good massage. It is useful in chronic constipation, dyspepsia, and sluggish liver. It removes rheumatism of legs, knee joints and hands, It reduces fat, energizes digestive system, and increases appetite. This is blessing for people suffering from gastrointestinal diseases. He who does *hatāsana, mayūrāsana,* and *dhanurāsana* will be full of energy, vigour and vitality.

1969 **धनुर्धारी-हस्त**

Dhanurdhārī hasta : a type of hand-gesture in iconography, not mentioned in *NS.*

1970 **धनुर्वेद**

Dhanurveda : science of archery, one of the *Upavedas* adopted in *NS.* It was used in the representation of fights (*NS,* Ch. I). the four acts relating to the bow are preparing, taking out the arrow, fixing the arrow and shooting the arrow.

1971 **धनुष्**

Dhanuṣ : the "bow" is considered as the foremost among the weapons of warfare, for it comprehends within itself the merits of all the four types of weapons : *mukta* with two sub-varieties, *pāni-mukta* (thrown by hand like discuss) and *yantra-mukta* (thrown by a device like arrow by the bow), *amukta* (retained in the hand and used like a sword), *muktāmukha* (with which the enemy is struck from a distance, like spear (cf. *Dhanurveda, dīkṣāpāda*). The bow is held in the hand, but the arrow is flung at the enemy. It is both an *astra* (because the arrow is shot from it) and a *śastra* (because the bow is retained in the hand).

Two varieties of bow are distinguished : *Śārṅga* and *vaṁśa.* The former is again of two types : the superior type measuring seven *vitastis* in length and fashioned by Viśvakarmā, which is one of the weapons in the hands of Viṣṇu; and the inferior type, measuring six *vitastis* and a half in length and used by human beings who ride elephants and horses. The cane-bow with nine nodes is called *kodaṇḍa.*

1972 **धनुष्-मुद्रा**

Dhanuṣ-mudrā : the gesture symbolizing the Vaiṣṇavite bow. Make the *śikhara* hand with middle finger hanging down to symbolize the bow (*VD*).

1973 **धम्मिल्ल**

Dhammilla : an ornamental hair-do of a woman, the braids would round with flowers tucked in, or decorated with jewels; dressed hair.

1974 **धर्मचक्र-प्रवर्तन**

Dharmacakra-pravartana : setting of wheel of Law in motion, the term which is used to denote the first sermon of the Buddha at Sāranāth. This happened on full moon in the month of Māgha (Jan-Feb.). This day is celebrated by the Buddhist as sacred.

Dharma is the righteous performance of one's traditional duty in life.

1975 **धर्म-चक्र-मुद्रा**

Dharma-cakra-mudrā : the gesture of "turning the wheel of *Dharma*" symbolizes the first discourse that Gautama, the Buddha delivered in Varanasi to the group of fie ascetics, after the obtainment of his enlightenment. This discourse is called "the *sūtra* that set into motion the wheel of *dharma* (*Dharma - cakra - pravartana - sūtra*). The gesture is also known as *vyākhyāna - mudrā* or the gesture of the exposition of , or discourse on Truth.

In this gesture, the hands are held on the chest and joined. The thumb and the fore - finger of the right hand are joined, and the palm is held up and shown. The same fingers on the left hand are joined, but the palm is held at a level lower than the right hand, and turned towards the chest.

The two hands are brought together so that the thumbs and the forefingers of the two hands are joined.

This gesture is to be seen in many images of the Buddha and Mahāyāna deities like *Prajñā-pāramitā,* where palms are placed near the breast in the mode of explaining something. (b) *dharma-cakra* is also one of the four nerve-cycles in the *tāntric* Buddhist conception. It is situated near the region of the heart and is connected with the *dharma-kāya* of Buddha. It is kindled by a female energy having the force of fire known as *caṇḍālī.*

1976 **धर्मज्ञ-मुद्रा**

Dharmajña-mudrā : Let three fingers hang obliquely and down-faced. Place the little-fingers over them and let all of them hang down together. Put the right thumb on them. This is the *dharmajña-mudrā* of *Piṅgalā* (*VD*).

1977 **धर्म-मुद्रा**

Dharma-mudrā : gesture of the tutelary deity of Religion. Place the right-hand so up-turned and the left hand below it, that nails of each hand should touch the other. It is the gesture of *Dharma* (*VD*).

1978 **धर्मध्वजिन्**

Dharmadhvajin : one practising piety just to show to others.

1979 **धर्मराज-हस्त**

Dharmarāja-hasta : hands waved by the arms represent the mythical king Dharmarāja (*Mirror of Gesture,* p. 47).

1980 **धर्मापेत**

Dharmāpeta : atheism, wicked. Vālmiki in his *Rāmāyaṇa* (*Ayo. Kan.* 108.1) has given a materialistic philosophy through Jābāli, a well-disciplined brāhmaṇa, which is known as *darmāpeta i.e.* the philosophy of atheism against the code of moral ethics of life. According to atheism narrated there none is relative to no body and none has a benefit from anyone :

कः कस्य पुरुषो बन्धुः

(*Ibid.* 3)

Since a person has none as dear and near, there is nobody as father, mother or relatives. If anyone feels having such relation with anyone, it is out of insanity :

तस्मान्माता पिता चेति राम सज्जेत यो नरः ।
उन्मत्तः इव स ज्ञयो नास्ति काश्चिद् हि कस्यचित् ॥

(*Ibid.* 4)

According to Jābāli, the attachment to father, mother, etc. are just like an attachment to a house outside our native place. One going outside may stay in a house there for a day. Next day he forsakes it not leaving any attachment for that house, even though till then he called it his own house. This being the real thing the wise do not get attached to relations :

यथा ग्रामान्तरं गच्छन्नरः काश्चित् क्वचिद्वसेत
उत्सृज्य च तमावासं प्रतिष्ठेतदपरे ऽ हनि ।
एवमेव मनुष्याणां पितामाता गृहं वसु
आवासमात्रं काकुस्थ सज्जन्ते नात्र सज्जनाः ॥

(*Ayo. Kan. 108.677)*

For a human being father is only an accidental cause of birth and it happens out of sexual relation of father with a catamenial mother :

बीजमात्रं पिता जन्तोः शुक्लं रुधिरमेव च ।
संयुक्तमृतुतन्मात्र पुरुषस्येह जन्म तत् ॥

(*Ibid. 11)*

Jābāli had no respect for the books on *Dharmaśāstra* that enunciates the sacrifice, *śrāddha,* etc. So he says that the performers of *yoga, dāna, dīkṣā, tapas* and the renunciation of everything in the *Dharmaśāstra* are to deceive the people. They were cunningly planned and written in those books by greedy people desirous of gaining the wealth and prosperity of others (*Ibid.* 108.16). Finally Jābāli concludes his preachings with an evocation not to believe in heaven and to accept only the perceptable and throw away all those non perceptable since pleasure in this world is the highest good.

Here Vālmīki was examining through the words of Jābāli whether the atheism can heel the wounds of Rāma and dissuade him from staying in the forest. The poet has examined whether the one suffering from great difficulties and troubles and doing nothing to get rid of that believing in destiny can be saved by atheism. It was merely an experiment, which failed. (K.C. Nair, 1990. 12-16).

1981 **धारण**

Dhāraṇa : attention consisting in fixing the mind on the desired object. It is the sixth discipline of *yoga.*

1982 **धारण-मातृकाकला**

Dhāraṇa mātṛkā kalā : art of remembering everything. One of the 64 arts given in *Kāmasūtra* (1.3-16). Lexicography and other devices for memory training.

1983 **धारण-यन्त्र**

Dhāraṇa-yantra : the *yantras* generally used as an amulet or talisman. These are drawn on leaves and dedicated in the name of different deities. Their use is regarded as efficacious for warding off evil spirits and in the attainment of merit (*Tantrasāra,* 585).

1984 **धारणा**

Dhāraṇā : exclusive attention to a present idea, the process of preferentially responding to a stimulus or range of stimuli. The adjustment of the sense organs and central nervous system for maximal stimulation.

1985 **धारणी**

Dhāraṇī : a conglomeration of syllables, occasionally containing one or two intelligible words, used as a charm or prayer by the followers of *tāntric* Buddhism.

1986 **धिक्कार**

Dhikkāra : reproach.

1987 **धीरा**

Dhīrā : a heroine who expresses her resentment in the presence of her husband or lover.

1988 **धूत-शिर**

Dhūta śira : slow rotation of the head, side bend of the head, slow sideways movement of the head, a variety of the head-movement; a slight hurling movement of the head expressing ideas of unwillingness, sadness, surprise, confidence, sideways, rejection, etc. It is a type of the Head twist. This is a half head shake. It is employed as no sign. It is more clearly related to the child's action of refusing food which is being pressed to the mouth. It is applicable in unwillingness, dejection, astonishment, confidence, looking sideways, emptiness and forbidding. Slow sideways movement of the head is *dhūta* while the same effected quickly is *vidhuta* (q.v.). *Vidhuta* is applicable in attack of cold, terror, panic, fever and the first stage of drinking.

1989 **धूनन**

Dhūnana : thrashing relevant sentiment and feelings through appropriate gesture (*NS*, IX. 175).

1990 **धूप-मुद्रा**

Dhūpa-mudrā: gesture of the scented burning stick. Place two palms upturned, keep six fingers in a curved position, extend two fore-fingers and join their tips. Then put two thumbs at the roots of fore-fingers. This is called *dhūpa-mudrā* (*VD*).

Dhūpa is an incense stick. When it burns it emits a fragrance. It is required in the worship of deities.

1991 **धूम्रपान**

Dhūmrapāna : smoking. when a group of Māhisya men (in Bengal) smoke together, the pipe is passed from hand to hand with the same posture; so that when the first smoker receives the pipe for the second time, it comes to him with the same gesture he used in giving away.

Younger boys do show formal respect to elders by avoiding smoking. They do not smoke *bīdis* in front of the elders. It is also true that these days, younger boys do smoke in the presence of the elders other than their fathers and elder brothers of fathers. A son of 40 years shares the *chilam* with the father of the sixty. These traits are criticized by older people.

While smoking *chilams* or *hukkās*, the circle starts from the eldest member sitting there.

1992 **धूर्तरचना**

Dhūrtaracanā : roguery, *thugee.*

1993 **धृति**

Dhṛti : one of the *vyabhicārī bhāvas.* self-command, contentment. (a) It is manifested by enjoyment of the objects attained, absence of regret for the unattained, impaired or lost, etc. (b) an aspect of *kṣamā* or mercy in philosophy.

1994 **धृतैकवेणि**

Dhṛtaikaveṇi : bearing a single braid of hair.

1995 **धृष्ट**

Dhṛṣṭa : haughty; and erotic hero who is rude and insolent, who is not afraid even when he has done an offence, who is unashamed even when he is reproached, and continues to speak lies even when his fault is manifest.

1996 **धेनुमुद्रा**

Dhenu-mudrā : a *yogic* pose which required to offer *naivedya* (food-offering) to god in the ritual of worship. It symbolizes a cow.

1997 **धैर्य**

Dhairya : self-control, or a state of mind free from inconsistency and boastfulness (*Daśarūpaka*, II. 37). It is the natural mental condition which is not affected by rashness and is free from boasting in all matters. One of the natural graces of women (*NS*). It is the ability to guide one's own behaviour, the ability to repress or inhibit impulsive behaviour or impulses.

1998 **धौतापाङ्ग**

Dhautāpāṅga : having the corners of the eyes illumined.

1999 **धौति**

Dhauti : washing.

2000 **ध्यान**

Dhyāna : undistracted attention, meditation and contemplation; Meditation is essential for all. Why? The mind is like a pond of water and even a little breeze of thought can disturb its surface. Constant thought-waves create tensions which bring in ageing, which in turn ebbs away the strength in a short time. Man is not a mere bottle of blood, a mass of flesh, and a bundle of bones; he is full of likes and dislikes, ideals, faith and feelings. From the cradle to the grave he goes on filling his basket of life with agreeable and disagreeable experiences. His mind thus becomes very much a lumber room of sensations, perceptions and conceptions. All these overpower his divine nature.

Had these experiences of one life only, it would have been easy to wipe out the impressions of mind and make it a "*tabula rasa*" again. But man is reborn to work out actions of his past lives. He comes with a rich store of *anādivāsanā* (beginningless instincts) which may be called his impressions and experiences of many lives. All these block his supreme awareness and it is his task in the new life given him to wipe them off.

Rājayoga is a branch of *yoga* which devises the technique of *dhyāna* for physical, mental and spiritual unfoldment. *Dhyāna* is a process of exhausting the hidden, latent and suppressed desires of unconscious. It is a tonic for every one. The mind feels relaxed during the practice of *dhyāna*. It calms and controls the astral body. It restores the vitality of mind. By deep meditation alone can we overcome mental, physical and emotional tensions and rid the world of its besetting maladies.

Dhyāna refers generally to that portion of the *sādhana* of the *Mahāyāna* Buddhism in which instruction is given as to the description of the deity with whom the worshipper is to identify himself. *Dhyāna* is also the name of a *mudrā* and an *āsana*. It is defined as steady contemplation of the object without break which reveals the reality of the contemplated object to the aspirant's mind. It is the seventh discipline of *yoga*.

2001 **ध्यानमुद्रा-हस्त**

Dhyānamudrā-hasta : single hand gesture, occurs often in iconography.

2002 **ध्यानयोगासन**

Dhyānayogāsana : type of sitting posture, state of fainting.

2003 **ध्रुवदर्शनम्**

Dhruvadarśanam : the ritual of seeing the pole-star by the couple after the completion of marriage ceremony (*Śiva*, II.46).

2004 **ध्रुवा गीति**

Dhruvā-gīti : a particular song to propitiate the gods.

2005 **ध्रुवा मुद्रा**

Dhruvā-mudrā : "in the palm of a hand, when a curved finger is taken tightly and the rest fingers remain there like a compressed lump, or in the way of *piṇḍa*, it is called the *dhruvāmudrā*" (*BT*).

2006 **ध्वज**

Dhvaja : a banner, the sign of the custom house (*A*, 2.21.1). The Symbolicity of *dhvaja* for Indra is depicted in *Ṛgveda* (X. 103.11). The banner is indicated by various names such as *lakṣma* (ensign), *cihna* (sign), *dhvaja* (banner) or *ketu* (flag). The fall of the banner, once hoisted was an evil sign (*Śiva*, 53.13). There were different banners for different gods.

2007 **ध्वजपात**

Dhvaja-pāta : want of erection of penis : also known as *dhvaja-bhaṅga*.

2008 **ध्वजमुद्रा**

Dhvaja-mudrā : if the fore-finger of the *kapiṭṭha*-gesture is taken by the *śikhara*-gesture, it is the *dhvaja* (*VD*).

2009 **ध्वजोच्छ्राय**

Dhvajocchrāya : (a) raising or unfurling a flag. (b) erection of penis.

2010 **ध्वनि**

Dhvani : power of word to convey the suggestible meaning, poetic work containing the suggestible element. *Dhvani* is the intuitive meaning of the poetry which is conveyed by the conventional words. *Dhvani* stands for (a) conventional symbol. (b) the articulate sound, (c) conventional meaning. Grammarians used the word *dhvani* for both the suggestive word and the suggestive meaning. *Dhvani* is sound, sounding overtone of meaning, resonance of sense. In the field of acoustics, ancient India reached a stage of development which was far superior to that in the contemporary cultures. It was, perhaps, due to the fact that the ears of the Indians were attuned to the phonetic niceties required in correctly reciting the *Vedic* hymns. The development of acoustics is discernible in the realm of Indian music. In this domain, we find distinctions of musical tones much closer and finer than those in other musical systems of the ancient times. Quite early we know of as many as twenty-two *śrutis* or quarter-tones. Their proportions are measured with great precision.

In the analysis of sound, Mīmāṁsakas distinguish between three elements, *viz.* (i) *nāda*, a quality of the air, which is the physical basis of audible sound. (ii) *dhvani*, audible sound, (iii) *sphoṭa* - transcendental or intelligible sound.

The early *nyāya* writers have expressed the view that the sound-wave (*śabda-santāna*) has its substratum in either (*ākāśa*) and not air (*vāyu*). According to later writers, sound is not a mode of motion (*parispanda*), because either, the substratum, is incapable of motion. In analysing vibratory motion, writers hold that molecules of a bell vibrate when the bell is struck. Echo (*pratidhvani*) was considered to be a reflection of sound. Different kinds of sounds were differentiated from one another by means of pitch (*tāra*, *manda*, etc.), intensity (*tīvra*, *manda*, etc.) and timbre (*asādhāraṇa dharma*). The pitch of a note was held to be inversely proportioned to the length of a wire.

न – Na

2011 **नकुल-परिरम्भण**

Nakula-parirambhaṇa : the embrace of *inchneumon* (Dāmodaragupta, *Kuṭṭanimatam,* 581), experienced by a slender lady. Nakula is known for its closed proximity. It sees everything white in the day.

2012 **नकुल-हस्त**

Nakula-hasta : *kaṭakahasta* represents Nakula, the Pāṇḍava (*Mirror of Gesture,* p.47).

2013 **नक्षत्र**

Nakṣatra : stars as objects of propitiation for their auspicious and inauspicious effect. The oldest lists of the stars and their presiding deities are found in *AV* (XIX.7.2-5; *Tait. Saṁ* IV.4.10. The stars play an important role in tribal life. The Daṇḍāmī Maria and other tribes of Bastar have firm belief with the scorpion (*vṛścika*). They call it *bāghmogā.* In Antagarh, Kondagaon and Jagdalpur regions the movement of the moon and the position of this constellation are sometimes watched when marriages are performed. The *mūr* is known in Halbi dialect of Bastar. The original form is *mūla,* a bad asterism. The child who is born in this nakṣatra is forsaken (*Skanda* IV. 82.23-25).

2014 **नक्षत्रपाठक**

Nakṣtra-pāṭhaka : astrologer. According to *Nārada Purāṇa* (23.38) an astrologer was not to be saluted, nor was he a fit person to be given gifts to :

पाषण्डं पतितं मूर्खं तथा नक्षत्रपाठकम् ।
तथा पातकिनं चैव कदाचिन्नाभिवादयेत् ॥

2015 **नख**

Nakha : nail. *nakha-nikṛntana* 'nail-cutter', *nakha-nirbhinna* 'split asunder with nails' (*KS,* XV.4), *nakhara* 'shaped like a claw' (*SBr.*), *nakhin* 'having nails (*SBr.*). It is common among the elite class college girls in India to have large nails to grow. This tendency is not found in village India.

2016 **नखखादि विनश्यति**

Nakhakhādi vinaśyati : the eater of the nails *i.e.* the person who cuts nails with this teeth is sure to meet disaster and destruction (*Agni,* 155.18).

2017 **नखक्षत**

Nakha-kṣata : nail-prints. A term used in *Kāmasūtra* (2.4.1) for the tactile movement involving partners in courtship or haptics to produce various types of arousals. Vātsyāyana defines it as follows: *rāgavṛddhau saṅgharṣātmakam nakhavilekhanam* which means that nails (M) come close to the skin (F) and produce visible friction. Vātsyāyana opines that the love of a woman, who sees the marks of nails on the private parts of her body, even they are old and worn out, becomes again fresh and new:

*Nakhakṣatāni paśyantasya gūḍhasthāneṣu yoṣitaḥ ।
cirotsṛṣṭāpyabhinavā prītirbhavati peśalā ॥* (*Kāmasūtra,* 2.4.27).

Kālidāsa (*Kumārasaṁbhava,* 9.29) has experienced the same in Pārvatī :

Priyeṇa datte maṇidarpaṇe sā
saṁbhogacihnam svavapurvibhājya
trapāvatī tatra ghanānurāgam
rōmañcadambhena bahirbabhāra

Vātsyāyana believes that "nothing tends to increase love so much as the effects of marking with the nails and biting:

*Nānyatpatutaram kiñcidasti rāgavardhanam
nakhadantasamutthānām karmaṇām gatayo yathā* (*Kāmasūtra,* 2.4.31).

Padmaśrī (*Nāgara sarvasva,* XXII) has enumerated eight types of *nakhakṣata.*

2018 **नखक्षतनितम्ब**

Nakha-kṣata-nitamba : nail-prints on the hips. Hips are another important place for nail-prints. Māgha (*Śiśu.* 10.85), Ratnākara (*Haravijaya,* 27.41), Dāmodaragupta (*Kuṭṭanimatam,* 402) and Kālidāsa (*Raghu,* 6.17) have depicted this type of tactile gesture.

2019 **नखक्षतभेद**

Nakha-kṣata-bheda : classification of nail-prints. On the body is a feature of sexiologists, where entire body was classified into many components. *Kāmasūtra* (2.4.4) has classified it into eight categories. The *Pañcasāyaka* (4. 50-56) accepts this classification, but adds *sansmarāka* instead of a 'tiger's claw': *churita, ardhendu, maṇḍala, śaśaplutakam, rekhā, mayūrapādam, paṅkajapatram* and *sansmarāka.* The *Anaṅgarāga* (9.23-28) narrates only seven types of nail-scratches: *Churitam, ardhacandram, maṇḍalakam, rekhā, mayūrapādam, śaśaplutam* and *utpalapatram.* It leaves the 8th one.

2020 **नखच्छेद**

Nakhaccheda : nail-cutting.

2021 **नखपद**

Nakha-pada : scratch made by nail (Kālidāsa, *Ṛtu.5.*63)

2022 **नखपादाङ्कितोरू**

Nakha-pādaṅkitōrū : nail-scars on laps. Kālidāsa has mentioned it: *ūrūmūlanakhamārgarājibhiḥ* (*Kumārasaṁbhava,* 8.87) and *nakhapadāṅkitoravaḥ.* (*Raghu,* 19.35).

2023 **नख-विलेखन**

Nakha-vilekhana : nail-prints show prosperity in sexual act-according to Dāmodaragupta: *nakhavilekhanamabhyudayaḥ* (*Kuṭṭanīmatam*, 377).

2024 **नख-विलेखन-स्थान**

Nakha-vilekhana-sthāna : one of the main parameters added in the tactile classification of kines, referring to where on the body-part a print is made. Vātsyāyana recognised the places that are pressed with the nails for communication correspond to the main physical divisions, *viz.* the armpit, the throat the breasts, the hips, the back and the thighs: *kakṣau stanau galaḥ pṛṣtham jaghanamūrū ca sthānāni* (*Kāmasūtra*, 2.4.5) *Suvarnābha* (*Ibid.*2.4.6) has opined that in *rati-atireka* there is no use of *sthānamasthānam* (*na vidyata it*). The whole body becomes the place of articulation. The *Ratirahasya* (8.1) has enumerated three more places after *Kāmasūtra.* They are the shoulders, the flanks and between the breasts: *kakṣākarorū jaghanastanapārśvapṛṣṭhahṛtkandhārāsu nakharāḥ. Anaṅgarāga* (9.22) gives one more place, *i.e.* the cheeks:

grīvākarorujaghanastanapṛṣṭhakakṣā
hṛtpāraśvagaṇḍaviṣāye nakharāḥ kharāḥ syuḥ

(b) It is said that one should not scratch the earth with nails, nor with an ember nor with the ashes (*Matsya*, VII.40): *Vilikhenna nakhairbhūmim, nāṅgāreṇa ṇa bhasmanā*

2025 **नखाकृतिविज्ञान**

Nakhākṛti-vijñāna : sign of the nails. It nails are thin like *chatt*, they indicate impotence; if curved and broken, they indicate poverty; if colourless, it is a sign of being guided by others; if they are reddish like copper, it is a sign of royalty (*Garuḍa*). If white and dry, they indicate grief and lack of power (*Bhaviṣya*, 27). Varāhamihira (*BS*, LXVIII) has the following comments; 'Those whose nails resemble husks, *i.e.* are rough and contain many lines, are impotent; with flat and split nails men become poor; with ugly and colourless ones, dependent on others; and with red ones, commanders of armies:

तुषसदृशनखाः क्लीबाश्चिपिटैः स्फुटितैश्च वित्तसन्त्यक्ताः ।
कुनखविवर्णैः परतर्कुकाश्च ताम्रैश्चमूपतयः ॥ (41)

2026 **नग्न-क्षपणक**

Nagna-kṣapaṇaka : naked ascetics. The term was often used for the Digambara jain monks.

2027 **नग्नता**

Nagnatā : nakedness (*A V.*X.33.2). *Nagnaka* (naked) and *nagna-bhāvuka* (becoming naked) are also *Vedic* terms. (b) sleeping being naked, is taboo (*Brahma*, 221.34; *Vāmana* 14.47). (c) nudity appears to be a characterstic in Śaiva mythology if we scrutinize the accounts of *Purāṇas.* According to one account, Śiva and Pārvati were playing at dica; but when he was defeated by her, he ran naked; नग्नो द्यूते विसर्जितः (*Padma Uttara.* 124.26-27). According to *Skanda Purāṇa* (1.1.6.4) Śiva was cursed by the sages for that uncivil act of his showing himself naked to their wives, and attracting them.

2028 **नग्न-शबरी**

Nagna-sabarī : Name of Durgā, worshipped by the forest-dwelling tribe known as *śabaras*, and visualized as a naked damsel belonging to this tribe. *arya-stava* (*Harivaṁsa* 3.3) describes Durgā as adored by śabaras, barbaras (savage aliens), and pulindas (tribal hunters). Another of her names mentioned in this work as well as in the Durgā-*stotras* in *Mahābhārata* (4.6 and 6.23) is aparṇa (meaning "one who does not have even a leaf as her garment, *viz* nude), which is synonymous to *nagna-śabari.* (Fig. 2028)

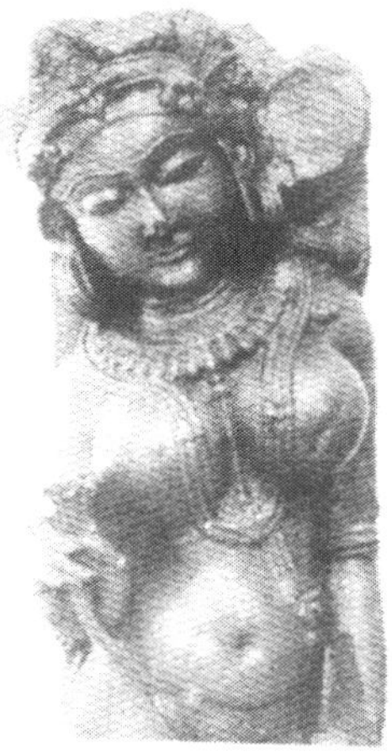

Fig. – (2028)

2029 **नग्निका**

Nagnikā : a girl attain puberty, a beautiful girl though nude, a girl who does not reach womanhood, a girl whose menstruation is imminent, a girl in whom sexual desire has not yet grown, a girl whose menstrual flow has not yet started and whose breasts are not yet fully developed. It is stated that a girl who begins the 'period' is called *nagnikā;* hence a girl should be married when she is an *"a-nagnikā"* (*Skanda*, IV. 40.42) to gain the real fruit of *kanyā-dānā. Śatapatha Brahmaṇa* (XIX. 6.) also prescribes the same, because she is *lagnikā* 'mature for copulation'.(Fig. 2029)

2030 **नट**

Naṭa : in modern India : actor, name of a tribe; *naṭa* is a word very commonly used in modern India for one who is proficient in the art of acrobatics, such as walking on ropes and doing several types of balancing feats. These

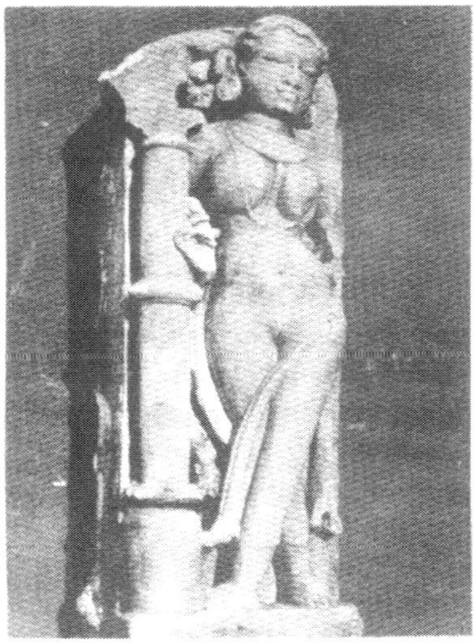

Fig.– (2029)

naṭas (Hindi *naṭ*) assume different names in the different states. In Maharashtra, they are known as *ḍomri,* doing all sorts of feats on ropes. In Bengal, they are called *bodiyās,* proficient in traits of dancing, singing and acrobatics. The *baghuliā* of Uttar Pradesh and the *naṭs* of Punjab and Madhya Pradesh have traits similar to those of Rajasthan in one way or the other.

The meaning of the word *naṭa* can be taken as an actor in ancient India. The passages in *Rāmāyaṇa* (II.69.4) which have references to *naṭas* have the claim to an early date of naṭas. Keith observes that the word *naṭa* occurring in Paṇini (IV.3.110) means pantomime. The special term *bhrūkuṁśa* (*Mahābhāṣya,* IV.1-3) was used for the actor playing feminine roles. It means that *naṭas* as a class existed in the *Rāmāyaṇa*-period. Bharata has included this class in the dramatic troupe. According to Bharata, be gesticulated the life of the people endowed with sentiments and states (*NS*).

2031 **नटसूत्र**

Naṭa-sūtra : a work on dramaturgy by Paṇini, probably composed *ca.*600. B.C. Although it has not survived, it is referred to by later dramaturgists.

2032 **नटी**

Naṭī : female dancer. The term applied to Śakti when the goddess dances out of delight at the performance of her rituals (*Niruttara,* XV). (Fig. 2032)

2033 **नट पाद**

Naṭapāda : leg is slightly bent down or one leg is slightly deflected to the back as in the Elura figure in Rāmeśvara cave.

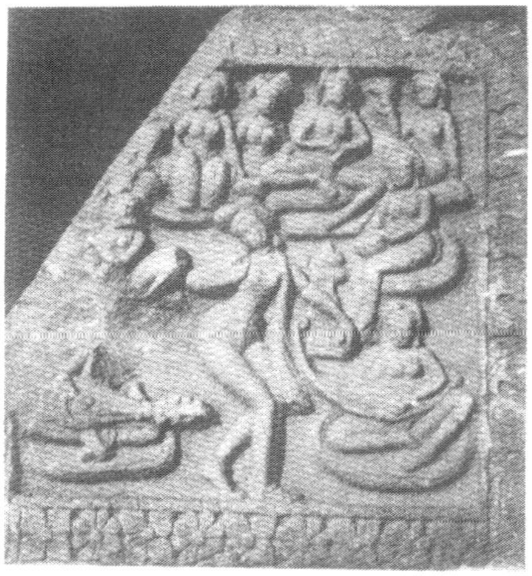

Fig. – (2032)

2034 **नट पार्श्व**

Naṭapārśva : side bending in the right-left direction. In the *naṭa*-pose, the waist is slightly bent and one shoulder is drawn away slightly. It is used in approaching any body (*NS,* X. 10-17).

2035 **नत-शयन**

Nata-śayana : a posture for lying down. The shanks should be slightly stretched and both hands loose. It is used in laziness, fatigue and distress (*NS*).

2036 **नतसंस्थान**

Natasaṁsthāna : the down-looking pose (*VD*).

2037 **नत स्थानक**

Nata sthānaka : a posture of lying down (*NS,* XII. 234).

2038 **नताकटि**

Natā-kaṭi : bending of the waist.

2039 **नता ग्रीवा**

Natā grīvā : neck bent down, bent low; of *adhogata* head-movement suggests embracing in *Ratnāvalī* (Act. III); It suggests to hold ornaments (necklace), flinging arms on one's neck, etc. (*NS,* VIII. 164-171); resulting when the face is bent down; used in wearing ornaments and embrace round the neck.

2040 **नताङ्गी**

Natāṅgī : a woman of supple body, of pilant or flexible limbs or body.

2041 **नताजङ्घा**

Natājaṅghā : the position when the knee touches the ground; the knee is bent in one front (*NS,* IX. 262b-263a); *naṭa* is a gesture of the lower leg in which the knee is shrunk.

It is used to take position, a seat and to start a motion of the body (*NS*, X.33-40). In this position the knees are bent in front: this shank and knee position is seen very often in tribal dance. *Naṭa* is used in several ways, in sitting, walking and various *sthānakas*; here the leg bends down.

2042 **नता नासा**

Natā nāsā : clinged nostrcs; frequent depressing and delating of nostrils; a type of nose-gesture in which lobes are clinging;the lobes of the nose clung frequently to suggest interruptedly fading with shy (*NS*, VIII. 123-129). Nostrils clinging together again and again; it is used in the persuasion of women, in slight weeping at intervals and in breathing and gentle throbbing.

2043 **नता भ्रकुटि**

Natā bhrukuṭi : knitting the eyebrows, only presented by *Bālarāmbharata.*

2044 **नति**

Nati : obeisance; humility: *natyupekṣā rasāntaraiḥ* (*DR* IV.68)

2045 **नदी-हस्त**

Nadī-hasta : river in general. The *patāka*-hand moving up and down indicates river in general (*Mirror of Gesture*, p. 48).

2046 **नन्दी**

Nandī : he praised all the world by sweet words of praise and salutation with auspicious rites. He pleased people in the performance of the play in ārious ways with Sanskrit and Prākṛit recitation (*NS*, IV. XXXV. 29)

2047 **नन्द्यावर्त स्थानक**

Nandyāvarta sthānaka : a type of posture. *nandyāvarta* means vessels for *argha.*

2048 **नपुंसक**

Napuṁsaka : eunuch, neither male non female.

2049 **नपुंसक चेष्टितम्**

Napuṁsaka ceṣṭitam : *napuṁsaka* eunuch's absorbed actions. *Ceṣṭitam* or absorbed actions are those which are unconsciously copied from other people. One is not aware when he first acquired it. However it varies from group to group, culture to culture and nation to nation.

The way we talk and stand, laugh and grimace, are all subject to absorbed actions. The case of eunuch in Indian context may be taken. Such a male learns from the society how to behave in a more feminine way. In origin these actions may be pseudo-female, but once they have become established in an eunuch group they go away from the typically female and, by repeated male-to-male transfer, become more modified until they develop a character of their own. In many cases they are now so distinct that a true female could, by miming them accurately, make it quite clear that she was not acting in a feminine way, but was instead pretending to be a male homosexual.

In India *hijrā* is a class of enuchs, who form a separate community, recruited by the admission of persons born with this deformity or reduced to the like condition by amputation. They are known as *khasuā* in Sagar. They wear female clothes and ornaments and assume the names of women. The *hijrās* usually mutilate themselves in the performance of a religious vow. As a further fulfilment of their vow the *hijrā* pull out their hair of the beards and moustaches, bore their ears and noses for female ornaments and effect female speech and manners. Their cutting of male genital organs is done ritually. Some of them make money by allowing spectators to look at the mutilated part of their body, and also by the practice of pederasty.

2050 **नपुंसक-मन्त्र**

Napuṁsaka-mantra : *mantras* which are neither male nor female. The *mantras* for male deities are known as *puruṣa-mantra* and those intended for female deities are known as *strī-mantra* or *vidyā*. The rest belonging to *napuṁsaka* category (*Śāradātilaka*, II. 57-58).

2051 **नपुंसकलिंग-हस्त**

Napuṁsakaliṅga hasta : neuter hands. *Bālarāmabharata* divides *asaṁyuta* and *saṁyuta hastas* into all three genders. It is one of them. (b) in Konkani women of low status (unmarried girls and widows) are referred to by neuter pronouns, while their married sisters are accorded to the feminine. Thus, gender classifications are based on a concept of relative value. Thus those languages which classify men with big animals and women with small ones, or men with gods and women with valued animals, followed by a class of devalued creatures, make use not directly of sex reference or the semantic features maleness and animacy, but of a commonsense ranking principle. It is of interest to note a clear parallel in several cultures which exploit the ranking'masculine, feminine, neuter' in their use of language in order to mark the inferiority of women to men.

2052 **नपुंसक-वर्ण**

Napuṁsaka varṇa : letters which are neither male nor female. To this category belong long 'r' and long 'l' (Rāghava on *Śāradātilaka*, II.5-7).

2053 **नभो मुद्रा**

Nabho-mudrā : *nabha* means 'sky'. *nabho-mudrā* is to direct the tongue towards the palate. In *nabho-mudrā* you have to look at the middle space of the eyebrows also. *Nabho-mudrā* is complete and perfect when you achieve *śāmbhav* and twist the tongue backwards and touch the palate.

2054 **नमत्-कन्धरा**

Namat-kandharā : lady whose shoulders are dropping, quality of the conch-lady (*Anaṅgaraṅga,* 1.17).

2055 **नमस्कार**

Namaskāra (*Bṛhaddevatā* 144.60) : salutation. form of speech and thought. It is a type of greeting. It occurs with establishing eye contact, eyebrow flashing, smiling, raising and joining both palms in *añjali-mudrā.* (b) *namaskāra-mudrā:* gesture of salute. When fingers, beginning from little ones and ending in forefingers are extended and near the chest, as an *añjali,* it is called *namaskāra* (*VD*). (c) bring two hands in front, join and extend them. This is the gesture for salutation and applied to please the Sun-God (*VD*). (d) *namaskāra-mudrā* is a gesture of politeness. The Hindu palms-together, thumbs about the level of the chin, is a greeting a "thank you", and a gesture of obeisance, depending on the context.

Namaskāra means joining the palms to show respect or for the purpose of salutation. It is also *mudrā* or hand-pose. The distinction between *abhivādana* and *namaskāra* is that in the former, one bows and utters some words while in the latter one only bows with folded hands. (e) there are certain taboos regarding saluting persons. The following persons are not to be saluted, nor are they to be greeted : an atheist, a law-breaker, sonless person, stupid one, villain, thief, *pāṣaṇḍa* (one who has not been duly initiated by *Gāyatrī*), *Veda*-seller, one who is quarrelsome, or always given to debate, a fierce person, a woman who is sterile, one holding faggots and flowers in hand, holding a water-jar, one who is fallen, a wanton woman, (*jārā*), a woman in her period, a pregnant woman, one who helps or performs abortion, an idol-monger, a sacrificer engaged in sacrifice, one who is offering *piṇḍas* in a ritual for the manes, one who is vomiting, one taking food, one sleeping, taking bath and one who holds alms (*Nārada.* 23.37). Also a person who does not return a greeting is never to be saluted (*Ibid*). In addition to these, according to *Nārada Purāṇa* (23.37), the following are not to be saluted -a village priest (*grāma-yāyaka* intoxicated person and one who has applied oil to his body.

2056 **नमोवाक**

Namo vāka : expression of respect (*Ś.Br.* I. 7.2.4) *sūktavākamuta namovākam;* one to whom respect is paid (*Ibid.* VIII. 25.23); *namaskāra* in later Sanskrit. See the following verse.

नारायणं नमस्कृत्य नरं चैव नरोत्तमम् ।
देवीं सरस्वतीं चैव ततो जयं उदीरयेत् ॥

2057 **नम्र बाहु**

Namra bāhu : slightly arched position of the arms.

2058 **नयन-चुम्बन**

Nayana-cumbana : kissing eyes (*Haravijaya,* 27.24); *Śiśupālavadha* (10.54) records: *upoḍharāge nayanāravindam vicumbati.*

2059 **नयनादिप्रसाद**

Nayanādiprasāda : brightness of the eyes. The nature of pleasure (*sukha*) is that it is characterized by a peculiar consciousness of gratification, a sense of favourableness (*anugraha*) and its specific effect are certain bodily expression such as the brightness of the eyes, the face etc. It is the physiological effect of pleasure (*Nyāyakandalikā*).

2060 **नयनोन्मीलन**

Nayanonmīlana : chiselling the eye of an image (*Mānasa-sāra,* LXX.1-14).

2061 **नर-नारायण-मुद्रा**

Nara-nārāyaṇa-mudrā : gesture symbolizing god Nara-Nārāyaṇa of Vaiṣṇavite cult. The *mukula*-hand with extended fore and middle fingers symbolizes Nara-Nārāyaṇa (*VD*).

2062 **नरनारी**

Nara-nārī : man and woman. About the mutual characteristics of woman and man, in *Varāha Purāṇa* (146. 38-39), it is said that woman is like fire-alter, while man is like a jar of clarified butter, the difference however is said to be that, by contact the clarified butter in the jar is melted; but man, when infatuated, melts by the mere sight of woman: *agnikuṇḍasamā nārī, ghṛtakumbhasamaḥ pumān,*

> and also ghṛtakumbhogniyogena-dravate natu darśanāt
> pumān strīdarśanādeva dravate yadvimohitaḥ

Though there is some division of labour between men and women, Bison-horn Maria women are much freer to share the work of men than are the women of many other tribes and castes. They are allowed, for example to plough-a thing strictly taboo to the Gonds of the central provinces. They may reap a crop. They may climb trees. They may fish, but not hunt. Men, on the other hand, may not husk rice or clean it in a fan; they should not grind, nor they should carry pitchers on their heads.

2063 **नरमेध**

Naramedha : human sacrifice.

2064 **नर्तनी-मुद्रा**

Nartani-mudrā : "this gesture of *nartanī* is especially applicable in the occasion of social or scholastic dialogues. This pleases divine beings and helps to gain a position, either in a place or an authority or country. Here one should perform a dance like a child and pose the mouth as if breathing out the wind from the mouth. It is a *mudrā* that may bring all the worlds under control" (*BT*).

2065 **नर्मकेलि**

Narma-keli : jesting, sport.

2066 **नर्मदा-हस्त**

Narmadā-hasta : the river Narmadā. *ardhapatāka* hand moving upward and downward indicates river Narmadā (*Mirror of Gesture*, p. 48).

2067 **नर्मद्युति**

Narmadyuti: bright with joy; a type of *sandhyaṅga*. In the view of Bharata and Abhinavagupta the laughter which is meant for concealing one's faults but produces laughter is*narmadyuti* (*NS*, 19.78); satisfaction caused by humorous remarks (*DR*. 1.58).

2068 **नर्मन्**

Narman : Joke, clever jesting, fun, pastime, humorous remark, dalliance, pleasantry.

2069 **नर्मसचिव**

Narmasaciva : jesting companion.

2070 **नर्मस्फूर्ज**

Narmasphūrja : outburst of affection; *narmasphūrjaḥ sukhārambho bhayānto navasaṅgame* (*DR*.II.80).

2071 **नर्मस्फोट**

Narmasphoṭa : disclosure of attention: *narmasphoṭastu bhāvānām sūcito' lparaso lavaiḥ* (*DR*.II.81).

2072 **नर्मालाप**

Narmālāpa : joking is a type of speech act. Joking or *narmālāpa* is a ritual of everyday life. There are no beginnings, middles, and ends as such, and people do not normally assemble explicitly to do joking. What is striking about joking in general is that it is in symbolic form. For a variety of reasons specific to particular cultures, structural relations exist between groups that are manifested in particular kinds of verbal behaviour, either between individual who are members of different structural groups or between people who differ on some other dimension than group membership but who nonetheless embody sets of roles that place them distinctly apart. Further more, these role-relationships are not random; there appears to be certain dyads in which ritual joking relationships are never realized anywhere in the world.

It means that joking occurs at a tension point in the social structure of a society, and it serves-as do many other kinds of social behaviour to maintain an equilibrium between conjuctive and disjunctive components of intrasocial relationships (Radcliffe-Brown 1952:95). According to Radcliffe-Brown, the conjunctive component of joking relationship is almost always associated with "friendship relations", at least, it is never associated with "solidarity" which is established by kinship or by membership of a group such as lineage or clan. On the other hand, in any "alliance" or "friendship" relation there is potential antagonism, which is the disjunctive component.

Joking relationships exist in Gwalior region (Madhya Pradesh) among the elderly persons and adolescent boys. Randhir Kirar (60) has observed asking Pītam (15), whether he indulged in masturbation (Mutalkar, 1978. 122).

The behaviour of a Korku towards her husband's younger brother is on the one hand more relaxed. A kind of joking relationship exists between them. They may be quite familiar with each other, eat and work together, and a younger brother is permitted to beat his elder-sister-in-law. If the elder brother dies, he may take her as his wife (levirate).

The relationship between the wives of brothers are carefully regulated in the Bison-horn Maria. Between an elder brother and his younger brother's wife there is an absolute taboo : there is no stronger rule of evidence in the primitive society. But the younger brother stands in a special and privileged relationship to his elder brother's wife : he can flirt her; he can make indecent jokes; he can become her lover; after her husband's death he has the first claim on her person and if she marries anyone else, he has a right to compensation (Shamrao Hivale, *The Devar-Bhauji-relationship, Man in India*, Vol. XXIII. 1943. pp. 157-67).

Joking behaviour's equivalent in Maria is *nālumātā* which is a part of everyday life, a frequent activity for a large segment of tribal populations. This type of joking behaviour is very common in India during marriage ritual. At all other times, sexual joking is literally a catch-as-catch-can affair, occurring in the interstics of daily activities, such as at chance meetings going to and from the village wells, or forest. Every such casual encounter is a small ritual, with prescribed sorts of stereotypes that serve to set the boundaries and the rules of the joking game. Within the rules, however, every player has the chance to use whatever creative resources he has in order to bring laughter, mock disgust, shame and anger, and/or incredulity from the other player or players. Although sexual joking does take place between same-sex players (about each other's sisters or mothers for example), cross-sex joking has a special piquancy and moreover, has potentially very real consequences if the players to choose at any time to back up their words with actions.

The joking episode takes place among young men and women who have grown up together. Somehow they are in preferred marriage relationship. In Bison-horn Maria society marriage is arranged through negotiations between representatives of the lineages of the prospective bride and groom. A man is prohibited from marrying anyone whose paltry membership coincides with his. Given tribal endogamy, all other females within a certain age range are potentially acceptable spouses. Within the group of women who may be acceptable is much smaller group who are definitely preferred as spouses. These are women who stand in the relation of first cross-cousin to a particular man. It is generally assumed that at the appropriate time the children of brothers and sisters will marry, and over a long period after a brother and sister have married and have established household of their own, discussions are carried on between the siblings and their spouses as to the bride-price to be paid, the length of the wedding, and other matters of concern to the families and lineages involved.

From the time of their early childhood children of cross-sex siblings understand that they are to be wed and behave toward each other in specified way. This behaviour includes a certain amount of deference toward and avoidance of each other in the presence of adults (especially their parents), as befits their future relationship as husband and wife. But it also includes a certain amount of overt sexual activity outside the purview of adults. This activity includes sexual joking and bantering as well as clandestine sexual contacts. The latter behaviour is sometimes verbally disapproved by adults but more often is indulged by them as being in the natural order of things.

Sometimes, when the time for the agreed-upon marriages comes about, the family of the groom or of the bride (and usually both) is not capable of paying the costs entailed in a marriage. For most Bison-horn Maria families the cost of marriage is the largest one-time capital outlay they will ever make. In these cases the prospective spouses are encouraged by their parents to elope, thereby alleviating the necessity of an expensive wedding. The young man and woman prearrange a meeting place—perhaps in the forest during the day, or outside the girl's house late at night—and then escape to the village and the house of some "neutral" and usually distant relative, although the house of a married sister is often preferred by the man. The couple stay at this house for a period of a week or a month until the feigned anger of the parents has cooled. They then return to the house of the husband and he pays a small fine to the father of the girl (and to her lineage), whereupon the two are free to set up a household as a married couple.

Thus the proximate cultural norms operative in the joking behaviour of Bison-horn Maria as the following,.

1. Cross-cousins are preferred marriage partners.
2. Joking is an expected part of the cross-cousin relationship.
3. If cross-cousins are in an appropriate situation, then they will joke.
4. The topic of the joking under this circumstance will be sexual-overtly as well as overtly-reflecting one of the primary functions of the conjugal union.
5. Marriages are arranged between the parents and lineages of the individuals concerned.
6. If a prearranged marriage cannot be formally held because of the financial burden placed on the parties, then the couple is encouraged to elope.

A few classes of kin behaviours appear to be more or less similar in all the castes and tribes in India. They generally have joking relationships with wife's younger sister, elder brother's wife, brother's wife's younger sister, sister's husband's sister, between grand children and parents, wife's brother's wife, etc. In these relations exist a mutual joking relationship, but all the relations have different degree of cutting jokes. But sexual relation is not legally permitted among these relations. It only gives over recognition and expression to sanctioned intimacies. The customs of *Devar-bhābhī*, and *Jījā-Sālī* joking relation signify the prevalence of lavirate and sororate. The relationship between *māmī* and *bhāñjā* is not of joking, but is of respectful and reverential as *māmī* touches the feet of *bhāñjā* along with her husband. Among the Harijans, often, a woman refers her husband's son as *bhanej devatā*, which means he is god-like.

2073 **नल-हस्त**

Nala-hasta : *mayūra hasta* represents the mythical king Nala. (*Mirror of Gesture*, p.47).

2074 **नलिनी-पद्मकोश-नृत्तहस्त**

Nalinīpadmakośa-nṛtta-hasta : the lotus-core dancing hands. When the two hands with the *padma-kośa* style are turned and altered, it is called the *nalinī-padmakośa* (*NS*, IX.176-197). The *padmakośa* hands are moved by turns with *vyāvartita* and *parivartita karaṇas*.

2075 **नलिनी-पद्मकोश-हस्त**

Nalinī-padmakośa-hasta : type of hand-gesture watering the plants. In Act I of *Abhijñāna-Śākuntalam* the stage direction *vṛkṣasīcanam rūpayati* (1.17). This is performed by *nalinī padmakośa hasta:* they are taken to the shoulder region. The body bends gracefully a little; hands are then brought down and released (*NS,* IX.207).

2076 **नवाङ्गुलिमितं लिङ्गम्**

Navāṅgulimitam liṅgam : whose sex-organ is nine *aṅgulas* in length, quality of a Bull-man (*Kāmasūtra,* 3.32-33).

2077 **नवान्न**

Navānna : The ceremony of first fruits; literally it means new rice. It is performed in the month of Mārgaśirṣa (Nov-Dec) after the harvest has been gathered.

2078 **नवोढा**

Navoḍhā : newly married wife.

2079 **नहुष-हस्त**

Nahuṣa-hasta : The moving hand represents the mythical king Nahuṣa (*Mirror of Gesture,* p. 47).

2080 **नागबन्ध-स्थानक**

Nāgabandha-sthānaka : elephant catcher posture, type of posture.

2081 **नागबन्ध-हस्त**

Nāgabandha-hasta : both hands gesture. When two hands with the *sarpaśirṣa* style are crossed together; it is the *nāgabandha.* It indicates a pair of snakes, a bower and some ancient magic spells.

2082 **नागरक**

Nāgaraka : highest priest of aesthetics who like a aesthete, though celebrate, used to enjoy fine arts in the company of beautiful women in his aesthetic surroundings; he was a class of connoisseurs and a touch-stone of arts (*Kāmasūtra,* 1.4.1); a gallant (*A,* 7.17.45). *Nāgaraka,* the city-dweller (in the Gupta era) began his day with a carefully executed toilet, the multiple phases of which were almost ritualistic. After cleaning his teeth by rubbing them with a root, he bathed his mouth and eyes, applied a salve to his eyelids, and chewed a few betel-quids.

When these preliminaries were accomplished, he devoted all his attention to the bath which he took each morning either in a special room provided with water installed in the house itself, or else in the river that flowed by just outside the town. The slope leading down to the river was provided with couches and all sorts of equipment for the use of those who went there to bathe. He began by rubbing his body thoroughly with a sort of wooden hand coated with a scented powder. Then he poured oil over his hair and rubbed oil into his skin, before relaxing on a couch and having himself massaged. After the massage, he performed a series of exercises designed to keep his muscles supple. Finally, he stepped into the water and soaped himself (every other day, only) with a frothy preparation (*phenaka*). Once the washing procedures were over, he combed his hair carefully.

Back home once more,he continued the long process of his morning toilet. First, he smeared the whole body with a sweet-smelling unguent, powdered his chest with a camphorated talcum, painted a decorative mark on his forehead with red arsenot and drew designs on his arms with civet powder, symbolizing good fortune. He rimmed his eyes with black cosmetic and smeared some red lac over his lips. Every three days, he smeared lac over his whole body; every four days, he shaved his beard and moustache; every five days, or every ten days, he plucked out all his body hair. When he had completed these lengthy preliminaries, he dressed himself in freshly laundered garments whose sweet smell was due to their having been fumigated in incense, adorned himself with jewellery, threaded flowers and strings of parts into the coils of his hair, and, often, trimmed his nails. Finally, he looked at himself in the mirror to make sure that everything was in order.

Thereafter leaving the house, he chewed a compound of mango, camphor, cloves and other ingredients, to sweeten his breath, and hung a garland of flowers around his neck. He placed on his head a turban-like hat, armed himself with a parasol and a walking stick, and strode off to attend to his business affairs. Since these required only the minimal presence expected of a wealthy scion, he was soon free to pass the rest of the day as he pleased. He took three meals, ones in the morning, one at midday and one in the evening. Before the midday meals, he played a few rounds of some gambling game with his customers or cronics. After this meal, he took an afternoon nap; then he visited the parrots and *mainās* in his aviary to teach them new words. Cock-fights, or fights between quails or pigeons, on which he betted enthusiastically.

After the evening meal, he received his friends in the reception room of his house. He enjoyed playing host to society and, while waiting for his mistress to appear, passed the time agreeably in their company, listening to music, making pleasant conversation, and sipping alcoholic drinks. When he thought the moment opportune, he bade his guests farewell, following the traditional code of politeness, and as they left he handed them flowers and betel.

Once alone with his mistress, he initiated a love play full of amorous propositions accompanied by delicate and tender caresses, to which she yielded willingly. After they had made love, each resumed a modest attitude. To spend their evening together, they strolled out on to the terrace to gaze at the star-lit sky, nibbled at sweetmeats of all kinds and sipped gruel, coconut milk, sweetened mango and lemon juice and fragrant wine. After she had retired happy and still languid from love-making, he prepared for bed, rubbing a scented ointment over his face and crowning himself with a wreath of flowers before lying down to sleep until the morning in his elegant bedroom.

2083 **नागरिक-वृत्ति**

Nāgarika-vṛtti : polite manners.

2084 **नागहस्त**

Nāgahasta : both hands gesture (*Abhinayadarpaṇa*), not mentioned in *NS.*

2085 **नागापसर्पितकरण**

Nāgāpasarpita karaṇa : hands in *recita* and head in *parivāhita,* release of one leg from *svastika* position of feet (*NS,* IV. 166-167, VIII. 27). The foot is moved from *svastika,* the head is in *paravāhita* and the hands are in *recita.* It is used in medium intoxication.

2086 **नाट**

Nāṭa : dance, *nāṭaka* 'dancer', *nāṭakam* 'typical form of drama'.

2087 **नाटकीया**

Nāṭakīyā : female dancer; she was extremely beautiful and had mastery over tempo, rhythm and sentiments.

2088 **नाटयन्**

Nāṭayan : acting as if (*Priyadarśikā,* 1.27) or 'acts as if' is about the best rendering for the stage-direction, *nāṭayan* or *nāṭayati* used to indicate that the actor is to represent or portray by some special conventional gesture or mood; 'mimicking, counterfeiting, would also convey the idea, but less satisfactorily. Special rules regarding these gestures, attitudes, and the like are given in *Abhinayadarpaṇa* (pp.152-172).

2089 **नाटकाख्यायिका-दर्शनकला**

Nāṭakākhyāyikā-darśanakalā : attending dramas and variety shows. One of the 64 arts given in *Kāmasūtra.*

2090 **नाट्य**

Nāṭya : drama, stylized, dramatic presentation with music and dance as the later synonym *Saṁgītakam* indicates; theatre is also the mother of the other visual arts; as the *VD* (1.3.2.3) defines. It is to Bharata and his *NS* that we have to go for a full appreciation of this conception of *nāṭya.*

"*Nāṭya* is the representation of the three worlds. Brahman devised this *nāṭya* as the mimicry of the ways of the world, endowed with various emotions and consisting of various situations (*NS,* 1.107,112)". According to Bharata, "when the nature of the world, possessing pleasure and pain, both is depicted by means of representation through gesture and the like (*i.e.* speech, dress, make-up and temperament), it is called *nāṭya*" (*Ibid*). Thus, the *nāṭya* becomes the art of representation in which speech, music and appropriate gestures are harmoniously blended. The *nāṭya* is the art of *naṭa.* From *naṭa* the word *nāṭya* is derived in the sense of (a) the practice of the *naṭas*: *naṭasya dharmaḥ,* or (b) the sacred traditional works of the *naṭas*: *āmnāyo vā.*

Thus, *nāṭya* is the enacting of a sequence of such meanings which are linked as a sentence: *Vākyārthābhinaya* (D.R.I.C). *nāṭya* is the articulate expression of connected meaning communicating *rasa.*

2091 **नाट्यकार**

Nāṭyakāra : he created the different roles of different types, as directed (*NS*).

2092 **नाट्यधर्म**

Nāṭyadharma : dramatic rules (*DR.*1.122)

2093 **नाट्यधर्मी**

Nāṭyadharmī : the abstract, stylized theatrical convention or style of production where suggestive gesture replaces props or other aids. It is the conventional style of performance. The two types of dramatic styles are the *nāṭyadharmī* and the *lokadharmī. nāṭyadharmī* is the practice in which the speech, activity and states are extra-ordinary as they are imagined by the poet. It has graceful *aṅgahāras,* dramatic conventions, embellishments of notes, characters represented not naturally (*i.e.* males representing as females and *vice versa*), and the words represented as having corporal form (*e.g.* in the play *Māyāpuṣpaka,* the entry of the curse of the Brāhmaṇa). The words spoken by a near characters are not heard by others. The speech which is not uttered is heard. The mountains, vehicles and aerial cars, the shield, the armour, weapon or banner are represented boldly. Due to the skill or necessity, an actor performs two roles in the same play. A woman with whom marriage is prohibited by *śāstra* is employed in the role of a woman with whom marriage is allowed or *vice-versa.* Dancing or walking with graceful movements of limbs and with raised steps is employed. All these are the illustrations of theatrical practice. The divisions of the stage with various procedures to be followed are also theatrical practice. The conventional is two-fold-that which is wholly meant for beautifying the representations, *e.g.,* the use of the four *karaṇas* of the hand and that partially indicating popular behaviour as the use of *tripatāka* and to represent words spoken aside. The dramatic representation should always be produced with conventional practice without the use of gestures and music etc. There would be no enjoyment to the audience.

2094 **नाट्यवेद**

Nāṭyaveda : the fifth *Veda* created by Brahman for the benefit of all the *varṇas;* the *NS* (Vol.I pp. 15-16) describes the origin of *nāṭya* in the first chapter. God Brahman created the *nāṭyaveda* for the benefit of all the *varṇas* (*Sārvavarṇika*) as the śūdra could not be instructed in the *Veda.* The four constituents of this *Veda* were adopted from the four earlier *Vedas,* namely the recitation from the *Ṛgveda,* the song from the *Sāmaveda,* the *abhinaya* from the *Yajurveda* and the *rasas* from the *Atharvaveda.* The *Upvedas* also were connected with it.

The nature of *nāṭyaveda* was explained by Brahman as follows "the *nāṭyaveda* treats both the good and the evil, showing that the good is rewarded and the evil punished. It takes into account acts and ideas of the demons as well as of the gods, as there is no exclusive representation in it, of either of them" the *Abhinayadarpaṇa* (p.2) also records the traditional view of Brahman giving the *nāṭyaveda* to Bharata.

2095 **नाट्यशास्त्र**

Nāṭyaśāstra : theatrics. The *Nāṭyaśāstra* of Bharata deals with theatre in the most comprehensive manner. It was written somewhere from c.500 B.C. to c.300 A.D. The work is encyclopaedic in character, but written for the most part in the highly technical language of the performing arts of the long vanished age.

2096 **नाट्याचार्य**

Nāṭyācārya : the teacher of the dramatic art, who instructed the pupils in *nāṭya.* He enjoyed patronage of the kings, etc. The teacher was an expert in vocal and instrumental music and the movements following the rhythm. He was to know what is reasonable. He was intelligent, study-minded and he possessed good memory (*NS*).

2097 **नाट्यायित**

Nāṭyāyita : dramatized, one of the physical gesticulations. It is the indicative histrionic representation which is employed in a drama with different practice for the sake of enlivening time, lasting till the coming together of the characters on the stage. The histrionic representation of the *dhruvās* relating to the states and sentiments effected by means of delineating joy, anger, grief and the like is also to be known as *nāṭyāyita. Abhinava* (*NS,* III. 172-173) explains it in the first case as when there is a play within a play also. As regards the *dhruvās* he says that there is no gesticulation of each and every word but there is gesticulation of major and minor limbs and temperament indicating joy, etc.

2098 **नाडी**

Nāḍī : nerves of the human body. These are supposed to be 72,000 in number ; 72 are major nerves and the most important 14 are: *iḍā, pingalā, susumnā, gāndhārī, hastijihvā, yaśasvinī, alambuṣā, kuhū, śaṅkhinī, sarasvatī, vāruṇī, puṣā, vṛvodarā,* and *payasvinī* (*Prāṇatoṣaṇī,* 1.4.32-33). The purification of nerves (*nāḍīśuddhi*) when done by *mantras* is known as *samāna* and when by physical exercises like *dhautā* etc. it is known as *nirvāṇa* (*Gheraṇḍa,* V.36).

2099 **नाद**

Nāda : sound. (1) In *Tāntrism,* the supreme being (Parā Śiva or Parā Śakti) is soundless without any vibration. when this Parā Śakti begins to express itself in creation, its first vibration is known as *nāda.* It is the manifestation of the consciousness of the supreme being revealed as sound. This manifestation is thought of in terms of the union of Śiva and Śakti (the static and kinetic aspects). the thrill of the pleasure of this union (*maithuna*) is also known as *nāda.* The condensed form of *nāda* is *Vindu* (*Śāradā-tilaka,* 1.6.). (b) the various aspects of sound are said to be efficacious in sorcery. Thus, *nāda* is said to be good for controlling the victim (*Śiva* V. 26.44-46). (c) noise. Anything which interferes with the messages in the channel is called noise.A verbal message travelling in the form of sound waves, may have to compete with many other messages and sound. But noise need not be sound. Noise is anything which disrupts the message in the channel.

2100 **नाद-ब्रह्म**

Nāda-brahma : eternal articulated sound corresponding to art of music. *Nāda* conceived as *brahman* in the form of primordial sound expressed in *parā, paśyantī madhyamā* and *vaikharī* (*Kāmakalāvilāsa,* IX).

2101 **नानादेश-वेष-भाषा-विचार**

Nānā-deśa-veṣa-bhāṣā-vicāra : *NS* (1.8) opines that while analysing the *loka-pravṛtti* one should have in mind different countries, their distinctive dresses, speech-patterns and manners. Four basic regions and style (*pravṛtti*) based on them have been recognized.

Two questions are explicitly raised : *yathā pṛthivyām nānādeśāḥ santi katham asmin caturvidhatvam upapannam samānalakṣaṇāśca pravṛttayaḥ* (*NS,* XIII, prose after world); how then can there be four fold division of the *vṛttis*? Besides, the employment of the *vṛttis* has common features, so why divide them into four? The point is that different countries of the world are distinguished by different modes of life. They differ in their dress, artefacts, language, conduct, secular and religious, or common and learned, mode of livelihood etc., and this distinctive way of life is called *vṛtti.* When it is known to others, it is called *pravṛtti: pṛthivyām nānā-deśah-veṣa-bhāṣā-ārcravārtaḥ khyāpayantīti vṛttiḥ pravṛttiśca nivedane* (*NS Ibid*). *Abhinavabhāratī* (*NS,* II, p. 205) Commenting on this writes: *deśe deśe yeṣveva veṣādayo naipatham bhāṣā vā ācāro loka śātravyavahāraḥ vārtā kṛṣi-pāśupālyādijīvikā ceti tān prakhyāpaynti pṛthivyādi-sarvaloka vidyā prasiddhim karoti pravṛttir bāhyārthe yasmān nivedane niśśeṣeṇa vedane jñāne prayṛttiśabdaḥ.*

On what basis are these life styles to be classified into four? In particular, since the *vṛthis* have common features and help in aesthetic generalization through revealing universal psyche factors of love, anger, infatutation etc. and thus supersede the reference to particularities of place etc; why bring in such coordinates now: *tathā ca lobha-krodha-mohaistu sādhāraṇī kṛta-jagaccintā dyāsu pradeśaḥ parakrīyate tathā prakṛtepi* ? (*AB*, Vol. II, 206).

The answer given is that the difference of regions are generally admitted and may be connected with broad psychic attitudes. Thus the four *vṛttis* may serve to represent regional styles. The southerners are, thus, particularly fond of song and dance and of clever, delicate and graceful gestures of limbs. They have an abundance of romance. Such a style is called *kaiśiki: tatra dākṣiṇātyāstāvad bahunṛtta-gita-vādyāḥ kaiśikīprāyāḥ catura-madhura-lalitā ṅgābhinayaśca* (*NS*, II. p.207). The eastern is *Oḍra-māgadhī* and is admixture of *bhāratī* and *ārabhaṭī*. It is marked by a bombastic use of words: *prācyām et.*

2102 **नानास्थान-नखप्रदान-रसिका**

Nānāsthāna-nakhapradāna-rasikā : lady who likes giving the nail-prints on various places, quality of the conch-lady (*Pañcasāyaka*, 1.8).

2103 **नान्दी**

Nāndī : the *svastika* mark (*A*, 2.19.16) benediction, prelude of a play.

2104 **नाभि**

Nābhi : navel. *Nābhi-sūtra* in iconography passes through the navel. It is in between the *Kakṣa-sūtras* (passing through the breast-nipples) when vertically reckoned.

2105 **नाभिवर्धन**

Nābhivardhana : cutting of the umbilical cord.

2106 **नाभ्यावर्तलक्षण**

Nābhyāvarta lakṣaṇa : sign of the navel pit. If spacious, indicative of pleasure; if deep, it indicates affliction; if spread in one side, it indicates long life; if low (turned downwards), it indicates wealth in cattle; if like the circle of lotus, it indicates royalty; if circular like the earth, it indicates lordship of wealth; if it is deep, it is good (*Garuḍa*, 26. 3-7).

Deep navel such as *nimnanābhi* and *trivalī* is appreciated in Sanskrit literature. If turning leftwards, or showing a knot, it is not good (*Sk.P.* IV. 37.44). Men become happy with a navel that is round, raised and broad; afflicted with trouble with one that is small, almost invisible and deep; poor and suffering from colic with one that is uneven and surrounded by folds of skin; rogues with one that is turned from right to left; intelligent with one that circles from left to right; long-lived with one that is elongated at the sides; lords with one that is elongated at the top; owners of cattle with one that is elongated at the lower end; and kings with one like the knob in the centre of a lotus (*Bṛhat-Saṁitā*, LXVIII). cf the unnamed authority:

वर्तुला विपुलात्युच्चा नाभिर्यदि नरेश्वरः ।
अल्पदृश्याः तथा निम्न नाभिः क्लेशावहा भवेत् ॥

2107 **नामकरण**

Nāmakaraṇa : the ceremony of naming a child (*Āp.Gr.*XV. 8-11; *Gobhila Gr.*II. 8.8-18). From the various instructions regarding the naming of a child, it appears that the names for the boy indicate freedom, while those of a girl indicate dependence. We know how the name of a boy is prescribed to have the prefix *su*; but what may appear rather curious is that the name of a girl with the ending *rakṣitā* or *dattā*, with a name of a deity as the first part was not favoured (*Vār. Gr. Su.*3; *Jain.Gr.Su.*1.19). There seems to be a double motif in naming. The first is that the name symbolizes the very person; and the name that is bad may render the person bad; or, the other way round. The belief that the name is the very presence of the person obtains widely.

The names of the aboriginals may fall into several categories. These are: (a) gods and goddesses, (b) harvest and crops, (c) colours and complexion, (d) place of birth, (e) days of the week, (f) months, (g) jewels, (h) plants, (i) animals (j) rivers, (k) stature, (l) nature etc. In the places where there are youth dormitories, we find two types of name of a person. One is the real name and other is the given name at *ghotul.* When the bachelors (boys and girls) are married, the *ghotul* names are entirely given up and it is a great insult to a married woman to call her by *ghotul* name. A married woman among the aborigines is not given a fresh name when she goes to her husband. Wives will not name their elders nor their husbands.

There is a widespread popular belief in India that given names can influence the development of self-image and personality. At the simplest level, it expresses itself in occasional parental concern about nicknames; or in felt need to change a name. As little is known scientifically about name effects in most societies; but the impact of naming on the tribal people has been studied and revealing. Some tribes give their children a "soul name" according to the day of the week they are born on. Their behaviour reflects their name-affected self-image. Astrological birth signs also have the same explanations.

2108 **नामग्राहम्**

Nāmagrāham : mentioning by name as Bhaṭṭi records: *"nāmagrāhamarodīt, sābharatarau rāvaṇāntike"*. Thus it means addressing by taking the name. One is to accost one's equals by the name with which they are styled to (*NS,* XVII. 65-94). A superior person, however, be addressed by name by inferior persons when the latter are privileged to do so. Men and women in their employment and artisans and artists are to be addressed as such (*i.e.* according to their status). The teacher as well as the father may take the names of their disciples or sons.

As a general rule it is said that a married woman should not utter the name of her husband *i.e.* she should not call him by his name, if she desires him to have a long life (*Skanda Purāṇa,* III. 2.7.18): *bharturnāma nagṛhṇāti.*

Addressing is a class sign. One of the functions of its service is the system of concepts by means of which the members of a given community provide themselves with a representation of their social relations and in this way it sanctions and imposes what it states, tactily laying down the dividing line between thinkable and unthinkable, thereby contributing towards the maintenance of the symbolic code from which it draws its authority. This was precisely how verbal deference functioned in ancient India (even in modern days), upholding semifeudal relationships between old and young, male and female, high caste, and low caste. These words were a way of entering into relations with persons. It was therefore essential that in a society which enjoined formal respect for senior kin on the part of their juniors there should be some rules of speech strictly to govern such behaviour. The latter are forbidden from mentioning any of the elders by their proper names in many communities, may be tribal or non-tribal.

2109 **नाममुद्रा**

Nāmamudra : seal-ring.

2110 **नामरूप**

Nāma-rūpa : name and aspect, words and images, the means of conventional discrimination, that by which the phenomenal universe is known. It is the fourth point in the chain of Buddhist doctrine of causation.

2111 **नामलिङ्गानुशासन**

Nāmaliṅgānuśāsana : rules regarding the gender of nouns.

2112 **नायक**

Nāyaka : the hero. A dramatist achieves much reputation by selecting a proper hero, who would lead or dominate (*nāyaka*) the other roles in a play. The heroes are classed, according to their nature as *dhīrodatta, dhīroddhāta, dhīraśānta* and *dhīralalita* (*SD,* III. 31-34). As regards *Śṛṅgāranāyakas* (erotic heroes) they are of four kinds: *anukūla, dakṣiṇa, dhṛṣṭa* and *śaṭha* (*Ibid.* 35). Thus, *nāyaka* was the hero of the dramatic representation, expert in dramatic art.

2113 **नायिका**

Nāyikā : heroine, woman. warious types of women are described in *NS* under the *abhinaya* as they are indeed the source of happiness. The types possess the nature of gods, demons, *gandharvas,* etc. and also birds, goblins, tigers, monkeys and such animals. After knowing a woman's nature one should approach her accordingly. According to dramatic convention, the enjoyment of love is two-fold: *ābhyantara* (relating to kings in *nāṭaka*) and *bāhyā* (relating to courtesans in *prakaraṇa*). the women are of three classes: *bāhya* (courtesan), *ābhyantarā* (noble, high-born) and *Tāhyābhyantarā* (purified courtesan). The king should be united with *ābhyantarā* and divine courtesan, others with courtesans. The signs of courtesan's love are casting sidelong glances, touching ornaments, itching the ears, scratching the ground with toes, showing the breast and the navel, cleansing the nails and binding the hair. Those of a high born lady are smiling eyes, steady gaze, concealed smile, and speaking slowly with downcast eyes, replying with a smile , concealing her sweat, lower lip throbbing and nervousness.

Various stages of love to be represented are longing, anxiety, recollection, enumeration of the lovers merits, distress, lamentation, madness, sickness, stupor and death.

Eight kinds of heroines are described according to *Kāmaśāstra: Vāsakasajjā, Virahotkaṇṭhitā, Svādhīnabhartṛkā, Kalahantāritā, Khaṇḍitā, Vipralabdhā, Proṣitabhartṛkā, Abhisārikā.*

The eight types of heroines are to be represented thus: *khaṇḍitā, vipralabdhā, proṣitabhartṛkā and kalahāntaritā* should gesticulate anxiety, sighs, dejection, burning of the heart, conversation with female friends, looking to one's own condition, weakness, depression, tears, appearance of anger, giving up ornaments, and toilet, sorrow and weeping. *Svādhīnapatikā* should have gaudy and brillant dress, face beaming with joy and excess of physical charm.

2114 **नारद**

Nārada : a *davarśi* or saint of the celestial class who often comes down to report what is going on in heaven and return with his account of what is being done on earth (*AV,* V. 19. 9). (b) Brahmā cursed Nārada to be young for ever, to make love in deserted forests, and to beget children in a śūdra woman. Nārada then cursed Brahmā to be without worship and to desire a woman who should not be desired. Because of this, Brahmā lusted for his own daughter and was ashamed (*Nāradapañcarātra* 10, 24-32). In this case, the cycle is completed: The final curse produces the primeval incest from which the central episode originally arose. The curse is both a way of moving from one face to another and a reinforcement of the natural development of myth: excessive desire for *tapas* ultimately results in excess lust. The character of a wanderer is particularly appropriate to Nārada, a notorious meddler and gossip, who frequently acts as a mediating agent in myths, catalysing the transition from one place to the next by inspiring anger, jealousy, or lust in characters formerly involved in the myth or temporarily inactive. The seven sages tell Pārvatī the story of Nārada: who even listened to Nārada's instructions and had a home to live in ? (*Śiva*, 2.3.25).

2115 **नाराच-मुद्रा**

Nārāca-mudrā : arrow-gesture. "If this is made by the curved right hand in standing position, it is called the *nārāca-mudrā*. It may also be *dūtī-mudrā* or *bhūti-mudrā*, that promises fertility" (*BT*).

2116 **नारी**

Nārī : woman. woman is Kali-age are described as being fond of jewels and ornaments; but if the ornaments are not available, they would entice men with their hair; for it is the hair that are source of their pride and beauty (*Brahma* P.229.16): स्त्रीणां रूपमदश्चैव केशैरेव भविष्यति

They would leave their husbands when the latter becomes poor (*Ibid.*17-21). Another marked characteristics of persons, including women, in the Kali-age is said to be that they would be covetous, short in stature, given to eating more,delivering many children, but less fortunate (*Ibid.*28). It is further said that girls would get conceived and produce children before they reach the age of sixteen (*Ibid.*23.10).

It would be wrong to think that Indian women in Kali-age has lost a sense of self-respect as the Purāṇakāra presents. On the contrary, her sense of indentity with the family and her role as a wife and mother gives her dignity and pride. Though they may be frustrated their ultimate role is to preserve unity and continuity in the society. Change from the joint to the nuclear system has not had any fundamental effect on this situation. "Hindu woman is given the opportunity to realise rather than to express herself. She is given the opportunity to be a woman...we do not identify freedom with self-assertion. ...The oriental woman is what she is , only because our social and religious culture has permitted her to be and remain essentially feminine, (Coomaraswamy, *The Dance of Śiva*, London.1924).

2117 **नालिक**

Nālika : (i) a measure of time and space. It was employed both for measuring space and time. According to Kauṭilya, 4 *arantis* made a *daṇḍa* or 1 *nālika* or 1 *apuruṣa* was equal to 96 *aṅgulas* or 6 feet. For measuring time, he noted 40 *kalās* were equal to 1 *nālika* or the times during which 1 *āḍhaka* or water passed out of a pot through an aperture of the same diameter as that of a wire of 4 *aṅgulas* in length and made of 4 *māṣas* of gold. According to him 2 *nālikas* made 1 *muhūrta* and 15 *muhūrtas* 1 day. One *nālika* has been taken to be equal to 24 minutes or quarter of an hour. (*Arthaśāstra*, pp. 117-119). This measures seems to have been current in Kashmir also during the reign of King Jayāpīḍa (762-63 A.D.). In *Rājataraṅgiṇī* (IV.571) it is stated how one of his ministers ,made a request to be permitted to stay outside for 2 *nālikas*. (ii) an enigmatical remark.

2118 **नालिका**

Nālikā : an enigmatical remark that gives rise to laughter. (*NS*,XVIII.118). It is one of the thirteen constituents of *vīthī* in which sportive answers are given to become the other.

2119 **नासा**

Nāsā : nose-gesture. Nose-gesture may be classified on the basis of different *rasas: Socchvāsā nāsā* (*Śṛṅgāra*), *Vikṛṣṭā nāsā* or *mandā nāsā* (bhayānaka), *Vikūṇitā nāsā* (*hāsya*), *Natā nāsā* (*karuṇa*), *Svābhāvikā nāsā* (*adbhuta*), *Vikṛṣṭā nāsā* (*raudra*), *Svābhāvikānāsā* (*vīra*) and *Vikūṇitā nāsā* (*bībhatsa*), Alike the eye and its relevant parts, the gesture of the nose also suggests some mental states. They are *natā* (drooping), *mandā* (dull), *vikṛtā* (deformed), *socchvāsā* (breathing heavily), *vikūṇitā* (contracted) and *svābhāvikā* (natural), *VD* (III.1.25/66-74) devised six by number: *natā, mandā, vikṛṣṭā, socchvāsā, vikūṇitā* and *svābhāvikā*. *NS* reads *vighūrṇitā* for *vikūṇitā*.

The nose-touch is an action associated with momentary stress. At times when a man's inner thoughts do not reflect his outward claim, he may leak the fact by touching, rubbing or squeezing his nose. The reason for this is still not clear.

2120 **नासापुट**

Nāsāpuṭa :'nostril' *suśr. nāsāpuṭa* is an agent of NV communication. In *Mālatī Mādhavam* (Act VI) Kapālakuṇḍala worships the deity entering the cemetery smelling the odour: This would be done by the *vikṛṣṭā* movement of the *nāsāpuṭa* (*NS*, VIII. 134).

2121 **नासाकृतिविज्ञान**

Nāsākṛti-vijñāna : signs on the nose. If it is like that of a parrot, the person is happy; if he has a dry nose he has an excess of life; if his nose is cut in the front, or if it resembles the opening of a well, he is given to sex in forbidden degrees; if he has a long nose, he is a fortunate; if the nose is short, he is a thief; if flat he is unfortunate and would meet death. If the nostrils are narrow, straight and well formed, it indicates royalty; if crooked to the right, the person is cruel; if one sneezes only once (at a time), he is full of vigour (*Garuḍa*, 65.59). According to *Bhaviṣya Purāṇa* a dry nose indicates long life; and a parrot nose indicates the person to be of auspicious speech. Fortune and piousness are indicated by straight nose; short nose indicates love for duty; a snub nose and a crooked one indicates sinful act; a nose like that of a horse, lion or elephant indicates success in trade (*Brahma*, 26.65-67; *Bṛhat Saṁhitā* 67.61). "With a nose resembling the parrot's beak, happy; long-lived with a dry nose; one comes to have sexual relations with forbidden women with nose that appears cut; becomes attractive or fortunate with a long one; a thief with a curved one; cruel and gluttonous with one turned to the right; and highly fortunate with a straight one with small nostrils and fine slopes;

शुकनासः सौख्यभागी शुष्कनासाश्चिरायुषः ।
छिन्नानुरूपा येषां स्यान्नासा ते ऽभ्यगामिनः ॥
दीर्घनासा भोगयुक्ता अग्रवक्रा धनान्विताः ।
क्रूरा दक्षिणवक्राश्च स्पष्टनासा नृपोत्तमाः ॥

2122 **नासावक्त्रविकूणन**

Nāsāvaktravikūṇana : contraction of the nose and mouth.

2123 **नासिका**

Nāsikā : (a) nose. (b) in temple architecture, the projected arched opening of Southern *Vimāna. alpanāsikā* or *kṣudranāsikā* is small, while *mahānāsikā* is large.

2124 **नासिक्य**

Nāsikya : nasal sounds.

2125 **नास्तिक**

Nāstika : unbeliever. (a) Manu (II.11) defines *nāstika* as a person who challenges the authority of *Vedas*. (b) according to Kumārila *nāstika* is one who does not believe in the soul. The Kāśikā on Pāṇini (IV. 4.60) holds that it means one who does not believe in the next world.

2126 **निःशब्द-चुम्बनम्**

Niḥśabda-cumbanam : kiss without sound. This division of kiss has been proposed by Padmaśrī. Kiss without sound has also been dealt by Vātsyāyana. It is divided into seven classes: *nipīḍitam, bhrāmitam, unnamitakam, sphuritam, saṁhatoṣṭham, vaikṛtam* and *nataganḍam* (*Nāgarasarvasva*, 25. 1-4).

2127 **निःश्रेयस**

Niḥśreyasa : liberation. Freedom from the bonds of birth and death and the complete cessation of all sufferings (philosophy)

2128 **निःसृत-जङ्घा**

Niḥsṛta jaṅghā : the leg is extended forward high, a type of the position of thigh.

2129 **निकुञ्चित करण**

Nikuñcita karaṇa : one leg in *vṛścika*, one hand across the chest, the other touches tip of the nose, one hand in *arāla* (*NS*, IV. 86-87). Moving the foot in *vṛścika karaṇa*, the left hand is bent at the side and the right is held at the tip of the nose. It is used in moving in the sky, guess and in deep meditation. (Fig. 2129)

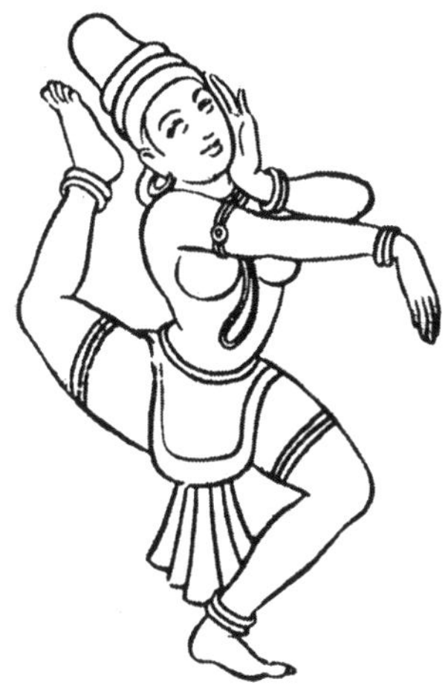

Fig. – (2129)

2130 **निकुञ्चित-मणिबन्ध**

Nikuñcita maṇibandha : an outward bend at the wrist.

2131 **निकुट्टक-करण**

Nikuṭṭaka karaṇa : this *karaṇa* can also be classified under the *pāda-karaṇa*. Arms bent with hands near the shoulders, feet in *udghaṭṭita* (*NS*, IV. 69). Each hand is moved near its respective shoulder, having *alapallava* gesture accompanied by the movement of the respective leg with *udghaṭṭita* foot. It is used in self-adulation.

2132 **निकुब्जपाणि**

Nikubjapāṇi : palm of the hand contracted to receive water.

2133 **निगद**

Nigada : sound, prose *mantras* of *Yajurveda*. (b) explained by mere saying. (c) speech.

2134 **निगम**

Nigama : pure *Vedic* tradition, *Veda, Vedic* texts, any word quoted from *Veda*, any auxiliary to *Veda*, precept, place of traders, way, town.

2135 **निगमन**

Nigamana : a conclusion drawn from valid premises; final conclusion.

2136 **निग्रह**

Nigraha : holding forcibly sentiments and feelings (*NS*, IX. 175).

2137 **निग्रहस्थान**

Nigrahasthāna : a flaw in an argument, a fault in a syllogism by which a disputant is defeated in an argument (philosophy), shift from one's own stand, confessional retort, irrelevant reasoning, irrelevant statement, defiance of the temporal order, causal fallacy etc. are called *nigrahasthāna* (*Caraka Saṁhitā,* 8.65). Sustaining defeat in philosophical disputation. It is one of the sixteen topics of *nyāya.*

2138 **निघात**

Nighāta : *anudātta,* low tone = negation of *udātta.*

2139 **नितम्ब**

Nitamba : buttocks, hips.

2140 **नितम्ब-करण**

Nitamba-karaṇa : derived from the *bhadrā cārī:Svastika* position of the feet. The arms are lifted high in the initial position and then fingers and the palms move in *vyāvartita karaṇas* of the hands: palms face the chest gradually and are finally in *patāka.* This is the complete movement of the *nitamba* hands (*NS,* IV. 145 b-146 a, IX. 217,X.21). Arms are thrown up and then have fingers of hands facing each other; *baddhācārī* is to be performed. (Fig. 2140)

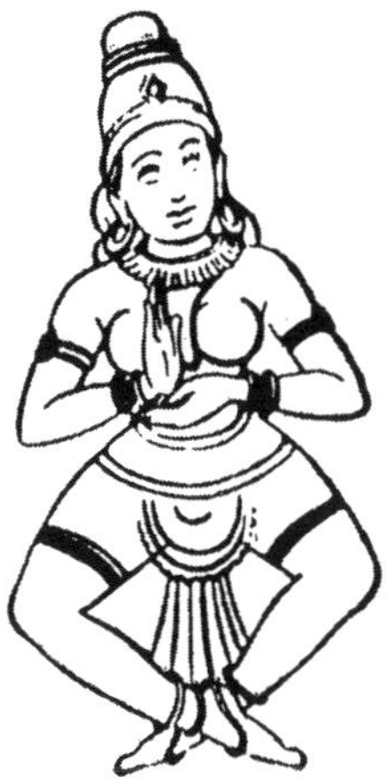

Fig. – (2140)

2141 **नितम्ब-नृत्तहस्त**

Nitamba-nṛtta-hasta : the buttock or the hip. A type of hand gesture in dancing given in *NS.* If two *patāka*-hands are taken from the shoulders to the hips, it is the *nitamba* (*NS,* IX. 176-196).

2142 **नितम्बाकृतिविज्ञान**

Nitambākṛti-vijñāna : sign of the buttocks, bony, poverty; fleshy , happiness; lion-like, royalty (*Garuḍa,* I. 65.19). normally it is prescribed to be soft, fleshy and devoid of wrinkles; but it is also desired to be rounded like the fruit of wood-apple. It is also desired to be endowed with tender soft hair(*Bhav.P.Brāhma,* 5.30).

2143 **नितम्बिनी**

Nitambinī : having large and rounded hips.

2144 **नित्यकर्मन्**

Nityakarman : to be observed daily: (i) *Sandhyā* (morning and evening prayer), (ii) *tarpaṇa,* (iii) *balivaiśvadeva,* (iv) *atithisevā,* (v) *vedapāṭha,* (vi) *homa.*

2145 **निदर्शक**

Nidarśaka : illustrator. One particularly well defined type of body-behaviour. It acts to modify and augment spoken messages. For instance, if you are asked to describe how to get your dormitory,you are likely to point in the appropriate direction. Similarly, if you were asked to describe how big a new radio is,you would probably illustrate its size by indicating its dimension in the air.

Compare *nidarśanā,* a figure of speech in which the connection of things implies a relation of type (*bimba*) and prototype (*pratibimba*) and that connection may either be possible or impossible.

Ekman and Friesen (1966) keeps the illustrator in the second category of NV behaviour. It is very much part of the speech and serves the function of emphasis. Examples are head and hand movements that occur more frequently with primary stressed words, pointing gesture , or other movements that redundantly draw a picture of the linguistic referent. Included in this category are those movements that seem to serve as added punctuation or emphases, such as pointing with hand or with a turn of the head, or tracing the contour of an object or person referred to verbally. (Fig. 2145)

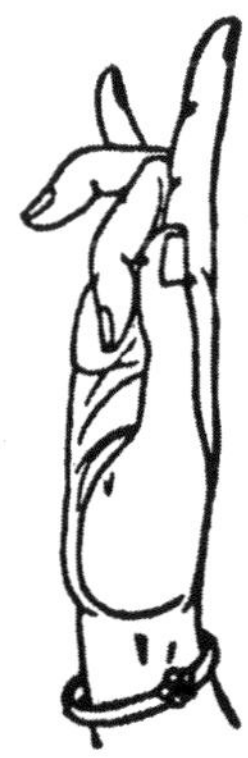

Fig. – (2145)

2146 **निदिध्यासन**

Nididhyāsana : constant meditation, with a concentrated mind (*Darśana*).

2147 **निद्रा**

Nidrā : state of drowsiness,sleeping. One of the thirty-three *vyabhicārī bhāvas.* It is occasioned by fatigue, exhaustion, intoxication etc. Yawning, closing of the eyes, breathing out, stretching and relaxing of limbs, etc. are its external manifestations (*Sāhityadarpaṇa,* III.157). It represents heaviness of the face, rolling of the body, rolling of the eyes, massaging of the body, deep breathing, relaxed body, etc. (b) sleep is a condition of the organism characterized by markedly reduced consciousness, inactivity, depressed metabolic processes, and relative insensitiveness to stimulation.

2148 **निद्रित हस्त**

Nidrita-hasta : sleeping hands. A type of hand gesture in iconography, not mentioned in *NS.*

2149 **निधन**

Nidhana : the process of the termination of the copulation (*Chāndogyopaniṣad,* 2.12.1-2). It is symbolic death of sexual desire. (b) the finale of *Sāman;* the earlier stages are *udgītha, pratihāra* and *upadrava.* (c) poor.Śūdraka has depicted the state of being poor in his *Mṛcchakaṭikam* (1. 9,13,35) as follows:

Swans and cranes would snatch up the daily offerings
From this threshold the minute they were offered;
Now at this threshold, sunken under weeds,
The gnawing worms leave offerings of his seed.
I am not saddened by the lose of riches,
For riches flow in and out with turns of luck.
This is what hurts : the golden prop removed,
Friendship grow suddenly feeble, start to totter.

When he has nothing, his words are nothing, even to family
Friends turn away, miseries bristle, then loom larger;
Substance melts off, the glow of reputation fades,
Even the rotter acts of others stick to him.
(Vātsyāyana and Mishra,155).

2150 **निधुवन**

Nidhuvana : coitus. *nidhuvana-līlā* (sport in coitus). see Kālidāsa (*Kumāra*).

2151 **निन्दा**

Nindā : (*Nirukta,* VII.3, *Bṛhaddevatā* 144-60, *Arthaśāstra* 11.10): blame; form of speech and thought, *garhaṇa* according to *NS* (18.26). The *nindā* form of speech could only effect its object in the society where great stress was laid on family relationships and where the rules of those relationships are strictly observed. It is just a man never does intrique with a forbidden relation that the accusation becomes effective and amusing. If a *Vedic* thought it was really true, he would not say so; for he was a decent fellow, and even in his hottest moments did not to cause trouble. The most significant thing about this speech is in its omissions. There were no religious oaths, for they would be too dangerous. There was no suggestion of unnatural offences--for they were practically unknown. There are no references to prostitution for there were no *Vedic* whores.

2152 **निबन्ध**

Nibandha : essay. Digests of conduct written by Hemādri, Raghunandana and others as supplements to the *Dharmaśāstra.* They were devoted to the regulation and conservation of social order. Glosses of important legal texts, comprehensive digests, manuals on special topics of law and various other works also pass under the name *nibhandha.*

2153 **निभृतक**

Nibhṛtaka : privacy. When a lover creates confidence, then he should say to her,"I have something to tell you in private (*Kāmasūtra,* 3.4.21) Amaruka describes an experience of a heroine who tells her friend thus: "I have a word for thee, he said and drew me to a lonely place, and as my heart was filled with eager longing, I sat close to him and was attentive. Then whispering something in my ear and smelling my mouth, he caught hold the braid of my hair and sipped the nectar from my lips."The Yakṣa of Kālidāsa was always is search of privacy (*Megha,* 105).

Thus privacy is a state in which one has control over other people's access to one's person or information about one's person. Most people have two potentially opposing needs: one is to be available to others for social contact; the other is to have privacy. Some people need more privacy, others more social contact.If we think about the environment, the possibility of closing or opening doors and curtains is a device for signalling privacy. Vātsyāyana has drawn attention to the prevalence of back (private) regions and front (public) regions both in domestic settings and in public settings. Back regions or *antaḥpura* are regions in which only intimates may penetrate without invitation. Front regions or *catuśśāla* or open to public. In fact the environment can be considered entirely from a territorial point of view,where the major distinction is between public and personal spaces. The widespread relationship between power and rank on the one hand, and the size of both the buffer zones and territory which the individual is permitted on the other. The more important the person, the less others are permitted to approach him closely, speak of him within earshot, and the greater the size and number of areas which he is permitted to control. Probably one of the most trying features of poverty is the lack of privacy that is typical of the living conditions of the poor.

Privacy is described as an "interpersonal boundary control process" where the person is made more or less accessible to others at various times, given the circumstances of the social situation. An individual's privacy may be considered in terms of the privacy desired versus the actual degree of privacy achieved. Crowding or intrusion occurs when desired privacy is discrepant from achieved privacy; where the reverse is true, a state of isolation is considered to exit. In particular, various NV behaviours are employed to regulate privacy including distancing, variation in the angle of orientation, and use of objects or areas for territorial defence.

2154 **निमन्त्रण**

Nimantraṇa : invitation. *nimantraṇa (Mahābhāṣya*, III.1.161) was an invitation to take food at sacrifices or a sraddha, the acceptance of which was obligatory. If rejected without a proper cause, it involved a sin while the *āmantraṇa* was a friendly invitation and could be rejected freely.

2155 **निमितकं-चुम्बनम्**

Nimitakam cumbanam : nominal kiss. "When a lady under compulsion touches only the mouth of her lover with her own, but does not herself do anything, it is called the nominal kiss: *balātkāreṇa niyuktamukhe mukhamādatte, natu viceṣtata iti nimittikam* (*Kāmasūtra*, 2.3.1).

Vātsyāyana adds that this kiss should be given to young girl. The lover in Māgha (*Śiśu.* 7.44) forcibly raises the mouth of a young girl and kiss her in this style: *Mukhakamalamunnamayya yūnā yadabhinava ūḍhavadhūrbalādacumbi.*

The writer of the *Śṛṅgāratilaka-Bhāṇa* (5.90) caught the hair of the maiden, raised her chin to kiss her lips. She offered him saying 'no no'.

Oṣṭham cumbitumunnamayya cibukam
keśe gṛhīte mayā
mā meti bhramitābhru vakrakamalam
pātum ca dadyātsvayam

In this nominal kiss the M is active while the F is passive.

2156 **निमित्त**

Nimitta : auspicious signs, omens. Auspicious signs for men appear on the right side of his body, whereas the reverse is true in the case of women, (*A*, 1.9.9). (b) happenings. According to *Amarakośa, nimittam hetulakṣaṇaḥ,* means 'cause or prognostic sign'. (*Manu* VI.50; *Mbh.* VI.2.16-17; *Rāmāyaṇa* II.4.17.19, *Gītā* 1.31; *Matsya* CCXLI). (c) target, motive, cause.

2157 **निमित्त कारण**

Nimitta-kāraṇa : efficient cause. For example in making a table, the carpenter is a *nimitta kāraṇa;* as the potter is who makes the jar.

2158 **निमित्त-ज्ञानम्**

Nimitta-jñānam : knowledge of omens, one of the 64 arts mentioned in *Kāmasūtra* (1.3.16). Indication of auspicious and inauspicious events. *nimittajñānam* was a form of protective response. While Indians were busy improving the technology of realistic, down-to-earth body protection, they were also perpetually occupied with the business of inventing curious magical acts of self defence. These were superstitions which appear in every epoch and every culture. They were so numerous and so varied that were studied as one of the arts. They are almost all totally meaningless and futile, except in one basic respect; namely, that they make the performers of the actions feel a little less insecure in a hostile and mysterious world. They all consist of some activity which, if performed, is supposed to prevent bad luck in the future. The fact that there is never any logical connection between the act and the outcome does nothing to deter the superstitions. They continue to protect themselves by continuously performing the acts, 'just in case'. It is easy to start them off. If you tell people that by throwing a coin in to Narmadā river will have good luck, they will make a silent wish come true, they will be happy to do this. Even if it does not work, it provides an attractive shared procedure which enhances the structure of a social occasion.

2159 **निमीलित दृष्टि**

Nimīlita dṛṣṭi : half-closed eyes.

2160 **निमेष**

Nimeṣa : shutting the eye, wink; *nimeṣatas* 'with regard to the closing of the eye (*VS*). The time required to pronounce a short syllable; a moment. The wink is symbolic according to Varāhamihira (LXVIII):

द्विमात्रस्पन्दिनो ये तु धनिनस्ते प्रकीर्तिताः ।
त्रिमात्रस्पन्दिनो ज्ञेयाः पुरुषाः सुखजीविनः ॥
चतुर्मात्रनिमेषश्च धनवान् परिकीर्तितः ।
दीर्घायुषो धर्मरताः पञ्चमात्रनिमेषिणः ॥

2161 **निमेष-पुट**

Nimeṣa-puṭa : closing of the eyelids; winking, downward accent, a type of eye-lid gesture, closing eye lids in fear, anger etc. (*NS*, VIII. 106-113).

2162 **निम्नसम्मुन्नतमूर्धा**

Nimna sammunnata mūrdhā : lady whose head is uneven, quality of the Mare-lady (*Ratirahasya*, 3.22-26).

2163 **निम्न-सुवर्तल-नाभि**

Nimnasuvartalanābhi : lady whose navel is deep and round, quality of the Mare-lady (*Ratirahasya,* 3.22.-23).

2164 **नियम**

Niyama : fixed law, cultivation of good habits. It is second discipline of *yoga.* It consists of *śauca, santoṣa, tapas* and *īśvarapraṇidhāna.*

2165 **नियोग**

Niyoga (*Bṛhaddevatā* 144-160) : (a) form of speech and thought. (b) assignation. This was remarriage by assignation, and was probably a survival of the ancient custom of compulsory marriage with childless brother's widow (levirate), but by the sixth century it was already becoming a thing of the past (Renou, p. 98).

2166 **निरीक्षण-हस्त**

Nirīkṣaṇa hasta : single hand gesture derived from the *bāṇa.* Only mentioned in *Bālarāmabharata.*

2167 **निरुक्त-मुद्रा**

Nirukta-mudrā : gesture symbolizing the *Nirukta,* a part of *Vedāṅga.* If the thumb goes to the middle of the forefinger, it is *Nirukta* (*VD*).

2168 **निर्ऋति-हस्त**

Nirṛti hasta : *Khaṭvā* with the right and *śakaṭa* with the left-hand, indicate *nirṛti,* one of the *Dikpālas* (*AD,* 211-215). The concept of *nirṛti* as the personification of evil, sin, misfortune, misery, decay, death and destruction is as old as the *Ṛgveda* (10.165.1). *Nirṛti* means decay, bad luck, destruction, death, dissolution.

2169 **निरोध**

Nirodha : check, suppression; contraceptive. Of the greatest importance to India's future will be the effects of the worldwide sexual revolution of modern times. Especially in India, the consequences of contraceptive facilities are, sooner or later, bound to have a chain reaction of profound significance, not only on the rate of population increase, but also on the pattern of social life between the sexes. Hitherto the latter has been circumscribed by taboos on pollution and sexual contact between castes, and concerning the status of woman. Decline in the appeal and effectiveness of religious curbs on mixed socialization under modern conditions, the pattern of co-education, and the use of reliable contraception, are already weakening the purist's case for retaining the strict rules which have been so much a feature of life in India during recent centuries.Nuclear family life leads to an equalization of the martial relationship and this is already visible among the Indian professional classes. More important still,the pattern of liberalization in sexual mores with which the west is now familiar, has already reached India,and with freer association between young men and women a new kind of emotional reciprocity is bound to develop. The negative effects of liberalization---coarseness, molestation, vulgarity in manners---are not likely to be permanent, even if they continue for many decades to be obtrusive. Today emotional reciprocity has appreciably changed the social atmosphere among the middle classes,though without actually dissolving their Indian cultural identity.

2170 **निर्णय**

Nirṇaya : decision. ascertainment of truth about something by means of any of the recognised methods or sources of knowledge.It is one of the sixteen philosophical topics of the *nyāya.* (b) demonstration of truth after stating reasons both for and against a certain thing (*DR*.1.101).

2171 **निर्धारण**

Nirdhāraṇa : ascertaining ;regulating,selection of one from a group by means of genus, quality, action or name (used in grammar). (b) the fourth category proposed by Ekman and Friesen (1966) of NV behaviour. It refers to acts that help to initiate and terminate the speech of participants in a social situation. These regulators might suggest to a speaker that he keeps talking, that he clarify, or that he hurry up and finish.

2172 **निर्भुग्न मुख**

Nirbhugna mukha : lowered face,lowering of face, lowering face long drawn, a type of mouth-gesture (*NS,* VIII.153-160); crooked too much. It is applied to look into depth of a thing, or a subject.

2173 **निर्भुग्न वक्ष**

Nirbhugna vakṣa : also known as *nirbhugnoru:* straight and erect torso; indicates a spinal stretch, erect, back depression, is the opposite position where the character of the torso completely changes by the erectness and tautness of the back. Here tension rather than relaxation is emphasized: the difference between the softer Mathurā figures and later Colā bronzes is this: the depression of the back so characteristic of the South Indian bronzes is result of the *nirbhugna* position of the *uras.* The *nirbhugna* style of the chest in a stand-still position with bent back and raised shoulder should be made. This is to look at something with wonder, to tell the truth, to speak something with pride and energy and to indicate one's self as "I am here" (*NS,*X.1-9).

2174 **निर्भुग्नोरस्**

Nirbhugnoras : same as *nirbhugna vakṣa.* The description of the back and stiffening of the torso leads to the *nirbhugna* position of the chest (*NS*, IX. 226). Breast is raised and stiff, back depressed, shoulders unbent. It indicates paralysis, accepting with respect, look of surprise, speaking truth, mentioning oneself in haughtiness and excess of pride.

2175 **निर्वाण**

Nirvāṇa : liberation. according to Buddhists, the highest bliss. It means purification of the mind, its restoration to its primitive sublimity or radiant transparency. Sometimes four kinds of *nirvāṇa* are distinguished.

2176 **निर्वाद-कथा**

Nirvāda-kathā : a talk of scandal (*Raghu*, 14.34). *Nirvādo janavādepi* (*Amara*.III.3.90), blame, censure, scandal, consummate, discussion.

2177 **निर्वेद**

Nirveda : disgust, loathing indifference, one of the thirty-three *vyabhicārī bhāvas*. Anxiety, tears, paleness of the face, deep sighs and low-spirits are its external manifestations (*Daśarūpaka*, IV.9).

(b) distinctive clues to disgust are: the upper lip is raised; the lower lip is also raised and pushed up to the upper lip, or is lowered and slightly protruding; the nose is wrinkled; the cheeks are raised; lines show below the lower lid,and the lid is pushed up but not tense; the brow is lowered, lowering the upper lid.

2178 **निवर्तनोरू**

Nivartanorū: going through the pair of heels. In the *nivartana* gesture of things, heels should go inwards in a dancing trot. It suggests welcoming, or going forward honourably, or to see some striking things worth visible (*NS*, X. 27-33).

2179 **निवर्तित पुट**

Nivartita puṭa : eyelids-returned, a type of eye-gesture.

2180 **निवृत्ता कटि**

Nivṛttā kaṭi : the turned-round waist; hips turning to the back, facing the front while the body is twisted sideways. A taut movement of the hips. This can be seen in Khajurāho and Koṇārka temples where waist is twisted completely. A turned-round position of the waist. It is used to display such feats in a dramatic event (*NS*, X.21-26).

2181 **निवृत्त ग्रीवा**

Nivṛttā grīvā : a taut position of the neck, a type of neck-gesture (*SR*, VII.329-334); a neck with the face-front. It indicates to look at a thing in the front (*NS*, VIII. 164-171). Return to its original position after having faced something.

2182 **निवृत्त्यङ्कुर**

Nivṛttyaṅkura : it occurs when one represents words spoken by other person by *sūcā*. *Nivṛtti* is cessation of action, quiescence, peace opposed to *pravṛtti*.

2183 **निवेष-करण**

Niveṣa-karaṇa : derived from *maṇḍala sthāna*. Hands on the chest. The chest is in *nirbhugna* and the sides are in *unnata* (*NS*, IV.156-157, IX.226, 236-38;X.65-66). The two hands are on the breast, the bosom is *nirbhugna* and the posture is *maṇḍala*. It is used in elephant-side.

2184 **निशुम्भितकरण**

Niśumbhita karaṇa : derived from the *nirbhugna* position of the chest and the *unnata* of the side, a movement of the *kuñcita* feet is indicated. The backward extended leg can also form a *vṛścika*. Hands are in *Kaṭakāmukha*,one of them touching the forehead (*NS*, IV.824b, IX.216, 239-40). Also known as *nistambhita*. The foot is bent towards the back, the breast raised high and the hand is at the *tilak* mark. It is used in the gesticulation of Śaṅkara.

2185 **निषध-हस्त**

Niṣadha-hasta : both hands gesture. If the left hand, holding the right arm above the elbow and the right hand touching the left arm with a clenched fist, it makes the style of *niṣadha*-gesture. This is used to suggest pride, obstinacy, decency, curiosity, courage, sprite, affection, motionlessness and weight (*NS*, IX.135-137). (b) the second style of *niṣadha* is as follows: "If two *haṁsapakṣa* styles of the *asaṁyuta-hastas* are joined together, from the opposite direction, it is also called the *niṣadha-hasta*. It is used to indicate opening the window-net, screen and door" (*Ibid*).

2186 **निष्कर्षणाधर**

Niṣkarṣaṇādhara : drawing out lips; a type of lip-movement suggested by *SR*.

2187 **निष्कलरूपा मुद्रा**

Niṣkalarūpā-mudrā : abstract gesture. When three fingers except the thumb and the little-finger are curved and upturned; the right thumb, tied with the left thumb should wrap the left thumb with fingers of the right and the fingers of the left -hand wrap similarly with the fingers of the right. Under the condition, curve both the fore-fingers of both the hands. This makes the gesture named *niṣkalarūpāṇi* (*VD*).

2188 **निष्क्रमण-दृष्टि**

Niṣkramaṇa dṛṣṭi : an eye-gesture. The movement along the thickness of the eyeball, which suggests a going out or a bulge of the eyeball. In *Mālavikāgnimitra* (Act V), the dwarf enters the stage. Mālavikā enacts fear. Here the eyeballs move in *niṣkramaṇa* (*NS*, VIII. 102) coming out the eyeballs in an emotion; also called *niṣkrama.*

2189 **निष्क्रम-तारा**

Niṣkrama-tārā : a type of pupil-movement suggested in *adbhuta rasa;* going out pupil-movement.

2190 **निष्क्रान्ता मध्या दृष्टि**

Niṣkrāntā madhyā dṛṣṭi : a type of eye-gesture.

2191 **निष्ठुर-मुद्रा**

Niṣṭhura-mudrā : gesture showing cruelty. Wrap the two curved thumbs with your fingers and place them to one's own front jointly. This is called *niṣṭhura* (*VD*).

2192 **निहञ्चित-शिर**

Nihañcita śira : movement of the head with raised shoulders, the *añcita* movement with raised shoulders; two shoulders are raised up with the neck slant by a side. It indicates the pride of the fair sex, erotic sense, affection, hysteric fears, silent love, affected anger, jealous, pretended anger, and affected indifference, etc. In it the two shoulders are raised up with the neck bent (*NS*, VIII.17-18).

2193 **नीच-अलङ्कार**

Nīca-alaṅkāra : low voice-embellishment. *Nīca* proceeds from the breast and is lower than *mandra* (q.v).It is used in natural speech, sickness, weariness, due to austerity, falling down in panic, fainting, etc. (*NS*).

2194 **नीप्रान्तर**

Nīprāntara : the distance between the eaves of neighbouring houses (*A*, 3.8.14).

2195 **नीराजन**

Nīrājana : waving of lights round a person. As the bridegroom arrived at the abode of the would-be father-in-law, he was greeted with *nīrājana* rite; and it appears that the bride herself used to do this (*Śiva*, II.46.3):

नीराजनार्थं शम्भोश्च दीपपात्रकरा सती

Omens are to be known from the *nīrājana* rite, an aspect of which is the waving of lights round the cows and other beasts. In the context of the rituals of the *Govatsa-dvādaśī* associated with the festival of lights (*dīpāvalī*) omens are mentioned.If the flames of the lamps turn right or remain steady the indication is of happiness; if otherwise it indicates sorrow. If the flames appear coarse,they indicate the loss of wealth; if they turn whitish the indication is of loss of grains; if they flicker and get enlarged, the indication is said to be war, and if they turn black the indication is of death(*Sk*.p.II.4.9.5-13).

Varāhamihira in his *Bṛhat-Saṁhitā* (XLIV) has presented a separate chapter on the lustration ceremony-*nīrājana-vidhi.* According to him *nīrājana* is lustration of arms, a kind of military and religious ceremony performed by kings or generals of armies in the month of Āśvina before they took the field. This is mentioned by poets like Kālidāsa (*Raghu* IV.25) and Śrīharṣa (*Naiṣadha*). Actually the word *nīrājanam* is derived thus: नीरेण जलेन अजनं स्पर्शनम् This is done by house-holders for cows during the Dīpāvalī and for tools etc. during the Dussera:

भगवति जलधरपक्ष्मक्षपाकरार्केक्षणे कमलनामे ।

उन्मीलयति तुरङ्गमकरिनरनीराजनं कुर्यात् ॥

Nīrājana, according to Kālidāsa, was the lustration ceremony performed especially before marching against an enemy (*Raghu.* 4.56).

2196 **नीवि**

Nīvi : the navel band. Navel is touched in the state of anxiety as we find in *Mālavikāgnimitra* (Act.III). Nīvi is some times a genital echo. In Sanskrit literature navel display is more 'genital' in terms of body mimicry. This does not mean that navels evolved their special shape as genital echos, but displaying more sexual like labial slit. (b) nīvi: a piece of cloth wrapped round the waist, petticoat (*AV*,VIII.2.16).

2197 **नूपुरकरण**

Nūpura-karaṇa : the *trika* is turned round gracefully with the hands in *latā* and *recita* respectively and the foot in *nūpura-pādā-cārī.* (Fig. 2197)

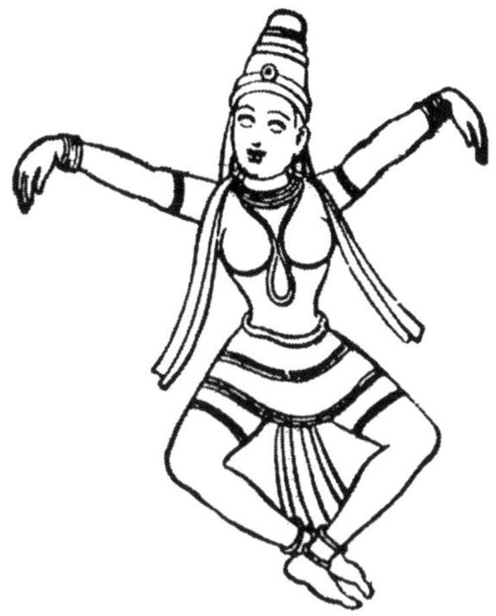

Fig. – (2197)

2198 **नूपुर-चारि**

Nūpura-cārī : initial position of *bhramarī cārī,* final position of *nūpurapādikā cārī,* the *hastas* in *latā recita* but both arms are above shoulder-level, a turn is suggested after the first position (*NS*, V.96b-97a, IX.35, X.45).

2199 **नूपुरपादिक करण**

Nūpurapādika karaṇa : the back crossing with the *kṣipta* position of the knees.

2200 **नूपुरपादिका चारी**

Nūpurapādikā cārī : both feet in *samapāda añcita;* an *añcita* foot is lifted and then taken to the back of the opposite thigh and finally the toes touch the ground; *udvāhita* or *parivartita* position of thighs; *nūpurakaraṇa.* Drawing one *añcita* foot backwards and then letting it fall on the ground quickly at the back of the other foot, with its forepart (*NS*, X.35). (Fig. 2200)

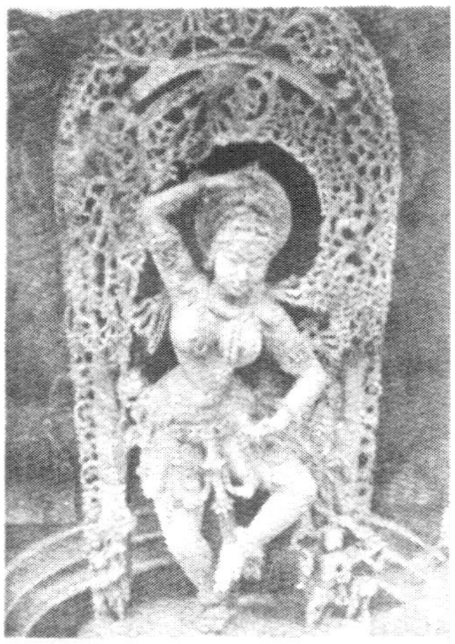

Fig. – (2200)

2201 **नृतु**

Nṛtu : dancer (*RV*, 1.92.4). In the *Ṛgveda nṛtu* occurs in the sense of the dancer. Uṣas is described as revealing her beauty like a dancer removing the garment in the form of darkness (*ibid*). In the *Ṛgveda,* Indra, the destroyer of enemies is addressed as *nṛtu* and the charming goddess of dawn also is addressed by the same word, indicating thereby, the vigorous and the gentle aspect respectively. The classical *nartakī* (dancer) has been presented in *Ratnāvalī* (I) as follows:

The wild hair has thrown off its beautiful binding of flowers; The anklets, drumming against her feet, wail higher and higher; The swinging necklace of pearl strikes her as if in revenge: Whirling, she risks being broken in half by the weight of those breasts.

2202 **नृत्त**

Nṛtta : pure dance. It simply denotes the movements of limbs in a definite rhythm and tempo: *nṛttam tālalā syāśrayam* (*DR*.1.10) It is taboo for the hill Marias to dance except on the night of Kaqsār and at weddings or at the rare visits of the officials. It may be stated that they dance only in the early summer, between the harvest - home and sowing. It is not the case with other tribes. They dance whole year. The Mill Maria dance is entirely different from that seen among other tribes of Bastar. The Hill Maria dance is known as *pāṭā endānā* which means "dance with the song ". Here also they are keener on song than dance.

The tribal dances are provocative to sexual emotions. The splendid parade of Māndrī dance, the intimacies of the Hulkī dance, the suggestiveness of some of the games are invaluable as a preparation for tumescence. There is a Maria proverb: *Relā Relā Bonde Pelā*-if you start with singing *relā,* you end with the satisfaction of desire. It must be noted that it is not the boy who by the energy of their play excite the girls, the girls' games and dances are equally stimulants.

Abhinava (*NS*, I.12.3) gives seven divisions of *nṛtta*: (1) *Śuddha:* in which *recaka* and *aṅgahāras* are present. (2) *Gītakādyābhinayonmukha:* in which there is a gesticulation of song in general manner. (3) *gānakriyāmātrānusāri-vādyatālānusāri:* that following the song and the rhythm of the instruments accompanying it, having the various movements of the body. (4) *uddhata:* forceful, the tribal dance. (5) *sukumāra.* (6) *uddhata-sukumāra*: forceful-gentle, and (7) *sukumāroddhata:* gentle-forceful. The first three are the popular (*laukika*) dance and in the satisfaction of deities. The last four are employed in the preliminaries.

Nṛtta is dear to the people and also regarded as auspicious: *prāyeṇa sarva lokasya nṛttamiṣṭam svabhāvataḥ māṅgalyamiti kṛtvā ca nṛttametat prakīrtitam (NS,*IV.269). Dance is often used in all festive and cultural occasions, hence used in *NS* too: *Vivāha-prasava-āvāha-pramoda-abhyudayādiṣu vinodakāraṇam ceti nṛttametat pravartitam (NS,* IV.270). It releases one of the tensions and worries that afflict the mind (*Ibid.* IV.270). Hence, dance is an integral part of drama. *Nṛtta* or pure dance in *NS* consists of the following elements: (1) *nṛttahasta,* (2) *sthāna* (posture), (3) *cārī* (*bhaumī* and *ākāśikī*), (4) *karaṇa* (movements of hands of hands and feet), (5) *aṅgahāra* (sequence of *karaṇas*).

2203 **नृत्त-अङ्गहार**

Nṛtta-aṅgahāra : dance-performance (*NS*, X). (Fig. 2203)

2204 **नृत्त-मूर्ति**

Nṛtta-mūrti : dancing aspects. The *nṛtta-mūrtis* of Sarasvatī, Kṛṣṇa and Durgā are all in the *tribhaṅga* pose in Indian sculpture. *Nṛtta mūrti* is a class of images of the gods and goddesses described in sculptural and the iconographical texts. Some gods or goddesses are occasionally represented in dancing postures (e.g. Śiva, Gaṇeśa, Sarasvatī, Kṛṣṇa and *apasaras*). The classification of postures is usually into standing (*sthānaka*), seated (*āsīna*), recumbent (*śayana*), mobile (*yānaka*) and dancing *(nṛtta)*.

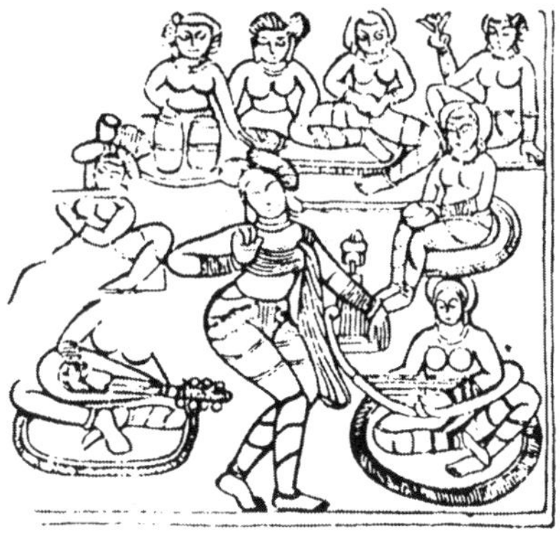

Fig – (2203)

2205 **नृत्त-हस्त**

Nṛtta-hasta : type of hand gesture in dancing. These dancing hands may be joined and disjoined applicable especially in the performance of dance and drama. They are *caturasra* (the square), *udvṛtta* (palm leaf fan), *talamukha* (slanting square), *svastika* (auspicious), *arālakaṭakāmukha āviddhavaktra* (fixed bent face), *sūcīmukha* (needle-pointed), *recita* (bent move), *ardharecita* (the half-bent), *uttanāvañcitau* (the flat-bent), *pallava* (the foliage), *nitamba* (the hip), *keśabandha* (binding up hairs), *latā* (the creeper), *karihasta* (an elephant trunk), *pakṣāvañcitaka* (the oblique sides), *pakṣapradyotaka* (contrary to the *pakṣāvañcitaka*), Garuḍa-*pakṣaka*(Garuḍa's wings), *daṇḍapakṣa* (standing swan's wings), *uromaṇḍalin* (the breast-circling), *pārśvamaṇḍalin* (the side-circling), *muṣṭikāsvastikau*(the first and the *svastika*), *Nalinī-padmakośa* (the lotus-core), *alapallava* (the lotus-leaf), *ulvaṇa* (the ups and downs), *lalita* (the delicate) and *valita* (the twisted). Thus they are twenty-seven in total enumerated by Bharata (*NS*, IX.176-197).

2206 **नृत्य**

Nṛtya : mime,gesticulation, dramatic dance, art-dance, dance giving expression to *rasa* and *bhāva*. *Nṛtya* had a profusion in *āṅgika*. The dancer expressed *emotional* states through the motion and disposition of his limbs. Hence, *nṛtya* has been described as *bhāvaśraya, i.e.* based on *bhāva* or feeling. Alternatively it has been described as *padārthābhinaya* or the representation of the meaning of a word, *i.e.* a self-content and static tableau. The purpose was the enactment of *rasa* by some narrative theme or lyrical literary composition.

2207 **नृत्य-अभिनय**

Nṛtya-abhinaya : a synonym of *āṅgika* used by Kālidāsa.

2208 **नृत्य-अभिनय-क्रिया**

Nṛtya-adhinaya-kriyā : gesticulation referred to in *Kumārasaṁbhava* (V.79).

2209 **नृत्य-गोष्ठी**

Nṛtya-goṣṭhī : one of the five types of *goṣṭhīs* mentioned in *Harṣacarita* of Bāṇabhaṭṭa. Other *goṣṭhīs* are as follows: *kāvyagoṣṭhī, galpagoṣṭhī, gītagoṣṭhī* and *vādyagoṣṭhī.*

2210 **नृत्य-प्रयोग**

Nṛtya-prayoga: practice of dance (*Ṛtusaṁshāra*).

2211 **नृत्य-मुद्रा (विचित्र-मुद्रा)**

Nṛtya-mudrā (or Vicitra-mudrā) : "'taking no dress or a dress that unfurls ten directions; a devout, when performs a single course of a dance circle with hands whirling round and catching the heads of his partner and doing the kissing sound, it is called the *nṛtya-mudrā* or *vicitra*" (*BT*).

2212 **नृत्य-रत्नावली**

Nṛtya-ratnāvalī : a work on dance written by Jayasenāpati, based on dramatic gestures. It also includes some important gestures of folk-drama.

2213 **नृत्योपहार**

Nṛtyopahāra: dance to welcome the messenger (*Pūrva Megha*, 36). It is still prevalent in the tribal regions.

2214 **नृसिंह-मुद्रा**

Nṛsiṁha-mudrā : gesture symbolizing the God Nṛsiṁha of the Vaiṣṇavite cult. Two hands of "*akāra*-symbol made separated (*VD.*). (b) two *dravya-mudrās* (9.V) along with *vanamālā mudrā* may be directed in between the leg-joints and the chin half-hanged. Open the mouth to hang down the tongue.

2215 **नृसिंह (वक्त्र) मुद्रा**

Nṛsiṁha (vaktra) mudrā : "fill the mouth with wind; make the eyeballs inside the eye-pits, curve the pair of knees; but the pair of hands down on the earth and then move them alternately. This is a great gesture called Nṛsiṁha" (*BT*).

2216 **नृसिंह-हस्त**

Nṛsiṁha hasta : style the *siṁhamukha mudrā* with the left hand and the *tripatāka* with the right; this is Nṛsiṁha (*AD*, 216-225).

2217 **नेति नेति**

Neti-neti : 'not this, not this'. It is a negative method of philosophical discussion.

2218 **नेत्रगोचर**

Netragocara : visible, within the range of sight.

2219 **नेत्रप्रदर्शितमुद्रा**

Netra-pradarśita : to guide one's eyes. If the middle and the forefinger of the left hand are raised up and the little and the ring fingers are crooked with the thumb; it is the *netra-pradarśita,* applicable to bring a cow and a bull (*VD*).

2220 **नेत्र-मुद्रा**

Netra-mudrā : (a) the eye gesture. "When the two fore-fingers of both the hand are kept extended and the rest fingers are placed at the bottom of two thumbs, it is called the *netra-mudrā.* It assures a look that determines the best knowledge and makes a devout all-knowing one". (*BT.*) (b) If the fore-finger is brought near the eyes and three fingers are curved and placed on the thumb of the said hand. Then it is *netra* (*VD*). (c) join the thumb and the fore-finger at their ends and extend all other fingers (*VD*).

2221 **नेत्र-मोहन**

Netra-mohana : confounding the eyes (*A*, 14.1.38).

2222 **नेत्रोन्मीलन**

Netronmilana : the ritual of marking the pupils in the icon's eyes (signifying the opening of the eyes) during the installation of the icon in the sanctum, is an important sequence of consecration of icons and rendering them fit for worship.

The ritual of 'opening the eyes' is followed by the elaborate and colourful ritual of infusion of life into the icon (*prāṇa-pratiṣṭhā*).

2223 **नेपथ्य**

Nepathya : inside or behind the path, decoration, part of a stage.

2224 **नेपथ्य-प्रयोगकला**

Nepathya-prayogakata : stage-playing, costume, one of the 64 arts enumerated in *Kāmasūtra* (1.3.16). Planning dress and decoration according to time and place.

By observing the dress worn, one can recognise the class of the people in which they belong. *Dhoti* (long cloth used as a garment for lower portion of the body) stands for the Indianized rich and complete gentlemen, but Full Pant symbolizes the westernized elite class. Usually poor people wear a *laṅgoṭī* or *laṅgoṭā* (a small piece of cloth tightly worn around the waist). The down-trodden wear *bhagvā* (a loose under-wear for male).

Bharata (*NS*) has divided male costume into three types: *śuddha* (white), *citra* (variegated) and *śyama* (soiled). *Śuddha* dress should be used when going to temples, while observing some auspicious rite or vow, at the time of conjunction of the particular day and stars at the marriage time and whenever any religious activity is to be performed. The *citra* dress should be used in the case of gods, demons, *yakṣas, gandharvas, rājās* and kings of amorous nature. *Śuddha* is meant for chamberlain, elderly Brāhamaṇas, merchants, ministers, priests, ascetics, kṣatriyas, vaiśyas and royal officers. *Malina* is meant for lunatics, intoxicated persons, travellers and those in calamity. Far *śuddha* and *citra* costume the lower and upper garments should be white and variegated respectively : and in *malina* they should be soiled. The sages, Jain and Buddhist monks should have their own dress according to their rules. Ascetics should wear tattered garments or bark or skin garments. Wandering ascetics and great sages should have *kāṣāya* (saffron-colour) garment. *Pāṣupata* should have variegated dress. The person guarding the harem and lower people should wear saffron-coloured tailored garment. Warriors dress should be suited for the battle, with brilliant weapons, armour, quiver and bow. Kings should have always variegated dress. When there is ominous appearance of any star or observance of auspicious rite their dress should be white.

2225 **नैवेद्य**

Naivedya: 'offering of food to an idol' (*Bhāgavata Purāṇa*) and a portion of which is returned to the offerer for eating. The person who refuses it is said to get into difficulties. (*Sk.P.*2.38.54.-60). It is regarded as the sixth *upacāra* (presentable articles). The others being *pādya, gandha, puṣpa, dhūpa* and *dīpa.*

2226 **नैवेद्य-मुद्रा**

Naivedya-mudrā : gesture of the food-offerings. Raise all the fingers of both the hands. They are to be affixed by the roots of the thumbs, joining each back with other. This is an auspicious *mudrā,* indicating a fruit (*VD*).

2227 **नैष्ठिक**

Naiṣṭhika : students who dedicate themselves to life long studentship. A Brahmacārin having carried out the vow of chastity.

2228 **नोदन**

Nodana : impelling; directing relevant sentiments and feelings through appropriate gestures (*NS*, IX.175).

2229 **न्याय**

Nyāya : the movement of the body in dance for simulated protection against weapons and for the simulated discharge of weapons is called *nyāya.* The *nyāyas* are to be employed with *cārīs* in discharging weapons. There are four *nyāyas* --the ways of fighting --to be employed in the use of missiles. They are (i) *Bharatanyāya* --the weapon should strike the waist.(ii) *Sāttvata nyāya*--the weapon should strike the foot. (iii) *Vārṣagaṇya nyāya*--the weapon should strike the chest and (iv) *Kaiśika nyāya*–the weapon should strike the head. With these *nyāyas* arising out of the various *cārīs,* various movements should be performed in the release of weapons.

According to the *Dhanurveda*, described in the *Śārṅgadharapaddhati* there are five *nyāyas*: *Kaiśika*, *Sāttvika*, *Vatsakaraṇa*, *Bharata* and *Skandhanāman*. (c) rules for the interpretation of *Sūtras* (*HC*, p.313).

(b) The system of logic which became the basis of one of the six traditional systems of Indian philosophy.

2230 **न्यास**

Nyāsa : feeling of the deity in different parts of the body (*Lalitāsahasranāma*, 1.4). It also serves as a protection against evil (*Tantrasāra;* p.93). Without proper *nyāsa* worship is meaningless (*Tārātantra* II.3). There are many types of *nyāsas*. (*Śāradātilaka*, VII).

प – Pa

2231 **पक्कण**

Pakkaṇa : 'hut of the Cāṇḍāla; village inhabited by barbarians' (*Mbh*); houses or village of Śabaras.

2232 **पक्ष**

Pakṣa : (a) a point under discussion; the subject of a syllogism or conclusion (minor term); the term with which one is concerned, alternative view. A way of presenting a matter. (b) plaint in a lawsuit.

(c) role-taking : understanding that others have a different point of view and set of perceptions about the world and that messages must take into account the decoder's perspective—the encoder will try to judge the characteristics of the listener and situation.

A known worth trait of the tribes and particularly of the Hill Maria is that they start talking together and don't understand that others have different points of view. This results in utter confusion and none can understand of any body. Three, four or more persons would talk at the same time. This trait in their character was seen everywhere but only one illustrative example may be given. At Dhurbābeṛā, when asked about the Bison-horn Marias, all the assembled people, who were about ten in number, started replying together and it was difficult to hear or understand them. They had to be asked to keep quiet and speak one by one, so that they could be understood.

Norohna had also noticed that all the Hill Marias start speaking at the same time. This is what he says in Tour Diary.

(d) fortnight, specially in relation to moon.

2233 **पक्षप्रद्योतक-नृत्तहस्त**

Pakṣapradyotaka—nṛtta-hasta : contrary to the *pakṣavañcita*. If the *pakṣavañcitaka*-figure is styled by the alternate direction, it is called the *pakṣapradyotaka* (*NS*, IV.17).

2234 **पक्षप्रद्योतक-हस्त**

Pakṣapradyotaka - hasta : a type of hand-gesture held on the waist in *patāka* (*NS*, IX.200-201). In a conflict situation, or when a female delivers a hostile verbal message, the verbal message is often accompanied by the hand-on-hip stance. This is the most aggressive stance that Indian females (uneducated) take, and it is executed in the following manner: first the feet are placed firmly in a stationary step, with the body weight concentrated on the heel of the rear foot; the buttocks are protruded; and, one hand is placed on the extended hip (the hip is extended because of the weight concentrated on the rear foot and the protrusion of the buttocks); the hand either rests on the hip supported by the fingers being spread, or it is supported by making the hand into a first and resting the knuckles against the hip. Sometimes, the body of the female will slowly rock to and fro during the stance, particularly while she is listening to the other person. If the stance is not taken while the female is listening, it is quickly taken when she delivers her hostile message. The stance can also be accompanied by rolling of the eyes and twitching of the nose to further punctuate the hostility of the female. The NV message communicated when female takes this stance is: "I am really mad, now. You better quit messing with me".

2235 **पक्षवञ्चितक-नृत्तहस्त**

Pakṣavancitaka-nṛtta-hasta : a type of hand-gesture in dancing (*NS*). One *tripatāka* hand is placed on the waist and the other hand on the head.

2236 **पक्षवञ्चित-हस्त**

Pakṣavañcita-hasta : the oblique sides; a type of hand-gesture; one hand raised to the head and the other on the waist: this is a common mode of standing and performing dances in Amarāvatī sculptures. When one hand of the *tripatāka* is placed on the head and the other on the waist, then it is formed (*NS*, IX.180).

2237 **पक्ष्मन्**

Pakṣman : eyelash; *pakṣmala* 'having beautiful eyelashes'.

2238 **पङ्कज-मुद्रा**

Paṅkaja-mudrā : gesture of a lotus. Upturn two palms with fingers extended. It is a *paṅkaja* (*VD*).

2239 **पङ्क्ति**

Paṅkti : row, a row of diners. Elaborate rules are given in *Dharmaśāstras* in regard to the manners to be observed. For example, a person in *paṅkti* should not take *ācamana* before others get up; he should not sit in the same row as undeserving persons or with persons belonging to a different caste. Persons in a row should not touch one another and so on.

2240 **पङ्क्तिपावन**

Paṅktipāvana : privileged to sit at dinner. Those who sanctify by their presence a company of diners. According to Hārīta they must be from a good family, be endowed with *Vedic* learning, and have good character and decent conduct (*Manu* III. 83-84). Again, commensality is restricted to castes ranked in alliances, while it is common to observe how caste groups who eat together at a village feast are separated from each other, and seated at graded distances. These are, in fact, two food systems of classification: (i) when it is a question of caste ranking, the simplest criterion concerns who may receive food and water from whom without incurring pollution, (ii) a triple gradation according to degrees of nourishment and quality: *sattva*, *rajas* and *tamas*. These three categories are called *guṇas*.

2241 **पञ्चकला**

Pañca-kalā : five aspects of *Śakti*. They are *nivṛtti, vidya, pratiṣṭhā, śānti* and *śāntyatītā* (*Śāradātilaka*, V.79).

2242 **पञ्चक्रिया**

Pañca-kriyā : five active expressions of *śakti*: *Sṛṣṭi* (creation), *sthiti* (maintenance), *saṁhāra* (destruction), *tirodhāna* (disappearance) and *anugraha* (favour). (*Tantrāloka* 1.121.)

2243 **पञ्चक्लेष**

Pañca-kleṣa : five fetters in form of *avidyā* (false knowledge), *asmitā* (self-conceit), *rāga* (attachment), *dveṣa* (hatred) and *abhiniveśa* (adherence).

2244 **पञ्चगव्य**

Pañcagavya : the mixture of five products of a cow, viz. milk, curd, ghee, cow's urine and cowdung (*Smṛti*), which is to be taken in by a sinner for his purification (*Yāj.* III. 314).

2245 **पञ्चगुणा**

Pañcaguṇāḥ : the five objects of senses: *rūpa, rasa, gandha, sparśa* and *śabda*.

2246 **पञ्चतत्व**

Pañca-tattva : also called *kula-dravya* or *kula-tattva*. In common parlance it is called *pañca-makāra*. The five *tattvas* or *makāras* are: *madya* (wine), *māṁsa* (meat), *matsya* (fish), *mudrā* (position of fingers) and *maithuna* (copulation). Tāntric esoteric ritualism constitutes this *pañcatattava*. Also known as *pañcamakāra, pañcamudrā, kuladravya* and *kulatattva*, etc., (b) five elements taken collectively: *pṛthvī, āp, tejas, vāyu* and *ākāśa*.

2247 **पञ्चनीराजन**

Pañcanirājana : waving five things before an idol and then falling prostrate before it; five things: lamp, lotus, cloth, mango and betel-leaf.

2248 **पञ्चभद्र**

Pañcabhadra : having five auspicious marks on: chest, back, face and flanks.

2249 **पञ्चभूत**

Pañcabhūta : the five material elements. Five states of existence are: *pṛthvi* (earth), *āppa* (water), *tejas* (fire), *vāyu* (air) and *ākāśa* (space) and they stand for solidity, liquidity, radiation, gaseousness and ethereality respectively. In iconography, *pṛthvi* is represented by a square or cube; *āppa* by a circle; water by aquatic plants and animals; *tejas* by radiation of light or stellate figures; *vāyu* by smoke, a globe flying bodies, etc.; and *ākāśa* by heavenly bodies such as the sun, moon, etc.

2250 **पञ्चम**

Pañcama : fifth note of musical scale, fifth.

2251 **पञ्चमकार**

Pañcamakāra : five rituals in *Tantra* towards the spiritual progress by means of *mūrti, maṇḍala, mantra, mudrā* and *manana*. See *Pañca-tattva*.

2252 **पञ्चमजन**

Pañcama - jana : the fifth caste. The *pañcamas* or the fifth are the outcastes who are not considered good enough by the castes even to serve them (like Śūdra). They are known in different parts of the country by different names. In the law-books they are mainly referred to as *Caṇḍālas*. The vast majority of the aborigines of India belong to the *pañcamas*, although certain hill tribes have a status higher than that of the majority of *pañcamas*. Progeny of unions between a man of one caste and a woman of a higher caste usually shrink below the level of either, and are treated as outcastes from both the communities.

Whatever the origin of the *pañcamas*, they have all along been the victims of social tyranny. We have seen, that although the Śūdras were allotted an unenviable position in society, they have all along enjoyed a better status: the same, unfortunately, is not true of *pañcamas*. They were not allowed to enter villages and towns except to do scavenging work. Their touch was considered defiling even by Śūdras.

Ingenious methods were invented to distinguish the unapproachables from others. During Fa Hien's visit he noticed that the unapprochables, on entering the city, had to go about striking a gong. Huien Tsang says that they were not allowed to use the public thorough fares but to keep to a certain footpath allotted for their exclusive use. In the Punjab, the sweeper castes had to go about always holding a broom. In the reign of the Peshwās the *Mahārs* had to drag a bush of leaves with them wherever they went. They were not allowed to enter the city of Pune after 3 P.M. as towards the evening they cast too long a shadow which falling on their superiors might defile them.

The *pañcamas*, as a rule, were not allowed to live in villages inhabited by the higher castes. They had to keep away from village wells and temples and certain main thoroughfares leading to the streets of the Brāhmaṇs. They were not allowed to build houses of stone or wood, but had to construct hovels of mud, reads and straw. The entrance to their houses were to be low so that a *pañcama* could not enter his house without stooping. The idea was that as a *pañcama* grew older he should learn to stoop lower. Wearing of clean clothes was forbidden to the *pañcama*. He was not allowed to own land. This law alone ensured his observance of other laws, as by this he became completely dependent upon the higher castes.

(b) *Pañca-Jana* was a demon. This demon is said to be living in the waters of the ocean. Kṛṣṇa killed the demon; from his bones a conch was prepared. It was called *pāñcajanya* (*Viṣṇu.* V. 21.24-28)

2253 पञ्चमुद्रा

Pañcamudrā : see *pañca-tattva.*

2254 पञ्चवीर-गोष्ठी

Pañcavīra-goṣṭhī : assembly of village head. A type of gathering mentioned in *Daśakumāracaritam* of Daṇḍin. There Rāgamañjarī is a woman of rare accomplishments: we have a description of a performance by her which citizens gather to look at with great expectations. Here she dances in a gathering called *pañcavīra*. The gathering here is the equivalent to the *janapada samāja* of the *Rāmāyaṇa* and the *goṣṭhī* of *Kāmasūtra.*

(b) *Pañcavīra* also means the five heroes of Vṛṣṇi family (a branch of Yādava clan), defied and worshipped by the *Bhāgavatās* since very early times, were iconically represented (*arcā*) and housed in stone-temples (*śaila-devagṛha*).

2255 पञ्चशिखा-मुद्रा

Pañcaśikhā-mudrā : the five-tip gesture. "Make two opposite hands (palms), twisted together into braid and two ring-fingers pressed by the middle and joined by the tips. Two hands, joined by the roots of thumbs and positioned with a little curvature, make the *mudrā* of *pañca-śikhā*. This is also called *mokṣadā* (that promises salvation), or *mahābhāgyadā* (one, that assures the greatest fortune)" (*BT.*).

2256 पञ्चसन्धि

Pañcasandhi : five junctures in a drama: *mukha* (opening), *pratimukha* (progression), *garbha* (development), *avamarśa* (pause) and *nirvahaṇa* (conclusion).

2257 पञ्चाग्नि

Pañcāgni : the five sacred fires; *viz. āhavanīya, gārhyapatya, dakṣiṇā, sabhya,* and *āvasathya. Pañcāgni-vidyā* was the knowledge of *Brahmaṇ* which Śvetaketu Āruṇeya learnt from Pravāhana Jaivalī. *Pañcāgni-sādhanā* was a type of penance. In it the person sits in the midst of four fires, the fifth being the sun above. This is to be performed in summer (*Skanda.* VII.1.40.5).

2258 पञ्चाङ्ग

Pañcāṅga : (a) a book containing details about days of the week, lunar mansions, stars etc. (b) five limbs of the body, a type of obeisance known as *pañcāṅga praṇāma.* These five parts of the body are two feet, two knees and the head which touch the ground while bowing down before a deity. Only *pañcāṅga*-method is prescribed for a woman: *pañcāṅgam eva nārī tu nānyathā munisattama.* The *Skanda Purāṇa* explains that the *pañcāṅga* comprises five units, namely arms, mind, speech, head and eyes, wherein only the standing position is enough:

> bāhubhyām caiva manasā
> śirasā vacasā dṛśā I.
> pañcāṅgoyam praṇāmah syāt
> pūjāsu pravarāvimau II.
>
> (*Sk.P.* II. 9.29.29)

(c) Feeling of the deity in the heart, head, central cerebral region, protective symbol (*kavaca*) and intestine is known as *pañcāṅga-nyāsa.*

2259 पञ्चाङ्गप्रणाम

Pañcāṅga-praṇāma : obeisance made with arms, knees, head, voice and looks. (Fig. 2259)

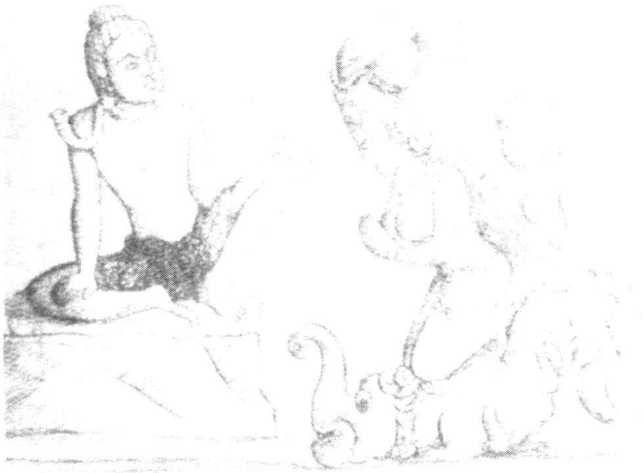

Fig. – (2259)

2260 पञ्चाङ्गवृक्ष

Pañcāṅga-vṛkṣa : five parts of tree: root, bark, leaf, flower and fruit.

2261 **पञ्चाङ्गभक्ति**

Pañcāṅgabhakti : five means of devotion: silent prayer, burnt offering, libations, bathing and feeding Brāhmaṇs. (Fig. 2260)

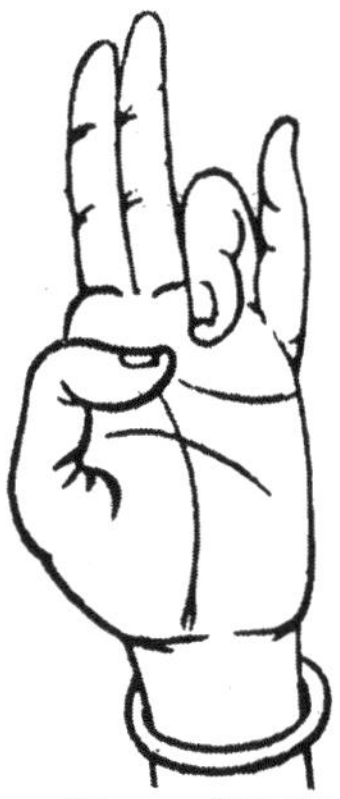

Fig. – (2260)

2262 **पञ्चामृत**

Pañcāmṛta : the five kinds of divine food, *viz*, milk, coagulated or sour milk, butter, honey and sugar.

2263 **पञ्चालिका**

Pañcālikā : a doll or image (*puttalikā*) made of cloth, ivory, wood, pith, clay or metal. It is also called *śāla-bhañjikā*, *pañcālī*.

2264 **पञ्चीकरण**

Pañcīkaraṇa : the mixing of five subtle elements: *ākāśa*, *vāyu*, *agni*, *āpa* and *kṣiti*—in different ways to produce the gross elements.

2265 **पञ्चेन्द्रिय**

Pañcendriya : five senses. Those who have written about NV communication are not in agreement on the categories Sanskrit scholars used for analysis. They thought that the easiest way to classify NV communication was on the basis of the channels used to pick up the "messages". The five senses, then, would give the categories for analysis. The only problem with this system, however, is that one important kind of NV communication does not fall neatly into five categories. In spite of this flaw in the system, these five types of NV categories are still relevant: (1) *sparśanam* (touching), (2) *āsvādanam* (tasting), (3) *ghrāṇam* (smelling), (4) *śravaṇam* (hearing) and (5) *darśanam* (seeing) and then note one multi-channel type.

2266 **पञ्चोपचार**

Pañcopacāra : five *upacāras* (materials) which are offered in worship. These are *pādya* (water as the symbol of the element *āpa*), *gandha* (sandal, etc., as the symbol of the element *pṛthvi*)—*puṣpa* (flower as the symbol of the element *ākāśa*), *dhūpa* (incense as the symbol of the element *vāyu*), and *dīpa* (light as the symbol of the element *tejas*). This *pañcopacāra* was later elaborated into ten (*daśopacāra*), sixteen (*ṣoḍaśopacāra*) and at times even to sixty-four (*Puraścaryārṇava*, III.224).

2267 **पट**

Paṭa : picture. Two dimensional painting or picture of a deity which often serves as a symbol of worship instead of the three dimensional image.

2268 **पटहप्रणाद**

Paṭahapraṇāda : tattooing. Tattooing is a global phenomenon where human body is marked with different pigments by puncturing the organs. It is the art of body-marking. The body is punctured with small needles put together, which are capable of holding colouring matter. In Hindu society, the females of *Naṭa* (tribal) caste visit the houses and after convincing the females of beautiful tattoo designs, they mark their bodies with different colours.

One of the important designs of tattooing is to make needle mark on the hands in such a manner that alphabets become apparent on the person and one can read the name tattooed. Marco Polo noticed this type of incision on the body. Mostly soldiers, sailors and robbers used to have their names marked on their hands. In Indian literature we find such references.

In India, blue colour was selected for marking. In central India the tribal people had many parts of their bodies tattooed and some females had a strong desire for tattoo marks all over the body. In northern India, the arm and the hand are open parts for body-marking. The limbs selected for this purpose do not have the uniform tattoo-marks but different parts have special designs which add beauty to the body.

The various designs of corporal marking may be divided into two classes. The first type is exclusively depicted for making the body more beautiful and other design is connected with religious and magical aspects of human life. The most prominent among the designs are animal forms which are copied from the existing social objects. Several animal designs such as—scorpions, bull, elephant, lion, etc., are known from the prehistoric seals and also depicted on ancient punch-marked coins. The ordinary people could not conceive of any other design but the so-called symbols and figures carved on the ancient Indian seals and coins. There was no underlying principle to guide the community regarding tattooing but each person was instructed to have a few marks.

After the animal designs, the second stage of development, in this art, was more or less advanced and it may be termed "geometrical" which reached its excellence in tattooing.

The third phase was religious and the theological signs which were punctured on different parts of the body. It was and still is a widespread belief that God will not admit those women in the heaven who had no tattoo marks. They may be in the form of symbol of different sects, *i.e. cakra* for *Vaiṣṇavas, triśula* for Śāktas and *Gaṇeśa* for others.

In Asian countries, tattooing is regarded as a puberty rite for the woman. In India, girls are tattooed after marriage and it is taken as a symbol of love and attraction. Tattooed black spot on the chin of women, denote their youth and puberty. It also helped in the investigation of the so-called criminal tribes and their psychological thinking. Some people believe that tattoo marks cure diseases or rheumatic pains. Thus, we can find out several social, psychological, religious and magic beliefs behind tattooing.

The scarring of skin is a special type of body adornment prevalent in tribal India and known as *godanā* or tattooing. This tattoo-mark persists for a lifetime, indicating the social status, the sexual condition, the group allegiance or some other quality of the decorated tribal body.

The Hill Maria girls are tattooed when they are eight or nine years old. In other regions there are professional tattooers, while in the Hilly regions it is the mother who performs this job. The tattooing operation is performed with the help of the brass wire used for the rings in the helix of the ear, sharpened into rough needles. After the prick, black charcoal powder is smeared on the spot. This initiation causes great pain and this pain is an important part of bonding. The pattern of tattooing consists of short horizontal and vertical lines. Dots are not a common feature in the design except the two dots on the forehead surrounded by a circle. Hill Maria women never seem to tattoo legs or arms. They now confine tattooing to only face and breast. Again of these two parts, it is the facial tattooing that is most common.

For the Hill Marias tattooing is just body adornment and that is all.

In Hindi literature and folk-songs, tattooing has been described in a very interesting manner. In a literary poem composed by Hindi poet Padmākar, the corporal marking is vividly described as a device to write the names of gods on various parts of the body by tattooing:

दे लिख बाहिन में ब्रजचन्द रु,
गोल कपोलन कुंजबिहारी ।
त्यों 'पदमाकर' याहि हिये हरि
गोद गोविन्द, गले गिरिधारी ।।
या बिधि ते नख से सिख लौं,
लिख नाम अनन्त भवै भव प्यारी ।
साँवरे के रँग गोद दे गात,
अरी गोदनान की गोदनहारी ।।

Here the poet says that the devotee of Kṛṣṇa requests the operator to incise the several names of the Lord, on the various parts of the body with dark colour; for instance *Braja Chandra* on the arms, *Kuñj Bihārī* on the cheeks, *Giridhārī* on the neck and *Hari* on the chest.

In one of the folk-songs, a woman insists on incising the tattoo marks beautifully, so as to have a fine combination of colours. The names of pigments are not given here but only selection of colours is pointed out:

गोरी गोरी बहियाँ गोरी, गोदना' रे गोदवली,
जे सुईंया साले अल्हर करेज ।
अइसन गोदना गोद रे गोदनरिया
जइसे चुनरी रँगेला रँगरेज ।।

In brief, it means that the needle marks should be obvious on the arms and the female operator should use different pigments so as to make the whole tattoo multi-coloured.

The following folk-songs give a picture of a lovely lady and the operator who is called *Naṭinī*, is requested to sit in the courtyard and write the names of Kṛṣṇa, Govinda and Giridhārī on the different parts of the body. Probably in this case, Kṛṣṇa, himself has taken the work of operation. In the disguise of a female operator, he begins the work of tattooing:

आवऽना गोदनहारी बइठऽमोरे आँगनवा से लिखि देहु ना ।
हमरा मन के गोदनवा, से लिखि देहु ना ।।१।।
गाल पर गोविन्द लिखऽ राधा के मिलनवा हो अँचरवा लिखि देऽ ना ।
माता कुन्ती के ललनवाँ, अँचरवा लिखि देहु ना ।।२।।
गले गिरिधारी, बाजू कृष्ण बनवारी हो किनारे गोदऽ ना ।
काली नाग के नथनवा, हो किनारे गोदऽ ना ।।३।।
इहे अरमनवा, तोहसे कहीला बचनवा
अलबेला मोर सजनवा, हो गोदनवा गोदऽ ना ।।४।।

This gives an idea of the mode of movement and style of the female operator who keeps the basket on her head and a stick in her hand. This is the real picture of a female *Naṭinī* in Northern India while she is engaged in tattooing. The following lines depict the love story of Rādhā and Kṛṣṇa in the form of the operator and the woman tattooed:

माथ पर दउरिया धइके,
हाथ में लकुटिया लेइके;
धइले नटिनियाँ के भेस;
गोदनहारी कहेले गोदाइले गोदना ।।
अपने महलिया से,
निकले ली रानी राधिका हो;
चरेले नटिनियाँ आपन नाम ।

गोदना हम गोदइबो हो ।
धइके राधा के कलाई,
राधा बोले झुंझलाई,
कहेले कृष्ण कन्हाई ।
त त हउब ऽ बाड़ा दागाबाज
गोदनवाँ हम गोदाइबि हो ॥

In Hindi literature, we find a large number of mystic sayings and riddles which have only one reply and that is tattoo. It shows that the society was well acquainted with the body marks and tattooing was generally known to everyone. The lines are but in the form of questions:

(a) करिया के बाजू, बहू के पखुरा पर दमकी

(b) ब्याह के निसानी, कबौ ना मिटानी

(c) नित धोवइ नित माँजइ, नित नयी होय ।
फाटइ ना फूटइ, पुराना कइसे होय ॥

(d) एक सोने के सलाई, ओमे मोती जड़ाई ।
ओके जिनिगि भरि चलाई ॥

(e) बारी कुँआरी सादा जाइ ।
बियही जाइ, तब दागी जाइ ॥

(f) हँसि के मँगाई, रोइ के लेइ ।
एक सखी एक सखी के देइ ॥

(g) गोर बदन करिया तन रेखा ।
लिखत सखी रोवत हम देखा ॥

Among the Baiga-riddles, tattoo-marks are described as "eggs laid by a black bird which can't pick up", "a black dog that casts no shadow", and "a Jacket that can never be taken off". These marks, said Phulmat of Elwin, "are the only things that are certain to go with us to the grave and beyond it". There is also a theory that the ornaments tattooed on the body can be sold after death. There is also no doubt that the tattooing greatly enhances a girl's beauty in the eyes of Baiga menfolk. "When she is well tattooed, then our sinful eyes declare her beautiful". Women like being tattooed, partly because they know it increases their attractiveness to their men, and partly because of its permanence. This, Elwin thought, is a quite genuine sentiment; one thing at least lasting in a world of changing husbands, changing settlements and shifting cultivation.

A *Dadariyā* declares:

If you buy bangles, my daughter
They will break in a few days;
But if you are tattooed;
It will last for ever.

on the whole, tattoos are permanent reminders of an impetuous moment—usually during the teenage or adoleocence.

2269 **पट्टिमुद्रा**

Paṭṭi-mudrā : gesture of a spear. Place the curved little finger on the thumb and extend the rest three fingers. It is *paṭṭi* (*VD*). It indicates the prescribed learning for each sect.

2270 **पणिस्सव**

Paṇissava : the clapper of hands, one who beats time (*Vidhura -paṇḍita-jātaka* -pp. 410-11).

2271 **पण्डक**

Paṇḍaka : a eunuch (*A*, 1.12.21), impotent.

2272 **पण्डित**

Paṇḍita : learned, clever (*Br. Ār. Up.*); scholar, teacher (MBh); an address form in modern India. Any Brāhmaṇa is commonly addressed by other castes as *mahārāj* (great king), or else as *paṇḍit* (a learned man). Even a *caparāsī* is addressed by the *mahārāj* or *paṇḍit* who is illiterate and low paid.

2273 **पण्णावणा**

Paṇṇāvaṇā : types of speech. The Jain text *Paṇṇāvaṇā* (Chapter XI) groups speech into four classes: true, false, mixed of true and false, neither true nor false (XI, *Sutta* 865, verse 196). The last is the ordinary communication. It occurs in twelve types: address (*āmaṁtaṇī*), order (*āpavaṇī*), request (*jāyaṇī*), question (*pucchāṇī*), announcement (*paṇṇavaṇī*), refusal (*paccakkhāṇī*), agreement (*icchā-nulomā*), non-understanding (*anabhiggahiyā*), understanding (*bodhavyā*), doubt (*saṁsaya-karaṇī*), clear (*voyaḍā*) and unclear (*avvoyaḍā*).

Āmantraṇa means terms of address. It is used to refer to, or to name a person directly in speech or writing. It includes titles, kingship terms, endearments and insults as well as first name, surname, and title and last name. Choice of forms, which clearly vary in degree of formality, is dependent upon the speaker's relationship with, and attitude towards, the audience, and the kind of situation in which the interchange takes place. In modern sociolinguistics it is argued that two main relations governing choice are power of status; and solidarity or social intimacy (Wales, New York, 1989.9).

2274 **पताक-कपित्थ-हस्त**

Patāka-kapittha-hasta : single hand-gesture.

2275 **पताकहस्त**

Patāka-hasta : single hand gesture, 'flag-hands', known as *tripatāka* in *Hastalakṣaṇa-dīpikā*; also known as *abhaya hasta* and *varada mudrā* in Indian iconography. The middle finger and the forefinger being placed near the chin (*NS*, XXV.

81b-82b). Widely used in Sanskrit dramas. The open palm is held facing upwards, the four fingers and thumb held all close together. It is used at the beginning of a dance, and to denote clouds, a forest, things, bosom, might, peace, a river, heaven, prowess, moonlight, strength, sunlight, wave, entry, silence, an oath, the sea, sword and a palm leaf. In it the thumb is bent, touches the root of the forefinger; the palm and fingers are outstretched and the fingers are pressed against one another. Fingers of a hand are raised up closely and the thumb is bent. It is used to thrash, to express joy, to show pride of "I am here" when placed on the forehead; but if fingers are closely joined and quivering, it indicates flames of fire, torrents of the rainfall, scattering flowers from the heaven. This is also suggestive of separating the *svastika* gesture, offering flowers foliage. grass and to indicate things scattered on the ground. Then again breaking the *svastika* position of the *patāka*-hand and pointing it out downwards, whatsoever are hidden, opened, worth obeying, covered and closed confidentially, are indicated. With the help of the fingers of the *patāka*-gesture, made downwards, expanded, upturned and moving; waves of the wind, the tide, the rolling of waves on the shore and the obedient servants are to be indicated.

By the curve (*recaka*) style of the *patāka*-hand, one may exhibit the idea of encouragement, many men, a great crowd, height, beating of drums and flying birds above. The rubbing gesture of the *patāka*-sign indicates: washing, rubbing, fasting, etc. This also enacts the idea of holding and uprooting a hill, or a heavy thing. This gesture further suggests a dual enactment of a man and woman (*NS*, IX. 18-26).

Variants of this gesture are *tripatākā-hasta* and *ardha-patākā-hasta*. The former signifies crown, tree, dart, fish, mirror dismissal and lighting of face, while the latter suggests banner, tower, a pair of persons, sprout and lamp.

2276 **पताका**

Patākā : flag, banner. It signifies success, victory and prosperity. According to *Prāsāda-maṇḍana* (4.48), a temple should not be without a banner, for the demons would reside in such temples: *asurāvāsam icchanti, dhvajahīnam na kārayet*. When the flag rises up high, the gods are pleased *dhvajocchrāyena tuṣyanti devāḥ*. A banner of flag eliminates the signs of the devotees (*pāpahārī*) and destroys the enemies (*Śatru-pakṣa-kṣayaṅkarī*).

The flag-post must not be bent (*vakra*), broken (*bhinna*) or have crevices (*suṣira*); it must be free from insects and worms (*Kāraṇāgama*, 141.42). It is best if the flag-post is made of bamboo (*vaṁśamayastu kārayet*); or wood that is free from disease and infirmity and untouched by fire (*Aparājita-Paripṛcchā*, 144.21). The wood for the flag must be perfectly round (*su-vṛtta*) and healthy; if it is bamboo must have an odd number of knots (*parvabhir viṣamaiḥ kāryaḥ*, *Prāsāda-Maṇḍana*, 4.44; *Dīpārṇava* 9.17).

The length of the banner must be equal to the length of flag-post (*dhvaja-daṇḍa*); its width must be one-eighth of the flag-post height. The bottom portion of the flag-post is said to be Śiva, and the top Viṣṇu.

2277 **पताकादि**

Patākādi : 64 hands-gesture in iconography.

2278 **पताका मुद्रा**

Patākā mudrā : gesture of a banner. From the clenched left fist make the forefinger up-stretched and the right-hand curved and moved with loosely set fingers, it is the auspicious gesture, called the *patākā*. It indicates a mundane being an ethereal one and a residence. It assures great fortune, gives power to fly in the sky and makes a devout all-knowing one (*BT*).

2279 **पताका स्थानक**

Patākā sthānaka : episode indication. An equivocal speech or situation in a drama, which foreshadows an event whether near at hand or distant. The element of dramatic irony was supplied through the four *patākā-sthānas*. When some matter is already taken in hand and another matter of similar nature is suggested through an accidental idea, it is known as *patāka-sthāna* due to its nature of indication like that of *patāka*, *i.e.* banner.

2280 **पति**

Pati : God or the Supreme soul (Tāntric concept). *Pati* means one who protects or controls *paśu* by a five-fold activity: creation, preservation, destruction, dispensation and emancipation. *Pati* is one of the three entities of most forms of Śaivism; the others are *pāśa* (fetters), *paśu* (jīva or soul, the (individual). (b) lord, ruler, husband. The husband is the holiest for a woman. The virtue that accrues after the performance of many sacrifices is obtained by a woman by serving her husband (*Padma Purāṇa, bhūmi*, 41.15):

सर्वतीर्थसमो भर्ता सर्वधर्ममयः पतिः ।
मखानां यजनात्पुण्यं यद्वै भवति दीक्षिते ॥
तत्पुण्यं समवाप्नोति भर्तुश्चैव हि साम्प्रतम् ॥

Bath with the water touched by the foot of the husband is equal to that at Prayāga or other holy place (*Ibid.*, 10-13):

सव्यपादं स्वभर्तुश्च प्रयागं विद्धि सत्तम ।
वामं च पुष्करं तस्य या नारी परिकल्पयेत् ॥
तस्य पादोदकस्नानात् तत्पुण्यं परिजायते ।
प्रयागपुष्करसमं स्नानं स्त्रीणां न संशयः ॥

In the conjugal life, the wife had full right to expect attention from her husband. In her 'period' she was entitled to have sexual intercourse, leaving the first four days. At other times, the husband was ordained to approach her only if she desired (*Skanda*, II.4.5.31). About the behaviour of a woman to her husband an important detail is that she is advised to drink the water touched by the feet of her husband. She is also ordained to taken the food that remains after her husband has partaken (*Brahmavaivarta*, 57.20-21). It is recorded that Pārvatī did drink the water touched by the feet of Śiva (*Ibid*., 39.34).

The husbands used to decorate their wives in various ways. Kṛṣṇa adorned Rādhā as follows (*Brahmavaivarta*, *Śrīkṛṣṇa*, 53.17-24). He combed and fashioned her hair and arranged it into *Kabarī* (a braid). He placed over it a wrath of Jasmine and *mādhavī*. He arranged a *tilaka* mark of *sindūra* below the bright sandal mark, along with a dot of musk. On her cheeks, he drew beautiful lines (*patrakam*) and applied collyrium to her eyes. He applied lip-dye (*adhara-rāga*) as per the wish of Rādhā, and placed the ear-ornaments. He tied jewel-studded anklets round her feet, applied the lac-dye to the toe-nails and arranged a cloak, to which was applied saffron and musk. In the love-sport Kṛṣṇa is said to have adorned Rādhā's breasts with the paste of sandal, musk and saffron, arranged *patrikā*-designs on her breasts and imprinted signs of lotuses on her thighs and breasts.

2281 **पतित-भ्रू**

Patita-bhrū : falling eyebrows.

2282 **पत्र**

Patra : written debate. The peak of the aggressive debate (see *sambhāṣā*) that how to achieve effect and victory can also be seen in Jain philosophy when they introduced written debate. They decided the written style for it, called as *patra* or letter. According to them, the word *patra* can be defined etymologically as: *padāni trāyante gopyante rakṣyante parebhyaḥ svayaṁ vijigīṣuṇā yasmin vākye tat...patram* (*Prameya-Kamala-Mārtaṇḍa*, p. 685) or such sentence is called *patra*, in which the inflected words (*padas*) are hided by a disputant (desirous of victory) from his opponent. The hiding of inflected words mean the hiding of its radical (*prakṛti*) and suffix (*pratyaya*) etc. (*Ibid*., p. 658). Such *patra*-writing, so far, has not been seen in the available texts of other systems of Indian philosophy. The above *patra* used to contain the following form: *pratijñā*, *hetu*, *udāharaṇa*, *upanaga* and *nigamana*. Thus, *patra* had all the five members of syllogism.

In modern days debates, especially the aggressive debates, are hardly seen. Although in India on rare occasions the aggressive debates are organised between two rival groups of same philosophical thought, the *patra*-writing is no more in practice. In the ancient days too it used to take place only between 9th to 11th centuries. Nevertheless, the friendly discussions which used to occur between teacher and pupils can still be seen and the *patra*-writing can also be seen in the form of modern examination system.

2283 **पत्र-पद्धति**

Patra-paddhati : mode of writing a letter. Vararuci in his *Patra-kaumudī* has designed the method of letter-writing. In a letter, first of all, an *aṅkuśa* (a hook) mark, with the figure '7' below and a dot inside, should be drawn as an auspicious sign. This is to be followed by the word *svasti*. Next will be written "*Śrī* " to precede the mode of address appropriate to the person written to. In the next place, one should enquire about the welfare (*kuśala*) of the addressee in Sanskrit. Then the message should be written in Sanskrit and Prākṛt. In the space below will be written a verse proclaiming the fame of, and causing delight to, the addressee. The next thing to be written is expressions like *kimadhikam* (what more) etc. In conclusion, a verse dealing with the dispatch of the letter and containing the date, month etc. should be written. From the top of the letter-paper, a space, measuring six fingers, should be left out. Below this space, a circular mark of *kasturī* (musk) and *kuṅkum* (saffron), resembling the moon's orb, should be put on a royal despatch. The mark should be of saffron alone for ministers, sandal for learned men, preceptor, father, son and anchorities, of vermilion for husbands, lac-dye for wives, red sandal-paste for servants and of blood for enemies.

2284 **पत्रभङ्गी**

Patrabhaṅgī : beautiful lines; drawing lines or figures on the forehead, cheeks, neck and breast with fragrant pigment of sandal, saffron, and musk etc, also known as *patrakam*. Kṛṣṇa used to draw beautiful lines (*patrakam*) on the cheeks of Rādhā (*Brahmavaivarta*, Śrīkṛṣṇa, 53.17-24).

2285 **पत्ररचना**

Patra-racanā : painting of leaves. South Indian women beautify their bodies especially bosom and cheeks with *patrāracanā*. They mix up different kinds of spicy articles and colours and use it to paint varied designs like the leaves and others. It is a kind of painting lasting for one day. Every day they decorate themselves with it. The term *makarikā-dīpta-racanā* is very common in Sanskrit literature (*Sarasakavi-Kulānanda bhāṇa*, p. 451) meaning the 'painting in the shape of leaves and that of small crocodiles. Various other shapes are also painted by ladies. This type of decoration has been in vogue since ancient times and is employed by ladies to attract their lovers. Nowadays also it is prevalent in South India. The *kucīpuḍī* dancers decorate themselves with this at the time of dance performance. Their skill in painting such designs is well brought out. Courtesans too decorate themselves with this sort of painting (*Ibid.*, p. 22). Often lovers enjoy with the pastime of mutually painting themselves with these designs.

2286 **पत्रलेखा**

Patralekhā : drawing lines or figures on the face of a person with fragrant pigments consisting of sandal, saffron, musk etc.

2287 **पत्रसूत्रम्**

Patrasūtram : chain-letters. Chain-letters are still current in many parts of India. Unsolicited and unknown origin as a rule, one of these bearing usually a religious (or occasionally, a religio-political) message would reach an addressee by post with the command that he should, on pain of dire consequences, make a stated number of copies of the text and send each of these to a friend or relative. The 'chain' in the case of this curious and as Majumdar (*The Sepoy Mutiny and the Revolt of 1857*, Calcutta, 1957:209) says, powerful device operates in just the same way as the *chapātis* did on the eve of the Mutiny, that is, by geometrical progression. But there are the similarity ends. The graphic character of the 'chain letter' keeps its meaning firmly tied to the text; in fact, the addressee is specially warned by his anonymous correspondent not to alter the message in the least, which is precisely what makes it the very reverse of the omen. The vague and indefinite character of the message carried by the latter keep it wide open to various degrees of semantic modification at each point of its passage between communicators.

2288 **पत्राङ्गुलि**

Patrāṅguli : drawing lines or figures with fingers on neck, throat etc. with coloured sandal, saffron and musk etc.

2289 **पत्रावलि**

Patrāvali : lines of painting made on the body to beautify it.

2290 **पथ्यनुसरण**

Pathyanusaraṇa : a wife going away with another man (*A*, 2.16, 24; 4.5.16, 7.17.59).

2291 **पद**

Pada : foot step, mark, sign, place, position. In the movements of the legs and feet, there are those of the feet planted on the ground, and the feet raised above and involving an aerial movement (*cārī*), stances (*sthānaka*) and actions of the legs (*maṇḍala*) and ways of walking on the stage (*gati*). The *VD* (III. 1.65) devises six styles of feet as *udghāṭita*, *sama*, *recita*, *añcita* and *kuñcita*. The *NS* adds one more, the *agratalasañcara*.

(b) word. *pada* or word is regarded as one of the six paths leading to the realisation of the Supreme Being according to the *Tantras*. In Vaiṣṇavism the *pada* stands for the steps of Viṣṇu. In *Tantra pada* or *padādhva* refers to words which are regarded as the body of *mantra* (*Śāradātilaka*, V.91).

2292 **पदक्रमाध्यायिन्**

Padakramādhyāyin : one reading by dividing *pada* and *krama*.

2293 **पदन्यास**

Padanyāsa : step, foot-prints.

2294 **पदपाठ**

Padapāṭha : the recension of *Vedic* stanzas with each word shown in its independent original position.

2295 **पदभञ्जिका**

Padabhañjikā : the commentary in which compounds are analysed.

2296 **पदवादिन्**

Padavādin : an empiricist who claims that the child is not born with special ability for language acquisition. *Padavādins* based the study of language on its analytical function. To the *padavādins*, the fundamental units of language are the distinctive sounds, the phonemes—*varṇas*. These sounds are combined into meaningful units, morphemes-*prakṛti* and *pratyaya*. Then we make *padas* (words) out of morphemes. Finally we make phrases and sentences out of words. Bhartṛhari on the other hand advocates the semantic unity of sentence.

2297 **पदविग्रह**

Padavigraha : separation of words.

2298 **पदवृत्ति**

Padavṛtti : hiatus between two words.

2299 **पदस्थितिप्रदर्शन**

Padasthiti-pradarśana : status displays. A status display is a demonstration of a level of dominance. In primitive conditions dominance is achieved by a show of brute force. In modern human societies physical strength has been replaced by other forms of dominance (such as money, intellect, costumes, dress, telephone, car, etc.)

The ranking of castes in rural India is nowhere more clearly seen than in the commensal rules of eating, drinking and smoking.

The positions of the members of the *pañcāyat* are most clearly marked when they sit as a judicial body. In the meeting pavilion the big men sit on mats clustered around the village headman, facing the public; in the school they sit on a bench, again facing the public. Litigants or the accused stand facing the *pañcāyat* members. The headman enjoins who will give testimony to speak truthfully, saying *pañca nārāyaṇa hari*, or very roughly, "where five men gather, god is present". If one man stands accused of a crime, he may be told to state his case touching the mat or bench upon which the *pañcāyat* sits. The implication of this gesture is that he speaks touching the seat of a god and might be stricken deed if lying. Such a gesture must be carried out in a reverential posture, slightly stooped, the upper part of the body covered by a cloth, the fingers of the left hand touching the right forearm and pointing towards the right hand. Such a posture is taken when making an offering to a Brāhmaṇa, receiving from a Brāhmaṇa the food (*prasād*) which has been offered to a deity, and in most transactions between the members of higher and lower castes.

It is derogatory for a high caste woman specially housewife to come out from her house or to talk to a man other than her kin groups, essentially a junior. She does never come before an outsider. A woman of upper caste should cover her head with *āñcal* before any elderly persons in her in-laws house. This shows a sense of respect.

2300 **पदानुशासन**

Padānuśāsana : science of words.

2301 **पदार्थ**

Padārtha : objects of knowledge or realities which according to Vaiśeṣika are of seven categories: *dravya* (substance), *guṇa* (quality), *karma* (action), *sāmānya* (generality), *viśeṣa* (particularity), *samavāya* (inherence) and *abhāva* (non-existence).

2302 **पदावग्रह**

Padāvagraha : dividing word for word.

2303 **पदघोष**

Padaghoṣa : sound of feet.

2304 **पद्म**

Padma : lotus. (a) it serves as emblem of deities belonging to different creeds. The blue lotus is designated by the word *utpala* or *nīlotpala*. In Tāntric terminology *padma* is the day lotus and *utpala* stands for night lotus. (b) *padma* also denotes lotus-seat of deities. (c) *padma bandha* is a decorative band. while *Padma-śilā* is a pendant of a ceiling. (d) The lotus appears most often in Sanskrit metaphors, and its connotations are somewhat ambiguous; the flower itself is usually likened to the face of a woman, and in Tāntric symbolism the lotus represents the *yoni* (the jewel is the lotus). Nevertheless, the stalk of the lotus appears in Śaiva *Purāṇas* in place of the *liṅga*, and the seed of Śiva which is placed upon a lotus leaf (the *yoni*) travels through its stalk (the *liṅga*). The latter aspect of the lotus symbolism is manifest in the symbolism of the tree of *Kāma*. (e) on the occasion of *phalasaptamī*-vow golden lotus is donated, the lotus being the symbol of sun-god (*Śiva*, 13.74-3-4).

2305 **पद्मकोश-हस्त**

Padmakoṣa-hasta : lotus-bud hand; upgoing hand-gesture (*NS*, IX. 79b-80a). In *Ratnāvalī* (Act I), Vāsavadattā holds her hands in the *padma-kośa* to show many flowers. In *Mālatīmādhavam* (V.21), Kapālakuṇḍalā worships the deity with *padmakośa*. We find examples of this gesture in *Buddha Carita* (IV. 2) and *Vikrama* (III). *Abhinayadarpaṇa* derives it from its own *Kaṭakāmukha* by raising the forefinger. The palm is hollowed and face outwards. The fore-finger is bent apart a little, and the thumb moved in towards the bent finger. It is used to express the idea of frisking about, fruit, mango flower, lotus bud, water-lily, bud, cluster of flowers, bell-shaped, brilliance, charm, coconut and blossoming of a bud. Thus, the gesture with all fingers including the thumb, separated and curved, having their tips raised and aloof is called the *padmakośa*. This gesture also indicates to show and take the breasts of women, to accept a piece of meat. If further indicates worshipping and food-offering to Gods; presenting fooding and clothing to departed souls, strewing flowers, etc. Moreover, joined with the wrist, the pair of hands, having quivering fingers, this gesture enacts blossoms.

2306 **पद्मबन्ध**

Padmabandha : artificial composition in which the words are arranged in the form of a lotus-flower.

2307 **पद्ममुकुल-हस्त**

Padmamukula-hasta : a type of both hands gesture mentioned in *Bālarāmabharata*.

2308 **पद्म-मुद्रा**

Padma-mudrā : the lotus-gesture. (a) "Make a skull-like pose with two hands, the right and the left; and curve two thumbs, this will make a *padma-mudrā*" *(Brahmayāmala-tantra)*. (b) "*Padma mudrā* is ordinarily to be made by this way with a little alternation. The previous gesture with the up-turned palm is *śūla* and with down-turned palms; it is a *padma*" (*Ibid*). (c) two symbols of "akāra" fixed together and touched with fingers symbolize the lotus (*VD*). (d) backs of both the hands should be so joined, that the little-finger and the fore-finger are to be joined together and the rest fingers are raised. This is a *padma*, the gem or divinity (*VD*). The *padma* indicates a spiritual seat with its eight petals indicating eight *aiśvaryas* (spiritual wealth) *i.e. aṇimā, laghimā, mahimā, prāpti, prākāmya, īśitva* and *vaśitva*; as explained in the *ṣaṭcakra* (six spiritual centres, or lotuses).

2309 **पद्मरेखा**

Padmarekhā : a figure on the palm of the hand indicating the acquisition of wealth.

2310 **पद्मासन**

Padmāsana : a type of yogāsana. Cross-legged meditation pose known as lotus-posture; Spread a blanket and sit on it with legs stretched in front of you. Then fold the right leg and place it on the left thigh. Similarly, fold the left leg and place it on the right thigh; adjust the heels in such a way that they almost meet in front of the pubic bones and each foot presses the portion of the abdomen adjacent to it. The position of the hands varies. Some find it convenient to keep them on their respective knees while others place the right palm over the left palm. Both the palms are upturned and cupped. While performing the *āsana*, the head and spine must be kept erect.

Padmāsana is an ideal *āsana* for meditation. Yogis maintain that the practice of meditation is facilitated by adopting positions in which the spine is held erect so that psychic energies may freely move. One can sit in this *āsana* for hours together. The erect position of the spine helps the nerve flow along spine and between vertebrae to be carried out uninterrupted. The erect spine also prevents the compression of the abdominal viscera and so frees the mind from the burden of the body. *Padmāsana* tones up the coccygeal and sacral nerves by sending extra supply of blood to those nerves. When a person sits in this posture for a long time, the lower portion of the body is compressed this interferes with the free circulation of blood and the coccygeal and sacral nerves get extra supply of the blood from abdominal aorta.

In short, *padmāsana* is a sitting posture for *yogis* in which the right foot should be placed on the left thigh and the left foot on the right thigh.

Padmāsana was a type of *brahmāsana* also. *Brahmāsana* was a posture of the body for profound meditation. It seems that *Brahmāsana* described in *Harṣacarita* (III) was a generic name applicable to any *āsana*—*dhyānayogāsane brahmāsanam* (*Amarakośa*). Some define it as *ekapādamurau datvā tiṣtheddaṇḍākṛtirbhavet.*

2311 **पद्मिनी (नायिका)**

Padminī (nāyikā) :the lotus-lady. That lady is lotus-lady, who is soft like lotus bud, whose mucus smells like a blossomed lotus, whose body contains divine fragrance, whose sides of eyes are red, whose beautiful breasts are attractive, whose secret part is like a blossoming lotus-bud, who walks softly and gracefully, who is slender, whose abdomen contains three fleshy folds, whose voice is like swan, who eats soft, clean and little food, who has self-respect, who is full of bashfulness and who likes white flowers and clothes (*Ratirahasya*, 1.11-13).

All the heroines in Sanskrit dramas or in poetry are mostly the Lotus-type of women. Kālidāsa depicts Pārvatī as a Lotus-lady by describing her feet as lotus (*Kumārasaṁbhava*, 1.33), her gait like that of royal swans (*Ibid*., 1.34), her thighs like plantain stalks (*Ibid*., 1.36), her sender waist as having three folds of skin (*Ibid*., 36), her yellowish white black-nippled breasts which have no space between them (*Ibid*., 40), her shoulders which are more delicate than *sirīśa* flower (*Ibid*., 41), her deep navel (*Ibid*., 1.38), her hair which are curly (*Ibid*., 8.45), her eyes which are long (*Ibid*., 8.56), and her face which is like lotus (Ibid., 8.43). Other women of Kālidāsa, such as Mālavikā (*Mālavikāgnimitram*, 2.3) and Yakṣiṇī (*Megha*, 84) are the Lotus-ladies. Sāgarikā and Damayantī have been treated like-wise. (b) Name of Lakṣmī carrying a lotus in her hand. As a woman she is distinguished by her eyes as lotus, small nostrils, tight breasts, slim figure, soft speech, and interest in music. (c) a lore called *Padminī* is mentioned in *Mārkaṇḍeya Purāṇa* (68.4).

2312 **पद्या**

Padyā : a foot-step, a foot-print (*A*, 2.210), road.

2313 **पन्नगी-मुद्रा**

Pannagī—mudrā : "Taking the right fore-finger with the left hand, when thumbs of the both hands are tied together". (*BT*). *Pannagī* is also called *Kandarpā*. She is *Vidyā-devī* and a snake goddess identified with *Manasā*.

2314 **परकीया**

Parakīyā : a female partner of the man other than his wife. The woman of the another man. *i.e.* an adulterous mistress, adultery.

2315 **परचित्तज्ञान**

Paracittajñāna : the power of reading the thoughts of others. It is mentioned as one of the *abhijñās* in the Buddhist texts.

2316 **परदेशी**

Paradeśī : others. the regional/tribal view of otherness was an element of territoriality in feudal India which was the main cause of the hool.

2317 **परमाणु**

Paramāṇu : atom, an indivisible base of all the aggregate bodies.

2318 **परमार्थ**

Paramārtha : ultimate significance, transcendental, absolute. Altruistic, altruism is the performance of an unselfish act. It is not merely a matter of being helpful, it is helpfulness at a cost to yourself. In particular it explains the phenomenon of dying for a cause, as in the mythical story of Dadhīci. There is some basic symbolism in each *paramārtha*. We tend to be more altruistic toward people that we like, and like people whom we perceive as altruistic. If people interact with each other on a regular basis, then the chance of receiving some benefit in return is fairly high.

2319 **परमिश्रा**

Paramiśrā : mixed with enemy: when one's allies join hands with one's enemies (*A*, 9.6.11,73; 7.14.28; 7.9.28).

2320 **परम्परा**

Paraṁparā : 'tradition, series' (*MBh.*), succession. *Paraṁpariṇa* 'one who has seen or experienced the succession., Abhinava Gupta (*Abhinava Bhāratī* VI, trans) has stressed the importance of tradition in the following lines.

> And what's new about telling a truth already
> Discovered, passed from mouth to mouth over
> The long haul of time? Nothing. Couldn't they
> Sue you—and win—if you said: 'I' ve said something new'?
>
> The mind is a great climber climbing higher
> To see what's really there, the thing itself.
> Why should it condescend to rest on ideas
> Which are more steps for spiralling up and up?
>
> I know-it's hard, hard and misty, those first
> Tries to see. Really to see. But this road
> Means trying again, again, till the archways loom clear
> The Bridges and buildings lift into lucid place.
>
> What was left behind by them, our father's fathers
> Isn't abandoned. It's carefully treated and saved.
> What was left behind, if carefully treated and saved,
> Is going to yield good things for those who will follow
>
> (Vātsyāyana and Mishra, 1983.173)

Tradition is a body of practices or social customs that has been handed down from previous generations.

2321 **परलोकविलोपवाद**

Paralokavilopavāda : the theory that there can be no such thing as the other world. One of the five basic principles of Cārvāka.

2322 **परलोकित-दृष्टि**

Paralokita-dṛṣṭi : a type of searching glance (*NS*, VIII. 109). Occurs in *Vikramorvaśīya* (Act. II).

2323 **परलोलित-शिरस्**

Paralolita śiras : a type of head gesture. The head moves on all sides; *viz. recita śiras.* It is used in fainting, intoxication and when one is possessed by a spirit (*NS*, VIII. 36-37, 86-87). In *Mālavikāgnimitra* (Act III), queen Irāvatī's state of intoxication is represented with this type of head-movement.

2324 **परशु-मुद्रा**

Paraśu-mudrā : the battle axe-gesture. "O Divine Lady, raise up your pair of hands and extend obliquely your body. In this position, when the pair of hands are exercised like a strike of an axe, it is called *Paraśu-mudrā* (a gesture of an axe). This removes bad omens of all good deeds" (*BT*). *Paraśu* is a weapon held in the hands of several male deities like Śiva and Gaṇeśa.

2325 **परशुराम-मुद्रा**

Paraśurāma-mudrā : gesture symbolizing God Paraśurāma of the Vaiṣṇavite cult. The *Kapittha*-hand represents Paraśurāma (*VD*). Paraśurāma is regarded as one of the *Vibhava*-manifestations of Viṣṇu, he is one among the principal *Vibhava*-forms assumed by Viṣṇu and one of the ten incarnations.

2326 **परशुराम-हस्त**

Paraśurāma hasta : frame the *ardhapatāka mudrā* and place it on the left waist. This represents Paraśurāma (*AD*, 211-215).

2327 **परसंश्रय**

Parasaṁśraya : protection. Somadeva (*Nītivākyāmṛta*) opines: *āyati kalyāṇe sati kasmiṁcit sambandhe parasaṁśrayaḥ śreyān* "Protection is to be sought only in case there be the prospects of an eventual good turning up in the future". That is, Somadeva does not advise the weak to seek protection of others under all circumstances. He must have to consider the pros and cons carefully and then when he decides upon seeking somebody's tutelage he has only to utilize it with a view to the long run effect. It is the conjecture of the circumstances that he has to study all the time.

2328 **परहस्त**

Parahasta : 'another's hand'.

2329 **परा**

Parā : form of sound or speech which corresponds the logos of the Bible. It is *Śabda-brāhmaṇ* (*brāhmaṇ* in the form of sound), *avyaktak* (unmanifested) *nāda* (q.v.) and can be experienced deep in sleep. (b) Distance.

2330 **परा-अपरा**

Parā-aparā : two divisions of art (kalā); *aparā* is bound with the five limiting powers and thus limited to the sphere of phenomenal and sensual world; *parā* is free from limiting powers and depicts metaphysical aesthetic relish.

(b) distance and proximity.

2331 **पराङ्मुखता**

Parāṁmukhatā : away from oneself, aversion. Though the Hill Marias are very hospitable and though they are extremely curious about the way of life and things used by the outsiders, they do not want that people should stay in their villages longer than is equally necessary. Though they welcome you heartily and serve you well, they all the time want in their hearts of hearts that you should go away as soon as possible and leave them alone. One can very clearly sense this and there is no case when they will ask you to stay on. Their send off is as hearty as the welcome. Also, much curiosity though they show about your things and your way of life, they do not want you to pry into their life, things and their ways. Because of the feeling of bitterness, wound and suspicion, the Hill Maria like many of his Indian brothers remains to confine to his dwelling.

Like all tribes and conservative Hindus of the region, the Korkus too observe certain rules and practical conventions which regulate social life in the family and eliminate the proximate occasions for prohibited familiarities: (a) Thus Korku women usually do not work together within men unless they are closely related. (b) They do not wander far away from their houses when alone; even for a call of nature they go in company or take at least a child along. (c) When a man goes to the house of his neighbour, he is supposed to go away immediately and not linger even for a short chat. If he were observed talking to the wife of an absent neighbour, he might be reported to the village council and warned by the elders or even fined. (d) In a joint-family certain rules of avoidance must be strictly followed (Fuchs, 1986: 167).

2332 **पराङ्मुख-हस्त**

Parāṁmukha hasta : away from one-self hand-gesture.

2333 **पराधि**

Parādhi : hunting. *Pāradhi* is also a name of the hunting tribe in Bastar.

2334 **पराभाषा**

Parābhāṣa ; also known as *parāvāk* : paralanguage. Nageśa (*Uddyota*, p.33) has defined *parāvāk* as follows:

svarūpajyotirevāntaḥ
parāvāganapāyinī /
tasyāṁ dṛṣtisvarūpāyā —
madhikāro nivartate //

Thus according to Nageśa, metalinguistic phenomena are the part of paralanguage. The relationship between language and paralanguage was nicely described by Trager (*Studies in Linguistics*, 1958, 3-4): "When language is used it takes place in the setting of an act of speech. Speech (talking) results from activities which create a background of voice set. This background involves the idiosyncratic, including the specific physiology of the speakers and the total physical setting; it is in the area of prelinguistics.... Against this background there takes place three kinds of events employing the vocal apparatus: language; variegated other noises, not having the structure of language vocalizations; and modifications of all the language and other noises. These modifications are the voice qualities. The vocalizations and voice qualities together are being called paralanguage".

The number of paralinguistic features may be listed as follows: vocal qualities of pitch, loudness, intensity, and amplitude, the speech disturbance categories of stutter, omission, repetition, filled pauses, and coherent sounds; such temporal dimensions as duration of utterance, reaction-time latency, and percentage of interruptions; measures of verbal productivity such as speech rate and verbal quantity (time spent in talking, number of words, number of clause units); silences as indexed by hesitations and unfilled pauses, and such conversational regulators as intonation changes, paralinguistic drawl, and drop in pitch or loudness.

Paralinguistic performances are particularly important in situations where communicators can be heard but not seen. In face-to-face situations, paralinguistic cues are likely to combine with facial, body, visual, and distance cues to create an impression.

Thus paralanguage is: NV voice qualities, modifiers and sounds produced or conditioned in the areas covered by the supra-glottal cavities (from the lips and the nares to the pharynx), the laryngeal cavity, and the infra-glottal cavities, down to the abdominal muscles, which consciously or unconsciously man uses supporting or contradicting the linguistic kinesic, or proxemic message mainly, either simultaneously or alternating with them.

The vocal aspects of speech other than words are called paralanguage. This includes loudness, speed of delivery, pitch, inflection, emphasis, breathiness, stretching or clipping of words, pauses, moaning, laughing, crying and so on. By using techniques of voice analysis we can eliminate higher frequencies from recorded speech. Although words become unintelligible, the paralanguage remains. People listening to these recordings can easily tell if the message conveys liking or disliking. Paralanguage is one of the main vehicles we use to express personality. A deep tone is perceived as a sign of confidence and sophistication. Women tend to be assessed on the basis of tone of voice for their sensitivity, enthusiasm and sense of humour. Studies have correlated breathiness with lack of self-assertion. Soft voices with little resonance have correlated with introversion.

Poyatos (1981: 112) has proposed the following taxonomy of paralanguage:

(a) *Primary Qualities* : timber, pitch level, pitch registers, pitch interval, intonation range, resonance, volume, syllable duration, overall tempo, and general rhythm of speech.

(b) *Modifiers : Qualifiers* : glottolic control, velar control, articulatory control, articulatory tension, pharyngeal control, laryngeal control labial control maxillary control, and respiratory control.

(c) *Modifiers: Differentiators* : forms and degrees of whispering, of loud voice, of crying, of laughing, etc., when they override words.

(d) *Alternants* : Consonantal (bilabial, labiodental, whistling, clicking, velar), vocalic (mainly glottolized voiced central vowel-like sounds, with up to five pitch levels and varying nasalization), inarticulated (pharyngeal, nasopharyngeal and narial frictions), and pausal (modified speech pauses with different meanings).

2335 **परामर्ष**

Parāmarṣa : deduction, ascertaining that the *pakṣa* or subject possesses the *hetu* which is concomitant with the *sādhya*; an inference made from formal premises or propositions.

2336 **परावाक्**

Parāvāk : contradiction, refutation, derogatory speech (AV, VI.13.2); *parāvākāya te namaḥ*; see *parābhāṣā*.

2337 **परा-विद्या**

Parāvidyā : transcendental knowledge, knowledge of *Brahman*; science leading to knowledge of Brahman; opp. to *aparā-vidyā*.

2338 **परावृत्त-ग्रीवा**

Parāvṛtta grīvā : turning back of the head (*Bālarāma-bharata*, pp.199-202),

2339 **परावृत्त-जङ्घा**

Parāvṛtta-jaṅghā : one leg is stretched backwards while the knee touches the ground. In any one of these positions one leg is bent forward at the hip-level and the other is stretched back. The knee of the stretched leg may touch the ground or both the knee and the lower leg may be in contact with the ground.

2340 **परावृत्त-शिरस्**

Parāvṛtta śiras : head turned backwards to indicate looking backwards; a type of head gesture, when the face is turned around backward turning back of the head (*NS*, VIII.27). In *Vikramorvaśīya* (Act I), bashful love-confusion is shown by *parāvṛtta* head. Śakuntalā's (*Śākuntalam*, I) aversion is depicted by an averting hand. This head-movement is used in turning away the face and looking back. Mālavikā in her anger (*Mālavikāgnimitram*, Act IV), turns away her face with *parivṛtta* movement of the head; movement of the head with the face turned round. It is used to look at a thing, turning round the face, looking back, etc.

It is a type of the Head Toss. The head is tilted sharply back and returns less sharply to the natural position. This is an inverted Head Nod, and is a special way of saying 'No'. Many signals work on the antithesis principle, and this is one of them. The principle states, quite simply, that if two signals mean the opposite of each other, then the actions are on which they are based will also be opposite in form and direction. For example, in a dominant posture, the body is held high, while in a submissive posture it crouches low. Similarly, if the Head Nod means YES, then one might expect the sign for 'No' to be the opposite of it. There are two ways of opposing the downward nodding movement— one is the sideways shaking action, the Head Shake, and the other is upward Head Toss.

Perhaps because it is less distinctive than the Head Shake, the Head Toss has a much more limited range.

2341 **परावृत्त-स्थानक**

Parāvṛtta sthānaka : a type of posture.

2342 **पराव्याध**

Parāvyādha : distance of a stone's throw.

2343 **परिकथा**

Parikathā : that *kathā* which is written to expound the beauties of a single *Puruṣārtha.*

2344 **परिकर्मन्**

Parikarman : 'perfuming the body after bathing' (*MBh.*) servant, assistant.

2345 **परिक्रमण**

Parikramaṇa : "walking around", one of the conventional acting techniques in which the actor suggests a journey from one locale to another, within the same scene, through a stylized walk around the stage.

2346 **परिग्रह**

Parigraha : acknowledgement of sentiments and feelings through the actions and functions of appropriate gesture (*NS*, IX. 175), cause of gestural creation.

2347 **परिचय**

Paricaya : acquaintance, habit: *idānīm paricayo mām viḍambayati* (*Cāru.* VIII), an activity that has become relatively automatic through prolonged practice, relatively consistent pattern of thought or attitudes, a characteristic form of behaviour; a trait; an acquired drive, such as *bhaṅga*-addiction.

2348 **परिचारिका**

Paricārikā : bed-room attendants (*śayyāpālī*), umbrella-bearers, fan-bearers, shampooers, mixers of perfumes, dressers (*prasādhikā*), or those who helped in putting on of ornaments or prepared garlands. All being female (NS, XXIV. 58-59).

2349 **परिचुम्बन**

Paricumbana : kissing passionately. In India, kissing is regarded as so intimate an activity that it is still very much restricted in public, and was not seen in Indian films until recent years-when it caused much controversy.

2350 **परिजल्पित**

Parijalpita : covert indication of his or her skill by a servant or the beloved or mistress:

Prabhor nirdayatāśāṭhya cāpalādyupapādanāt

Svavicakṣaṇatā vyaktir bhaṅgyā syāt parijalpitam (Ujjvalamaṇi).

2351 **परिणाम**

Pariṇāma : transformation, assuming new characteristics. For example, curd is the *pariṇāma* of milk. It is the *Sāṅkhya*-theory of *pariṇāmavāda.* According to this theory, when an effect is produced, there is a real transformation of the cause into effect. *Pariṇāma* is of two kinds: *svarūpa* (or change into homogenous) and *virūpa* (change into heterogenous). A figure of speech allied to *rūpaka* wherein the properties of any object are transferred to that with which it is compared *Pariṇāmaḥ kriyāthaścedviṣayī viṣayātmanā* prasannena dṛgābjena vīkṣate madirekṣaṇā (*Candrāloka*, V.18).

2352 **परिदेवना**

Paridevanā (*Nirukta*, VII. 3, *Bṛhaddevatā* 134-139, *NS*, 18.36): form of speech and thought; lamentation.

2353 **पारिधर्षण**

Paridharṣaṇa : lit. treatment, non-person. The most extreme historical example of *paridharṣaṇa* is to be found in erotic art (*mithuna-mūrti*) of India, which depicts couples blithely disregarding their servants as if they were non-persons. This depicts the bombard or assault in our sensory stimuli. It is possible that we may over-adopt western way of life and completely ignore anyone who is not relevant to our life.

2354 **परिधान**

Paridhāna : clothing signals. It is impossible to wear clothes without transmitting social signals. Every costume tells a story, often a very subtle one, about its wearer. Even those people who insist that they despise attention to clothing, and dress, as casually as possible, are making quite specific comments on their social roles and their attitudes towards the culture in which they live.

For the majority of people, clothing signals are the result of a single daily event—the act of dressing, performed each morning. At the top and bottom of the social scale this activity may lose its once-a-day frequency, with rich socialities changing several times daily as a matter of course, and poor vagrants sleeping rough in the same clothes they wear by day. Between these two extremes, the once-a-day-routine is usually only broken for the donning of specialized clothing. The man who gets dirty wears working clothes, the sportsman wears high-activity clothes. People attending special ceremonies change into the appropriate costumes. But although these pursuits mean the doubling of the once-a-day act of dressing, the change is nearly always from 'everyday' clothes into 'special' clothing. The old pattern, in which social rules demanded the changing from 'ordinary dress 'to 'dhoti' as a dining dress has now virtually vanished.

Basically, clothes have three functions: comfort, modesty and display. In India clothing was simply a matter of comfort and protection. Garments were also worn to switch off certain body signals. The 'full frontal' body might have created problems, so the 'loin-cloth' was culturally the most widespread of all garments. It is the last clothing barrier to fall on the tribal folk.

The human body is a mass of gender signals, and every curve of flesh, each bulge and contour, transmits its basic signals to the eyes of interested onlookers. The female breasts, the buttocks, the hips, the thighs, the waist, the slender neck, the rounded limbs, and the male chest, the body hair, the broad shoulders, the muscles of the arms and legs, all these visual elements are potentially arousing to the opposite sex. If their messages are to be reduced, then they too must be hidden by enveloping garments.

At different times and indifferent epoches, the social rules of modesty have varied, but the basic principle has remained the same. The more anti-sexual the demands of society, the more all-covering has been the clothing. Extreme examples are the heavily veiled females of Haryana, peering through the tiny slit in her heavy veil, such a female could be either a raging beauty or a hideous hag, and only her husband knows the truth, for she never appears in public, in any time in her life, in a more revealing costume. This is the case with the Muslim women in India.

In medieval India clothing and social status were intimately linked. Nowadays, people are trying to improve their status by the wearing of costumes typical of superiors. Now the legal rules are replaced by rules of etiquette.

In tribal societies clothing signals have certain connotations. The Hill Marias of Bastar are the least-clad people of India. Persons of both sexes have nothing on their bodies except a loin cloth. The children go naked up to the age of seven years. After this age the boys cover their private parts by a small piece of cloth suspended from a waist-cord and one end of which hangs as the square piece in front. When the girl is in this age, the mother ties a waist-cord and a smaller piece of cloth covers her private parts but no piece hangs in front. This cloth worn by small girls is known as *mudāng* and she wears this for the rest of her life below loin-cloth.

Objects of wear are still status markers. It was 'out of respect to the higher castes' that no woman of the Bharia caste of farm-servants and agricultural labourers in Madhya Pradesh would wear an upper garment. Gumperz (41) reports that in U.P shoemaker women have been prevented by Rajputs to wear clothes similar to those of Rajput women.

However, of all things worn on the person it is clothes which are the most semioticized. For the body 'is purely sensuous, is without significance' (Hegel, 1975:745), and it is clothing, writes Barthes (1967:261) following this Hegelin dictum, which 'ensures the passage from the sensuous to the meaningful: it is one could say, the signified par excellence'. Nowhere is this more explicit than in the countryside where the distinction between peasants and others—townsmen, officials, gentry, etc— is often perceived as one of dress in the first instance. "Dress is a fundamental element of distinction", said Gramschi (272) about Italy. Indeed, this was true of most societies, especially of those vegetating for long under colonial and semi-feudal condition. It is known, for instance, that dress was a means of publicity manifesting the status of the person in the urban India. In India, castes, classes and ethnic groups were often differentiated by the clothes their members wore and the manner of wearing them. The Bengali *bhadraloka* was utterly self-conscious about his dress, for no self-respecting person could go about his business in society wrapping himself up in a dirty knee-length *gamchā*, wrote the *Sādhanā* in a clear reference to typically lower-class garment (Anon. 1891:78).

In south India it was obligatory for a low-caste man to approach anyone of the upper castes or indeed for a servant his master by first stripping himself to the waist as a mark of respect (Logan, 127-8). In Gujarat, the so-called impure '*Mahārs* were not allowed to tuck up their loin-cloth but had to trail it along the ground' while in central India among the Kurmi the difference in length between the peasant's jacket, *banḍī* covering the trunk only up to the hips and the landlord's long coat, *angarkhā*, reaching down to the knees, was indicative of the difference in social standing (Russell and Hira Lal, IV: 91, 143). And among the tribes of Bastar of the phrase *dhotīmārā* referred not only to alien Hindu landlords, but also, any Indian wearing *dhotī*, which later on became contemptuous.

In rural India dress which discriminated so clearly between the elile and the subaltern as a matter of course, Sanyasis acquired an added significance in the eyes of both the parties in periods of serious confrontation between them. The Rangpur *dhing* of 1783, for instance, broke out at a time when widespread disturbances were not uncommon in that part of Bengal, thanks to gang robberies and incursions of *fakirs*, Sanyasīs and predatory soldiers of the East India Company's army. When, therefore, a large gathering was reported from Kedagaon and Magurrah, its character as a mass of rebel peasantry was identified, among other things, by the dress worn by the members of the crowd. "Each of these peasants has a stick or bamboo in his hand", reported an official witness, "their dress is like that of the ryots or villagers, they are neither *sepahis*, *fakirs* or night robbers" (Kaviraj : 37). In yet another historic struggle, that of the tenant cultivators of Pabna in 1873, the manner of dress was recognised by all concerned as an index of class divisions made explicit by antagonism over the rent question. The officer in charge of the subdivision most affected by the *vidroha* put it in unmistakable terms in a report to the higher authorities : "This class feeling was so universal that the opinion of any native on the agrarian question may be told to a certainty by looking at his dress. If he wore a light *chādar* on his shoulder, used shoes on his feet and carried an umbrella, one could make sure that he was a zamindar's man. If merely clad in the *dhoti* and *gamchā* he was at heart an unionist" (Saha, III. 108).

Dress had a place in the Santhāl hool, too, as an element of the idiom of that revolt. At the battle of Maheshpur, said Sido afer his capture, 'many of the Manjees were dressed in red clothes'. Neither he nor his brothers had taken to wearing red until then. It was indeed a signal turning things upside down. (Guha 1986).

There was a common knowledge when to wear a dress and when to avoid new cloth. In every caste a new cloth is put on specific days and after sprinkling a little *haldī* (turmeric) over it; this is considered to be auspicious.

2355 **परिधावन**

Paridhāvana : going round and round in combat.

2356 **परिपाटी**

Paripāṭī : method, usage, succession, order: *upāyaparipāṭīghaṭiṭa-pāśamukhī* (*Mudrā* VI.). (b) turn, arrangement.

2357 **परिभाषण**

Paribhāṣaṇa : conversation (*Kāmasūtra*, 5.3.31) One of the 64 *sandhyaṅgas* in dramaturgy. Bharata defines it as the talk full of censure (*NS*,19.99). According to Abhinavagupta it is disclosing of one's own faults. Dhanañjaya defines it as the mutual conversation in which one or more characters participate. Abhinavagupta and Dhanika illustrate it with the same example of *Ratnāvalī*. (b) a reproof, a reprimand (*A*, 2.5.19, 2.14.37)

2358 **परिभाषा**

Paribhāṣā : talking with one another, censure, technical term, any definition which is applicable throughout: *Ikadeśasthitā sāstrabhavane yāti dīpatām* ।
parito vyāpṛtām bhāṣam paribhāṣam pracakṣate ॥ (Nāgeśa on Pāt. II.1.1).

2359 **परिमाण**

Parimāṇa : a set of measurement, the measure of the girth or periphery of the body. The expression used in iconography is taken to mean simply measurement (*Bṛhat Saṁhitā*, 57.3), measurement of width (*Ibid*., 16). Height of the men. Varāhamihira (*BS*, LXVIII) records, 'The height of the best type of men is 108 digits in themselves, that of the medium type, 96 digits, and that of the inferior one, 84 digits'. Here the digit is not a standard measure, as it varies from person to person.

2360 **परिलुठन**

Pariluṭhana : rolling on the ground. In Tirupati and other religious centres some devotees are described to be rolling on the ground accompanying the chariot (on the occasion of some festival, in case of Tirupati, *Vaiśākha*-festival) led by a procession: अं खलु खरतरमपि आतपं अविगणय्य धरातले परिलुठन् रथं अनुसरति (Rasodara-*bhāṇa*, p.12). This act of rolling was done all over India in order to fulfil their oath taken in the past. For the fulfilment of their cherished desire they take different oaths, one of them being rolling on the ground. Some do this such that they may be blessed by good fortunes.

2361 **परिलोलित-शिरस्**

Parilolita śiras : the head is moved to all directions. It indicates sickness, drowsiness, haunted by evil spirits, confusion, giddiness, etc.

2362 **परिवर्त्तनी-मुद्रा**

Parivarttanī-mudrā : revolving gesture. "Both the forelegs should be joined together. The waist (*kaṭimārga*) and the back of the body should also be affixed with the stomach by the way of making a triple circle with a cyclic movement. Then by offering a salutation with eight limbs they are to be brought in a very close contact with an opposite direction" (*BT*).

2363 **परिवर्तित-ग्रीवा**

Parivartita-grīvā : inverted neck, a circular half-moon movement of the neck (*Abhinayadarpaṇa*, 79-87); not mentioned in *NS*. *Parivartita* is another style of the neck. It is used to move the neck from right to left, like a half-moon. It is also used to dance, suggesting amorous love and to kiss on both the cheeks.

2364 **परिवर्तित-जङ्घा**

Parivartita-jaṅghā : inverted thigh; turned back position of *jaṅghā*. This position is attained when the thigh is stretched backwards and the leg is bent at a right angle. The *SR* (VII. 265) defines this as a movement of one who moves along a curved path.

2365 **परिवर्तित-शिरस्**

Parivartita śiras : inverted head, the movement of the head in a circular half-moon movement.

2366 **परिवर्तित-हस्त-करण**

Parivartita-hasta-karaṇa : a type of movement. The external contra-round up; when fingers beginning from the little one are rounded up one after another from the out-side, it is called the *parivartita karaṇa* of hands (*NS*, IX. 198-204). It means that the fingers, beginning with the little finger and ending with the forefinger open outwards.

2367 **परिवाहित-शिरस्**

Parivāhita śiras : the sideways movement of the head, a side to side movement is actually a neck movement (*NS*, VII. 28). See *paralolita*; the head turns alternately on both the sides and it is used to demonstrate a thing; joyful memory, thinking, intolerance, surprise and sportive play, etc. It is a type of the Head sway. The head tilts rhythmically from side to side, describing an arc as if it were an inverted pendulum. To modern Indians, this action would mean "may be yes, may be no", with the head mimicking the alternating actions of going, 'this way or that way'. In Bengal, this rocking movement of the head is reputed to be a replacement for the more familiar Head Nod. Here it is said to mean yes, rather than may be and the movement is sufficiently similar to the more common head shake to cause some confusion.

2368 **परिवृत्त-करण**

Parivṛtta karaṇa : derives its name from the *parivṛtta* movement of the *trika*. One foot in *sūcī* and the movement of the *baddhā cārī* is performed. The movement of the head is described in *ūrdhvāpaveṣṭita nṛtta hasta* (*NS*, IV. 13b-133a, 236-238, X. 262b-263a). The hands are raised up in *apveṣṭita* and with the foot in *sūcī trika* is turned round.

2369 **परिवृत्त -जङ्घा**

Parivṛtta-jaṅghā : crosswise movement of shanks, turning the shank in an opposite direction. In this gesture shanks are turned in opposite direction and raised up, indicating use of such movement in *Tāṇḍava* and group dance (*NS*, X. 33-40). It is also used in class dance and the like.

2370 **परिवृत्त-संस्थान**

Parivṛtta saṁstnāna : the revolving position. The pose would suggest a con raction or a revolving position of a feature, drawn in style either standing, or looking-up, or front-facing (suggesting a revolving mood). In both the portions—the upper and lower parts of the figure, appropriate to the play of light and shade should find due touch. The figure would ordinarily come to sight by parts and it may represent sometimes a r istic and gross look. The middle-part of it, particularly g fted with charming look and necessary diminution, should take prominent position with a crafty curve of colours and brushes (*VD*. 3.39.26-29).

2371 **परिसंख्या**

Parisaṁkhyā : restriction relating to a part when the whole may be applicable. For example, when all five-toed animals may appear to be edible, the injunction permitting the eating of five species of five-toed animals only—*pañca pañcanakhā bhakṣyāḥ* is *parisaṁkhyā*.

2372 **परिस्वज**

Parisvaja : embracing from all sides, closely embracing (*AV*, VI. 75.3).

2373 **परिहस्त**

Parihasta : hand-amulet for birth of a son=put round the hand: *parihasta vidhāraya yonim* (*AV*. VI. 81.2).

2374 **परिहार**

Parihāra : avoidance, shunning. One way to protect the self is to stay clear of situations that are the most likely to threaten our self concept. We all, at times, feel the urge to avoid source of unpleasant information about ourselves saying *sāntam pāpam*. Many people walk the long way home to avoid the prospect of meeting a person who acts in a belittling manner toward them.

Avoidance operates even where social contact cannot be prevented. Avoidance ranks among the most common of all defensive tactics. It is the source of least resistance. Continuous avoidance involves retreat, which in turn prevents us from being touched by the experiences of others.

2375 **परिहास**

Parihāsa : amorous jesting, ridiculing, mirth; see *narmakeli*.

2376 **परिहास - सम्बन्ध**

Parihāsa-saṁbandhah : joking relationship. Privileged familiarity is permitted and encouraged between certain relations. These relations are between whom marriage is also possible. The *devar-bhābhi* relationship is such an example which is all pervading in the Indian—social, tribal and non-tribal both.

The Hill Maria society permits joking relationship between the wife of elder brother and the younger brother or between the elder sister's younger sister and the husband of the elder sister (*Sālī-Jījā*). It is also prevalent in other tribal and non-tribal societies. Joking relationship also exists between a man and his daughter's daughter and between a women and her son's daughter like the Bengālī society.

Because of the system of cross-cousin marriage, a boy has special licence to joke and flirt with his mother's brother's daughter or his father's sister's daughter (both referred to as *mandāṛi* in the Hill Maria. A girl can be equally free with her father's sister's son or her mother's brother's son (both referred to as *marrio*). This freedom, however, only lasts so long as they are not engaged themselves in which case they begin avoiding each other. However, if the girl standing in the aforementioned relationship is engaged elsewhere or she is already married, the joking relationship persists.

The place where the joking and fun most commoly occurs is at the *kaqsār* festival and at a marriage. There can be no restriction in a house of marriage. Everywhere in India, it is a common joking region. Both these occasions are the occasions when the boys and girls of different villages and different clans assemble together. Everyone feels free to fool about. No one is going to be offended. Everyone is slightly drunk.

2377 **परिह्वाल**

Parihvāla : gentle speech (KŚS, VII. 5.6); stammering, faltering (*Ś.Br.* III. 2.3.27) *tad yat prihvālam vācam vadati.*

2378 **परीप्सा**

Parīpsā : hate; accentuated (Pāṇini: *Aṣṭādhyāyī*, 4.1.42) rule of accent, paralanguage. *Parīpsā* is a strongly aversive attitude involving anger, ill-will, and the desire to inflict injury on the object of hatred. *Contr.* to *īpsā* (love).

2379 **परेक्ष**

Parekṣa : to stand and look *parekṣate tatraiva tiṣṭhannīkṣate.*

2380 **परुषा वृत्ति**

Paruṣā-vṛtti : the diction characterized by consonants suggestive of floridity (*Kāvyaprakāśa*, IX. 80).

2381 **परोक्ष**

Parokṣa : beyond the range of sight. Cp. *parokṣe liṭ* (Pāṇini, III. 2.215).

2382 **परोन्मेष-जिज्ञाषा**

Paronmeṣa-Jiñjāṣā : eagerness to excell other's poetic faculty.

2383 **परोपकार**

Paropakāra : helping others; one who wishes for universal love or popularity should help others. Varāhamihira (LXXV) thinks that the whole world renders help to a man who is ever engaged in helping the people. The fame that is won by helping enemies in their distress cannot be acquired by a small measure of religious merit:

सर्वोपकारानुगतस्य लोक सर्वोपकारानुगतो नरस्य ।
कृत्वोपकारं द्विषतां विपत्सु या कीर्त्तिरल्पेन नसा शुभेन

This reminds us of Vyāsa's dictum:

श्लोकार्धेन प्रवक्ष्यामि नतु ग्रन्थकोटिभिः ।
परोपकारः पुण्याय पापाय परपीडनम् ॥

2384 **परोपजाप**

Paropajāpa : the act of rousing others to rebellion.

2385 **पर्यङ्क**

Paryaṅka : The word means a cot or a wide stool, and also a posture of sitting (*āsana*). The posture is also called *vīrāsana*, where the right foot rests upon the left thigh and right thigh upon the left foot, so that the upper part of the body is held erect (*sthira-pūrva-kāyam*). Many deities, especially the male ones, are shown in this posture. The important illustration is the cot upon which the goddess Lalitā sits. (b) Cloth worn round the waist.

2386 **पर्यस्त -मुद्रा**

Paryasta-mudrā : thrown round gesture. Make the hand oblique, curve all the fingers and cover the thumb with the middle one. This indicates the gesture of *paryasta* (*VD.*).

2387 **पर्यस्तिका**

Paryastikā : 'sitting on the hams' *Suśr.*

2388 **पर्यायवाचक**

Paryāya-vācaka : synonym.

2389 **पर्युक्षण**

Paryukṣaṇa : dropping of holy water on the head of the bride during marriage ceremany (*Śiva*, II.46.55), sprinkling around water muttering a *mantra*.

2390 **पर्युदास**

Paryudāsa : proviso or exception, prohibitive rule, a kind of restriction. In it stress is laid on what should be done rather than on what should not be done. For example, *abrāhmaṇam ānaya.* Here, the stress is on who should be brought and not on who should not be brought. So, the negative particle in *abrāhmaṇam* is in sense of *paryudāsa.* When a particular rule is given in negative, it is *paryudāsa.* To take another example, *Yāj* (1.132) provides that one should not say anything to a man or woman that would be painful. This does not altogether prohibit speaking of what is painful.

The famous prohibitive rule, "*nekdṛṣed ud yāntam ādityam, na astam yāntam* (one should not see the sun rising and setting), as it occurs in the text, does not seem to have any idea of sin attached to it, or of any danger to *snātaka*. Further, it has been taken as a case of *paryudāsa*, as noted in *pratiṣedha* (q.v.), stating that the idea is not prohibition, but of some definite resolve (*saṅkalpa*), which is positive.

2391 **पर्युपास्ति**

Paryupāsti : courtesy, politeness: *paryupāstiranunayaḥ* (*DR*. 1.61). The following Santhāl-folksong is an example of Indian way of politeness:

Din doy calvena belay hasurena.
Strangers are coming.
Strangers have arrived.
Bring the cot and bring the pirhā.

Proceed with potful of water and an oil-pet keeping on a metal. Wash their feet and smear with oil O girl?

Bring the cot and *Māci* for their seat. We shall please the strangers.

Nawa pera debon manot

2392 **पर्येषण**

Paryeṣaṇa : investigation, examination (*A*, 7.6.19).

2393 **पल**

Pala : a measure of time = 1/60 part of a *daṇḍa* (q.v.).

2394 **पलल - गन्धि - रतसलिला**

Palala-gandhi-rata-salilā : lady whose mucus has the smell of meat, quality of the mare-lady (*Nāgara-sarvasva*, 14.6).

2395 **पल्लव**

Pallava : twigs and leaves considered to be auspicious: *āmra, aśvattha, vaṭa, plakṣa*, and *udumbara*. These are also called *pañcabhaṅga*.

2396 **पल्लव - हस्त**

Pallava-hasta : single hand-gesture.

2397 **पल्लव - नृत्तहस्त**

Pallava-nṛtta-hasta : the foliage. a type of hand gesture in dancing (*NS*, IV. 46). When the two *patāka*-hands are joined by the wrist, it is called the *pallava*.

2398 **पल्लीहस्त**

Pallīhasta : if in the style of the *mayūra*, the middle finger is placed on the back of the forefinger, it is called the *pallīhasta*. This gesture indicates also a *pallī*. The word *pallī* implies so many senses; as a village, particularly of the cowherd community, composed of so many huts, cottages and a kind of small creature (*Abhinayadarpaṇa*, Verses 170-171). *Pallī* is the small village.

2399 **पवित्र**

Pavitra : loop or ring, made of *darbha grass*; to be worn on ring fingers in religious rites. (b)*Pavitraka* was a sacred cord placed on idols. The cord was cut and fashioned by a brāhmaṇa woman. The length of such a cord may be up to the knees, thighs or the navel (*Garuḍa*,. II.24.13).

2400 **पशु**

Paśu : fettered individual. To this category belong men, animals and even gods (*Pāśu-patasūtra*, 1.1;V.7). In *Tantra*, *paśu* is divided into two classes: *sabhāva* (when influenced by knowledge) and *vibhāva* (when knowledge leaves a mark on it). *Kaulāvalīnirṇaya* (XI. 187) records this classification. It is also divided into *adīkṣite* (uninitiated) categories (*Niruttara*, XII).

2401 **पशुपाशक**

Paśupāśaka : a mode of coitus.

2402 **पशुबन्ध**

Paśubandha : immolation of an animal in sacrifice. Six priests are required to perform the sacrifice. The procedure is as follows: (a) selecting a tree and making a *yūpa* (sacrificial post) and a *caṣāla* (head piece) for the post; (b) preparing a *vedī* (altar) and a raised platform on it (*uttaravedī*) and a square hole thereon called *nābhi*; (c) invocation of Indra, Agni, Sūrya or Prajāpati; (d) by employment of eleven *prayāja* offerings and verses from *āpri* hymns; (e) animal is to be bathed and touched with *kuśa* blade and *plakṣa* branch; (f) its right foreleg and right horn is to be bound with a girdle of two strands; (g) Hotṛ's recital; (h) killing of the victim; (i) limbs are cut off for *puroḍaśa* and cooked in *ukhā*; (j) its omentum is offered in the *āhavanīya*. (*Baud*, *Sr.* IV).

2403 **पशु - भाव**

Paśu-bhāva : the ordinary human state. (*Rudrayāmala*, VI. 50-51).

2404 **पशुमानभङ्ग**

Paśumānabhaṅga : animal insults. Animal signals are often used as insults. Almost any animal will do, so long as it has a bad reputation and is generally considered to be stupid, clumsy, hostile, lazy, dirty, or in some way laughable or unpleasant. If an animal has become a symbol of stupidity, like the donkey, then making 'donkey-ears' becomes insulting. Perhaps the most popular and widespread animal sign is the 'cock's-comb' gesture called 'cocking a snook', 'thumbing a nose', or 'making a long nose'.

2405 **पशुयोनिमैथुन**

Paśuyonimaithuna : sexual act with the beasts, a type of abnormal sexual act (*Skanda Purāṇa*, 1.2.41.57). It is also known as *prakīrṇa maithuna* and causes impotence according to *Brahma Purāṇa* (225. 51-52).

2406 **पश्चिम - आम्नाय**

Paścima āmnāya :The western Tāntric zone.

2407 **पश्चिमोत्तानासन**

Paścimottānāsana : Sit on the ground with the legs stretched out. Bend the trunk forward and catch the toes with the index finger. There should be no jerk while bending and do not use any force. After a few day's practice it should be possible to touch the knees with your forehead. Retain the breath till you take the fore head back to its original position. Breathe in when you have come to the original position.

This *āsana* is excellent, since it stimulates the gastric fire. It reduces fat in the abdomen and is specific for corpulence, enlargement of spleen and lever. It stimulates the kidneys, liver, pancreas, etc. and increases the peristalsis of the intestines. It relieves constipation, removes sluggishness of liver, as well as dyspepsia and gastritis. Lumbago and all sorts of myalgia and other diseases of the back muscles are cured. This *āsana* also cures piles and diabetes.

2408 **पश्यतोहर**

Paśyatohara : stealing before one's eye, thief.

2409 **पश्यन्ती**

Paśyantī : one of the constituents of sound regarded as the second stage of its development. This form of the sound belong to the region around the navel. It has little vibration and is connected with *nādatattva* (*Prapañcaśāstra*, II. 43). Speech to be felt by mind alone. (b) Visible speech. From the point of view of the sender, this element is physical activity—the use of body to convey meanings. From the point of view of receiver, it is visible stimuli. These cues are taken in through the eyes of the receiver. How the receiver sends or sits (posture or stahce), what gestures are used, the expressions of the face—the entire body really transmits impressions (messages) to the receiver.

2410 **पाकशाला**

Pākaśālā : kitchen.

2411 **पाङ्क्तेय**

Pāṅkteya : fit to sit in the same row in dinner.

2412 **पाञ्चाली-प्रवृत्ति**

Pāñcālī-pravṛtti : northern local usage. The people in Northern India like Pāñcāla, Śauraśena, Kāśmīra, those residing on Himalayas and countries to the northern side of Ganges have this *pravṛtti*. They have *sāttvatī* and *ārabhaṭī* styles (*NS*).

2413 **पाटच्चर**

Pāṭaccara : thief, robber; worn out cloth.

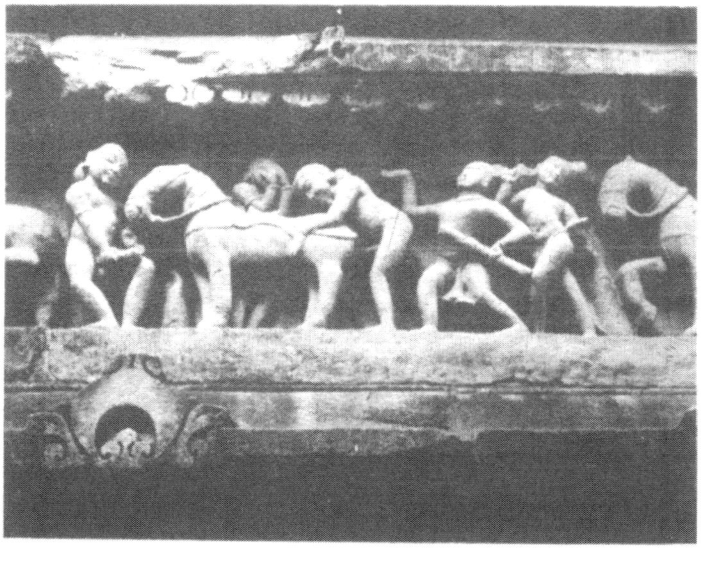

Fig. (2405)

2414 **पाटलिक**

Pāṭalika : (a) one who appreciates time and place. (b) one who knows other's secrets. (c) a pupil.

2415 **पाठ**

Pāṭha : recitation, study, text, a reading.

2416 **पाठक्रिया**

Pāṭhakriyā : paralinguistic functions. Abhinava (*NS.* Vol. II, p. 390) states that *varṇas* (accent) accelerate the function of paralanguage: पाठक्रियाबिस्तारकाः ।

2417 **पाठान्तर**

Pāṭhāntara : variant, another reading.

2418 **पाठीन**

Pāṭhīna : public reciter of *Purāṇas.* It is known as *pāṛhī* in Halbi.

2419 **पाठ्य**

Pāṭhya : text, the recitation, paralinguistics. Even though the language of the play may be perfect, without its impressive utterance the effect would not be fully communicated. Not only this, but the difference in utterance would cause a change of meaning, which would be out of place in that situation. It is possible to have the contrary feelings like respect and contempt to be produced by the help of modulation of voice. All this comes under *pāṭhya,* a subdivision of *vācikābhinaya,* according to Bharata. *Pāṭhya* in known asparalanguage in modern western linguistics and the science which deals it is known as paralinguistics.

2420 **पाठ्यगुण**

Pāṭhyaguṇa : qualities of speech, paralinguistic features. According to Bharata, there are, to begin with, three registers of the voice — low, middle and high — corresponding to chest, throat and head resonation, which are used corresponding to the nature of the character, the situation, and the feeling. The high vocal register is used when calling or addressing one at a distance. The middle and lower registers are used for those within greater degrees of proximity. An utterance starting in a lower register may also wax louder.

Pāṭhya (paralinguistics) is described to possess six qualities essential for the effective performance. They are *svaras, sthānas* (voice-registers), *varṇas* (manner of uttering notes), *kāku* (intonation), *alaṅkāras,* and *aṅgas.* In utterance of a language *virāma* (pause) is the main thing. All other qualities help the effective modulation.

2421 **पाणि**

Pāṇi : hand. *Pāṇi* stands primarily for 'palm of the hand' (from *maṇibandha* to *aṅgula*). There are a number of expressions which are used to refer to taking of the hand of the bride in marriage and other similar compound formations are employed to refer to wife etc. In this context, the word *pāṇi* is much preferred to *hasta* or *kara.* Expressions like *pāṇigrahaṇam, pāṇipīḍanam, pāṇi-praṇayinī, pāṇigrāha* are very common in Sanskrit literature. As against this, we have a very few expressions with *hasta* and *kara* — *hasta-grābha, hasta-graha, kara-pīḍanam, karagrahaṇam,* but are not very commonly used and have later disappeared. Since 'taking the hand' does not involve the whole arm but primarily the palm and fingers, can one not say that the distribution is understandable and logical. Thus this suggests that the term *hasta* emphasizes the physical aspect while *kara* is more elegant expression signifying the beauty, the grace of the arm. The word *pāṇi* primarily stood for arm. The prevalence of expressions like *cakra-pāṇi, khaḍga-pāṇi,* perhaps now can be explained by arguing that a dagger or a disc is held in the palm and does not need the whole arm directly. (b) hand: *saṁvṛttāṅguli pañcakaḥ pāṇiḥ ghūṁsā* in Hindi.

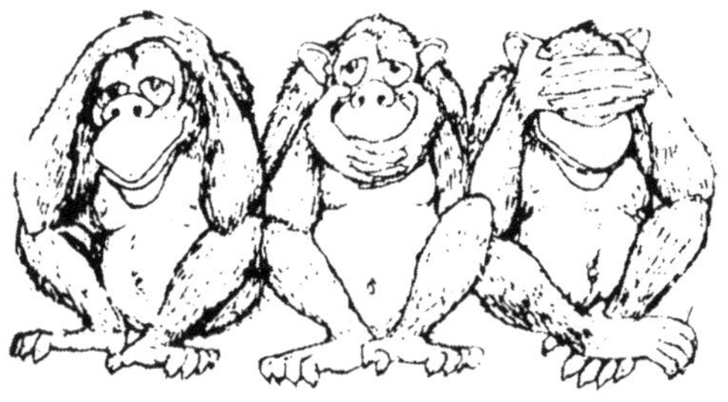

(Fig. 2421)

2422 **पाणिगृहीती**

Pānigṛhītī : legally wedded wife. Indian wives often face the state of solitariness. The following Bhili folk song depicts the loneliness of the tribal woman:

> In my husband's small dark hut
> I live all, all alone.
> I pass sleepless nights with thoughts
> of a husband who has gone to work
> Far away to a town Sankali.
> I grind the corn all, all alone
> without the help of my *Jeṭhānī.*
> I clean the cowshed all, all alone
> Without the help of my *Nanad.*
> I make the bread all, all alone,
> without the help of my *Jeṭhānī.*

I fetch the water all, all alone,
without the help of my *Nanad.*
In my husband's small dark hut
I live all, all alone.
Long the hours of my sleepless nights.

2423 **पाणिग्रहण**

Pāṇigrahaṇam : holding of the hand; symbolizes marriage between the male and female. In all the *varṇas* the marriage between parties of the same *varṇa* is marked with only the holding of hand (*Agni,* 154.1.3; *Skanda,* IV. 38. 8-9); main marriage rite. Other related terms are *pāṇigrāha, pāṇipīḍana, pāṇibandha, pāṇidharma,* etc.

2424 **पाणिग्राह**

Pāṇigrāha : husband. *pāṇigrahītṛ.*

2425 **पाणिघ**

Pāṇigha : striking hand (in music), playing upon an instrument with hands; *tabalcī* in Hindi.

2426 **पाणिघात**

Pāṇighāta : boxing.

2427 **पाणि-चापल्य**

Pāṇi-cāpalya : snapping of fingers; also *pāṇicāpalam*

2428 **पाणितल**

Pāṇitala : palm of the hand.

2429 **पाणिध्म**

Pāṇidhma : one who claps his hand (*T.Br.* 111. 4.15); *pāṇimdhama,* the way where one walks striking hands: darky path.

2430 **पाणिपात्र**

Pāṇipātra : folded and joined hands for drinking water.

2431 **पाणिवाद**

Pāṇivāda : clapping the hands; *tālī bajānā* in Hindi.

2432 **पाणिस्वनिक**

Pāṇisvanika : one who claps his hands, keeping time with hands.

2433 **पात-दृष्टि**

Pāta-dṛṣṭi : a relaxed normal position of the eyeball, has a downward accent. Occurs in *karuṇa* and *jugupsā.* Those lost in deep thought walk with their heads lowered, often lower the eyebrows.

2434 **पातन (भ्रू)**

Pātana (bhrū) : lowering the eyebrow: loose position of the eyeball, a type of glance by movement of the eyeball (*NS,* VIII. 92-105); lowering down eyebrows alternately and simultaneously suggests envy, disgust, smile, smelling, etc.

2435 **पाताल-भञ्जिनी-मुद्रा**

Pātāla-bhañjinī-mudrā : breaker of the lower-most world. Make both the hands down-turned and fix the look downwards (*VD*); (b) If in the *rahasya-mudrā la* and *sa* are repeated with *e* and *s mudrās,* it is *pātāla-bhañjinī* (*VD*). *Pātāla* means nether regions which are generally understood as being seven. The names differ in the *Purāṇas.*

2436 **पात्र**

Pātra : begging bowl or bowl generally found in the images of Buddhas. Sometimes *kapāla* is used to designate a bowl (*Sādhana-mālā*).

2437 **पाद**

Pāda : (1) foot-gesture. (2) portions. The five positions of the feet mentioned in *NS* are the basic positions, and eight others mentioned by *SR* and repeated by *Naṭyaśāstra Saṁgraha* are combinations of movements arising out of these. The five gestures of feet mentioned by *NS* (X. 40-51) are: *udghaṭṭita* (firstly standing on the fore-feet then touching the earth by heal), *sama* (resting on the natural step), *agratalasañcāra* (the heel-up, the big toe bent and other toes shrunk), *añcita* (heels on the floor, fore-foot raised and toes extended) and *kuñcita* (heels raised up and toes and hind foot bent).

All the gestures, feats and styles, related to the thigh, the fore-leg and feet should be exercised in an equal rhythm. No feat attains success, if it is not symmetrically corroborated with functions of the thigh and the fore-leg. All the actions of feet in a *tāṇḍava* performance should always rhythmically follow the action of the thigh and the fore-leg. It is, therefore, an imperative, that an action of the thigh should always symmetrically follow the same of the fore-leg. An equal rhythm should be maintained among the gaits; the three lower parts of the body: the thigh, fore-leg and the feet (*NS,* X.40-51).

2438 **पाद-करण**

Pāda-karaṇa : derives its name from the position and movement of the feet.

2439 **पादगृह्य**

Pādagṛhya : seizing by the foot (*VS,* IV.19.22) *yat prākṣiṇāḥ* *pitaram pādagṛhya pādamātra* : one foot long; *pādaka*: little foot (*Ibid.*, VIII. 33.19).

2440 **पादक्षेप**

Pādakṣepa : step.

2441 **पादग्रहण**

Pādagrahaṇa : respectful salutation, prostration; *pādavandanam.*

2442 **पाद-चारी**

Pāda-cārī : types of walking (*Abhinayadarpaṇa*, 259-260). One of the basis of the movements of the separate part of the human body. Bharata discusses and analyses the fundamental units of movement. The *cārī* is the most important single unit of movement in the *nṛtta* technique as enunciated by Bharata. A movement of the lower part of the body consequent upon a movement of one foot from the *sama* position of the feet is termed as *pāda-cārī.* Bharata devotes one chapter to this and says that "whatever has been prescribed as *nāṭya* is included in the *cārī* and no part of it can take place without the same" (*Abhinayadarpaṇa* 42-45, *SR*, VII. 37-41) *Nāṭyaśāstra Saṁgraha*, pp. 40-42, *NS*, X.5). Since *cārī* is also a part of a system of exercise, its various forms are related to one another and cannot be considered in isolation. The *cārī* results from movement with one foot. (b) Walker. The Indian tribes are great walkers. The men carry heavy loads balanced at either end of a carrying stick borne on their shoulders. Women carry the heavy baskets on their head generally supporting the burden with their left hand, or with their right hand if they are carrying a baby, and proceed at a jog trot for 15-16 kilometres at a stretch without halting. The Hill Marias of Bastar like going up and down the hilly terrain and do not like walking on plains. While in group they walk in a single file.

pāda-cāra means 'on foot' (*Skanda*, III. 2.32.69).

2443 **पादतल**

Pādatala : 'sole of foot' (*MBh.*), *pādamūlam.*

2444 **पाद-त्राण**

Pāda-trāṇa : foot-wear, meant to protect the soles of the feet while walking. It may take the form of leather sandals with straps or wooden sandal with a knot. At present shoes have become symbolically female. The high-heeled shoe is feminine because it causes women to take smaller steps and resembling again *gajagāminī.*

2445 **पादधावन**

Pādadhāvana : washing the feet; *pādaprakṣālanam.* The rite of washing the feet of the bride and bridegroom at the marriage ceremony is still prevalent among all the castes and tribes alike. It is known as *pāyn pakharī* in Aryan dialects and *kālk dāynā* in Gondi.

2446 **पादन्यास**

Pādanyāsa : foot-work (*Megha*), step, measured step, dance. In Dantewāṛā tahsil I recorded five different steps used by the Bison-horn Maria women:

(a) The circle moves anticlockwise singing '*Nonile-Vāyale*' and the steps are: right foot to right, left foot swings back behind with a pause in mid-air while the dancing stick is thumped twice on the ground. Then right foot again, and three thumps of the stick. This step is also done to refrain '*so-lo rela re relā*' and '*so rela re relā* '

(b) A very simple anticlock wise circular movement. Right foot to right and left foot to right behind it. The song is about cattle and the fields.

(c) Another circular dance with the steps going right to right, left behind to right, right to right, then left over in front of right.

(d) The feet go: left, right, left to right, a pause, the right is wagged over in front on the left and towards the left for three beats on the stick, then it is put back on the ground to the right of the left and then left right left quickly.

(e) Left in front of right, right to right behind it, then the left in front of the right and son on. In this dance the sticks are not thumped with three beats at a time, but with single beats.

2447 **पाद-पतन**

Pāda-patana : touching the feet (*Kāmasūtra*, 2.10.42). Touching the feet of the beloved was very popular in Sanskrit literature. Agnimitra, when caught red-handed, touches the feet (*Mālatīmādhavam*, 3.22). Udayana touches the feet of Vāsavadattā (*Priyadarśikā*, p.40; *Ratnāvalī* 3.40). Bilhaṇa also touched the feet of his beloved (*Caurapañcāśikā*, 36). Amaruka (34) depicts *pādapatana* as follows:

Sutanu jahihi maunam paśya pādāpatam mām
na khalu tava kadācit kopa evam vidho bhūt
iti nigadati nāthe tiryagāmīlitākṣyā
nayanajalamanalpam muktamuktaṁ na kiñcit

The Yakṣa in *Meghadūta* (107) tries to bow before the drawing of his beloved. Thus, bowing down to the feet of beloveds is a very common and popular way to console the angry woman.

2448 **पादं पादेन नाक्रमेत्**

Pādam pāden nākramet : the *Agnipurāṇa* (155.28) records a belief that one should not sit cross-legged. (Fig. 2448)

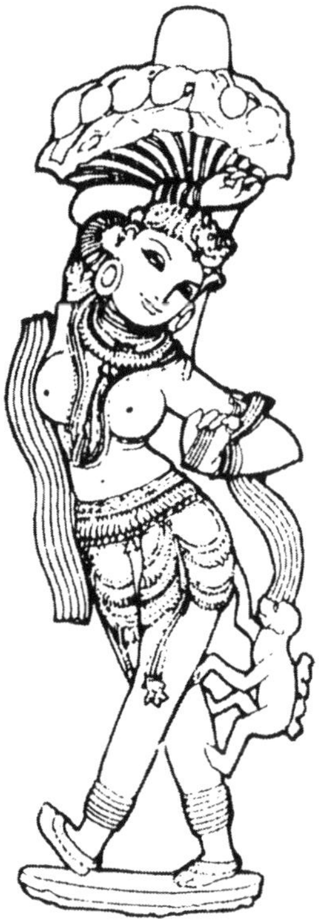

Fig. – (2448)

2449 **पादप्रहार**

Pādaprahāra : a kick; *pādāghāta, lāt mārnā* in Hindi.

2450 **पादमुद्रा**

Pāda-mudrā : feet gesture of icon. In the *pādamudrās* are included *mudrās* which are used in iconography of India. The *pādamudrās* of iconography are known as *āsanas* in yogic literature and *śarīra mudrās* in dramaturgy. *Yogic pādamudrās* are as follows: *yogāsana* or *padmāsana* or *svastikāsana* (2) *baddha-padmāsana* (3) *ardha-paryaṅkāsana* or *sukhāsana* (4) *bhadrāsana* or *lalitāsana* (5) *utkaṭāsana* (6) *gopālāsana* (7) *vīrāsana* (8) *pretāsana* (9) *kūrpāsana* (10 *siṁhāsana* (11) *paryaṅkāsana.*

2451 **पादरजस्**

Pādarajas : foot-dust.

2452 **पादरेचक**

Pādarecaka : going from side to side with wavering feet or with differently moving feet is called their *recaka* (NS). It is one of the four *recakas.*

2453 **पादसंवाहन**

Pādasaṁvāhana : massaging the feet. Village Indians walk barefoot and feel the sensations under foot. The foot-massage in this way is very common as an art of reflexology. They say that for every internal organ and part of the body there is a corresponding point on the feet.

2454 **पादाकृतिविज्ञान**

Pādākṛti-vijñāna : auspicious and inauspicious signs of feet. If feet are shaped like the winnowing basket, if it is dry, then the person becomes poor and full of grief (*Garuḍa,* 63.3). If they are soft, fleshy reddish, without perspiration, elevated and devoid of protruding veins, it is an indication of kingship. If the lines on the lower portion are clear they indicate happiness (*Bhaviṣya,* 24. 15-17). If the finger of the foot, next to the toe is longer, it indicates enjoyment of women (*Ibid.,* 25).

Legs like lotus are appreciated in Sanskrit literature such as *pādakamala.*

A woman or a girl should not shake or move her hanging feet while sitting on a chair or cot. By doing this, one multiplies the family debt.

The feet should not be placed on the floor causing sound while moving or walking. By this one becomes poorer day by day.

"If possible, feet should not be stretched towards a fire, water, a Brāhmaṇa, a cow, images of the gods, a door, or against the wind (*Āpastamba,* 1,2.31.22).

If the feet are even-soled, of the hue of a red-lotus, it is a sign of enjoyment for women (*Bhav. P. Brahmakhaṇḍa,* 5.12); they should be fleshy, soft, warm, and not given to perspire (*Sk.P.*IV.37.10). Dry, pale, having of the shape of winnowing basket, coarse and having mutilated reflection are not good. (*Ibid*). The nails should be reddish, and on the feet there should be such signs as that of a plough, disc, fish, goad and lotus (*Ibid.*). If all the toes be wellset, long and slender, it is a sign of royalty; if they are short they indicate good life; if thick and parted, they indicate loss of wealth (*Bhav. P. Ibid.*). According to another belief, if the toes are long, the woman is prone to be faithless; if very thin she would be poor, she would have a short span of life; if bent, she would be lovely; if flattened, she would be a maidservant; and if separated she would be wretched (*Sk.P.* IV. 37. 15-16). Other welcome signs on the feet are arrow, barley-grain, *tomara* (javelin), flag, *camara* (hair of yak), wreath, mountain, earring, conch, umbrella, *svastika* and chariot. These may also be on the palm (*Garuḍa P.,* 1.65. 97-98; Sk.:P. IV. 37. 12-14)

2455 **पादाङ्गुल्याभरण**

Padāṅgulyābharaṇa : ornaments of toes, for women only (*NS*). Toe-rings and *tilaka* for the big toe.

2456 **पादापविद्ध -करण**

Pādāpaviddha-karaṇa : feet are first in *sūcīviddhā cārī* and are then moved to the *atikrāntā cārī* position. Hands are in *kaṭakāmukha* near the navel (*NS*, IV. 90b-91a, IX.279, X.39). It is also known as *pādāpaviddhaka*. The *kaṭakāmukha* hands are placed with their back touching the navel and the feet are in *sūcī* and *apakrāntā cāris*.

2457 **पादारविन्द**

Pādāravinda : lotus-like feet; *caraṇa-kamala*.

2458 **पादावनेजनी**

Pādāvanejanī : water meant for washing foot; *pādāvanejya*: washing the feet (*TMB*,VI.I.II); *pādaprakṣālana* in classical Sanskrit, also *pādāvanejana* 'washing feet'.

2459 **पादावर्त**

Pādāvarta : a field measured by strides.

2460 **पादुका**

Pādukā : wooden sandals worn while walking. They may be seen on the feet of Vīra-bhadra, Bhairava, Dakṣiṇā-mūrti, Sudarśana, Dattātreya and Bhikṣāṭana-mūrti, Ep. *pādukāḥ dārunirmitāḥ upānaha-ścarmanirmitāḥ*. The establishing of feet in stone had been a custom. The sight of sandals in dream is said to be inauspicious (*Brahmavaivarta. Śrīkṛṣṇakhaṇḍa*. 82.19).

2461 **पादुकाधारणसंकेत**

Pādukā dhāraṇa-saṅketa : shoe symbol. Shoes have been jealously guarded symbols in colonial India. Shoes, too, could offend if worn in the presence of one's superiors. Members of the lower castes, particularly if they were women, had to take these off on meeting a highcaste man and in some villages even while going past an uppercaste residence or through caste Hindu wards (Fuchs, *The Children of Hari*, Vienna, 1950: 81). Indeed, umbrellas or shoes could be so suggestive of power that often under conditions of growing antagonism between the peasant and his enemies both sides regarded these as symbolic sites of conflict. The ban imposed on their use by the *diku* landlords was felt to be an unbearable tyranny by the Mundas as they became increasingly politicized. Conversely, the Tamil Nadu landlord who identified shoe feet as the symptom of rebelliousness among agricultural labourers at the time of the Kilvenmani massacre, spoke up against what was, to his class, a real affront: "Things used to be very peaceful here some years ago. The labourers were very hard-working and respectful. But now... the fellow who used to stand in the backyard of my house to talk to me comes straight to the verandah wearing slippers and all.... These fellows have become lazy and arrogant, thanks to the communists. They have no fear in them any more" (Anon., 1973: 926-7).

A Gond is thought to be unlucky enough to be hit with a leather sandal and becomes subject to pollution irrespective of the status of the person who hit him or the cause of assault.

Before the abolition of Zamiṁdari, the women from the lower layers in the caste hierarchy could not pass in front of the *thākurs* houses with the shoes on. She had to take shoes in her hand. Even now a few *Korī* and chamār women of middle age (in the Gwalior region), who have seen the Zamindari days, while passing in front of the *Baṅgalā*, take their shoes in hand. After going out of the village, they wear it again. The *Kacchī* and Gaḍariā women no more pay respect in this manner (Mutalkar, 1978: 123)

2462 **पादोदक**

Pādodaka : literally the water from the feet of the guru or *Jaṅgama* which is regarded sacred by the Vīra-Śaivas. The custom of touching or drinking the water touched by the guru with his feet is not confined to the Vīra Śaivas only. Kālidāsa has used it in the sense of water offered to the guests for washing their feet (*Śāk.*, 1.73).

2463 **पादौ कुरु, पृष्ठं कुरु**

Pādau kuru pṛṣṭham kuru : wash your feet and wash your back.

2464 **पाद्य**

Pādya : water used for washing feet.

2465 **पान**

Pāna : drinking, kissing, drink, wine. *Pāna* in the sense of *adhara* (lips) is much used in Sanskrit literature. *Kāmasūtra* recommends passing wine from one mouth to the other as part of love-play.

2466 **पान-पात्र**

Pāna-pātra : the bowl containing liquor or blood, held in one of the hands of a fierce deity (like Kālī, Durgā, Pratyaṅgirā, Bhairava and Vīrabhadra). It is classed among the thirty-six "weapon" (*āyudha*) in *Aparājita Sūtra* (235), ascribed to Viśvakarma.

2467 **पानीय**

Pānīya : water, beverage, drinkable. In Sanskrit literature, woman is symbolically equivalent to water. The bathing motif is connected with erotic attraction and impregnation; *vagina dentala* represents the dangerous, destructive aspect of women, and the *yoni* is ambivalent.

2468 **पानीयसंकेत**

Pānīya-saṁketa : water-signal. In north India the use of *jala* and *pānī* for water has different connotation. *Jala* is used in a more purified or dignified way, while *pānī* is used commonly. A glass of water crossed over by someone should not be taken because it may cause throat trouble.

The iconic feature of Pānaka Narasiṁha in Guntur's Maṅgala-giri is distinguished by gaping mouth into which the jaggery-water is poured.

2469 **पाप**

Pāpa : sin, a sinful act, guilt. Sin is said to be of two types, namely (I) *buddhipūrvam kṛtam karma* (done knowingly); and (II) *anyam* (done unknowingly). Sins are further said to be mainly ten in number and are divided into three varieties: *kāyika* (bodily), *vāṅmaya* (of speech) and *mānasa* (of the body). A survey shows that the main concept behind sin has been the expectation of good and responsible behaviour, performing one's ordained profession and morality. Also see *pātaka, mahāpātaka, anupātaka, kṛccha* and *prāyaścitta*. There is the mention of anthropomorphised image of sin in *Padma Purāṇa* (125. 69-74). This idol of *pāpa* should be terrible to look at and should be shown as wearing fearful clothes; a sword should be shown in its hand, and it should have iron-jaws. It should be placed on a measure of sesame and should be covered with black cloth. Red flowers should be placed upon it and it should have shining golden ear-rings. It should be worshipped and asked to pardon the sins. This ritual is fixed for the full-moon-day of the month of Kārtika at a holy place. (b) *pāpa* is a complex feeling that we should atone for something we have either done or thought of doing. It has developed as a force for preserving society by giving humans the means to deal with the constant temptation to put their own interests and immediate gratification before the needs of the community. To be effective, such a force must be very strong, and it is therefore not surprising that *pāpa* is probably the most oppressive of all emotions. However, within limits, it is valuable both to the individual and to society. No human relationship is free from guilt. As a result, guilty feelings are an important feature in most relationships: *Śāntam pāpam.*

2470 **पापनाशिनी-मुद्रा**

Pāpanāśinī-mudrā : name of a river. The *Śukatuṇḍa* hand moving up and down indicate this river (*Mirror of Gesture*, p. 48).

2471 **पारतल्पिक**

Pāratalpika : an adulterer (*A*, 4.5.1). Indra is a notorious adulterer, famed for the seduction of Ahalyā, the wife of Gautama. the *Mahābhārata* (XII. 14.1) relates the reaction of Gautama, who curses Indra to wear a green beard, or, in another version, to bear the marks of a thousand *yonis* (female sexual organs). This punishment is the reversal of Indra's manhood. Afterwards the curse is modified and the marks are changed to eyes, so that Indra is called *sahasrākṣa* (having a thousand eyes) or *Netrayoni* (having Eyes for Female organs). The punishment of Indra reflects the traditions of Hindu law which ordained that a man who had violated his guru's bed must be branded with the *yoni* (*Manu*, 9.237).

2472 **पारदेशिक**

Pāradeśika : foreigner.

2473 **पारावत-गूहनम्**

Pārāvata-gūhanam : embrace of dove, experienced by a slender lady (Dāmodaragupta, *Kuṭṭanīmatam*, 581).

2474 **पारावत-मुद्रा**

Pārāvata-mudrā : gesture of a pigeon. The *kapotaka* hand move horizontally indicates a pigeon (*Mirror of Gesture*, pp. 50-51).

2475 **पारिपार्श्विक**

Pāripārśvika : one attending his master. He was of middling type possessing the qualities of *sūtradhāra* in a lesser degree. Sometimes he assumed secondary role in the play. He is also not mentioned separately in the troupe.

2476 **पार्वती-हस्त**

Pārvatī-hasta : *ardhacandra* held up with the right hand and the same with the left held down; represented in the styles of boon-offering (*varada*) and fear-removing (*abhaya*) indicates *Pārvatī* (*AD*, 205-210). Legends describe this goddess as the daughter of Dakṣa-prajāpatī or of the mountain Himālayas (hence the name Pārvatī) and consort of Śiva; she is the mother of Gaṇapati and Kārtikeya; and she is sister of Kṛṣṇa (*Viz.* Viṣṇu). She has numerous names: Haimavatī, Dākṣāyaṇī, Umā, Gaurī, Bhavānī, Śārvaṇī, Kātyāyanī, Aṁbikā, Āryā, Satī and Mahāmāyā. She is usually worshipped as *Śakti* and hence her devotees are called *Śāktas.*

2477 **पार्श्व**

Pārśva : region of ribs, sides. There are five styles of the side-gestures. They are (1) *nata* (the bent), (2) *unnata* (the raised up), (3) *prasārita* (the extended,) (4) *vivartita* (the turned round) and (5) *apasṛta* (drawn away). These are the gesture of the body as a whole (*NS*, X. 10-17).

Varāhamihira (LXVIII) has presented some characteristic

feature of men according to their *pārśva-lakṣaṇa.* Thus, according to him, "Men with fleshy sides become wealthy; with sunken and crooked ones, devoid of the pleasures of life;

अविकलपार्श्वा धनिनो निम्नैर्वक्रैश्च भोगसंन्त्यक्ता : ॥

2478 **पार्श्वक्रान्त करण**

Pārśvakrānta-karaṇa : performing the *pārśvakrānta cārī,* the foot is made to fall in front, the hand is kept in conformity with the foot movements. It is used in the movements of Bhīmasena and others in the Furious Sentiment.

2479 **पार्श्व- क्रान्ता-चारी**

Pārśva-krānta-cārī : the movement about in the sky (*NS,* X.30) both feet in *samapāda kuñcita.* The *kuñcita* foot is lifted with the knees pointing sideways. The foot is brought to the thigh-level and then dropped to the ground with the heel touching the floor. *Kṣipta* position of the knee which is lifted. *Pārśvajānu karaṇa.* Lifting up a *kuñcita* foot so that the knee would be on the level of breast and then making it fall on the ground with the *Udghaṭṭita.* According to Bharata (*NS,* X.32) "the *kuñcita* foot is lifted up on its own side and dropped by the heel on the ground, and thus by the *udghāṭṭita* movement the *pārśvakrāntā* is formed."

2480 **पार्श्वगत-संस्थान**

Pārśvagata-saṁsthāna : the side-exposed position. Limbs, movements and other prominent parts of a body are almost diminutive. Only a single eye will catch the vision along with diminished parts of lips, nostrils, ears and eye-brows. When only an ear of the figure with a requisite quantity of hairs and a part of the chin are added to appropriate measurement, sweatness and beauty it called either the *pārśvagata* or the *bhittika* (*VD.,* III. 39. 18-20).

2481 **पार्श्वगत-हस्त**

Pārśvagata-hasta : going sideways at any high, low or middle level, the side-traced hands (*NS,* IX. 175). One of the three types of the movements of hands. All these styles of hands are to be exhibited with the expression of eyes, eye-brows, and appearances of the face. An expert in the art of gesture may devise different styles of hands in accordance with the particular *karaṇa,* the place of action, the mode of movement and the actions of dance. To show the gesture of respect to honourable people, the position of hands in a gesture should move in the region of the head-part, for the middle-class people, it is advised to place by the breast part and for the lower grade, nothing is especially indicated. People of higher and middle status should frame gestures of hands as indicated in the treatise, but lower grade people should devise them as prevalent in local behaviours (*VD,* Pt. III, ch. 36).

2482 **पार्श्वग-पाद**

Pārśvaga-pāda : the foot is placed sideways. Going sideways with the help of the foot-sides. It is used in dancing styles. Also known as *pārśvaga-caraṇa* (*SR,* IV.7.324).

2483 **पार्श्वजानु-करण**

Pārśvajānu-karaṇa : walking sideways: both the knees are bent to the same side. Feet as in the *pārśvakrānta cārī.* Hands to accord with the feet which are moved in front (*NS,* IV. 123b-124b, x.32). One foot is in *sama* position and the other placed at the back of the thighs and the hand in *muṣṭi* is held on the breast. It is used in fights and personal combats.

2484 **पार्श्वजानु-चारी**

Pārśvajānu-cārī : a type of knee-movement, the knee is taken to the level of the side.

2485 **पार्श्वतो दृष्टिम्**

Pārśvto dṛṣṭim : looking sideways.

2486 **पार्श्व-निकुट्टित-करण**

Pārśva-nikuṭṭita-karaṇa : hands in *svastika.* Feet and legs in *nikuṭṭita* (*NS,* IV.109-110). Also known as *pārśvanikuṭṭaka.* The hands in *svastika* are held on one side and the foot is in *nikuṭṭita.* It is used in concealing or revealing something.

2487 **पार्श्वपरिवर्तन**

Pārśvaparivartana : turning round from one side to another in the bed.

2488 **पार्श्व-मण्डलिन् नृत्तहस्त**

Pārśva-maṇḍalin nṛtta-hasta : a type of hand-gesture in dancing; the side-circling dancing hands; when the *haṁsapakṣa* gesture is in the style of circling by sides, it is called the *pārśvamaṇḍalin* (*NS,* IX. 176-197).

2489 **पार्श्वसूचिमण्डल**

Pārśva-sūcī-maṇḍala : a type of posture.

2490 **पार्श्वसूत्र**

Pārśva-sūtra : the vertical drawn from the side of forehead, the cheek, the side, the side of the arm, the centre of the thighs, the centre of the knee, and the centre of the ankle-joint; used in sculpture. One of the five *sūtras* employed for making icons (others being *Brahma-Sūtra, Madhya-Sūtra, Kakṣa-Sūtra and Bāhu-Sūtra*).

2491 **पार्श्वाभिमुख-शिरस्**

Pārśvābhimukha-śiras : neck bent with face turned sideways. If the head is moved sideways, it is a gesture of the head as named here, indicating to look at on both the sides (*SR,* IV.7.78).

2492 **पार्श्वासन**

Pārśvāsana : latéral position.

2493 **पार्ष्णि**

Pārṣṇi : 'heel' (*RV*).

2494 **पार्ष्णिग-पाद**

Pārṣṇigapāda : walking backwards on the heels, going back rapidly on the heels. It is used in the speedy dance. Also known as *pārṣṇiga-caraṇa* (*SR*, VI.7.325).

2495 **पार्ष्णिपार्श्वगत-स्थानक**

Pārṣṇi-pārśvagata-sthānaka : a type of posture.

2496 **पार्ष्णिविद्ध-स्थानक**

Pārṣṇividdha-sthānaka : a type of posture.

2497 **पार्षद**

Pārṣada : also known as *pāriṣada*. The term means those who are in the assembly. It signifies the followers of a deity, members of his troop (*gaṇa*) or attendants. It has larger connotation with *parivāra* and includes the devotees (*bhakta*) and worshipping sages (*pūjakamuni*).

2498 **पालागल**

Pālāgala : runner, a messenger; also known as *pālākala* (*Satyāṣāḍha-śrauta sūtra*, XIII.4); one who touches the feet of the man to whom he carries a message saying पा लागै. Obviously a very late term intruding into Vedic works (*Kātyāyana-Śrautasūtra*). The following Chhatisgarhi *suā-git* refers to the touching of the feet of the Sun and the Moon:

> *painyā mai lāgavna candā suruj ke,*
> *suanā tiriyā janam jhani dey* ||

A man of low caste meeting a Brāhmaṇa says, *"pāyn lāgī"* or "I fall at your feet" and touches the Brāhmaṇa's feet with his hand, which he then carries to his own forehead to signify this.

Pālāgan is also an act of prostration; obeisance by touching the feet, laying one's head on anothers feet, a mark of reverence or veneration, especially to Brāhmaṇs.

2499 **पालित्य**

Pālitya : greyness of hair.

2500 **पाशमुद्रा**

Pāśa-mudrā : the noose-gesture. "Join two tips of thumbs with the tips of two-fore-fingers and make a knot of the two, this will frame the gesture of a noose" (*Brahmayāmalatantra*). (b) "Inside the fist of the fore-finger and the ring-finger, both the thumbs should be kept. With the right fist of the same position, the little finger should be tightly caught. This is the gesture of noose, which may be appropriated in all the purposes" (*Ibid.*).

2501 **पाशहस्त**

Pāśahasta : both hands gesture. Showing a clasping of the fingers (*Abhinayadarpaṇa*, 46), not mentioned in *NS*. If the fore-fingers of the *sūcī* style are enchained together, it is the *pāśa* style, that indicates a quarrel between the two men or parties and to join two strings. *Pāśa* is the noose or lasso that is found in the hands of some deities like Gaṇapati and some forms of Devī. It signifies the power to bind, and is always associated with goad, held in the corresponding hand on the other side, which symbolizes ability to control. The background imagery is that of the binding of the elephants for purposes of taming (noose) and of the employment of goad to control and regulate its movements when tamed (goad). *Pāśa* also denotes fetters. These are generally considered to be eight in number (*Paraśurāmakalpasūtra*, X.70). A list of sixty-two fetters is also found in different texts (*Lalitāsahasranāma*, 129).

2502 **पाशुपतव्रत**

Pāśupatavrata : the *Pāśupata* custom of besmearing the body with ashes. *Pāśupata* was a sect which came into existence sometime around the beginning of the Christian era (Ingalls, 1962.295). The *kāpālikas* were derived from them (Auboyer, 1960.62), and both sects are closely linked with *yoga* and *tantra*. It is as a *Pāśupata* or a *Kāpālika* that Śiva enters the *dāruvanam*. The *Pāśupata* was instructed to 'play the lecher' in order to stimulate slander, acquiring *tapas* by this means: 'He should take up his stand by a group of women... Turning his attention to one of them that is young and pretty he should stare at her and act as though he were setting his desire upon her and honouring her. When... she looks at him, he should act out the symptoms of love such as straightening his hair, etc. Then everyone, women, men and eunuchs, will say, "This is no man of chastity; this is a lecher? By this false accusation their merit comes to him and his bad *karma* goes to them' (*Pāśupata-sūtra*, 3.6-19). Thus by the erotic appearance and gestures *Pāśupata* used to excite women.

2503 **पिकरवा**

Pikaravā : lady whose voice is like that of a cuckoo, quality of the Deer-lady (*Anaṅgaraṅga*, 3.20-21).

2504 **पिङ्गला**

Pingalā : one of the major nerves. It rises from the *mūlādhāra* and ends in the right nostril. It symbolizes waking state and leads individual to violent actions (Rāghava on *Śāradā*, XXV. 38).

2505 **पिङ्गाक्षी**

Piṅgākṣī : lady whose eyes are red, quality of the Elephant lady (*Anaṅgaraṅga*, 3.24-25).

2506 **पिच्चक-मुद्रा**

Piccaka-mudrā : occurs in BT. "Making a fist with right-hand and encircling it over the head continuously, it poses the *mudrā* of *piccaka*."

2507 **पिण्ड**

Piṇḍa : lump of food offered to dead ancestors and kings. the size of the lump varies in accordance with the length of time of the ancestors. Ball of rice (*piṇḍa*) represents the body of the dead at *śrāddha*-rite (*Agni*, 117.20).

2508 **पिण्डदान**

Piṇḍadāna : presentation of rice balls to the manes. पितरों को पिण्डदात

2509 **पिण्डी**

Piṇḍī : mass, cluster, dance-symbol, grouping with song and instrumental music. *Piṇḍī* literally means the cavity in the plinth of an idol into which the latter's lower portion fits snugly for stability. In the end, it indicates prime attribute, the root cause etc. *Piṇḍī* may also mean the *aṅgahāras* and *karaṇas* introduced in dance to signify a particular deity. The meaning now expands to include *vāhana*, weapon and other implements of that deity. *Piṇḍī* also means the favourite *karaṇa* of a deity, with which it is appeared. Finally *piṇḍī* appears to stand for any characteristic attribute of a deity. Although iconographic representations of the gods are not referred to, characteristic symbolizations in dance for their worship are known as *piṇḍīs*. We hear of the *piṇḍīs* or worshipful dance-symbols of Śiva in the form of the *liṅga*, or Nandī in the form of the Trident, of Caṇḍikā in the form of *Simhavāhinī*, of Viṣṇu in the form of *Garuḍa*, of Brahmā in the form of the lotus, and of Indra in the elephant *Airāvata*. *Kāma*, the lord of love, has fish as his dance-symbol, Kumāra has the peacock, Lakṣmi has form (*rūpa*), Ganga has *dhārā* or the stream, Yama has the noose, Varuṇa a river, Kuvera a *yakṣī*, Balarāma a plough, the Nāgas a snake, and the Rudra the trident.

2510 **पिण्डीबन्ध**

Piṇḍībandha : emblems; four varieties are mentioned: *piṇḍī*, *śraṅkhalikā*, *latābandha* and *bhedyaka*. *Piṇḍībandha* meant at first, the concrete symbol which was created in the course of deity's dance and therefore came to be associated with and to signify that deity e.g., *liṅga*. *Piṇḍībandha* is the formation indicating the characteristic of the deity. The form of *Śivaliṅga* for Sankara, the lionriding for Caṇḍikā etc. are the formations mentioned. Bharata says that the *piṇḍībandhas* were to be used as flags or emblems. This confirms that the representation of gods was still primarily symbolic, not iconographic. In short, *piṇḍīs* are said to represent well-marked emblems of the various gods (*NS*, IV.257). Emblem, according to Ekman and Friesen (1966), is the first category of NV behaviour which refers to the small class of NV acts that can be accurately translated into words (for example, a handshake, a smile, a frown). Ekman and Friesen (Hand Movements, *Journal of Communication*, 1972.22.253-374) define emblems as such: "those NV acts (a) which have a direct verbal translation usually consisting of a word or two, or a phrase, (b) for which this precise meaning is known by most or all members of a group, class, subculture, or culture, (c) which are most often deliberately used with the conscious intent to send a particular message to the other person, (d) for which the person who sees the emblem usually not knows the emblem message but also knows that it was deliberately sent to him and (e) for which the sender usually takes responsibility for having made the communication. A further touch-stone of an emblem is whether it can be replaced by a word or two, its message verbalized, without substantially modifying a conversation... Emblems, as we have defined them, are communicative and interactive acts."

2511 **पितृ**

Pitṛ : father. In our country the father is still not a family friend, but a dictator... culturally we expect the father to be a sort of authority, and every member of the family must try to keep him happy. The family is ready to accept this type of dictatorship. We still feel that we are not able to speak frankly or discuss all our desires with our fathers. Whenever children want to ask something they speak with their mothers. This is because of fear of dictatorship, and not fear of the father as a person. The father is head of the family. Sometimes he is used as a policeman over all the activities of the children, and I think that is the reason for the relationship I have observed in many families. The children are never free in activities and speech in the company of their fathers. But though the child is always in its mother's company, it still likes to follow the father's mannerisms. The father thinks that to look after the child's training is not his field and so he should not waste his time with the child. Many fathers do not even know what their children are learning in the school.

2512 **पितृ-हस्त**

Pitṛ-hasta : gesture indicating a father. If in the gesture of *mātṛ-hasta* (q.v.) the gesture of *sikhara* is held with the right hand, in lieu of *ardhacandra*, it is *pitṛ-hasta* - that indicates either a father, or a son-in-law (*AD*, 231-244).

2513 **पित्ताधिका**

Pattādhikā : lady whose body contains more bile; quality of the Mare-lady (*Nāgarasarvasva,* 14.6).

2514 **पिबतखादता**

Pibata-khādatā : eat and drink.

2515 **पिष्टपेषण**

Piṣṭa-peṣaṇa : to grind what is already ground, repetition. Repetition in behaviour is another aspect of human activity that deserves attention. In Sanskrit, *āmreḍita* is used when a morpheme is repeated in a compound. Repetition can be seen at all levels of behaviour and throughout the developmental stages, from infant acquisition of Communication to Kālidāsa's 'mandam mandam'. It is not unusual for children to repeat an expression half a dozen time and more. Repetition occurs in conversational behaviour to emphasize. We find repetition in tribal music. Yet again, some people cannot tolerate the repetition in the speech. In trauma, people are known to repeat a phrase or a particular movement, as also in eating or drinking the *bhāng*. Some activities may be repetitious, and helpful in their monotony, because, by following habits, the brain can be freed to other creative productivity, as in the recitation of a *yogic* formula. But when repetitious activity is important, a person may balance novelty with repetition. *Piṣṭapreṣaṇa* is also a logical formula: Siddhi vastu kī siddhi ko vṛthā jatan jahan ṭhān kahat piṣṭapreṣaṇa tihīn kavijan buddhinidhān (Bhanu: *Kāvyaprabhākara*).

2516 **पिहित-पुट**

Pihita-puṭa : closed eyelids, fully contracted eyelids, almost covered in thinking, dreaming, eye-sore, etc. (*NS*, VIII. 105-113); suggests sleep, faint, affliction due to storm, heat, smoke, rains, collyrium and eye-disease.

2517 **पीठकेलि**

Pīṭha-keli : male confident.

2518 **पीठमर्द**

Pīṭhamarda : the associate of hero in the episode of a drama. He is a little less qualified than the hero, and helps him in sentiments other than erotic. (DR.II.12). *Pīṭhamardikā* is an attendant, a lady assisting the heroine in securing her lover.

2519 **पीडितक**

Pīḍitaka : pressing position in coition seen in the Elephant-lady (*Kāmasūtra,* 2.6.14).

2520 **पीडितकम् आलिङ्गनम्**

Pīḍitikamāliṅganam : pressing embrace. *Kāmasūtra* (2.2.13) explains that "when on a particular situation (dark, public resort, lonely place) two lovers meet, one of them presses the other's body forcibly against a wall or pillar, it is called pressing embrace: *tadeva kuḍyasandeśena stambhasandeśena vā sphuṭamavapīḍayediti pīḍitikam.* The pressing embrace has been described by Kālidāsa (*Kumārasaṁbhava,* 8.14) while narrating the honey-moon scene of Śiva and Pārvatī:

> Sasvaje priyamuronipīḍanam
> prārthitam mukhamanena nāharat |
> mekhalā praṇayalolatā gatam
> hastamasya śithilam rurodha ||

2521 **पीत-पलगन्धि-सुरताम्बु**

Pīta-palagandhi-suratāmbu : lady whose mucus is yellowish and smells like meat., quality of the Mare-lady (*Ratirahasya,* 3.22-26).

2522 **पीताम्बर**

Pītāmbara : yellow garments. It is customary for a newly girl to put on yellow (in some parts as in Mithila red) *sāṛī* as this colour is omenous.

The colours of garments differ according to the rituals. *Pītāmbara* is a yellow silk cloth lower-wearing, whiee-worship Brahmā it is put on (*Brahma.* 61.7.8). Yellow is primarily the colour of stimulating body, intellectuality, hope and productivity. Those who wear it are interested in new ideas.

2523 **पीन-कठिन-कुच-कलशा**

Pīna-kaṭhina-kuca-kalaśā : lady whose breast-pitchers are hard and full of flesh, quality of the Mare-lady (*Ratirahasya,* 3.22-26).

2524 **पीन-घ्राण-कपोल-कर्ण-गलक**

Pīna-ghrāṇa-kapola-karṇa-galaka : lady whose nose, cheeks, ears and neck are big, quality of the Elephant lady (*Pañcasāyaka,* 2.14).

2525 **पीनोत्तुङ्ग-कुच**

Pīnottuṅga-kuca : lady whose breasts are plumb and protruding, quality of the Lotus-lady (*Anaṅgaraṅga,* 1.11-12).

2526 **पीनोरू**

Pīnorū : strong thighs, quality of the Horse-man (*Ratirahasya,* 3.34-35).

2527 **पीनोरू-कामालय**

Pīnorū-kāmālaya : the lady whose thighs and sex-organ are fleshy; quality of the Deer-lady (*Anaṅgaraṅga,* 3.20-21).

2528 **पीवर**

Pīvaraḥ : stout, quality of the Bull-man (*Ratirahasya*, 3.32-33).

2529 **पुंलिङ्ग**

Puṁlliṅga : masculine gender.

2530 **पुंलिङ्ग-हस्त**

Puṁlliṅga-hasta : masculine hands. *Bālarāmabharata* divides *asaṁyuta* and *saṁyuta hastas* into all the three genders. It is one of them.

2531 **पुंवेशनायिका**

Puṁveśanāyikā : women dressed like men. According to the *Brahmavaivarta-Purāṇa* (II.4.180-181) the Gōpīs were seen in the Goloka as wearing men's clothes.

2532 **पुंव्यञ्जन**

Puṁvyañjana : male organ. Male-fingers pointed directly at his genitals is the gesture of the aggressive sexuality.

2533 **पुंश्चली**

Puṁścalī : demi monde corrupting young men; running after men (*Śuklayajurveda*, XXX. 5-6, 22). It is known as *maṭakko* in colloquial Hindi that means one who wantons in her gait. *Pumāṁsam pumāṁsam prati calati.* 'unchaste woman'.

2534 **पुंसवन**

Puṁsavana : ceremony leading to the birth of a male child. Time of menses: *snātā puṁsavane śuciḥ* (*Mbh.* 1.13).

2535 **पुंस्कामा**

Puṃskāmā : wishing for a husband; *garmāī* in Hindi.

2536 **पुट**

Puṭa : eyelid. Movement of the eyelids. There are nine types of eyelid-movements enumerated by Bharata (*NS*, VIII. 110-14): *unmeṣa* (opening the eyelids), *nimeṣa* (closing the eyelids), *prasṛta* (eyelids well extended), *kuñcita* (contracted eyelids), *sama* (normal eyelids), *vivartita* (eyelids moved up), *sphurita* (throbbing eyelids), *vitāḍita* (upper eyelid suddenly striking the lower). Gestures of eyelids are guided by the meaningful movement of the eyeballs. They give appropriate exposures of mental waves in special relation to their respective impulses.

2537 **पुटपाक**

Puṭapāka : a particular method of preparing drugs, in which the various ingredients are wrapped up in leaves, and being covered with clay and roasted in the fire (*Āyurveda*).

2538 **पुण्ड्रलांछन**

Puṇḍra-lāñchana: *puṇḍra*-marks. *Skanda Purāṇa* (II. 5.2.20) prescribes various *puṇḍra* marks for various *varṇas*. For a brāhmaṇa twelve *puṇḍras*, for the kṣatriya four *puṇḍras*, for the vaiṣya two *puṇḍras*, for the śūdra and women one, at fore-head only. The black *puṇḍra* is for pacification, red for control, yellow for wealth, white for release (*mokṣa*).

The *puṇḍra* is the symbol of the *kālātman* (time that is the soul of the universe), and one who holds the *tripuṇḍra* symbolically holds this universal soul (*Kūrma*, 1.2.103-105).

2539 **पुण्य**

Puṇya : meritorious acts which, according to the *Dharmaśāstras*, consist in performing the prescribed rituals, *saṁskāras*, *dānas*, five daily sacrifices, going on pilgrimage and so forth. There are nine kinds of *puṇya* and forty-two ways in which the reward of *karma* can be reaped according to Jainism. The Buddhist term for meritorious act is *kuśala-karma*.

2540 **पुत्र**

Putra : the son. The word 'putra' means 'he who protects from going to hell'. Having a son not only assures a man social dignity and status, but through their functional solidarity father and son are jointly and successfully responsible for the maintenance of all other members of the family. In fact, the relationship is one of mutual dependence. The son must obey his father unquestioningly, pay him formal respect, for example, touching his father's feet on parting or reunion, and offer him the complete support in every need, both in life and after death. Likewise, the father owes his son support, a good education, the best possible marital arrangement, sound caste and kinship relations and inheritance of property. Much of the interaction between father and son takes place in the context of caste and kin dispute, factionalism, and distrust for outgroups. The principal aspect of paternal socialization is the transmission of information to sons on the various feuds, alliances, and friendships in which the family has been involved from generation to generation, thus reflecting its status image within the community.

We may assume that the rigid, formal system of obligations with its culturally prescribed alienation (on personal level) between father and son acts as a control on the son's unconscious oedipal wishes. Probably because of sexual connotations, fathers in many parts of India were only supposed to hold, play, or interact with their nephews, never their sons. Disciplining might also, for the same reason, be permitted to the father in the privacy of the home and not among his adult male peers. Similarly, even the general welfare of sons used frequently to be the responsibility of the grandfather or uncles. At the same time the aloofness of the father would suggest unconscious resentment of the son. The duty of the son to perform his father's last rites, accentuates the father's dependence on the son. The manifold restrictions placed on intimacy between father and son control their feelings of ambivalence to each other. An external, disciplined paternal training and an internal, oral aggressive mechanism help to circumvent, or altogether avoid, conflict. The strong overt hostility to the father by rebellious sons which is so much a feature of Western patriarchal societies, is checked in the Indian joint family not only by plural discipline and the code of formal respect, but also by the narcissistic streak which gives the father a strong sense of identification with his son, preventing excessive authoritarian rule of the kind the Westerners associate with, for example, ancient Roman families.

Various types of *putras* (sons) are discussed in the Sanskrit texts. They are (1) *aurasa* (born from legally wedded wife). (2) *putrikāsuta* (son of the brotherless daughter). (3) *kṣetraja* (son born of one's wife from one's younger brother). (4) *gūḍhaja* (son born of a woman, when her husband is absent, the real father being unknown). (5) *kānīna* (son of an unmarried woman). (6) *paunarbhavaḥ* (the son of a widow remarried). (7) *dattaka* (son given away by his parents). (8) *krīta* (son bought from his parents and adopted). (9) *kratrima* (artificial son adopted giving the temptation of property, etc.) (10) *dattātman* (an orphan or a son who being deserted by his parents offers himself to persons prepared to adopt him as a son). (11) *sahoḍhaja* (son of a woman pregnant at marriage). (12). *apaviddha* (son deserted by his parents and adopted by another).

2541 पुत्रक

Putraka : the son, a disciple or a son is to be addressed by the guru (teacher) as *putraka, vatsa, tāta* or by name or clan name (*NS*, XVII. 65-94). Those who have been initiated into *viśeṣa-dīkṣā* of *Āgama-Śaivism*. They are so called because they belong to the *sāmīpya* stage of spiritual progress in which they feel them to be the son of God.

2542 पुत्रमन्थ

Putra-mantha : copulation. One of the *pañcāgnividyās*. Copulation gestures are of two kinds, those that emphasize insertion and those that represent pelvic thrusting.

2543 पुत्रहस्त

Putra-hasta : the gesture of a son. Placing the gesture *sandaṁśa* on the belly, moving it round over there and then framing the *śikhara* gesture with the left; are the symbol of a son (*AD*, 231-244).

2544 पुत्रिका

Putrikā : daughter, puppet. These are small figures with exaggerated limbs, the eyes and nose being disproportionate in the anatomy of body compared with earthly beings. The language of these creatures is the whistling, squeaking voice which accompanies all movements and which is interpreted by the person, who gives the rhythm. Puppets have limited vocabulary, therefore the movements play a more important part than the spoken word. Conversation is shown by bringing the mouth of one puppet to the ears of another by jerking the strings of both puppets. Anger is shown by a quick jerk of the puppet done with a slight movement of the hand. Laughter is shown by jerking the puppet in such a way that the shoulders make quick upward and downward movements. Indifference or rather contempt, is shown by turning one puppet away from another puppet, bringing the latter round to face of the first puppet, and repeating this movement several times. Fighting puppets are moved towards each other with great speed, and with sword and other weapons in their hands. The lifting of a weight is done in a very humorous way. The puppet is bent over with the help of its strings, until it touches the object to be lifted.

Sound effects are given from the back of the stage, with jerks to the puppet, as well as the object. Delivery of inspiring speeches is made by moving the hands of the puppets in an upward direction and giving a little jerk to it. Greeting and saluting is done by handling the puppets and leaving their arms to hang loosely. Rebuking and beating is done by throwing one puppet on the other. An affectionate meaning is shown by bringing the shoulders of two puppets together.

These are only a few examples from the code language used by the puppeteers.

2545 पुद्गल

Pudgala : atom. According to Buddhists, something endowed with *sparśa, gandha* and *varṇa*. It is of two kinds, *viz. aṇu* and *skandha*. In the early Buddhism *pudgala* denotes *attā* or soul. It is matter in the Jain cosmic conception.

2546 पुनरुक्ति

Punarukti : repetition. Repetition in tribal behaviour is an aspect of activity which deserves attention. Repetition can be seen at all levels of behaviour and throughout the developmental stages. Repetition occurs in conversational behaviour to an astonishing degree. Tribal people have a remarkable tolerance to repetition in their folkmusic. Tribal activities are always repetitious, and helpful in their monotony, because, by following habits, the brain can be freed to other creative productivity.

2547 **पुनर्विवाह**

Panarvivāha : remarriage. In Indian society remarriage was allowed if the husband is lost (for many years), is dead, has become a medicant, is a eunuch or he has fallen low. In the event of husband being dead, she may be given to the *devara* (younger brother); and in his absence she may be given to any body according to the elders' desire (*Agni*, 154.5.6): *Manu* (IX. 64) and other texts on *Dharmaśāstra* did not give further sanction to this custom referring it as an old custom and not favouring it in the Kali-age.

2548 **पुमर्थता**

Pumarthatā : aim of man.

2549 **पुरश्चरण**

Puraścarana : (a) repeated recitation of a *mantra*, form of *sādhanā* in *Tantra*. In it the *sādhaka*, after taking of *haviṣyānna* or *pañca-gavya* recites with a concentrated mind a particular *mantra* many times. The purpose of *puraścaraṇa* is to attain *mātṛsiddhi*. (b) a preparatory rite (*A*, 4.5.7).

2550 **पुरः पश्चात् स्थितोरू**

Puraḥ-paścāt-sthitorū : crossing of the thighs (*Bālarāmabharata*).

2551 **पुराण**

Purāṇa : the *Purāṇas* occupy a very important place in ancient Indian literature. They are the source-books of modern popular Hindu religion and philosophy. It is the *Purāṇas*, which are instrumental in carrying the Indian civilization and culture to the door of the common man. It would be no exaggeration to say that *Purāṇas* are the encyclopaedia of Hindu religion, philosophy and culture. Their deep knowledge is absolutely necessary for the exposition of the *Vedas*. It is truly said that the *Vedas* fear that foolish people who are quite ignorant of *Purāṇic* lore may not deceive them while explaining their meaning. A Brāhmaṇa, who might be well-versed in all the six branches of the *Vedas* and may also be expert in the study of the *Upaniṣads* can never be termed as a scholar, unless he has mastered the *Purāṇas* (*Vāyu Purāṇa*, 1. 200-201). One may be a *Vedic* scholar and may have studied all the *Śāstras*, cannot possess a true vision of things until he has heard or studied the *Purāṇas* (*Padma Purāṇa*, 105. 12-13).

The message of the *Purāṇas* is the most sublime. It is inspiring and prompts us to greater and greater action. There can be no better and timely message than is recorded in the *Padma Purāṇa*. A sacrificer prays, 'O God! the donors in our country may increase; the study of the *Vedas* and *Śāstras* may be popularised; let our descendants march on the path of progress and prosperity; may our faith increase in the performance of the sacrifices and pious and virtuous deeds; may we possess riches, so that, we may distribute them among the poor and the needy; may the corn grow in our fields in large quantity, and may we have enough of food and drinks; may guests favour us with their visits; may the beggars and the poor come to us, but we never beg of anybody (*Padma Purāṇa, Sṛṣṭi-khaṇḍa*, 9. 117-18).

Thus, the *Purāṇas* are an important body of literature in Indian tradition, comprising theology, mythology, cosmogony, and chronology into one elaborate structured whole. This mythological bias of the Indian mind has often been a target of mockery. The Western 'scientific' approach has been almost obsessed with history and the historical obligation of man, an attitude essentially linked with a view of time as undirectional, irreversible and 'deathward' set. It is only in recent years that modern man in the West has gradually reawakened to the value of myth not only in the enrichment but even the survival of human personality. The Indian mind has always conceived of change within a frame-work of continuity, a new event is regarded not as a historical product of preceding events but rather as a re-enactment of the first event of creation.

(b) A story or implied account of the characteristics of nature, or of beings with superhuman powers and qualities, the commerce of gods with men, and the fate of gods. In contradistinction to a fairy tale, a myth is taken as true by its narrators and hearers, and formulates the world-view or conception of history of a community or society, even though — in rational and casually explicative terms, — it seems improbable and nonsensical.

The basic heuristic problem of research into myths is that the "experienced" and "living" myth requires and allows of no interpretation.

Myth provides a closed picture of the world which, in contrast to the scientific world-view, recognizes no open questions, and therefore embodies one stage in the historical development of thought.

Myth's functional role in the primitive society has been accepted and analysed by anthropologists and folklorists. According to Malinowski Myth "expresses, enhances and codifies belief; it safeguards and enforces morality; it vouches for the efficiency of the ritual and contains practical rules for the guidance of mass. Myth is thus a vital ingredient of human civilization, it is not an intellectual explanation or an artiotic imagery, but a pragmatic charter of primitive faith and moral wisdom" (1926:19). LeviStrauss also believes that the myths of primitive people reveal a kind of truth about the nature and working of human mind. Myth's importance in the Indian society hardly needs any analysis as it is a recognized fact having a long history of voluminous treatises known as the *Purāṇa.* Myths, in fact, constitute a significant part of religious beliefs, customs and performances of the Hindus and socalled tribes.

Biardeau has applied the following method to Hindu mythology: "As our texts shed little light on this point, we may look for some similar stories where the symbolic meaning would be made more explicit. What appears to many people as an unmanageable growth of myths in epics and *Purāṇas* is actually an invaluable source of information for a better understanding of each of them.... The regional variants are all authentic as long as the overall significance of the epic remains... 'The major variations in the text are likely each to have its own significance fitting into the whole' (1970.293).

2552 **पुराणिक**

Purāṇika : the bard who recited the *Purāṇas,* the reader of *Purāṇas.* The *Purāṇic* cult is still prevalent in the village India. According to the *Purāṇas,* he is well-versed. He should finish his preliminaries up to bath prior to the break of the day. He is to face the north, while the audience the east (*Bhāgavata P.* 40.25). By the side of the reader, there should be another learned person who would explain the difficult portions, or elucidate certain important portions and concepts (*Ibid.* 25): *paṇḍitaḥ samśayacchettā loka-bodhana-tatparaḥ.* On the day previous to the starting of the *saptāha* the reader should have his head tonsured (*Ibid*). On the first day the *purāṇika* is said to be worshipped, and so the *Purāṇa*- manuscript (*Padma P., Uttarakhaṇḍa* 29.2.3-26). The reading of a *Purāṇa* is said to start on any auspicious day in the bright half of a month (*Ibid. Pātālakhaṇḍa* III.22). The seat of the *purāṇika* was called *dharmāsana* (*Ibid.* 27). At the end of the session the *purāṇicka* was to be honoured with gift of a new silken clothes and other things (*Ibid. 28*). The *purāṇika* was never to bow to anybody once he takes his seat on this *āsana.* He is called *Vyāsa* and the seat *Vyāsāsana* (*Sk.P.* III. 3.22.25).

Purāṇikas have acquired special status and money. Some of the *purāṇikas* of Chhattisgarh have even weilded power and have entered into the politics.

2553 **पुरुकुत्सु-हस्त**

Purukutsu-hasta : *alapadma-hasta* represents the mythical king Purukutsa (*Mirror of Gesture,* p. 47).

2554 **पुरुरवस्-हस्त**

Pururavas-hasta : *muṣṭi-hasta* represents the mythical king Pururavas (*Mirror of Gesture,* p. 47).

2555 **पुरुष**

Puruṣa : a measure, same as *chāyāpuruṣa* (*A,* 2.33.3). (b) male being, person. Generally meaning 'person'. The word is of *Vedic* origin and derived from the *Sāṁkhya* ideology, to distinguish the principle of life and consciousness from the inanimate but evolving *Prakṛti* (*Lakṣmi-Tantra,* 16.15). In the traditional texts, the word signified godhead, usually Viṣṇu. Etymologically, the meaning would be "the spirit that is hidden in the body" (*puri śete*), the spirit that fills the universe and makes it complete (from the root *prū*) (c) *puruṣa-lakṣaṇam* 'signs of men'. This an important chapter in *Bṛhat-Saṁhitā* (LXVIII) dealing with the physiognomy of man. The origin of this science is traced to Lord Śiva, one of His numerous names being *Samudra,* and to a sage called *Samudra.* Hence the popular name of this lore is *Sāmudrikaśāstra.*

2556 **पुरुष-केशरचना**

Puruṣa-keśaracanā : male hair-dressing. To the Hindu, the mode of dressing hair has a deep religious significance. Shaving is something of a ceremony and the barber a priest. The caste and religion of a man is known mainly by the manner he dresses his hair. The easiest way to recognize a Sikh is by his long hair and beard. The generality of Hindus in North India shave their heads and faces clean, leaving a small tuft of hair, known as *coṭī,* at the back of the head. The *coṭī* is dear to the Hindu and even those who crop their hair in western fashion take care to see that the *coṭī* is not cropped off.

Hair dressing among men has not developed into so elaborate an art in North India as in the South. The Brahmins of South India shave the front portion of the head but grow long hair on the back which is tied into a knot at the back of the neck. Others think this practice unclean; hence while they shave the front part of the head, they crop the hair at the back low. The Brahmaṇs and Nayars of Malabar are contemptuous of the taste of the Tamils in the matter of hair dressing; they shave the back of the head and leave the hair to grow long at the front of the head in a circle, shaving off the sides which fall beyond the radius of the circle. Men in the south are as much proud of their hair as women, and take great care in combing and oiling it, and assiduously practise the art of tying the end of the hair into a beautiful knot.

During days of mourning, and certain periods of ceremonial impurity the Brahmaṇ will not shave. But when this period is over, he shaves from head to foot excepting his *coṭī* or its equivalent. The only persons who are allowed to shave off their *coṭī* are *sannyāsins* who, as a sign of having attained emancipation from all bonds, may discard both the sacred thread and the *coṭī*. Some *sannyāsins*, on the other hand show their spirit of emancipation by not shaving at all, and leave the hair and beard to grow into dirty glued locks. Among the ordinary run of Hindus, the western method of cropping is becoming exceedingly popular and people have now begun to crop off their *coṭis*.

Hindus shave their beards but some of them keep moustaches. Among certain communities, moustaches are shaved off in times of mourning. It is said that during the life-time of father, one should not shave his moustaches. The Hindus of Bengal and Malabar love to shave their faces clean.

2557 **पुरुषत्वं योषितत्वं च**

Puruṣatvam yoṣitatvam ca : sociology of gender. The *Kāmasūtra* (2.7.21) distinguishes between manhood and womanhood. According to Vātsyāyana, manhood consists of roughness and impetuosity, while weakness, tenderness and inclination to turn away from unpleasant things are the distinguishing markers of womanhood:

> *pāruṣyam rabhasatvam ca puruṣam teja ucyate* I
> *aśaktir ārtivyāvṛttir abalatvam ca yoṣitaḥ* II

Vikrālā has the same concept of womanhood when she suggests her friend as follows:

*anubandhamānukūlyam vāmatvam prauḍhatama sāmarthyam*I
surateṣu darśayiṣyasi kāmukabhāvam sphuṭam buddhva¯II
(Dāmodaragupta, *Kuṭṭanīmatam*, 159).

"At the time of sexual act, having understood the emotions of your partner you should show your love, co-operation, skill, maturity and weakness'. Further she opines that weakness of the females encourages the males at the time of love-union:

Yāvad yāvadśaktim prathayati lalanāhi mohanākrāntā I
tāvattāvat puṁsāmutsāhaḥ pallavān samutsṛjati II
(*Ibid.*, 1053)

But Vikaṭanitambā instructs a lover not to show mercy due to her delicateness during the coition:

> bālā tanvī mṛduriyamiti tyajyatāmatra śaṅkā
> kāñcid dṛṣṭvā bhramarabharato mañjarībhajyamānām I
> tasmādeṣā rahasi bhavatā nirdayam pīḍanīyā
> mandrākrāntā visṛjati rasam ikṣuyaṣṭisamagram II
> (*Ibid.*, 1033).

2558 **पुरुष-परिधानम्**

Puruṣa-paridhānam : men's dress. The generality of Hindus practice economy of wearing clothes. In South India, throughout the year and in North during the hot season, men in their houses wear loin cloths and leave the upper part of the body and head bare. Those young men who consider the loin cloth too scanty for modern ideas of modesty wear the *dhoti* at home, which, as a rule, is used only out of doors. The *dhoti* is a single piece of white cloth, about five yards long and three to four feet broad. It is passed round the waist up to half its length and the other half is drawn between the legs and tucked at the waist behind. The aristocrats in Bengal wear unusually long *dhotis* which leave, when worn, about a yard of cloth in front which is passed over the upper part of the body and thrown over the shoulders somewhat like the toga of the Roman aristocrats. While walking about, the Bengali holds this portion of the *dhoti* in his hands. Inside the house all Hindus walk about barefoot, sandals made of leather being considered unclean.

The generality of Hindus in South India wear only *dhotis* and go barefoot and bareheaded, the upper part of the body uncovered. The better classes, especially on ceremonial occasions, wear long coats and turbans. In Malabar, however, aristocracy is measured in proportion to the amount of bareness of the body, and the less a Hindu is covered the more aristocratic is he considered. Some of the Nambudiri Brāhmans wear just a narrow piece of cloth in front when inside the houses, and a loin cloth when going out of doors. The Malabar Brāhmaṇ usually protects himself with an umbrella made of the leaves of the talipot palm. In North India, except in Bengal, the Hindus wear head-dresses. These vary in shape and size according to the caste and social position of the wearer. The turban is the favourite head-dress of the Sikhs and the Rajputs. All turbans are not however alike. The turban of the Madrasi aristocrat is a neat affair in white with a bright band binding up the sides to the crest, symmetrical in shape. When worn, it leaves the ears free and becomes the head very well. The turban worn by the lower classes in Bombay, Gujarat, Rajasthan and Kutch is a long narrow piece of thin white or coloured cloth wound loosely round the head, covering up at least one of the ears and a good part of the brow, and sits on the head like a crushed basket. The better classes in these parts of India wear their turbans neater, but the design is the same and the turban must cover half of one ear and a good part of the brow. The Punjabi Hindus' turban, a model borrowed from the Muslim, is martial in appearance. It is of white or coloured muslin wound beautifully round a small peaked cap of bright material, one end of the muslin rising up in a flowery crest in front and the other end hanging at the back of the neck as a tail. When worn by a well proportioned man, it looks very impressive.

Before passing from the subject of headdress, a word may be said about the Gandhi cap. This is a plain white cap made of the thick *Khaddar* which, when not required, can be folded and kept in the pocket. Instead of pure white, some people prefer brown and dark hues but the shape and material are the same. The Gandhi cap is generally worn by Congressmen and those who profess sympathy for Congress ideals, and its use by Hindu clerks in government offices was, during the British period, considered by Englishmen as an offence against official etiquete. It is the white cap that was objectionable, and not the dark and brown ones. The cap, it may be mentioned, was invented and popularised by Gandhiji as the best for Indian climate and pocket, hence its name. It's one great advantage over other caps is that it can be washed while other kinds of caps are worn till they stink. Gandhiji, by the way, never wore the Gandhi cap.

The Hindus as a rule do not care much for the tailored clothes. But in the Punjab some Hindus have adopted the *salwar* or the baggy trousers of the Muslims. Throughout Nothern India, out-of-doors the Hindus wear tight jackets or loose shirts. In Bengal and U.P., in spite of centuries of Muslim domination, the preference for the *dhoti* prevails. The Rajputs wear tight breeches of thin linen. The Sikhs do not care much for *dhotis.* They wear loose shirts, breeches and turbans. For the Sikh the turban has a religious significance, and no Sikh is allowed to discard his turban for a cap. Well-to-do Hindus who wish to appear aristocratic, wear long coats like the Rajas and Nawabs. The long coat known as sherwānī, has been standardized and is the dress recognized by the Government of India for official and ceremonial wear.

Now most of the modernized Hindu males have adopted the European costume in their outdoor life.

2559 पुरुषभाव

Puruṣabhāva : *Nar.Manu Smṛti* (XII.9 and 10) describes "an eligible male". The joints of his shoulder, his knees and his bones are well built. His neck and his shoulders are well-shaped. His neck and the skin of the body is thick. His department and his voice is unbroken. His excreta does not float on water, and his urine is full of bubbles and noisy (*rāvi*). These are external signs of manhood and they do not have much significance in deciding manhood in the eyes of modern science.

2560 पुरुषमेघ

Puruṣa-medha : human sacrifice. There are actually some instances of human sacrifices (*Taitt. Br.* II. 4; *Vāj. Saṁ.* XXX-XXXI) and there is reason to believe that in the earliest stage of *aśvamedha* human beings were sacrificed and the custom was later substituted by the sacrifice of horse.

2561 पुरुषाञ्जलि

Puruṣāñjali : the palm of a man (*Mānasāra,* XVIII. 6-7).

2562 पुरुषाभरणम्

Puruṣābharaṇam : men's ornament: The craze for ornaments is common to all Hindus. This applies to the male of the species. In addition to the ring, which men all over the world love to wear, a Hindu gentleman delights to wear wristchains and bangles. In most parts of India, men wear ear-rings, studded with glittering stones, and for this purpose the ears of the Hindu boy is bored at an early age. Boys and grown-up men, when they can afford it, wear gold chains and lockets round their necks. The craze for ornaments is greatest among South Indians, and here many an ebony coloured, pot-bellied male may be seen in the street with his bare trunk adorned as a black idol of Krishna. He wears glittering ear-rings, gold wristchains in many folds, a huge locket round the neck hanging from a massive gold chain, and a gold girdle worn round the waist over the dhoti.

The poorer classes imitate the rich. Among them, the males have to be contented with cheap silver ear-rings and a silver or brass locket tied from a string.

2563 पुरुषायित

Puruṣāyita : opposite of the usual custom of cohabitation when the female plays the role of male. It is also known as *viparīta rata,* i.e. the woman acting like the man (*Kāmasūtra,* 2.8.1). Sanskrit poets have given much importance to *puruṣāyita* and have described it in various way (*Subhāṣita-ratnabhaṇḍāra,* p. 320; *Sārṅgadhara—paddhati,* 3698; *Mukundānanda bhāṇa.* 192; *Hammīrakāvya,* 7.73; *Caurapañcāśikā,* 12; *Amarukaśataka* 3; *Śrīkaṇṭhacarita* 15.35; *Vikramāṅkadevacarita,* 7.23; *Kuṭṭanīmatam* 389; *Gīta-Govinda,* 12.4; *Naiṣadha,* 16.15; etc.). (b) a type of penance said to have been performed by the daughters of Dakṣa to propitiate Śiva:

पुरुषायितेन संज्ञेन तप्तं यत्तपसाधुना ।
(*Skanda.*IV. 16.13.5) (Fig. 2563)

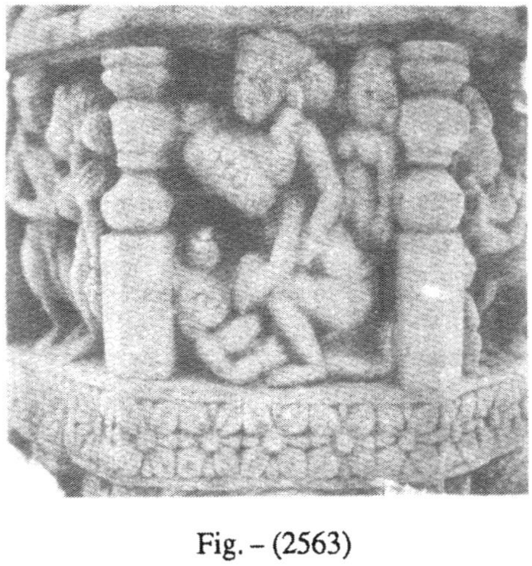

Fig. – (2563)

2564 **पुरुषार्थ**

Puruṣārtha : value, the aim of life, the meaning or purpose of life; the four ends or values of life, that is, *dharmārthakāmamokṣa,* the advantage to be derived from the accomplished work as from *kratvārtha,* the good of the work to be done. These are *dharma, artha, kāma* and *mokṣa.* The first three are collectively known as *abhyudaya* and the last one as *niḥśreyas.* The acceptance of *puruṣārtha* was basic to membership in Indian society. The individual who did not pattern his behaviour after them, was regarded as a deviant. These were the parts of cultural norms and expectations for the Hindu society.

2565 **पुरोनतहस्त**

Puronata hasta : single hand gesture mentioned in *Bālarāmabharata* but absent in *NS* similar to *candrakalā.*

2566 **पुलक**

Pulaka : bristling of hair.

2567 **पुष्कलाभिधान**

Puṣkalābhidhāna : having words or sentences indicative of their meanings, or having words or sentences indicative of vast meaning.

2568 **पुष्प**

Puṣpa : (a) flower. (b) remark in relation to excellent qualities: *vākyam viśeṣavat* (*DR.* 1.62).

2569 **पुष्पकर्म**

Puṣpa-karma : worship with flowers. "Whoever with devotion offers me a leaf, a flower, a fruit or water, that I accept — the devout gift of the pure minded" (*Bhagavatgītā,* IX.26).

2570 **पुष्पगण्डिका**

Puṣpagaṇḍikā : subdivision of gentle dance in which men act as women and women as men (*SD,* VI. 21).

2571 **पुष्पपथ**

Puṣpapatha : the vulva, way to monthly course, the external genitalia of the female.

2572 **पुष्पपुट-हस्त**

Puṣpapuṭa-hasta : the flower-plate hands. If the fingers of the *sarpa-śiraḥ* gesture are very close and the second finger is by the side of the same gesture on the other hand, it is called the *puṣpapuṭa* gesture. It is used to express the idea of a heap of paddy, a deposit of water, a bunch of flowers, various edible things, accumulating money lawfully and to fetch and pass water (*NS,* IX. 140-141).

2573 **पुष्पभङ्ग**

Puṣpabhaṅga : festoon of flowers-वन्दनवार.

2574 **पुष्प-मुद्रा**

Puṣpa-mudrā : upturn two hands, curve little and ring fingers of them, extend two middle fingers and join fore-fingers with thumbs. This is *puṣpa-mudrā* (gesture of a flower) and may be treated as a style of *dravya* (*VD*). (b) gesture of a flower. All the fingers collected and curved together; make the second gesture for flower (*VD*).

2575 **पुष्पवती**

Puṣpavatī : menses, *rajasvalā.* About the menstruation the popular *Purāṇic* belief is that it was the result of a part of Indra's sin taken up by women, on the suggestion of Bṛahaspati. Indra killed Vṛta, the son of Tvaṣṭṛ, which act was a *brahmahatyā*— When Indra was afraid of this deadly sin, Bṛhaspati divided the sin among women, the trees, and the rivers, which release it at certain periods, and respectively in the form of menstruation — fluid, gum and the yellowish flood water in the rainy season (*Skanda,* 1.1.16.4). At another place, the division is said to have been accomplished by Brahmā (*Ibid,* V. 3.118.30), where it is said that half of the sin was given to women and is experienced by them on the second day of the period, and that the sin lasts for four days. According to another version (*Brahmāṇḍa,* 2.4.9. 24-25) it was Viṣṇu who divided the sin, and that the reward of this sin of Indra was that they would give birth to progeny after uniting with their husbands, immediately after the period of four days and during the period.

2576 **पुष्पशकटिका-कला**

Puṣpaśakaṭikākalā : fortune-telling by a flower-choice. One of the 64 arts given in the *Kāmasūtra.*

2577 **पुष्पास्तरणकला**

Puṣpāstaraṇa-kata : decoration of halls and assemblies with flowers and foliage. One of the 64 arts enumerated by Vātsyāyana. Bharata in his *NS* has enumerated *puṣpālaṅkāra* as a component of *alaṅkāra* which is a part of *āhāryābhinaya. Puṣpālaṅkāra* or the flower garlands have been classified under the following categories: (I) *veṣṭima:* In this along with flowers, leaves and green grass are woven decoratively. Abhinava explains it as उपरि जतुसिक्थादिना वेष्टस्तेन निर्वृत्तो वेष्टिमः (II) *vitata:* In it many garlands are mutually put together. (III) *saṅghātya*: In it the thread is woven through the flowers, or many bunches of flowers are woven together. (IV) *granthima*: In it the flowers are knitted together with knots. (V) *prālambita*: It is long garland hanging down.

2578 **पुष्पिका**

Puṣpikā : mucus of penis; *phūsī* in Bagheli.

2579 **पुष्पिता**

Puṣpitā : woman in menses. Female pheromores—copulins—are related to vaginal secretions and increase at ovulation.

2580 **पुष्परथ**

Puṣparatha : carriage for pleasure drive, prevalent as a rite at Dussura festival in Bastar.

2581 **पुस्त**

Pusta : the model work. One of the varieties of *āhāryābhinaya*. *Pusta* is again three fold: (I) *saṁdhima:* joined. It is the model work which is made up of birch, bamboo, skin, cloth and the like. (II) *vyājima:* mechanically devised. It is made by means of the *yantra* — a mechanical device (*NS*, II. 100). (III) *veṣṭima:* wrapped. Abhinava explains it as व्याजः सूत्रस्याकर्षादिरूपः क्षेपस्तेन निर्वृत्तो व्याजिमः *i.e.* formed by pulling the rope, etc. (NS, III. 110). Thus it is produced by wrapping. Hills, carriages, celestial cars, shields, armours, banners, elephants or trees which are constructed for use in a dramatic performance, are called model works.

In general, mountains, vehicles, *vimānas*, shields, armours, flags, etc. were included in *pusta* (*NS*, XXI.9). Thus, in *Śākuntalam*, the king enters seated on a chariot; in the *Mṛcchakaṭikam* a clay toy-cart gives the name to the play. In the *Bālarāmāyaṇa* we have mechanical dolls. Mythical animals and monsters could be made of bamboos and cloth.

2582 **पुस्तक**

Pustaka : book or manuscript held in the hands of some forms of deities (like Brahmā, Dakṣiṇā-mūrti, Gaṇapati, Sarasvatī, Haya-grīva, Hanumān and Vyāsa) is technically recognised as *āyudha* (weapon) belonging to the *sāttvika*-type. It is included among the thirty-six *āyudhas* listed in *Aparājita-Sūtra* (2.35) ascribed to Viśvakarmā. It is usually accompanied by other *āyudhas* like *akṣa-mālā* and *kamaṇḍalu*. The stance in which the book as an *āyudha* is carried is often seated one in *yogapaṭṭa* or *padmāsana*. According to *VD* (3.77.5) the book symbolizes scriptures (*āgama*) and the *akṣa-mālā* symbolizes time: *akṣamālā smṛtaḥ kālaḥ pustakam cāgamam smṛtam.*

Sacred books are objects of worship in India.

2583 **पुस्तक-वाचनम्**

Pustaka-vācanam: reading of different types of compositions. One of the 64 arts given by *Kāmasūtra.*

2584 **पूग**

Pūga : any combination or body of persons: an association, corporation, union. Assembly or group of families in the same village; assembly of townsmen *(Smṛiti);* a communal gathering (*A*, 1.13.2). (b) betel-nut. *pūga-puṣpikā* 'betel-nut and flowers given to guests at a function'; known as *patra-puṣpa.*

2585 **पूजा**

Pūjā : worship. It is of two kinds: *bāhya* (external) and *abhyantara* (internal). It may be *sādhāra* (with object) or *nirādhāra* (without object). It is often classified into *Vedic, Tantric* and *miśra* (*Gīta*, XI.57.7) Among the other classifications we have *nitya, naimittika,* and *kāmya; sāttvika rājasika* and *tāmasika; uttama, madhyama* and *adhama* (*Mahānirvāṇa*, XIV.122).

Pūjā was open to all while *homa* was restricted. Generally *pūjā* comprises sixteen acts or *upacāras*, namely *āsana* (seat), *pādya* (foot-wash), *arghya* (offerings), *snānīya* (washing material), *anulepana* (unguents), *dhūpa* (incense), *dīpa* (offering of light), *naivedya* (food-offering), *tāmbūla* (betel-leaf), *śītalajala* (cool water), *vasana* (cloth), *bhūṣaṇa* (ornament), *mālya* (wreath), *gandha* (sandal-paste), *ācamanīya* (water to sip) and a charming bed (*Brahmavaivarta*, 1.23. 53-54).

2586 **पूर्ण-कुम्भ**

Pūrṇa-kumbha : pot filled with water; (also known as *pūrṇa-ghaṭa* or *pūrṇa-kalaśā*) is a sacred symbol of prosperity. It is sometimes included in the group of *aṣṭa-maṅgala*, hence called *bhadra-kumbha.*

Sculptural representation of *pūrṇa-kumbha* are frequently seen in temples from very early times. They occur on walls and pillars in a variety of decorative arrangements.

Pūrṇa-kumbha occurs in *Kādambarī* as *pūrṇa-pātra* which means 'vessel filled with valuable things'. When a stranger brought some good news, it was customary to give him or her a vessel (*pūrṇapātra*) filled with valuable things such as clothes and ornament etc. cf. कदा ते तनयजन्म-महोत्सववानन्दनिर्भरो हरिष्यति पूर्णपात्रं परिजनः ? (*Kādambarī*) and also तत्कामं भवति पूर्णपात्रवृत्या स्वीकर्तुं मम हृदयं जीवितं च (*Mālatimādhavam*, IV). *Pūrṇapātra* is defined as

हर्षादुत्सवकाले यदलङ्कारांशुकादिभिः ।
आकृष्य गृह्यते पूर्णपात्रं स्यात्पूर्णकं च तत् ॥
वर्धापकं च यदानन्दालङ्कारादिकं पुनः ।
आकृष्य गृह्यते पूर्णपात्रं पूर्णानकं च यत् ॥

This practice is still prevalent in village India, particularly at the time of the news of the birth of a son.

2587 **पूर्ण-गण्ड**

Pūrṇa—gaṇḍa : raised (cheek muscles probably); a type of cheeks gesture in *vīra rasa*; fully expanded cheeks; the style of gesture of the cheek suggests pride, energy and joy (*NS*, VIII. 129-134).

2588 **पूर्णचन्द्र-हस्त**

Pūrṇacandra—hasta : single hand gesture mentioned in *Bālarāmabharata.*

2589 **पूर्णोदर**

Pūrṇodara : the full belly. The full belly is indicative of breathing out, fat-belly, stomach-disease, drowsiness and heavy eating (*NS*, X. 17-20).

2590 **पूर्वकाय**

Pūrvakāya : upper part of the body, above the navel. Taking the navel as a natural dividing line, the body has been into two sections. The *pūrvakāya* can be seen as an extrovert — for the functions of the upper half involve reaching out with the arms to express love, anger, to direct others and to perform all the intricate and symbolic gestures with our hands. Our upper part also houses the lungs and brair, and so is essential for our very being.

2591 **पूर्वपक्ष**

Pūrvapakṣa : the opponent's view, views of the opponents. In the Indian method of logical discourse it is the general rule that the views of the opponent will be introduced first in clear undistorted terms and then each point be refuted. Also known as *pūrva-koṭi* (starting point of debate).

2592 **पूर्वनिपात**

Pūrvanipāta : irregular priority of a word in a compound; opp. *paranipāta.*

2593 **पूर्वरङ्ग**

Pūrvaraṅga : preliminaries, prelude of a drama, the prologue (*SD*, VI. 22).

2594 **पूर्वराग**

Pūrvarāga : incipient love, pre-union love. *Pūrvarāga* is a love between two persons which results before their meeting. It is love at the first sight or on first hearing about the valour or virtues of a person. The lovers may see each other in person, in a picture, a dream etc. *Pūrvarāga* is a peculiar mental condition of mutual longing aroused at first acquaintance, direct or indirect; maiden alone can be its subject or object; love between two persons which springs before their meetings:

> Śravaṇād darśanādvāpi mithaḥ saṁrūḍharāgayoḥ ।
> daśāviśeṣo yo prāptau pūrvarāgaḥ sa ucyate ॥
> (*SD*,II.14)

2595 **पूर्ववाक्य**

Pūrvavākya : one of the 64 *sandhyaṅgas* in Indian dramaturgy. Bharata (*NS*, 19.103) defines it as showing the *artha* stated before. Dhanañjaya terms it *pūrvabhāva* and defines it as foreseeing of the *kārya* (denouement).

2596 **पूर्व-हस्त**

Pūrva-hasta : sometimes also referred to as *nija-hasta.* The term signifies the two normal hands of a four-armed deity, the extra hands being referred to as *para-hasta.*

2597 **पृच्छा**

Pṛcchā (NS) : question, form of speech and thought; questioning, asking, enquiring.

2598 **पृथग्जन**

Pṛthagjana : 'man of lower caste', the common people, (*Manu*). (b) Buddhist term for the ordinary individual. A person who labours under the delusion of "I-ness" or "Mine-ness" and thinks that he has *rūpa, vedanā,* etc. Not knowing the true law, he develops attachment to things and thereby increases the flowing inpurities (*āśrava*) of wordly desires, desire for re-existence and ignorance (*kāma, bhava* and *avijjātanhā*).

2599 **पृथु-कुच-युगला**

Pṛthukucayugalā : lady whose breasts are wide, quality of the Deer-lady (*Pañcasāyaka*, 2.12).

2600 **पृथु-कुचा**

Pṛthukucā : lady whose breasts are big, quality of the Elephant-lady (*Anaṅgaraṅga*, 3.24-25).

2601 **पृथ्वल्पनीलालका**

Pṛthvalpanilālakā : lady whose hair are thick, small and blackish; quality of the Elephant-lady (*Anaṅgaraṅga*, 3.24-25).

2602 **पृथ्वी-मुद्रा**

Pṛthvī-mudrā : gesture symbolizing the Earth of the Vaiṣṇavite cult. The *patāka*-hand up-turned symbolizes the Earth (VD).

2603 **पृष्ठ**

Pṛṣṭha : back. It is a common gesture in India that to say someone (of the same sex) bravo or encourage, the speaker pats his back. The Hindi idiom *pīṭh ṭhoknā* conveys the same meaning, *i.e.* to pat on the shoulder. This patting is not prevalent among cross-sexes. The shoulder is tabu-zone in the tribal society. One can touch the breast of a woman, but one can not touch her shoulder. The backs communicate in different postures like gracefully upright, rigid or bowed.

2604 **पृष्ठगत – बाहु**

Pṛṣṭhagata bāhu : the back-going arm (*NS*, IX. 205-206).

2605 **पृष्ठगत संस्थान्**

Pṛṣṭhagata saṁsthāna : standing-on-back position; also known as *ṛjvāgata saṁsthāna.* A figure, in this position should be direct, clear to dimensions and long drawn. The position will exhibit a front-look, distinct measurement, engrafted with requisite art qualities; like all-roundness, perfectly distributed limbs of the physique, suggestive to a tender rhythm, exposed with correct harmonious lines and having no weak limb or part of the art piece. The text represents two names of the position (i) *pṛṣṭhagata* and (ii) *ṛjvāgata* (*VD,* III. 39. 2-6). The first elicits negative response while the next is a more positive response in most situations.

2606 **पृष्ठमांसं खादति**

Pṛṣṭha-māṃsam khādati : indulges in backbiting (*Mbh*).

2607 **पृष्ठवाह**

Pṛṣṭhavāha : carrying a load on the back.

2608 **पृष्ठ-स्वस्तिक-करण**

Pṛṣṭha-svastika-karaṇa : arms and hands in *svastika,* but completely turned, so that back faces audience, feet and legs are in *apakrāntā cārī* and *ardhasūcī cārī* (*NS,* IV. 76-77, X.3.34). The legs come together in *svastika* with *apakrāntā* and *ardhasūcī cārīs* and the arms are thrown up and down and brought together in *svastika.* Its use is similar to that of *svastika.*

2609 **पृष्ठस्वस्तिकचारी**

Pṛṣṭhasvastika-cārī : a type of movement.

2610 **पृष्ठोत्तानतल-स्थानक**

Pṛṣṭhottānatala sthānaka : a type of posture.

2611 **पेचक-मुद्रा**

Pecaka-mudrā : gesture of an owl. The *gajadanta* hand indicates an owl (*Mirror of Gesture,* pp. 50-51).

2612 **पेल**

Pela : penis, too delicate, *pelhar* in Bagheli.

2613 **पेशल**

Peśala : lovely, charming (A, 2.25. 15).

2614 **पेशलवचन**

Peśala-vacana : soft-words win the heart (*Kuṭṭanīmatam,* 396).

2615 **पोटा**

Pota : a woman having the signs of man and woman, impotent.

2616 **पोत-मुद्रा**

Poṭā-mudrā : the gesture of a ship. "Make the fingers of palms a little curvingly extended; keep the two fore-fingers straightly up and place below the two thumbs. This is called a *pota-mudrā* (gesture of a ship). Divine beings dance with it. It assures enjoyment and salvation and removes all sorts of bad omens." (*BT*). (b) With the style of quivering fingers and the half-slant hand, when diving beings are attended to, it is called the *pota-mudrā,* which is applied to beg mercy of God" (*Ibid.*).

2617 **पौराणिक**

Paurāṇika : one belonging to the past, one reciting the *Purāṇas.*

2618 **पौरुष**

Pauruṣa : (a) height, length (*A,* 2.20.10; 17.18.19); (b) human energy, manhood, manliness. Manliness is the quality of one superior to weakness. *Bṛhaspati Sūtra* (III.1) tells us that it also means that manliness comes through conquest of difficulties and troubles:

जितक्लेषस्य पौरुषम्

The arrow does not shoot out of the bow of itself from the hands of the man who depends on *daiva* (chance or luck), says Somadeva (*Nītivākyāmṛta,* XXIX). It is to the person who depends on *pauruṣa* that there is the problem of gain or loss: पौरुषावलम्बिनोऽर्थानर्थयोः सन्देहः । But the fellow depending on *daiva,* loss is certain. the relationship between *daiva* (luck, chance, fate) and *pauruṣa* (human energy, exertion, manhood) are those between life and medicine. It is with such philosophy of faith in the efficiency of *pauruṣa* as capable of deciding the issue between success analyzes the relationship between man and man. In his treatise, then we are to encounter action, active life, the ability to transform external conditions, activism.

2619 **पौर्वापर्य**

Paurvāparya : relation of cause and effect, proper sequence.

2620 **प्रकटदशना**

Prakaṭa-daśanā : lady whose teeth are protruding, quality of the Elephant-lady (*Nāgarasarvasva,* 14.7).

2621 **प्रकम्पिताकटि**

Prakaṁpitā - kaṭi : hip in the trembling movement; the trembled hips; hips moving up and down obliquely. It is used to walk of a hunch-back, a dwarf and to indicate the way of inferior people (*NS,* X.21-26).

2622 **प्रकम्पितग्रीवा**

Prakampita-grīvā : a forward and backward movement of

the head (*Abhinayadarpaṇa*, 78-87), not mentioned in *NS*. *Prakampita* is a style of the neck that moves like the neck of a pigeon. It indicates the first person and the second person in a *deśī*-dance; the movement of the palanquin and the tinkling sounds of ornaments.

2623 **प्रकम्पितवक्ष**

Prakampita vakṣa : trembling chest, when the torso is thrown upwards and slightly shaken; a type of chest-movement. The *prakampita* style of the chest is indicated by breathing the chest as up and down incessantly. It suggests to laugh too much, to weep heavily, to be afraid, to feel fatigue, to lagour, to feel ill and to suffer from any disease (*NS*, X.1-9). The breast is heaving up and down incessantly. It is used in laughter, weeping, exhaustion, fear, heavily breathing, asthma, hiccup and misery.

2624 **प्रकम्पित - शिरस्**

Prakampita—śiras : forward and backward movement of the neck mentioned by *Abhinayadarpaṇa*.

2625 **प्रकर**

Prakara : theatrical dress.

2626 **प्रकरण**

Prakaraṇa : context. understanding of a context or the intention (*tātparya*) of the speaker which is necessary if a *śabda* or verbal statement is to yield knowledge. (b) subject under discussion, point at issue in a valid discussion. (c) a form of minor drama (*SD*, IV.306). (d) meaning is a sensation plus the context of the mental images that form around the core of sensation giving it meaning. Communication does not take place in a vacuum. It always occurs within a context, and that environment affects the communication process. Other word for *prakaraṇa* in Sanskrit is *prastāva* or setting. We all communicate in a wide variety of situation each day, and we must adapt to these different communication settings. Each communication context (*prakaraṇa*) has three aspects or dimensions: the physical context, the social context, and the cultural context. Physical context has to do with when and where the communication event takes place. It occurs within the boundaries of time and place and is also known as *prasaṅga*. The social context is determined by the relationship between (or among) the communicators. There are probably three aspects of social relationships: *bhūmikā* (role), *padasthitā* (status) and *sambandha* (social relationship). The third aspect of *prakaraṇa* is cultural context which brings the influences of the groups to which communicators belong. They may be *nāgara, upanāgara, grāmya* or *āraṇyaka*.

2627 **प्रकरी**

Prakarī : episodical element in a drama.

2628 **प्रकर्मन्**

Prakarman : sexual intercourse (*A*, 3.15.11). According to one tribe, fire originated from the intercourse of two dirty people (Elwin 1949.113). A similar tale is told among another tribe: 'Agnisur Dano (the demon god of fire) lived in a cave in the depth of the forest. A Baiga woman fell in love with him, for he was beautiful and light came from all parts of his body. (She slept with him, and then she wanted to take fire from his mouth. When she bathed, he opened his mouth and fire issued from it. Thenceforth there was fire in the world, (*Ibid.* 108). These tribal tales are supported by the Vedic symbolism of the two fire-sticks, the upper one male and the lower one female, whose friction (*prakarman*) is described in anthropomorphic terms (*RV*, III.29.1-3). This symbolism was manifested in Hindu thinking by the identification of ritual heat, *tapas*, with sexual heat *kāma*, and *Agni* was called *Kāma* (*Atharva veda*, III. 21.4).

2629 **प्रकर्षण**

Prakarṣaṇa : to draw and take hold for squeezing. Cp.

akṛṣya kroḍīkaranạm prakarṣaṇamudāhṛtam |
ākarṣaṇam līlayaiva sammukhīkaraṇam smṛtam ||
puraḥ paścāt pārśvayoścābhyākarṣo bhramaṇam tathā
paścāt prapātanam vegād vikarṣaṇamudāhṛtam ||

(Nīla on *Mbh.* IV.13.32).

2630 **प्रकाश**

Prākāśa : aloud talk, the talk to be heard by all, interpersonal, communication one of the three ways of presenting the matter in Sanskrit-stage (*Daśarūpaka*, I.63-64): Some matter is to be heard by all, some by certain persons, and some is supposed not to be heard by anyone. *Prakāśa i.e.* 'aloud' is not mentioned by Bharata. It comes after *svagata*.

If communication takes place between human beings, then the interaction level is interpersonal. *Prākāśam* is person-to-person communication; two people are involved in the process. *Prākāśam* is person-to person communication. The person is both a receiver and a transmitter.

In *prākāśam* or interpersonal communication, when there are two people communicating, there are two transmitters of messages and two receivers of messages. One person is not the actor and other the reactor; the two people are interacting. That is what *prākāśam* is all about.

There are three levels of *prākāśam* in Sanskrit literature. (I) one level of *prākāśam* occurs when a person sends a message to a group of receivers at the same time. When the teacher talks to the class, person-to-group communication is taking place. (II) when a group of people send a message to a single person, it is group-to-person communication. The class reacts as a group to teachers, lecture. (III) communication can occur at group-to-group level. A country sends a message to another country.

2631 **प्रकाश्य**

Prākāśya : things to be revealed. There are nine things to be revealed: a sin committed in secret, non-wicked behaviour (*akutsitam*), a good performance (*prāyogyam*), freedom from debt, birth of a son, sale, purchase, gift of a daughter in marriage, and one's own qualifications:

नवैतानि प्रकाश्यानि रहः पापमकुत्सितम् ।
प्रायोग्यमृणशुद्धिश्च सान्वयः क्रयविक्रयौ ॥
कन्यादानं गुणोत्कर्षो नान्यत्केनापि कुत्रचित् ॥

(*Sk.P.* IV. 40.80)

There are said to be nine secrets that are not to be made public or revealed. They are one's own birth-constellation, sexual union, *mantra*, family defect, deception, one's age, one's wealth, an insult and one's woman:

जन्मनं मैथुनं मंत्रो गृहच्छिद्रं च वञ्चनम् ।
आयुर्धनापमानं स्त्री न प्रकाश्यानि सर्वथा ॥

(*Ibid.* 79)

2632 **प्रकीर्णा-मुद्रा**

Prakīrṇā-mudrā : "When with the fingers of both the hands, one plays (beats) on the earth of the floor in the position of *visarjani-mudrā* (q.v), it is termed as the *prakīrṇā mudrā*" (*BT*). *Prakīrṇā* means unspecified.

2633 **प्रकृति**

Prakṛti : (a) stem or root in *vyākaraṇa*. (b) primary material or form of rite. According to *Sāṁkhya* the equilibrium of the qualities of *sattva, rajas* and *tamas*. According to *Mīmāṁsā*, *prakṛiti* is that for which all the accessories are ordained. For example, the chief sacrificial rites like *darśa* and *pūrṇamāsa* are called *prakṛti*. Among the followers of *Vedānta*, the school of Śaṅkara divides *prakṛti* into *māyā* and *avidyā*. The followers of Vallabha take *prakṛti* to mean matter which is a part of God. According to the followers of Madvācārya, *prakṛti* is two fold, viz. *cit-prakṛti* and *jaḍa-prakṛti*, the former is Lakṣmi or will of God, the latter is the entire immovable world like earth, stone, etc. (c) in grammar the word means the base-form of a word or root before the addition of suffixes. (d) in *Āyurveda*, it means the condition of the body. (e) in *Rājadharma*, the following seven limbs of a state are called *prakṛti*: king, minister, ally, treasury, territory, fortress. (f) in the *Vedānta* and in the theistic systems associated with it, *prakṛti* has been equated with *māyā* or *avidyā* conceived variously as the energy of Brahman. (g) in *NS* (XXIV.1) *prakṛti* means the nature of a person. It is one of the most characteristic basis of the division of men and women in *NS*. Briefly, the nature of men and women is recognised to be three fold: *uttamā* (superior), *madhyama* (middling) and *adhama* (inferior). These types are distinguished by their *śīla* (character). This converts a typology of "character" into a social hierarchy. High, middle and low are not merely moral and cultural standards, but also social ranks, that is to say, they come to signify the norms of behaviour expected of or imparted to the different rungs of the social hierarchy.

Emotional states involve bodily changes and thoughts. The bodily changes are largely changes to do with states of arousal, that is changes in heart rate, blood pressure, skin conductance, and a whole range of other changes which are variously detactable to people. They are controlled by the actions of the autonomic nervous system, and they get body into a state of readiness to take action. In some emotional states the physiological changes are quite dramatic as in extreme fear or rage or sexual arousal. In others they are quite slight as in generalized euphoria or faint nostalgia. Psychologists are not entirely in agreement about the extent to which physiological changes are really different in such different states as anger and fear and sexual arousal, and whether, if they are different, they are perceptibly different. But perception of bodily states is only one component of the information that leads up to describe ourselves as feeling one emotion rather than another.

2634 **प्रकृति-चपला-दृष्टि**

Prakṛīti-capalā-dṛṣṭi : lady whose glances are naturally unsteady, quality of the Art-lady (*Ratirahasya*, 1.14-15).

2635 **प्रकृति-विकार-भाव**

Prakṛti-vikāra-bhāva : relation of cause and effect. This retrospective modality is as fundamental as the non-sequential thought-process of which it is a part. It will be recalled that the Indian syllogism is the reverse of the Western; the notion of effect is formed first, and that of cause is retrospectively inferred and stated afterward. *Phalahetu* means 'effect and cause' — in that order, not the other way round. The Indian logic works from effect to cause, just as Indian myth traces. In India the myth of the Golden Age has been employed to disastrous political effect.

2636 **प्रकोपक-सन्देश**

Prakopaka-sandeśa : rebel-messages. The rebel messages were circulated more by spoken utterances than by writing, a phenomenon which constituted a distinctive feature of this genre of conflict in rural India. It also made for the use of some traditional and relatively archaic forms of communication which, rooted as they were in a culture unfamiliar to the colonial authorities, helped merely to emphasize the distance between the latter and the mass of the native population. Not infrequently therefore the British officials felt perplexed and mystified as much by the speed of an uprising as by the mode of its transmission. Occult symbols were used to flow from village to village.

All rebel messages had the dual function of informing and mobilizing at the same time.

Insurgency spread by verbal and non-verbal means. The latter were of two kinds — aural and visual. Thus the non-verbal messages were relayed by sight and sound both (*A*, 9. 4.11).

Vālmiki records that the rebellious tendency arises due to unfavourable behaviour and ill-treatment:

आराधिता हि शीलेन प्रयत्नैश्चोपसेविता: ।
राजान: सम्प्रसीदन्ति प्रकुप्यन्ति विपर्यये ॥

(*Ayo. Kān.* 20.35)

2637 **प्रकोष्ठ**

Prakoṣṭha : 'forearm' (*Suśr.*), court in a house, open space surrounded by houses.

2638 **प्रक्रम**

Prakrama : place of articulation of sounds.

2639 **प्रगण्ड**

Pragaṇḍa : the upper part of the *arm* from elbow to shoulder.

2640 **प्रगमन**

Pragamana : response. (a) first advance in courtship. (b) response in a drama: *uttarā vāk pragamanam* (*DR*, 1.59). When we look at *saṁvāda* (communication event), we always pick up the story in the middle. Something has always gone before—no matter where we start. We have chosen to start by looking at the sender's response to some stimulus. That makes sense to the auidence or hearer. The sender is reacting to something - he or she sees, hearer, tastes, smells, touches, or feels. The stimulus may be what someone else says or does. Or the stimulus may be some internal state; the person might feel hungry or sad or in pain. In any case, something stimulates the sender to respond. That person's response will be determined in part, of course, by the nature of the stimulus. (c) the recognition that direct speech is out of place in courtship must not be regarded as a refinement of civilization. Among so-called primitive people everywhere it is well recognized that the offer of love, and its acceptance or refusal, must be made by action symbolically, and not by the crude method of question—answer.

2641 **प्रगल्भता**

Pragalbhatā : boldness, courage. One of the twenty *sāttvika alaṅkāras* of the heroine. It consists in being bold and fearless.

2642 **प्रगल्भा**

Pragalbhā : bold, mature, and well-versed in the art of love. According to *Kāmasūtra,* she is well-versed in the art of sex-sport. She is also known as *praudha.* Viśvanātha describes her: "She makes her husband a servant by embracing when she is embraced, by kissing when she is kissed, by biting when she is bitten (*Sāhityadarpaṇa,* 3.122). Māgha (*Śiśu.* 3.122) has shown the skill of a *pragalbhā.* Kālidāsa has described Pārvatī who attained boldness (*Kumārasaṁbhava,* 8.17). Generally, *pragalbhā* takes pleasure in being decorated by her lover. We see such a picture in *Gīta-Govinda* (12.9) in which Rādhā as a *pragalbhā,* tells her lover, the Lord Kṛṣṇa: "Put the leaves on the breasts, draw the picture on the cheeks, tie the girdle to the waist, braid the hair which are dishevelled, put the bangles and anklets on the hands and the legs." The above division of the heroine is based on the basis of her behaviour in cohabitation.

2643 **प्रचार**

Pracāra : movements (*A*, 4.8.3), sphere of activity (*A*, 2.8.24).

2644 **प्रच्छन्दक**

Pracchandaka : a loafer, a tramp (*A*, 4.4.3).

2645 **प्रच्छेदक**

Pracchedaka : a song sung by a wife who thinks that her husband is not faithful to her, form of *lāsya* (*SD*, VI. 218).

2646 **प्रडीन**

Praḍīna : the act of flying forward, flying rapidly.

2647 **प्रणति**

Praṇati : salutation, humility, courtesy. Those who are torn apart by grief, or humbling themselves before a deity, usually lie face down with eyes closed, thereby cutting themselves off from everything.

2648 **प्रणम्य शिरसा**

Praṇamya sirasā : bowing the head down. (a) on entry into the court, the nobles bowed and made three salutes — with their right hand nearly touching the ground: *avanitala* *niveśitalola-śiras* (Bāṇa). The prince rose up in his seat if the noble was *tazimi.* The noble made three salutes again when he came to the middle of the hall. When the noble came near the ruler he again bowed down and made three salutes (*Prabodha-candrodaya,* 47) in the manner of *kornish* of the Mughals. The noble placed his sword in front and bowed down to touch them of the coat of the ruler. The prince touched his shoulder with his right hand and when the noble stood up straight, prince moved his hand to his bosom. This was treated a sign of acceptance of his salute. The noble then presented the *nazar* and offered *nazrānā* after which the prince requested him to take his seat in the flank to which he was entitled (In every court seats and flanks were fixed for principal nobles of the state).

2649 **प्रणयनिवेदन**

Praṇayanivedana : love-making.

(a) How does a person single out his victim in Sanskrit literature? What body language does a person at a party use to say, "I am available. I am interested. I can be had"? There must be a definite set of signals because characters rarely make a mistake.

A girl in our society has an additional problem in this game of sexual encounters. No matter how available she may be, it's considered pretty square to let anyone know it. This would instantly put her value down and cheapen her. Nevertheless, her love whose course is checked by modesty, is neither fully revealed nor fully concealed (*Abhījnāna Śākuntalam,* 2.11). And yet, unconsciously, she must let her intent be known. How does she do it?

A big part of the way she transmits her message is dropping the mask before her lover. Incidentaly, instead of using body to signal this message, these characters use voice volume (*Kāmasūtra,* 3.3.30). In *Setubandha* (10.70) the lady utters something to her friend, when her lover is looking at her. Here we have the unusual technique of having two messages transmitted by one medium, the meaning of the words transmit one message to her friend, and the loudness of the voice transmits another to her lover. Sound is a very definite part of the approach. It is not always what she says, but the tone of her voice, the invitation behind the words, the pitch and the intimate, caressing quality of the sound.

But lovers have more gestures than sons. They have dozens of little gestures, perhaps unconscions ones, that send out elaborations of their sexual messages. Does she avert her eye when he tries to catch it? Yes, Śakuntalā does not meet the eyes of Duṣyānta in *Abhījnāna Śākuntalam* (2.11). She withdraws her glance from her lover's face. Śakuntalā is using sideways glances —expressing her intense love, "I can be approached and I am readily available."

Preening behaviour is also patterned in love-making. A woman will bite her lower's lip (*Kuṭṭinīmatam* 693) or braid her hair (*Ibid.* 693; *Setubandha* 10.70), or rearrange her clothes (*Ibid.,* 10.70), or push her hair away from her face (*Ibid.*) or loosen her waist-knot (*Kuṭṭinīmatam* 693) or play with bangles (*Setubandha,* 10.70), draw ornamental marks on female servants (*Kāmasūtra* 3.3.34), embrace or kiss a child before him (*Kuṭṭinīmatam* 693), smile and laugh to attract him (*Śākuntalam* 2.11), while a man sits near her (*Vikrama.* 1.3), try to be in privacy with her (*Meghadūta* 105) or touch her (*Kāmasūtra* 3.4.21).

(b) Love-making in tribal societies begins with laughing, smiling and dancing together. Then the lovers arrange to meet in the fields or forest, perhaps by a stream. The boy gives her a carved comb. She steals a little money from her parents, and buys beads to make him a necklace. When it is dark she gives it to him. He wears it at night, but in the day he keeps it carefully hidden. (Fig. 2648)

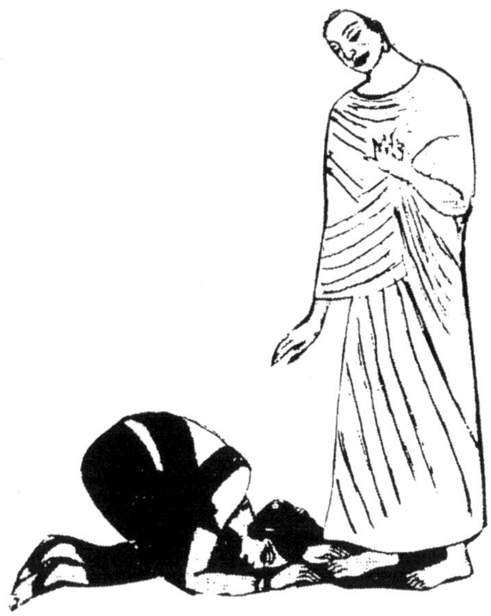

Fig. -(2648)

In the remote approach to the beloved, gifts play an important part. The boy makes hair-pins, wooden block for the back hair, pretty little combs and a small tobacco-pouches. The girl responds with bead-necklace, head-bands, ear-pendants, and even mats. Mirrors are popular gifts on either side. Some girls accumulate a great number of these ornaments. It does not necessarily mean that they have many, but rather that they have devoted lovers.

Many of these gifts promote a boy's suit not only by pleasing the girl, but by a more direct solicitation. The boys carve tiny symbols of the vagina or of a penis in erection, they draw breasts and even the pimples round the areola. They make these drawings or carvings on combs or tobacco-pouches, and on the walls or pillars of the buildings and on trunk of trees in the forest. Sometimes they carve breasts on the wooden pillows they use at night. These symbols, they say, often make it easier to open a conversation.

When girls fall in love with boys, they show their devotion by doing things for them. They take their dirty clothes to the stream for washing. They do their hair with special attention. They carry their drums. They bring secret presents of liquor or tobacco from their homes. They go to the jungle for little gifts of fruit. Such attention quickly wins the boy's heart.

The pangs and sorrows of frustrated love are rarely in the Muria region. I think, and Elwin experienced (1947 : 434). Even where desire is strong, it is tempered by the great range of sexual opportunity. 'Is there a lack of tigers in the jungle?' A girl who was attracted by a boy but who, for some reason, could not win him, said philosophically enough, 'what is the use of rice in someone else's grain-bin?' and found another lover. A boy says, 'If not today, I will plough the field tomorrow'.

Kālidāsa had also realized the heart beats of this wanton. Even the rhetorical device in the verse: स्त्रीणामाद्यं प्रणयवचनं विभ्रमो हि प्रियेषुं । has the same content, *i.e.* 'wanton wiles' are the first (unspoken) word of endearment which a woman addresses to her beloved, which, in strictly logical parlance, would amount to a generalisation in the guise of the concrete, but is, in reality, a unique expression for which, as Collingwood would say, 'nothing will serve as a substitute'.

2650 **प्रणव**

Praṇava : the mystical and sacred syllable '*Om*'. The *praṇava* (*om*) is said to be of two types (I) subtle; and (II) gross. The three letters, a, u and m or *aum* (*om*) represent the three guṇas — *sattva, rajas* and *tamas* — are supposed to be embodied in Viṣṇu, Brahmā and Śiva.

2651 **प्रणाद**

Praṇāda : loud noise, expression, approbation or delight.

2652 **प्रणाम**

Praṇāma : reverent salutation, obeisance. The *Purāṇas* mention various ways to bow down before a deity. The *Skanda Purāṇa* (II. 9.29.6) gives three types of obeisances in the context of bowing down before Vāsudeva Viṣṇu: (a) *daṇḍavat* (falling like a staff), (b) *aṣṭāṅga* (eight parts of the body touching the ground) and (c) *pañcāṅga* (five parts of the body touching the ground).

2653 **प्रणाम-मुद्रा**

Praṇāma-mudrā : "Make the upside down hands like matted hairs and keep the tips of fingers outside from the roots of thumbs. This is the *praṇāma mudrā* that draws near all divine beings" (BT).

2654 **प्रणिता मुद्रा**

Praṇitā mudrā : In the context of the worship of the goddess *Tvaritā* certain *mudrās* are mentioned by the *Agni Purāṇa* (310.34). Among them *praṇitā* is said to be important, and has five varieties. The first variety is called *praṇitā* itself, the palms are to be set together placing the thumb inside, the *tarjanī* (index finger) should be placed up on the head; and then gradually the hand should be brought to the heart. The other *mudrā* is called *bhedanī*, and it is ordained to be held at the navel. The other *mudrā* is called *bhedanī*, and it is ordained to be held at the navel. The *karālī* called also *mahāmudrā*, is to be joined at the heart; then there is the *vajratuṇḍā*, and the last is *vajramudrā*. In the *bhedanī mudrā* the two index fingers (*tarjanī*) are to be joined together, and in between them the tip of the *jyeṣṭhā* (middle finger) is to be inserted. In the *vajratuṇḍā* and the *vajramudrā* both the wrists are to be caught hold of by the opposite hand.

2655 **प्रणिपात**

Praṇipāta : prostration before the image (*A*, 9.7.83), reverent salutation.

2656 **प्रतल**

Pratala : open hand with extended finger: *vitalāṅguli hasta.*

2657 **प्रतिकृति**

Pratikṛti : portrait, *ākṛti, ākāra, pratirūpa, pratibimba* means an image, a replica; and it is usually synonym of *pratimā* or *vigraha*. It is a term used as early as the days of Pāṇini (*Aṣṭādhyāyī*, 5.3.96 and 99).

2658 **प्रतिगणिका**

Pratigaṇikā : a deputy courtesan (*A*, 2.27.1.2).

2659 **प्रतिघात**

Pratighāta : a counterblow (*A*, 9.7.55), repulsion, warding off, resistance.

2660 **प्रतिच्छाया**

Praticchāyā : reflection, image.

2661 **प्रतिज्ञा**

Pratijñā : a proposition which is to be proved. It is one of the five steps of Indian syllogism.

2662 **प्रतिदान**

Pratidāna : gift in return (Pāṇini), restoration, giving back: *priyādānasya pratidānamidam śarīram* (*DKC*,II.2).

2663 **प्रतिपक्ष-भावना**

Pratipakṣa-bhāvanā : thinking of the opposite views which the *Yogasūtra* (II. 33-34) advocates as a method of weeding out one kind of disposition by cultivating mentally the converse disposition.

2664 **प्रतिपुरुष**

Pratipuruṣa : effigy of a man pushed by the thieves into the interior of a house before entering it.

2665 **प्रतिपूर्वभाषिणी**

Pratipūrvabhāṣiṇī : reporting to the guest that the food is ready (Sītā reporting to Rāvaṇa, *Rāmāyaṇa* III).

2666 **प्रतिप्रश्न**

Pratipraśna : question asked in return.

2667 **प्रतिबिम्ब**

Pratibimba : reflection, substitute.

2668 **प्रतिबिम्बवाद**

Pratibimbavāda : the view of Madhva School that Brahman is independent and maker of all, the *bimba* or source, and that which it makes is *pratibimba* or a reflection. The latter is not independent of the former, nor an illusion. The world is real, essentially *paratantra* (dependent) having derived reality from Brahman. If it is unreal there is no occasion to find out and conceive Brahman as the source of all that exists. Therefore to understand the World as *pratibimba* or *paratantra* is the only way to understand its principle which is Brahman.

2669 **प्रतिबोधन**

Pratibodhana : awakening, music played to awaken a king.

2670 **प्रतिभा**

Pratibhā : intuition, genius, inspiration. *Pratibhā* is a capacity to grasp a situation and to act (*Vākyapadīya*). All activity is the direct outcome of *pratibhā* which makes us intuitively grasp a meaning-situation instantaneously (*Ibid.* II. 145). Bhartṛhari holds the view that a man is born with *pratibhā*—an ability to think, to learn, to act. Just as a cuckoo inherits the ability to sing a note in spring or just as spiders inherit the ability to weave their web, so also man inherits the ability to use language. Even the NV infant is initially equipped with *pratibhā* which plays a vital role in language acquisition. Bhartṛhari probably claims that we have no adequate theory other than *pratibhā* to explain how the child comes to possess abstract linguistic systems. Language develops in the human child because it is equipped with innate *pratibhā* — a capacity for acquiring language system.

Pratibhā is absolutely necessary for the composition of poetry: काव्यं तु जायते जातु कस्यचित् प्रतिभावतः । (*Bhāmaha*). It is found in someone only, and in him also not at all times (*jātu*). It is only in a few happy hours, when a man is fired by poetic genius of a superior kind, that he is able to compose what deserves to be called poetry.

Mammaṭa also places *pratibhā* which he calls *Śakti* as the first and the most important of all the requisites for composition of poetry (*KP*, 1.3). Now *pratibhā* is intelligence that buds forth in new and newer sprouts. The verse which defines it, defines also *Kavi* and *Kāvya* as under:

> प्रज्ञा नवनवोन्मेषशालिनी प्रतिभा मता ।
> तदनुप्राणनाजीवद्वर्णनानिपुणो कविः ॥
> तस्य कर्म कृतं काव्यम्
>
> (*Hemacandra*, p.3)

In the opinion of Hemacandra a poet is one who is skilled in the description animated by poetic genius; and his composition is known as poetry. (b) *pratibhā* is thus direct or immediate knowledge without consciousness of having engaged in preliminary thinking.

2671 **प्रतिभाषा**

Pratibhāṣā : speaking in reply, answer.

2672 **प्रतिभू**

Pratibhū : surety. *pratibhūs* are generally of three kinds, *viz.* (i) *darśana-pratibhū*: one who stands guarantee for production of a man.

(ii) *pratyaya-pratibhū*: one who creates confidence in the mind of the creditor etc. about the debtor and the like.

(iii) *dāna-pratibhū*: one who gives assurance.

2673 **प्रतिमा**

Pratimā : an image. It is a creative device to an image to an idea. A poet exercises the *upamā* (simile) to represent his thought but an artist follows the *pratimā* to draw an image of thought. Whenever Kālidāsa thinks that his literary technique is insufficient to give his exact idea a true expression, he takes help of painting methods (*Kumāra.* 1.32; *Śākuntala* II. 9, *Mēgha, uttarā*). The panoramic description of Pārvatī's beauty in *Kumārasaṁbhava* (1.49), as well as the pen-picture of Urvaśī in the *Vikramorvaśīya* (1.10); when could not satisfy his imagination, he tells that the creator, having been collected all the best materials of similitudes and putting them proportionately in the appropriate places, perhaps has made his most beautious figures. (b) in Jainism, *pratimā* means the eleven stages of right conduct of a householder.

2674 **प्रतिमान**

Pratimāna : weight (*A*. 2.7.2), model, idol, match, counterpart.

2675 **प्रतिमाला**

Pratimālā : a game generally called *antyākṣarī* which starts from the last syllable of a verse quoted by the opponent party (*Kāmasūtra,* 1.3.16).

2676 **प्रतिमुख**

Pratimukha : (a) standing before the face. (b) development of germ in drama (*DR*. 1.51).

2677 **प्रतिरागिन्**

Pratirāgin : over sensitive to colour (*A*, 2.13.23).

2678 **प्रतिराधस्**

Pratirādhas (*Bṛhaddevatā* 144-60) : form of speech and thought, obstacle.

2679 **प्रतिरूप**

Pratirūpa : effigy. The practice of making effigies of enemies and torturing them. With a view to torture the enemies, prevalent from very early days. The *Atharvaveda* mentions it, and it continued later. The *Matsya Purāṇa* (92. 150-51) mentions a practice of preparing an effigy of the enemy, and cutting it with a knife: प्रतिरूपं रिपोः कृत्वा क्षुरेण परिकर्त्तयेत् ।

2680 **प्रतिलेख**

Pratilekha : a document in reply (*A*, 2.10.38, 45).

2681 **प्रतिलोम**

Pratiloma : the reverse order, usually applied to marriage between a male of the lower caste and a female of the higher caste.

2682 **प्रतिवर्णक**

Prativarṇaka : a sample (*A*, 2.21.12).

2683 **प्रतिवर्णिका**

Prativarṇikā : a sample test (*A*, 2.13.57).

2684 **प्रतिवाक्यम्**

Prativākyam : reply, response (*Mahābhārata,* 10.4.6.8), form of speech and thought (*Bṛhaddevatā* 144-60). No *vākya* (communication) can occur until there is a *prativākya* (response) — a reaction. There are three important kinds of *prativākyam*: feedback, signal response, and symbol responses. Feedback (*pratipuṣṭi*) is a response from the receiver of the message that affects the transmission of sender. It may be positive or negative, verbal or nonverbal. Signal (*lakṣaṇa*) responses are reactions to signs. The recognition of the signal triggers the response. These signals stand in a one-to-one relationship so there is no misconception. With signals persons always react the same way to the same signal. With symbols, whether verbal or nonverbal, persons do not always react the same way to the same symbol. Responses are determined by the context of the symbol.

2685 **प्रतिवाच्**

Prativāc : censuring others and extolling one's own self.

2686 **प्रतिवाचिक**

Prativācika : answer.

2687 **प्रतिशब्द**

Pratiśabda : echo.

2688 **प्रतिशिरस्**

Pratiśiras : crowns and masks, etc. (a) *mukuṭa*: crowns should be used for gods and kings. They are of three types according to Bharata: *pārśvagata, mastakin* and *kirīṭa*. The first is to be used in the case of Gods, Gandharvas, Yakṣas, Pannagas, and Rākṣasas; second in the case of middling gods and the third in the case of superior gods. In the case of inferior gods *pārśvagata* should be used. The *mastakin* should be employed in the case of kings. The *keśamukuṭa* (with locks of hair tied) should be used in the case of Vidyādhara, Siddha and Cāraṇa. For the superiors amongst the demons, *pārśvagata* should be used. Crowns are to be used when the head is shaven as in the case of sacrifice and when the hair are not long. Half crowns should be used in the case of commanders, princes and *mahāmātras.* Ministers, leaders of the guilds of merchants, *kañcukīya* and priests should have turbans (*NS*). (b) masks should be employed in the case of Rākṣasas and Demons. Masks are to be used when characters with two or three heads, etc. are to be represented or when the character covering his own face manifests that of the other. As regards the artificial hands and legs, they should be prepared according to the necessity. The *ghaṭī* of the mask should be 32 *aṅgulas* in measure or of appropriate measure and should be prepared out of *bilva* paste and cloth or bark of trees, etc. The masks should be made with ashes or husk of paddy mixed with *bilva* paste. The *ghaṭī* should not be too thick nor too thin nor too slender. After drying it, the holes are to be made (for ear, nose, etc.) dividing it into two halves. The opening forehead should be six *aṅgulas* by one-half *aṅgula* (or one) having angles at the two ends; and for cheeks two *aṅgulas* by $1^1/_2$ *aṅgulas*. The hole for the ear (and also for the mouth) should be three *aṅgulas*. The symmetrical portion of the neck should be 12 *aṅgulas*. (c) the different weapons like *kunta, śataghnī* bow, etc. are described as the accessories (*NS*).

2689 **प्रतिषेध**

Pratiṣedha : taboo; obstruction of one's own desired object (*NS*, 19.93). One of the 64 *sandhyaṅgas* according to Bharata; form of speech and thought (*Bṛhaddevatā* 144-60, *Arthaśāstra* 2.10.8). Also known as *niṣedha*. It is the term for proscription or abstinence. This is also clear from the statement: *nāprasaktasya pratiṣedhaḥ*. The word *prasakta* does not mean so much as "enjoined"; it means "adhered to". Hence, many *niṣedhas* do not have an earlier statement of injunctions, we have straight *niṣedhas*. The meaning of the statement, then, would be, "There cannot be any negation or prohibition of a matter, which does not imply probability, or adherence". In the words of the *Mīmāṃsā-nyāyaprakāśa*, "*prāptisāpekṣyatvāt pratiṣedhasya*". Thus, even without an injunction, as such, negation implies only *prāpti*, and *prāpti* can be from a *vidhi*-context, or from the *rāga*. *Pratiṣedha* should not be confused with the *paryudāsa*, the essence of *paryudāsa* is positive, though there is the mention of negative *na*.

The following verse points out the difference between *paryudāsa* and *niṣedha*:

> paryudāsaḥ sa vijñeyo yatra pūrvapaden nan' ।
> pratiṣedhaḥ sa vijñeyo yatrottrāpadena naṅ ॥

From among the various rules indicative of negation, those with an idea of sin to be conveyed come under the sphere of toboo. (b) In the western Anthropology, taboo refers to the social custom of isolating and forbidding reference to an object or person considered to be either sacred or accursed. Each society and each period has its different objects or subjects to be avoided. Sex and pregnancy were more openly talked about in the *Vedic* Age than in the modern times.

2690 **प्रतिसंसर्ग**

Pratisaṁsarga : contact, association (*A*, 1.16.7).

2691 **प्रतिस्पन्दन**

Pratispandana : throbbing. Omens are indicated by the throbbing of a particular limb of the body. Generally the throbbing of the right limb is considered to be an auspicious omen; and various fruits are mentioned to be indicated by the throbbing of various limbs. (See *prasphuraṇa*).

2692 **प्रतिहार**

Pratihāra : lying upon the woman for copulation (*Chāndogyopaniṣad*, 2.12. 1-2).

2693 **प्रतीक**

Pratīka : a symbol, such as *liṅga* in the case of Śiva or *śāligrāma* in the case of Viṣṇu or *yantra* in the case of Śakti, or *stūpa* in the case of Buddha. (b) sound also serves as a symbol, e.g., *om* representing the undifferential brahman. (c) the deity is worshipped not as the symbol, but through the symbol. The aim is to recognise in the limited presence of the all-pervading spirit which trancsends all limitations of time and space. (d) the *pratīka* may be internal like the mind, intellect or soul of the worshipper or it may be external — it may be any token object which serves as a substitute or suggestion for the real object. (e) in modern semiotics, symbol is a sign, whether visual or verbal, which stands for something else within a speech community. For Barthes (1970) the symbolic code is one of the Frames of Reference we draw upon for our understanding of a text, which enables us to work out thematic oppositions, such as good v. evil, life v. death. A text which has a systematic level of meaning other than the narrative is often an *rūpaka* or *dṛṣṭānta* (allegory). Modern symbolism is frequently associated with it.

(f) tribal society of India is much more of a symbolic milieu than ours is. There is no hiatus between poetic symbolism and social communication. Tribal culture is loaded with symbols. A symbol is readiest — Cure for embarrassment, and can smooth over a business transaction or a hitch in one's love-making with equal facility. So when emissaries go on the delicate business of arranging a girl's betrothal they do not state their purpose directly, but say they have come for merchandise, or to quench their thirst for water, or seek a gourd in which to put their seed. Similarly, the whole intricate absorbing business of daily love is carried on with symbols. Women by the well ask each other, "Did you have your supper last night?" "Are you weary from yesterday's rice-husking?" Men speak of digging up their fields, getting water from the well, entering a house. Not only the solicitations of the seducer but the domestic arrangements of wife and husband cannot be decently conducted without verbal stratagem. (g) appearance, face, surface (*Āpastamba-Gṛhyasūtra* (VI. 50.8): *Uṣaso na pratīkam*.

2694 **प्रतीकोपासना**

Pratīkopāsanā : idol-worship.

2695 **प्रतीति**

Pratīti : self-intelligibility, clear intuition, awakened, manifestation of *rasa.*

2696 **प्रतीत्यसमुत्पाद**

Pratītyasamutpāda : inter-dependence; a Buddhist doctrine which means that the existence of everything is conditional, dependent on a cause; nothing happens fortuitously or by chance.

2697 **प्रतीपदर्शिनी**

Pratīpadarśinī : looking sideway, a woman; *apāṅgadarśinī.*

2698 **प्रत्यक्ष**

Pratyakṣa : before the eye, visible, evidence, objective, perceptible, empirical observation, like the model, true to nature. Perception, is the direct knowledge of objects produced by their relation to our senses. It may be external (*bāhya*) or internal (*antara*), according to whether the sense concerned is external like the eye and the ear, or internal like the mind (*manas*). In Cārvāka-philosophy perception alone is acceptable (*pratyakṣa-prāmāṇyavāda*).

2699 **प्रत्यङ्ग**

Pratyaṅga : in every limb; a synonym of *upāṅga* according to Bharata (*NS*, VII. 12-14), but *Abhinayadarpaṇa* (42-45) and *SR* (VII. 37-41) classify neck, arms, abdomen, shanks and knees under the category of *pratyaṅga.*

2700 **प्रत्यभिज्ञा**

Pratyabhijñā : recognition. Knowledge produced through sense-organs. The *pratyabhijñā—śāstra,* founded by Somānanda, is a class of literature belonging to the Śaiva philosophy of Kashmir. (b) method of perception which, according to the *Nyāya,* is the cognition of an object as what was cognised before. (c) while the *Naiyāyikas* treat *pratyabhijñā* as a single act of cognition, the Buddhist treat it as a combination of perception and memory.

2701 **çत्यभिवाद**

Partyabhivāda : answer to the salutation, returning a salutation. *pratyabhivāde aśūdre* (Pāṇini, *Aṣṭādhyāyī,* 8.2.83); a case of accentuation and intonation of a sentence. It is a paralinguistic/colloquial aspect of Sanskrit.

2702 **प्रत्यवसित**

Pratyavasita : an ascetic who reverts to the life of a house holder.

2703 **प्रत्याख्यान**

Pratyākhyāna : (*Arthaśāstra* 2.10.6): form of speech and thought, taboo zones. A taboo zone is an area of the body which a companion may not touch. Each of us has a sense of body-privacy, but the strength of this varies from person to person, culture to culture, and relationship to relationship. Above all, it varies according to the part of our body which is experiencing physical contact. If a companion touches a 'public zone', such as the hand, then no problem arises; but if the same companion reaches out to make contact with a 'private zone', such as the genitals, then the result can be anything from embarrassment to anger. Only lovers and parents with babies have completely free access to all parts of the body. For everyone else there is a graded scale of body-contact taboos. In general, tribal societies are far freer with their body-contacts than urban civilizations and a great deal of the clamping down is due to the crowded, stranger-infested environments of big cities and towns. With further population increases, all forms of privacy, including body-privacy are likely to become more and more carefully guarded, and it is unlikely that the phenomenon of taboo zones will show any decline in intensity in years to come. The Indian society as a whole has retained its general mood of body-privacy and contact-taboo.

2704 **प्रत्यालीढ**

Pratyālīḍha : the reverse of the *ālīḍha.* Here the right leg is bent (*kuñcita*) and the left one is spread. The posture in which the legs prominently involved: the left leg is thrown forward and kept firmly while the right leg is slightly bent; it is the reverse of posture known as *ālīḍha.*

A posture of sitting in which the left leg is outstretched while the right is slightly bent and placed under it. The weapons aimed at the target in *ālīḍha sthāna,* are actually to be thrown now in assuming the *pratyālīḍha-sthāna* (*NS*, X. 70-72) Bharata has not mentioned the name of the presiding deity for the *pratyālīḍha* and Śārngadeva has given it as Rudra, the same as that of *ālīḍha* (*SR*, Vol. IV. 1052-53). (Fig. 2704)

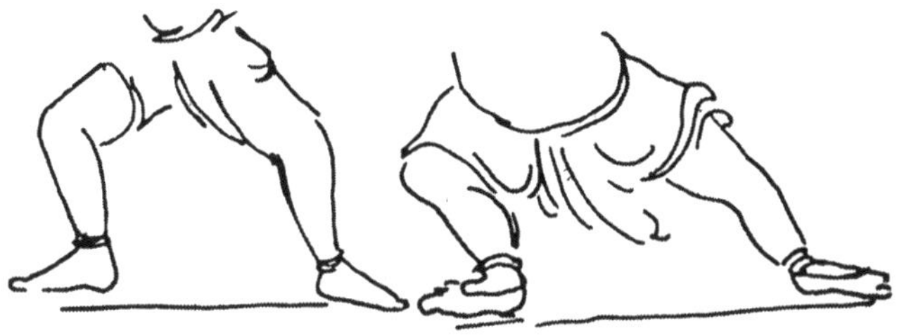

Fig. – (2704)

2705 **प्रत्यालीढ-मण्डल**

Pratyālīḍha-maṇḍala : a type of static posture.

2706 **प्रत्यालीढ-स्थान**

Pratyālīḍha-sthāna : a type of standing posture prescribed for men by Bharata (*NS*,X.51). This arises out of different positions of legs and the feet to lead a posture. *Samapāda* feet in *tyaśra* placing, but sometimes one foot is in *kuñcita,* one knee in *kṣipta* position. It is also the extreme opposite posture where a full leg extension is indicated. It is used in throwing or releasing of weapons, etc. Right foot is bent and the left extended to *ālīḍha.*

2707 **प्रत्यावरोहण**

Pratyāvarohaṇa : a rite performed to mark the giving up of the use of cot for sleeping.

2708 **प्रत्यासत्ति**

Pratyāsatti : proximity.

2709 **प्रत्युत्थान**

Pratyutthāna : rising up to receive; to honour by rising from one's seat. One need not rise to receive a brāhmaṇa who has not studied the *Veda* unless the old.

2710 **प्रदक्षिणा**

Pradakṣiṇā : circumambulation. The practice of walking round an object, person or sacrifice to influence, to honour or to purify, is ethnic in nature. The practice of walking round an object of reverence with the right hand toward is mentioned in the marriage-ceremony of Vāsavadattā in *Kathāsaritsāgara*(Vol.I, p.80). This practice of circumambulating the gift is yet presently prevalent in the North India in one of the pre-marriage ceremonies known as "*lagun*" where bride's parents send the money and precious clothes after the ceremony of circumambulating around them which in return is spent by the bridegroom's parents for the ornaments and *saris* of the bride herself when actual marriage takes place. The references to *pradakṣiṇā,* which have occurred in the stories of Sanskrit and Prākṛt literatures are given below: *Pārśvanāthacarita*(Vol.VI. 997) story of Madanarekhā and her son Nāmi, written by Bhavadatta Sūri; *Kathāmahodadhi* (pp. 14,30, 1.137), 43.214, 63.83, 100.54, 106.84, 107.126) written by Samacandra; *Daśakumāracarita* (1,37, II. 1); *Jātakas* (193, 251, 276, 457); and *Kathākośa* (pp. 27,27) edited by Tawney.

Pradakṣiṇā literally means turned rightward; making reverential salutation by circumambulation from left to right (*AV*,VII. 50.3)

2711 **प्रदर्शनम्**

Pradarśanam : display-rules are the implicit rules that govern a given situation or interpersonal relationship regarding the appropriateness of showing a particular emotion by means of facial expressions (*Anaṅgaraṅga*, 4.16). These display-rules are learned as a part of childhood socialization experience as children's cognitive abilities and control over their facial masculature increase. These rules prescribe different procedures for the management of affect displays in various social settings, roles, etc. We can distinguish at least four display rules. One rule is to de-intensify the appearance clues to a given affect; for example, when one is extremely fearful he must attempt to look only moderately or slightly fearful. A second display rule is to over intensify for example, when one is slightly fearful he must attempt to look extremely fearful. A third display rule is to look affectless or neutral; for example, when one is fearful, he must attempt to look as if no affect were being experienced. A fourth rule is to mask the affect as completely as possible by dissimulating it with another affect; for example, when one is fearful, he must attempt to look happy.

Facial expressions can be reduced for analysis into sets of 'displays'. Displays are behaviour patterns modified in form and/or employment to provide information to other individuals whose actions are pertinent for the communicator. That is, displays have become formally structured to function indirectly. Most facial displays are employed in diverse circumstances and vary in form within wide limits. For instance, a study of 'smiling' would require observation of its use in human behaviour ranging from suffering to exultation, from anger to terror, from casual to intense, and would have to account not only for its contribution to such events, but also for its wide variability in form and its intergradation into other facial expressions.

2712 **प्रद्युम्न-मुद्रा**

Pradyuman-mudrā : join both the fore-fingers in an upper position, along with the thumbs joined parallely and if a fist is so made; it is *pradyumṇa* (*VD*). Pradyumna is one of the five adorable heroes of Vṛṣṇi clan, who were responsible for the spread of *Bhāgavata* cult.

2713 **प्रपञ्च**

Prapañca : mutual praise through false matter, expertness etc, in the women of others. Bharata defines that when comic and untrue words purporting to be the mutual praise of two persons are uttered in the interest of one person, it is *prapañca* (*NS*, XVIII. 120-121). Abhinava accepts it and illustrates it with the example of *Ratnāvalī.*

It is one of the thirteen constituents of *vīthī* in which untrue words of mutual praise of two are uttered in the interest of one creating laughter.

(b) *prapañca* also means phenomenal order and also for the universe and its constituents.

2714 **प्रपत्ति**

Prapatti : whole-hearted submission or complete surrender of the devotee to God, a trait that leads one to seek and accept the domination of others.

2715 **प्रबोध**

Prabodha : awakening. One of the *vyabhicārī bhāvas.* It is the state of regaining normal consciousness after sleep. It is accomplished by yawning, stretching and relaxing of the limbs, closing of the eyes, and looking at one's own limbs, etc. (*Sāhityadarpaṇa*, 3.151). (b) threat signal. Threat signals are warnings of aroused aggression. They are actions which, if carried through, would lead to actual assault, but because they are stultified, remain visual displays. The movements are checked in three main ways: First, there are intention movements of attack — actions which begin but are not completed. The most familiar of these is the raised — arm threat. Second, there are vacuum gestures such as the hand chop, the neck wring, the head chop and the eye stab. The third category of checked attack movements is made up of a colourful variety of redirection gestures, in which the assault is carried through. Again there are regional varieties such as biting his own lip, shaking the head violently, tense body, exaggerated breathing, compressed mouth, deep frowning and some degree of skin pallor. One common threat display is hair erection. The beard is a striking masculine gender signal, and erecting it towards a rival is saying, as it were, 'I throw my masculinity at you'. The Indian threatens his rivals with verbal onslaughts, bangs drums, and brandishes his weapons. Like other animals, we are much more of a threatener than an attacker. (Fig. 2715)

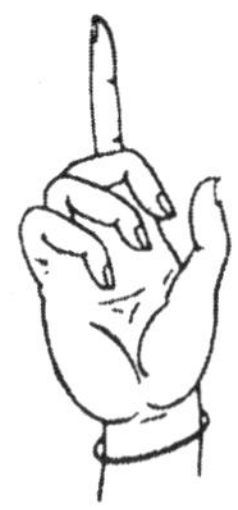

Fig. – (2715)

2716 **प्रभक्षणी-मुद्रा**

Prabhakṣaṇī-mudrā : "Knitting the opposite fingers with others turn them into the opposite direction and placing one's own head on it wait in a style of *praṇāma* (bowing down one's own head). When in the style of *patāka* one opens his mouth with an air of taking food, it is called the gesture of *prabhakṣaṇī*" (*BT*).

2717 **प्रभामण्डल**

Prabhā-maṇḍala : It is the arch of effulgence surrounding the deity, the solar orb stylistically represented in icons meant for worship. It is usually elliptical in shape, sometimes but very infrequently round, and rises above the pedestal of the icon, slightly at the back of the icon, and encompasses the icon's body completely, going above the tip of the icon's crown. The *Tantras* suggest that the deity is to be visualized as seated within, or as emerging out of the solar or lunar orb (*sūrya-maṇḍala, candra-maṇḍala*) and this idea has been translated here. (b) every living creature is surrounded by a force field of bio-magnetic energy which *Tāntrics* have called *prabhāmaṇḍala,* the aura. A number of western scientists have produced pictures of this force-field, and are busy in further research.

2718 **प्रभावाङ्कनम्**

Prabhāvāṅkanam : impression formation. The process through which we combine and integrate diverse informations about others into unified impressions of them. When we meet someone new our natural impulse is to size them up at once — by our quick glance. Thus our first glance takes in selected features of appearance and manner. Voice, smell and content are other factors likely to influence us. We match these features against the stereotypes — mental pictures of different sorts of persons — and choose the one that seems to fit best. The stereotypes at once prompts us to assume the existence of other characteristics.

2719 **प्रभुशक्ति**

Prabhuśakti : the power of material resources (*A*, 6.2.33), authority. Of the NV expressions of authority which come under attack in all uprisings, there are those which are paralinguistic in character and operate as kinesic and proxemic systems under the sign respectively of gestures and body movements and that of distances in space and time.

2720 **प्रमदाप्रमथनम्**

Pramadāpramathanam : lady-killing. Sporting activities are essentially modified forms of hunting behaviour. Lady-killing is such an sport. This type of sport is also known as 'amorous dalliance'. The pursuit of females has often been likened to a hunt. The normal courtship sequence of the human species has many of the characteristics of a symbolic chase (popular in Hindi as *śikār*), culminating in the climax of copulation as a symbolic kill. In real sexual relationships this climax heralds the development of a grip-bond, a deep bond of attachment between the mated pair that will see them through the rigours of a breeding cycle that lasts, in our species, for many years and makes heavy demands on both parents. In the pseudo-sexual relationships of 'girl-hunting' the reaching of the climax of copulation virtually ends the sequence. The male who uses females as substitute pray and who talks of scoring rather than of adoring, quick loses interest once the prey has been successfully 'speared' with the symbolic weapon. He must now move on and search for a new prey. He may, of course, find himself succumbing during the chase to the influences of normal pair-formation, and what stated out as a sport may grow into a true courtship despite his intentions. But, tragically, he may simply create a one-sided pair-bond and leave his female victim stranded with a loving attachment to her pseudo-hunter. Worse, he may accidentally fertilize her prey and leave her with the beginnings of a 'parental sequence' in which he feels no emotional involvement. As a sport, girl-chasing, like war, has dangerous consequences for society.

2721 **प्रमदा-मुद्रा**

Pramāda-mudrā : The gesture of *añjali*, placed by the heart and directed hurriedly right-wards, in the way of salutation, is called the *pramādamudrā* (*VD*).

2722 **प्रमा**

Pramā : accurate knowledge; valid presentative knowledge which, according to the *Nyāya*, is definite or certain (*asandigdha*) faithful or unerring (*yathārtha*) and non-reproductible experience (*anubhava*) of the object.

2723 **प्रमाण**

Pramāṇa : (a) set of measurement, measurement of the length and breadth of body in Indian sculpture, proportion, arrangement of the line and the mass, perspective and design. (b) a form of painting. Vātsyāyana in his *Kāmasūtra* divided painting into six main heads. It is one of them. In this (*pramāṇa*) category, he described about the measurement of the face of woman and the man so that distinction should be clearly drawn in the painting. Woman's body should be seven times more than the measure of his countenance. The eyes, nose, ears, mouth, hands and feet should also be proportionate to the whole size of the body. The size of the body of the noble-man and the low-born man should also vary in painting. (c) principle, ideal symmetry, aesthetic conscience. (d) the knowledge of anything truly which includes all the ways of knowing, namely perception (*pratyakṣa*), inference (*anumāna*), comparison (*upamāna*) and testimony (*śabda*).

Anumāna is the process of deduction, of working something out, of making explicit what is unspoken or unwritten, is recognized in modern text linguistics and the conversational analysis as an important element in the understanding of other's speech, and in the making of textual coherence.

2724 **प्रमाद**

Pramāda (*Bṛhaddevatā* 144-60) : form of speech and thought, negligence, intoxication.

2725 **प्रयोग**

Prayoga : the theatrical production (*Kūmārasaṁbhava*, 8.91), performance, practical (*Mālavikāgnimitram*, 1.15); application, actual presentation of the dramatic art. The development of disciplines like discourse analysis, pragmatics, sociolinguistics and speech-act-theory has led to more serious attention being paid to performance, though Chomsky's (1956) generative grammar had more emphasis on the competence. Kālidāsa's main stress was on the aspects of linguistic behaviour which was largely ignored by Chomsky.

2726 **प्रयोजन**

Prayojana : use, application, purpose, intent, theme. An end to achieve for which one acts or avoids acting. It is one of the sixteen philosophical topics of *Nyāya*.

2727 **प्रलम्ब – हस्त**

Pralamba — hasta : single hand gesture, only mentioned in *Bālarāmabharata*, derived from the *bālacandra*, and becomes a variation of *mayūra* of *Abhinayadarpaṇa*.

2728 **प्रलय**

Pralaya : death or unconsciousness, the last extreme physical reaction caused by a sudden outburst of overwhelming emotion. It is the result of unbearable grief, pain, ecstasy or wrath. It is manifested by motionlessness, breathing gently (unnoticed), falling on the ground.

(b) The dissolution or the closing down (*nimeṣa*) of the world at regular intervals. Whole *sṛṣṭi* or creation is nothing but the self-manifestation of the supreme being, and may be described as opening out (*unmeṣa*) like a flower from the bud, *pralaya* is the reverse process. Thus *pralaya* is doom. It is said to be of four types: (I) *nitya* (regular destruction), (II) *naimittika* (at the destruction of the whole world), (III) *prākṛta* (destruction of elements), (IV) *ātyantika* (dissolution of the self into supreme self). *Kūrmapurāṇa* (II, 43. 5-12) has given a vivid description. It is the *naimittika pralaya* that is most notable. The symptoms thereof are lack of rain. Then occurs flood. At the *prākṛta* doom the qualities (*gandha, rasa, rūpa, sparśa, and śabda*) merge successively. Then *prakṛti* merges with *puruṣa*.

2729 **प्रलाप**

Pralāpa (*Bṛhaddevatā* 144-60) : form of speech and thought; prattle, useless talk, lamenting, a stage of *vipralambha*.

2730 **प्रलोकितदर्शन**

Pralokita - darśana : looking sideways; a type of eye-gesture with the movement of the eyeball, the movement of the eyeball along the horizontal plane is suggested; looking an object from the side (*NS*).

2731 **प्रलोकित -दृष्टि**

Pralokita- dṛṣṭi : the glance with eyeballs moving side to side (*NS*, VIII. 92-105).

2732 **प्रवर**

Pravara : chief; also called *ārṣa* or *ārṣeya*. It denotes one or more illustrious *Ṛṣis* who are ancestors of a person and are associated with his *gotra* (q.v.).

2733 **प्रवह्लिका**

Pravalhikā (*Bṛhaddevatā* 144-60) : form of speech and thought, riddle, enigma, enigmatical statement.

2734 **प्रवातचुम्बनम्**

Pravāta-cumbanam : the air kiss. The man makes a kissing movement with his lips, in the direction of the girl. This is done for the benefit of his companion, to indicate what he would like to do the girl, because she is so beautiful; and it is most likely to be performed at a moment when the girl cannot observe him.

2735 **प्रवालमणिरद**

Pravālamaṇi-rada : the bite indicating the line of coral; the cheeks are the place of this bite (*Kāmasūtra*, 2.5.8).

2736 **प्रविलोकित -दर्शन**

Pravilokita - darśana : a type of glance.

2737 **प्रवृत्ति**

Pravṛtti : (a) local usage, regional usage and style. There are four types of local usages as discussed by Bharata (NS, XIII). Among the *pravṛttis*, *dākṣinātya* is abundant in *kaiśikī* favouring various kinds of dance, song, music and clever and graceful gestures. *Āvantī pravṛtti* depends on *sāttvatī* and *kaiśikī* styles. In *pañcālī pravṛtti*, *sāttvatī* and *ārabhaṭī* are known to predominate. Application of this requires paucity of song and excessive movement and extraordinary gait and steps.

From the dress, language, manners and profession one can distinguish the individual as belonging to the particular region. This is called *pravṛtti*. The dramatic action of the character is in harmony with the impression we gather about him. Hence, corresponding to the four styles of actions, *pravṛttis* related to the people of different regions are described as four. The regions are divided broadly into four divisions taking into consideration the common characteristics possessed by them and overlooking the minor differences. They are *oḍhramāgadhī* (Eastern), *āvantī* (Western), *dākṣinātya* (Southern) and *pañcālī* (Northern).

(b) Literally *pravṛtti* means one's mental inclination. According to the *Nyāya-Vaiśeṣika*, *pravṛtti* means striving for a thing which belongs to the category of *yatna* (*Siddhāntamuktāvali*, 150). In *Pūrva-Mimāṁsā* it is the term for volition. In Madhva's system *pravṛtti* is the function of a thing. In Buddhism the group of kinetic forces is called *pravṛttivijñāna*.

(c) Bharata mentions four *pravṛttis* which reflect the diversity of regional usage and styles (XIII. 37). It has been agreed that while *vṛttis* are principally concerned with expression, the *pravṛttis* are concerned with communication (*Ibid.*). Actually it would be more accurate to think of *pravṛtti* as regionally fashionable styles of theatric representations. These styles are a mixture of social and linguistic usages with NV conventions.

(d) Action, involvement, energy. Opposed to *nivṛtti*.

2738 **प्रवेशक**

Praveśaka : It is a device used for indicating some matter in a drama. It is inserted in between two acts. In it low characters speaking Prākṛt take part.

2739 **प्रवेशन-दृष्टि**

Praveśana - dṛṣṭi : movement of the pupil suggested in *hāsya* and *bībhatsa*.

2740 **प्रव्रजिता**

Pravrajitā : a woman who has left home (*A*, 2.23.2), literally going out from one home to another.

2741 **प्रशंसा**

Praśaṁsā : (*Nirrukta* VII.3, *Bṛhaddevatā* 134-39, *Arthaśāstra* (10.11): form of speech and thought; also known as *guṇa-kīrtana* (*NS*, 18.34). An anonymous Sanskrit author records:

> Virtues are only virtues
> When someone is there to prize them.
> The lotus only a lotus
> When the sun lauds it with light.

Complimenting someone on his or her appearance allows everyone to sustain a reasonably civilized social front and avoid obvious conflict.

2742 **प्रशमन**

Praśamana : gliding down to a low key in speaking.

2743 **प्रशस्ति**

Praśasti : (a) It is the concluding part of a Sanskrit play and it is also termed as '*bharatavākyam*'; because it was recited by the actors at the end. It has been a general mode with Sanskrit play-rights from Bhāsa up to present day dramatists to end their plays with *praśasti* or *bharatavākyam.* (b) praise and mode of address. *Patra-kaumudī* of Vararuci deals with different kinds of *praśastis* to be used in the letters meant for different persons. The *praśastis* are so lengthy to be reproduced here. Hence, we shall simply indicate the principal features of the *praśastis.* The *praśasti* for a king should contain extravagant references to his suzerainty, prowess, generosity, learning etc. The eulogy of a minister stresses his efficiency, and that of a preceptor lavishly speaks of his devotion to gods, proficiency in the various branches of learning, observance of rites and customs appropriate to his stage of life etc. The *praśasti* of a husband should emphasize his great and exemplary love, and that of a wife should speak of her deep attachment and exquisite beauty. In eulogising the father, the son should set forth his own deep regard and obedience. To the son the father should mention the former's learning, good qualities and his being an ornament to the family. To a recluse one should write lavishly about the former's detachment to worldly objects, great learning and possession of many disciples. The praise of a servant consists in stressing his devotion to gods, protection of cattle and efficiency in service. To praise any enemy, his heroism should be spoken of. To a wise man, one should write about his generosity and great merits accrued from the worship of gods, etc.

2744 **प्रश्न**

Praśna (*Bṛhaddevatā* 144-60) : form of speech and thought; also known as *pṛcchā* (*Arthaśāstara* II. 10.3; *NS*, 18.21). Pāṇini has formed rules regarding the question, or praise or narration, according to which a particular type of accent is to be used in a particular type of situation (*Aṣṭādhyāyī*, 8.2.10).

2745 **प्रसङ्ग**

Prasaṅga : name of the principle by which an act done in connection with one thing is helpful in another also. For example, expiation for a grave sin is capable of washing off a light sin also committed by the same person (*Smṛti*). *Prasaṅga* is a *Mīmāṁsaka* term denoting that which occurs when something done in one place becomes of help in another place. (b) deep attachment, intercourse, having recourse to a thing again and again, (c) mentioning one's elders on drama (*DR*, I. 8). (d) occasion.

2746 **प्रसज्य-प्रतिषेध**

Prasajya-pratiṣedha : the negative of a positive statement, a kind of restriction. In it stress is laid on what should not be done rather than on what should be done. For example, in the grammatical rule *na nirdhāraṇe* (II. 210), the emphasis is on the prohibition: *prsjyastu niṣedhakṛt.*

2747 **प्रसन्न-मुख-राग**

Prasanna-mukha-rāga : natural colour of face in *Śṛṅgārarasa.*

2748 **प्रसर्पितकरण**

Prasarpita — karaṇa : the movement is circular but the feet are in *agratalasañcara* here; hands are in *latā* and *recita* (*NS*, IV. 148b-149a, X. 198). Also known as *prasarpitaka.* One hand is in *recita* and the other in *latā* and the feet moving slowly with the soles rubbing the ground. It is used in movements of those going in the sky.

2749 **प्रसाद**

Prasāda : one of the 64 *sandhyaṅgas* in dramaturgy. According to Bharata (*NS*, 19, 101), it is the gratification caused by attendance, etc. Danañjaya regards it as the act of pleasing or showing courtesy. (b) one of the three excellences of poetry, creates mental-state of *ātma-dīpti*, resides in all *rasas.* Mammaṭa defines *prasāda* as '*sādhāraṇaḥ samagrāṇām*'(8). Bhāmaha thinks that a poem with *prasāda* must be such as can be comprehended by all, from the learned right up to women and children – आविद्वङ्गनाबालप्रतीतार्थं प्रसादवत् (2.3). Simplicity and lucidity are acknowledged by all nations to be the first essentials of excellent poetry. Out-of-the-way words and involved constructions must be shunned. Unlike Bhaṭṭi, Bhāmaha is of opinion that poetry should be so lucid that it might be understood buy all, not by the learned alone.

(c) God's grace to the faithful (*DR*. 1.103). (d) the term also means consecrated food.

2750 **प्रसादनव्यवहार**

Prasādana-vyavahāra : submissive behaviour, appeasement behaviour. If a man is threatened with attack, and there is no one to come to his aid, then appeasement is the only solution. It is at such moments that submissive behaviour occurs. The most important aspect of submission is making oneself appear small. The language itself is full of references to symbolic bigness and smallness. Lowering of body is also an act of submission. When a subordinate leans his body slightly forward as he talks to a high-status companion, we may judge this behaviour. The bower aims his display straight at the dominant figure, who may reciprocate with a milder version of the same action.

Among the Muslims, the *salām* appears to be an abbreviated form of the kowtow, just as a dip of the head is a modern token gesture for the full kneel.

Traditionally, when low-rank meets high-rank, he must lower his body in some way; but if high-rank enters a room where low-rank is sitting, low-rank must rise. Rising to greet a visitor is still widespread in India. Masters sit and servants stand, attending to their master's needs.

The greatest weapon we have against this is irreverence and disrespect. Any culture which loses these qualities will soon be dangerously awash with submissive behaviour.

2751 **प्रसारित -कटि**

Prasārita kaṭi : extended movement of the waist.

2752 **प्रसारित -ग्रीवा**

Prasārita-grīvā : extended neck movement. Extending look with eagerness indicates a glance to a thing (*VD*, III. 1.61).

2753 **प्रसारित -पार्श्व**

Prasārita - pārśva : stretching of both sides, extended side movement, sides taken to the extreme point in space right left direction; the stretched side, both the sides are stretched. In the *prasārita* pose, the sides are to be stretched in their respective directions. It is used to suggest joy and similar things (*NS*. X. 10-17).

2754 **प्रसारित-पृष्ठग-बाहु**

Prasārita-pṛṣṭhaga-bāhu : indicates the movement of the arms in relation to the thickness of the body, where the arms are stretched out in front and are then taken to the back — either over the shoulders or otherwise.

2755 **प्रसारित-बाहु**

Prasārita - bāhu : extended torso. In Deogarh temples Lakṣmaṇa holds a tuft of Svarūpanakhā's hair firmly and the extended torso provides the tension suggesting her discomfiture. When the arms proceed up, it is *prasārita* (*SR*, IV. 7.335-347). The commentary names it *apasārita*.

2756 **प्रसारित-शयन**

Prasārita-śayana : a posture for lying down. One arm is used as pillow and the knees stretched. It is used in sleeping happily (*NS*).

2757 **प्रसारित-स्थान**

Prasārita-sthāna : the recling posture.

2758 **प्रसारित-हस्त**

Prasārita-hasta : the extended or outstretched hand. It is one of the attitudes of the hands employed in dance and shown in sculpture.

2759 **प्रसृत दर्शन**

Prasṛta-darśana : eyelids are well extended.

2760 **प्रसृत-पताक-मुद्रा**

Prasṛta-patāka-mudrā : gesture of the unfurled flag. Make the left fore-finger circular and place it on the thumb and put the right fore-finger in the mouth (Joint of the circle) of the former. Then again making the right one curved, extend three left fingers. Make a *muṣṭi* by the left, raise the thumb and collect it with the help of the thumb. This makes the *patākaprasṛta* (*VD*).

2761 **प्रसृत—पुट**

Prasṛta-puṭa : expanding the eyelids; eyelid movement, the movement of the eyelid on the horizontal plane (*i.e.* side to side); suggests *Vīrarasa;* spreading eyelids wide in joy. wonder and bravado (*NS*, VIII. 106-113).

2762 **प्रसृता**

Prasṛtā : leg spread.

2763 **प्रसृति**

Prasṛti : extension or spreading of the hand contracted to receive water for drinking. (b) handful (a measure) also known as *nikubjapāṇiḥ*.

2764 **प्रस्तरण**

Prastaraṇa : bed, couch, seat.

2765 **प्रस्ताव**

Prastāva : request made by a male to a female for copulation (*Chāndogyopaniṣad*, 2.12.1-2). (b) preface, beginning, appropriate time, context.

2766 **प्रस्तावना**

Prastāvanā : prologue in which the chief actress and *Vidūṣaka* etc. converse with the stage-manager relating to their own work or the plot of the drama.

2767 **प्रस्थानकौतुक**

Prasthāna-kautuka : auspicious things done at the time of departure (*Mbh.* XII).

2768 **प्रस्थूल-लम्बौष्ठिका**

Prasthūla-lambauṣṭhikā : lady whose upper lip is long and big, quality of the Elephant-lady (*Pañcasāyaka*, 2.14).

2769 **प्रस्फुरण**

Prasphuraṇa : throbbing; *pharaknā* in Hindi. **Throbbing**

of the particular limb of the body has message to convey. Generally throbbing of the right limb is considered to be an auspicious omen. However, a throb in the case of the left portion of the back and the heart is considered good:

aṅgadakṣinabhāge tu śastam praspharaṇam bhavet |
atha śastam thathā vāme pṛṣthasya hṛdayasya ca ||

(*Matsya* P. 240.2)

The *Purāṇa* further refers that if there is throbbing at the head, it indicates the gain of kingdom (*Ibid.*). If it is at the forehead there is indication of promotion, if at the eye-brows and the nose, the indication is of union with a beloved person; if the eyes throb the indication is of getting servants to attend upon; if the inner ends of the eyes throb it indicates gain of wealth; if the middle part of the eye throbs the indication is curiosity or eagerness regarding something; if there is a mixture of the parts of the eyes in throbbing the indication is quick victory; and if outer ends of the eyes (*apāṅga*) throb the indication (in the case of a male) is that he would get enjoyment of women. If the ends of the ears throb that indicates tidings from a beloved person. The nose-throb indicates pleasure of love, if the lower lip throbs it is an indication of the gain of issues; a throb at the throat indicates enjoyment; and increased enjoyment is indicated by a throb at the shoulder:

pṛthvīlābho bhavenmūrdhni lalāṭe ravinandana |
sthānam vṛddhimāyāti bhrūnasoḥ priyasaṅgamaah ||

(*Ibid.* 4)

The throb of the arms indicates love from friends and that at the palms gain wealth. A throb at the back is indicative of defeat; but that of chest indicates success. In the case of women a throb at the abdomenal side indicates love gain, and that at the breast indicates delivery. A throb at the navel-pit indicates loss of position, but at the intestines gain of wealth. If there is a throb at the feet the king (or any person) attains a higher position (*Ibid.* 8-11):

bhṛtyalabdhiścākṣideśe dṛgupānte dhanāgamaḥ |
utkaṇthopagamo madhye rājan vicakṣaṇaiḥ ||

The *Vāmana Purāṇa* (42-15) mentions the throbbing of the whole right, up to the nails, of Śiva as a good sign as he advanced in the battle against the demon Andhaka:

dakṣiṇāgam nakhāntam vai
samakapata sūliṇaḥ ||

2770 **प्रहणनं अङ्गम्**

Prahaṇanamaṅgam : the places of strike during intense love. *Kāmasūtra* (2.7.2) enumerates the following body-parts: shoulders, head, space between the breasts, back thighs and the sides.

2771 **प्रहर्ष**

Praharṣa : excessive joy, erection of hair and penis, exultation. *cp. praharṣo bījasya.*

2772 **प्रहसन**

Prahasana : ridiculing, mocking, one-act play, a farcial or comic satire. It is characterized by exuberant gaiety and brilliant imagination, causticity, and humour and the objects of satire are sensuality and hypocrisy.

Mimic gestures are those in which the performer attempts to imitate, as accurately as possible, a person, an object or an action. Here we leave our animal heritage behind and enter an exclusively human sphere. The essential quality of mimic gesture is that it attempts to copy the thing it is trying to portray. In Sanskrit stylized conventions are applied. A successful mimic gesture is therefore understandable to some one who has never seen it performed before. There are four kinds of mimic gestures: social mimicry, theatrical mimicry, partial mimicry and vacuum mimicry. (b) a type of Sanskrit *rūpaka* enumerated by *NS.* It has two varieties. The *śuddha* (pure) variety has comic disputations by Bhāgavatas, ascetics, Brāhmaṇas and others and also abounds in jocular remarks by low persons. The parts of the story in it are possessed of the particular states with language and behaviour natural to them, giving uniformity to the plot. The *Saṁkīrṇa* (mixed) variety has courtesans, servants, eunuchs, parasites, rogues, and unchaste women as its characters. These appear with their immodest dress, movements and behaviour. Some popular scandalous topic or hypocritical incident should be introduced in it through the disputation of pretenders. The elements of *vīthī* should be judiciously used.

2773 **प्रहस्त**

Prahasta : open hand with fingers extended.

2774 **प्रहास**

Prahāsa : derision, accentuated (*Aṣṭādhyāyī*, 8.1.46), rule of the accent.

2775 **प्रहेला**

Prahelā : unrestrained behaviour.

2776 **प्रहेलिकाकला**

Prahelikā-kalā : riddle and puzzle of words, sentences and verses, etc. One of the 64 arts given by *Kāmasūtra.* (b) entertaining story. Cp. *nālikā*. Also known as *pravalhikā*. It is a saying with hidden meaning, based usually on a pun (double entendre) *e.g. pānīyam pātum icchāmi tvattaḥ* kamalalocane (I want to drink water from you, oh Lotus-eyed one) *yadi dāsyasi* (if you are a slave-girl, and if you give) *necchāmi* (I do not wish to) *na dāsyasi pibāmi* (if you do not give/if you are not a slave-girl, I shall drink).

2777 **प्राकृत**

Prākṛta : The imprint of hierarchical divisions within a speech community is perhaps most clearly witness in the diglossic situations of Sanskrit dramas. These two phenomena were in the co-existence of 'high' (Sanskrit) and 'low' (Prākr∞it) varieties of *bhāṣā*. The first and more prestigious of the two was used for religious sermons, academic or political lectures and in the elite-class situations etc, and the second for instructions to servants, for conversation among female friends, colleagues and members of one family, for use in regional cultures, and so on.

Diglossia of this kind has been a traditional feature of many of the later linguistic communities in India. For instance, the well-entrenched caste division between Brāhmaṇa and non-Brāhmaṇa in parts of southern India has been found to correspond to dialectal differences. This situation in a different setting may also be seen in the Hindi-region.

There is yet another aspect to differences of this kind. The same speaker would often vary his speech between the 'high' and 'low' dialectal modes depending on the solemnity of an occasion or the importance of the person addressed. Even a person of high status could use the *moṭi bōlī* in speaking to his servants or junior kin, while he would almost invariably adopt the *sāf bōlī* as a vehicle of discourse on elevated political or religious topics. Such switching between a formal and informal style, corresponding by and large to a literary and colloquial style, is common to speakers of many Indian languages. However, the feedom of switching from one to the other, especially from low to high, is far from absolute. Whether this is permitted at all, and if so, to what extent, depends on the speakers standing relative to the addressee's: this is all right when a person is speaking to his subordinates or equals, but anathema if the addressee happens to be of superior status. For the formal or high style is often closed associated with education, and in a land where most people are illiterate and far too poor to pay for schooling of any kind, this appears, by contrast, as an unmistakable sign of elite culture and authority. To adopt that mode of speech is therefore to claim an elite standing which is, of course, denied subaltern. This is why in a UP village the Chamār may not imitate Rajput speech for fear of incurring the displeasure of the higher castes.

2778 **प्राकृत दृष्टि**

Prākṛta dṛṣṭi : the normal relaxed position of the eyeball, natural glance, natural position of the eyeballs, a type of glance by the movement of the eyeballs (*NS*, VIII. 92-105).

2779 **प्राकृत-पातन**

Prākṛta pātana : normal position of the eyeball.

2780 **प्रागल्भ्य**

Prāgalbhya : boldness. It is the absence of agitation or nervousness in practice of love, such as embrace, etc. One of the natural graces of women (*NS*).

2781 **प्राञ्जलि**

Prāñjali : folding the hands as mark of humility and respect (*Mahābhārata*), folding the hands in a posture of reverent salutation.

2782 **प्राणनाथ**

Prāṇanātha : lover, husband.

2783 **प्राणायाम**

Prāṇāyāma : breath-control; name of the three breath exercises, *viz. pūraka, kumbhaka* and *recaka*, to be performed during daily prayers. By it the vital breath is supposed to be controlled. The *Tāntric* worshipper believes that this practice secures for him rousing of the energy, freedom from disease, aversion to objects of sense and bliss.

Prāṇāyāma is the regulation of breath which is the fourth discipline of *yoga*. A *prāṇāyāma* is defined thus:

सव्याहृतिं सप्रणवां गायत्रीं शिरसा सह ।
त्रिः पठेदायतप्राणः प्राणायामः स उच्यते ॥

Vyāhṛtis are seven in number. The *gāyatrīśiras* is *āpo jyotī raso, amṛtram brahma bhūrbhuvaḥ svarom*. A *prāṇāyāma* consists of three parts: *pūraka* (filling in), *kumbhaka* (retention) and, *recaka* (evacuation).

2784 **प्रातिपदिक**

Prātipadika : crude form of a noun: *arthavadadhāturapratyaḥ prātipadikam* (Pāṇini, 1.2.45).

2785 **प्रातिभासिक**

Prātibhāsika : concept of illusory creation; just as a shell is mistaken for silver. The term is specially used to suggest that everything other than *brahman* is perceptual, having no existence outside perception (*ajñāta-sattva*).

2786 **प्रादेश**

Prādeśa : the span between thumb and the last finger.

2787 **प्रादेशिक संकेत**

Prādeshikasamketá : regional signals. Regional signal is one that has a limited geographical range. It is the way signals change from country to country and district to district. It is a topic of gestural geography which is still unexplored.

2788 **प्राप्ति**

Prāpti : a consideration whether a person during the talk is nervous or whether his manner of speaking is composed and unruffled: *prāptiḥ dvidhā.... jalpataḥ sākṣobhyamāsākṣobhyām vā* (*Asahāya* on *Nar.* 1..143) Viśvarūpa and Aparārka take the expression. (b) attainment of happiness in drama (*DR.* 1.44).

2789 **प्राप्तफला**

Prāptaphalā : lady who has attained puberty (*A*, 4.12.3).

2790 **प्रायश्चित्त**

Prāyaścitta : expiation.

The institution of *prāyaścitta* is as old as, if not older than, the *Vedas* (*Atharva veda,* 6.112.3; *Sāmaveda*; 1.5.6-9). There are so many references to expiation in the different *Vedas* which go to show that the nucleus of the institution was conceived and followed from a very early time in Indian society.

Almost one-third of the *Dharmaśāstra* of Gautama has been devoted to the treatment of expiation. The first question obviously with which Gautama begins the subject emphasises the necessity or occasion of observing penances. Thus according to him man in this world is indeed polluted by vile acts, such sacrificing for men unworthy to offer a sacrifice, eating prohibited food, speaking what ought not be spoken, neglecting to perform the prescribed duties and delighting in doing what is forbidden. This is, no doubt, a statement of the circumstances which have given rise to the necessity or occasion for the performance of penances. They have been similarly stated by *Manu* (XI. 44,51) and *Yājñavalkya* (III. 219,220) also. Gautama opines that expiation is competent to remove the evil consequences of sinful deeds. The general rule that was generated by Gautama was that great sins entail great penances and small sins small penances.

After having discussed the most general doctrines in connection with the penances, Gautama goes on to discuss the two important factors of penances, namely, excommunication and readmission to the society. These refer to the social aspects of penances. Whenever a sin is committed the most visible punishment is that he is driven out of the society. The other consequence that occur is to take place after death in the form of hell and rebirths.

The processes of excommunication (*Manu,* IX.183-185) and re-admission (*Manu,* X. 187-188) to the society have been described in details by Gautama (XXI. 227) and they have been essentially accepted by the subsequent authors also. These provisions for ex-communication and readmission are followed in substance even today in the tribal societies. As a matter of fact these are the most visible and effective instruments in the tribal society with reference to the very ancient institution of *prāyaścitta* which has otherwise undergone substantial changes in the urban and rural society.

In *Taitt. Saṁ* (II. 1.2.4), the word *prāyaścitti* occurs in the sense of 'doing something by which one would get rid of some accidental happening'. Most digests and commentaries derive the word from *prāya* and *citta.* The former means 'sin' and the latter 'purification'.

2791 **प्रार्थना**

Prārthanā : a type of *sandhyaṅga* in dramaturgy. According to Bharata (*NS,* XIX.84), it is the request for love's enjoyment, rejoicing festivity and the like. See and compare *prastāva.*

2792 **प्रार्थनाविधि**

Prārthanā-vidhi : rules of requesting. To comment or someone's possession, *e.g.* rare food or precious things, is felt to contain a demand towards the possessor to share. In some instances the strangers to the tribal way of life misbehave considerably in that respect, especially in situations when a group of village folk came back home from the field laden with string bags full of mangoes. Talking about these things is not proper. One should keep mum. The basis for this 'silence behaviour', as we may call it, is the very mechanism: to openly comment on something precious must be avoided. Otherwise it would induce the possessor to give of his wealth. Many things are rare. It is difficult to get them. The possessor therefore must not be urged to share, he must be allowed to secure his load in his hut. He will often keep not a single piece for himself. But he will share according to his own decision. Sharing is so much an everyday pattern in tribal life that in particular situations possessors have to be protected from the demands of others.

Particular relationship ties require particular generosity. The mother's brother, *māmā,* for instance, is expected to give more often than other relatives to his sister's children. The father of the married daughter should not go to the village where she is married. If he does it, he should neither eat nor drink in her daughter's house and in return-visit he should pay for the journey.

2793 **प्राश्निक**

Prāśnika : judge. The audience also included experts who acted as judges in the theatrical production (*NS,* XXVIII.

50-53, 64-67). One who decides: *jayāpayajaya - nirṇāyakaḥ* (*Mbh.*).

2794 **प्रासङ्गिक**

Prāsaṅgika : subsidiary (*NS*, XIX. 1-2).

2795 **प्रास-मुद्रा**

Prāsa-mudrā : the missile-gesture. "If the fore-finger, the ring finger and thumb are joined together; two little-fingers are kept in the bending position and the two middle fingers are jointly extended; it is called *prāsa-mudrā*. This makes senseless all the species of semi-ghostly beings like *bhūtas* and *vetālas*" (*BT*).

2796 **प्रियतोषण**

Priyatoṣaṇa : particular posture in coitus.

2797 **प्रियप्रवणा**

Priyapravaṇā : lady who loves her lover, quality of the Mare-lady (*Ratirahasya*, 3.22-26).

2798 **प्रियवचन**

Priyavacana : gentleness and agreeableness of speech (Vātsyāyana).

2799 **प्रिये**

Priye : beloved. In *śṛṅgāra* the wife may be addressed by the king or the others as *priye* (NS, XVII. 65-94).

2800 **प्रियाख्यान**

Priyākhyāna : agreeable speech.

2801 **प्रेक्षक**

Prekṣaka : spectator (*NS* III, XXVI). The true spectator becomes possessed of the states represented in the play. Normally the young people are pleased with love, the old with *Purāṇic* legends and tales of virtue, the learned with religious or philosophical instruction, seekers of money with the topic of wealth, the brave with the heroic, the furious and the personal combats and fights and the passionless with salvation. The children, women, and the uncultured are pleased with the laughter and costume.

Spectators express their appreciation of a successful performance by such exclamations as 'well done', 'how pathetic', 'how wonderful', etc. Smile and laughter according to propriety, and swelling uproar at times, manifest their approval. Signs .f success expressed physically are horripilation, rising up from seat, giving away clothes or waving garments (Abhinava, *NS*, III. 308) and moving up fingers, raising the hand. The success is divine when the performance abounds in temperaments and states and is not marred by any untoward incident.

2802 **प्रेक्षणक**

Prekṣaṇaka : street play, a type of *uparūpaka* mentioned by Śāradātanaya. Whatever is performed in street, assembly, squares or temples by many characters is called *prekṣaṇaka.*

2803 **प्रेक्षणिक**

Prekṣaṇika : actor, one who sees.

2804 **प्रेक्षणीयक**

Prekṣaṇīyaka : show, spectacle.

2805 **प्रेक्षा**

Prekṣā : a show, a theatrical performance (*A*, 2.27.26, 3.3.21, 2.10.37, 5.1.43); seeing, *Karuṇaprekṣāsu puraraprav ṛttiḥ syāt* (Abhinavagupta).

2806 **प्रेक्षाव्यापार**

Prekṣāvyāpāra : dating; see *milanavelā;* meeting grounds, meeting places. Many poets have sketched the meeting of lovers in accordance with the instructions of Bābhravya as follows:

(a) *devatābhigamane yātrāyām* (at the time of going to the temple of deity), (b) *udyānakrīḍāyām* (garden parties), (c) *jalāvataraṇe* (taking bath in a river), (d) *vivāhē* (marriages), (e) *yajñavyasanotsaveṣu* (sacrifices, festivals and funerals), (f) *agnyutpatti* (at the time of fire-calamity), (g) *cauravibhrame* (fear of robbers), (h) *janapadasya cakrārohaṇe* (hostile aversion of the country), *prekṣāvyāpāreṣu teṣu teṣu ca kāryeṣuviti bābhravyīāḥ (Kāmasūtra,* 5.4.11). Agnimitra meets Mālavikā in *pramadavana* and *samudragṛha*. Jīmūtavāhana sees Malyavatī near the temple of Gaurī. Mādhava shields Mālatī in a cemetery. Mahāsvetā beholds Puṇḍarīka when she is going to the river to take bath. Vasantasenā visits Cārudatta at the festival of Kāmadeva.

Dating is still taboo for most lower middle classes in the modern sense, but the ancient type of dating is still prevalent in village and tribal societies. The concept of dating among modern societies is as follows.

Dating is still taboo for most lower middle class parents in India, although a few have become more flexible about the time their daughters return home. Romance on the sly, has, ironically, had to go to public. Today's lovers are not really embarrassed, nor the onlookers. Indian society now seems to accept dating as a new fact of life. Bombay with its cosmopolitan character and large force of working women set the trend. But the rest of the country is quickly catching up. Romance seems to be fading even while dating is on.

Young girls are looking for thrills because they are bored or in search of affection. There is also pressure in schools and colleges. Many girls from these backgrounds like to imitate the upper classes. Many girls are now seeking relationships before marriage — preferring to defer marriage. But it is still clandestine. Why the sudden crush for courtship? The widespread phenomenon of dating in this social strata is a reflection of changes in the urban middle class society. The information explosion is one of the catalysts for this new openness. Usually, economic hardship or the inability of parents to arrange marriages, compels girls to date in the hope of finding husbands. Clearly, there is an increase in the dating phenomenon. Cupid is now increasingly busy as permissiveness elbows aside tradition and fathers forget to lock up their daughters.

Apart from the urban society, the sexual relationship with the boy and girl in the tribal society is free. Relations between Hill Maria boys and girls belonging to *akomāmā* cleans a socially sanctioned and are not frowned at. The various *Jātarā* festivals, marriage ceremonies, occasional visits to markets, and the roaming about in the forests and so on give ample opportunity to the Hill Maria youth of both sexes to meet and develop intimate friendship and very few Hill Maria or Gond girls remain virgin till their marriage.

2807 **प्रेक्षित**

Prekṣita : gaze, look, glance, (b) seen. Here is a mythical account on the gazing behaviour. Brahmā, Viṣṇu and Śiva gazed at each other. Thus, their sight became one, from which was born a girl of divine lustre. This girl had threefold complexion — black, white and yellow; and was named *trikalā* (*Varāha* , 90.18-22):

त्रिवर्णा च कुमारी सा कृष्णा शुक्ला च पीतिका ।

The colours indicate the traditional quality-colours of the three gods, *sattva, rajas, tamas* (= Viṣṇu, Brahmā and Śiva in order).

2808 **प्रेक्षित दर्शन**

Prekṣita darśana : a type of glance (*NS*, VIII. 90-92).

2809 **प्रेङ्खोलित–करण**

Preṅkholita—karaṇa : derived from the *dolāpāda cārī.* Initial position of the *dolāpāda* is continued into *bhramarī cārī* with a jump. The *trika* is turned round, *i.e.* the sides are in a *vivartita* movement (*NS*, IV. 144b-145a, IX. 236-238, X.36, 45). After performing *dolāpāda* the foot falls with a jump and the *trika* is turned round.

2810 **प्रेत**

Preta : ghost, spirit of a departed person, dead. The *Garuḍa Purāṇa* (II. 25.4) states that the dead body be laid on the carrier (*śibikā*), with hands and feet tied. A dead body should not be taken out in the night for fear of trouble with nightly spirits (*Ibid.* 42). A dead body should not be left alone, for if someone touches it, calamity will befall. Food should not be taken while corpse is in the locality. The *Purāṇa* mentions that four effigies made of *darbha* grass should be burnt with the corpse:

शवस्य तु समीपे च क्षिप्यन्ते पुत्तलास्ततः ।
दर्भमयाश्च चत्वार ऋक्षमंत्राभिपूजितः ॥

(*Garuḍa* II. 25.23)

According to *Agni-Purāṇa* (157.36) at the place of cremation after the body is consigned to the flames, a close relation should go round the pyre from the left; then all should walk round and should take bath with their clothes on.

2811 **प्रेतपटह**

Pretapaṭaha : drum beaten at funeral. This practice is still prevalent in the Dravidian tribes of Bastar.

2812 **प्रेतहार**

Pretahāra : one who carries a dead body.

2813 **प्रेतासन**

Pretāsana : the deity with corpse as seat or the corpse as a seat for deity. Some of the violent forms of Devī, especially of *Tāntric* nature, are described as dwelling in burning grounds (*Śmaśāna-vāsinī*) and as seated upon corpse, *e.g.* Kālī, Cāmuṇḍā, Some forms of Tārā, Bagalā and some yoginīs. The four legs of the cot are also regarded as *pretas.* The symbolism is that they are immobile and devoid of power unless the Devī enlivens them. When associated with *Śakti,* Śiva is what he is, all-powerful, but bereft of Śakti, he is only 'sava' (corpse).

2814 **प्रेय**

Preya : desirable things for pleasure or enjoyment as opposed to *śreya* or those desirable for better ends.

2815 **प्रेरण**

Preraṇa : a variety of *uparūpakas.* It is full of laughing and enigmatic expression. (b) impelling, inciting, impulse, passion. *Preraṇa* is an act directed by the id or by another instinct, it is a sudden incitement to act, a motive or propensity, an awareness of a tendency toward action.

2816 **प्रेरित–मण्डल**

Prerita-maṇḍala : a type of posture.

2817 **प्रेषण**

Preṣaṇa : sending a communication (*A*, 1.16.33).

2818 प्रैष

Praiṣa (*Bṛhaddevatā* 134-39): form of speech and thought; injunction, command, distress, madness or frenzy.

2819 प्रोत्कण्ठ

Protkaṇṭha : stretching out neck, very keen.

2820 प्रोल्लास

Prollāsa : perception: *prājyam prollāsa mātram* (Abhinava). Perception, according to Abhinava, is a process by which we try to make sense out of reality. It is the awareness of something. It is a process that goes on inside. Perception is the process of gathering information, selecting what to notice from that information, mixing that selected information with previously gathered information and beliefs, organizing the mixture into some pattern, and interpreting the organized mixture as meaning something. The *prollāsa* starts when we take some information. From the world inside our skins, we collect data though the senses — seeing, hearing, tasting, smelling, touching.

2821 प्रोषित-भर्तृका

Proṣita-bhartṛkā : is one whose husband has gone away (*Manu Smṛti*, IX. 74). She is to wear a white dress and tie her hair on one placid. Kālidāsa in his *Śākuntalam* (VII) describes Śakuntalā as wearing white dress and single plaid. According to *NS*, *Proṣtitabhartṛkā* is a heroine whose husband has gone abroad on account of various duties. She wears her hair hanging loose. Also known as *proṣita-patikā*.

2822 प्रोषिता

Proṣitā : a woman who has gone away from home (A, 2.23.11).

2823 प्रौढ-निद्रालषा

Prauḍha-nidrālaṣā : needs more sleep, quality of a Horseman (*Ratirahasya*, 3.34-35).

2824 प्रौढवाद

Prauḍhavāda : bold or defiant speech.

2825 प्रौढा

Prauḍhā ¯: a bold and grown up woman no longer timid in the presence of her lover.

2826 प्रौढिवाद

Prauḍhivāda : bold assertion. *Prauḍhi* means maturity, full growth, pride or arrogance, boldness, zeal, discussion.

2827 प्लवक

Plavaka : a rope-dancer (*A*, 2.27.25; 7.17.34; 11.1.34), frog, monkey.

2828 प्लुत

Pluta : designation of a word having three *mātras* (moras). The vowels of words used to express calling from afar, used in singing and weeping receive this name (*Vyākaraṇa*).

2829 प्लुति

Pluti : protraction of a vowel.

फ – Pha

2830 **फक्किका**

Phakkikā : a thesis to be maintained, a preconceived opinion, a difficult or tortuous problem (specially in grammar, as the *paṅki* of *acīkamat*). Thus one may postulate a thesis that Śiva is a yogi, and the antithesis would be 'Śiva is the lover of Pārvatī'. The synthesis, however, is more complex than appears to be the case with the cultures studied by Levi-Strauss, for it involves the actual tempering of each of the first term— the realization of elements of *Kāma* in *tapas* and *tapas* is *Kāma*--as well as an interaction between them in so far as they are opposed. One statement of the synthesis of this particular options would be: Śiva's wife is *yoginī*. This synthesis then give rise in turn to new oppositions: her *tapas* is necessary in order for her to be able to bear his son/her *tapas* is so great that it is too dangerous for her to bear a son. Almost always, different poles may be somehow incorporated in one another even before they are mediated. In this way a great many of Indian themes may be analysed in terms of oppositions and resolutions.

2831 **फर्फरीक**

Pharpharīka: the palm of the hand with the fingers extended.

2832 **फल**

Phala : fruit held in the hands of some deities like Gaṇapati and the yakṣas and yakṣirṇis of the Jain pantheon. It is usually *kadalī* (plantain), *āmra* (mango), *panasa* (jack-fruit) or *dāḍima* (promagranate) in the case of form of Gaṇapati, and *matuluṅga* (citrus) and *bahu-bīja* in the case of yakṣas and yakṣiṇis. The fruit in the hands of deities symbolize the gift of fecundity, prosperity and success.

(b) the motif of fruit-birth is to be seen in the *Padma Purāṇa* (Bhūmikhaṇḍa, 103.134;104.4) in the account of King Āyus. The god Dattātreya is said to have given him a fruit to be given to his wife to eat. His wife,indumatī ate and conceived :

सा च इन्दुमती राज्ञी गर्भमाप फलाशनात् ।
दत्तात्रेयस्य वचनात् (आ) दित्यतेजः समन्वितम् ।।

2833 **फलकोष**

Phalakośa : scrotum or covering of testicles.

2834 **फलागम**

Phalāgama : attainment of result in a drama.(*DR*,1.21).

2835 **फलाहार**

Phalāhār : living on fruits.

2836 **फुल्ल—गण्ड**

Phulla-gaṇḍa: full blown cheeks; bloomed cheeks, expresses the feeling of joy and contentment (*NS*, VIII.129-134). It is used in great joy.

2837 **फुल्ल लोचन**

Phulla-locana : eyes dilated with joy.

2838 **फुल्लाम्भोज-सुगन्धि-कामसलिला**

Pullāmbhoja-sugandhi-kāmasalilā: lady whose mucus smells like a blossomed lotus, quality of the lotus-lady (*Anaṅgaraṅga*, 1.11-12).

2839 **फुल्लेन्दीवरलोचना**

Phullendīvaralocanā : lady whose eyes are blossomed like night-lotus, quality of the Deer-lady (*Anaṅgaraṅga*, 3.20-21).

2840 **फेला**

Phelā : remnant of food.

SEMIOTICA INDICA

Encyclopaedic Dictionary of Body-Language in Indian Art & Culture

H.L. Shukla

Volume II

Aryan Books International
New Delhi

SEMIOTICA INDICA
Encyclopaedic Dictionary of Body-Language
in Indian Art & Culture

ISBN: 978-81-7305-045-9 (Vol. II)
978-81-7305-046-6 (Set)

First Published: 1994

Reprinted: 2022

Published by:

Aryan Books International
Pooja Apartments, 4B, Ansari Road, New Delhi-110 002 (India)
Tel.: 23287589, 23255799; Fax: 91-11-23270385
E-mail: aryanbooks@gmail.com
www.aryanbooks.com

Printed in India

ABBREVIATIONS

A	:	Arthaśāstra
AB	:	Abhinayabhāratī
AD	:	Abhinayadarpaṇa
AK	:	Amarakośa
AS	:	Aśvaśāstra
AY	:	Āyurveda
BP	:	Bhāvaprakāśa
BT	:	Brahmayāmala Tantra
C	:	Chandaḥśāstra (prosody)
D	:	Darśana Śāstra (philosophy)
DR	:	Daśarūpaka
G	:	Gajaśāstra (elephant-lore
HC	:	Harśacarita
J	:	Jyotiṣaśāstra (astronomy and astrology)
K	:	Kāmaśāstra (erotics)
Kr	:	Kṛṣiśāstra (agriculture)
Mbh	:	Mahābhārata
MR	:	Mudrārākṣasa
NC	:	Naiṣadha carita
ND	:	Nāṭyadarpaṇa
NLR	:	Nāṭakalakṣaṇaratnakośa
NP	:	Nāṭyapradīpikā
NS	:	Nāṭyaśāstra
Raghu	:	Raghuvaṁśa
Ram	:	Rāmāyaṇa
S	:	Saṅgītaśāstra (music)
SD	:	Sāhitya darpaṇa
SK	:	Śākuntalam
SM	:	Smṛtiśāstra
SR	:	Saṅgītaratnākara
Sy	:	Śyainikaśāstra (hawking)
T	:	Tantraśāstra
U	:	Udbhid-vidyā (botany)
V	:	Vāstuvidyā (architecture)
VD	:	Viṣṇudharmottara
VK	:	Vikramorvaśīya
VS	:	Veṇīsaṁhāra
Vy	:	Vyākaraṇa (grammar)
Fig. – (X)	:	Fig. for Entry No. X

ब – Ba

2841 **बकुर**

Bakura : (a) thunderbolt. (b) a kind of tree, said to put forth blossoms when sprinkled by young ladies with mouthfuls of wine. Also known as *bakula*. Such conventions are summarized in the following verse quoted by Mallinātha on *Meghadūta* (II-17) :

> स्त्रीणां स्पर्शात् प्रियङ्गुर्विकसति बकुलः सीधुगण्डूषसेकात्
> पादाघातादशोकस्तिलककुरबकौ वीक्षणालिङ्गनाभ्याम् ।
> मन्दारो नर्मवाक्यात्पटुमृदुहसनाच्चम्पको वक्तवातात्
> चूतो गीतान्नमेरुर्विकसति च पुरो नर्तनात्कर्णिकारः ॥

2842 **बत**

Bata : interjection expressing pity or regret, ah ! oh! alas! (*Kāṭhaka-Saṁhitā*, x.10.13). It is still used in Bagheli-Hindi while in conversation, such as *batāo* : alas !

2843 **बद्धजिह्व**

Baddhajivha : a tongue tied.

2844 **बद्धदृष्टिव्यवहार**

Baddha dṛṣṭi vyavahāra : gaze behaviour. When two people meet and make eye contact, they find themselves in an immediate state of conflict. They want to look at each other and at the same time they want to look away. The result is a complicated series of eye movements, back and forth, and a careful study of gaze behaviour can reveal a great deal about their relationship.

To understand why the rules of human 'glancing' are so complex, it is necessary to appreciate that there is not one, but several reasons why we may want to look at someone, and several other reasons why we may want to look away. In the case of young lovers experiencing the first intense emotions of mutual attraction, there are some very noticeable patterns of gazing. If both boy and girl are acutely shy, they may spend a lot of time looking far away from each other. As they talk, they exchange only the briefest of glances. For most of the time they will stare down at the ground or gaze in opposite directions. Sometimes their deflected gaze as so intent that it seems there must be something fascinating lying on the ground near their feet. Their eyes are rivetted there, as if concentrating hard on some tiny speck of dust. Internally, it is the conflict between fear and sexual attraction that is creating the problem of where to direct their eyes. As the courtship progresses, there is less fear and the lovers meet each other's eye's more often.

Summing up this highly-charged scene of love, it can be said that a direct stare indicates intensely active feelings of an amorous, hostile or fearful kind, while a deflected gaze is linked with shyness, casual superiority, or down-cast submissiveness.

2845 **बद्धपद्मासन**

Baddha padmāsana : place the right foot and right leg on the left thigh and left foot and leg on the right thigh. Cross your hands along your back and catch your toes. *baddha padmāsana* eliminates all diseases.

2846 **बद्धमुष्टि**

Baddhamuṣṭi : having a closed fist, covetous.

2847 **बद्धमौन**

Baddhamauna : keeping silence.

2848 **बद्धलोचन**

Baddha locana : looking with a steadfast gaze (100 per cent eye contact). It may be contrasted with *viprekṣaṇa* or looking away where there is zero eye contact. Such extreme variations in the visual behaviour of the confederate can facilitate the experimental control of his behaviours and are likely to maximize the effects of eye contact on the various dependent measures.

2849 **बद्धवाच**

Baddhavāca : maintaining silence.

2850 **बद्धाञ्जलि**

Baddhāñjali : (a) folding the hands together in supplecation, with the hands joined in humble entreaty or raised to the forehead as a mark of respect. (b) Yogeśvara, the Sanskrit poet, suggests some new concept in the cupping hands :

> "Tell me, Mother, what does my father hide in his cupping hands"
> "A luscious fruit he's not going to give me.
> Take it yourself!"
> Urged by his mother, Gaṇeśa wrestles his father's fingers.
> Breaking his dawn meditation.
> So Śiva smiles.
> May that smile preserve us.
>
> (Vātsyāyana and Mishra, 1983.180)

2851 **बद्धानुराग**

Baddhānurāga : manifesting love.

2852 **बद्धाचारी**

Baddhācārī : crossing of the thighs, both feet in *samapāda* positions, *svastika* position of the shanks and thighs. *Svastika* of the knees, used in several *karaṇas* (*NS*, X.21). In

Vikramorvaśīya (Act IV), the king moves in this position. The *baddhācārī* position is also depicted in the sculptures of Sāñcī and Bhuvaneśvara temples.

The two shanks are crossed to form *svastika* with the sideways movements of the thighs, or the two thighs make the *valana* movements and the shanks are crossed in *svastika*. (Fig. 2852)

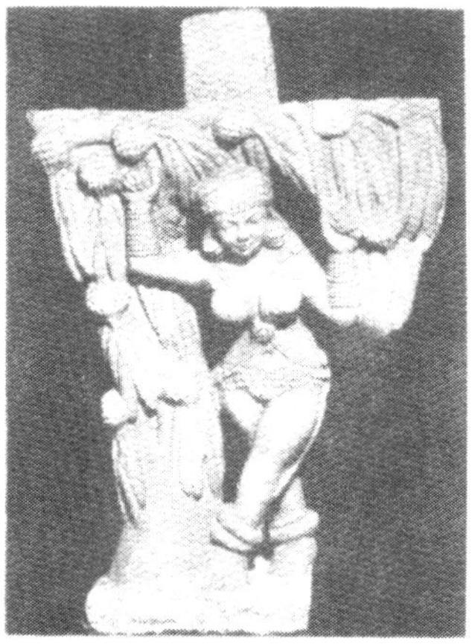

Fig.– (2852)

2853 **बन्ध**

Bandha : flexion, bondage; *bandhas* are internal flexions and form the *yogic* technique of controlling and exercising the involuntary organs which are connected with the nerves in the body. Their effects on the nervous plexuses which are groups of nerves are salutary. They possess remarkable curative value in many physical ailments concerning organic and functional disorders. Their psycho-physiological utility is remarkable.

In *yoga*, four *bandhas* are known and practised down the ages. They are *jālandhara, uḍḍiyāna, mūla* and *mahābandha*. (b) the term is generally used in Jainism meaning bondage : There are two kinds of bondage: *bhāva-bandha* (caused by passion or bad disposition) and *dravya-bandha* (caused by the influx of matter which the *jīva* takes up in accordance with its *karma*).

2854 **बन्धक**

Bandhaka : (a) pledge, mortgage (*Smṛti*). (b) catcher.

2855 **बन्धकी**

Bandhakī : a prostitute attached to many men, harlot.

2856 **बन्धु**

Bandhu : relative or friend. *bandhu* is friend or kin : *bhinnagotra sapiṇḍa* (*Mit.* on *Yaj.* II. 135) who is involved in with funeral impurities by virtue of his relation to the departed one. *Bandhus* are of three kinds : *ātmabandhu, pitṛbandhu* and *mātṛbandhu*. A *bandhutva* - theory is found in *Brāhmaṇa* literature which is based on the association of certain common characteristics of the gods and the rituals connected with them.

2857 **बन्धु-वर्ग**

Bandhu-varga : kinsmen. Manu has argued that 'kins should help each other'. It is the genitic tendency towards altruistic behaviour.

2858 **बलदेव-मुद्रा**

Baladeva-mudrā: gesture symbolizing Baladeva, the Vaiṣṇavite God. *Tripatāka* symbolizes Baladeva (*VD*).

2859 **बलराम-हस्त**

Balarāma-hasta : *patāka* with the right hand and *muṣṭi* with the left; represent Balarāma (*AD*, 216-25).

2860 **बलात्कार**

Balātkāra : rape. Rape is the frustated need to display dominance. A man who is sex-starved can, after all, find a prostitute to satisfy his need without too much trouble. What the rapist wants is not so much sexual relief as the total, subjection of his victim, her humiliation and her degradation. Only if this is extreme can he experience a temporary status-boost. This is status Sex, and it is not by any means as species of primate as a method of displaying dominance. All that is important is that one on top is dominant and the one beneath is subjected to domination. Thus rape is a redirected activity.

Rape is one of the most stressful events that it is possible to experience one in which a woman's body is invaded, and she suffers a massive loss of control over her environment and worst of all, fears for her life.

2861 **बहिर्गत – जङ्घा**

Bahirgata—jaṅghā : the movement of the knee where the sideways movement is indicated.

2862 **बहिर्मुख-हस्त**

Bahirmukha hasta : outward movement of the palm, fingers and wrist.

2863 **बहुल**

Bahula : used in connection with a rule, affix or the like. It denotes four kinds of operation, *viz.* applicable, not applicable in certain cases, optionally applicable in some cases and quite something else in others (*Vyākaraṇa*).

2864 **बाण-सन्देश**

Bāṇa-sandeśa : icon of the arrow of war. Tribal folks in

India made up a number of visual signs for the propogation of insurgency. The best known example of iconic sign was the arrow of war used by the Kol and the aborigines of Bastar. Its role as a means of rebel mobilization was made widely known by Dalton in his *Descriptive Ethnology of Bengal* published forty years after the event : "An arrow passed from village-to-village is the summons to arm and sent to any one in authority it is an open declaration of war". On the eve of 1832 uprising such arrows circulated 'like the fiery cross' in that region, so that by the time it got under way by the middle of January that year the Mundaris and Oraons had all entered with zeal into the spirit of the insurrection. (Dalton : 171-72).

Arrow or dart is shot with the help of a bow. The deities that carry bow (*dhanus*) in right hand invariably carry arrow in the left, for they go together (*dhanur-bāṇa*). Arrows may be made of metal, when they are called *nārāca.*

The fixing of the arrow in the jar during rituals (*Śiva* IV. 12. 37.) is the symbolic union of female and male organs :

गिरिजां योनिरूपां च बाणं स्थाप्य शुभं पुनः ।
तत्र लिङ्गं च तत्स्थाप्य पुनश्चैवाभिमन्त्रयेत् ।।

2865 **बाण-हस्त**

Bāṇa-hasta : the arrow hand. The palm faces upwards and is slightly hollowed. The little finger is extended; the three other fingers are bent to touch the thumb at fingers tips. It is used to express the number six, contentment and perseverance.

2866 **बादरायण-सम्बन्ध**

Bādarāyaṇa-sambandha : far-fetched relation.

2867 **बान्धव (बन्धु)**

Bāndhava (***bandhu***) : the following three classes of relatives. (a) *ātmabandhu*—son of one's father's sister, mother's sister, and of one's maternal uncle. (b) *pitṛbandhu*—son of one's father's sister, father's mother's sister and one's father's maternal uncle. (c) *mātṛbandhu*—son of one's mother's mother's sister, mother's father's sister and of one's mother's maternal uncle.

2868 **बालचन्द्र-हस्त**

Bālacandra-hasta : a type of single hand gesture mentioned in *Bālarāmabharata*, derived from the *sūcī*. Crescent moon as an ornament on the head of some deities, principally Śiva, Durgā and Gaṇapati.

2869 **बाला**

Bālā : a girl below sixteen years, evernew. Sexual intercourse with a *bālā* (younger woman) is said to be invigorating (*Garuḍa*, I.31.33). The physical charm of a *bālā* is depicted in the following verse :

iyaṃ vyādhāyate bālā
bhrūrasyāḥ kārmukāyate ।
kaṭākṣāśca śarāyante
manome hariṇāyate ।।
"This damsel doth as an archer serve,
The bow she handles is her eye-brow curve,
Her side-long look is the arrow aimed,
My mind the deer, is the target maimed."

2870 **बाहु**

Bāhu : the arm, shoulder. The styles of the arm in a *karaṇa* of hands (in a dance-drama) are ten in numbers : *tiryaggata, ūrdhvagata, adhomukha, āviddha, apaviddha, maṇḍala, svastika, añcita, kuñcita* and *pṛṣṭhagata.* Arms have no independent action. They are to be exercised in ten styles mentioned above, as an auxiliary to a *karaṇa* and a gesture. They are the scanting, the up-going, the down-facing, the closed tightly, the loose, the circling, the crossed, the curved, the recoiled and the back-going (*NS*, IX. 205-06). *SR* (IV. 7.335-47) enumerates all the ten styles of *NS*. The first eight are almost common but the last two differ a little. *SR* names them as *prasārita* and *udveṣṭita.*

Idiomatic arm-gesture in Hindi are as follows: (a) *bāhn pakaṛnā* 'to take under one's protection', as evident from the following saying :

baṛe na būṛan det hain
jāke pakṛe bāhn ।
jaise lohā nāv meṇ
tirat phire jalamāhṇ ।।

(b) *bāhn gahe kī lāj* 'It is shame to cast off one whom you have taken under wing'. (c) *bāheṇ caṛhānā* 'to tuck one's sleeves for work, to threaten'.

Varāhamihira (*BS*, LXVIII) has given some of the characteristics of the shoulders through which men were assessed. Thus according to him a poor man's shoulders are full of hair , split, small and without flesh, while those of the happy and the powerful are large, unsplit and compact. Vide the following :

कदलीस्तम्भसङ्काशा अजस्कन्धाश्च ये नराः ।
राजानस्ते विजानीयुर्महाकोशा महाबलाः ।।
करिकरसदृशौ वृत्तावाजान्ववलम्बिनौ समौ पीनौ ।
बाहू पृथिट्टवीशानामधमानां रोमशौ ह्रस्वौ ।।

'Kings have arms that resemble the trunks of elephants, that are round, equal, muscular and touching the knees; whereas the poor have hairy and short ones.' Vide the following :

उद्बद्धबाहू पुरुषे वधवन्धमवाप्नुयात् ।
दीर्घबाहूर्भवेद्राजा समुद्रवचनं तथा ।।
प्रलम्बबाहूरैश्वर्यं प्राप्नुयाद् गुणसंयुतम् ।
ह्स्वबाहूर्भवेद्दासः परप्रेष्यकरस्तथा ।।
वामावर्त्तभुजा ये तु ये तु दीर्घभुजा नराः ।
सम्पूर्णबाहवो ये तु राजानस्ते प्रकीर्त्तिताः ।।

2871 **बाहु-करण**

Bāhu-karaṇa : the movement of the arm. The movement of the arms in drama and dance are ten - oblique, raised upward, turned downwards, bent, moving round, thrown off, in *svastika,* turned to back, extended and in the position of *udveṣṭita karaṇa.*

2872 **बाहु कुचन**

Bāhu-kucana : contraction of the arm *(Kāṭhaka-Saṁhitā,* XX.13); *bāhu saṁkocana, bāhu-kuṇṭhatā.*

2873 **बाहुपाश**

Bāhupāśa : the arm-link. Perhaps the most obvious and publically displayed of all Tie-signs, the arm-link is basically a signal of co-ordinated walking, embracing, with one partner expressing mild control over the other. The support and protection are largely symbolic. As a tie-sign it could almost be described as a signal of mutual ownership.

When two Gond friends or relatives meet, they clasp each other in their arms and lean against each other's shoulder in turn.

2874 **बाहुमूल**

Bāhumūla : the arm-pit.

2875 **बाहुमूल-नख-क्षत**

Bāhumūla-nakha-kṣata : nail-scratches on arm-pits. Generally the nail-scratches on arm-pits are referred to by the poets at the time of the description of plucking and gathering of flowers, as they appear at that time clearly. Bilhaṇa pictures an angry wife of the king, who unaffected even by the desire of plucking flowers, became attentive to see the nail marks in the arm-pits of many women :

mānapriyā kāpi nṛpasya patnī
spṛṣṭā na puṣpoccayavāñchayāpi ॥
anekanārījanabāhumula-
nakhakṣatāvekṣaṇa tat parābhūt. ॥
(*Vikramāṅkadevacarita,* 10.51).

2876 **बाहुमूलाकृतिविज्ञान**

Bāhumūlākṛti-vijñāna : signs of the arm-pit. If arm-pit is even, it indicates enjoyment; if sloping down, poverty; if raised up, kingship; if un-even, crookedness (*Garuḍa*).

2877 **बाहुसंरम्भ**

Bāhusaṁrambha : stroking the arms. Stroking the arms or objects is obvious symbolic signal to an interested observer. This gesture of attraction is often blatantly exaggerated by tribal dancers.

2878 **बाहुसूत्र**

Bāhusūtra : one of the five principal vertical axes (*sūtra*) enumerated by the *Śilpaśāstra* texts. The *brahmasūtra* is the vertical axis on the imaginary line passing through the centre of the image and represents the direction of the pull of gravity. The *bāhusūtra* is the vertical drawn from the shoulder-joint to the ground.

2879 **बाहूत्क्षेप**

Bāhūtkṣepa : raised or tossed up arms, lifting up the arms.

2880 **बाहूत्सार**

Bāhūtsāra : repelling as with arms *(A,* 10.2.4; 10.4.13).

2881 **बाहूपपीड**

Bāhūpapīḍa : clasping the arms.

2882 **बाह्यभ्रमरिका-करण**

Bāhyabhramarikā-karaṇa : ascending movement (*NS,* p.222). In Act VI of *Śākuntalam,* the heavenly *apsarā* is shown ascending to heaven by this *karaṇa.*

2883 **बाह्य-सम्भोग-रक्ता**

Bāhya-saṁbhoga-raktā : lady who has interest in external coition, quality of the Art-lady (*Ratirahasya,* 1.14-15).

2884 **बाह्यासन**

Bāhyāsana : seats for common man (*NS*). In society and in one's home, according to Bharata, one should have seats according to his will. The seats for ascetics and sectarians should be according to their order of vows. While pouring *ghee* into the sacrificial fire or performing the sacrificial duty or offering libation of water to the dear departed, one should sit on a seat made of *kuśa* grass, *muṇḍa* seat or cane seat. The local persons of noble birth and possessed of learning should be greeted by offering a seat by the kings. The equals should be offered equal seat, middling medium and the superiors more elevated seat and the inferiors the ground. Wise persons should sit on the ground or on wooden seat before the preceptor, the king and the elderly persons. They should sit together with him when going in a boat, riding an elephant or a chariot.

2885 **बार्हपत्य**

Bārhapatya : a doctrine akin to the views of the *lokāyatas* and *cārvākas*; named after Bṛhaspati. This doctrine upholds a materialist worldview.

2886 **बिन्दु**

Bindu : dot or mark on the body; *bindī*(Hindi) mark (usually red) put on the forehead by a married woman; *bindī ṭikiā, ṭiklī, bottu, pottu* is unique in a-Hindu woman. Indian culture has given it an importance of its own which has made it a basic beauty aid for the *suhāgan* and an indispensable part of her life itself.

In the South, when a *Sumaṅgalī* (whose husband is alive visits a house, even if she is too busy to sit and chat or partake of any refreshments, she has to be offered *kumkum* by the hostess white parting. The custom is overlooked only in a mourning house. Again, in the South, there are *haldī-kumkum* festivals, during *Dussehra, Sāvan, Makara Saṅkrānti*, etc. which are exclusively meant for women. Here women are invited and offered *kumkum* being the most prominent of gifts. The silver *kumkum* container that a girl gets from the in-laws is one of her most valuable gifts.

History has it that the Dravidians practised the custom of sacrificing on animal when a new bride entered her marital home for the first time. They made a dot on her forehead with the blood of the animal. Another custom which is responsible for the *bindī* being linked with marriage, and the life of the husband, originated due to the lopsided supply and demand position of girls and boys among the Āryans. Since girls were less in number, brides from non-Āryans, who were considered inferior had to be taken. Hence an animal was sacrificed and the bride was purified by applying a dot of its blood on her forehead. Later, this dot of blood was replaced by red powder. Again, at a time when society was less civilized and when might was considered to be right the bride was forcibly taken away by the suitor. Other suitors had to be defeated and kept at bay. To establish the winner's right over the bride, a red mark was smeared on her forehead.

Thus the red dot on the forehead became the first sign of the married state and is revered as a sacred symbol. But of late, seeing the variety and types of *bindīs* and *bindī* materials available in the market, one wonders whether the aesthetic aspect has replaced all other considerations. Today, it is donned by one and all, and is more a beauty aid than anything else.

Matching *bindīs* for each dress are now in vogue in the urban India, while the traditional red mark is even preferred in the rural India.

The exact spot prescribed by the scriptures for the application of the *bindī* is in between the eyebrows because this place is considered to be the abode of intellect, consciousness and wisdom—in short, the abode of the 6th sense and hence has to be protected by the *bindī*. But today, the place for the *bindī* is a matter of personal choice.

Bindīs are considered to be one of the *solaha śṛṅgāras*, the 16 adornments and, of course, colours, especially red do have their own charm. Till a few decades ago, especially in the South, *bindīs* were not the prerogative of women alone. Even men used to decorate their foreheads with *bindīs* of various hues, depending upon personal choice.

The materials used varied from *kumkum, candan, vibhūti* or holy ash or even the black liquid derived by splashing a few drops of water on the soot-stained wall of the kitchen which used firewood. All this, apart from warding of evil was supposed to give a dignified look to the wearer. But the advent of the Western mode of dress and way of life restricted this practice to formal functions and *pūjās*.

Perhaps the pathetic side of the *bindī* is revealed in the custom of denying its application to a woman as soon as her husband dies.

(b) the seed which according to *Tāntric* ideas issues from the creative union of Śiva and Śakti. (c) drop, semen (d) expansion, the sudden development of a secondary incident which , like a drop of water in water, quickly diffuses itself and thus supplies important elements of the plot. It is the source of intermediate object, while the *bīja* is that of the principal one (*SD*, 319; *DR*, 1.28). *Bindu* which can be subsumed under *bīja* was the name given to narrative devices by which an action showing signs of going astray was brought in line with its goal.

2887 **बिन्दु-धारण**

Bindu-dhāraṇa : the process of checking the down-ward flow of the semen (*Tantra*). *Tantras* refined the doctrine of ritual chastity to allow the man who had conquered his desire to perform the sexual act itself, merely retaining his seed to demonstrate the complete control of his senses. This further confuses the subtle between free license and controlled release, for with this sanction *rati* or *mahāmaithuna* becomes the complete demonstration of the control of passion. This is the ultimate variation upon the theme of temptation, for in physiological terms the 'extreme temptation' is the erotic impulse that stirs the seed so that it can rise through the spinal cord to the brain (Pott 1966.8.); a process which renders the *yogī* immortal : 'Loss of semen is loss of power, Exposure to sexual stimulation arouses this power controlled, the power is like steam in a boiler, no longer random' (Dimock, 1966. 157). The seed must be stirred sexually before it can be absorbed mentally. The model *brahmacārin* is a man whose virile energy has been stirred up (*Majjhima Nikāya* 1. 145).

2888 **बिन्दुमाला-रद**

Bindumālā-rada : the line of points bite. The throat, the arm-pit and the thighs are places on which this bite is made (*Kāmasūtra*, 2.5.15). The line of points is to be impressed on the forehead (*Ibid*).

2889 **बिन्दुरद**

Bindurada : the point bite. Lower lip is the place on which the point bite is made (*Kāmasūtra*, 2.57).

2890 **बिब्बोक**

Bibboka : affected coldness; coquetry. showing indifference towards a beloved object through pride : *manākpriyakathālāpe bibboko anādarakriyā (Pratāparudrīyam)*, haughty indifference in general, playful or amorous gesture. It is the indifference which women show on account of vanity and pride after they have realized their cherished desire, *i.e.* winning the lover's heart. Cp. *kuṭṭamita* 'pretended anger'.

2891 **बिम्ब**

Bimba : (a) perfect imitation, subject, presentation, semblance : *darpanaṣya yathā bimbamasat sadiva dṛṣyate tathā lekhasya bimbāni kurvanti kuśalāḥ narāḥ*

"Clerver fingers will easily make an image, *i.e.* the perfect imitation of a writting and thus it may just be linked to the perfection in a mirror which though unreal seems to be real." (b) an image, an effigy (*A*, 13.2.19). The word is used to signify an icon made in stone, metal or clay. The *bimba* is of seven kinds (*bimbam saptavidham smṛtam*) considering the material employed. There is another division of *bimbas* into three types : *niṣkala* (formless), *sakala* (with form) *miśra* (mixed). All the three types are symbolic in nature: the object of worship has significance beyond what is seen and handed. Still another classification of *bimbas* is into *acala* (non-mobile), *cala* (mobile) and *calācala* (partially mobile and partially not). *Bimbas* are also classified into sculptures in the *citra* (round), *ardha-citra* or *ardhāṅgadarśana* (relief sculptures) and *citrābhāsa* (paintings). *Vāśiṣtha-Saṁhitā* (4.59-60) speaks of a two-fold division of *bimbas* : *saumya* or those which are pacific in nature and *āgneya* which are violent in nature. (c) that which causes reflection (*Vedānta*).

2892 **बीज**

Bīja : symbol (*Śiva*). (b) semen (c) seed. In *Tāntric* belief. It signifies the germ syllable which takes the form of deity. (d) origin. (e) cause of denouement in a drama. It was the general principle, the ideal governing the construction of a plot which was to grow organically. The end to be contained in the beginning. It was to grow from a small beginning to great fruits.

2893 **बीजन्यास**

Bījanyāsa : making know the germ of the plot of a play (*DR*, 1.39).

2894 **बीज-मन्त्र**

Bīja-mantra : seed-spell; abbreviated letters or words, symbolic of the tenets of the creed, which are conveyed by the teacher to his disciple after initiation. These *bījamantras* are regarded as microcosms of the actual *mantras* and the meanings suggested by them. These are mystical syllables with which a *mantra* begins.

2895 **बीज-मुद्रा**

Bīja-mudrā : gesture of the seed. Frame *mudrās* of *sa* and *ha* divide it by *sva* and *ta* and join it with the middle finger. This is *bījamudrā* (*VD*). The hands to be turned in the fashion of the half-moon; the index-finger and the thumb of both hands should be joined; the middle finger to be taken below the little finger; at the bottom of these, a bit curved, the ring-finger (*anāmikā*) be arranged (*Brahmāṇḍa*, II.4.42.2).

2896 **बीजाक्षर**

Bījākṣara : the germ-syllable; seed letters like *hrīm*, *krīm* etc. These letters or rather sounds have well-defined meanings and are rationally planned. It is the germ-syllable or syllable containing the primary principle.

2897 **बीभत्स**

Bībhatsa : odious; the sentiment of disgust, one of the eight of nine sentiments in literature. Its consequents are spitting or vomitting, turning away in disgust, sickness, fatigue, death, etc. form its accessories. The art of disgustful experience is suggested by the ghostly images and sketches of the burial or burning grounds, gruesome events, heinous works, dreadful scenes, which particularly create a hateful and hair-startling sensation (*VD*, 3.43.8). It is to be represented by consequents such as stopping movement of all the limbs, narrowing down of the mouth, vomitting, spitting out, shaking the limbs in disgust and the like. Bharata suggests two types of *bībhatsa* : pure, caused by *kṣobha* and, impure (*udvegī*) caused by *udvega* (excitement).

According to Bharata *udvegī* (exciting) arises from the sight of stool and worms, etc. and the *kṣobhaja* arises from the sight of blood, etc. Abhinavagupta (*Abhinavabhāratī*, VI) comments that odious sentiment or the disgust may be due to various causes, subjective, objective or both. Something may be disliked by a person because of his cultural peculiarity as Brāhmaṇs have natural disgust for garlic. *Apriyam* (not pleasant) means that an object may be disliked on account of inequilibrium in three humours, as milk is disgusting to a man suffering from phlegmatic disorder. 'Impure' indicates an object becoming disgusting because of its having been enjoyed to satiation. In Abhinava's opinion the *bībhatsa* arising from the sight of the blood etc. is pure because it agitates the mind. The odious sentiment arising from the foul smelling excrement like stool etc. is *udvegī* as it troubles the mind, so it is impure because of the impure *vibhāvas*.

2898 **बीभत्स्यदृश्य**

Bībhatsya-dṛṣya : the odious scene. Padmākara, the mediaeval Hindi poet has presented the odious scene of the *yoginīs* performing love and war:

पढत मंत्र अरु यंत्र, अंत्र लीलत इमि जुग्गिनि ।
मनहुँ गिलत मद मत्त गरुड, तिय अरुण उरुग्गिनि ॥
हरबरात हरषात प्रथम, परसत पल पंगत ।
जहँ प्रताप जिति जंग-रंग, अंग अंग उमंगत ॥
जहँ पदमाकर उतपति अति रन, रकतन नद्दिय बहत ।
चख चाकित चित्त चरबीन चुभि, चकचकाइ चंडी रहत ॥
रिपुन अंत्रन की कुंडली, करि जुग्गिनि जु चबाति ।
पीबहि में पागी मनो, जुबति जलेबी खाति ॥

2899 **बीभत्स-मुद्रा**

Bībhatsa-mudrā : "make a mat with fingers of both hands, keep two thumbs outside, look downwards and laugh loudly with tongue outside and ugly face". This is called the *bībhatsa-mudrā;* the favourite of Bhairava (*BT*).

2900 **बीभत्सा-रसदृष्टि**

Bībhatsā-rasadṛṣṭi: corners of eyes are shrunk and shut with eyelids, eye-balls disturbed and disgusted and eyelashes are closed together motionlessly. It is used in the odious sentiment.

2901 **बुद्धि**

Buddhi : pure intellect (the habit of first principles). *Buddhi* is not only involved in perception, it also assumes the form of the object. This is an instance of the influence of metaphysics in the analysis of mental processes. As Hiriyanna writes, "the *buddhi* itself assumes the form of the object, when a suitable stimulus is received from outside. The modification of the evolvement *buddhi, viz vṛtti,* is a characteristic not only of perception but also of all forms of consciousness, and when it is inspired by spirit, experience results. The psychic apparatus as a whole meditates between the *puruṣa* and the outside world thereby security for the former experiences of life (*bhoga*) or, if the time for it is ripe, final freedom (*apavarga*) through right knowledge (*viveka*)" (p.285). The *Sāṁkhya-yoga* systems hold that space and time are categories of the *buddhi.*

2902 **बुध-मुद्रा**

Budha-mudrā : gesture of Mercury. The gesture of *sandaṁśa* with the raised little finger (*VD*).

2903 **बुध-हस्त**

Budha-hasta : if *muṣṭi* with the left in a slanting way and *patāka* with the right hand, it is *Budha* (*AD*, 216-25).

2904 **बृहस्पति-मुद्रा**

Bṛhaspati-mudrā : the gesture of *sandaṁśa* with the root of little finger represents Jupiter (*VD*).

2905 **बृहस्पति-हस्त**

Bṛhaspati-hasta : making the *śikhara* gesture with both the hands, if the sacred thread is demonstrated, it indicates the sage*Bṛhaspati* (*AD*, 216-225).

2906 **बोधक**

Bodhaka : indication, index. One of the *Sāttvika Alaṅkāras* of the heroine. It consists in the clear indication of time and place of assignation by the heroine to the hero or vice *versa*, through bodily movements and other signs, in a way that others present may not know their secret love adventures.

Thus *bodhaka* is an index in Peirce's (1931-1958) semiotic approach, which is one of the three major types of sign (the other two being icon and symbol). It is related to referent by relations of contiguity or proximity or causality. Human attributes are often interpreted indexically: a staggering walk indicating love-lorn or drunkenness; a stutter nervousness. Watching a play performed on stage we are especially alert to such indexical signs from gestures, postures and voice quality and tone, for characterization, emotions and plot. So too in the novels: as well as physical attributes.

2907 **बोधि**

Bodhi : perfect wisdom, enlightenment. According to Buddhist philosophy, the sole Absolute embracing this consciousness which in its turn, includes in itself all psychic processes, is *bodhi.* It is the one and only truth attainable to him who practices *yoga,* and even to him only in stages, after he has gone through all the ten stages (*daśabhūmi*) of the career of *Bodhisattva.*

2908 **बोलन**

Bolana : talk (*A*, 2.14.53). It is instructive to look at some of the ways in which Indians use talk, or sometimes the absence of talk, i.e., silence, to communicate. Talk among Indian tribes helps to maintain peaceful social relationships by allowing people to keep in touch with one another about how they are thinking and feeling. Silence is maintained until each person once again becomes accustomed to the presence of the others. The initial stage of courting behaviour also requires silence; in this case, silence is taken to be proper indication of the shyness that is expected between two people attempting to enter into a close relationship. Silence is also used as a kind of sympathizing device. Silence is also required during curing ceremonials. Indians resort to silence when they are confronted with ambiguity and uncertainty in their social relationship; they do not try to talk their way out of difficulty or uncertainty as people with other cultural back-grounds sometimes try to do:

रहिमन निज मन की व्यथा
मन ही राखे गोय ।
सुन अठलैहैं लोग सब
साथ न दैहैं कोय ।।

2909 **ब्रह्मचारिन्**

Brahmacārin : one who practices *brahmacarya,* the first of the four stages of life, a chaste young student. The *brahmacārin* is one who tries to be useful to his preceptor by learning (*Matsya,* 144-23-24). Some of the taboos for *brahmacārin* are as follows : He should not cut the nails or the hair on the body; he should not wash teeth in excess (*Skanda,* II.9.21.6), nor should he wash his clothes, he should not apply the decorative dye to the body (*Ibid,* 10) nor should he use flower-wreaths or ornaments; nor apply oil to his body; nor should he put collyrium to his eyes. He should studiedly avoid the contact of wine and flesh. He should avoid looking at the women, their touch, speech with them or playing with them. He should not even draw the sketch or the picture of the women (*avalekhanam, Ibid,* 12). Except for the image of a goddess, he should not even touch the idol etc. of a woman, nor should he look at it with desire (*Ibid.* 13). He should never look at the copulation of all creatures (*Ibid.* 14). Even the wife of his own preceptor he should not touch while bowing down, nor should he be even with his own mother, in seclusion :

प्राणिमात्रं च मिथुनीभूतं नेक्षेत कर्हिचित् ।

Brahmacarya is the first stage of life, literally 'moving in *brahma',* usually it merely denotes chastity.

Chastity was characteristic of Indian asceticism from the very start (*Śatapatha Brāhmaṇa* XI.5.4.16; *Manu* 5.15.9; *Mbh.* XIII. 74). Sexual excitement represented a threat against which the student must constantly be on gaurd. When Brahmā desired his daughter, he lost all the *tapas* which he had amassed in order to create, and a nymph fell from heaven when she destroyed her *tapas* by falling in love with a mortal man (*Matsya,* 14.1-8).

(b) Any *brahmacārin* who has shed his seed in violation of his vow of chastity must put on the skin of an ass and go to seven houses, begging and proclaiming his misdeed (*Manu,* 11.123). A *brahmacārin* who seduces his *guru's* wife must spend a year wearing bark garments and performing *tapas* in a lonely forest (*Manu,* 11.106).

2910 **ब्रह्म-तेज (ब्रह्म-शक्ति)**

Brahma-teja (brahma-śakti) : the concept of pollution was utilized symbolically. It is soul-substance or spiritual energy, which grew up. The Brāhmaṇs were not to be polluted by untouchables. If they were, their soul-substance or spiritual energy (*brahmateja, brahmaśakti*) would burn up the presumptuous untouchable.

2911 **ब्रह्म-मुद्रा**

Brahma-mudrā : the gesture of *padma* (*VD*).

2912 **ब्रह्म-विद्या**

Brahma-vidyā : knowledge of the *Veda,* knowledge of *Brahman.*

2913 **ब्रह्मा-विष्णु-महेश्वर-मुद्रा**

Brahmā-Viṣṇu-Maheśvara-mudrā : gesture symbolizing the trinity of god. The ring-finger of the *mukula*-hand is extended to symbolize *Brahmā, Viṣṇu* and *Maheśvara* (*VD*).

2914 **ब्रह्म-हस्त**

Brahma-hasta : hold the *catura*-gesture by the left and the *haṁsāsya* by the right. It makes *brahman,* the principal God (*AD,* 205-210).

2915 **ब्राह्मण**

Brāhmaṇa : Brāhmaṇa still stands a symbol for virtue and goodness and wisdom among the common masses. Brāhmaṇa type of saintliness is still focus of attention and adoration in Indian politics. Brāhmaṇa is a priest, member of the four classes. In view of the ritual status supremacy of the Brāhmaṇa in the *varṇa* system was established. All purification after pollution is, in a sense, imitation of Brāhmaṇa purity. Just as all etiquette observed in relation to members of inferior to superior castes is a dramatization, an imitation.

2916 **ब्राह्मण-हस्त**

Brāhmaṇa-hasta : frame *Śikhara* gestures with two hands, and indicate the sacred thread with the right hand, it indicates a *brāhmaṇa,* the intellectual class (*AD*, 226-231).

2917 **ब्राह्म-स्थानक**

Brāhma-sthānaka : a kind of posture.

2918 **ब्राह्माश्रम**

Brāhmāśrama : stage of life based on the *brāhma* sect. The believers of *brāhma* show a *tilaka* mark (round mark).

2919 **ब्राह्मी**

Brāhmī : (a) Sarasvatī. (b) speech leading to the realisation of *Brahman.* (c) the *Brāhmī* script of 46 letters, worked out in India on phonetic principles, existed by 500 B.C.

भ – Bha

2920 **भक्त**

Bhakta : (a) boiled rice, food, wages. (b) devotee, loved, attached to, distributed, allotted, cooked. The traditional dietary system is based on food categories which are 'heating' and 'cooling', foods which either inflame the passions or cool them. Food directly affects the body, so here in India, body image is projected on social organization. It has *sattva, rajas* and *tamas* aspects. Food is 'cooked' in the stomach, yielding to *rasa*, and this in turn gives blood, and from blood forms semen. Any pollution reaching the inside of the body via the mouth will therefore contaminate the vital essence itself.

2921 **भक्ति**

Bhakti : devotion, worship, faith. Loving devotion of the worshipper to the god and tender love of the god for his devotees. It is said to be of three types: (i) *mānasī* (mental), (ii) *kāyikā* (bodily) and (iii) *vāk-saṁbhavā* (involving speech). The nine aspects of devotion are *śravaṇa* (hearing), *kīrtana* (singing the praise), *smaraṇa* (remembering), *sevana* (service), *dāsya* (servitude), *arcana* (worship), *vandana* (bowing down), *sakhya* (always being near) and *ātmanivedanam* (offering of the self; (*Śiva*, IV. 41. 20-22). (b) loving faith in God and surrender to him. Śāṇḍilya defines *bhakti* as *sāparānuraktirīśvara*. This means either the highest form of *bhakti* is 'affection fixed on God or *bhakti* is the highest affection fixed on God'. It is also explained as the state of mind having the Supreme being as its object. The *Gītā* derives the word from the root *bhaj* meaning 'to resort to'. *Bhakti* is again divided into *lauḳikī* (of the common people), *vaidikī* (laid down by the *Veda*) and *ādhyātmikī* (philosophical) or *mānasī* (mental), *vācikī* (verbal) and *kāyikī* (done with body); or into *sāttvikī, rājasī* and *tāmasī* (*Padma-Purāṇa*, V.15. 164-168). The theory propounded in the *Bhagavad-gītā* and other works on *bhakti* is that it leads to the *prasāda* (grace or favour) of God which enables the devotee to attain liberation.

Bhakti is historically one of the main agencies of social fusion developed in India. In origin it is a non-Brahmanic movement of popular religiousity which emerged in South India among classes which were resistant to the pressures of caste hierarchization; it is still very much a living force. True, as soon as any *bhakti* sect gained social influence it was incorporated into the social body; inter-caste as each successive wave has been, and emotionally appealing among low castes for this very reason, the *bhakti* sect which does not find a very large number of adherents tends to become just another caste.

Thus *bhakti* is a powerful source of appeal to the sentiment of inter-caste fraternization, which focused attention less on particularistic caste ethics than on the universal ethico-social ideal of harmonious equilibrium.

Kosāmbi (1962: 32) regards *bhakti* as 'the basic need in feudal ideology' to make total dedication to one's superiors, divine as well as human, a matter of spiritual commitment. There were the consecrated memories of legendary low-born servants who had died for their high-caste masters.

Bhāgavata mentions nine characteristics of *bhakti* (1) *śravaṇa* (listening to God's glory); (2) *kīrtana* (chanting); (3) *smaraṇa* (recalling); (4) *pādasevana* (service); (5) *arcana* (worship); (6) *vandana* (eulogizing); (7) *dāsya* (servitude); (8) *sakhya* (friendship); and a *ātmanivedana* (self-dedication).

2922 **भक्तिच्छेद**

Bhakticcheda : a *mark* on forehead, nose, breast or any other part of the body for decoration (Kālidāsa, *Megha.* 47; *Kum* 7.118).

2923 **भक्ष**

Bhakṣa : eatable food. Levi Strauss (1969) has discussed considerable connection between eating and sexual activity, and it is of great significance to Hinduism: " *Vīrya* (seed) is generated inside the body of a man and *rati* (the seed of a woman) is generated in the body of a woman after the intake of food. Food is converted into blood and from the blood itself are generated *vīrya* or *rati*' (Sinha, 1961. 194-6). This is based on the *Upaniṣadic* concept of the generation of seed from rain through the medium of ingested plants (*Chāndogya Upaniṣad*, 5.10. 3-6), and it is related to the general belief in the interdependence of the digestive and reproductive tracts. In this way, *Śukra*, trapped inside Śiva's stomach after having been eaten , emerges as seed from the *liṅga* (*Mbh.* XII. 278. 1-38). Lust and hunger are closely related in Indian mythology. In a tribal myth Śiva supplies a sexual penance to satisfy hunger; 'A man saw so beautiful maiden and he wanted to devour her, for he had no penis and he could only find pleasure in swallowing. Mahadeo came there and between her legs with his nails he made an oval opening. He made a penis and testicles for the man out of his own thumb and the two swellings on his ears. The world was saved' (Elwin, 1949. 261). The reversal of this situation - food used to satiate a sexual appetite - appears in the *Rāmāyaṇa* (V. 22. 8-9), where the demon Rāvaṇa threatens to eat Sītā if she refuses to satisfy his desire. Thus it seems that sexuality and hunger are interwoven in Indian myths.

2924 **भग**

Bhaga : vagina; female generative organ (q.v. *yoni*). The word later came to mean different qualities of a human being. In a special sense it is applied to the six qualities or types of non-material wealth (*Ṣaḍaiśvarya*): fulness of sway, manliness or energy, glory, auspiciousness, knowledge and indifference to worldly objects: *aiśvaryasya samagrasya dharmasya yaśasaḥ śriyaḥ* | *jñānavairāgyayoścaiva ṣaṇṇā bhaga itīriṇāḥ* ||. (b) vagina is the passage leading from the uterus to the exterior of the body.

2925 **भग-मुद्रा**

Bhaga-mudrā : gesture of the female organ. When two *vitastis* (measurement from the thumbs to the end of the little fingers) are joined together, it is the *bhaga-mudrā* (*VD*).

2926 **भग-लिङ्ग-क्रिया**

Bhaga-liṅga-kriyā : actions involving female and male genital organs in the cult of the Female principle.

2927 **भगवती**

Bhagavatī : an address form prescribed by Bharata. Wives of the great sages are to be addressed as *bhagavatī* (*NS*, XVIII. 65-94). Female ascetics and goddesses are to be addressed as *bhagavatī*.

2928 **भगवन्**

Bhagavan : an address form in Sanskrit. The great sages even adored by gods should be addressed as *bhagavan* (*NS*, XVII. 65-94) For example Kaṇva is addressed so by his disciple, and Mārica by Duṣyanta in *Śākuntalam*. Gods, persons wearing sectarian marks, teachers and persons very learned should be addressed as *bhagavan* by men and women.

2929 **भगिनी**

Bhaginī : an elder sister is to be addressed as *bhaginī* and the younger as *vatsā* (*NS*, XVII. 65-94).

2930 **भगीरथ-हस्त**

Bhagīratha-hasta : *ardhacandra hasta* styled like *tripatāka* represents the mythical king *Bhāgīratha*.It also indicates a solar or lunar eclipse (*Mirror of Gesture*, p. 47).

2931 **भगोस्**

Bhagos : signifies vocative.

2932 **भग्नप्रक्रमता**

Bhagnaprakramatā : violation of the uniformity of expression; broken uniformity (*Kāvyaprakāśa*, VII. 243).

2933 **भङ्ग**

Bhaṅga : deflection from the vertical axis or *sūtra*. Different aspects and moods of gods can be depicted by employing different types of *bhaṅgas*. Various types of deflected stances are also commonly translated as pose; the pose or deviation from the vertical median. Four major types of *bhaṅgas* have been enumerated: *samabhaṅga, abhaṅga, tribhaṅga* and *atibhaṅga*. Each type of *bhaṅga* stands for a corresponding spiritual and emotive quality, closely related to the manipulation of space in relation to the vertical median (*sūtra*) and measurements along the different planes in the manipulation of weight which results in the deflections of different parts of the body from the vertical median. All human movements are classified into four *bhaṅgas* in both sculpture and dancing.

Bhaṅga meaning the bends or inclinations of the body. The term refers to the poses and postures in which an image, especially a standing one, is seen. The poses are stylized in Indian iconography, and there can hardly be found an image which does not answer to one or the other of the conventional poses.

Mānasāra (ch. 57) mentions four possible bodily poses while standing : (1) *sama-bhaṅga* (equally inclined on both sides; equipose, balance); (2) *abhaṅga* (a slight bend, especially of the upper part of the body, to one side); (3) *tri-bhaṅga* (three bends) and (4) *ati-bhaṅga* (excessive bend).

Some texts recognize only two types; with *bhaṅga* (*sa-bhaṅga*) and without *bhaṅga* (*abhaṅga*). (b) *bhaṅga* is the bending of a limb.

(c) hemp; hallucinogenic drug, heterodox techniques for attaining ecstasis, the experience of hallucinogenic drugs. We know that Patañjali himself puts samples (*auṣadhi*), together with *samādhi*, among the means of obtaining *Siddhis* (magico-ecstatic powers). *Auṣadhi* can mean either ecstasy - inducing narcotics or the 'herbs' from which the elixir of longevity was extracted. In any case, hemp and similar drugs produce ecstasy... and not the *yogic samādhi*....; These mystical means properly belong to the phenomenology of ecstasy and they were only reluctantly admitted into the sphere of classic *yoga*. And in fact a certain number of *śāktas* and members of other ecstatic and orgiastic movements used, and still use, opium and *haśīśa*. The majority of these ecstatics are in more or less direct dependence upon Śiva - in other words belong to an aboriginal cultural substratum.

That the ineffable state of ultimate revelation can only be attained in a semi-doped condition has never been seriously advocated. Drugs are regarded as a crude and uncertain aid; they are referred to in texts as dangerous because the *yogin* cannot, under artificial stimulus, obtain complete control over the body.

There is a Chhattisgarhi song depicting the effects of different intoxicants:

> *Gānjā* colour is red as a rose
> Opium appears as black as a ghost

Liquor is just a thorough-going rascal
When the drunkard sleeps he cares for nothing
A dog pisses in his month and runs away.

Gānjā or Indian hemp (*Cannabis sativa*), which is the same as *haśiśa*, is generally taken in the form of *bhānga* (also called *Indrāsana* or *Vijayā*), a drink made from its flowers. This, like opium is one of the sacred drugs: it turned Mahādeva's throat blue; it is popular among ascetics who pour a few drops on the ground in the name of Śaṅkara; for it was he who brought it from the Himālayas and gave it to the mankind; there appears to be little social censure on those who take it. A song addressed to *Vijayā Mātā* sings its praises:

She is the giver of virtue and wisdom;
In drinking is honour and glory
who doth evil to the hemp-juice
May his father become a cat
His mother a she-ass
To wander laden with the hemp-juice
who calleth thee *bhānga* is a fool
who calleth *Vijayā* is a liar
The home is Kamalāpati
That dwells with thine eyes filled.
Saints drink it
Sages drink it
Kanhyaya drinks it
Who speaketh evil or Vijayā
Him will mother Kālkā destroy

(Punjab Notes and Querries, 1883)

A medical book perhaps of the seventeenth century, the *Rājavallabha* of Narayanadasa Kaviraja, says, 'Indra's food is acid, it produces infatiation and destroys leprosy. It is a desire-fulfilling drug begetting joy and destroying every anxiety (*IA*, XXIII. 261). In the ancient folk songs of India, says Grierson (*Ibid*), *gānjā* or *bhānga* is the invariable drink of heroes before performing any great feat. At the village of Bauri in Gaya there is a huge hollow stone, which is said to be the bowl in which the famous hero Lorik mixed his *gānjā*. The epic poem of *Ālhā* and *Ūdala* contains numerous references to *gānjā* as a drink of warriors (*Ibid*).

2934 **भङ्गि**

Bhaṅgi : mode, style, way of saying.

2935 **भङ्गिमन्**

Bhaṅgiman : incurvature, waviness, a winning posture.

2936 **भङ्गिविशारद**

Bhaṅgiviśārada : deft in the use of equivocation. See *vakrokti-nipuṇa*.

2937 **भट्ट**

Bhaṭṭa : an overlord (*sārvabhauma*) king should be addressed by his servants as *bhaṭṭa* (*NS*, XVII. 65-94). Form of address from low-born to superior. (b) bard.

2938 **भट्टिणी**

Bhaṭṭiṇī : queen other than the chief queen. In Sanskrit dramas, *bhaṭṭiṇī* is often used by the maid servants in addressing a queen or a princess (*NS*, 17.86). In a play king's wives are to be addressed by servants and attendants as *bhaṭṭiṇī*, *svāminī* and *devī* (*NS*, XVII. 65-94).

2939 **भट्टारक-वार**

Bhaṭṭāraka-vāra : day of forced labour; later on *kavār* signified the same meaning due to back-formation. Back-formation is the creation of new word by deletion of longer words.

2940 **भणिति**

Bhaṇiti : speech. *vidagdha-bhaṅgī bhaṇitiḥ.*

2941 **भद्रमुख**

Bhadra-mukha : inferior persons are to be addressed as *bhadramukha* and *somya* preceded by he (*NS*, XVII. 65-94).

2942 **भद्रवाच्**

Bhadravāc : speaking auspiciously (*T. Br.* VI. 28-26) *bhadram gṛham kṛṇutha bhadravācaḥ.*

2943 **भद्रवाच्य**

Bhadravācya : congratulations (*VS*, XXI. 61); known as *sādhuvāda* in classical Sanskrit, *vadravācyāya preṣitaḥ.*

2944 **भद्रसूत्र**

Bhadra-sūtra : one of the three horizontal axes through the navel, commonly used in *Śilpaśāstra* texts.

2945 **भद्र-हस्त**

Bhadra-hasta : a type of single hand gesture derived from the *siṁhamukha hasta.*

2946 **भद्रासन**

Bhadrāsana : a golden throne with cushions. It is also a bodily posture.

2947 **भय**

Bhaya : fear, terror. It is one of the eight or nine basic emotions. The inborn instinct latent in all minds. It is aroused at the sight of beasts such as tigers and lions that cause extreme disaster. It may also be aroused on noticing disastrous calamity, of a terrific power. It is the basic instinct in *bhayānaka rasa.*

Accompanying many of the threat gestures there are several characteristic facial expressions, a tense body and exaggerated breathing. The expressions vary according to the shifting balance between the urge to attack and the urge to retreat. For both fear of injury and the urge to inflict it are present in every threatener. If one mood starts to get the upper hand, then the expressions begin to change slightly. The very hostile man, whose urge to attack is stronger than his urge to retreat, will be more likely to display a tightly compressed mouth, a thrust-forward head, deep frowning, and some degree of skin palor. If he begins to feel more frightened of his opponent, his face will change, the mouth showing a snarl that exposes more teeth than before, and he will have a more withdrawn neck, eyes that are wide-open and staring, and skin that is perhaps beginning to redden. One common mammalian threat-display is hair-erection. He threatens his rival with verbal onslaughts, he puts on war-paint, he dresses up in gaudy uniforms (*laḍāībānā*), bangs drums, chants, stamps and dances, and brandishes his weapons. At a national level his threat displays reach the complex proportions of military parades. At a more informal level they express themselves in the form of protest marches, with banners, slogans, badges, and ritual salutes.

The terrible is to be represented by (the *anubhāvas* such as) trembling of the hands, the feet and the eyes, horripilation, change of colour, loss of voice, palpitation of the heart, paralysis, dryness of the mouth, licking lips, perspiration, tremor, apprehension of danger, seeking for safety, running away, loud crying and the like.

The character should move with faltering, quick and near steps, eyes moving and wide, head shaking with frightened looks cast on both sides, hands in *kapota*, the body trembling and lips dry. When a person is pursued by enemy, etc. threatened or frightened and when he sees any dreadful creatures or hears any dreadful sound, the same gait should be resorted to. This should be used by men and women showing prowess at times with successive *eḍakākrīḍita* steps, sometimes fallen near and sometimes far; and the hands are to follow the foot movements.

(b) *bhaya* is a strong emotional reaction involving subjective feelings of unpleasantness, agitation, and desire to flee or hide, and accompanied by widespread sympathetic activity. Fear is a reaction to a specific present danger: anxiety to an anticipated danger. Phobia is persistent, irrational fear.

Fear is a basic human emotion that occurs in the face or real or imagined danger. It prepares us to take action in a crisis, and it is adaptive because it makes us feel like avoiding or running from the things that can harm us. But sometimes we attempt to overcome fear. We may specially want to overcome fear when it is irrational—when it does not warn us of any danger at all but unproductively interferes with our lives.

2948 **भयदृष्टि**

Bhayadṛṣṭi : a type of *bhāvadṛṣṭi* enumerated by Bharata.

2949 **भयानक**

Bhayānaka : the sentiment of terror, one of the eight or nine sentiments. Its basic urge is fright or terror (*bhaya*) and its cause of object is anything that is terrific or fearful. Ladies and low-class characters are proper subjects of the terrific. Its colour is dark. Palour, hoarseness, swoon, perspiration, horripilation, trembling, glancing, away, etc. are its consequents. Disgust, agitation, unconsciousness, piteousness, distress, fatigue, suspicion, confusion, death, etc. are its accessories. The art of the fearful experience finds best exposure through the images and sketches of wild animals, phenomenal disaster, mid behaviours, wild life, tight and similar terrible things (*VD*, III. 43.7).

2950 **भयानक-भावदृष्टि**

Bhayānaka-bhāvadṛṣṭi : It is expressible with widely opened eyes and eyeballs moving in fear, but not fixed in the centres. It suggests fear, awe and horror (*NS*, VIII. 52-53).

2951 **भयानका-रसदृष्टि**

Bhayānakā-rasadṛṣṭi : It is indicated with the eye-lid fixed and drawn up. Eyeballs in this gesture should remain gleaning and turning up. The eyelids are drawn up and fixed, the pupils gleaming and turning up. It indicates a great fear and is used in the Terrible sentiment.

2952 **भयान्विता-भावदृष्टि**

Bhayānvitā-bhāvadṛṣṭi : Both the eyelids are expanded fully, the pupils tremulous in fear and the central part, as it were, coming out of the eye. It is used in fear.

2953 **भरत**

Bharata : actor. Through him the play was raised up with various types of roles. He was like a leader and his representation was accompanied by instrumental music (*NS*). (b) son of Duṣyanta.

2954 **भरत-मुद्रा**

Bharata-mudrā : the *Śikhara* hand held on the right shoulder denotes Bharata, the mythical king (*Mirror of Gesture*, p.47).

2955 **भरतवाक्य**

Bharatavākya : the concluding verse of a drama. It was so called because it used to be recited by Bharatas or actors. In it we find prayer to God or benediction to the spectators.

2956 **भर्तृदारक**

Bhartṛdārakā : princes other than the crown princes should be addressed as such (*NS*, XVII. 65-94).

2957 **भर्तृदारिका**

Bhartṛdārikā : unmarried princesses are to be addressed by their handmaids as *bhartṛdārikā* (*NS*, XVII, 65-94).

2958 **भर्त्सन**

Bhartsana : (*Arthaśāstra*, 2.10.12): form of speech and thought; scolding, threat. It occurs for wrong conduct. It is expressed through the paralinguistic technique prescribed by Pāṇini in his *Aṣṭādhyāyī*, 8.2.94). In the same manner, the word *aṅga*, when joined with the five verbs, is used as a threat (*Aṣṭādhyāyī*, 8.2.9). *Bhartsanā* is threat according to *Amarakośa*.

2959 **भवति**

Bhavati : a vocative used in respect of different *varṇas* in the alms-begging. The ritual alms-begging with the use of the word *bhavati* in respect of different *varṇas* is, respectively, with the word first, in the middle and at the end (*Agni*, 153.9-10) *Manu* (II. 49) also prescribed as a series of syntactic variations on a string of words to make beggars identify themselves by their respective castes while calling for alms: "An initiated Brāhmaṇa should beg, beginning his request with the word *bhavati* (lady); a Kṣatriya, placing the word 'bhavati' in the middle, but a Vaiṣya, placing it at the end (of the formula)."

This meant in effect that if ABC could be said to represent the sequence of the three words in the sentence '*bhavati bhikṣām dehi*' as uttered by a Brāhmaṇa beggar, a Kṣatriya's call was to be construed BAC and a Vaiṣya's BCA.

Here again one can find the elements of a linguistic discrimination between castes entrenched in *Agni Purāṇa* and *Manusmṛti*. *Vāśiṣtha-Dharmasūtra* (XI. 68-70) also records the same: "A brāhmaṇa shall ask for alms placing the word *bhavati* (lady) first. A kṣatriya placing the word *bhavati* in the middle. A vaiṣya placing the word *bhavati* at the end of the formula." According to *Baudhāyana Dharmasūtra* 11.2.3. 16-7) "Let him beg employing a formula consisting of seven syllables, with the word *bhavat* in the beginning, with the word *bhikṣā* in the middle, and with the verb expressing the request at the end; and let him not pronounce laudly the syllables *kṣā* and *hi*.

The brāhmaṇa shall ask for alms, placing the word *bhavat* first, a kṣatriya placing it in the middle, and a vaiṣya placing it at the end of the formula from men of all castes. *Baudhāyana* (II. 10.18.6) also instructs that one should stand begging no longer than the time required for milking a cow.

2960 **भवती**

Bhavatī ¯: the queens and her maids are to be addressed by *Vidūṣaka* as *bhavati*¯ (*NS*, XVII. 65-94). Wives of respectable seniors and of King's officers or respected women and a little old ones are to be addressed as such (*DR*, II. 104).

2961 **भवनविन्यास**

Bhavana vinyāsa : design of a house. The concept of territoriality or proximics was well analysed by Vātsyāyana. The *Kāmasūtra* (1.4.2-15) directs a *Nāgaraka* "to build a house in a city or large villages or in the vicinity of good peoples. This abode should be situated near some water and surrounded by a lovely garden. It should contain different compartments for different purposes: two parts be there for dwelling. The inner part is for females. The outer part, sweet smelling with rich perfumes, should contain a soft bed which is low in the middle part with a white clean cloth to cover it. There should be pillows one at the top and the other at the bottom. A stool should be at the head on which are placed pigments, perfumes, garlands, bark of citron, betel and a box of cosmetics. A spittoon should be there on the ground near the couch. There should be lute hanging from a pig, books, drawing-board, a vessel containing perfumes and some garlands. Not far from the couch and on the ground, there should be a round seat and a board for playing dice. There should be cages of birds outside the room. Separate places should be left there for spinning, carving, etc. In the garden, there should be whirling swing and a common swing as well as a bower of creepers full of flowers, in which a raised parterre should be there for sitting." Really this points out the widespread relationship between power and rank on the one hand, the size both of inner part and outer part territory. Here the *Nāgaraka* is the more important person (in the social sense), so the design of the house is such that less others are permitted to approach him closely, speak of him within earshot, and the greater the size and number of areas which he is permitted to control. Probably one of the most trying features of poverty in India is the lack of privacy that is typical of living conditions of the poor and village folk allocated to them.

The construction of a house in the village at present is in keeping with the social and domestic notions of the Hindus. In front of the house there is usually a spacious courtyard where untouchables and other low-born visitors may stand

and speak to the male members of the family who occupy the verandah of the house for the purpose. At the foot of the verandah there is a low platform for the accommodation of 'touchable' visitors of low social status who cannot be admitted into the verandah which is open only to men of equal status. These may sit with the male members of the family on terms of equality and transact business, the visitor and the host usually squatting on the same mat, when they are of equal age, and chewing betel leaves. A door leaves from the verandah into the house proper. The entrance usually is into a hall which opens into an inner courtyard on the sides of which are built the rooms in which the members of the family live. The male members occupy the more spacious and airy rooms and the hall nearest to the front verandah, and the ladies occupy the darker and smaller rooms away from the verandah and near the kitchen. Only very intimate male relatives are allowed to cross the verandah into the house proper.

The *Matsya Purāṇa* (255.16) gives a set of omens—both good and evil—indicated by certain birds and beasts at the time of construction depending upon their side.

2962 **भवसन्तति**

Bhavasantati : Buddhist term for denoting the continuity of existence.

2963 **भसत्**

Bhasat : *pudendum muliebre*, hind quarters, the region of the hips (*VS*, X. 867); known as *bhosrā* or *bhoshyī* in Bagheli-Hindi *bhasadvartī* situated in the region of hips (*AV*, 11.33.5) *yakṣamam bhasadyam.*

2964 **भस्म**

Bhasma : ashes, particularly the ashes from the funeral pyre, placed upon the bodies of certain sectarians. Ashes have been associated with great efficacy and magico-curative value from very ancient times. With *bhasma, tripuṇḍraka* is to be marked on the fore-head. The use of *bhasma* for purificatory purpose was a general custom. The belief behind the curative properties of the *bhasma* is, obviously due to its being produced from the fire and its contact with Rudra-Śiva (*Vāmana*, 17.14.16). *Bhasma* was used as a territorial marker. Those who sat in one line, but could not touch one another due to some social restrictions were divided by the lines of ashes; thus there was no contaminational 'mixture' among them. The other alternative for such demarcations were fire, water, sprinkling, door and pole (*Kūrma*, II. 16. 31-32). (b) *bhasma* is the inner intuition which reveals the self and destroys by burning illusion. As an outer symbol of the *Pāśupata*, the *Liṅgāyata* and other forms of Śiva religion enjoin *bhasmadhāraṇa* or besmearing the body with ashes. (c) the image of the ash as seed, as the essense of the dead lover, the pyre as a bed, and ashes as sandlewood paste — all of this is present in a verse expressing the erotic longing for union with god:

Let me become a pyre of sandlewood;
Light it with your hand.
And when it burns to a heap of ashes,
Apply it to your body.
Paraśurāma Caturvedi, *Mīrābāī Padāvalī, pada* 46)।
Classical Sanskrit writers transfer one step further:
May the breasts of the Mountain daughter save you,
Swelling like the temples of Indra's elephants,
coated with ashes for cosmetic
from the pressure of her tight embrace of Śambhu.
(*Subhāṣitaratnakośa*, No. 69)

2965 **भस्म-मुद्रा**

Bhasma-mudrā : to paint the holy ash. Make the palm upturned, curve four fingers to join the thumb with the side. This is *bhasma mudrā* (*VD*). The *bhasma-mudrā* indicates taking *bhasma*, or something of the same nature, prescribed for the particular sect, for painting on the fore head and other parts of the body after the daily bath.

2966 **भस्मस्नान**

Bhasma snāna : purification by ashes, a type of *bathing*.

2967 **भाण**

Bhāṇa : monologue; a type of Sanskrit *rūpaka* enumerated in *NS*. It is to be acted by a Single character narrating one's own experiences or describing those of others. Other characters, though they are not present on the stage, are made to speak through one only, that is present — he is *dhūrta* or *viṭa*. This is done by making him repeat the words that are supposed to be addressed to him, together with his replies in the course of *ākāśa-bhāṣitas*. He thus develops the story through this manner of speech and appropriate physical movements, in a gradual manner. It should have one act and should include many movements, expressive of the various conditions of *dhūrta* or *viṭa*.

2968 **भाण्डब्रह्माण्डतत्त्व**

Bhāṇḍa-brahmāṇḍatattva : the theory that the body (*bhāṇḍa*) is the microcosm of the universe (*brahmāṇḍa*).

2969 **भामिनी**

Bhāminī : pretending anger, beautiful woman.

2970 **भारत**

Bhārata : reciters of the Epics; modern *bhāṭas*. Bhāratas were the rhapsodes of Bharata tribe. *Mahābhārata* is the great Epic of the family. With the passage of time, the rhapsodes took upon them the newer art of drama. Keith says that, hence the term *Bhārata* meant a comedian in later texts. (b) name of the country (India) relating to Bharata:

uttaram yatsamudrasya himādreścaiva dakṣiṇam ।
varṣam tad bhāratam nāma bhāratī yatra santatiḥ ॥

(*Viṣṇu Purāṇa*)

(c) According to one interpretation, Bhārata-*varṣa,* the ancient name of India, literally means 'land of the actors'. Here the perspective of life is seen as one vast drama, in which the actors assume a succession of masks in accordance with the laws of *karma* without the essence of self-being affected by the taint of impersonation. There is no freedom in the individualistic sense, but the very word 'freedom' begs the question. The idea of like as a masquerade may to some extent mitigate the feeling of hopelessness on the face of inexorable destiny; it equally reduces the significance of any effort to escape from the grip of fate in the wordly sense, but not in the ultimate sense of liberation into 'a perfect state of happiness beyond human understanding'.

2971 **भारत-न्याय**

Bhārata-nyāya : striking the waist. The shield is to be held in the left hand and the weapon in the right. The shield should be moved round by extending the hand and then drawing back. The sword should be brandished round the head or near the cheek. Again by turning the wrist gracefully the sword and the shield should be moved round the head.

2972 **भारती**

Bhāratī : eloquent style, a particular style of theatrical presentation in which the word predominates. It is mainly adopted by males and has four varieties: (a) *prarocanā:* arousing expectancy through praise; (b) *vīthī* : a gay mode indicating eros mixed with other sentiments; (c) *prahasana:* the mode of force; (d) *āmukha* : a device of introducing the writer, the theme etc. at the beginning of a drama. *Bhāratī vṛtti* prevails where the action of words dominates; it is generally used by male characters excluding female characters, it is used in Sanskrit speeches, and it is employed by the actors when they are in their own capacity and they have not assumed the roles of characters (*DR*, III. 7).

2973 **भारतीयम्**

Bhāratīyam : Indianness. The idea of national identity — the self-awareness of the nation, its self-image, and its values - springs from a desire for fixed points of reference in the enlarged world of today. The self-image of India is tentative in character and has evolved from the way it perceives its history from ancient times through many centuries of decline and foreign domination to the decades of its recently achieved status as an independent sovereign state. The difficulties in forming a contemporary national self-image may be more clearly appreciated when it is realized that while India is now building a modern secular state, its traditions are permeated by a sophisticated religious sensibility. One of the primary concerns of India's leaders is consequently to build up a cohesive, integrative and secular nationalism from the sundry particularistic forces which are so strongly engrained. It is inevitable that the emotional needs of a newly independent nation have prompted influential persons to focus national energies more on an idealized image than one which emerges through a discrimination insight into history. However, until the contradictions end what is less often appreciated, the affinities between India's pluralistic cultural traditions and the new elements of contemporary civilization are frankly faced, and until a clearer image of its identity is thereby obtained, it will be difficult for the nation to define its place and role in a fast-changing world. Because of these contradictions and affinities the individual also remains divided within himself. The search for clearer definition and constant redefinition has to be conducted within the continuous sequence of actions and choices in response to very grave economic and political problems. Yet if it is not undertaken with concerned objectivity, India is in danger of failing to set itself consistently and with determination to any major undertaking (see, Dube 1986).

2974 **भारती-हस्त**

Bhāratī-hasta : a type of both hands gesture mentioned by *Bālarāmabharata.*

2975 **भारवाह**

Bhāravāha : carrying a load. The Indian male (tribal as well as non-tribal) does not carry load over his head. He carries it over his shoulders. It is the Indian girls and women who carry heavy loads on their heads. They bring water from the streams and carry their children. The practice of carrying load on the woman was also prevalent in the *Purāṇic* period. *Skanda-Purāṇa* (1.1.23.75) records:

हैम कलशमादाय शिरसा बिभ्रती स्वयम् ।

In the Hill Maria society it is taboo for men to carry any load on their heads. He carries it over his shoulders. It is the Hill Maria girls and women who carry heavy loads on their heads.

2976 **भाल**

Bhāla : forehead. *bhālatilaka* '*tilaka* on the forehead'; *bhālapaṭṭa* the plate on the forehead': *nijabhālapaṭṭa likhitam* (*Bhartṛ. Nīti.* 40).

2977 **भाव**

Bhāva : (a) emotion, moods, mental state, emotional disposition. (i) one of the twenty *sāttvika alaṅkāras* of the heroine. It has been defined as the first touch of the erotic emotion in a mind which had no such experience in the past (*Sāhitya-darpaṇa*, III.93). (ii) a single undeveloped emotion. In Indian aesthetics, *bhāvas* have a broad scope. Psychologically sometimes they indicate feelings, sometimes imagination, sometimes views and ideas, etc. Even a hero or heroine are not men of blood land flesh. They are the image-bodies of poet's imagination. Their excitants, ensuants, functions, expressions of temporal and oormant feelings, emotion, sentiment and temperament are the different exuberances of a poet's own imagination. Indian dramaturgy defined and classified psychological natures and characteristics of human-feelings, appropriate to express the dramatic performances; what should reflect on life-like pictures of a blessed artist. The first exposure of the spontaneous psychic change is a *bhāva;* but a *bhāva* is an acquired device of conscious mind to give best exposure of the mental waves with the help of some voluntary actions, like a side-glance, a studied smile etc., which add extra beauty to a physique (*NS*, XXIV. 3-5). The display of non-voluntary and acquired feelings with the help of curves of a brush is indicated by *bhāva-lāvaṇya-yojanā* (adding extra lustre to a picture with the exposure of feeling). Lustre of such feelings on a body is relished as beauty or *lāvaṇya*, like a flash of the light on a pearl bead (*Ujjvalanīlamaṇi*, 1.17). The net-work of sweat-drops on Śakuntalā's countenance, the loose scarf on her shoulder etc. add extra lustre to her beauty. In the same way, the king's sweating finger-prints, the spots of his tear-drops on the portrait are suggestive to his sincere love (*Śākuntalam,* Act IV).

(b) a type of address form according to Bharata. A *Mārṣa* (respected person) is to be addressed as *bhāva* (*NS*, XVII, 65-90).

(c) the environment plays some role in modulating our emotional responses to their people.

(d) dispositions according to which mankind in classified in *Tāntrism*. These are *divya* or the man with a divine disposition; *vīra* or the man with a heroic disposition; and *paśu* or the man with an animal disposition. In *Vaiṣṇavism*, *bhāva* is the mode of approach to devotion like *dāsya* (servant-like), *sakhya* (friend-like), *vātsalya* (filiar), *kānta* or *madhura* (romantic) etc. The *Gītā* explains the term as 'tendency' and classifies it into *sattva, rajas* and *tamas*. In philosophical tradition it denotes existence, positiveness and so on.

(e) *bhāva* has been defined by Viśvanātha (III. 118) thus:

निर्विकारात्मके चित्ते भावः प्रथमविक्रिया

Bāhulaka has extensively explained it as follows:

लीला विलासो विच्छित्तिर्विभ्रमः किलकिञ्चितम् ।
मोट्टायितं कुट्टमितं बिब्बोको ललितं तथा ॥
विहृतं चेति विज्ञेया दशा स्त्रीणां स्वभावजाः ।
तथा च
वागङ्गालङ्करणैः श्लिष्टैः प्रीतिप्रयोजकैर्मधुरैः ।
इष्टजनस्नायुकृतिर्लीला ज्ञेया प्रयोगज्ञैः ॥
स्थानासनगमनानां हास्यभ्रूकर्मणां चैव ।
उत्पद्यते विशेषो यः श्लिष्टः स तु विलासः स्यात् ॥
मालाच्छादनभूषणविलेपनानादरन्यासः ।
स्वल्पोऽपि परां शोभां जनयेद् सा तु विच्छित्तिः ॥
विविधानामर्थानां वागङ्गाहार्यसत्वयुक्तानाम् ।
मदरागहर्षजनितो व्यत्यासो विभ्रमः प्रोक्तः ॥
स्मितहसितरुचितभयपुलकरोषगर्वश्रमाभिलाषाणाम् ।
सङ्करकरणं हर्षादसकृत् किलकिञ्चितं ज्ञेयम् ॥
इष्टजनस्य कथायां हेलालीलादिदर्शनेनापि ।
तद्भावभवनकृतं तन्मोट्टायितमभिख्यातम् ॥
केशस्तनादिपीडनरागादतिहर्षसम्भ्रमोत्पन्नम् ।
कुट्टामितमनुवदन्ति हि सुखस्य दुःखोपचारेण ॥
इष्टानां भावानां प्राप्तावभिमानगर्भसम्भूतः ।
स्त्रीणामनादरकृतो बिब्वोको नाम विज्ञेयः ॥
हस्तपादादिविन्यासे भ्रूनेत्रौष्ठे प्रयोजिते ।
सौकुमार्यं भवेद् येन ललितं तत्प्रकीर्तितम् ॥
वाच्यानां प्रीतियुक्तानां प्राप्तानां यदभाषणम् ।
व्याजात् स्वभावतो वापि विहृतं नाम तद्भवेत् ॥

Viśvanātha enumerates 18 *alaṅkāras* of women including the ten mentioned here.

(f) the emotionally constrained interpersonal relationships which we still find in the typical rural joint family have had decisive consequences for every aspect of life in India. The emotional control essential to this collective life — in other words the celebrated 'serenity' and 'impassive calm' — can be traced to the conditions under which the vast majority of population have lived since ancient times.

(g) emotion has been variously defined by psychologist of different theoretical orientations, but with general agreement that the emotional state is a complex reaction involving a high level of activation and visceral changes, and accompanied by strong feelings or affective states. cf.

"Na devo vidyate kāṣthe
na pāṣāṇe na mṛnmaye ।
Bhāveṣu vidyate deva-
stasmādbhāvo hi kāraṇam ॥

2978 **भावकरण**

Bhāva-karaṇa : indication of intention. Action is revealed through certain preparatory movements. These can act cues, revealing what we intend to do, and they are called *bhāvakaraṇa*.

2979 **भाव-करुणा**

Bhāva-karuṇā : pathetic sentiment. In *Vikramorvaśīya* (Act IV), the king picks up a pebble to throw it into the pond, stops and enacts *bhāva karuṇā;* to depict this *bhāva*, he would use the appropriate glance, *i.e. karuṇā dṛṣṭi*, where the upper eyelid is lowered; the eyeball is at rest, the gaze is fixed on the tip of the nose, and a tear is held in the eye (*NS*, VIII., 49).

2980 **भावग्राहिन्**

Bhāvagrāhin : appreciating the sentiment, accepting the essence or sense.

2981 **भावजननम्**

Bhāvajananam : reaching the climax of pleasure in co-habitation (*Naiṣadha*, 18.166).

2982 **भावत्व**

Bhāvatva : the term for 'being'.

2983 **भाव-दृष्टि**

Bhāva-dṛṣṭi : glances suggesting relevant emotions, 8 gestures enumerated by Bharata.

2984 **भाव-देह**

Bhāva-deha : There are two *bhāvas*, transient *bhāvas* which manifest and disappear: permanent emotion stays till the intensity of love is culminated into *rasa*. This is only a inherent emotion. This permanent state with permanent emotion is known as *bhāvadeha*.

2985 **भावना**

Bhāvanā : impression; the suitability of the activity of the creator corresponds with the suitability of the created thing (*Sāhitya*). (b) one of the constituents of the Jain concept of *bhāvasaṁvara*. It is meditation or contemplation on twelve aspects of Jain dogma. (c) in *Pūrva-mīmāṁsā bhāvanā* means a particular operation or activity of an agent which initiates the desired result. It is of two kinds: *śābdī* (word-force) and *ārthī* (result-producing force.) (d) in Buddhism *bhāvanā* is a comprehension which is regarded as one of the two ways or *mārga* leading to salvation, the other being *darśana* (e) *bhāvanā* is a phenomenological observation or an unanalyzed sensation. It is a vague judgement or conculsion. Our impressions of others and the implicit predictions we make about them are produced partly by our observations of them, and other available information about them, and partly by our theories of how personality is organized and structured.

2986 **भावना-व्यापार**

Bhāvanā-vyāpāra : one's own continuous state of emotion, cultivation of sensibility.

2987 **भावम्**

Bhāvam : secretion of semen from men or women on sexual arousal, ejaculation in coition, orgasm, discharge of 'spermat' (*Kāmasūtra*, 2.1.32-34). (b) to think of again and again or constantly. (c) orgasm is a pattern of involuntary movements of the genital organs and associated movements of the voluntary masculature, accompanied by intense pleasure and strong sexual feelings and culminating in the ejaculation of semen by the male. It is normally the climax of coitus.

2988 **भाव-लक्षणम्**

Bhāva-lakṣaṇam : sign of enjoyment and satisfaction of women have been depicted by *Kāmasūtra* (2.8.8) as such: 'Her body relaxes, she closes her eyes, she puts aside all bashfulness and shows increased willingness to unite as closely as possible: *gātrāṇām sranśanam netranimīlanam vrīḍānāśaḥ samadhikā ca ratiyojaneti strīṇām bhāvalakṣanam.* According to *Ratirahasya* (10.44) *Srastatā vapuṣi mīlanam dṛśo mūrchanā ca ratibhāva-lakṣaṇam.* Kalyānamalla also gives the same description but adds that she prespires and pays attention to her clothes and hair: *Keśavastrādi saṁvṛttiḥ* (*Anaṅgaraṅga*, 10.46-47). Sanskrit poets have taken great pleasure in describing the stage of sexual satisfaction of women (*Śiśu.* 10.82; *Caurapañcāśikā* 22; *Daśakumāracarita*, p. 115; *Naiṣadha*, 8.119; *Kuṭṭanīmatam* 161).

2989 **भावशबलता**

Bhāvaśabalatā : chain of emotions, mixture of feelings, varied emotions, union of emotions.

2990 **भावशान्ति**

Bhāvaśānti : pacification or calming down of feeling.

2991 **भावसन्धि**

Bhāvasandhi : conjunction or conflict of feelings. (b) a figure of speech where several feelings are strung together (*Alāṅkāra sarvasva*, 84).

2992 **भावस्थिति**

Bhāvasthiti : stagnant feeling, a group of imperceptible order of suggestion.

2993 **भावानुकीर्तन**

Bhāvānukīrtana : exemplification of the inner reality of the whole of life (*NS*., 1.106-107).

2994 **भावाभाव**

Bhāvābhāva : being and non-being.

2995 **भावाभास**

Bhāvābhāsa : illusion of an emotion, pseudo-emotion. An emotion or feeling which is inappropriate in a particular context.

2996 **भावावस्था**

Bhāvāvasthā : emotional states involve bodily changes and thoughts. The bodily changes are largely changes to do with states of arousal, that is changes in the heart rate, blood-pressure, skin conductance - and a whole range of other changes which are variously detectable to people. They are controlled by the action of the automatic nervous system, and they get the body into a state of readiness to take action. In some emotional states the physiological changes are quite dramatic, as in extreme fear or rage or sexual arousal. In others they are quite slight as in generalized euphoria or faint nostalgia. Perception of bodily states is only one component of the information that leads us to describe ourselves as feeling one emotion rather than other. We can perceive the difference between feeling angry and feeling frightened because our apprehension of situations informs us of the difference.

2997 **भाविक**

Bhāvika : imflaming, inciting. *Bhāvikam* is the being activity present of the poet's interest throughout his work (*Kāvyaprakāśa*, II. 364). (b) gesticulation or movements of the body calculated to bring out, or contributing to the manifestation of a feeling (*Mālavikā.*, I).

2998 **भावुक**

Bhāvuka : disposed to be, having a taste for poetry, appreciating beauty.

2999 **भावैकरस**

Bhāvaikarasa : having love as the sole essence.

3000 **भावोदय**

Bhāvodaya : the dramatic moments of augmenting, diminishing, and muting an emotion (*Kuvalayānanda,* 105-107).

3001 **भाषण**

Bhāṣaṇa : one of the 64 *sandhyaṅgas* in dramaturgy (*NS*, 19. 102). It is full of conciliatory words, gifts, etc. according to Bharata. Dhanañjaya interprets it as the 'acquisition of honour, etc: *mānādyāptiśca bhāṣaṇam* (*DR*. 1.107).

3002 **भाषा**

Bhāṣā : (a) language. (b)plaint in a lawsuit (*Smṛti*). (c) social use of language. Social differences were reflected in speech, dress, hair-styles etc., also. The rulers were supposed to speak in chaste Sanskrit termed *āryabhāṣā*, but the spoken language of the common people was called *Jātibhāṣā* and could be either of the bordering areas which have many barbarian words (*mlecchaśabda*) or of the *Bhāratavarṣa* (*NS*, XVII. 28-30). The *Jātibhāṣā* itself could be Prākṛt or Sanskrit (*NS*, XVII. 31-32):

jātibhāṣāśrayam pāṭhyam dvividham samudāhṛtam
prākṛtam saṁskṛtam caiva cāturvarṇyasamāśrayam

The heroes were to speak in Sanskrit normally but could use Prākrit for some reason. Ascetics of diverse kinds including mendicants and Bhāgavatas, women and those belonging to the low *jātis* were to speak in Prākṛt. So also those who did not have the opportunity of studying on account of poverty or were sunk in poverty or were spoilt rich people or were uneducated people of the upper class (*NS*, XVII. 34-35):

dāridryā dhyanābhava-yadṛcchā dibhireva ca
aiśvareṇa pramattānām dāridryeṇa plutātmanām
anadhītottāmānām ca Saṁskṛtam na prayojayet

Educated ascetics, queens, hetairas and women versed in arts and crafts could speak in Sanskrit (XVII. 39):

Śilpakāryāstathaiva ca.

It follows thus, that Sanskrit was primarily the symbol of education, high social position and office. The people, especially when uneducated, extremely poor or low social strata spoke dialects called Prākṛt. These dialects differed according to regions and *NS* mentions seven *bhāṣās* and seven *vibhāṣās,* the former being well-known varieties of Prākṛt while the latter were dialects of non-Aryan languages (*Ibid.*, XVII. 49-50).

3003 **भाषिक–स्वर**

Bhāṣika-svara : the accent used in the Brāhmaṇs; *uccanīcasvaram prāhuḥ* (*TS*, 1.1.3.4). It indicates the quality of vowel sound, pitch, or length etc. cf. *deśamākhyāti bhāṣitam.* "Speech tells the native country of the speaker".

3004 **भाष्य**

Bhāṣya : commentary, elucidation. That which sets out the meaning of the *sūtra* or an aphorism which follows the text of the *sūtra* and makes its own contribution to the elucidation of the subject of the *sūtra.* Commonly the term is used in the sense of commentary.

3005 **भिक्षा**

Bhikṣā : begging; alms obtained by begging. It was the duty of householders to give alms to the *Brahmacāris* (students) and *yatis* (ascetics). Food might be begged from all the *varṇas* except from those who are *abhiśapta* (guilty of grave sins) and *patiṭa* (outcasted). Food obtained by begging was supposed to be pure and was to be placed before the teacher. Apart from the students, begging was allowed to the diseased and those oppressed by hunger and to such persons who did it for the teacher, for one's marriage, for a sacrifice, and anxiety to support one's parents, and to ward off the sin caused by the non-observance of the duties expected of a worthy person and so on (*Āp. Dh. S* 1.1. 3. 25-44, *Manu,* II. 182-189).

(b) giving alms to beggars symbolises prosperity in the land and the generosity of the householder. There are also cases where there is streak of quaint romance, as the following Bhili folksong suggests:

> My *nanad* and I went to the foot of the hills,
> To gather grass where we had sown the seeds.
> Two *sādhūs* appeared and said, "Beautiful girls,
> Are you married? Please give us some grain."
>
> One of us give them grain, saying,
> "O Sage, here is a handful of grains."

(c) begging is the traditional occupation of *Jogīs* in India, but they have now adopted others. The *kanphaṭas* beg and sell a woollen string amulet (*gaṇḍā*), which is put round the necks of children to protect them from the evil eye. They beg only from Hindus and use the cry *alakha,* the invisible one. The Nāndiā *jogīs* lead about them a deformed ox, an animal with five legs or some other malformation. He is decorated with ochre-coloured rags and cowrie shells. They call him *Nandī* or the bull on which Mahādeva rides, and receives gifts of grain from pious Hindus, half of which they put into their wallet and give the other half to the animal. They usually carry an a mare profitable business than other classes of beggars. The ox is trained to give a blessing to the benevolent by shaking its head and rising its legs when its master receives a gift. Some of the *jogīs* of this class carry about them a brush of peacock's feathers which they wave over the heads of children afflicted with the evil eye or of sick persons, muttering texts. This performance is known as *jhāḍanā* (sweeping), and is the commonest method of casting out evil spirits (Russell and Hiralal, II. 253).

3006 **भिक्षाचर्य**

Bhikṣācarya : going about for alms, rules of begging. Manu has laid down the rules of begging in his law book. Different sects and groups in India have evolved their own methods of begging. The *Gosāīn* sect of mendicants have various rules of begging. "Some will never turn back to receive alms. They may also make a rule only to accept the surplus of food cooked for the family, and to refuse an: of special quality. One *Gosāīn* noticed by A.K. Smith, always begged hopping, and only from five houses; he took from them respectively two handfuls of floor, a pinch of salt, and sufficient quantities of vegetables, spices and butter for his meal, and then went hopping home. Some carry bells of bullocks which they tie round the waist, so that the tinkling of the bells may announce their coming. A common begging cry is *Alakha Niranjana,* which is said to mean 'apart', and to refer to themselves as being apart or separated from the world. The beggar gives his cry and stands at the door of the house for half a minute, shaking his body about all the time. If no alms are brought in this time he moves on." (Russell and Hiralal, II. 1916: 154).

The other sect of Daṇḍīs live in the forest and only come once a day to beg at a Brāhmaṇa's house for a part of such food as the family may have cooked. "He should not ask for food if any one else, even a dog, is waiting for it. He must not accept money, or touch fire or any metal. They repeat the phrase *Śivoham,* which means 'I am Śiva' (*Ibid.,* 155).

Rāvanvansi Gosaīn smear vermilion on their forehead and beg only at twilight and never at any other time, whether they obtain food or not. In begging they will never move backwards, so that when they have passed a house they cannot take alms from it unless the householder brings the gift to them (*Ibid.,* 156).

During their visits to villages they used to engage in intrigues, and a rebald Gond song sung at the Holi festival describes the pleasure of the village women at the festival of a Gosāīn owing to the sexual gratification which they expected to receive from him.

3007 **भिक्षु**

Bhikṣu : beggar. (a) representatives of the *sannyāsa* order. The *Bṛhadāraṇyaka upaniṣad* (III. 5.1, IV. 2.22) defines *bhikṣu* as those who give up desire and practise begging in order to realize *Brahman.* (b) in Buddhism the term received a special significance. It came to denote the monks residing in *Saṅgha* under certain definite rules and regulations. The status of a *bhikṣu* had to be attained through a prolonged course of religious exercises and after going proper initiation. The nuns were called *bhikṣuṇīs.*

3008 **भिक्षुचर्या**

Bhikṣucaryā : worn out clothes. *Bhikṣu* means a beggar or monk who wears the torn clothes.

3009 **भित्तिक-संस्थान**

Bhittika—saṁsthāna : the side-exposed position, same as *pārśvagata saṁsthāna* (see).

3010 **भिन्नगति**

Bhinnagati : of flattering gait.

3011 **भिल्ल**

Bhilla : a mountain tribe in the Vindhyas. *Bhillapallī* 'village of the Bhils; cf. *sun kol-bhillini kī girā* (*Mānasa*, 2.250.1), *bhillini jimi chāṛan cahat, vacanu bhayankar bāju* (*Mānasa*, 2.28).

3012 **भीमरथी-हस्त**

Bhīmarathī-hasta : name of a river. The *arāla* hand moving up and down indicates this river (*Mirror of Gesture*, p. 48).

3013 **भीम-हस्त**

Bhīma-hasta : *muṣṭi-hasta* flung forward represents Bhīma, the Pāṇḍava (*Mirror of Gesture*, p. 47).

3014 **भुक्ति**

Bhukti : experience of enjoyment akin to the experience of *savikalpa-yoga.*

3015 **भुक्तिवाद**

Bhuktivāda : according to this view of Bhaṭṭa Nāyaka, *rasa* is enjoyed, and it is neither inferred nor produced.

3016 **भुक्तिसिद्धि**

Bhukti-siddhi : material success (*Tāntric* concept).

3017 **भुग्न—मुख**

Bhugna—mukha : stooping mouth, somewhat long drawn face; a type of facial gesture in *sṛṅgāra*; also known as *udvāhimukha* or *vivṛta mukha* or slightly expanded (*NS*, VIII. 153-160); half-opened mouth. It suggests bashfulness, impatience, anxiety, shame, summoning, ascetic mood, despondency, longing, discipline and consultation.

3018 **भुग्नग्रीवा**

Bhugnagrīvā : of arched neck.

3019 **भुज**

Bhuja: arm : Although gestures using the upper arm and forearm as points of reference appear in India, no minimal pairs exist to demonstrate their emic status. Two analogous pairs do appear, however. In 'strong' the open hand graps the biceps: but in 'They caught him' the open hand seizes the lower arm or wrist area. The reason that this contrast is analogous rather than minimal is that the pair also differs in dynamics of movement; specifically, 'they caught him' involves more forceful contact. In another analogous opposition, a grasp of the upper arm in 'strong' contrast with a grasp of the wrist in 'bracelet'. Again the nature of the grasp differs slightly.

Configuration of designator features appearing uniquely in Hindi include total and partial arm extension and divergent, parallel and convergent arm alignment. Cf. *bhuj uṭhāi ūnce caṛhi ṭerat* (*Mānasa* 2.14.1).

3020 **भुजङ्ग-त्रासित-करण**

Bhujaṅga-trāsita-karaṇa : (a) derived from the *cārī* of that name: one *kuñcita* foot lifted up, the thighs in *vivartana.* There is an oblique turning of the entire body specially knees, thighs and waist: the hand positions are not indicated; one arm is in *karihasta* (*NS*, IV. 84-85, IX. 199, 255-56; 275; X. 42). Raising up the *kuñcita* foot, the thigh should have an oblique movement, the waist and the knee should be turned.

This is one of the 108 *karaṇas,* well-known to the dance-texts and found in sculptural representations, as for instance in the temple complex of Cidambaram. The dance-pose, known as "frightened by the serpent" involves the lifting of one foot (*kiñcit pādam utkṣipya*) suddenly, as if a serpent has been discovered in very close proximity (*viz.* near the foot). The lifted foot may be held on the same side of the body or thrown across to the other side. In either case, the posture is unsteady, the weight of the body balanced on one leg only. In this pose, the arm hangs freely (*ḍolā-hasta*), or thrown across (*gaja-hasta*); the hand points down. The other hand assumes the *kaṭaka*-gesture. (Fig. 3020)

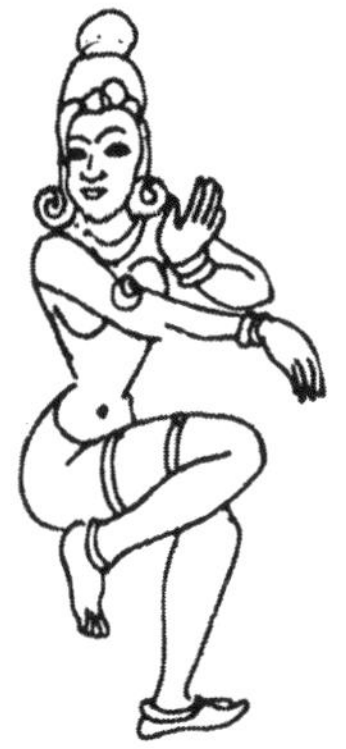

Fig. – (3020)

3021 **भुजङ्ग-त्रासिता-चारी**

Bhujaṅga-trāsitā-cārī : gait of the person afraid of snake nearby; feet in *sampāda cārī*, lifted but sideways turning of the waist also. The *kuñcita* foot is lifted and the knee of this leg touches the other knee. *Vivartita* position of knees and thighs. Lifting up a *kuñcita* foot (up to the region of the top of the thigh of the other), turning round the waist and the knee and the thigh also turned round. Abhinava explains thus: 'a *kuñcita* foot is raised, taken to the joint of the other thigh, then due to the *vivartana* of the waist *i.e.* turning the *trika* and the knee, the heel of this foot faces the other hip, then the thigh in this oblique position is turned; thus the knee moves to its own side, the sole of the foot facing upwards. It is used in showing the gait of a man afraid of a snake nearby."

3022 **भुजङ्ग-त्रासित-रेचित-करण**

Bhujaṅga-trāsita-recita-karaṇa : is derived from the *cārī* of that name. The *karaṇa* can also fall into the category of the *recita karaṇas* for the circular movement is emphasized here (*NS*, IV. 95b-96a). After performing the *bhujaṅga trāsitā cārī* the hands in *recita* are placed on the left side. It is a dance-pose described in Bharata's NS used in the portrayal of Śiva as dancing. In this *karaṇa* the *bhujaṅga-trāsita-karaṇa* pose is slightly altered, both arms being thrust to the left side: *vāma-pārśva-sthitau hastau.*

3023 **भुजङ्गाञ्चित-करण**

Bhujaṅgāñcita—karaṇa : derived from the *cārī* of that name. The *kuñcita* foot crosses at the thigh level. Right hand in *recita* and left hand in *latā* (*NS*, IV. 100b-101a). The foot is in *bhujaṅga trāsitā*, right hand in *recita* and the left hand in *latā.*

3024 **भुजङ्गासन**

Bhujaṅgāsana : lie down flat on the ground, face downwards, and relax. Place the palms on the ground besides the shoulders. Raise the head and the upper portion of the body slowly like a cobra. Bend the spine backwards, then slowly bring the head down. This process of raising the head and bringing the same down may be repeated, while breathing slowly through the nose. The breath may be retained till you raise the head and bend the spine; then exhale. Again retain the breath while bringing the head down.

This is particularly useful for ladies in toning up the ovaries and uterus. It relieves various utero-ovarine diseases. Deliveries become normal and easy.

3025 **भुजङ्गिनी-मुद्रा**

Bhujaṅginī-mudrā : drink in air by opening and expanding the mouth a little. This is *bhujaṅginī-mudrā.* All the disorders of the stomach and its chronic ailments are cured by this *mudrā.*

3026 **भुजबन्ध**

Bhujabandha : the arm-link. It is one of the most obvious and publicaly displayed of all tie-signs among the tribal female-folk. The arm-link is basically a signal of co-ordinated walking, with one partner expressing mild control over the other. In the majority of cases it symbolizes support and protection. It is a visual display of emotional linkage. In other words, it is done for others to see, rather than for the pair themselves. As a tie-sign it could almost be described as a signal of mutual ownership.

3027 **भुज-स्पन्द**

Bhuja-spanda : throbbing of an arm. In the case of men, the throbbing of right arm is believed to predict good fortune (*Raghu*, XII. 90).

3028 **भुजाकृतिविज्ञान**

Bhajākṛtivijñāna : signs of the arms. If arms are touching the knees and fleshy, they indicate kingship; if they are hairy and short, they indicate poverty (*Garuḍa*, I. 65). If they are like the trunk of an elephant, they indicate royalty; if uneven and stubby the indication is that the person is thief (*Ibid.*, 30-31). The long arms are a sign of good fortune and high position (*HC*, I).

3029 **भुजाभुजि**

Bhujābhuji : fight with arms. It represents the failure of threat displays.

3030 **भुषुण्डी-मुद्रा**

Bhuṣuṇḍi-mudrā : missile-gesture; a type of weapon gesture. "As the gesture of an axe is posed; so is nearly *bhuṣuṇḍī mudrā.* The only difference between the two is that in case of a *bhuṣuṇḍī* the front part of the mouth of *paraśu mudrā*, should be extended forward instead of raising it up. This is applicable to win the favour of *vetālas.* It may also be applied to all destructive rituals—*abhicārika karmas*" (B.7).

3031 **भूतबलि**

Bhūta bali : offering to creatures, as a part of the householder's duty.

3032 **भूत-भाषा**

Bhūta-bhāṣā : people's language. Guṇāḍhya's *Bṛhatkathā* witnessed that there was a people's language of wonderful literary beauty. All these languages gradually went on decaying as a result of growing popularity of Sanskrit language indicated by the pathetic episode of Guṇāḍhya's burning *Bṛhatkathā*, written in people's language, with his own blood. Bāṇabhaṭṭa in his *prastāvanā* of *Kādambarī* records: *bhūta-bhāṣāmayīm prāhuradbhutārtham bṛhatkathām.*

3033 **भूत मात्रा**

Bhūta-mātrā : five elements (*agni, vāyu, āpa, pṛthvī, ākāśa*) of phenomenal being; shape; pictorial factor (*citra*) in art.

3034 **भूत-शुद्धि**

Bhūta-śuddhi : a process by which the five elements of the body are supposed to be purified (*Tantraśāstra*). These five elements are: earth, water, fire, air and space — of which the body is constituted. (*Tantrasāra,* 85-87)

3035 **भूतापसारण**

Bhūtāpasāraṇa : chasing away evil spirits, and disturbances with the help of *mantras*. During sacrifice, it is done by sprinkling white mustard seeds around the alter (*Tantrasāra,* 616)

3036 **भूमि**

Bhūmi : territory. In the midst of all the internationalizing ideologies Somadeva's geopolitics teaches the world to remain awake to the one great reality of the life, namely, that it is nothing but nationalism that rules mankind and that the eternal problem of today as our *Mahābhārata* has taught for all ages, to study the science and art of *Śakti* or power. In geopolitics the student of Hindu societal theories will thus come across the dicta of Somadeva's *Nītivākyāmṛta* as न हि कुलागत कस्यापि भूमि-and वीर भोग्या वसुन्धरा. "It is by the powerful that the Earth can be enjoyed." And that is why even the "small man" or the ruler of a small territory, furnished with *upāyas* (diplomatic methods) and power, became the *sārvabhauma* or universal monarch.

The Gonds link *būm* (territorial divisions) to descent, in a way that is familiar to anthropologist. Like Hindus they follow the agnate rule of descent. The *būm* is the territorial division as well as administration division. Many of these territories were also the territories of Gond clans. The custom was that those who lived on one territory should behave towards one another as brothers. They were required to observe three rules. First, the clans were exogamous, so that a man should find his bride from the woman of another clan and another territory, and the girls of the clan should go elsewhere in marriage. Second, those who belonged to the same clan were expected to protect one another and the clan territory against outsiders. Third, they were linked by a common dependence on the Earth, a deity which controlled the fertility of their land and of themselves.

So far as concerns Gond culture, this pattern of descent regulated territorial relationships throughout the region. Clan territories other than a man's own contained either enemies (whose women he might marry or who could take his own clan sisters in marriage) or brothers, who would give him land if he settled there, with whom he should not fight, with whom he had a common observation of the cult of the Earth, and whose sisters were his sisters and therefore not available for marriage.

To the Hill Maria the *būm (bhūma)* is almost a living being who produces and who sustains. At the sowing and other ceremonies the *kaser-gāytā* chants his mysterious formula: *Bhūm Kenji, Talur Kenji* (Hearken Earth, Hearken Mother). It is also sometimes stated that *bhūm* is the supreme, paramount entity. It becomes clan-god in its dealing with the clan and becomes village Mother in its dealing with the village. The *Bhūm* as clan-god is the god of nourishment and reproduction, and of life itself. The Hill Marias are her children sustained by her.

To the *Purāṇas* also, *bhūmi* is the woman. In the *Brahmā Purāṇa* (219.71-115) we have an interesting account about the earth being pregnant. It is said that Viṣṇu, in the form of the boar (varāha) performed a *śrāddha,* where he invited the brahmaṇs. His wife the earth, also called Chāyā, took part in it. He gave the plate of the *piṇḍa* (rice-ball to be offered to the manes) to Chāyā (=Earth); and she divided it into two and again each into three. The middle *piṇḍa* was then taken up by Viṣṇu—varāha who gave it to Chāyā (=Earth) whereby she became pregnant, when she ate it.

According to *Bhaviṣya Purāṇa* (*Brahmakhaṇḍa,* 79. 4-8), Earth has to go through menses. After her menstrual bath (dark seven of the month Māgha), She takes the seed from the Sun and becomes pregnant.

In Chattisgarhi songs, woman is the earth: she is the field filled by man:

Sweet-smelling earth
Where grass grows quickly
Beneath storm and cloud
I drove my plough
The rains came in torrents
My earth was fertile
My plough was strong
Is there any beauty
To compare with the ripe harvest.

Earth as the mother is worshipped in a score of different forms. 'Woman is like earth: you may dig again and again, but she remains firm. But man is like the wall of a house: once it is loosened, it falls'. It is a very common way of talking. A youth says, 'We cannot dig in a field that is not ready or the plough-share will be damaged' - that is, it is not advisable to attempt intercourse with an immature girl.

3037 **भूमिका**

Bhūmikā : role. The impersonation in the play according to Bharata (*NS*,XXVI) was of three types: (1) *anurūpā bhūmikā:* Similar role, *e.g.,* when women act female roles and men, the male roles, of the same age and condition. (2) *rūpānurūpa* *bhūmikā*: imitating the role, befitting the form, *e.g.*, when the male actor takes the female role and the woman the male role, skilfully. (3) *Virūpā bhūmikā*: dissimilar role, *i.e.*, when the child enacts an old person or an old person, the role of a child, etc.

The roles of gods should be enacted by actors who are young, graceful, lustrous, and faultless in appearance. They should have sweet voice. The roles of Rākṣasas, Dānavas and Daityas should be presented by tall and large - bodied actors, who possess thunder-like voice, fierce eyes and naturally crooked eye-brows; those of princes and kings by actors having beautiful eyes, forehead, nose, lips, cheeks, face, neck and other limbs and graceful appearance; they should be tall, proportionate in body, learned and of good character. The roles of commanders and ministers should be taken by actors with faultless body, with clarity in speech and action. They should be neither too tall, nor too fat and should be skilled in perfect reasoning. They should be bold and capable of proper decision at the right time. Chamberlains and the learned Brāhmaṇs should be enacted by actors, short or tall, with tawny eyes and long nose. The servants should be presented by actors who are short, slow, hunch-backed, deformed, ugly-faced, squinted in eyes, fat, flat-nosed and ill-tempered.

(b) The stages of realization in the *Yoga*-system.

(c) Social role is one of the three aspects of our culture. The other two are social situations and physical environment.

Bharata has asserted that the creation and maintenance of a role or identity is a critical component of social interaction, and failures in this regard produce embarrassment and damage interaction. These roles or identities are ones which individuals create for themselves during their encounters with others and which are sustained in collusion with them.

What is a *bhūmikā* or social role? First, social roles are slots or positions in social systems, slots that exist for anyone to occupy and are independent of any particular occupants. The second and most important aspects of role positions, however, is that expectations exist about the behaviour of the occupants. Finally, there is of course the actual behaviour of the role occupant. It is the actual behaviour of any particular occupant.

Social roles do not exist in isolation; they constitute social systems or role sets. Any occupant of a social role will have role partners, that is, the other member of the role set. The role of husband is predicted on the existence of the role of wife, the role of son on the role of parent, teacher on pupil, and so on. Each role partner will have particular expectations about another role occupant in the role set. It should be clear from Bharata's exposition that the occupation of a social role can be a major determinant of one's behaviour and experience, and therefore of the type and quality of one's interactions with others.

Roles do not entail just behavioural expectations; they also entail norms and stereotypes. Many of the expectations that we have of roles develop a moral quality. This is particularly clear when we think about some more general roles generated by age and gender. It feels to us morally wrong for people to behave like teenagers once they are middle-aged, and the sight of a middle-aged person behaving like a teenagar regularly. Frequently a dance for teenagers is likely to call forth a moral response; Equally pervasive are the stereotypes of masculinity and feminity which many people hold.

Many of the more specific roles have stereotypes associated with them. We expect *sādhus* and *sannyāsīs* to be different kinds of people to *nartakas* and *naṭas*. We expect older people to be more conservative than the young.

3038 **भूमिस्पर्श**

Bhūmisparśa : a *mudrā* or hand pose characteristic of Buddha images. The right hand exhibits this *mudrā;* the palm turned inward and the fingers outstretched with the tips touching the ground. Also called *bhūmisparśana* or *bhūsparśa*.

3039 **भूषण**

Bhūṣaṇa : ornaments.

3040 **भूषण कला**

Bhūṣaṇa-kalā : the art and crafts of making ornaments (*Śukranītisāra* 4.308-11).

3041 **भूषण-योजन-कला**

Bhūṣaṇa-yojanakalā : adorning with ornaments. One of the 64 arts given in *Kāmasūtra* (1.3.16). The wearing of clothing is only one of many ways in which the human animal decorates itself. In addition, skin may be scarred, flesh pierced, hair lopped, necks scented, nails painted, faces powdered, and teeth filed. Some of these body adornments persist for a lifetime while others last for only a few hours; but they all act as important human displays, indicating the social status, the sexual condition, the aggressiveness, the group allegiance, the playfulness, or some other quality of decorated body.

The permanent adornments - those involving some form of body mutilation - are more typical of tribal societies, where allegiance to the group is of massive importance. These are badges (or the sacred thread) that can never be taken off, and that set their owners apart from all other groups until the day they die. Frequently the application of the decoration is performed at a special ceremony. *Godnā* (tatooing) is one of them, which initiates suffering great pain in the process. This pain is an important part of the bonding - a physical horror that binds her even tighter to those who share it with her. Acquiring the status of belonging to the group is made such an ordeal, so difficult to endure, that forever afterwards it will be felt as something vitally important in her life. The very intensity of the experience helps to widen the gulf between her and those who have not shared it. The best way to study these adornments, both temporary and permanent, is to look at each part of the body in turn, and see what kind of attention it receives. Starting from the hair, there are obviously enormous possibilities for decorative modification, but always of a temporary kind, since whatever is done is soon undone by the death of old hairs and the growth of new ones.

The head-hair of mankind has for centuries been a vital decorative organ, often being employed as an additional gender signal by dressing it differently on males and females. The next region to consider is the face. Make-up does several things to human face. Tatooing of body is widespread in tribal societies. Tatooing means that they are married and are not to be molested. Apart from tatooing, piercing of ears and nose (of women) are also common in India.

There are, of course, a thousand other ways in which Indians seek to adorn their bodies and enhance their display qualities. Taken together they amount to a set of wide-ranging 'frozen' gestures, items of display that are long lasting and highly efficient in relation to the actions that produce them.

3042 **भूषा**

Bhūṣā : ornaments (*DR*, II. 63).

3043 **भृकुटि**

Bhṛkuṭi : contraction of eyebrows; also known as *bhṛkuṭī*, *bhrakuṭi*.

3044 **भृत्याचार**

Bhṛtyācāra : devotee's attitude of complete humility to the lord (*Vīra-Śaiva*-concept).

3045 **भेद**

Bheda : incitement (in a drama): *bhedaḥ protsāhanā matā* (*DR*, I. 50). (b) different, dualism.

3046 **भेदन**

Bhedana : breaking, splitting, dividing. disclosure; penetrating relevant sentiment and feelings through appropriate gesture (*NS*, IX. 175). *gūḍhabhedana* 'disclosure of something previously hidden' (*DR*, 1.48).

3047 **भेरुण्ड-हस्त**

Bheruṇḍa-hasta : frightful hands. both hands gesture mentioned in *Abhinayadarpaṇa*. If wrists of *kapittha*-hands are joined together, it is the *bheruṇḍa* hand, that denotes a pair of birds of the same name (*Abhinayadarpaṇa*, verse 186-187). Bheruṇḍa is a minor form of goddess and also *yakṣinī*. The goddess Kālī is also called bheruṇḍā in her aspect as a *Vidyeśvarī* and *Kula-sundarī*.

3048 **भैरव-मुद्रा**

Bhairava-mudrā : "The little fingers of both the hands, when extended by half and both the fore-fingers of both the hands, extended by the opposite direction; are to be joined together. Keeping closed both the lips; the upper and the lower; one should maintain this position sometimes with the mouth opened and the tongue out by turn. The votary should also join both of his hands like a bud of a flower and the waist-knot (*nīvī-bandha*), resting on the right hip, should be redoubled" (*BT*). *Bhairava* means 'one with a frightening cry' (*bhīr bhyānako ravo yasya*), and it refers primarily to Rudra (*viz.* Śiva). In fact Bhairava is regarded as one of the violent forms of Śiva, associated with his fights against demons. Initially *Bhairava* was a human teacher who seems to have attained complete spiritual emancipation and became almost Śiva. Their views are reflected in Tāntric *yāmala* literature.

3049 **भैरव-संज्ञिका-मुद्रा**

Bhairava-sañjñikā-mudrā : "standing on the one toe of a leg and moving it repeatedly in circles, sometimes by opposite direction, we may frame the gesture, *bhairava-sañjñikā* or *bhairava* by name. The middle finger and the ring finger of both of the hands should rest on the roots of the thumbs. All other fingers are to be made half-slant." (*BT*).

3050 **भैरवी-चक्र**

Bhairavī-cakra : a *Tāntric cakra*—ritual in which the *pañcatattva* are used. The male and female aspirants sit together and perform the rites which include drinking of wine and sexual intercourse (*Mahānirvāṇa* VII. 54-206; *Kulārṇava* VIII; *Kaulāvalinirṇaya*, VII).

3051 **भैरवी-मुद्रा**

Bhairavī-mudrā : gesture of the Mother-Godess. Two hands are to be so wrapped, that the left may cover the right (*VD*); (b) the *bīja-mudrā* in the opposite way (*VD*). Bhairavī is feminine counterpart of Bhairava. She is identified with Cāmuṇḍā. She is the Supreme being of the *Śākta-Tāntric* cult.

3052 **भोग**

Bhoga : enjoyment; particulary of sensual pleasures or food. Where there is *rasa,* it consists of enjoying it because of suggestion and predominance of *sattva* state of mind. (b) an ideal of perfect enjoyment other than literature includes the following: woman, bed, drink, clothes, incense, unguents, betel-leaf are indicative of royal enjoyment. The *Skanda-Purāṇa* (IV. 10) mentions good clothes, good fragrance, good bed, good woman, a wrath, good food, *tāmbūla* and drinks as enjoyments:

सुवासांसि सुवासाश्च सुशय्या सुनितम्बिनी ।
स्रक् ताम्बुलान्नपानाश्च भोगाः स्वधर्मिणाम् ॥
suvāsāṁsi suvāsāśca suśayyā sunitambinī ।
srak tāmbulānnapānāśca bhogāḥ svadharmiṇām ॥

(c) trials and troubles of common life, experience, etc. *bhoga-bhūmi* is the term for material world. (d) the term *yoga* and *bhoga* appear often in Tāntric texts to represent the extremes of two paths: 'If a man is *yogī,* he does not enjoy (sensual pleasures); while one who enjoys them does not know *yoga.* That is why the *kaula* doctrine, containing the essence of *bhoga* and *yoga*, is superior to all other doctrines (*Kulārṇava Tantra* 2.23): This *Tantra* goes on to explain its central doctrine: "In the *kaula* doctrine *bhoga* turns into *yoga* directly. What is sin, becomes meritorious. *Saṁsāra* (worldly life) becomes Release' (*Ibid*). 'Sexual union is an auspicious *yoga* which, though involving enjoyment of sexual pleasures, gives Release' (*Ibid.*)

On one level, this is a simple conjunction of opposites enhanced by a felicitous assonance (*bhoga-yoga, bhokṣa-mokṣa*). Compare:

Guṇam pṛcchasva mā rūpam
Śīlam pṛcchasva mā kulam ।
siddhim pṛcchasva mā vidyām
bhogam pṛcchasva mā dhanam ॥
Here *bhoga* means the living-norm.

3053 **भोग-शयन**

Bhoga-śayana : one of the four varieties of the recumbent form of Viṣṇu, the other three being *vīra, yoga* and *abhicārika* varieties. This is distinguished by a large assembly of gods and sages around the god, who lies upon the folds of the serpent Ananta, and from whose navel springs forth a lotus carrying golden hued Brahmā seated upon it.

3054 **भोगहस्ता-मुद्रा**

Bhogahastā-mudrā : "sitting down on the *svastikāsana* and the similar *āsanas* and keeping the neck and the head straight and erect, both the hands should be placed on the ground and the eyes should remain open. This is *bhogahastā-mudrā* that grants all sorts of good omens" (*BT*).

3055 **भोगीकरण**

Bhogīkaraṇa : an activity of aesthetic fruition, aesthetic appreciation, *āsvāda* the power of enlivening (from *bhāva* or emotion) to the enjoyment, experience like *yoga pratyakaṣajā pratīti. Bhogīn* or *bhogi* is one who enjoys sensual pleasures or food.

3056 **भोजन**

Bhojana : eating, partaking of a meal. This was raised to the level of a sacred ritual. In the *Vedic* literature great importance was attached to the purity of food and there were elaborate rules about every aspect of eating. For example when food was to be eaten, the direction in which one had to be seated to eat, the vessels to be used, preliminaries before eating (such as *ācamana, prāṇabutis,* etc.), the posture at the time of eating, how much to eat, how *paṅktis* (rows of dinner) were distinguished, and who were the *paṅktipāvana* Brāhmaṇs and etiquette while eating. Occasions like eclipses were specified for abstaining from taking food, or what food should or should not be taken and various grounds on which the food was forbidden. Flesh-eating was never taboo but there were elaborate rules about the flesh of beasts, birds and fishes. Exhaustive lists of persons are found from whom food may not be accepted by Brāhmaṇs and there are great variations in these rules. All intoxicants were forbidden to the Brāhmaṇs from the time of the *sūtras* but these were allowed to the *kṣatriyas* and others (*RV*,I. 187. 1-7), *Ch. Up.* VII. 26.2; *Taitt. Br.*, 1.4.9, II. 1.115, III. 1.3; *Śat. Br.*, II. 4. 2-6; *Ap. Dh. S.*, 1.11.31, etc.; *Baudh. Dh.S.*, II. 7-31; *Manu,* V.1. etc.).

There are various taboos regarding food in Indian Society. They also serve to give glimpses of social behaviour. As a general rule, it is said that a respectable person should not take food from a king, a prostitute, a castrated man (*Ṣaṇḍa*), a thief, washerman, pot-maker, smith, money-lender, goldsmith, physician, a staff-bearer of an officer, a convict, one born of a woman remarried, umbrella-bearer, an actor, hunter, non-believer, dog-cooker (*śvāpaka*), a person controlled by his wife (*bhāryājita*), a eunuch, an ascetic, one who is afraid, one intoxicated, one infatuated (*matta* or *unmatta*), an artisan, one's father-in-law, and such others (*Kūrma,* II. 17.4).

Also under general food—taboo are included onion, garlic of any type, milk of the cow in the first seven days of her delivery (*gopīyūṣa*), *kavaka* (a kind of mushroom), rice-gruel (fermented), milk of a cow whose calf is dead, flesh not consecrated and offered at a divine ritual or at the ritual for the manes, milk of a one-hoofed beast, camel-milk, and milk of a she-goat (*Skanda,* IV. 40. 9-11).

Among the varieties of flesh that of the following birds

is taboo - *ṭiṭṭibha, kālavinka, haṁsa,* crane, cock and others of the sort (*Ibid.,* 12-15).

Also in the period of eclipse food is taboo (*Kūrma,* II. 19.115). Also it is said that food should not be taken at exact mid-day or mid—night; nor standing, nor sitting, nor sitting on a broken vessel, nor placing it on the bare ground, nor in one's hand; while eating one is enjoined not to touch his head (*Ibid.,* 21). At a *śrāddha* (ritual of the manes) certain types of food are taboo, such as cucumber, *musūraka,* gourd, brinjals, buffalo-milk, pepper and black gram; also taboo is betel-nut (*Ibid.,* 46-48). For taking food in a plate made of bell-metal (*kānsya-pātra*) is strictly prohibited (*Brahmavaivarta, Śrīkṛṣna Khaṇḍa,* 75.61); also is taboo a copper-plate, or a copper-vessel, on various days in certain months various objects of food and drink are mentioned to be taboo (*Ibid.,* 26-43); and as a general precaution against bad health eating of curds - mixed malt is taboo (*Skanda,* VII. 3. 29. 46).

The Singo-legend prevalent among the Gonds records that initially Brāhmaṇs and Gonds were one and the same, but because Gonds broke the food—taboo, they were separated. They never discriminated between eatable and non-eatable:

How did the Gonds conduct themselves?
Whatever came across them they must needs kill and eat it;
They made no distinction. If they saw a Jackal they killed
And ate it; no distinction was observed;
They respected no antelope, Sambhar and the like.
They made no distinction in eating a sow, a quoil, a pigeon,
A crow, a kite, an adjunct, a vulture,

A lizard, a frog, a beetle, a cow, a calf, a he and she buffalo,
Rats bandicoots, squirrels - all these they killed and ate.

So began the Gonds to do. They devoured raw and ripe things;

(*Lingo-legend,* Russell and Hiralal, III. 50)

Food may be classified under four categories: *cūṣya, carvya, lehya* and *peya* c.f. *cāni bhānti bhojan vidhi gāī* (*Mānasa,* 1.329.4).

3057 भोजन-कण्टक

Bhojana-kaṇṭaka : one stopping eating while others are still eating.

3058 भोजन-विधि

Bhojana-vidhi : the ritual of eating. The ritual of eating followed precise rules in ancient India. Before the meal, the children washed their father's feet as a sign of respect, and then their mother's feet. The wife personally served her husband's meal, which he took alone, sitting on the ground or on cushion. She filled a clean pot with water so that he could rinse his hands, after using it, he emptied it and placed the empty pot by his side (*Mahā Unmagga Jātaka,* No. 546, V. pp. 183-84). A large banana leaf had been laid before him, and on this wife heaped the different foodstuffs, one after the other. He carried the food to his lips with his right hand only, never even touching it with his left hand. After eating and drinking, he rinsed his mouth without swallowing the water (*Ibid.*). When he had finished, his wife ate in turn, observing the same proprieties, and served by her children who only ate afterwards. This practise is still followed. A woman does not eat along with her husband and she takes food only after feeding the children and her husband.

In different tribes and castes, people go away when the visiting official or guest sits for meals but not the Hill Marias. They keep on sitting in the very room and may even take the liberty of lighting the *biḍī* or pipe from the hearth.

3059 भोस्

Bhos : in addressing : sir, hello; cp. *bhagos.*

3060 भौम—मण्डल

Bhauma—maṇḍala : The earthly *maṇḍalas* arise out of the combination of *bhaumī-cārī.* They are as follows: *bhramara, āspandita, āvarta, samotsarita, eḍakākrīḍita, aḍḍita, śakaṭāsya, adhyardha, piṣṭakuṭṭa* and *cāṣagata.*

3061 भौमी—चारी

Bhaumī-cārī : earthly movement. One of the two kinds of *cārī.* There are sixteen *bhaumī-cārīs.* In these *bhaumī-cārīs* the foot movements are more related to the ground. These are to be used in personal combat, and in *karaṇas* Abhinava (*NS,* Vol., II p. 101) explains that these *cārīs* are used since time immemorial in personal combat, *karaṇas,* and *aṅgahāras* and then in dramatic representation.

3062 भौम-स्नान

Bhauma-snāna : smearing the body with loose earth; also known as *pārthiva-snāna.*

3063 भ्रङ्गीश्यामलकुन्तला

Bhraṅgī-śyāmala-kuntalā : lady whose hair are black like bees, quality of the Art-lady (*Anaṅgaraṅga,* 1. 13-14).

3064 भ्रमण

Bhramaṇa : walking, roaming, touring. Note:

bhramaṇam sātatyenāniyatadeśaparyaṭanam valganam niyatadeśagamanam udbhramaṇam parivartanam.

Walk communicates NV messages in different situations. Tribes have their own way of walking. Observing young tribal males walking down streets, one can't help noticing that they are, indeed, marching to the tune of a different drummer. The "different drummer" is a different subculture; the NV message of their walk is similar to the NV message of young non-tribal males, but not quite the same.

The young non-tribal walk is usually brisk, and they walk on the balls of their feet with strides of presumed authority. Both arms swing while they walk. The NV message is: "I am a strong man, possessing all the qualities of masculinity, and I stride through the world with masculine."

The young tribal males' walk is different. First of all, it's much slower - it's more of a stroll. The head is sometimes slightly elevated and causally tipped to the side. Only one arm swings at the side with the hand slightly cupped. The other arm hangs limply to the side or it's is tucked in the liṅgoṭī. The gait is slow, casual and rhythmic. The gait is almost like a walking dance, with all parts of the body moving in rhythmatic harmony. This is referred to as "walking that walk".

The walk of young tribal males communicates the same NV message as that of young non-tribal males. In addition, the tribal walk communicates that the young tribal male is beautiful, and it beckons female attention to the sexual prowess possessed by the walker. Finally, the tribal walk communicates that the walker is "cool"; in other words, he is not upset or bothered by the cares of the world and is, in fact, somewhat disdainful and insolent towards the world.

The description of the walk is a general description, and it includes all the components that can be present in the walk. All the components are not always present in each individual's walk, because each individual must impose a certain amount of originality onto the general pattern. Thus, some young tribal males will vary the speed or swing of the head or effect a slight limp or alter anyone or a number of components of the tribal walk to achieve originality. The general "plan" of the walk, however, is recognizable even with the imposed originality. The imposed originality also communicates the individualism of each young tribal male.

The tribal walk is used for mobility (as any walk is) and to arrive at a destination. Sometimes, however, one gets the feeling that where the young tribal male is going is not as important as How he gets there. There is great deal of "styling" in the walk. The means are more important than the end.

The walk is also used as a hostile rejection of another person in a conflict situation. For example, after a person in an authority role has reprimanded a young tribal male, the person with authority can tell whether his reprimand has had positive effects by the way the young tribal male walks away from the authority figure. If the young tribal male walks away in a "natural manner", then the reprimand was received positively; if he walks away with a "pimp strut" it means that the young tribal male has rejected the reprimand and in fact is non-verbally telling the authority person to "go to hell".

Young tribal females communicate the same NV message when walking away from a person in an authority role after a conflict situation by pivoting quickly on both the situation by pivoting quickly on both feet and then walking briskly away. Sometimes the pivot is accompanied by a raising of the head and a twitching of the nose.

When either the young tribal male or the young tribal female walks away from the authority person in the above manners, the knowledgeable authority person will angrily tell the young tribal person to "come back here and walk away right". To walk away "right" means to walk away without communicating the negative, disrespectful, insolent message. This is proof that these walks are sending a message.

3065 **भ्रमण-दर्शन**

Bhramaṇa—darśana : turning round glance. (a) a circular movement of the eyeball, eyeball movements are used to express states and sentiments, also known as *bhramaṇa,* rolling movement of the eyeballs, a type of gesture of the glance by movement of the eyeball.

3066 **भ्रमणोरस्**

Bhramaṇoras : a right-to-left movement of the chest which seems to indicate a grotesque movement (*Bālarāmabharata*).

3067 **भ्रमर**

Bhramara : a curl on the forehead; *bhramaraka* 'humming top', 'hair falling on the forehead'.

3068 **भ्रमरक-करण**

Bhramaraka-karaṇa : with the *svastika* foot in *ākṣiptā cārī* and hands in *udveṣṭita,* the *trika* is turned round. It is employed in haughty movements.

3069 **भ्रमर-चारी**

Bhramara—cārī : this is a movement where the knees and the feet continue to be in the *ākṣipta* and *svastika* positions. The hands are in *udveṣṭita* when the fingers beginning with the fore-fingers open outwards. Only *trika* is turned and thighs are in *valana* position (*NS,* IV. 98b-99a, IX. 216, X. 37, 45).

3070 **भ्रमर-मण्डल**

Bhramara—maṇḍala : the going round in all the four directions (*NS*, XI. 44b-47a).

3071 **भ्रमरहस्त**

Bhramarahasta : the bee-hand, a kind of hand-gesture used for plucking of a flower from the stem (*NS*, IX. 101, 112-116). In *Karpūramañjarī* (Act II), Susaṅgatā brings lotus leaves and makes coils of the long lotus stalks. It is possible that real lotus stalks were used, but if not, this may have been represented in *abhinaya* with the *bhramara-hastas* and the *nalinīpadmakośa-hastas.* It is synonymous to the *arāla hasta.* Occurs often in iconography. The palm is very slightly hollowed, and the third and little fingers are separated and bent a little. The second finger is bent parallel to the base of the palm, and the thumb bent to touch the tip of the second finger. The first finger is bent to touch the first joint of the thumb. It is used to express the bee, parrot, cuckoo and wing. Join the tips of the thumb and the middle-finger and make the fore-finger curved. Then raise up other fingers in a loose order. It makes the *bhramara.* This gesture is framed to hold any flower with long stalk; like the lotus, the blue lotus, the night-lily etc. and similar ornaments as ear-rings, armlets etc. This gesture, if disconnected with a sound, suggests scolding and similar actions. This also indicates the chatting of young ones, hurriedness, keeping marks in a song, or a dance and to bring somebody else into confidence (*NS*, IX. 95-99). Here the middle finger and the thumb crossing is related to each other. The first finger curved and the remaining two are separated and pointing upwards.

3072 **भ्रमरी**

Bhramarī : the spiral movement or turn. Nandikeśvara mentions seven types of *bhramarī, viz. utpluta, cakra, garuḍa, ekapāda, kuñcita, ākāśa* and *aṅga* (*Abhinayadarpaṇa*, 281-298).

3073 **भ्रमरी-चारी**

Bhramarī-cārī : feet in *sampāda kuñcita.* Initial position of the *atikrāntā cārī.* Foot lifted and the entire body turned around. *Udvāhita jaṅghā* position, *bhramara karaṇa* and *maṇḍala, bhramara angarahāra.* With the foot in *atikrāntā cārī* (the *kuñcita* foot lifted up), the entire body is to be turned round, moving on the sole of the foot; thus the *trika* is turned round (*NS*, X. 45).

3074 **भ्रमि**

Bhrami : movement.

3075 **भ्रमिकण**

Bhramikaṇa : a little of dalliance, graceful gait.

3076 **भ्रातृ-हस्त**

Bhrātṛ-hasta : the gesture of a brother. If the *mayūra* gesture is demonstrated in front and two sides; it symbolizes either of two brothers - the elder or the younger (*AD*, 231-244).

3077 **भ्रान्त**

Bhrānta : having wandered, confused, mistaken, perplexed, gone astray, in error. Cp. *udbhrānta* 'frenzy'. Note:

maṇḍalākārataḥ kaṅgabhrāmaṇam bhrāntamucyate |
tadeva bāhumudyamya kṛtamudbhrāntamīritam ||
bhrāmaṇam svasya piritaḥ kaṅgasyākviddhamucyate |
paraprayuktaśastrasya vāranārthamidam trayam ||
śastrorākramaṇārthāya gamanam tvāplutam matam |
khaṅgasyāgreṇa taddehasprasanam prasṛtam matam ||
vañcayityā ripau śastrapātanam gaditam sṛtam |
parivṛttam bhavecchatrorvāmadakṣiṇamāgataḥ ||
paścāt padāpasaraṇam nivṛttam sampracakṣate |
anyonyatāḍanam prāhuḥ sampātamubhayorapi ||
ādhikyamātmano yattat sumudīrṇamudāhṛtam |
aṅgapratyaṅga deśeṣu bhrāmaṇam bhāratam smṛtam ||
(Nīla *on Mbh.*, VII. 191).

3078 **भ्रामर**

Bhrāmara : going round, walking round from left to right, see *pradakṣiṇā. dayitā bhrāmara* is depicted in *Karpūramañjarī* (4.2), known as *bhānwara* in Hindi.

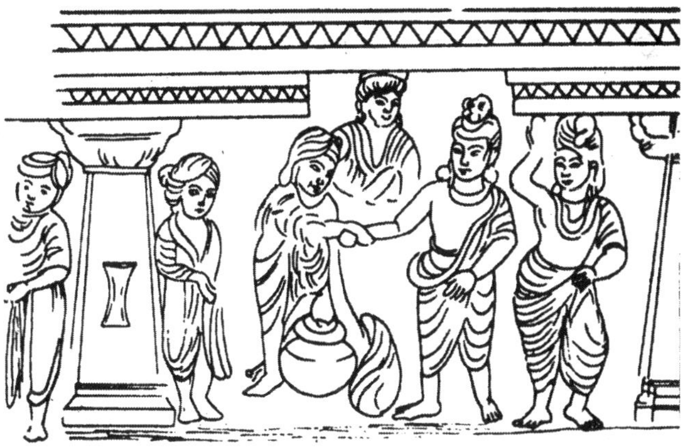

Fig. - (3078)

3079 **भ्रामित—मणिबन्ध**

Bhrāmita—maṇibandha : the rotative movement of the wrist.

3080 **भ्रू**

Bhrū : eye-brow. The movement of the eyebrows in relation to a certain *rasa* are the following: *bhrū-sahaja* or *bhrū-utkṣepa* (*Śṛṅgāra*), *kuñcita-bhrū* (*hāsya*), *sahaja-bhrū* (*adbhut*), *bhrukuṭi* (*raudra*), *bhrū-utkṣepa* (*vīra*), *pāta-bhrū* (*bībhatsa*) and *sahaja-bhrū* (*śānta*).

The seven movements of the eyebrow take into considerations all movements possible physically. This can be reclassified according to the directions of movement and the positions of the eyebrow. Bharata is fully aware of this when he discusses anyone of these movements, and this pattern which seems to abstract can be understood in its entirety only by an awareness of the interrelationships of the movement of different parts of the eye. The movements of the eyebrow along the vertical plane are *unmeṣa, utkṣepa* and *ullokita* with an emphasis of an upward movement: *pāta* (eyebrow) has a downward accent. The movements along the horizontal plane (*i.e.* side to side) are *catura, sācī* and *pralokita*. The circular movements can apply to the eyebrow and the *recita-bhrū* movement belongs to this category.

Contraction, expansion and throbbing, corresponding to the tense and relaxed positions of the other limbs have also been classified. This, the *kuñcita* eyebrow and the *bhrukuṭi* eyebrow denote contraction, the *sahaja* eyebrow denotes relaxation. The normal position is termed as *sahaja* eyebrow.

The nine movements of the eyebrow which the *Bālarāmabharata* enumerates are in fact only combinations of the movements described by Bharata and Sārṅgadeva, and can be reclassified easily under the six basic movements.

NS (VIII. 118-123) mentions the following movements of the eyebrow: *utkṣepa* (raising of the eyebrow), *pātana* (lowering the eyebrow), *bhrukuṭi* (knitting the eyebrow) *catura* (when the eyebrow is pleasantly extended) *kuñcita* (contracted), *recita* (moving gracefully), and *sahaja* (natural). The *VD* makes *svābhāvika* for *sahaja.*

The eyebrows and their movements form an important part of the description of facial expressions: Thus the women of Ujjain of large eyes (*cakita netra)* and through graceful movements they allure the cloud-messenger *(Pūrva-Megha,* 29). They are unlike the women described earlier (*Ibid.*, 6), who do not know how to use their eyebrows for amorous purposes (*bhrūvilāsa*). The cloud can have a drink from the river Vetravatī: she is compared to a woman with beautiful attractive eyebrows (*Ibid.*, 26). The maidens of Daśapura have dark eyebrows (*Ibid,* 51). The favourites of Agnivarṇa are of course adept in the use of eyebrows. (*Raghu,* XIX. 17).

3081 **भृकुटि**

Bhrukuṭi : knitting the brows, a frown, raising up of the root of eye-brows; eyebrow-gesture, used for dazzling light and for objects of anger, etc.; raising up the roots of eyebrows to look at the dazzling light and object of anger occurs in *Buddhacarita* (13.25) in *raudrarasa* (*NS*, VIII. 123b-126); also pronounced as *bhrukuṭi. Bālarāmabharata* (p. 154) has given some additional movements of *bhrukuṭi* as follows: *valitā, calitā, stabdhā, āyatā, avakuṇṭhitā, vivartitā, natā, vakritā* and *lalitā*;

In the odious dancing of Māra and his retinue (*Buddhacarita*, XIII. 25), there is the *bhrkuṭi* which is used for dazzling light and for objects of anger (*NS*, VIII. 123b-126). Here the brow is wrinkled horizontally by the scalp being drawn forward. The eyebrow tilts down at the outside corner.

3082 **भ्रूक्षेप**

Bhrūkṣepa : knitting (contraction of) the eyebrows. In *Mṛcchakaṭika* (Act I), Vasantasenā enacts knitting her eyebrows to answer her friend: this is the *utkṣepa* movement of the eyebrows of the *NS* (VIII. 123-124).

3083 **भ्रूबन्ध**

Bhrūbandha : bending or knitting the eyebrows.

3084 **भ्रूभङ्ग**

Bhrūbhaṅga : contraction and knitting of the eyebrows, a frown. The *bhrūbhaṅga* of the eyebrows in *Śākuntalam* (Act II) is in response to the king's loving attentions. It occurs in *Meghadūtam* (24).

3085 **भ्रूभङ्गवीक्षित**

Bhrūbhaṅga vīkṣita : gentle looks (*Viṣṇu-Purāṇa*, V. XIII). "The Mādhava conciliated some with soft speeches, some with gentle looks".

3086 **भ्रूभेद**

Bhrūbheda : contraction or knitting of the eyebrows, a frown.

3087 **भ्रूरचना**

Bhrū racanā : bending or knitting the eyebrows.

3088 **भ्रूलक्षण**

Bhrūlakṣaṇa : sign of the eye-brow. If a person has uneven eyebrows, She is wretched; if long and disjointed, he is wealthy; if like a crescent and raised, he is rich; and if a person is with broken eye-brows (*khaṇḍa-bhrūḥ*), he is penniless (*Garuḍa*). Eyebrows which meet were deemed unlucky in *Vedic* period.

Curved eyebrows are an ideal beauty in Sanskrit literature: *asitabhrū, natabhrū*. Varāhamihira (LXVIII) has given certain features of the eye-brows which enumerate the personalities of men. Thus, 'lofty brows lead to a short life; large and lofty ones, to great happiness; unequal ones to poverty; bent ones resembling the crescent to wealth; long and unconnected one to affluence; cut ones to penury; and those that are bent in the middle to addiction to forbidden women'.

The Gond and Pardhān have special love for the eyebrows like sesamum: your eye-brows like sesamum

Like the stripped seed the parting of your hair.

Stripped-seed is the *ghunghucī* -

a black seed with a straight white stripe, a good smile for the enchanting line of a girl's hair-parting.

3089 **भ्रूवञ्चित**

Bhrūvañcita : arched eyebrows. Aśvaghoṣa has described some movements of the women as follows: "The ladies of the place allure the prince by their arched eyebrows and they cast on him half-shut, half-stolen glances (*Buddhacarita*, II. 31).

3090 **भ्रूविकार**

Bhrūvikāra : contraction of the eyebrows.

3091 **भ्रूविक्रिया**

Bhrūvikriyā : contraction of the eyebrows.

3092 **भ्रूविक्षेप**

Bhrūvikṣepa : contraction of the eyebrows, contracting the eye-brows. *Bhrūvikṣepam kathayati. Bhrūvikṣepa* is also an innate greeting phenomenon. This friendly signal occurs spontaneously as we make visual contact with someone we know, and seems to be body shorthand far pleased surprise. The eyebrows are raised far a fraction of a second, usually accompanied by a wellcoming smile.

3093 **भ्रूविचेष्टितम्**

Bhrūviceṣṭitam : graceful movement of the eyebrows.

3094 **भ्रूविभ्रम**

Bhrūvibhrama : graceful or playful movement of the eyebrows, amorous play of the eyebrow.

3095 **भ्रूविलास**

Bhrūvilāsa : graceful movement of the eyebrows. According to Kālidāsa (*Megha.* 16) *vanecara* (tribal) ladies are ignorant of this type of gesture which is used for amorous purpose (1.24). It is a type of raised eyebrows gesture to attract. In *Śrīmad Bhāgavata* (XXXIII. V. 2), the eyebrows of *Gopīs* are raised to attract Kṛṣṇa.

3096 **भ्रूसमुन्नयनम्**

Bhrūsamunnayanam : knitting of the eye-brows.

म – Ma

3097 **मकर**

Makara : crocodile, emblem of the god kāma.

3098 **मकरमुद्रा**

Makara-mudrā : (a) the gesture indicating a shark. The *patāka* hands are crossed and held apart to indicate a shark (*Mirror of Gesture,* p.51) (b) the extended thumb placed obliquely symbolizes the *Vaiṣṇava*-deity (*VD*).

3099 **मकरहस्त**

Makara hasta : the shark-hands, both hand-gestures with *patāka hastas* (*NS*); when the *patāka*-gestures are to be so framed by both the hands, so as to raise up the pair of thumbs and to lower down the rest fingers of those gestures, it is known as *makara-kara.* This is to be used to see and show ferocious beasts, and reptiles; like the lion, the snake, the shark, the crocodile, big fish and such creatures which live on eating the dead animals (*NS,* IX. 142-143).

3100 **मकराख्या-महामुद्रा**

Makārākhyā—mahāmudrā : the paramount gesture in other process. "The *makārākhyā* and the *mahāmudrā* are practically two *mudrās* nearly of the same nature. The *mudrā* so named is a very auspicious one to assure success in all respects. O Goddess of Divine-beings, press both the palms with two thumbs. The fore-finger is on their back and the ring-finger, too, should press them in an expanding position. This makes a *makāra-mudrā* (*BT*).

3101 **मकार**

Makāra : see *pañca-makāra.*

3102 **मकुति**

Makuti : a government order addressed to the *śūdras;* also known as *śūdrānuśāsanam.*

3103 **मङ्गल-मुद्रा**

Maṅgala-mudrā : gesture of the Mars. The gesture of *sandaṁśa* with the raised ring-finger (*VD*).

3104 **मङ्गल-शब्द**

Maṅgala-śabda : a benedictory expression, greetings. In principle, a greeting must occur between any two persons who are visible to each other. Out on the road, in the fields, or if someone is entering the compound yard, a greeting must occur, even one party must make a wide detour to accomplish it. In the village centre, a large open plaza which usually has many people sitting about (on the *paṭiyā* in Bhopal), one must greet all those whom one passes within a distance of about a hundred feet. Actually, it would be more accurate to say that the village plaza contains a number of activity zones that determine which persons are to be considered near enough to greet : the main market area; the secondary market area; the well; loading areas outside of shops; the low-caste launging area; the gathering area for the temples; the area for secular public meetings; and other small shady lounging areas. These zones have boundaries which are very clear even if unmarked, and they do not overlap. As one walks through the plaza one must greet all those persons occupying zones contiguous to one's path. If a zone is empty, one must greet persons in the zone beyond it, and so on to the limits of visibility. But if the nearer zones are occupied, the people in more distant zones need not be greeted. This practical limitation can be called an "attention rule" (following Gottman). It also limits the number of people who need be greeted if a zone is occupied by a large crowd; one greets first those nearest oneself, perhaps up to some twenty others in the crowd.

One important than physical distance, however, is the similar attenuation rule which provides for omitting people on grounds of social status. (Bauman and Sherzer, 1974. 168-169).

Greetings, which may most simply defined as an exchange of actions by which two individuals acknowledge that they have seen each other and by which each provides the other with information about how the other will be treated, have received lesser attention. They offer themselves as a seemingly well-defined unit of interaction and they are, of course, functionally important. It is through the ritual of the greeting that people define their social access to one another.

3105 **मङ्गलसूत्र**

Maṅgalasūtra : a string of golden and other beads which is worn round the neck by brides.

3106 **मङ्गल-हस्त**

Maṅgala-hasta : if the gesture of *sūcī* with left and the *muṣṭi* with the right hand, this is *maṅgala* (*AD,* 216-225).

3107 **मङ्गलाचार**

Maṅgalācāra : repeating a prayer for success. Compare the following verse :

lābhasteṣām jayasteṣām
kutasteṣām parābhavaḥ.
yeṣāmindivara'syāmo
hṛdayastho Janārdanaḥ.
Success is theirs and God send theirs,
To humble them no person dares-
Those are the men who lodge the Lord
Within their heart—that darked-hued God.

3108 **मञ्जु-गमन**
Mañju-gamana : having a lovely gait.

3109 **मञ्जुघोष**
Mañjughoṣa : uttering a sweet sound.

3110 **मञ्जु-वक्त्र**
Mañju-vaktra : beautiful face, handsome.

3111 **मञ्जुवाक्**
Mañjuvāk : sweet speech; *Ṛtusaṁhāra* (5.74, 12.39).

3112 **मठ**
Maṭha : solitary residence, residence of ascetics, monastery, student's residence.

3113 **मठर**
Maṭhara : intoxicated. The loss of usual controls on behaviour can cause aggressive outbursts.

3114 **मणिबन्धाकृति विज्ञान**
Maṇibandhākṛti-vijñāna : sign of the wrist. Wrist well proportioned and the bone on it not visible, it indicates royalty; if it makes a crackling sound, it indicates poverty; if covered and bent, it is a sign of wealth; if it is endowed with a raised palm, the person is fond of giving gifts; if it is uneven, it indicates unevenness in nature (*Garuḍa*, I.65.37). According to *Bṛhat-Saṁhitā* (LXVIII), wrists that are hidden, firm and of well-knit joints make men kings; deficient ones indicate severance of the hands; and loose and sounding ones, poverty :

मणिबन्धनैर्निगूढैर्दृढैश्च सुश्लिष्टसन्धिभिर्भूपाः ।
हीनैर्हस्तच्छेदः श्लथैः सशब्दैश्च निर्द्रव्याः ।।

3115 **मणिबन्धाभरण**
Maṇibandhābharaṇa : ornaments of the wrist (*NS*). (a) males : *rucaka* (bracelet) just on the wrist and *cūlikā* above it, *keyūra* (armlet) and *aṅgada* (armband).

3116 **मणिमाला**
Maṇimālā : wrist-movement. *SR* enumerates five types of wrist-movements. *Bālarāmabharata* gives a different classification in terms of *sthira* and *asthira*. In total there are twenty five types of wrist-movement. All these movements are, of course, combinations of five basic movements of the *SR*.

3117 **मणिमाला-रद**
Maṇimālā-rada : the line of jewels bite. The throat, the armpit and the thighs are places of this bite (*Kāmasūtra*, 2.5.15).

3118 **मण्ट्**
Maṇṭ : to dally, (*T.Br.* 11.3.8).

3119 **मण्डल**
Maṇḍala : (a) a technical term used in many contexts, but especially with the motif of the circle. In dance, it is the static position, akin to the grand pile of Western classical ballet. Three or four *karaṇas* constitute a *maṇḍala* (*NS*, X 3.4). There are ten aerial and eight earthly *maṇḍalas*. (b) a kind of mystical diagram used in invoking a divinity. (c) in dance, *maṇḍala* is the name given to a particular combination of *cārīs*. *Maṇḍalas* are twofold : *bhaumaja* (terrestrial) and *ākāśika* (aerial). Each class comprises ten *maṇḍalas*. These are employed in discharging weapons.

The *maṇḍalas* arise out of the combination of *cārīs* in dance. They are to be employed also in fights, personal combats and moving about on the stage with graceful and sportive movements of the limbs and in accompaniment of instrumental music. They are described in detail in the *NS* (II. 118-128).

Mhaumaja maṇḍalas are : *bhramara, āspandita, āvarta, samotsarita, eḍakākrīḍita aḍḍita, śakaṭāsya, adhyardha, piṣṭakuṭṭa,* and *cāṣagata*.

ākāśika maṇḍalas are : *atikrāntā, vicitra, lalitā-sañcara, sūcīviddha, daṇḍapāda, vihṛta, alāta, vāmaviddha, lalitā* and *krānta*.

(d) a magic, protective circle representing the unity of self. This concept was taken by the psychologist Jung from Hindu writings that show the *maṇḍala* as a square in a circle; it is a symbol for meditation. (Fig. 3119)

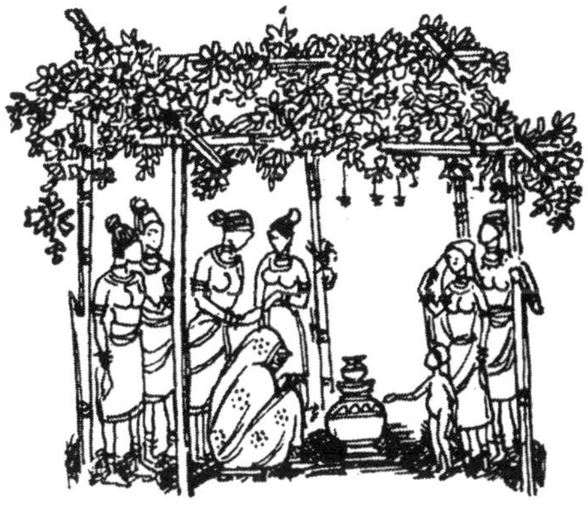

Fig.–(3119)

3120 **मण्डल-बाहु**
Maṇḍala-bāhu : the circling arm (*NS*, IX.205-206).

3121 **मण्डल-स्थान**

Maṇḍala-sthāna : standing posture for men. *Samapāda* feet are placed in a *tryaśra,* pointing sideways but four *tālas* apart. *Kaṭi* and *jānu* in natural position. Indra presiding deity. The feet are 4 *tālas* apart and obliquely placed with toes facing sideways; the waist and the knee are in natural position. It is used in the employment of weapons like bow and thunderbolt, riding on elephants and looking at large birds (*NS*, X.65-67). According to Śārṅgadeva the feet are at the distance of only one *tāla* each other. But he further says that according to some feet are kept at a distance of four *tālas* probably hinting at the Bharata (*SR*, Vol. IV. 1046).

3122 **मण्डल-स्वस्तिक-करण**

Maṇḍala-svastika-karaṇa : *svastika* position of feet and hands are derived from *maṇḍala sthāna* (*NS*, IV. 68-69, X.65). The hands with their palms turned upwards pointing in front and *sama,* are moved in *svastika* position and the posture is *maṇḍala.* It is used in indicating insult.

3123 **मण्डूक-प्लुति**

Maṇḍūka-pluti : frog-leap. A kind of *adhikāra* in which a *sūtra* or a part of it is to be understood in a remote *sūtra* without being applicable in the intervening *sūtras.* Pāṇini's 'adhikāras' sometimes skip over a *sūtra* or *sūtras* and reach further *sūtra* or *sūtras.* Jagannātha Prasād Bhānu records: *Viṣaya calata aure kachū aure kachu batrāt. maṇḍūkapluti nyāya so kahat sumati avadāt.*

(Kāvyaprabhākara : 600)

3124 **मण्डूक-मुद्रा**

Maṇḍūka-mudrā : the gesture of a frog. Double *cakra* hands are used to indicate a frog. The thumb and the fore-finger go in. The middle-finger is bent and the little finger is extended (*Mirror of Gesture,* p. 51).

3125 **मतानुज्ञा**

Matānujñā : when a *pakṣin,* being unable to answer objections raised on his *pakṣa,* starts finding out defects in his *pratipakṣina's* view then he comes to *matānujñā.*

3126 **मति**

Mati : idea, thought, talent, a state of mind characterized by self-confidence and determination. One of the thirty-three *vyabhicārī bhāvas. Mati* is the state of mind in which one arrives at a firm decision in conformity with the rules of moral conduct. Smiling, feeling confident and satisfied, and holding one's ownself in high esteem are the external manifestations of this state of mind (*NS*). It is also represented by instructing pupils, ascertainment of meaning, removal of doubts, etc. (b) *mati* a form of knowledge according to the Jain conception belongs to the category of *parokṣa* (indirect knowledge of existing things acquired through the senses and mind).

3127 **मतिप्रविवेक**

Matipraviveka : a difference of opinion (*A,* 1.15.44).

3128 **मत्तलीकरण**

Mattalīkaraṇa : leg-movement as in *cārī.* Here the circular movement is emphasized. Arms in *apaviddha.* The hand form an *udveṣṭita* movement (*NS*, IV.87-88, IX.276, X.28). A whirling movement is made with the feet turned alternately and the hands are in *udveṣṭita* and *apaviddha.* It is used in intoxication.

3129 **मत्तली-चारी**

Mattalī-cārī : both feet in *agratalasañcara* positions. *Svastika* and going back in a circular movement without lifting of the lower leg. Half-crossing of the legs and then proceeding backwards, hands *udveṣṭita, mattalīkaraṇa.* Moving in a circular manner (forward or backward) with the feet closely touching (*SR,* VII., 938) the ground and shanks in *svastika* and the hands in *udveṣṭita.* It is the final *bhaumī-cārī.* According to Bharata there is the "*apasarpaṇa* of feet in a circular fashion", (*NS*, X.28). Abhinava explains thus— "The feet with the sole touching the ground are crossed in *svastika* at the shanks and slightly oblique. Then with a circular movement they either come together or move away from each other. It is used to indicate slight intoxication (*NS, Ibid*).

3130 **मत्सर**

Matsara : envy, jealousy. Unpleasant feeling or emotion aroused by the desire to have what another possesses.

3131 **मत्स्य**

Matsya : fish. It is one of the *pañcamakāras.* Symbolically *matsya* is described as that which destroys the felters and lead to the way of salvation (*Prāṇatoṣaṇī,* VII. 2.508). Fish as a sex or fertility symbol is very old. The double fish is found on bronze bowls, bells and gongs imported from Eastern Tibet into the Brahmaputra Valley. This is a Buddhist symbol, one of the eight auspicious signs. The same sign was regarded lucky when put on the walls of huts in Orissa. The kings of Madurai adopted a fish or a pair of them as their family crest. In respresentations of the late Buddhist deity Hāriti found in Bengal she has been shown with four hands, one holding a fish, one a drinking bowl and the other two a baby. This appears to be a fertility symbol. The place of *matsya* (as stated above) in Tāntric ritual is well known. The famous archery competition for the hand of Draupadī was the attempt to pierce the eye of a metal fish hung high in the air, through a revolving disc.

Coming to tribal India we find certain Gondi songs symbolizing fish as a girl :

I You go to the river
And try to catch fish
A lovely girl
Has slipped through my hands.

II The ducks settle on the bands of Seoni
What great love there once was between us
But now you have wearied of me
Great fish swim in the Seoni river
Queen of my garden, let me take you to the bank.

Oraon uses fish as symbols for marriageable girls :

The fish sport in the pools
The fish sport in the pools
The fish sport
The bride sits in the mother's lap
The bride sits on the father's knees
The bridegroom catches fish
The bride jumps in the corners.
Jumps, holding herself with glee
In the corners.

The expression 'the bridegroom catches fish' means that the marriage has been settled and a fish has been caught.

Among the Chongli, a youth proposes marriage with a girl by offering her parents a catch of fish taken by himself. The Mongsen boy does the same after betrothal has been settled (Mills, *The Ao Nagas,* 270). The presentation of fish is the formal sign that an Ao marriage is complete (Mills, *The Lhota Nagas,* 168). Among the Palaung of Burma fish is also part of the bridegroom's to his bride's parents (*Ibid.,* 168).

The Lhota Naga use cooked fish as one of the ingredients of an aphrodisiac. Crooke records that during a Lohār marriage in Uttar Pradesh the bride holds a fish made of flour in front of the bridegroom who attempts to shoot it and explains this as an obvious form of fertility magic. In Madhya Pradesh the ritulistic use of fish is more common at funerals.

3132 **मत्स्य-मुद्रा**

Matsya-mudrā : the fish-gesture. "The left palm is placed opposite to the flat palm; the right palm is placed in the same position on it and all other fingers of both the hands are joined among themselves (the right palm is placed upturned over the left palm with fingers joined together), then move the two thumbs like fins. This makes *matsya mudrā* (the gesture of a fish). It is used to purify a thing, helps to make fortune in all respects and assures enjoyment and renunciation" (*BT*). (b) gesture symbolizing *matsya* of the *Vaiṣṇavite* cult. The *ardhacandra*-hand indicates the incarnation of *Matsya* (*VD*).

3133 **मत्स्य-हस्त**

Matsya-hasta : both hands gesture (*Abinayadarpaṇa*), akin to *makara-hasta* of *NS.* If one hand is placed on the back of the other with their thumbs out-stretched; it is the *matsya-mudrā* and is used to indicate a fish and to cover things for the ritual functions. (Fig. 3133)

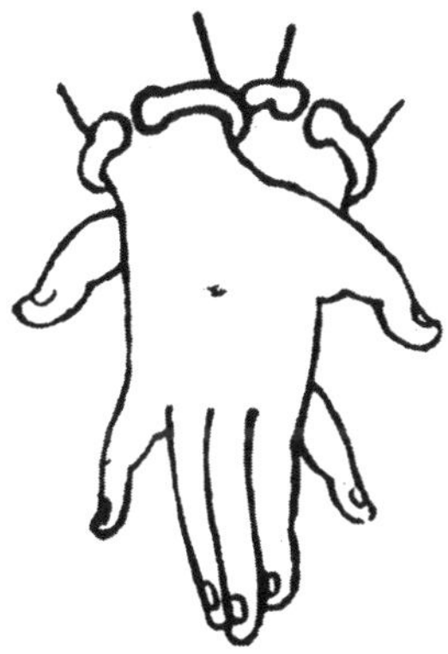

Fig. - (3133)

3134 **मत्स्यासन**

Matsyāsana : sit in *padmāsana,* bending gradually, lie flat on the back resting the top of the head on the ground on one side and the buttocks on the other, making an arch of the trunk. The hands may be placed on the thighs or else catch the toes. This is one variety. The other is lying flat on the back, the head may rest on the crossed forearms. When you have done this *āsana,* slowly release the head with the help of the hands and sit up. This supplements *sarvāṅgāsana.* It destroys many diseases and removes constipation. This is also useful in asthma, consumption, and chronic bronchitis.

3135 **मद**

Mada : hilarity, intoxication.(a) feeling of pride. One of the eight *sāttvika alaṅkāras.* It is a feeling of pride due to one's youth, good fortune and the like (*Sāhityadarpaṇa,* III, 105). (b) intoxication. The fifth among thirty-three *vyabhicārī bhāvas. Mada* or intoxication is a mixed state or confusion and delight due to drinking. When in such a state, a person of refined make-up would go to sleep, a man of average culture would laugh and sing, and a ill-bred person would hurl abuses and weep (*Ibid.,* III. 146-147).

Mada has a class character according to *NS.* In the case of superior persons—sleeping, middling ones—crying and using coarse words. Following stages of *mada* have been enumerated: (i) *light* : smiling face, pleasant feeling, slightly flattering words, delicately unsteady gait. (ii) *medium:* drunken and rolling eyes, arms drooping or restlessly thrown about, irregularly unsteady gait. (iii) *excessive:* loss of memory, in capacity to walk due to vomiting, hiccup, thick protruding tongue and spitting. When there is panic, grief and increase of terror due to some cause, intoxication is to be stopped by effort.

(c) pride, egoism and the like. It is regarded as one of the six internal enemies (*ripu*) of man.

3136 मदन

Madana: passion; the highest aspect of *mahābhāva* or supreme love according to followers of Caitanya. It is maddening ecstasy felt by Rādhā and nobody else, not even by Kṛṣṇa himself. It is the experience of embrace, kiss and union simultaneously in an instant caused by a single touch or sight of Kṛṣṇa. At the same time it is tempered with an acute feeling of separation from Kṛṣṇa despite his proximity (*Ujjvalanīlamaṇi, sthāyībhāva* 155, 160). (b) physical beauty. In *Kumārasaṁbhava* the limitation of physical beauty is symbolised by the defeat of the God of love. The third canto holds out a rich pageant of the senses: sheer physical charms, luxurious infatuation, floral adornment, the ogling from love-intoxicated eyes, the concentrated offerings of the spring, and the elaborate preparations of the Love-god to launch an all-out offensive. There was no room there to catch even a fleeting glimpse of the ascetic *Aparṇā*, seated on a stone, lost in the ecstasy of her austere meditation—a feast reserved for canto V. It was to set Umā's penances in bolder relief that blatant desire had to be burnt out by cosmic anger which reduced *madana* into a handful of ashes : भस्माशेषं मदनं चकार.

(c) the god of love and husband of Rati (*Brahmāṇḍa*, II.4.11.30).

(d) the *mainā* bird. The *mainā* bears a family resemblance to the European starling. 'No bird', says Eha, 'is a more characteristic feature of Indian life than the *mainā*.' It is everywhere, in town or village, field or garden, sometimes walking after cattle, and catching the grasshoppers. They startle, sometimes patrolling a field on its own account, nodding its head at every step. It is always among the scarlet flowers of the coral tree when they are in bloom. *Maināś* are eminently sociable. They go in pairs, or small parties, talking a great deal. They sleep in company like crows and Jabber incredibly while getting to bed. The suitability of the bird as a woman-symbol in the following *suā-geet* needs no emphasizing :

> O playful *mainā*, don't go to that village
> She shouldn't go there, should she, parrot?
> The Rājā's son there is too free a lover.
> Don't flirt with me, boy, I'll tell my father.
> I'll make your father drunk, parrot
> And carry you away
> She shouldn't go there, should she, parrot?

About the *mainā* a tale comes from Raipur. The *mainā* was born in the Gondwānā and the parrot in the Hindwana. Raja Kuhimansha had a daughter called Ramo; She was twelve years old and very lovely. She and Māra Kshattri loved each other, but he did not come for her. So Ramo made a *mainā* from the dirt of her body. She told it everything and sent it to Māra. When Māra saw it, he caught it and shut it up in a golden cage. There it told him so much about Ramo that Māra thought it was Ramo herself and refused to let it go. But at last he was persuaded to go with it for his bride (Elwin, 1946: 137).

In fact, the *mainā* is after the parrot, probably the most popular bird among the villagers of Chhattisgarh. It is often kept as a pet and is charming and entertaining in captivity. In folk-tales the *mainā*, like the parrot, is sometimes a go-between of lovers.

Like the parrot, the *mainā* is often the home of the life-index of hero or villain of a story. Like the parrot also it sometimes acts as a messenger and in one of stokes' (*Indian Fairy Tales*, 1880, 149) stories it tells the hero the sorrows and misfortunes of the heroine.

3137 मदनकण्टक

Madanakaṇṭaka : horripilation due to passion.

3138 मदनबाधा

Madanabādhā : love-pangs.

3139 मदन-महोत्सव

Madana-mahotsava : great festival in honour of *Kāma* (god of love). It is said that while Śiva was observing the Pāśupata vow, Madana, the god of love shot him with an arrow made of flowers. Śiva got angry and reduced him to ashes. Rati, Madana's wife wept bitterly; and Śiva said, though it was impossible to restore Madana with the same body, he would stay in the minds of people. But especially on the bright 13th of the Caitra, he would regain his form, symbolically. The rite associated with this festival is as follows. One should draw the Aśoka tree with *sindūra* and other colours. Near it one should draw a picture of *madana* along with *vasanta* (the personified spring season), having a face of a horse and the banner of a fish (*Bhaviṣya, Uttarakhaṇḍa,* 135.1) वाजिवक्त्रं झषध्वजम्। The figures may be in wood or in gold. In accompaniment should be drawn the nymphs. He should be worshipped. A lady should worship her husband, on this day, thinking him to be the god of love. The night should be spent in joy (not in sleep) in this abode of god of love (prepared in the house). Dances with lights are mentioned in this connection.

3140 **मदनललित**

Madanalalita : love play . It is common between mothers and infants (in the broadest sense) and also common between lovers (in the sexual sense) where a great deal of kissing, hugging, rocking and tickling takes place.

3141 **मदनलेख**

Madanalekha : love-letter.

3142 **मदन-लीला**

Madana-līlā : love-play, graces of love (*Ratnāvalī*, 1.12.13). Love-play in the narrowly sexual sense is common between lovers, where a great deal of kissing, hugging and tickling takes place.

3143 **मदन-वेदना**

Madana-vedanā : love-sickness. In *Vikramorvaśīya*, Urvaśī enacts love-sick.

3144 **मदनातुर**

Madanātura : love-sick.

3145 **मदनायुध**

Madanāyudha : pundendum; *yoni, madanālaya, madanagṛham.*

3146 **मदनावस्था**

Madanāvasthā : love-sick state. In the beginning of the Act III of *Śākuntala*, the king appears in a love-lorn state and represents *madanāvasthā*. This love destruction is represented by the *lolita* head, the *śūnya dṛṣṭi* used in anxiety, indicating motionless and *dolahasta*. Thus the whole state is represented by a circular movement of the head, with vacant staring and shoulders drooping with arms released in the *dola hastas*, a most appropriate rendering of love-distraction.

3147 **मदस्खलित-करण**

Madaskhalita-karaṇa : derived from the *āviddha cārī*. Initial position of feet in *svastika*. The head moves in the *parivāhit* and the arms hang down (*NS*, IV.159b-160a, VIII.27, X.38). With the hand hanging down and the head in *parivāhita*, the feet are turned in *āviddha cārī*. It is used in intoxication due to wine.

3148 **मदालस**

Madālasa : languid with lust. A man should perform *tapas* if he feels lust (*Mbh.* XII.207.13), a clear suggestion of the sexual nature of the ascetic; and if an ascetic makes love to a woman because of lust, he must torture himself with yogic breathing exercises, while another kind of breathing exercise, together with a fast, is prescribed for the ascetic who spills his seed by looking at a woman (*Vāyu*, 18.7.8).

3149 **मदालसासन**

Madālasāsana : a type of sitting posture.

3150 **मदावेशिनी**

Madāveśinī : lady who is passionate, quality of the Conch-lady (*Anaṅgaraṅga*, 1.15.16).

3151 **मदिरा**

Madirā : wine, particular type of glance.

3152 **मदिराक्षी**

Madirākṣī : a woman with intoxicating eyes.

3153 **मदिरा-दृष्टि**

Madirā-dṛṣṭi : intoxicated glance (*NS*, VIII.94).

Irāvatī's state of intoxication is shown in *Mālavikāgnimitram* (Act III) through *madirā-dṛṣṭi;* a glance in which the mid-eye is rolling, the eye-ends are thin; eyes bent and corners of eyes are flashing, is the *madirā*. It suggests an intoxicated look of a drunkard, exhibits the complete set of aesthetic experiences, suggested through a series of glances of the same manner. To indicate light intoxication the pupils are rolling, eyes bent and the corners widened; to indicate medium intoxication the eyelids are slightly contracted, the pupils slightly moving, look somewhat unsteady; the excessive intoxication is indicated by the pupils slightly visible, look turned downwards, the eyes winking and unwinking.

3154 **मद्य**

Madya : spirituous liquor; The first of the five *makāras*. It is wine of various types. Symbolically *madya* is described as the nectar-essence of the union of *Śiva-Śakti* flowing from the highest cerebral region (*Kulārṇava*, V).

3155 **मधुकर-मुद्रा**

Madhukara-mudrā : gesture of a bee. The *bhramara* hand fluttered indicates a bee (*Mirror of Gesture*, pp.50-51).

3156 **मधुकरी**

Madhukarī : begging of an ascetic, collecting alms by begging from door to door.

3157 **मधुपर्क**

Madhuparka : a mixture of certain delicious substance offered to deities in religious rites or to distinguished guess. Now-a-days used in the worship of deities only. It consists of a mixture of curd, ghee, water, honey and sugar (*Baud.*

Gr. Sū., 1.2.65; Yāj., 1.110; Aśv., Gr., 1.24, 25-26). The king Bali is said to have welcomed Vāmana (dwarf Viṣṇu) with *madhuparka*, along with a cow (*Skanda*, VII. 2.18.237). This offering had to be partaken of, or even smelt (*Ibid.*): आघ्राते च मधुपर्के During the period of Kālidāsa *madhuparka* was used for a compound of honey, milk and curd etc., which was presented to the bridegroom by the father of the bride (*Raghu.* 7.108).

3158 **मधुर-दर्शन**

Madhura-darśana : sweet appearance. (*Śākuntalam*, p.10) *aho madhuram āsām darśanam.* (How beautiful?). Here the source of pleasure is the new experience checked against all other previous experiences in its particular category.

3159 **मधुर-भाव**

Madhura-bhāva : loving attitude. One of the five kinds of personal loving relationships. The others are *śānta, dāsya, sakhya,* and *vātsalya.* The attitude is *madhura-bhāva*, the corresponding emotion is called *madhura-rasa* and the application is called *madhura rati.*

3160 **मधु-विद्या**

Madhu-vidyā : (a) the highest state of experiencing beauty in *ānandamayakośa.* (b) the science which turns poison into nectar. The *Chāndogya* (III. 11.5) defines it as knowledge of highest excellence which should be imparted by the father only to his son or to a worthy pupil. (c) Science of bee-keeping, known to the Vedic Āryans and still practised in the villages of Bastar. (d) science of distilling wine.

3161 **मधु-सुरभि-रताम्बु**

Madhu-surabhi-ratāmbu : lady whose mucus odour is like that of honey, quality of the Art-lady (*Ratirahasya*, 1.14.15).

3162 **मध्य:**

Madhyaḥ : hips, waist.

3163 **मध्यमा**

Madhyamā : a special type of sound. It lives between *paśyantī* (q.v.) and *vaikharī* (q.v.) and forms the third stage of its development. It is within and connected with the intellect. It is also called as state of equilibrium of *parā* (q.v.) and *paśyantī* (*Kāmakalāvilāsa*, XXVI). (b) middle finger. (c) a girl arrived at puberity. (d) one of the three *vṛttis*, the other two being *nāgarikā* and *upanāgarikā.*

3164 **मध्यमा-प्रकृति**

Madhyamā prakṛti : the middling nature is known for its proficiency in conducting social business (*lokopacāra*), skill in practical arts (*Śilpasūtras*), professional knowledge and pleasing manners (*vijñāna-mādhuryayutā NS*, XXIV.4).

The middling women have *uttamā prakṛti* (q.v.) in a limited manner and only slight blemishes.

3165 **मध्य-सूत्र**

Madhya-sūtra : the medical line drawn from the centre of the crown of the head, through the centre of the chest, the navel, the knees down, down to the inner side of the feet. One of the five principle vertical axes (*sūtra*) enumerated by the *Śilpaśāstra* in making of images.

3166 **मध्या**

Madhyā : (a) a variety of the amorous heroine. *Madhyā* is one whose characteristics are smiles and side-glances (*Kāmasūtra*, 8.13-14). According to *Sāhityadarpaṇa* (3.59),"*Madhyā* is one who exhibits some novely at the time of coition, whose interest in the pleasures of youth has fully developed, who is in the prime of her youth, whose speech is the tinged with a little audacity, and who has overcome the initial stage of bashfulness." Kālidāsa (*Kumāra*, 8.13-14) pictures Pārvatī as *madhyā*. In her full bloom, the woman becomes adept at caressings. She becomes somewhat bold in speech. In this youthful condition she is called *madhyā*. Her passion and bashfulness are equal, as it were, she may be quite rough in her indignation. Her lust becomes full and well rounded. She has restless eyes with the flash of side-long glances. She shakes off her maiden coyness. Love gets possession of her whole being. She is yet somewhat shy. When her lover looks at her, she conceals her smile and her eyes look down. But when he looks in another direction, she casts her eyes on him.

(b) One of the *śrutis* in music.

3167 **मध्यार्ध-संस्थान**

Madhyārdhasaṁsthāna : the mid-half pose (*VD*).

3168 **मनस्**

Manas : mind. It is the central organ of perception, according to *Sāṅkhya*. Together with *buddhi* and *ahaṅkāra* it constitutes the internal group (*antaḥkaraṇa*) while the senses of sight, hearing, etc., and the organs of action are the external (*bāhyakaraṇa*). It interprets the indeterminate sense-data supplied by the external organs into determinate perception. The *Sāṅkhya* view of *manas* differs from those of other systems.

According to *Nyāya-Vaiśeṣika, manas* should be regarded as a sense-organ because it perceives pleasure and pain. It holds the dictum that perception is always a sensuous origin. The *Vedāntins* point out that according to the *Vedas*,"the objects are greater than sense-organs, and the *manas* is greater than the senses." The Jainas also disagree with this position. According to them *manas* is *anindriya.* It is not a sense organ. As noted above, *Sāṅkhya* also speaks of eleven *indriyas,* including *manas.*

3169 **मनसालिङ्गन**

Manasāliṅgana : embrace through minds. Anantabhaṭṭa

(*Campūbhārata*, 3.89) has suggested this for heat-lorn lovers who are unable to hug.

3170 **मनोहर-मुद्रा**

Manohara-mudrā: "by *makarākārasaṁstha (makara*-position on a thing), when the middle finger is pressed hard, the little finger is out and the thumb in the root is visible; is a great *mudrā, manohara* by name; which may hold a control of this world" (*BT*).

3171 **मन्त्र**

Mantra : chants. *Mantras* are not just verse from the *Vedas* or folk-poetry; they are bits and pieces from the *Vedas* or the folk-poetry used ritually. This ritual use of *mantras* is very different from the ordinary use of a natural language. Even if *mantras* derive from straightforward and intelligible sentences, their ritual uses are often unintelligible and "crooked" (*vakra*). A verse is taken, but before it is half over, the reciter inserts a long O and breathes; he then continues, but dose not stop at the end of the line, linking it instead with the following and inserting other vowels and nasalisations. The ritual meaning or function of such *mantras* dose not lie in their themes and variations, repititions, inversions, interpolations and the particular distribution of their elements. All these transformations are executed in accordance with fixed rules. However, these rules are musical rather than linguistic, *mantras* resemble music more than language. Oral expression of devotion. The list of things that might disturb normal peace and quiet and destroy routine was almost limitless. To ward off these dangers, the inhabitants of ancient India had on their disposal an imposing series of magical practices which were infallible methods of keeping at a distance all the disquieting influences that lurked everywhere. The most effective measure was to murmur formulas (*mantras*), taken mostly from the domestic treatises (*Gṛhya Sūtras*) which provided long lists, classifying the spells according to the problem, they were intended to solve. In addition, a great number of more or less harmless stratagems were in popular use when it was desired to grant blessings, to lay a curse or to compel someone to do something. And there were more or less complicated magical acts designed specifically to cure ailments, to induce the woman one loved to surrender to one, to ward off diseases of cattle, to bring success in a difficult enterprise, to win one's case in a law suit or to come out top in a business bargain, and innumerable other objectives. Sometimes figures were moulded of clay, wax, wood or edible paste, representing a specific enemy, and then pierced with a sharp point, or burnt, or eaten.

In the Tāntric traditions *mantra* is the *Śakti* (power) in the form of sound, words and letters. It is the culture of true knowledge necessary to get rid of worldly fetters. The *mantras* constitute the backbone of *Vajrayāna* worship. When the *mantra* becomes powerful, the vibrations let loose by the worshipper reacting on the universal *śūnya*. According to *Mahāyāna*, the power and efficacy of *mantras* is beyond dispute.

Mantras are magical formulas that are verbal. These are, of course, readily analyzed grammatically and semantically, yet their meaning—if we define meaning as the effect of a message on those to whom it is addressed—is quite distinct—in fact, often directly opposed to the covert literal sense of constituent sentences. Until quite recently, modern linguistics dealt only with the literal sense of isolated sentences, and our theories of grammar, especially those of Chomsky and most other theoretical linguists, reflect this limitation. The question of speaker's interpretation of context-bound messages and the role of grammatical rules in this interpretation are still, in large part, unresolved.

3172 **मन्थरपाततारा**

Mantharapātatārā : slow relaxed normal position of the eyeball given by *Bālarāmabharata*.

3173 **मन्दगा**

Mandagā : lady who walks slowly, quality of the Conch lady (*Anaṅgaraṅga*, 1.17).

3174 **मन्दा-नासा**

Mandā-nāsā : depressed nose, gentle or slow movement of inhaling and exhaling; a type of nose-gesture suggesting *karuṇā*, the lobes of the nose in a resting position; suggests detestation, curiosity and anxiety (*NS*, VIII.123-129), steady nostrils; it is used in despondency, longing and sorrow.

3175 **मन्दालापा**

Mandālāpā : lady who speaks slowly, quality, of the Deer-lady (*Pañcasāyaka*, 2.12). The Bhil bride is also *mandālāpā* when she desires :

> As I enter the house
> My *pāyals* they jingle.
> O! bridegroom, I speak softly and tread slowly;
> For my *sasaro* is asleep and *sasuḍī* awake.
> O ! bridegroom, speak softly and tread slowly;
> My *jeṭh* is sleeping, but his wife lies awake.
> O ! bridegroom, speak softly and tread slowly;
> My *devar* is sleeping and his wife is awake.
> O ! bridegroom, speak softly and tread slowly;
> My *sāsū* is sleeping in the cowshed nearby,
> So I must speak softly to you.

3176 **मन्दावेग**

Mandāvega : small passion (*Kāmasūtra*, 2.1.13).

3177 **मन्द्र-अलङ्कार**

Mandra-alaṅkāra : grave voice embellishment. *Mandra* proceeds from the breast register and is used in despondency, weakness, anxiety, longing, low spiritedness, sickness, deep wound from weapon, fainting, intoxication and communication of secret words, etc. (*NS*).

3178 **मन्वन्तर**

Mavantara : period, crisis in history. There were a number of crisis in our history which they called *manvantara.* These had to be accounted for. Besides after the crisis the streams again looked placid. Great man had intervened, the *avatāras* who appeared at every crisis but on the whole, there was a sort of social entropy, a dispersion of energy, a loss in quality in time. Such a state of affairs could be met by the concepts of *kalpas* and *yugas, manvantaras, avatāras* and the doctrine of *karma*: a doctrine be it noted which is different from that of *kriyā śakti.* In short the people's philosophy of time was a variation of the theme of predestination and recurrence. For the Indian people, the curve of history was cyclical, sociologically speaking, it was unilinear, and, therefore, quantitative. Its equality was related to the individual but for the people it offered no quality other than patience, which is another name for taking it as a static, objective unity, that is, time as it is. This will not do for the Indian of today. So the second requisite for the new philosophy will be such a concept of time that it will not be along one direction, that it will not be cyclical; it will be neither the Greenwich time nor the twinkle of *Brahma's* eye but that it will be open, responsive to deliberate changes of collective efforts and living, very human, dialectical and materialist in the first instance. Through this change from transcendental to human time, philosophy will become one with history; or if that appears to be a bold statement, philosophy will be worthy of history in making.

According to the *Purāṇas*, an era presided over by each of different Manus is called *manvantara.* (different Manu). These fourteen Manus are identified with 14 letters (*Skanda,* 1.2.5.71). Every *manvantara* consist of seventy-one *yugas* (eras).

3179 **मयूरपदक**

Mayūra-padaka : the peacock's foot. Vātsyāyana (*Kāmasūtra,* 2.4.19-20) defines when a curved mark is made on the breast by means of five nails, it is called the peacock foot. *Pañcabhirapi nakhairlekhā cūcakābhimukhī mayūrapadakam.*

Ratnākara *(Haravijaya,* 27.70) has described this type of nail-mark. A scratch made by a lover in the form of peacock's foot.

3180 **मयूरललितकरण**

Mayūralalita-karaṇa : a type of movement. *Vṛścika* of one leg, but crossed thighs, hands in *recita* and movement freely. *Trika* in *vivartana* (*NS,* IV.140-141), with the foot in *Vṛścika* (*i.e.* performing the *vṛścika karaṇa*) and hand in *recita, trika* is turned. (Fig. 3180)

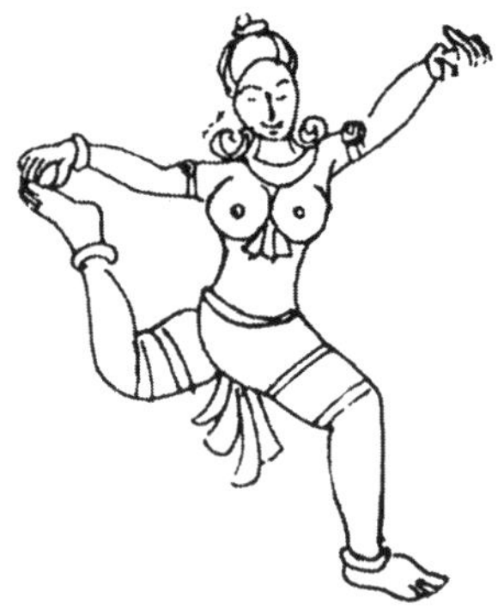

Fig. – (3180)

3181 **मयूर-स्वना**

Mayūra-svanā : lady whose voice is like that of a peacock, quality of the Art-lady (*Anaṅgaraṅga,* 1,13-14).

3182 **मयूर-हस्त**

Mayūra-hasta : single hand gesture described in *Abhinayadarpaṇa.* If the thumb and the ring-finger are joined together and the rest are extended; it is the peacock-gesture. It is used to indicate the beak of a peacock, a creeper, a bird, to root out a forehead hair, to paint the mid-forehead, to throw something into the river — water and to an intellectual talk (*Abhinayadarpaṇa,* verse 108-110, *Nāṭyaśāstra Saṅgraha* and *Bālarāmabharata*). It dose not occur in *NS*.The hand is raised with the palm upwards. The first, second and little fingers are extended straight, the third finger is bent to touch at the tip. It is used to express the peacock's beak, wiping away something,wiping away tears, stroking the hair, the forehead mark, etc.

3183 **मयूरासन**

Mayūrāsana : peacock-posture. This pose resembles a peacock. Kneel on the ground and squat on the toes. Place the palms of the hands on the ground, projecting towards the feet. Now bring down the abdomen slowly against the conjoined elbows and support the body upon the elbows which should be pressed against the navel. This is the first stage. Then stretch your legs and raise the feet straight in level with the hands. When this *āsana* is in full manifestation the head, trunk, buttocks, thighs, legs and feet will be in one straight line and parallel to the ground.

This *āsana* is wonderful for improving the digestion. It cures dyspepsia and diseases of the stomach and reduces enlargement of the spleen and liver. The lungs are properly toned. It improves the appetite, removes diseases caused by excess of wind, cures diabetes, piles and strengthens the muscles of the arm.

3184 **मरण**

Maraṇa : (a) death, one of the (31st) transitory states. It is mainly represented through two ways : (1) *from sickness*: looseness of the body, motionless of the limbs, closed eyes, hiccup, deep breathing, not looking towards surrounding people, indistinct words, etc. (2) *due to accidental injury* : (i) *wounded by weapons* : suddenly falling down on the ground, tremor, throbbing, etc. (ii) *snake bite or poison* : gradual development of the following symptoms—thenness of the body, tremor, burning sensation, hiccup, foaming mouth, breaking of the neck, paralysis and death.

The following verse compares between the death signs and begging signs :

> Gaterabhaṅgaḥ svare hainyam
> gātre svdo mahad bhayam,
> marṇe yāni cihnāni
> tāni cihnāni yācane

> "A feeble voice, a stumbling gait,
> A sweting body, horror great—
> Those signs you find while dying, true,
> you find in men while begging too.

(b) death. The Abujhmāriā's ideas of man's fate after death are vague, and it would seem that various notions adopted from their Hindu neighbours have not been incorporated into a consistent body of eschatological beliefs. There is no definite idea that a person's fate after death depends on his deeds in this life, even though some of their stories contain references to reincarnation. More widespread is the belief that a person's *Jīva* (life-force) is derived from the god, and it returns to him after death. The nearest approach to a belief in some sort of retribution is the vague notion that the *Jīva* of a man having guilty of repeated acts of violence, quarrelsome behaviour and frequent intrigues with married women, may be unacceptable to the god and hence forced to roam the earth as an evil ghost, dangerous to his former kinsmen and without hope of final rest. While this idea seems to contain the germ of a belief in supernatural retribution, it cannot with any certainty be attributed to traditional Abujhmāriā view. There is the strong likelihood that the whole concept of a life-forces, and its emanation and eventual return to god, a belief common to various Indian populations, stems from casual contacts with Hindus, and thus represents a comparatively new element in Abujhmāriā thinking. There is certainly no trace of any idea that morally desirable action leads to an accumulation of merit determining man's fate after death, and the belief in the possible ill effect of evil deeds has thus no positive counterpart, and appears unassimilated to the general Abujhmāriā world view. (c) the Bison-horn Marias believe that the dead are reborn.

3185 **मराल-स्वना**

Marāla-svanā : lady whose voice is like a swan, quality of the Lotus-lady (*Anaṅgaraṅga*, 1.11-12).

3186 **मरिच**

Marica : paper corn (*Āpastambha śrautasūtra*) *mirc* in Hindi. If the arrow-head bunch of chillies representing name of a village is seen it symbolizes to the Hill Marias that they have to assemble at such and such village in so many days (according to the number of chillies) and they should be prepared for the war.

3187 **मरुत्वान्-मुद्रा**

Marutvān-mudrā : *mukula,sūcī* and *ardhapatāka*,twisted upward and touching the body in order to denote the mythical ruler *Marutvān (Mirror of Gesture,* p.47).

3188 **मर्दन**

Mandana : squeezing; also known as *upapīḍam (Śisupālavadha* 10.47), *grahaṇa (Haravijaya,* 27.20), *mardana (Naiṣadha,* 16.103), *pīḍana (Naiṣadha,* 18.100). Some references are as follows: *Kucamardanam guṇavardhanam* breast squeezing creates sex' (*Nāgarasarvasva,* p.102), *niṣpīḍitastanataṭam* 'kneading breasts (Mankhaka, *Śrīkaṇṭhacarita,* 15.11), *Stanamardanam* ''breast squeezing' (Nayacandrasūri, *Hammīrakāvya,* 7.95). Jayadeva (*Gīta-Govinda,* 5.2) depicts Kṛṣṇa whose hands are expert in squeezing the breasts of Gopīs :

> *gopīpīna-payodhara-mardana*
> *cancala-kara-yugaśālī*

Anantabhaṭṭa *(Campū bhārata,*3.25) refers to the *Kucamardana* of *Ulūpī* performed by Arjuna.

3189 **मर्दित-पाद**

Mardita-pāda : a type of foot gesture. The foot is placed sideways, when the toes point sideways. Striking the floor obliquely with the mid-foot. This is used in rapid dance (*SR*, IV.7.324).

3190 **मर्यादा**

Maryādā : limit exclusive (*Vyākaraṇa*), boundary-mark. It is of two kinds relating to time and space.

3191 **मल-संकेत**

Mala-saṅketa : dirt—signals. Gestures connected with dirt are obviously insult signals in India. Most of these signals related to human waste-products—spittle, snot, urine, and faeces, but occasionally they involve the dung of other animals. Picking one's public hair means 'go to hell'. Spitting on the floor in urban India conveys the same meaning. Holding the nose as if protecting oneself from a bad smell is also recognized as the insult. Throwing the saliva means the same. (b) according to *Śaiva* school, *malas* are fetters which cover knowledge and action of the individual. It is the same as *pāśa*, the cause of worldly existence and suffering. (c) *malamāsa* is the intercalary month in which *kāmya* rites cannot be performed.

3192 **मलापसार**

Malāpasāra : natural defilement. "When a Brāhmaṇa, to remove a natural defilement, is to make five applications of clay, a Kṣatriya is to make four, a Vaiṣya three; and a Śūdra and a woman two" (*Manu*). The castes in India do wash after defecation, but the tribes, particularly the hill marias of Bastar do not wash after defecation. Rather they wipe the anus with leaves or soil.

The Bison-horn Marias usually give an impression of cleanliness; the women especially, with their carefully-dressed hair and gleaming ornaments, often look very smart. But I have noticed that many of them do not wash their hands before meals, and many continue their old habit (shared by Baigās and most of the tribes) of wiping themselves with leaves after defecation. But now there is a change. The change in defecatory habits symbolizes an advance in culture. I noticed that in a Baster school, new boys are treated with the question, "Do you wash or wipe?.' If a boy wipes, he is regarded as coming from an inferior social stratum. Likewise, in public schools, if a boy washes he is regarded as coming from a definitely inferior class.

3193 **मलिना-दृष्टि**

Malinā-dṛṣṭi : it is a *sañcārī-bhāva-dṛṣṭi*. A glance with motionless and pale ends, indicated by half-shut eye-lids suggesting awe, melancholy and content (*NS*,VIII.69-92). The ends of eyelashes are throbbing, the eyelids slightly closed, corners of the eyes pale and pupils rolling. It is used in dejection and loss of colour.

3194 **मल्लयुद्ध-हस्त**

Mallayuddha-hasta : a type of both hands gesture mentioned by *Bālarāmabharata*.

3195 **मषक**

Maṣaka : gnat-like elevated mark on the body, the mole. The *maṣaka* or *tilaka* or any other dot in between two eye-brows is said to be indicative of kingship; if it is reddish and on the left cheek, the indication is getting good and sweet food; reddish and at the right breast it is indicative of giving birth to four daughters and the three sons; if the same is at the left breast, it indicates one son and then widowhood; if it is on the right side of the vagina, it is indicative of queenship; A sign of *tilaka* or *maṣaka* on the hand, ear, cheek, throat and below the navel is auspicious (*Sk.P.*, IV.37.121).

3196 **मस्तक**

Mastaka : the head, skull. *Cakram bhramati mastake,* forehead or the highest part of the anything; compare : *tulasī ke māthe par hāth phero (*Tulasīdāsa, *Hanumannāṭaka* 33). When we are talking, we use our heads in the same ways as hands- to add weight and drama to what we're saying. This type of body language is more often used by men, when seem to nod more than women when they are speaking. We do'nt just nod our heads when we mean yes, we also use this movement to encourage the other person.

3197 **मस्तिष्क**

Mastiṣka : brain. Research into the functions of the brain has found that the left brain seems to specialize in verbal activities while the right brain is the storehouse of NV activities.

3198 **महांकुश-मुद्रा**

Mahāṅkuśa-mudrā : the two *anāmikās* to be pointed down like a goad (*Brahmāṇḍa*, II.2.46.9).

3199 **महातार्क्षी-मुद्रा**

Mahātārkṣī-mudrā : "Making the fingers disconnected and curved the left hand should be down-turned and placed on the right hand and the middle finger joining with the left-middle finger is to be placed on the fore-finger. The rest fingers should remain curved sideways. When the thumb is put on that; it is called the gesture of *Mahātārkṣī.* It is to be appropriated in a war activity in the midst of enemies and in the royal and judicial courts" (*BT*).

3200 **महादशा**

Mahādaśā : influence of the dominant planet.

3201 **महानाद**

Mahānāda : same as *śabda-brahman (brahman* in the form of sound) and its constituent *anāhatanāda* (so-called because this sound has a spontaneous origin and is not produced by friction or percussion).

3202 **महापातक**

Mahāpātaka : great sin (*Manu*, XI.55).

3203 **महापुरुष-लक्षण**

Mahāpuruṣa-lakṣaṇa : the characteristic signs of a god or Buddha or Jina when represented in images.

3204 **महाप्रभा-मुद्रा**

Mahāprabhā-mudrā : "on the opposite and upturned left hand put the little finger on the fore-finger. Then join it with the thumb from the very root with the upturned, interlocked and curved left hand. This is called *jyeṣṭha* or the *mahāprabhā mudrā*" (*BT*).

3205 **महाप्रलय**

Mahāpralaya : the *Purāṇic* concept of the great dissolution of the universe which takes place after each *kalpa*. During the period of dissolution *Śakti* or creative force is supposed to return at its source and stay there until it manifests again in new creation.

3206 **महाप्रसाद**

Mahāprasāda : food offered to idols:

pādodakam ca nirmālyam naivedyam ca viśeṣataḥ ।

mahāprasāda ityuktvā grāhyam Viṣṇoḥ prayatnataḥ ॥

3207 **महाप्रस्थान**

Mahāprasthāna : starting on a great journey with inevitable death before the end is reached. The term is used in particular for the Pāṇḍavas after their renunciation of worldly life.

3208 **महाप्राण**

Mahāprāṇa : aspirates.

3209 **महाबन्ध**

Mahābandha : sitting in *padmāsana* achieve *jālandhara* and *mūla bandhas* simultaneously and hold the breath outside.

It controls the secretions of the endocrine glands. Bestows good health and vigour.

3210 **महाभाव**

Mahābhāva : supreme love, divine love which is developed to its fullest degree, like the love of Rādhā to Kṛṣṇa. It is culmination of several stages: *prema (*attachment), *sneha* (affection), *māna* (jealousy), *praṇaya* (feeling of respect), *rāga* (excessive eagerness) *anurāga* (feeling of attractiveness every moment) and finally *mahābhāva* (supreme love in which the distinction between subject and object disappears (*Ujjalanīlamaṇi, sthāyībhāva*, 57).

3211 **महाभूत**

Mahābhūta : gross elements, the sense-particulars of the *Sāṅkhya*, the five gross elements emanating from the *Tanmātras* according to the *Sāṅkhya*. These are *ākāśa* (ether), *śabda* (the essence of sound), *vāyu* (air), *sparśa* (the essence of touch) plus that of sound; *tejas* (fire), *rūpa* (the essence of colour) plus that of sound and touch; *āpa* (water), *rasa* (the essence of taste) plus that of sound, touch and colour; and *kṣiti* (earth), *gandha* (smell) plus that of sound, colour, touch and taste. (b) according to *Skanda Purāṇa* (VII. 1.208.10) a jar was called *mahābhūta* which was donated on the auspicious day.

3212 **महामाया-मुद्रा**

Mahāmāyā-mudrā : "conjoin two hands by the opposite direction and the fingers, coming out of the backside of the palms. Then in the same position of nudity and a complete self-controlled state, get your sitting position fixed with the legs; coming out to the east and the south by the opposite direction. This is the process of *mahāmāyā* "(*BT*). *Mahāmāyā* is the body of glory and power. It is the transfiguration of the ordinary body caused by purging all the impurities by the several ways and means prescribed in the *siddha* tradition. *Mahāmāyā* is also an epithet for female principle conceived as the supreme being owing to her impersonation of the forces of *Prakṛti* or *Māyā*.

3213 **महामायूरी**

Mahāmāyūri : prayer for exorcism.

3214 **महा-मुद्रा**

Mahā-mudrā : the paramount gesture; "two hands clenched, and joined together is to be fixed, facing upward. Fingers of both heads to be joined separately with the right thumb up. All other fingers should remain inter-woven. This is the *mahāmudrā*, one of the best kinds of gestures and this may grant a devotee the status of a *Khecarin* (a spiritual elevation)" (*BT*). (b) "Make two thumbs in one side, and in the same way the ring and the little fingers. Then making the middle ones curved place them on the backs of ring-fingers and adding there fore-fingers, cover the middle ones. This is called *mahāmudrā*. This indicates so many styles, senses, applications and utility as per the difference of treatise (VD). *Mahāmudrā*, then, is a form of bodily posture intended to maintain physical fitness and mental alertness. In this the fingers of both hands are specially utilised in forming different shapes. (*Gheraṇda*, III.1-3). (c) *Mahāmudrā* also stands for women and female organ. (d) *Mahāmudrā* is *mahāmaithuna*, which means 'great' or 'complete' intercourse, including ejaculation.

3215 **महायान**

Mahāyāna : the great vehicle for *nirvāṇa*, the other, *i.e.*, *hīnayāna* is the 'shorter vehicle' for *nirvāṇa*.

3216 **महायोनि**

Mahāyoni : female sex organ. It is the supposed triangle of the *sahasrāra-cakra. (Kaulamārgarahasya*, 256).

3217 **महाराज**

Mahārāja : the king should be addressed as *mahārāja* (*NS*,XVII.65-94); (b) a salutation used to address the *Gurus*, venerable saints, and ascetics since they are considered to be great kings of the spiritual world.

3218 **महावाक्य**

Mahāvākya : great sayings, especially in relation to doctrine of *Vedānta*. Most of the post-Śaṅkara *Advaitavādins*, except Vācaspati have given prominence to these sayings as the means to the realisation of *Brahman* by holding that not only the senses but words also have the capacity to produce perception in certain cases.

3219 **महावेध-मुद्रा**

Mahāvedha-mudrā : *Mahāvedha mudrā* will be easy to practise if all other *bandhas* have been learnt and mastered well. *Mahāvedha* is practised with *kumbhaka* and other three *bandhas*.

3220 **महाव्यसन**

Mahāvyasana : deadly vice, sevenfold:*mṛgayā* (hunting, *akṣa* (gambling), *strī* (other's wives), *pāna* (drinking liquor), *vākpāruṣya* (harsh speech), *arthadūṣaṇa* (prodigality) and *daṇḍapāruṣya* (infliction of unduly harsh punishment).

3221 **महाव्याहृति**

Mahāvyāhṛti : name of the mystical formula: *bhūr bhuvaḥ svaḥ*.

3222 **महाव्योम-मुद्रा**

Mahāvyoma-mudrā : "Make the middle and the ring fingers stretched upward, place them in the opposite direction and join alternately on back sides of both the palms in a position of a seat. This is styled as the *mahāvyoma-mudrā*" (*BT*).

3223 **महासमया-मुद्रा**

Mahāsamayā-mudrā : "When the little finger holds the finger joined by the left hand, having a firt of clenched fingers, it is one of the best type of *mudrā* known to everybody by the name of *samayāmudrā*" (*BT*).

3224 **महिलाकृति-विज्ञान**

Mahilākṛti-vijñāna : sign of a female. If a woman is very tall, she would be *kulaṭā* (unchaste); if she is thin, she would be poor; if short, she will be a short span of life; if she is flat-nosed, she will be a servant; if she is not compact, she would be wretched; if she is curved, she would be crooked; if her toes rise from one another, she would kill many husbands and would resort to others (*Skanda*, IV. 37.16-17). A woman who raises dust while walking, will be of low character (*pāṁsulā*) and would destroy three families. She, whose little toes dose not touch the ground when she walks, will kill her husband and have another (*Ibid.*, 19-20). About the various limbs of woman also there are instances of devinations. For example, it is said about the feet that if the upper side of the feet is depressed in the middle, the woman will be wretched; and if it has protruding veins, it indicates that the person will always be a wanderer; if it is fleshless, she will be unfortunate (*Ibid.*, 37.25). If the back of feet is thick, the person would be unfortunate; if it is raised, she will be *kulaṭā* (adulterer); if it is long she will be sorrowful. About the knees, it is said that, if they are devoid of flesh, she will be adulteress; if they are loose she will be wretched. About the thighs, it is said, that, if they are hairy, they indicate widowhood; if they are flat, the person will be unfortunate. About the waist, it is said that, if it is short and hairy, it indicates widowhood. And if the vagina has circle like conch, she would be issueless.

Elwin (1947:428) has presented a description of a Muria youth under the definition of a beautiful woman: "Her legs and feet should not be too long; they should be neither thin nor fat. The toes must not be big or crooked. She should have a slim waist, so that when she ties her cloth round it, buttocks and waist will be level. A long stomach is ugly; so are buttocks that stick out behind. The nose may be small but not snub. A big head or ears, or fat cheeks are ugly. When the hair is combed it should lie flat on the head. A girl will not be very tall. Her eyes should not be black, and she should never put lamp-black in them or she would look like a witch. The most important thing is that she should dress well and work well. If a girl wears a good cloth she looks sweet, but with loss of ornaments she is entranching. Even an ordinary girl can be beautiful with popular ornaments. But however sweet her face may be, if she is idle or slovenly, we think her ugly."

It will be of interest to compare these ideas with the estimate of classical Indian beauty made by Coomaraswamy. In the Rajasthani and Pahari paintings, he points out, are all Hindu woman-ideals, both physical and spiritual. "The heroine's eyes are large as any lotus flower, her tresses fall in heavy plaits, her breasts are firm and high, her thighs are full and smooth, her hands like rosy flowers, her gait as dignified as any elephant's, and her demeanour utterly demure" (*Rajput Paintings*, Oxford, 1916:8).

Muria songs sometimes make reference to a quality in woman which they call *sapoṭā*, meaning that her physical characters are balanced and in proportion. Such a girl is neither tall nor short, fat nor thin; she has straight hands and feet, a slim waist, round breasts that are not too large. Her 'eyes are dark and bright'. The songs also refer to a type of girl they call *jalmalko*, which seems to describe the way a girl carries herself. 'She struts about like a peacock with tail erect'-many *motiarī* resemble the male rather than a female bird. A *Tutumri Pāṭā* refers to a girl as :

neka jalkemaima

One who goes swinging her hips to attract the eyes of man. A *bāi cikan khosā*, a girl with hair parted and combed with care is always beautiful.

Trench gives the expression '*Singrī-mingrī*' for a well-dressed and ornamented girl.

3225 **महिला-केशरचना**

Mahilā-keśaracanā : female hair-dressing. Hair is the pride of a young lady. Black, glossy, luxuriant hair is the delight of the Hindu. Hindu women anoint their heads with oils and rub the hair with herbs at the time of bathing which promotes the growth of the hair and keeps it black. Some young ladies have hair which, when left loose, reaches down to the heels. Such long hair is greatly valued and considered the principal symbol of feminine attraction. Bobbing the hair is an abomination to the orthodox.

The usual method of dressing hair among Hindu ladies is to comb it well and tie it behind the neck. The method of tying the knot differs with different communities but a casual observer will find all knots alike. The ladies of south India adorn the knot with petals of jasmine or some other sweet smelling flower which adds to the beauty of hair. The ladies of Maharashtra make regular garlands of flowers which they pit to the knot of the hair; and these give the head the appearance of gaudy over decoration. In other parts of India the hair being generally covered, woman wear no flowers on the head.

Children and unmarried girls plait their hair and let it fall to the back and tie the tail and with bright pieces of ribbon. Those who follow Western methods bob the hair of their children, and this practice is at times continued by the ultra modern even after marriage. Such cases are very rare. Among the lower classes too, long hair is much valued. But they tie it in stiff knots, for better freedom of movement, and as they have very little time to attend to their hair. Hence the hair of the working class woman often gets glued up, and is a regular forest teeming with insect life. On these holidays these poor women may be seen at the doors of their huts sitting in a circle and hunting in each other's heads with knives and sickles.

3226 **महिला-परिधानम्**

Mahilā-paridhānam : women's dress. The dress of a middle class lady of Mahārāṣtra and the south is a bodice and a *sārī*. The *sāṛi* may be of silk or of cotton according to the purchasing power of the wearer. The conventional *sārī* is a coloured robe with bright borders twenty to thirty feet in length and three to four feet broad. The orthodox method of wearing the *sārī* is to pass it round the waist so as to divide it into two unequal parts. The longer part falls as a skirt and its end drawn between the legs and tucked behind the waist; the shorter part is passed across the upper part of the body and thrown over the shoulders. When worn well, the lower portion has the appearance of breeches falling in graceful folds when viewed from the front, but the back view is not equally attractive. For obvious reasons, a *sārī* so worn does not permit of the use of a petticoat and Hindu lady walking in this attire often exposes her legs to thighs. Among the lower classes this is always the case; but the better classes, by dexterously arranging the lower part, manage to expose nothing above the knees while walking.

Among the poorer classes, and the old woman of the middle class, a bodice is not worn but the upper part of the *sārī* is made to serve this purpose. In this case the *sārī* is very long and the upper half is passed across the front portion of the body, brought behind the back and the end tucked to a convenient spot. Widows manage to cover their heads also with their *sārīs.*

Among modern ladies, it is considered inartistic to draw the lower end of the *sārī* between the legs, and the *sārī* they wear are of different design. The modern *sāṛī* is smaller, five to six yards long, made of silk with bright detachable or printed borders along its whole length on either side and at one of the ends. It is worn over a petticoat, half of the portion falling as a skirt, and the other half rising in graceful folds, supported by the shining borders, from the left foot of the right shoulder across the whole figure of the lady. The modern *sārī* well worn, can compare favourably with the fashionable clothes of European women. The Parsis and the Indian Christians have been the leaders of fashion in the matter of wearing the *sārī* and educated young Hindu ladies follow the lead. The Hindu lady is extremely loyal to her *sārī.* While most of the modernized Hindu males have adopted the European costume in their outdoor life, no Hindu lady, however, emancipated from conventions, has known to have given up her *sārī* for the European frock. A modernized lady may move freely in the society of Europeans, but always in the *sārī.*

In Rajasthan and Uttar Pradesh, women wear skirts and jackets with wrappers to cover the head and, if need be, the face. The *sārī,* however, is slowly ousting the skirt. Among *Purdah*-observing Hindu ladies one end of the *sārī* is used as a veil to cover the head and face. In the Punjab, mainly through Muslim contact, young ladies consider it fashionable to wear long shirts and breeches with a coloured muslin wrapper to match. Those who wish to appear modest use the wrapper to cover their heads, others throw it over the shoulders. The Punjabi costume, because of the freedom of movement it gives, is becoming fashionable among unmarried young ladies, and very well suits a slim figure. Sikh ladies set the fashion in this costume and they seldom wear anything else, except when some modern Sikh lady shows a preference for the Parsi or Indian Christian *sārīs.*

In North India, including Bengal, for a lady to appear in public without covering her head is considered immodest. Hence a wrapper or the end of the *sārī* is invariably used for covering the head. Young coquettes who are proud of their hair leave it bare, but if they happen to come across some elderly personage they immediately draw the wrapper or *sārī* over the head. On the other hand, if her head is covered and if she meets some young gallant whose attention she wishes to attract, she, as if by accident, drops the wrapper of the *sārī* from her head. The convention regarding covering the head is not observed in Maharashtra where young ladies decorate their hair with flowers, and strut about, like dancing peacocks. In South India only widows with shaven heads are expected to cover their heads. There is no convention of covering the head in the Chhattisgarh of Madhya Pradesh.

Inside and out of doors, the generality of women in South India walk barefoot. In North India they wear slippers. None except the modernized lady wears high-heeled shoes, and even these would not care to wear stockings. Poor women all over India walk barefoot.

3227 **महिलाभरणम्**

Mahilābharaṇam : women's ornament. The Hindus will starve themselves in order to buy ornaments for their womenfolk. Among orthodox classes, what is most admired in a woman is not good looks, figure or health but ornaments. A middle class Hindu lady carries a fortune about her person by way of ornaments. She may not have enough to eat or feed her children, but she must have her trinkets. The minimum equipment of jewellery a middle class Hindu lady is expected to possess are two ear-rings of good size studded with diamonds, a nose-stud, ten rings for the ten fingers, an additional ten for the toes, two or three gold chains for the neck and a dozen gold bangles for the wrist, and anklets for the ankles. With this paraphernalia she can appear in society as a properly clad person. In South India, the ladies of the upper classes wear girdles made of gold over their *sārīs,* which when worn by a slim-waisted lady, beautifully divides the figure into two. The nose rings worn by orthodox ladies in Kaccha are too massive to be supported by the nose and to prevent the ring from tearing the nose they bring down a few hairs from the crown of the head across the brow and tie the nose rings.

Ladies of the aristocrats and courtezans wear ornaments on their heads. These consist of pearl or gold chains worn at the side and centre of the head, after the hair has been properly dressed. A jewelled crest go with these chains and is worn at the front of the head. By far the most lavishly adorned person is the Hindu bride. The wedding is a Hindu lady's day of days and the most burning thirst for jewellery is quenched on this day. From head to foot, a Hindu bride is literally loaded with gold and precious stones.

The poorer classes imitate the rich. Among them, the males have to be contented with two cheap silver earings and a silver or brass locket tied from a string. But his wife must have all the ornaments her more fortunate sisters wear. As it is impossible for her to have them made of the same metal or stone, she goes in for the inferior quality. Gears bangles are greatly admired by them and the poor Hindu woman has often her arms covered with them from wrists to the elbows. As ear-rings, she hangs two small iron hooks from the lobes of her ears. Around her neck she wears a twisted metal bar. In addition she has garlands of cowries and the inevitable locket hung from a string. The ankles and toes must also be adorned with metal even if base. Nor should the nose be neglected. A small iron hook, like her ear-rings, adorns the nose. Lower class women have small green marks tattooed at the centre of the brow and at the wrists.

Objects of wear too were seen as status markers. It was 'out of respect to the higher castes' that no woman of the Bharia caste of farm-servants and agricultural labourers in Madhya Pradesh would wear a nose-ring, as Russell and Hiralal had noticed (II. 249-50). Many decades later social inferiority still continued to be denoted in much the same way in Uttar Pradesh by means of sanctions against the use of jewellery by outcastes: "Shoe-maker women, for example, report having been prevented by Rajputs from wearing ornaments and cloths similar to those of the Rajput women" (Gumperz, *Language in Social Groups,* California, 1971: 41).

3228 **महिष-मुद्रा**

Mahiṣa-mudrā : indication of a buffalo. The hands touching the wrist, the left-hand *muṣṭi* and the right hand *mudrikā,* making the *muṣṭi-mudrā* hand indicate the buffalo (*Mirror of Gesture,* pp. 49-50).

3229 **मांसपेशी**

Māṁsapeśī : muscles.

3230 **मागधी**

Māgadhī : the Prākṛta of Magadha.

3231 **माणव**

Māṇava : a criminal such as a dacoit, adulterer, etc. (*A,* 4.5.1.); boy; *māṇavikā* 'girl'; *māṇavya* 'company of boys, boyhood'.

3232 **माणव-विद्या**

Māṇava-vidyā : magical arts useful for dacoits, etc. (*A*,4.5.1.).

3233 **मातृका**

Mātṛkā : (a) two *karaṇas* constitute a *mātṛkā.* (b) source (*A,* 7.6.41). (c) the mother prostitute (*A,* 2.23.2, 2.27.5).

3234 **मातृमुख**

Mātṛmukha : having the face like that of his mother, foolish.

3235 **मातृ-हस्त**

Mātṛ-hasta : the gesture indicating a mother. If a woman, holding the *ardhacandra* in the left hand and *sandaṁśa* in right, places her left hand turning round on the belly, it is called the *mātṛ-hasta*. It is used to indicate a mother, as well as a maiden (*AD*, 231-244).

3236 **मात्रा-संसर्ग**

Mātrā-saṁsarga : contact with the senses such as eye etc. (*TS*, II. 2.6); also known as *mātrā-sparśa* : *mātrā-sparśāstu kaunteya, śītoṣṇa sukhaduḥkhadāḥ* (*Gītā*, II.14).

3237 **मात्सर्य**

Mātsarya : envy, jealousy, malice, an attitude of envy toward another because of affection that individual shows to a third person.

3238 **मात्स्य-न्याय**

Mātsya-nyāya : the rule of might; anarchy, oppression of the weak by stronger persons. The analogy is drawn from the finny world in which a big fish devours smaller ones (*Arthaśāstra*, 1.4.13, 1:13.5). The law of fishes, where a large fish devours a smaller one.

3239 **मादन**

Mādana : exhilarating; it is the highest aspect of maddening delight which is possessed by Rādhā alone and so it is also called *Rādhā-mahābhāva*. Its unique feature is that even a touch or sight of Kṛṣṇa is attended with the thrilling delight of being kissed and embraced, etc.

3240 **माधुर्य**

Mādhurya : delicacy, sweetness. One of the three excellences of poetry creates mental state of *druti* and exists in *Śṛṅgāra*, *Karuṇa* and *Śānta*. (b) one of the involuntary graces in women. It results when the movement of limbs is moderate in conditions, which are *dīpta* and *lalita*. (c) self-possession. One of the temperamental aspects in men. When even in the great changes the natural harmony of sense organs is unchanged due to practice (of warfare, exercise, etc.), it is called *mādhurya*. (d) one of the five kinds of personal relationship with God in which the latter is seen as loving consort of the devotee (*Caitanyacaritāmṛta*, II.8). The term is also used to denote the sweetness of God, a feature greatly emphasized by the later Vaiṣṇavas.

(e) grace (of women: *śobhā* 'beauty', *vilāsa* 'delight', *mādhurya* 'equanimity', *lalita* 'lolling', *audārya* 'dignity', : *slakṣṇo vikāro mādhuryam*, *DR*. II.11.) (f) the two major departures of *bhakti* are the introduction of the ideas of spiritual grace and love, which are quite alien to Vedic culture in feeling. The normative Hindu concept of cyclical time is rigidly deterministic, whereas the more pragmatic *bhakti* sects concede that the individual can perform spontaneous actions by means of grace and devotion, hence ignoring, or reversing the normative, preordained *kārmic* time-cycle.

3241 **माधूक**

Mādhuka : of honeyed speech. No two people sound exactly alike, and sound of voice is an important part of personality. *Mādhūka* is a seductive voice that increases our attention to what is being said.

3242 **मान**

Māna : (a) one of the six different sets of measurement of body in *Śilpaśāstra*. The *māna* is the measurement of the length of body. (b) self-respect. Somadeva (*Nītivākyāmṛta*) opines: *apamānena varam mānino maraṇam*. "For a person with the sense of self-respect, death is preferable to disgrace."

3243 **मानक-हस्त**

Mānaka-hasta : both hands gesture.

3244 **मानभङ्ग**

Mānabhaṅga : loss of honour.

3245 **मानस-जप**

Mānasa-japa : when the mutterer fixes his mind in the meaning also of the *mantra* as he utters letters and words, it is said to be "mental muttering", as against *vācika* (*Linga*, 1.85.20).

3246 **मानस-काव्य-क्रिया**

Mānasa-kāvya-kriyā : art of composing poems in mind, one of the 64 arts given in *Kāmasūtra* (1.3.16).

3247 **मानसी-कला**

Mānasī-kalā : observation test, memory training to discriminate between a seen and unseen. One of the 64 arts given by *Kāmasūtra*.

3248 **मान्धाता-मुद्रा**

Māndhātā-mudrā : *mukula*, *sūcī* and *ardhapatāka*, twisted upward, touching the body in order, to indicate *māndhātā*, the ruler of mythical age (*Mirror of Gesture*, p.47).

3249 **माया**

Māyā : illusion, the Indian concept of time. The mysterious process that creates and sustains the great game of life is called *māyā*, a term pregnant with multiple meanings and itself the primordial matrix, the womb of time. It variously means: illusion, cosmic, creative illusion, becoming, magic, and art. The flux of *māyā*, recreating the 'many' and dissolving itself back into the primordial unity, or unmanifest condition or Brahman, studies the cosmic cycle. The phenomenal world is made of the same stuff as dreams; both are *māyā*. Creation is conditioned by time: everything is born only to die, for the life-urge not only contains the seeds of its own decay but also is magnetically attracted to the primal source. Man can reverse the outstreaming course of creation. The Vedic sacrifices re-enact creation in reverse, fusing multiplicity back into the primordial unity which centrifugal creation has burst as under.

"Life is sorrow", as the Indian philosophy says, but man must escape from the anguish of time. Suffering is a fact which must be dissociated from its connotation of pain; it arises from the instinct libido, or 'desire'; it is but one part of a larger reality, the 'playfulness' of the divine itself. From the point of view of one who has freed himself from phenomenal existence (*māyā*), the whole of creation is seen as a paradisal vision, a state of divine play, in which he recaptures the innocent vision of the child. In a normal state of mind the phenomenal world appears concrete, real, profane; only in an exalted state it is no longer what it had seemed to be - it is something more not less than real - it is magical, it is sacred. At such moments (in the recapture of the festival, for instance) the sense of time is annulled, the flux of the life is no longer experienced as a pain but ecstasy.

It should now be possible to view the usual definition of *māyā* as 'illusion' in its proper perspective. It does not mean that most Indians, "see life as unreal". Only in the metaphysical system is the world viewed as unreal. Obviously the term *māyā*, which covers the whole of phenomenal existence, has been interpreted in many different ways. Since it is temporality it must be sacramentalized, or melt into Great Time, the cyclical cosmic rhythm.

The influence of this concept of *māyā* is incalculable importance to patterns of thinking today. It is positive in the sense that it expresses India's sense of transience of life, of mutuality, and that this provides solace to those who can look forward to nothing but suffering. It is negative in the sense that the brute fact of life are, in the final analysis, either illusory or of secondary importance and that nothing one does can alter them for the better. While *māyā* is, therefore, a consolation in the face of sorrow because it implies that life need never be taken too seriously, it also serves as a rationale for apathy. (b) deceiving, magic, sorcery.

3250 **मायागत**

Māyāgata : creation of illusions, jugglery (*A*, 1.12.1).

3251 **मायायोग**

Māyāyoga : application of magical arts.

3252 **मायायोगविद्**

Māyāyogavid : an expert in magic (*A*, 1.19.32; 4.3.11).

3253 **मायावचन**

Māyāvacana : false or deceitful words.The best way to deceive may be seen in *Rāmāyaṇa*, where Rāvaṇa restricts his signals to words and facial expressions.

3254 **मायावाद**

Māyāvāda : doctrine of illusion, according to Śaṅkara this world is the seeming product of illusion.

3255 **मारण**

Māraṇa : killing; the black act of killing through rites and spells. (b) for killing brāhmaṇa, a cat, a lizard, an ichneumon or a frog expiation is prescribed (*Garuḍa*, 1.105.34); for killing an elephant five black bulls are to be released (*Ibid.* 35).

3256 **मारिष**

Māriṣa : title of the Sūtradhāra's assistant, noble, my worthy friend.

3257 **मारुति-मुद्रा**

Māruti-mudrā : if the *vāruṇī* (q.v.) gesture is placed obliquely, it is *Māruti* (*VD).*

3258 **मार्गण**

Mārgaṇa : an enquiry, an investigation (*A*, 4.6.20; 4.7.24).

3259 **मार्गदर्शनम्**

Mārgadarśanam : guide-signs. Guide-signs are actions which indicate direction. They guide the attention of on-looker, or his actual movements. In a word, they are pointers. The most popular form of deliberate guide-signing in India is undoubtdly the Fore-finger Point. When someone stops us in the street and asks the way, we may give a perfectly adequate verbal answer, but we rarely omit to add a Fore-finger-Point in support of those words.

Instances of road-signals are very often seen in the tribal-village-complex. Whenever a person is ill, the healing-ceremony takes place where two roads cut each other.

3260 **मार्ग-विरूढ-दृष्टि**

Mārga-virūḍha-dṛṣṭi : eyes fixed on the path (*Pañcasāyaka*, 5.34).

3261 **मार्जारकरणम्**

Mārjārakaraṇam : a kind of coitus or mode of sexual enjoyment.

3262 **माला-मुद्रा**

Mālā-mudrā : the wrath gesture."Join close two hands, the left and the right; make a pot with both of them and go on touching from head to knee; it is called the *mālā* or *vanamālā-mudrā*" (*Brahmayāmala-tantra*).

mālā 'garland'; *mālyakṛta* 'maker of garlands' (S).

3263 **मिताक्षर**

Mitākṣara : (a) short yet comprehensive. (b) name of a commentary of Manu.

3264 **मित्राचार**

Mitrācāra : conduct to be observed towards friends. We can observe an elaborate philosophy of friendship among the Gonds and other communities in central India. The Gond, who in most cases has his first experiences with a girl long before the age of puberty, would be horrified at the very idea that is one of the things they do in cities. But it is not for the *madhubana.* These friendships bind primitive society together and even triumph over the barriers of castes: they are ever lasting than marriages and are a unique feature of village life. There are endless grades and types of friendship, each with its own name, its initiation ceremony and its special obligations. The five most important form an ascending series. First is the *bhojlī,* or 'pal' who stands by you in trouble. Then comes the *sakhī,* a more religious and sacred bond, and the *Janwārā,* the romantic friendship, initiated when the friends place sprouts of green corn round each other's ears. The most intimate of all are *mahāprasāda* and *gaṅgājala.* A man may have many a *sakhī* or *Janwārā,* but only one each of these. Nothing can break these friendships; there is no divorce, and they last beyond the grave. There are also a number of less serious, more sentimental, relationships —*tulsīdal, govardhan, gondāphūl gulābphūl* (flower of the rose), the *kelāpān* (leaf of the plantain), the *amarbel* (the immortal creeper), and so on. These friendships are normally, but not necessarily, between members of the same sex, but husband and wife share each other's friends. This is known as *mitānī* in Chhattisgarh.

"Leaf of the plantain" or "kelāpān" friendship is depicted in the following Gondi song:

I am looking out my house:
The sun is but a bamboo's length above the hills,
where can you go now it is grown so late?
Leaf of the plantain, lover in whom my heart is wound,
Like a dry leaf in the wind,
You are ever blown to and fro away from me.
Where can you go now it has grown too late.

The *Gajabel* is one of the many types of ceremonial friendship, as depicted in the following *Sailā* song :

Gajabel, Gajabel
Your flowers come out in clusters
But when my *arhar* pulse born
Its flowers will be like yours.

Gajabel is actually the name of a creeper. *Lālbhājī* and *Jāmun-ḍārā* are also the names of ceremonial friendships as in the following lines of Gondi song :

Your are my *lālbhājī*
and I your *Jāmun-ḍārā.*

To call one's beloved 'red spinach' or a 'koilar flower' (used as vegetable) or 'kader fruit' is considered entirely appropriate by the Gond and Pardhān, for 'love is eating'. A girl says, 'How I wish I could eat him?' 'When a girl has a man she eats him, for he goes into her stomach'. It is notable that such terms of endearment as, for example, Chaucer uses for 'sweet Alisoun', are also connected with the imagery of eating—'honey-comb', 'fair bird', 'sweet cinnamon'.

O *Gajabel,* take me in your swing
And let us swing together.
Singing the while.
How sweet you look
With *dhoti* underneath
And cloth above
May I cling into your swing?
Swing me, swing me with you.
If I don't see you every moment
I am filled with longing
But how can I climb into your swing?
Swing me, swing me with you.

Here, a girl stands by while her *Gajabel,* a boy-friend, swings on his swing. The *Gajabel,* as stated above, is one of the many types of friendships made by villagers in Central India. It is usually established between members of the same sex, but many sometimes exist between a boy and a girl. The word is used aptly here, for the swinging creeper and its associations of love and friendship blend with the idea of swinging, which is symbolical of the sexual act.

3265 **मिथुन**

Mithuna : pair. A pair is believed to be auspicious. It is generally termed *mithuna.* It has been mentioned that a human couple in privacy should not be seen; if one does, he incurs sin (*Sk.P.* VI. 152.22-23). It is also said that one should not go in between a couple (*Ibid.,* I. 2.41.142) : *antareṇa na gacchet.*

A man and woman engaged in love-sport of any kind are not to be disturbed (*Brahmavai. P.* 42.10-11).

3266 **मिथुनीकरण**

Mithunīkaraṇa : method of ritual coupling in Vedic literature and erotic sculptures in the cave temples. Sex was not erotic in Vedic culture. It developed afterwards in the second century B. C. in terracotta form.

3267 **मिथुनीकृत**

Mithunīkṛta : paired, practising copulation (*Mbh.* XII. 165.26).

3268 **मिथ्याचार**

Mithyācāra : false or improper conduct. (*Suśr*). The word *mithyā* in Śaṅkara's commentary means *anirvacanīyatā* (indefinable ignorance) and not *ahpahnava* (negation). According to Padmapāda, anything that is neither existent (*sat*) nor non-existent (*asat*) is false. Prakāśātman adds to this definition two others. (1) whatever is destroyed by true knowledge is false and (2) whatever can be negated for all time on its own ground or where it was known to exist is false. Many lies are attempts to cover up negative or aggressive feelings, and hand-gestures often reveal them. Different facial expressions may express lies.

3269 **मिथ्यादृष्टि**

Mithyā-dṛṣṭi : false doctrine, atheism.

3270 **मिथ्यापवाद**

Mithyāpavāda : false accusation.

3271 **मिन्मिन**

Minmina : one speaking through nose.

3272 **मिर्मिर**

Mirmira : blinking (of the eyes) *T.Br.*, III. 4.17; *Sat.*, XVII.3.

3273 **मिलिता-दृष्टि**

Militā-dṛṣṭi : a type of eye-gesture. Closing and turning away from the objects, suggests *Jugupsā. Abhinayadarpaṇa* means by it a half-opened look, indicating the *japa* (counting names of Gods); meditation, salutation, madness, the subtle or inner look, subjugation and the fear of a snake (*Abhinayadarpaṇa*, 66.8-9).

3274 **मीलन**

Mīlana : closing the eyes.

3275 **मुकुट**

Mukuṭa : crown; *mukuṭakāra* 'maker of various types of crown (*NS*).

3276 **मुकुर-हस्त**

Mukura-hasta : single hand gesture; *mukura* means 'looking glass.' Cf. *nij mukh mukur vilocanhi jāī* (*Mānasa*, 1.135.6).

3277 **मुकुल-हस्त**

Mukula-hasta : bud-hand, single hand gesture. A type of *asaṁyuta hasta* according to Bharata (*NS*, IX. 117), where fingers bent and close to each other's meet: it is used for worshipping a deity, a lotus bud, etc. (*NS*, IX.118). Kālidāsa (*Kumārasaṁbhava*, VIII) has described this gesture in which Pārvatī holds the rosary. Often occurs in iconography. The palm is raised facing outwards. The four fingers are bent forward together, and the thumb is bent to touch the tips of the fingers. It is used to express a cock, writing or drawing, camel, calf, the number three, *Vedas*, a leaf, etc. The fingers with their ends are brought together close to one another and raised up like *haṁsāsya*. It represents offering of oblation and worship of deities, bud of lotus and water lily, throwing a kiss (as by a *vita*), contempt, scattered objects, taking meals, gold, counting, narrowing of mouth, gifts, quickness and buds of flowers.

3278 **मुकुलक-हस्त**

Mukulaka-hasta : the young bud-hand, same as *mukula-hasta*. When all the fingers of *haṁsamukha* (q.v.), stretched up flatly with their tips bent, it is called the *mukulaka* gesture. It is to be used to worship Gods and offering things to them, to indicate blossomed lotuses, to style a *viṭa's* (go-between) kiss, to show an ugly performance, to scatter things. In addition to them, this may also be used to take food, to count gold, to deform face (*mukha-saṅkocana*), to give, to make hurry and to indicate buds of flowers (*NS*, IX. 111-113).

3279 **मुकुला-दृष्टि**

Mukulā-dṛṣṭi : the bud-like glance, a type of *sañcārī bhāva dṛṣṭi*, a glance with lightly quivering eyelashes, the upper eyelids in a bud-like pose and the eyeballs opened in joy, is called the *mukulā* glance suggesting the sense of sleep, dream and happiness (*NS*, VIII. 61-92). The eyelashes tremble and the eyeballs are opened in happiness. The eyelashes are united and throbbing, the upper eyelids bent in the budlike manner and pupils opened in happiness. It is used in sleeping, dreaming and happiness.

3280 **मुकुला-मुद्रा**

Mukulā-mudrā : the gesture of a bud (a) "To style the gesture of *mukula*, join the palms in the heart region and make the two elbows always bent equally in a line. This is *mukula*, which assures success citing sacred lores and inviting deities" (*BT*); (b) upturn two palms with fingers in a curved position, this makes the gesture of *mukula* (*VD*).

3281 **मुकुलिताक्ष**

Mukulitākṣa : with eyes closed.

3282 **मुकुलिता-दृष्टि**

Mukulitā-dṛṣṭi : a type of glance. The eyelashes trembl and the eyeballs are opened in happiness. It is used in sleeping, dreaming, sexual enjoyment etc. (*NS*, VIII, 70).

3283 **मुकुलिता-शंकिता-दृष्टि**

Mukulitā-śaṅkitā-dṛṣṭi : a type of glance for showing fear.

3284 **मुकुलीकृत-हस्त**

Mukulīkṛta-hasta : a type of hand-gesture in *Kumārasaṁbhava* (5.63), same as *mukula hasta.*

3285 **मुक्तग्रीवा**

Mukta-grīvā : loosened neck; a type of neck-movement given by *VD* (III.1.61). The *recita* neck becomes *mukta* by circumambulation. This is to be used in meditation and swooning.

3286 **मुक्तकण्ठ**

Muktakaṇṭha : weeping aloud. The idea that weeping aloud can do good is very old one (sea *Uttararāmacaritam).* And now it has scientific validity, for recent research into tears has shown that tears contain a natural painkiller called enkaphalin.

3287 **मुक्तजानु-आसन**

Muktajānu-āsana : a type of sitting posture.

3288 **मुक्तरोधोनितम्बा**

Muktarodhonitambā : quitting the hip-like bank.

3289 **मुक्तलज्ज**

Muktalajja : one who has cast away modesty.

3290 **मुक्तवसन**

Muktavasana : one who has put off clothes.

3291 **मुक्तसङ्ग**

Muktasaṅga : free from attachment.

3292 **मुक्तहस्त**

Mukta hasta : having open hands, generous.

3293 **मुक्ताचार**

Muktācāra : lack of social manners.

3294 **मुक्तासन**

Muktāsana : one who has left his seat.

3295 **मुख**

Mukha : mouth. The face (mouth) is rich in communicative potential. Bharata mentions that it is the primary site for communicating emotional states and thus classifies it as follows: *udvāhi* or *bhugna* or *vivṛta* (*śṛṅgāra*), *vivṛta (bhayānaka) vivṛta* or *vinivṛta* (*hāsya*), *bhugna* or *nirbhugna* (*karuṇa*), *udvāhi* (*adbhuta*), *vinivṛtta* (*raudra*), *vidhuta* or *udvāhi* (*vīra*), *vinivṛtta* or *nirbhugna* (*bībhatsa*). Movement of the mouth is classified according to the muscular possibilities of the movement of the mouth. Physiologists have estimated that the facial masculature is such that over twenty thousand different facial expressions are somatically possible. At the initial stage of investigation, Bharata could isolate sex kinemes in the mouth area : *vidhuta, vinivṛtta, nirbhugna, bhugna, vivṛta* and *udvāhi* (NS, VIII. 147-154). The *VD* (III.1.61) accepts the first of them and replaces the *udvāhi* by *ṛju.* It is the normal position of the face, indicating the natural state of the face part.

In the area of upper face, Indian emblems demonstrate a distinction between the forehead and the eyes. In 'unfortunate fool' the hand covers the whole face, while on my eyes' it covers on the eye. In 'think' the hand or index touches the forehead.

The village India presumes that the face is the mirror of heart: *jī kā dukh, dikhāve mukha* 'The heart's woe, the face doth show'. The face contributes more information about emotional meaning than either vocal intonation or the words people use.

In total, seven kinemes of mouth have been enumerated by Bharata (6) and *VD* (+1). These seven kinemes make up the circumoral complex. Only continued research will give us confidence that these represent the complete assessment and that the list is composed of equivalent categories. Here it is worth mentioning that Birdwhistell (1970 : 193-200) has also counted seven mouth kinemes. The list includes "compressed lip", "protruded lips", "retracted lip", "apically withdrawn lips", "snare", "lax open mouth" and "mouth overopen". He is particularly doubtful about the first two of these. According to Birdwhistell, both may belong to some general midface category which he has thus far been unable to isolate. To this list, he adds "anterior chin thrust", "lateral chin thrust", "putted cheeks" and "sucked cheeks". "chin drop" may gain kinemic status (Birdwhistell. *Kinesics and Context,* Philadelphia, 1970, 100-101).

3296 **मुखकाम**

Mukhakāma : one who is exited by copulation in mouth; *mukhamaithuna.*

3297 **मुखचपेटिका**

Mukhacapeṭikā : slap on the face.

3298 **मुखज**

Mukhaja : of the face, that which originates in the face, facial, also known as *upāṅga,* a type of *āṅgika abhinaya.* The following parts constitute the *upāṅga* : eyebrows, eyeballs, nose, lips, chin and mouth; movement of these minor limbs.

Facial expressions, and micro-expressions, are constantly changing in response to inner, and outer stimuli. And when we look at someone's face we are quickly able to tell whether the person is interested, bored, cheerful or downcast. In turn, we consciouly or unconsciouly use our facial signal to convey a wide range of emotions and give emphasis to what we are saying.

There are many idioms in Hindi derived from the face, such as : *mukh cūmnā* 'to kiss', *mukhāgar* face to face, *muhn boltī mūrat* 'a speaking statue', *muhnphaṭ* 'foul-mouthed, abusive', *muhn tāknā* 'to stare or gaze at one', *muhn chupānā* 'avoidance', *muhn sīnā* 'to keep silence' etc.

3299 **मुखज-अभिनय**

Mukhaja abhinaya : that which originates in the face, facial gesture. The *mukhajābhinaya* is very specific. In this sense facial expressions lie towards the communicative end of the scale. Facial expression is perhaps the area in non-verbal communications research that comes closet to the more traditional concerns of Indian dramaturgy. The question of nature versus nurture as the origin of behaviour is much more present here.

Thus several reasons why the face is an important NV channel include the amount of information it can convey (especially in a short period of time) and the kind of information (*e.g.*, emotional, attitudinal) conveyed.

There are five classes of facial expression : nose, cheeks, lips, chin, mouth, and the colour of the face. Movements of the mouth, nose, cheeks, chin and lips are classified in the *NS*, the *SR*, the *Nāṭyaśāstra Saṅgraha* and the *Bālarāmabharata* according to the muscular possibilities of the movement of these parts of the face. The *NS's* classification is followed to a large extent by the other texts. The *SR* adds a few more movements in the case of lips such as *udvṛtta*, *āyata* and *recita* and two more movements, *grahaṇa* and *niṣkarṣaṇa*, in the case of chin (classified as teeth-movement). The tongue-movements (*jihvābhinaya*) are enumerated only by the later texts (*i.e. SR*, *Nāṭyaśāstra Saṁgraha* and *Bālarāmabharata*) and have not been mentioned by Bharata in *NS*. There is scant evidence in the literary works of Sanskrit literature of the popular usage of these movements of the nose, cheeks, chin, etc. : the *dṛṣṭis*, the movements of the eyeball (*tārā*) and the eyebrow (*bhrū*) are, however, frequently mentioned by the creative writers. *Bālarāmabharata* mentions many more movements of these parts of the face which seem to derive their validity from the oral rather than the academic tradition; nevertheless, most of them can be analysed in terms of their *vyabhicārī bhāva* etc. and thus form an integral part of *āṅgikābhinaya* of classical dancing.

Grant, (*Human Facial Expression, Man*, 1969, 4.526-536) has suggested an "ethnological check list" for human facial expressions. He considers the face to be divided into three relatively independent expressive areas : "gaze, eyebrow position and mouth position." To these he adds body posture. The lower part of the face, "with the extreme mobility built into the lips and mouth has the greatest number of expressive positions. In determining a procedure for describing behaviour, he questions whether a minimal element exists in nature. But the description must go on, so he weighs the validity of patterns built up from muscle contractions against "functional" designations, "bits of behaviour which fulfil a particular function". He prefers the latter, since "many recognisable patterns of behaviour can be adequately described and may yet vary considerably in terms of mascular contraction, as, for example, a pecking bird will use different muscles according to the positioning of its prey, but that it is pecking is incontrovertible. He chooses, then, cutaneous, "functional" descriptions rather than muscular ones.

3300 **मुखप्रेक्ष**

Mukhaprekṣa : watching the face (not intent on work).

3301 **मुखभूषण**

Mukhabhūṣaṇa : betel.

3302 **मुखमण्डल**

Mukhamaṇḍala : face-orb.

3303 **मुखमार्जन**

Mukhamārjana : washing the mouth.

3304 **मुखमुद्रण**

Mukhamudraṇa : to make one silent : *asahṛdayānām mukhamudraṇāya.*

3305 **मुख-मुद्रा**

Mukha-mudrā : facial expression. Of the diversity of formalized, visible acts with which humans communicate are among the most consistently important in Indian dramaturgy. Indeed, the range and subtlety of facial expressions is basic in the conduct of what Bharata has designated *Mukhajābhinaya.* Bharata has reduced facial expressions for analysis into sets of displays. Most facial displays are employed in diverse circumstances, and vary in form within wide limits. For instance, a study of 'smiling' would require observation of its use in human behaviour ranging from suffering to exultation, from anger to terror, from casual to intense, and would have to account not only for its contribution to such events, but also for its variability in the form and integradation into other facial expressions. *Bālarāmabharata* has rightly presented this insight.

With regard to face as a designator the following affect displays appear: 'pleasure' (a smile), 'anger', 'alarm', 'doubt', 'pain', 'grief' and 'sour'. 'Pleasure' and anger contrast in a joking vs. a serious shaking of the index finger. Presence or absence of the smile does cause the information to assign a different gloss to the gesture. Displays of surprise appear in Hindi, but without evidence of shared performance or of contrast. Several informants gave a similar performances for 'doubt' and for 'surprise', raising the eyebrows and protruding the lips slightly. 'Grief' contrasts with 'pleasure' when the singer places his palm on the chest. The former expression conveys 'worry' but the latter conveys the message 'I am your servant' (as a greeting or farewell). Finally 'sour', a tight closing of the eyes and smacking of the lips, contrasts with 'delicious', a smacking of the lips with smile and open eyes. 'Disgust' differs strikingly from 'sour' in that it involves contraction of the nose and upper lip area than closed eyes and smacking lips.

Expressions of affect displays involve all the features of the face, but individual features also signal emblematic meaning. Blowing from the mouth appears in chase away 'evil spirits after prayer'. The cheeks move in for 'weak' and out for 'fat'. Contrasting eye positions include the wink in 'let's go' and 'I'm kidding' closed eyes in 'sleep', and 'death' and squint in 'I didn't understand'. Raised eyebrows appear in 'surprise', 'doubt' and 'no', lowered brows appear in 'anger' and 'disgust' and lowered brow raised slightly in the centre appear in 'pain'.

3306 **मुखयुग्मक**

Mukha-yugmaka : facial deceit - refers to several techniques through which individuals attempt to control their facial expressions, and so mislead others with respect to their present emotional state.

3307 **मुखर**

Mukhara : talkative. *Mukharā khalveṣā dāsī* (*Ratnāvalī* Act II). Talkativeness is censured. The belief is that ghosts, demons, and the dead enter (the mouth of) those who talk nonsense. Whatever auspicious a talkative person does or eats, it is for the satisfaction of the ghosts, etc. (*Skanda P.* 1.2.63.28-30).

3308 **मुखराग**

Mukharāga : the complexion of face; the colour of face. Bharata has stressed that the colour of face changes with the change in the sentiment (*rasa*). It explains the states of mind which are expression of *rasas*. Thus he has classified *mukharāga* as follows (four): *prasanna* or *svābhāvika* (*śṛṅgāra*), *śyāma* (*bhayānaka*), *prasanna* (*hāsya*), *rakta* (*karuṇa*), *prasanna* (*adbhuta*), *rakta* (*raudra*), *rakta* (*vīra*) and *śyāma* (*bībhatsa*) *NS*, VIII.161.

Rāma (*Raghu*, 12.8) had such control over himself that he did not undergo any mental change at the time of prosperity or adversity. People are flushed red when they are in prosperity and become pale or swarthy when in adversity; but as quoted in *Raghu* (21.8), Rāma was *sthitaprajña*. Such persons may not display the change.

Gestures of all the parts of the face have a very close relation with the colour. No gesture can be successfully exhibited if it is not approximately added to the requisite colours of the face that suggests appropriate sentiments or *rasas*. Four colours are appreciated as to be the media of eight *rasas* as mentioned above. (a) *svābhāvika* : natural (the climatic natural colour of a man living in various parts of the world). Colour should be maintained in enacting the natural habit and behaviour of an artist. It may also be maintained to suggest one's own indifferent feeling. (b) *prasanna* : (clear) bright colours of the face suggests the erotic, the cosmic and the wonderful. (c) *rakta* : red colour suggests the heroic, the furious, the pathetic and some accessory feelings like pride, blushfulness, etc. (d) *śyāma* : black (dark) colour suggests the terrible and the disgustful.

Colours are also responsible to add extra lustre to any kind of gesture, shown with other parts, limbs and sublime of the body. Even some insufficiencies in the physical representation of gestures may be waived with the help of colours. They redouble the beauty with appropriate gestures. It is must for the gesture of the eye and its relevant parts. A drama attains success when it is added to the glory of face (*NS*, VIII. 155-163).

Six emotions—happiness, sadness, anger, fear, surprise and disgust—are found both in tribal and non-tribal settings. My study has demonstrated that the same facial expressions are associated with the same emotions, regardless of the language.

3309 **मुखलिङ्ग**

Mukhaliṅga : a class of *mānuṣaliṅga*. They are conventional in character. They denote those emblems which show on their *rudra* or *pūjābhāgas* one or more human faces. *Rūpamaṇḍana* mentions thirty one four-faced *mukhaliṅgas*.

3310 **मुखवासन**

Mukhavāsana : a thing which makes the mouth fragrant, betel etc.

3311 **मुखव्यादान**

Mukhavyādāna : opening the mouth wide.

3312 **मुखशब्दम्**

Mukhaśabdam : making sound with mouth. In *Sūtra*-period (800 B.C.-300 B.C.) some rules of etiquette were that a person should not make sound with his mouth and should not speak while taking his meals (*Ap. Dh. Sū.*, 2.8.19, 10-16).

3313 **मुखाकृति-विज्ञान**

Mukhākṛti-vijñāna : sign of the face and mouth. If even, closed, pleasing, and clear, kingship; if contrary to what has been noted above, grief; if like that of a woman, gain of son is indicated; if circular or round, pride; if long, lack of money; if the mouth is haunted with fear, it indicates the person to be sinner; square-face, cunning; if short, it indicates the person to be a miser; if full and lustrous, it indicates enjoyment (*Garuḍa*). If the face is big, it indicates misfortune; if like a woman, it shows death of sons; if roundish, it indicates happiness (*Brahma*, 26. 44-46).

Face like the moon and lotus are the standards of ideal beauty in Sanskrit literature : *candramukhī, kamalamukhī.*

The face, according to tribal norms, should not be too thin. It should slope straight downwards. The nose must be straight. A snub nose is bad. The forehead should be broad. The lips should not be very thick. The ears must be thin and fine, the throat slender. The eye should not be so big as a cow's, not yet so small as a frog's. The eyelids should not be very big. Eyebrows must not join in the middle. This may be taken as an authoritative and representative statement of what the tribes expect of the human face (Elwin, 1939.248).

(b) facial feedback hypothesis. One of the most intriguing implications of the universality notion in emotional expression is the *mukhākṛti-vijñānam*— that facial expressions not only reflect emotional experience, but are important in determining how we actually experience and label emotion. (c) the facial signs according to Varāhamihira (LXVIII) as follows: 'The mouth being pleasant, round and closed, soft and even, makes men monarchs; being contrary, miserable and penniless; and a very big mouth belongs to the unfortunate'. A feminine face belongs to those who are issuless; a round one, to rogues; a long one, to the poor; a timid one, to those who commit sinful acts; a quadrilateral one, to the treacherous; a sunken and crooked one, to the childless; a very small one, to misers; and a full, fleshy and attractive one, to those who enjoy pleasures :

स्त्रीमुखं निरपत्यानां मण्डलं शाठ्यसेविनाम् ।
दीर्घं मुखं च निःस्वानां भीरुवक्त्रा दुराशयाः ॥
चतुरस्रं तु धूर्त्तानां निम्नं सुतविवर्जितम् ।
कृपणानां तथा ह्रस्वं चिपिटं परजीविनाम् ॥
यन्मुखं मांसलं स्निग्धं सप्रभं प्रियदर्शनम् ।
वर्णाढ्यं सन्धिविश्लिष्टमजस्रं सुखभागिनाम् ॥

3314 **मुखादारभ्य नाभ्यन्तरं चुम्बनम्**

Mukhādārabhya nābhyantaram cumbanam : kissing all the limbs from face to navel (*Naiṣadha*, 20.92).

3315 **मुखाभिनय**

Mukhābhinaya : mouth-gesture. Sāgarikā's love-lorn state in *Ratnāvalī* (Act II) is shown through this gesture.

3316 **मुखावलोकनम्**

Mukhāvalokanam : display of mouth; known as *mukha-dikhāī* in Hindi; the present given generally by the female relations of the bridegroom on the first visit to the bride. (b) seeing the reflection on auspicious occasions. One of the rites about the marriage ritual is that after worshiping the goddess Lakṣmī the couple should see their reflection in liquid clarified butter (*Sk.P.* III.2.18.54):

rātrau jāgaraṇam kāryam suvāsinīm ca pūjayet /
mukhāvalokanam cājye kurvītām ca dampatī //

Seeing one's reflection in a mirror is enjoined as a daily duty (*Agni.P.*, 236.5): *anulipto alaṅkṛtaścamukham paśyecca darpaṇe.* But seeing one's reflection in a sword was prohibited: *khaḍge na paśyed vadanam* (*Ibid.*, 245.27).

3317 **मुखेभगा**

Mukhebhagā : a woman satisfying the carnal desire of a man by mouth (*Kāmasūtra*).

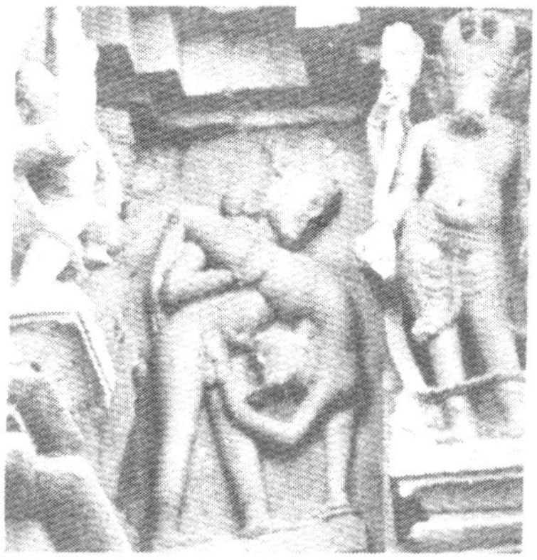

Fig. – (3317)

3318 **मुग्धभाव**

Mugdhabhāva : foolishness.

3319 **मुग्धा**

Mugdhā : inexperienced; a variety of heroine. *Mugdhā* is one who has just stepped into the domain of youth and love, who shrinks from sexual union, who is gentle in her indignation, and who is extremely bashfull (*Sāhityadarpaṇa*, 3.58). *Mugdhā* is so innocent that she does not understand even the fact that she is entering the youth. Śakuntalā, having seen Duṣyanta thinks, "why I, having seen this person become susceptible to an emotion opposed to a penance-grove" (*Śākuntalam*, p.19). The second epithet of *mugdhā* is her non-cooperation in sex-sport. Kālidāsa describes Pārvatī as a *mugdhā* where he states, "Although she did not reply when addressed to, desired to go away when held by her upper garment, and slept on the bed with her face turned aside, still she gave delight to Śiva (*Kumāra*, 8.2). Bashfulness which is one of the characteristics of *Mugdhā* is seen in the literature ever and anon. Śarmiṣṭhā having seen Yayāti diverts her glances (*Yayāticaritam*, p.8). Mālavikā having heard the words of her lover gesticulates bashfulness (*Mālavikāgnimitram*, p.68). Thus, every heroine of the *mugdhā*-type shows her bashfulness at the first sight of her lover:

prathamāvatīrṇa-yauvanamadana-vikārā ratau vāmā /
kathitā mṛduśca māne samadhika-lajjāvatī mugdhā //

(*SD*, 3, 58)

Mugdhā means the artless girl. She shrinks from caress and is extremely shy. She is averse to amorous dalliance. At the first blush of youth, the girl changes in her appearance. Her waist becomes thin, her loins become bulky; her belly is depressed and her breasts are developed. Her glances fall into a side long habit. Her face beams and her eyes become bright. The pupils of her eyes become a little restless. She feels a desire to look at her admirer. However, she shrinks from the caress of her lover and casts down her eyes when he looks at her. She is silent. She will not reply when her lover speaks to her. She is extremely shy and does not know how to communicate her indignation.

3320 **मुण्डन**

Muṇḍana : shaving the hair on the head as well as the moustache and beard. The tonsure, or cutting of hair at holy places has been enjoined. It is also known as *vapanam* (*Skanda*, V.3.34.16). It is also said that tonsure and fast is a common ritual at all holy places:

मुण्डनं चोपवासश्च सर्वतीर्थेष्वयं विधिः ।

(*Ibid.*, V.3.27.31)

The initial ceremony was known as *kṣaura*. It is associated with new creation; and this belief indicates hair to be endowed with life whence comes both new forms of life. Hence hair-cutting in rituals comes to symbolize ritual-death which was necessary for a symbolic new birth prior to performing sacrificial or other religious rituals. Thus, at initiation (*upanayana*) or sacrificial consecration (*dīkṣā*) it was necessary to tonsure the head of the initiate. According to the old tradition, gods themselves helped in the symbolic tonsure (*Ibid*).

3321 **मुद्गर-मुद्रा**

Mudgara-mudrā : the club-gesture. "Make two palms of hands like buds and join them together up to the elbows. When this fist is repeatedly brandished, it is called the *mudgara-mudrā*. This *mudrā* removes all sorts of fear of a devout" (*BT*). *Mudgara* is hammer, staff, mace used as weapon by gods.

3322 **मुद्रा**

Mudrā : (a) from the viewpoint of linguistics, *mudrā* is a code-language of the beloved of ancient India who were illiterate to communicate through letters. It is one of the scripts also. It is the NV means of communicating 93 per cent of the messages (b) sign-language. In *Kathāsaritasāgara* the heroine shows one finger to her lover Devadatta which means "come near". (c) gesture in *Tantrayoga*. The use of mudrās or positions of hands or fingers in connection with *saṅgīta*, particularly dance, appears to betray *Tāntric* influence. It may be added that *mudrā* is regarded as a means of *Tāntric sādhanā*. (d) hand-gesture. It falls into a separate category and there are literally hundreds of *mudrās*, some taken from conventional poses of mediative practice and some from the ritual gestures of ancient sacrificial ceremonies. A few are fixed symbolic poses formed by positions of hands and fingers but the majority of dance *mudrās* are fluid and changing. (e) pose in Indian sculpture, a particular attitude of human form in sculpture. We may recall the different dancing *mudrās* of Śiva. The king in *Ratnāvalī* (Act III) sits in one corner in the thinking *mudrā*. (f) pose. This can be static or active and corresponds to expression. Poses can be composed, relaxed, leisurely, passive, leaning, seductive, snuglling. Bodies can be vertical or horizontal. An individual can use another to act as a shield or as an object to lean against, or rest hands or legs on. Pose is also related to social position and status, hence women are often seen in a lower position than men, for instance sitting at their feet. (g) a gesture employed in dancing or in iconography. They are described at length in *NS* and also in other texts. The most common are the *añjali* (prayer), *varada* (gift) and *abhaya* (protection) *mudrās*. Less common are the *patāka* (flag), *padma* (lotus), *mukula* (bud) and *muṣṭi* (fist). They are also employed in Buddhist and Jain imagery. In Buddhist iconography, they are only the manifestations of Intellectual Enlightenment (*bodhicitta*). Thus, if protection was required, the *bodhicitta* was expressed in the *abhaya mudrā;* if a boon or gift was desired, the *varada* was depicted. When instruction in the Buddhist Law was necessary, the *dharmacakra* or *vyākhyāna* (first shown by the Buddha when practising his first sermon at Sāranātha) and so forth. In Buddhist iconography the following ten are the most important *mudrās: bhūmi-sparśa* (earth-touching or witness), *dharma-cakra* (teaching), *abhaya* (blessing or refuge), *Jñāna* or *padmāsana* (contemplation), *tarka* (right hand raised to the chest), *vīra* (enchanting), *śaraṇa* (protection) and *uttara-bodhi* (highest perfection).

In the Jain-Iconography also the *mudrās* occur though not many in the case of their Tīrthaṅkaras, but quite a number in connection with their *yakṣas* and their counterparts, the *yakṣiṇīs*. All the *mudrās* mentioned in Jain texts do not appear in their iconography. Among these the *Jina*, *yoga*, and *varada* are the most prominent. In the *Jina mudrā*, the ascetic stands erect like Bāhubalī in the *kāyotsarga* posture (letting the limbs loose and keeping the feet four finger's breadth between the toes and a lesser width between the heels). In the *yogamudrā*, the sage sits keeping the palms of his hands in the shape of lotus buds besides his stomach. The *varada* and *vīra mudrās* are identical showing the ascetic setting at ease and spreading his right hand opened, in the posture of granting a boon. (h) fried or consecrated rice and some other savouries of the kind in a certain stream of esoterics is called *mudrā* (*Skanda* P. 89-1.38). (i) In ritual and spiritual spheres, *mudrā* is used in *pūjā* (worship) *japa* (chanting names of god), meditation, bath, welcome, celebration, protection, offering things etc. (j) but in the sphere of behaviourism *mudrā* is the symbolic gesture for suggesting various human feelings and thoughts, inexplicable through words. (k) in the *yoga* system, sometimes it indicates *āsana* (spiritual feat and position) like *kṣurikā mudrā, mahā-mudrā*, etc. (l) in fine arts *mudrās* suggest poses, postures and positions, like *gīti-mudrā, piṇḍī-bandha-mudrā, aṅguli-mudrā, grīvā-mudrā*, etc. (m) it is a seal in social and political science, money in economics, a ring in literature, a type of scripts in palaeography. (n) In the *Vāmakeśvara Tantra* (43.2) *mudrā* is defined as a symbolic gesture for the purpose of ascertaining Joy and Safety. (o) from early childhood, each of us has been almost harassed by admonitious regarding "correct" posture, and not without any justification. Thus posture carries the strongest connotation of guilt. Whether walking, standing, sitting or lying down, body is all too frequently abused, twisted, distorted into all sorts of unproductive and even ugly shapes. Not only are the abused positions harmful to the development and efficiency of our internal organs, but they also act as "signals" to our contemporaries revealing such matters as state of health, possible motivation, and nature and strength of belief. For many years, our seers noted that persons experiencing certain mental and physical states characteristically assume discrete positions whether standing or sitting. But even without these notices, most individuals can distinguish the relaxed person and the tense, uncomfortable one by the position of their legs and arms. (p) one finds mention of *mudrās* in many books, but of their actual representation in human ceremonial there is very little record. And yet the subject is profoundly interesting from several points of view, cult, history, mysticism—all of which require attention in order to arrive at a complete understanding of the meaning of these symbolic gestures.

The *mudrā* or symbolic hand-gesture is the physical presentment of the same *mantra* or magic formula, which is first recalled by the mind and articulated by the mouth. By this threefold manner of expression, the three constituents of human personality are simultaneously brought into activity—body (*mudrā*), soul (speech: sound) and spirit (memory). In examining these *mudrās*, it must be borne in mind that they represent only one, and the lowest, of the three possible means of expression which form the complete rite.

The *mudrā* illustrates visibly and materially a formula. The formula or *mantra* is composed of short extracts from the *Vedas* on the names of spiritual powers, benevolent, or hostile, preceded or terminated by words of power; or lastly, of a series of unmeaning syllables, so selected and related that, when rapidly repeated in the prescribed manner, they set up definite vibrations in the body and the brain, producing well-defined and calculated states of consciousness. Many of the syllables thus employed are considered to possess magic properties, as for instance, in the ceaselessly—muttered *Hill Māṛia mantra,: Oṁ maṇi Padma him*, which is believed to resound through the Six Regions of Beings, helping towards their liberation from the wheel of Rebirth.

Here in India, Viśvakarmā, the architect of the Gods, was thought to have created and delivered to man the holy *Devanāgarī* (Sanskrit) alphabet. Letters, their uttered sound and their simulation by interlacements of the fingers, were on this account conceived to possess equally divine properties, as produced from that Divine mind with which the Devotee sought union by the practice of the *yoga*- ritual.

It does not seem an unreasonable assumption to suppose that in the mystery—schools of India, where the aspirant was trained by the severest excercises and symbolic drama for eventual union with the cosmic spirit, that the formula (*mantra*) of the exercises, the physical positions necessary, and the due enunciation of the Divine syllables, should have received their crowning "seal" (*mudrā*) by an actual representation of letter or symbol upon the fingers, or by some gesture symbolising the particular power contained in the idea of the *mantra*, or in the God under meditation.

Mudrā formed a *franca-lingua*, like the notes of music or the figures of mathematics understood by all, and thus often has been the most authentic expression of the site.

The language of the hands is probably the oldest in the world, its tradition reaching further back than those of the spoken word. As a means of expression there probably existed a symbolic and conventional art of gesture, before any artistic attempts in stone, clay, wood, or colours had been made.

In some parts of the world this symbolic language of gesture still survived, after the human mind had gone the way to express itself also through words, art and music, and it continued to develop a parallel with the other means of expression. It is certain that in the most ancient rituals hand—movements played a great role. In India they developed through the ages into the system of the so-called *mudrās.*

Mudrā is a Sanskrit word means 'seal'. The designation of ritual hand-gesture by this word originates from a time, when the priests used to pronounce certain *mantras* (which were supposed to produce a magic effect), at the same time accompanying the sound by imitating the corresponding Sanskrit characters with their fingers, thus sealing the magic. With the higher initiates this grew into a complicated and secret language, for, after having abandoned the Sanskrit motif, the *mudrā* system diverged into different forms in different regions. (Fig. ·3322)

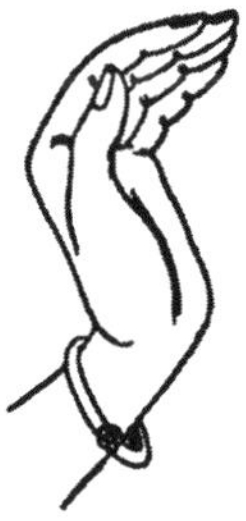

Fig. – (3322)

3323 **मुद्राख्य-हस्त**

Mudrākhya-hasta : single hand-gesture.

3324 **मुद्रा-लिपि**

Mudrā-lipi : gesture-script, kinegraph, kinegraphic symbol. The *VD* deals with the *mudrā-lipi.* With the help of the gesticulatory movements of major and minor limbs of the body, first some words are framed with the help of the gesture-scripts (*mudrā-lipi*). As we build a word with letters, similarly people frame some words of their interest which compose a sentence (*VD,* ch.32, pp.110-111).

Mudrā-lipi was a type of pictorial notation system for coding kines. Birdswhistel developed it in 1970 called kine-graphs. In this system the body is divided into eight different areas and movement in each body area is transcribed in a different type of kinegraphic symbol. An observer trained in this system can easily record the movements quickly without the use of mechanical equipment.

3325 **मुद्राशास्त्र**

Mudrāśāstra : gesturology. Alike *tantra, mudrā* suggests scores of sense in reference to appropriate context. In spite of the ripe heritage, no earlier documentary evidence of the same has come to our hands till the discovery of *mudrādhikaraṇas* of the *Picumata* and *Piṅgalamata* had been made. Literally *mudrā* means a gesture, that conveys the message of one's mind through the movements of the limbs. The *mudrās* discussed in *Picumata* and *Piṅgalamata* may be classified into five groups: (i) the ritual, (ii) the spiritual, (iii) the socio-cultural, (iv) the dramaturgic, and (v) the musical. Thus we may appreciate the *mudrādhikaraṇa* as to the first complete work in Indian Gesturology (second century B. C. to fourth century A.D.). *NS, Abhinayadarpaṇa* and *VD* may be appreciated on all-round complete work on Indian Gesturology. *Arthaśāstra* and *Mahābhārata* deal with the secret gestures.

3326 **मुद्रिका**

Mudrikā : ring bearing the wearer's name.

3327 **मुष्टि**

Muṣṭi : fist, clenched hand: *muṣṭibandhaniḥ sārita rasaḥ; muṣṭika* 'pugilistic encounter'; *muṣṭi-ghaṭanā* 'to get in one's hand'; *muṣṭighātam* 'striking with fists'; *muṣṭibandha* 'taking into fist'; *muṣṭimeya* 'to be measured by the palm of the hand'. (b) *muṣṭi* indicates the vulva and penis in *Śiva-dīkṣā. Agni-Purāṇa* (27, 31-37) while describing the process records that the *muṣṭi-mudrā* of a vulva and penis is made by the *guru.* Then he touches the jar (Śiva) with the thumb, and with the fist (symbolizing vulva and penis):

> भगालिङ्गसमायोगं विदध्याल्लिङ्गमुद्रया ।
> अंगुष्ठेन स्पृशेत्कुम्भं हृदा मुष्ट्याऽस्त्रवर्धनीम् ॥

(*Ibid.,* 37)

Compare the following passage :

> *cukai na ghāt mār muṭhbherī* (*Mānasa,* 2.133.4)
> *muṭhikā mār mahā dhuni garjā* (*Ibid.,* I 4.8.2)

3328 **मुष्टिक-स्वस्तिक-नृत्त-हस्त**

Muṣṭika-svastika-nṛtta-hasta : a type of hand gesture in dancing; the fist and the *svastika;* when the two hands at the end of the wrists are styled curved, they are called either the *muṣṭika-svastika* or the *kaṭaka* (*NS,* IX. 167-197). The two *kaṭakāmukha* hands are bent at the wrists and moved round.

3329 **मुष्टि-हस्त**

Muṣṭi-hasta : fist; single hand gesture can be used for holding spears, club and other objects (*NS,* IX. 55-56). a clenched fist. Fingers other than the thumb are placed tightly with their ends on the palm and the thumb is pressed over them. Then it is called the *muṣṭi*-gesture. It is used to indicate, to strike, to exercise physically, to go out, to press hard, to brandish a rod and a sword and to take hold a *kunta.* It is used often in iconography, though the fingers are not so closely fisted. It depicts the four fingers bent into the palm and the thumb set on them. It is used to express steadfastness, holding or grasping things, stronghood, holding a book, holding a shield or spear, order, imprisonment, to represent blows, exercise as in fights, exit, pressing (as the pressing of teats in milking a she-buffalo), shampooing and holding sword or staff.

People make fist in our culture and they know that they are using it an emblem for anger or hitting, and yet be quite unaware of having done so.

3330 **मुषल-मुद्रा**

Muṣala-mudrā : occurs in *BT.* "Make a fist with right hand and place it upward. Here is the *muṣala-mudrā.* " (b) make two wrists well-joined and fingers of both the hands concealed among themselves. Then move it round upward. It is the *muṣala-mudrā*" (*BT*). (c) a pair of *karkaṭa* hand symbolizes the Vaiṣṇavite deity (*VD*).

3331 **मुहूर्त**

Muhūrta : measure of astrological time = ten *daṇḍas* or 1/6 part of a day or night. According to some it is 1/16.

3332 **मूक**

Mūka : dumb, silent. *vācā mūkitam* 'kept silent' (*Mṛccha.* IX).

3333 **मूढ**

Mūḍha : superstition, superstitious ignorance in Jain terminology. It is of three types: (i) *loka-mūḍha* : general belief among people that by performing certain acts one acquires sanctity. (ii) *deva-mūḍha* : belief regarding the efficacy of propitiation of gods. (iii) *pāṣaṇḍī-mūḍha* : superstitions regarding false ascetics and so-called godmen. (b) *mūḍhatā* is a tendency to ascribe events to supernatural causes. It is the tenaency to assign cause-and effect relationships to events because of temporal association or connections that are supposed to exist between them.

3334 **मूत्रत्याग**

Mūtratyāga : urination. According to *Atharvaveda* (VII. 102), a man who urinates when standing erect, commits a sin which requires expiation, as it offends the gods of Heaven and Earth, and those of atmosphere and Death, and hence the Indian peasants adopt the squatting position when urinating. Anyone urinating facing the Sun will be hewn off at the root. The *Viṣṇu-sūtra* (LX. 1) includes a number of rules regarding urination and defecation, among which are the following: not facing the wind, fire, moon, sun, or before a woman, *guru* or a brāhmaṇ.

The tribal/Chhattisgarhi men and women stand to urinate, while the women of other regions of Madhya Pradesh sit to urinate. I have often seen Bison-horn Marias, both men and women, standing to urinate. The custom is also common among the northern Murias, and even among so advanced a tribe as the Santals I have seen women standing to urinate against a fence or wall.

The high or low force in the process of urination has been a subject of *sāmudrika.* According to Varāhamihira (LXVIII), those who urinate noisily become happy; without any sound poor. Utpala writes

मूत्रधारा पतेद् देहाद् दक्षिणावलिता यदि ।।
पार्थिवः स तु विज्ञेयः समुद्रवचनं यथा ।
द्विधारं च पतेन्मूत्रं स्निग्धं शब्दविवर्जितम् ।।
भोगवान् स तु विज्ञेयो गवाढ्यो नात्र संशयः ।
बहुधारे तथा रूक्षे सशब्दे पुरुषाधमः ।।

Here there is slight difference between the views of Varāhamihira and Utpala.

If a person passes urine in a garden or a temple and in the temple proper, the expiation mentioned is *cāndrāyaṇa,* and the cutting of a portion of his penis:

देवोद्याने तु यः कुर्यान्मूत्रोच्चारं सकृत् द्विजः ।
छिन्द्याच्छिश्नं तु शुद्ध्यर्थं चरश्चान्द्रायणं तु वा ।।
देवारतने मूत्रं कृत्वा मोहाद् द्विजोत्तमः ।
शियश्नस्योत्कर्तनं कृत्वा चान्द्रायणमथाचरेत् ।।

3335 **मूर्छना**

Mūrchanā : the rising of sounds, an intonation, duly regulated rise and fall of sounds, conducting the air and the harmony through the keys in a pleasing manner, changing the key or passing from one key to another. *Mūrchanā* is also called *mūrchā. Mūrchā* comprises the gradual raising and subsequent lowering of tunes. These tunes, called *svara,* are seven in number. They are further divided into three *grāmas,* the total number of *mūrchanā* is twenty-one.

3336 **मूर्छना-मुद्रा**

Mūrchanā-mudrā : "The middle fingers and the ring-fingers of both the hands should be made curved and other fingers should remain alternately in an extending position. This makes the *mūrchanā-mudrā* which is a gesture to control every living being" (*BT*).

3337 **मूर्च्छा**

Mūrchā : congealment, fainting, contraction, melody; a temporary condition bordering on loss of consciousness with dizziness, weakness and sometimes nausea. (b) *Mūrchā* is one of the eleven stages of *Viyoga* :

दशा नियोगहि की कहत, जू है मूर्छा नाम
जहँ न रहत सुधि कौन हूँ, कहाँ शीत कहाँ घाम ।।

(*Kāvyaprabhākara,* 416)

3338 **मूर्छित**

Mūrchita : fainting. Fainting of the king in *Vikramorvaśīya* (Act IV) is depicted by closing *(pihita)* the eyelids, by performing a *kuñcita* movement of the eyebrows; the head is in the *añcita* position and the hands in *ḍola hastas;* the mouth and face follow other approriate gestures.

3339 **मूर्छितं वाक्**

Mūrchitam vāk : the murmuring sound produced by the female during coition (Dāmodaragupta, *Kuṭṭanīmatam*, 572).

3340 **मूर्त**

Mūrta : formal, in a likeness, contrasted with *amūrta*, imageless, transcending form.

3341 **मूर्ति**

Mūrti : image, incarnation (*avatāra*), solidity, body, any solid body, form, shape, figure, person. cp.

mūrtiraṣṭarūpa : *bhūmyambuvahnivāy vākāśasūrya-candra-yajamānātmikā. mūrtimaya* possessing form.

3342 **मूर्तिकला**

Mūrtikalā : the art of image-making (*Śukranītisāra*, 4.320-22).

3343 **मूलकर्मन्**

Mūlakarman : a magical rite performed with the help of herb-roots (*Arthaśāstra*); bewitching anyone through medicine and spells.

3344 **मूलबन्ध**

Mūla-bandha : sit in *padmāsana*, breathe out and contracting the anus draw it inside. Try to maintain the contraction as long as you can.

It strengthens the sphincter muscle. cures maladies like piles, fistula and disorders of the urinary tract.

3345 **मूलाधार**

Mūlādhāra : name given in *Tantras* to a mystical circle supposed to exist above the organ of generation; the mystical circle situated above the generative organ (in *yoga*). It is the base on which a person sits. It has a lotus of four petals. The element is *pṛthvī*, earth, and the sensation connected is smel. The motor organs are the feet. The four petals have four letters of the alphabet. *Mūlādhāra* is the seat of dormant cosmic energy. It is also the seat of *parāvāk*. It is the seat of massive pleasurable sensation and voluminous organic sensation of repose.

3346 **मूलाधिष्ठान**

Mūlādhiṣṭhāna : the anus.

3347 **मूषक-मुद्रा**

Mūṣaka-mudrā : the fore-finger of the *mukula*-hand is fully extended to indicate a mouse (*Mirror of Gesture*, pp. 49-50).

3348 **मृग(पुरुष)**

Mṛga(puruṣa) : the Deer-man, whose organ is seven *aṅgulas* and the man who is given pleasure to Art-lady (*Pañcasāyaka*, 6.17). (b) in Purāṇic literature the deer symbolizes a person who is attracted towards various types of enjoyments. He is joyous at the sweet words of his and others. But he is unaware of the days and nights, which pass on quickly and deprive him of his like the wolves. The hunter is Death. The world is a garden.

3349 **मृग-मुद्रा**

Mṛga-mudrā : indication of a deer. The *candramṛga* hand, or the fore-finger of the *mṛga*-hand is raised which indicates a deer (*Mirror of Gesture*, pp. 49-50).

3350 **मृगतृष्णा**

Mṛgatṛṣṇā : deer-thirst, mirage, delusion, a false belief that cannot be modified by reasoning or a demonstration of facts. Delusion should be distinguished from illusion which is a distorted perception, and from hallucination, which is a false perception.

3351 **मृगनयनी**

Mṛganayanī : deer-eyed, having large and tremulous eyes.

3352 **मृगयायान**

Mṛgayāyāna : hunting expedition. A taboo about hunting says that a beast sleeping or having union with its mate, sucking or suckling milk, or drinking water should not be killed (*Skanda*, VI.10.12):

> सुप्तं मैथुनसंयुक्तं स्तनपानक्रियोद्यतम् ।
> हत्वा मृगं जलासक्तं नरः पापेन लिप्यते ॥

3353 **मृगशायिका**

Mṛgaśāyikā : sleeping like a hunter, a feigned sleep.

3354 **मृगशीर्ष-हस्त**

Mṛgaśīrṣa-hasta : deer-headed gesture (*NS*, 9X.86). The hand-gesture which is the supplement of the *hariṇapluta*-cadence. In it, three fingers are extended (away from the palm), and the thumb and the little finger are at right angles while the palm faces away from the body. This lively piece of miming can be seen in *Śākuntalam* (Act IV).

NS derives this gesture from *Sarpaśiras*. It is *siṁhāsya of Bālarāmabharata* and is related to *catura*. It is rarely used in iconography. The palm is raised facing outwards. The little finger is extended straight, the three other fingers are bent parallel to the base of the palm, and thumb tip touches the centre of the first finger. It is used to express fear, the face of a deer, discussion, drawing lines on the brow, cheek, patterns on the ground etc. All the fingers would remain down-turned with the thumb and the little finger raised upturned. This will make the gesture of the *mṛgaśīrṣa*. This is to suggest the sense (a) "It is enough", (b) It could be done now; to nourish, to play the game of chase, to remove sweat, to play caquetish devices, to walk and to move.

3355 **मृगी-मुद्रा**

Mṛgī-mudrā : "tips of two thumbs are joined together. The middle finger and the ring-finger are joined similarly. The fore-finger and the little finger are then to be raised up separately. This is one of the great gestures and is called *mṛgī-mudrā*" (*BT*).

3356 **मृगी(स्त्री)**

Mṛgī (*strī*) : Jyotirīśa in his *Pañcasāyaka* (2.12) calls her as Deer-lady who has tender limbs and long eyes, whose shoulders are long and delicate like fibrous stalk of creeper, whose waist is slender, who has good hair and loins, whose hands bear the beauty of the red lotus, whose neck is like conch, whose breasts are wide and whose vagina is six *aṅgulas* in depth." She is also known as lotus-lady, having interest in arts. She is also the Art-lady. (Fig. 3356)

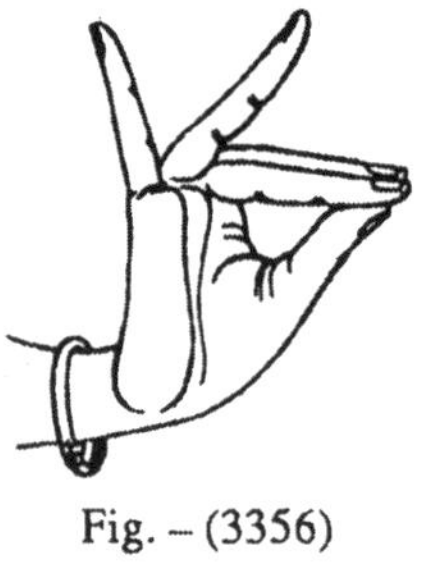

Fig. – (3356)

3357 **मृत्युञ्जय**

Mṛtyuñjaya : (a) Śiva. (b) spell warding off death.

3358 **मृत्युञ्जय-मुद्रा**

Mṛtyuñjaya-mudrā : occurs in *BT*." the *mudrā*—which is applicable also for the "ocean of milk" and an 'ox', too is called *mṛtyuñjaya*."

3359 **मृत्युसंकेत**

Mṛtyuaṅketa : death-indication. Various indications of death may be noted from the *Purāṇas*. If breath goes out and in, the right nostril continuously, the person may die within three years. If one sees a group of serpents in the sky, he may die within six months. If a person is unable to see the tip of his nose, his death is near. If he sneezes during or at the end of sexual inter course, he may die in the fifth month. If a chameleon climbs the body and speedly rises to the head, death is sure during six months. If the shadow trembles, even when the body is steady, death comes within four months. If a person sees the reflection of his body, without the head, he may die within a month (*Skanda*, IV.43.3-23).

Death-indications from dreams are also noted. If one sees himself seated singing in a vehicle, he dies soon (*Mārka*, V.25.15). The person who is led in his dream by a woman, laughing and singing, he also dies (*Skanda*, 1.2.55.74-75). Other indications in dream are seeing hair, embers, ashes, serpents and a dry river, which indicate death prior to eleven months. Falling in a hole and its suddenly closing up indicates death.

The person who could forecast the death was known as *kālavādin* (knower of time).

It is stated that after death the soul has to cross the river *Vaitaraṇī*. Now, if a cow is gifted away at the advent of death the soul can catch the tail of the cow and cross the *Vaitaraṇī* (*Skanda*, VI. 26.59):

मृत्युकाले समुत्पन्ने धेनुं यच्छन्ति ये नराः ।
तस्या लांगूलमाश्रित्य तारयन्ति सुखेन च ॥

3360 **मृदव**

Mṛdava : reversal, demerits are considered as merits, and merits as faults. According to Bharata when due to an altercation, one represents another's merits as demerits by showing cause for it and *vice versa*, it is called *mṛdavam* (*NS*, XVIII.121-122). (b) one of the thirteen constituents of *vīthī*. The merits are turned into defects and *vice-versa*, in repartee.

3361 **मृदु**

Mṛdu : one of the *śrutis* of music. (b) soft, mild, weak, patient. *Mṛdula-vāc* of gentle speech:

3362 **मृदुवाक्**

Mṛduvāk : gentle speech. Quality of the Deer-man (*Pañcasāyaka*, 2.9).

3363 **मृद्वङ्गी**

Mṛdvaṅgī : woman of tender limbs, quality of the Deer-lady (*Pañcasāyaka*, 2.12).

3364 **मृद्वारक्तं करमतिललितम्**

Mṛdvāraktam karamatilalitam : soft and red hands with beautiful fingers, quality of a Hare-man (*Ratirahasya*, 3.30.3).

3365 **मेखला**

Mekhalā : a girdle. It is given to initiate at the time of *upanayana*.

3366 **मेधा**

Medhā : retention (*NS*, XXVI.35-37), capacity for learning, intelligence. *Medhāvin* 'having retentive memory, intelligent'. The persistence of a learned act or experience during an interval of no practice. The most widely used measure of retention are (i) recall, (ii) recognition, (iii) reproduction, (iv) relearning.

3367 **मेलापक**

Melāpaka : an assembly, a fair, a union (BT), a particular ritual function of the *Tāntric* culture. *nāyakamelakam.*

3368 **मेषकुक्कुटलावक-युद्धविधि**

Meṣakukkuṭalāvaka-yuddhavidhi : fighting of cock, bull and ram etc. one of the 64 arts given by *Kāmasūtra.*

3369 **मैथुन**

Maithuna : congress, sex, copulation. *Tantra* teaches *maithuna* as one of the essential means of *Sādhanā*. Copulation gestures are of two kinds, those that emphasize insertion and those that represent pelvic thrusting. Phallic insertion is the key to the age-old Fig Sign, in which the 'male' thumb is squeezed between the female fingers. This is done with a closed hand, the thumb protruding from between the fist and second fingers, like a penis inserted through labia. Copulation signals other than the Fig Sign nearly always include the element of pelvic thrusting. There are many variants of this, some one-handed and others two-handed.

The *Skanda-Purāṇa* (V.3.22-32) says that everything in this world is marked by *bhaga* and *liṅga* (the female and male-organ, respectively).

Maithuna or sexual intercourse is regarded as one of the *pañcamakāras* in Tāntric cult (*Mahānirvāṇa*, VI.10; *Paraśurāmakalpasūtra* X.63; *Yoginītantra*, *pūrva*, VI). *Mahāmaithuna* is the 'great' or 'complete' intercourse, including ejaculation.

(b) *maithuna* is an interaction between two individuals or groups. It is then coitus or sexual intercourse.

3370 **मोक्ष**

Mokṣa : final release, salvation (*Mbh.*, XII).

3371 **मोक्षण**

Mokṣaṇa : releasing relevant sentiment's and feelings through appropriate gesture (*NS*, IX. 175)

3372 **मोक्षणी-मुद्रा**

Mokṣaṇī-mudrā : "join at first both of your hands, with clenched fists and then open gradually both the clenched fists as done before. It is the *mokṣaṇī*" (*BT*).

3373 **मोटित-उत्प्लवन**

Moṭita-utplavana : one of the five types of *utplavana.*

3374 **मोटित-मण्डल**

Moṭita-maṇḍala a type of posture.

3375 **मोट्टायित**

Moṭṭāyita : manifestation of affection; involuntary expression of affection towards an absent lover. One of the twenty *sāttvika alaṅkāras* of heroine as enumerated by Bharata. One of the natural graces of women. It occurs through the sportive imitation, amorous gestures and the like when at the mention of the lover one gets absorbed in his thoughts.

3376 **मोह**

Moha : distraction of mind, bewilderment, delusion. One of the thirty-three *vyabhicārī bhāvas* enumerated by Bharata. This transitory state is expressed by want of movement, excessive movement of a particular limb, falling down, reeling, and dazed condition (*DR*, IV.32).

(b) in philosophy, *moha* is regarded as one of the six enemies of man. In Buddhism it is regarded as belonging to the category of four universal bad properties. According to Jainism it is an *āvaraṇa* (cover) which generates worldly attachments and passions. (c) psychologically *moha* or delusion includes error, doubt, pride and negligence. Vātsyāyana and Viśvanātha have included seven tendencies under illusion which is cognitive as well as emotional. They influence action which leads to maladjustment.

3377 **मोहन**

Mohana : enchanting action suggesting relevant feelings (*NS*, IX.175); delusion, enchantment, mental error.

3378 **मोहन-कार्य**

Mohana-kārya : love-sport (*Kuṭṭanīmatam*, 392); *mohan-līlā* 'copulation-sport'.

3379 **मौन**

Mauna silence : Silences are indicated in literature as breaks in speech, which the author may fill by describing the still continuing paralinguistic (sighs, hesitation, ingressions), kinesic (gesture, postural shifts), or proxemic (distance shortening, or orientation shift) behaviours. If he does not indicate silence verbaly (*niḥśvasiti, viramati*), he can resort to a varying and eloquent series of suspension points that may take up to several lines.

Only from an acoustic point of view is silence the opposite of speech, but it is not complete as long as it is filled with consciously or unconciously displayed paralinguistic sounds (hesitation clicks, naseal egession of contempt) that simply replace verbal expression. If there is a total absence of sound, however, the semantic context of that silence is then built up and defined by its duration and by the concomitant kinesic and/or proxemic behaviours; and those interactive breaks can carry meanings, from the minimal pause of surprise or hesitation to the prolonged one that can become unbearable, or the infinitely expressive silences between Śakuntalā and her lover, in which case there is acoustic silence, but not communicative one, since Kālidāsa tells us that they speak with the flash of glances and smiles. We could refer to non-acoustic, non-visual silence, and yet time would grant that silence its meanings, and we would respond to our interlocutor according to our decoding of it. The incisive narrator recognizes the semantic importance of silences, and uses them as interactive elements—in fact, as part of the repertoires of certain characters—and differentiates what we might call paralinguistically-filled silences, kinesically—filled silences, and proxically—filled ones.

The study of the use of silences in different authors and in different types of narration is, therefore, an interesting topic that can reveal various realistic, communicative and technical functions of psycholinguistic silences, interactive silences, and socio-cultural silences; c.f.

> *ātmano mukhadoṣeṇa*
> *badhyante śukasārikāḥ* /
> *śukāstatra na badhyante*
> *maunam sarvārtha-sādhakam* //

> "In talking too much e'er engaged
> Are mynas, parrots—all encaged,
> But none confines a stark, believe
> There's nothing silence can't achieve."

3380 **मौन-कवि**

Mauna-kavi : Rājaśekhara classifies poets into two major grades: the speaker and the thinker. Not only that he locates a special cadre of poets called the *mauna-kavi* or the silent poets (*Kāvya-mīmāṁsā*, IV.pp.14-19), he denotes to an artist who draws a *pratibimba* or reflection. There is still a sect of *maunī bābā* in village India.

3381 **मौनमुद्रा**

Maunamudrā : the attitude of silence.

3382 **मौनव्रत**

Maunavrata : vow of silence, still prevalent in village India. There is a special festival *maunī amāvasyā* to observe this vow of silence. *Maunin* 'observing silence'. cf. *Mauninaḥ kalaho nāsti* 'be silent and then none of quarrel is there'.

3383 **मौलि**

Mauli : headgear. various type of headgears are found in icons. These have been described in the *mānasāra* as *jaṭā-makuṭa, kirīṭa-makuṭa, karaṇḍa-makuṭa, śirastraka, kuntala, keśabandha, dhammillaa* and *alaka-cūḍaka.*

3384 **म्लाना-दृष्टि**

Mlānā-dṛṣṭi : faded glance; a type of *sancārī-bhāva-dṛṣṭi* enumerated by Bharata.

3385 **म्लेच्छ**

Mleccha : foreigner. One who speaks an indistinct or barbarious language, one not speaking the Sanskrit language or conforming to Āryan institutions. *Baudhāyana* says:

> *gomāṁsasvādako yastu viruddham bahu bhāṣate* /
> *sarvācāravihīnaśca mleccha ityabhidhīyate* //

Foreigners were placed in the same category as the outcastes, but were not subjected to the same indignities even though they were "untouchable" by the very fact of not belonging to the *dharma* and not being initiated into the *Veda.* They were called *mleccha,* a term which means literally "Jabberer" and was used to designate all "barbarians". Many of these foreigners were ordinary travellers, others were enterprising traders or adventurers in search of fortune; but the term was applied equally to ambassadors and official delegates, as well as to monks and scholars and men of letters who had come to India either to teach or to study, mostly in Buddhist universities. The term *mleccha* was applied more specifically to invaders, and since most of these penetrated into India through the north-eastern passes, it was traditional in iconography to represent them dressed in the style of the 'cold' regions, that is to say, like the Parthians who were under Iranian or Hellenistic influence. In the same way, they were depicted with pronounced features intended to make clear their distant origin.

Although foreigners of noble rank were treated with appropriate honour and respect, it was still impossible for certain essential rules to be broken on their behalf: when they were received in the home of a brāhmaṇa family, for instance, the rites of hospitality could never be carried out fully, and no man of good caste could take a meal in their company. But special annual feast-day was reserved for the *mlecchas,* on which they all assembled together, a fact which leads up to suppose that many of them must have been long-established residents. It was, also, by no means unknown for foreigners to be absorbed in Hinduism, introduced into an appropriate caste, sometimes a high one, and assimilated into Indian society.

The *Liṅga Purāṇa* (II.3.36) mentions that the *mlecchas* had carried away one idol of Kṛṣṇa :

प्रतिमां च हरेश्चैव म्लेच्छाहत्वा ययौ पुनः ।

This incidence and such others created bias against them.

3386 **म्लेच्छभाषा**

Mleccha-bhāṣā : a foreign language, any indistinct language. Yājñavalkya in his *Yājñavalkya-smṛti* records that one should neither learn the foreign language nor bear the foreign costumes : म्लेच्छवेशो न कर्त्तव्यो म्लेच्छभाषा तथैव च । न मलेच्छभाषां शिक्षेत्' । *mleccha-bhāṣā* is known as *giṭ-piṭ* in northern village India. Talking English' so-called by the villagers unacquainted with the language: "गिटपिट गिटपिट गोरा बोले" "The English talks *giṭ-piṭ giṭ-piṭ*.

Padma-Purāṇa (Ādikhaṇḍa, 55.61) also records that there was a taboo regarding the learning of the *mleccha*-language: न म्लेच्द्भाषां शिक्षेत् ।

The word *mleccha* for a language is used for that of the Āndhra, Drāviḍa, etc. at *Tantra vārtrika* (a work of the 7th century A.D.) X.1.3. see also A. Burnell in *Indian Antiquary* (Vol. I, 1982), p. 309-310); cf. Tulasidāsa: *jimi malech bas kapilā gāī* (*Mānasa,* 3.29.8).

3387 **म्लेच्छित-विकल्प-कला**

Mlecchita-vikalpa-kalā : speaking by changing the forms of words, one of the 64 arts given in *Kāmasūtra* (1.3.16). Learning of various foreign codes, symbolic scripts and languages.

य – Ya

3388 **यक्षग्रह**

Yakṣagraha : being possessed of *yakṣa* or evil spirits.

3389 **यक्षगान**

Yakṣa-gāna : operatic plays on mythological or religious themes which are popular in south India.

3390 **यजुर्वेद**

Yajurveda : one of the four *Vedas*; The *NS* records that God Brahman adopted *abhinaya* (a gesticulation) in *nāṭya* from the *Yajurveda*. About the adoption of *abhinaya* from the *Yajurveda* we can explain in the manner of Abhinava (*NS*, I: 15-16) by saying that in the sacrificial ritual of the *Yajurveda*, the priests have to go through various actions and the mental state was produced in the priests performing the various rituals of the *Atharvaveda* having the dress such as the red turban and the like.

The *Yajurveda* consists of sacrificial formulas. It is two-fold: *Black* and *White*.

3391 **यजुर्वेद-मुद्रा**

Yajurveda-mudrā : gesture symbolizing the *Yajurveda*. Extend the ring-finger and curve the thumb at the roots (*VD*).

3392 **यज्ञ**

Yajña : sacrifice: Vedic religion; when it was systematized, became mainly a religion of sacrifices. The Brāhmaṇs attached to the *Vedas* give detailed instructions on how to perform sacrifices, what hymns are to be repeated at each stage of proceedings, what types of altars, and sacrificial pits are to be constructed for each kind of sacrifice. The killing of animals constituted on important items of Vedic ritual. On the regeneration of Hinduism after the decay of Buddhism, animal sacrifice lost much of its importance in the cities and villages, but remained as a part of tribal life in the forest. Though Brāhmaṇs then generally disapproves of animal sacrifices (except in Tāntric rites), these are widely prevalent among the lower castes and the aborigines. In annual village festivals knows as *Jātrās*' it is customary to sacrifice a buffalo. The shrines of *Kālī* even now claim a large number of victims in several parts of India. The animal generally sacrificed being sheep or goats. Of the species of birds, the goddess has a preference for chicken.

Manu (1. 88-90) thinks that *yajñas* are to be performed by all those who are twice-born. A house holder, according to Manu, possesses as it were five slaughter houses. They are the hearth, the grinding stone, the broomstick, the pestle and mortar and the water pitcher (III. 68). In order to expiate the sins committed by the householder, on account of using these objects, he should daily perform five "sacrifices". (Fig. 3392)

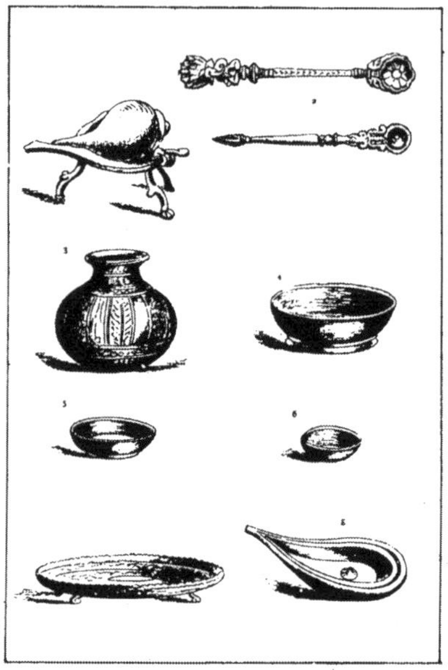

1. Shell for pouring libations. 2. Brass and Copper Sruvas or Spoons. 3. Lota, or Ewer. 4. Sampatni. 5. Katori. 6. A smaller Katori. 7. Tali. 8. Arghya Patra.

Fig. – (3392)

3393 **यज्ञोपवीत**

Yajñopavīta : sacred thread worn by the brahmacārin during his *upanayana* or initiation into student life. It is a symbol of *dvijatva* or rebirth (being consecrated) which is to be used throughout life. Consisting of nine strands in a set of three, its size varies according to caste status. Each strand is a symbol of a deity. Religious acts done without wearing *yajñopavīta* are futile. Taking meal without wearing it makes one liable to expiation (Kālidāsa, *Māl.* 4.67). Cf. *dvij cihna janeu ughār tapī* (*Mānasa*,7.101.7).

3394 **यति**

Yati : pause, caesura. a short pause in reading or reciting the line, pause in metre, pause in a song. (b) an ascetic, medicant, that has no fixed home, one who wanders or goes *yo yāti sa yatiḥ proktaḥ* (*Sk. P.* VI 185.33). (c) as many, as often, how many (pronoun). (d) the paradox of *yati* and *pati* is widely accepted in Hindu mythology. This problem was intensified by uncertainties regarding Śiva's place in the historical development of Hinduism. The two roles of Śiva are enacted simultaneously. Śiva wears the garb of a *yogī*, but his behaviour is that of a lover in separation. In fact, he is *yati* because he is *pati*. This may be read as a contradiction but psychologically it is entirely logical.

So completely are the roles of ascetic and lover combined that the myth-makers themselves often confuse them. The seven sages say to Pārvatī, 'How can you enjoy the pleasures of the body with an ascetic (*yati*) like him, so terrifying and a disgusting?' (*Matsya*, 154,332). But in another version of the same text they say, 'How can you enjoy the pleasures of the body with a husband (*pati*) like him, so terryfying and disgusting? (*Matsya*, 154.332). The sense remains the same in both readings, for the two roles are being compared and in fact interchanged.

3395 **यथा नृत्ते तथा चित्रे**

Yathā nṛtte tathā citre : as indicated in dances, so it be utilised in painting (*VD*).

3396 **यथारसं रसानुकूलं अभिनयति**

Yathārasam rasānukūlam abhinayati : Mālavikā (*Mālavikāgnimitram*, Act II) does the *abhinaya* according to the proper *rasa*, which is *śṛṅgāra*.

3397 **यदृच्छा**

Yadṛcchā : accidental as opposed to *svabhāva* or natural. *Tarka-rahasya-dīpikā* (15) defines *yadṛcchā* as a denial of causation altogether according to which various pleasures and pains of people appear suddenly, just as the flying of a crow has no connection with the falling of a palm—fruit (*Kākatālīya*).

3398 **यदृच्छालाभ**

Yadṛcchālābha : gain by chance; *yadṛcchāvāda* 'doctrine of chance which maintains that the words is attracted by chance alone and there is no outside agent to control. Cp. *Śvetāśvataropaniṣad.*

3399 **यदृच्छाशब्द**

Yadṛcchāśabda : a word used for one's desire for a thing.

3400 **यदृच्छा-संवाद**

Yadṛcchā-saṁvāda : accidental meeting, accidental likeness.

3401 **यन्त्र**

Yantra : (a) image (architecture), symbol of deity, a diagrammatic image, a symbol key to vision of unity, icon, device, machine, geometrical representation of a deity. (b) a mystical diagram painted with minerals on something or on the ground at the time of worship. The worshipper imagines that the deity, which is being worshipped by him, for the time being resides in the diagram in accordance with his prayer. The diagrams differ in form according to the forms of the desired deity (*Tantra*). *Yantras* are drawn or engraved on cloths, paper, leaves, stones and metals (*Kulārṇava*, VI, XVII; *Saundaryalaharī* XI, *Tantrasāra* 312). (c) *yantra* has been adopted in the Western psychology which means "a visual pattern used in meditation". (Fig. 3401)

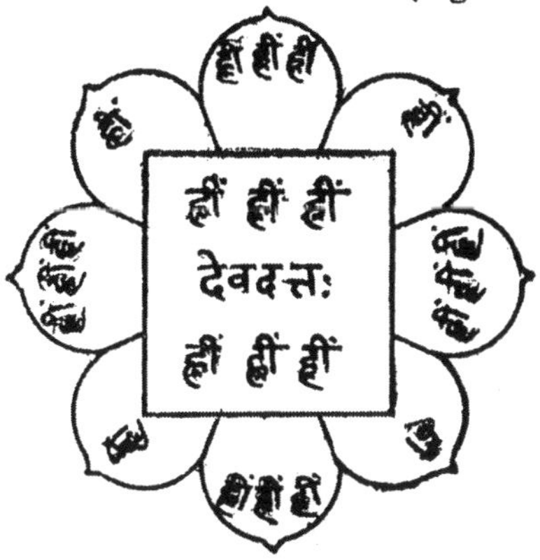

Fig. – (3401)

3402 **यन्त्रमातृका-कला**

Yantramātṛkā-kalā : framing mystical diagrams, one of the 64 arts given in *Kāmasūtra* (1.3.16).

3403 **यन्त्रित-वाच्**

Yantrita vāc : tongue-tied, forced to be silent.

3404 **यभ्-युम्**

Yabh-yum : goddess-in-union-with-god. It is a characteristic feature of Tibetan Buddhist iconography. *Yabh* means father and *yum* mother; hence the combined word means the father in the embrace of the mother.

3405 **यमपट्टिका**

Yamapaṭṭikā : a piece of canvas on which internal torments were depicted.

3406 **यममुद्रा**

Yamamudrā : (1) ascending seven notes of music (*Sāma-Veda*). (2) *pāśa* with the left and *sūcī* with the right hand, indicate *Yama*, the death God.

3407 **यमुना-हस्त**

Yamunā-hasta : the river Yamunā. The *rekhā*-hand moving upward and downward indicates river Yamunā (*Mirror of Gesture*, p. 48).

3408 **ययाति-हस्त**

Yayāti-hasta : *tāmracūḍa hasta* represents the mythical king Yayāti (*Mirror of Gesture*, p. 47).

3409 **यवनानी**

Yavanānī : script of the *yavanas*.

3410 **यशः पटह**

Yaśaḥ paṭaha : drum.

3411 **याञ्चा**

Yāñcā : (*Bṛhaddevatā*, 144-60, *NS* 18.19): begging, request; form of speech and thought; also known as *arthanā* (*Arthaśāstra*, 11. 10.5).

3412 **याज्य-मन्त्र**

Yājya-mantra : formula of sacrifice (*Smṛti*).

3413 **यातुधान**

Yātudhāna : one who employs black-magic, the sorcerer. It is clear that the help of the sorcerer was sought in Vedic period at the time when the individual was confronted by disease or danger or when he desired the fulfilment of some intense wish or when he wished to ensure health and prosperity. It is still common in the tribal folk. It is also clear that the incantations and amulets give one the courage to face the struggle, overcome the danger and attain the objective desired - to attain the *aihikaphalas* here and now.

The mental diseases referred to in *Atharvaveda* are still common in the aborigines. They can be classified into (a) severe mental disorders like *unmāda*, insanity; and (b) mild deviation generated by *krodha* (rage), *moha* (sexual and other delusions), *śoka* (depression), *īrṣyā* (jealousy) and evil dreams. It is pointed out that while the hymns of *Atharvaveda* are rich in therapy, they are poor in terms of description of symptoms.

3414 **यात्रा**

Yātrā : literally it means setting out or going from one place to another (*Kāmasūtra* 1.4) and as such it also means procession. Derivatively, it has come to mean a festival, as in *snāna-yātrā* (ablution-festival), *hindola-yātrā* (swing-festival) *rāsa-yātrā* (festival of circular dance), *ratha yātrā* (car-festival), *dola-yātrā* (holi-festival) etc. Subsequently the term came to mean theatrical performance on mythological and religious themes such as *Kṛṣṇa-yātrā*, *Rāmayātrā*, etc. Bhavabhūti refers to *yātrā* of *Kalāpriyanātha* when his *Uttararāmacarita* was going to be presented. *Yātrā* in the sense of an open air performance of *nāṭakas* was used commonly as a means of mass contact by the Vaiṣṇavas.

The *Arthaśāstra* (13.5.1) mentions *yātrā* held in honour of deities. Various matters used to be represented as superhuman (*Ibid.*, 5.2.30) It is still prevalent among the tribes of Bastar with the word *Jātrā*. In the Hill Maria it has the Gondi equivalent *Kaqsār*. It is one of the greatest religious journey. It is celebrated from the end of January till April or so on. Apart from the religious significance, this journey-festival has lot of social significance. The year of hard and constant labour in the productions of crops has ended and before the another begins, there is time for joy and festivities. Since boys and girls of different clans meet in the *Jātrā*, they begin friendship and search their partner in life. Also, meeting of different villages in the festival strengthens the feeling of unity and oneness.

The formal announcement that *Jātrā* is to be held in a certain village on a certain date is conveyed by three young boys or messengers. They go from blowing their hunting-horns.

Clan-gods of other clans are brought to the village where the *Jātrā* is to be held. Those are accompanied by villagers of concerned villages. On the next morning the clan-gods are taken to the stream where young boys proceed them with their drums and receive the gods there with drum sounds. The *Pen-Waddai* then bathes the gods, their teeth are ritually cleansed and they are dressed with coloured cloths and peacock feathers and then taken back to the village in a procession.

Liquor is consumed quite liberally and by the time it is afternoon, all are quite high in their spirits. Slowly the males reassemble at one open field and wild and vigorous dancing starts. Some become possessed by gods. People also smear one another with the red substance known as *lālī*.

Parties of young boys and girls from different villages start coming by about sunset. They are already-well-dressed and decorated having taken care to appear their best just before entering the village. When all village parties assemble, they also enter the open field and start dancing. This is a night-long affair. It is quite a flirtatious one rich with lot of sexual gestures. The songs are in honour of the gods and the couples occasionally slip away to the jungle to have more intimate body contact. The most colourful celebration is that of Orchā, where the clan-god is brought from Japaguṇḍā. From miles around, the villages send their youth to dance at the Orchā Kaqsār.

(b) mime, religious mime. Prof. Hillebrandt traces the origin of drama in Vedic *yātrās*. In the *yātrā* performances of Bengal, or *Jātrās* of Bastar; music, song and dance are as important as the dialogue. Formerly the *yātrās* had their themes concerned with *Śakti*.

3415 **यान**

Yāna : vehicle, journey: It was a custom to perform religious rituals while one was prepared to go for a journey. When Kṛṣṇa is said to have started on his journey with Akrūra, on his left side was a jar with leaves and fruits in it and decorated with sandal-paste and other marks; to the right stood a brāhmaṇa, fire and a lamp. There was also a woman, with a son and her husband alive. There were also *dūrvā*-shoots, white flowers and grains. He had his reflection in the ghee, honey, silver, gold and curd (*Brahmavaivarta*, II. 71. 6-10). (b) vehicle, or the way which carries an adept to the highest goal. Two general divisions of Buddhism are known as *hīna-yāna* and *mahā-yāna*.

3416 **यायावर**

Yāyāvara : wandering ascetic.

3417 **युक्तपिप्पलक**

Yuktapippalaka : with teats raised.

3418 **युक्तिशास्त्र**

Yuktiśāstra : pragmatics, the science of what is suitable. *Yukti* means justification or reason or critical intelligences. *Mahābhārata* (V. 30.49) mentions the concept of pragmatics, : appropriateness of action in drama is also the subject of *yuktiśāstra* (*DR.* 1.43). It is termed as *kāryayukti.*

3419 **युग**

Yuga : four ages in Indian mythological tradition. In the first *yuga*, called the *Kṛta* or *Satya*, the duration of which is computed to be 4,800 years of god (each year of gods being 360 years of men), there is perfect righteousness and the *dharma* is said be on all its four feet. The next three *yugas*, viz. *Tretā*, *Dvāpara* and *Kali*, consisting of respectively of 3,600, 2,400, and 1,200 years of gods, *dharma* gradually decreases by one-fourth and so does righteousness. These four *yugas* together make a *mahāyuga* or a *manvantara*, and 2000 such *manvantaras* make a *kalpa*. However there are divergent views in the texts in counting the *yugas*. In astronomical texts a *yuga* denotes a very limited span of time.

3420 **युगधर्म**

Yugadharma : concept of *dharma* caused by time and age which introduces the element of adaptation and adjustment with the changing demands of time and space (*Manu* X. 98; *Mbh.* XII. 35. 266)

3421 **युगनद्ध**

Yuganaddha : iconic representation of god and goddess symbolising the male and the female principles. The *yuganaddha* symbolises unique harmony and interpretation of masculinity and feminity. For a man, woman is the material object of concentration, a goddess for meditation, and a symbolic truth for comprehension.

3422 **युगबोध**

Yugabodha : The Hindu idea about social progress was quite the reverse of modern theory. The Hindu sages did not accept the modern theory that civilisation advances as time marches forward. They thought that in the earliest period, social life was full of virtues and deterioration of social virtues and moral values take place as the society passes from one age to another. According to them, the *Kṛtayuga* was full of virtues. In *Tretā* the society passed three-fourth virtues and one-fourth vice; in *Dvāpara* virtues and vices were equal, and in *Kaliyuga* virtue is only one-fourth.

3423 **युगान्तबन्धु**

Yugāntabandhu : companion in distress.

3424 **युग्मचारिन्**

Yugmacārin : copulating. *Joṛī* is yoke-fellow, friend, ally and above all husband or wife, and *jānwar-joṛī*, means a friend of the same age, sharing the same interests and delights.

3425 **युवजन**

Yuvajana : younger generation. In this century Indian women have undergone a social revolution rather more far-reaching and radical than that of men. In fact this quiet revolution is the most important element in the social changes which have occurred in modern India. Women have proved themselves more than equal to their counterparts, as yet, only partially accompanied emancipation, and have not cost their essential feminity. Even when they become highly competent in professional life Indian women show no sign of acquiring those masculine traits of behaviour which are familiar in their counterparts in Anglo-Saxon countries. Their sense of power is already sufficiently deeply rooted in, and identified with, the family, especially in those women who are over forty-five, for them to feel no need to resort to the kinds of aggressive assertion which intensely competitive, male-dominated Western societies demand. This is one more reason why mother-dependence does not automatically assume the character of a neurosis in the Indian male; the balance of masculinity and feminity is less distorted by the emancipated woman. The prudent woman takes care not to contravene society's most basic ideas of what a woman should do and be, but even then many have acted with courage to defy conventions they thought outmoded or unnecessarily restrictive.

3426 **योग**

Yoga : (a) in philosophy it means the restraint of the functions of the mind; concentration of the mind;. (b) in *Smṛti* literature it means acquisition of what has not been acquired, trick, connection, relation, power and zeal. (c) *yoga* means union and identification. Identity with the joys and sorrows of everyone, extend your horizons, live above the pettiness of life. *Yoga* stands for both physical and mental well-being. It comes to suffering humanity as a blessing in the guise of psycho-somatic treatment. It comes to the seekers of truth as the shortest cut to God-realization. Indeed *yoga* is a blueprint of perfection. You can consider it as a programme, a method, and a philosophy. It is a programme in so far as it assumes the shape of a movement with definite aims and objects. It is a method in the sense that *yogic* practices are methodically pure. (d) the practice of asceticism by physical mortification and meditation. (e) one who performs the *yoga*, is known as *yogī* (*jogī*). The *jogī* is a familiar figure in the life of the people and there are various sayings about him. *Jogī jogī laṛen, khopṛan ke dām*, or 'when *jogīs* fight skulls are smashed', that is, skulls which some of them use a begging-cups, not their own skulls, and with the implication that they have nothing else to break; *jogi jugat jāne nahīn, kapṛe raṅge to kyā huā*, 'If the *jogī* does not know the magic, what is the use of dyeing his clothes'? *Jogikā laṛkā khelegā to sānp*, or 'If a snake-charmer's son plays, he plays with a snake'.

3427 **योगक्षेम**

Yoga-kṣema : (a) sacrificial acts performed with *śrauta* or *smārta* fire and charitable gifts such as construction of tanks, parts etc. (b) royal minister and *purohita* who bring about the welfare of the people. (c) umbrella, chowrie, weapons, shoes and the like. (d) comfortable life or easy and happy way of maintenance or annuity descending from the father (to the son) at a royal place. (e) *yoga* means ship and *kṣema* means fort. (f) the wealth gained by a learned Brāhmaṇa resorting to a rich man for his maintenance. (g) acquisition of what has not been acquired and the preservation of what is acquired (*Gītā*, IX. 22). (h) welfare. The main functions of the king according to Kauṭilya was to ensure the *yogakṣema* (*A*, 1.4.11) of the people. Kauṭilya was of the opinion that state should not only protect the people from anarchy but it should also ensure *yogakṣema. Yoga* meant successful accomplishment of an object and *kṣema* meant peaceful, undisturbed enjoyment of that object and protection was necessary for both. It implies the idea of welfare, well-being including the idea of prosperity, happiness and so on.

3428 **योगचूर्ण**

Yogacūrṇa : a chemical powder referred to in Sanskrit literature, the inhalation of which induces stupor. *Yogadhūli* is a mystic dust (*Agni.*, 123, 27-28).

3429 **योगमाया**

Yogamāyā : cosmic-power.

3430 **योगमुद्रा**

Yogamudrā : one of the four *hasta-mudrās* known to Indian Iconography in the context of meditation. "Tie the middle-finger with the ring-finger and the thumb. Making the middle finger extended, curved and up-turned with the two, affix it to the rectum point chanting the *mantra* in the state of a nude and prostrate before the God with eight limbs. This is called *yogabandha* or *yogamudrā*." (*BT*). (b) Sit in *padmāsana* with crossed legs and place the palms on the heels. Slowly bend forward while exhaling and touch the ground with your forehead or chin. Retain this pose as long as you can comfortably remain, while breathing in and out as usual. Breathe out and come back to the former position while breathing in. You can also keep the hands at the back, catching hold of the left wrist with your right hand. This pose removes abdominal disorders and helps in concentration.

3431 **योगवर्तिका**

Yogavartikā : chemically prepared stick for generating light without fire.

3432 **योगविभाग**

Yoga-vibhāga : a device by which a portion of a grammatical rule is cut off and treated as an independent rule. This has been adopted in the School of Pāṇini. For example, Pāṇini's rule *Saha Supā* (II.1.4) has been split up into two, *viz. Saha* and *Supā.*

3433 **योजना**

Yojanā : union, connection, grammatical construction, any linking between two phenomena, whether physical or mental. Cf.

amantramakṣaram nāsti
nāsti mūlamanauṣadham
ayogyaḥ puruṣo nāsti
yojakastotra durlabhaḥ ||

"No word is there that's not a spell,
No root as herb that does not serve.
No man is there that doesn't deserve,
We need that one who wields them all."

3434 **योनि**

Yoni : a figure representing the female genitals, serving as the formal symbol under which the female power in nature is worshipped; vagina: *Madhyā kṛśā* - middle part which is small is supposed to be a factor of ideal beauty in Sanskrit literature.

Like Sanskrit literature, a small vagina is admired in Baiga society. The Baiga distinguishes between a vagina that is *tip-tip* or small and right, and one that is *gus-gus*, enlarged by frequent intercourse and child-bearing. There are many folk—tales on penis and vagina among the tribes of Madhya Pradesh.

The best shape of the vagina is said to be that of an *aśvattha* - leaf (*Garuḍa P.*, 1. 64.15). Other characteristics mentioned are, that it should be well set (not floppy), elevated like the back of a tortoise (*kūrmapṛṭhonnata*), of the shape of a jar (*kalaśa*), of the hue of the orb of the moon (*Bhav. P., Brāhma Khaṇḍa*, 30-31). In addition to these, other characteristics mentioned are that it should have hair like that of mouse (*ākhuroma*) with the glans covered, having the hue of a red lotus or the interior of an oven, and the "nose" visible (*dṛśya-nāsa*), looking like the hoof of a deer (*Sk.P.*, IV. 37.37). A woman who has her pudenda with a whirl like the conch is said not to hold a foetus; likewise the pudenda flat like the pot-sherd, like the leaf of a bamboo or a cane, having the "nose" elevated, having the hair like that of an elephant (*gajaroma*), curved in shape, and ugly, is bad (*Ibid.* 40-41):

शंखवर्तो भगो यस्याः सा गामिह नेच्छति ।
चिपिटः खर्पराकारः किंकरोपपदो भगः ॥

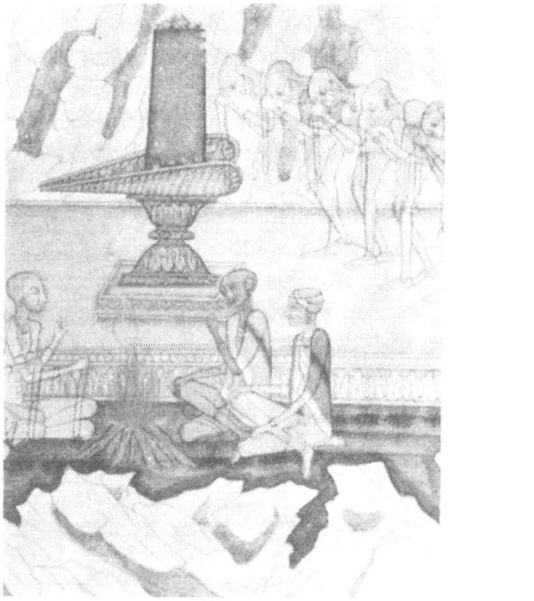

Fig. – (3434)

One with the hue of the flower of seasame, having a protrusion like a hoof, of the shape of a mortar, with a wide opening and such other defective characteristics is said to indicate poverty, sorrow or even death. (*Bhav. P.*) If the upper portion (*bhāla*) of the pudenda, having a turning to the left is fleshless and curved, it indicates widowhood (*Sk.P.*). It is said that the vagina which is devoid of hair (*aromaka*) and well set indicates that the woman would be a queen (*Bhav. P.*, 30). (Fig. 3434)

There are archaeological evidences of the cult of generative organs and numerous references to sex rites designed to secure fertility of the fields seemed to belong to the special competence of women who were the first cultivators of the soil and whose power of child-bearing had, in primitive thought, a sympathic effect on the vegetative forces of the earth. The woman was not only the symbol of generation, but the actual producer of life. Her organs and attributes were thought to be endowed with generative power, and so they were the life giving symbols. In the earliest phases of social evolution, it was this maternity that held the field, the life producing mother being the central figure of religion. This primitive empirical and analogical belief in the equation of earth and woman, of natural and human fertility has connected the mystery of nature with that of human body in tantrism and tribalism which hold that the birth of the universe is the result of the same, or a similar process as the birth of the human beings.

3435 **योनिकण्डम्**

Yonikaṇḍam : itching, itch for sex in women in the vaginal part. *Padma-Purāṇa* (*Pātāla-khaṇḍa*, 108. 23-24) indicates about self-sex in the case of widows. *Kalā*, a widow, says that many are the ways of a woman. In widowhood, once a woman resorted to a concealed place, when she had an itch for sex: *yonikaṇḍam samāsādya divā yadi vā niśi;* she released her wearing cloth, widened her vulva with her hands at its lips and censured the vagina saying, "What have you started, O vagina?" or is the male organ sinful if it enters you?" When the itch did not yet stop, she inserted her finger inside the vagina and acting various movements thereof, she smote the vulva getting it yet wider, ultimately she embraced the foot of her bedstead pressing her breasts against it (*Ibid.*, 25-29):

अतोऽपि कण्डूसम्भूतौ प्रवेशयेदथाङ्गुलीम् ।
विचित्रचेष्टारं कृत्वा तु कण्डूबुद्धेरतः परम् ॥
मर्दयित्वा कराभ्यां तत् संताड्य च विवृत्य च ।
असकृद्धुन्वती पादौ विवृतास्याति दुःखिता ॥
खट्वाकाष्ठमथालिङ्ग्य स्तनपीडं यथाप्रियम् ।
अथो विचित्रचित्तत्वं ततस्तद्घृष्टता भवेत् ॥

3436 **योनिपुष्प**

Yonipuṣpa : black *aparājitā* flower serving as *maithuna* (sexual inter course) symbol (*Paraśurāma-kalpasūtra*, X. 63).

3437 **योनिमुद्रा**

Yonimudrā : (a) a particular position of fingers in Tantra-*śāstra*. "Place the little finger down-faced on the up-stretched left palm and put three extended right fingers over it. Next, place the two, the little finger and the forefinger, on the thumb and other fingers should remain joined among themselves. This makes a *yonimudrā*." (*BT*). (b) female obscene signs are less common than phallic gestures, but a number of them do exist. Many people employ the "squashed-circle" gesture. The circle is made by the thumb and forefinger, making it more reminiscent of the outline of the female genitals. According to *Brahmāṇḍa-Purāṇa* (II. 4.42.2) in *yoni-mudrā* the tips of the middle fingers to be a bit curved and posed on the index-finger; the little-fingers to be in the midst of the *anāmikās*. All should be joined together and present by the thumb.

3438 **योन्यन्तरी भाषा**

Yonyantarī bhāṣā : language of non-human beings (*NS*, XVIII. 25-63). One of the four languages occurring in Sanskrit dramas. It is used by the rustics and foresters and has its origin in animals—domestic or wild and in birds of various species. It follows the conventional practices (*nāṭyadharmī*).

3439 **यौवन**

Yauvana : youth, bloom of youth, puberty, host of young women. The youth is portrayed as the unstable period in life. The *Śukanāśopadeśa* episode in *Kādambarī* confirms the same. According to a Chhattisgarh proverb youth regards no caste or out-caste:

> *bhūkh na mānay jūṭhā bhāt*
> *piās na mānay dhobī ghāṭ*
> *nīṅd na mānay marghaṭ khāt*
> *javānī na mānay jāt-kujāt.*
>
> (Hunger regards not unclean food,
> thirst minds not the washing place;
> sleep objects not to the bier as a bed
> and youth regards not caste or out-caste.

3440 **रक्त**

Rakta : coloured, red, passionate (song, blood); *rakta-kaṇṭhin* 'of pleasing note or sound, sweet-voiced'; *raktacūrṇa* vermillion' *raktadantikā*: having red teeth, Durgā; *rakta-dṛś* red-eyed, *kapota*; *rakta-nepathya* clad in red garments; *raktapa* 'drinking blood', mosquito; *rakta-paṭa* 'having red garment, ascetic in red garment'; *raktapāta* 'blood-shed'; *rakta-bhāva* 'red'. Red colour is both ascetic and erotic. It is the traditional colour for a bride's dress, indicating *śakti*.

3441 **रक्त-मुखराग**

Rakta-mukharāga : red colour of face in *karuṇa* and *vīra rasas.*

3442 **रक्तलोचन**

Raktalocana : having red eyes, the pigeon.

3443 **रक्तवर्ण**

Rakta-varṇa : red colour. The colour red frequently appears in Indian poetry of every kind. It is said that its popularity among the Hindus is due to the fact that it is the colour of blood, and that the *sindūr* or virmilion powder, so often used in Hindu worship, on the parting of the woman's hair and in marriage ceremonies, is a blood-substitute. The vermilion is part of what is known as *sohāg*, the lucky gift which is given at the marriage of a Hindu girl in parts of India and which also includes *kumkum* or red powder, and *mahāwar* or red balls of cotton wool.

The aboriginals also are very fond of the red colour. A poem from *Amarakaṇṭaka* depicts the same:

> You of the red jacket
> And shining armlets
> Why did you enchant me
> With the magic of your eyes
> My mind bids me go
> But my heart is sad
> I stand in the midst of water
> And yet I die of thirst.

But the aboriginals do not use either *sindūr* or *kumkum* unless they have come into contact with civilization. They are not accustomed to throw red-coloured water at *Holī*, nor do they use red in the marriage ceremonies. Yet there is no doubt that they, like the Hindus, are very fond of this colour, and it is said that a red *sārī* or a red turban at once awakes desire. It is possible that among a people who have no need of a blood-substitute, since they offer actual blood in sacrifice, the affection for this colour is purely a practical one. The *sārīs* supplied by the Baniās to this part of India are generally of only two kinds, white and red; the majority of Gond and Pardhān women wear white, but when a girl is enterprising enough to buy a red *sārī* or fortunate enough to have a lover who will give her one, she at once becomes an object of excited admiration.

3444 **रक्त-वसन**

Rakta-vasana : clothed in red, a Brāhmaṇa in the fourth order of life. It symbolized creative female power, sexuality and all the energy of passion and positive emotion.

3445 **रक्ताक्ष**

Raktākṣa : red eyed, fearful.

3446 **रक्षण**

Rakṣaṇa : protecting or maintaining relevant sentiments and feelings through appropriate gesture (*NS*, IX. 175).

3447 **रक्षाकरण्डक**

Rakṣākaraṇḍaka : amulets. Wearing of amulets is a special category of Protective Behaviour (*Śākuntalam*). There are literally hundreds of different 'lucky symbols' that have been carried or worn by Indian people over the centuries. We have a reference in *Śākuntalam* of Kālidāsa in which Bharata is shown as wearing an amulet. Again the practice is still alive almost everywhere, despite the scientific age in which we live. As before, people smile and admit that it is all 'a lot of nonsense', but *tābīja* (in Hindi) is still prevalent and they do this nonsense.

3448 **रक्षाबन्धन**

Rakṣābandhana : the custom of tying a knot on the wrist of another denoting solicitation of protection, usually a sister from brother. It falls on the day of full moon in Śrāvaṇa (Aug. - Sept.) and is observed both by the Hindus and Jains.

3449 **रघु-मुद्रा**

Raghu-mudrā : *ardhapatāka* twisted upward, touching to body, placed by the side, to indicate the mythical ruler Raghu (*Mirror of Gesture,* p. 47).

3450 **रङ्ग**

Raṅga : colour. Colours have messages to deliver (*DR.* III. 4). White colour implies the purity of the soul. Perhaps the most interesting messages are sent out by red. In terms of traffic signals, the colour of course means stop. But when we come to social arena, red is a colour of joy, worn by brides and forbidden to widows.

The three colours that are most associated with sex are, it appears to be, black, red and white. The first shows sophistication and mourning - somewhat contray impressions, since a widow's black implies no more legitimate outlet for sex. The next colour shows joy, and the promise of an initiation into sex in one culture, and an invitation to the illicit in another. The last is almost universally held to mean purity and hence virginity, but in this country it is also the colour of mourning and grief.

This does not mean that all other colours are thrown into shades by the big three. Green, for instance is commonly associated with fertility and its rites. Pink sends off messages of a diluted red, asking for sexual attention in a less obvious way.

Amidst all this theorising, it is interesting to note that men have taken to wearing brighter colours in the office atmosphere, hardly the traditional repository of sexual activity. Conversely, women who want to make it in a man's world tend to wear duller clothes so as to tone down any sexual messages.

(b) colour prejudice in India may be seen while selecting a spouse. The new bride is an object of prying and pawing curiosity, every detail of her costume, ornaments and behaviour loudly commented on, the colour of her skin the source of discussion among the men. (c) despite the fact that the racist theory for the origin of the caste system has been disproved, there is no doubt that the white Āryan despised the black *dāsa*. There are contemptuous references to the black colour of the Indigen in many ancient and classical texts. The connotation of black skin with menial status has never charged since ancient times. Indians are extremely conscious of the gradations in skin colour, from the so-called "fair" (*gaurā*) and 'wheaten' (*geṅhuā*) to the dark (*kālā*), as may be seen from the matrimonial advertisements which are a common feature of Indian newspapers.

3451 **रचना**

Racanā : making, style in literature. Cp. *ākalpa-racanā* 'arrangement of adornment' (*DR,* II. 62).

3452 **रजक**

Rajaka : dyer, a member of the dramatic troupe (NS).

3453 **रजकी**

Rajakī : woman of the washerman caste who serves as a female partner of the Tāntric aspirant. (b) any woman in the third day of her menstruation (*Tantrasāra,* 627). (c) why there is *rajakī* and no *rajaka*? It is a question which has haunted the tribal minds. They have conjectured it in different ways. The Bison-horn Maria of Bastar have the curious belief that men (*rajaka*), not women, were originally subject to menstruation or menstrual period. They used to tie hollow bamboos to their organs to catch the discharge. Once - according to one legend - a girl was laughing at a man in this distressing and inconvenient condition, and he lost his temper and threw the bamboo at her. Yet other legends ascribe the origin of menstruation to a wound. There were formerly teeth in the vagina and when these were removed, the wound was not wholly healed. Once the vagina was in the crick of leg behind the knee - you can still see its shape, - but a hen pecked at it and the frightened organ jumped for safety to its hiding place between the thighs. But it was heart and still bleeds every month at the recollection.

3454 **रजस्**

Rajas : the second attribute; that constituent of *prakṛti* which is of the nature of pain and is mobile (*cala*) and stimulating (*upastambhaka*). It gives rise to wrath, greed, egoism, worldly activity and boastfulness. (b) dust, pollen, small particle, darkness, mid-region, impurity, menses, sin, impure, passion, anger. The vernacular of menstruation in Sanskrit as well as in modern Indian languages and dialects may be grouped under the following subheadings: impurity, periodicity or time, explicit or implicit (reference to blood or colour red), reference to visitors, mention of persons, illness, inconvenience or disability, references to material culture, blossoming of flower, burst of a pitcher, untouchability, and sexual unavailability. Menstruation is "call to water" (*yete artā*) in Gondi and 'the blossoming of flower' (*phūlasundarī*) in Halbi.

3455 **रजस्वला**

Rajasvalā : full of dust, menstruous, menstruation. The Hindus have many superstitions connected with menstruation in women. Women are considered ceremonially impure during this period. Even a Brāhmaṇ woman degenerates into *cāṇḍālī*, the lowest of the low, once her period starts. It is only proper that such a woman should be excluded from descent society during her uncleanliness. Hence she is not allowed to enter the house, cook meals or touch a clean person. She lives in solitude during this period. In villages, every Hindu household has an outhouse set apart for this purpose, and women, during their periods of uncleanliness, live in these houses. Their meals are served here and they are expected not to show themselves about as their sight may bring calamity to all people. In the cities this seclusion is not possible among middle classes who live in small flats and they usually set apart a corner of a room for unclean women. Such women are not allowed to use clean clothes or good furniture but must squat on torn or dirty mats as untouchable outcastes. In houses, which have no servants, the male member or children do the cooking as the unclean woman is not allowed to enter the kitchen or cook food. It is very common for school boys and girls to stay away from classes and for clerks to ask leave on the ground that the lady of the house is "out of home" which is the euphemistic way of expressing the monthly troubles of women of India. So much for ceremonial uncleanliness of women.

The same rule applies with the tribal women. During her period a woman may neither cook nor enter the kitchen, she may not fetch the water, touch a grain-bin or a grinding stone. She must not go near any cultivated field lest the crops will fail. She may have no sexual intercourse, and must sleep apart from her husband. Any breach of these prohibitions is believed to have disastrous supernatural consequences, even if it remains hidden from human witnesses. Verrier Elwin quotes the case of a Baiga magician whose powers were destroyed by his wife's inadvertent infringement of a taboo. One day she went to clean his shrine not knowing that her period had begun. Suddenly the central pillar of the shrine broke of its own accord and the place became foul and stinking. The terrified woman ran to her husband, but when he approached the shrine, the voice of a god threatened him with destruction and death of his children. Though he fasted and purified the shrine, the prophesied disaster overtook him and his family. All his children became insane and died, and the magician himself lost most of his knowledge and skill. This case demonstrates the automatic action of supernatural sanctions which may set in motion by mere mischance, and without any moral guilt on the part of those affected.

Grigson (1937) has studied in detail the custom of Hill Marias in regard to menstruation, pregnancy and birth, but his notes on the Bison-horn Marias, as he says, are 'considerably supplementing. The Bison-horn Marias have the curious belief that men, not women, were originally subject to a menstrual period. They used to tie hollow bamboos to their organs to catch the discharge. Once - according to one legend - a girl was laughing at a man in this distressing and inconvenient condition, and he lost his temper and threw the bamboo at her; in an another story a sister wanted to help her brother, who could not cut his clearing properly on account of the bamboo tagged in front of him, and offered to take it instead. Yet other legends ascribe the origin of menstruation to an wound. There were formerly teeth in the vagina and when these were removed, the wound was not wholly healed. Once the vagina was in the crick of the leg behind the knee - you can still see its shape - but a hen pecked at it and the frightened organ jumped for safety to its hiding place between the thighs. But it was hurt and it still bleeds every month at the recollection.

Purāṇas have different logic about the four days period of menstruation. They record that during these four days the face of a woman is not to be seen by anyone. On the first day such woman is termed *cāṇḍālī*; on the second she is termed *rajakī* (washerwoman) and on the fourth she is purified (*Garuḍa*, II. 22. 7-9; *Padma, uttarakhaṇḍa*, 234. 31-32). She may be allowed to take part in the ritual for the gods or for that of the manes only on the fifth day (*Skanda*, VII. 1.206. 51; *Agni*, 156.13), or after seven days (*Garuḍa*, II. 22.10). For women, according to the favour of Brahmā conception was caused by sexual union with a man, during the period after four days. But, in the case of Pārvatī, no conception took place, as Śiva copulated with her daily:

प्रत्यहं रमणाद् देव्या नाभूद् गर्भो हराद् बत ।

(*Skanda*, II. 7. 9. 56-57)

According to *Mārkaṇḍeya Purāṇa* (49.9) prior to the *Tretā* age, women did not have the monthly period; hence no conception was ever possible even though sexual union took place:

मासि मास्यार्तवं यत्तु न तदासीत्तु योषिताम् ।
तस्मात्तदा न सुषुवुः सेवितैरपि मैथुनैः ॥

It is only at the advent of the *Tretā* age that conception took place, because of the monthly period (*Ibid.,* 29).

3456 **रजस्वला-कुटीर**

Rajasvalā-kuṭīra : the menstruation room or the menstruation-hut is common in the tribal folk of India. Non-tribal women have not such separate rooms, instead they keep themselves aloof. The different types are used for menses room. In Gondi, *kurma lon* is more popular.

There may be only one menstruation-hut in the village used in common by all menstruating women of the village or there may be menstruation-hut in each house. There may also be a mixture of the two types.

The common menstruation-hut is slightly bigger and may sometimes have two rooms separated from each other by a partition. One room is used by the menstruating women and the other may be used by a companion.

It is taboo for men and boys to enter the menstruation-hut or to come anyone nearer to it. Special cooking pots and utensils are kept in the menstruation-room for the use of the women in seclusion or else the woman's food is cooked outside and left at the door for her. The roof of the menstruation-hut is often covered with the seed-bearing twigs of the castor-oil plan which symbolizes fertility. The castor-oil plant is also regarded to be efficacious against magic. It is in the menstruation-room that child-births also take place.

All the Gond tribes are very strict about the menstrual taboos, in this contrasting sharply with the Orissa Bondos, Gadbas and Saoras, who are at similar stage of culture and not live very far away. Grigson has described the extreme rigorism of the Hill Marias and has rightly suggested that the Bison-horn Marias are some what less apprehensive of the dangers of menstruation. They do not usually build menstruation-huts, but sometimes where there is a girls-dormitory, menstruating women sleep on one side of the hut and unmarried girls on the other.

Elsewhere part of varandah and the ordinary living-house is screened off or a little hut is built in the compound for the use of a woman at this time. At the "blossoming of the flower" (*kumor utta* in the Bison-horn Maria and *puṣpavatī* in Sanskrit having the same meaning), however, a special hut is built for the girl by women outside the village. A woman of the house hold brings her food and sleeps with her at night; she must bathe whenever she returns to the house. In some villages, the Marias still make a platform up a tree for the girl, who during the day must hide herself in the forest.

3457 **रजस्वला-धर्म**

Rajasvalā-dharma : duties and impurities of a *rajasvalā* (q.v.) laid down in *Taitt. Saṁ.* (II. 5.1), *Taitt. Br.* (III. 7.1.), *Baudh. Dh. S.* (1.5.139), *Mit.* on *Yāj.* (III. 20).

3458 **रत**

Rata : pleased, fond of *ratam* 'sexual intercourse'.

3459 **रतकूजित**

Ratakūjita : sound in sexual intercourse.

3460 **रति**

Rati : sentiment of love, pleasure, love, affection, erotic state, sexual pleasure, love-sport, sexual union; the basic instinct or erotic sentiment. In the broad sense, it is a longing or desire for an object which attracts the mind. In poetics, however, it is restricted to sexual passion that forms the basic instinct (*sthāyī bhāva*) of eros or the erotic sentiment (*Śṛṅgāra rasa*). (i) In union the *anubhāvas* to be represented are clever movements of the eyes and eyebrows, soft and delicate movements of limbs, sweet words, etc.; whereas those to be represented in (ii)separation are despondency, weakness, apprehension, envy, weariness, anxiety, yearning, sleep, dreaming, awakening, illness, insanity, epilepsy, inactivity, death and other conditions. The permanent state of *rati* represents such *anubhāvas* as smiling face, sweet words, contraction of eyebrows, sidelong glances and the like.

NS has also dealt with the gait in the sentiment of love: (a) In ordinary love-making the actor is to enter the stage with the female messenger showing the way. He should indicate his intention by *sūcā*. He should walk with graceful steps in the *atikrāntā cārī* and the body in *sauṣṭhava*, in proper tempo and *tāla*. His hands should follow the feet. (b) in secret love-making: with the female messenger only as guide and with the lamp put out he should enter, without much decoration and with garments in harmony with the time. He should move with slow and quiet steps, apprehensive of any sound, anxious, looking around alertly, with body trembling and stumbling often.

(c) *rati* also means sexual intercourse. (d) In Vaiṣṇavism it is called *premāṅkura* or the first stage of divine love. *Rati* ripens successively into *prema* (sense of belonging), *sneha* (idea of mineness), *māna* (love-jealousy), *praṇaya* (confidence in love), *raga* (excessive eagerness for union), *anurāga* (fresh charms) and *mahābhāva* (supreme love); *Ujjvalanīlamaṇi, sthāyī,* 102). There are five kinds of *rati*:

śānta (preliminary which develops up to *prema* stage), *dāsya* (love of servants which develops up to *sneha*), *sakhya* (love of friends which develops up to *rāga*), *vātsalya* (love of parents which develops up to *anurāga*), and *madhura* (love of Gōpīs which develops into *mahābhāva*).

3461 **रतिकर्मन्**

Ratikarman : sexual union. compare the following verse:

anavasare yatpaṭhitam
subhāṣitāmapi bhavati hāsāya
rahasi prauḍhavadhūnām
ratikāle vedapāṭha iva //

"Our words though wise
If contest should despise,
Make us a butt
Of ridicule in others' eyes;
As a sacred line
Should one to chant incline,
In raptures sweet
when grown up maids in their clasp entwine".

3462 **रतिकला**

Ratikālā : the art of love and sex (*Śukranītisāra*, 4. 308-11). To try to have a girl before she is mature, is as hard as for a pig to dig up roots. But after a girl's first menstruation, everyone plans to be first in the Muria region. Even now, however, the girl must not be forced or hurried; she must be wooed, persuaded, loved into yielding. Girls who are afraid of intercourse succeed in resisting the Chelik for a long time. Often the first serious sexual experience of a girl is during a marriage, when everyone is excited and perhaps a little drunk, and no one asks questions or notices what is going on.

The ghotul leaders do not interfere unduly with the young children, but they see that they receive proper sexual training and instruction. As a young bullock is broken to the plough, so a young boy is taught'. A big girl teaches a little boy by letting him fondle her breasts and hug her. Then she opens and spreads her legs and makes the little boy lie on her breasts. She shows him how to open her clothes, and insert the little penis with his hand. The first time the boy doesn't know what to do and the juice comes out too soon.

Thus from a very early age the boys and girls are trained in *kāma-kalā*, both by example and actual instruction. A boy does not approach his marriage bed a virgin, and so is the girl.

3463 **रतिकुहर**

Ratikuhara : *pudendum muliebre*; also *ratyaṅgam*, *ratigṛham*, *ratimandiram*, *ratibhavanam*.

3464 **रतिक्रिया**

Ratikriyā : intercourse. The tribe discuss the sexual act simply and naturally; they are neither embarrassed not excited. The method of intercourse is similar to that of Trobriand Islanders.

They lie down together and the man holds his girl tightly in his arms; their legs are interlocked, he rubs his face against hers. The woman may sing quietly to her lover a refrain from a *karmā* such as:

Let up sleep together in a beautiful bed.
Hold me so tightly that no air can pass between our bodies. And:

These two are playing together.
Thigh to thigh, breast to breast.
Their legs are intertwined.
Slowly, slowly he presses into her.

There is little conversation; the tribe have practically no vocabulary of endearment; almost directly after the clothes are removed, the normal healthy man enters the state of tumescence, and commences the sexual act.

The woman lies on her back, her legs apart and raised, the knees bent. The man squats or kneels in front of her, taking her legs under his arms and against his waist. Then "he swings to and fro, as the green bamboo swings in the wing" on "his body wriggles to and fro like rice-stalks in the breeze."

The tribe sleep on the separate beds. The Gond always sleep in each other's arms, not so the Baiga. If a man goes to sleep without doing it his girl wakes him up. "What are you sleeping for? she asks. "whom have you been with today?" But if he is awake, they wait till all is quiet. Then a ripple passes between them. She coughs to show she is ready. They go on to the floor together. She does not remove all her clothes. She lies on her back with her legs in the air. The man kneels against her. It knows its place; it makes no mistake. Like an arrow it goes straight to its home. If it misses, the man is impotent. She puts her legs round his waist. She makes no response. She wants it, but she must not show it. So long as her breast is round like a fig, they hold and press it; when it is loose as a sack, they let it go. Once they are there, they want to live there, stuck there, pressed to her, forever.

It is naturally very difficult to discover what the woman feels about these things. But some of the *Karmā*-songs, all composed and sung by women, provide us with a few authentic documents:

1. Long, long are the pumpkins !
   The yare milky and long.

He sleeps all night with me,
But in the day he calls me sister.
Often, often he plays with my firm breasts.
They are his playthings.

2. The brinjal is growing round the borders of my court.
O I am a young calf, and he is a bull.
He is pushing me against my will.
He is tugging at my breasts.

3. O Wheaten is the bread, from the coconut oil!
He has filled his belly with thick wheaten bread.
He is playing roughly with me
Now he has attacked my breasts.

4. I asked him for a little love.
But he gave so much that he wore me out.
Even the crows began to talk outside.
For he wouldn't let me leave the bed.
The whole night long
He hugged and hugged and hugged me.

5. The *chuṭney's* made of mango,
The curry's made of *bohar* flowers.
My lover's lust is up.
Come let us go to bed.
The curry's made of *karelā*
The *pej* is made of *kuṭkī*
All night my lover slept with me.
Now take me to the big bazar.
He gave me *paiṛī* at the big bazar.
And that night too my lover slept with me.
All night the *paiṛī* tinkled, tinkled.
Now take me to the river for a bathe.

There are interesting riddles pertaining to sexual congress in Muria: (a) *Melā* and *Jelā* swing to and fro outside; the iron rice-husker is at work within. (b) three are dancing in a thick jungle.

3465 **रतिखेद**

Ratikheda : the languor of sexual enjoyment.

3466 **रतिदूती**

Rati-dūtī : a love messenger, *ratidūtipadeṣu kokilām* (*Kumāra*, 4.16).

3467 **रति-दृष्टि**

Rati-dṛṣṭi : a type of *bhāvadṛṣṭi* enumerated by Bharata.

3468 **रतिनाग**

Ratināga : mode of coitus.

3469 **रतिपाश**

Ratipāśa : mode of coitus.

3470 **रतिबन्ध**

Ratibandha : mode of coitus.

3471 **रतिमित्र**

Ratimitra : mode of coitus.

3472 **रतिरस**

Ratirasa : sexual pleasure.

3473 **रतिरहस्य**

Ratirahasya : the secret of sex, an erotic work by Kokkoka popularly known as *Kokaśāstra.*

3474 **रतिलम्पटा**

Ratilampaṭā : a lustful, lady who is coutous of sex, quality of the Deer-lady (*Anaṅgaraṅga*, 3. 20-21).

3475 **रतिसर्वस्व**

Ratisarvasva : the all-in-all of sexual pleasure, *pibasi ratisarvasvamadharam* (*Śiśu.*, 1.23), name of an erotic work.

3476 **रतिसुन्दर**

Ratisundara : a mode of coitus.

3477 **रथक्रान्त**

Rathakrānta : name of one of the three regions into which India is divided in certain *Tantras.* It extends from the Vindhya hill to *Mahācīna* including Nepal.

3478 **रथयात्रासङ्केतक**

Rathayātrāsaṅketaka : chariot-fair-signals. Evil omens are mentioned in the case of chariot-fair. If the pole gets broken it is inauspicious to the *brāhmaṇs;* if the axle breaks it is inauspicious to the kṣatriyas; if the balancing-pole breaks the vaiṣyas get into trouble; and if the yoke-pin breaks, the śudras get into calamity. If the yoke breaks it indicates lack of rain for the year; and if the seat breaks it is inauspicious for all people. The same is the case if the chariot turns up-side down; and if the flag-staff breaks, it indicates death of the king (*Bhav. P.* 56. 7-10; *Sk.P.*, II. 2.25. 61-65).

The association of the temple and the chariot is an interesting example of the interaction of classical and village/tribal India. The Vedic Āryan mythology of chariot - riding gods became a common feature of Hindu iconography-Vedic hymns ascribe symbolic significance to various parts of the chariot - e.g. time with the wheel. It is a custom to carry sacred village images during religious processions. The carved wooden *ratha* of colossal size, like the famous chariot of Purī is common in Bastar.

3479 **रद**

Rada : biting (*Anaṅgaraṅga,* 9.30) (a) at first used during the explorations of the environment by a solitary child. Most small children bite and chew new things to find out as much as they can about them. (b) later used during aggressive confrontations, but declines rapidly because of adult disapproval. (c) it is also used in sexual act. Jayadeva says: *Janaya radakhaṇḍam* (*Gīta- Govinda,* 10.2).

3480 **रमणीयता**

Ramaṇīyatā : beauty in a work of art, especially as seen in disinterested contemplation. From aesthetic point of view, lover is lost in the emotional contemplation of the beloved, that absorption brings charm which is akin to the experience of beauty. (b) no clear-cut concept of beauty can be ascertained from the tribal society. They are always moved by the loveliness of natural scenery, but they are not very articulate and find it hard to express themselves except when the words of a song or proverb provide them with a ready means of utterance. In human beings the tribes seems to admire loveliness, animation, vigour more than perfection of colour or feature. They apply their universal test of hard work not only to assess a persons morals, but even his erotic attractiveness. (c) aesthetic behaviour is the pursuit of beauty. This is easy to say but difficult to explain, because beauty is such an elusive quality especially when viewed biologically. It bears no obvious relationship to any of the basic survival patterns, of the human animal, such as feeding, mating, sleeping or parental care. And yet it cannot be ignored because any objective survey of the way people spend their time must include many hours of beauty-reaction. There is no other way to describe the response of men and women who can be found standing silently in front of paintings in an art gallery, or sitting quietly listening to music, or watching dancing, or viewing sculpture, or gazing at flowers, or wandering through landscape, or savouring wines. In each of these cases the human sense-organs are passing impressions to the brain, the receipt of which appears to be the only goal involved.

It is true to say that virtually every human culture expresses itself aesthetically in some way or other, so the need to experience the beauty-reaction has a global importance. The hard truth is that beauty is in the brain of the beholder and at every time, it creates joy:

If this is so, then how can any statement be made about the biology of beauty? The beauty-objects are group phenomena. The human brain experiences new every time. And it is the environment which regulates the human brain. Take the instance of the Baiga society. "Beauty, however, does not always, spell enjoyment. "Her face is lovely as a parrot. But her vagina is wide as well! or again: 'What is the use of pretty face, if she has the brains of a buffalo'. And the Baiga cynic sums up his experience of womankind. Outside, how beautiful? But go in and there is nothing but a mouse's hole.' But this is no argument against romance. Necessity drives everyone. When Mithu took his elderly leprous wife to his bed, they said, "when you are hungry, you will make a full meal of a cucumber. When you are burning hot, you will have even an old woman" (Elwin., 1936: 70).

3481 **रमल**

Ramala : sort of astrology.

3482 **रविमुद्रा**

Ravi-mudrā : gesture of the Sun. The gesture of *sandaṁśa* with the raised ring-finger (*VD*).

3483 **रस**

Rasa : flavour, sap, taste, colour, elixir, residual essence, joyful consciousness, the major aesthetic goal of Sanskrit theatrical performance, sentiment, the aesthetic experience. To recall the explanation of the term given by *Bharata*, *rasa* is so-called because it is tasted, relished (*NS,* VI.) - *āsvādatvāt.* It appears therefore that the very essence and existence of *rasa* consists in its being relished, the relish leading to enjoyment and delight, which is supposed to be the main function and purpose of art-presentation; when the *rasa-sūtra* mentions the *niṣpatti* or creation of *rasa*, the 'creation' is to be understood rather metaphorically, because, as Abhinavagupta points out, the *vibhāva* and other factors which enter into the construction of an emotional experience are not operative causes; they do not actually create *rasa* like *śṛṅgāra* etc.; but rather the flavour or taste (*rasanā*) associated with the particular *rasa* (*Ibid.*). Further, the flavour or relish in art experience is not that of a material thing or product; the analogy of *anna-rasa* or *pānaka-rasa* (a delicious dish or drink) is used only to explain the nature of *rasa* in art-experience. But just as he taste or flavour or even a delicious dish or drink is different from the taste of the individual ingredients mixed into its preparation, so the aesthetic relish too is different from all the elements of art-construction, including the basic emotion; and it is this flavour (*rasanā*) that the art creates and which we relish. Thirdly, the enjoyment is not *bhoga* as Bhaṭṭanāyaka understands it, but a consciousness, an awareness of a special kind. *Rasa* is emotional experience visualised, mentally realised vividly, by this kind of tasting or relishing. Thus, *rasa* must be regarded as "an emotional experience, essentially of relish, to be taken by perception freed from all impediments: *Sarvathā rasanātmaka-vītavighna-pratītigrāhyaḥ bhāvaḥ eva rasaḥ* (Abhinavagupta, *Ibid.* comm. *NS*). (b) gesture is always with the accordance of proper *rasa*. Kālidāsa (*Māl.* 2.6) says: "*yathārasam rasānukūlam abhinayati* ", Mālavikā does the *abhinaya* according to the proper *rasa*.

(c) in Tāntric cult, *rasa* is conceived in terms of intense emotional attachment between the male and female principles, symbolising two aspects of *Śakti*, embodied by the aspirant and his partner (*Lalitā-Sahasranāma*, 106). This conception is very popular among the aboriginal tribes.

(d) according to *rasesvara-darśana*, the use of chemical drugs, especially those prepared from mercury, makes possible the renovation of the body, and is conductive to *jīvanmukti* (*Sarvadarśanasaṅgraha*, IX. 1).

3484 **रसचित्र**

Rasacitra : which expresses the emotion through colours (realism).

3485 **रस-दृष्टि**

Rasa-dṛṣṭi : glances suggesting sentiments; glances corresponding to sentiments (*rasa*), glances according to the dominant states (*sthāyī bhāva*), glances corresponding to the transitory states (*vyabhicārī bhāva*). There are eight *rasa dṛṣṭis* enumerated according to different *rasas*: *kāntā* (*rati*), *bhayānakā* (*bhayānaka*), *hāsyā* (*hāsya*), *adbhutā* (*adbhuta*) *raudrī* (*krodha*), *vīrā* (*vīra*) and *jugupsitā* (*bībhatsa*) etc.

3486 **रसपिच्छल**

Rasapicchala : having all the constituents of sentiments.

3487 **रसभावव्यञ्जन**

Rasabhāvavyañjana : flavour, mood and implied significance. Cp. *nṛtya;* a combined experience from the olfactory, gustatory and cutaneous senses.

3488 **रसवत्**

Rasavat : possessing *rasa*, said of a work of art by imputation or projection; (b) juicy, savoury, moist, impassioned.

3489 **रसव्यक्ति**

Rasavyakti : (a) fall of semen in coition, orgasm, discharge of 'spermat' (*Kāmasūtra*, 2.1.42). (b) the consummation of *rasa*. The following anonymous poem is based on consummation:

> My limbs were not tangled in his,
> My lips didn't touch his, my friend.
> I kept looking at his lotus face
> And knew the loving consummation.
> (Vātsyāyana and Mishra, 1983. 198)

3490 **रससिद्ध**

Rasasiddha : that poet who is consummate in the manifestation of *rasa*.

3491 **रससिद्धान्त**

Rasasiddhānta : theory of *rasa*.

3492 **रसात्मक**

Rasātmaka : having *rasa* as the soul of poetry.

3493 **रसान्तर्य**

Rasāntarya : disturbance in aesthetic-experience is aesthetic distance.

3494 **रसाभास**

Rasābhāsa : the semblance or mere appearance of a sentiment, touch of *rasa*.

3495 **रसास्वादन**

Rasāsvādana : tasting of aesthetic-experience (*rasa*).

3496 **रसिकत्व**

Rasikatva : notion of taste given be Abhinavagupta. *Rasika* is the lover of literature, also known as *sahṛdaya*. Hemacandra (p.3) defines him. "The *sahṛdaya* is one whose mind-mirror being made spotless by practice is studying poetry, he has with a sympathy of heart a fitness for identifying himself with the matter described;" and he adds 'the poet himself, who according to Bhoja's commentator likewise (*Sarasvatī-kaṇṭhābharaṇa*,1.2), is also a spectator (*sāmājika*) of his own work, has taste of the sentiment (*rasa*) only in his enjoying phase, since being poet is apart from being enjoyer'. The anthologies express vividly the victorious effect of a good poetry, as in *Subhāṣitāvali* (163):

> What a poetry is that should not stir the heart, as if it had drunk much wine,
> should not by force of its sentiment thrill the hair even of those with minds befogged by envy.
> Make the head tremble, the cheeks redden,
> the eyes fill with tears,
> Mainstay the voice intent on chanting out the imagined theme?"

3497 **रहस्यमुद्रा**

Rahasyamudrā : secret gestures. *Arthaśāstra, Mahābhārata* and *VD* mainly deal with the secret gestures. *VD* in its chapter titled "*rahasya-mudrādhyāya*" (deals with secret gestures for Sanskrit alphabet, beginning from A to H) devises gestures for each letter of the alphabet which may build a word and thereby a sentence; implying any sense, that any other sentence, composed of literary words can express. Reference to the use of such secret scripts and languages is traceable in the *Mahābhārata* and early Indian Literature for the purpose of communicating secret messages to the men engaged in the military and intelligent services. They used some symbolic scripts and languages in the guise of gestures. What we know about the *mudrā* in general is that it must be a two-way process. But *rahasyamudrā* is a one-way process. The mystic-poet does not expect anything from other mystics. Moreover, the receiver perhaps lives in a distant future. And of course there is no agreement between the emitter and the receiver explicitly or implicitly. The code-book is then just the similarity of the spiritual experience between the two. Therefore, Western definition of communication should cover also the communication among mystics; this communication may be a one-way process, and not necessarily a two-way process.

3498 **राक्षस-हस्त**

Rākṣasa-hasta : if two hands with *śakaṭa* styles are placed near the mouth; they indicate a *rākṣasa, i.e.* a demon (*AD*, 226-231).

3499 **राग**

Rāga : colour, passion, affection, sexual feeling, attachment, (*dṛṣṭirāga, cakṣurāga*), musical mode, melody (*gitarāga*), (b) light tints indicate happy characters, kings and "western" races; darker tints were used for characters coming from the south, barbarians, rival kings, and so on. (c) there is no word for love in Gondi. The Muria uses the Chhattisgarhi word *mayā* and sometimes Oriya word *pirīti* or *prem*, which are equivalent to Sanskrit words *māyā, prīti* and *preman.* But neither do they have any word for lust or desire, and for erotic excitement use expressions that are only descriptive of the physical sensation of sex - *penda hohalla* said of a girl menas that her 'vagina is itching'; *boṇḍe ḍokalta* that the 'penis is quivering'. The expression *girdā kiyānā* is sometimes used for 'making love'; *girdā* means pleasure or liking. *Girdā ātor* can be used in the sense of 'being in love'. But abstract and emotional terms are rare in Gondi, as in most primitive languages. (d) *rāga* develops into *anurāga* in which object of love, even though realised, is relished always and appears to be clothed in fresh charms and attractiveness every moment (*Ujjala-nīlamaṇi*, 102). (e) *rāga* is also known as *guṇa-ślāghā-rāga* which means the love of excellence and celebrity which arises competitive keenness (*NS*, XXVI. 35-37). (f) concept of colour is very exhaustive in Sanskrit literature. There are as many as 13 synonyms for white in *Amarakośa; arjuna* among these being somewhat uncommon. *Hariṇa* is yellowish white, off-white being *dhūsara Aruṇa* is blush pink and *pāṭala* is rose. *Kadru, kapila* and *kedāra*, with two other synonyms, means tawney, *kapiśa* is black-red. *Kirmira, karbura or kalmāśa* is dapped.

(g) *rāga* or *anurāga* is an emotional attractions or dependence between two persons. (h) attachment. Vātsyāyana has included under *rāga* (attachment) the following as the springs of action: sex love (kāma); covetousness (*matsara*) the desire for what belongs to others; desire for acquisition (*spṛhā*); will-to-live (*tṛṣṇā*), the hankering for continuation of life; and greed (*lobha*), insatiate longing for food, wealth, etc.

Viśvanātha, another commentator on Gautama's *Nyāya-sūtra*, in his *Nyāya-sūtravṛtti*, adds two more to Vātsyāyana's five, *viz*, fraudulence (*māyā*), the desire to deceive other and boastfulness (*dambha*), the desire to display one's superiority in possessions, etc. Praśastapāda in his *bhāṣya* mentions eight kinds of attachment. He enumerates sex, food, desire to realise a remote end (*saṅkalpa*), compassion (*karuṇā*), dispassion (*vairāgya*), desire to deceive others (*upadhā*) and concealed desire (*bhāva*), that is not manifest in organic expression or speech, besides attachment (*rāga*), itself. Śaṅkara Miśra adds three more to the list of eight, viz., desire for acquisition (*spṛhā*), greed (*lobha*) and miserliness (*kārpaṇya*). (i) rāga has, thus, different manifestations. Bhānu opines: *Rāga prem kī khāni hai rāga raṅg ko mūl rāg-raṅg te hot hain sakal deva anukūl.*

3500 **रागदीपनं चुम्बनम्**

Rāgadīpanam cumbanam : kiss that kindles love. When a woman looks at the face of her lover while he is asleep and kisses it to show her intention or desire, it is called a 'kiss that kindles love.': *Suptasya mukham avalokayantyāḥ svābhiprāyeṇa cumbanam rāgadīpanam* (*Kāmasūtra*, 2.3.26). *Amarukaśataka* (32) has a vivid description of this type of kiss:

> *suptoyam sakhi supyatāmiti gataḥ sakhyastato nāntaram*
> *premāveṣṭuyā mayā taralayā mukham tanmukhe /*
> *jñāte alīkanimīlane nayanayordhūtasya romāñcato*
> *lajjāsīnmama tena sāpyahṛtā tatkālayogyaiḥ*
> *kramaḥ //*

There is another version of this type of kiss, where the poet describes: "Finding herself alone in the bed-room, the young bride raised herself gently and slowly from her couch and for a long scanned the face of her lord, who feigned deep sleep, and she imprinted a kiss on his face without any shyness; but as she perceived the thrill of the pleasure of his cheeks, she bent down her head in bashfulness, while her laughing lord rained kisses on her" (*Ibid.*, 74). In both these cases, there is a pretention of deep sleep from the M-side, while the F kisses.

3501 **रागबन्ध**

Rāgabandha : manifestation of feeling, interest created by a proper representation of various emotions. There are different techniques of manifestation of feelings which are symbolically loaded. The first type of symbolic Technique may be seen in the following Oraon poem:

> When the paddy stalks are full of sap
> The grains mature and ripen,
> The pigeons come crowding.
> I have a grown-up daughter,
> And friends and relatives
> Even from distant villages
> Come crowding to my house.

In the above poem, the entire statement is through symbol, without any clue. It is only at the end of the poem that one or two lines occur that suggest what the symbol stands for. No parallelism is worked out. In the following Muṇḍāri poem., until the dire consequences are mentioned, we do not suspect that the "mad dark bees" are love-lorn voung men:

> The glisterning white *mallikā* flowers
> Blossoming in your garden
> Invite the mad dark bees;
> When the flowers fade
> And the aroma is no more
> The bees will vanish;
> If they are caught send them
> To the Keonjhar Cutchery.

While analysing the symbolic structure of the tribal poetry we will do well to remember the essential social purpose they serve. Since tribal society is much more of a symbolic milieu than ours is, there is no hiatus between poetic symbolism and social communication.

3502 **राजन्**

Rājan : an address form. The king may be addressed either by name or *rajan* by the Brāhmaṇs and that is to be accepted, for the Brāhmaṇs are to be adored by the kings (*NS*, XVII. 65-94). The king is to be addressed by the sage or Vidūṣaka as *rājan* or by patronymic name.

3503 **राजसभा-विनयरीति**

Rājasabhā-vinayarīti : court etiquette. A definite courtly culture had established itself in India since long. *Śukranītisāra* (II. 187-188, 209, 210, 267-68, 211-13, 215-219) describes the court etiquettes of entry to the court and how it was regulated, how salutations were performed and how the ruler was addressed. It also laid down the behaviour of the ruler and his mode of taking decisions to the Court (*Ibid.*, II. 271-72, 275). The Mughals developed a very advanced court culture. The Hindu rulers of north India learnt much from them and adopted it in their own courts. In the States like Gwalior of Madhya Pradesh this influence was considerable while in Indore and Rewa is was prominent. In Mewar (Rajasthan) much of old court etiquette was retained. By the eighteenth century a definite Court culture and Court etiquette had come into existence in India. It was not a mere copy of the Mughals but had much of the original *Rājpūt*-system blended with the Mughal Court culture. Barring minor regional and local variations the etiquette and system of the Courts in India were mostly similar throughout.

In Rājpūt Courts some traditions were faithfully followed till recently. It is now possible to trace how these traditions came into vogue. However these traditions have helped to establish a sound relationship between the chiefs and their rulers. Most of these traditions came to be established in earlier part of the history and some were mere imitations of the traditions followed in the Mughal court. These traditions were:

1. The courtiers (including nobles) were required to dismount at a fixed point from their *pālkīs,* horses or elephants and from there to move to the assembly hall on foot (*Bikaner State*: Golden Jubilee, 1937:79).

2. The nobles would not attend the Court except on *Dassura* or when it was their turn to serve with their armed quotas, unless they received official call known as *khās rukkā*. It was written in a definite format and a fixed phraseology was used. The first grade nobles got *khās rukkā* from the Prince (ruler) himself written by his personal scribe and imprinted with the special sign manual *viz. sahī* or *hukum se* by the ruler. These *rukkās* were put into envelopes and sealed with the signet finger ring of the ruler. The nobles of the lower ranks got such summons on behalf of the ruler and imprinted with the office seal of the *Dīwān* or some other officer of equal rank who was assigned this job (Tod, I: 150).

2. When *khās rukkā* of the ruler was delivered to the noble, he received it with due respect and after taking it in his hands, he raised it to his head. It was then opened and read (Kaviraja Shyamaldas's collection, RSAB, Nos. I 10, 57, 60, 66, 67, 74, 81, 84; II. 100).

4. Such summons of *khās rukkā* had to be complied with immediately. The nobles on receipt of this urgent call

repaired to the ruler's Court without much loss of time. The quick compliance was appreciated. (Tod, I: 328-329).

5. The nobles of Rājpūt origin and the *muttsadis* performed *mujrā* when they came to the Court and/or received a gift. When a Brāhmaṇa appeared in the Court instead of performing *mujrā* (salute) he gave *āśīrvāda* (blessings) to the ruler (*vīra-vinoda*, I: 130).

6. Every courtier presented his *nazar* to the ruler. The *nazar* offered by the *Cāraṇas* and the Brāhmaṇs was touched by the ruler and returned to the person concerned. They were exempted from the payment of *nazars*. The *nazars* of all others were accepted (Tod, I: 377,493, 577).

7. The Court proceedings were closed with offering of the betel-leaf. The nobles of the first grade got it from the ruler and others got it from the superintendent concerned (*Ibid.*).

The betel-leaf when presented personally by the ruler was received with due etiquette. The noble received the betel from the Prince in both hands standing. The prince rose in his seat while giving the betel. The noble after receiving the *bīṛā* or *pān* performed *mujrā* (salute) and left the hall.

8. When the Mahārājā received some gifts or new commodities from abroad, he distributed a part of it among his nobles. The produce of the royal garden was also shared among the courtiers in a garden party or was sent to the *havelīs* (residences) of the nobles.

9. Like the Mughal Emperors the Rājpūt rulers bestowed robes of honour on their nobles from time to time. The Mughals called it *khilat* but in Hindu states it was known as *siropāo i.e.* from head to foot - a complete dress (Tod, I: 212).

Presentation of such a dress was considered a great honour. The receivers put on this dress and performed *mujrā* to the ruler as a token of gratitude for bestowing *siropāo*.

Whenever the ruler wanted to banish a prince or a noble from his country he sent to him a *siropāo* consisting of sable (black) coloured dress, black vestments, a sable shield and a sword of the same colour with a black horse. This was a definite hint that his presence was not required and banishment from the country had been pronounced on him. He left before the next sunrise with such of his retainers as chose to accompany him. The banished prince or noble was free to go anywhere he liked and seek his fortune (Tod, II. 34,212).

On festivals the rulers bestowed on a noble or the *purohita* the dress which they had worn on a particular occasion.

10. Whenever some difficult expedition was at hand the Mughal emperors held out a *bīṛā* or *pān* (betel) in a platter and circulated it among their nobles and generals. The one who picked it up accepted to lead the expedition and was appointed commander of the armies going on this errand. Sawāī Jaisingh repeated the same custom of holding out the *bīṛā* in this court for taking revenge from the Gaur Chief of Deoti (*Ibid.*, II. 295).

11. When the ruler rode on elephant, especially in a procession, his rear seat was occupied by the nobles of the first or the second grade who waved the fly-whisk over the prince (*Vīra Vinoda*, I: 31)

12. The ruler often paid visit to his courtier either on invitation or on some festive occasion, *viz.* marriage etc. When the ruler was to visit the *havelī* or the town of the noble, elaborate arrangements were made of his reception was received at some distance from the *havelī* or the town. He was accorded a warm reception at the door of the noble's *havelī* with *maṅgalācāra* and *maṅgalakalaśa*. Red strip of cloth was spread for the prince to walk on and enter the *havelī*. In the courtyard or hall a crimson canopy with silver or gold plated pillars was raised under which was placed crimson cushion or royal throne. The prince occupied. His feet were washed and large amount of money in *nazar* and *nichāvar* were offered by the noble and his follower.

The singers and dancers performed their arts to amuse the prince. A banquet was held in his honour. The prince bestowed presents and *siropāos* on the noble, his family members and his followers. The noble accompanied the ruler up to a long distance to bid him farewell.

3504 राजसिक

Rājasika : secondary quality; classification of human form according to the secondary quality.

3505 राधाकृष्णतत्त्व

Rādhākṛṣṇ-tattva : intense emotional attachment between the lover and beloved is symbolised by the principle Rādhā-Kṛṣṇa. In Vaiṣṇava poetry Rādhā is a symbol of yearning for the Eternal. Even without postulating a fleshy existence for Rādhā is possible to interpret the vast corpus of Vaiṣṇava lyrics as an expression of a form of mysticism in which the love of Rādhā is a symbol in transcendental awareness, so that in a moment of rare illumination Rādhā may declare, "Kṛṣṇa is lost in sleep in the temple of my heart, but love keeps vigil". In that inseparable awareness the duality of matter and spirit is completely obliterated. "He is no more the beloved, than I (Rādhā) am an adoring woman". The *sūfīs* call this state *tauhīd*, or a feeling of oneness.

3506 रामचन्द्र-हस्त

Rāmacandra-hasta : make the *Kapittha* gesture with the right hand, the *śikhara-mudrā* with the left and raise up both of them; this makes *Rāmacandra-mudrā* (*AD*, 216-225).

3507 **राममुद्रा**

Rāmamudrā : the *Śikhara* hand denotes Rāma and other mythical kings who bear bows (*Mirror of Gesture*, p.47).

3508 **राम-लक्ष्मण-मुद्रा**

Rāma-Lakṣmaṇa-mudrā (*Dāśarathau-mudrā*) : gesture symbolizing Rāma and Lakṣmaṇa. Two hands joined symbolize Rāma and Lakṣmaṇa (*VD*).

3509 **रावण-हस्त**

Rāvaṇa-hasta : *patāka*-fingers spread and feathered represent the mythical demon king Rāvaṇa (*Mirror of Gesture*, p. 47).

3510 **रास**

Rāsa : a pastoral festival, a dance festival enjoyed by Kṛṣṇa, sport, sound, *sītkāra* in coition.

3511 **रासभोक्ति**

Rāsabhokti : speech like an ass, quality of the Conch-lady (*Ratirahasya*, 1.16-17) and the quality of an Elephant-lady (*Pañcasāyaka*, 2.14).

3512 **रासलीला**

Rāsa-līlā : cosmic play, mystic play, where passion-feelings are elevated and sublimated and the circle of *mahārāsa* shows the beginningless and endless cosmic-play of transcendentals; it is the condensed form of nine permanent emotions which are acted and enjoyed accordingly. *Rāsalīlā* is an expression of the manifestation of divine love.

3513 **राहु-मुद्रा**

Rāhu-mudrā : the thumb at the root of the fore-finger (*VD*).

3514 **राहु-हस्त**

Rāhu-hasta : *śarpaśirsa* with the left hand and *sūcī* with the right, make the symbol of *rāhu*, the planet-god (*AD*, 216-225).

3515 **रीति**

Rīti : also called *mārga*. It is defined as *viśiṣṭa padaracanā* *i.e.* a particular mode of composition or arrangement of words. There are several *rītis*.

3516 **रूक्षनिष्ठुरवाद**

Rūkṣaniṣṭhuravāda : harsh and rough language.

3517 **रूक्षभाव**

Rūkṣabhāva : harsh and unfriendly behaviour.

3518 **रूक्षस्वरा**

Rukṣasvarā : lady whose voice is rough, quality of the conch-lady (*Anaṅgaraṅga*, 1. 15-16).

3519 **रूढि**

Rūḍhi : conventional usage of words.

3520 **रूप**

Rūpa : form, figure, visual representation, plays, appearance; *cakṣurmātragrāhya-jātimān guṇo rūpam* (*Tarka*); any visible object or thing. *Manu* (8.45) says: *deśam rūpam ca kālam ca vyavahāravidhau sthitāḥ*. (b) also called *rūpaka*: the *NS* describes ten *rūpakas* - *nāṭaka, prakaraṇa, samavakāra, ihāmṛga, ḍima, vyāyoga, aṅka, prahasana, bhāṇa* and *vīthī*. It is obvious that the author of *NS* had a large body of plays available to him for such a classification. (b) the first impression we form of someone depends on the first information we receive. This might be physical appearance, behaviour or name. As often as not, our first information about someone is their appearance: अहो अस्या- रूपम्. We are likely to notice sex, bright, build, facial expressions, clothes, their general manner and who they are with, as in the case of Rāma depicted by Vālmīki. Research has shown that if someone is physically attractive we will get the impression that they also have and attractive personality and possess a wide range of desirable attributes. They are expected to be kind, interesting, sensitive, responsive and modest, for example. How distinctive someone is has a strong impact on our impression of them.

Compare the following passage; *rūp nihārat palak na prerat* (Tulasidāsa, *Gītāvalī* 2.14.2).

3521 **रूपक**

Rūpaka : drama or dramatic representation, (b) metaphor: where there is non-difference between the object 'compared to' and the object 'compared' *tadrūpakamabhedo yad upamānopameyayoḥ* (*Kāvyaprakāśa*, X.93).

3522 **रूपकार**

Rūpakāra : a sculpture, imager (maker of images).

3523 **रूप क्रिया**

Rūpakriyā : to display. Ekman and Friesen (1966) proposed five major categories of NV behaviour that illustrate some functions of implicit behaviour. Affect display, according to them is the third major category. Happiness, anger, surprise, fear, disgust, sadness and interest are primary affects.

3524 **रूपग्रह**

Rūpagraha : the eye.

3525 **रूपजीवा**

Rūpajīvā : a prostitute (*A*, 1.20.20; 2.4.11; 2.23.2; 2.27.27).

3526 **रूप-दर्शन**

Rūpa-darśana : appearance as a communication tool. *Anaṅgaraṅga* (6.4) suggests the following forms: (a) *age*: The age of the people is a crucial focus of identification and an important factor. (b) *gender*. This again is a most important source of identification. The display of a character's gender refers to the conventionalized portrayals of culturally established correlates of sex. Analysis of sculpture suggests that gender is routinely protrayed according to traditional cultural stereotypes: women are shown as very feminine, as 'sex' objects, as house-wives, mothers, homemakers; and men in situations of authority and dominance over women. Feminity and masculinity are prototypes of an essential expression which can be conveyed fleetingly in any social situation and yet something which strikes at the most basic characterization of an individual. (c) *territoriality* and *caste:* These characteristics are usually related to stereotypical views of 'other' people and are frequently used in dramas. (d) *hair*. This is one of the most potent symbols in cultural communication. Female hair, in particular, is considered to be seductive and narcissistic, meaning an object of love or self-admiration. The colour, length, texture and style of a person's hair are important qualifiers of their overall appearance. (e) *body:* This can be then thin, fat, short, tall, clothed or partially closed. The naked body is, of course, not value-free, carrying meanings according to a particular society's norms. Iconography has been quick to exploit the perennial meaning of human, particularly female bodies. (f) *size:* Size is an important signifier of meaning. Relative size can convey social weight and superior status, power, authority, rank, etc. (g) *looks:* Looks are related to the overall class, age, style and expression created by a character.

3527 **रूपदासी**

Rūpadāsī : a female slave possessed of beauty (*A*, 2.27.17).

3528 **रूप-परिकल्पना**

Rūpa-parikalpanā : the assuming of a shape.

3529 **रूप-लावण्य**

Rūpa-lāvaṇya : exquisiteness of form. It furnishes information about sex, age perceived status and attractiveness.

3530 **रूप-विपर्यय**

Rūpa-viparyaya : disfigurement, morbid change of bodily form.

3531 **रूपशब्द**

Rūpaśabda : metaphorical expression.

3532 **रूप-शोभा**

Rūpa-śobhā : represented beauty.

3533 **रूपान्तर-परिणत**

Rūpāntara-pariṇata : transferred to another meaning.

3534 **रूपावली**

Rūpāvalī : a list of series of variations of grammatical forms.

3535 **रूपिका**

Rūpikā : deceiving men by appearance.

3536 **रूपेन्द्रिय**

Rūpendriya : the organ which perceives form and colour, the eye.

3537 **रूपोपजीवन**

Rūpopajīvana : gaining of a livelihood by a beautiful form.

3538 **रूप्य**

Rūpya : beautiful, shapely, formal.

3539 **रेखा**

Rekhā : straight position of all limbs in dancing, correct position of all limbs in dancing (Sten Konow(ed), *Karpūramañjarī*, p.280). *Rekhā* is the name given to a particular position of the body, attractive to the mind and the eyes. In it, there is a harmonious combination of the various poses of the major limbs, *e.g.*, head, eyes and hands. (b) lines on the palms. Varāhamihira (*Bṛhat-Saṁhitā*, LXVIII) has certain predictions on the basis of the lines on the palms: "The wealthy possesses glossy (clean) and deep lines on their palms; the poor, rough and not deep ones. The fingers of the poor are far removed from one another, while those of hoarders of wealth, thick." *vide* Prahlāda:

> रेखासमाकृतौ शस्तंवैकृते विकृतं फलम् ॥
> रेखैव माहेश्वरी मुद्रा शरीरं हि समुद्रकम् ।
> एतत्सामुद्रिकं शास्त्रं सङ्ग्रहेण समीरितम् ॥

Three lines starting from the wrist and going towards the palm make one king. One with a palm marked with a pair of fish performs sacrifice daily (or feeds the worthy); those who have the figure of the weapon *vajra* become rich; of fish-tail, learned men; of conch, umbrella, palanquin, elephant, house and lotus, kings; of a pitcher, lotus-stalks, flag and goad, very rich with buried treasure; of rope, wealthy; of *svastika*, lords; of discuss, sword, axe, lance, spike, bow and spear, commanders of armies; of mortar, sacrificers; of a crocodile, banner and store-room, blessed with immense wealth. Those whose root of the thumb is shaped like an altar, become worshippers of the sacred fire; men with the figures of the quadrangular tank, temple and the like as well as of a triangle, performers of religious and meritorious acts. Conspicuous and slender lines at the root of the thumb indicate sons and daughters respectively. Three lines touching the fore-finger make one live for 100 years; and for shorter ones proportionate reduction in the years will have to be made. If the lines are in the middle, the person will have a fall from a tree. Those who have either too many lines or no lines at all on their palms becomes utterly penniless.

The following verses from the *Harigaurī-sāmudrika* are interesting:

यस्य मणिसमा रेखा कर्मसिद्धिश्च जायते ।
धनाढ्यस्तु स विज्ञेयो बहुपुत्रो न संशयः ॥
तुलाग्रामौ तथा रज्जुः करमध्ये च दृश्यते ।
तस्य वाणिज्यसिद्धिः स्यात्पुरुषस्य न संशयः ॥
शङ्खचक्रध्वजाकारो माषाकारश्च दृश्यते ।
सर्वविद्याप्रदानेन बुद्धिमान्स भवेन्नरः ॥
अंकुशं कुण्डलं चक्रं यस्य पाणितले भवेत् ।
तस्य राज्यं महच्छ्रेष्ठं सामुद्रवचनं तथा ॥
यस्य पाणावूर्ध्वरेखा कनिष्ठामूलसंस्थिता ।
न नरः परदेशेषु दीर्घमायुश्च विन्दति ॥
रेखैका मणिबन्धे तु राजभोगी भवेन्नरः ।
यदि द्वे स गुणी वक्ता धनवांश्च भविष्यति ॥

3540 **रेखायते**

Rekhāyate : praises.

3541 **रेचक**

Recaka : rotation, spinning, piroutte, circular movement of limbs, *cakkar* in contemporary *kathak* terminology. The *NS* describes *recaka* of *pāda* (feet), *kaṭi* (waist), *hasta* (hand) and *grīvā* (neck). Thus *recaka* is a component of the *karaṇa*. There are four types of *recaka: kaṭi-recaka* (waist-movement), *hasta-recaka* (hand-movement), *grīvā-recaka* (neck-movement) and *pāda-recaka* (foot-movement).

Thus, particular movements of the feet, hands, waist and neck are called *recaka*. The continuous movement of the foot in between the heel and the tip of the toe and then onwards, involving bending and stretching, is the *recaka* of the foot. A swift circular movement of the hands inward and outward alternately is the *recaka* of the hands. Turning round the waist in all directions along with the vertical rotation of the toe slightly spread out is the *recaka* of the waist. Shaking and moving the neck around is the *recaka* of the neck.

(b) a part of *prāṇāyāma* (breath control). It is the exhaling of breath.

3542 **रेचित**

Recita : as a general term, only means moving the limbs round separately, almost all the movements of the limbs and the face, there is one movement called *recaka*. The four *recakas* are described as follows: (a) *pādarecaka*, (b) *kaṭi-recaka*, (c) *hastarecaka* and (d) *grīvārecaka*.

3543 **रेचित-अधर**

Recita-adhara : rotating lips (*SR*).

3544 **रेचित-कटि**

Racita-kaṭi : rotating the hip on all sides, a circular movement of the hips; the moved-about position of the waist. It is used in an one-sided twisting gesture of common movements (*NS*, X. 21-26) or moving round on all sides.

3545 **रेचित-करण**

Recita-karaṇa : indicating *recita* or *recaka* of either the hands or feet or waist or neck.

3546 **रेचित-ग्रीवा**

Recita-grīvā : shaking and moving around; rotating movement of the neck. It has something in common with *paralolita* head-movement (*NS*, VII. 171-75); moved and shaken neck. It suggests some accessory feelings churning cream and dancing.

3547 **रेचित-निकुट्टितकरण**

Recita-nikuṭṭita-karaṇa : feet in *udghāṭita*. The knees are bent to form *nikuñcita* (*NS*, IV. 89-90, X. 265). The right hand in *recita*, the right foot in *nikuṭṭita* and the left hand in *ḍola*. It is used in swing like movement.

3548 **रेचित-नृत्त-हस्त**

Recita-nṛtta-hasta : the bend-move, a type of hand-gesture in dancing. When two *haṁsapakṣa*-hands moving swiftly in an upturned style with extended flat-palms, it is called the *recita* (*NS*, IX. 176-197).

3549 **रेचित-भ्रू**

Recita-bhrū : graceful up and down movement of brows, eyebrows moving gracefully. The *recita* of the eyebrows is the lifting of the one eyebrow and is used for amorous sporting (*NS*, VIII. 119); raising up one of the eyebrows in lovely manner to indicate some pleasant affair like a dance, a song, etc. Raising up one eye-brow amorously, used in dance.

3550 **रेचित-हस्त**

Recita-hasta : rotating hands, it is a type of *nṛtta hasta.* The two *haṁsapakṣa* hands move swiftly with the palms facing upwards.

3551 **रेणु**

Reṇu : unit of measurement of the human form in sculpture.

3552 **रेतस्**

Retas : semen, seed, stream, flow (*T.Br.*, IX 74.1); *raitasa* 'relating to semen'. (a) *ūrdhva-retas* is the upward movement of the seed. It represents the challenging of the life forces, and in order for the ritual to be effective, it was essential for the *yogī* to restrain his seed. Tāntric texts describe the manner in which the *yogī* may even control the seed after it has been emitted (*Haṭhayoga-pradīpikā* 3. 82-96). In the mythology, this takes the form of numerous incidents in which the seed of the *yogī* is swallowed, or cast into a fire, or redirected in other unnatural ways (*Bṛhaddevatā* 5.97; *Harṣacarita* 9. 196; *Kathāsarit-Sāgara* 3.6.81; *Kumārasaṁbhava* 1.51, *Vāmana* 28.50; Elwin 1949. 203).

(b) *retapīta* 'one who has drunk semen.' In spite of the thematic importance of the motif of the drinking of the seed (*Vāmana*, 28.50; *Brahmavaivarta* 10.5.2. 11-12), in anthropomorphic sense drinking of seed is a sin. Śiva says to Agni, 'you did a perverse thing to drink my semen' (*Śiva*, 2.4.2.46). The law-books prescribe an expiation for a man who has unwittingly swallowed semen (*Manu*, 4.222) and even the permissive *Kāmasūtra* (2.9) has nothing but blame for this particular perversion, which confined to eunuchs and prostitutes.

Impregnation by drinking semen is a world-wide theme, and it is particularly well developed in India. In a tribal tale, Pārvatī is said to have miscarried and thrown the embryo into a stream; the Seven daughters of Jālandar guru bathed there and became infected with various diseases including syphlis, gonorrhoea and menstrual problems (Elwin, 1949, 349).

3553 **रोदन-विधि**

Rodana-vidhi : weeping ceremony. The marriage of capture has this ritual in the tribal society of India. This type of marriage is known as *rākṣasa-vivāha* in *Garuḍa-Purāṇa* (1. 95.11), where weeping is sanctioned. In Wardhā the bride is expected to cry continuously for a day and night before the wedding to show her unwillingness to leave her family.

In Kānker it is said that before marriage the bride is taught to weep in different notes, so that when that part of the ceremony arrives in which weeping is required, she may have the proper note at her command (Russell and Hiralal, III. 79).

This weeping ceremony is also prevalent in the village India.

3554 **रोम**

Roma : public hair. Symbol of joyful copulation. Indra seeing Romaśā asks, "do you have hair or not?" (*romāṇi te santi na santi rājñi*) she replies," come near and examine, then you will come to know: *sā tam jagāda upopa me śakra paramṛśeti* (*Bṛhaddevatā*, 4.2.3). Sign of puberty in Vedic period.

Indian classics show that men with a lot of body hair were no 'sexier' or more potent than men with little hair. The distribution of body hairs varied from individual to individual and is a matter of genitics.

However, it's certainly true that many women had strong preferences about the amount of body hair a man had. Hairy chests, backs, arms and legs appealed to some and not to others. These preferences were based not only on aesthetics and experience with other men, but on fantasy on some levels, royal women associated hairy men with a primitive Rāvaṇa who would overwhelm and carry them off. For some women this kind of fantasy heightened the erotic attraction, others found such an association brutish and animal - like and were repelled by it.

The sensual aspect of a man's hairiness also played a role in women's response. Some women loved the feeling of playing with a lover's body hair, smoothening it out, curling it around their fingers. Others preferred smooth, silky skin against their own.

3555 **रोमककूप**

Romakakūpa : pore of the skin.

3556 **रोमजन्मकृत्**

Romajanmakṛt : public-hair, hair on the private parts (*Agni*, V. 303. 25-27).

3557 **रोमहर्ष**

Romaharṣa : bristlling of hair, thrill (*Gītā*, 1.29); also *romaharṣaṇa.*

3558 **रोमाञ्च**

Romāñca : horripilation. the third natural sensation in deep emotion. It is generally caused by ecstasy, surprise, fear or disgust aroused suddenly to its climax: *harṣādbhutabhayādibhyo romāñco romavikriyā* (*Sāhityadarpaṇa*, 1.67). It is manifested by repeated thrills, hair standing on end, touching the body, etc. *Sit-bhīti haraṣāditen uṭhe romasamudāy. tāhi kahat romanc hai Sukavin ke samudāy.*

(Bhanu: *Kāvyaprabhākara*)

3559 **रोमावलि**

Romāvali : row of hair below the navel; also known as *romāliḥ*.

3560 **रोमशा**

Romaśā : a woman whose secret part is full of hair, a woman of blossoming youth (*Ṛgveda*, 1, 126.7). (b) having the lots of hair. Note that in later Vedic period, it denoted beard, as Pahlavas were called *Romaśā* due to their heavy beard.

3561 **रोहिणी-मुद्रा**

Rohiṇī-mudrā : tie the ring-fingers and the little-fingers in a upturned position and the ring-fingers and middle fingers should be joined and extended. The thumb should remain joined and hidden. This is called the *rohiṇī-mudrā* (*BT*).

3562 **रौद्र**

Raudra : the sentiment of wrath or ferocity. It is developed from the basic instinct of wrath (*krodhasthāyībhāvaḥ*), is red in colour (*raktaḥ*) and has Rudra as its presiding deity (*rudrādhidaivataḥ*). The art of furious appeal should suggest stern and stubborn pride, aversed actions and behaviours; anger, poisoning of food, drink etc. deadly attack and wound from an enemy, natural calamities, sudden fall of arms and ornaments (*VD* III. 43.5). In the view of Bharata. (*NS*, VI) it is created by determinants such as anger, rape, abuse, insult, untrue allegation, exercising, threatening, revengefulness, jealously and the like. Its actions are beating, breaking, crushing, fighting, drawing of blood and similar other deeds. It's representation should be by means of consequents such as red eyes, knitting of eyebrows, biting of the lips, movement of the cheeks, pressing one hand with the other and the like. Transitory psychological states in it are: presence of mind, energy, excitement, indignation, restlessness, fury, perspiration, trembling, horripilation, choking voice and the like. In the view of Abhinavagupta (*Abhinavabhāratī*, VI), the violation of the principles of morality and social laws (*anyāyakāritā*) is mainly the object of anger, *i.e.* it excites the wrath of all right-minded persons and they wish to suck the blood of anyone who violates such laws and principles.

3563 **रौद्री-रस-दृष्टि**

Raudrī-rasa-dṛṣṭi : wrathfull feelings through glances; a *mudrā* with eye-balls red, rough and raised; eye-lids motionless and eye-brows frawned. It suggests the furious sentiment. The glance is pitiless, the eyelids still, the pupils red and raised and the eyebrows knitted. It is to be used in furious sentiment.

ल – La

3564 **लक्षण**

Lakṣaṇa : (a) mark, sign, a lucky or auspicious mark on the body which numbers in thirty-two (*TS*, 1.2.1) (b) the science of the interpretations of signs (*A*, 1. 12.1), semiotics; *lakṣita* 'having a mark or sign'. (c) *NS* (ch. 16) enumerates thirty-six *lakṣanas* in a drama. These *lakṣaṇas* appear to be a miscellaneous collection logically since they include figures of speech and thought as also types of feelings and situations. (d) thus *lakṣaṇa* is a term of wide significance: on the one hand it denotes observation, sight and seeing and on the other a mark, sign, symbol, characteristic line ment, attribute and illustration (in all the disciplines), a symptom (of a disease), an auspicious or inauspicious marks on the body. Some of the definitions of *lakṣaṇa* are as follows: (i) लक्ष्यते येन तल्लक्षणम्, धूमो लक्षणमग्नेरिति वदन्ति *Lakṣaṇa* (icon) means by which something is perceived; as for example, smoke is the *icon* of fire (Śabara). (ii) Vātsyāyana explains *lakṣaṇa* as *abhidhāna* of the *bhāva* which distinguished the name.

(iii) *Agni Purāṇa's* definition is two-fold:

सामान्यं च विशेषश्च लक्षणस्य द्वयो गतिः।
सामान्यं सर्वविषयं विशेषः क्वापि वर्तते।। (338.4)

(iv) In Āyurveda *lakṣaṇa* stands for manifested signs and symptoms of disease. *Ākṛit, cihna, saṁsthāna, vyañjana, rūpa* and *liṅga* stand as synonymous of *lakṣaṇa:*

प्रादुर्भूतलक्षणं पुनर्लिङ्गम्। तत्र लिङ्गमाकृतिर्लक्षणं
चिह्नं संस्थानं व्यञ्जनं रूपनित्यनर्थान्तरम् ।।

(*Caraka* 1.9)

Thus *lakṣaṇa* is primarily a sign. Al-George (1972) is also of the view that *lakṣaṇa* stands for sign.

Compare the following passages from Tulasidāsa: *rām bhagat kar lacchan ehū* (*Mānasa*, 1.104.6); *sab lacchan sampanna kumārī* (*Mānasa*, 1.67.3).

3565 **लक्षणभ्रष्ट**

Lakṣaṇa-bhṛṣṭa : deprived of qualities. *Jāyante lakṣaṇa bhṛṣṭāḥ daridrāḥ* (*Baudhāyana*, 4.3.217).

3566 **लक्षणा**

Lakṣaṇā : metaphor, implication, a function of words. By it a word expresses a sense other than its primary sense with which the former is connected. One of the most fundamental qualities of human signalling is the use of *lakṣaṇa*. Hindi rhetorian Bhanu has defined it as follows:

mukhya artha ke bādhten, puni tābī ke pās.
aur artha jāten bane, kahen lakṣaṇā tās.

3567 **लक्ष्म**

Lakṣma : mark, sign (*AV*, I.23.4).

3568 **लक्ष्ममार्ग**

Lakṣmamārga : series of definitions (*DR*, III. 65).

3569 **लक्ष्मण-मुद्रा**

Lakṣmaṇa-mudrā : (a) the *śikhara* hand placed on the left shoulder denotes *Lakṣmaṇa*, the mythical ruler (*Mirror of Gesture*, p. 47).

3570 **लक्ष्मी-मुद्रा**

Lakṣmī-mudrā : the symbol of Goddess of wealth. The curved thumb symbolizes Lakṣmī (*VD*).

3571 **लक्ष्मीहस्त**

Lakṣmīhasta : in *kapittha* hands, held near shoulders, they indicate Lakṣmī (*AD*, 205-210).

3572 **लक्ष्य**

Lakṣya : secondary meaning to be expressed, mark.

3573 **लग्नपत्रिका**

Lagna-patrikā : marriage-invitation-card. The *Śiva Purāṇa* (II. 37. 4-9) indicates that invitation card was to be written. Thus, it is stated that at the marriage of Śiva and Pārvatī, the latter's father, the mountain Himālaya got the *lagnapatrikā* written by his preceptor Garga; it was then forwarded to Śiva, placing a *tilaka*-mark on it (*Ibid.*, 4.6): तिलकं सम्विधाय च. Then he invited the relations: ततो निमंत्रणं चक्रे (*Ibid.* 9).

3574 **लघुतरनयना**

Leghutaranayanā : lady whose eyes are small, quality of Elephant-lady (*Pañcasāyaka*, 2.14).

3575 **लघुसमदशना**

Laghusamadaśanā : teeth small and equal, quality of a Hare-man (*Ratirahasya*, 3.30-31).

3576 **लघुसुरतरत**

Laghusuratarata : a little desire for sex-sport, quality of a Hare-man (*Ratirahasya*, 3.30-31).

3577 **लज्जा**

Lajjā : bashfulness. *lajjām nāṭayati* : stage direction (*Śākuntalam*, Act I; *Mudrārākṣasa* 2. 16) enacting bashfulness.

3578 **लज्जान्विता–दृष्टि**

Lajjānvitā-dṛṣṭi : bashful glance. This glance is described

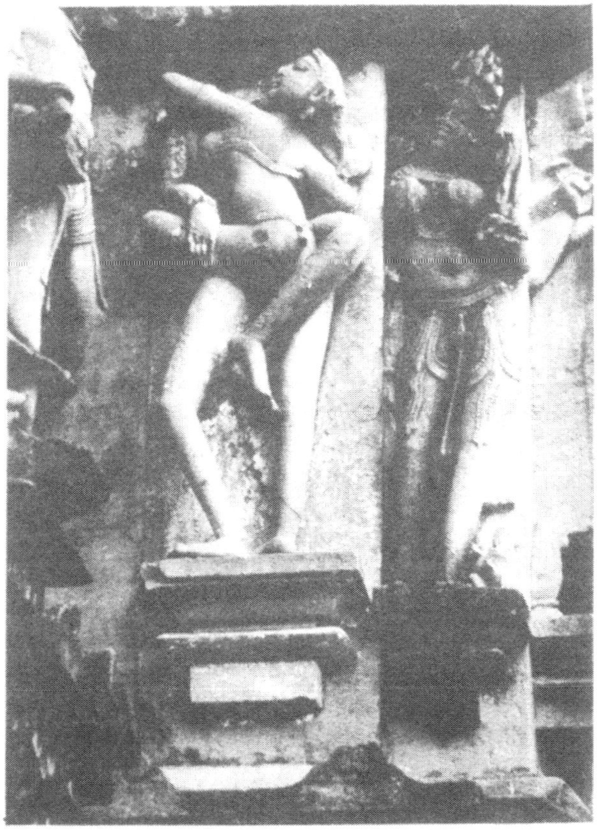

Fig. – (3581)

as the glance in which ends of eye-lashes are slightly curved. The upper eyelid is lowered. The eyeballs look down (*NS*, Nirnayasagara, p. 40). This blushful glance is enumerated under *sancārī-bhāva-dṛṣṭi*. It is a glance with slightly down eye-lashes, the upper eye-lids coming down in shyness and eyeballs dropping in a shameful way. It suggests bashfulness and mental weakness (*NS*, VIII. 61-92); same as *lajjitā—dṛṣṭi*. The ends of eyelashes are slightly curved, the upper eyelid fallen in shyness and eyeballs lowered in bashfulness. It is to be used in shyness.

3579 **लज्जिता-दृष्टि**

Lajjitā-dṛṣṭi : bashful glance (*NS*, VIII. 66). It is described as the glance in which ends of the eyelashes are slightly curved, the upper eyelid is lowered, the eyeballs look down. Same as *lajjānvitā dṛṣṭi*.

3580 **लण्ड**

Laṇḍa : penis.

3581 **लण्डवेश्म**

Laṇḍveśma : a particular posture in coition. (Fig. 3581)

3582 **लतानृत्त-हस्त**

Latānṛtta-hasta : the creeper, a type of hand gesture in dancing; Two hands (with the *patāka* gesture) stretched obliquely to both sides in a dance-drama, is called the *latā* (*NS*, IX. 176-197).

3583 **लताबन्ध**

Latā-bandha : a type of *piṇḍībandha* dance-composition which suggests a dance composition where the dancers put their arms around each other.

3584 **लता-वृश्चिक-करण**

Latā-vṛścika-karaṇa : a type of movement. One leg in *vṛścika*, hands in *latā* (*NS*, IV. 104-105). The foot in *añcita* is turned backwards and the left hand in *latā* with its palm and fingers bent and turned upwards. It is used in falling down from the sky.

3585 **लतावेष्टितक-आलिङ्गन**

Latāveṣṭitaka-āliṅgana : twinning of a creeper-like embrace. When a woman clinging to a man as a creeper twines round a tree, bends his head forward to hers with the desire of kissing him, slightly makes the sound of *śītkāra*, embraces him and looks lovingly towards him, it is called "twinning of a creeper". (*Kāmasūtra*, 2.2.16). Śrīharṣa refers to this type of embrace when he described the legs of Damayantī (*Naiṣadha*, 7.97). In the *Mukundānanda Bhāṇa* (192) a lover narrates his experience of this type of embrace: "His beloved, standing on the toes with difficulty, having placed her hands on his shoulders, writing with her breasts on his chest, having touched his cheeks as if to kiss him sprinkled the nectar of words in his ears."

3586 **लता-हस्त**

Latā-hasta : a type of hand gesture. One hand swinging across the body (*NS*, IX. 198).

3587 **लम्बमान**

Lambamāna : a measurement of the human form along the vertical axes.

3588 **लय**

Laya : making the mind inactive, rhythm, tempo. The tempo of the movement is given by Bharata for several situations. The gait (*gati*) in particular, should be integrated with the rhythm of the background instrumental music. In Bhavabhūti's play *Mālatīmādhava*, the lovelorn hero, Mādhava, enters with a languid gait described by the onlooker Makaranda as *gamanam alasam* (1.20) and in explaining this, the commentator Jagaddhara, who is also a writer on music, dance and drama, says that Mādhava's entry is in *dvipadī*-

laya tempo, a slow measure composed of long *mātrā*, suited to situations like the present one. (b) *laya* or tempo in music is of three kinds: *druta* (fast), *madhya* (medium) and *vilambita* (slow). The serial recurrence of sounds or other phenomena marked off by time intervals is *laya*.

3589 **लयसंकेत**

Layasaṅketa : baton signal. Baton signals beat time to the rhythm of spoken thoughts. Their essential role is to mark the points of emphasis in our speech, and they are so much an integral part of our verbal delivery that we sometimes gesticulate even when talking on the telephone. The palm up baton of the speaker who implores his audience to agree with him. His hands adopt the posture typical of a begging man. The fore-finger Baton is usually employed assertively by a domineering speaker. The palm baton is used by gesticulators attempting to embrace a concept. The hands appear to embrace an invisible companion.

3590 **ललाक**

Lalāka : penis, also known as *lāmu*.

3591 **ललाट**

Lalāṭa : forehead. (a) auspicious marks on the forehead are the following: *gorocana* (cow-bile) with cow's urine, warm cow-dung; these two along with curds and sandal be marked on the forehead. This *tilaka* is conductive to prosperity and health; and it is also the favourite of the goddess Lalitā (*Matsya*, 61.6).

Another auspicious material is *kuṁkum* (saffron). *Sindūra* is another auspicious powder for married women. It is said that putting the *tripuṇḍra* on the forehead is equal to putting the *kālātman* (soul-of-time). (b) the forehead is very important and various signs in it are noted to divide the nature of a man.

3592 **ललाटतिलककरण**

Lalāṭatilaka-karaṇa : after performing *vṛścika karaṇa*, the *tilaka* sign is made on the forehead. With the toe of the foot. It is used in the movements of *vidyādharas*.

3593 **ललाटतिलकासन**

Lalāṭa tilakāsana : one knee is bent outwards with a side facing, the other leg is thrown back with the knee touching the ground; but the calf is so raised that the foot practically touches the head. We find this pose in the Śiva temple of Śrīśailam. It also belongs to *vṛścika* variety: the *vṛścika* leg is taken to its extreme position when the toe touches the forehead. The hand of the uplifted leg is in *patāka*. The other hand with uplifted toe in the forehead region (*NS*, IV. 110-111).

3594 **ललाटफलक**

Lalāṭaphalaka : fore-head picture. It is the Indian belief that a man's fortune is written in his forehead. If the *lalāṭa* is like the crescent, it is an indication of being wealthy; if it is uneven, it indicates poverty; if it is broad and like a pearl, the person is a scholar; if the veins on it are prominent, it indicates sinfulness; if the forehead is low (depressed), the person may commit an offence; if the forehead is covered by hair, he is miserly; and if it is raised, he is to be a king (*Garuḍa*, 65-67).

If a person has three well-knit lines on his fore-head, it indicates that he is happy with his family, and would live for sixty years, if two lines are seen, he would live for forty years; if one line is seen, the age would be twenty years; and if the only one line stretches to both the ears, the person would die early. Likewise, with two extending lines, the person's life will be seventy years; if the lines are clear in certain parts, and unclear in certain parts, they indicate twenty years life. If the lines are invisible he would live for forty years; and if the lines are broken, it is an indication of sudden and immature death. If there be a sign of a *triśūla* on the forehead, the person lives a hundred years. In the same three clear lines on the forehead also indicate a hundred years life, if there are four, it is indicative of royalty and life of ninetyfive years. If there are no lines at all on the forehead, the life is for ninety years; if the lines touch the border of hair on both sides, the life is for eighty years.

"An uneven forehead leads to poverty; one resembling the half-moon, to opulence; one large like a shell, to the position of preceptors of men; one full of veins, to addiction to unrighteous act; one filled with raised veins as well as with those shaped like the *svastika* figure, to great affluence; a depressed forehead, to imprisonment, foul death and cruel deeds; a raised one, to commandership of armies; and a round and small one, to miserliness."

'Three horizontal lines on the forehead indicate a life of hundred years; four such lines, kingship and a life of 95 years; cut lines or absence of lines, addiction to forbidden women and a life of 90 years, the lines touching the hair on the both sides, a life of 80 years; five lines on forehead indicate a life of 60 years; many lines (*i.e.* six), a life of fifty years; crooked ones, one of 40 years; those touching the brows, one of 30 years; those bent towards the left, one of 20 years; slender and small ones, a short life; those short of above number (*i.e.* one or two), a short life; and for any number in between the given ones, a life that is to be proprotionately calculated' (Varāhamihira, *BS*, LXVIII).

3595 **ललाटाभरण**

Lalāṭābharaṇa : ornament of the forehead for women

only : *āvarta lalāṭikā*. It occurs in *Kumārasambhava* (V.55) ललाटिकाचन्दनधूसरालकां:-Mallinātha explains *lalāṭikā* as ललाटस्थालंकारः तिलकः। *Śabdakalpadruma* gives it as स्वर्णादिराचितलटाभरणम्।

3596 **ललाटिका**
Lalāṭikā : one who looks at the forehead of his master from a distance, and keeping himself aloof does not do any work; a care-free servant. The expression *lalāṭikā* is formed by the Pāṇinian rule *sañjāyām lalāṭa-kukkuṭyau paśyati* (4.4.6). The suffix *ṭhak* is added in the sense of 'who sees that'. So *lalāṭam paśyati* forms the noun *lalāṭikā*.

3597 **ललाटिकालिङ्गन**
Lalāṭikāliṅgana : embrace of forehead.

3598 **ललित-करण**
Lalita-karaṇa : from the *karihasta* position one hand and arm move from side to side in *utsārita*. Feet in *kuṭṭita* or *nikuṭṭa*, *i.e.* bent knees and *tāḍita* movement of the feet. The left hand is in *karihasta* and the right hand variously and the foot is moved up and down repeatedly. It is used in graceful dance.

3599 **ललितगमना**
Lalitagamanā : beautiful gait, quality of the Deer-lady (*Pañcasāyaka*, 2.12).

3600 **ललित-नृत्तहस्त**
Lalita-nṛttahasta : a type of hand-gesture (*NS*, IX, 209); the delicate dancing hands; Two hands with the *pallava*-gesture placed on the head, is called the *lalita* (*NS*, IX. 176-197).

3601 **ललित-भाव**
Lalita-bhāva : (a) amorous gesture of women. occurs in *Buddhacarita* (VIII. 53). *Lalita-bhāva* is not one of the transitory emotions *(vyabhicārī bhāva)* but is related to *rati* and *śṛṅgāra* (*NS*, IV. 25). It is, however, included into ten natural glances (*alaṁkāra*) of women. Thus it means where graceful movement of hands, feet, brows, eyes, lips, etc. are made by women' (*NS*, XXII. 22). (b) sportiveness. One of the temperamental aspects in men. The amorous movements which are not deliberate and are tender nature, constitute *lalita* as in the following verse:

> मृदु मुसकाय उठाय भुज, क्षण घूंघट पटपटारि।
> को धनि? ऐसी जाहि तू ! इक टक रही निहारि।।

3602 **लास्य**
Lalita lāsya : graceful dancing.

3603 **ललित हस्त**
Lalita hasta : a type of hand gesture in iconography.

3604 **ललिता दृष्टि**
Lalitā dṛṣṭi : amorous glance. Used for love (*NS.*, VIII. 74) a type of *sancārībhāva dṛṣṭi*; a sweet glance, contracted at the end with the love-loaded eye-brows and the smile, showing an amorous air, is called *lalitā*. This suggests joy and contentment. The glance is sweet with ends contracted, smiling with knitting of eyebrows and showing sign of love. It indicates contentment and joy in sporting, amorous moods.

3605 **ललिताभिनय**
Lalitābhinaya : manifestation of love can be represented through *lalitābhinaya* of various kinds. It is the graceful gesture of women. It is mentioned under 'Basic Representations' (*sāmānyābhinaya*) where in describing *helā*, the phrase *lalitābhinaya* is used: "emotion which depends on the erotic sentiment and expresses itself in graceful movements is called *helā* 'passion' (*NS*, XXII. 22).

3606 **ललिता-भ्रुकुटि**
Lalitā-bhrukuṭi : a type of movement of the eyebrow given by *Bālarāmabharata.*

3607 **लवणोदधि-हस्त**
Lavaṇodadhi-hasta : the *mukula* hand moved up and down denotes salt ocean (*Mirror of Gesture*, p.48).

3608 **लाक्षणिक**
Lākṣaṇika : word expressing the secondary meaning.

3609 **लाङ्गूल**
Lāṅgūla : penis, tail. (a) The rather bizarre Freudian elements of sexual myths are an anthropomorphic form of the episode in Sanskrit versions of the myth in which Śiva's phallus moves about causing a damage to the sages. The following Baiga myth also expresses the basic concept underlying the corpus (*Padma*, 5.17. 269-71) of seduction myths: that the sexual act is dangerous, causing the loss of power and sometimes of life itself: "Two Baiga discovered their wives having an intrigue with a *Brāhmaṇ* beggar (*i.e.* Śiva), and decided to make a trap for him. They made nooses of their hair and tied these in the organs of their wives. The noose of the first woman tightened round his penis and cut off, but he did not cry out; he said to one of the women, 'I have dropped my medicine on the ground,' Give it to your husband to eat and he will get strength. The man swallowed it whole. That night it broke out of his stomach and entered his wife's vagina. He went to her and the double-lengthed killed her" (Elwin, 1949. 392).

3612 **लाञ्छन**

Lāñchana : emblem.

3613 **लाटिका**

Lāṭikā : a particular style of composition.

3614 **लाला**

Lālā : saliva, spittle.

3615 **लावण्य**

Lāvaṇya : reflected fluidity in the pearl which flushes beauty; charm that has saline effect.

3616 **लावण्ययोजना**

Lāvaṇya-yojanā : outward painting which is in harmony with mental images while expresses beauty in painting.

3617 **लास्य**

Lāsya : feminine dancing, also known as *sukumāra nṛtya.* The lady who performs the *lāsya* is called *lāsikā.*

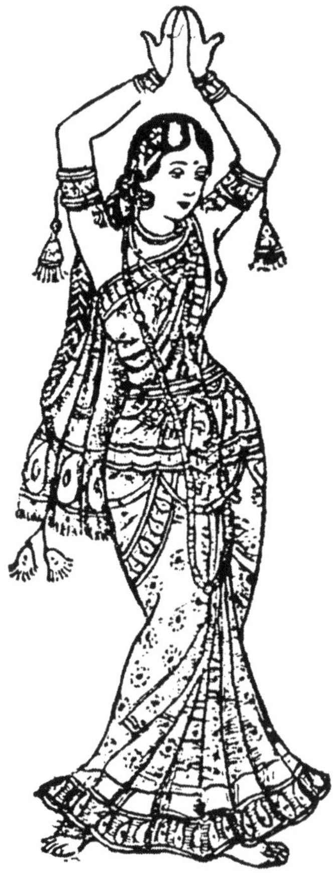

Fig. – (3617)

3618 **लिङ्ग**

Liṅga : a distinguishing mark, badge, symbol, genital organ (*Mānasāra* L.III. 1-376). emblems. Eforn (1941) used the term 'emblem' for the first time only for those gestures which are not morphologically related to what they signify; emblems could only be arbitrarily, not iconically coded. Ekman and Friesen (1972) have defined emblem: "Emblems are those NV acts (a) which have a direct verbal translation usually consisting of a word or two, or a phrase, (b) for which this precise meaning is known by most or all members of a group, class, subculture or culture, (c) which are most often deliberately used with the conscious intent to send a particular message to other persons, (d) for which the person who sees the emblem usually not only knows the emblem's message but also knows that it was deliberately sent to him and (e) for which the sender usually takes responsibility for having made that communication. A further touchstone of an emblem is whether it can be replaced by a word or two, its message verbalized without substantially modifying the conversation." (f) *Liṅga* is the most important emblem of Śiva: *liṅgam Śivaliṅgam jñeyam* (*Sk.P.,* 1.1.31). But the most prominent belief is that *liṅga* is the penis of Śiva. (g) In the *Mīmāṃsā* tradition *liṅga* means the suggestive or indicative power of a word. (h) *Liṅga* or *lingo* cult is widespread among the Muriās of Bastar and is coterminous with the Śiva-Mahādeva cult, better known in *Pūskolāṅg* dances. For Muriās, *lingo* is the originator of *saṅgīta.* The *lingo*-legend has been elaborately studied in *The Muria and Their Ghotul* (Chapter VIII). (i) Sometimes *Liṅga* the phallus, particularly of Śiva.

3619 **लिङ्गपरामर्श**

Liṅgaparāmarśa : perception of *hetu, i.e.* smoke, etc. the basis of inference: *liṅgaparāmarśo numānam.*

3620 **लिङ्गपुष्प**

Liṅga-puṣpa : the *raktakaravi* flower. It is used as a substitute for *maithuna,* the other item being *yonipuṣpa* which is blue *aparājitā* flower (*Paraśurāmakalpasūtra,*X. 63).

3621 **लिङ्ग-मुद्रा**

Liṅga-mudrā : (a) occurs in *BT.* "placing the thumb of left hand into the right first and the left-ring finger. Extending by the right, surround one fist by another." (b) the penis, make the palm unturned, carve four fingers and raise up the thumb. Then it is *liṅga* (*VD*); (c) gesture of the penis. The upturned right thumb should be wrapped with the left thumb and fingers. This is *liṅga* (*VD*); (d) when two fists of the two hands are rubbed together, it is the *liṅga-mudrā* (*VD*). (d) phallic signs are the simplest and most popular, requiring no more than some form of symbolic erection.

In different regions this is done in a variety of ways, employing several part of the body. The symbolic phallus may be the tongue, the second finger, the middle finger, the thumb, or the forearm. A more impressive phallus is made by jerking upwards with the whole forearm, the head of the symbolic penis being formed by the clenched fist. This, the forearm jerk, is extremely common today in India, France, Italy, Spain and Greece, where it is employed almost exclusively as a threatening insult by one male towards another.

3622 लिङ्गशरीर

Liṅgaśarīra : the subtle body. The *Sāṅkhyas* admit the existence of the 'subtle body' composed of 'intellect' with other rudimentary principles. It is constant and does not change throughout the cycles of life and death; however, it is not eternal, for it is eventually re-absorbed into the elements of which it is composed; it consists of eighteen elements, *viz.* Intelligence *(buddhi)*, Mind *(manas)*, etc. It is also called *sūkṣma śarīra,* q.v., op. *sthūla śarīra.*

3623 लिंङ्गसंकेत

Liṅga-saṅketa : gender signals. Gender signals are clues that enable us to identify an individual as either male or female. At birth the only obvious gender signal of the human baby is the shape of its genitals. (Penis means boy and vagina means girl and that is all the layman has to go on'. As the child grows, society prepares them for the gathers and gives them a gender identity long before they need it for reproductive activities). This trend has the effect of widening 'gender gap' between the sexes. Artificial, invented gender signals may come and go, but those stemming from human genitic inheritance may prove stubbornly resistant to social progress.

The male genital symbols are depicted in the Muria riddles:

(a) The pole is long, its bottom is black.

(c) The fish that has no eyes.

(c) Touch it and up it goes

(d) There are two witnesses to this thief's escapades (The testes and penis).

Śiva Purāṇa (IV. 12.6) also symbolizes the male genital organ in Muria way of life: *yonirūpeṇa malliṅgam dhṛtam.* The *Agni Purāṇa* (217. 2-10) mentions thirty-six types of *liṅgas.*

3624 लिंङ्गाकृतिविज्ञान

Liṅgākṛti-vijñāna : sign of the penis. The position of the generative organ is said to be indicative of progeny and potency. It is said that if the penis is turned slightly to the right, it indicates the gain of male issue. If leftward, it indicates female issues. A thick, yet curved and veiny penis indicates poverty and wretchedness; if straight and round it indicates the gain of male issues. If the penis touches the ground in the seating position with knees up, the person is wretched; if, in this position, it touches the ankles, the person is dear to women and is prone to become a leader. If the penis is like that of a lion or a tiger and short, the person is a master enjoyer. If the prepus (fore-part of the penis, when uncovered) has minute lines, it is indicative of royalty (*Bhaviṣya,* 25. 1-6).

'A Man with small genital organ becomes rich, but issueless; one with a stout organ, poor; with one bent towards the left, devoid of issue and wealth; with one turned towards the right, blessed with sons; with one bent on the lower side, poor; with one full of veins, father of few children; with one having a thick knot, happy; and with a soft one, dies of gonorrhoea and the like (*Bṛhat-Saṁhitā,* LXVIII). Men with the genital organ covered with sheath become kings:

लिङ्गह्स्वे महाभोगी लिङ्गाधिक्ये दरिद्रता ।

Men with a red tip (*maṇi*) of their generative organs become very rich; with a whitish and dark tip, penurious; those who urinate noisily become happy (*saśabda-mūtrāḥ*); without any sound poor;

3625 लिङ्गाग्रच्छेदनम्

Liṅgāgracchedanam : circumcision. Circumcision is, in fact, the only really severe form of primitive mutilation to have resisted the modern trend towards abhorrence of body-violation. If, as used to be the case, it was performed at puberty instead of infant, that too would not doubt have vanished long ago, swept away by the outrage of the initiates. But the protests of babies are more easily ignored, and with the false accolade of medical hygiene to help it on its way, the genital deforming of young males continues still in the Muslim communities of India. Mutilation of female genitals may still be seen in some sections of Muslim society, but its survival is not confirmed. (b) there are various castration motifs in Sanskrit literature. Indra was castrated and was branded with the mark of *yoni.* Moreover, Indra is said to have created a male organ on every limb of the Brāhmaṇa Sumitra so that the Brāhmaṇa could marry a domoness who had a female organ on every limb and who refused to marry him until he could match her (*Jaminīya Brāhmaṇa,* 1.162).

3626 लिङ्गानुशासन

Liṅgānuśāsana : a treatise laying down genders for words.

3627 **लिङ्गिनी**

Liṅginī : Abhinava meant painter but it might simply mean the woman living in religieux (*NS*, XXIV. 30).

3628 **लिङ्गायत**

Liṅgāyata : an influential and powerful Śaiva sect, also known as *Vīra-Śaiva*. The members of this sect in Bastar worship Śiva in his phallic form, reject the authority of *Vedas*, deny the doctrine of rebirth, object to child-marriage and approve of the remarriage of widow.

3629 **लिपि**

Lipi : script (Kālidāsa, *Raghu*. 3.43, 18.264).

3630 **लीन-करण**

Līna karaṇa : feet are in *samapāda*. There is no bend of the knees. The hands are moved and brought together in *añjali saṁyuta hasta*. The head is slightly bent *nihañcita* (*NS*, IV. 66-67, IX. 128). The two *patāka* hands are in *añjali* placed on the breast, the neck stretched and shoulders bent. It is employed in request to the beloved.

3631 **लीला**

Līlā : one of the twenty *sāttvika alaṅkāras* of the herione as enumerated by Bharata. Imitation of the hero in manners, dress, ornaments and speech by the heroine out of sheer love is *līlā* (*Sāhityadarpaṇa*, 3.99). It is one of the natural graces (*lalitābhinaya*) of women. It is imitating the behaviour of the beloved persons by means of speech, gestures, and ornaments, which are delightful and inspired by affection. It is the sportive mimicry. It is a type of *sāmānayābhinaya*. vide:

tiya baiṭhī piya ko pahiri
bhūṣaṇa-vasana-viśāla.
samujhi paṛat nahi sakhi ko
ko tiya ko Nandalāl.

(b) sport, charm; celestial sport, the playful spirit in which Śiva participates in meaningless actions. Play-acting, erotic play.

3632 **लेख**

Lekha : letter, document, article, line, signature, god.

3633 **लेखक**

Lekhaka : clerk (*NS*, XVII. 53-57).

3634 **लेखिनी**

Lekhnī : pen. cf.

lekhinī pustakam rāmā
parahastam gatam gatam/
athavā punarāyāti
bhraṣṭam naṣṭam ca cumbitā//

"A pen, a book, a maiden fair
When out of hand are out fore'er;
If once per chance they come back missed.
They do so worn out, torn and kissed"

(A maiden coming back kissed in India means coming back fallen in morality.)

3635 **लेहन-चिबुक**

Lehana-cibuka : licking by teeth; a type of chin-movement in *hāsya rasa* (*NS*, VIII. 148).

3636 **लेहित-चिबुक**

Lehita cibuka : licking with tongue. It is expressed to indicate greediness (*NS*, VIII. 141-146). It takes place when the lips are licked by the tongue. Licking movements are not uncommon; many occur in situations not characteristic of tongue showing, and although in many other cases they may combine the display with the act of wetting dry lips. We did not tally any cases in which it appeared that the tongue could be serving directly to cleanse or wet the lips. In the vast majority of our observations there was no reason to suspect any direct function for the act of protruding the tongue.

3637 **लोक**

Loka : sphere, world, universe; three *lokas* are commonly enumerated, but a fuller classification gives seven worlds, society. Bharata has defined the *loka* or society as an order based on human nature (*svabhāva*) and established usage or *vārtā* (*NS*, II, p. 214). *Vārtā* has two meanings *viz*., livelihood and news or social currency. Cf. *Amarakośa* (1.6.7; 2.9.1, 3.3.75): *vārtā vṛttau janaśrutau*. Abhinava says that in this context: *lokavārtā* is *lokaprasiddhi*.

The general assumption was that the constituents of human nature are universal, though each individual has a specific character formed by his own actions (*karma vipāka* and *āśaya* are specific). It is recognized, however, that social positions also reflect the level and quality of a persons, conduct, but this quality is cultural rather than ethical.

The broad division of *loka* or society in the *NS* may be said to comprise of classes, castes and professions. The *NS* like all ancient works viewed society as a hierarchical organisation in which men were grouped in different strata and ranked as high and low. This was done in several ways, according to *prakṛti, varṇa, jāti* and *śilpa*, that is to say, culture, character (nature), caste and profession were the principle variables on which social ranking depended. It is noticable that wealth as such is not so recognised formally, although it must undoubtedly have played a prominent part just as the formal ranking of the Brāhmaṇs by *varṇa* must have been in practice often suspended by the actual position of the royalty. The *Pañcatantra* gives expression to the social recognition of wealth. The superiority of the kṣatriyas was upheld by the Buddhists and even the *Bhagavadgītā* exalts the king over other men.

Briefly, then, society or *loka* is conceived as a moral order at human and cosmic in which nature or *svabhāva* is regulated by revealed and immemorial norms. Men are ranked as high, middling and low on the basis of character, caste, social position and profession. The superior person is held to set a standard for the rest. A secular and humanistic outlook pervades social life although a picturesque religion of diverse gods, rituals and superstition serves as a background. Asceticism and devotionalism play only an extremely limited part. Activity motivated by duty, gain and romantic desire is held to be the stuff of social life. While tradition is respected, innovation is valued. Adventure is at a premium.

3638 **लोकधर्मी**

Lokadharmī : belonging to the society, The naturalistic or realistic theatrical convention or style of production, where it is permissible to be representational and to use props. The embracing of child, the child's entering with the bow, etc., are like those in the last act of *Śākuntalam*, are all performed in the *lokadharmī* tradition.

Lokadharmī abhinaya is a realistic practice of gesticulation. The dramatic representation which has natural behaviour and has activities of the ways of the world, devoid of graceful artificial movements of the limbs and has natural acting based on men and women of various types is *lokadharmī*. Abhinava (*NS*, Vol. II, 25-26) explains further that the realistic gain is two fold - (a) that expressive of mental condition, *e.g.* as in arrogant reference to one's ownself the *patāka* hand raised on a level with the forehead, and (b) that indicative of some external object, *e.g.*, the *padmakośa* hand used to represent lotus.

According to Abhinava *lokadharmī* consists of *svabhāva-bhāvopagatam* (natural feelings and conditions), *lokavārtā-kriyopetam* (social usage and behaviour) and *svabhāvābhinayo-petam* (natural acting).

Thus *lokadharmin* drama would naturally stress the treatment of the common, secular aspects of life. As its widest, such drama might embrace the whole range of theatre that presents man's circumstantial and appetitive life in all its heights and depths. In which case, it would appear that the entire Aristotelian tradition is *lokadharmin*? In any event, thi: might well be an instance of Bharata's catholicity and open-mindedness that is evident everywhere. He never makes the mistake of equating the common with the low in quality by definition.

3639 **लोकधर्मी-अभिनय**

Lokadharmī-abhinaya : acting methods of the folk. Methods of presentation in the folk theatre are considerably influenced by the limitations imposed by the amateur and seasonal nature of the folk activities; a great deal is left to the audience's imagination. The conditions under which the actor performs does not permit much refinement whether of movement, gesture, speech or general delivery. Obviously, no theatrical building or proper stage is available for them. The nature of the space upon which they are limited to perform can vary not only from year to year but from day-to-day or performance to performance. It is performed in the open air.

Although some attempts are made by folk actors to convey various emotions by means of vocal inflection and facial expression. This is not developed to any great degree. Emphasis and point is, however, often given to speeches, particularly those of a belligerent nature. When a character rushes on stage wildly flourishing a weapon of some sort this is accepted as a sign of extreme displeasure and is usually the preface to a challenge and duel. Stamping the feet on its own may be used simply to add a note of authority or to stress an important speech.

If the actions of the actors show a certain lack of subtlety, the same can also be said of their manner of speech. All those taking part in the performance try to speak as loudly as possible. In general the voices of the actors tend to lack the natural inflections, adopting instead a strangely monotonous intonation, faster than normal speech and with a rising and falling tone reminiscent of a chant.

3640 **लोकपालन**

Lokapālana : preservation of society (*Mahābhārata*).

3641 **लोकप्रचार**

Loka-pracāra : that can be broadcast among people, synonym of *saṁvṛtti* (*Śikṣāsammucaya*, p. 256, lines 5-10, Bendall's edition). The sphere of knowledge of Buddha may be described in *saṁvṛtti* and *paramārtha* (knowledge of public dissemination).

3642 **लोकयात्रा**

Lokayātrā : ways of the world (*A*, 1.2.5, 5.4.1) (b) orderly maintenance of the people (*A*, 1.4.4), the course of worldly life, maintenance of society.

3643 **लोकवाद**

Lokavāda : common talk, public rumour.

3644 **लोकवृत्तं न वर्तेत**

Lokavṛttaṁ na varteta : one should not go to the way of the world, should not indulge in gossip, etc. It is often said in Sanskrit literature that villagers are more prone to gossip in the blander sense of the world that citizens. Enlightened gossip is a sort of communal novel-writing; it can suggest motives and delineate character as well as describe event. The only reason city-dwellers do not gossip is that they seldom think for a long or deeply about other people. Their main topics of conversation are money, politics and sport. When they can think of nothing more to say on any of these subjects, they resort to telling jokes.

Gossip is the voice of envy, and envy is a growth industry. The moderately prosperous are made restless by the presence of people with larger houses and more leisure time than they themselves enjoy. As the distance between the idol and his devotee decreases envy does not diminish; it becomes greater. In the same way, no one will ever be capable of stopping newspapers peddling malicious gossip if readers can be found who enjoy it.

It we do wish to engage in gossip, there is one rule that we must obey; we must never tell the victim of gossip what is being said about her or him. If gossips cannot trust one another, then all is lost. Those who transgress this fundamental law do nothing to ameliorate their sin by adding "I" am only telling you this for your good or "I" tell you this so that you will know who your real friends are. Infact these wicked people are *kamikaze* pilots; unwelcome news will always be more closely associated with those from whom we actually hear it than from those who originated it.

If we wish to avoid the temptation to gossip, we must, of course, strike envy from our hearts. We must not think of ourselves as deprived.

Gossip harms not only those whose reputations it defiles and those who indulge their lust for exposing the weakness of others, it harms everybody. By exposing the clay-feel of public idols, gossip has deprived us all of, one of the human spirit's deepest needs - the opportunity for unconditional admiration.

3645 **लोकवृत्तानुकरण**

Lokavṛttānukaraṇa : imitation of social reality. The conformity of *nāṭya* to social reality is what Abhinavagupta understands '*lokavṛtta*'. It is not the reference to any specific locality. When a person uses language in accordance with the current social idiom, he cannot be said to be imitating anyone. His conformity to social usage is merely a precondition of social communication.

3646 **लोक-व्यवहार**

Loka-vyavahāra : business of daily life (*Siddhāntavāgīśa, Vyavahāraloka*), a popular expression, a common usage, social usage, action patterns. *Lokavyavahāra* depends on natural drives (*karma*) as well as the norms of moral law (*dharma*). This is the implication of the doctrine of *svadharma*. Cf. the remarks of fisherman in *Śākuntalam*, in the *Viṣkambhaka* between the 5th and 6th Acts.

3647 **लोकशोषक**

Lokaśoṣaka : the sucker of the world, the exploiter, hence a tormentor (*Raghu*, 12.29).

3648 **लोकश्रेय**

Lokaśreya : social good as the moral standard (*Mahānirvāṇatantra*).

3649 **लोकसिद्धि**

Lokasiddhi : realization of social good, social stability (*Nyāyamañjarī*).

3650 **लोकस्थिति**

Loka-sthiti : maintenance of social Equilibrium (*Nyāyamañjarī*). There are only three essential moral predicates: *dāna* (to give others their due); *dayā* (to sympathize with one's fellow creatures) and *dama* (to restrain one's passion) which (all three *d*s) comprise a model conservation policy, an intense desire to preserve the equilibrium, a subsistence ethic which is never permitted, so to speak, to upset the social ecology. In sum, the cardinal virtue is *ahiṁsā*, non-violence.

3651 **लोकस्वभाव**

Lokasvabhāva : human nature. Human nature is not considered to be intrinsically constituted or determined by social development. It was believed to be the result of a unique and timeless tradition. The timelessness is with respect to ordinary empirical history. The cosmic history of *yugas* does transform human nature and *dharma* (*NS*, 1.8). cf *Lokarīti phūṭī sahahin ānjī sahai na koi* (*Dohāvalī*, 423).

3652 **लोकानुकरण**

Lokānukaraṇa : social representation. It was an acknowledged primary object of drama, although it intended to communicate an inner experience through its medium (*NS*, IV.10).

3653 **लोकानुग्रह**

Lokānugraha : favour to the universe or pity on the people.

3654 **लोकापवाद**

Lokāpavāda : public scandal.

3655 **लोकायत**

Lokāyata : the materialistic system of Bṛhaspati (*A*, 1.2.10) Literally that which belongs to the masses. The term includes religious customs based on folklore and popular beliefs. The term has a broad significance. This *lokāyata* system was very much akin to *tāntric* system.

3656 **लोकित-दर्शन**

Lokita-darśana : a type of sight (*NS, VD*).

3657 **लोकोत्तराह्लाद**

Lokottarāhlāda : where state of mediator gets lost in the philosophic contemplation of Brahman on intended objects - a word, stone, colour and gesture.

3658 **लोकोपचार**

Lokopacāra : social business (*NS*, XXIV. 4).

3659 **लोचनगोचर**

Locanagocara : being within range of sight.

3660 **लोचनाञ्चल**

Locanāñcala : side-glance.

3661 **लोप**

Lopa : zero sign of utterance; elision as prescribed by Sanskrit grammatical rules. The ancient recipe for dealing with verbal delinquency by destroying the organs of speech offers some idea of linguistic control in an authoritarian society (see under *sāhasa*). And what was sought to be controlled was not the spoken word alone, but also the zero sign of utterance.

This conceptualization of prescriptive silence as the zero degree of utterance is based on Pāṇini's dictum: *adarśanam lopaḥ* (1.1.60) and some of the subsequent rules, such as VI. I. 66, VI. 4.118, etc. As Vasu has explained it in his edition of the *Aṣṭādhyāyī*: "This *lopa* is considered as a substitute or *ādeśa*, and as such this grammatical zero has all the rights and liabilities of the thing which it replaces. This blank or *lopa* is in several places treated as having a real existence and rules are made applicable to it in the same way as to any ordinary substitute that has an apparent form. The grammarians do not content themselves with one sort of blank but have invented several offers...which like different sorts of zeroes of a Mathematician have different functions" (Pāṇini: 56).

This zero sign of utterance means silence, used formally and yet eloquently enough as 'a significant absence' of speech. It was as if language was made to operate in a state of Pāṇinian *lopa* and was known only by virtue of its elision so that the ban imposed by custom on various kinds of discourse could announce and display the subordination of junior kin to senior, of wife to husband, of low caste to high caste and generally of the underdog to the elite. In village India a youth is not to initiate conversation in the company of his elder as it is rebuked as *choṭe munh baṛī bāt*. To keep silence in the husband's house is the songster teaching to the bride. Thus silence was a sign of subordination to authority in other spheres too (See *Maunam*). In Orissa, a Bauri untouchable was not to speak to a high caste person until spoken to, while in a UP village one frequently finds a lower-caste individual sitting or standing at a slight distance from a higher group engaged in discussion, listening to what is said, but not participating (Gumperz: 194). In parts of Southern India a servant would cover his mouth while receiving his master's command in a sort of metalinguistic acknowledgement of the latter's power over himself (NNQ: 80). In Bengal a landlord would feel it an affront if a peasant were to speak up to him.

3662 **लोपामुद्रा**

Lopāmudrā : the *mantras* of *Srīvidyā* consisting of fifteen symbolic letters (*Tantrasāra*, 242-43) (b) wife of Agastya. *Lopāmudrā* significantly means "Breaker of the seal". Lopāmudrā seduces Agastya eventually, but it is not clear whether he merely yields to her desire, or actively desires her (*Bṛhaddevatā*, 4.57-58). Lopāmudrā merely convinces Agastya to abandon his chastity sooner than he had intended. Agastya speaks several times of the need of progeny, while Lopāmudrā's whishes are purely sensuous, here, sexuality and fertility are combined or rather confused.

3663 **लोभिलिङ्ग**

Lobhiliṅga : addicted to coitus.

3664 **लोम-संहर्षण**

Loma-saṁharṣaṇa : horripilation, thrilling. see *romānca*. Tulasīdāsa describes the thrilling as 'Syāmala gāt roma bhoye ṭaṛhe. Benipravīra has a case of horripitation:

कौतुक एक अनूप लख्यो, सखि ! आजु अचानक नाथ गये छ्वै।
श्रीफल से कुच कामिनी के दोऊ फूल, कदंन के फूल गए ह्वै।।

3665 **लोल करण**

Lola-karaṇa : derived from *vaiṣṇava sthāna*. The arms are in *recita* and the hands are in *añcita*. The head is *lolita* (*NS*, IV. 165-66, VIII. 37. X.52).

3666 **लोलगति**

Lolagati : lady who moves rolling, quality of the Conch-lady (*Pañcasāyaka*, 1.8).

3667 **लोल-नेत्र**

Lola-netra : unsteady eyes, quality of the Bull-man (*Pañcasāyaka*, 2.10). Kālidāsa, while describing Ujjayinī presents a breath-taking spectacle of the artful daughters of Mālavā. Full of amorous gusto, they are masters of the language of the eye. To look is for them to kill with a lethal glance. Intended as a foil to village women to whom love is no art, these extremely sophisticated products of urban refinement, which included an anvanled course of erotics, have been elaborately taught to exploit their resources. The cloud must be wary; to avoid a flirtation with such provoking specimens of female allure would be no easy matter. But the cloud must bear in mind the plight of the Yakṣa's beloved. He cannot afford to tarry for dalliance:

> विद्युद्दामस्फुरित चकितैस्तत्र पौराङ्गनानां
> लोलापाङ्गैर्यदि न रमसे लोचनैर्वञ्चितोऽसि ।।

Even Hindi poet Behari feels alike:

> अमी हलाहल मदभरे
> सेत श्याम रतनार।
> जियत मरत झुकि-झुकि परत
> जिहि चितवत इक बार।।

3668 **लोलितकरण**

Lolita karaṇa *:* The hands are in *recita* and *añcita* and the head *lolita* and *vartita* on both the sides.

3669 **लोलित-शिर**

Lolita-śira : movement of the head, turning of head on all sides. The love-distraction in *Vikramorvaśīya* (Act III) is represented by the *lolita* head (*NS*, VIII. 36). In it the head is moved on all sides. *Lolita* is a type of the Head shake. The head turns horizontally from side to side, with equal emphasis left and right. This is the most common form of negative response, covering a wide range of NOS. It can also signify disapproval or bewilderment. Like the Head Nod, the Head Shake is vertually common in Indian literature except in Marāthī. It is thought to stem from the infantile action of rejection of the breast, when the parent tries to persuade the baby to feed, the negative response to the offering is to twist the head first to one side then to the other, turning the head away from the unwanted object. This alternate turning is seen as the starting point for the adult Head Shake, and explains why, wherever it occurs, it is always a negative signal.

Lolita is used in fainting, sickness, power of intoxication and drowsiness due to being possessed of evil spirit.

3670 **लोलित स्कन्ध**

Lolita-skandha : rotation of the shoulder in the circular movement.

3671 **लोष्ट्र-मुद्रा**

Loṣtra-mudrā : the stone-gesture. "Making the right hand up-stretched; the thumb, in a position of hidden inside, should cling other fingers. Thus placing all the fingers on the thumb, makes a *loṣtra-mudrā* (gesture of throwing stones). This gesture brings under control all the worlds and destroys all sorts of enemies" (*BT*).

3672 **लौकिक**

Loukika : worldly, mundane; literally 'local' Cf. the concept of deceipt hanging between *Vedic* and *laukika:*

> *yatra vaidikāstatra laukika*
> *yatra laukikāstatra vaidikāḥ*।
> *yatra cobhayam tatra nobhayam*
> *yatra nobhayam tatra tūbhayam*।।

"When lo! We meet great Vedic men of parts
We greet as scholars in the worldly arts;
When Savants in the latter field we meet
As scholars of the Holy wit we greet;
When both are there, we say we neither are
When neither's there, we claim that both we are."

3673 **लौकिक-प्रत्यक्ष**

Laukika-pratyakṣa : ordinary perception. According to the *Nyāya* it is of six kinds: *cākṣusa* (visual), *śrauta* (auditory), *sparśana* (tactual), *rāsana* (gustatory), *ghrāṇaja* (olfactory) and *mānasa* (mental).

व –Va

3674 **वंशनर्तिनी**

Vaṁśa-nartinī : a pole-dancer. In the *Taittirīya Brāhmaṇa* (III. 4.2.1) we get reference to *vaṁśanartinīnām* about which Sāyaṇa explains as *vaṁśāgra-nṛtta-jīvinām* (one who has livelihood by the dance on the pole-end, a pole-dancer or an acrobat. Thus in dance, acrobatics had a significant place.

3675 **वंशावलिरचकः**

Vaṁśāvali racakaḥ : genealogist. Genealogists (generally known as *bhāṭ)* form amongst themselves a microcosm of the wider society. To a considerable extent they are divided commensally and endogamously by the status of the castes and tribes they serve. In general, the genealogist ranks lower than his patron; the latter will eat only *pakkā* food from his hands; whereas he will take *kaccā* food when visiting the villages.

The *bhāṭ* is the most important of the genealogists. Genealogists in pilgrimage-places keep the records of the every family of the India-villages. Their books record the visit of the ancestors of at least ten generations. The pilgrim-genealogist provides a reflection of the unilineal structure of the society, since he is believed to have records of the agnates to whom worship is at the same time made.

3676 **बक-मुद्रा**

Vaka-mudrā : gesture of a crane. The mingled *haṁsa* hand indicates a crane. The fore finger and the thumb are joined, the second and third fingers extended and the little finger touchs the palms (*Mirror of Gesture,* pp. 50-51).

3677 **बकवृत्ति**

Vakavṛtti : hypocricy, false devotion.

3678 **वक्तव्य**

Vaktavya : blameworthy, unfit (*A*, 3.1.47), to be said, censurable. *vaktavyatā* blamable.

3679 **वक्तृ**

Vaktṛ : speaker, orator; *vaktṛtā* : ability to speak, eloquence. Cf.

kim kariṣyanti vaktāraḥ
śrotā yadi na vidyate /
nagne kṣapaṇake deśe
rajakaḥ kim kariṣyati //

"What can great gifted speakers do
If there be not one listener too;
In places where nude people live
How can a launderer hope to thrive?"

3680 **वक्त्र-मुद्रा**

Vaktra-mudrā : mouth-gesture; occurs in *BT.* "holding up the mouth place or join it with the another. This is called the *vakra-mudrā* and none should hesitate to make it."

3681 **वक्र -परिहास**

Vakra-parihāsa : startric words in love (*Kuṭṭinīmatam,* 396).

3682 **वक्र-रुचिर-जघना**

Vakra-rucira-jaghanā *:* lady whose hips are beautiful and big, quality of the Mare-lady (*Ratirahasya,* 3.22-3).

3683 **वक्रा**

Vakrā : a beautiful woman.

3684 **वक्रास्थिग्रन्थि**

Vakrāsthigranthi : lady whose bones of ankles are tortuous, quality of the Mare-lady (*Nāgarasarvasva,* 14.6).

3685 **वक्रिता-भ्रुकुटी**

Vakritā-bhrukuṭi : a type of *bhrukuṭī* given by *Bālarāmabharata.*

3686 **वक्रोक्ति**

Vakrokti : indirect mode of expression, evasive speech or reply, obliquity, ingenious speech implying cleverness and charm, 'pleasant poignancy', *equivoque* base on punning and intonation: *yaduktamanyāthā vākyamanyathātvena yojyate śleṣeṇa kākvā vā jneyā sā vakroktiḥ* (*Kāvyaprakāśa*, IX. 79; *SD.* X. 9). The following verse from Bhāmaha is quoted by many writers such as Ānandavardhana, Mammaṭṭa, and Hemacandra.

सैषा सर्वत्र वक्रोक्तिरनयार्थो विभाव्यते।
यत्लोऽस्यां कविना कार्यः कोऽलंकारो ऽनया विना।। (2.85).

Here *vakrokit* means a charming and suggestive expression. It is synonymous with *lokātikrāntagocaram vacaḥ* which Bhāmaha uses in defining the figure *atiśayokti* (2.81), which says that when words are used in an ordinary manner in which people in general without a poetic turn of mind use them, there is no *vaicitrya,* no charm, and consequently no figure of speech. It is only when they are used in a charming sense, in an extraordinary manner which remotedly suggests something very charming, that we have what we call a figure of speech. *Vaicitrya* of word and sense which Bhāmaha means by *vakrokti* is essential to constitute an *alaṅkāra* (2.66).

In modern linguistics *vakrokti* means "indirect speech act". It is in recognition of the fact that in speaking we often say one thing and mean or implicate something else. So one illocutionary act is performed indirectly by what appears to be another. A lot depends on the context in *vakrokti.* Compare the following verse from Mānasa:

> मैं सुकुमारि नाथ बन जोगू।
> तुमहिं उचित तप मोकहँ भोगू।।
> धर्मशीलता तुम जग जागी।
> पावा दरश हमहुँ बड़ भागी।।

3687 **वक्रोष्ठि**

Vakroṣṭhi : a gentle smile.

3688 **वक्रोष्ठिका**

Vakroṣṭhikā : a gentle smile.

3689 **वक्ष**

Vakṣa : the gesture of the trunk, breast, chest: The style of the chest are of five kinds: *ābhugna* (the little broken) *nirbhugna* (the full broken), *udvāhita* (the raised up), *prakampita* (the trembling) and *sama* (the natural). (b) The hand-on-heart. The man places his right hand flat on to his chest in the heart region. This symbolism indicates that the woman is so beautiful that she makes his heart-beat faster with emotion (*NS,* IX. 224).

Varāhamihira (*BS,* LXVIII) has also portrayed the signs (*lakṣaṇa*) on the chest through which the nature of men can be perceived. According to him "only kings possess a heart (*hṛdaya*) that is raised, broad, muscular and not convulsive, while the penniless have one that has contrary features, and is full of veins and rough and thick hair

> हृदयं समुन्नतं पृथु न वेपनं मांसलं च नृपतीनाम् ।
> अधमानां विपरीतं खररोमाचितं शिरालं च ।।

People with an even chest become wealthy; with a muscular one, heroes; with one deficient in flesh, penniless and with an uneven one, indigent and meet their end by weapons:

> समवक्षसोऽर्थवन्तः पीनैः शूरा ह्यकिंचनास्तनुभिः ।
> विषमं वक्षो रोषां निःस्वा शस्त्रनिधनाश्च ।।

Cf. the same source:

> अर्थवान् समवक्षाः स्याद् दीर्घैः शूरा धनान्विताः ।
> अल्पैश्च विकलाः दीनाः विषमैः शस्त्रमृत्युवः ।।

3690 **वक्षःस्थल**

Vakṣaḥ-sthala : breast, bosom.

3691 **वक्षस्वस्तिक-करण**

Vakṣasvastika-karaṇa : the legs are in *svastika* and the *recita* hands are brought on the breast which is bent. It is used in repentance and sense of shame.

3692 **वक्ष-स्वस्तिक-रेचित-करण**

Vakṣa-svastika-recita-karaṇa : hands in *svastika.* The chest is bent in *nikuñcita.* Feet are in *svastika* and all alternatively opened and crossed (*NS,* IV. 73-74, IX.224).

3693 **वक्षाभरण**

Vakṣābharaṇa : ornaments of the breast (*NS*). (a) males: *trisara* (pearl necklace with three strings) and *hāra* (necklace). The suspended pearl necklace and the flower garland are meant for the body. (b) females: necklaces of artistic variety.

3694 **वचनशक्ति**

Vacana śakti : speech competence (*Caraka Saṁhitā,* Vimāna, 8.14-15). Bhāravi in his *Kirātārjunīyam* (XIV) portraits the speech that lifts all men to its praise:

> Lucid, cleanly uttered, and good to hear,
> Winning even a mind that came to attack;
> Straight, fluent, but also grave with sense,
> A speech issuing from act on scrupulous act.
>
> There are those, it's true, so facile and well-schooled
> There talk exactly proclaims their adequate minds;
> And then a few, a masterly few, whose words
> Flash, of a sudden, down through the dark of sense.
> Some find powerful plainness is best, and some
> Allusion, finely worked until it's exact;
> Different stations, different tastes. Most coveted
> And rare the speech that lifts all men to its praise.
> (Vatsyāyana and Mishra, 1983. 124).

cf. the following example of speech competence:

> कल करील की कुंज में, रह्यो अरुझि मो चीर।
> हे बलवीर अहीर के, हरत क्यों न यह पीर।।

3695 **वचोविग्रह**

Vacovigraha : quarrel, *vākkalaha.* Quarrels are an important part of Indian mythology, not only because they demonstrate the conflict between the characters, but also because, in the Hindu view, quarrels, violence and separation are an essential part of any sexual relationship, enhancing rather than impending it (*Kāmasūtra* 2.4-5; *Subhāṣitaratnakośa,* part 22, vv. 700-51). The lover's infidelity and the subsequent quarrel and separation provide a more ardent spur to love, and the theme of love in separation is used by the court poets to heighten the erotic mood (*Ibid*). Physical violence and sex are closely intertwined in the *Kāmasūtra,* which devotes an entire chapter to the technique of biting and scratching, and Kālidāsa explicitly mentions this part of the love-play of Śiva and Pārvatī: although when he first made love to her there was no biting of her lips and scratching of her breasts, later her hands were tremulous with pain, her lips marked with bites, and her thighs scored with the traces of his nails (*Kumārasambhava*, VIII. 9, XVIII. 87).

Quarrel in cross-setting is therefore a sexual stimulus. This may be illustrated by the Kālī argument: "Śiva called Pārvatī 'Kālī' and a terrible quarrel took place." (*Skanda*, 5.2.18.34-4) Thus, the quarrel between cross-sexes produces the symbol of sexual union which prevents quarrels, a most concise example of the workings of sexual mythology. After a quarrel there is reconciliation which brings ultimate union and the starting point for new separation. Śiva quarrels with Pārvatī in his ascetic aspect and reunites with her in his erotic aspect; the myth begins with fasting and ends with feasting.

3696 **वज्र**

Vajra : thunderbolt shaped in the form of a weapon. It serves as an emblem of certain Buddhist deities (*Prajñapāya*, III. 9). (b) a penance in which barley grains fried in clarified butter and mixed with cow's urine are required to be partaken (*Atri*, 164). (c) name of nerve situated within *Susumnā*. (d) rude remark made to one at his face in drama (*DR*, 1. 69). (e) adamantine.

3697 **वज्रपञ्जरमुद्रा**

Vajrapañjara mudrā : "keep your wrists separately and raise up the thumbs and little fingers of both the hands. It is the gesture of *vajrapañjara* that assures great strength" (*BT*).

3698 **वज्रपर्यङ्कासन**

Vajraparyaṅkāsana : also known as *dhyānāsana*. It is the meditative pose. Two legs are firmly locked in a seated posture with both the soles apparent. It is the characteristic sitting attitude of *dhyānī Buddhas*. *Dhyānāsana* should be distinguished from the *paryaṅka* attitude in which case the legs are crossed but the feet are tucked under and both the soles are invisible.

3699 **वज्र-मुद्रा**

Vajra-mudrā : "Make two arms as good as two lances, elbow visible distinctly; and the fingers of both the hands matted themselves. This is called the thunderbolt-gesture (*BT*)". (b) "Two hands are to be placed in an opposite order and the extended fingers are to be kept joined together. All the fingers are to be so tied that the thumb and the little finger should remain entwined. This is the *Vajra-mudrā*, that revives the spiritual strength of a devout, accumulated previously. It is also an indicative of the great union between the worshipper and the worshipped" (*BT*). (c) With the help of two tips of two fore-fingers, the left and the right, hold the left-fore-fingers tip by the right and the right by the left, in turn. Curve the rest six fingers, three of each hand and put each fore-finger to each thumb of the same hand. This is the gesture of *vajra* (*VD*). (d) Keep your palms on the flat position, curve two ring-fingers, place both the thumbs and fore-fingers also with the curved way and lastly place those two, the ring and the little fingers to a certain side. All these make the gesture, known *vajra*, which controls all evil powers (*VD*).

3700 **वज्रसूची-मुद्रा**

Vajrasūcī-mudrā : "turning upward the palms with interlocked fingers and twisting them to the opposite direction, the devout seated on the *svastikāsana* should affix them upward. This is called *vajrasūcī-mudrā* applicable to bid farewell to Gods" (*BT*).

3701 **वज्रहुङ्कारमुद्रा**

Vajrahuṅkāra-mudrā : an iconic *mudrā*. The wrists are crossed at the chest with the two hands holding the *vajra*, and the bell, both of which are turned inwards. If the two symbols and the hands are turned outward the *mudrā* is called *Trailokyavijaya-mudrā*.

3702 **वज्रासन**

Vajrāsana : the soles of the feet may be kept on both the sides on the buttocks, calves touching the thighs. The whole burden of the body is put on the knees and ankles. The knees should be kept quite close and the hands should rest straight on the knees. Keep the trunk, neck and head in one straight line.

Sitting in this *āsana*, even after food, is helpful for digestion. The stomach works vigorously. Myalgia in the knees, legs, toes and thighs disappears and sciatica vanishes.

This *āsana* alone can be done after taking food. No other *āsana* should be practised after food.

(b) Throwing thunderbolt.

3703 **वज्रोलि-मुद्रा**

Vajroli-mudrā : a method for prolonging the duration in sexual-intercourse for Tāntric purposes. It is supposed to confer a long life on *yogin* even after indulgence in sexual orgies (*Haṭhayogapradīpikā*, II. 82-96).

3704 **वञ्चनाशास्त्रम्**

Vañcanāśāstram : political economics, science of cheating, *arthaśāstram* (*Mbh.*).

3705 **वंचिताक्ष**

Vañcitākṣa : avoidance (*Ratirahasya*, 6.2).

3706 **वडवा**

Vaḍavā : the Mare-woman. According to Kokkoka. "She is called a mare-lady whose head is uneven, whose hair are thick, straight and compressed, whose eyes are unsteady like the petals of blue lotus, whose face and ears are big and wide, whose teeth are strong and lips are attractive, whose breast-pitchers are hard and full of flesh, whose shoulders are beautiful and fleshy, whose stomach is small, whose hands are soft like lotus, whose chest is wide and voice is sweet, who is anxious due to jealously, whose navel is deep and round, whose hips are beautiful and big, thighs are long and straight, whose waist is thin, gait is nice, heart is fickle, limbs are soft, who loves meals, sleep and lover, whose body contains *vāta* and *kapha*, whose mucus is yellowish and smells like meat, who is satisfied with the Bull-man and whose sex-organ is nine *aṅgulas* in depth (*Ratirahasya*, 3. 22-26). (b) a mare, particularly the submarine mare-fire.

3707 **वत्स**

Vatsa : a disciple or a son is to be addressed by the *guru* (teacher) or the father as *vatsa, putraka, tāta* or by name or clan name (*NS*, XVII, 65-94), lit. means 'the age when one picks up speech (*vad*); form of address.

3708 **वत्सल**

Vatsala : parental affection. Natural affection for children is its basic impulse. Children—sons, daughters, etc. are its stimulating objects. Their activities, learning, valour, etc. excite it further. Embracing, fondling, caressing, or kissing on the head, etc. Constitute its consequents, while ecstasy, pride, fear of possible evil represent its accessories. Its colour is like the interior of red lotus and its presiding

3709 **वत्सा**

Vatsā: younger sister is to be addressed as *vatsā,* while the elder sister is addressed *bhaginī (NS*, XVII, 65-94).

3710 **वदन-चुम्बन**

Vadana-cumbana : kissing of face. Throughout the kissing round, it is the face of the female that appears to function as a regulator, modulating the approaches and orientation of male. Thus Kālidāsa names Śiva a the lotus of Pārvatī's mouth: *Pārvatī-vadana-śaṭpadaḥ* (*Kumāra,* 8.23). Other references such as *vadanam dayitāyaḥcumbati* (*Kirāta*, 9.47) and *ānane paricumbya* (*Naiṣadha,* 18.41) are numerous in Sanskrit literature.

3711 **वदनपरिपाटी**

Vadanaparipāṭī : facial expression, hint, sign, manner of speaking.

3712 **वधू-नाटक-सङ्घ**

Vadhū-nāṭaka-saṅgha : theatre meant for women (*Rāmāyaṇa,* 1.5.12).

3713 **वधूप्रधर्षण**

Vadhūpradharṣaṇa : molestation of a woman.

3714 **वध्यपटह**

Vadhya-paṭaha : drum struck at the time of execution.

3715 **वनमाला-मुद्रा**

Vanamālā-mudrā : gesture symbolising *vanamālā* of the Vaiṣṇavite cult. Two *śikhara* hands kept separated symbolise the *vanamālā* (*VD*). (b) if the *Vahni-mudrā* in left hand and *Śikhara-mudrā* in the right, meet together, it is called *Vanamālā* (*VD*).

3716 **वनेचर**

Vanecara : forest-dweller, the tribe. According to Indian thought, *vānaprastha* is a compromise between the *gṛhastha* and *sannyāsa.* This myth and reality makes the Hindu aware of the struggle and of its futility. They show him that his society demands of him two roles which he cannot possibly satisfy fully-that he becomes a householder and begets sons, and that he renounces life and seeks union with god. The myth shows the untenable answer arrived at by compromise—the *vanecara* with his wife—and suggests a solution finally in the re-examination of the nature of the two roles, of the presence of each in the other, so that a balance may be sought without any of the unsatisfactory accommodations necessary in real life. The myth makes it possible to admit that the ideal is not attainable (Douglas, p. 52).

3717 **वनौकस्**

Vanaukas : foresters (*NS*, XVII. 53-57).

3718 **वन्दनी-मुद्रा**

Vandanī-mudrā : 'bowing' with the palms placed at the heart (*Garuḍa Purāṇa*, I.II.26.33).

3719 **वन्दिन्**

Vandin : panegyrist, bard: *dūtavandī-sakhīmukhāt* (*SD*, III. 189). In the Gond community the whole story of epics and *Purāṇas* have come from *Pardhāns* and they are known as *pāṭādi* being the reciters of songs. They are the carriers of Gond culture. The Gonds have become familiar with Hindu gods and mythical characters through these songs. Garbed and very incorrect versions of *Rāmāyaṇa, Mahābhārata* and *Purāṇas* are still sung by these *Pardhāns* which have reached into the cultural consciousness of Gonds.

3720 **वयस्य**

Vayasya : friend of the same age; persons of equal status are to be addressed as *vayasya* (*NS*, XVII, 65-94). The king may be addressed by Vidūṣaka as *vayasya.* The Vidūṣaka should be addressed by the king as *vayasya* or by name.

3721 **वर**

Vara : lover, suitor, husband, bridegroom (Kālidāsa, *Śāk.* 5.389). *Upayantṛ* is the synonym of the bridegroom (*Kumāra.*, 5.81).

3722 **वरद-मुद्रा**

Varada-mudrā : single hand gesture in iconography. Known as *patākahasta* in *NS.* Right hand hangs down over the knee and the palm is turned outward showing chastity. *Varada-mudrā* depicts the hands of gods while conferring boons. The hand showing this gesture is pendant with its palm outward and fingers all stretched. Sometimes a jewel is seen stamped on the hand showing this *mudrā.* In this case it is known as the *ratnasaṁyukta-varada,* that is, the gift bestowing attitude together with a jewel.

3723 **वरद-हस्त**

Varada-hasta : a type of hand gesture. We can see the *varada hasta* of Naṭarāja.

3724 **वरयात्रा**

Varayātrā : procession of bridegroom. While the bridegroom's party is absent at the bride's house, the village women who remain behind enjoy amusements of their own. One of them strips herself naked, tying up her hair like a religious mendicant, and plays the sexual game. It is known as *jindbā* in Baghelkhand. In this state she romp with her companions in turn, while the other laugh and applaud. Occasionally some man hides himself in a place where he can be a witness of their play, but if they discover him, he is beaten severely with beens or wooden bread-rollers. This is a type of mock-drama (see also Russell and Hiralal, III. 5).

3725 **वरारोहा**

Varārohā : having winsome buttocks, a beautiful woman.

3726 **वराह-चर्वितक**

Varāha-carvitaka : the biting of the bear. Breasts are suitable places chosen for this bite (*Kāmasūtra*, 2.5.16-17).

3727 **वराह-मुद्रा**

Varāha-mudrā : Indication of a boar. The *saṁkīrṇa-makara*-hand held down with fingers apart indicate a boar (*Mirror of Gesture*, pp. 49-50) (b) gesture symbolizing the Vaiṣṇavite deity *varāha.* The *śikhara* hand with the stretched little finger down symbolize *Varāha* (*VD*); (c) gesture of the Boar-God. Make a *sampuṭa* (a cup-like pose) with two hands and raise a little the left one. This is *varāha* (*VD*).

3728 **वराह-हस्त**

Varāha-hasta : both hands gesture. It is represented in Lakṣmaṇa temples of Khajurāho. The style of the *mṛgaśirṣa* of one hand, when placed on the same of the other; it is the *Varāha,* that represents the third incarnation of Viṣṇu. (Fig. 3728)

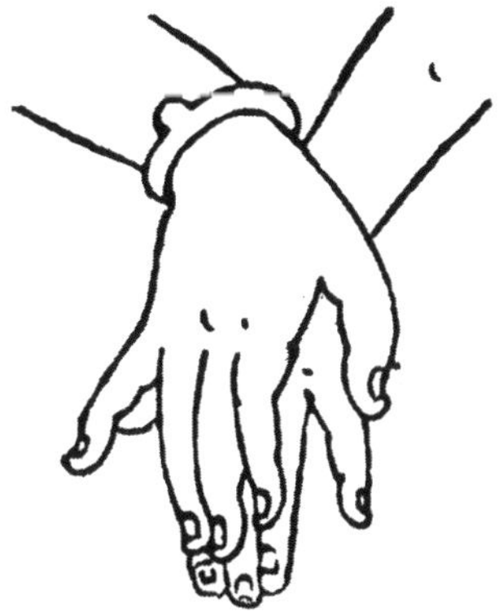

Fig. – (3728)

3729 **वरुण-हस्त**

Varuṇa-hasta : *patāka* with the right and *śikhara* with the left hand, indicate *Varuṇa,* one of the *Dikpālas* (*AD*, 211-215).

3730 **वर्कराट**

Varkarāṭa : side-glance, marks of a lover's finger-nails on the bosom of his beloved.

3731 **वर्ण**

Varṇa : modulation, colour, quality of sound, scale, letter, palette; Lit. colour. Voice modulation is related to emotion. In a situation of love or laughter, raised and shaking; in pathos, fear, or disgust, it should be lowered, mixed, and shaking. The vehicle of an abstract idea is a *varṇa,* what in Indian languages means the both; letters of alphabet, as well as a colour. Possibly letters had been used to be drawn by painting (*lepana*) colours, they are called *lipi*; which is appreciated as the visible forms of the invisible divine energy. (b) in *Ṛgveda* (III. 34.9; II. 12.4) the word *varṇa* has been originally used to signify skin-colour and has been applied to distinguish the two main tribes likes *āryavarṇa* (white colour) and *dāsa-varṇa* (dark colour). In the classical Sanskrit texts, skin-colours like *sveta, switnya* and *gaura* have been used to denote the people of white skin. The Yavanas, Śakas, Vāhlīkas, Khasas, Kulinds, Daradas, Kuṣāṇas and Hūṇas of Northern India are included with in this group. The complexion of human both, as is well known, is more or less influenced by the climatic condition though heredity is a primary criterion. The tropical climate has a tendency to darken the skin colour. (c) *Varṇas* are accents in *NS.* Abhinava (II.390) explains that they are *svaradharmas, i.e.,* qualities of sound. They are so-called because they make clear the special meaning. They are *udātta* (acute), *anudātta* (grave), *svarita* (circumflex), and *kampita* (quivering). *Svarita* and *udātta* are to be used in the comic and the erotic; *udātta* and *kampita* in the heroic; the furious and the marvellous; and *anudātta, svarita* and *kampita* in the pathetic, the odious and the terrible. (d) Letters, also called *mātṛkās*, symbolising different manifestations of *Śakti*..

(e) *NS* like all ancient works viewed society as a hierarchical organisation in which men were grouped in different strata. This was done also on the basis of *varṇa*. *Varṇa* was thus a social variable. The *NS* was the *cāturvarṇya* to indicate the universe of characters, or the concourse of the four *varṇas* as is the usual meaning (*NS*, XVIII. 82; 1.86). The Brāhmaṇs could be found among ministers and officials advising and assisting the king. Their characteristic roles which drama represented were those of teachers, priests and councillors. The protrayal of the *Vidūṣaka* (jester) possibly represents a satire on the Brāhmaṇcial dependence on patronage. While kings, warriors and officials are prominently represented on the stage, the Kṣatriyas as such find little mention. The Vaiṣyas included householders engaged in agriculture as well as business. The Śūdras are mentioned as one of the four *varṇas* who constituted the spectators in the theatre (*NS*, II. 49-50). The four *varṇas* are symbolised by the four pillars which support the theatre. Each had a distinct contribution—wisdom, energy, wealth and hardihood respectively. (f) body-complexion. 'A glossy and shining complexion belongs to kings; a medium one, to those that have wealth and children; a rough one, to the poor; a clean complexion is always auspicious; and not so, a mixed one (*Bṛhat-Saṁhitā*, LXVIII).

3732 **वर्णक**

Varṇaka : *A* touch (*A*, 2.13.15,16). Kauṭilya knows little about the conditions under which a person will permit another to touch him, the meanings people attach to touching and being touched, the loci of the acceptable touch, and little of the consequences of body contact; while Vātsyāyana is an expert advisor. It is as if the touch-taboo most of us learned in childhood has produced a scotoma of our professional vision, making us describe man in our texts as if he did not get closer to his fellows than a food or so. Vātsyāyana and the Tāntrikas tried to break the touch-taboo, while the law-givers adhered to it.

Kauṭilya thinks that *varṇaka* (touch) can communicate like letters, while Vātsyāyana thinks it to be a device of physical arousal. Touching in relation to status or *varṇa* (e.g.; sex, colour, age, socio-economic level, caste) was studied by the law-givers.

Heslin (1974) has proposed five categories of touching in the interpersonal relationship: (a) at the functional/professional level, use of touch is an impersonal 'manipulator-to-object' level, as during a physician's examination where the motivation is to do something to the other person who is regarded largely as an object. (b) touches such as handshakes represent the Social-Polite level, where physical contact occurs on a very restricted, socially prescribed level. (c) touches that convey Friendship/warmth are often the most difficult for persons to interprete because the relationship is close enough for love or sexual attraction to develop. (d) love/intimacy touches (*e.g.*, hand on cheek) also require an appropriate interpersonal context if they are not to disturb others by conveying sexual intentions. (e) the touch level of sexual arousal is obviously the most intense, and the kinds of touches which convey this meaning are probably somewhat indiosyncratic among partners.

3733 **वर्णना**

Varṇanā : description.

3734 **वर्णमयी दीक्षा**

Varṇamayī-dīkṣā : initiation by infusing the spirit of letters in different parts of the candidate's body (*Śāradātilaka*, V. 116-21).

3735 **वर्णमाला**

Vrṇamālā : series of letters, alphabet.

3736 **वर्ण-विपर्यय**

Varṇa-viparyaya : change in the position of letters: *siddho varṇaviparyayāt.*

3737 **वर्ण-वृत्ति**

Varṇa-vṛtti : letter-repetition, alliteration. Example of paralanguage.

3738 **वर्णव्यतिक्रान्ता**

Varṇa-vyatikrāntā : a woman enjoying sexual intercourse with a man of lower caste.

3739 **वर्णसंहार**

Varṇasaṁhāra : a type of *sandhyaṅga* in dramaturgy. Bharata (*NS*, XIX.82) defines it as the 'meeting of four *varṇas* in a drama; a case of proximity, coming together of the four *varṇas* in a drama (*DR*, 1.65). (b) songs and catches about the different castes always go swell in India. Take for example the following poem from Chattisgarh:

> On every roof the flowering gourds are swinging
>
> The *kewat* boy is strong
> With what force he pushes the *pelnā* trap through the water

The *Dhuliā* boy is strong
How vigorously he weaves his baskets
The *Lohār* boy is strong
With what might he hammers the iron
The *Pankā* boy is strong
How deftly he threads the warp
The *Gond* boy is strong
With what power he ploughs his field.

This is probably an apt characterization of the boys of the different castes. Songs about the girls reflect rather on their morals:

A *Telī* girl is smooth and oily
A *Pardhān* girl has a straight parting to her hair
A *Pankā* girl goes visiting from house to house
An *Ahīr* girl spreads gossip everywhere.
A Teli girl is smooth and oily
A Gondin's hair is always tousled
A Panka girl is highly coloured
She soon calls you indoors.

The words used are expressive.The Telin is *Cikan-Cākan*, with hair smooth and glossy with the oil that it is her profession to extract. The Gondin is *jhingrī*, wild and dishevelled. The Pankin is *rangrailin*, exciting and colourful. The Pardhanin is *māng-ciknin*. Finally the Ahirin is *cuglī-batain*.

The Panka, who is not only a weaver but did hold the post of village watch-man, is a stock figure of mockery. The Gond is regarded as a bysmally stupid. His untrustworthiness is also reflected in the proverbs: 'A Gond, a woman, or a dream: never claim that these are yours'. His manners is also notorious. There is none more generous than the Gond—but he won't part unless you kick him'. The Gond are so united, 'they even share a little bit of bread with one another'. The Ahīr too are given the worst of reputations:

Ahir and Gaḍariya are a dirty lot
They excrete at midday
And wash their asses at night.

3740 **वर्णसंकर**

Varṇasaṅkara : mixing of the castes, born of parents belonging to different castes.

3741 **वर्णानां आनुपूर्वेण पूर्वनिपातः**

Varṇānām ānupūrveṇa pūrvanipātaḥ : the castes are placed according to their order (*Aṣṭādhyāyī*, II. 2.34, *Vārtika*). It is a well known Pāṇinian rule which was interpreted in such a way as to make the words standing for four *varṇas* replicate the *varṇa* hierarchy in itself of the *dvandvasamāsa*, which would then read ब्राह्मणक्षत्रियविट्शूद्रा : The *Sūtra alpāchtaram* (II. 2.34) has the above *Vārtika*. This *Vārtika* puts the four *varṇas* together in their ascriptive order descending from Brāhmana to *Śūdra*.

Thus deference in speech was to a great extent in the domain of caste and class relationship where feudal authority prevailed in its most explicit and effective form. Here again one finds the element of a linguistic descrimination between castes entrenched in *Aṣṭādhyāyī*.

3742 **वर्णाश्रम**

Varṇāśrama : the scheme of a society based on four *varṇas* (vocational classes) and four *āśramas* (stages of life).

3743 **वर्तन**

Vartana : attitude: *rasikasyaiva vartanāt* (*DR*, IV.47). *Vartana* is a relatively stable and enduring predisposition to behave or react in a certain way towards persons, objects, institutions, or issues. Looked at from a slightly different point of view, *vartanas* are tendencies to respond to people, institutions or events either positively or negatively. The source of attitudes are cultural, familial, and personal. That is, we tend to assume the attitudes that prevail in the culture in which we grow up. A large segment of these are passed on from generation to generation within the family structure.

Vartana reflects the fact that we use language not only to communicate factual information, but also feelings and attitudes. Prosodic and para-linguistic features in speech are important indicators of attitudes: loudness, voice quality, and intonation can show boredom, exitement, anger or sarcasm. Attitudes in face-to-face interactions can also be conveyed by body language; facial expression of disgust, pleasure, etc.

In dramatic theory the study of *rasika's* attitude to the representation being performed can be seen as an important aspect of the study of point of view.

3744 **वर्तना**

Vartanā : (a) Pāli; *vartanā*; shading, that is: plastic modelling in painting. (b) *vartanā* (in dance terminology) means a particular movement of the arms. By resorting to various movements of arms, separately and collectively, and adopting the tempos *druta*, etc. innumerable *vartanās* can be produced. Śārṅgadeva does not enumerate *vartanās* of which twenty-four varieties are described by Kallinātha following Kohala.

3745 **वर्तिका**

Vartikā : brush.

3746 **वर्तित-करण**

Vartita-karaṇa : *āvartita* and *parivartita* of hands. The initial position is of *svastika* hands. One foot is in *agratalasañcara*; a *svastika* of the wrists also mentioned (*NS*, IV.62; IX.218, 273). The hands are in *vyāvṛtta* and *parivartita*, bent at the wrist and then placed on thighs. It is used in gesticulating jealousy with upturned *patāka* hands, and anger, with downward *patāka* hands.

3747 **वर्तुलास्य**

Vartulāsya : round face, quality of a Hare-man (*Ratirahasya*, 3.30-31).

3748 **वर्धमानक-हस्त**

Vardhamānaka hasta : greeting posture. It is formed by *mukula* and *kapittha hasta. NS* describes the formation of *vardhamāna* through the *haṁsapakṣa* hands facing outward (*NS*, IX. 158) (a) when the gesture of the *mukula* style is rounded up by the *kapittha hasta* (q.v.), it is called the *vardhamānaka.* It is used to collect and accept things desire, taking up an oath, or a term and to tell the truth. They are to be exhibited in a little alteration, pressing of the *avahittha* gesture (b) turning the two *haṁsa-pakṣa* gestures in from the opposite direction we may also make the second style of *vardhamāna* gesture. It is stylized to indicate a latticed-window (*NS*, IX. 148-150). Also known as *vardhamāna-hasta.* The *haṁsa pakṣa* hands inverted in *svastika* position or without *svastika* also. It indicates opening of the latticed windows, etc. (Fig. 3748)

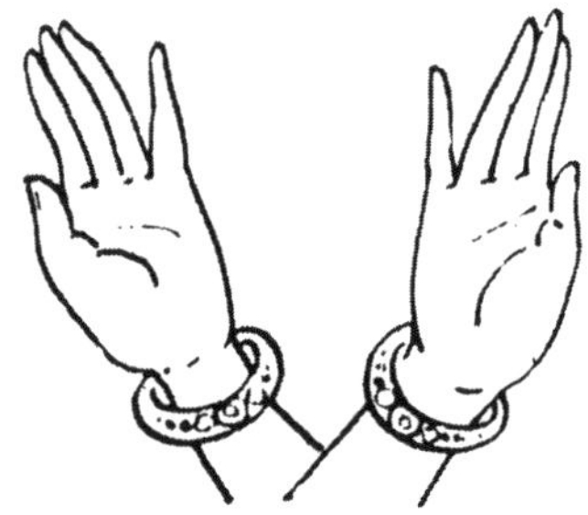

Fig. – (3748)

3749 **वर्धमान-स्थानक**

Vardhamāna-sthānaka : type of posture.

3750 **वलन (तारा)**

Valana (tārā) : moving the eyeballs obliquely. A type of eye-gesture. Movement of the pupil in *krodha* (anger). Diagonal or oblique movement of the eyebal. In *Mālavikāgnimitram* (Act V), the dwarf enters the stage. Mālavikā enacts fear. The eyeballs she uses for this is *valana* (*NS*, VIII.102); oblique movement of the eyeballs, a type of glance by movement of the eyeballs.

3751 **वलनोरू**

Valanorū : this is really a crossing of the things even though it is not clearly stated in the NS. It is a gesture of the thigh; when knees are drawn inward in a process of going on and used in the movement of women's going at ease (*NS*, X.27-33). It is used in the easy gait of women. Bharata describes *valana* as the movement of knee inwards. But from its description in the 108 *karaṇas* and from Abhinava's commentary it becomes apparent that *valana* is actually the crossing of the thighs.

3752 **वलित-करण**

Valita-karaṇa : *sūcīmukha hasta: sūcīmukha* in initial position and *bhramarī* in final (*NS*, IV. 92; IX. 191). With the hand in *apaviddha* and foot in *sūcī*, the *trika* is turned round.

3753 **वलित-नृत्त-हस्त**

Valita-nṛtta-hasta : a type of hand-gesture in dancing; the twisted. When two hands in the *latā*-gesture are crossed by the elbows, it is called *valita.* The *NS* also reads it *lalita.*

3754 **वलित–संस्थान**

Valita saṁsthāna : the crooked moving pose *(VD).*

3755 **वलिता-ग्रीवा**

Valitā-grivā : turned sideways; A type of neck movement. Circular half-moon movement. Turned to look sideways. Cf. *Privāhita* head movement and also *dhuta* (Nāṭyaśāstra *Saṅgraha,* pp. 420-427); resulting when the face is turned sideways; used in looking with bent neck.

3756 **वलिता-भ्रुकुटी**

Valitā-bhrukuṭī : a type of *bhrukuṭī* movement presented by *Bālarāmabharata.*

3757 **वलितोरू**

Valitorū : this is really a crossing of thighs even though it is not clearly stated in *NS.* In the description of the *karaṇa* the movement is described and this position is implied.

3758 **वलितोरू-करण**

Valitorū-karaṇa : from the *valita* entwining of thighs. Both the hands are in *Śukatuṇḍa* and they make a *vyāvartita* and *parivartita* movement (*NS*, IV. 112b-113a). It is also called *valitoruka-karaṇa.* The thighs are *valita* and the *Śukatuṇḍa* hands are in *vyāvṛtta* and *parivartita.* This is used in the case of a *mugdhā* (a coy pretty maiden).

3759 **वली (वलि)**

Valī (vali) : lines on the stomach. If one, it is indicative of a hundred years of life; if there are two lines, it is indicative of enjoyment of women; three lines are indicative of lordship of the earth; straight indicates the person to be preceptor; if curved the person has forbidden sex-relationship (*Garuḍa,* 26. 3-7). Persons with one, two, three, four and no folds at all on their belly become slain with weapons, enjoyers of many women, preceptors or teachers of men, fathers of many sons, and kings respectively. Those who have unequal folds become sinners and addicted to forbidden women; and those whose folds are straight enjoy happiness and hate other's wives:

शस्त्रान्तं स्त्रीभोगिनमाचार्यं बहुसुतं यथासंख्यम् ।
एकद्वित्रिचतुर्भिर्वलिभिर्विन्द्यान्नृपं त्ववलिम् ॥
विषमवलयो मनुष्या भवन्त्यगम्याभिगामिनः पापाः ।
ऋजुवलयः सुखभाजः परदारद्वेषिणश्चैव ॥

About *paradāra* Kālidāsa's statement is noteworthy.

षीणां तु परपरिग्रहसंश्लेषपराङ्मुखी वृत्तिः ॥

Vide the unnamed authority:

एकवलिः शस्त्रमृत्युः स्त्रीभोगी द्विवलिः स्मृतः ।
त्रिभिराचार्य इत्याहुश्चतुर्भिः स्याद्बहुप्रजः ॥
अवलिस्तु नृपः प्रोक्तो यज्वा दानैकतत्परः ।
विषमा वलयो येषु ते चागम्याभिगामिनः ॥
ऋज्वस्तु वलयो येषु ते नराः सुखभागिनः ॥

3760 **वशीकरण**

Vaśīkaraṇa : hypnotism. One of the six black acts. It is to hypnotise someone (*Śāradātilaka*, XXVII. 123) various *mantras* and *tāntric* rituals are recorded for the purpose of conjuring. In one *mantra* the god Kāma and the goddess Cāmuṇḍā are invoked to fulfil all desires and help control the whole world; the *mantras* are invariably preceded by the mystic syllable *Oṁ* and other mystic utterances. The *mantra*, *'Oṁ Rhīm*, bow to Kāma, the one who favours all and conjures all, the brilliant one! Render the hearts of all in my control, Oṃ!:

ॐ ह्रीं ॐनमः कामाय सर्वजनहिताय सर्वजनमोहनाय प्रज्वलिताय सर्वजनहृदयं ममात्मगतं कुरू कुरू ॐ

(*Agni*, 302.6)

Most of the *mantras* and remedies centre round conjuring in the sphere of sex, though other cases obtain. It is said that if a person takes his semen by the left hand and anoints the left foot of a women, he becomes darling for the woman:

निजशुक्रं गृहीत्वा तु वामहस्तेन यः पुमान् ।
कामिनीचरणं वामं लिप्येत स्यात् स्त्रियः प्रियः ॥

(*Garuḍa.*, 1.185. 15)

It is also said that if at the time of coitus the man holds his penis with his left hand and licks the left hand of the woman in close embrace, she becomes soley his (*Ibid.*, 3). According to another passage the *mantra*: *pari priyā hi vaḥ kāri* (Indeed she has been made dear to you?) causes the desired woman to ooze (*samasrāvayet*). (b) hypnosis: a sleeplike state induced artificially by a hypnotist and characterized by greatly heightened suggestibility. For this reason the hypnotized individual shows extreme responsiveness to suggestion made by the hypnotist.

3761 **वस्तु**

Vastu : theme, subject (*DR*, 1.113).

3762 **वस्तूत्थापन**

Vastūtthāpana : elevation of the plot, a type of *ārabhaṭī*. The deed which either includes panic or is without it or which is being connected with as giving shelter to anyone and includes a combination of all sentiments in brief, is called *Vastūtthāpana* (*SD*, VI. 134).

3763 **वस्त्रगोपनकला**

Vastragopanakalā well-dressing with clothes of any length. One of the 64 arts given by *Kāmasūtra*. The body bneath the clothes makes the first statement to others. Vātsyāyana attached different personality traits to different body types. In modern days these have been broadly classified as ectomorph, mesomarph and endomarph. Protection, modesty, status and magic have all been proposed as reasons why human beings wear clothes. And the motive for doing so is probably the mixture of all four, these criteria still exist today.

3764 **वहिनीदधि**

Vahinīdadhi : curd of that cow which is yoked to a cart or plough (Vedic); Marias of Bastar still yoke cows to a plough.

3765 **वाक्**

Vāk : speech. Speech is of four types namely *parā*, *paśyantī*, *madhyamā* and *vaikharī* (*Sk.P.*, VI. 259. 64). Speech is generally called *vāk* or Sarasvatī and is believed to be the goddess of learning. She is said to be tongue of Viṣṇu - *viṣṇor jihvā sarasvatī* (*Mārk.P.*, 23.48). In other words, creation is analogous to an act of speech. *Vāk*, Goddess of speech, was the embodiment of creative energy and the abstracted reality of all realities in early Indian thought. For this reason incantation, recitation and effective speech were regarded as amongst the highest achievements of man. From meticulously preserved mnemonic evidence, we know that elaborate rules of correct pitch and intonation had been formulated as early as the 8th century B.C., when most of the early Vedic works on phonetics were composed. Good speech was the outward manifestaion of the true nobility of man. The act of good speech was an act of purification and simultaneously an act of recognition. The seer-poet continuously regenerated the world.

Speech is the act of producing audible, visible and verbal symbols. Speech is something we do. It is an action; it is an activity. The action involves something that our bodies do (so there is *parā* factor); something produced that can be heard (so there is a *vaikṛta* factor); and something produced that can be seen (so there is a *paśyantī* factor). In a very real sense, *madhyamā* is a series of words made audible and visible.

The four steps of *vāk* are (a) consciousness desire to speak, (b) *citta* - memory of what has already passed, (c) *manas* - *saṁkalpa* - *vikalpa* and (d) *buddhi* - final decision to speak out.

3766 **वाकोपवाक (वाकोवाक्य)**

Vākōpavāka/Vākovākya : dialogue, conversation, speech and reply. A figure containing remark and reply (*Agni-Purāṇa*, 342. 32-33). (b) *Veda* in the form of question and answers.

3767 **वाक्कलह**

Vākkalaha : quarrel.

3768 **वाक्केलि**

Vākkeli : speech-play, speech and counter speech, It is a series of questions and answers of speech and counter speech, producing comic effect (*Sāhityadarpaṇa*, VI.36). In the words of Bharata, *Vākkeli* arises from a single or two-fold reply (*NS*, XVIII. 120), repartee in drama.

3769 **वाक्चापल्य**

Vākcāpalya : idle-talk.

3770 **वाक्छल**

Vākchala : an evading reply, fraud in speech, equivocation.

3771 **वाक्-दीक्षा**

Vāk-dīkṣā : the common form of initiation with *mantras* (Rāghava on *Śāradā* V. 127-40); *Puraścaryārṇava* X. 391). See *Vācikī*.

3772 **वाक्पटुता**

Vākpaṭutā : linguistic competence : is the highest level of linguistic ability a person can master, and it is reflected in the initial formulation of a message. *Sadaṣi Vākpaṭutā* is well known maxim.

3773 **वाक्पारुष्य**

Vākpāruṣya : a verbal violence; offences committed through utterance of inculpating words - vilification, defamation, intimidation, etc. *Manu* (VIII. 267-68) has laid down the following rules "If a Kṣatriya utters insulting defamatory or arrogant words at a brāhmaṇa, the offender shall be punishable with fine which may extend to one hundred *paṇas*, the same offence committed by a Vaiṣya shall make him liable for time extending up to one hundred and fifty or two hundred *paṇas* (according to the gravity of the insult or defamation). A Śūdra committing the same offence shall be liable for physical punishment. When a Brāhmaṇa is found guilty of having insulted or defamed a Kṣatriya, the punishment is that of a fine extending up to fifty *paṇas*. By committing the same offence against a Vaiṣya, the Brāhmaṇa offender shall be punished with a fine not extending twenty-five *paṇas*, and if the person vilified or defended is a Śūdra, the maximum punishment to which a Brāhmaṇa offender may be sentenced, is twelve paṇas." (*Viṣṇu* IV. 31. 35-39) makes progressively enhanced punishments according to gradation of castes of the offenders.

Rudradeva in his *Śyainika Śāstram* (ed. by H.P. Shastri, Delhi 1982, Chapt. II. verse 4, p. 73) has defined *Vākpāruṣyam:*

> *aślīlā karkaśā coktiḥ*
> *vākpāruṣyam itīṣyate* ।

"rudeness of speech means indecent and abusive utterances."

The abuses, insults and, generally speaking, breaches in the norm of social discourse are often far too numerous and figure for too integrally in such cases. Indulgence in 'bad' language is taken for granted on these occasions. Indeed the violence against person and property dominates events of this kind to such an extent as to make a verbal violence relatively unimportant for purposes of administrative or judicial intervention. Since official records constitute the principle source of our information about such conflicts, it is easily understood why the Kauṭilyan category of *vākpāruṣyam* had so little to do with the historical evidence on rural crimes. *Vākpāruṣyam* inversion was homologous to the reversal brought about by the *Saṁkṣhobha*.

Yājñavalkya quotes different *Smṛtis* to explain *vākpāruṣya* as follows:

> देशजातिकुलादीनां क्रोशनं न्यङ्गसंज्ञितम् ।
> यद्वचः प्रतिकूलार्थं वाक्यपारुष्यं तदुच्यते ॥ (नारदः)

> देशाक्षेपो यथा गौडं प्रति कलहप्रिया गौडा इति । जात्याक्षेपो यथा विप्रं प्रति नितान्तलोलुपा विप्रा इति । कुलाक्षेपो यथा क्रूरचरिता वैश्वामित्रा इति । न्यङ्गम् असभ्यवचनम् ।

> हुंकारं कासनं चैव लोके यच्च विगर्हितम् ।
> अनुकुर्यादनुब्रूयाद्वाक्पारुष्यं तदुच्यते ॥
> निष्ठुराश्लीलतीव्रत्वात्तदपि त्रिविधं स्मृतम् ।
> आक्षेपो निष्ठुरं ज्ञेयमश्लीलं न्यङ्गसंज्ञितम् ॥
> पतनीयैरुपाक्रोशैस्तीव्रमाहुर्मनीषिणः ।
> यस्त्वसत्संज्ञ कैरङ्गैः परभाक्षिपति क्वचित् ॥ (नारद)

3774 **वाक्प्रलाप**

Vākpralāpa : excellent discussion.

3775 **वाक्य**

Vākya : sentence. *Vākya* in Ancient India has been defined variously in different branches of knowledge from diverse points of view. It is, therefore, quite natural that emphasis should have been laid in them on different aspects according to the particular need felt in that particular branch. For example, *Mīmāṁsaka* emphasized the points of अर्थैकत्व(syntactical unity) and आकांक्षा (expectancy), while the grammarian laid stress on formal aspect. Amara gives a general description, while the *Naiyāyika* attached importance to प्रमाणत्व aspect thereof. Among the earliest *Munitraya*, Pāṇini held the ordinary view of *vākya*. Kātyāyana thought *vākya* to be *ākhyāta* (verb). Patanjali emphasized on *ekatin*.Three elements are required for constituting words into a sentence according to rehetorians, *viz.* expectancy (*ākāṅkṣā*), compatibility (*yogyatā*) and proximity (*sannidhi*). According to Annambhaṭṭa, the author of *Tarkasaṅgraha*, a sentence is a collection of words - *vākyam padasamūhaḥ*.

3776 **वाक्यग्रह**

Vākyagraha : difficulty in speaking.

3777 **वाक्यदण्डक**

Vākyadaṇḍaka : long sentence.

3778 **वाक्यपदीय**

Vākyapadīya : work dealing with a word in a sentence, written by Bhartṛhari.

3779 **वाक्यपद्धति**

Vākyapaddhati : diction.

3780 **वाक्यविप्रेक्षण**

Vākyaviprekṣaṇa : looking away during another's speech (*A*, 1.21.8). It is a type of "reluctance" to look another person directly in the eye. Thus, the stereotyped view of Kauṭilya has even some truth. That is, many subordinate people don't look the dominant person in the eye. To look another person in the eye (in the context of the dominant culture) is a NV way of communication reveals trustworthiness, forthrightness, masculinity, truthfulness, sincerity etc. In the subordinate cultural context, avoiding eye contact is a NV way of communicating a recognition of the authority - subordinate relationship, of the participants in a social situation.

Many lower class children are taught not to look another person in the eye. In India females were taught not to look a male in the eye because this communicated equality resulting in sexuality. Thus, not to look males in the eye was really a survival pattern in India and perhaps this was the main cause of veiling.

Note how "culture clash" can occur because of the avoidance of eye contact: in the dominant culture, eye contact is interpreted one way, while it is interpreted in another way within the subordinate culture. Avoidance of eye contact by a subordinate person communicates, "I am in a subordinate role and I respect your authority over me," while dominant cultural member may interprete avoidance of eye contact as,"Here is a shifty unreliable person I am dealing with."

Avoidance eye contact to communicate respect and acknowledgement of one's being in a subordinate role is a common pattern in India. This pattern is also found in the Japanese culture. It could well be that this particular pattern within the village and tribal societies has its origin in the post-Vedic culture (particularly the Rāmāyaṇa-age).

3781 **वाक्याभिनय**

Vākyābhinaya : speech gesture in drama, gesticulation of words, one of the six-fold of physical gesticulation. It is the recitation of Prakṛit and Sanskrit speech composed in verse and prose, possessing meaning full of various sentiments.

3782 **वाक्यावक्षेपण**

Vākyāvakṣepaṇa : cutting short another's remark (*A*, 5.4. 10).

3783 **वाक्शल्य**

Vākśalya : harsh speech.

3784 **वाक्सङ्ग**

Vāksaṅga : hesitation in speech (*A*, 1.21.8), faltering of speech.

3785 **वाक्संतक्षण**

Vāksaṁtakṣaṇa : biting speech, speech with a bite of acid.

3786 **वाक्सिद्धि**

Vāksiddhi : power of speech (*Ṣaṭ-Siddhi; Yukti-dīpikā*, 164. 14-15), one of the six varieties of spiritual powers. Thirdly, by the loss of power of vision, an issue was born by mere utterances of an expression like uttering - lets have a child (*Vākya-siddhi*). This also we can see today has been survived in the lower biological order, as has been in the female conch conceives an issue by uttering a shrill sound. The *Śaṅkara-bhāṣya* (on *Brahmasūtra*, II. 1.25) writes : *Valākās ca stanayitra rava śravaṇād garbhaṁ dhatte* - that the female crane conceives by hearing the roaring of the clouds and thunder.

3787 **वाक्स्तम्भ**

Vākstambha : paralysis of speech. In *Uttararāmacarita* (VIII. 7) Mālatī enacts paralysis of the tongue: *Vākstambham nāṭayati*, This is done by enacting a sudden motionless and pulling a smileless face with a stiff body (*NS*, VII. 155).

3788 **वागपेत**

Vāgapeta : dumb.

3789 **वागर्थ**

Vāgartha : words and meaning.

3790 **वागापहारक**

Vāgāpahāraka : a stealer of speech, liar, a reader of prohibited text.

3791 **वागोजस्**

Vāgojas : speech-power (Vedic).

3792 **वाग्जाल**

Vāgjāla : bombast.

3793 **वाग्जीवन**

Vāgjīvana : a professional story-teller (*A*, 1.12.9, 1.18.12, 2.1.34). Compare the following verse:

asya dagdhodarasyārthe
kiṃ na kurvanti paṇḍitāḥ ।
vānarīmiva vāgdevīm
nartayanti gṛhe gṛhe॥
"What may not a learned scholar do
If cursed belly true?
Like a monkey he his wisdom makes
Dance everywhere he takes."

3794 **वाग्दण्ड**

Vāgdaṇḍa : rebuke, restraint in speech.

3795 **वाग्दान**

Vāgdāna : betrothal, the betrothal ceremony is more or less a solemnization of the forthcoming marriage contract. The astrologers and the priests of the two families, the male parents of the boy and the girl and a few friends congregate on the occasion. The parents in presence of the friends who act as witnesses give their solemn word, that they are willing to perform the marriage of the boy and the girl on the date to be fixed later, and the priests ratify the contract by repeating sacred verses. In certain cases a written contract is drawn up, in others a promise by word of mouth is considered sufficient. The ceremony is called, *Nisbet* in Hindi and *maṅganī* in Punjabi. Once the betrothal is performed, the parties are expected to stick to their contract, but under extraordinary circumstances it can be broken up. A betrothed girl, however, is not widowed by the death of the person to whom she is betrothed and there is no objection to her being married again. (b) In the tribal society, betrothal-talks are initiated by the boy's side. The betrothal ceremony in the Hill Maria society is known as 'talq-dāynā' which means 'going to ask' and is very similar to the Sanskrit word *Vāgdānam*. *Talq-dāynā* is divided into two parts. In the first visit the talks are of preliminary nature though the betrothal is finalised in the first visit itself. It is this first visit that the talks are symbolic.

When a youth and his girl have become friends and have fallen for each other, each tells his or her parents. Then the youth's parents go to the girl's village accompanied by the village elders but without the boy. They usually take with them four to five bottles of *Mahuā* liquor. They so arrange their visit that they reach the girl's village in the afternoon. The father of the boy places the liquor bottles inside the threshhold of the girl's house and he and his fellow-men sit silently outside a little distance away. The girl's father, on seeing the bottles, asks them who they are and why they have come. The two sides are usually well-acquainted and it is known beforehand that the party is to come even then the talks start in a symbolic language.

On being asked the boy's father or his fellow-villagers say that they are from such village. They have lost their calf who used to come for grazing this side and they have just come to find out if there calf was there. There are may more ways of saying the same thing. Another way is to say that they were travelling through the jungle and were feeling thirsty. From a distance they saw birds flying over there and thought there should be water. So they had come in search of water. Yet another way of saying is that they were passing by the village and smelt a flower and they just come wandering to locate that fragrant flower in that house. It is also sometimes said that they have lost something and came searching for it. There are such other symbols also through which they ask for the girl.

If the girl's father is not willing then his reply may be simple ignorance (negative). If so, the boy's party pick up the bottles and leave without any animosity. If the girl's father is affirmative and he says that he has seen the calf grazing, or there is water nearby, or they are right in smelling the flower, it is proof that girl's father has given his consent. But it is equally necessary to know the will of the girl. If father and his daughter are willing, then in the third stage the local group is equally important. The consent of the local group is also thus obtained. If the elders of the village say that they have enough liquor and don't want this, then the betrothal cannot happen. If everything is settled, they all drink the liquor and the first step in betrothal is completed.

The second and final part of the betrothal is held after about a year. Now boy's parents go alone to the girl's village. They take with them bottles of liquor. This time the date of marriage is fixed, which is generally held in the month of Phālguna.

(c) Kols go to the girl's village, and addressing her father say that they have come to hunt. He asks them to what jungle they wish to hunt, and they name the *sarnā* or sacred grove in which the bones of his ancestors are buried. If the girl's father is satisfied with the match, he then agrees to it (Russell and Hiralal, II. 511).

3796 **वाग्दुष्ट**

Vāgduṣṭa : speaking harsh.

3797 **वाग्भावुक**

Vāgbhāvuka : a critic assessing the words, language and style; opposed to *hṛdaya-bhāvuka.*

3798 **वाग्डम्बर**

Vāgḍambara : bombast, grace or splendour of speech.

3799 **वाग्मिन्**

Vāgmin : good speaker, orator.

3800 **वाग्याम**

Vāgyāma : dumb.

3801 **वाग्वज्र**

Vāgvajra : biting speech.

3802 **वाग्व्यवहार**

Vāgvyavahāra : verbal discussion, oral conversation.

3803 **वाग्व्यापार**

Vāgvyāpāra : speech behaviour (Dhanañjaya, *Daśarūpaka,* III, 4-5), cf. *bhāratī saṁskṛtaprāyo vāgvyāpāro naṭāśrayaḥ* (*Bhāratī* is a speech behaviour, chiefly in Sanskrit, employed by actors).

3804 **वाच्**

Vāc : voice, vocal speech, exterior word, Logos, wisdom, a word which expresses something. Its substratum is *śabda* or sound which indicates a slight stir, throb or vibration in reality, the self-expression of which is called *parā-vāc* or the supreme word. The other aspect is *artha* or meaning. *Vāc* has four forms: *parā, paśyantī, madhyamā* and *vaikharī* (q.v.). The stages preceding *para* (q.v.) are *śūnyā, saṁvit* and *sūkṣmā.* The first is the vibrational stage, the next is that when the sound is about to form and the third is that when it is forming. (b) *vāc* is the vocal element of speech which relates to human voice. The voice itself (apart from the words used by the sender) sends us messages. There are four aspects of voice that can be varied: pitch (highness or lowness), volume (loudness or softness), rate (fastness or slowness), and quality (tone, colour, or character or texture). One can change these aspects of voice and the changes will send messages to the listener.

3805 **वाचक**

Vācaka : (a) speaker, (b) meaningful word, dictionary meaning of the word. Bhanu has feined it as such:

> Śabd kahat phagaṭai arth, vācak soi pramāṇ
> Jāti-yadṛcchā-guṇa-kriyā, nām cāri pahcān

3806 **वाचक-वाच्य**

Vācaka-vācya : *śakti* or power of *mantra.* The former is the denoting or signifying aspect, while the latter is the basic. *Vācya* is contained in the *vācaka* and formerly there is no distinction between them - *janyajanakayor bhedābhāvāc vācyasya vācakenāpi* (*Varivayasyārahasya,* 11. 81).

3807 **वाचन**

Vācana : reading, reciting.

3808 **वाचनिक**

Vācanika : verbal (*Manu Smṛti,* 5.1). Verbal symbols are words. Words are spoken symbols that stand for ideas. The verbal element of speech communication is that element that uses spoken symbols to represent concepts. It is the word component of the transmission. One who knows Sanskrit - or any language - has to understand two things: its symbols or vocabulary, and its syntax or grammar.

3809 **वाचाघात**

Vācāghāta : aphasia. A speech disorder which occurs as a result of localized brain lesions, especially in the so-called speech-areas of the dominant cerebral hemisphere (in right-handed people the left hemisphere). It is the partial or complete loss of ability to use language as a result of cerebral damage. Many specific types of aphasia are distinguished in the Āyurvedic literature.

3810 **वाचाट**

Vācāṭa : talkative (*Veṇīsaṁhāra,* Act. III).

3811 **वाचादत्ता**

Vācādattā : verbally given. The *Smṛtiśāstra* prescribes this phrase in the matter of *kanyādāna* (marriage). It is the second stage of gift. The first stage is *manasādattā* and third one is *dhārādattā.*

3812 **वाचालिङ्गन**

Vācāliṅagana : embrace through words. Anantabhaṭṭa (*Campū-Bharata,* 3.89) has seen this imaginative embrace during the summer, when hugging is avoided.

3813 **वाचिक**

Vācika : verbal, message, statement in words, words *(A,*

2.10.22.23) verbal voice. Bharata confines his discussion of voice (*vācika*) to five short chapters beginning with the chapter 15. A good part of his initial remarks are devoted to linguistic considerations rather than the oral interpretations. It is important to note that characters were distinguished, one from another, by the language which they spoke. From a practical point of view, this permitted the spectators to easily identify one character type from the other. For example, the heroic characters speak Sanskrit and only on special occasions resort to Prākṛt. Bharata says that ordinary characters speak natural languages which fall into one of two categories; regional languages spoken by the inhabitants of the various parts of the country, and dialects spoken by tribals and foreigners. Bharata suggests that different regional languages and dialects were suitable to characters depending on their rank and temperament. Women and inferior characters were to use Prākṛta dialects, except for the courtesans who might on occasion converse in Sanskrit, as Vasantasenā does in the *Mṛcchakaṭikam.*

Bharata provides detailed examples of the various models of addresses that are proper for people of the same or different stations in life. (b) According to *Amarakośa*, *vācika* is message, *rustaī* is bad news, *kalya* being good news.

3814 **वाचिक-जप**

Vācika-japa : vocal muttering. The utterance of a *mantra* is termed vocal sacrifice: जपयज्ञैः सवाचिकैः (*Liṅga,* 1.85.20). In the method of *japa* the *mantra* is to be uttered very softly, almost mutely with only the movement of the lips being visible.

3815 **वाचिक-अभिनय**

Vācika-abhinaya : verbal gesture. Speech is defined as the body of drama and *vācika-abhinaya* is central: *vāci yatnastu kartavyo nāṭyasyeṣā tanūḥ smṛtā* (*NS,* XIV.2) The dialogue or recitation may be in Sanskrit or Prākṛta and the author of the play as well as actor used to pay due attention to the sounds, grammar, prosody and figures of speech of the language concerned. Equally important was the attention given to *kāku* (q.v.). Dramatic speech required not only the realistic rendering of natural speech in all variety of situations but the manner in which speech was effected by sickness, old-age, childhood, death-bed, dream, fight, hurry etc. was also to be carefully represented. When long speeches and narrations were to be made they were to be rendered vivid, intelligible, and effective by constant attention to gestures, movements and modulations of the voice. Conventional gestures were used to convey that the speech was a soliloquy (*svagata*) or a whisper (*karṇe*) or an aside (*janāntika*) or a secret shared by a character with the audience (*apavāritaka*). *Ākāṣa-bhāṣita* meant a conversation with a character supposed to be invisible present (*NS,* XVII. 25). The *lāsyāṅgas* and the *vīthyaṅgas* were special contexts in which the use of words and their rendering contributed to beauty or to witty repartee, amusement and humour.

3816 **वाचिकम्**

Vācikam : oral message.

3817 **वाचिकी**

Vācikī : the common form of initiation with *mantras* (Rāghava on *Śāradā* V. 127-40; *Puraścaryārṇava* V. 391). See *vāk-dīkṣā.*

3818 **वाचोयुक्ति**

Vācōyukti : skilled in speech (*Mālatīmādhavam,* 1.2). In the tribal society of India, there are three types of specialists who display a skill in language use. These are the Shaman, the mediator, and the maker. Chief among the repositories of tribal memory are the Shamans. "Some of our old men carry around a thousand years of history in their heads", says the young Muria of Bastar. They are called upon to recite it on certain occasions and stories are told of enormous feats when a man may sing and recite for four or five days at a stretch with only brief periods of rest.

Besides the Shaman the *sirahā* (mediator) is a specialist in language. The mediator, like the Shaman, has mastered a great deal of text to which he could refer in his reasoning and in giving his judgements.

In Bastar there is a special place for makers, the poets and singers. Among the tribes, musical specialization is part of the specialization of the Shaman. But the singing and making of songs is not his prerogative alone. There is also a specialization among lay people based on skill and on individual differences in musical ability. In the tribal culture, women and even children, as well as men are the best singers. So they are the makers.

3819 **वाच्य**

Vācya : (a) mode of address (*NS,* XVII. 66). Structured by *prakṛti, varṇa, jāti* and *śilpa* the society of *NS* was divided into a hierarchy of ranks. This can be seen most clearly by attending to that modes of address which are prescribed in *NS* (*Ibid*). At the top are placed the sages who are the gods of the gods themselves. They are to be addressed as *bhagavān* (lord). Gods, ascetics and great scholars are to be similarly addressed as *bhagavān.* The Brāhmaṇa is to be addressed as *ārya* (noble man). The ruler is to be addressed as *mahārāja* (great king). The teacher should be called *upādhyāya* and older people *tāta.* The Brāhmaṇs could address the king by his name or as just King. This should be acceptable to the kings because the Brāhmaṇs are superior (*NS,* XVIII. 70): *yasmāt pūjyā dvijāḥ smṛtāh.*

The minister (*saciva*) is to be addressed by the Brāhmaṇs as *amātya* or *saciva,* but the others of lower rank must address him always as *ārya*. Among equals the address is to be by name; the superior is to be addressed with the surname joined to the name. Where men and women hold office, they are to be addressed by their office. Artisans and craftsmen are to be addressed by their profession. These modes of address are indicative of a socially egalitarian sense. Those who are a little inferior are to be addressed as *mārṣa* or *bhāva*. An equal may be addressed as friend or *vayasya*. An inferior may be addressed as *haṃho, haṇḍā*. The charioteer is to address the passengers as *āyuṣman*. Ascetics are to be addressed as such *viz. tapasvin* or *sādho*. The heir-apparent is to be addressed as *svāmin*, other princes as *bhaṭṭāraka*. The ascetics of the Buddhist and Jain orders are to be addressed as *bhadanta*. The other ascetics are to be addressed according to their respective sects. The king is to be addressed by the people as *deva*, but emperor is to be addressed as *bhaṭṭa* (*NS*, XVII. 80).

The husband was to be addressed by the wife as *āryaputra* when young, and *ārya* otherwise. The wife was to be called as *āryā* or the daughter or mother of such and such. Women ascetics and goddesses were to be addressed as *bhagavatī*. Ladies were to be called *bhadrā* and elderly ones *ambā* (mother). Queens were to be addressed as *bhaṭṭinī, svāminī*, and *devī*. Maidens were to be addressed by servants as *bhartṛdārikā*. Women were to address each other as *halā* and their maids as *hañjā*.

This system of social addressing reaffirms, the general principles of hierarchy emerging in the Indian society. The sages and ascetics enjoyed the highest status, the Brāhmaṇs came next and then the kings. Below them came the officials, traders and bankers. Artisans and craftsmen were given due respect except when they happened to be menials or servants. It is curious that *NS* does not refer to the guilds at all. This could be due to the fact that their belonging to a guild probably made no difference to the representation of traders and craftsmen on the stage (*NS*, XVII. 91).

3820 **वाच्यता**

Vācyatā : blame, infamy.

3821 **वाच्यवाचन**

Vācya-vācana : pleonasm, redundancy of expression.

3822 **वाडवक**

Vāḍavaka : the Mare's position in coition, seen in the Elephant-lady (*Kāmasūtra*, 2.6.14).

3823 **वाजपेय**

Vājapeya : primitive sacrifice for food (*vāja*) and drink (*peya*) which was later transformed into the consecration for overlordship. The number 17 predominates in it. It requires 17 cups of *soma*, 17 cups of *surā*, 17 chariots and 17 drums. A mock chariot race is held in which the sacrificer is declared victorious. A ladder is raised against the *yūpa* on which the sacrificer climbs and hods a ritual dialogue with his wife. Animals for *Prajāpati* are offered at the time of midday *soma*-pressing. The *adhvaryu* declares the *yajamāna* to be *samrāṭ* (universal monarch). After *Vājapeya* a king should perform *Rājasūya*. (*Śat.Br.* , V. 1-2).

3824 **वातकेलि**

Vātakeli : low whispering of lovers.

3825 **वात्सल्य**

Vātsalya : paternal or maternal affection. The instinct which prompts it is called *vātsalya-rasa* and the emotion is called *vātsalya-rati*.

3826 **वाद**

Vāda : a mode of argumentation in philosophy. It consists in a number of declarations put forward by various speakers purporting to be reasons in support of several theories, leading ultimately to the acceptance of one of these theories and the demonstrated truth. The sole object of *Vāda* is to ascertain truth.

(b) one of the three kinds of debate (*kathā*). The main business of *vāda* was to ascertain the metaphysical truths, therefore, it rarely included the controversial subjects. Generally, *vāda* took place between a preceptor and his pupils and occasionally took the shape of a conference, including some *prāśnika* or doubters. In this *vāda*, own thesis is established by the evidences, the thesis of the opponent is refuted by logic, but consistent according to the dogma of the components and also consists of the five-membered syllogism: *pramāṇa-tarka-sādhanopālambhaḥ-siddhāntā-viruddhaḥ-pañcāvayopapannaḥ-pakṣa-pratipakṣaparigraho vādaḥ* (*Nyāya-sūtra*, 1.2.1). The discussion between Naciketas and Yama in *Kaṭhopaniṣad* is an example of *vāda*. Thus *vāda* means discussions and controversies through which the exponent and opponent parties each try to establish their own position. It is one of the sixteen philosophical topics of the *Nyāya*.

3827 **वादी**

Vādī : the note that manifests the form of a *rāga*. The principle note in music to which other notes are determined. (b) a speaker, an expounder, or teacher of any doctrine or theory.

3828 **वानप्रस्थाश्रम**

Vānaprasthāśrama ; the third stage of life; life away from the locality in the forest. The state of the *brahmacārin* on the one hand and of the *vānaprastha* on the other are similar, in that both are devoid of the regular joys and responsibilities of the house-holder. The *vānaprastha* is ordained to keep the hair long and Oilless, in the form of *jaṭā*; he should not cut nails and the body-hair. He should study his *śāstra* and control his speech. He should offer *havis* to the gods, prepared from some wild material; he should eat salt prepared by himself (*Kūrma*, II. 27.6). He should discard wine and flesh and mushroom. He should not eat anything at night. Though his wife is allowed to be with him, he should always be celibate, and he should not have union even with his wife. He should move with beasts, and should sleep either on sand or on a stone-slab. He should follow the way of a pigeon. He should sustain himself by eating fruits ripened at seasons. He may prepare a living room from grass or leaves. He should wear either skins or bark.अजिनवल्कलम्.

The Hill tribes in India are *vānaprasthī* in the literal sense. Take the example of the Hill Maria of Bastar. Because he lives the life of shifting cultivation, so there is no permanency in his life. When there is no permanency, no attachment. This non-attachment makes him live wholly in the present. They argue that when there is no certainty about the next moment and when one cannot do anything about it, and again when everything is shifting, everything is fleeting, why look back and be sorry about it or look ahead and hope. This is a very pragmatic approach to the life.

3829 **वानर**

Vānara : monkeys provided a constant theme for popular legend, in which they played the role of turbulent, empty-headed creatures, living in troops, commanded by brave chiefs, and committing various misdeeds which were, nevertheless, treated indulgently. They were also judged capable of prodigious feasts, several of them achieving lasting fame in brāhmaṇic mythology. One such was the virtuous Hanumān, son of the wind, a solar hero and a messenger who flew like an arrow through the space. Hanumant is celebrated by an epic poem in the *Rāmāyaṇa;* he was the object of a cult in which his image was represented by a vaguely anthropomorphic raised stone. (b) There is Chhattisgarhī saying: *ghoṛā kā rog bendrā me jāy.* This saying appears to have originated in the belief that if a monkey is tied in the stable of a horse, any disease which may be likely to attack the horse, will go to monkey instead. The saying is now repeated when one person has to suffer for the offences of another. It may be that in time this practice will be discontinued and forgotten and the saying will still be current and will arouse questions as to its origin.

3830 **वानर-मुद्रा**

Vānara-mudrā : indication of a monkey. The thumb and the second finger of the *muṣṭi* are joined together to indicate a monkey (*Mirror of Gesture*, pp. 49-50).

3831 **वामदेव-मुद्रा**

Vāmadeva-mudrā : if the *sadyojāta* (q.v) gesture is styled in the reverse way, *i.e.* the left fixed by the right, it is the gesture of *Vāmadeva* (*VD*).

3832 **वामन-हस्त**

Vāmana-hasta : form the *muṣṭimudrā* up and down with two hands. This represents the *Vāmana* incarnation (*AD*, 216-225).

3833 **वामन-मुद्रा**

Vāmana-mudrā : gesture symbolizing the Vaiṣṇavite deity *Vāmana*. The alphabetic symbol of "*Om*" indicates *Vāmana* (*VD*).

3834 **वामा**

Vāmā : agreeable women. (b) coy in love = *ratau vāmā* (*DR*, II. 26). It should be made clear that social aversion (*vāmācāra*) does not necessarily imply dislike or negative reaction. This has been appreciated especially by Dhanañjaya in an analysis of NV signals used by the lady in coy or shy poses of flirtation. This is why an agreeable woman's aversion makes her *Vāmā*. Coyness seems to involve mixed messages of affiliation and aversiveness, and portrays a peculiar social relationship combining eager approach tendencies with tendencies to avoid. The individual is at once strongly attracted to the partner and yet fearful of approaching. Anxiety is high (rapid heartbeat, low GSR), and auto-manipulations are frequent (especially preening activities), gaze alternates between looking at the partner and gazing downward, and smiles or ambivalent smiles (smiling-tongue-show, compressed-lips-smile, smiling-lip-bite) are performed. Except for smiling and periods of direct gaze, the flirting display is identical to more purely aversive performances.

3835 **वायस-विद्या**

Vāyasa-vidyā : the interpretation of the crow's cries (*A*, 13. 1.9).

3836 **वायु-मुद्रा**

Vāyu-mudrā : gesture symbolizing the Air of the Vaiṣṇavite cult. The *patāka*-hand in the moving pose symbolizes the Air (*VD*).

3837 **वायु-सङ्केतक**

Vāyu-śaṅketaka : the wind-signal. Omens are seen from the wind also. The wind is said to be fire when it rises up, and *varuṇa* when it blows down; and if it is steady in the middle of the quarters, it is said to belong to Indra. It is usually said to blow to the left in the bright half of the month, and to the right in the dark half, for three days in the beginning. Now, if the wind blows following the gait of the sun in the morning and with that of moon at sunset it is conducive to the growth of good qualities; if otherwise it indicates calamities (*Garuḍa P.*, 1. 200. 2-5). It is said that the total changes of wind are sixteen during the day and night. When the wind changers at half of the duration, it indicates loss of health. Likewise the breath from the right nostril is good at taking food or sexual intercourse: *dakṣiṇe ca puṭe vāyur hito bhojana - maithune.* At war, or when one is wielding a weapon the blowing of the wind to the left is excellent. The wind is the aspect of *Mahendra* or *Varuṇa*. Hence if it blows to the East or the West, there is no fault; but if it blows to the right, it indicates lack of rain; while it indicates the gain of rain if it blows to the left (*Ibid.* 8-9):

> *vāmena gamanam śreṣṭham*
> *sarvakāryeṣu bhūṣitam*
> *māhendre vāruṇe vāte kopi doṣo na jāyate* ।
> *anāvṛṣṭirdakṣavāhe vṛṣṭiḥ syādvāmavāhake* ॥

3838 **वायु-हस्त**

Vāyu-hasta : *arāla* with right and *ardhapatāka* with the left hand, denote *vāyu* one of the *Dikpālas* (*AD*, 211-220).

3839 **वार**

Vāra : appointed time or place (*Rāmāyaṇa*).

3840 **वारणार्थ-पद**

Vāraṇārtha-pada : prohibitive words uttered during coition by the female-partner. Māgha (*Śiśu.*, 10.70) has used these words:

> *vāraṇārthapada-gadgadvācāmīrṣyayā muhurapatrapayā ca* ।
> *kurvate sma sudṛśāmanukūlam pratikūlikatayaiva yuvānaḥ* ॥.

3841 **वाराङ्गना**

Vārāṅganā : a woman taken in turn, the prostitute.

3842 **वाराही-मुद्रा**

Vārāhī-mudrā : "the arm is by the left; or the left arm should be made curved. Place the face inside it and make the right eye big. The lower part of the body is to be made visible. The arm should be caught hold with the left elbow, lowered down by an embrace. This is the *mahāvārāhī-mudrā* which may be applied in an intercourse and similar feats" (*BT*); (b) gesture of the Boar-goddess. Let the gesture of *la* and *sa* be repeated with *ca*, *la* and *ka*. Then join them by opposite way (*VD*).

3843 **वारुणी-मुद्रा**

Vāruṇī-mudrā : if fingers are stretched of the up-turned (right) hand, it is called the gesture of *Vāruṇī* (*VD*).

3844 **वार्षगण्यन्याय**

Vārṣagaṇya-nyāya : the *sāttvata* way of fighting with missiles. It is similar to *sāttvata;* but the weapon and the shield should be moved round the head or the weapon should be moved with the chest or the shoulders.

3845 **वावदूक**

Vāvadūka : very eloquent.

3846 **वासकसज्जा**

Vāsakasajjā : dressed up for union. a woman who dresses herself in a befitting manner and keeps herself (and her house) ready to receive her lover; one of the several classes of heroines. The lady is known as *Vāsakasajjā* whose limbs are beautified by garlands, sandals and ornaments, whose eyes are fixed on the path of lover's arrival and who is reclining on the bed in her beautiful house' (*Pañcasāyaka*, 5.34). Jayadeva describes the activities of Rādhā when she was waiting for Kṛṣṇa at night (*Gīta-Govinda*, 6.3.). *NS* terms her as *vāsaka sajjikā*.. "When the conjugal union is due, the heroine in the eager expectation of love's pleasure, decorates herself joyfully:

> साजि सेज भूषन वसन, सबही नजर बचाय।
> रही पौढ़ि मिस नींद के, दृग दुवार से लाइ।।
> (*Kavyaprabhākara*, 215)

3847 **वासगृह**

Vāsagṛha : living room (*A*, 1.20.2) Many Sanskrit poets have given a vivid description of the houses and bed-rooms of the elite class of people, which differs from the village abode. Śūdraka's (*Mṛcchakaṭikam*, Act IV) elaborates description of Vasantasenā's house resembles that of modern city building. Kālidāsa's Yakṣa describes his house in the same manner (*Megha*, 78, 80, 81, 87). Bāṇa describes the bedroom (*Harṣacarita*, p. 248). He describes the holy place of Goddess Pārvatī, which was full of smoke due to continuous burning of resin (*Kādambarī*, p. 108). Daṇḍī also similarly describes the bed-room of Kalpasundarī (*Daśakumāracarita*, p. 113).

3848 **वासताम्बूल**

Vāsatāmbūla : betel-leaf with fragrance put in.

3849 **वासना**

Vāsanā : (a) latent impressions, particularly impressions unconsciously left on the mind by past deeds and experiences. According to *NS*, eight basic instincts - emotions or mental states, called *sthāyī bhāvas*, exist in the human psyche. They are inborn in a man and exist permanently in the form of latent impressions (*vāsanā*) derived from actual experiences of the present life or form the instincts inherited from the past lives. Under appropriate stimuli they emerge into man's consciousness and are experienced in the form of emotions. (b) potential memory, that subconscious unity which underlies specific remembrances of a giving thing (actual memory). *Vāsanā* can be used to refer to the smell that clings to a cloth that has been perfumed with fragrant smoke. A vessel of unbaked clay retains the smell of whatever it first contained, and in the same way the subtle body is pervaded by the *Vāsanā* (fragrances, perfumes and subtle-residues) of all its earlier *karmas.* These *vāsanās* tend to cause *saṁskāras,* permanent scars that go from life to life. So *Vāsanās* are latest memories of the past experiences and consequent present sensibility. (c) according to *Yogasūtra* (IV. 9) the mind is differently equipped with instinctive cravings in different kinds of beings in accordance with the type of their embodiment. (d) in Jainism *vāsanā* is a predisposition which repeatedly originates in human life from ignorance, passions of attachment and hatred. (e) the word *vāsanā* generally refers to the tendencies of past lives most of which lie dormant in the mind. Only those appear which can find scope in his life. But *saṁskāras* are the sub-conscious states which are being constantly generated by experience. *Vāsanās* are innate *saṁskāras* not acquired in this life.

The term *vāsanā* indicates the operation of desires or drives at the biological as well as social, the unconscious as well as the conscious level. Vidyāraṇya speaks of three kinds of *vāsanās,* namely, (i) *loka-vāsanā* (conformity to custom and desire for name, fame and respect). (ii) *deha-vāsanā* (desire for various kinds of food, drinks, cloths, cosmetics, ornaments and such other material goods). (iii) *śāstra-vāsanā* (a kind of addiction to study as many books, in as many subjects as possible, and fastidious observance of injunctions laid down in religious books: (*Pañcadasī* IX. 104, and *Jivanmukti viveka* p. 263).

The term *vāsanā* appears to have two connotations. First, it stands for biological urges like the need for food, sex, rest, etc., which mankind shares with animals. Secondly, it connotes the way in which our life experiences influence our attitudes, our likes and dislikes, etc. Though we may not be aware of their influence on our behaviour, feelings and thoughts overpower us.

3850 **वासुदेव-मुद्रा**

Vāsudeva-mudrā : the left fist with its thumb raised up and the right fist with its thumb tightening the fist, are to be styled first. Then bringing two fists in the particular position; they should be raised jointly. This symbolizes *Vāsudeva* (*VD*).

3851 **वासू**

Vāsū : young girl.

3852 **वास्तुकला**

Vāstukalā : architecture.

3853 **वाहन**

Vāhana : a vehicle, a conveyance (*Mānasāra,* LX. 1). The traffic-rules were observed in ancient India in accordance with the order of precedence. The king, the *snātaka,* women and persons carrying heavy loads were given precedence in the use of roads (*Mitā.* (*ācāra*) 1.117). (b) *vāhana* also means the mounts of gods. The mount may be any animal, or sometimes men, demons and corpses. Occasionally, even gods of an alien faith serve as *vāhanas.*

The idea of animal 'vehicles' for Hindu deities and animal incarnations is probably totemic, as are tree and snake worship. 'Tree-marriages' performed among both tribes and higher castes, and the numerous instances in Purāṇic myths of animals who gave birth to human beings or *vice-versa.* Gaṇeśa, the elephant headed deity, and Śiva's horrendous dance in the skin of a flayed elephant both suggest tribal Shamanism. In Hindu mythology, the Kṛṣṇa cult, *yoga,* and *Tantra* are replete with magical lore and symbolism of tribal origin. Robert Redfield summed up the process: "rural (*i.e.* caste) India is a primitive or tribal society rearranged to fit a civilization."

Different types of vehicles also act as status symbols and have a part to play in the negative articulation of rebel consciousness. Some of these are means of transport identified with rank in many feudal societies and subject to the shocks and tremors of agrarian disturbances. In a well known incident of the Peasant war in Germany the rebels used this symbolism for a particularly dramatic act of reversal: forcing a wicked countess to sit in a dungcart they mocked her, "In golden carriage camest thou to Weinsberg, in a dungcart must thou depart" (Zimmermann: 1.394). The Human Movement, reported by Mao tse-tung, saw a good deal of smashing of sedan-chairs (Mao: I: 28). And in the period of the civil war in England fraught with so many threats to *status quo,* "the wisest of men saw it to be a great evil that servants should ride on horses: an evil now both seen and felt in this unhappy kingdom" (Hill: 1974: 200).

3854 **वाहितग्रीवा**

Vāhitagrīvā : a neck turned sideways with the face. It indicates to look at sideways and turned round (*NS,* VIII. 164-171).

3855 **वाहेयिका-गाथा**

Vāheyikā-gāthāḥ :Songs or stories to be sung or told at the death of a hero.

3856 **विकटघोरा-मुद्रा**

Vikaṭaghorā-mudrā : "make the mouth opened and bring down the tongue, as long as one can. The belly is to be shown as dried up and the breast-nipples also hanging down.

The pair of hands should be joined together and the worshipper should do all those things in a nude state. This makes the gesture of *Vikatāghorā*" (*BT*).

3857 **विकटदशना**

Vikaṭadaśanā : lady with beautiful teeth, quality of the Deer-lady (*Pañcasāyaka* 2.12).

3858 **विकट-नितम्बा**

Vikaṭa-nitambā : lady with beautiful hips, a heroine of *Subhāṣitaratnabhaṇḍāra.*

3859 **विकटोद्‌बद्धपिण्डिक**

Vikaṭodbaddhapiṇḍika : having very prominent calfs.

3860 **विकत्थना**

Vikatthanā : boasting. Bhavabhūtiś boast is well-known to an Indologist:

> Are there any around who mock my verses?
> They ought to know I don't write for them.
> Someone somewhere sometime will understand.
> Time has no end. The world is big.
> (*Mālatī-Mādhavam* 1.6)

Boast, in this usage, means 'being assertive'. In day-to-day Indian life, a principal form of proclamation of self is 'boasting'. It is a routine which shows up in a number of different conversational genres. Cross-culturally boasting varies greatful in its meanings, from our own concerns with 'reticence' and 'blowing your own horn' to the heroic boasting of Paraśurāma in *Rāmacaritamānasa.* Boasting is a basic form of humour in the tribal societies. Boasting is also an essential form of defence against all forms of attack or criticism. The appropriate response to a tease or challenge is a boast, a show of strength.

3861 **विकरण**

Vikaraṇa : modification, (b) producing a change, the conjugational sign placed between the root and the terminations.

3862 **विकर्ष**

Vikarṣa : the drawing of bow up to ears.

3863 **विकर्षण**

Vakarṣaṇa : reaction of sentiment and feelings by action and function of the appropriate gesture (*NS*, IX. 175). (b) delay, drawing the bow up to ears, fasting (*Mbh.*).

3864 **विकल्प**

Vikalpa : rational knowledge, determination. It consists of conceptual unification of the many into "one", distinguishing between one object cognition and another, between "this" and "not-this" and accepting one among the many stimuli received from outside. It is the opposite of *nirvikalpa* (apprehension devoid of determination) and discrimination in which the limited "I" of the individual is united with the unlimted "I" of its own higher self and in which the difference between "this" and "not-this" does not arise. (b) In *Mīmāṁsā* tradition *vikalpa* means option especially where the contents of two texts are irreconcilable. (c) alternative, either this or that, doubt, hesitation, (d) a figure of speech arising in juxtaposition of two hostile things of equal strenght. *viz:*

> कै तन प्राण कि केवल प्राणा।
> बिधि करतब कछु जातन जाना।। (*Mānasa)*

3865 **विकल्पक**

Vikalpaka : (a) adjective. (b) thought opposed to direct sense-apprehension. (c) creating, making, causing, disturbance (Caraka), putting separately.

3866 **विकसित**

Vikasita : blown, opened (said of the eyes), blossomed.

3867 **विकांक्षा**

Vikāṁkṣā : lack of respect.

3868 **विकार**

Vikāra : (a) the transformation of *prakṛti.* It means the assumption of a different form after giving up the original form. For example, curd, sprout earring are the *vikāras* respectively of milk, seed and gold. (b) a rite in which not all subsidiaries are directly prescribed. (c) modification of a word-base or an affix, caused generally by the addition of suffixes.

3869 **विकाश**

Vikāśa : unfolding; manifestation; development. In a cosmogonical sense the term denotes evolution as opposed to *saṅkoca* or involution.

3870 **विकास**

Vikāsa : growth (in drama).

3871 **विकुञ्चितभ्रूलता**

Vikuñcitabhrūlatā : with contracted eye-brows.

3872 **विकूणिता-नासा**

Vikūṇitā-nāsā : contracting nose, contracted nostrils; a type of nose-gesture in *hāsya.* The contracted lobes of the nose suggest laughter, disgust, hatred, envy, disease, etc. Also known as *vighūrṇita* (*NS*, VIII. 123-129).

3873 **विकृति**

Vikṛti : same as *vikāra*, obscure or adapted subject-matter (*DR*, IV. 90).

3874 **विकृष्टा-नासा**

Vikṛṣṭā-nāsā : extremely dilated nostrles, a type of nose-gesture in *bhayānaka rasa*. Lobes are blown. In *Mālatīmādhava* (IX.4), Kapālakuṇḍalā enters the cementary smelling the odour: this would be done by the *vikṛṣṭa* movement of the nose (*NS*, VIII. 134). The blown lobes of the nose suggest the strong smell, the drawn up breathing, anger, fear and disease (*Ibid.*, 123-129). Nostrils blown; it is used in powerful smell, anger, fear and in the Furious and Heroic.

3875 **विकोशा-दृष्टि**

Vikośā-dṛṣṭi : full-burst glance, a type of *sañcārībhāva dṛṣṭi* a joyous dance with the wide and open eyelids and the immobile eyeballs is called *vikośā* (*NS*, VIII. 61-92). It is used to suggest arrogance, cruelty, assurance, etc. Both the eyelids are wide open, fully blown without winking and pupils unsteady. It is used in awakening, pride, indignation, fierceness and determination.

3876 **विक्रिया**

Vikriyā : modification, transformation, change. *aṅgavikriyā* 'alternation of the body'. The motif of changing from man to woman is associated with many gods. Indra fell in love with a demon woman and went to live among demons, as a man among men and a woman among women (*Atharva veda*, VII. 38.2). An Indian folk-tale expands this motif and relates it to Śiva and Pārvatī (Kindcaid, 119). Other forms of transformation are also associated with Indra. He is said to have taken the form of a Brāhmaṇ guest or of Gautama himself (*Padma* 1.56.15-33) in order to seduce Ahalyā. Śiva also assumes the role of a Brāhmaṇ guest when he seduces the wives of the sages.

3877 **विक्षिप्त-करण**

Vikṣipta-karaṇa : the kneess are in *kṣipta*. Feet and both hands are in *vikṣipta* away from the body. The extended outward movement of the hands is emphasized. The commentary mentions the *vidyutbhrāntā cārī* (*NS*, IV. 118b-119a, IX. 257-58). The hands and feet are thrown backwards or sideways. It is used in gaits of the haughty. (Fig. 3877)

3878 **विक्षिपाक्षिप्त-करण**

Vikṣipākṣipta-karaṇa : the hands and the feet both are thrown out. One hand in *vyāvartita* movement and the other in *catura hasta*. The movement is preversed in the final position. Abhinavagupta adds that it should be used for going and coming (*NS*, IV. 82). Hands and feet are first thrown out and then drawn near. It is used in going and coming.

3879 **विक्षेप**

Vikṣepa : power of projection or transformation, throwing variously, distraction.

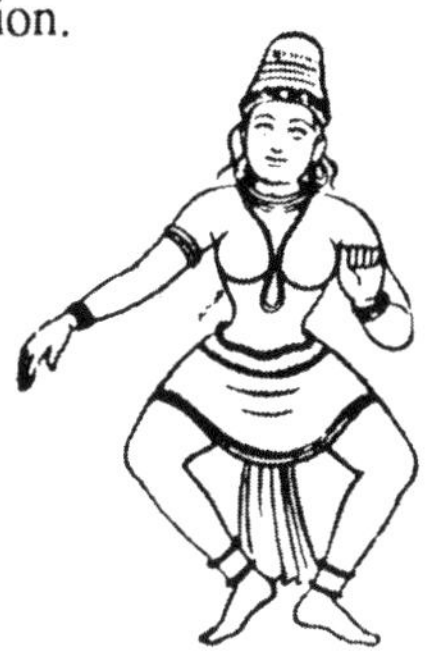

Fig.– (3877)

3880 **विक्षेपक**

Vikṣepaka : that which causes distraction. These are nine: (i) *vyādhi* (disease). (ii) *styāna* (non-activity of mind). (iii) *Saṁśaya.* (doubt). (iv) *avirati* (greed). (v) *pramāda* (negligence) (vi) *ālasya* (laziness. (vii) *bhrānti* (delusion). (viii) *alabdha bhūmikatya* (non-obtainment of *samādhi*). (ix) *anavasthitatva* (fickleness of mind).

3881 **विक्षेपण**

Vikṣepaṇa : throwing away relevant sentiment and feelings through appropriate gesture (*NS*, IX. 175).

3882 **विक्षेपण-शक्ति**

Vikṣepaṇa-śakti : projective power of *māyā* or ignorance.

3883 **विगता**

Vigatā : a girl in love with a person unfit for marriage.

3884 **विग्रह**

Vigraha : a figure, a form, a shape, an image, an idol (*Mānasāra*, LIV. 180). The word is constituted by *vi* and *gṛha* which means 'to grasp firmly'. Hence *vigraha* is a representation which helps the mind to grasp an idea. *Vigrahas* used for worship may be *arūpa-vigrahas* (formless ones) or *sarūpa-vigrahas* (Those with anthromorphic forms). (b) analysis of the secondary element in a word.

3885 **विघटन-संघटन**

Vighaṭana-saṅghaṭana : disuniting and uniting.

3886 **विघूर्णिता-नासा**

Vighūrṇitā-nāsā : contracted nostrils, (*NS*, VIII. 131-132), same as *vikūṇitā-nāsā*

3887 **विघ्नराज-मुद्रा**

Vighnarāja-mudrā : if the middle-finger or the *Skanda* (q.v) gesture is bent a bit and the thumb is placed on the fore-finger, the styles indicate Vighneśa or Vighnarāja and this removes all sorts of evil mens (*VD*).

3888 **विघ्नसिद्धि**

Vighna-siddhi : removal of obstacles.

3889 **विघ्नापसारण**

Vighnāpasāraṇa : the clearance of all evil elements with the help of *mantras.* Also known as *bhūtāpasāraṇa* (*Puraścaryārṇava,* III. 154; Rāghava on *Śāradātilaka* IV.10).

3890 **विचलन**

Vicalana : one of the 64 *sandhyaṅgas*; a self-panegyric statement (Dhanañjaya), boasting, *boastfulness* (in drama).

3891 **विचार**

Vicāra : discussion or enquiry to get rid of ignorance. *Vicāra* is also called *kathā* or controversy (—*kathā*—which is of three kinds; *vāda, jalpa* and *vitaṇḍā*) and *tadvidyā—saṁbhāṣā* (discussion with people versed in the relevant science).

3892 **विचारणा**

Vicāraṇā : reflection on the nature of self and the world (*Yogavāśiṣtha,* III. 118.2-16), investigation, enquiry.

3893 **विचालित-पुट**

Vicālita-puṭa : when the upper eyelid suddenly strikes the lower, this type of eye-gesture is seen (*SR.* VII. 440-445, *Nāṭyaśāstra Saṅgraha,* pp. 534-540).

3894 **विचिकित्सा**

Vicikitsā : doubt; a mental state according to *Bṛhadāraṇyaka* (1.5.3). In *Kaṭhopaniṣad* (1. 20) the word has been used in the sense of philosophic doubt as to man's existence after death.

3895 **विचित्त**

Vicitta : unconscious, perplexed (*DR.,* IV.32). Characterizing an activity for which the individual does not know the reason or motive of the act; pertaining to the state of an individual who has suffered a loss of consciousness, such a person in a faint or coma; pertaining to all psychic processes that cannot be brought to awareness by ordinary means;

3896 **विचित्र-मुद्रा**

Vicitra-mudrā : "Raise up two middle-fingers and fore-fingers and ring-fingers should come to roots of each separately. The little-finger and thumbs are to be made raised up. This is the gesture known by the name of *vicitra* that helps to satisfy all sorts of desires' (*BT*).

3897 **विचेष्टित**

Viceṣṭita : action: *madhurāṅga viceṣṭitaiḥ* (*DR.,* II.60).

3898 **विच्छित्ति**

Vicchitti : a careless toilet, one of the natural graces of women. The great charm which arises out of the slightly careless placing of garlands, dress, ornament and unguents. (*Dhvanyāloka* III.19), disregard for adornment. *Viz.*

तनक बनकही में जहाँ, तरुणि महाछवि देत ।
सोई विच्छिति हाव है, वरणत बुद्धिनिकेत ॥

3899 **विच्छेद**

Viccheda : pause or stop in speaking.

3900 **विच्यवा-चारी**

Vicyavā-cārī : both feet in *samapāda* positions. The description indicates a movement: a jump from the *samapāda* feet is suggested. The feet touch the ground in the final position as *kuñcita.* The feet are separated from the *samapāda* position striking the ground by their force or from the *samapāda* position the feet are lifted up and the foreparts are brought down (*nikuṭṭana*) on the ground (*NS,* X.19).

3901 **विजयादशमी**

Vijayādaśamī : the tenth day of the bright fortnight in Āśvina (Sept.-Oct.). Which concludes the Durgā Pūjā festival. It is regarded the day of victory because on this day Rāvaṇa was killed by Rāma.

3902 **विजया-मुद्रा**

Vijayā-mudrā : "make two hands up-turned and flat and place them like a *tomara* (a kind of weapon), then make your eyes flushing, hands uplifted, and face smiling and happy; this makes a *Vijayā-mudrā.* All these are the favourite *mudrās* to please mother Gods and *Yoginīs* (*BT*).

3903 **विजल्प**

Vijalpa : idle talk.

3904 **विजातीय भेद**

Vijātīya-bheda : *bheda* or difference between alien species (*Vedāntic* school).

3905 **विजृम्भा**

Vijṛmbhā : yawning. Yawning has a sexual suggestion too. Bala, the son of demon Maya, yawned and from his yawn were produced three women—Kāminī, Svairiṇī and Puṁścalī. All these three names are indicative of free sexual indulgence. These women caught men and gave them to drink *hāṭaka,* which made them strong. The women then had prolonged sex with them (*Bhāgavat Purāṇa,* V.24.16).

3906 **विजृम्भित**

Vijṛmbhita : the yawning position in coition, prescribed for the Deer-lady (*Kāmasūtra*, 2.6.7).

3907 **विज्ञान**

Vijñāna : correct undestanding, consciousness, science, *Vijñāna-vāda* is a philosophical stream of Mahāyāna Buddhism which believes in the reality of thought-waves and denies the objective existence of all perceived through the gross sense-organs. For distinction between *Jñāna* and *Vijñāna* cp. *Bhagvad-gītā* (VII).

3908 **विट**

Viṭa : paramour, passionate rogue. Associate of a king or a characterless young man. Accomplish of a prostitute.

तासन सब विट कहत हैं
जो हब कला-प्रवीन ।
लायो मोहाने को मना
सुना माधुरी बीना ॥

(*Kāvyaprabhākara*, 260)

3909 **विडम्बना**

Viḍambanā : imitation, (or action), insult, deriding, copying the actions of another intentionally.

3910 **विडम्बितगामिनी**

Viḍambita-gāminī : of slow and winning gait.

3911 **विडाल-मुद्रा**

Viḍāla-mudrā : indication of a cat. *ardhamukha*, or the thumb and the third finger of the *muṣṭi*-hand are joined to indicate a cat (*Mirror of Gesture*, pp.49-50).

3912 **वितण्डा**

Vitaṇḍā : cavil, that form of discussion in which only the opponent's views are contradicted without supporting one's own view is called *Vitaṇḍā* (*Caraka Saṁhitā*, 8.28). One of the three types of *kathā* (debate). When the *jalpa* (q.v.) is converted into discredit and repudiates the rival's dogma and tenets as a main object of contestants, without any direct effort to justify and fortify his own, then it is called *vitaṇḍā* (cavil): *sa pratipakṣa-sthāpana-hīno vitaṇḍā* (*Nyāyasūtra*, 1.2.3.). The repudiation of Advaitic *upādhi* of *māyāvāda* and *mithyāvāda* by Śri Mādhava are known as *vitaṇḍā*.

Thus, *vitaṇḍā* is a kind of debate in which the opponent does not establish his own position but only tries to refute that of the exponent. It is one of the sixteen philosophical topics of *Nyāya*.

3913 **वितण्डावादिन्**

Vitaṇḍāvādin : a section of the followers of the Cārvāka school who used to engage themselves constantly in refuting the views of others.

3914 **वितर्क**

Vitarka : conjecture, arguement. One of the transitory states. It represents various discussions, non-settling of the problems, concealment of the counsel, movement of the head and eyebrows,etc. (b) *vitarka* is the basic perceptual functioning at the *manomaya* level by which a particular object is differentiated from all other objects. At this level, there is the most elementary form of reasoning, while *vitarka* isolates a particular object from all other objects, *vicāra* is at the conceptual level, the *vijñānamaya* level. While commenting on *Yoga-sūtra* (II.19) Jaimini warns, "It may be pointed out that the simple mental process of *vitarka* or *vicāra* which may engage in during the course of our studies and thinking should not be considered equivalent to the corresponding mental process as they take place in the state of *samādhi* " (p.182). (c) *Vitarka* is one of the varieties of the *Sañcārī-bhāvas*, cf. *Kāvyaprabhākara* (390):

उर उपजत संदेह जहँ, कीजै कछु विचार ।
ताहि वितर्क विचारहीं, जे कवि सुमति विचार ॥

3915 **वितर्क-मुद्रा**

Vitarka-mudrā : an iconic *mudrā* represented by the right arm bent, all fingers erect except either the index or the ring-finger which touch the thumb so as to resemble a ring. If the hand is extended forward with palm outward, it denotes a discussion.

3916 **वितर्किका-दृष्टि**

Vitarkikā-dṛṣṭi : argumentative glance, a type of *sañcārī bhāva dṛṣṭi*, a glance with the turned up eye-lids and the full blown eye-balls, moving downwards; is known as *vitarkikā*. It breaths an air of deliberation, pondering, doubts and recollection. Eyelids are turned in guess, pupils full blown and moving downwards. It is used in recollection and deliberation.

3917 **वितस्ति**

Vitasti : a long span measured by the extended thumb and little finger.

3918 **विताडित-पुट**

Vitāḍita-puṭa : when struck; a type of eye-gesture, when the upper eyelid suddenly strikes the lower, driven in accident and other calamities (*NS*, VIII. 107).

3919 **वितान-मण्डल**

Vitāna-maṇḍala : canopy. In both the hands, expand both the fingers (*i.e.* thumbs and little fingers of both the hands). They are to be placed, in a position of a square to the aim of performing the particular purpose prescribed in the *Tāntrika* rituals as advised in constructing a *bhadramaṇḍala.* This is called the *vitāna-maṇḍala*, which is a great hide of *mantras.* (*BT*).

3920 **विदूषक**

Vidūṣaka : a character in a drama, the jester. The hero's confident and devoted friend. He is a Brāhmaṇa ludicrous in dress, speech and behaviour. He is generally represented as a dwarf, bald-headed, with projecting teeth and red eyes. He evokes laughter in his silly chatter in Prākṛta, and his revenous greed for food. The traditional foolery in Sanskrit dramas used to serve as a safety-valve for ancient Indian society releasing tension and making the social order 'perhaps that much more tolerable'.

3921 **विद्धक-आलिंगन**

Viddhaka-āliṅgana : piercing embrace. "When a woman in a lonely place bends down as if to pick up something, and pierces, as it were, a man sitting or standing, with her breasts, and the man in turn takes hold of her, is called *viddhaka* : *prayajyam nāyikā sthitamupaviṣṭitam vā vijane kiṁcid gṛhṇāni payodhareṇa viddhyennāyakopi tāmavapīḍya gṛhṇāditi viddhakam* (*Kāmasūtra*, 2.2.10). The *Ratirahasya* (2.2) defines this embrace thus: "When a woman under the pretext of taking something, pierces her lover who is either standing or sitting with her breasts, and if her love clasps her in his arms, then it is called *viddhaka* :

yadgṛhṇāti kiñcana yañcitākṣam
sthitopaviṣṭam puruṣam stanābhyām /
nitambinī vidhyati tām ca gāḍham
gṛhṇātyasau viddhakamucyate tat //

Such type of embrace is depicted by many poets, such as Māgha (*Śiśu.*, 6.13), Bhāravi (*Kirāta.*, B.46), Gaṅgādevī (*Madhurā-Vijaya*, 6.58) and Bilhaṇa (*Vikramāṅkadevacarita*, 10.54).

3922 **विद्या**

Vidyā : studies, knowledge; female deities and their *mantras*; the female partner of the aspirant; certain forms of *tattvas* and *kalās* ; *Vimarśa-śakti* expressed in the idea of I-ness; the name of school and sects, and so on.

(a) As knowledge, *vidyā* is of two kinds; viz; *parā-vidyā* (spiritual knowledge) and *aparā-vidyā* (material knowledge).

(b) The Buddhist concept of *vijā* (*vidyā*) denotes faculty. It is of three kinds.

(c) Fourteen or eighteen disciplines have been enumerated:

aṅgāni vedāścatvāro mīmāṁsā nyāyavistaraḥ /
arthaśāstram purāṇam ca vidyā hyetāścaturdaśa //
āyurvedo dhanurvedo gāndharvaśceti te trayaḥ /
arthaśāstram caturtham ca vidyā aṣṭādaśaiva tāḥ //

compare the following *śloka* on the significance of *kṛtavidyāḥ* :

śūraśca kṛtavidyaśca
rūpavatyaśca yoṣitaḥ /
yatra yatra gamiṣyanti
tatra tatra kṛtādarāḥ //

"A warrior bold, a scholar deeply read
A maid in prime of life enchanting, sweet
These three, Be sure, where'es they wish to tread
Them do good cheer, applause, honour and greet".

3923 **विद्यारम्भ**

Vidyārambha : a rite at the commencement of learning the alphabet in the fifth year of the child. It is not mentioned in the *Gṛhyasūtras* and *Smṛtis.*

3924 **विद्यालापरता**

Vidyālāparatā : lady who has interest in studies and discussion, quality of the Art-lady (*Pañcasāyaka*, 1.7).

3925 **विद्युत्-भ्रान्त-करण**

Vidyut-bhrānta-karaṇa : feet as in *cārī* one leg is taken back and extended high so that the foot touches the forehead: the other foot is in *samapāda* : weight of the body is on the *sampāda* foot. The arm-movement is given as *maṇḍalāviddha*, i.e., *maṇḍala* (circular) movement and *āviddha* movement when the hands are turned inward towards the body from an outer point in space (*NS*, IV. 125b-126a, IX. 220-21, X.40). The foot is turned backward and extended on all sides close to the head in a circular manner. It is used in haughty gait.

3926 **विद्युत्-भ्रान्ता-चारी**

Vidyut-bhrāntā-cārī : foot in *samapāda kuñcita* or *samapāda* positions. The lifted foot taken back on the flexed position where it touches, the hips and then the head, etc. Thus the movement is in all directions. *Parivartita jaṅghā, alātaka karaṇa* and *maṇḍala*, also *aṅgahāra* by the same name.

In the Vimal Visāhi temple of Ādinātha, we observe an accurate illustration of *vidyut-bhrāntā cārī* ; the back flexing of one leg clearly sculptured and it is this movement which can result in the final position of the *vidyut-bhrāntā-karaṇa*, where toes of the foot touch the *karaṇa.*

The foot is turned to the back and extended to touch the head moving all round. It is one of the *ākāśikī cārīs.* According to *NS* (X.40) 'the foot is taken back, touches the head, is turned round in all the directions then stretched'.

3927 **विद्रव**

Vidrava : tumult, flight. One of the 64 *sandhyaṅgas* in dramaturgy. Bharata (*NS*, 19.88) mentions it as the panic caused by apprehension (*śaṅkā*), fear (*bhaya*) and uneasiness (*trāsa*). Abhinavagupta understands by it the apprehension from the object which causes fear and trembling. Dhanañjaya states it as a slaying, tacking prisoner and the like (*DR*, I.85).

3928 **विद्राविणी-मुद्रा**

Vidrāviṇī-mudrā : other fingers posed as in the *saṁkṣobhinī*, the middle fingers are to be straight (*Brahmāṇḍa*, II.4.42.2)

3929 **विद्वेषण**

Vidveṣaṇa : rite for creating bad blood (*Śāradātilaka*, XXIII. 124), causing to hate.

3930 **विधवा**

Vidhavā : the widow. The lot of the widow who survived her husband was far from enviable. The disappearance of her husband placed her in an inferior position, legally as well as socially. Not only might she no longer take part in the family's sacremental life, she had also to remain absent, thence forward from social reunions and ceremonies, where her presence would have struck a note of ill omen. She no longer wore jewellery or perfumes, her face was no longer made up, her hair was no longer tanned or dressed or even combed (Upadhyaya, *op.cit.* p.204). Her fate was simply to live in a chaste and austere life, sleeping on the ground, taking only a single meal each day, one without honey, meat, wine or salt, dividing her time between prayer and religious rites and possessing only one hope: to be married to her husband again in a future life, and meanwhile to satisfy his soul by her faithfulness and good conduct until the moment of her own death. Furthermore, she was now subject to the direct authority of her eldest son in his capacity as head of the family. There was no question of her leaving her home and setting down elsewhere, for, by her marriage, she had become part of her husband's *gotra*. In the same way, she was strictly forbidden to remarry, under pain of endangering the soul of the man to whom she had been indissolubly bound by the sacrament of marriage (many social reformers including Gandhi, preached the remarriage of widows, which has since been authorized by the constitution). In any case, a woman had to be a virgin in order to get married, so that the only possible grounds on which she might receive permission to remarry were if her union with her husband had remained unconsummated.

In general, she accepted unhesitatingly her new condition of life and resulting austerities. Neither her temperament nor her education had conditioned her to envisage widowhood as a liberation which would have allowed her live at last according to her own inclinations, after so many years spent following her husband's orders and advice.

The widow is not particularly praised in Indian literature. She is described in rather dark words. Even a glance at her should be avoided, much less her touch (*Skanda.*, II.9.22.11). If a widow is seen when one is starting out one should turn back; for if one goes he is sure to die:

> प्रयाणकाले विधवादर्शनं सन्मुखे यदि ।
> स्यात्तदा नैव गन्तव्यमन्यथा मरणं ध्रुवम् ॥
> (*Skanda*, II.9.22.12)

The blessing of widow is said to be like the hissings of poisonous serpents; hence a house-holder should be afraid of their blessings, as he should be afraid of demonness (*Ibid*,13). A widow is ordained to spend her time in the worship of Viṣṇu. She should never hear any news regarding love or love-sport, nor should see any beasts copulating (*Ibid*,61-65), nor should sleep on a bedstead (*Ibid*,66). Decoration or looking into a mirror is forbidden for a widow (*Brahmavaivarta*, III.83.94). They should not decorate their hair or she should completely remove her hair (*Skanda*, IV.4.76)

Self-burning by widow on the death of her husband was a common practice which can be seen under *Satī*.

Remarriage of a widow is also allowed. She may be given to the younger brother (*devara*); and in his absence she may be given to any body according to the elder's desire (*Agni*, 154.5.6.). This is an old custom that is referred to in the *Agni-Purāṇa*. According to the texts on *Dharma-Śāstra* this custom is not favoured in the Kali age (*Manu*, IX.64).

(b) The remarriage of widow is freely permitted in the fourth *varṇa* and the tribal society. As a rule it is considered suitable that she should marry her deceased husband's younger brother. After her husband's death she resides with her parents, and a price is usually paid to them by any outsider who wishes to marry her. In Bastar widow was considered the property of the state, and sold by auction for the benefit of treasury (Russell and Hiralal, III. 81).

3931 **विधान**

Vidhāna : conflict of feelings: *vidhānam sukhaduḥkhakṛt* (*DR*, 1.46).

3932 **विधि**

Vidhi : injuction; ritual, the ways to achieve the end; the fourth category of the *Pāśupata* system. The important *vidhis* are known as *caryās* which are again subdivided into *vratas* (vows) and *dvāra* (door). (b) *vidhi* is also the term for *injunction*. (c) *vidhimārga* meas the way of injunctions and prohibitions or the path of duties. (d) *vidhi* is an *exhortation* that is meaningful on account of enjoining a matter that has a useful purpose and that prescribed somthing which does not follow from any authority. (e) *vidhis* are variously classified as *apūrva*, *niyama* and *parisaṅkhyā* or into *puruṣārtha* and *kratvartha*. (f) *vidhi* is used in the sense of procedure to be adopted in the performance of ceremonies, (Kālidāsa, *Vikrama.* 5.120). A *vidhi* is a perfunctory, conventionalized act through which an individual portrays his respect and regard for some object of ultimate value to that object of ultimate value or to its stand-in.

3933 **विधुत मुख**

Vidhuta-mukha : mouth expanded obliquely. A type of mouth-gesture in *Vīrarasa.* Mouth opened face turned from side to side (*NS,* VIII, 153-160); opened obliquely. It suggests envy, jealousy, anger, contempt and blushfulness of a woman. It is also used in warding off, saying 'not so' etc. (b) non-observance of the lover's request is *vidhūta* (*SD,* VI.90).

3934 **विधूत शिर**

Vidhūta śira : A type of head-movement, side bent of the head (*NS,* VIII.26), a violent movement. This type of head-movement (*Ratnāvalī,* Act. III) also indicates acute fear; the move of quick action of *dhuta* (q.v.) to indicate an attack of cold, terror, fever, panic and a newly addicted drunkard.

3935 **विनति**

Vinati : bowing down, modesty.

3936 **विनयपिटक**

Vinayapiṭaka : basket of discipline, the Etiquette system (*Mbh.,* XII.122.33) The entire etiquette system is perhaps best summed up and symbolized in the way Indians use their language. In Sanskrit it is nearly impossible to say anything without indicating the social relationship between the speaker and the listener in terms of status and familiarity. Status is determined by many things—wealth, caste, education, occupation, age, kinship and nationality, among others, but the important point is that the coice of linguistic forms as well as speech style is in every case partly determined by the relative status (or familiarity) of the converserers. The difference is not minor, a mere *tvam* and *bhavat* difference. To greet a person lower than oneself Manu prescribes a particular formula, but one greets a superior in the different formula. As a result, several words may denote the same normal linguistic meaning but differ in the status connotation they convey. Thus, for 'house' we have a dozen of forms (*gṛham, sadanam, niketanam, mandiram, bhavanam, āyatanam, dhāman, garbhāgāram, vāsagṛham, kuṭajaḥ, veśman, āvāsaḥ* etc), each connoting a status of the listener with respect to the speaker.

It will be discussed later on how etiqutte patterns tend to be regarded by the Indians as a kind of emotional capital which may be invested in putting others at ease. Politeness is something one directs towards others; one surrounds the other with a wall of behavioural formality which protects the stability of his inner life. Etiquette is a wall built around one's inner feelings, but it is, paradoxically, always a wall for one of two reasons.

3937 **विनिगूहन (अधर)**

Vinigūhana (adhara) : drawing in lips, drawing the lips inside. A type of lip-movement suggested in *raudra.* Folding lower lip in the mouth (*NS,* VIII. 145-46) Śakuntalā's aversion is depicted by folding lips in the mouth (*Śākuntalam,* Act III); concealment; suggests amorous devises to hide love sign, used in making efforts.

3938 **विनियोग**

Viniyoga : application (*Darśana*), employment, separation.

3939 **विनियोग-विधि**

Viniyoga-vidhi : that which conveys the relation between the prinicipal act and its subsidiaries (*aṅgin-aṅga* ; *śeṣin-ṣeṣa*)in religious rites.

3940 **विनिवृत्त-करण**

Vinivṛtta-karaṇa : derived from a movement of the sacrum. The feet positions are as in *sūcī cārī* (*NS,* IV. 122b-123b): feet are placed in *sūcī cārī* in the initial position and are moved to a *svastika* position in the final situation. The *trika* is turned round, *i.e.* the side is in the *vivartana* movement. The two *haṁsapakṣa hastas* move in a fast tempo in *recita* (*NS,* IV. 122b-123a; IX.193, 236-238; X.34). Performing the *sūcī cārī,* the *trika* is turned with the hands in *recita.* It is used in gaits of the haughty.

3941 **विनिवृत्त-मुख**

Vinivṛtta-mukha : turned away face; face turned sideways; a type of mouth gesture in turning the face away (*NS,* VIII. 153-160); checking or altering talks by expanding mouth. It indicates either a check or a side-tracking in conversation. Also used in women's envy, anger, contempt and bashfulness.

3942 **विनेयता-संकेत**

Vineyatā-saṅketa : docility. The Hindus strike the Europeans as an exceptionally docile race. Of the present day Hindus this is somewhat true. But that the Hindus had not always been so is evident from their history and literature. Continued foreign domination is mainly responsible for the docility of the Hindus. From the 12th century of the Christian era to the present day, the Hindus have been a subject race and nothing so thoroughly induces docility as long-standing dependence upon others. The decay of the Kṣatriyas and the martial ideal they stood for also added to the inertia of the Hindus. Under the supremacy of the Brāhmaṇs, intellectual and spiritual attainments came to be considered superior to the martial. The martial philosophy of *Gītā* was interpreted by Brāmaṇs as a school of thought rather than as a guide to conduct. Its importance was shifted from the battlefield to the study rooms and discussion halls of philosophers. Then there came the feudal age. The tradition of using language as a register of caste status was still very much alive when Logan came across it in the late nineteenth-century Malabār. A man's deference towards those ranked higher than himself was demonstrated in explicit verbal acknowledgements of his own inferiority. In any conversation he had to debase himself by stigmatizing whatever he had. Convention required him to refer to his own food not simply as rice, but as 'stony or gritty rice', his money as nothing more than 'cowrie', his house as 'dungheap' (85.127). The indigenous perception of the structural cleavages in Malabār society of a century ago was recorded in a list of words for houses, as given by Logan. He wrote: "The house itself is called by different names according to occupant's caste. The house of a Pariah is a *cheri*, while the agrestic slave—the Cheraman—lives in *chal*. The blacksmith, the goldsmith, the carpenter, the weaver, etc., and the today-drawer (Tiyan) inhabit houses styled *pura* or *kudi*; the temple servant resides in a *variyan*, the ordinary Nāyar in *vidu* or *bhavanam*, while the man in authority of this caste dwells in an *idam* ; the Raja lives in a *kovilakam* or *kottaram*, the Namūdiri in an *illam*". (85). This all created discrimination and docility.

3943 **विन्दु**

Vindu : a term used in variety of senses. (a) as a dot it denotes Śiva and as a double dot (*visarga*) *Śakti*, both being alphabetical signs. (b) In *Śāradā* (II.6), the former stands for solar power, the latter for lunar. (c) In Śaiva conception, *vindu* is an evolute of *nāda* which is produced owing to the *kriyāśakti* of Śiva (*Śivapurāṇa, vāyavīya, uttara*, V.18). (d) In Kashmir Śaivism *vindu* is one of the ten *vidyātattvas* (*Tantraloka* I.216). (e) According to *Śārdātilaka* (1.7) *vindu*) by which *parāśakti* is characterised, becomes divided into three parts as *vindu, nāda* and *vīja*. *Vindu* is Śiva-oriented. *Vīja* Śakti-oriented and *nāda* is combination of both. (f) *Vindu* also stands for male organ while its complementary principle *visarga*, stands for the female.

3944 **विन्दु-चक्र**

Vindu-cakra : taññtric diagram with *vindu* as the central point. The elevation of *vindu* is said to form a triangle or *trikoṇa* (*Kāmakalāvilāsa*, XXII).

3945 **विन्यास**

Vinyāsa : touching with hands limbs while reciting *mantras*.

3946 **विपक्ष**

Vipakṣa : disputant, opponent. when one wants to censure an opponent worsted in argumentation, there is a particular rule prescribed by Pāṇini (*Aṣṭādhyāyī*, 8.2.94) which regulates type of the accent to be used.

3947 **विपरीत-रतासन**

Viparīta-ratāsana : the female partner of the couple is in the thighs-up pose. In one terracota *mithuna* from the Tamluk, we have a typical *mithuna* in a chair. The nude man is recling face upwards with legs stretched down in ease; and a woman also nude is sitting face to face upon, in his middle in a coital fixture, with thighs astride. This position of the *puruṣāyita* type is very akin to *viparīta rati*.

3948 **विपर्यय**

Viparyaya : (*NS*, 18.21): form of speech and thought, false knowledge, inverted order, reverse.

3949 **विपर्यास**

Viparyāsa : reverse : *strīpuṁsayorviparyāsa ceṣṭitam puṣpagaṇḍikā* (*SD*, VI. 217) contrariety. A Chhattisgarhī proverb records: *ulṭā pulṭā bhau saṁsār, tab nāū ke mūṛ muṛaī lohrā* "when the world is turned upside down the blacksmith will shave the barber".

3950 **विपल**

Vipala : a measure of time=1/60th *pala* (q.v), a moment.

3951 **विपुला-कटि**

Vipulā-kaṭi : lady whose hips are big, quality of the Mare-lady (*Ratirahasya*, 3.22-26).

3952 **विप्रकीर्ण**

Viprakīrṇa : distributed in due order (*DR*, 1.96).

3953 **विप्रकीर्णक नृत्त-हस्त**

Viprakīrṇaka-nṛtta-hasta : a type of hand gesture in dancing. If the *talamukha* hands are crossed by the wrist in a *svastika* style, it is called the *viprakīrṇaka* (*NS*, IX, 176-197). It is also known as *svastika*. Also known as *viprakīrṇa*.

3954 **विप्र-चरणामृत**

Vipra-caraṇāmṛta : he more orthodox Śūdras carry their veneration for the priestly class to such an extent that they will not cross the shadow of a Brāhmaṇa, and it is unusual for them to be under a vow not to eat any food in the morning before drinking Brāhmaṇa's nectar, or water in which the toe of a Brāhmaṇa has been applied (Russell and Hiralal, *The Tribes and Castes of Central Provinces of India*, Vol.II. p.383).

3955 **विप्रयोग**

Viprayoga : separation. It is one of the two aspects of *śṛṅgāra* or love; the other being *saṁyoga* or union (*DR*, IV.58).

Others have divided it into three aspects: *ayogo viprayogaśca saṁbhogaśceti sa ·tridhā.*

3956 **विप्रलब्धा**

Vipralabdhā : the deceived. The heroine whose lover having given appointment, does not come in time. She finds pleasure in the nectar-like words relating to her lover (*Pañcasāyaka*, 5.36). "She is a lady whose lover does not come to her for a certain reason even though the appointment was made through the female messenger (Fig. 3956) (*NS*). Jagannāth Bhānu has characterized her as follows:

> *vipralabdha akulāy, piyavihin saṅket lakhi*
> *kahān gayo piya hāy, sajaphūl ab śūlasam.*

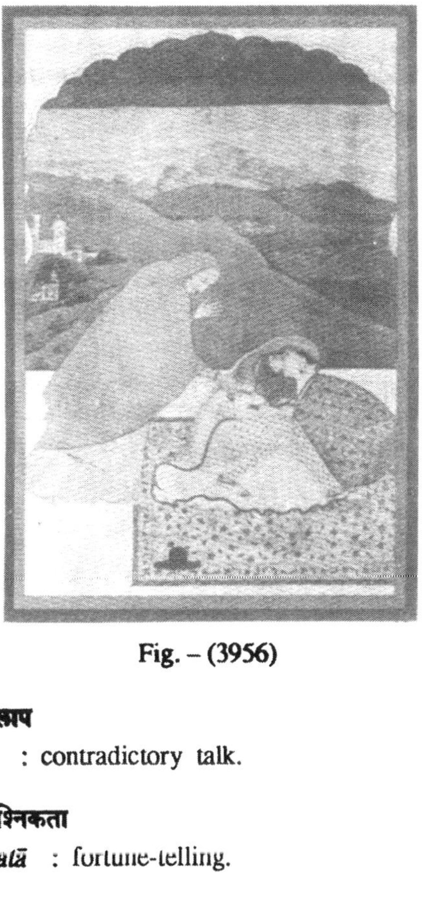

Fig. – (3956)

3957 **विप्रलाप**

Vipralāpa : contradictory talk.

3958 **विप्रश्निकता**

Vipraśnikatā : fortune-telling.

3959 **विप्रिय**

Vipriya : faithfulness, offence cp. *gūḍha-vipriya-kṛt* (*DR*, II.9).

3960 **विप्लुता-दृष्टि**

Viplutā-dṛṣṭi : disturbed glance; a type of *Sañcārī bhāva dṛṣṭi* ; In a *viplutā* glance the eyelids first tremble and then stand fixed and the eyeballs look disturbed. It suggests insanity, in-consistancy and sorrow in demise (*NS*, VIII. 61-92). The eyelids are throbbing first and then become steady and fall down, pupils are disturbed and turned up. It indicates restlessness, madness, affliction and death.

3961 **विबोध**

Vibodha: awakening. One of the transitory states of mind. It is represented by yawning, rubbing the eyes, leaving the bed, etc: *vibodhaḥ kāryamārgaṇam* (*SD*, VI.110). cf. Padmākara:

> अधखुली कंचुकी उरोज अध आधे खुले
> अध खुले वेष नख रेखन के भलकैं ।
> कहैं पद्माकर नवीन अध नीवी खुली
> अध खुले छहरि छराके छोर छलकैं ।
> भोर जगि प्यारी अध ऊरध इतैकी और
> भाषी झिकि झिरखि भिझखि उचारि अध पलकैं ।
> आँखे अधखुली खिरकी है अधखुली
> अध खुले आनन पै अधखुली अलकैं ।

3962 **विब्बोक**

Vibboka : affection of indifference towards beloved through pride. see *bibboka*:

> रहीदेख दृग दै कहाँ, तुहिन लाज कछु छूत ।
> मैं बेटी वृषभान को, तू अहीर को पूत ॥

3963 **विभक्ति**

Vibhakti : division, inflections, a bending or change in the shape of a curve, change in word forms to express grammatical modifications.

3964 **विभाव**

Vibhāva : cause of poetic emotion, one of the three main divisions of *bhāva*, the other two being *anubhāva* and *vyabhicārī bhāva* ; determinants or stimulants; that division of the stimulus serving to arouse the permanent or basic emotion (*sthāyī bhāva*) is *ālambana-vibhāva*; the stabilizing factors are *uddīpana-vibhāva*. *Vibhāva* is used for the sake of vivid knowledge. It determines words, gestures and representation of the *sattva*. *Vibhāva* is the means of expression. It is physical stimulant to aesthetic reproduction. It is the exterior manifestation of emotion. It is the temporary state of emotion and physical and involuntary product.

3965 **विभावना**

Vibhāvanā : manifestation; a figure of speech where effects arise without causes: *kriyāyāḥ pratiṣedhepi phalavyaktir vibhāvanā* (*Kāvyaprakāśa*, X. 107).

3966 **विभाषा**

Vibhāṣā : (a) tribal dialects. In the dramatic composition there are besides *Vibhāṣās*, such as the speeches of the *Śakāra, ābhīras, caṇḍālas, śabaras, dramiḍas, oḍras* and the lowly speech of the foresters. Abhinavagupta (*Abhinavabhāratī*, XVII.372) thinks that *bhāṣā* is the *Apabhraṁśa* of Sanskrit, and the *Apabhraṁśa* of *bhāṣā* is *vibhāṣā* and it belongs to persons living in caves and open: *bhāṣā Saṃskṛtāpabhraṁśaḥ, bhāṣāpabhraṁśastu sā tattaddeśa grānamnivāsinām ca.*

Depending on sex and age, there are at present sharp differences in adaptation to dialect variation and in attitudes to it. Dialectal and diatypic varieties of the tribal languages are viewed with considerable sophistication by young men. They could often locate a visitor's village and always his general area by hearing him speak. The speech of some villages and clans is said to be beautiful and that of others "crow-like" and "rattling" (as of the Hill Maria). Certainly the tribal area presents extraordinary dialectal complexity in India. Elwin's description (1947) of the uncompromising terrain of Bastar gives the geographical rationale for the classic situation of speech communities separated from one another by areas of low density of communication.

Elwin (1960) writes: "For centuries the real ruler of the tribal people has been environment; it has shaped their bodies, directed their art, forced Babell on their tongues.... (b) alternative, optionality of rules (Pāṇini, 1.1.44): *naveti vibhāṣā.*

3967 **विभूति**

Vibhūti : astonishment; miraculous power which is acquired by a *yogin* in the course of his progress towards concentration; while to the novice, these powers prove intoxicating, the adept is advised to treat them as mere signs of spiritual progress and not as the real attachment (*Yogasūtra* III.46; *Haṭha-yogapradīpikā* II.78).

3968 **विभ्रम**

Vibhrama : confusion. (a) Physical grace; confused or disordered; especially the flur of mind caused by love. One of the twenty *sāttvika alaṅkāras* of the heroine; physical grace which is inclusive of gesture, speech, dress, make-up and the rest (*NS*, XII, 42), (b) a disturbance, a revolt (*A*, 3.11.13, 3.16.30, 4.12.38). (c) confusion: It is the inversion of various things such as speech, gestures, costume and temperament due to intoxication, passion and joy (*SD*, III.104). Compare the following lines:

> पहिरि कंठ बिच किंकिणी, कस्यौ कमर बिच हार ।
> हरबराय देखन लगी, कबते नंदकुमार ।।

3969 **विभ्रम-दृष्टि**

Vibhrama-dṛṣṭi : graceful glance (*NS*, VIII.93), coquettish glance.

3970 **विभ्रान्ता-दृष्टि**

Vibhrāntā-dṛṣṭ : eye-gesture showing confusion (*NS*, VIII. 93b) There is a reference to it in *Ratnāvalī* (Act II). The agitation and fear of two, friends caused by the sudden appearance of a monkey is shown through this gesture; confused glance, a type of *sañcārī bhāva-dṛṣṭi*; a glance with inconsistent eyelids and eyebrows and full-blown middle-eyes is called *vibhrāntā*. This suggests a mental state of hurry, agitation and confusion. The pupils are unsteady with looks confused and perturbed and eyes wide and full blown. It is used in agitation, confusion and hurry.

3971 **विमर्ष**

Vimarṣa : deliberation. The vibrating, dynamic, or kinetic aspect of power (*Śakti*) of the Absolute, the starting being known as *prakāśa* (*Tantraloka*, III.2). (b) deliberation, pause (in drama).

3972 **विमलीकरण**

Vimalīlkaraṇa : processing of *mantra* (*Tantrasāra*, 54).

3973 **विमान-मुद्रा**

Vimāna-mudrā : the gesture of an aeroplane. "Making the two thumbs curved sufficiently and frawing them near the ears, position the two middle fingers by their upper knots. When they are well-balanced, it is called the *vimāna-mudrā*. It is a kind of *mahā-mudrā* (the great gesture) and is always favourite of *Ḍākinīs*. This is applied to fly over the sky, practice penance to attain the above power (flying in the air) and meant especially for the great congregation of *Tāntrikas* (*Mahāmelāpaka-Vidhi*)" *BT*. *Vimāna* is also the main shrine where the deity is installed.

3974 **विमुक्तासन**

Vimuktāsana : type of sitting posture.

3975 **वियोग**

Viyoga : substracting or separating relevant sentiments and feelings through appropriate gesture (*NS*, IX. 175). (b) separation in the erotic sentiment with the eleven stages:

3976 **वियोगिनी**

Viyoginī : "she is *viyoginī*, whose husband is out of station and whose body sufferes even due to the moon, the lotus and sandal, etc. (*Anaṅgaraṅga*, 10.67). Kālidāsa's Yakṣiṇī, whose husband is far from her on account of the curse, is the example of this type of woman.

3977 **वियोनिमैथुन**

Viyonimaithuna : the sexual act with a woman not involving her vagina; a type of abnormal sexual act (*Skanda Purāṇa*, 1.2.41-57) This type of variation in sex is also known as *prakīrṇa maithuna* which brings impotency (*Brahma-Purāṇa*, 225.51-52).

3978 **विरोहोत्कण्ठिता**

Virohotkaṇthitā : distressed by separation. She is a heroine whose lover does not turn up due to his pre-occupation with many other engagements and makes her sad (*NS*):

उत्का सोच सहेट मैं, क्यौ आयो नहि कंत ?
रात जात सियरात सब, पिय बिलमें कंह ंत ॥
(*Kāvyaprabhākara*, 210)

3979 **विरक्तिसंकेत**

Viraktisaṅketa : boredom signals. If one is disintered, the response is to display boredom. A favourite signal employed in India is the mock-one. Alternatives include deep sighing, a glazed far-away expression, or repeated examination of the wristwatch. This may also lead to a variety of postures. (b) boredom is very close to the indifference sought by the devotees. The explanation which Edward C. Dimock (1966.156) offers for the Viśvanātha story illuminates one aspect: "If one is continually exposed to a given sexual situation, passion gradually drains away; desire loses its significance, perhaps even being replaced by boredom". Dimock (*Ibid.*53) has pointed out the importance of self-temptation in *Tāntric Sahajiyā* sect of Bengal: "It is necessary to transform desire into true love, or *prema*, before ritual union can be effective. And the *Sahajiyās* consider the chastity, especially under extreme temptation, has the power to transform desire into love....Desire, called *kāma*, is dangerous only when it is considered as the end. The truth is that *kāma* is the beginning". The initial impulse to chastity is a sexual impulse.

3980 **विराग**

Virāga : disaffection (*A*, 7.5.27). Kauṭilya points out that disaffection is a step behind rebellion. Impoverishment (*kṣīṇa*) causes greed (*lobha*) and greed causes disaffection (*virāga*). The greedy and dissatisfied subjects because of greed willingly respond to the enemy's instigations.

3981 **विराम**

Virāma : pause, when handling a verse, the actor on the stage uses a pause according to the line's meaning, not according to prosodical rules. A pause may, according to situation, be of one to six *kalā* (approximately one second); it should not exceed the limit of six *kalās*, except in cases where special situations, like illness or a swoon, require longer pauses. Sometimes, in situations where, as in the illustrative verse given by Bharata, an offended lady is brushing aside the approaches of an erring lover through gestures, the words uttered are to be as few as possible (*NS*, 17.32).

The pause should be after completion of meaning and not accordance to the metre as the meaning depends on the pause. It is found in practice that there occurs pause even after one, two, three or four syllables. In a play, words occur containing small number of syllables in cases of *sūcā* and *aṅkura*. That is why, care should be taken about pause. When the two hands are busy, the recitation should be with proper eye movements and with pause expressive of meaning. In the heroic and furious, the hands are mostly busy with weapons; in the odious they are contracted; in the pathetic, hanging; in the comic, pointing to something; in the marvellous, motionless due to wonder and in the terrible, motionless due to fear. When the hands are thus employed in these and other movements the meaning of the words is made definite by *alaṅkāras* and pauses. Pauses prescribed in verses require *alaṅkāras*. They should be used when the word meaning is complete or breath is exhausted, or when there is a long compound, quick utterance or confusion of many meanings. Pause should be observed at the end of the foot of a verse or according to breath. Otherwise, the pause should be observed according to meaning alone. The long syllables with *ā e ai* and *au* are to be used in sadness, argumentation, questioning, or indignation with one *kalā* time. In the *vilambita* pause, the syllables should not be of more than six *kalās*. On taking into consideration the particular incident etc. the pause should be observed in a verse to suit the sentiments and the state.

In the recitation of verse, the pauses arising out of foot divisions are to be used; but the learned should adjust them according to the meaning.

Ungrammatical word should never be recited and metre never spoiled. One should not pause where it is not prescribed and should not have excited utterance where sorrow is to be expressed.

The *alaṅkāras* and the pauses which are prescribed in the recitation of Sanskrit should be resorted to by women in the recitation of Prākṛt.

3982 **विरुत**

Viruta : moaning (of women). Vātsyāyana in his *Kāmasūtra* (2.7.4-5) has described that in sexual situation women moan due to their tenderness (*ārtivyāvṛtti*) and weakness (*aśakti*). The *Kāmasūtra* (7.7.8) further suggests that the moaning sounds made by women all the time of cohabitations should sound like the calls of the dove, the cuckoo, the green pigeon, the parrot, the bee, the gallinule, the swan, the duck and the quail. Śriharṣa (*Naiṣadha*, 18.17) has depicted this type of moaning. Dāmodaragupta (*Kuṭṭanīmatam*, 157) has discussed this mode of weeping. Anantabhaṭṭa describes this paralinguistic feature in a poetic way. (b) cries of birds and beasts. It is really remarkable that the ancient sages had observed minutely the different cries of birds and beasts, as well as their psychological background. Varāhamihira (LXXXVIII) has classified these sounds as *dīpta* (malignant), *sāmānya* (moderate) and *pūrṇa* (auspicious). Some of these sounds are as follows with different suggestions; *ā* (stag, deer), *iśi* (*pingala* bird), *o* (spotted deer), *kara-kara* (*karāyikā* bird), *kaha-kaha* (*karāyikā* bird), *kilkili* (hawk, parrot), *kuṭukli* (*karāyikā*), *koṭikili* (*karāyikī*), *kiṣkisi* (*karāyikā* bird), *keka* (cāṣa bird), *kekra* (*cāṣa* bird), *kvakva* (*aṇḍīraka* bird), *krakra* (myna), *kuku* (cocks, crows), *kulu-kulu* (*chippikā* bird), *kuśa-kuśa* (*pingala* bird), *kucā-kucā* (*pingala* bird), *gum* (*karāyikā* bird), *guggu* (hārīta bird), *guglug* (mating sound of owl), *ciccid* (musk-rat), *cirilu-irilu* (*pingala* bird), *cikciki* (*bhāṇḍaka* bird), *cacca* (female cuckoo), *cikcik* (female cuckoo), *cicit* (female cuckoo), *ṭi* (*aṇḍīraka* bird), *ṭiṭṭi-ṭiṭṭi* (*aṇḍīraka* bird), *ṭaṭaṭṭaṭa* (owl), *tittiḍ* (hawk, heron), *ṭiṭṭiḍ* (musk-rat), *tretre* (myna), *deśi* (*pingala* bird), *bala-bala* (owl) and *hum-hum* (mating sound of owl).

3983 **विरुतभेद**

Virutabheda : eight type of moaning has been discussed by Vātsyāyana in his *Kāmasūtra* (2.7-4-5) as follows:

aśaktiḥ-ārtivyāvṛttiḥ-abalatvam cayoṣitām
ududbhavam ca śītkṛtam tasyāti rūpatvāt
tadanekavidheyam virutāni cāṣṭau bhavanti

These moanings are known as *śītkāra*. These *śīkāras* are as follows: (1) *hiṁkāra* (the sound of Hiṃ) (2) *stanita* (the thundering sound), (3) *sūtkṛta* (the sound of *sūt*) (4) *dūtkṛta* (the sound of *dūt*) (5) *phūtkṛta* (the sound of *phūt*) (6) *kūjita* (the sound of cooing) (7) *rudita* (the sound of weeping) and (8) others. Under others, Vātsyāyana (*Kāmasūtra*, 2.7.6-7) quotes words like mother (*ambārtha śabdaḥ*), and those that are prohibitive (*vāraṇārthaḥ śabdaḥ*), desire of liberation (*mokṣanārthāḥ*) and sufficiency (*alamarthāḥ*).

3984 **विरुद**

Viruda : citation, byrd; poetic titles of the rulers describing achievements and sacrifices of their ancestors and reminding them of their duties and tasks again. *Sāhityadarpaṇa* (5.70) defines it as follows: *gadya-padyamayī rājastutirvīrudamucyate.*

Whatever the ruler moved towards the assembly hall, his arrival was duly announced by the *kañcukī* or *cobadār* through set phraseology which was known in the mediaeval India as *nazar daulat* that whosoever got the kindness became the rich. The sound of *kham-kham* resounded in the hall and those present in the hall stood up. They bowed to the ruler on his entry in the hall and said, *kṣamasva bhagavan* (*khama annadātā*: forgive us, O! giver of food).

Whenever a noble entered the *darbār* the herald (*Kañcukī*) made an announcement known as *salāmatī* (welfare) which indicated the name, rank and status of the incoming noble. Just after it the byrd of the noble's clan or family was pronounced in the emphatic terms reminding the ruler of his privileges and of the services and sacrifices rendered by his ancestors to the crown. Different clans had different byrds. These byrds were often chanted by the family bards (*bhāṭa*). These byrds had a historical background and pointed to the sacrifices and heroic deeds performed by the particular clan to the ruling house. By hinting to the past it reminded the nobles to act likewise in the future to keep up the reputation of their houses. It served as a check on wanton behaviour of the nobles. No doubt they sacrificed much to uphold the traditional honour of their clan (Tod, II.90).

3985 **विरूपाक्ष-मुद्रा**

Virūpākṣa-mudrā : the hand is made down-turned with all its fingers curved, except the extended middle one. It is the gesture of *Virūpākṣa* (*VD*).

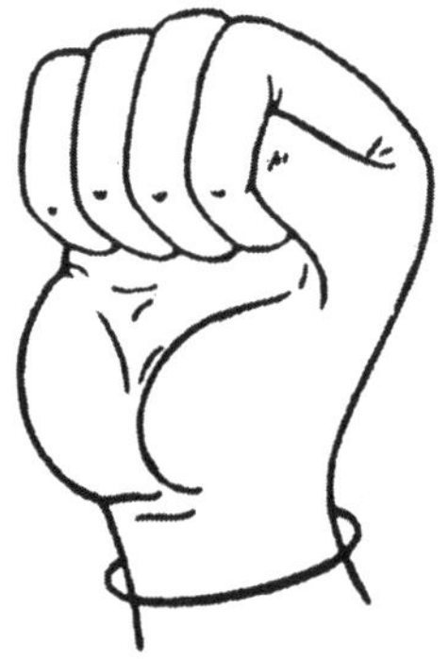

Fig. – (3986)

3986 **विरोध**

Virodha : strife, hostility. (b) contradiction: when something is spoken of as contradictory even when there is no contradiction: *virodhaḥ so' virodhe'pi virudhatvena yad vacaḥ* (*Kāvyapakāśa*, X.110). (b) *virodha*, in social context, means the tendency to wish to inflict harm on others; the tendency to feel anger toward others; trying to force others to behave in such a way as to prove the correctness of one's constructs in the face of evidence to the contrary.

3987 **विरोधन**

Virodhana : besieging. One of the 64 *Sandhyaṅgas* (*NS*, 19.93). Dhanañjaya defines it as the opposition of excited and angry persons. Dhanika interprets it as the proclamation of their powers by excited persons.

3988 **विरोधोक्ति**

Virodhokti : expression of hostility. Overt expression of hostility between castes is common enough, but the resolution of conflict arising from hierarchical inequality by aribitration could never remove the ultimate cause of hostility—the prinicple of hierarchy itself. Such expression of protest as was permitted to those who remained dissatified with formal rearrangement within the hierarchy occurred on ritual occasions and was thought to have mystical benefit. The anthropologist, Max Gluckman, is of the opinion, "that the licensed ritual of protest and rebellion is effective so long as there is no querying of the order within which the ritual of protest is set, and the group itself will endure" (1955.130). It is perhaps more appropriate, in the Indian context. We drop the term 'rituals of rebellion' and refer, as Edward Norbeck (1953) does, to 'rituals of expressing and relieving, if not resolving, conflict'. Such conflict-management is to be found in many societies all over the world, and it is characterized by a great variety of institutionalized departures from everyday practice—role-reversal, utterance of protest by oracles in a state of possession, great annual festivals that provide the occasion for the airing of grievances. These do not permit rebellions against authority but they do serve as dramas of conflict. Commonly, such festivals in India reveal how society tolerates, indeed insists on, the temporary reversal of rules of sexual behaviour, sanctioned sexual play through promiscuity and adultery, reversal of women's everyday behaviour, transvestism, lifting of restraints on eating of certain foods, and institutionalized outlets for hostilities against the village headman, the Brāhmaṇ, or the landlord. All the above traits are to be found in *Holī*, the spring festival of India. *Holī* provides outlets for repressed personal drives. Marriott's account of *Holī* is an example: "The idiom of *Holī*..... differed from that of ordinary life both in giving explicit dramatization to specific sexual relationships that otherwise would not be expressed at all and in reversing the differences of power conventionally prevailing between husbands and wives...... Aside from the *Holī* festival, each of the other thirteen major festivals of the year seemed to me to express and support the proper structure of patriarchy and gerontocracy in the family, of elaborately stratified relations among the castes, and of dominance of landowners in the village generally' (*Marriott*, 1966.206).

Marriott goes on to list examples of role-reversal and rebellious acts (some of them violent) that occurred in the village during *Holī*. The men beaten by wives of low-caste labourers and menials were Brāhmaṇs and peasant proprietors; six Brāhmaṇ elders were belaboured by a sweeper of their latrines; four specialists in purification—a barber's son, a water-carrier, and two Brāhmaṇ-priests—heaped mud and filth on the heads of the leading citizens; the police headman poured diesel oil over the head of his arch-rival and cousin, the village land lord. Marriott concludes: "under the tutelage of Kṛṣṇa, each person plays and for the moment may experience the role of his opposite: the servile wife acts the domineering husband and *vice versa;* the ravisher acts the ravished; the menial acts the master; the enemy acts the friend; the strictured youths act the rulers of the public.... Each actor playfully takes the role of others in relation to his own usual self. Each may thereby learn to play his own routine roles afresh, surely with renewed understanding, possibly with greater grace, perhaps with a reciprocating love" (Marriott in Singer., 1966.212).

In similar spirit of catharsis, the village tribunal traditionally settled caste disputes by arbitration and cutomary law, though it was less concerned to find "truth" and give "justice" than to abate conflict and promote harmony.

Scaste disputes, then, may be described as ritualized realignments, not rebellion against the caste system itself. Their functions are not to be sought in their relation to emotional needs alone, but in the need to dramatize and uphold the prinicple of inequality in social relationships. The very fact that they are disputes indicates that they are institutionalized deviations from everyday norms. Gluckman and others have shown how ritualized conflicts are built into social life by the nature of social rules themselves" (Gluckman, 1962.46).

3989 **विलपित**

Vilapita : wailing, mourning (*Bṛhaddevatā* 134-39); also *vilāpa (Bṛhaddevatā* 144-60): Form of speech and thought; crying. It occurs because of pain, in grief over someone or something lost, after being wronged by somebody. Mourning is the process through which we incorporate the event and circumstances of bereavement into our day-to-day experience. It is an acknowledgement of loss but in most cases it is also a healing process. Different societies observe the process of mourning in different ways. In Hindu society, widow, in particular dresses in white *saree.* If the deceased is well known, the national flag may fly at half-mast to show society's sense of loss.

The thought of change and decay, of death and mortality is constantly present to the aboriginal mind. Life is short, 'it lasts only for two days' and every child is familiar with the sight of death and the melancholy ritual of the disposal of the body. It is curious how often sententious songs about the transitoriness of life and loneliness of death are sung to the gayest *karmā* dance turns and movements:

> After this life of two days is passed
> We must travel onward alone.
> Again and again the gay children swinging to and fro in the rhythm of the dance foretell the day when,
> On my chest grass will grow
> My bones will burn like Jungle wood
> And my hair like Jungle grass.

They delight in reflecting how this warm and breathing loveliness of human flesh will pass away:

> What is man's body ? It is a spark from the fire
> It meets water and it is put out
> What is man's body ? It is a bit of straw
> It meets fire and it is burnt
> What is man's body? It is a bubble of water
> Broken by the wind.

The real mourning of the aboriginal, however, is to be found in often beautiful and moving spontaneous poems that are sung by the bereaved husband and wife, parent or child, on the day of a loved one's death. Such songs are not, of course, altogether spontaneous. As for love-making, so for death, there is a great reservoir of poetic cliches on which the singer can draw, rearranging his material to suit the circumstances. But often, too, where greef is deep and genuine, - as usually is - the singer produces from the strength of intense emotion some beautiful images and ideas:

So long as my lord breathed
I lived upon the throne
But since he died
How worthless are my bangles
And the world is empty.

The song of a widow. A woman's bangles are broken after her husband's death and sometimes thrown into his grave.

Indians mourning the death of a relative or national leader show their grief in a hand-on-heart gesture that signals deep sorrow. The woman internifies this with a backward lean. Her companion shows distress mainly through his facial expression but in addition feels a need to touch somone.

3990 **विलम्बित**

Vilambita : slow voice embellishment. *Vilambita* proceeds from the throat in slightly low pitch and is slow. It is used in love, pathos, deliberation, discrimination, jealousy, anger, envy, speaking, something indistinctly, bashfulness, anxiety, threatening, surprise, telling faults, prolonged sickness and harassment, etc. (*NS*).

3991 **विलास**

Vilāsa : (a) graceful manners of the heroine indicative of amorous sentiment, coquetry. One of the twenty *sāttvika alaṅkāras* of the heroine, as enumerated by Bharata, and the second among the ten *svabhāvaja alaṅkāras*. The graceful changes in the manner of sitting, in appearance, or in actions of the heroine at the sight of the beloved constitute *vilāsa* (*Sāhityadarpaṇa*, III. 99-100). (b) it is discussed by Bharata under *sāmānyābhinaya* and is a variety of *lalitābhinaya*, one of the natural graces of women. *Vilāsa* means amorous gestures. These are the relevant changes of the special kind relating to the standing and sitting postures as well as to gait and movements of hands, eyes and eyebrows which occur at the sight of the beloved person. (c) grace. One of the temperamental aspects in men. When the eyes move steadily, gait is like a bull, and there is smile on the lips while speaking, it is *vilāsa*. (d) the natural beauty of a country woman has an uncommon appeal of sweetness according to *Bharatamallika* (Com. on *Megha* 16):

विलासा नागरस्त्रीणां न तथा रमयन्ति नः ।
यथा स्वभाव-शुद्धान्ति वृंत्तानि जनयोषिताम् ॥

3992 **विलासकुशला**

Vilāsakuśalā : lady who is expert in dalliance, quality of the Lotus-lady (*Pañcasāyaka*, 1.6).

3993 **विलोकन-दृष्टि**

Vilokana-dṛṣṭi : a circular movement of the eyeball given by *Bālarāmabharata* (pp. 137-139).

3994 **विलोकित-दर्शन**

Vilokita-darśana : a type of look in *vismaya*. The diagonal or oblique movement of the eyeball. Looking an object behind turning (*NS*, VIII.105-107).

3995 **विलोकिता-दृष्टि**

Vilokitā-dṛṣṭi : glance by the special movement of the eyeball; the glance with eye-balls looking back (*NS*, VIII.92-105).

3996 **विलोभन**

Vilobhana : allurement, mentioning of the good qualities of the hero (*DR*, 1.2).

3997 **विलोल-नयना**

Vilola-nayanā : lady whose eyes are tremulous, quality of the Elephant-lady (*Nāgarasarvasva*, 14.7); the loving glance.

3998 **विवर्त**

Vivarta : false knowledge of a substance, when the real thing remains unchangd. For example, the mistake of a rope for a serpent. Non-existence: *atattvato'nyathāprathā vivarta ityudīritaḥ.*

3999 **विवर्तवाद**

Vivartavāda : the theory, favoured by *Advaita-Vedāntins*, that the effect is a mere transfiguration of a cause, or that it is of the nature of an illusory modification of any substance. It holds that the change of cause into an effect is only apparent.

4000 **विवर्तन (अधर)**

Vivartana (adhara) : narrowing down, twisting of the lips in an awry fashion. A type of lip-movement in *hāsya;* shrinking of lips, suggest envy, appeal, laughter, shame, laziness, contempt, pain, etc. (*NS*, VIII, 134-140).

4001 **विवर्तन (तारा)**

Vivartana (tārā) : turning sideways in a sidelong glance; A type of pupil-movement in *śṛṅgāra*, pupil moves to one side, the sideways movement with open eye-lid is called *Katākṣa* also; eyeballs are moved to one side and not up; turning the eyeballs sideways, a movement used in expressing the erotic sentiment (*NS*, VIII.98b-100a). The women of Ujjain look at the cloud with *Vivartana (Pūrva Megha,* 38-

39). Here the eyeballs are contracted and there is a sideways movement of the eyeballs. Turning the eyeballs side-ways and side-longs, a type of glance by the movement of the eyeballs.

4002 **विवर्तनोरू**

Vivartanorū : thighs turning round, turning of heels inward, circular movement of the thighs. It results when the heels are drawn inwards. It is used in moving about in confusion or in circular movement (*NS*, IX. 252).

4003 **विवर्तितक-करण**

Vivartitaka-karaṇa : the name derived from the circular movement of the side and the sacrum *(trika)* termed *vivartita*. The knee and the calf of one leg are in contract with the ground in an outstretched position of the thigh (*NS*, IV 127b-128a, IX.239-240). The hand and foot are thrown out and the *trika* is turned round and the other hand is in *recita*. (Fig. 4003)

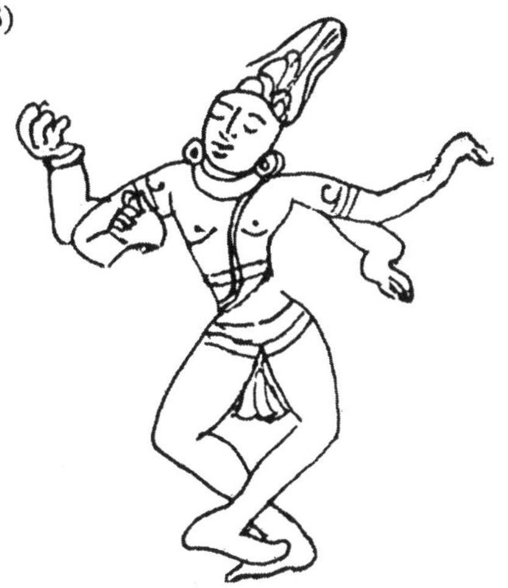

Fig. – (4003)

4004 **विवर्तित-पार्श्व**

Vivartita-pārśva : turning of *trika* or sacrum; Upward movement of the sides, sacrum turned around (*NS*, IX.236-238): In the *vivartita* pose of the side; the *trika*-part of the waist (sacrum) is to be made turned round. It indicates in turning about.

4005 **विवर्तित-पुट**

Vivartita-puṭa : turned up; a type of eye-gesture showing the movement of eyelid, the movement of the eyelid along the vertical plane with an emphasis on an upward movement, eyelids moved up, raising up in anger, wonder, etc. (*NS*, VIII. 105-113).

4006 **विवर्तित-शयन**

Vivartita-śayana : a posture for lying down. It is lying down with face downwards. It is used when wounded, dead, thrown, intoxicated and mad (*NS*).

4007 **विवर्तित-स्थान**

Vivartita-sthāna : a type of reclining posture.

4008 **विवर्तिता भ्रुकुटि**

Vivartitā bhrukuṭi : a type of *bhrukuṭi* movement given by *Bālarāmabharata*.

4009 **विवर्तितोरु**

Vivartitoru : thighs turning round, a circular movement of the thighs, twisted movement of the thigh; turning round thighs; *vivartana* is drawing knees inwards in a moving condition. It is used to go round in a hurry (*NS*, X.27-33).

4010 **विवाक**

Vivāka : judge. Cp. *prāḍvivāka*.

4011 **विवाचस्**

Vivācas : speaking in various ways.

4012 **विवाद**

Vivāda : dispute, discussion. Caste-disputes may be described as ritualized realignments, not rebellion against the caste system itself. Their functions are not to be sought in their relation to the emotional needs alone, but in the need to dramatize and uphold the principle of inequality in social relationships. The very fact that they are disputes indicates that they are institutionalized deviations from everyday norms. Gluckman (1962:46) and others have shown how ritualized conflicts 'are built into social life by the nature of social rules themselves.' Here conflict tends to become a *tamāśā* - a play. Traditionally, the mediator was the priest, the king, or the *guru*, whose role to restore peace through exercise of self-restraint originated in the sacrificial structure of the Vedic religion; this was eventually delegated in the majority of cases to the *pañcāyata*, which has, ever since, settled dispute by the consensual process as distinct from the adversary process.

4013 **विवादी**

Vivādī : the note that causes loss of charm to a *rāga*. If, between two notes, there exists one *śruti*, then those two notes are *vivādī* of each other. (b) disputing, litigant.

4014 **विवाह**

Vivāha : marriage; eightfold: (i) *brāhma*, (ii) *daiva*, (iii) *ārṣa*, (iv) *prājāpatya*, (v) *āsura*, (brideprice). (vi) *gāndharva*, (love), (vii) *rākṣasa* (forceful)., (viii) *paiśāca* (assault). Marriage is looked upon as a sacred link in the life of man in his journey towards perfection. A worthy and fortunate partner, therefore, would greatly help him in accomplishing his earthly ambitions as well as those of other world. A knowledge of feminine psysiognomy stood one in good stead in the selection of a suitable bride. Varāhamihira (LXX) while presenting the suitability of the maiden writes:

स्निग्धोन्नताग्रतनुताम्रनखौ कुमार्याः
पादौ समोपचितचारुनिगूढगुल्फौ ।
श्लिष्टाङ्गुली कमलकान्तितलौ च यस्या-
स्तामुद्वाहेद्यदि भुवोऽधिपतित्वमिच्छेत् ॥

One wishing to become the lord of the earth must marry a maiden whose feet are glossy, arched, pointed at the tip, and red, the ankle-joints, equal, fleshy, beautiful and hidden; the toes, close-touching; and the soles, as lustrous as a lotus. Prahlāda says :

स्फुरच्चन्द्रमुखी नारी पद्मपत्रायतेक्षणा ।
अर्धेन्दुनिटिला वक्रभ्रूलताकुटिलालका ॥
चाम्पेयनासिका कुन्दरदना कोमलाङ्गिका ।
बिम्बोष्ठी कम्बुकण्ठी च कृशाङ्गी सूक्ष्ममध्यमा ॥
शातोदरी पृथुश्रोणी रम्भोरुर्भाग्यशालिनी ।
पद्मसन्निभपाण्यङ्घ्रिः सुशीला सुगुणान्विता ॥
सुगन्धा सत्कुलोत्पन्ना लज्जाविनयशालिनी ।
दयालुधर्मनिरता पातिव्रत्यपरायणा ॥
यत्र स्यादीदृशी नारी तत्र लक्ष्मीः प्रसीदति ॥

4015 **विवाहकौतुक**

Vivāhakautuka : auspicious thread worn on the occasion of marriage.

4016 **विवाह-प्रस्ताव**

Vivāha-prastāva : marriage proposal. Even though language is a possible modality to convey information, there are times when it is impossible or ill-advised to use it. Information which is overwhelming and too powerful cannot be conveyed by verbal means. Anthropologists have commented on the use of language in marriage proposals. The recognition that direct speech is out of place in courtship must not be regarded as a refinement of civilization. Among so-called primitive peoples in India it is well recognized that the offer of love, and its acceptance or refusal, must be made by action symbolically, and not by crude method of question and answer. In the Hill Maria society of Bastar, the talk of marriage is at no time branched upon. The entire gossip is always symbolic. One example of the marrige proposal from the boy's side is as such: "We were passing through this side and smelt a fragrant smell. We thought that the fragrant flower may be here and came here just to investigate."

The betrothal ceremony is called in Gondi *puṅgār mihcnā* (the plucking of flower), *puṅgār kurki* (looking at the flower) and *tālk dāynā* (going to beg). These expressions indicate the *flower* (future bride) whom the boy will pick and put in his turban.

When the boy's party reaches the destination the girl's father says, "Have you come on any business." They answer, 'we hear that a flower has blossomed in your house; we have come to pluck it'. 'Why do you want to pluck it ?' asks the girl's father. 'So that we may stick it in our hair'. (Elwin, 1947:87).

W.G. Archer has made a careful study of these symbolic dialogues during marrige negotiations. The flower symbolism does not seem to be used by Oraon, but Russell and Hiralal notice it for the Kond (III.467) and give some charming sentences used by the Ṭurī: "I hear that a sweet-scented flower has blossomed in your house and I have come to gather it." To which the bride's father may reply: You may take my flower if you will not throw it away when its sweet scent is gone (*Ibid.* IV.590). The same symbolism is known to the Kharia and I have recorded its use among the Bison-horn Maria, the Kuruk and the Dhurwa in Bastar.

Such symbols vary from society to society. Mundas go to the girl's village and addressing her father say that they have come to hunt. He asks them in what jungle they wish to hunt and they name the *sarnā* (sacred grove) in which bones of his ancestors are burried. If the girl's father is satisfied with the matter, he then agrees to it (*Ibid.*, 511).

In the Khond society, a proposal for marriage is made by placing a brass cup and three arrows at the door of girl's father. He will remove these once to show his reluctance, and they will again be replaced. If he removes them second time, it signifies his definite refusal of the match, but if he allows them to remain, the bridegroom's friends go to him and say, "We have noticed a beautiful flower in passing through your village and desire to pluck it" (*Ibid.*, 467).

When a man wants to propose a girl in the Hill Maria, he approaches his father and says, "I have started work in my fields and I have need of a cow (they use cow in ploughing). I hear you have a good one in your shed and I have come to buy it from you." He normally uses the symbolism of a flower in the betrothal dialogues, saying "I have come to pick a flower and put it in my hair."

Four Gaḍaria castemen of standing carry the proposal of marriage from the boy's father, and the girl's father, being forewarned, sends others to meet them. One of the ambassadors opens the conversation by saying, "We have the milk and you have the milk-pail, let them be joined." To which the girl's party, if the match be agreeable, will reply, "yes, we have the tamarind and you have the mango, if the *punces* agree, let there be marriage" (*Ibid.*, 5).

When the father or a boy in Agaria community whishes to arrange a marriage, he sends emissaries to the father of the girl. They open the proceedings by saying, "So and so has come to partake of your stale food *(bāsī).*" If the father of the girl approves he gives his consent by saying,

"He has come on foot. I receive him on my head". (*Ibid.*, Vol. II).

Having selected a bride for his son, the boy's father in the Kanwar community sends some friends to her village, and they address a friend of the girl's family saying, "so-and-so (giving his name and village) would like to have a cup of *pej* (rice-gruel) from you; what do you say." The proposal is communicated to the girl's family, and if they approve of it, they commence preparing the rice-water which is partaken by the party and their friends. If the bride's people do not begin cooking the *pej*, it is understood that the proposal is rejected (*Ibid.*, III. 393).

4017 **विवाह-संस्कार**

Vivāha-saṁskāra : marriage ritual. In a brilliant analysis of the marriage ritual of Bihari Kayastha, W.G. Archer takes a comparison from modern art. 'If we are to find an analogy for this wedding ritual, the nearest would be a surrealist poem, ballet or novel. In a surrealist work the action has a strange power and a mysterious charm. Strange persons develop their intriguing contacts and the action has an air of irrational urgency. On analysis it is seen that many of the actions are symbolic and the poem, novel or the ballet generates its power from the semi-conscious associations with it dialogue, gestures, scenary and action evoke. In the ritual of a Kayastha wedding, there is a similar use of irrational action, a similar use of persons with a strangely inflated power, and a similar use of semi-conscious symbols. The meaning of ritual may be submerged and for many, may be scarcely comprehended but its basis is in a symbolic system and it total effect is overpowering" (quoted from Elwin, 1247:137).

This will apply also to a tribal and non-tribal wedding in India. The consummation of marriage is everywhere a matter of absorbing interest to the villagers. There does not seem to be any custom of formal wedding of the bridal pair; but there are strict conventions of behaviour. The bride must resist all she can; she must try to escape, she must weep, she must beg to be let off for a few days. The older women say, 'silly child, let him husk the grain properly', or 'A tree canot grow without water, nor can love'. The husband's share is described symbolically: 'his medicine has gone down her throat', 'his shadow has pierced her', or 'his knife is hollowing out the guard'.

The most intimate aspects of married life are described in songs, and are sung with gusto at marriges and festivals.

4018 **विवृत्त-करण**

Vivṛtta-karaṇa : this lis extreme position of the *kṣipta* knees, where one fore-leg rests on the ground. The side is turned round in *vivartita* movement. The arms are extended and move in *recita*. The commentary also mentions the *bhramarīcārī* (*NS*, IV. 121b-122a, IX. 239-240, 257-258, X. 45). Hands and feet are first thrown out and then the *trika* is turned round and the two hands are in *recita*. It is used in the haughty gait.

4019 **विवृतजघना**

Vivṛtajaghanā : open thighs calling eroticism in F (Kālidāsa, *Mēgha*).

4020 **विवृत-मुख**

Vivṛta-mukha : Open with lips apart, mouth movement in *hāsya* (*NS*, VIII. 153-160); widely opened mouth. It is used in laughter, fear and sorrow and the like.

4021 **विवृता-कटि**

Vivṛtā-kati : hips turning to the back.

4022 **विवृताक्ष**

Vivṛtākṣa : rolling the eyes. Rolling the eyes is the same as *caṭula-netra* of Bhavabhūti. Rolling the eyes is a NV way of expressing impudence and disapproval of the person who is in the authority and of communicating every negative label that can be applied to the dominant person. The movement of the eyes communicates altar wsparts as the message. The main message is hostility. The movement of the eyes - rolling the eyes - is performed in the following way. First, the eyes are moved from one side of the eye-socket to the other, in a low arc (usually, the movement of the eyes - that is rolling - is preceded by a stare at the other person, but not an eye-to-eye stare). The lids of the eyes are slightly lowred when the eye-balls are moved in the low arc. The eye-balls always move away from the other person. The movement is very quick, and it is often unnoticed by the other person, particularly if the other person is not tribe. Sometimes, the eye movement is accomplished by a slight lifting of the head, or a twitching of the nose, or both. Rolling the eyes is more common among tribal women that it is among tribal men.

This movement of the eyes is different from the movement of the eyes which is called "cutting the eyes", in the dominant culture. In "cutting the eyes", the movement of the eyes is always toward another person. Furthermore, after the eyes are focused on the other person (following the cutting) they usually remain focused in a stare. In other words, the stare follows the cutting action.

Tribal people (particularly females) will often roll their eyes when being reprimanded about some infraction of a rule. After the person who is in the authority role has continued the reprimand for a while, the tribal person in the subordinate role (the receiver) will roll the eyes. Rolling the eyes can also be used to express a kind of general disapproval. For example, if two women are together and the third woman enters their social sphere wearing a *sāree* that the two women know costs Rupees 200 and obviously giving the impression that she not only looks good but that the *sāree* is much more expensive, then one of the two women will roll eyes. In this situation the message communicated is "She thinks she is cute but she doesn't look like nothing, because that *sāree* cost Rupees 200".

Rolling the eyes is probably partly responsible for the saying used by many tribal people: "Don't look at me in that tone of voice". In fact, one of the indications that rolling the eyes is hostile impudent NV message is that when it is done the tribal person in the authority role will stop reprimanding and say, "Don't you roll your eyes at me". Sometimes, this command is punctuated by a slap.

Often non-tribals will miss the message communicated by tribals when they roll their eyes. It's just as well, because rolling the eyes gives the tribe an opportunity to non-verbally release his hostility and endure the reprimand with a minimum amount of conflict. Tribals, on the other hand, usually recognize the action and properly interprete the message. As mentioned before, this sometimes causes them to punish the child, thus escalating the conflict and worsening the situation.

It is well known that rolling the eyes is also a NV pattern in Vedic culture.

4023 **विवृता-ग्रीवा**

Vivṛtā-grivā : the circular movement of the neck in relaxed position (*NS*, VII. 175-79). Constant movement of the neck indicates amorous action (*VD*, III. I. 61), taking place when the face is towards the front; used in going towards one's place.

4024 **विवृतोरु**

Vivṛtoru : expansion of thighs (*Bālarāmabharata*); Kālidāsa *Meghadūta*) calls it *vivṛatajaghanā.*

4025 **विशकलितार्थ**

Viśakalitārtha : speech whose content is well analysed.

4026 **विशदाक्षरेण**

Viśadākṣareṇa : in plain words.

4027 **विशल्या मुद्रा**

Viśalyā mudrā : gesture of an arrow head. "Make your pair of palms flat (upturned) in the way of opposite direction. This is called the *Viśalyā mudrā* which grants fulfilment in the *yogakarman* — the spiritual exercises" (*BT*).

4028 **विशालाक्ष**

Viśālākṣa : larg eyed.

4029 **विशाला (ऋद्धिपाला) मुद्रा**

Viśālā (ṛddhipālā) mudrā : This is supposed to be a very secret gesture of the obscure cult. By an esoteric devout, in the state of nudity and engaged in some confidential esoteric service with a face in a very happy pose and hairs scattered round in joy, it is called either the *Viśālā* or *ṛddhipālā mudrā* (*BT*).

4030 **विशेष धर्म**

Viśeṣa-dharma : code of conduct specific to various *varṇas* and *āśramas* (*Arthaśāstra*, 3.1.40).

4031 **विशेषक**

Viśeṣaka : distinguishing feature, a mark.

4032 **विश्वमुखी-मुद्रा**

Viśvamukhī-mudrā : "Make the two middle fingers up-turned by the back. The ring-finger should be made moving. The ring-fingers are to be kept bending and the little-fingers should remain in their own hands. All the rest fingers, but the thumb are to be styled back-side. This is the *Viśvamukhī-mudrā* that grants all desires and boons" (*BT*).

4033 **विश्वमुद्रा**

Viśva-mudrā : gesture of the universe. Make hands like a lotus with their middle fingers clasped and the figure should be held on a certain finger (*VD*).

4034 **विश्वयोनि-मुद्रा**

Viśvayoni-mudrā : "Fingers of both the hands matted among themselves in a loose style with the positon of joining the former fingers and coming out of the back of the left hand and then going to the mid-points of the right-hand fingers" (*BT*). "Bend your own left hand along with the middle finger and the ring finger and place the thumb on the tip of the middle finger. This is called the *Viśvayoni-mudrā*, that grants the very nearness of Gods" (*BT*).

4035 **विश्वसूची (घोरपराक्रमा) मुद्रा**

Viśvasūcī (ghoraparākramā)mudrā : "Both the thumbs should be made curved in a moving position; the little fingers are to be made flat or upstand and the rest of the fingers should remain in the interlocked conditions. This makes the *viśvasūcī-mudrā*" (*BT.*).

4036 **विश्रब्धालाप**

Viśrabdhālāpa : confidential talk (*Veṇīsaṁhāra*, Act. II). Lover's talk is always the confidential talk. Bhavabhūti in his *Uttararāmacaritam* (1.27) has presented the situation:

> Slowly and so close our faces touched,
> We talked: without stopping disconnected,

Arms in each other's arms relentlessly locked.
We didn't think about time, but the night did end.

The warmth and enthusiasm in the voice is the indication of happiness.

4037 **विश्रान्ति**

Viśrānti : repose.

4038 **विश्वास**

Viśvāsa : faith. It is the basis of all forms of spiritual aspiration. Both hands behind the head signals faith.

4039 **विषकन्या**

Viṣakanyā : poison-girl; a poisoned woman with whom an enemy is induced to cohabit and die as a result (*Arthaśāstra*). A girl who has been administered poison from her childhood in regular quantity becomes a poison-girl. (b) closely related to the motif of a sexual death (see *Śiśnākṛtivijnāna*) is the theme of the 'Poison Damsel' in Indian literature. She is a young girl fed on poison and sent to destroy an enemy who would die in her embrace, the poison being transferred by a kiss, a bite, a scratch, or by the sexual act. This motif of the snake-maiden (Tawney and Penzer, ii, Appendix 3) has been explained in terms of the fear of snake-bite. The story of *Āḍi* in *Śiva Purāṇa* (4.68-69) has the same bearing. *Āḍi* takes the form of serpent to enter Śiva's bedroom before assuming the form of a woman to kill him. Perhaps the most famous example of this theme in India is the tale in which the goddess of snakes becomes a female black cobra to bite a young man on his wedding night. The cobra weeps when she sees the beauty of the bridegroom's body, and does not wish to kill him, but his foot strikes her fang and he dies (*Manasāmaṅgala,* 1949. 250-55). The motifs of the *Libestod* are obvious here.

4040 **विषण्णा दृष्टि**

Viṣaṇṇā dṛṣṭi : a type of glance used in despair. *Śakuntalā* (*Śākuntalam*, Act. II) enters with her friends in the bower. She is sorrowful and dejected: *Viṣādamnāṭayati.* She uses the glances of despair to show this. In *Vikramorvaśīya* (Act II) also, this glance has been used by Urvaśī (*NS*, VIII.89); dejected glance, a type of *sañcārī bhāvadṛṣṭi*, a bewildered look with the eyelid down in dejection and no winking and the eyeballs slightly motionless. It suggest despair. It is also known as *viṣādinī dṛṣṭi*. The eyelids are wide apart in dejection, the corners upset, eyes closing and pupils slightly motionless. It is used to indicate despair.

4041 **विषम-सूचीस्थान**

Viṣama-sūcī-sthāna : a type of posture.

4042 **विषम-स्थान**

Viṣama-sthāna : a type of posture (*VD*, 1.39, 1-32).

4043 **विषय**

Viṣaya : object; that which is perceived by the perceiver. *Viṣayā* is subject. *Viṣayī-viṣaya-bhāva* is subject-object-relation. *Viṣayatā* is a term used by *Nyāya-vaiśeṣikas* which means a distinct external relation. Thesis. Subject of an argument, the first division of a topic (*adhikaraṇa*, q.v.).

4044 **विषयाभिमुख-तारा**

Viṣayābhimukha-tārā : a circular movement of the eyeball, but *SR* and *Nāṭyaśāstra-Saṁngraha* call it *darśana*; it clearly denotes the variation in the position of the pupils in different kinds of observtions and thus called the object of pupil.

4045 **विषाद**

Viṣāda : helplessness and despair, agony, displeasure. The nineteenth among the thirty-three *vyabhicāri bhāvas* as enumerated by Bharata. *Viṣāda* is the feeling of helplessness and despair occasioned by lack of means to attain the desired end. Singing, breathing out, mental distress, seeking for aid, etc. are its external manifestations (*Sāhityadarpaṇa*, 3.167). In *Śākuntalam* Act III), Śakuntalā enacts despair: *Viṣādam nāṭayati.* She represents this through an enactment of thinking (*NS*, VII.104), a loss of energy and the like: the *dṛṣṭi* she uses for this is the *viṣaṇṇā.*

One of the transitory states of mind. It is manifested by looking for allies, thinking about means, loss of energy, absent-mindedness, deep breathing and like in the case of superior and the middling types. In the case of the inferior type -- running away, looking down, drying up the mouth, licking the corner of the mouth, sleep, deep breathing, meditation and the like. (b) *Viṣāda* is depression. Arjuna felt depressed in the beginning of the Great War. His depression was a range of feelings and a tendency to behave in a certain way. When he was depressed his feelings were negative. Depression sapped his mental and emotional energy - he felt empty, sluggish and understimulated. He felt loosing contact with other people. He was physically and emotionally distressed.

People who are depressed typically stop mixing with other people. This reinforces the depressed person's feeling of being abandoned. A sense of helplessness is characteristic of depression. Dejected people have a shuffling step, with bowed posture and heavy feet.

4046 **विषादशून्यादृष्टि**

Viṣādaśūnyādṛṣṭi : it is used in *Kādambarī* (p.61) for fear (*NS*, VIII.67, 70). The movement of the eyebrows is also mentioned (*Ibid.*, 174), but this is a more generalized reference.

4047 **विष्कम्भक**

Viṣkambhaka : a device in a drama, placed in the beginning of an act, which serves as a connecting link between what has happend and what is going to happen.

4048 **विष्कम्भ करण**

Viṣkambha karaṇa : knees are bent in *nikuṭṭita*: feet are in *kuñcita*. In the final position, one foot is in the *sūcīpāda cārī* (*NS*, IV. 162b-163a, IX. 191, X.34). The right hand is moved in *sūcīmukha* touching the other, the left placed on the bottom and the foot is in *nikuṭṭita*.

4049 **विष्कम्भितासन**

Viṣkambhitāsana : a type of sitting posture.

4050 **विष्टि**

Viṣṭi : labourers who work for things instead of wages; sappers and miners (*Arthaśāstra*).

4051 **विष्णुक्रान्त**

Viṣṇukrānta : name of one of the three regions into which India has been divided in certain *Tantras*. The tract of land from the Vindhya hill to Chittagong is called *Viṣṇukrānta*.

4052 **विष्णुक्रान्त-करण**

Viṣṇukrānta-karaṇa : the leg is extended out high on its own side without a knee bend: this is an extreme position of the *daṇḍapādā cārī*, where the foot is lifted from the ground to the level of the waist. The two hands are in *recita* (*NS*, IV.160b-161a, X.44). In *Śākuntalam* (Act. VI), the flowing of Gaṅgā has been represented through this *karaṇa* with a shift: the *viṣṇukrānta karaṇa* and *tripatāka hastas* are held over the uplifted foot to show Gaṅgā flowing. One foot is stretched forward and bent as if rising upwards and the hands are in *recita*. It is used in the gait of Viṣṇu.

4053 **विष्णुधर्मोत्तर**

Viṣṇudharmottara : It is the all-round complete work of Indian Gesturology. The special emphasis of this work is to devise significant gestures for Indian alphabets, the code language, symbolic gods, materials applicable in worship and similar rites; along with the common gestures, utilized for literary and dramatic purposes, referred to in the *NR* and *Abhinayadarpaṇa*. The *VD* aims to cover the entire span of Indian Gesturology with the greater emphasis to ritualistic and scientific gestures and nominal attention to socialistic, literary and dramatic gestures.

4054 **विष्णु-मुद्रा**

Viṣṇu-mudrā : gesture symbolizing Lord Viṣṇu. *Śikhara*-hand symbolizes Lord Viṣṇu (*VD*).

4055 **विष्णु-हस्त**

Viṣṇu-hasta : *tripatākas* by two hands indicate *Viṣṇu* (*AD*, 205-210). (Fig. 4055)

4056 **विसंवादक**

Visaṁvādaka : one who does not keep his words (*A*, 13.5.6).

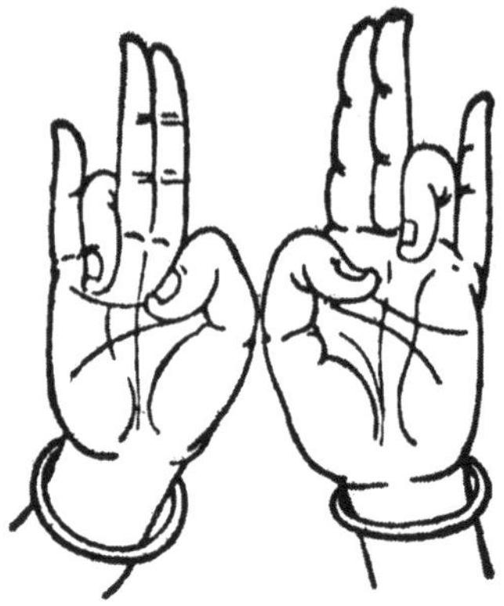

Fig. – (4055)

4057 **विसंवादी**

Visaṁvādī : not agreeing (with the model or prescription).

4058 **विसङ्केतक**

Visaṅketaka : decoder. The person receiving the message.

4059 **विसर्ग**

Visarga : (a) gradual release from the *arpaṇa*, leading to a finale in speaking. (b) giving up relevant sentiment and feelings through appropriate gesture (*NS*, IX. 175). (c) alphabetical sign of the double dot which is symbolically regarded as the female organ (*Tantrāloka*, III.120).

4060 **विसर्ग-अधर**

Visarga-adhara : protruding lips; a type of lip-gesture in *śṛṅgāra* and *hāsya;* hiding or spreading out lips; suggest lady's vanity, tricky devises (*bibboka*), painting (lips), affected indifference, and others (*NS*, VIII. 134-140).

4061 **विसर्जन-मुद्रा**

Visarjana-mudrā : gesture of farewell. The upturned right thumb should be wrapped with the left thumb and fingers. Then it should be moved with the thumb in a circular position. Then it makes *visarjana-mudrā* (*VD*).

4062 **विसर्जनी (वज्रसूची) मुद्रा**

Visarjanī (Vajrasūcī) mudrā : "Place two hands with their fingers wide extended and then tie each other correspondingly. They are to be directed upwards on the both sides. This is called the *Visarjanī* or *Vajrasūci-mūdrā*" (*BT*).

4063 **विस्तीर्णा-गण्डश्रुति**

Vistīrṇā-gaṇḍaśruti : lady whose ears are wide, quality of the Deer-lady (*Anaṅgaraṅga*, 3.20-21).

4064 **विस्तृत-हृदयकवाटा**

Vistṛta-hṛdayakavāṭā : lady whose chest is wide, quality of the Mare-lady (*Ratirahasya*, 3.22-3).

4065 **विस्तृतोरू**

Vistṛtorū : expansion of the thighs (*Bālarāmabharata*).

4066 **विस्मय**

Vismaya : (a) wonder, marvellous, astonishment. It is the basic instinct, underlying the *adbhutarasa*, the sentiment of wonder. It is aroused by a variety of things, supernatural beings or persons that appear to transgress the natural limits of the moral world. It results in an expansion of the mind. Jugglery, magic, conjugation are some of its excitants. (b) form of speech and thought (*Bṛhaddevatā* 144-60). (c) distinctive cue to surprise are: the brows are raised, so that they are curved and thin: the skin below the brow is stretched; horizontal wrinkles go across the forehead; the eyelids are opened; the upper lid is raised and the lower lid drawn down; the white of the eyes shows above the iris, and often below as well; the jaw drops open so that the lips and teeth are parted, but there is no tension or stretching of the mouth.

Vismaya is to be represented by (the *anubhāvas* such as) wide opening eyes, looking with fixed gaze, horripilation, tears, joy, perspiration, uttering words of approbation, making gifts, crying (incessantly) hā-hā-hā, waving the end of *dhotī* or *sāṛī*, moving the head to and fro, the cry of "well done" and the like.

The gait in *Vismaya* is also typical. *NS* records that the middling and inferior characters should have quick steps in different direction in wonder and joy.

4067 **विस्मय-दृष्टि**

Vismaya-dṛṣṭi : a type of *bhāvadṛṣṭi* enumerated by Bharata.

4068 **विस्मय-हस्त**

Vismaya-hasta : a type of hand-gesture in *Śilpaśāstra*, not mentioned in *NS*.

4069 **विस्मयोत्फुल्ल-लोचन**

Vismayotphulla-locana : wonder in the eyes (*Buddhacarita*, 4.18) We observe that when the prince in *Buddhacarita* is taken out to the grove and women came out to greet him, there is wonder in the eyes of women: *Vismayotphullalocanaḥ*; and they pay him homage with *padmakośa* hands. The *vismita* glance of the *NS* (VIII.60) used on such occasions is also not very different.

4070 **विस्मिता-दृष्टि**

Vismitā-dṛṣṭi : astonishment (*Vismaya*) in *Mālavikāgnimitra* (Act V) is enacted by opening the eyes without a wink (*NS*, VIII.61). It is a wonder-striking look. Eyelids are opened fully, eyeballs turned upward and eye-lids stand still. It suggests a feeling of wonder and surprise. The glance in level, fully widened and has pupils greatly turned up with the curve of both the eyebrows lost due to being widened. It is *bhāvadṛṣṭi* and is used in wonder.

4071 **विहत-पुट**

Vihata-puṭa : eyelids fully contracted.

4072 **विहसित**

Vihasita : laughing gently, gentle smile. *Madhurasvaram vihasitam* (*Priyadarśikā*, Act IV) laughing is making soft sound. A gentle laugh in appreciation or mockery. Unlike the first two silent types, this type of laugh is accompanied by a sweet and soft noise. It is the first type in which middle-class persons indulge for expressing appreciation of humour.

Vihasita is the symbol of the middle class people. This laughter is always suitable to the occasion. It represents slight sound and sweetness, face joyful, eyes and cheeks contracted.

Bhānuji Dīkṣita on *Amarakośa* (1.7.35) quotes and defines *vihasita:*

> *ākuñcitakapolākṣam sasvanam nisvanam tathā* /
> *prastāvottham sānurāgam prāhurvihasitam budhāḥ* //

4073 **विहितसगोत्रता**

Vihitasagotratā : ritual kinship. There are several ways in which Indian people of different castes and tribal groups can be linked as kin through ritual acts. It is termed as *gōtī* (Bagheli), *goinyā* (Bagheli), *gaṅgā-bārū* (Bhatri).

There are several ways in which people can be linked as kin through ritual acts. In Malwa the ritual act occurs on the full-moon day of Āṣāḍha (June-July) when groups of young people 'hear Rama's name' together from a teacher (*guru*), and are then considered to be ritual brothers (*guru-bhāī*) and sisters (*guru-bahin*). The main manifestations of the link are those exchanges of presents which are also prescribed for real kin.

Another ritual tie is the relation between a woman and her ritual father (*dharam kā bāp*). These ritual kin ties provide a means by which differences of castes or tribal groups or ward membership can be bridged. In theory, ritual kin ties should be as binding as real ties. Each of the members of the household has more than four ritual links, and this makes him tied to very many other households in the village.

4074 **विहृत**

Vihṛta : want of response. One of the ten modes of indicating love by women. One of the *Sāttvika alaṅkāras* of the heroine as enumerated by Bharata. If the damsel does not speak because of modesty, even when there is an occasion to speak, the *vihṛta alaṅkāra* is manifested (*Śāhityadarpaṇa*, III. 106). It occurs when women do not make any reply to the lover even though they have heard his words, due to bashfulness or pretence, hesitation or reluctance to show feelings to a lover. Dvijadeva has depicted this mode of beshfulness

बोलि हारे कोकिल, बुलाय हारे केकीगन
सिखै हारी सखी सबजुगत नई नई ।
आननि समैं में दुखदाइनि भई सी लाज
चलन समय में चल पगन दगा दई ॥

4075 **वीक्षण**

Vīkṣaṇa : seeing, looking at. *vīkṣam* 'glance'.

4076 **वीज**

Vīja : seed, sprout, semen, one of the seven limbs of *mantras*, a single-lettered *mantra* in which the deity is revealed in subtle form (*Śāradā* 1.57; *Tantrasāra* 182).

4077 **वीतत्रपा**

Vītatrapā : lady who is shameless, quality of the Elephant-lady (*Anaṅgaraṅga*, 3.24-25).

4078 **वीत-लज्जा**

Vīta-lajjā : lady who is shameless, quality of the Elephant-lady (*Ratirahasya*, 1.18-19).

4079 **वीतोच्चटाबन्धा**

Vītoccaṭābandhā : with her girdle-knot loosened.

4080 **वीथी**

Vīthī : a dialogue with two participants. The material presented being based on words, and with two speakers trying to excel in outwitting each other. A type of Sanskrit *rūpaka* (drama). It may contain all the sentiments and has one actor or also two. It has the characters of three types—superior, middle and inferior. It has the use of thirteen constituents: *udghātyaka, avalagita, avaspandita, nālikā, asatapralāpa, vākkeli, prapañca, mṛdava, adhibala, chala, trigata, vyāhāra* and *gaṇḍa* (*DR*, III.13). (b) gait of the horse :

valganam nīcairgatam laṅghanam dhoraṇam nāroṣṭamityaupavāhyam vīthi pañcakam, and also *caturasram kāṅkam māyuramardhamāyū ramiti sāṁnāhyam vīthicatuṣṭayam.*

4081 **वीप्सा**

Vīpsā : repetition, entirety, successive order, arrangement of things each by each.

4082 **वीर**

Vīra : the sentiment of heroism. The basic instinct (enthusiasm) is aroused in a magnanimous heart. It is golden in colour and presided over by Mahendra. The art of heroic appeal gives expression of resolution, vanity, bravado, strength, nobility, proud, smile and all sorts of such expressions, which suggest energy, valour and noble courage (*VD.* III. 43.6). Bharata divides it in three types: *dīanavīra* (heroism arising from making gifts), *dharmavīra* (heroism arising from fulfilling one's duty) and *yuddhavīra* (heroism arising from fighting).

(b) Tāntric aspirant of the second grade whose mental faculties are advanced. The spiritual exercises of a *vīra* are known as *vīrācāra* (*Prāṇatoṣaṇī,* VIII. 1.495).

(c) man, husband, son, the male of an animal, the root of *uśīra.*

4083 **वीर-रसदृष्टि**

Vīra-rasadṛṣṭi : it is suggested by a glance opened, bright, serious and energetic. The eye-ball should remain centred in the mid-points of eyes. The glance is bright, eyes fully open, agitated and serious, the pupils are at the central part blooming fully. It is used in the heroic.

4084 **वीरासन**

Vīrāsana : yogic *āsana.* It is a posture of *kṛcchra* and *aghamarṣaṇa* observances. Comp. *jāgan lage baiṭh vīrāsana* (Tulasīdāsa, *Mānasa,* 2.90.2).

4085 **वृक्षाधिरूढक**

Vṛkṣādhirūḍhaka : climbing a tree-like embrace. "When a woman, having placed one of her feet on the foot of her lover and the other one of his thighs, passing one of her arms round his back and the other on his shoulders, makes slightly the sounds of singing and cooing and wishes as it were to climb him up in order to have a kiss, it is called *Vṛkṣādhirūḍhaka*" (*Kāmasūtra*, 2.2.17). Kālidāsa (*Raghu*, 19.29) draws it depicting the amorous activities of Agnivarṇa. Māgha (*Śiśu.* 7.46) describes it in a different context.

4086 **वृत्तान्त**

Vṛttānta : established usage, conversation (*Śākuntalam* II; *DR.* 1.112).

4087 **वृत्ति**

Vṛtti : (a) tendency, manner of mode; style of speech and action, a style in composition. It is man's activity in the direction of achieving the aim of life. An old element of dramatic theory mentioned by Bharata which seems to signify the basic context of the play in so far as it determines a style of representation, similar to Shakespeare's "tragical-comical-historical-pastoral". Literally it means "existence" or "specific mode of existence". It is the theme of all literature. Hence, the *vṛttis* are called the mothers of *nāṭya.* Anandavardhana says that *vṛtti* of Bharata is a function of the meaning (*vācya*), while that of other writers is a function of the outward shape of the words (*vācaka*). Dhanika has divided the *vṛtti* into four types: *kaiśikī, sāttvatī, ārabhaṭī* and *bhāratī.* The *vṛttis* are really the styles or modes of conduct that a character, mostly, the hero or the heroine adopts in a play and these modes depend upon the mood or sentiment (*bhāva*) that occupies the whole personality of the hero in the particular kind of a play. These *vṛttis* also decide the form of a play. (b) modification based on previous impression, the word 'previous' denotes the prior in a sense of past moments and previous births as well. (c) in grammar it means that in which a word, besides expressing its own meaning, also declares the meaning of another. Grammatical *vṛttis* are five, *viz. kṛt, taddhita, samāsa, ekaśeṣa* and roots taking the affixes like *san, yañ* etc. (d) attitude in social semiotics. The attitude and character of the Hill Marias of Bastar to live entirely alone in the present and not remember the past or worry for the morrow is born in his environment, his habitat and his way of life. There is nothing permanent in his life; everything is transient; everything is shifting in nature. The *peṇḍā* sites are changed and so do the village sites. With every change the house changes and a new one is constructed, the old grave-yards are abandoned, the ponds of drinking water are given up, the beautiful *ghoṭul* building is left to be eaten of by white ants.

So there is no permanency and when there is no permanency there is no attachment.

4088 **वृद्धत्व-संकेत**

Vṛddhatva-saṁketa : ageing signals. *Vasiṣtha-Dharmasūtra* (XXX.9) records that the hair of an ageing man shows signs of age, and the teeth of an ageing man show signs of age, (but the desire to live and the desire for wealth do not decay even in an ageing man.).

4089 **वृश्चिक-करण**

Vṛscika-karaṇa : indicating an arch of the leg like a scorpion's and utilizes a back-flexed position of the leg. The left leg is planted and the right leg is thrown back and bent so as to resemble the uplifted tail of scorpion and the arms bent (*Kuñcita*) at elbow and held upwards (*NS*, IV. 107-108). The two hands are bent and held near the shoulders and the leg bent and turned towards the back. Back is bent. It is used in aerial movements and to indicate *Airāvaṇa*.

4090 **वृश्चिक—कुट्टिक—करण**

Vṛscika-kuṭṭika-karaṇa : one leg in *vṛscika* taken back; the arms bent in *nikuñcita* : *alapallava* hands are held in the shoulder-region (*NS*, IV. 102-103). *Vṛscika karaṇa* is performed with the hands in *nikuṭṭita*. It is employed in wonder and desire for going in sky.

4091 **वृश्चिक-रेचित-करण**

Vṛscika-recita-karaṇa : *Viprakīrṇa nṛtta hastas* in *recita* are suggested (*NS*, IV.106-107, IX.187). The foot is in *vṛścika* and the two hands in *svastika* to be moved in *recita* and *viprakīrṇa*. It is used in moving through air.

4092 **वृश्चिक-लता-करण**

Vṛscika-latā-karaṇa : a category of movement. Its characteristic feature is that while one leg is bent in front, the other is extended back. This can be seen in *Śākuntalam* (Act IV).

4093 **वृष (नायक)**

Vṛṣa : the bull-man. The man whose organ is nine *aṅgulas* in length (*Kāmasūtra*, 2.41). (b) one that sprinkles semen, bull. (c) sign of the zodiac Taurus (d) bull of Śiva. (e) chief, excellent.

4094 **वृषभ**

Vṛṣabha : The bull is believed to be auspicious in Indian culture and is a symbol of prosperity (*Vāmana-Purāṇa*, 14.36). The economic condition of a farmer is indicated by the number of bullocks in his possession. A farmer who keeps one bullock is looked as a pauper, possessor of two bullocks is independent in agricultural work, possessor of the three bullocks is hated by the co-villagers. A farmer who keeps four bullocks is able to level his field independently; six bullock-owned farmer has to employ a supervisor. A farmer who owns eight bullocks can walk with umbrella and stick like a pretty zamindar. There are many proverbs related to this bullock-symbol. (b) The bull is also the symbol of sexual power. Śiva's mount is the bull and he himself is called a bull.

4095 **वृषभ-क्रीडा-करण**

Vṛṣabha-krīḍā-karaṇa : derived from the *alātācārī*. The arms move in *recita* with a *vyāvartita* movement of the hands (*NS*, IV. 164 b - 165 a, X.41). Performing *alātā* first, the hands are in *recita* and afterwards they are in *kuñcita* and *añcita*.

4096 **वृषभ-मुद्रा**

Vṛṣabha-mudrā : gesture of a bull. The *talasiṁha* represents a bull. The *Siṁhamukha* with the back of the hand in the horizontal plane indicates a bull (*Mirror of Gesture*, pp.49-50).

4097 **वृष-मुद्रा**

Vṛṣa-mudrā : gesture of an ox. If all the fingers of *jaṭā*-style are stretched and made curved like horns, it is an ox (*VD*).

4098 **वृषभासन**

Vṛṣabhāsana : a type of posture.

4099 **वृषायते**

Vṛṣāyate : burns with sexual desire.

4100 **वृष्टि**

Vṛṣṭi : rain. Omens are associated with rain. It is said that if torrential rains come off season it is fearful; rains when no clouds are visible indicate death of the king; red rain indicates war and blood-shed; rain accompanied by dust-winds are said to be harmful to fruits (*Matsya Purāṇa*, 232.1-9, *Bhāg. P.*, III. 19.18-21). (b) The motif of the seed as rain appears in an incident during the wedding of Śiva and Satī; " Brahmā looked at Satī's face and was filled with lust. As he became excited, his seed fell upon the earth and turned into thundering clouds which covered the sky, releasing their water. Śiva was looking at Satī and was fiercely excited by *Kāma,* but nevertheless ne raised his trident to kill Brahmā (*Kālikā*, 11.27). A longer version of the story elaborates upon the nature of clouds:" Brahmā lifted the veil from Satī's face and was overcome with desire. He spilled four drops of his seed upon the ground like a mound of snow. Fearing (Śivas) *tapas,* Brahmā concealed the drops of seed with his feet, but Śiva saw everything with his divine eye, and he said in anger, Evil one, you have done a reprehensible thing, to gaze with passion upon the face of my bride at my wedding. Did you think to deceive me? At first he raised his trident to kill Brahmā, but then calmed by Viṣṇu, he instructed Brahmā to wander on earth in human form, as expiation. Then Śiva said, 'these four drops of seed will become the clouds of doomsday in the sky.' Immediately the seed became the four doomsday clouds, roaring and releasing water, covering the sky. Then Śiva was satisfied." (*Śiva.*, 2.2.10).

(c) In order to stop excessive rain, a naked bachelor collects water from the caves in a new earthen pots among the Gond, covers the pot with a lid or with mud, and buries it beneath the earth; or the pot may be filled with salt. Here it may perhaps be supposed that, as the water dries up in the pot or the salt gets dry, so the rain will stop and the world generally become dry. The reason for employing women to produce rain (see *maṇḍūka*), and men to stop it, may be that women, as they give milk, will be more potent in obtaining the other liquid, water. Nakedness is a common element in magic, perhaps because clothes are considered a civilised appendage, and unsuitable for a contest with the powers of nature; a certain idea of impurity may also attach to them (Russell and Hiralal, II. 107). (d) The wind and rain are widely used in the poetry of the world as emblems of the act of love. There is a charming poem from Maikal Hills:

> How can I tell the love I have for you
> At midnight my life burns
> Before my eyes in a dream I see my love
> In July the rain falls *rimjhim rimjhim*
> But in August it is deep and silent as river
> So when I desire you
> Water flows from my eyes
> As a deep and silent river.

W. G. Archer has given some beautiful poems from Bihar which show that, because rain is a poignant image of the male act, the rains are necessarily a period of sexual strain:

> June is the month of parting, friend
> The sky glowers with gloom
> Leaping and reeling the god rains
> And my sweet budding breasts are wet.
> All my friends sleep with their husbands
> But my own husband is a cloud in another land.

4101 **वेणी**

Veṇī : braided hair. *Veṇī* comprised the long streaming hair tied unceremoniously with a single string at the end. No oil was to be applied to the hair in this condition, and the hair became coarse, some dangling onto the cheeks. The condition of the *yakṣa's* wife is the same (*Megha, Uttara* 31). Hair in this condition would dangle down and the condition of Vāsavadattā, who is the *proṣitabhartṛkā* is said to be the same (*Svapnavāsavadattam,* V.10). This was the *ekaveṇī,* which is only another form of the dangling hair but for a single knot somewhere, may be at the end or just at the start of the hair. This explains the *dīrghālakam mukham* of Vāsavadattā or the *vilola-kabarīkam-ānanam* of *Sītā* at the *Uttararāmacaritam* (III. 4). This type of *ekaveṇī* would not hinder the *proṣitabhartṛkā* from taking bath upon the head when necessary. The *ekaveṇī* suggests a partial and time-bound, separation from the husband, the *mukta-veṇī* (completely loose hair without any knot) denoted total separation from her husband, which is widowhood. Thus, we hear about the loosely flowing hair of *Gāndhārī's* daughters-in-law and the wives of the dead warriors (*Mbh. Strī.*, 16.18; 17.25;18.2; 21.6, 23.25, 24.7). Draupadī is *mukta-veṇī,* as she decidedly wants to show that she is without her husbands for the time they do not avenge her insult (*Veṇisaṃhāra*, 1.18).

It will be seen that the untying of the hair of the bride at the marriage ritual, and the symbolic parting of the wife's hair by her husband has a long tradition of symbolism. The hair of the Muria girls have a very close association with not only the existence of their lovers but also with their special privilege.

4102 **वेणीप्रमोक्ष**

Veṇīpramakṣa : loosening of hair (worn in a singular plait) as a sign of mourning.

4103 **वेणीसंहार**

Veṇīsaṁhāra : tying the braid, a Sanskrit drama.

4104 **वेताल-सिद्धि**

Vetāla-siddhi : kinds of psycho-physical attainment through which the adepts are supposed to be able to maintain a certain amount of control over departed souls and other subtle-bodied beings using different types of mental practices.

4105 **वेत्रवती-हस्त**

Vetravatī-hasta : the river Betawa. *Sūcī*-nand moving upward and downward indicates river Betwa (*Mirror of Gesture*, p.48).

4106 **वेदना**

Vedanā : feeling or sensation. It is one of the five *Skandhas* or constituents of a being, most generally any conscious state or experience, specifically an affective or emotional state. The primary dimensions of *vedanā* is pleasantness-unpleasantness.

4107 **वेदमुद्रा**

Veda mudrā : gesture symbolizing four *Vedas*. Spread the four fingers and curve the thumb at the roots. (*VD*).

4108 **वेदिविलग्नमध्या**

Vedivilagnamadhyā : slender hip, slender in the middle like the middle part of an alter.

4109 **वेदी**

Vedī : sacrificial alter. Its different parts have special names, for example, the eastern corners are called *aṁśa* and the western *śroṇī*.

4110 **वेपथु**

Vepathu : trembling of the body. The fifth physical sensation consequent upon sudden outburst of deep emotion.

4111 **वेश्या**

Veśyā : seducing others by dress, the prostitute. The prostitute is said to have a definite social importance, and in rituals she had a unique importance. One of the ways how women became prostitutes is stated in the *Padma Purāṇa* (*Sṛṣtikhaṇḍa*, 23.86). A prostitute is said to be that woman who has sexual relations with four men (*Brahmavai. P.*, 75-64): *nārī veśyā pratijñeyā catuṣpuruṣa-gāminī.*

To see a prostitute while going out on an errand is said to be an auspicious sign; and actually among such auspicious things arranged, a prostitute is also included. It is said that if one sees a prostitute in dream he is sure to gain wealth (*Ibid.* 77.21): *veśyām dṛṣtvā śriyam-āpnuyāt.* But it is said to be sin to touch a prostitute: *sparśane ca mahāpāpam.*

In the festival known as *Kaumudī-mahotsava*, a prostitute along with other women of her group, goes from house to house pronouncing 'auspicious words'; and women wash her feet and worship her:

वेश्या विलासिनीसार्धं स्वस्तिमङ्गलकारिणी ।
गृहाद् गृहं व्रजन्ती च पादाभ्यंगप्रदायिनी ।।
(*Bhaviṣya.* Uttarakhaṇḍa, 140.31)

4112 **वेष**

Veṣa : appearance, costume; see *nepathya*. The different costumes in ancient India identified the wearers' rank or quality. The brown-skinned peasants wore-loin-cloths and turbans, while their wives wore simple straight skirts and twisted their hair into a large coil worn on the neck. The young nobles, dawdling languidly, and ostentatiously adorned and perfumed, sheltered nonchalantly under a palm-leaf and bamboo umbrella. The brāhmaṇs were half naked, their hair gathered up in a knot on top of the head, the sacred thread across the chest, a bundle and a gourd hanging from one shoulder holding a stick to ward off evil spirits; they wore sandles as a mark of precedence, and they, too, possessed an umbrella to emphasize their dignity; they sometimes led a fighting-ram or a trained monkey from whose antics they would make a little money. *Sādhus* (religious mendicants) were also to be seen, almost naked, their bodies smeared with ashes; and emanciated beggars bent double under the weight of some real or feigned misery; and snake-charmers and monkey-trainers in search of generous audience; and sellers of tame mongooses, sprightly young servants, neat-looking and carefully dressed, hurried fast to deliver a note or fetch a jar of perfumed wine from the nearest tavern. Buddhist monks with shaven skulls made bright patches in the crowd in their swaying yellow or garnet-red robes; they walked with downcast eyes for fear of meeting a woman's glance, forbidden to them by their rules. And everywhere there were housewives, carrying a young child astride on hip, buying provisions which were then placed in a basket with a handle carried on the arm, or a plain basket that was balanced on the head.

A light coloured dress signified a feast or pious occasion; gaudy costumes were worn by kings, lovers, gods and guardian spirits; a dark costume indicated that the bearer was the mad man, a traveller or an invalid. The system of make up was made on colour symbolism which did not necessarily reflect natural appearances.

Bharata has mentioned the name of *veṣakāra* (*NS*) among the group forming a dramatic company.

In appearance the upper two *varṇas* were represented as fair in complexion, while the vaiśyas and śūdras were represented as dark in the drama (*NS*, XXI.113). *Brahmacārins*, mendicants, *amātyas* and priests shaved their beard completely while kings, princes and those dependent on the kings trimmed their beard in diverse ways. Those in trouble or engaged in austerities let the beard grow even though it had been shaved earlier. Sages and ascetics engaged in long vows kept long beard (*Ibid.*, XXI. 115-120).

Kings had gorgeous dresses, but old men, Brāhmaṇs, *śreṣtis, amātyas, purodhās,* traders (*vaṇijāḥ*), chamberlains (*kañcukīyas*) and ascetics donned clean clothes (*Ibid.*, XXI. 125-127). Both the garments, the lower (*vāsas*) and the upper (*ūrdhvāmbarāṇi*), were to be either pure (white) or red (*Ibid.*, XXI.129):

śuddha-rakta-vicitrāṇi
vāsāṁsyūrdhvāmbarāṇi ca.

This choice of colour could only be a theatrical convention or else, *rakta* probably meant as 'pleasing' or 'striking' colour. The mendicants put on ochre-coloured robes. The servitors in the inner apartments of the palace wore ochre-coloured coats (*kañcukapaṭa*):

kāṣāyua-kañcukakapaṭāḥ kāryāstepi yathāvidhi I vicitra-śāstra-kavaco baddhatūṇo dhanurdharaḥ II (*Ibid.*, XXI. 135).

The warriors donned armours, quiver and bow. Kings wore a crown, the higher officials like the *senāpati* or *yuvarāja* used only a half crown (*ardha-mukuṭa*). The ministers, chamberlains, bankers and priests donned turbans. In fact, this can be seen in the sculptures of Bharhut and Sāñcī (*Ibid*). Cf. *veṣu dekh bhaye nipaṭ dukhāre* (*Mānasa*, 2.270.5).

4113 **वेष्टितक**

Veṣṭitaka : twining position in coition seen in the Elephant-lady (*Kāmasūtra*, 2.6.14); also known as *Veṣṭanaka* 'particular posture of entwing in coitus'.

4114 **वैकृत**

Vaikṛta : the actual sound spoken by the speaker and hearer and heard by listener. It includes all the various differences in intonation, tempo, pitch, etc., depending on individual speaker. It is a paralinguistic feature. (b) one of the three kinds of *ahaṅkāra* connected with the *sāttvika* quality, out of which the eleven organs issue forth according to *Sāṅkhya* account of mind.

4115 **वैखरी**

Vaikharī : indirect speech, extraordinary speech. One of the four ingredients of sound, others being *parā*, *paśyantī*, and *madhyamā*. It is said that sound is carried by the wind inside the body and becomes articulated in the throat. It is the gross sound. According to Rāghava (on *Śāradātilaka* 1.1) *parā* is unmanifested sound, *paśyantī* reveals letters, *madhyamā* words and *vaikharī* sentences (Setubandha on *Nityaṣoḍaśikārṇava* ,VI. 10-11).

4116 **वैदग्ध**

Vaidagdha : skill.

4117 **वैदर्भी**

Vaidarbhī : name of a *rīti* or particular mode or arrangement of words in a literary composition. It is regarded as the *rīti* par excellence. It consists of ten *guṇas*, viz. *śleṣa*, *prasāda*, *samatā mādhurya*, *sukumāratā*, *arthavyakti*, *udāratva*, *ojas*, *kānti* and *samādhi*.

4118 **वैनायिकी-कला**

Vaināyikīkala : art of discipline. One of the 64 arts given in *Kāmasūtra* (1.3.16).

4119 **वैराग्य**

Vairāgya : cultivation of dispassion or detachment which is the indispensable condition for all spiritual advancement (*Yogasūtra*, 1.12-14; *Bhagavadgītā*, VI.35). *Vairāgya* is of two kinds: *aparā* (lower) and *parā* (higher).

The concept the *vairāgya* is different in the tribal world. *Bairāgī* or *sādhū* or *jogī* though supposed to be the very embodiment of renunciation and chastity, often appears in folksongs as the symbol of a lover:

Never fall in love with a *jogī*
For any day he may go on pilgrimage
Leaving you in tears behind your house.

At a marriage, the bridegroom is abused by his mother-in-law as a *jogī* with matted hair full or scorpians. The symbol is appropriate not so much because the ascetic often has a very bad reputation among the aboriginals but rather because he is always wandering on from place to place and never remains attached to a fixed abode. So too the aboriginal lover changes from girl to girl and can never remain in one place. Compare the following folksong:

To which hamlet has the *jogī* come, *bhauji*
Where has he made his camp.
He has come to the Dhīmar's hamlet, *bhaujī*
O how I long to see him

Tari O nānā o de mor nānā
re suā tari nāwāwa nānā.

4120 **वैराग्य-मुद्रा**

Vairāgya-mudrā : gesture symbolizing asceticism. Two thumbs and little-fingers when extended jointly, this makes the gesture of *vairāgya* (*VD*).

4121 **वैरस्य**

Vairasya : absence of sentiment, *rasābhāva: vairasyāyaiva tatpoṣaḥ* (*DR*,IV.45).

4122 **वैवर्ण**

Vaivarṇa : palour, paleness, colourlessness, loss of colour. The sixth physical sensation, consequent upon outburst of deep emotion. The person, particularly his face, loses all brightness and vitality and appears ghastly pale and yellow. This temperamental state is manifested by alternation of the colour of face with effort by putting pressure on the artery.

4123 **वैशाख-रेचित-करण**

Vaiśākha-recita-karaṇa : hands and feet both in *recita*, derived from the *sthāna* of that name (*NS*, IV. 97-98, X.61-62). Hands and feet are in *recita* and so also the waist and the neck. The posture is *vṛścika*. This is used in carrying one forward.

4124 **वैशाख-स्थान**

Vaiśākha-sthāna : a type of standing posture for men. *Sampāda* but both feet in *tyaśra* with toes pointing sideways, and three *tālas* and a half apart. The thighs are motionless in *sampāda*. Presiding deity *Skandha*. The feet are $3^1/_2$ tālas apart, obliquely placed pointing sideways and the thighs steady. It is used in riding horses, in exercise, exit, imitating large birds, bending the bow, throwing of arrows, fighting, riding horses and the *recakas* (*NS*, X. 61-65).

4125 **वैश्य-हस्त**

Vaiśya-hasta : if the *haṁsāsya* is the left hand and the *kaṭakāmukha* with the right one; it is the hand for a *vaiśya*, the mercantile class (*AD*, 226-231).

4126 **वैष्णव-आलीढ**

Vaiṣṇava-ālīḍha : a type of posture of men.

4127 **वैष्णव-स्थान**

Vaiṣṇava-sthāna : the standing posture for men. *Samapāda* in *tyaśra* position. Two *tālas* apart. Shank bent in *nata*. The term used in *añcita*. Other limbs in *sauṣṭhava*. It is used in *śṛṅgāra* and *vīra rasa*. Presiding deity Viṣṇu. The feet are $2^1/_2$ talas apart, one foot in the natural posture, and the other obliquely placed with toes pointing sideways, the shank is bent a little and the limbs are in *sauṣṭhava*. It represents the characters of superior and middle class people when they are in conversation with the various duties. It is to be used in throwing a disc, holding bow, in patient and stately movements of limbs and in anger. In the pretended anger of love it is to be used in the reverse position. It is to be assumed in rebuking, distress, apprehension and envy etc. It is to be used prominently in the erotic, the marvellous, the heroic and the odious sentiments. Abhinava (*NS*, II.108) mentions its use in the performance of *Sūtradhāra*. It is one of the six *sthānas*.

4128 **वैष्णवाश्रम**

Vaiṣṇavāśrama : the Purāṇas give a variant classification the *āśramas* (stages of life based on sects). Those belong to *vaiṣṇava* sect show the sign of a lance on their forehead, arranged with fragrant water on sandal-paste.

4129 **वैष्णवी-मुद्रा**

Vaiṣṇavī-mudrā : the *vaiṣṇavite* gesture. Make both of the hands upturned and place one on the other. Six fingers of them (excluding two thumbs and two little ones) are to be equally and proportionately fixed. This is *Vaiṣṇava-mudrā* (*VD*).

4130 **व्यंसित-करण**

Vyaṁsita-karaṇa : derived from the *ālīḍha sthāna* : arms in *recita* and hands in *viprakīrṇa nṛtta hasta*. *Udveṣṭita* movement (*NS*, IV. 108-109, IX. 187, 216; X.67). In *ālīḍha* posture the two hands are in *recita* and held on the breast. Then moved up and down in *viprakīrṇa*. It is used in moving round on the stage in confusion or hurry.

4131 **व्यक्ताङ्गवैकृत**

Vyaktāṅgavaikṛta : one who shows the disfigurement on his body to others (*DR*, II.90).

4132 **व्यंग्य**

Vyaṅgya : meaning to be suggested, product of the poet's mind and an unexpressed sense.

4133 **व्यञ्जक**

Vyañjaka : indicator, signifier, suggesting. (b) dramatic action.

4134 **व्यञ्जन**

Vyañjana : a mark (*A*, 2, 2, 12), sign.

4135 **व्यञ्जना**

Vyañjanā : suggestion; a function by which a word expresses a suggested sense which is other than its primary sense.

4136 **व्यत्यस्तोरू**

Vyatyastorū : incoherent thighs; a type of position of thighs (*Bālarāmabharata*).

4137 **व्यत्यास**

Vyatyāsa : (a) inversion, inverted position or order. (b) touching with right hand the left foot and with left hand the right foot of the teacher. (c) *Vyatyāsa* is a transposition, upside down or right to left, or both, of a variable. It is a change in the direction of a curve. It can also be the assumption of opposite role as we find in *Uttararāma caritam*.

4138 **व्यभिचार**

Vyabhicāra : incest. Incest is condemned in a number of myths, and the very frequency of the motif of incestuous unions seems to indicate that they are considered a possibility and a danger to the normal pattern of family relationships. One Baiga story describes how a man lives with his own daughter pretending that she is his young wife. But one night his cow speaks to him; 'you have lived with your own daughter; you will become a leper'. And so he does, and worms devour his feet till he dies. Another story tells of a man who seduces his daughter-in-law, whereupon his son in revenge rapes his own sister, who being very small dies of the injuries. Finally, both father and son are siezed by madness, and mutilate their sexual organs. The son's wife continues to live with the two impotent men, but soon she dies by drowning. The father falls down from a tree and the son is eaten by a tiger. Thus the crime of incest wipes out a whole family.

Although these myths have a clearly moral tone, and strongly condemn incest, the Baigas' attitude to concrete cases is less severe, and their general opinion is that even brother-sister incest can be atoned by giving a feast. Elwin quotes a case of a young married woman, who had intercourse with her brother and eloped with him. But her father and her husband brought her back, and paid for an expense feast which effected the girl's readmission to the tribal community.

In the Hill Maria society, the sexual relationship between boys and girls belonging to the same clan are viewed with the strictest disfavour and held to be incest which offence is believed to enrage the deities who in turn punish the village by sending tigers to devour them.

Original creation involves incest in all the myths of the world. All the tribal myths have the same content that in the beginning there were brother and sister. In the Gond myth Lingo (Śiva) encourages the incestuous union by means of a horrible rather than an erotic element. Thus Śiva appears in the popular tradition as an incestuous creator (Ruben, 1939, 213). The motif of Śiva's initial disinclination towards incest is retained in Gond mythology (Elwin, 1939, 325), where the Śiva figure, Liṅgal, is accused of incest with his sister. Although in some versions the incestuous contact is purely accidental, Liṅgal sometimes foresees the consequences. He objects that such a contact would be a sin, but his sister replies, 'I shall teach you the means to blot out the sin' (Von Furer-Haimendorf, 1948.283). Thus even in these tales Śiva retains his anti-incestuous attitude, however much his participation in original creation necessitates his involvement in the act of incest. The original myth regarded Brahmā and his daughter is well-known (*RV.* X.61.7). (b) *Vyabhicāra* is sexual relations between persons of the opposite sex who are closely connected by blood relationship. The degree of relationship is governed by law (*Dharmaśāstra*) and social custom (*Smṛti*).

4139 **व्यभिचार-दोष**

Vyabhicāra-doṣa : fallacy of extreme limitedness.

4140 **व्यभिचारी-दृष्टि**

Vyabhicārī dṛṣṭi : corresponds closely to the names of the *vyabhicārī-bhāva* and sometimes identical.

4141 **व्यभिचारी-भाव**

Vyabhicārī-bhāva : transcient emotions as contrasted with *sthāyībhāva,* transitory feelings or state, one of the three constituents of *rasa,* the other two being *vibhāvas* and *anubhāvas.* It connotes general expression of moods like anger, envy, etc. Bharata has enumerated thirty-three *vyabhicārī bhāvas.* These thirty-three transitory psychological states are *nirveda* (discouragement), *glāni* (weakness), *śaṅkā* (apprehension), *asūyā* (envy), *mada* (intoxication), *śrama* (weariness), *ālasyam* (indolence), *dainyam* (depression), *cintā* (anxiety), *moha* (distraction), *smṛti* (recollection), *dhṛti* (contentment), *vrīḍā* (shame), *capalatā* (inconstancy), *harṣa* (joy), *āvega* (agitation), *jaḍatā* (stupor), *garva* (arrogance), *viṣāda* (despair), *autsukyam* (impatience), *nidrā* (sleep), *apasmāra* (epilepsy), *suptam* (dreaming), *vibodha* (awakening), *amarṣa* (indignation), *avahittha* (dissimulation), *ugratā* (cruelty), *mati* (assurance), *vyādhi* (sickness), *unmāda* (insanity), *maraṇam* (death), *trāsa* (fright) and *vitarka* (deliberation).

4142 **व्यभिहास**

Vyabhihāsa : laughing in front.

4143 **व्यवहार**

Vyavahāra : speech. *Vyavahāra-mātram:* 'merely a matter of speech' (*Śikṣāsamuccaya,* p.256, Bendall's edition). (b) legal procedure consisting of four stages, viz. *bhāṣā* (plaint), *uttara* (reply), *kriyā* (proof or evidence) and *nirṇaya* (judgement). It occurs in *Smṛti* literature. (c) administration of justice. (d) competency to manage one's own affairs, majority. (e) dealings (*A,* 3.2.1). Cf. *jathā vansa vyavahāru* (*Mānasa,* 1.286). The *vyavahāra* or decision by proof is one where the judge and assessors put forward some principles of the *Dharmaśāstra* while deciding the cases. That is why Nārada says that decision by *vyavahāra* depends upon witnesses, as they are the principle instrument of proof.

4144 **व्यवहारनियामकतत्त्व**

Vyavahāraniyāmakatattva : factors conditioning human communication *:* The total conditioning background of communication behaviour are *biophysiopsychological* (biological configuration, sex, age, physiological state, medical state, nutritional habits, psychological configuration, and emotional states), environmental (natural environment, built or modified environment, objectual environment and socio-economic environment), the degree of shareness (performer-spectator borrowing, that is, from an actor or public figure by others, the cohabiting couple, the nuclear or extended family, the social or occupational group, and the geographic or subcultural variety), cultural patterns (religious and moral values, relationships and role-expectations, etiquette norms and aesthetic values), and socio-economic levels (the supe refined, the average educated, the average middle-income employee, the low-income worker, the pseudo-educated, and the rustic). This would of course lead us to the different interpretation of the narrative work by the various types of readers, and their specific relationship with both the author and the characters.

4145 **व्यवहार-पद**

Vyavahāra-pada : subject matter of speech, subject-matter of litigation (*Smṛti*).

4146 **व्यवहारिक**

Vyavahārika : empirical. The term is prefixed to many concepts.

4147 **व्यसन**

Vyasana : calamity (*Arthaśāstra,* 8.1.2-3). Kauṭilya is of the opinion that *vyasana* is so-called because it throws out a person from his good. Inversion of excellence, absence of any of the constituent, a defect or spoiling or deteriotion of a constituent, addiction or affliction to the constituent constitute *vyasana.* Calamity or *vyasana* can be of both origins—human and divine and the former ensues from bad policy and the latter from ill luck (8.1.2-3). He elaborately discusses the comparative seriousness of different calamities befalling the state and suggests measures to remedy them.

According to *Manu* (VII.47-48) there are twelve components of *vyasana*: *mṛgayā* (hunting), *akṣāḥ* (gambling), *divāsvapna* (sleeping in the day), *parivāda* (censure), *striyaḥ* (addiction to women), *mada* (drinking), *tauryatrika* (dancing, singing and instrumental music), *vṛthābhramaṇa* (idle roaming), *paiśunya* (tale-bearing), *sāhasa* (violence), *droha* (insidious injury), and *īrṣyā* (envy).

4148 **व्यस्तोरू**

Vyastorū : a sideways movement of the thighs. *Vyasta* "distance between two feet."

4149 **व्याकरण**

Vyākaraṇa : grammar, analysis. Note *mano vyākaraṇātmakam* (*Mbh.* XII., 252.11).

4150 **व्याकरण-मुद्रा**

Vyākaraṇa-mudrā : the gesture symbolizing grammar, the part of *Vedāṅga.* Join together the thumb and the fore-finger to symbolize *vyākaraṇa* (*VD*).

4151 **व्याख्या-मुद्रा**

Vyākhyā-mudrā : symbolizing the explaining attitude which is referred to in the case of goddess Sarasvatī. (*Brahmavaivarta, prakṛtikhaṇḍa* 1.35): व्याख्यामुद्राकरा शान्ता वीणापुस्तकधारिणी.

4152 **व्याख्यान-मुद्रा**

Vyākhyāna-mudrā : one of the four *hasta-mudrās* known to Indian iconography. Hand gesture in the context of exposition.

4153 **व्याघ्र-मुद्रा**

Vyāghra-mudrā : indication of a tiger. *Ardhacandra* held downward indicates a tiger (*Mirror of Gesture,* pp.49-50). (Fig. 4153)

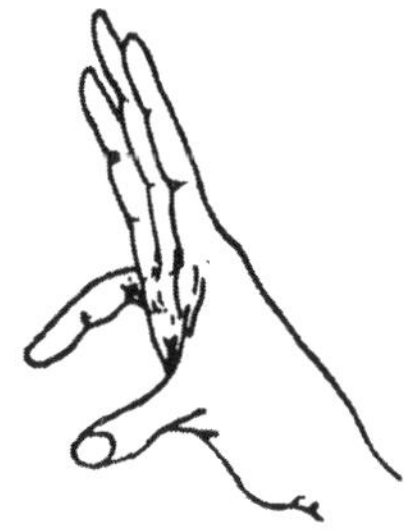

Fig. – (4153)

4154 **व्याघ्र-हस्त**

Vyāghra-hasta : single hand gesture (*Abhinayadarpaṇa,* verse 166-67). It does not occur in *NS.* If the thumb and the little-fingers are to be made down-turned in the *mṛgaśīrṣa* style, it is called the *vyāghra-hasta* by authorities on the *Bharataśāstra.* It is used to indicate a tiger, a frog, a monkey and some such sour things.

4155 **व्याजोक्ति**

Vyājokti : dessembling expression. A figure of speech in which a thing, though clearly known, is concealed artfully (*Kāvyaprakāśa,* X.118).

4156 **व्याधि**

Vyādhi : sickness. one of the (29th) transitory states of mind. It is manifested in three ways: (i) *fever with a feeling of cold:* shivering, tremor of the entire body, bending the body, shaking of the jaws, desire for heat, horripilation, movement of the chin, narrowing down the nasal passage, dryness of the mouth, lamentation, etc. (ii) *fever with a feeling of heat:* throwing out clothes, the hands and the feet, desire to roll on the ground, use of unguents, desire for coolness, lamentation, dryness of mouth, crying. (iii) *other types of sickness:* narrowing down the mouth, dullness of the body, downcast eyes, deep breathing, making peculiar sounds, crying, tremor, etc.

4157 **व्यापक**

Vyāpaka : omnipresent. A thing which pervades another (*vyāpya*). In *Parvato vahnimān dhūmāt, vahni* is *vyāpaka.*

4158 **व्याप्ति**

Vyāpti : pervasion. (a) invariable correlation or concomitance between two things (*vyāpya* and *vyāpaka*) (b) a general proposition. For example, the relation of smoke to fire is one of *vyāpti.* (c) the Buddhists base the knowledge of *vyāpti* on the principles of causality and essential identity while the vedantists hold that *vyāpti* is the result of an induction by simple enumeration. (d) *Nyāya* school establish *vyāpti* or a universal proposition on the particular ground of the observation of particular facts, the methods being known as *anvaya* (agreement in presence), *vyatireka* (agreement in absence), *vyabhicārāgraha* (absence of contrary instance), *upādhinirāsa* (elimination of condition), *tarka* and *sāmānya-lakṣaṇa.*

4159 **व्याप्य**

Vyāpya : to be pervaded. A thing that is pervaded by something else (*vyāpaka*). For example, in *parvato vahnimān dhūmāt,* smoke is *vyāpya* while fire is *vyāpaka.*

4160 **व्याभाषण**

Vyābhāṣaṇa : conversation.

4161 **व्याभुग्न-मुख**

Vyābhugna-mukha : a type of face movement (*NS,* VIII. 153-160).

4162 **व्यालि-मुद्रा**

Vyāli-mudrā : gesture of a snake-like bird. The fore-finger and the middle-finger are bent like a bow; the third finger is placed at the base of the thumb and the little finger is bent to indicate a *vyāli* (*Mirror of Gesture,* pp. 50-51).

4163 **व्यालोल**

Vyālola : fickle man, quality of the Bull-man (*Anaṅgaraṅga,* 3.17).

4164 **व्यावर्तित-हस्त-करण**

Vyāvartita-hasta-karaṇa : the contra-round-up. When fingers beginning from the little one are turned downwards one by one inside, it is called *vyāvartita karaṇa* of a hand (*NS,* IX. 195-205), *i.e.* the fingers beginning with the little finger point inwards gradually (the fingers are bent as in *āveṣṭita,* but commencing with the little finger and ending in fore-finger).

4165 **व्याहत्वम्**

Vyāhatvam : inconsistency (*SD,* VIII, *Kāvyaprakāśa* VII. 25).

4166 **व्याहार**

Vyāhāra : the speech uttered vividly bordering on the comic sense (*NS,* 18.125). Abhinava (*Ibid*) understands by "*pratyakṣa*" the further happening. Dhanañjaya (*Daśarūpaka,* III. 20) deviating a little from Bharata, defines it as a remark made for someone else causing laughter and desire: *Vyāhāro yat parasyārthe hāsyakṣobhakaram vacaḥ.*

4167 **व्याहृति**

Vyāhṛti : speech act, Utterance, spoken word, the mystical utterance of the names of the seven words, viz. *bhūḥ, bhuvaḥ, svaḥ, mahaḥ, janaḥ, apas* and *satya.* One thing that many utterances do is make proposition: they do this mainly in the form of either statements or questions but other forms are also possible. A different kind of proposition is ethical or magical proposition. Just like an ordinary proposition, an ethical proposition may be true or false, although not in the same sense. But truth or falsity are not the real purpose of ethical propositions; their real purpose is to serve as guides to behaviour is some world or other. We employ such utterances not for their propositional content but rather for their affective value as indicators that one person is willing to talk to another and that channel of communication is either being opened or being kept open. Phatic utterances do not really communicate anything; rather, their use allows communication to occur should there be anything of consequence to say.

Once we begin to look at utterances from the point of view of what they do, it is possible to see every utterance as a speech act of one kind or other, that is, as having same functional value which might be quite independent of the actual words used and their grammatical arrangement.

4168 **व्युत्पत्ति**

Vyutpatti : poetic talent full of knowledge and culture and is capable of receiving aesthetic experience.

4169 **व्योमचारिणी-मुद्रा**

Vyomacāriṇī-mudrā : "In the hand, joined with the wrist and raised up with the folded hands, when there drops a finger, it makes the gesture of *vyomacāriṇī*" (*BT*).

4170 **व्योम-मुद्रा**

Vyoma-mudrā : curve two fore-fingers as well as (both of) the little fingers and so place them in the middle to the hands that their nails should touch the middle hands. The rest of four fingers (the middle and the ring fingers of the hands) should be raised towards back sides. Then the thumbs are to be so arranged on one side that it would look like a *nāla*- a lotus-stalk (*VD*); (b) *gesture of hemisphere.* Place two hands with interlocked fingers in front and join the little fingers and fore-fingers with middle fingers on one's own chest. It may be placed on the other hand to indicate Śikhābandha (*VD*). According to *Bhaviṣya Purāṇa* (*Brahmakāṇḍa,* 49.25.29), the *vyoma-mudrā* is to be accomplished as follows: "the palms are to be stretched and joined at the little finger; then each of the fingers up to the index-finger (near the thumbs) are to be joined up; the fingers (excluding of the thumb) may be straight or bent down".

4171 **व्रत**

Vrata : Hindu propitiatory ritual, vow. *Vrata* comprises a rule of behaviour based on tradition : *Śāstrodito hi niyamo vratam* (*Agni P.*, 175.2). *Agni Purāṇa* (175.10) mentions a ten-fold behaviour:

> क्षमा सत्यं दया दानं शौचमिन्द्रियनिग्रहः ।
> देवपूजाऽग्निहरणं सन्तोषोऽस्तेयमेव च ॥

Vrata and *saṅkalpa* (mental resolve) go together; a *vrata* without a *saṅkalpa* is lame. In many *vratas* there are relics of primitive magical beliefs and practices.

4172 **व्रात्य**

Vrātya : (a) any one born of the mixture of *varṇas* or castes. (b) one born to a member of the regenerate class by a wife of his own caste, on whom or on whose ancestors the sacrement of *upanayana* has not been performed (*Smṛti*). (c) fallen un-Vedic. (d) an early ascetic, probably Āryan but non-Vedic.

4173 **व्रीडा**

Vriḍā : bashfulness or shame which is taken to be a sign of modesty. The thirteenth among the thirty-three *vybhicārī bhāvas* as enumerated by Bharata. Change of colour of face, hanging down of the head, etc. are the external manifestations of *vriḍā*. Also, it is manifested by covered face, thinking with downcast face, drawing lines on the ground, touching clothes and ring, biting the nails, etc. The feeling of shame is related to public humiliation as embarrassment about a misdeed or to real or imagined inadequacy in ourselves. For example 'posing face' is a main motive of law-abiding behaviour, for wrong-doers are publicly humiliated.

श - Śa

4174 **शक**

Śaka : (a) the term *Śaka* was used in a vague way to denote all foreigners from the other side of the passes without clear distinction of race or tribe. It may have included both squat, narrow-eyed Mongols and handsome races like the Turks, who resemble the traditional Aryans in physique. (b) the *Śakas* came into India from Central Asia in the second century B.C. They founded kingdoms in the Punjab, at Mathurā and Kāṭhiāvāḍa. (c) low and barbarous (*Mbh.*, XII.65). (d) 'foreigners' in Jain literature. Cp. *Śakāriḥ Vikramādityaḥ*.

4175 **शकट**

Śakaṭa : cart. *Śakaṭikā* a small cart, toy cart, cp. *Mṛcchakaṭikam*.

4176 **शकट-हस्त**

Śakaṭa hasta : both hands gesture (*Abhinayadarpaṇa*), not mentioned in *NS*. If the middle finger of the *bhramara*-style is stretched, it makes a *śakaṭa*. It is used to play a role of a demon.

4177 **शकटास्य-करण**

Śakaṭāsya-karaṇa : derived from the *cārī* of this name: It also uses the *agratalasañcara* foot and the *udvāhita* chest. The *karaṇa*, however, seems to be an acrobatic one like the *Cakra-maṇḍala*. The *Kaṭakāmukha* hands are in from the chest level (*NS*, IV.167b-168a, IX.231, 275; X.16). After having the body at rest the *talasañcara* foot is extended and the breast is in *udvāhita*. It is used in sportive movement of the child, in *Bhāṇkā* etc.

4178 **शकटास्य-चारी**

Śakaṭāsya-cārī : foot in *samapāda agratalasañcara* position. The *agratalasañcara* foot put forward and distance of about 2 *tālas* postures. *Udvāhita* chest movement. *Śakaṭāsya karaṇa* and *maṇḍala*. The body is held up right. One *agratalasañcara* foot is put forward and the breast in *udvāhita*. It is one of the *bhaumī cārīs*. The upper part of the body is held firmly, one foot in *agratalasañcara* is stretched forward, and the chest is kept in *udvāhita* (*NS*, X.16).

4179 **शकुनिरव**

Śakunirava : sound of birds.

4180 **शकुनविद्या**

Śakunavidyā : the science of omens and portents. Belief in omens is universal among the Hindus. An omen seen on getting up in the morning is believed to be an index to the day's happening. On going out of the house, the Hindu looks for omens which are supposed to give an indication of what is in store for him. The method of determining the desirability of otherwise of an omen is somewhat arbitrary. A crow on the left side or a kite on the right, a snake, hare, an empty vessel, smouldering fire, a widow or a man with one eye or a big nose, is bad omen. A cow, a clear fire, a virgin, two or more Brāhmaṇs, etc. of good omens. Sneezing once is good; twice is evil. A pregnant woman must not go inside an empty house or one with an upper storey; nor should she sit with her feet turned back, or sleep during day light or lie awake at night. Her husband must be equally cautious. "He must not build a house; for that might rouse the wrath of the earth spirit. He must not bathe in the sea for the sea shore is thick with ghosts. He must not attend a funeral." Nor he should travel or shave his head.

In Malabar the craze for good omens has developed into an art, and for Vishnu, the new year day, every Hindu household prepares the *kani* or good omen at night for the members to look at as they get up in the morning. The *kani* is prepared in a spacious room, close to a wall facing east. A mystic design is drawn on the floor and a circular metal piece with rice in it is placed inside the design. Behind the plate a mirror is placed with its back propped up against the wall. Flowers and fruits are strewn on the floor on all sides of the design and a wick lamp is lighted on either side of the mirror. The *kani* is now ready to be gazed on. To see this early in the morning is believed to bring luck for the whole year.

There are literally hundreds of different 'lucky symbols' that have been carried or worn by people of India.

In Abujhmar the following birds are believed universally as omens: *Usi, Karmadi, Kondo, Kewadi, Jegdo* and *Kākar*. While going for settling marriage as also while going to undertake some important work, if anyone of the above brids are met on the left side, it is considered to be a good omen, while if the birds are met on the right the omen is bad. The sound of these bird coming from the right is taken as bad omen. If the omen bird is sitting on a green branch; it is better omen, while if it is found sitting on a dead tree, it is not that good. Any of the bird sitting on the right side on a dead tree is taken to be a definitely worse omen. The Bison-horn Maria and Dorla consult the clan-priest (*Waddai*) before confirming themselves.

Thus the omen is a signal in which true signal is hidden, masked or distorted by noise creating, among other things, a sense of indefiniteness about it. Omens are very much semioticized.

4181 **शक्ति**

Śakti : power, genius. In India the social hierarchy could be manipulated into conformity with the structure of power.

The foreign rulers in India knew this and exploited the countrymen. Indians, of course, had different notions of social status. (b) *Śakti* is generally the anthromorphozed power of Śiva - the female generative organ, counterpart of the phallus, believed to be a female deity. (c) the emblem of Skanda is the *Śakti* (power) and it is indicated that it is represented by a lance at certain places. (d) power of the supreme. Being conceived as the Female Principle through which the manifestation of the Universe is effected. (e) Female partner of the aspirant in *Tantra*. She can be of three kinds: *svakīyā* (aspirants's wife), *parakīyā* (wife of another) and *sādhāraṇī* (common woman). Women of the lower castes and despised professions are regarded as excellent partners (*Tantrasāra*, 627). (f) one of the six limbs of *mantra* (*Tantra*). (g) Placation, i.e. allaying of disagreement in drama (*DR*.1.17). (h) the power or signification of a word. These are three: *abhidhā, lakṣaṇā* and *vyañjanā*. (i) the cult of political power and the cult of mystical power were rooted in a single tradition: *yoga*. Kauṭilya's idea of disciplined manipulation of kingly authority is indeed chilling. *Mahābhārata* and *Manusmṛti* also propounded the doctrine of power through *daṇḍanīti*.

4182 **शक्तिका-मुद्रा**

Śaktikā-mudrā : "two ankles and elbows are joined together and two hands are interlocked with fingers. If two extended middle fingers kiss each other in a slightly bending position, it is called the *śaktikā-mudrā* (*BT*).

4183 **शक्तिकूट**

Śaktikūṭa : technical name of *śakti-vīja* or symbolic letters (*Śāradātilaka*, 1.1).

4184 **शक्तिचालनी-मुद्रा**

Śakticālanī-mudrā : a *mudrā* which bestows great success. (*Haṭhayogapradīpikā*, III. 6-7). The process is as follows. The aspirant has to sit in *siddhāsana* posture. Through both his nostrils he inhales air and sends to the spinal cord. Until it reaches there he contracts his anus and stops inhaling by *kumbhaka* process. The confined wind will then push the *kuṇḍalinī* and send it upwards.

4185 **शक्तिमुद्रा**

Sakti-Omudrā : same as *śaktyākāra-mudrā*. (b) when fingers, beginning from little ones and ending in fore-fingers, are extended, one after another; this is called the *śaktimudrā* (*VD*).

4186 **शक्ति-वर्ण**

Śakti-varṇa : the vowels (*Śāradātilaka*, VI.2).

4187 **शक्त्याकार-मुद्रा**

Śaktyākāra-mudrā : energy in form. Join the thumb of one hand, with the thumb of the other and similarly one little-finger with another. Then bring together the rest six fingers of two hands. When these six fingers are placed inside the palm in a contracting order; it is the *śaktyākāra-mudrā* (*VD*).

4188 **शक्र-मुद्रा**

Śakra-mudrā : two hands are stretched up turned and the left thumb and the fore-finger are joined. It indicates *Śakra* (*VD*). *Śakra* means *Indra*, the strong one.

4189 **शक्ल**

Śakla : sweet in speech (*A*, 6.1.6), speaking sweetly.

4190 **शङ्का**

Śaṅkā : apprehension, doubt. The third among the thirty-three *vyabhicārī bhāvas* as enumerated by Bharata. One of the transitory mental state which is represented by constantly looking about, hesitating movment, dryness of the mouth, licking the lips, change of facial colour, tremor, dry lips, change of voice and the like. Concealment of appearance to be characterized by adoption of clever gestures according to some authorities. (b) apprehension is the act of becoming aware of something, anxiety about the future. Lightly scratching or rubbing the side of the neck indicates doubt about what's heard.

4191 **शङ्किता-दृष्टि**

Śaṅkitā-dṛṣṭi : it is used for apprehension (*NS*, VIII. 89a). In *Ratnāvalī* (Act III), the glance of the queen is *śaṅkitā*, a timid glance, a type of *sañcārī bhāvadṛṣṭi;* a glance moved and rested. Sometimes slightly raised and obliquely opened with timid eye-balls, suggesting apprehension. The glance is concealed, alternately moving and steady, slightly raised, widened obliquely and pupils apprehensive. It is to indicate apprehension.

4192 **शंख**

Śaṅkha : temple, conch. (1) The temple and ear are emically distinct in Indian gesture. In 'intelligence' the index finger taps the temple, but in 'deaf' the hand contacts the ear. The emic status of the tabulae is doubtful, however, as the two gestures involve different hand configurations. (2) The custom of blowing the conch (*Cāturīcandrikābhāṇa*, p.42) and ringing the bell (*Ibid.* p.30) at the time of a festivity is still prevalent all over India. Both blowing of the conch and ringing of the bell in the temples at regular timings is resorted to for announcing the time for all. This custom is observed almost in each and every temple. Some devotees believe that by observing both these customs, the Lord wakes up and receives the things offered. They are also used to symbolize the fact that noon offerings to the Lord are made. Certain devoted brāhmaṇs and kings used to take their meal only after hearing these bells. (3) Kings and great persons were aroused from sleep in the morning by blowing the conches (HC, III). (4) Signs of temples. "With broad and raised temples men become wealthy; with sunken ones, bereft of children and wealth. Cf. the following:

उन्नतैर्विपुलैः शङ्खैर्धनिनः सुखजीविनः ।
सुतार्थरहिता निम्नैर्मानुषा दुःखभागिनः ॥

4193 **शङ्ख-मुद्रा**

Śaṅkha-mudrā : (a) on the well-placed wrists, where fingers are inter-locked inside the fingers, two thumbs are to be made joined together and the two little fingers are to be extended. This is called the gesture of a conch-shell (*śaṅka*) which is the most powerful gesture to remove all sorts of bad omen" (*BT*). (b) The thumb fixed on the fingers symbolizes the conch-shell (*VD*); (c) the fore-finger and the middle finger are joined with the middle knots of other fingers and the ring finger is made joined to the back. This is the *śaṅkha*-gesture (*VD*). (Fig. 4193)

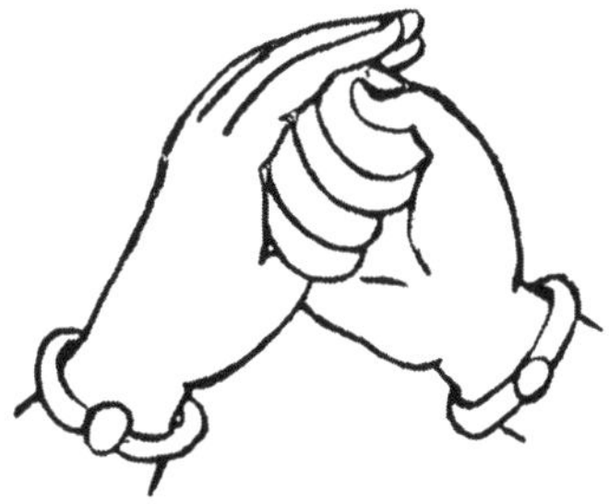

Fig. – (4193)

4194 **शङ्ख-हस्त**

Śaṅkha-hasta : both hands gesture (*Abhinayadarpaṇa*), not mentioned in *NS*. The thumb of a *śikhara* hand, if meets the other thumb and clings the first tightly with other finger, it makes a *śaṅkha* gesture. It is used to suggest blowing of the conch-shell.

4195 **शङ्खिनी**

Śaṅkhinī : conch-lady. "She is neither slender nor fat. Her body, feet and waist are long. She likes red flowers and red clothes. She is wrathful. Her tabular vessels are not concealed. She has a deep secret part which has huge public hair. Her mucus has pungent odour. She makes many nail-prints in co-habitation and ejaculates a small quantity of mucus. Her limbs are slightly hot by mature. She neither eats more nor less. She is bellious by health. Her mind is wicked and impure and she speaks like an ass" (*Ratirahasya*, 1.16-17). The *Pañcasāyaka* describes this lady as follows:

tanvaṅgī kuṭilakṣaṇā laghukucabhogā madāveśinī
prāyo dīrgha-kacā svabhāva-piśunā kaṣṭopabhogyā rate ।
piṅgā lolagatiśca gharghararavā raktāmbarā hlādinī
nānā sthānanakhapradānarasikā seyam matā śaṅkhinī ॥

4196 **शठ**

Śaṭha : (a) crooked, deceitful, indifferent or having no attachment. (b) a type of hero.

4197 **शत्रुघ्न-मुद्रा**

Śatrughna-mudrā : The *śikhara* hand placed on the face denotes *śatrughna*, the mythical ruler (*Mirror of Gesture*, p. 47).

4198 **शनि-मुद्रा**

Śani-mudrā : gesture of the Saturn. The thumb at the root of the middle finger (*VD*).

4199 **शनिश्चर-हस्त**

Śaniścara-hasta : *Śikhara* with the left and *triśūla* with the right make the symbol of *Śaniścara* (*AD*, 216-225).

4200 **शपथ**

Śapatha : (*Nirukta*, VII.3): oath, form of speech and thought; compare the following passages from Tulasīdāsa:

satya kahaun sankaru sākhi ˉ(*Mānasa*, 2.31.6),
pāvak sākhī dei kari jorī prīti dṛrhāi (*Ibid* 4.4).

(b) taking oath is a very common method of proving oneself cleared from a sin. It is resorted to not only in judicial proceedings but also in everday life to prove the purity of one's character. Nārada says that taking of oath even by gods and sages is on record.

4201 **शबर**

Śabara : an aboriginal tribe lviing in jungles (*Smṛti*). According to *Mbh.* Śabara country was in Dakṣiṇāpatha. According to Cunningham it extended as far southward as the Pennār river. (b) low and barbarous (*Mbh.*, XII. 65). (c) sinful people in South (*Mbh.*, XII.207). (d) 'foreigners' in Jain literature. Śabarāḥ 'inhabitants of the *Śabara* country. (d) a story from the *Padma-purāṇa* (*Pātālakhaṇḍa* 20.45-75) indicates that the aboriginal Śabaras became devotees of Viṣṇu. According to the account a Śabara was a devotee of Viṣṇu, and wore the *Śālagrāma* on his chest and the leaves of the Tulasī plant on his head. When he was about to be taken away to the other world by the attendants of Yama, he was left by them because of these two objects.

Suicide was a common practice among Śabaras according to *Skanda Purāṇa* (V.3.57. 29-31). Here the *Purāṇa* speaks about the practice of committing suicide at *Sūlabheda-tīrtha* situated on the southern bank of Narmadā, by falling from a precipice. According to this account a Śabara couple had committed suicide in the manner noted above.

4202 **शबरोत्सव**

Śabarotsava : a ceremony of festive character, consisting of obscene songs and gestures, associated with Durgā-worship (*Kālikāpurāṇa*). *Śabarotsava* is said to be in autumn (Śarad). There is another festival of the same nature known as *bhūtamātṛkā*, which is celebrated in spring (*Vasanta*). It is a Purāṇic festival celebrated by every town and every village people. The goddess of this festival is *bhūtamātṛkā* (*Skanda*, VII. 1.167.1). The festival comes on the 14th dark of the month of Mādhava (Spring-time, March-April). The speciality of the festival is that people go about dancing, singing and yelling as if they have turned intoxicated and are frenzy. They smear earth and even urine over one another, and enter muddy water:

गायन्नृत्यन्हसँल्लोकः सर्वत्र परिधावति ।
(*Skanda* , VII. 1.167.3)
उन्मत्तवत्प्रलपते क्षितौ पतति मत्तवत् ।
(*Ibid.*, 4)
सुखभङ्गाश्च कुरुते लोको वातगृहीतवत् ।
(*Ibid.*, 5)

4203 **शबलाङ्गिका**

Śabalāṅgikā : lady whose character is bad, quality of the Elephant-lady (*Anaṅgaraṅga*, 3.24); lit. it means 'spotted woman'.

4204 **शब्द**

Śabda : (a) *śabda* stands for voice in music. It is the basis of songs. It is divided in *ŚR* (*Prakīrṇaka* 39-57) into four main kinds: *khāhula*: arising from phlegm, *nārāṭa*: arising from bile; *bombaka* arising from wind, and *miśraka:* arising from the admixture of above three. In accordance with qualities, *śabda* is divided into fifteen kinds, e.g. *komala* (soft), *karuṇa* (evoking pity) etc. The capacity of *śabda* or voice for manifesting *rāgas* without practice is called *śārīra* (born with body). (b) word according to grammarians. (c) in the sense of sound, *śabda* has a different religio-philosophical significance. See under *Śabdabrahma.* (d) verbal testimony; knowledge derived from the statements of authoritative persons. It is sometimes regarded as valid source of knowledge. There are two ways of classifying *śabda*: *dṛṣṭārtha* (that relating to perceptible objects) and *adṛṣṭārtha* (that relating to imperceptible objects). There are two sub-divisions of testimony: *Vaidika* (scriptural) and *laukika* (secular). The latter is not always regarded as valid. (e) in rhetorics, word is threefold: *vācaka* (expressive), *lākṣaṇika* (indicative) and *vyañjaka* (suggestive). (f) *Vijñābhikṣu* maintains three kinds of word: *varṇa*, sound, and *spoṭa.*

4205 **शब्दचित्र**

Śabdacitra : poem having fanciful words, a class of poetry wherein the charm lies in the use of words which please the ear simply by their sound.

4206 **शब्द-पाक**

Śabda-pāka : maturity of words resulting from the best mode of diction (*vaidarbhī*). *Śabda-pāka* occurs when the words are so chosen that they cannot bear an exchange of synonym. *Pāka* consists of the composition of word and sense proper to the development of *rasa*. Ripeness of fruits analogically explained with the idea of *śabda-pāka* which bear different kinds of taste after ripeness. This ripeness corresponds to egg-plant (*vṛntaka-pāka*) or grapes (*drākṣā*), coconut (*nārikela*), mango (*sahakāra*), wood-aple (*kapittha*), jujube (*badara*), cucumber (*trapasa*), tamarind (*tintidi*) and *nimba* (neem) even.

4207 **शब्दपातिन्**

Śabdapātin : an arrow falling on the target the sound of which is only heard, hitting an invisible mark, the sound of which is heard.

4208 **शब्दब्रह्म**

Śabdabrahma : *Brahman* convceived as the substratum of sound. See under *parā*, *paśyanti*, *madhyamā* and *vaikharī.* It is the *caitanya* (tendency towards manifestation in all beings) pervading all creation, and is the source of the letters of the alphabet, of words, and of other sounds through which thoughts are exchanged. From *śabda* arises the ethereal region. See under *śabdāvaita* and *sphoṭa.* (b) *Veda*, consisting of words.

4209 **शब्दयोनि**

Śabdayoni : the sky.

4210 **शब्दलक्षणचक्षुस्**

Śabdalakṣaṇacakṣus : thc grammarian.

4211 **शब्दवित्**

Śabdavit : linguist or grammarian (*NS*, XVII. 53-57).

4212 **शब्दवृत्ति**

Śabdavṛtti : function of a word (in rhetorics).

4213 **शब्दशासन**

Śabdaśāsana : science of word.

4214 **शब्दाद्वैत**

Śabdādvaita : a monistic interpretation of the theory of *sphoṭa* advocated by Bhartṛhari and others. See under *sphoṭa*.

4215 **शब्दानुशासन**

Śabdānuśāsana : grammar, grammatical rules.

4216 **शब्दार्थ**

Śabdārtha : word and its meaning. A word has more than one meaning, but in a particular context, only one meaning is taken due to: (i) *saṁyoga* (connection), (ii) *viprayoga* (disjunction), (iii) *sāhacarya* (association), (iv) *virodhitā* (opposition), (v) *artha* (purpose), (vi) *prakaraṇa* (context), (vii) *liṅga* (peculiarity), (viii) *anyaśabdasannidhi* (proximity of another word), (ix) *sāmarthya* (capacity), (x) *aucitī* (appropriateness), (xi) *deśa* (place), (xii) *kāla* (time), (xiii) *vyakti* (gender) and (xiv) *svara* (accent).

4217 **शब्दालङ्कार**

Śabdālaṅkāra : a figure of speech depending for its charm on words and disappearing as soon as the words, which constitute the figure, are replaced by others of the same meaning.

4218 **शमनी-मुद्रा**

Śamanī-mudrā : gesture of tranquillity; "When one bows down his body with folded hands and upturned legs, it is called the *Śamanī-mudrā*" (*BT*).

4219 **शमीक्रिया**

Śamīkriyā : peace-making: *asya rūkṣasya vacasaḥ pariśvaṅgaḥ Śamikriya* (Bhāsa, *Pañcarātram*, 1).

4220 **शम्पा**

Śampā : girdle, a particular *tāla*.

4221 **शम्बर-मुद्रा**

Śambara-mudrā : gesture of a *Śambhara;* "The esoterically initiated devout; in the same state of nudity, having been besmeared with all sorts of scents and dressed with loosely scattered hairs, should make a sound of *sītkāra* (kissing sound) with the mouth. Then sitting on the *kukkuṭāsana* and recalling eight hundred of *vidyās*, should meditate the lotuses inside the body. This is called *śambara-mudrā* that brings complete success in the great reunion of *Tāntrikas*" (*BT*).

4222 **शम्बलम्**

Śambalam : envious talk; also *jambūlam*; the ridiculous talk of the women of bridegroom's party: *varapakṣīyastrīṇām upahāsavacanam*.

4223 **शयन**

Śayana : reclining pose, posture for lying down. There are six reclining postures enumerated by Bharata in his *NS: ākuñcita, sama, prasārita, vivartita, udvāhita* and *nata*. (b) during the chariout-fair at Purī, there was a ritual known as '*Śayanotsava*' 'the festival of sleep' (*Skanda.*,II. 2.29.30).

4224 **शयन-रचनाकला**

Śayana-rachanākalā : preparation of beds for different times and seasons. One of the 64 arts given by Vātsyāyana. In a Gondi poem the bed is compared to a bullock with a bell round its neck because when it is shared it is never silent. Here the girl singer has arranged that when she is mature (the reference to her first bath is to the menarche) her lover will come to visit her:

> My bed is a bullock with a sounding bell
> But when you leave me it is quiet
> Ignorant ploughman, when I first bathed
> You were to come in ten day's time
> Instead you took a month
> And yet my Raja, though you are away
> From me everyday
> Your memory stands like a pillar.

4225 **शयनागार**

Śayanāgāra : dormitory. The climate of psychological dependence in which a higher-caste child grows up is unknown in tribal life. The most characteristic tribal institution, common to many, but perfected by the *Muriā's*, is the village youth-dormitory, a highly sophisticated organization which compares favourably with any similar adolescent institution. Known as *Ghoṭul* among the Muriā of Kondagaon, it is as complete a form of audio-tactile social education as man could devise. Aesthetically, the youth-dormitory served tribal India as Sanskrit drama and the cave sanctuary served classical India; socially, it was of fundamental importance, and caste society had no equivalent institution. It was in the youth-dormitory that the subtle aesthetic culture of tribal India was formed. It has had no direct influence (at least, none that has been recorded) on the development of Indian civilization, but in terms of resultant character and sensibility its role as the basic educational agent of the tribes, (together with other adolescent customs of the tribes) has, in my view, imbued the flagging cultural vitality of India with a new sensuous exuberance at critical moments in history. When the Great Tradition was on the verge of sterility, when asceticism and dry scholasticism threatened the general health of Hindu society, waves of fresh energy seem to have coursed upward from the tribes, inspired by culture heroes nurtured among pastoral folk with wholly different ideas on the upbringing of the young. This is not a point that can easily be substantiated. Nevertheless the Krişņa-cults and even the imagery of the Ajanta frescoes were evolved in periods when tribalism was still a major cultural force, suggesting an affinity with the cultivation of balanced interplay among the senses, the total togetherness of the Ghoṭul. (Lannoy, 1971.184).

The Ghoṭul is not only a club but a self-governing commune where the two sexes develop tribal solidarity, train for the adult duties of social and economic life independent of adult control, and give assistance to the tribe on payment of certain specified fees. The boys assemble at the dormitory in the evening for dancing, games, and social and sexual training unhampered by the interference of elders; they sleep there after the departure of the girls. Each girl is paired off with a boy, combs his hair, massages his limbs, dances and sings with him, and is initiated into sexual life with him. According to Elwin, sexual congress is regarded by the Muriā's as natural and healthy, and countinence is not admired; while consumation is the goal of Ghoṭul attachments, pregnancy is exception rather than rule. He finds the divorce rate far lower than in tribes without youth-dormitories, and comes to the conclusion that the discipline and social sense taught in the Ghoṭul is responsible for creating a psychological attitude favourable to stability in marriage. Instruction is given in mimetic dances depicting the various adult skills in work and craft, love play, and sexual intercourse. "While ideas about the sanctity of tribal discipine, social approbation, social justice, reciprocity of obligations, law and order in society, as well as the relations between effort and reward, between crime and punishment, are inculcated through stories and anecdotes which graphically describe individual doings and their repercussions on the social life of the community" (D.N. Majumdar, *Races and Cultures of India*, Bombay 1961, pp. 278-79).

Furer-Haimendorf suggests that the institution of youth-dormitories was diffused over the Indian sub-continent by a neolithic agricultural civilization spread over a very wide area including Assam, the Himalaya, Burma, Malaysia, and Indonesia. The migration into India of these tribes, who lived in more or less permanent agricultural settlements, originated, he believes, in the Naga Hills of Assam. One movement followed a course westwards along the southern Himalaya slopes as far as Garhwal, the other south-westwards into the hills of Bihar and Orissa, probably penetrating into the western Ghats, and as far south as the Malabar and Nilgiri hills, Youth-dormitories are to be found among the Nāgas of Assam, a number of Munda and Dravidian-speaking tribes of Bihār, Orissa, and Bastar, semi-nomadic forest tribes of south-west India, the Kotas and other tribes of the Nilgiris, and the cattle-breeding, semi-nomadic Bhotias of Garhwal and Almora.

The heterodox sects had strong tribal connections, both ethnic and cultural; their institutions of *vihāra* (assembly hall, with a village-hall character) and *saṁgha* were derived from the tribal council and men's club; the origins of much their symbolism and their architectural prototypes must be sought in tribal culture, their segregation of the unmarried reveals a cultural nostalgia for the life of the food-gatherer, and a preference for choosing retreats near tribal cult-sites endorses this trend.

4226 **शयनासन**

Śayanāsana : bed.

4227 **शयनासन-भागज्ञा**

Śayanāsana-bhāgajñā : woman expert in arranging beds seats (*NS*, XXIV.30).

4228 **शयनीयम्**

Śayanīyam : bed.

4229 **शयनोपचार-कला**

Śayanopacāra-kalā : arts which are performed on the bed, 16 in number (*Kāmasūtra*, 1.3. 17-18).

4230 **शय्या**

Śayyā : bed, couch, (b) the unchangeableness of words is known as *maitrī*, *pāka* or *śayyā* in Sanskrit poetics. Vidyānātha's (*Pratāpa*.p. 767) definition of *śayyā* is: या पदानां परान्यौन्यमैत्री शय्येति कथ्यते it is the repose of words in their mutual favourableness like the repose of the body in a bed. The mutual friendship of words so close that they cannot be replaced by their synonymous constitute what is called *sayyā*. Mallinātha explains it as under:

> पदानां परिवृत्तिर्वैमुख्यं विनिमयासहिष्णुत्वम् ।
> एतदेव मैत्री शय्याति चाख्यायते यथास्मदीयश्लोके चन्द्रोदये
> निशाकरस्पर्शान्निशया निर्वृतात्मना ।
> अमी स्तम्भादयो भावा व्यऽन्ते रज्यमानया ॥
>
> Here we cannot replace निशया by क्षपया अत्र निशादीपदस्थाने क्षपादिपदान्तरप्रक्षेपे पदानां परस्परमैत्रीभङ्गः ।

This is one sort of *pāka*, viz. *sabdapāka* or maturity of expression that comes from a long study of good poetic works. But this felicity of expression, *Vāg-vidagdhatā*, as Bhāmaha calls it, is useless without a high poetic power, which comes very rarely to some one only from poetic genius of high order. By itself it is like possesing wealth without modesty and hight without the moon:

> विनयेन विना का श्रीः का निशा शशिना विना ।
> रहिता सत्कवित्वेन कीदृशी वाग्विदधता ॥

गुरोरादेशादध्येतुं शास्त्रं जडधियोऽप्यलम् ।
काव्यं तु जायते जातु कस्यचित् प्रतिभावतः ॥
(*Bhāmahālaṅkāra*, 1.4-5).

Thus what is wanted in poetry is not *śabda-pāda* alone, but *artha-pāka* also. *Arthapāka* is *arthagambhīrimā*—depth of sense. It is of various sorts, of which *drākṣāpāka* and *nārikelapāka* are mentioned by Vidyānātha (*Ibid.*, p.67).

आर्थगम्भीरिमा पाकः स द्विधा हृदयंगमः ।
द्राक्षापाको नारिकेलपाकश्च प्रस्फुटान्तरौ ॥

These varieties are brought about by different tastes of different poetic sentiments, like varieties of food. Without *pratibhā* or poetic genius such a charm in expression and sense (*śabdacamatkāra* and *arthacamatkāra*) cannot be brought about, and Bhāmaha, therefore, very rightly says:

काव्यं तु जायते कस्यचित् प्रतिभावतः ।

4231 **शरण**

Śaraṇa : literally means taking refuge; protection.

4232 **शरणागति**

Śaraṇāgati : complete self-surrender (*Gītā*, XVII.66) which is due to individual's feeling of utter helplessness.

4233 **शर-मुद्रा**

Śara-mudrā : occurs in *BT.* "Make the two palms upturned and bring the right one near the right ear. Then uphold the left one and extend it forward. The thumb and fore-finger should be made joined by tips in a pose of a circle and the other fingers are to be extended in another. This will make a *śara-mudrā*—a gesture of an arrow". (b) The gesture symbolizing an arrow. Making loosely joined the thumb fore, middle and ring fingers to symbolize an arrow of the vaiṣṇavite cult (*VD*).

4234 **शरीर**

Śarīra : the body *per se* is the medium of movement in acting and conversation. Therefore, the analysis of the action of different limbs, which Bharata does, is the only way of studying the role of bodily action. As has been observed in contemporary acting theory in the west: "The purpose of dividing body into individual units is twofold: to discover out of the total number of things the body can communicate by movement what kind of pantomimic action each can best project and by capitalizing on this knowledge, to increase by practice the expressiveness of each part.... the human body is singularly susceptible to division. the units are legs and feet, arms and hands, head and face, and torso and shoulders.... the most utilization of all divisions of body, the arms and hands have many functions and serve many purpose". (Jerry Blunt, *The Composite Art of Acting*, 1956, pp. 379, 383). (b) *Kaṭhopaniṣad* (1.3) treats body as a chariot: *Śarīram rathameva tu.* The Upaniṣadic idea symbolizes body with a chariot and the soul the charioteer. *Purāṇas* have explained this in detail. Thus, the body is the chariot, driven by five horses of five sense-organs. Merit and demerit are its two wheels; *sattva, rajas* and *tamas* its benners. The five breath are its support. Mind is its whip and intellect its charioteer. Heart is seat. Happiness and unhappiness are its axis.

4235 **शरीरज**

Śarīraja : one of the three divisions of *āṅgika* (body gesture).

4236 **शरीरधातु**

Śarīradhātu : chief constituent of body.

4237 **शरीराकृतिविज्ञान**

Śarīrākṛtivajñāna : body sign—auspicious and unauspicious.

Physical characteristics were often regarded as indicative of rank both by non-elites and elites in the society. The brāhmaṇical nightmare of a catasysmic upheavel, as evoked by the *Vāyu Purāṇa* (58:59), had in it the image of Śūdras with teeth as white as those of members of the higher *varṇas.* Even under less mythical circumstances the rural elite have been known for their aversion to shaling any of their own distinctive physical style with their social inferiors.

Many minute physical characteristics of a woman have been mentioned by the *Purāṇas.* Body, turning, smell, countenance, disposition, voice, gait and complexion are the points mentioned in this context:

वपुरावर्तगन्धश्चच्छाया सत्वं स्वरो गतिः ।
वर्णश्चेत्यष्टधा प्रोक्ता बुधैर्लक्षणभूमिका ॥
(*Sk. P.*, IV. 37.2)

A praiseworthy woman is expected to be beautiful and attractive in all her limbs, she should have the gait of an infatuated female elephant; her buttocks should be fleshy and large, eyes like infatuated pigeon; she should be slender without hair on her body and her hair should be profuse and dark; her feet should be even and touching the ground; her breasts should be close-built (and not hanging down); her navel should be whirling to the right side; the private organ should be like the leaf of the *aśvattha* tree; ankles should be concealed; her navel-pit should be as deep as to get in the thumb; her stomach should not be hanging loose (*Agni. P.* 244.1-4). A good woman is not given to harsh talk; she has no veins protruding; her eye-brows are not joined together (*Ibid.* 5-6).

The *Garuḍa Purāṇa* (1.64.3) mentions various disqualifications for a woman and says that with them her husband would die. They are: crooked hair; rounded eyes; hairy breasts and sides; the little toe and the next toe not touching the ground when she stands; gait causing tremor in the ground.

4238 **शलभासन**

Śalabhāsana : a posture in *yoga*' after *bhujaṅgāsana* comes *śalabhāsana*. Lie on the ground, face downward, and the hands under the thighs. Stiften the body, raise the legs and also the head as in *bhujaṅgāsana*. Lift the legs, thighs, and lower portion of the abdomen. While raising the head and legs, you must inhale, and retain the breath until you finish the *āsana*. This may be repeated five or six times.

This *āsana* gives a posterior curvature to the spine and is a counterpose of *sarvāṅgāsana* and *halāsana*. It gives good exercise to the abdomen and relieves constipation. It tones up the abdominal organs, viz. liver, kidneys, etc., and removes several diseases of the stomach and bowels. The digestive fire is increased and dyspepsia removed.

4239 **शव-मुद्रा**

Śava-mudrā : gesture of corpse. "Make the eyes half-shut, face deformed, the pair of arms extremely loose and the neck in the same position. This is the *śava-mudrā*, that checks immature death" (*BT*).

In Bastar, a dead body whether male or female is taken round the pyre three times before it is placed on it.

4240 **शवासन**

Śavāsana : This is an *āsana* for relaxation of all the nerves and muscles. This should be performed after all the *āsanas*. as a last item.

Lie flat on the back keeping the hands on the ground by the sides, and stretch the legs quite straight. Keep the heels and toes separated. Close the eyes and breathe slowly. Now relax all muscles, nerves and organs. The relaxation process should start from the toes and proceed upwards, through all the organs, heart, chest and brain.

It gives rest to the body, mind, and soul. Relaxation is a very important factor in the regime of *yoga* exercise. The organs that are put on severe strain while performing *āsanas*, demand relaxation and rest. In *śavāsana*, prompt and efficient relaxation is ensured.

4241 **शशक-मुद्रा**

Śaśaka-mudrā : the *talapatāka* hand is moved horizontally to indicate a hare (*Mirror of Gesture*, pp. 49-50).

4242 **शश-कर्णी-मुद्रा**

Śaśakarṇī-mudrā : making two hands upturned, join both the thumbs with fore-fingers and press both the wrists together. This is called *Śaśakarṇī*. (*VD*).

4243 **शश (नायक)**

***Śaśa* (*nāyaka*)** : the Hare-man. The man whose organ is six *aṅgulas* in length who is a good mate for a lotus-lady is the Hare-man (*Kāmasūtra*, 2.1.1).

4244 **शश-प्लुतक**

Śaśa-plutaka : the jump of a hare-nailprint. The *Kāmasūtra* (2.4. 19-20) explains 'when five marks with the nails are made close to one another near the nipple of the breast, it is called "the jump of a hare". Ratnākara (*Haravijaya*, 27.70) has used this mark. Dāmodaragupta (*Kuṭṭanīmatam*, 403) has seen this mark on the lips, throat and breasts of a lady named Ketakī:

adhare binduḥ kaṇṭhe maṇimālā
stanayuge śaśaplutakam ।
tava sūcayanti ketaki
kusumāyudha-śāstrapaṇḍitam ramaṇam ॥

4245 **शशाङ्क-मुद्रा**

Śaśāṅka-mudrā : gesture of the Moon. If the thumb of the *jaṭā* (q.v.) style is extended flat and joined with the head, it is *śaśāṅka* (*VD*).

4246 **शशाङ्कासन**

Śaśāṅkāsana :sit in the posture of *vajrāsana* and take both the hands above your head in a straight line. Breath in. Bend forward, releasing the breath slowly. The forehead and hands should reach the ground simultaneously. Breathe in, come back slowly to the original position. This posture cures dysentery. Liver and kidney disorders are also cured. Backache is relieved.

4247 **शाक्त**

Śākta : (a) worshipper of *Śakti* , teacher, (b) a sentence rich in compounds, where the sense of case-endings is expressed by compounds themselves. (c) pertaining to the worship of Devī.

4248 **शाखा**

Śākhā : branching out. *Āṅgika* is divided into *mukhaja*, *śarīraja* and *ceṣṭākṛta*. The *ceṣṭākṛta* has further three divisions. One of them is *śākhā*. The *śākhā* type of *āṅgikābhinaya* belongs mostly to the sphere of dancing, for here the theme is represented through the use of the head, face, thighs, feet and hands (*NS*, XXIV.45). What Śakuntalā and her friends present through descriptivity miming the watering of plants showing the diverse vegetation of the garden with their whole bodies and movements of their limbs is called branching out" (*śākhā*).

In a way, the whole gesticulation is *śākhā*. Kālidāsa refers to the acting of Mālavikā as *śākhāyoniḥ* (resulting from the gestures of various limbs). *SR* (VII.37) defines *śākhā* as *vicitra karavartanā* (i.e. the striking graceful movements of hands). This limited meaning of *śākhā* is not found in *NS*. The meaning of *śākhā* limited to the graceful hand gestures can be understood in the following manner. The single and double hand gestures were used to indicate more and more things and ideas as we find, in the *Cākyār* tradition the whole story is expressed by hand gestures i.e. *mudrās* alone. Hence, the importance of hand gestures in the *śākhā* became so great that *śākhā* denoted hand gestures only.

4249 **शाखासन्देश**

Śākhāsandeśa : bough message, bough-symbol helped to expand semantic range of the message in tribal areas. Kol used this symbol in the period of insurgency. Muria and other tribes used it in Bastar in their rebellious moods. Known as *dheori* in the Kol-region, this was despatched from one party of Kols to another as a signal from them to join expeditiously and to engage in any contemplated exploit. The receiving party was then expected to unite with the one issuing the summons before the leaves of the branch faded away.

It was the mango tree which Kols and the tribes of Bastar preferred for this purpose. By contrast, the Santals of Birbhum and the Saora of Jeypore taluk in the Koraput were to use *sāl* and jack branches to rally their fellow tribesmen for rebellion. Diversity such as this did nothing however to weaken the symbolism common to all of them. Verrier Elwin identified the Saora jack branch as "a well-recognized form of the fiery cross summoning villagers. to assemble at a fixed time and place", and the anonymous author of the *Calcutta Review* (1856) article at the hool described the *sāl* bough as "a symbol which like the fiery torch in old Highland gatherings, appears to have held, either by a general ancient custom, or more probably a preconcerned recognition, a secret attached meaning" (Elwin:254). The sign in both instances was categorized as one that had its meaning assigned to it by convention, that is a symbol and as such, was evocative, for all British observers, of the most celebrated symbol of that kind within their own tradition.

The circulation of a branch was a commonly understood signal for communal action. Its use in the course of the hool emphasized, once again the character of the uprising as a form of corporate activity.

4250 **शाण्डिल्य-विद्या**

Śāṇḍilya-vidyā : the secret knowledge taught in *Chāndogya* (III.14).

4251 **शातोदरी**

Śātodarī : of slender waist.

4252 **शान्त**

Śānta : (a) calm, quality of the Hare-man (*Anaṅgaraṅga*, 3.16) (b) spiritual quetitude, serenity, Bharata mentions detachment (*nirveda*) as its basis. The art of the quetistics. The images and sketches, which are suggestive of meditation, placid look, saintly behaviour, pious mood etc. suggest of the quetistic sentiment (*VD*, III, 43-10). (c) the relationship of quietness with God. It is one of the five *ratis* and *ratas* i.e., emotions and instincts. At the lowest stage the attachment of God which may enable the realisation of god is *śānta-rati*, which further develops into *prema* or love (*Caitanya-caritāmṛta*, II.19).

4253 **शान्त-मुद्रा**

Śānta-mudrā : "one should style this most powerful *mudrā* sitting by the style of *svastikāsana*. Placing flat the left palm on the navel region and the two thumbs over there, it makes one of the best *mudrā* called *śānta*, which may control the three-fold worlds" (*BT*).

4254 **शान्तरसदृष्टि**

Śāntarasadṛṣti : the placid look *(VD*, III.1.30-31).

4255 **शान्ति**

Śānti : rites performed to counteract inauspicious effect. (b) pacification, tranquillity, peace, welfare, happiness, bliss. (c) peace, the state in which the passions are extinguished. (d) quiescence. is not the end, not the final goal; it is merely the temporary goal for one who is involved in activity. It is the ultimate solution to the problem of cycles of activity. It has been suggested that the appearance of stillness resulting from two equal and opposite forces underlies the symbolism of the mathematical zero, which the ancient Indians invested: 'Zero is the transition-point between opposite, it symbolizes the true balance within divergent tendencies. Zero has now taken on, in a more deepened and philosophical way, the functions earlier assigned to the number three. Zero is the productive of all and none, the matrix of positive and negative, of addition and substraction, of generating and destroying capacities. It is the productive point of indifference and balance. between the two opposites of extreme greatness—*aṇu—ākāśa* and extreme greatness—*aṇu* (Heimann, 1964.97-98). In Indian mythology too, quiescence is an apparent calm which is in fact a perfectly balanced tension. The famous *śānti-mantra* of *Atharva Veda* (XIX.9) runs as follows:

Now let the earth still, and the air, the sky,
The waters, the herbs, the trees be still.
And let the gods give me stillness, and quiet come from
These calls for quiet.
With these quiet calls that assure everything,
I give peace to the terrible here,
To the cruel here, to the evil.
Let them, now quiet, mean well;
Let everything be good to us.

4256 **शापः**

Śāpaḥ : imprecation, curse. It occurs in situations of positive or negative surprise, using mainly obscene and sacred words. *Śāpaśāsanapaṭa* 'a scroll of cursing' *śāpita* 'bound by oath'. Mainly there are two types of curses in Sanskrit literature: (a) homoeopathic curses are those in which a character is cursed to experience an exaggeration of that aspect of his nature which prompted the curse. (b) heteropathic curses being a reversal of aspect and/or experience. Reversed roles occur in passages in which a character plays a role directly opposed to his usual nature, or in which two characters exchange roles; reversed episodes are those which appear out of their usual sequence in the myth, often in place of episodes of a similar structure or symbolism. Some of the more significant curses are indicated below: sex curses lust, curse of rebirth, curse of destruction, curse to be young, curse to be static like stone, curse to become eunuch, curse to be impregnated, etc.

A cursing is a verbal dispute. It requires a public setting—an audience—and one of the participants is thus usually on the road, directing at someone. The main content of cursing turns out to be interchanges of 'teasing' and 'boasting'. The aim is to shame the person publicly (even though the cursing is officially a personal interchange) by unveiling some private behaviour he wished kept hidden or that is talked about but never to his face. Sometimes between younger women things will turn into a fight, in which case the aim is still to shame by unveiling tearing off clothes—thus giving entertainment to the men.

As with boasting (*Vikatthanā*), cursing exhibits, a nice combination of the expressive and the rhetorical. In general one is felt to resort to cursing when carried away by strong feelings so that one can't help it. In general it is women's behaviour, as 'argument' is men's. One breaks away into it. That it is in fact deeply embedded can be seen in the fact that some middle-class town women will subject themselves to public ridicule for engaging in this lower-class behaviour when the provocation is great enough. On the other hand all cursings are fundamentally theatrical and public events, and as such they are highly stylized. The public theatrical quality of cursing is supported by the fact that it is a learned behaviour in which one may take pride. In neither cursing nor argument does anyone stoop to answer directly to other's accusation or position. There is a kind of scanning process at work which listens with multiple attention and which ultimately determines which voice will prevail.

4257 **शाब्दबोध**

Śābdabodha : verbal knowledge. Common sense takes verbal knowledge to be less reliable than perception and inference. For in acquiring verbal knowledge we have to depend essentially upon the reliability of speaker, upon his honesty, competence and authority. Such a person is called *āpta.* (b) knowledge derived from word is twofold: *abhihitānvayavāda* and *anvitābhidhānavāda.*

4258 **शाब्दिक**

Śābdika : a grammarian.

4259 **शाब्दी-भावाना**

Śābdī-bhāvanā : verbal impression, verbal experience, peculiar activity of some productive agent which tends to make a person act.

4260 **शाम्भवी-दीक्षा**

Śāmbhavī-dīkṣā : a higher form of initiation which is conducted by the touch, or a glance, or the will of the *guru.* It is connected with the secret cult of Kāmeśvarī (*Nityotsaya*, 9).

4261 **शाम्भवी-मुद्रा**

Śāmbhavī-mudrā : direct your eyes towards the middle of the eyebrows and meditate upon your own self. This practice controls the thoughts and the breath. The mind is suspended within a short time and entrance into the psychic world becomes easier. It is a very important technique for passing into the astral domain. Insomnia is cured by the practice of this *mudrā.*

4262 **शारीर**

Śārīra : of the limbs, that which relates to the body. The second division of physical gesticulation, (*āngika abhinaya*). In this division, the *NS* treats the movements of hand, breast, sides, waist and legs with their parts, i.e. shanks, thighs and feet. In this division the hand gestures are vey important. The hand is very eloquent in the physical gesticulation. The number of hand poses is sixty-four in all.

4263 **शार्मेय-मुद्रा**

Śārmeya-mudrā : The little finger of the *patāka*-hand (*madhya patāka*) is bent to indicate a dog (*Mirror of Gesture*, pp. 49-50).

4264 **शालभञ्जिका**

Śālabhañjikā : statue, engraved idol, prostitute. Cp. *Viddhaśālabhañjikā.* (Fig. 4264)

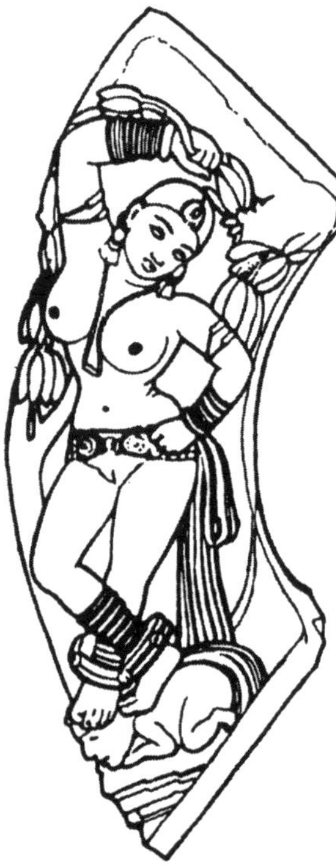

Fig. – (4264)

4265 **शालाक्यतन्त्र**

Śālākyatantra : science dealing with the upper limbs of the body (ear, eyes, nose, etc).

4266 **शाली**

Śālī : wife's younger sister=*kelikūcikā* 'black cumin'.

4267 **शासन**

Śāsana : a communication (*A*, 2.9.27, 2.28.20, 12.3.13). In its broadest sense, the word *śāsana* refers to process in which a response is evoked (or elicited or induced) by a message sent and received. There are three elementary elements, according to that definition: sending a message, receiving a message, and responding to that message.

4268 **शिक्षा**

Śikṣā : one of the six *Vedāṅgas* teaching place of articulation and other things regarding vowels and consonants.

4269 **शिक्षा-मुद्रा**

Śikṣā-mudrā : gesture symbolizing *śikṣā*—one of the *Vedāṅgas.* if the hand of the *Sāmaveda* (q.v.) is made down turned, it is *śikṣā* (*VD*); (b) framing a fist on the thumb make its head oblique and the fore-finger touch the fist. This makes the gesture of *śikṣā* (*VD*).

4270 **शिखण्ड**

Śikhaṇḍa : tuft of hair left on sides or on crown of head at tonsure, the knotted point of *śikhā.*

4271 **शिखर-हस्त**

Śikhara hasta : spire, the thumb of the *muṣṭi* is raised; same as *kartarīmukha* but the thumb position is different (*Hastalakṣaṇadīpikā*). It is used in iconography for holding weapons. The palm is raised outwards. The four fingers are bent into the palm, and thumb is extended straight out. It is used to express silence, questioning, sound of a bell, pillar, husband, saying no, embrace, stead fastness, hero, friend, sapphire and intensity. When the gesture of *muṣṭi* is raised up with the thumb, it is called the *śikhara* (*NS*, IX.50). It is also used to represent holding of reins, whips, goad and bow; throwing a javelin or spike; dyeing the lower lip and feet and raising up hair. (Fig. 4271)

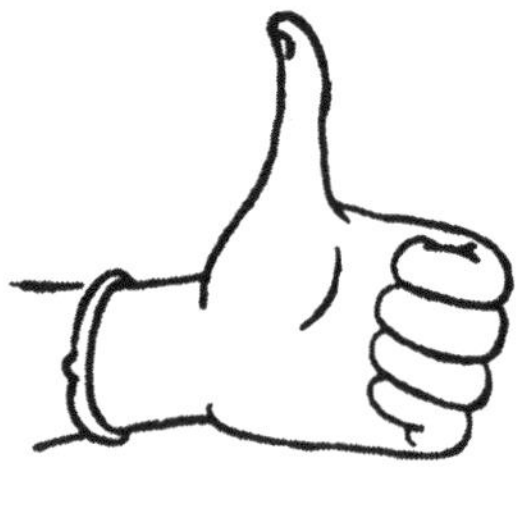

Fig. – (4271)

4272 **शिखरिदशना**

Śikharidaśanā : lady whose teeth are sharp (*Megha.*, 84).

4273 **शिखाज**

Śikhā : top-knot with locks of hair. Elaborate rules about keeping locks of hair according to *gotra* are laid down in *Dharmaśāstra.* (b) pig-tail. There seems to be a custom of the sale of a son. The sale of the son is indicated in the story of the sage Viśvāmitra (*Bhrahmavaivarta, Prakṛtikhaṇḍa.* 30.14). The custom reflected in the sale is that the person to be sold was to be tied by pig-tail at the neck:

गले वध्वा मध्यमं पुत्रं औरसं शिखया ।
तं तु गले वध्वा विक्रीतम् ।

4274 **शिखा मुद्रा**

Śikhā-mudrā : make a round fist, hide all but the middle fingers inside it and raise the middle one. This is *śikhā* (*VD*).

4275 **शिञ्जा**
Śiñjā : tinkle, tinkling of ornaments.

4276 **शिथिल समाधि**
Śithila-samādhi : imperfect concentration of the artist.

4277 **शिबिका**
Śibikā : the palanquin. The palanquin was a privileged form of transport in India. Some of the foreign powers who had acquired territorial bases in the subcontinent used this to indicate their superior standing as rulers. In Bombay under Prtuguese occupation no native was ever allowed to ride in a palanquin except with the Viceroy's permission, a practice which the British kept in force in their turn at least until 1788 (Russell and Hiralal, III.253). In rural India the native elite, especially the big landlords, continued for a long time to treat the palanquin as a part of the insignia of their authority and on one of inferior standing was allowed to ride in it through their residential villages. If a Zamindar was really powerful, even some junior white officials could risk being thrown out of his village for violating this code (C. Datta, *Purnakathā*, Vol.I, Calcutta 1962. 4-5). It was therefore symptomatic of a radical inversion in rural society that the peasants should publicly appropriate such vehicles. They did so when during the Rangpur insurrection they carried around their leader, Dirjanarain, in a palanquin. Nothing could have been more topsy-turvy than that. For as we know from Ratiram's ballad on this event, no one could pass through the hated Debi Sinha's estate in that district in any form of transport whatsoever without being beaten up by his *paiks* and that too in the most defiling manner—that is, with shoes (*pāike mārejūtā*).

In colonial India, there was a professional class of the litter-bearer known as *kahār.* When carts could not travel owing to the absence of roads, the litter was the regular mode of conveyance of those who could afford it and did not ride. Buchanan (*Eastern India,* ii.426) remarks: "Few or not except some chief native officers of Government kept bearers in constant pay: but men of large estates give farms at low rent to their bearers who are ready at a call and receive food when employed". A superior kind of litter used by rich women had a doomed roof supported on eight pillars with side-boards like Venetian blinds; and was carried on two poles secured to the sides beneath the roof. It was called *kharakhariā* in imitation of the rattling of the blinds when in motion. The *pālkī* or ordinary litter consisted of a couch slung under a long bamboo, which formed an arch over it. Over the arch was suspended a tier made of cloth, which served to screen the passenger from sun and rain. A third kind was the *caupāl* or square both open at the sides and slung on a bamboo; the passenger sat doubled up inside this. It was sometimes the case that the *caupāl* was hung considerably beneath the bamboo and the passenger was miserably dragged by dust and mud. Afterwards *Regular litters* were so little used that they became the rare commodity in villages; but when required, they were readily improvised by slinging a native wooden cot from two poles by strings of bamboo-fibre.

Under the native government the privilege of riding in a planquin was a mark of distinction; and it was enforced that no native could thus enter into the area of Madras and Bombay without the permission of the Governor; such permission being recorded in order book at the gates of the fort and usually granted only to a few. Who were lame or otherwise incapacitated. When General Medows assumed the office of Governor of Bombay in 1788 some Parasīs waited on him and begged for the removal of this restriction; to which the Governor replied: "So long as you do not force me to ride in this machine he may who likes it"; and so the rule was abrogated (Moor, *Hindu Infanticide,* 91). A passage from *Hobson-Jobson*, however, shows that the Portuguese were much stricter in this respect: "In 1591 a proclamation of the Viceroy, Matthias 'Alboquerque ordered 'that no person of what quality or condition' soever, shall go in a palanquin without my express licence, save they be over sixty years of age, to be first proved before the Auditor-General of Police. and those who contravene this shall pay a penalty of 200 cruzados, and persons of mean estate the half, the palanquins and their belongings to be forfeited, and the *bois* or *moucos* who carry such palanquins shall be condemned to His Majesty's galleys'. The meaning of the last sentence appears to be that the bearers were considered as slaves, and were forfeited to the king's service as a punishment to their owner. As the unauthorised use of this conveyance was so severely punished it would appear that riding in a palanquin must have been a privilege of nobility.

As a means of conveyance the litter is still held sacred in the tribal society. It is known as *ḍoli* in the tribal regions of Madhya Pradesh. Tribes carry their gods on this litter during the occasion of *jātrā* festival. Crooke gives an instance of the regard paid to it.

In the feudal India there were many restrictions regarding the use of *ḍhol* (drum) and palanquin for carrying bride and bridegroom by the low-castes. In the Gwalior-region, the *camār* used *camār-nāts,* special kind of small drums instead of *ḍhol* (big drum). These restrictions, after Zamindari abolition could not last long. The conflict of the *Kacchī* and the *Ṭhākur* on the use of *ḍhol* was there for a short time.

Now the *ḍhol* and palanquin can be used by all castes. *Ḍhols* are used by all the castes, but the *camār* and *korī* do not use palanquin, as they do not get any body to lift and carry it (Mutatkar, R.K., *Caste Dimensions in a Village*, Pune 1978, 121).

4278 **शिरस्**

Śiras : movement of the head. The *NS* (VIII. 18-37) mentions thirteen basic movements of the head. The *Abhinayadarpaṇa* (49-62) mentions nine movements of the head. The *SR* (VII.43-72) follows the *NS* closely and repeats the thirteen movements mentioned in the *NS*. The *Mirror of Gesture* enumerates twenty-four movements of the head. Thirteen gestures of the head enumerated in *NS* are as follows: *ākaṁpita, kampita, dhūta, vidhūta, parivarta, udvāhita, avadhūta, añcita, nihañcita, parāvṛtta, utkṣipta, adhogata* and *parilolita*. The *VD* accepts those thirteen gestures of the head with an exception of *nikuñcita* in the place of *nihañcita*, implying also the same idea (Part III,Vol.I, pp. 60-61).

4279 **शिरसाकृतिविज्ञान**

Śirasākṛtivijñāna : head sign. If the head is like a canopy (*chatrākāra*), the person would be a king; if it is flat, the early death of his father; if it is flat, the early death of his father, if it is circular, or round (*parimaṇḍalākāra*), the person is given to sin and is poor (*Garuḍa*. 65.67). A full moon-shaped head indicates kingship; an uneven one indicates poverty and a long head indicates sorrow. *Purāṇas* appear to copy the idea from *Bṛhat-Saṁhitā* (LXVIII) of Varāhamihira which records "Men with round head become rich in cattle; with one resembling an umbrella—kings; with a flat one, murderers of parents; with one like a turban (lit. skul), long-lived; with a pot-like head, wanderers or tourists; with a double head, sinners and penniless; with a depressed head, illustrious; and with a too much depressed one, miserable. Vide the following:

उत्क्रान्तिदो निम्नशिरा अल्पोपहत एव च ।
छत्राकारशिरा राजा गवाढ्यः परिमण्डलैः ।
विषमं तद्दरिद्राणां शिरो दीर्घं चिरायुषम् ।
नागकुम्भशिरा राजा समं सर्वत्र भोगिनाम् ॥

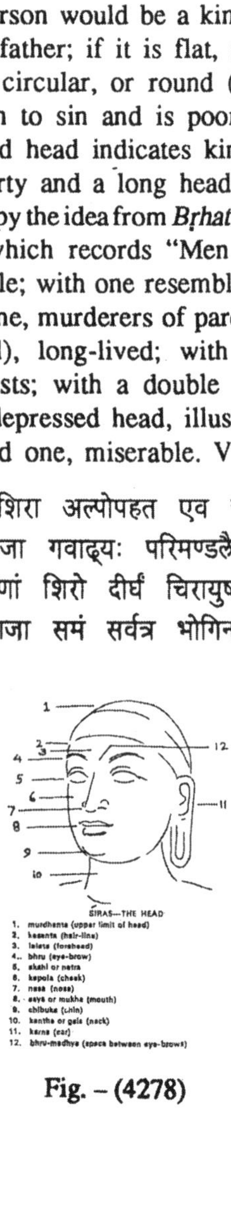

Fig. – (4278)

4280 **शिरः कम्पेन प्रतिवचनम्**

Śiraḥ kampena prativacanam : head nod; Replies by shakes of head (*Kāmasūtra*, 3.2.18). Śiva was assiduously asking Pārvatī a question in order to start a conversation even on some irrelevant topic. Pārvatī looked at him and gave a reply consisting on a nod of the head: *Pārvatī mūrdhakampanamayam uttaram dadau* (*Kumāra*, 8.6). This is a type of the Head Nod. Here the head moves vertically up and down one or more times, with the down elements stronger than the up elements. Essentially this is an incipient bowing action, with the head starting to make a bow and then stopping short. Since bowing is part of a classical system of submissive body-lowering, it is no surprising to find that the Head Nod occurs almost everywhere in Indian literature and that whenever it does occur, it is always a 'yes' sign, never a 'no except in Maharashtra. Even remote tribes, such as the Gonds, are found to using the Head Nod for yes. So the Head Nod is a Vedic symbol, thousands of years old. In addition to the Indians, the Head Nod has also been recorded in the Amazonian Indans, Eskimos, Fuegians, Papuans, Samoans, Balinese, Malaya, Japanese, Chinese, and a number of African tibes. It is also used by nearly all whites in Europe, north and south America, Australia, and New Zealand.

The occurrence of eyes' (*ām*) and head nods in conversations convey respect towards, and agreement with, a listener; that is serve as social reinforcers. These cues may also be used to regulate another's speech - suggest that the speaker continue, or prompts the listener to take over when the speaker stops talking. Thus, nodding is one of the most important ways in which a conversational partner's speech is reinforced.

4281 **शिरस्त्र**

Śirastra : head-dress.

4282 **शिरस्त्राण**

Śirastrāṇa : turban, helmet. The turban formed an important part of the attire; but it was a taboo to hear the *Kathā* (purāṇic exposition) with a turban on (*Skanda*., II. 1.27.4; *Śiva Māhātmya*. 6.42):

सोष्णीषमस्तका ये च कथां शृण्वन्ति पावनीम् ।
ते बालकाः प्रजायन्ते पापिनो मनुजाधमाः ॥

(*Skanda*., *Ibid.*)

सोष्णीषमस्तका ये च शृण्वन्तीमां कथां नराः ।
तत्पुत्राश्च प्रजायन्ते पापिनः कुलदूषकाः ॥

Śirastrāṇa is a common accessary which speaks volumes. But in recent times it is no longer so voluminous, instead it is generally relegated to weddings, formal events, eccentrics and business-men. Possibly this indicates a more egalitarian society.

4283 **शिरा**

Śirā : vein, nerve.

4284 **शिरोऽभिषेक**

Śiro'bhiśeka : sprinkling of the holy water on the couple's head during marriage ceremony (*Śiva*, II.46).

4285 **शिरोरुह**

Śiroruha : hair of the head. Hair has magical significance in India as in many other parts of the world. It is shaved at a funeral or when someone is to be readmitted into caste after excommunication. It is dangerous to allow hair-clippings to fall into the wrong hands. In the *Ālhākhaṇḍa,* Indul cuts off the hair of Sema the witch and thus destroys her power. On the other hand, women in South India sometimes sow seed with their hair hanging loose so that the rice may grow luxuriantly and have long stalks (L.K.A. Ayer, *The Mysore Tribes and Castes*, 1935.I.265). And there is a tradition in Mandla (M.P.) that until hair grew on the bodies of men, the crops did not grow in their fields (Elwin, 1946. 46).

Elsewhere in aboriginal India, there is an association of hair with the dangerous, the spiritually electric, the taboo. The Juang believe that woman originally had a hair growing from her tongue and so went about cursing people.

But here of course, it is the erotic appeal of hair, and especially of a woman's hair, that interests us. In seventeenth century England, hair was a noose or net to catch the heart. The countess, in Marston's *Fawn*, when bidden to put up her hair before execution, exclaims,

> O these golden nets
> That have ensnared so many wanton youths.
> The tresses of Milton's Eve were long and not displeasing to Adam:
> She, as a veil down to the slender waist,
> Her unadorned golden tresses wore
> Dishevelled, but in wanton ringlets waved,
> As the vine curls her tendrils.

T.S. Eliot loves hair: his hyacinth girl has 'her hair over her arms and her arms full of flowers'; and there is a lovely picture of

> Brown hair over her mouth blown
> Lilac and brown hair;
> Distraction.

In classical Indian opinion the five beauties of women were hair, flesh, bone, skin and youth (Penzer, VIII.228). In Kālidāsa's *Raghuvaṃśa*, Aja laments over his dead wife crying:

> Your bee-black hair from which the flowers are peeping,
> Dear, wavy hair that I have loved so well,
> Stirs in the wind until I think you sleeping,
> Soon to return and make my glad heart swell.

In the Bengal ballads there are many references to the beauty of hair. Sen (III.XI) has suggested that perhaps Bengal and Orissa owe their artistic manipulations of the hair forming into knots and Chignons of various fashions, to the Tibeto-Burman races in the north. A very superb description of manifold arrangements of the long and curly hair of women in which it is made to imitate scenes from human society and animal-life is found in the Maynāmati-songs (*Ibid.*).

The exiled princess Sannamala has long flowing hair that seems to kiss her feet. It is so beautiful that one could stake a lakh of rupees for that hair alone (Sen, III.210). And in the beautiful 'Shyam Ray' ballad we are shown the poor Dom girl reflecting how unworthy her wretched hut is for her princely lover. 'You will have to give up your golden bed and couch. But should you feel pain I will spread my long and flowing hair in the bed to make it easy for you. But afraid am I, since even a bed of flowers seems rough to you, that my hair may be found stiff. But should you dislike the bed of hair that I will spread for you, my breast may be found soft to lodge you in' (Sen, III. 210).

In South India, there is a famous story of a Morasu Okkalu girl of extraordinary beauty, whose hair was so luxuriant that she used it as a rope to lead her pet calf (Nanjundayya and Iyer, *Ibid.*, IV. 227).

In Chhattisgarh, hair is equally important as a means of erotic attraction, though the stress is not so much on its length or luxuriance as on the way it is tied. Hair should indeed be 'long and glossy as a horse's tail', but even so it looks best when it is well oiled, carefully parted and tied tightly on either side. A large bun, bound with gay-coloured woollen ribbons is much admired:

> Gently, gently, *mainā*, gently
> Carefully untie your long long hair
> Some take care to make the parting
> Some take care to tie the bun
> See it for a moment and the mind is taken
> Your body is the moon
> Your eyes are antelopes
> Long long is your hair
> My mind is for you
> Give me a quick embrace
> Take a bamboo comb

In your hand and tie the bun
Tie it with ribbons
Go with your uncovered head
Gently, gently, *mainā*, gently.

4286 **शिरोवेष्टनम्**

Śirovesṭanam : the head dress-display.

The clothing has three main functions: modesty, comfort, and display. The basic function of the head dress is to display the status, slotting the wearer neatly into a particular social category. This is the most ancient use of clothing, and it remains today of supreme importance.

In the colonial India it was not a matter of style or taste but of law laying down firm rules concerning the head dress permissible for each social class. There was a striking instance of the use of dress - the turban (*pagṛī*), to be precise - as a means of higher social status. This form of headgear carries much weight in many regions of rural India, with some local communities, such as the Balahi, it is only the headmen who have the right to wear this. In Gujarat this used to be an exclusive privilege of the dominant caste of Patidar, so that anyone of a lower caste risked being severely punished if he was tempted publicly to try it on. In Bastar, it was a matter of prestige to wear a *pagṛī* and the Raja used to confer it to the Majhis. It was the symbol of the chief rank of the pargana.

4287 **शिलीमुख-हस्त**

Śilīmukha hasta : gesture of the bee; Single hand gesture only mentioned in *Bālarāmabharata*. Similar to *Sandaṁśa* but with difference in finger position.

4288 **शिल्प**

Śilpa : icon, sculpture, art (Pali:*sippa*), any art or work of art, the practice of art, art as vocation taught by a master (*ācārya*), one who lives by his art, a professional. (b) the *NS* like ancient works viewed society in different strata. The *śilpa* was one of them. The bulk of the society was described as consisting of house-holders (*kuṭumbinaḥ*) who would be distinguished from the kings and religieux (*NS*, 1.118) on the one hand and the slaves and barbarians on the other. The real division amongst them was in terms of professions. It is the characteristics of these that the producer has to study carefully: *aneka-śilpajñātāni naika-karma-kriyāṇi ca* (*NS*, XIX.148).

The profession as found in the *NS* may broadly be divided into two categories viz., the *antaḥpura* (the service of the king in palace) and the *bāhya* (or outside).

4289 **शिल्पकम्**

Śilpakam : a form of *uparūpaka*.

4290 **शिल्पशास्त्र**

Śilpaśāstra : iconography. Lotman say: "The cultural function of the tension between the inner (closed) and the outer (open) spaces is clearly revealed in the structure of house (and other buildings). In making a house, man thereby partitions off a part of space which--in contrast with the outer sphere--is perceived as culturally assimilated and required. However, this initial opposition acquires cultural significance only against a background of continual breaches in the opposite direction". Thus, on the one hand, the close 'domestic' space begins to be perceived not as the antipode of the outside world, but as its model and analogue (for example, the temple as an image of the universe). In this case the regularity of the temple space is transferred to the outside world, suppressing the sphere of irregularity (the aggression of the inner space against the outside). On the other hand, some properties of the outside world penetrated into the inner world. Related to this is the attempt to distinguish 'the house within the house' (for example, the alter space is an inner sphere within an inner sphere). "A building acts as a man. It needs food as a man. It can fall ill and recover many times, and it will die. The architect is the mother and in even or eight months he will generate it".

4291 **शिव-मुद्रा**

Śiva-mudrā : put the right thumb into the left fist and join its nails on the back of the left fist. This gesture is named after *Śiva* (*VD*).

4292 **शिवलिङ्ग-हस्त**

Śivaliṅga-hasta : both hands gesture (*Abhinayadarpaṇa*), not mentioned in *NS*. Place the left hand flat in the *ardhacandra* style and put the right hand on it with the *Śikhara* style; it makes the gesture of *Śivaliṅga*. It is used to see and worship the same image. (Fig. 4292)

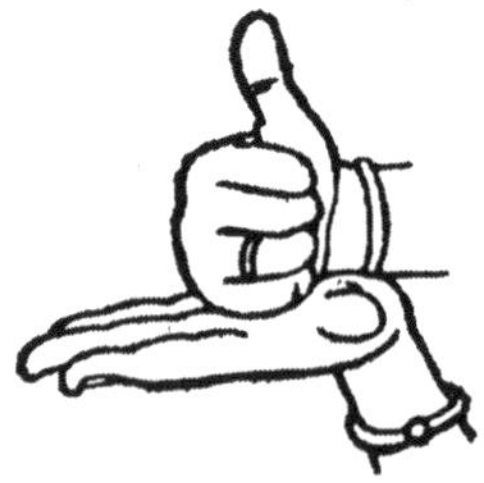

Fig. – (4292)

4293 **शिवहस्त**

Śivahasta : the hand of the preceptor which is purified by *mantras* when it is used to initiate someone in *Sparśa-dīkṣā* (Rāghava on *Śāradātilaka*, V.127-40).

4294 **शिवा**

Śivā : Pārvatī; female fox. This animal going to the left from right, or being at the left side is held to be a good sign by the *Vāmana Purāṇa* (42.14): *Śivā sthitā vāmatare ca bhāge.* According to *Garuḍa Purana* (1.67.20) the female fox may be passing by the left or the right side; while according to the *Brahma-vaivarta Purāṇa* (70.23) the female fox at the left is auspicious.

Varāhamihira has devoted a separate chapter on *Śivāruditam (Bṛhat-Saṁhitā,* XC). Accordingly, jackals are similar to dogs in effect, with the difference that dogs get passion for mating in the *Śiśira* (winter). The sound of *hū-hū* at the end of their howling, and *ṭā-ṭā* thereafter are auspicious; and all other sounds are said to be burning:

> श्वभिः शृगालाः सदृशाः फलेन
> विशेष एषां शिशिरे मदाप्तिः ।
> हूहूरुतान्ते परतश्च टाटा
> पूर्णः स्वरोऽन्ये कथिताः प्रदीप्ताः ॥

4295 **शिवि-हस्त**

Śivi-hasta : *kapittha hasta* waved forward represents the mythical king *Śivi* (*Mirror of Gesture,* p. 47).

4296 **शिशुक्रन्दीय**

Śiśukrandīya : a treatise dealing with the cry of children: *Śiśukrandanamadhikṛtya kṛto granthaḥ.*

4297 **शिश्न**

Śiśna : penis. *Śiṣ hiṁsāyām bhedane vā.* Trees and pillars are phallic symbols in Sanskrit literature.

4298 **शिश्नदेव**

Śiśnadeva : a non-Āryan worshipping phallus or indulging in sexual pleasure. Gods worshipped in phallic symbol and phallic worshippers. In *Ṛgveda* (VII. 27.5; X.99.3) Indra is depicted as crushing and exterminating the *Śiṣnadevas* or phallic worshippers.

4299 **शिश्नाकृतिविज्ञान**

Śiśnākṛtivijñāna : sizes and shapes of the penis. *Kāmasūtra* and the later erotic works have classified the males on the basis of the measurement of different lengths of the penis. A large penis is admired in the tribal society. Elwin (1949:360-61) gives several tribal versions of the myths of *vagina dentala* and *penis aculeatus* and relates them to the natural sadistic element of sex, (particularly the kind of biting and scratching described in *Kāmasūtra,*) to castration, impotence, defilement by menstruation blood, etc., several of these themes being pertinent to Śaiva mythology. Certainly the motif is related to the fear of harm or defilement by sex which plays such an important part in Hindu chastity and closely related misogyny of Hindu asceticism. These types of motifs of sexual death are common in the tribal as well as non-tribal societies.

4300 **शिष्ट**

Śiṣṭa : civilized. *Baudhāyana-Dharmasūtra* (1.1.6) has defined it as follows: "*Śiṣṭas,* forsooth, are those who are free from envy, free from pride, contented with a store of grain sufficient for ten days, free from covetousness, and free from hypocrisy, arrogance, greed, perplexity and anger. Those are called *śiṣṭas* who, in accordance with the sacred law, have studied the *Veda* together with its appendages, know how to draw inferences from that, and are able to adduce proofs perceptible by the sense from the revealed texts."

4301 **शिष्टाचार**

Śiṣṭācāra : etiquette. The relations of the various characters were governed by a series of rules of etiquette which were, no doubt, analogous to those prevailing in the society of the time: the names and titles given to the king, for example, varied according to the status of the character addressing him. Social freedom between the sexes being prohibited, a stranger is not allowed to speak to a lady who is not well acquainted with. Similarly it is considered immodest on the part of a woman to approach or speak to a stranger on any matter whatsoever. The only exception to this rule is when the lady is in peril of her life and the help of a man is needed to save her. It will be considered an insolence on the part of a stranger to help a lady out of a vehicle or a boat; and the lady and her husband, if he is with her, will resent it. On the part of a friend, such an act will be considered officious. An orthodox Hindu lady, offered a seat in a bus by a stranger, may frown upon him instead of thanking him. A wayfarer asking his way of a Hindu lady in a street may receive a rude answer or no answer at all.

Among the conventional it is considered immodest for a lady to walk abreast of a man even if he is her husband or brother. For a young lady to take the hand of man who is not her husband is very objectionable. A couple to be seen walking hand in hand is scandalous, and among the very orthodox may lead to anything short of ex-communication. Bold, emancipated ladies may dare to indulge in dancing with their husbands. But for a Hindu lady to dance with anyone who is not her husband is considered improper. Because of these conventions which, still rule Hindu society, the orthodox Hindu has a low opinion of the morals of Europeans, and they guard their young sons and daughters against the "corruption" of the West.

The Hindus are chivalrous and when women are in danger or their honour threatened, they will not hesitate to risk their lives to save the women folk. But in daily and social relations, the subordinate position of women is maintained. Men are given precedence and places of honour in all walks of life. If a man and a woman go shopping it is the woman who is expected to carry the parcel. It is improper for a woman to sit in a bus, while her husband is standing. A woman may eat only when her husband is fed. Cash is always kept with men and for all domestic expenses and for shopping, the womenfolk are to go daily to their husbands and get the money necessary for the day. A man who allows his wife to get the upper hand in any of these things is considered henpecked by the orthodox.

In the villages, one often comes across a man of middle class, walking along the highway unencumbered by anything but an umbrella or a walking stick while his wife struggles along at a respectable distance behind him with a child sitting astride her right hip, a load on her head, the hot Indian sun beating mercilessly on her. If, on the other hand, the man were to carry the baby and the load, and his wife to walk about protected by the shade of the umbrella, the party would be the laughing stock of every passerby and children may throw stones at them. In orthodox Hindu households young ladies are not allowed to open their mouths in presence of elderly male members of the house, and the mother-in-law or some other elderly lady alone may speak on their behalf to the head of the family.

It is an offence against good manners for a man to address a woman by her name. Nor may a woman address a man by name. This code of etiquette is more rigidly observed among husbands and wives than among others. A woman always refers to her husband as "the child's father" or by some other euphemistic term. The husband, likewise, refers to his wife as "so-and so's mother". Europeans may wonder how in a family man and a woman are able to pull on without addressing each other by name. But there are children handy who may be made to call their mothers and fathers. It is true that at times difficult situations arise when a man has to call his wife direct: in such cases he calls her as one would call a stranger whose name he does not know, by making a noise.

The Hindus have superstitions connected with names and ladies are very careful not to give out theirs: besides the obvious familiarity a name inspires, a man who knows a lady's name is believed to possess power over her. Hence a stranger is never allowed to know the secret of a lady's name and he who asks for it is suspected to possess evil designs.

On a woman getting married, she does not change her name for her husband's as the Europeans do. Very few Hindus have surnames and even those who have, do not attain much importance to them. A Hindu is generally known by his personal name, his father's name, his caste, and the name of the village he lives in, surnames being insignificant, a married woman retains her own name and in documents her personal name appears as the wife of such-and-such a person.

Speaking of names, it is customary to add to the names of the Hindus the affix "*jī*" as a mark of respect. Thus Gandhi in polite speech becomes Gandhiji. The word "*jī*" is more respectful than Mr. and is often used in conversation while assenting or dissenting from the views of others. Thus when a person wishes to show his approval of another's opinion he says, "*hān jī*" meaning Yes Sir; to show disapproval he says "*nā jī*" meaning No Sir. In Bengal *Babu* takes place of Mister. In North India the word *Babu* is understood by all, but in South India it is neither understood nor appreciated. In polite correspondence and in invitation cards South Indians and the Maharastrians often use the Sanskrit prefix *Śrīman* for men and *Śrīmatī* for women. This is however, now used all over India by Hindus and is now enforced by the Government of India; the prefix Mr. is now replaced by *Śrī*: in all official correspondence. Among the Maharashtrians it is fashionable for a person to be known by the name of the town or the village from which he hails. This stands in place of the surnames of the Europeans, the personal name, father's name and the subcaste name (when one wishes to include this also), being indicated by the initial letters that precede, much in the manner of Europeans.

4302 **शीघ्र-कम्पित-शिर**

Śīghra-kampita-śira : it is mentioned by *Bālarāmabharata*. It corresponds to *kampita* of *NS*.

4303 **शीघ्रपातदर्शन**

Śīghrapātadarśana : a type of eye-gesture in which the quick falling of eyeballs is suggested.

4304 **शीत्कार**

Śītkāra : sounds produced by the women while in copulation with the men (*Ratirahasya*, 1.4).

4305 **शीत्कृति**

Śītkṛti : also known as *śītkāra* or *śītkṛta*. A type of moaning sound made by the female partner during cohabitation. Dāmodaragupta (*Kuṭṭanīmatam* 155) says that a woman moans when she is marked by nails. Bhāravī (*Kirāta*, 9.50) mentions *śītkāra* of women when they are crushed in secret place; *Pāṇipallavạ-vidhūnanāntaḥ sītkṛtāni.* Anantabhaṭṭa describes the *sītkāra* when he portrays the dalliance of Arjuna and Ulupī: *Phūtkāra eva sphuṭa sītkriyāsīt* (*Campū-Bhārata*, 3.24). Vātsyāyana thinks that the exact reply of the male-kiss is *sītkṛtam* (*Kāmasūtra*, 2.7.8). Māgha has applied this in his *Śiśupālavadha* (8.13): *Sītkāram samucitam uttaram taruṇyāḥ.* He also mentions in which situations women develop the technique of *sītkāra: sītkṛtāviṣkṛtānām* (*Ibid.*, 11.54). Here, the *sītkāra* is the reply for scratching, biting and dragging the hair. The *sītkāra* is an answer given by a beloved to her lover when he expresses his passion in love-union: *Sītkṛtāni sudatī vitanvatī* (*Naiṣadha*, 18.104).

4306 **शीर्षासन**

Śirṣāsana : this is the king of all the *āsanas*. To perform this efficiently, spread a four-fold blanket and sit on the knees. Make a finger lock and place it on the ground. Now keep the top of your head on this finger lock between the two hands. Slowly raise the legs till they are vertical. Stand on the head for five seconds in the beginning and gradually increase the period. Slowly bring the legs down. This *āsana* should be done very very slowly and carefully. Avoid lerks while standing on the head. Breathe slowly through the nose.

By doing this *āsana* you can sublimate sex-energy and keep up celibacy. The seminal energy is transmuted into spiritual energy and forms a spiritual force used for meditation. Memory increases. You will find real plrasure and exhiliration of spirit. The advantages derived are incalculable. It brightens the intellectual and psychic faculties. All diseases of the eyes, nose, throat, stomach, liver, spleen, lungs, renal colic, deafness, gonorrhoea, diabetes, piles, asthma, consumption, syphilis, etc. are cured. It augments digestive fire. Utero-ovarian diseases are cured. Sterility disappears.

4307 **शुक**

Śuka : the parrot, traditional confident of young lovers, had the power to cure certain diseases, including jaundice, by tranferring them magically to another object. There are endless tales about the parrot in the village and tribal India. One kind of green parrot regards the earth as his father-in-law and never sits upon it as a mark of respect. Even if it wants to drink water from a stream, it first brings a twig in its claws and sits on that, but never directly on the ground. The parrot is the traditional go-between of lovers. In the tale of prince *Ḍholā*, so popular in Chhattisgarh, the Princess *Mārū* ties her message of love round the parrot's neck and sends it to her beloved. When the parrot has fulfilled its task she gives it sugar and a golden cage. In colonial India, parrot was the symbol of slavery which was tied by the English in the golden cage. Appāśāstrī has written a symbolic poetry entitled "*pañjarabaddha śukaḥ*" in the Sanskrit journal *Sanskrit-candrikā.*

The parrot is famous in Indian folklore as a bird of learning, a go-between of lovers and a sex symbol. The parrot does in fact have a larger brain than other birds and its thick tongue enjoys a sense of taste. There is learned parrot in *Kathāsaritsāgara;* another called *Vaiśampāyana* in Bāṇa's *Kādambarī.* In *Kathāsaritsāgara* again we find a continent king of the parrots named *Hemprabha*, rich in the chastity it had practised in the former birth. It helps the foolish parrot Cārumati, enslaved by its passions, to renounce the society of females. King Vikrama Kesarin had a parrot of *Śāstras* and ever assisted him by its discernment. According to *Viṣṇupurāṇa* the wife of the sage Kaśyapa was the mother of all parrots. In a story recorded by Steel and Temple a parrot is the companion and helper of the hero and assist the heroine (As in the story of Ḍholā - H.L. Kavyapadhyaya, *A Grammar of the Chhattisgarhi Dialect*, Calcutta, 1921, 198).

Although in the Madhya Pradesh the parrot is the go-between of lovers, the classical view of this bird is that it has the lowest opinion of women. King Vikramakesarin's parrot, for example, declares that 'females are of intolerable audacity, immoral and wicked and the talking parrot is often represented as warning the deceived husband. Even in the story of Ḍholā, where the parrot proves itself so useful a go-between, the heroine while admitting its intelligence diplores its infidelity.

Crook says that the bird seems to have been a sort of marriage totem among certain tribes: images of it made of the wood of the cotton tree or of clay were hung up in marriage shed by the *Kol* and others (II.252). In Central Indian poems, as well as in W.G. Archer's collections, the parrot is often associated with sex and marriage; it is used both as a male and a female symbol.

Padmāvatī, the daughter of King Gandharva Sen of Sri Lanka, had a parrot called Hīrāmaṇi which could understand the speech of human beings. It escaped and was caught by a fowler who sold it to Raja Ratan Sen of Chittor. When the parrot described Padmāvatī's beauty to its master, he renounced the throne and went on foot with the parrot to Sri Lanka

When he reached there he sent the parrot as his messenger and at last married the princess. This story, which is told in a sixteenth century Hindi poem by Malik Muhammad Jāysi, is illustrated by the delightful picture of the Jaipur School.

The *Śuka* is *Suā* in Chhattisgarh. The *Suā*-dance is famous in this region. It is like the movement of a parrot.

4308 **शुकतुण्ड-हस्त**

Śukatuṇḍa hasta : parrot's beak; single hand gesture,

derived from the *arāla hasta* (*NS*, IX.53-54). When the ring-finger of the *arāla*-gesture is curved, it is *śuka-tuṇḍa.* This is to indicate in a dramatic performance in the sense of (a) 'neither I nor you' and (b) 'it is not'. It also suggests welcome, biding fare-well and defying a thing hatefully. Used in inconography but not frequently. The palm is raised facing outwards. The second and little fingers are stretched, and the third and the first fingers are curved forward, while the thumb is bent a little beside them. It is used to express the sense of shooting an arrow, mystery and anger.

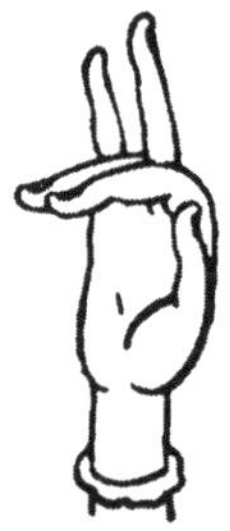

Fig. – (4308)

4309 **शुक-निरुत-ज्ञानकला**

Śuka-niruta-jñānakalā : art of parrot-speech (Bāṇabhaṭṭa, *Kādambarī*, p. 126).

4310 **शुक-मुद्रा**

Śuka-mudrā : gesture of a parrot. The *śukatuṇḍa* hand fluttered indicates a parrot (*Mirror of Gesture*, pp. 50-51).

4311 **शुकसारिकाप्रलापनकला**

Śukasārikāpralāpanakalā : teaching parrots and starlings to speak. One of the 64 arts given in *Kāmasūtra* (1.3.16).

4312 **शुक्र**

Śukra : (a) planet Venus (b) semen, sperm. *Varāhamihira* (LXVIII) has given the characteristics of men on the basis of the smell of their semen, following Vātsyāyana. According to him "With their semen having the smell of *flowers*, men become kings; having the smell of *honey*, very rich; of *fish*, fathers of many children; of *flesh* enjoyers of all kinds of pleasures; of *liquor*, performers of sacrifices; and of *salt*, very poor. Those whose semen is thin, beget only daughters; those who have too frequent sexual congress (or who experience orgasm too soon), live long; or those who have it rarely are short lived." Cf Prahlāda as follows:

> क्वाचिद्रतिः क्वचिन्निद्रो भुंक्तेऽल्पं क्षिप्रमेव यः ।
> चिरस्नायी दीर्घलक्ष्यो भाग्यवान्भवति ध्रुवम् ॥
> निःस्वोऽतिस्थूलस्फिक् समांसलस्फिक् सुखान्वितो भवति ।
> व्याघ्रान्तोऽध्यर्धस्फिग् मण्डूकस्फिग् नराधिपतिः ॥

Cf. the unnamed authority:

> पुष्पगन्धो भवेद्राजा बहुस्वा मधुगन्धिनः ।
> मत्स्यगन्धः पुत्रवान्स्यात् स्त्रीप्रजास्तनुरेतसः ॥
> मांसगन्धो महाभोगी याज्ञिको मदिरासमः ।
> गन्धो येषां क्षारसमस्ते निःस्वा मनुजाः स्मृताः ॥

4313 **शुक्र-मुद्रा**

Śukra-mudrā : gesture of the Venus. The gesture of the *sandaṁśa* at the root of the ring finger (*VD*).

4314 **शुक्र-हस्त**

Śukra-hasta : if *muṣṭi* with the raised left hand and the same with the right, placed downwards; it is *Śukra* (*AD*, 216-225).

4315 **शुण्ठ**

Śuṇṭha : hair in armpit.

4316 **शुद्ध**

Śuddha : soliloquy in Sanskrit dramas presented by one or two middle class characters (*DR*, 1.117); true, correct.

4317 **शुद्धकेश**

Śuddhakeśa : sinless: *yāni kāni ca pāpāni keśānāśritya tiṣṭhanti.*

4318 **शुद्ध-देह**

Śuddha-deha : where only love for God exists which is transformed by *nāma-mantra.*

4319 **शुद्धि**

Śuddhi : a comprehensive term meaning *purification* of a person after *aśauca* (q.v.), after contact with any impure object or certain evil occurrences and purification of food, pots, wells, temples, etc., after they are deemed to be polluted. (b) *Śuddhi* also denotes reconversion into Hinduism.

4320 **शुष्क-रुदित**

Śuṣka-rudita : 'artificial weep'. Māgha (*Śiśu.*, 10.69) describes that some beautiful ladies weep artificially in coition.

4321 **शूद्र**

Śudra : the fourth *varṇa.* Though the religious thinkers of India had a separatist tendency towards Śūdras, yet the political thinkers understood the importance of power in state politics and in their view power is a dividing rod in the society. *Mahābhārata* (12.79.13) goes to the extent of saying that if a powerful person of Śūdra caste comes to rescue of the people (protects *dharma*) and protects their lives and properties, he should be accepted as king.

Generally it is understood that the ritual of *upanayana* is not prescribed for Śūdras, but *Varāha Purāṇa* (127-128) prescribed it. Thus according to it, the skin should of black-goat (*nīla-chāga*), a bamboo-staff of eight cubits, and a bluish black umbrella; also a cloth of *nīla* colour is prescribed for them: The various colours are symbolically traditioned. Also, about the Śūdras are various emotions, praising him, sympathising with him and criticizing him if he follows the vocation of the first three *varṇas.* In spite of the critical views there are instances where a Śūdra is advised to practice penance; and when he practices it, he is elevated in the scale of the *varṇa.* Thus, there is the account of a Śudra who wanted to kill a Brāhmaṇa. Afterwards he changed his mind. The Brāhmaṇa told him to practice penance, which he did. Later, the sage Durvāsas came to test him. When the sage was satisfied with the integrity of the Śūdra, the former names him *Satvatapas* and said that the *Vedas* and the ancillary texts (*Vedāṅgas*) would come easy to him, along with all other lores:

> उवाच वेदाः साङ्गास्ते सरहस्य-पदक्रमाद्ध .... प्रत्यक्षा भवन्तु ते ।।
>
> (*Varāha.*, 38.20-28)

A pious Śūdra is believed to become a person of any of the first three as *varṇas* as is clear from the account of Śaśabindu (*Skanda.*, VII. 1.39.15-46). Some, Śūdras are termed *Sacchūdra* (good Śūdras); they are cowherds, barbers, Bhils, Modaka, a beter-vendor, a gold-smith and the trader. Other mixed castes are numerous (*Brahmavaivarta.*, *Brahmakhaṇḍa.*, 10.17-21). Among these mixed castes are mentioned a large number, some being called *śilpin* (artisans). Among them are also actors, singers and picture-drawers (*Skanda.*, VI. 242. 14-16).

4322 **शूद्र-हस्त**

Śūdra-hasta : If the *Śikhara* in the left and the *mṛgaśīrṣaka* in the right, it is the hand of a Śudra, the service class (*AD*, 226-231).

4323 **शूद्राः धर्मं चरिष्यन्ति युगान्ते पर्युपस्थिते**

Śūdrāḥ dharamam cariṣyanti yugānte paryupasthite : Śūdras will be practising *dharma* in the manner of upper *varṇas* as a sign of the cataclysmic advent of Kali (*Vāyu-Purāṇam* 58:59). This is why the slaying of Śambūka was instigated by the Brāhhmaṇs and applauded by the gods as a great deed on the part of its eponymous hero in the *Rāmāyaṇa* (*Uttara Kāṇḍa,* LXXXVI).

In the feudal India, religion constituted the most expressive sign of the elite culture in many of its essential aspects, the peasants defiance of the rural elite often involved an attempt to appropriate the dominant religon or to destroy it. To those who were high up in society the emulation of their culture by the lower strata seemed always fraught with danger.

There have been occasions when Sanskritizing movements among the lower castes to upgrade themselves by adopting the rituals and religious idioms of their superiors were resisted by the latter and generated much social tension and even some actual violence. We have the example of Guru Ghāsīdās of Chhattisgarh. He adopted all the religious idioms of the superiors.

Such an open and energetic avowal of *dharma* on the part of a lowly, unclean tanner peasantry could not have been regarded by the Hindu elite as anything but subversive. For it was an integral aspect of their dominance that they should consider it threatened by and unauthorized affiliation to the ruling culture. Thus they underminded the dominant culture in its most important, that is, religious aspect by emulating it.

Before the abolition of zamindari, a number of restrictions were imposed on low caste regarding formal aspects. At the beginning of the 20th century, string cots of low castes were not to be seen by the *ṭhākurs* of Gwalior region. Cots were kept in the house and were visible only on such occasions as marriage or at nights in summer season. The practice was abandoned by the thirties when the *kori* left their traditional occupation. If the *thākurs* visited low-caste localities, they were offered cots to sit and were offered new *chilam* and tobacco (Mutalkar, 1978:123) (b) *Śūdras* are the lowest of four classes.

4324 **शून्यवाद**

Śūnyavāda : the doctrine of vacuity. This doctrine of the *Mādhyamika* school of Buddhism advocates negatively the non-existence of substances and positively the ever changing flux of *saṁsāra* (*darśana*). They teach that there is nothing real, as everything is devoid of its innate or independent nature. That being the case any appearance is conditioned and as such it is in its imposed form (*āropita*) and not in its own form (*svarūpa*). It is *grāhya-grāhaka-bhāvarahita* (marked by the absence of subject-object relation). The doctrine of *śūnyatā* therefore implies simply the rejection of all sorts of impositions (*sarvāropa-nirākriyā*) and declares anything, external or internal, that appear to be existing, as unreal, like the imagery town in the sky (*gandharva-nagara*).

4325 **शून्यादृष्टि**

Śūnyādṛṣṭi : motionles glanec. a type of *sañcārī-bhāvadṛṣṭi*; eye-gesture suggesting anxiety (*NS*, VIII.65 and 87a). In *Ratnāvalī* (Act III), the eyes of king are *śūnyā* in anxiety. This is the conventional description of a love-sick person. *Śūnyā* (vacant) is *sañcārībhāva-dṛṣṭi.* It is a weak, vacant and motionless glance with the eye-balls and eye-lid in an ordinary position and inattentive to external objects. It suggest anxiety and a paralytic bearing. It symbolizes the conventional description of a love-sick person (*NS*, X.148-149). The glance is soiled, motionless and has pupils and eyelids in ordinary position; the look is vacant, unattentive to external objects. It is used in anxiety and paralysis.

4326 **शूर्पमुद्रा**

Śūrpamudrā : "in the joining points of fingers and hands, palms of hands are to be positioned with thumbs kept separated. They should remain extended and straights. This makes the gesture of a willow (*śūrpa*)" *BT*.

4327 **शूल-मुद्रा**

Śūla-mudrā : "make the *śūla-mudra* with the *trināḍī-baddhayoga*, that goes up to the end of twelve (fingers) and moves like flames of fire, having so many sparks. Then think of the palms joined together with the help of the little fingers, having their two tips high up proportionately". (*BT*). (b) gesture of the lance, join both hands inter-locking the thumb and the little finger and extend them jointly. This is a *śūla* (*VD*).

4328 **शृङ्खला**

Śṛṅkhalā : a dance where chain-formation is suggested and the partners hold hands. (b) chain. Sometimes used as an emblem in representing certain Buddhist deities especially of *Vajraśṛṅkhalā*. (c) chain or string as the base of three *alaṁkāras*.

4329 **शृङ्खला-बन्ध**

Śṛṅkhalābandha : that *śloka* in which the last two letters of the previous line stand at the beginning of the succeeding line.

4330 **शृङ्खला-मुद्रा**

Śṛṅkhalā-mudrā : occurs in *BT*. "When those two hands in the same position are to be enchained together, this will make the gesture of chain".

4331 **शृङ्खलिका**

Śṛṅkhalikā : a type of *piṇḍībandha*.

4332 **शृंगार**

Śṛṅgāra : eros, the erotic sentiment, love, one of the nine *rasas*. Images suggesting the erotic relish should be made of bright and beautiful nature, flashing, lustre and reflecting grace and beauty. Figures are to be dressed with serene decency, dignified and bright white attires; that should immediately fire up the love-feeling of any kind to one's own heart and melt it away to shine forth in a profuse brilliance. Bharata observes whatsoever is serene, pious and bright, that should be equated with the erotic. Bharata (*NS*, VI.300) mentions that *śṛṅgāra* is caused by the durable psychological state of *rati* or in other words, it proceeds from love. It consists of bright and pure attire. Whatever is seen pure, bright and beautiful in this world is compared to *śṛṅgāra*. It has two bases—*saṁbhoga* (union) and *vipralaṁbha* (separation). The *saṁbhoga śṛṅgāra* is represented on the stage by consequents (*anubhāva*) such as clever movements of eyes, eyebrows, glances, soft and delicate movement of limbs and sweet words and similar other things. The erotic sentiment in *vipralaṁbha* should be represented by consequents such as indifference, languor, fear, jealousy, fatigue, anxiety, yearning, drowsiness, sleep, dreaming, awakening, illness, insanity, epilepsy, inactivity, fainting, death and other conditions.

4333 **शृंगारचेष्टा**

Śṛṅgāraceṣṭā : erotic movements (*Raghuv*, 6,12).

4334 **शृंगार-रस-दृष्टि**

Śṛṅgāra-rasa-dṛṣṭi : a type of glance in *śṛṅgāra rasa*.

4335 **शेष-मुद्रा**

Śeṣa-mudrā : fingers of the *makara*-hand extended symbolize *śeṣa-nāga* (*VD*).

4336 **शैव्या-हस्त**

Śaivyā-hasta : *sūcī hasta* with twist fingers represents *śaivyā*, the mythical queen (*Mirror of Gesture*, p.47).

4337 **शोक**

Śoka : sorrow, pathetic, grief. *Śoka* is the basic instinct of pathos (*karuṇa rasa*). It is aroused by the loss of a desired person or thing and results in a mental dejection or depression. In Act IV of *Vikrama*. Urvaśī enacts sentiment of *śoka*. She expresses it by a copious shedding of tears, a change of colour etc. (*NS*, VII.19). The king then enters in a state of love-distraction: he addresses himself to the sky *(unmukhaḥ)*; his gait is unsteady, represented through irregular steps; his body covered with dust and his hair dishevelled. He talks to himself: sometimes he sings and sometimes he laughs: sometimes he dances in joy and sometimes he stands still. Bharata gives an elaborate description of the persons in this state and a reading of Act IV of the *Vikramorvaśīya* shows us how perfectly this description fits the king (*NS*, XII.123-130).

Śoka is to be represented by (the *anubhāvas* such as) shedding tears, lamentation, bewailing, dryness of the mouth, change of colour, drooping limbs, falling on the ground, crying, deep breathing, paralysis, insanity, loss of memory, death and the like.

The gait is also changed in the grief. According to *NS*, the actor should move with steps in slow tempo, with eyes filled with tears, drooping limbs, arms thrown up and down and crying. This is the gait of women and inferior persons. The superior characters should move patiently, having tears, with deep sighs and looking upwards. The *sauṣṭhava* of the body should not be resorted to. In case of middling type, the gait should be according to mental mood. In case of the death of the dear one the actor should move with steps not raised much high, with his energy lost, breast depressed, and with the consciousness lost due to grief. When struck severely the steps should be raised moderately and fall strongly. The shoulders and arms should be drooping and the body unsteady. When attacked by cold and torrential rain, women and inferior type should have slow steps, with limbs contracted and shaking, placing hands on breast, the body bent, teeth and lips clattering and the chin quivering.

Grief has been analyzed in different ways but many researchers agree that we experience grief in four main stages. The first stage is time of shock and disbelief, following by the second when we feel, the acute pain of loss. The third is characterized by anger and guilt, while reintegration is the fourth and final stage. It is important to remember that there may not be clear divisions between one stage and the next and that no two people have exactly the same experience of bereavement as Bharata has visualized. However, understanding the typical progression of grief can help us understand the intense and sometimes conflicting emotions that we experience when we mourn. It can also help us support people we care about when they are bereaved.

Bereavement is the most extreme term of loss but it is of course not the only kind. People who undergo other severe losses - such as separation, the loss of a home or the loss of a job—will experience many of the same feelings.

4338 **शोकदृष्टि**

Śokadṛṣṭi : a type of *bhāvadṛṣṭi* enumerated by Bharata; a strongly unpleasant emotional state associated with loss or deprivation accompanied by sobbing or weeping.

4339 **शोकाकुल**

Śokākula : overwhelmed with sorrow. When some close to us dies, our immediate reaction will be one of shock and disbelief. This stage is quite short, lasting from the time of death until after the funeral. As the shock passes and the bereaved person begins to accept what has happened, they enter the *sokākula* stage. This is very necessary and helpful part of grieving. We are unlikely to accept the reality of loss unlike we can allow ourselves to vent our anguish. Most survivors experience intense crying fits, and physical symptoms, such as restlessness, insomnia, poor appetite, and weight loss, become noticeable. This is the period of desperate yearning and yet the bereaved is often given little emotional support during this stage. This stage can last from a few weeks to a few month (up to one year) and, again, it is seen that mourners should not be alone too much.

4340 **शोधन**

Śodhana : purification. In *Tāntric* language it is the establishment of a thing in its real form. It is done by *mantras* and rituals.

4341 **शोभा**

Śobhā : (a) beauty, one of the involuntary graces in women. It is the decoration of limbs due to beautiful forms, youth and loveliness heightened after the enjoyment of love. (b) brilliant character. One of the temperamental aspects in males. Expertness, heroism, energy, aversion to mean acts, ambition to acquire great merits constitute *śobhā*. (c) what do the common man of India consider beautiful ? It is not always possible to say, for India has inherited a heavy burden of poetic diction from the Sanskrit past. As D.C. Sen (*I.L* VIII) rightly points out: 'The same stereotyped and hackneyed comparison without one word of original observation is to be met with everywhere. The face was to be like a lotus, the ear like those of a vulture, the neck of the form of a conch; the gait of a lady was compared to the grace of an elephant's movement; the lips were alway like the *bimba* fruit in the delicacies of their colour, the eyebrows like the bow of cupid or the rainbow. In case of a man his arms must reach the knees, the eyes should be so large as to stretch up to the ears, the nose to be like the beak of Garuḍa - the king of birds. What one poet writes, the other poets repeat. The elegant poets tell all this in an attractive language; those who are not so gifted use a commonplace and stale language; but the same thing recurs in the descriptions; and so stereotyped the accounts are that the readers might altogether omit many passages without the risk of losing any poetical treat, however great the poet whose work they might be reading. This is the characteristic of all poets of the Renaissance School.

But the folk-tales and folksongs of India have managed to a certain extent to break with this old tradition. The eyes of a lovely girl, says D.C. Sen, are compared in '*Kamala*', 'to the beautiful *aparājitā* flower. This flower grows abundantly in the countryside and offers a striking likeness to the dark eyes of the Bengali women. It is certainly curious that the Bengali poets have so often stumbled over the huge blocks of Sanskritic figures, when there was such a simple patch open to them near their own village-homes. The freshness of a *mahuā* flower, the emblem of health and undecayed charm, which is a familiar sight here, never struck a Renaissance poet who seemed to see everything through the eyeglass of classical culture. In these songs the face of a woman is often compared to the *mahuā* flower with great effect. Jayadeva, the Sanskrit poet, who had a great knowledge of his rural country than the poets who followed him, once referred to this flower and called it *madhūka*, and in *Kṛṣṇa-kīrtana* of Chanḍidāsa, which is full of rural charm, we find references to it.

Chhatisgarhi poetry is notable in describing men as well as women. 'He is handsome as a constable', said a romantic little girl:

When the moth
sees the beautiful lamp
It forgets the world
And dies.

'His eyes' - here is another description - 'are beautiful as the sliced halves of a mango.' his nose is straight as a *mahua* bud; his eyes are black; he has a *much-much* moustache and curly hair; his calves swell so that they appear ready to shoot awav from his body; his teeth are like cucumber seeds.'

But 'a man's beauty is only for a few days, then it is lost; but a woman's beauty endures till the withering of the tree.'

In the assessment of woman's beauty, the people seem to pay most attention to her hair, her ornaments and her figure. Their attitude to the breasts is tender and beautiful, worthy of a land of poets. No student of the court paintings or rock carvings of India need be reminded of the delicate and absorbed attention given to the female breast in antiquity. In the folk-tales of the *Kathāsaritsāgara* cycle, we read of the 'lovely full bosom' of *Upakośā*, of Madanamanchukā with her breasts like 'clusters of *mandaras*', of Mandanasenā whose breasts were like 'pitchers half revealed'. Penzer (VII.5) notes that the Hindus have always admired the full breast, while the Arabs admired firmness rather than fulness.

There is an elaborate classification of breasts, both according to their beauty and the quantity of milk that they secrete. Admiration for the breast requires something more than beauty: it demands and rich store of milk which will nourish a strong and handsome child. This is an important point. A great deal of village aesthetics has a utilitarian basis. The most lovely girl is not long admired unless she has a good look; she may have a perfect figure, but if she is lazy at her grindstone, she will not keep her lovers long. Perhaps the most admired breasts of all are compared to those of a tigress whose milk is strong and plentiful and which produces a child strong as a tiger-cub.

Then there are the breasts small and round as a deer's, those that are full of rich milk like a cow's, those that the lover compares to a gourd and are said to give great pleasure. The 'monkey breasts' stand up like those of a monkey and have a long tip to the nipples. The rice-pounder breasts are long and thick. There are breasts that sway like a child's swing, breasts like a silk-cocoon, breasts like sour limes. Both in ordinary speech and in song the breasts are compared to guavas, mangoes, oranges and mushrooms. The little nut-like *sarai*-fruit to which the breasts of young girls is compared is much admired.

Finally, is the 'pair of maiden worlds unconquered', the 'breasts so lovely that no one dare touch them but must gaze at them from a far.'

There is no doubt that this is the supreme form of erotic attraction. All night, sings a girl in Raipur:

All night you ate the *bel* stone
And were drunk at dawn.

And this was interpreted to mean "All night you fondled my breasts in ecstasy'. But I have nowhere found the thought so vivid in Shakespeare's England, that he who holds a girl's breasts will feel tumultuous beating of her heart.

But the figure is not everything. 'The most satisfying girl', said a Binjhwār, 'is one who has broad shoulders and slender hips. A gril who goes straight from head to legs gives no pleasure.'

In some places, a girl's body is regarded an index to her character and this too is important to people whose ideas of beauty are often utilitarian. 'A girl whose breasts have broad bases' - it is a Gond opinion - 'and good nipples will be faithful.' 'A girl with long breasts and a hidden nipple, who puts her legs tightly round a man in intercourse, who washes her loin-cloth daily is a wanton'. 'A woman with broad forehead and arched instep either kills her father-in-law or always stays in her mother's house, refusing to join her husband.'

Colour should usually be light. The typical skin-colour of the Brāhmaṇ is that which is most admired. But the rich golden brown of many Gond women, especially when it is set off with silver ornaments and bright coloured ribbons in the hair, is equally attractive. Ornamnets are always necessary; without them a woman looks 'like a rice-pounderer'.

The eyes are not often mentioned. When they do occur in a poem, it is their fire that seems to strike the observer.

'your eyes are fireflies', says one singer and another refers to the eyes that shoot arrows and subdue the lover.

The waist should be slender, swaying like a thin bamboo, and the hands and feet should be neither too large nor too small but should be just right and always decorated with ornaments.

On the whole, the descriptions in the folk-songs are astonishingly simple and austere. In many cases, of course, the poet feels that no description is necessary. When he calls a girl parrot he expects his hearers to realize that he means something lovely and coloured. When he calls a lover an *amarbel* creeper he has in his own mind a picture of the beautiful yellow creeper hanging like a mass of golden hair from the fresh green tree and he does not feel it necessary to elaborate this in detail, since everyone of his hearers will have the same picture in his mind. To say that a girl is tiger-breasted is sufficient. All his hearers know what he means. They have seen many such girls and they can see this is how with her splendid round firm breasts and erect carriage, a girl who will be a perfect mother and will bear a noble child.

In the end, the supreme beauty of a woman is her child. 'woman's beauty is hidden under seven coverings. Her beauty is like nature; it dies and is renewed with every child she bears. How quickly a barren woman's beauty disappears! Her breasts shrink and soon only a nipple is left.' :

Look at the dark girl
with a necklace of black beads
Round her sweet dark throat
A red *sari* on her dark body
A red flower in her black hair
Look at the dark girl
When she sees a boy
Her mind is filled with pleasure
She talks *lahar-lahar*
Her mouth is very smooth
But peep from below
There is no *ras* in her.

Surmā and *kājal* are the eye-salves of village India: *Kājal* is prepared from lamp black, *Surmā* is bought in the bazzars. The repulsive habit of staining the teeth with red or black *missī* or with red *pān* aims at improving beauty: it is not perhaps much worse than the use of powder and lipstick. The *bindiā* is a beautiful ornament tied across the forehead, and is attached at either end to the silver *ḍhār*-shields with their hanging chains. *Toda, rulai, pairi, paijan* are different kinds of anklets, of which the *pairī* with its tinkling bells are the most popular. *Bahunṭā* are the thick silver armlets. *Kaknā* and *banwariā* are broad silver bangles decorated with sharp protrusions. The *mūngā* necklace is of red beads; the *hawel* is a string of silver coins.

To the Gond girl a song which consists of nothing more than a catalogue of covered ornaments - the *ḍhaṛ* shield for her ears, the *Raibajan* anklets the *bindiā* to frame her face in silver beauty, the *sawatdigai* armlets, necklaces, bangles, rings - is fully as exciting in poetic appeal as the 'business song' of Autolycus :

My dark love is walking slowly
Come, wild berry, bare your arms
Show your feet adorned with anklets
Give me your hand
With its nine hundred rings
Open to me your breast
Your love, your body
Open your dark body.

(*Karmā* from Bilaspur)

The colour most admired in India, as I have said, is the pale brown of the Brāhmaṇ's skin, and by contrast the heavy black of the typical aboriginal is regarded with dīstaste and fear. But many aboriginals are far from dark: Some are a beautiful golden brown, some have an almost Mongolian hue; these are greatly admired.

Finally, it is the youth which is greatly admired :

Her Juvescence shows
Under the thin cloth
Wet with rain
And blown by the wind against her body.

'Juvescence', T.S. Eliot's word, is an exact translation of the original *Joban*, youth as expressed in the firm strong breasts. Girls treasure their youth: it is a fleeting prize, and they would enjoy it to the full. It is the dearest gift that they can give a lover. So in the Bengali ballad of Shyam Ray, when the Dom girl begs her lover to come again, she says, 'Be pleased to come to my house tomorrow also, and I will gather all the flowers from my garden to present you a cup of honey and all that my youth can give you will be for you!' (Sen, III.211)

Compare also the song by Amaru, translated by E. Powys Mathers :

Her robe clung close to her body
And the tissue of it became transparent
I thank you, rain,
You were, Sanabavi, as if you were naked.
But when the rainbow broke in flower
Who warmed your little shivering breasts for you ?

4342 शौच

Śauca : purity, the act of cleansing. Purity in the caste system is an empty or negative state characterized by the absence of impurity. The opposition between the pure and the impure should be formulated as an opposition between the impure and the non-impure, a positive value being attached to the negative state of the not-impure.

The organic aspects of life are the chief source of impurity so that avoidance of impurity requires a withdrawal from life itself. Higher castes are by definition less impure than lower castes. They are, therefore, required to divest themselves to a greater degree of the qualities associated with organic life, and the progressive restrictions on choice of occupation and diet in the upper reaches of the hierarchy derive from this requirement. The logic of the caste hierarchy rests on a fundamental opposition to life itself on the basis of the following equivalences:

impure: not impure: life: not life: low status: high status.

Purification is somewhat different from *prāyaścitta*. Purification may be of two different types; regarding the person or regarding things. Personal purification can be obtained by sipping water etc. and the purification of things depends on the nature of the things such as wood, thread, stones, etc. (*Manu*, VI. 111-112,115,122). Impurities in the shape of *aśauca* should be differentiated from sins or expiations. Sins are the results of acts whereas impurities are the result of event. No shaving or washing of clothes were permissible according to Gautama. These practices are followed even today also to a great extent specially in the villages. Worship, marriage and some social transactions are suspended during this period of impurity arising out of death and birth, both in tribal and rural society.

The general method of purification is bath, may be water or an "ash-bath". The *Skanda-Purāṇa* (VI. 238.17) has enumerated two types of purification : external and internal. The external purification is water (or other purifiers), while the internal one is faith:

> *śaucam tu dvividham grāhyam bāhyamābhyantaram sadā* /
> *jala śaucam tathā bāhyam śraddhayā cāntaram bhavet* //

Śauca differs in degree according to *āśramas*. Cleansing at night requires half the time prescribed for it in the day time. The internal is subdivided into five parts: *mānasa* (mental), *cākṣuṣa* (of the eye), *ghrāṇya* (of the nose), *vācya* (of speech) and *svādya* (of the tongue).

4343 **शौचभाजः**

Śaucabhājaḥ : one who is clean, quality of a Hare-man (*Ratirahasya*, 3.30-1).

4344 **श्मशान**

Śmaśāna : place for burning the dead bodies, cemetery.

4345 **श्मश्रु**

Śmaśru : the moustache. (a) Men may not use make-up, but they can always grow some facial decorations. Beards and moustaches seem to have a life of their own, sending out a complex set of messages to everyone who sees them. At various times in Indian history they have proclaimed political affiliations. Today, moustaches are symbols of masculinity—*binā mūch ke jawān.* (a) the moustache twist. The thumb and fore-finger are squeezed together in the cheek region and twisted round, as if twindling the tip of an imaginary moustache. The symbolism derives from the male's need to preen himself in preparation for his advances towards the girl, stimulated by her beauty. It services into modern times despite the absence of moustache and symbolizes "manliness." (b) keeping moustache is not peculiar at all in tribal setting, but it is prevalent among the older people only. (c) the curled, upturned moustache represents the distinctive style for upper-class males in village India. When a member of the traditionally labouring community of Barelas was found sporting such a moustache in a Gujarat village dominated by rich and politically powerful Patidars, he was forcibly shaved, beaten up and driven out beyond its boundaries. This anecdote was recorded by an anthropologist as evidence of 'greater concern with caste order in the past' (Pocock, 28), presumably in colonial times and before. However, in the light of the facts published by the Elayaperumal Committee's report, it seems that ban on the up-turned moustache continues to be a feature of the outcaste's subalternity even in India today (Hiro, Dilip. *The Untouchables of India, Minority Rights Group Report*, No.26, London 1975:9). (d) keeping moustache is not popular among the Hill Marias of Bastar. (e) Varāhamihira (*BS*, LXVIII) has tried to depict the personality of men on the basis of moustaches and beard. "The moustaches and beard being smooth, soft, well-bent and having unsplit, are auspicious; being red, hard and short or sparse, they make men thieves:

> स्निग्धमस्फुटिताग्रं च सन्नतं श्मश्रु चेश्ट्यते ।
> रक्तैरल्पैस्तथा रूक्षैः श्मश्रुभिस्तस्कराः स्मृताः ॥

(f) there is a wide-spread tradition—it exists also among the tribes, for example that women formerly had beards and moustaches. The following Baiganī-song also suggests this:

> As you blew on the fire
> Your moustache was burnt
> Fie on you, virile woman
> As you were cooking
> Your beard was burnt
> You are lucky, virile woman
> The black cat
> Always eats the little dove.

4346 **श्याम मुखराग**

Śyāma mukharāga : black colour of face. It is suggested in *bhayānaka* and *bībhatsa* *rasa.*

4347 **श्यामा**

Śyāmā : sixteen years' lady of dark complexion who has not yet borne children (*Pañcaśayaka*, 2.12). A lady who gives pleasure according to the season (*Ibid.*, 6). Bhaṭṭi (5.18) portrays the characteristics of the lady :

> *Śīte sukhoṣṇa-sarvaṅgī grīṣme tu sukhaśītalā /*
> *tapta-kāñcana-varṇābhā sā strī śyāmeti kathyate //*

This interpretation shows that black absorbs everything (light) into itself, giving nothing back. It dipects a person for whom conventional morality is meaningless.

4348 **श्येन**

Śyena : hawk; *chacān* in Halbi.

In *Ṛgveda śyena* is mentioned seventy times. It means 'eagle' according to Bloomfield. Keith, Macdonell and Bloomfield hold that in the *Ṛgveda śyena* denotes eagle and in the post-Vedic age it meant hawk. Bloomfield refers to a legend where the eagle is depicted as the bringer of *soma* from heaven (*JAOS*, XVI. 1-15). The legend existed in the *Purāṇas* which record that the *garuḍa* (eagle) brought a *soma* plant to the earth. In later times especially in the *Purāṇas śyena* came to be regarded as an inauspicious bird for its cruel nature and ugly outlook. *Matsya Purāṇa* prescribes the bones of *śyena* in *navagrahaśānti*-ritual (XC III.152). We also know that since *Atharvaveda*, the *śyena* was associated with the inauspicious rites. In *śyenayāga* the bird was sacrificed to bring a person under control. *Matsya Purāṇa* (XCIII.152) refers to this sacrifice. Both in the *Ṛgveda* (II.42.2) and the *Atharvaveda* (III.3.4) the *śyena* is described as the swiftest and a source of terror to the smaller brids. Being the strongest of birds, the *Śatapatha Brāhmaṇa* (XII.7.1.6) describes *śyena* as the king of the birds. The *Purāṇas* state that *śyeni* was the mother of the hawk. According to *Matsya* (VI.30-31) and *Vāyu Purāṇas* (LXIX.325-26) she is the wife of Aruṇa and mother of Sampāti and Jaṭāyu. This shows that many legends and sociological notions were attributed to this bird which has acquired a specal significance in the tribal culture of Bastar. Aboriginal tribes of Bastar use it as a bird of prey. The ancient playright Bhāsa describes hawk pouncing upon the prey. He observed hawks in houses (*Cārudatta*, III.1.) Bāṇa and Śrīharṣa usually refer to the hunting traits of the bird. Raja Rudradeva of Kumaon wrote *Śyainika śāstram* (Delhi, 1983) which is a unique work on hunting and the hawk.

Śyena Yāga is a rite or sacrifice to injure others. It is a general term for black acts.

4349 **श्रम**

Śrama : fatigue, weariness. It is the sixth among the thirty-three *vyabhicārī bhāvas* as enumerated by Bharata. It is the feeling of fatigue caused by coition, or even by exertion due to travelling, etc., and is manifested in gasping and drowsiness (*Sāhityadarpaṇa*, 3.146). It is represented by gentle rubbing of the body, deep breathing, contraction of mouth, belching, massaging of limbs, very slow gait, contraction of the eyes, making hissing sound.

4350 **श्रद्धा**

Śraddhā : faith (in God and scriptures) which is evidently the basis of (spiritual) aspiration. It is not identical with *bhakti* or devotion.

4351 **श्रवण**

Śravaṇa : hearing. We get two kinds of messages through hearing: sounds and silence. We have already discussed *parāvāk* (para language) - the vocal characteristics that are part of speech communication. We are not talking here about the sound of the human voice: We are talking about the other, NV messages we get from the sound.

Many sounds, of course, are used for signals. In our temples, bells signal the beginning and end of the worship. Bell may also indicate the school hours. We can use buzzers for signals.

Just as the presence of sound communicates information to us, so also the absence of sound (silence) communicates information to us or at least, it can communicate to us. The message we get may be a mistaken message; our received messages are inferences (guesses), after all, and we may guess wrong. But we do attach meaning to silences, don't we ?

We often interpret silence from other people to mean withdrawal or coldness or hostility. Sometimes we use silence intentionally to convey exactly that impression.

There are different kinds of silences; we are silent for different reasons; such as the silence of isolation, dog-matism, anger, grief or pain, reverence, contemplation, confusion and compassion. Some silences are positive and some are negative.

Sravaṇa also means listening to scriptures. It is a precondition of valid knowledge and is necessary for firmness and purity of devotion (*bhakti-dārḍhya, bhakti-pariśuddhi*).

4352 **श्रवणं स्पृशेत्**

Śravaṇam spṛśet : catching one's own ear. The ear comes in a magical device also, as a protection from evil. Ear was also a symbol of female organ (Karṇa born from Kuntī). It is said that if one sneezes or vomits in the way, one should catch hold of one's right ear (*Skanda*, I.2.4.41).

Other symbolic ear-gestures are clapping and rubbing the ear, pulling the earlobe, putting the finger inside the ear, and even bending the whole ear.

In Kerala, it is customary to apply betel-leaf ends to the ear-lobes, while eating betel-leaves; "to catch one's own ear" is a saying, the original idea being to be free from any sin committed.

4353 **श्रव्य**

Śravya : audible literature, audo-visual importance of art is felt by Bharata who divided whole literature into audible and visual (*śravya* and *dṛṣya*). (b) aural transmission. The drum, the flute and the horn were the popular instruments for aural transmission. They are the interpretations of verbal sign by means of signs of NV sign systems. As such they acted as a surrogate of human speech and were independent enough of the latter to permit the decoding of messages directly rather than through linguistic symbolism. The sound of the buffalo horn, flute and drum was the aural sign.

4354 **श्राद्ध**

Śrāddha : ritual for the spiritual welfare of departed ones accompanied by desire to keep in constant touch with the dead by means of ceremonials. The *Mit.* on *Yāj.* (1.217) defines *śrāddha* as the *offering* with faith of an article of food or some substitute thereof, intended it for the benefit of the departed. The distant ancestors are known as *pitṛs* and those who have lately departed as *pretas*. The first finds expression in the daily *pitṛyajñas*, the monthly *śrāddha* and the *aṣṭakā* and *anvaṣṭakā* rites in all of which the *pitṛs* are honoured and receive oblation like gods. The second finds expression in the funeral rites following immediately after and in the *ekoddiṣṭa* and *sapiṇḍikaraṇa śrāddhas*.

4355 **श्रान्तादृष्टि**

Śrāntādṛṣṭi : pale-glance. a *sañcārī-bhāva-dṛṣṭi*. A glance of fatigued look with tired eye-lids, fallen eye-balls and narrowed eye-ends. It suggests weariness and depression (*NS*, VIII. 61-92). The eyelids are languished due to fatigue, the corners are emaciated and contracted, the lense bent down and the pupils depressed. It is used in weariness and perspiration due to the fatigue.

4356 **श्रावक**

Śrāvaka : 'a sound audible from afar' (*Śiśu*). (b) *Śrāvaka* also means persons of average intellect who are capable of attaining perfection only by listening to and practising the *dharma* promulgated by beings of extraordinary intellect like a Buddha. In Jainism *śrāvaka* and *śrāvikā* means laymen and laywomen repectively who follow the precept of the *nirgrantha* religion preached by the *Tīrthaṅkaras* under the guidance of an organised system.

4357 **श्राविका**

Śrāvikā : high tone heard from afar.

4358 **श्रीप्रयोग**

Śrīprayoga : Vararuci in *Patrakaumudī* (6.40), written at the direction of King Vikramāditya, lays down a rule regarding the number of times the word "*Śrī*" (an honourable prefix) is to be used before the name of a person addressed, according to his/her rank." To a preceptor, there should be six "*Śrīs*", to husband five, to a servant two, to a foe four, to a friend three and one each to son, and wife. The higher the individual in social system, the more he tends to receive greeting from the persons of lower strata. Bhānu (*Kāvyaprabhākara* 672) records the rule regarding the use of *śrī*:

> devam gurum gurusthānam Kṣetrādevatām
> Siddham siddhādhikārānśca śrīpūrvam samudīrayet.
> Śrī likhiye ṣaṭ gurun ko, pānc svāmi ripu cāri
> tīn mitha dvai bhṛtya ko, ek putra aru nāri.

4359 **श्रीमुद्रा**

Śrīmudrā : a particular mark made on the forehead by the worshippers of Viṣṇu.

4360 **श्रीयन्त्र**

Śrīyantra : the most important Tāntric diagram connected with the cult of *Śrīvidyā*. It is also known as *Śrīcakra* and *Tripura-cakra*. This diagram symbolises the body of the goddess. It consists of nine triangles (*yonis*), five in the name of Śakti and four in that of Śiva. The Śakti triangles are pointed upwards and Śiva triangles downwards (*Kāmakalāvilāsa*, XXXVI). (Fig. 4360)

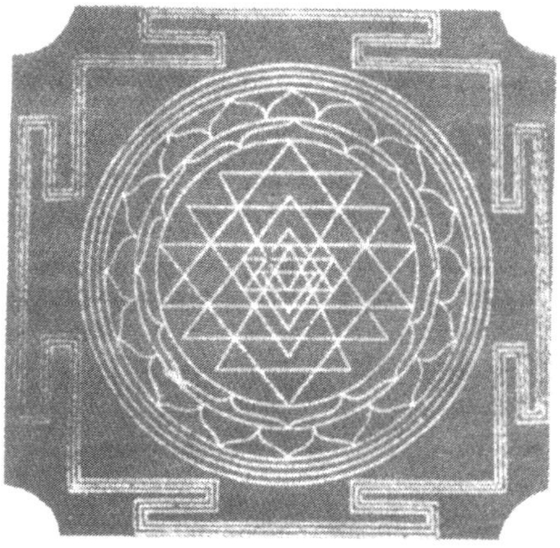

Fig.– (4360)

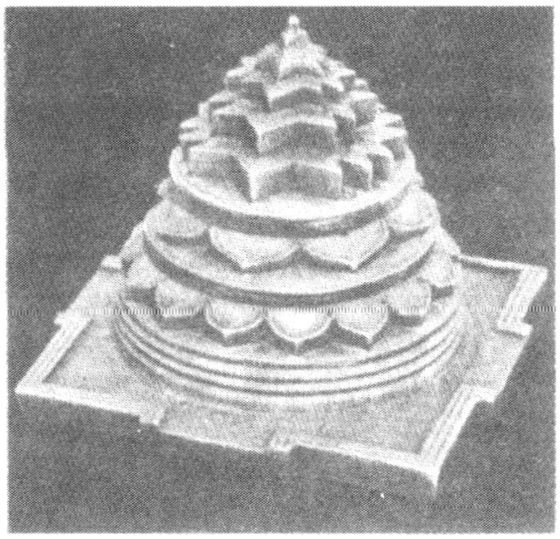

Fig. – (4360)

4361 **श्रुतार्थापत्ति**

Śrutārthāpatti : one of the two kinds of *arthāpatti* or postulation is used to explain the meaning of the words heard. It implies uncovering the figurative meaning, of understanding by words or certain sentences are omitted, in short the *hidden meaning* rather than the overt. Compare the following verse:

śrutvā dharmam vijānāti
śrutvā tyajati durmatim /
śrutvā jnānamavāpnoti
śrutvā mokṣam ca vindati //

"Hark and then your duties know;
Hark and vice away then throw;
Hark and then all knowledge gain
Hark, beautitude attain."

4362 **श्रुति**

Śruti : heard, audition, revelation, immediate authority, fame, scripture, the *Vedas*, course, path, hearing, listening to, the sacred tradition, knowledge. Etymologically that form of knowledge which is transmitted orally. Kullūka in his commentary on *Manu* (II.1) defines *Śruti* as traditional knowledge and says that it is two-fold: Vedic (*Vaidikī*) and Tantric (*Tāntrikī*). In a specific sense *Śruti* denotes the Vedic texts and the Vedic tradition. When any school of thought refers to *Śruti* to prove something it implies that it refers to a form of divine knowledge which cannot be questioned. The law-makers like Manu etc., claim to have based their works on *Śruti*, which has been characterized by them as of divine inspiration, and hold that if there is any conflict between *Śruti* and *Smṛti* (the contents of their own works), the former is to be taken as a more authoritative. (b) in Jainism *Śruti* is a form of knowledge which belongs to the category of *parokṣa* (indirect) to be acquired through reasoning and study. (c) *Śruti* is an audition: the sense of hearing. The receptors are the ears. The sense cells are hair cells located along the basilar membrane. The hair cells are capable of converting mechanical energy into nervous impulses which are transmitted to the primary auditory area in the temporal lobes. (d) we often receive our first impression of someone before we actually meet them, for example by their *Śruti*, as Damayanti formed her impression of Nala in *Mahābhārata*. A woman is generally better than man at forming accurate impressions of others. She is more likely to cry if she sees someone else crying, or winces if someone herts her. (e) *Śruti* has been defined by Jagannāth Prasād Bhanu as following:

jo dhvani ṭhahre kān men
soī śruti abhirām
bodh śrutī aru yog men
tāhī ko svar nām.

4363 **श्रुतिपरुषा**

Śrutiparuṣā : harsh to ear.

4364 **श्रुतिमण्डल**

Śrutimaṇḍala : the outer circle of the ear.

4365 **श्रुत्यनुप्रास**

Śrutyanuprāsa : alliteration, repetition of the sound or *varṇas*. As a deliberate phonological device, it is associated mostly with literary, especially poetic language, but it is also found in popular idioms. In poetry alliteration is characteristically used for emphasis, and to aid memorability. It is also used for onomatopoetic effects, to suggest by the association of sounds what is beihg described.

4366 **श्रोणि**

Śroṇi : hip and loins, buttocks. *Śroṇitaṭa* 'slope of the hips'. *Śroṇiphalaka* 'hips". *Śroṇibimba* 'round buttocks'. Resting one hand on the hip is more feminine, and centuries ago was the characteristic gesture of the *śālabhañjikās.*

4367 **श्रोता**

Śrōtā : audience. In Purāṇic literature there are two types of listeners: *pravara* and *avara (Skanda*, II. 6.4.10). The first type is like the birds *cātaka*, swan, parrot and fish; the second type is like the wolf, *bhuruṇḍa* bird, bull, camel etc. The person, who leaving all other things is intent on hearing is the *cātaka*; the swan is one who takes the essence; the parrot is one who goes on saying "well-well", thereby encouraging the speaker, and the fish is the loving person. One who curves his nose is the wolf, the *bhuruṇḍa* is one who teaches others, but does not practice himself; the bull is one who practices all that he hears without giving thought to it, as a bull enters the sweet grape-orchard and also the cornless field of *kathā*, the camel is one who leves the several sweat and takes interest in the opposite:

> प्रवरा अवराश्चेति श्रोतारो द्विविधा मताः ।
> प्रवराश्चातको हंसः शुको मीनादयस्तथा ।
> अवरा वृकभूरुण्डवृषोष्ट्राद्याः प्रकीर्तिताः ॥
> (*Skanda*, II. 6.4.10).

In its basic collective sense *śrotā* is the listner. Speakers will adjust their language to suit the social role of their audiences as reported in the *Skanda Purāṇa*.

4368 **श्रोत्र**

Śrotra : the ear (AV, X.86.11), the organ that contains the receptors for hearing. It is divided into three main parts: the outer, middle and inner ears.

4369 **श्लाघ**

Ślāgha (*Bṛhaddevatā*, 144-60) : form of speech and thought.

4370 **श्लिष्ट-शाखा**

Śliṣṭa-śākhā : curly hair (*Ratirahasya*, 3.30-31).

4371 **श्लेष**

Śleṣa : double-entendre, the real subject is intimated by puns or double meanings (*Kāvyaprakāśa*, IX.84). (b) a composition having *krama, kauṭilya, anulbaṇatva* and *upapatti* (*SD.*, VIII).

4372 **श्वसुर-हस्त**

Śvasura-hasta : gesture indicating father-in-law. If in the *Śvaśrūḥ-hasta* (q.v); a man holding the *śikhara* gesture with the right hand catches the hand of a woman; it indicates a father-in-law (*AD*, 231-244).

4373 **श्वश्रु**

Śvaśru : mother-in-law. The women of the house live under the tyranny of the mother-in-law. This personage is the terror of all the young ladies, and her genius for ill-treatment has become proverbial in India. Too old and dry to have any interest in mattrers relating to sex, she insists that every daughter-in-law of hers be as virtuous as herself. It is her duty to see that every young lady of the household drudges from sunrise to sunset; that no young girl speaks to any male-member of the household. Not even to her husband during daytime; and that no young lady has any time for keeping herself clean and attractive. If a young daughter-in-law puts on a presentable appearance the old woman calls her a prostitute; if she is slovenly, she calls her mother's names for not knowing how to bring up presentable children. Any slackness or oversight in the matter of domestic drudgery is pointed out by the mother-in-law as a reflection on her daughter-in-law's breeding.

Kālidāsa (*Raghu* .,14.20, 6.13) uses *Śvaśrujana* for the mother-in-law.

4374 **श्वश्रूहस्त**

Śvaśrūhasta : gesture indicating a mother-in-law; placing of the *haṁsāsya* gesture in the neck, holding the *sandaṁśa* with the right hand and skimming the left hand on the belly; if a woman catches the hand of a man; it is the hand of a mother-in-law (*AD*, 231-244).

4375 **श्वेतकाकीय**

Śvetakākīya : one who believes in a wrong thing.

4376 **श्वेतमण्ड**

Śvetamaṇḍa : the white part of the eye of an image (*Mānasāra*, LXV. 68).

ष - Ṣa

4377 **षट्-कञ्चुक**

Ṣaṭ-kañcuka : six veils which are the causes of human bondage (*Tantrāloka*, IX. 164.204).

4378 **षट्कर्ण**

Ṣaṭkarṇa : heard by six ears, i.e., by a third person.

4379 **षट्कर्म**

Ṣaṭkarma : six purificatory practices of *Haṭhayoga: dhautī, vasti, neti, laukikī, trāṭaka* and *kapālabhātī* (*Haṭhayogapradīpikā*, II. 24-35). (b) the term is also applied to denote six black acts: *Śānti, vaśya, stambhana, vidveṣaṇa, uccāṭana,*and *māraṇa* (*Yoginītantra*, IV). (b) a Brāhmaṇa performing six duties: study of the *Veda*, teaching of *Veda*, offering sacrifices, conducting them for others, giving and accepting gifts. (c) in *yoga, ṣaṭkarmāṇi* means *dhautī, vastī, netī, trāṭaka, naulika* and *kapālabhātī.*

4380 **षट्कल**

Ṣaṭkala : time measured by six *ghaṭikās.*

4381 **षट्प्रज्ञ**

Ṣaṭprajña : one knowing six subjects: four *puraṣārthas*, nature of the world, and the supreme spirit.

4382 **षडङ्ग**

Ṣaḍaṅga : six principal parts of body (b) *Kāmasūtra* refers to *Ṣadaṅgas* of painting as (i) *bhāva* (expression of mood), (ii) *lāvaṇyayojana* (embodiment of charm), (iii) *sādṛśya* (points of view with reference to stance), (iv) *varṇika bhaṅga* (preparation of colours); etc. (c) aboriginal tribes have the concept of eight principal parts of body. W. G. Archer gives an interesting Oraon song about 'the carving of the eight parts', the development of the body after its conception by the parents:

> Image, image, image, *bābū*
> Image of a face with hair
> when was the carving of the eight parts?
> of the father its creation
> of the mother was its birth
> out of the future were the eight parts.

4383 **षडङ्ग-न्यास**

Ṣaḍaṅga-nyāsa : *nyāsa* for feeling the deity in six parts of the body: heart, head, top of the head, protective amulet, eyes and intestines.

4384 **षडिग**

Ṣaḍiga : having six fingers in a hand.

4385 **षड्ज**

Ṣaḍja : the first note of the Indian gamut, like the cooing of a peacock.

4386 **षड्रस**

Ṣaḍrasa : having six flavours: *āmla, lavaṇa, kaṭuka, tikta, madhura* and *kaṣāya.*

4387 **षड्वर्ग**

Ṣaḍvarga : aggregate of six: five senses and *manas* : or (b) *kāma, krodha, lobha, harṣa, māna* and *mada* or (c) *prāṇavarga* along with mind.

4388 **षण्डक**

Ṣaṇḍaka : eunuch, sterile, impotent who lies like a woman in copulation.

4389 **षण्मुद्रा**

Ṣaṇmudrā : the torque, the bracelet, the jewel, the girdle, the ashes and the sacred thread which represent the six *pāramitās.*

4390 **षोडशदल-पद्म**

Ṣoḍaśadala-padma : Tāntric concept of sixteen-petalled lotus; each petal has a vowel symbolising a *mātṛkā* (*Kāmakalāvilāsa*, XXXIII). It is also conceived as existing in the *Cakra.*

4391 **षोडशदान**

Ṣoḍaśadāna : giving away sixteen things: earth (*pṛthvī*), seat (*āsana*), water (*Jala*), cloth (*vastra*), lamp (*dīpa*), food (*anna*), carriage (*yāna*), umbrella (*chatra*), perfume (*sugandhi*), flower-garland (*puṣpamālā*), fruits (*phala*), bed (*śayyā*), shoes s(*pādatrāṇa*), cow (*gau*), gold (*svarṇa*) and silver (*rajata*).

4392 **षोडशोपचार**

Ṣoḍaśopacāra : sixteen articles required for worship: They are *āsana, svāgata, pādya, arghya, ācamanīya, madhuparka, punarācamanīya, snānīya, bhūṣaṇa, gandha, puṣpa, dhūpa, naivedya,* and *vandanā* (*Mahānirvāṇa*, XII. 203-4).

4393 **ष्ठीवन**

Ṣṭhīvana : spitting. If a person spat or uttered haughty words before the images of gods or before the sages, the expiation was to give away gold, or burning of the tip of the tongue with a firebrand:

> देवर्षिणामभिमुखं ष्ठीवनाक्रोशने कृते ।
> उल्मुकेन दहेजिह्वां दातव्यं च कहरण्यकम् ॥

(*Kūrma.* II. 33.87)

स-Ṣa

4394 **संयम**

Saṁyama : restrained, self-controlled, constraint. It is comprised of *dhāraṇā, dhyāna* and *samādhi* according to the *Yogasūtra* (III.4). One who has restrained his passions is *saṁyamī* (*Raghu.*, III.20)

4395 **संयुक्त**

Saṁyukta : connected, furnished, married to.

4396 **संयुक्त-पताक-हस्त**

Saṁyukta-patāka-hasta : a type of hand gesture (*NS*, XXV. 81b-82a) In *Mṛcchakaṭikam* (Act II), the house is suggested by using *saṁyukta patāka* hands.

4397 **संयुत**

Saṃyuta : joined with, mixed with, attached,

4398 **संयुत-पल्लव-हस्त**

Saṃyuta-pallava-hasta : both hands gesture mentioned by *Bālarāmabharata.*

4399 **संयुत-हस्त**

Saṃyuta-hasta : combined hands movements. There are twenty *viniyogas* of *saṃyuta hasta. Añjali* is the most common *saṁyuta hasta* used in Sanskrit literature.

4400 **संयुत-हस्त-अंजलि**

Saṁyuta-hasta-añjali : a type of hand gesture.

4401 **संरब्धम्**

Saṁrabdham : quarrel : *saṁrabdham toṭakam vacaḥ* (*DR.*,1.77).

4402 **संलाप**

Saṃlāpa (*Bṛhaddevatā* 144-60) : (i) form of speech and thought, conversation, discussion; *mithobhāṣaṇa, saṁkathā.* (ii) talk. There are various ways in which people in the ancient India used to talk. Those ways, of course, derived entirely from the norms our ancestors internalized or from others with which they had become familiar. The main varieties are as follows : (a) *sūnṛta* is talk that is both pleasing and true. (b) *sāntva* is very sweet talk. (c) *saṅgata* is coherent talk, a synonym being *hṛdayaṅgama.* (d) *saṅkula* or *kliṣṭa* is contradictory speech. (e) *grasta* is elliptic speech, while speech rattled of is. (g) *nirasta.* (h) *ambukṛtam* is talk with saliva dripping. (i) *abhadram* is nonsense. (j) *anakṣara* is what should not be said. (k) *āhata* is a fallacy. *kliṣṭa* is indistinct speech (*Amarakośa*). (iii) Hymes (1974) has proposed an ethnographic framework which takes into account the various factors that are involved in speaking. We will now consider those factors one by one : (a) The setting and scene of speech are important. Setting refers to the time and place and scene refers to the abstract psychological setting, or the cultural definition of the occasion. (b) The participants include various combinations of speaker-listener, addressor-addressee, or sender-receiver. (c) Ends rfers to the conventionally recognized and expected outcomes of an exchange as well as to the personal goals that participants seek to accomplish or particular occasions. (d) Act sequence refers to the actual form and content of what is said : The precise words used, how they are used, and the relationship of what is said to the actual topic at hand. (e) Key, the fifth term refers to the tone, manner, or spirit in which a particular message is conveyed: light-hearted, serious, precise, pedantic, mocking, sarcastic, pompous, and so on. *Amarakośa* has provided key to the talk. (f) Instrumentalities refers to the choice of channel, e.g., oral, written, or telegraphic, and to the actual form of speech employed, such as the language, dialect, code, or register that is chosen. Formal, written, legal language is one instrumentality; spoken Hindi is another; code-switching between Hindi and English is a third, and the use of the dialect of Hindi is still another. (g) norms of interaction and interpretation refers to the specific behaviours and properties that attach to speaking and also to how these may be viewed by someone who does not share them, e.g., loudness, silence, gaze return, and so on. (h) genre, the final term, refers to clearly demarcated types of utterance; such things as poems, proverbs, riddles, sermons, prayers, lectures and editorials.

4403 **संल्लापक**

Saṁllāpaka : a dialogue containing passionate words of abuse whether these arise from contempt or not is called *saṁllāpaka.* It is also known as *saṁāpaka;* a type of *sāttvativṛtti. DR* (II.54) defines it as *gabhīrokti.*

4404 **संवदन**

Saṁvadana : the winning of love by occult means (*A*, 4.4.14, 4.5.1, 4.13.28), controlling by magical rites. *Saṁvad* means 'to converse' and *saṁvadana* is a type of conversation.

4405 **संवर**

Saṃvara : the way in which the *āśrava* or influx of *karma* is stopped. (b) covering, restraint, forbearance. *Saṁvaraṇa* 'stopping, shutting, covering, enclosure'. *Saṁvargaṇa* 'worship, respect, collecting'. *Saṁvarṇa* 'of the same colour'.

4406 **संवाच्**

Saṁvāc : argument. *Saṃvāda* 'conversation, agreement : *varṇasaṁvāda* (*Mudrā.* Y). Participants in a conversation were expected to produce informative remarks without being irrelevant, remarks that are believable; the impression is that speakers will conform to some prevailing cultural sense of politeness (*vinayarīti*) and regularity in their speech.

The child must learn normative constraints about who can speak first or next, when to stop speaking, and when an interruption is feasible.

The child learns to assume that he or she shares the same social settings as others. Learning to treat a range of appearances and utterance types as "obvious", despite the possibility of noticable differences becomes critical for adult in deciding that children are becoming more "mature".

In effect, Sanskrit texts stress that we must learn not only what to say, but also what to omit.

4407 **संवाद**

Saṁvāda : communication, dialogue. The social structure of the Indian community affects the pattern of communication in the village to a large extent. There is a traditional network of personal word-of-mouth. Communication and there are builting channels and blockades for communication in the village social system itself. Communication tends to be channelled along the traditional grooves of caste and kinship groups. Within the village there is far more social communication among the members of a caste than between castes, because of the traditional norms of intercaste commensality. There is usually a much faster flow of information horizontally, that is among the members of a caste, than vertically, that is, across caste lines in the village. As the social interaction among kinsmen is intensive as well as extensive, there is a much greater flow of communication among the kinsmen. However, sometimes communication is equally hampered due to quarrels and confrontation.

Fairs and festivals provide good opportunities for communication with the villagers and the tribes.

4408 **संवादनकला**

Saṁvādanakalā : the art of entertaining in conversation (*A*, 2.27.28). We are mostly aware of our talk and its effects. The idea of training people in the art of conversation is hardly new and is an important component of education for upper-class people. Language has the dual function of carrying information about the immediate situation and the relationship between the participants, as well as that of carrying the ideational content. Our capacity to utilize the resources of our language to narrate, explain, instruct, persuade, and generally divert cannot be underestimated, since it probably accounts for more social competence than any other single factor. The skilled talker is a formidable person in any situation. The development of verbal skills was a crucial factor of ancient educational curriculum. Talk is an art in the sense that, if it is to be successful, the speaker must reveal sensitivity to and awareness of each of the factors. Since we acknowledge that there are 'better' speakers and 'poorer' speakers, we may also assume that successful talk is a piece of 'skilled work'.

4409 **संवादिप्रवृत्ति**

Saṁvādīpravṛtti : purposeful action (in *Nyāya*).

4410 **संवादी**

Saṁvādī : agreeing with, comfortable to the model or prescription, purposeful action (in *Nyāya*). (b) a note that helps to develop a *rāga* manifested by the *vadī-svara* in *Saṅgīta*.

4411 **संवाहन**

Saṁvāhana : massaging; *Saṁvāhikā* 'a masseuse'. Cf. *cārana cānpi kahi kahi mṛdu bānī* (*Mānasa*, 2.198.3), *lage carana cāpan dou bhāī* (*Mānasa*, 1.226.3).

4412 **संवाहन-केशमर्दनादि-शिल्पकला**

Saṁvāhana-keśamardanādī-śilpakalā : hairdressing, massage, etc. One of the 64 arts given by *Kāmasūtra*. Gentle stroking, rubbing, squeezing and exploring of the partner's body with the hand, or occasionally with some other organ such as the nose, tongue, or foot, is nearly always sexual and can easily lead to physiological arousal according to Vātsyāyana. The Muria of Bastar are expert in this art (Elwin, 1947).

4413 **संवाहन-कौशल (कला)**

Saṁvāhana-kauśala (kala) : proficiency in massaging, one of the 64 arts enumerated in *Kāmasūtra* (1.3.16). In the tribal societies, particularly the Muria society, massaging is the first step to courtship. The Moṭiārī of the ghoṭul are expert in the technique of massage. Beginning with great vigour, almost roughly, it goes gentler and gentler until at last the girl's hands are moving caressingly, tenderly over the arms and bodies of their boys, rousing affection. Certain types of massages are specially exciting. The girl stands above the boy, bending over him, and rubs downwards, passing her hands over the stomach down to the specifically erogenous region, which thus receives a powerful tonic; sometimes she massages the legs, pushing her hands right to the groin.

4414 **संवृतक**

Saṁvṛtaka : terrible fires or clouds at the time of *pralaya* (dissolution of the world).

4415 **संवृति**

Saṁvṛti : a convention, a popular usage, a mere name accepted by people, something that exists only by name and not back by any reality. We are reminded of a Marathi proverb; *bolā cīca kaḍhī bola cāci bhāta* which means "soup or rice which one, only in words, promises to give, but it is never backed up by any real action". Pāli : *sammuti* (*Suttanipāta*, 897). (b) a social custom that is not rigidly binding but is widely observed is *saṁvṛti*.

4416 **संवेग**

Saṁvega : excitement, hurry due to excess joy, etc. *Saṁvega* is a highly emotional state characterized by motility, impulsive, verbal and motor behaviour, and feeling or tense anticipation. The Pāli word *saṁvega* is often used to denote the shock or wonder that may be felt when the perception of a work of art becomes serious experience. The emotional stimulus of painful themes may be evoked deliberately when the will or mind (*citta*) is sluggish; then he stirs it up (*saṁvajēti*) by a consideration of the Eight Emotional themes (aṭṭha saṃvega vatthūni); in the result of state of distress, he then "gladens".

4417 **संवेशन**

Saṁveśana : lying down, sleeping, copulation, sexual intercourse.

4418 **संव्यवहार**

Saṁvyavahāra : mutual transaction (Aparārka on *Yaj.* 2.92), social calls. Social calls among the Hindus lack the intimacy and pleasantness of such functions in the west. For one thing, the number of people a respectable Hindu gentleman can mix freely with are very few; for another, men never converse or move freely with women of even their own household. It is not considered proper for a man to eat or talk with one's own wife in the presence of other people, and it is nothing short of scandalous for women of a household to appear before male guests and converse with familiarity. As such, social calls among the Hindus are generally a matter of embarrassment rather than of pleasure. I must, however, make it plain that this applies only to orthodox families and not to the modern imitators of Western manners whose percentage of the Hindu population is still negligible.

Again, leisured classes are very few among the Hindus, especially in the villages and the women have always some household duties or religious ceremonies to perform. Men too have their daily work in the fields or in the shops, and the routine of domestic worship has to be gone through. Hence social visits have not, among the Hindus, developed into a social art. Men, however, visit other households very often on matters of business, and when these are not of a pressing nature indulge in petty talk, partake of refreshments and play indoor games with the hosts. Women occasionally get a holiday, when they visit other households, or there are occasions, however, it is made a wholetime job and they spend hours in gossip. Women usually take their children with them and the occasion is made use of to adorn the children with all their ornaments and display the wealth of the parents of the children. Sickness, petty ceremonies, etc., are made good excuses of by women for visiting neighbours and relations. Men folk as a rule discourage women from leaving their households for any purpose, whatever, least of all for making idle social calls, which they consider a waste of time and energy. But if some member of a family falls ill, or some ceremony is near at hand, which requires the assistance of a number of women for the preparation of the large quantities of sweetmeats which are indispensable for all Hindu domestic ceremonies, permission is readily granted to women to visit the sick person or the family needing their assistance, and the women take full advantage of the opportunity.

When men and women together visit a household, the men are conducted to the *mardānā* or men's apartments, and the women to the *zanānā* or women's apartments. Children are privileged to enter both and they often perform the office of messengers between the *mardānā* and *zanānā*. During social calls, if the guests are allowed to interdine with the hosts, light refreshments are served. These vary according to the localities, but nowehere in India will respectable Hindus think of entertaining their guests with liquor. Drinking is universally considered by high class Hindus as a bad habit, and even those who indulge in it will seldom drink in their own houses when guests or women folk are about. Sweetmeats, milk, coffee and tea are usually served. As far as women are concerned, the privilege of making social calls is confined to elderly ladies and children. Girls of marriageable age and young ladies newly married are at times allowed to accompany the elderly women, but widows never.

The generality of Hindus consider social calls a nuisance, and the most respectable person is he who never visits another man's house without sufficient reason.

4419 **संशय**

Saṁśaya : (Bṛhaddevatā) form of speech and thought; doubt, which arises when there is the suggestion of different alternative views about the same thing. It is regarded as a positive state of cognition (*Nyāyasūtra*, 1.1.23). Śivāditya defines doubt, *Saṁśaya* as cognition which is not certain (*anavadhāraṇam jñānam*) and error, *viparyaya*, as cognition which is false but carries with it certitude. According to him, all right knowledge is characterized by certainty. If there is uncertainty, it is due to incorrect apprehension. In the case of doubt (*saṁśaya*), there are two or more alternatives which are predictable. When an object is seen from a distance there is a doubt whether it is a post or a man. In the case of error (*viparyaya*), there is certitude, but it is wrong certitude as in the case of mistaking a rope for a snake.

4420 **संश्लेष**

Saṁśleṣa : embracing or summing up relevant sentiments and feelings through appropriate gestures (*NS*, IX. 175).

4421 **संश्लेषण-संकेत**

Saṁśleṣaṇa-saṁketa : tie-sign. A tie-sign is any action which indicates the existence of a personal relationship. If two people walk arm-in-arm down the street, their linked-arm action is a sign to onlookers that they are personally 'tied' to each other in some way. There are many different tie-signs of this kind and, as social mammals we are actually responsive to every subtle variation, Judging not only that a personal link exists, but also the nature of that link. Tie-signs indicating the bond between a woman and her absent husband in India may be referred here. The woman wears white from the time of her husband's death and continues to do so for the rest of her life, displaying a permanent bond with her departed male. In India, an unmarried girl neither wears the *mangalasūtra* nor applies *sindūra* in her fore-head, while the married woman displays it. Here it is possible to distinguish at a glance between the bonded and unbonded females in this group. (Fig. 4421)

4422 **संसर्गविद्या**

Saṁsargavidyā : the art of association (*A*, 1.12.1, 13.1.2).

4423 **संसारतरु**

Saṁsārataruḥ : the tree of birth and rebirth, worldly involvement, world-tree. The concept of *saṁsārataru* occurs in *Bhāgavat Purāṇa* (XI. 12.21-22), stating that the world is like the *paṭa* (cloth) in every thread of which (*tantuvitāna*) the divine ultimate reality is woven. It is also likened to a tree that gives flowers and fruits according to the action. It has two seeds, hundred roots; it has three stalks and five stems; five juices ooze from it. Its branches are eleven; on it are two nests for two birds (*dvisuparṇaniḍaḥ*). It has three layers of barks and two fruits. This tree has entered the sun : *arkaṁ praviṣṭaḥ*.

In the social semiotics of the tribes, the tree is the house of a man who has a number of marriageable daughters. The girls can also be sweet smelling *mallikā* flowers. The two girls of a village are compared to *ludam* and *champak* flowers:

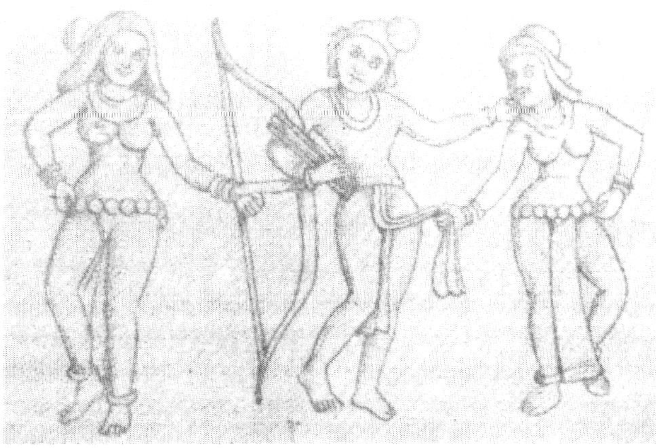

Fig. – (4421)

How nicely they bent down
The *ludams* of Diuri
How sweetly they wave in the breeze
The *champak* of *surmali*
When moving in a line or running in a curve
What a necklace do they weave.

This kind of hidden symbolism in what is called the "clue" poems is quite common in Muṇḍārī and Oraon folk songs but not in Kondha or Parjā songs.

4424 **संस्कार**

Saṁskāra : personal sacraments, forty or more—which accompanied the smallest events of an individuals life, from birth to death. Etymologically the term signifies "putting together", "forming well", "making perfect", "accomplishment", "embellishment". "purification", "cleansing", "preparation", "dressing" "refining", "polishing", etc. From religious point of view it denotes sacrements, rituals, purificatory acts, etc. Śabara (on *Jaimini* III.1.3). explains *saṁskāra* as that which being effected makes a certain thing or person fit for certain purpose. (b) *Saṁskāras* or ritual acts are in large part NV. (c) The term *saṁskāra*, appears to have three connotations in philosophical works. First, it connotes the impressions left on mind by experiences, which help us to recall the past experiences. Secondly, it indicates that our past experiences enrich us so that the later perceptions are influenced by the past assets, as it were. Thirdly, some of the past experiences, particularly, the highly emotional experiences, become latent, unconscious, that is not available to the consciousness, which nevertheless influence our behaviour.

4425 **संस्कृतक**

Saṁskṛtaka : artificial *(A*, 2.13.42).

4426 **संस्कृति**

Saṁskṛti : culture. The first use of the world *saṁskṛti* in its present meaning may be seen in *Aitareya Brāhmaṇa* 800 B.C.) where it is said that : आत्मसंस्कृतिवावि शिल्पानि Arts indeed are the culture of the soul. Again it is recorded that वा एतैर्यजमान आत्मानं संस्कुरुते The *yajamāna* receives the culture of the soul through all these arts.

A panoramic view of Indian culture reveals that there is an obstinate and unyielding continuity, a marvellous and ceaseless vitality and a rare activity on all its own. Here continuity does not mean a mere mechanical inert, mountain-like existence. It is continuity of living and vibrant existence with an unmistakable identity in spite of all the intermediate changes. The hoary *Ṛgveda* was composed by seers thousands of years ago. It is chanted today by thousands with the same - not merely similar—intonation and emphasis and is being interpreted in terms of modern thought and expressed in today's idiom. The *Upaniṣads* carried on for centuries in the *āśramas* in remote forests are today inspiring not only Indians but savants and saints abroad. Moral standards set by epics like *Rāmāyaṇa* and *Mahābhārata* are current coin for the whole population of the day.

The main characteristics of vitality is to breathe and live vigorously, continuously, rejecting what is not healthy and assimilating what adds for energetic activity. There have been ups and downs in the history of the culture of India, as high and low as the contours of the Himalayas. In spite of invasions by cultures of Persia, Greece, Islam and now of Europe, Indian culture, while exchanging some traits here and there, has been projecting itself and fighting its way to assert originality and identity. Its vitality is also visible in dealing with rebellious and reformist elements within itself. By yielding to the reformist trends, necessary for its own life and growth Indian culture has shown its plasticity as well as adaptability : अविद्यया मृत्युं तीर्त्वा विद्ययाऽमृतमश्नुते ।

4427 **संस्थान**

Saṁsthāna : position (of a form in sculpture).

4428 **संहत-जङ्घा**

Saṁhata-Jaṅghā : It is the position of perfect equilibrium which corresponds to the *sampāda* position of the feet.

4429 **संहत-स्थानक**

Saṁhata-sthānaka : a type of posture.

4430 **संहिता**

Saṁhitā : code, coding. The code which describes how meaning is contained in a NV act, that is, the rule which characterizes the relationship between the act itself and that which it signifies, may be extrinsic or intrinsic. An extrinsic code is one in which the act signifies or stands for something else, and the coding may be arbitrary or iconic. An intrinsic code is in a sense no code in that the act does not stand for but is its significant; the meaning of the act is intrinsic to the action itself. Ekman and Friesen have characterized these as three coding principles: arbitrary (extrinsic) codes, iconic (extrinsic) codes, and intrinsic codes.

4431 **सकल-मुद्रा**

Sakala-mudrā : making the two thumbs to a side like a lotus-stalk of the above hand, frame the *sakala-mudrā*, which may bring into control of all the spirits (*VD*).

4432 **सख्य**

Sakhya : the kind of devotion in which God is looked upon as a friend, as between Kṛṣṇa and Subala. *Sakhya bhaktas* are comerades who consider themselves equal to God in every respect. *Sakhya* is one the five kinds of *rasas* and *ratis* i.e., devotional instincts and experiences which develops into *anurāga* (intense love). *Caitanyacaritāmṛta* (II. 23).

4433 **सगन्ध**

Sagandha : kindred (*A*, 1.8.17, 7.11.27).

4434 **सगर-हस्त**

Sagara-hasta : *alapadma* on the head symbolizes the mythical king Sagara (*Mirror of Gesture*, p.47).

4435 **संकर्षण-मुद्रा**

Saṅkarṣaṇa-mudrā : when in both the hands, the thumb and the little finger are concealed and others are joined and extended, it makes the gesture of *saṅkarṣaṇa* (*VD*).

4436 **संकल्प**

Saṅkalpa : concept, conception, imagining, mental formulation, form of speech and thought (*Bṛhaddevatā* 144-60). (b) one of the essential elements in any gift or dedication to the public. (c) it also means to 'resolve'and is necessary in every religious life. (d) *Saṅkalpa* denotes a formula in *vrata* as well. (e) *Saṅkalpas* are formed by process of abstraction, which is then followed by a process of generalization. A Vedic hymn desires that a man's resolves should be auspicious : *Tanme manaḥ Śiva saṅkalpamastu.* In the *Upaniṣads,* we return to explore the depths of the inner world (Radhakrishnan, Vol. I, p.43). *Saṅkalpa* is the essence of mind. *Saṅkalpa* and *vikalpa* (indecision) are the two facets of the mind. The seer prays that his mind should not only be of firm resolve but also of auspicious (Śiva) resolve, that is constructive and growth-oriented. *Saṅkalpa* is autotherapy. It is based on auto-suggestion. It brings about auto-strength. When the self is energetic and determined, there cannot be any disintegration of personality.

4437 **सङ्कीर्तन**

Saṅkīrtana : singing the name of God in chorus to the accompaniment of musical instruments.

4438 **सङ्केत**

Saṅketa : (a) calling gestures, codes (*Nāgarasarvasva*, 1.16). (b) sign (*A*, 12.4.21). The concept of *saṅketa* is central to Indian erotics as well as to modern semiotic analysis. The formation and understanding of messages (encoding and decoding) is made possible by codes—a set of rules or an interpretative device known to both transmitter and receiver, which assigns a central meaning or content to certain sign. We recognize the signifier, long-blonde-hair for example, as a sign of feminity when we interpret it through the code of feminity as the signifier of a certain signified woman. Within that code there is a sub-code which assigns this long-blonde-haired woman a particular meaning—a particular kind of healthy sexuality. Codes are forms of social knowledge which are derived from social practices and beliefs although they are not laid down in any stature. Codes organize our understanding of the world in terms of 'dominant' meaning patterns' which vary from time to time but which we largely take for granted and which are uppermost in our minds when we interpret things or think about them.

An icon could be said to be 'semiotically thick'; it comprises a heterogeneity of signals and is characterized by its spatial as well as temporal dimensions. Each image operates spatially, whilst linguistic messages and unfolding of the text-messages is temporal.

(c) convention. Theorists differ as to the locus of convention in the case of words. Some think that convention lies in *jāti* (genus), *guṇa* (quality), *kriyā* (action) and *saṁjñā* (name). Others think that it lies in the genus alone. (d) sign. Indeed, signs are like the trees as described by Tagore, as efforts trying to speak to the listening sky. (e) Western semioticians seem to be in agreement that a sign is an object of some sort that 'stands for' something else. There seems to be little disagreement about the constitutes of the sign: (1) It must be something, (ii) It must represent, (iii) It must be based on convention. (f) a *saṅketa* is defined as *saṅketo gṛhyate jātau guṇakarmadravyakriyāsu ca* (*SD*, VII.5). It is a *saṅketa*, for instance, to imagine that the 'colour' of *yaśas* (fame) is white. As whiteness is sign of purity, it produces in our mind a pleasing impression. So does *yaśas*. Hence it is white. Similarly *apakīrti* or notoriety is black in colour. It is a type of poetic convention (*kavi-samaya*) for which the reader is referred to *Kāvyamīmāṁsā* of Rājaśekhara. (g) thus code is a set of symbols used to transform sets of data into another form; cf. *Sayanahin raghupati lakhanu ne vārī* (*Mānasa*, 1.254.4), *kahā anuj san sayan bujhāī* (*Ibid.*, 3.17.20), *nij pati kaheu tinhai siya sayanani* (*Ibid.*, 2.117.7), *barajatu sain nain ke koe* (Tulasīdāsa, *Kṛṣṇagītāvalī*).

4439 **सङ्केतक**

Saṅketaka : encoder; a person sending the message. Varāhamihira (505 A.D.) has used the term *Saṅketa-hetu* meaning occasions in close contact. Nocturnal recreation or walking, vigils, professing illness, staying in another's house, consultations with sooth-sayers, taking part in congregational mournings, and festivals were the occasions when women used to come in close contact with other men :

रात्रीविहारजागररोगव्यपदेशपरगृहेक्षणिकाः ।
व्यसनोत्सवाश्च सङ्केतहेतवस्ते रक्ष्याश्च ॥
(*Bṛhat-Saṇhitā, LXVIII*)

Kāśyapa also enumerates the same meeting places :

दुष्टसङ्गरता या तु सा क्षिप्रं नाशयेत् कुलम् ।
तीर्थयात्राटनं भेदे परवेश्मसमागमम् ॥
देवालये रात्र्यटनं परस्परनिवासिभिः ।
पितृवेश्मनिवासं च न श्रेयः स्वामिना बिना ॥
घृतकुम्भोपमा नारी पुरुषवह्निवर्चसः ।
संश्लेषाद् द्रवते कुम्भस्तद्वत् या स्त्रीपुंसि भविता ॥
निर्जने तु विविक्ताङ्गं या स्त्री पुरुषमीक्षते ।
तस्याः प्रस्विद्यते गुह्यमनुग्राह्येच्छयान्विता ॥

A loving damsel would at first evince no desire, but would not give up amorous talk; in the beginning of the sexual act, she would be bashful and languid; in the middle, she would be free from bashfulness, and at the end, bashfully hand down her face. Then again she would show, during coitus, various graceful expressions of sentiment,

आदौ नेच्छति नोज्झति स्मरकथां व्रीडाविमिश्रालसा
मध्ये ह्रीपरिवर्जिताभ्युपरमे लज्जाविनम्रानना ।
भावैनैकविधैः करोत्यभिनयं भूयश्च सा सादरा
बुद्ध्वा पुम्प्रकृतिं च यानुचरति ग्लानेतरैश्चेष्टितैः ॥
(*Bṛhat-Saṇhitā*, LXVIII)

4440 **सङ्कोच-विकास**

Saṅkoca-vikāsa : involution and evolution and *vice-versa* which characterize the world-process.

4441 **सङ्क्रान्ति**

Saṅkrānti : day of transition from one month to another which is held to be sacred.

4442 **संक्रोश**

Saṅkrośa : an outcry (*A*, 1.17.39, 2.7.10).

4443 **संक्षिप्तक**

Saṅksiptaka : condensed representation of the plot, a type of *ārabhaṭī vṛtti.* It includes relevant crafts such as many kinds of model works, drawings, and dresses for a condensed representation of the plot; (*NS*, XX).

4444 **संक्षोभ**

Saṁkṣobha : upheavel (*Vāyu Purāṇam*, 58.38, 41-43). *Manu* (7.20-21) fears that "if the king does not exercise his power of punishment relentlessly enough, the crow would eat the sacrificial cake, the dog lick up the food put out for ritual oblation and no right of ownership would be there for anyone to retain" in short, we are warned, the lower would become the higher: प्रवर्त्तेत अधरोत्तरम् ।

This braŚhminical dread of the inversive process was to be systematized later into a chiliastic image of total cataclysm in the *Vāyu Purāṇam.* It envisaged a great upheavel with the advent of *kali* at the *yugānta* (epoch end). Among the many reversals characteristic of that topsy-turvey age, Brāhmaṇs, it predicts, would behave like Śūdras and Śūdras like Brāhmaṇs, kings would take to the vocation of thieves and thieves to that of kings, women would be faithless to their husbands and servants to their masters.

4445 **संक्षोभिणी-मुद्रा**

Saṁkṣobhiṇī-mudrā : the middle finger of both hands are to be touched by the little fingers and the thumb; the index finger should be straight like a staff, and the *anāmikā* should be above the middle fingers (*Brahmāṇḍa*, II. 4.42.2).

4446 **सङ्गीत**

Saṅgīta : vocal music, instrumental music and dance are together designated by this term. The *saṅgīta* played a very important part in the rituals. The employment of music was not only for gaity; it had an emotional basis, and worked as a magic-charm (*Mān. Gr. Sū.*, 1.9.29; *Pār Gr. Sū.*, 1.7.2; *Sāṅkha Gr. Sū.*, 1.22. 11-22). The custom obtains even today in folk-songs. (Fig. 4446)

4447 **संगीतरत्नाकर**

Saṅgītaratnākara : a work on musicology written by Śārṅgadeva which deals with those common feats of gesture which enliven a dramatic performance.

4448 **सङ्घ**

Saṅgha : a collective body or tribe, or assembly.

4449 **सङ्घटना**

Saṅghaṭanā : one of the nineteen items in *pūrvaraṅga* (the preliminaries). In it there was employment of hands in different manners to indicate the time beats (*NS*). (b) the poetic structure; the well-known concept of poetic structure propagated by Udbhaṭa.

4450 **सङ्घातज**

Saṅghātaja : stroke. Using two strokes in *vīṇā*-playing; a type of *vistāra.* (b) stroke is the most loving, sexual, and pleasant behaviour.

4451 **सचिव**

Saciva : the minister is to be addressed by Brāhmaṇs as *saciva* or *amātya* and by other persons inferior to Brāhmaṇss always as *ārya* (*NS*, XVII. 65-90).

4452 **सजातीय-तत्त्व**

Sajātiya-tattva : general quality, or generalized value.

4453 **सजीव / सज्जीव**

Sajīva : the entrance of the animals on the stage (*NS*). According to Bharata animals are four-footed, two-footed and footless. Abhinava explains that when the *nāgāstra* is to be used the image of serpent should be shown, in the *nṛsiṁhāstra* the man-lion form should be represented etc. (*NS*, III.135).

Sajīva meant the forms of living beings such as snakes, birds, animals and men (*NS*, XXI.162) These were represented in scenes of fighting, siege, etc. Thus, when the use of *nāgāstra* or snake weapon was shown, the forms of snakes were to be represented (AB on *NS*, XXI.164).

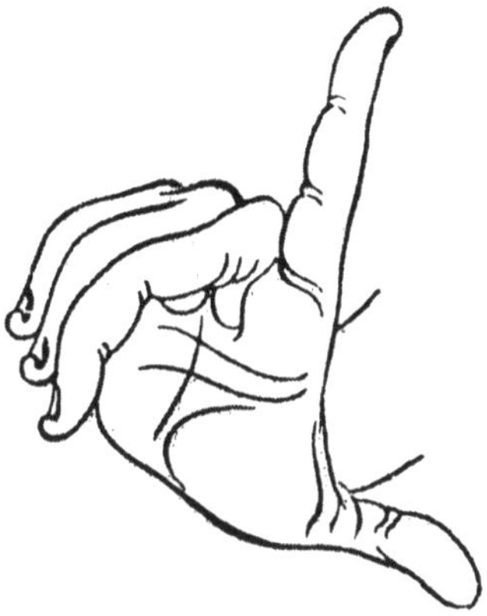

Fig. – (4446)

4454 **सञ्चार**

Sañcāra : movement (*A*, 2.9.26), Communication (*A*, 1.12.11). Walking to and from the speaker's platform, shifting weight from side to side or back and forth, and pacing about the platform are examples of bodily movement. The only rule governing total physical behaviour is that movement be communicative.

4455 **सञ्चारिका**

Sañcārikā : woman who kept watch over different halls, gardens, temples, pleasure-palaces, and also kept time. They were also used as messengers (*NS*, XXIV. 58-59).

4456 **सञ्चारी**

Sañcārī : one of the four types of *varṇas* (musical exercises). Notes employed in ascent and descent in a mixed manner (*NS*). (b) accessory feelings.

4457 **सञ्चारीभावदृष्टि**

Sañcārībhāvadṛṣṭi : glances pertaining to accessory feelings, glances suggesting temporal feelings; Bharata enumerates twenty *sañcārībhāvadṛṣtis.*

4458 **सञ्चारी-भाव**

Sañcārī-bhāva : transitory emotions, accessory or component feelings that rise and fall within the basic emotional states. A sentiment cannot be shown in abstract; it is developed and ramified through the portrayal of accessory or component feelings which rise and fall within the basic emotional state. The text and the incidents and motifs devised by the playright embody these feelings. The incidents, the dialogue, the scenes, in fact, the whole story or plot are of value or relevance only as embodiments or vehicles of these feelings and of basic emotion. Bharata thus describes thirty-three accessory feelings. See *vyabhicārī bhāva*, a synonymous term.

4459 **संज्वर**

Saṁjvara (*Bṛhaddevatā* 104-60) : form of speech and thought.

4460 **सती**

Satī : also called *sahagamana. Satī* is the designation of a woman who burns herself in the funeral pyre of her husband along with him. A woman committing *satī* is given a holy bath, adorned with ornaments, is made to put collyrium in the eyes, flowers and sandal-paste; she is asked to wear the holy-thread (*maṅgala-sūtra*); feet are decorated with lac-eye. She is required to be smiling, and should give various gifts. (*Padama P., Pātāla khaṇḍa,* 102.70-73).

The self-immolation of the widow. Although condemned by the brāhmaṇic caste, suicide by a widow was becoming increasingly fashionable during 200 B.C. to 700 A.D. especially among the Kṣatriyas, where it was perhaps the consequence of polygamy. The first dated mention of this custom goes back to A.D. 510, when such an incident was commemorated by the erection of a slate at *Eraṇ* (*Corpus Inscriptionum Indicarum*, III. p.92), and the custom became widespread subsequently, especially, in Southern India. The voluntary sacrifice on the part of the widow was spectacular indeed: during the cremation of her husband's corpse, she climbed on the blazing pyre and allowed herself to be burnt alive. This act was considered the supreme sign of conjugal fidelity, which is why a woman who performed it was named a *satī* or true wife (Upadhyaya, *Op. cit.* p. 189; *The Cambridge History of India,* I, pp. 292-93).

Widows respecting the Indian tradition of *satī* now no longer sacrifice themselves on their husbands funeral pyres, but they withdraw permanently from normal life. Even in social circles where women are regarded as liberated, a widow may have to make special efforts to establish a new and independent social status.

4461 **सत्य**

Satya : true, real, essential, sacred, hieratic (painting) Truth is of two kinds: conventional (*saṁvṛti*) and ultimate for transcendental (*pāramārthika*). There is another kind of truth known as *prātibhaṣika.* (b) *satya* or truthfulness is one of the five *yamas* in *yoga*, one of the ten *yamas* of *Yāj.* (III. 312) and one of the five duties enjoined by *Manu* (X.63) on men of all *varṇas.* (c) in later Vedic texts the term *satya* came to denote *ṛta*, meaning order, natural and moral. Signal and analytical truths are known as *lakṣaṇa* and *vibhāga.*

4462 **सत्त्व**

Sattva : the mental state transmitted to consciousness extends to body—*dehamātraniṣṭhāḥ* (Abhinavabhāratī, 22.154); purity; simplicity, quality of essence, being in itself, the first of the three *guṇas.* (b) the constituent of *prakṛti* which is of the nature of pleasure and is light (*laghu*) and illuminating (*prakāśaka*). It gives rise to happiness and love, tranquillity and modesty, health and lightness of body, patience and forgiveness, courage, magnanimity, self-restraint and the illumination of knowledge.

Sattva is temperament, the mental mood which pervades even the body. The *sāttvika,* as the attribute of body, is seen in the superior characters only. The excellence of woman results in the Erotic and that of men in the heroic. *Sattva* partakes the nature of body, and *bhāva* (feeling) arises from temperament (*sattva*), *hāva* (emotion), from feeling (*bhāva*), and *helā* (passion) from *hāva* (emotion).

4463 **सत्त्व-रजस्-तमस्-मुद्रा**

Sattva-rajas-tamas-mudrā : the gesture symbolizing *triguṇa* of the Vaiṣṇavite cult. The ring-finger of the *mukula*-hand is extended (*VD*).

4464 **सदस्य**

Sadasya : seventeeth priest whose services are required in the *Soma* sarifices (*Baud. Sr.*, II.3).

4465 **सदाचार**

Sadācāra : good manners, source of *dharma.* According to Yājñavalkya : *sadācāraḥ śiṣṭācare ityuktam. Śiṣṭāḥ khalu vigatamatsarāḥ nirahaṅkārāḥ kuṁbhīdhānyaḥ.*, according to *Manu* (2.18) :

> *yasmin deśe ya ācāraḥ pāramparya-kramāgataḥ* /
> *varṇānām sāntarālānām sadācāraḥ sa ucyate* //

At the household level the pattern of communication is directed by the traditional social norms of respect, distance and indulgence among members of a familial group. For instance, according to village norms, the daughter-in-law is expected to maintain a respectable distance from her father-in-law, as a result, communication between them is very restricted. Further, wife and husband are not expected to be very free with each other in the presence of others. This is carried to the extent that the wife covers her face and does not talk to her husband in the presence of elders.

Thus, *sadācāra* means usages and practises of *śiṣṭas* (elites or decent peoples). They are intricate questions about the relative merits of *Śruti* (the Vedic way) and *Smṛti* (the way prescribed by the *Dharmaśāstras*) in regard to *sadācāra.* According to Kumārila those usages are alone authoritative that are not opposed to Vedic texts, that are practised by *śiṣṭas* in the belief that they are part of *dharma* (right path) and for which no obvious motive can be predicted.

4466 **सद्गुण**

Sadguṇa : good human quality. The human qualities most highly valued in tribal societies are helpfulness, generosity, courage and amiable temper. The emphasis on helpfulness is understandable in a society where no one keeps a store of food and a person unable to go out collecting food must starve unless other members of the small group of families living in the same locality give him a share of the roots they have gathered. Usually this is done as a matter of course, and I knew a group where a man crippled by yaws and hence unmarried (among the Hill Marias of Bastar) was permanently maintained by his kinsmen and neighbours. Old people and orphans too are usually well looked after, and stories and myths provide divine approval of such socially desirable action. They tell how deities assuming human form cared for the weak and lonely, and thus set an example for the behaviour expected from Abujhmāriās. Conversely greed, cowardice and quarrelsomeness are condemned, and there are stories which in the manner of morality tales show how those exhibiting these obnoxious qualities come to a bad end.

4467 **सद्योजात-मुद्रा**

Sadyojāta-mudrā : make a fist by the right hand with its thumb raised, place it on the left thumb and wrap the right fist with leftfingers. This is the gesture of *sadyojāta,* which removes all bad omens (*VD*).

4468 **सद्-विद्या**

Sad-vidyā : same as *śuddha-vidyā. see śuddha-māyā.*

4469 **सधवा**

Sadhavā : a married woman. A married woman should not have bare hands but always with two pairs of bangles in both hands, if not ornaments. She also wears a *maṅgalasūtra* around her neck. This is for the welfare of her husband.

4470 **सन**

Sana : seated pose.

4471 **सनातन-धर्म**

Sanātana-dharma : a title of modern coinage to designate Hinduism as an eternal and ever-existing religion. The word occurs in *Brahmāṇḍa Purāṇa* (II. 33, 37-38 and *Mahābhārata* (1.128.28).

4472 **संदंश**

Saṁdaṁśa : climax of love; lit. closely adhered.

4473 **संदंश-हस्त**

Saṁdaṁśa-hasta : clasping hand; the pincers hand derived from *arāla.* Used for picking of a flower from the stem (*NS*, IX, 112.16). The palm is raised facing outwards. The first finger is bent down to touch the thumb at the tip, and the other three fingers are extended forward and very slightly bent at the joints. It is used to express generosity, sacrificial offerings, worship, the number five, small bud, gentle dance, sprout blades of grass, eclipse, fly, garland, pointing, snow, etc. When the thumb and the fore-finger of the *arāla*-gesture are joined like a tong and the middle finger is adjacent to the palm in a curving order, it is called the gesture of *saṁdaṁśa.* The pincers gesture is of three kinds, as per the use of aesthetic appeal : (a) the fore-facing (b) the front-facing and (c) the side-twisting. The fore-faced pincers is used to wreath flowers; to take grass, leaves and hair-strings. The front-facing pincers is to be applied to draw a lance, to take hold the same and to pull it out, pierced into something, to pluck flowers from branches, to fill up a wick and a lamp-stick (with oily things), to utter words of censure like *dhik* etc. in anger. The side-twisting pincers is to be applied to suggest the sacred thread, penetrating a hole, a bow-ring, fineness of an object of an arrow, practising penance, study, very small thing; but if this gesture is styled with the left hand; it indicates fatness, badnames, envy and hateful talks, etc. In case, the side-pincers is styled with turned out tips of the left hand, they may suggest a picture, colouring eyes, argument, wreathing twigs, newly opened leaves and extracting the vermilion (*alaktaka*) for the use of women (*NS*, IX. 104-110).

(b) the fore-finger and the thumb of the *arāla* hand are crossing and the palm little hollowed. According to sentiments and moods, it is three-fold: (i) held in front: in this position it represents the plucking of flowers, arranging them, holding grass leaves, hair and thread, holding or pulling out dart or thorn. (ii) near the mouth: In this pose it indicates plucking of flowers from the stem, completing the decoration by collyrium stick and the word fie upon in anger (iii) by the side: with the left hand held on one side having the end turned slight to represent *saroṣabhāṣaṇa* according to *SR* and *sadoṣavacana* according to *NS*, i.e. words of censure, delicacy, abuse and jealousy. It is also used to indicate painting, colouring the eyes, deliberation, stem, drawing designs and squeezing of the lac dye by women. Combined with other hand, it represents wearing sacred thread, piercing a hole in pearls, etc., bow-string, fineness, arrow, targets, concentration, meditation and small quantity.

4474 **सन्दष्टक-अधर**

Saṁdaṣṭaka-adhara : pouting of lips, a type of lip-gesture in *raudra rasa;* biting of lips by teeth; this sense is expressed in Hindi idiom : *Oṇṭh cabānā* "to bite one's lips with regret or vexation", bitten by teeth, biting lips by teeth; suggests an exposure of anger (*NS*, VIII. 134-140).

4475 **सन्धान**

Sandhāna : accomodation. The technique for making verbal encounters run more smoothly, which many people adopt, apparently without realizing it, as *sandhānam* (accomodation). Speakers may attempt to enhance their value for another speaker by drifting towards the other's mode of speech. This can be at the level of accent. It can be at the level of style, teachers who hope to 'get on' with their pupils may speak about their subjects in exaggeratedly 'inarticulate' style. It can involve simply the use of some phrases that aspiring social climbers associate with the class or caste to which they would like to belong.

The capacity to modify one's speech, whether at the level of accent or register, to fit in a situation or a group of people is an important one. Note the word "capacity" — as with any social skill it is important to have the ability to do something even though one might not choose to exercise that ability. Because of the strong association between language use and caste in India, any situation where an individual is bound to confront people from different castes, the capacity to modify speech needs to be acquired.

4476 **सन्ध्या**

Sandhyā : literally twilight. The term indicates the act of prayer at day-break, noon and sunset. (*Manu*, II. 101).

4477 **सन्ध्या-भाषा**

Sandhyā-bhāṣā : twilight language. A curious language used by the saints of *Śaiva-Siddhas* in the sectarian literature in the time of Kramāditya (7th century A.D.). It was a kind of code language also known as *sandha-bhāṣā*. It was prevalent among the various schools of *tāntrikas* (Śaiva, śākta and Bauddha etc.)

4478 **सन्नत-करण**

Sannata-karaṇa (dola-hasta) : feet in *svastika* in initial position with a slight jump as in *hariṇpluta cārī*. The final position is attained. Thighs and knees are spread out in *kṣipta* (*NS*, IX. 148). After a jump, the two feet are put forward in *svastika* and the two hands in *dola*. It is used in forward movement due to the words of the inferior.

4479 **सन्निकर्ष**

Sannikarṣa : contact of senses with objects. According to *Nyāya* thinkers, perception depends upon *sannikarṣa*, some sort of an intercourse or dynamic communion between the object and as particular sense-organ. They describe six kinds of *sannikarṣa*. But they appear to be more logical than psychological. It is sufficient to note the nature of the first two kinds. When there is a visual perception of a jar, there is *saṁyoga*, union between the substance, the *dravya* and the sense-organ. That is, *saṁyoga* is a direct relation between the sense-organ and the object. Secondly, there is *saṁyukta samavāya* or united inherence which gives rise to the perception of the quality which inheres in the object. That is, this differentiates between the perception of the object as such and the perception of the quality of the object, the quality which infers in the object (Sinha, I, 76).

4480 **सन्निधि**

Sannidhi : proximate (*Naiṣadha*, 18.40; Viśvanātha, *Sāhitya-darpaṇa*, 3.108) Proximity of both place and time. (b) one of the conditions of a sentence in Sanskrit grammar; juxtaposition. The utterance of the words should be consecutive without any interval between them. When the words are uttered at intervals, they cannot make an impression on the mind. If the interval is long, we may forget the first word when we hear the second.

4481 **सन्निधिविज्ञान**

Sannidhivijñana : proximics. Initiated by the anthropologist Edward T. Hall (1966), proximics can be defined as peoples' conception, structuration and use of space, from their natural built surrounding to the distances consciously or unconsciously kept in personal interaction. Proximic behaviour covers a very wide range of manifestations, both culture-specific and universal, but first of all biological that is, displayed by human beings as living organism claiming, delimiting and maintaining their own territory of occupying someone else's. As a body-originated system of communication in personal interaction, proximic behaviour seems to be patterned along with other message-conveying activities as a motorbased modality, perceived through vision, touch, olfaction, and also kinesthetically and exercised as what is actual: / kinesic activity.

The analysis of proximic behaviour in the character's interaction would reveal not only a specific psychological context, but often a cultural one as well, and it would be part of literary anthropology. Hall (1968) reviewed proximics on an inter personal level as "a constellation of sensory inputs...coded in a particular way". He formulated a comprehensive "proximic notational system" that covers the following eight different "dimensions": (a) postural-sex identifiers (sex and postural status of the interactants, (b) sociofugal-sociopetal axis (face-to-face vs. back-to-back positioning of shoulders, (c) kinesthetic factors (the different distances between persons that provide a capability for touching one another), (d) touch code (e) visual code (based on the retinal areas used, e.g., foveal for direct gaze), (f) voice loudness, (g) thermal code (the heat transmitted by a human body), (h) olfaction code (the presence and degree of undifferentiated breath and body odour).

4482 **सन्यासी**

Sanyāsī : sometimes *sanyāsī:* an ascetic, one engaged in the fourth stage of life. When the *gṛahastha* broke his first links with society by leaving the hermitage and becoming an anchorite, he required great force of character and determination to sustain his new existence : from now on he considered himself entirely to asceticism and contemplation, attaining thus the highest possible human estate on the spiritual plane, and achieving the most complete detachment, qualities that would ensure him deliverance from the contingencies of transmigration. This action made him a *Sanyāsin* and automatically divorced him from society, to take his place among the 'outcastes' while still preserving unanimous respect. This was the ideal proposed by the Brāhmaṇism to its best adepts, and many did their utmost to approach this ideal. Bāṇa has left a remarkable portrait of a typical recluse in his historical novel, the *Harṣacarita* (Cowell and Thomas, III.12). In this account, he describes his emaciated and deeply wrinkled features, his hollow eye-sockets, the pupils of his eyes as red 'as drops of wine', his aquiline nose, the distended lobes of his ears, his prominent teeth and jutting jaws. He carried all his worldly possessions with him. The only outer garment he wore was a tattered old rag, coloured red knotted around his chest; a red scarf hung from one shoulder or was draped around him. In one hand, he held a bamboo cane; with the other he balanced on his shoulder a yoke from the ends of which dangled multifarious objects tied together in a complicated manner by means of cord made of woven hair. These included an instrument for scraping encrusted dirt from the skin, a bamboo-wood sieve, a spare loin-cloth, a begging bowl carried inside a box made of *kharjūra* wood, a water pot held upright in a triangular-shaped framework of three sticks meeting at the top, sandals, a bundle of manuscripts tied together with a strong cord. Thus encumbered, the holy man wandered the length and breadth of the country, begging his daily food, and walking long distance to obtain a supply of salt . During the rainy season, he withdrew to some retreat, and emerged again at its end to continue his never ending pilgrimages and visits to holy places. The king sometimes invited a *sanyāsin* to attend his presence. Some *sanyāsins* put an end to their life committing ritual suicide, often by submerging themselves in a sacred river and remaining under water until they died.

The goal of ascetic striving is conceived in Hinduism as an "emptying" or undoing of life. The continuation of life is negatively valued as the source of suffering and opposed to a negative or empty state of not-life, which is positively evaluated. In consequence the values which were once associated with the renunciation of the world are often chiefly evident as "symbolic strategies" in support of social exclusiveness and other-worldly interests.

4483 **सपत्नी-हस्त**

Sapatnī-hasta : the gesture of a co-wife. Demonstrating the gesture of a *pāśa* (snare) at first; if two hands of a lady are held, it is called the gesture of a co-wife (*AD*, 231-244).

4484 **सप्तपदी**

Saptapadī : the seven steps, It is walking seven steps together. To the north of the Fire seven steps are marked with rice and bridegroom makes the bride step on these starting with right foot. *Saptapadī* according to *Skanda-Purāṇa* is to take seven steps stepping in seven circles specially drawn : *saptamaṇḍalānām ca gamanam* and perform the ritual of *karagrahaṇam* (holding the hand). It is a symbol for their cooperation in married life. The motif of friendship and cooperation brought about by taking seven steps together is to be noted in *Atharvaveda* (11.9) also; and the saying *satām hi sāpta-padīnām sakhyam* is quite famous. The seven steps at the marriage-ritual, obviously, stand as a symbol for continued friendship, and this for the whole life, in happiness or sorrow. This would also show that the marriage for the Hindu was never subservience, it was a tie of friendship, which presupposes equality. The number seven in such contexts indicates totality. The number seven indicated totality for the ancient Indians.

In the Gond-community of Kānker (Bastar) the concept of *saptapadī* is as such. On the day fixed for marriage the pair accompanied by the priest proceeds to a river and the priest lays down on the bed. The bride and bridegroom jump seven times over his body and thus *saptapadī* is performed (Russell and Hiralal, *Tribes and Castes*, -III).

4485 **सप्तशिखी-मुद्रा**

Saptaśikhī-mudrā : "on a fist, in which fingers are clung to the back-side of the palms; when two little fingers are to be made curved and the hairs of the head should be dressed in the style of upturned and scattered, it is called the *saptaśikhī-mudrā*" (*BT*).

4486 **सभक्षता**

Sabhakṣatā : messmateship (*SA*, VIII. 1).

4487 **सभङ्ग**

Sabhaṅga : *Sabhaṅga* has five varieties : *sthānaka* (standing), *āsīna* (seated), *śayana* (recumbent), *yānaka* (moving) and *nṛtta* (dancing). Of these five varieties, the first three have sub-varieties : *yoga, bhoga, vīra* and *ābhicārika*. Each of these in turn is 'superior', (when accompanied with consorts retinue and attendants), 'middling' (accompanied only he consorts), and 'inferior' (alone):

> *uttamam parivāra-yuktam*
> *madhyamam śakti-yuktam*
> *adhamam kevalam*

4488 **सभा**

Sabhā : assembly hall (*Śatapatha Brāhmaṇa*, VII. 12.ii). Men and women used to sing and dance in *Brāhmaṇa* period. They used to gather in *Sabhā* which was a recognised place for social interaction. (b) courts. Bṛhaspati describes four kinds of *Sabhā; pratiṣṭhitā* or established in a place; *apratiṣṭhitā* or moving from place-to-place; *mudritā* or the court in which the chief judge is an appointee of the king and has the royal seal; and *śāsitā* or the court headed by the king himself (1.57).

4489 **सम**

Sama : the point of perfect balance of human body; used in dance, calm, natural position, reclining posture. *Sama* means even, equal, proper, etc.

4490 **सम-अधर**

Sama-adhara : a type of lip-gesture in *Adbhuta rasa.*

4491 **सम-करण**

Sama-karaṇa : indicating stable position.

4492 **सम-गण्ड**

Sama-gaṇḍa : normal cheeks, natural position, natural cheeks; a type of cheeks gesture in *adbhuta rasa;* the natural pose of the cheeks suggests all other feelings (*NS*, 129-134).

4493 **सम-चिबुक**

Sama-cibuka : normal chin, slight contact of teeth, this is accepted as the natural, a type of chin gesture in *vīra rasa;* natural position, or slightly separated two sets of teeth. It indicates the usual position of the mouth (*NS*, VIII. 141-146). It results when the lips are slightly closed; it is used in natural position.

4494 **समता**

Samatā : equality. It should be observed that in social atmosphere, *Bārhaspatya Sūtra* and *Nītivākyāmṛta* are as the poles asunder. In Somadeva (chapter I) the message is one of equality. 'The highest of all social dealings and attitudes consist on sameness or equality to all beings : सर्वसत्वेषु हि समता सर्वाचरणानां परं चरणम् । (*Nītivākyāmṛta*, I), says he. It is the farthest removed from Bṛhaspati's prejudices of all sorts. We are all here led to the doctrine of equality vis-a-vis not only men but all sentient beings. And so far as human beings are concerned, Somadeva (950 A.D.) is equally precise and positive. Among the ways of acquiring *dharma*, he attaches first importance to आत्मवत् परत्र कुशलवृत्तिचिन्तनम् i.e. the cultivation of thought regarding other peoples welfare as one's own. In his analysis of ***dharma***, he propogates the doctrine of *tyāga* i.e. self-sacrifice or gifts and charities as well as of *tapas* i.e. the control of mind and senses. Last but not least, the doctrine of *ahiṁsā* (non-injury) to animals finds its proper place in his moral system. The conduct of person who does not perform *vratas* but whose minds are not given to killing can lead to heaven: आजिघासुगनसां वृतरिक्तमपि चरितं स्वर्गाय जायेत ।

The deep philosophy of Gītā is the philosophy of *Samatvavāda*. Though it is at present a rarity in the masses, but it can be very well perceived in the behaviour of the tribal folk. In the eyes of Hill Marias all are equal. There is no class consciousness in these people. When *bīḍis* are being distributed, they will give the *bīḍi* even to non-smokers and children. Asked why they give it to children, they say that they are entitled to receive it since they are also sitting in the group and if the child does not smoke, his father or elder brother will. Similarly, if any eatable is distributed everybody gets equal share respective of his or her age. That they regard all as equal is also seen from the fact that they do not hesitate in talking about any subject even before children. Among many other people, some distance is maintained between elders and children, but among the Hill Marias all are equal except when the *pancāyata* sitting takes place.

4495 **समत्व**

Samatva : co-ordination. The harmony of the movements of major and minor limbs; accompanying song and instrumental music.

4496 **समदन्तपंक्ति**

Samadantapaṁkti : equal teeth-rows, quality of the Deer-man (*Pañcasāyaka*, 2.9).

4497 **सम-दर्शन**

Sama-darśana : a type of normal look given by *NS*.

4498 **सम-दृष्टि**

Sama-dṛṣṭi : gentle look; eyelid in perfect balance in *rati*, normal eyelids; the eyeballs in a level position, the level glance (*sama-dṛṣṭi*) is that where the eyeballs are raised in wonder, and when the eyelashes are just a little curved. It is the *adbhuta rasa* (*NS*, VIII.51). The eyeballs are in a level and resting position.

4499 **समधि-कफा**

Samadhi-kaphā : lady who contains phlegm more, quality of the Deer-lady (*Pañcasāyaka*, 2.12).

4500 **समन**

Samana : the assembly in *Yajurveda* time where young people gathered to find their marriage partners (*Kaṇva-Saṁhitā*, 34.5).

4501 **समनख-करण**

Samanakha-karaṇa : the natural position. Feet are in *Samapāda* and the hands hang naturally in *latā*. The body in natural position (*NS*, IV.65, IX.198). It announced the commencement of the dance.

4502 **सम-पाद**

Samapāda : the foot rests on the ground in a natural way. Resting on the natural step. Walking in steadly equi-distant steps. Feet are obliquely placed. When the whole feet is placed on the ground with the leg in the normal position, then it is called *sama*. *Sama* is applied to various *recakas* in a *tāṇḍava* and natural position of a standing pose (*NS*, X.40-51). The feet are naturally placed on the ground in even manner. They are kept unmoved in connection with various karaṇas, but in the *recita*, they should be moved.

4503 **समपाद-चारी**

Samapāda-cārī : feet in *samapāda* position, lower limbs close together, toes facing front posture. *Samanakha* and *samapāda sthāna* are associated *karaṇa* and *maṇḍala*. Standing with the two feet close together, and nails of the toes even and then in *samapāda sthāna*. The two feet close together, toes at one level facing front and *samapāda* posture (X.14). *Samapāda-cārī* is walking in a more confident way—that is with a relaxed, upright posture. It aids breathing and voice projection.

4504 **समपाद-स्थान**

Samapāda-sthāna : equibalanced posture for men, natural position. *Sauṣṭhava* of limbs, presiding deity Brahmā. Weight is equally divided and limbs are in natural position (*NS*, XII. 79-86); a type of standing posture. The feet are in natural position and kept a *tāla* apart; the body is in natural *sauṣṭhava*. It symbolizes accepting the blessings from the Brāhmaṇas and imitating birds. It is to be assumed by the bridegroom at the marriage ceremony, persons in the sky, in chariots and in the aerial car, persons of sects with indicatory marks and observing vows (*NS*, X.58-61).

4505 **समपाद-स्थानक**

Samapāda-sthānaka : a type of posture.

4506 **सम-पुट**

Sama-puṭa : natural eyelids; normal eyelids. normal position of eyelids, brightly opened eyelids in the sense of love (*NS*, VIII. 106-113).

4507 **सम-भङ्ग**

Sama-bhaṅga : it is the position of equipose or perfect balance. It is used to show the calmer, more reposeful moods and attitudes. All the *sāttvika mudrās* whether standing, seated or reclining are shown in this pose. The *dhyāna* images of Śiva, Viṣṇu and Buddha are in the *sama-bhaṅga*.

The right and left of the figure are disposed symmetrically, the *sūtra* or plumb-line pressing through the navel, from the crown of the head to a point midway between the heels. In other words, the figure, whether seated or standing, is poised firmly on both legs without reclining in any way to right or left..... The dispositions or attitudes of the limbs and organs on either side are made exactly, similar, except that the *mudrā* or symbolical posing of the fingers is different. (Fig. 4507)

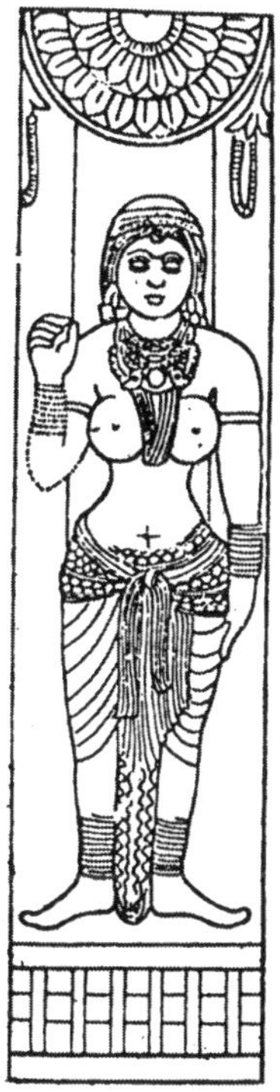

Fig. – (4507)

4508 **सम्भ्रान्त-करण**

Sambhrānta-karaṇa : hand in *āvartita* is placed on the thigh which is in *āviddha cārī*. It is used in movements in confusion.

4509 **सम-मणिबन्ध**

Sama-maṇibandha : the normal position of the wrist.

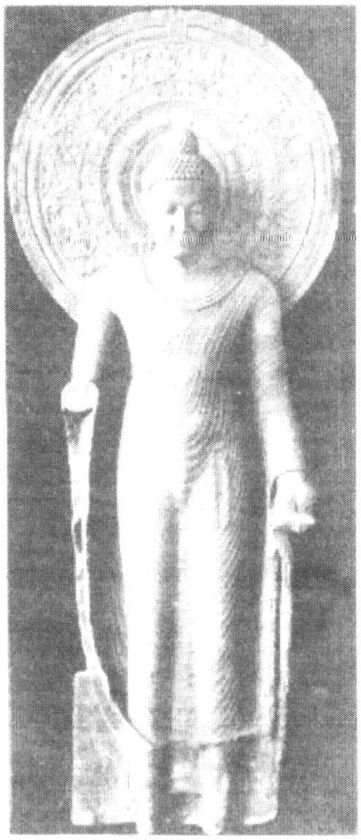

Fig. – (4507)

4510 **समय**

Samaya : social union, assembly, interaction, social function according to *Tāntras;* time, oath, division of time. Time is a part of NV code. The way we use time communicates. We operate on rigid time schedules. We give important people and important matters more time. People who have no time for you make you feel unimportant. Those who are close to you drop in any time. Another important matter is being "on time". Differences in time systems cause countless interpersonal conflicts. Lateness also communicates. Keeping someone waiting three minutes usually requires no apology and creates no offence. Keeping someone waiting 45 minutes is an insult which requires an apology. People sometimes use lateness to gain attention. Some people always arrive late because they want to be special or important.

4511 **समय-मातृका**

Samaya-matṛkā : measurement of time (*Kāmasūtra's* commentary written by Kṣemendra).

4512 **समय-मुद्रा**

Samaya-mudrā : occurs in *BT*. Both the ring-fingers and the little fingers, tied like a mat and the two middle fingers should be made up-turned, hidden-tipped and extended to the back. Two fore-fingers should kiss both the middle fingers. This is called the *samaya-mudrā,* which may be made in the eve of the *Tāntric* culture. (b) "Two palms turned upwards with two middle finger-tips hiding back and two fore-fingers clinging the next. It is designed to practice penance to preach the code of conduct" (*Ajanta Cave paintings*).

4513 **समयाचारिक**

Samayācārika : concerning proper behaviour (*A,* 7,15.21).

4514 **समरत**

Samarata : equal union in copulation (*Kuṭṭanīmatam,* 396) a type of the best union (*Kāmasūtra,* 2.1.9).

4515 **सम-लघूरू**

Samalaghūrū : lady whose thighs are long and straight (*Ratirahasya,* 3.22-23).

4516 **समलिङ्गता**

Samaliṅgatā : homo-sexuality. Homo-sexual practices are believed to be distinctly rare among Hindus, and common among the Muslims. The Hindu sacred books, however, do not attach severe penalties to this act. According to *Manu* (XI) "a twice-born man who commits an unnatural offence with a male, shall bathe, dressed in his clothes; and all these are reckoned as minor offences. "*Agni Purāṇa* (169.37) also indicates the homo-sexual behaviour.

Homo-sexual males display a number of actions peculiar to their social group, and due to their actions they are also termed as *mehrā,* which means that they acquire unknowingly womanish manners. Women may also become homo-sexuals. A homo-sexual of either sex will, in certain social contexts, find it easier to indulge in his or her privateties if he or she presents a public set of heterosexual Tie-signs. A marriage of convenience is an obvious solution. Sexual reactions have been tested. Pin-up pictures of naked males and naked females have been shown to both men and women, and the findings are that homo-sexuals on the whole show a positive pupil response— that is, their pupils enlarge-when they see the naked body of a member of their own sex, while heterosexuals show a strong response to the opposite sex.

After masturbation, the second type of non-risky activity is homo-sexuality in India. One may sleep with one's own sex. But it is not a type of sodomy which is prevalent in the west. If a man (villager or forester) cannot get a boy, there are goats and mares, sows and cows to be had everywhere; for the urban woman there is the dog. But if one is caught with an animal, one is a social outcaste. Children from the age of six to sixteen, must make experiments. A child knows very little about its own body, let it explore.

Homo-sexuality was common phenomenon in India particularly in traditional *pāṭhaśālās* and *madarasās.* Curzon in his time had grimly drawn up a list of princes with homo-sexual tastes. He blamed Indian customs : "I attribute it largely to early marriage. A boy gets tired of his wife, or of women, at an early age, and wants the stimulous some more novel or exciting sensation." (*Curzon to Hamilton,* 3.12.1902, *Mss Eur F* III/161).

Homo-sexuality was present in India at the time of the *Kāmasūtra.* Varāhamihira, an astrologer and expert in *āyurvedic* medicine who was a contemporary of Vātsyāyana, has mentioned it in his *Bṛhat Saṁhitā* that a person born when mars and venus are placed in a particular manner will satisfy his or her passions with a member of the same sex acting as the opposite sex.

(b) Home-sexuality is sexual intercourse between members of the same sex; sexual attraction for members of the same sex. Homo-sexuality may involve the entire range of behaviour from overt sexuality — that is, mutual mastur-bation, cunniliction, fellatio, or anal intercourse — to repressed desires towards members of the opposite sex. Overt homo-sexual practices are still regarded as perversions.

4517 **सम-वक्ष**

Sama-vakṣa : normal position of the chest; also know as *samauras. Caturasra* pose and *sauṣṭhava* of limbs, indicative of natural position. The *sama* style of the chest indicates an all-square position of the body, quite fit and all chivalrous and this style is to be made to express an air of such behaviours (*NS,* X.1-9). All the limbs are in *Caturasra* and with the breast in *sauṣṭhava.* It is used in natural positions.

4518 **समवायज**

Samavāyaja : using three strokes in *vīṇā*-playing; a type of *vistāra.*

4519 **सम-शयन**

Sama-śayana : a posture for lying down. The face should be turned up and hands free, dropping downwards. It is to be used in deep sleep (*NS*).

4520 **सम-शिरस्**

Sama-śiras : normal position of the head given in *SR* (IV.7.77). The natural position of the head to indicate an 'at ease' position.

4521 **सम-सूची-मण्डल**

Sama-sūcī-maṇḍala : a type of posture.

4522 **समस्त-व्यस्त-कम्पितोरू**

Samasta-vyasta-kampitorū : raising and lifting of the thighs (*Bālarāmabharata*).

4523 **समस्तोरू**

Samastorū : motionless position of the thighs (*Bālarāmabharata*).

4524 **सम-स्थान**

Sama-sthāna : a type of posture.

4525 **सम-हस्त**

Sama-hasta : used by Vedic reciters to remember the accent and stress of the sacred chant in the absence of musical instruments. The thumb connected of the phalange of the fingers which represents the notes, timings and accompanying actions. They, therefore, serve as cues to assisting in remembering the order of the ceremonial.

4526 **समा-ग्रीवा**

Samā-grīvā : natural neck; normal position of neck. It is styled to indicate meditation, counting names of God (*japa*), natural position of the neck (*NS*, VIII. 164-171), natural poses and muttering of incantations.

4527 **समाज**

Samāja : (a) one of the social institutions described in *Kāmasūtra* (1.4.35-36) where discussions and demonstrations were held. The other institution was the *goṣṭhī*. In *Kaṇavera Jātaka* (IV.III), there are references of *samāja* and *Samājamaṇḍalī*. (b) a festive gathering of people (*A*, 2.21.28, 2.25.36, 5.2.39, 10.1.15, 13.3.56). (c) society, assembly, party. *Samāja* was a type of group meeting. By group meeting we mean any group of persons sitting and informally discussing something. One still finds such groups at various convenient and strategic places such as teashops, street corners, and *baithaks* (men's quarters). They may be playing cards, putting a *hukkā*, taking tea or just basking in the Sun, but even so they are usually engaged in some sort of informal discussion. Someone makes a point, others strongly contradict it, others support either of the views expressed during the course of discussion. Occasionally all burst into laughter and then again proceed with chit-chat. Such group meetings are common features of social life and serve important functions of dissemination and, to an extent, assimilation of information in the Indian community. The tribals often cite some folk or other cultural story to make their points. This facilitates greatly the process of communication. Hence, *samāja* occupies a vital placing among the communication channels in India.

4528 **समाज-सम्प्रेषण-वस्तु**

Samāja-sampreṣaṇa-vastu : social communicative content. (*Anaṅgaraṅga*, 6.4). It is the degree to which people take into account the characteristics of the audience to when they are speaking and produces message which is understood in the way they intend for it to be understood. Social dialects in India had a social communicative content. The existence of social dialects in ancient India is perhaps implied by the form of the classical Sanskrit dramas, in which the higher ranking characters speak Sanskrit and the lower ones speak various Prākṭs.

4529 **समाधि**

Samādhi : concentration of particular emotion in *citta* is that contemplation which attains identity of object with the subject. (b) the mind's perfect absorption in the object of contemplation. It is the eighth discipline of *yoga*. The mind loses itself in the object and has no awareness of itself (*Yogasūtra*, 1.1).

4530 **समाधि-मुद्रा**

Samadhi-mudrā : a posture of the hands while in meditation. Same as *dhyāna-mudrā*. The hands with palm upwards lie one upon the other on the lap with all fingers extended. It is the characteristic *mudrā* of *Amitābha*.

4531 **समानत-संस्थान**

Samānata-saṁsthāna : the equibalanced position. The position of the buttock and feet are opened to the vision. The upper half of the figure by half and the hip slightly are to be made visible. Legs and toes are missing. A beautiful look is indicative of four dimensions. Arms are distinct and the face with the shoulder and the thigh would go out off the sight (*VD*, 3.39. 29-32).

4532 **समापत्ति**

Samāpatti : accomplishment.

4533 **समा-यति**

Samā-yati : evenly regulating of the duration of words. It has the same tempo in the beginning, the middle and the end. It has predominance of instrumental music (*NS*).

4534 **समावर्तन**

Samāvartana : return home of a student after completion of Vedic studies in the preceptor's house. Literally, return; the return of the student to his paternal home.

4535 **समाश्लेष**

Samāśleṣa : embrace.

4536 **समासोक्ति**

Samāsokti : concise speech.

4537 **समीपार्थकता**

Samīpārthakata : solidatory semantic. This choice of address is based up what Brown and Gilman (1960) have called the power semantic and solidatory semantic. The solidatory semantic refers to the degree of shared social experience between two people. It operates to allow greater familiarity between people who, for example, are close neighbours or friends or attend the same class.

In Sanskrit, pronoun *tvam* and the reverential *bhavat* correspond respectively to the French *tu* (T) and *vous* (V), and stand for what has been described as the 'nonreciprocal power semantic'. They are equivalent to Hindi *tū* and *āp*. According to this notion the more powerful of any two interlocutors says T and receives V, all relations such as 'older than', 'parent of', 'employer of', 'stronger than', 'nobler than' and other hierarchical expressions which can be assimilated to these being subsumed for the purpose of this generalization under the term 'more powerful than'. Brown and Gilman who have done much to investigate the T-V index of authority in many cultures, past and present, have observed that it is "associated with a relatively static society in which power is distributed by birthright and is not subject to much redistribution. In India, the truly feudal pronominal pattern, part of a long-standing tradition, still largely operates in the T-V expressions used in the Gujarati and Hindi languages non-reciprocally between elder brother and younger brother as well as between husband and wife. The series could of course be extended to the entire range of power relations including those of caste and class in many of the other Indian speech communities too.

4538 **समुदाचार**

Samudācāra : polite manners, decorous conduct (*Veṇīsaṁhāra*, Act V).

4539 **समुद्ग-अधर**

Samudga-adhara : contracted lips used in *śṛṅgāra*.

4540 **समुद्गक-अधर**

Samudgaka-adhara : rounded cheeks; contracted lips. suggests the sense of kiss, pity, greeting, welcoming, etc. (*NS*, VIII. 134-140).

4541 **समुद्गक-कवाट**

Samudgaka-kavāṭa : the artificial stanza, the two halves of which exactly correspond in sound though differ in meaning.

4542 **समुद्देश**

Samuddeśa : topic.

4543 **समुद्वृत्त-तारा**

Samudvṛtta-tārā : raising of the eyeballs. A type of eye-gesture in which there is the movement of *tārā* (eyeball). It suggests fear and anger. Eyeballs move in the up-down direction. The movement of the eyelid and the eyebrow along the vertical plane raising of the eyeballs. Turning upward the eyeballs in a wonder, a type of glance by the movement of the eyeballs (*NS*, VIII. 92-105).

4544 **समुन्नत-पार्श्व**

Samunnata-pārśva : same as *unnata-pārśva*, raising a side: this is said to be the reverse of *nata-pārśva* (*NS*, IX. 236).

4545 **समोत्सरित-मण्डल**

Samotsarita-maṇḍala : a type of *maṇḍala*.

4546 **समोत्सरित-मत्तलि-चारी**

Samotsarita-mattali-cārī : both feet in *agratalasañcara* positions. Circular movement of the lifted leg and a movement indicating going back; *samotsarita-maṇḍala*. Moving in a circular manner (*SR*, VIII. 936, 937), forward or backward with *talasañcara* feet forming *svastika* of the shanks. Bharata records "Both the feet in, where *agratalasañcara* is kept behind the other foot making a *svastika* at the shank. Then the other foot is made *talasañcara* and in this fashion the feet make circular movements." (*NS*, X. 27). This *cārī*, says Abhinava, is used to indicate moderate intoxication.

4547 **समोरू**

Samorū : motionless position of the thighs (*Bālarāmabharata*).

4548 **सम्पाठ्य-कला**

Saṁpāṭhya-kalā : art of showing intelligence, one of the 64 arts given in *Kāmasūtra* (1.3.16); group-reading, recitation, etc.

4549 **सम्पुटक**

Sampuṭaka : clasping position in coition prescribed for the Elephant-lady (*Kāmasūtra*, 2.6.14). Half joint, forming a half opening.

4550 **सम्पुट-हस्त**

Sampuṭa-hasta : both hands gesture (*Abhinayadarpaṇa*) not mentioned in *NS*. If fingers of the *cakra* style are curved, they make the gesture of the *sampuṭa*. It is used to indicate covering of a secret thing and representing costly boxes or packets.

4551 **संप्रतीक**

Sampratīka : emblem, visible representation of an idea or quality. Emblems are body-movements that replace spoken language. They tend to be specific to particular culture, and they are understood by most members of a culture in the same way that everyone understands the verbal language.

4552 **सम्प्रदाय**

Sampradāya : sect, community, group, etc., upholding different religious ideas.

4553 **संप्रयोग-काल**

Samprayoga-kāla : time of sexual union (*Kāmasūtra*, 2.1.13).

4554 **संप्रलाप**

Sampralāpa : lamentation, wailing, incoherent talk. The love-lorn person, unable to bear the pangs of agitation, begins to wail aloud. In the absence of mental peace, his or her remarks often become incoherent. It is the sixth stage in the lovelorn condition.

4555 **संप्रवेशण-दर्शन**

Sampraveśaṇa-darśana : the movement of the eyeballs in the up-down direction, has a downward accent. When the eyeballs are drawn inside so that the pupil is practically invisible, drawing in the eyeballs, a type of glance by movement of the eyeballs (*NS*, VIII. 92-105).

4556 **सम्प्रवेषण-दृष्टि**

Sampraveṣaṇa-dṛṣṭi : drawing in glance (pupils).

4557 **संप्रेषण-सरणि**

Sampreṣaṇa-saraṇi : communication channel. The term channel refers to the various paths along which messages flow. For example, facial expressions, eye-gaze, body movements, and even such less obvious behaviours as the positioning of the eyebrows can be conceptualized as separate channels of communication.

4558 **सम्फेट**

Sampheṭa : conflict, a type of *ārabhaṭī*. It is known to include excitement, many fights, personal combats, deception, betrayal and much striking of weapons. (*NS*, XX). (b) the application of *sampheṭa* theory to the Indian style has rather been neglected. According to this classic exposition of conflict theory, reciprocal 'repulsions' maintain the total Indian social structure by creating a balance of claims by rival castes. The pluralist society here in India tend to coher by multiple conflicts between groups, and that interdependence of these conflicting groups prevents deep cleavages along a single axis. The antagonistic interests of a multiplicity of conflict groups tend to cancel each other out. The absence of revolutionary movements and the rarity of overt class struggle in India originate in this multiplicity of conflict groups. Rivalries in castes have not drawn the total energies and allegiance of the low caste into a single area of class-conflict, except in those regions where a multiplicity of gradations between the dominant and the low castes is absent.

4559 **सम्बन्ध**

Sambandha : connection, and may be one founded on descent, caste, marriage, friendship and social intercourse: *anvaya-jāti-vaivāhya maitrayekavyavahārataḥ yujyate dravya sambandho niḥsambandho na yujyate* (Asahāya on *Nar.* 1.144).

4560 **सम्बोधन**

Sambodhana : mode of address. (a) the ruler was addressed, whenever necessary, in a prescribed manner in set phrases and according to the traditional etiquette. Different castes used different modes of address. In pre-modern India, Kṣatriyas addressed their ruler as *annadātā* (giver of food). The Brāhmaṇs called him *gaubrāhmaṇa-pratipālaka.* Different castes addressed the prince differently. This mode of address revealed the caste of the person, addressing so was treated accordingly.

(b) the bards addressed the rulers in a very interesting manner. If the ruler was busy and was short time, the *cāraṇas* pronounced the short addressed (byrds) and if time permitted the larger byrd was recited.

(c) vocative. In Sanskrit it refers to a special case form of the noun used in direct address. All the Sanskrit examples reveal, the vocative is typically used to attract someone's attention, and as such most typically occurs initially to keep someone's attention, to invite *Turn-Taking;* or to express a feeling or attitudes. Titles and first names and surnames are commonly used in this way as terms of address indicating degrees of formality from polite respect to familiarity. They are also traditionally used in invocations to the gods of Muses; and are still a feature of liturgy.

4561 **सम्भवा-दृष्टि**

Sambhavā-dṛṣṭi : the *saumya dṛṣṭi* or the peaceful look (*VD*, III. 1.30).

4562 **संभाषा**

Saṁbhāṣā : debate, dialogue, discussion. The *Caraka-Saṁhitā* (*Vimāna-sthāna*, VIII) gives a detailed discussion about the debate which is known in *Nyāya-sūtra* (1.2.1) as *vāda*. Caraka has used the word *saṁbhāṣā* for debate. It is divided into two parts: (a) *sandhāya-saṁbhāṣā* (positive or friendly discussions (VIII. 16) and. (b) *Vigṛhya-saṁbhāṣā* (*Ibid.*, discussions involving quarrels or conflicts). The former one is also called *anuloma-saṁbhāṣā*, can be translated as - friendly discussion and the latter as aggressive debate. According to Caraka, one should not enter into *vigṛhya-saṁbhāṣā* with one's preceptor or men of similar position; *sandhāya-saṁbhāṣā* with them is recommended for augmenting one's knowledge.

4563 **सम्भोग-घटना**

Saṁbhoga-ghaṭnā : sexual sequence. The ascending scales of intimacies - the sexual sequence - varies from case to case but a typical sequence is : (1) *Eye to body*: the looking stage. (2) *Eye to Eye*: the mutual gaze condition - catching the other's eye. (3) *Voice to voice*: the talking stage - and exchange of personal information and attitudes. (4) *Hand to hand*: the first touching stage - often started with a disguised act of 'supporting aid', 'body protection' or 'directional guidance', the partner helps to take off or put on a coat, lingering a little too long in the process, or takes a hand to guide the other across a street or through a door. (5) *Arm to shoulder:* the bodies come into slightly closer contact, again often starting with a body 'guidance' subterfuge. (6) *Arm to waist*: a slightly more intimate action, bringing the male hand nearer to the female sexual regions. (7) *Mouth to mouth*: the kiss - the first seriously arousing intimacy. If prolonged, it may lead to female genital secretions and male penis erection. (8) *Hand to head:* caresses are added to the kissing, with the hands exploring the partner's face and hair. (9) *Hand to body*: the hands start to explore the partner's body surface, fondling and stroking. If this stage is passed, the courtship sequence has reached the pre-copulatory stage, and the chances are that arousal will be so great that copulation will occur. (10) *Mouth to breast*: now, in a strictly private context with clothing removal, the partners begin to explore with their mouths the naked skin surfaces of each other's bodies. Elaborate embracing occurs at this stage and, in particular, the exploration of the female breast by the male lips. (11) *Hand to genitals*: finally the hands move to the genital region, where they explore and stimulate. By this time both the male and female genitals are fully aroused and ready for intromission. (12) *Genitals to genitals*: genital contact is made, accompanied by rhythmic pelvic thrusting from the male until orgasm is reached.

Naturally, this sequence of sexual behaviour varies considerably. Preliminary stages may be shortened or omitted, especially in cases where the partners are well known to each other and have mated many times before. Between puritanically minded partners the final genital-to-genital contact may be made before the more arousing preliminaries have been performed.

4564 **सम्भ्रम**

Sambhrama : one of the 64 *sandhyaṅgas* according to Dhanañjaya which includes apprehension and uneasiness. It is in the lims of *avamarṣa*. (b) embarrassment syndrome. It occurs with alternating smiling, establishing eye contact on the one side and cut-offs, face-hiding, self-embracing, finger-biting, and shaking-off movements on the other.

4565 **सम्भ्रान्त-रेचित-करण**

Sambhrānta-recita-karaṇa : the name of the *karaṇa* is derived from the circular movement it implies. The movements of the hands in *parivartita* and *vyāvartita*, they rest on the thighs in the final position (*NS*, IV. 161-162, IX. 217-218, X.38).

4566 **सम्मुखागत-हस्त**

Sammukhāgata-hasta : hands coming towards oneself, i.e, right-back, or left-back, or high-back or down-back.

4567 **सम्मुखीन**

Sammukhīna : face to face (*Raghu*, 15.17).

4568 **सरयू-मुद्रा**

Sarayū-mudrā : the name of a river. The *padma*-hand moving up and down indicates *sarayū* (*Mirror of Gesture*, p.48).

4569 **सरल-बाहु**

Sarala-bahū : slightly arched position of the arm.

4570 **सरलाङ्गुलि**

Saralāṅguli : lady whose fingers are straight, quality of the Deer-lady (*Anaṅgaraṅga*, 3.20-21).

4571 **सरस्वती-मुद्रा**

Sarasvatī-mudrā : the river Sarasvatī. The *patāka* and *catura* hand moving upward and downward indicate river Sarasvatī (*Mirror of Gesture*, p.48).

4572 **सरस्वती-हस्त**

Sarasvatī-hasta : sūcī with the right hand and *kapittha* with the left, raised on an equal level with shoulders make Sarasvatī (*AD*, 205-210).

4573 **सर्पशिरस्-हस्त**

Sarpaśiras-hasta : snake-head hand. Single hand gesture mentioned in *NS* and *Abhinayadarpaṇa.* It is rare in iconography. The palm is hollowed, slightly raised and faced outwards. The fingers and the thumb are closed together, extended and bent a little at the top. It is used to express a snake, sandal paste, sprinkling, cherishing, giving water to the gods, washing the face; short man, shoulders, image, water and very true. If all the fingers of a hand with its thumb and the palm are joined and curved a little, it is called the *sarpaśiraḥ.*

4574 **सर्पित-करण**

Sarpita-karaṇa : the feet are in *añcita* and moved apart in semi-circular movement of snake; the head follows the feet in *parivāhita* movement: the hands and arms move in *recita* (*NS*, IV. 141b-142a, VIII.27, IX.275). It is used in intoxicated walk.

4575 **सर्पि-सागर-मुद्रा**

Sarpi-sāgara-mudrā : butter-oil-ocean. The *catura* hand moved up and down denotes the butter-oil-ocean (*Mirror of Gesture,* p. 48).

4576 **सर्व-कर्तृता**

Sarva-kartṛtā : supreme sovereignty and omnipotence. It is one of the five expressions of God's perfection.

4577 **सर्वज्ञता**

Sarvajñatā : omniscience.

4578 **सर्वतोभद्र-मण्डल**

Sarvatobhadra-maṇḍala : a geometrical diagram on which the *pūrṇakumbha* is placed during a festivity.

4579 **सर्वत्र-चलन-(तारा)**

Sarvatra-calana-(tārā) : The tremor of the eyeballs given in *NS.*

4580 **सर्वदा-कष्टसाध्या**

Sarvadā-kaṣṭa-sādhyā : lady who gets climax with trouble, quality of the Elephant-lady (*Pañcasāyaka,* 2.14).

4581 **सर्वभाषासु कौशल (कला)**

Sarvabhāṣāsu kauśala (kalā) : art of knowing all the languages (*Kādambarī,* p. 126).

4582 **सर्वलिपिकौशलकला**

Sarvalipiṣ-kauśala-kala : art of knowing all the scripts (*Kādambarī,* p. 126).

4583 **सर्वशक्तिमुद्रा**

Sarvaśakti-mudrā : upturn two hands, curve all the fingers and move them placing the thumbs up, again and again. This indicates the gesture of *sarvaśakti* (*VD*). Names of *Śaktis*, according to *VD* are nine. They are : *Dīptā, Sūkṣmā, Jayā, Bhadrā, Vibhūti, Vimalā, Amoghā, Vidyutā* and *Sarvatomukhī.*

4584 **सर्वसम्पत्करी (शूकी) मुद्रा**

Sarvasampatkarī (śūkī) mudrā : "This particular *mudrā* is to be framed by fixing the middle finger (in the mouth) along with other fingers joined to the tip of the thumb in the mouth. The fore-finger of one hand should be placed there in a bending position. It is the *mudrā, Sarvasampatkarī* by name, that grants great courage and valour" (*BT*).

4585 **सर्व-स्त्री-सुभग**

Sarva-strī-subhaga : liked by all women, quality of a Bull-man (*Ratirahasya,* 3.32-33).

4586 **सर्वाङ्गासन**

Sarvāṅgāsana : lie flat on the back. Slowly raise the legs, first left and then right, then both legs together. Supporing the back with the two hands, lift the trunk, hips and legs vertically, resting the elbows on the ground. The chin may be pressed against the chest. The back, the shoulder portion and the neck may be allowed to touch the ground. Do not move the body, keep the legs straight. Retain this pose as long as convenient. When the *āsana* is finished, bring down the legs very slowly without any jerk.

The *āsana* nourishes the thyroid glands and keeps you in perfect health with wonderful results. It supplies a large quantity of blood to the spinal column and keeps the spine elastic, which means everlasting youth. It helps in maintaining celibacy, checks wet dreams, and is powerful blood tonic and blood-purifier. It tones the nerves and removes constipation as well as other gastrointestinal disorders. This *āsana* is very useful for ladies, as it removes sterility and genito-urinary disorders.

4587 **सर्वात्म-मुद्रा**

Sarvātma-mudrā : make a fist by the left hand, extend its fore-finger and take it by the right fist. This is the gesture of *sarvātman* (*VD*).

4588 **सवर्ण**

Savarṇa : double, substitute.

4589 **सशब्द-चुम्बन**

Saśabda-cumbana : kiss with sound. This has been proposed by Padmaśrī. It is discussed in the seventh chapter of *Sāmprayogikādhikaraṇa* of *Kāmasūtra*.

4590 **सशब्द-ताल**

Saśabda-tāla : the *tāla* as indicated by hands was *niḥśabda* (without sound) and *saśabda* (with sound). *Saśabda* was four-fold: *Śamyā* : clapping by the right hand, (b) *Tāla* : clapping by left hand (c) *Sannipāta* : clapping by both hands together, and (d) *Dhruvā* : the movement of the hand with the snapping of the fingers according to the three-fold *kalā*.

4591 **सहज**

Sahaja : easiest and most natural. (a) the *mārga* or way of spiritual exercise. It is also the term for those who believe in this *Sahaja-mārga*.

4592 **सहज-भ्रू**

Sahaja-bhrū : natural position of brows, eye-gesture in which eyebrows are in normal position; natural position of eyebrows to indicate an easy-going life *NS*, VIII, 113-123).

4593 **सहजयान**

Sahajayāna : offshoot of *vajrayāna*, which holds the truth is something which can never be found through the prescribed codes of study, discipline, conduct, worship, and ritual. What is natural (*sahaja*) is the easiest, and hence there is no need for religious formalities, austere practices of discipline, reading, philosophising, fasting, constructing temples and images and so on. The followers of this school lay greater emphasis on the imperative necessity of making the body sufficiently strong and fit before starting yogic processes and believe in the existence of an internal female-force in the *nirmāṇa cakra*. The *sahajayāna* considers the human body itself as the seat of all human experience including that of *sahaja-mahāsukha*.

4594 **सहदेव-हस्त**

Sahadeva-hasta : *Śikhara hasta* represents Sahadeva, the Pāṇḍava (*Mirror of Gesture*, p. 47).

4595 **सहृदय**

Sahṛdaya : persons of similar sensibility, the ideal audience and the proper poetic-context. The connoisseur participates in the consensus of mind and is one who has perceived the natural appropriateness of what is represented. His mind has become lucidly receptive like a mirror through effort and constant practice of poetry. Appreciation of *rasa* is all too rare and is opened only to the privileged few, gifted with a refined sensibility by birth. These Ānandavardhana called by the name *Sahṛdayas* or 'those with kindered hearts' because they can respond fully to the heart-throb of a poet which finds expression in his poetry. Other names for *Sahṛdaya* are *rasika* or *rasajña*. One who is blind to the aesthetic experience of *rasa* in poetry is no literary critic, however learned he might be in the diverse branches of learning. In this new approach of Ānandavardhana, we see for the first time poetry valued as an art, and not as a unique supplement of science. To understand poetry means to understand its *rasa*.

4596 **सहृदयतत्व**

Sahṛdayatatva : social perception. The process through which we come across to know and understand the persons around. The notion of aesthetic susceptibility. given by Abhinavagupta which expresses his belief in the distinct quality of the aesthetic experience. *Self-actualization* is a state where we recognize other's needs and feelings. A *sahṛdaya* is more sensitive and responsive to his own words and feelings, and finds it easier to recognize those of others. Empathetic rather than competitive or demanding, he is prepared to reveal more of his inner selves, and enjoys the mutual explorations of true intimacy.

4597 **सुभद्र-ताल**

Subhadra-tāla : Abhinava (*NS*, II.142) states that it is to be used in secret love as per the view of Kohala and others. It is used in the Furious and the Heroic sentiments.

4598 **सुषिर**

Suṣira : the flute. It was the most ancient instrument. It was the leading instrument in ancient India. In many dance panels in the ancient Indian sculptures flute is seen though *vīṇā* is absent. The flute gave very sweet notes. As regards the flute-playing, the manner of producing different notes is described by Bharata. The four *śruti* notes were to be produced by keeping the hole fully open; the three *śruti*-notes, with fingers shaking; and two *śruti* notes by covering half of the hole with fingers. (b) *Mārkaṇḍeya Purāṇa* (50. 82.93) records that evils do not enter a house where there is a flute.

4599 **स्रोतगता-यति**

Srotagatā-yati : current-like *yati*. In it the playing is sometimes stopped and sometimes continued in a running manner, like the water-current (*NS*).

4600 **साक्षराः राक्षसाः**

Sākṣarāḥ rākṣaāḥ : literates are demons, a popular saying in Sanskrit signifying hatred to the graphic form. There was hardly a peasant uprising on any significant scale in colonial India that did not cause the destruction of large quantities of written or printed material including rent rolls, deeds and bonds and public records of all kinds.

It is the objectification of the illiterates hatred to the literates. Writing is this is the sign of enemy and favours the exploitation of human beings rather than enlightenment. Want of literacy bars him access to it as a secular, intellectual aid to remembering, learning, understanding. In order therefore to use it for insurgency, for purposes of reversing the world, he appropriated it symbolically. He had been conditioned by his own subalternity and the elite monopoly of culture to look upon writing as a symbol of dominance.

4601 **साक्षात्**

Sākṣāt : present to the eye; also known as *pratyakṣa.*

4602 **साक्षी**

Sākṣī : witness. Literally means a person who has seen something with his eyes. In broader sense it means a person who has obtained knowledge of any fact through the agencies of knowledge, that is through anyone of the five senses, the eyes, the ears, the nose, the tongue, and the skin or in other words, the senses of sight, hearing, smell, taste and touch. (*Arthaśāstra,* 4.6.8).

4603 **साचीकृत-दर्शन**

Sācīkṛta-darśana : a type of sight (*NS, VD*), sidelong look, with the eyeballs covered by the eyelashes.

4604 **साचीकृत-देह**

Sācīkṛata-deha : bending body obliquely, body orientation. In *Reghu* (6.13), the princes bends his body obliquely to adjust his shawl. In areas where men still use shawls, the adjusting of the shawl is a method of token submission. *Sācīkṛta-deha* is one of the clearest clues of the emotional state. If someone with whom we are conversing faces us directly and leans forward, this is usually a clear sign that he or she likes us. In contrast, if another individual orients his or her body away from us and leans back while we interact, this creates the impression that he or she dislikes us.

4605 **साचीकृत-संस्थान**

Sācīkṛta-saṁsthāna : the bending-aside position. The beauty of the *sācīkṛta-saṁsthāna,* as described by Kālidāsa, is a slight curvature of the neck suggesting shy love in Pārvatī: "Placing the wrath of lotus seeds on the neck of Śaṅkara, she stood before him in a position of the slight curvature of her neck, with her thrilling limbs and a wistfully wide glance. This is the sign of love in courting - a mental feeling (*Sāttvika-bhāva*) and this particular thought-provoking position adds extraordinary lustre to her blooming beauty (*Kumāra.* III): *Sācīkṛtam cārutareṇa tasthau.* In this position, the side-glance of the image should be prominently fixed on the earth and the rest angles of vision would be fair and attractive. The body would look slim and beautiful in all respect. The eye-brow, the forehead, the nostril etc. would be visible through the thicket of hairs. The eyebrow line, dimnuted by a part, would be curved in a tender line. It should neither be shaded, nor suggestive of a strong position (*VS,* III, 39. 10-13).

4606 **साची-दृष्टि**

Sācī-dṛṣṭi : a type of glance where the pupil moves from side to side along the horizontal plane. The side-long glance in which the pupil is taken to the corner of the eye. In *Vikramorvaśīya* (4.51), the king delienates the idea of sound of birds calling by *sācī* glance (*NS,* XXII. 76b-77a); the side-glance with eyeballs half-shut by eye-lashes.

4607 **साची-हस्त**

Sācī-hasta : bent hand. The palm is raised outwards. The third and little fingers are extended and bent very slightly, the first finger stretched straight, and the second finger bent to the tip of the thumb and the thumb bent a little towards. It is used to express saying 'this or that', threatening, astonishment, explaining, rod, braid of hair, beating the drum, life, solitude, lotus-stalk, etc.

4608 **साजात्य-भेद**

Sājātya-bheda : one of the three kinds of *bhedas*; literally 'difference within the same species'. According to this doctrine both Brahman and *jīva* are *cit* (conscious) in essence and hence they belong to the same species. So the difference between Brahman and *jīva* belongs to the *sājātya* category according to the *acintya-bhedābheda.*

4609 **साञ्जलि**

Sāñjali : folded hands; *hāth joṛnā* in Hindi. Folding of hands is common in India at a meeting place. Even the politicians of India fold their hands to the commoner when they go for election campaign. After getting the power they leave this practice for five years but keep on folding hands to the persons whom they think more powerful. This tradition was reverse in the feudal age. In those days superiors did never fold their hands. Instead it was the gentry which used to urge the superiors folding its hands.

In ancient days only the Mahārāṇā of Udaipur folded his hands whenever he spoke to the nobles of the first grade. The sixteen nobles of the first grade also folded their hands whenever they had an opportunity to speak to the sovereign. It was probably done to show regard so as to impress upon their nobles that the rulers regarded them as equals. Such a tradition does not seem to have been in vogue in any other state. The nobles of all other ranks when they spoke to their ruler folded their hands and kept them folded till they had finished (*Hakiki Bahī*, RSAB, No.5, V.S. 1848; *Pṛthvīrājarāso*).

4610 **सात्त्वत-न्याय**

Sāttvata-nyāya : striking the foot. It is similar to *Bharata-nyāya;* but the weapon (and the shield) are to be moved at the back.

4611 **सात्त्वती-वृत्ति**

Sāttvatī-vṛtti : grandiose style. The style which is endowed with the quality of the *sattva,* the *nyāyas* (proper) and the *vṛtta,* and has exuberance of joy and suppression of the state of sorrow (*NS*, XII, 41-44). It is known to have the four varieties: *utthāpaka* (challenge), *parivartaka* (change of action), *sallāpaka* (harsh discourse) and *saṅghāṭya* (breach of alliance).

4612 **सात्त्विक**

Sāttvika : virtuous (*Ratirahasya*, 3.32-33). Bharata (*NS*, XXII. 33) mentions *śobhā* (brilliant character), *vilāsa* (graceful bearing), *mādhuryam* (self-possession), *sthairyam* (steadiness), *gāmbhīryam* (gravity) *lalitam* (sportiveness), *audāryam* (nobility) and *tejas* (spirit) are the different aspects (male's *sattva*).

4613 **सात्त्विक-अभिनय**

Sāttvika-abhinaya : graceful gesticulation which portrays mental condition. The fourth aspect of acting is *sāttvika.* This relates to the presentation of light special involuntary physical manifestations that occur when an emotion reaches a high pitch. *Sattva* means the mental capacity of the actor to identify himself with the character and his feelings. Relying upon such identification alone the actor can show the emotional reaction of perspiration, hairs standing on end, limbs becoming benumbed, the voice breaking or faltering, trembling, pallor, tears and immobility. One who is not truly, or deeply, in sorrow cannot shed tears; one who does not feel excitement or fear does not prespire. It is because of this special quality of these manifestations that they are separately dealt with. In chapter seven, where they are described along with the emotions, Bharata gives the circumstances under which each rises and the way to act them. Later, when describing actions of limbs, he says, that in situations of deep emotion, gestures of hands and other movements naturally subside and the appropriate type of representation is through the eight *sāttvikas* (*NS*, IX. 173-178).

Sattva has been described by Bharata as the inner poise and concentration of mind (*Ibid.*, Vol. I, p. 374-75). The *sattva* enables the actor to indicate the signs of joy and sorrow even he is not effected by them. It has also been defined as the inner unmanifest source of emotion or *bhāva* (*Ibid*): *avyaktarūpam sattvam hi vijñeyam bhāvasaṁśrayam.* Still another definition identifies *sattva* with the body or rather physical vitality and declares that from *sattva* arises *bhāva*, from *bhāva* comes *hāva,* and from *hāva* arises *helā* (AB on *NS.* Vol. III, p.152).

Abhinava explains that these emotions arise naturally and spontaneously in different types of persons, e.g. of love in cultured women: *bhāva-hāva-helāstu sarvā eva sarvāsyeva sattvādhikāsūttāmaṅganāsu bhavanti (Ibid.)*. *Sattva*, thus joins the psyche and the body as their vital link finding expression in their emotions.

4614 **सात्त्विक-भाव**

Sāttvika-bhāva : physical and involuntary products as horripilation, sweating, fainting etc; *physical sensations;* natural reactions of overwhelming emotion; external indications of depth of feeling. Unlike other sensations, *sāttvika bhāvas* arise out of only *sattva guṇa* (quality of goodness and purity) which brings peace and enlightenment to the soul. Sentiment, at its best, results in the excitement of *sattvaguṇa,* and its consequent reactions appear on the body in the form of these sensations. These are eight in number and are common to all emotions. They are described, not singly, but in groups of three or more. They are as follows: stufication (*stambha*), perspiration (*sveda*), horripilation (*romāñca*), chocked voice (*svarabhaṅga*), tremor (*vepathu*), palour (*vivarṇa*), tears (*aśru*), unconsciousness (*pralaya*) and death (*mṛti*). Unlike other consequents (*anubhāvas*), they arise in a state of purity of mind and hence are called *sāttvika* (Nagendra, 1987, 161). (b) *Sāttvika bhāva* is the elementary process or experience aroused when a stimulus has excited a receptor. It is the process of sensing, with images and feelings, one of the three elements of consciousness. It may be called discriminable experience.

4615 **सात्त्विक-मुद्रा**

Sāttvika-mudrā : used to show the calmer, more reposeful mood and attitudes.

4616 **सादृश्य**

Sādṛśya : parallelism, fidelity of representation, *upacāra* or a metaphor consists in suppressing the differences of two paradoxical objects by representing one common quality (*sādṛśya*) between both. *Sādṛśya* or parallelism is a common technical device constantly employed by the ethnic poets. Ladākhī poetry, for example, 'makes use of the rhyme of sentence, generally called parallelism when occurring in European poetry. In *karmā* and *sailā* songs of the central India, two or more sentences are constructed accordingly:

> Come with me to Mungeli
> And I will give your bangles
> Come with me to Lāmnī
> And I will give you anklets
> Come with me to Lormī
> And I will give you ear-rings.

There is an interesting use of the same technique of parallelism.

4617 **साधक**

Sādhaka : spiritual aspirant.

4618 **साधन**

Sādhana : the middle term in *anumāna* (q.v) in the Indian logical system of inference. Also known as *hetu.*

4619 **साधनदेह**

Sādhanadeha : purified body for *sādhanā.*

4620 **साधारण-धर्म**

Sādhāraṇa-dharma : the common duties of man, the duties that are obligatory on all man equally irrespective of individual capacity, social status, nationality or creed.

4621 **साधारणी**

Sādhāraṇī : female partner of the aspirant, drawn from public women.

4622 **साधारण्य**

Sādhāraṇya : It is another aspect of that 'consent' which is already recognised as *sādṛśya, sāhitya* or *sārūpya* and *tadākāratā.* It is an aesthetic sympathy which can be said as ideal-sympathy. *Sādhāraṇīkaraṇa* is the process of idealization by which the reader passes from his troublous personal emotion to the severity of contemplation of a poetic sentiment. It is an emotional attitude characterized by feeling with another person who is undergoing an emotional experience.

4623 **साधु**

Sādhu : what is good and right in a work of art (opposite of *anyathā*) as an exclamation 'well done'. (b) a sage, holy person whose life is dedicated to the search for God. *Sādhus* are often compared to cotton. Their lives are pure as the whiteness of cotton, as dry (i.e. unattached) as the cotton-pad and as useful for protecting common men as cotton-clothes for the body. *Sādhu* means one who attains - *sādh* 'to attain'.

Religion is the corner-stone of life and culture in India. For over 5000 years the country has been the home of the largest body for organized monks. Known as *sādhu* or as *sanyāsī, yogī, muni, svāmī, ṛṣi, tapasvī, tyāgī,* and *guru,* they are the votaries for the Vedic spiritual heritage and present the essence of Hindu spiritualism.

A *Sādhu* is easily recognisable by the *tilaka,* the sanctified marking he carries on his forehead, and by the robes and apparel prescribed by the sectarian code. The unique *nāgās* belonging to the two principal Hindu sects are, however, expected to remain stark naked, though they may cover their genitals when they move in society. They follow a strict code governing the body's hair. And there are only two options: either they grow hair on the all five parts of the body or they get themselves fully shaved and do not allow any hair to grow at all. The colour of a *Sādhu's'* robe and the design of his *tilaka* will define the sect to which he belongs.

Kumbha-melā is a sight that provides immense inspiration for the thousands of devotees who line up on either side of the pageant. And after the *Sādhus* have crossed, the faithful who worship them lie and roll in salutation upon the ground that the holy men have trod and adorn their foreheads with the dust of the holy feet. (fg. 4623).

The hypocracy of *Sādhus* is well known in Sanskrit literature. An anonymous Sanskrit verse portraits them as follows:

> Having spent half the morning
> raking over the king and upper classes,
> Their hands washing the alters,
> gathering flowers or *kuśa* grass.
> They spend their day
> pretending holy breathing and meditation.
> Their half shut eyes
> devoted to watching the breast of bathing girls.
> (Trans. Vātsyāyana and Mishra, 181)

4624 **साधो**

Sādho : an ascetic or who has attained beautitude is to be addressed as *sādho* (*NS*, XVII. 65-94).

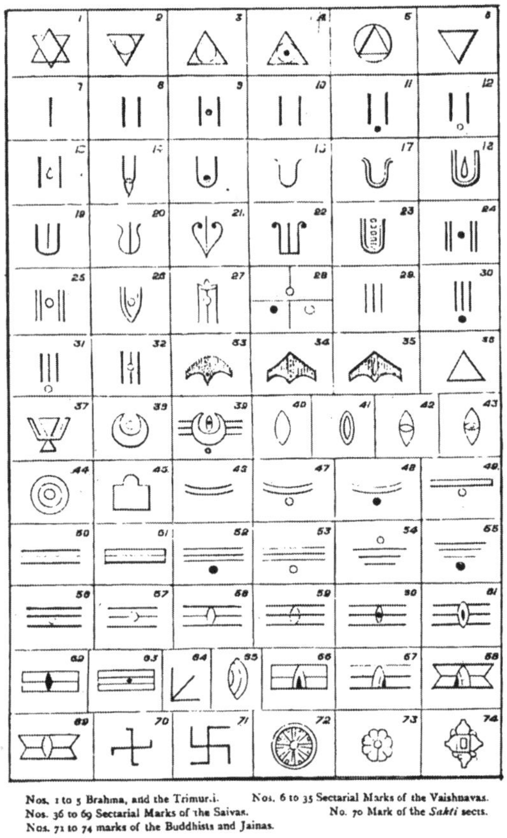

Nos. 1 to 5 Brahma, and the Trimurti. Nos. 6 to 35 Sectarial Marks of the Vaishnavas.
Nos. 36 to 69 Sectarial Marks of the Saivas. No. 70 Mark of the *Sakti* sects.
Nos. 71 to 74 marks of the Buddhists and Jainas.

Fig. - (4623)

4625 **साध्य**

Sādhya : the major term, the object which one wants to know in relation to *pakṣa* (q.v.) or the inferable character of the letter. See under *anumāna*.

4626 **सान्त्व**

Sāntva : form of speech and thought. (*Arthaśāstra*, 2.10.10).

4627 **सान्द्र-कुञ्चित-कुन्तल**

Sāndra-kuñcita-kuntala : lady whose hair are compressed and thick, quality of the Deer-lady (*Anaṅgaraṅga*, 3.20-21).

4628 **सामन्**

Sāman : a melody that is sung at sacrifices. It is said to have the power to fulfil any desire. Each *sāman* chant is linked with a particular Vedic verses and has its own tune, prescribed handpose and is meant for a specific purpose. (*Jaimini*, II. 1.36; IX. 2.34-38).

4629 **सामरस्य**

Sāmarasya : complete *harmony.* Any form of discipline needs a complete state of harmony according to *Śāstras.* (b) The *union* of the female and male principles. Same as *yuganaddha.*The *equilibrium* between Śiva and Śakti. Very often the equilibrium is conceived in sexual terms. Complete understanding of this equilibrium lead to the sense of non-duality (*Tāntric* concept). (c) The achievement of a balance between two opposed forces.

4630 **सामवेद-मुद्रा**

Sāmaveda-mudrā : gesture symbolizing *Sāmaveda.* Extend the middle finger and curve the thumb at the roots (*VD*).

4631 **सामाजिक**

Sāmājika : same as *Sahṛdaya* (q.v.).

4632 **सामान्य-धर्म**

Sāmānya-dharma : generality. Code of conduct common to all castes and stages, such as speaking truth, etc. (*Arthaśāstra* 3.1.39). (b) according to Buddhism, generality is only a name because the individual (*svalakṣana*) alone is real, and there is no class or universal other than the particular objects of experience. (c) according to the Jains and the Vedāntins, generality is constituted of the essential common attributes of all the individuals, and hence both are related by way of identity. (d) according to the *Nyāya-vaiśeṣikas, sāmānya* of the universal is a real entity, which is eternal (*nitya*) and distinct from, but inherent in, many individuals (*anekānugata*). Universals may be distinguished as *parā* or the highest and all pervading, *aparā* or the lowest, and *parāparā* or the intermediate.

4633 **सामान्याभिनय**

Sāmānyābhinaya : basic representation. The *sāmānyābhinaya* is defined as that which is presented by the head, the hand, the waist, the chest, the shanks and the thighs simultaneously. It is produced by the representation of speech, gestures and temperament. The superior historionic representation has the exuberance of temperament; in the medium, the temperament is adequate and in the inferior, it is lacking. Temperament is something invisible but it is the basis of states and endowed with proper sentiments by means of qualities like horripilation, tears and the like.

4634 **सामीप्य**

Sāmīpya : proximics. The Pāṇinian rule *uparyadhaydhasaḥ sāmīpye* (Aṣṭādhyāyī,8.1.17) prescribes the repetition of the indeclinables *upari, adhi* and *adhas*, when they express uniterrupted nearness.

The *Kāśikā vṛtti* explains the concept of *sāmīpya* as *pratyāsatti* (close proximity) which can be of two kinds, viz: (1) *Kālakṛata* (in point of time) and (ii) *deśakṛta* (in point of space).

Deśakṛta (varying from region to region) distances of higher-caste people, their dwellings, etc. are depicted in Sanskrit literature. It developed, later on, in the form of 'untouchability' which refers to a set of provisions in traditional Hindu law which specified harsh penalties for members of the lowest castes who approached within certain distances.

4635 **सामुद्रिक**

Sāmudrika : the science of palmistry. Ancient Indians made notable progress not only in palmistry but also in physiognomy. They also tried to read the character and fate of women from the signs of their limbs. Palmistry and physiognomy, were applied in detecting criminals and in selecting brides. The *Yājnavalkya-Smṛti* (II. 13-15) lays down the following signs as indicative of a perjurer and a wicked plaintiff: licking the lips, perspiring forehead, discoloured face, indifference to other, words, not looking at one who looks at him, curving the lips. *Manu* (III. 8.10) and *Viṣṇu-dharma sūtra* (24.12.16) hold the following bad signs of a girl who should not be married: tawney hair, extra limb (e.g. six fingers), devoid of one limb (four fingers instead of five), hairless, too hairy, talkative, yellowish eyes. According to *Viṣṇu Pūraṇa* (III. 10.18.22), crow-like-voice, too hairy legs or ankles, dimples on cheeks while laughing, dwarfish, too tall are evil signs. The following are the good signs according to Manu and *Viṣṇudharma sūtra* stated above: limbs free from defect, gait like that of a swan or an elephant, slightly grown hairs on body, small teeth, delicate body. The *Garuḍa-Purāṇa* (1.63-65) also deals with good and bad signs in men and women. It is an extensive description.

The *Sāmudrika-śāstra* is very extensive and exhaustive science in *Bṛhat-Saṁhitā* (LXVII) containing every detail, internal and external of man. There are 13 items a physiognomist is expected to observe. All these points are explained by Varāhamihira himself in the course of *puruṣa lakṣaṇam.*

This science has three branches viz. palmistry, physiognomy and feminine features. The marks on the body are of three kinds, viz. natural, temporal and causal. The lines are nothing but the writing of the creator on the human body which can be read by experts. The whole body should be measured with a tape with a limb-count-mathematics.

4636 **साम्यावस्था**

Sāmyāvasthā : the state of equilibrium of the three *guṇas* which in the *Sāṅkhya* are collectively known as *prakṛti.*

4637 **सारसभेद-मुद्रा**

Sārasabheda-mudrā : gesture of a curlew. The *alapadma* hand is bent to touch the palm to indicate a curlew.

4638 **सारस-मुद्रा**

Sārasa-mudrā : the *śukatuṇḍa*-hand indicates a hawk (*Mirror of Gesture,* pp. 50-51).

4639 **सारूप्य**

Sārūpya : co-aspectuality, conformation, coordination, correspondence. (b) models in *NS. Sārūpyāṇi* (models) may be created of straw, bark, gourd, etc. Diverse shapes resembling the original may be made of clay, gourd, cloth, wax, lac, bits of mica, *atasī, śaṇa, bilva*, etc. (*NS*, XXI. 205).

4640 **सालक्ष्य**

Sālakṣya : having like features, similarity, common denotation.

4641 **साश्रु-कण्ठ**

Śaśru-kaṇṭha: with the throat (choked) with tears (*Mahābhārata,* 4.6.9.10). How can the throat be possessed of tears? The idea is that the lachrymal moisture finds its way into the throat and hinders utterance, cf. *vāṣpa-kaṇṭha.*

4642 **साहस**

Sāhasa: (a) punishment (b) violence, rape, felony (*Smṛti*). *Arthaśāstra* (III. 17-19) has defined it such contemptuous talk as a measure of the sensitivity of the elite to unauthorized speech that an expression such as 'a bad Brāhmaṇa' was to be regarded as 'contemptuous and punishable. It is known from the text that the lower the status of the speaker relative to that of the object of his insult the higher the penalty. One could hardly improve on that as an instance of the correspondence between language and social hierarchy. Thus as *Manu* (VII. 267) says, the penalty for speaking ill of a Brāhmaṇa increased with the hierarchical distance between him and the speaker: 100 *panas* for Kṣatriya offender, 150-200 for a Vaiṣya, and a corporal punishment (*vadham*) for a Śūdra. The latter could be imposed in one of the three ways depending on the precise character of the Śūdra's crime; he could have his tongue cut, or get an iron nail ten fingers long, thrust red-hot into his mouth, or have hot oil poured into his mouth and into his ears (*Manu*, VII. 270-72).

4643 **साहित्य**

Sāhitya : unity of *śabda* and *artha* and their inseparability concomitance of sound and sense. But this unity brings about a special beauty in a poetry which is not found elsewhere. Special *Śabdārtha* are known as *Sāhitya-viśiṣta-pada-racanā* (Vāmana), *Viśiṣtam eva sāhityam abhipretam* (Kuntaka.)

4644 **साहित्य-विद्या**

Sāhitya-vidyā : criticism on poetry (10th cent. A.D. by Rājaśekhara) in *Kāvya-mīmāṁsā*).

4645 **सिंहकरणहस्त**

Siṃhakaraṇa-hasta : a type of *kaṭakāmukha hasta* only seen in iconography.

4646 **सिंह-पदक्रम**

Siṃhapada-krama : walking style like a lion, quality of a Bull-man (*Ratirahasya,* 3.32-33).

4647 **सिंहमुख-हस्त**

Sirhhamukha-hasta : lion-head hand. Single hand gesture commonly used by women in Dilwārā temples. The face is raised facing outwards. The first and the little fingers are straight; the second and the third fingers are bent parallel to the palm, and the thumb touches the tips. It is used to express a lion's head, a lotus garland, stroking the hair, fragrance, appeal, hare and elephant. If the thumb is joined with the fore and the middle fingers and rest fingers are extended; it is the hand of the *sirhhāsya* (a lion's mouth). It is used to indicate a sacrifice, a horse, an elephant, to handle a *kuśa*-grass, the lotus plant, the face of a lion, to extract a drug and to purify something else (*Abhinayadarpaṇa,* verse 142-143). (Fig. - 4647).

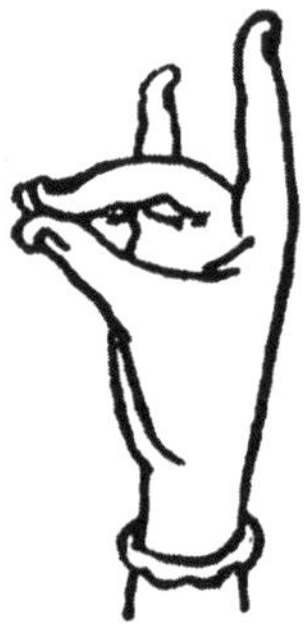

Fig. - (4647)

4648 **सिंह-मुद्रा**

Siṃha-mudrā : indication of a lion. *Sim§hamukha* and *patāka* applied to the back of the right with fingers moving freely indicates a lion (*Mirror of Gesture,* pp. 49-50).

4649 **सिंह-विक्रीडित-करण**

Sirhha-vikrīḍita-karaṇa : derived from *alātā cārī.* Movements similar to *alāta karaṇa,*but in performing the *alātā cārī,* the other foot is moved quickly, with the hands following the feet. It is used in the gait of the furious.

4650 **सिंहाकर्षित-करण**

Sirhhākarṣita-karaṇa : *Vṛścika* of one leg. Arms bent in *nikuñcita.* Hands in *padmakośa* or *ūrnābha* (*NS,* IV. 150-151). It is used in gesticulating lions and others.

4651 **सिंहासन**

Sirhhāsana : lion-seat or throne on which images of deities are installed in iconic representations or the kings used to sit. The lion-throne was a symbol of Buddha.

4652 **सिंहास्य-हस्त**

Sirhhāsya-hasta : single hand gesture.

4653 **सिद्ध**

Saddha : saints who have received *siddhi* or perfection.

4654 **सिद्धान्त**

Siddhanta : a view that a certain thing is such-and-such and accepted as a true in a system. It is one of the sixteen philosophical topics of the *Nyāya.*

4655 **सिद्धासन**

Siddhāsana : the cross-legged posture. Same as *dhyānāsana.* Place one heel at the excretary organ and then place the other one above the generative organ. Press the chin against the chest. Control the sense organs, keep the eyes fixed at one place and look at the space between the two brows.

It resembles the cross-legged posture. The sense organs are to be controlled through the control of mind. This *āsana* is very important as this takes you off the world. The mind is controlled and gets merged into the absolute if this *āsana* is practised for long hours ruthlessly for years.

It is the yogic posture adopted by seated Tirthāṅkaras.

4656 **सिद्धि**

Siddhi : the aesthetic process achieved by the actor while *rasa* in the form of sympathy and enjoyment is achieved by the spectator. (b) success. In traditional societies success was measured in conspicuously displayed property, hospitality and a multiplicity of wives and offspring. (c) miraculous power. Eight in number: *aṇimā* (atomisation), *laghimā* (levitation), *mahimā* (magnification), *garimā* (greatness), *prāpti* (power of getting anything), *prākāmya* ? (non-obstruction of desire), *vaśītva* (power of charming), and *īśitva* or sovereignty overall things (*Āp. Dh.S.,* II. 9.23. 6-7; *Prapañcasāra,* XIX. 62-63).

4657 **सिद्धिरोहा-मुद्रा**

Siddhirohā-mudrā : when the *viśālā-mudrā* (q.v.) is recalled in the *devī-cakra* (a kind of Tāntrika ritual function arranged in a circle made by a group of devouts in pair initiated particularly for the purpose) in the position of nudity and the devout in the circle offer oblation with wine, fish, meat, etc. to the appropriate fire, the devout duly inspected with the power of that rite is called the performer of *Siddhirohā* " (BT).

4658 **सिन्दूर**

Sindūra : zinc oxide, vermilion. The custom of applying *sindūra* on the head by married women is described in *Matsya*

Purāṇa (61. 20-21). When a cattle or a vehicle is bought, a little portion of vermilion is applied to it. This indicates the abode of goddess of money.

4659 **सीमन्तोन्नयन**

Sīmantonnayana : parting of the women's hair in the middle during the fourth or seventh month of pregnancy. The husband attaches to the wife's neck an *udumbara* twig and parts her hair from the front across the crown, first with *darbha* blades, then with a silver of *vīratara* wood, probably for ensuring fertility (*Baud. Gr.*, 1.10; *Āp. Gr.*, XIV. 1-8). It is obvious that the details of the ritual of *sīmantonnayana* indicate the gain of the power of fertility. In fact, the act of parting of the hair of the wife is symbolic ploughing; and the rite of symbolic ploughing obtains among certain tribes in the context of marriage (Thurston, E. *Castes and Tribes of Southern India*, Madras 1909, Vol. I, p.144; III, p. 103). It has been noted that the things used at this rite for parting the hair are long.

4660 **सुकुमार-नृत्य**

Sukumāra-nṛtya : synonym of *lāsya*, graceful dance. In *Kumārasaṁbhava* there is the mention of graceful dance performed by Pārvatī.

4661 **सुकुमार-प्रयोग**

Sukumāra-prayoga : graceful performance.

4662 **सुकुमारोद्धत-नृत्त**

Sukumāroddhata-nṛtta : one of the seven types of *nṛtta* (dance); gentle-forceful dance (*NS*).

4663 **सुकृत**

Sukṛta : well and truly made (of the world, as God's art) perfect.

4664 **सुकेशी**

Sukeśī : having good hair, quality of the Deer-lady (*Pañcasāyaka*, 2.12).

4665 **सुखासन**

Sukhāsana : this is the easiest of all the *āsanas* and is intended for those who are too old or too stiff to be able to perform the other *āsanas*. In this case, after crossing the legs, raise the knees eight or nine inches above the ground. Then pass a scarf on folded cloth round the small of the back and round the legs below the knees and knot it in front so that the weight of the knees is supported by the cloth. The hands may then be put together palm to palm and rested on the cloth between the knees. (b) blessed position. Those who are blessed possess the following quality:

श्रान्तस्य यानमशनं च बुभुक्षितस्य
पानं तृशापरिगतस्य भयेषु रक्षा ।
एतानि यस्य पुरुषस्य भवन्ति काले
धन्यं वदन्ति खलु तं नरलक्षणज्ञाः ॥

(*Bṛhat Saṁhitā*, LXVIII)

and also

अर्थागमो नित्यमरोगिता च प्रिया च भार्या प्रियवादिनी च ।
वश्यश्च पुत्रोऽर्थकरी च विद्या षड् जीवलोकस्य सुखानि राजन् ॥

4666 **सुखा (सशान्ता) मुद्रा**

Sukhā (Saśāntā) mudrā : "Seated on the *svastikāsana* with his head, neck and breast erect clenching two fists and keeping two thumbs out, in the navel region, make a joint of the left and right thumbs. This is a *mudrā, sukhā* by name which may grant a man eight kind of *siddhis* (attainments) namely, *aṇimā, laghimā* etc.

4667 **सुचिह्न**

Sucihna : emblem. Bhrata defines *piṇḍī bandha* as *sucihna* (*NS*, 258-262). Abhinavagupta states that emblem (*piṇḍībandha*) is a complex formation using three elements viz *ādhāra, aṅga* and *prayoga* (AB on *NS*, Vol. I, p.401). The term *ādhāra* would mean basis. This representation of the emblems of the different deities was apparently done within a framework of cosmic symbolism. Thus, it was limited not only to the emblems, but perhaps also accompanied with the representation of cosmic dimensions of space and time. The emblems served to symbolize the deities, and cosmic space and time imparted a befitting context to them (*Ibid.*, 402). The latter are, therefore, know as *ādhāra* or basic constituent. The medium of expression is *aṅga. Prayoga* means rendering.

4668 **सुतीक्ष्ण-दशना**

Sutīkṣṇa-daśanā : lady whose teeth are sharp, quality of Elephant-lady (*Anaṅgaraṅga*, 3.24-25).

4669 **सुतुङ्ग-स्तनी**

Sutuṅga-stanī : lady who has high breasts, quality of the Deer-lady (*Anaṅgaraṅga*, 3.20-21).

4670 **सुदर्प**

Sudarpa : man having pride, quality of a bull-man (*Pañcasāyaka*, 2.10).

4671 **सुदीर्घ-कण्ठ**

Sudīrgha-kaṇṭha : Long neck, quality of the Deer-man (*Pañcasāyaka*, 2.9).

4672 **सुनख**

Sunakha: good nails, quality of the Horse-man (*Ratirahasya*, 3.34-35).

4673 **सुनेत्र**

Sunetra : charming eyes, quality of the Deer-man (*Pañcasāyaka*, 2.9).

4674 **सुन्दर**

Sundara : which that pleases, pretty, handsome, balance in volume, weight and shape of all the limbs and their assemblage that gives the impression of unity that is *saundarya* as said in Ujjvala-*nīlamaṇi* quoted in *Śabda-kalpadruma.* (b) the concept of beauty is utilitarian in the tribal society. Complexion does not form an item in the Hill Maria's conception of beauty. The Hill Maria males prefer short-statured girls to long ones and they say that tall girls 'wither' away faster whereas a short girl retains her figure longer. A thin skinny girl is positively disliked. Good proportioned body, well-developed breasts, hips and limbs are the principal items of beauty in girls. Breasts do not seem to have any fascination of that. However, well-developed full breasts are liked in girls for they say that such girls would be better mothers and will be better able to feed their children. Fat people are nowhere seen in Abujhmārh, but as informed by the Hill Maria youth, they will give negative points to girls who are fat.

Actually speaking, the Hill Maria do not seem to have any eye for female beauty as we understand it. With almost the whole body devoid of clothes, such arrogance centres as breasts, do not form any item in their judgement. If they had any idea of beauty, it is not understood why they have no hesitation in choosing any girl. According to them, all girls are alike and the main consideration that they weigh in selecting a girl for marriage is her ability to bear children and bring them up and her capacity for hard work (see *Sundarī*).

In Muria, "its the ornaments that matter. It's the hair and necklaces and the combs that matter. He must have all the ornaments, round his head, at his ears, about his neck, and his waist; how beautiful he looks them! He must have combs in his hair, and clean clothes. Let the nose be as it is, let the eyes be as they are, let the mouth be as it is; they were made by God and will be what they are." When a boy is in love he borrows all he can, sticks feather in his hair, covers himself with coloured beads, ties bunches of little bells at his waist.

4675 **सुन्दरी**

Sundarī : beautiful woman. Hindu women like their sisters all over the world wish to appear attractive to men. But social codes have restricted the cultivation of beauty among the orthodox and certain traditions and usages have even perverted their notions of beauty. Hindus prohibit free social intercourse between the sexes, and respectable women are considered those who hide away from men. Women are allowed to appreciate good looks and good taste only among themselves. The generality of women being unable to correctly judge beauty among themselves, what is more valued among them is the financial position of the husband and not the personal charms of the wife. Hence it is the cost of the ornaments and clothes a lady wears. That is more interesting in the society of women than her good looks. Most of the Hindu women love to load themselves with silver and gold ornaments from head to foot not to enhance their good looks but to cow down other women by a show of their husband's wealth.

Modern notions of beauty is in keeping with the social life. Men do not want a lady to be active and flit about like a fawn, but to shuttle about like a swan. Men do not care much for a slim body but delights in hips like an elephant's. They value long, black glossy hair reaching up to the ankles when left loose, and have a horror of red or golden hair. As regards eye, it is the shape more than the colour that counts. Blue eyes, so dear to the European, is detested by the Indian who calls them "cats eyes". According to Indian standards the eyes should be of the shape of fish, and the eye brows arched like a bow with long lashes to match as arrows. Thus the eye of the lady should be Cupid's bow complete with arrows.

Though women of respectable classes have neglected beauty culture, the courtesans in India from very early times have been most careful in studying and cultivating those arts that enhance beauty and please men. In the girls the tribal youths admire vitality and beauty, but expect them to be well dressed and decorated. The concept of a Muria about a *Sundarī* is as follows: Her legs and feet should not be too long; they should be neither thin nor fat. The toes must not be big or crooked. She should have a slim waist etc.

4676 **सुन्दरी-ग्रीवा**

Sundarī-grīvā : neck-movement horizontally without turning of the face (*Abhinayadarpaṇa*, 78. 86-87). *Sundarī* is a curved movement of the neck. It is used to indicate the first appeal of love and affection, tender care, to assert a right idea and thought, to extend anything; and to appeal any aesthetic experience. It does not occur in *NS*.

4677 **सुप्त**

Supta : asleep. It is the twenty-third among thirty-three *vyabhicāri bhāvas*, enumerated by Bharata. It is also known as *svapna* (dreaming). It is manifested by deep breathing, dullness of the body, closing the eyes, superfaction of all senses, dreaming, tálking while asleep, closing eyes softly.

4678 **सुप्तवज्रासन**

Suptavajrāsana : after sitting in *vajrāsana* lie down flat on the back, resting the hand on the palms. More strain and force are exerted on the knees in this *āsana.*

4679 **सुप्त-स्थान**

Suptasthāna : sleeping or reclining posture.

4680 **सुप्त-स्थानक**

Suptasthānaka : a broad variety of posture.

4681 **सुप्रौढ-वक्षस्थल**

Suprauḍha-vakṣasthala : expansive chest, quality of the Bull-man (*Anaṅgaraṅga,* 3.17).

4682 **सुभ्रू**

Subhrū : having beautiful eyebrows (*Mahābhārata*).

4683 **सुमांसल-श्रुति**

Sumāṁsala-śruti : strong ears, quality of a Bull-man (*Ratirahasya,* 3.32-33).

4684 **सुरक्त-पाणि**

Surakta-pāṇi : red hands, quality of the Deer-man (*Pañcasāyaka,* 2.9).

4685 **सुरक्षात्मक व्यवहार**

Surakṣātmaka-vyavahāra : protective behaviour. Like any other species, the human animal tries to protect itself when danger threatens. The basic protective response, when time permits, is to hide body from attack. When it is impossible to hide from a physical attack, the typical response is to shield the face and head and curl up the body. At moments of savage physical attack the victim usually remains silent, but in associated moments of feeling, panic or temporary respite, another protective response often occurs - the scream. This is an alarm cry which we share not only with apes and monkeys but also with many other species to mammals. As a signal alerting others either come to the rescue or to protect themselves, it is perhaps the most non-specific in the animal world. It is so uncharacteristic of anyone species that we ourselves can recognize its meaning, regardless of the animal that is producing it. It varies from case to case, of course, sometimes sounding more like a squeal and sometimes more like a shriek, but there is no confusing its message of pain and fear. In the human species there appears to be a sex difference not only in the pitch of the screaming, but also in the frequency of its use. Adult males are less likely to use it in the moments of panic and fear, children and adult females use it.

People still dwellon ancient terrors such as slithering, creeping, crawling animals, pests and insects, thunder and lightning, enclosed spaces and great heights. The greatest fear by far is that of snakes. Other strong animal hatreds include spiders and rats, and any small crawling pests that invade the home. Lions, tigers and crocodiles rate moderately high in the lists of most hated animals by children, they never approach the intense feelings aroused by snakes and spiders.

A form of protective response unique to man is superstition. One special category of protective behaviour is the wearing of an amulet, talisman, charm or mascot.

4686 **सुरत-लीला**

Surata-līlā : coition-drama (Rājaśekhara, *Viddhaśālabhañjikā,* 1.1). sexual signals; the courtship and pre-copulatory sequences. Sexual signals function in four important ways: finding a mate, choosing a mate, arousing a mate, and bonding with a mate (such as Rādhā and Kṛṣṇa). First, finding a mate. With the arrival of sexual maturity there is a sudden increase in certain special kinds of social activity. In addition to fixed events, such as dances and goṣṭhīs, teenage males and females develop a powerful urge to go out 'on the prowl' in the absence of parental supervision. In most tribal societies there are informal arrangements for the coming together of young unmated males and females, which take on the quality of an 'Arena Display'. The fixed occasion, such as the dance, speeds up the process by giving a social reason for making contact with a member of the opposite sex. For many urban young adults, these mate-finding problems arc solved by virtue of modern co-education arrangements, or work situations involving a similar mixing of the sexes. Choosing a mate depends on many factors. Physical appeal is obviously important, with the various gender signals playing a role, but behaviour is also vitally significant. 'Warm into the eyes; making small touching movements, looking in turn at different parts of the other body; nodding the head vigourously in agreement, sitting directly falling the other, eyebrows high up on the forehead.

Once a bond has started to form between a male and female, there follows and escalating sequence of bodily intimacies. Contraceptive techniques have enhanced the courtship sequences.

The ascending scale of intimacies - the sexual sequence - varies from case to case. Between puritanically minded partners the final genital-to-genital, contact may be made before the more arcusing preliminaries have been performed.

The whole object of courtship, of the mutual approximation and caresses of two persons of the opposite sex, is to create the state of sexual tumerscence.

How then is tumerscence achieved under the rather unfavourable circumstances of *Ghotul* life. The buildings and surrondings of dormitory are powerful stimulants. These little huts, rise with tender and romantic association, the waving forest trees, around the stillness of the night, perhaps a moon, the bright fire in the courtyard, the tinkling bells tied to *chelik's* waist, the distant song of *moṭiārī* on their way — cannot fail to make the hearts of boys and girls beat faster.

The routine of a Ghotul-evening is carefully devised preparation for intercourse, a tonic to deficient libido. First of all, the sense of touch is vividly stimulated by the combing and messaging.

The auther of *Anaṅgaraṅga* believed that passion resides in the woman's right side during the bright fortnight of the lunar month, from new moon to full. The reverse is the case during the dark fortnight. The shifting of passion is believed to take place by the action of light and darkness.

Sculptures of Indian dancing girls often depict them with one hand on the hip in the traditional pose of the sex initiatness inviting erotic intimacy.

4687 **सुरतासन**

Suratāsana : posture in congress or coition, congress is the final goal of love. The lovers feel pleasure by lying in various postures. Different kinds of postures have been mentioned by Vātsyāyana (*Kāmasūtra,* 2.6.22) Kokkoka (*Ratirahasya,* 10.13-14) describes thirty-one types of postures. Kalyāṇamalla (*Anaṅgaraṅga,* 10.3) divides them into five categories: two types of supine postures (*uttānakam*), three types of side postures (*tiryak*), ten types of sitting postures (*āsītākhyam*), three types of standing postures (*sthitam*), and five types of bowing postures (*ānatakam*). The *Pañcasāyaka* (5.7-22) presents seven types of supine positions, three types of side positions, two types of sitting positions, two types of standing positions, and many bowing positions. The *Nāgarasarvasva* (28.32) depicts twenty-one types of supine postures, two kinds of sitting postures, two types of bowing posture and seven types of standing postures.

4688 **सुरभि-मुद्रा**

Surabhi-mudrā : "Make two hands joined together with their fingers matted themselves and put the left fore-finger through the fingers of the right hand. Then extend the left middle finger and right fore-finger. Again put the little finger on the tip of the ring finger and ring finger of the little finger. Thus framing the *surabhi-mudrā* one should think the cerebral nectar dripping down (from the cerebral lotus). It makes a *yogin* like Lord Śiva within the limit of six months." (*BT*).

4689 **सुरभि-रत-जल**

Surabhi-rata-jala : semen having good smell, quality of Hare-man (*Anaṅgaraṅga,* 3.30-31).

4690 **सुरासागर-हस्त**

Surā-sāgara-hasta : the wine-ocean. The *saṅkīrṇa* and *patāka* hands moved up and down denote the wine ocean (*Mirror of Gesture,* p.40).

4691 **सुरोहा-मुद्रा**

Surohā-mudrā : as described in the *vicitra-mudrā* (q.v.) when in the down-turned pair of palms all fingers are arranged like matted hairs and the pair of thumbs tied hard together, it is called the *Surohā-mudrā.* (*BT*).

4692 **सुललित-मांसलबाहु**

Sulalita-maṁsala-bāhu : lady whose shoulders are beautiful and fleshy, quality of the Mare-lady (*Ratirahasya,* 3.22-26).

4693 **सुवर्णमुखी-मुद्रा**

Suvarṇamukhī-mudrā : name of a river. The *ardha-catura* hand moving up and down indicates this river (*Mirror of Gesture,* p. 48).

4694 **सुवाच**

Suvāca : nice speech, quality of a Hare-man (*Ratirahasya,* 3.30-31).

4695 **सुवेष**

Suveṣa : wearing good dress, quality of a Hare-man (*Ratirahasya,* 3.30-31).

4696 **सुशिर-मुद्रा**

Suśira-mudrā : if the fist is placed on the waist, it is *suśira* (*VD*).

4697 **सुश्रोणि**

Suśroṇī : having good hips, quality of the Deer-lady (*Anaṅgaraṅga,* 3.20-21; *Pañcasāyaka,* 2.12).

4698 **सुषमा**

Suṣamā : the aggregate of the propriety and proportion.

4699 **सुष्ठु**

Suṣṭhu : excellent (in praise of a work of art).

4700 **सुसान्द्र-शिरोरुहा**

Susāndra-śiroruhā : lady whose hair are thick, quality of the Deer-lady (*Pañcasāyaka,* 2.12).

4701 **सूक्ष्म**

Sūkṣma : subtle (mental, as opposed to physical).

4702 **सूक्ष्माभिव्यक्ति**

Sūkṣmābhivyakti : micro-expressions. Extremely brief facial expressions lasting a small fraction of a second which reveal an individual's true emotions when he or she is attempting to conceal them. *NS* terms it as *sūcā.*

4703 **सूचक**

Sūcaka : an informer (*A*, 2.8.29, 32), symbol; cf. *Bharat āgaman sūcak ahahī* (*Mānasa*, 2.7.5).

4704 **सूचा**

Sūcā : micro-expression (*NS*, XXIV.45), a type of *ceṣṭākṛta* (physical) gesticulation. When the meaning of the sentence is first indicated by temperament and gestures and then there is *Vākyābhinaya* (q.v.) it is called *sūcā.*

4705 **सूची**

Sūcī : "Pointing out" The *NS* (XXII.43) defines the *sūcī* as a technique which conveys and foreshadows, through gestures and temperament, the meaning of a sentence before it is sung or recited. Thus *śākhā* is always followed by *sūcī*, as we observe Śakuntalā's (*Śākuntalam*, 1.5) first showing, through movement, the disturbance caused by the bee—what Bharata calls— "pointing out first through gestures" (*sūcī*)—and then describing it through speech.

Sūcī is the guide signal. It guides the attention of onlooker, or his actual movements. In a word it is pointer. When we point at something it seems such a simple thing to do that we tend to take this type of action for granted. Pointing is, in fact, speciality of human species and we perform it in many different ways.

The most simple Guide sign is the body point, and this is the only form of pointing which we do share with other species. If some sudden stimulus alerts one animal in a group and it swings its body quickly to face the stimulus, this action may guide the attention of its companions so that they do turn to face in the same direction, even though they themselves may not have spotted the source of interest.

Human body-pointing can be observed at any social gathering where an important personage is present. We can detect his position as we enter the room by the cluster of bodies surrounding him and all facing towards him. Street clusters of this type also arouse our curiosity, when we form a circle of inward-facing bodies obscuring some focal point of interest. When there has been an accident, people run towards such a cluster, guided by the inward-pointing, so that the clamp of onlookers quickly swell to a dance crowd.

Sūcī is only an incidental gesture. We do not do it as an intended signal—it is secondary to what else is going on. The most popular form of deliberate guide-signing is undoubtedly the fore-finger point. When someone stops us in the street and asks the way, we may give a perfectly adequate verbal answer, but we rarely omit to add a fore-finger point in support of those words. Even when the pointing is clearly superfluous we still feel compelled to do it, and it is an action that is observable in almost all countries in the world.

Thus, a pointing relationship is one in which some part of the body, usually the fingers or hand, points to some person, to some part of the body, to an object or place. Or, the referent may be a more abstract attitude, attribute, affect, direction, or location. Pointing is always intrinsically coded; the act means 'to show something'; the something is the target or referent of the point and, of course, can vary.

4706 **सूची-अभिनय**

Sūcī-abhinaya : a type of gesticulation. Bharata defines *sūcī-abhinaya* as that in which the meaning of the sentence is indicated first by gesticulation and then by words (*NS*, XXII.43). It occurs in *Ṛtusaṁhāra* (2.24). In *Śākuntalam* (1.7), the *sūta* and the king both do the *sūcī* type of *abhinaya*, for the movement expresses the mood first and then the words are used.

4707 **सूची-करण**

Sūcī-karaṇa : feet as in the *cārī*, the *kuñcita* foot is lifted and placed forward. In the initial position it touches the knee of the stationary leg, in the final the toe touches the *samapāda* foot. No specific hands are prescribed (*NS*, IV.136b-137a, X.34).

4708 **सूचीकृतमुख-संस्थान**

Sūcīkṛtamukha-saṁsthāna : the slightly curved-cheek pose (*VD*).

4709 **सूची-चरण**

Sūcī-caraṇa : same as *sūcī-pāda* (q.v.) The left foot is in natural position. The other is resting on the floor by the tip of the thumb-toe. It is used to wear the *nūpura* (*SR*, IV.7.318).

4710 **सूची-चारी**

Sūcī-cārī : a type of posture, both feet in *samapāda kuñcita. Kuñcita* foot lifted and brought to knee level. The leg there is stretched at the level and then the foot is lowered and the toes again touch the floor. *Udvāhita jaṅghā, sūcī, ardhasūcī* and *sūcīviddham karaṇa* and *sūcīviddha maṇḍala.* Throwing up a *kuñcita* foot and extending it up to the knee or above the knee of the other and then letting it fall on its forepart. According to *NS* (X,34) "the *kuñcita* foot is raised, the knee in level with the chest, the shank is stretched fully and then dropped to the ground on its forepart."

4711 **सूची-पाद**

Sūcī-pāda : forefront of the toes of the foot touches the ground. The *NS* (X.10-17) reads an extra foot, called *Sūcī-pāda.* When one stands on the toes, lifts up the heel and rests the left foot as it is, it is *sūcī-pāda.* This is to be used to dance with *nūpura* (belled anklet), to cross, or to jump over a fixed mark, or limit etc.

4712 **सूचीमुख-असंयुत-हस्त**

Sūcīmukha-asaṁyuta-hasta : a type of gesture. The hand is the most important pointer. There are some variants there, too. In addition to the fore-finger point, there is also the hand point, in which all five digits are aimed, flat-handed and with the fingers together. The difference between the fore-finger point and the hand point is subtle. If I ask someone in the street "Where is the station"? and he replies, "It is down there," he is likely to point with his fore-finger. If I ask 'How do I get to the station'? and he replies 'you walk down there', he is more likely to indicate the direction of my walk by pointing with the whole of his hand. In other words, the pointing hand is guide sign indicating the course to be taken.

4713 **सूचीमुख-नृत्त-हस्त**

Sūcīmukha-nṛtta-hasta : the needle-pointed. A type of hand gesture in dancing (*NS*, IV.187) also occurs in sculpture. When two hands in the *sarpaśiraḥ*-style with thumbs joining middle fingers are stretched in a bending way, it is called the *sūcīmukha.*

4714 **सूचीमुख-हस्त**

Sūcīmukha-hasta : the point of a needle; single hand gesture. Hands facing each other and held on the right side (*NS*, VII.156). When the fore-finger of the *kaṭakāmukha* (q.v.) is stretched, it is *sūcīmukha.* The *sūcīmukha* gesture may indicate a lot of things by different applications; like (a) raising up, (b) lowering down, (c) quivering, (d) gaping or displaying, (e) dwindling and (f) moving. (i) The raised up *sūcīmukha* indicates; a discuss, lightning, bunches of flowers, the hair-locks by the ear-side, zigzag walking, praise, and thanks-giving. (ii) The bent-ordered *sūcīmukha* styled by turning upwards indicates: a small snake, a down-turned twig, a bride, an earthen lamp, a crawling, creeper, a peacock, falling down, curving etc. (iii) The upturned *sūcīmukha* indicates: stars, the nose-rod, the rod etc. (iv) The down-turned *sūcīmukha* styled as a down-faced one, suggests all sorts of ferocious animals. (v) The *sūcīmukha* in a circular style indicates: to take for granted everything, what a man may desire. (vi) The *sūcīmukha* gesture in the bowing down style suggests: pondering over a thing in urge of a certain cause. (vii) This is by the mouth in a curved position indicates: yawning and frowning or devising sentence. (viii) The *sūcīmukha* in a curved style by the ear indicates: yawning and the mouth, speaking sentences. (ix) The same gesture in a joined position suggests: either 'it is she', or in the state of beating or sounding. (x) This in the position of flat, widened and extended styles suggests: an expression of anger with trembling lips and limbs sweating, hairlocks, ear-rings, armlets and other decoratives of the cheek. (xi) This is placed on the forehead to indicate the sense of pride, 'Its I am', pointing an enemy and angry temper, itching an ear and to indicate, 'Who is there'. (xii) By joining this gesture with both the hands it indicates: joining and disjoing it suggests separation. (xiii) By the *svastika* position it indicates: quarrelling and by pressing them tightly each other it suggests binding hard. (xiv) By the double *sūcīmukha* gestures it indicates: left-turning, or going to and fro; by the left and by the south facing, drawing near, turning back and splitting up. It indicates the close of the day and the night. (xv) Moving the tip of this gesture in a cyclic order it indicates: beauty, moral whirling and hills. (xvi) The lowered-down position of the gesture suggests: distribution of service. If this is placed on the forehead with the same position it may indicate the image of Lord Śambhu. (xvii) The slanting pose of the gesture suggests hoisting up *Indradhvaja.* (xviii) By the double representation it represents the moon-disc. (xix) By moving in a cyclic order it may also indicate the moon-disc. (xx) Placing it on the forehead by the upturned bent it may further suggest the pair of Śiva's and a series of Indra's eyes (*NS*, IX.58-73).

Bālarāmabharata derives it from *śikhara* and prescribes in *Bharatanāṭyam.* It is common in iconography and is also known as *tarjanī-hasta.* The fore-finger of *kaṭakāmukha* (q.v.) is stretched. It represents a discus, lightning, banner, blossoms, ear-ring, zigzag movement like that of a fish, cry of approbation, young serpent, sprout, smoke, lamp, various creepers.

4715 **सूची-मुद्रा**

Sūcī-mudrā : "an intelligent votary in a nude condition should make the pairs of his hands joined—folded, like a bud of flower by the way of a crooked feat of the great spiritual culture (*kuṭilena mahāyogena*). The elbow and the wrist of the right hand should come out from the bottom. Raise up the left hand and join tightly two legs and then again check or finish it by the left hand. In the same way the equal time should also be kept in the right hand. By the three movements of legs or leg-bones, one should observe the *sūcī-mųdrā*. These are the strictly *haṭhayoga* feats and very difficult to explain and practice without the direct demonstration of seasoned teachers" (*BT*).

4716 **सूचीविद्ध-करण**

Sūcīviddha-karaṇa : this is the extreme position of the last movement of the *sūcīcārī*.The *kuñcita* foot pierces into the heel of the other foot. Hands are on the hips and the chest: the commentary adds that the hand on the hip is *ardhacandra* and the one on the chest is *kaṭakāmukha* (*NS*, IV.138b-139a). It is used in anxiety.(Fig. - 4716).

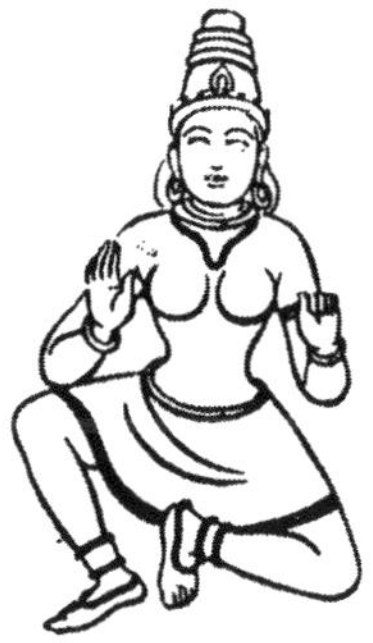

Fig. - (4716)

4717 **सूची-हस्त**

Sūcī-hasta : fore-finger is held upright.

4718 **सूत**

Sūta : the reciters of the *Purāṇas*. According to the account of the *Cākyārs*, the dramatic art was taken to Kerala by a *sūta* family.

The *sūta* is said to be given the duty of reciting or composing the *Purāṇas*, the poetic folk-traditions of ballads. He is differentiated from the *bandin, māgadha* and the *cāraṇa* in as much as these later are said to be devoid of the study of the *Vedas* (*Skanda*, VI.194.72). They are also termed *stāvaka* (prisers), which probably points out an important difference from the *sūta*, who is also a composer. The *kāyastha* is keeper of records but he is censored.

4719 **सूतक**

Sūtaka : child-birth; impurity of parents consequent upon the birth of their child or miscarriage (*Smṛti*). *Sūta* is one that is born or begotten, hence the basic meaning of *sūtaka* is birth or production. As the process of birth is always attended with faith, this eventuality came to be looked upon as 'filthy'. (b) among the Maria Gonds of Baster the father is impure for a month after the birth of a child and dose not go to his work. A Muria Gond father is impure until the navel-cord drops; he may reap his crop, but cannot thrash or sow. This is perhaps a relic of Hindu custom.The rules for the treatment of the mother resemble of the Hindus, but they do not keep her so long without food. On some day from the fifth to the twelfth after the birth the mother is purified and the child is named. On this day its hair is shaved by the son-in-law or husband's or wife's brother-in-law. The mother and child are washed and rubbed with oil and turmeric, and the house is freshly whitewashed and cleaned with cowdung. They procure a winnowing-fan full of *Kodon* and lay the child on it, and the mother ties this with a cloth under her arm (Russell and Hiralal, III. 85-86).

4720 **सूत्र**

Sūtra : axes, the plumb-line. The *Mānasāra* (LXVII) enumerates as many as eleven *sūtras* and lays down the relative distance of each part of human figure from each of these lines for various types of deflected stances. These *sūtras* are also helpful in trying to decipher the language of the iconic body or the structure of the psyche. Research into the functions of the brain has found that these *sūtras* seem to specialize in different activities.

4721 **सूत्रधार**

Sūtradhāra : director of the play. His natural qualities were intelligence, good memory, generosity, steadiness in speech, good health, sweet nature, tolerance, self-control, sweet-tongue, calmness, truthfulness, politeness and holiness. He was the knower of *sūtra* (thread) which brings about the unity of songs, *Śāstric* instruction. He was important in the preliminaries. Sometimes he played the main role in the play (*NS*). (b) one who holds the puppets by threads is *sūtradhāra*, rope-holder hence might be associated with rope-dance also. The *naṭa* in north India even today walks on the rope stretched from the summit of the cliff.

4722 **सेवा**

Sevā : public service. In ancient India, *sevā* was the way of devotion without any thought of benefit, but now it has become individual merit. Here motives are mixed. Here the traditional service of the superior by the inferior has been changed into the social service of the inferior by the superior—superior because it is service which brings merit and liberation. It is a trained way from orthodox religious observances towards social service as the major religious activity. *Nitiśataka* of Bhartṛhari has raised certain problems of *sevāvṛtti*:

> If quiet, he's dumb, but if articulate, a loud mouth;
> Impudent if near at hand, but shiftless if he keeps his distance.

If patient, he's a mouse; vulgar if he shows a little flare.
The rules for serving are such not even *yogis* master it.

4723 **सैन्धवाक**

Saindhavāka : one of the elements of *lāsya*. This is in *Saindhavī* language. Abhinava explains that it is devoid of all softness. It is popularly known as spectacles (*prekṣaṇīya*), designated (*ḍombika*) and *bījaka-prasthāna*, etc. (It seems that this sort of an *uparūpaka* enacted out in the local Sindhi dialect). Abhinava says that there is not the slightest *pāṭhya* or recitation (*NS*, XXI. 358-60).

4724 **सैरिन्ध्र**

Sairindhra : a class of men who used to arrange the dress of rich people.

4725 **सोच्छ्वासा-नासा**

Socchvāsā-nāsā : drawn air nostrils, inhaling of air by nostrils i.e. deep breathing; a type of nose-gesture expressing sweet scent, deep breathing, etc. (*NS*, VIII. 123-129). It is used in powerful smell, anger, fear and in the Furious and Heroic.

4726 **सोपाधिक**

Sopādhika : conditioned.

4727 **सोम-मुद्रा**

Soma-mudrā : gesture of the moon. The gesture of *sandaṁśa* with raised middle finger (*VD*). *Soma* is also the elixir of immortality, food of gods, used in Vedic ritual.

4728 **सोम्य**

Somya : inferior persons are to be addressed as *somya* (*NS*, XVII. 65-94).

4729 **सोलपद्म-हस्त**

Solapadma-hasta : full-blown lotus hand. The palm is faced outwards and hollowed. It is used to express the idea of full-blown lotus, the hair-knot, anger, praise, full moon, a round face, a ball, beauty etc.

4730 **सौन्दर्य-शिरस्**

Saundarya-śiras : a type of head-movement given by *Abhinayadarpaṇa*.

4731 **सौभिक**

Saubhika : a juggler, a puppet-player (*A*, 2.27.25, 7.17.34, 11.1.34). It also occurs in *Mahābhāṣya* (III.1.26) as *Śobhanika*, which means the teacher who trained the *naṭas* (actors) in the matter of actual dancing: They demonstrated how Kaṃsa is killed by Kṛṣṇa or Bali is fettered. This demonstration was a visible demonstration given by the instructors while superintending over the acting of their disciples.

4732 **सौम्य-शिरस्**

Saumya-śiras : a type of head movement given by *Abhinayadarpaṇa*.

4733 **सौष्ठव**

Sauṣṭhava : the *sauṣṭhava* of the limbs is defined by Bharata as the position of the body where there is complete equilibrium (*NS*, X. 56-58). *Sauṣṭhava* of the limbs is an important technical phrase from Bharata: He refers to *sauṣṭhava* at various places, and defines it "as the completely natural position of the limbs, when the person is neither too upright nor bent, and is at ease; when the waist and the ears as well as the elbow, the shoulder and the head are in their natural positions (*sama*) and the chest is slightly raised." These performing the exercises in the *nṛtta aṅgahāras* must be careful of this (*NS*, X. 89 and 91-93). In *Mālavikāgnimitra*, Parivrājikā wants to see the movements of all her (Mālavikā's) limbs, and her *abhinaya* is to be clear and precise: *Sarvāṅgasauṣṭhava*. The *sauṣṭhava* of the limbs is the indicative of the accuracy of training, and trappings would necessarily conceal it. Even today, in contemporary classical dance, we can observe that the dance loses its charm and restraint the moment this *sauṣṭhava* is lost sight of; negligence in this respect leads to indiscipline in movement, and the body bends where it is not necessary and desirable. Mālavikā then appears on the stage with all her limbs in the *sauṣṭhava* position (*Sarvāṅgasauṣṭhava*), a dance performance must begin from this position of poise, complete control and balance. When the waist and the ears as well as the elbow, the shoulders and the head are in their natural position and the breast is raised, it is called *Sauṣṭhava*.

4734 **स्कन्द-मुद्रा**

Skanda-mudrā : if styling the *śaktyākāra* (q.v.), it is placed down-turned with three curved fingers, it indicates Skanda (*VD*).

4735 **स्कन्ध**

Skandha : (a) shoulder. (b) feelings; the Buddhist term for five elements, namely *rūpa* (matter), *vedanā* (sensation), *saṁjña* (perception) *saṁskāra* (impressions) and *vijñāna* (consciousness). (c) the term is also used by the Jains to denote the minute aggregates of the *paramāṇus* or atoms. (d) Buddha Ghosha in his work *Visuddhimagga* recognises three kinds of feelings: pleasure, pain and mental feeling (*upekṣā*). Pleasure is agreeable, pain is disagreeable, and mental feeling is neither pleasant nor painful. Feelings arise with *sparśa*, contact with sense-object. There are six kinds of contact five connected with the five sense organs and the sixth is connected with the mind.

4736 **स्कन्धनत-शिरस्**

Skandhanata-śiras : a type of head-movement given by *Abhinayadarpaṇa* and *SR* (IV. 7.75). The head placed on the shoulder indicates slope, pride, fatigue and thinking. In this head signal, the head turns to the shoulder and back again to the neutral position. This is half a head shake and means much the same.

4737 **स्कन्धाकृतिविज्ञान**

Skandhākṛti-vijnāna : if bony and hairy, they indicate poverty (*Bhaviṣya*, 26.21); but if they are robust, raised and fleshy, they indicate bravery.

4738 **स्कन्धाभिनय**

Skandhābhinaya : movement of the shoulder; five movements are enumerated. They are the Nod, the Shake, the Twist, the Sway and the Toss. These are the ways in which we signal agreement and acceptance, or denial and refusal.

4739 **स्खलित-करण**

Skhalita-karaṇa : derived from *dolāpāda cārī*. The hands follow the feet. *Recita* and *ghūrṇita* hands are used: in the initial position the *haṁsapakṣa recita* hands are used. It leads to a series of postures and movements (*NS*, IV. 146b-147a, IX. 193, X. 36). After performing *dolāpāda*, both hands, following the foot movement should be in *recita* or turned round.

4740 **स्तन**

Stana : breast. Bosom is shown by the *mudrā* which is formed by touching the tip of the first finger of the right hand with that of the second finger of the left hand and *vice versa* in a crossed position and the last finger of each hand touching the third finger of the other hand. (b) about the breasts of a woman it is said that they are warm in the winter season, while in the hot season, they are cool:

शीतकाले भवेदूष्णं ऊष्णकाले च शीतलम्
(*Garuḍa*, 1.101. 32)

The Indian attitude to the breast is a case in point. Once upon a time, breasts were a symbol of maturity and maternity. We can see the large breasts in iconic representations, such as the heroines and Khajuraho. In sculptures of ancient India there is an obvious admiration for women with large breasts and buttocks. Even today large bosoms may be admired as a measure of sexual potency.

4741 **स्तन-जघन-विशाला**

Stana-jaghana-viśālā: lady whose breasts and hips are broad, quality of the Art-Lady (*Ratirahasya*, 1.14-15).

4742 **स्तनाकृतिविज्ञान**

Stanākṛti-vijñāna : shape and design of the breasts. Breasts which are big, fleshy and like pot, which are high and hard are supposed to be beautiful in Sanskrit literature: *gurustanī, pīnastanī, ghaṭastanī, kumbha-stanī, tuṅgastanī, kaṭhinastanī.*

Among the secondary sexual characters, the breasts must have first place. Before anything else, a Baiga looks at a girl's breasts. The Baiga distinguishes different kinds of breasts: *bajar dūdh* (firm and hard), *kumha-kumha dūdh* (strongly erected and straight), *ūncā dūdh* (the high and prominent), *bhoir dūdh* (small and undeveloped), *oram dūdh* (breasts that fall down) and *buṛhyā dūdh* (wrinkled and flabby breasts).

4743 **स्तनालिङ्गन**

Stanāliṅgana : embrace of the breasts. Vātsyāyana explains that "When a woman places her breasts on the chest of her lower and presses it, letting him feel the weight of her own breasts, then it is called the embrace of the breasts" (*Kāmasūtra*, 2.2.26). Hemādri says: "*Āliṅganasukhe stanayoreva prādhānyam.* Kālidāsa (*Raghu.* 19.32) has described the queens of Agnivarṇa in this type of embrace.

Breasts do not seem to have any erotic significance to the Hill Marias and they do not embrace the breasts.

The breasts play an important part in the mechanism of intercourse. The fondling of the breasts is generally the only tactile contact that precedes intercourse." "We do not kiss. We just press the breasts till she cries out "stop"! Stop! I cannot bear it any longer." The posture adopted by the Baiga also gives them every opportunity to observe and handle the breasts. They do so. "As long as they are firm and rounded as a fig; but when they fall like a sack, we leave them alone" (Elwin, 245).

The development or growth of the breasts in Hindi is known as *ubhār* or *uṭhān*. Breasts are known as *Chātī*. *Chātī pakaṛnā* means squeezing a woman's breasts. *Chātī piṭna* means cry aloud. *Chātī masalnā* means squeezing a woman's breasts. The following Chhattisgarhi Dadariyā (Janakpur, Surguja) symbolizes the nipples as 'ink on the youth':

हाथी पर हौदा घोड़े पर जीन ।
जोबन पर स्याही कौन धर दीन ॥

hāthī par haudā ghoṛe par jīn /
joban par syāhī kaun dhar dīn //

4744 **स्तुति**

Stuti : form of speech and thought (*Nirukta*, VIII. 3; *Bṛhaddevatā*, 134-139).

4745 **स्तोत्र**

Stotra : chant of hymns required in the performance of sacrifice. These are of two types: *pavamāna* and *dhurya*. There are definite rules about place, time, chanting priests and their movements, accents and method of introduction. Each *sāman* in a *stotra* has five parts: *prastāva, udgītha, pratihāra, upadrava* and *nidhana.*

4746 **स्तोभ**

Stobha : musical interjections added or introduced in chants, such as *hān, hāi, i, u, huṁ* (*Chāndogya*, 1.13. 1-3).

4747 **स्त्री**

Strī : woman. pre-Manu India accorded women equality with men in the Vedic sacrifice. At that time women could become priests; there was no immolation of the widow on her husband's funeral fire (*satī*), and widows were allowed to remarry. The Vedic age was liberal in its attitude towards women than the long period following the composition of the *Law of Manu,* which became the canon of Hinduism. Though destitute of virtue, or seeking pleasure elsewhere, or devoid of good qualities, yet a husband must be consistantly worshipped as a god by a faithful wife. The husband cannot be displaced even though he be devoid of good qualities, addicted to evil passion, fond of spirituous liquors or diseased. "To Śūdras, women and servants' the *Vedas* are so sealed. No sacrifice, no vow, no fast must be performed by women apart from their husbands; if a wife obeys her husband, she will, for the reason alone, be exalted in heaven."

Manu draws a distinction between the woman as sexual partner and the woman as mother; the latter is accorded very high status. This duality of her role has continued to be an important feature of Indian society. As a wife she seduces her husband away from his work and his spiritual duties, but as a mother she is revered.

In the tribal society, the woman stands at a par with the Vedic society. They enjoy full freedom. Even the young girls are not checked to meet a stranger, once the initial ice is broken and once the suspicion lurking in their minds is removed, there are few women who may become as free with the outsiders as the Hill Maria women.

woman, says the Pardhān poet, is *nārī, nāhar* and *nāgin:*

> Woman, shew your wisdom
> you have two arrows
> of mercy and of scorn
> The black-faced and hooded snake
> Has two tongues
> You have the knowledge of a *panch*
> And a learned Pandit
> Woman, shew your wisdom
> Yet like a little child you pickup leaves
> And in a moment make them into a plate
> To give the hungry food.

A woman is a snake because, 'once she desires a man, she chases him and bites him, thus making him love her'. 'To love a girl is like poison in the body'. There is story of that a Raja had a lovely daughter, so beautiful and auspicious that she was like Lakṣmi herself. One day four rich men came at the same time wishing to marry her, and the father angry at their importunity made his daughter into four girls, one her original Lakṣmi-like self, one a cobra, one a bitch and one a cat, and to each married one of the four suitors. So it is said that there are four kinds of women. Some are like Lakṣmi, fortunate, beautiful and adored, some are bitches, some are cats and some are cobras.

The subject is very large one and has been studied at length elsewhere. There are several stories in *Folktales of Mahakoshal* which are based on the motif of a snake inhabiting a woman's body, and the idea goes back as far as *Atharva Veda.*

4748 **स्त्रीपुष्प**

Strīpuṣpa : a woman's menstrual fluid (*A*, 14.2.32). Seeing or touching a women in menstruation is said to be a great sin (*Agni*, 155.25; *Śiva Māhātmya*. 7.14). It is said that if a person touches a woman in menstruation and touches the idol of a deity, he would drink the vile blood for a thousand years, and become blind (*Varāha*, 132.19.20). After touching such a woman one is required to take bath (*Garuḍa*, I. 205.107). If a woman in menstruation herself gets touched by a woman of a lower *varṇa* she gets purified by taking her normal purificatory bath (*Agni*. 170. 34); but if she is touched by a person of the *antyajāti* (the last caste) or by a *cāṇḍāla*, she gets pure only after performing penance for three nights after her normal purificatory bath (*Ibid.*, 41).

A girl's first menstruation is always an occasion. If it is delayed, the neighbours tease her - 'As soon as you'll touched, you'll be pregnant', 'When is the pot going to break?' and so on. Two girls of the same age may kick another to hasten the process.

When the fact is known (and it seems always to be known atonce), the news flies round the village. There is no reticence about it: why should there be? 'It is a beautiful thing: the girls tree bears red blossoms; she is a woman now'. Boys and even older people in a joking relation to the girl, shout, 'The mouth of the new pot is open', 'The pot is broken',

'The stream is flooded', and so on. Songs are improvized: they usually discuss the matter with entire frankness and some obscenity:

The red flower
Has blossomed
The lake
Has broken its banks
The lemons
Have ripened
The tender wheat-cake
Is ready for dinner.

4749 **स्त्रीभाव**

Strībhāva : womenhood (*Jaimini-Gṛhya-Sūtra,* 1.20). The role of Hindu woman in orthodox society is one of subordination to man. They are not allowed to move or speak freely with men. A woman shall not sit in the presence of a man of her age and social position, but must always stand. She shall not look him in the face, but must turn her face away from him even when necessity demands that she speaks to him. This applies to the conversation between husband and wife also, especially in presence of others. While walking a woman must walk behind her husband at a respectable distance. Modern means to transport had compartments or seats apart for women as a concession to this ancient Indian prejudice. In states where Muslim influence has been considerable the higher classes of Hindu women observe *purdāh.* They seldom move out of the *zanānā:* when necessity demands their moving about, they take care to cover their faces with the end of their *sārīs.* The Hindu ladies do not wear a veil proper like the Muslims, but make use of their *sārīs* to serve as a veil in case of necessity. In social functions and feasts, men are served first and women afterwards.

4750 **स्त्रीलिङ्ग-हस्त**

Strīliṅga-hasta : femine hands. *Bālarāmabharata* divided the *asaṁyuta* and *saṁyuta hastas* into all the three genders. It is one of them.

4751 **स्त्री-वर्ण**

Strī-varṇa : the long vowels are known by this name (Com. on *Śāradā,* II. 5-7).

4752 **स्तब्धा-ग्रीवा**

Stabdhā-grīvā : stiff neck-movement. Stiff and cold indicate a cold and stiff action (*VD,* III. I. 61).

4753 **स्तब्धा-भ्रुकुटी**

Stabdhā-bhrukuṭī : a type of *bhrukuṭī* given by *Bālarāmabharata.*

4754 **स्तब्धोरू**

Stabdhorū : a still motionless position of thighs. It is also known as *stambhana-ūrū* (*NS,* IX. 252).

4755 **स्तम्भ**

Stambha : inactive. One of the temperamental states. It is manifested by being inactive, smileless, being like an inert object, limbs drooping.

Harakh-lāj-bhaya-āditen,
jabai aṅga thakijāt.
tāhi kahat stambha sab
rasa granthani sarasāṭ

(Bhanu: *Kāvyaprabhākara*)

4756 **स्तम्भन**

Stambhana : arresting the efforts, one of the *ṣatkarmas* (q.v.).

4757 **स्तम्भन-चूर्ण**

Stambhana-cūrṇa : a powder paralysing sensory and motor-organs.

4758 **स्तम्भनी-मुद्रा**

Stambhanī-mudrā : paralysing. If the middle finger is extended of the *kapittha*-gesture, it is the *stambhanī* (*VD*); (b) *kṣa* and *ta* are to be joined with the middle of *i* and *ra* (*VD*).

4759 **स्तम्भनोरू**

Stambhanorū : the stand-still gesture of thighs indicating suspension of movement, used in perturbation and despair (*NS,* X.27-33). A still motionless position of the thighs. It takes place when the knee is drawn inwards. It is used in the easy gait of women.

4760 **स्तम्भिताश्रु**

Stambhitāśru : it is a common experience that the news of the death, etc. is not imparted to a person suddenly. So when the messangers were sent to inform Bharata, they were instructed to check their tears and thus they did not inform him of his father's death, till be came back to capital. Any show of tears would have aroused Bharata (*Raghu,* 12.12). (b) tears are symbolized as seed in both tribal as well as non-tribal myths. In a tribal myth, tears are the substitute for the seed: 'She objected that she could not marry him because they were siblings. This she followed with taunting remarks about his ugly face. He wept and she picked up the tear-drops. The tears penetrated the womb and she became pregnant.' (Elwin, 1949.7). Creation by tears is particularly central to the early mythology of Śiva: 'After his first unsuccessful creation, Prajāpati wept, and his tears became Rudra, with his hundred heads and thousand eyes, and all the other Rudras. Rudra sought food and the gods were afraid of him. They gathered food and appeased him.' (*Śatapatha Brāhmaṇa*, 9.1.1. 6-7). Usually it is Rudra who wept until he is fed or name (*Kūrma*, 1.10. 22-7), his name is said to be derived from rud, to weep (*Taittirīya Saṁhitā*, 1:5.1.1) Another tribal myth describes the creative power of Śiva's tears: 'There never used to be tears when Sahadeo, the father of Mahādeo, went to his wife, he was able to continue for six months without rest. As a result Sahadeo's wife conceived. When she gave birth she was in pain and her eyes flashed fire. Sahadeo threw magic water into her eyes and water began to flow from them. Mahādeo was born. After that people began to cry' (Elwin, 1949. 257). The traditional motifs are here deprived of their causal relationship, but the fiery liquid (tears, sweat, seed, or *soma*) still results in primeval creation.

4761 **स्थान**

Sthāna : (a) the standing posture, stances, attitudes, static positions or poses, posture of body. Postures indicate the distance of the feet from each other and the exact direction in which the feet are placed. It indicates the poses for the most part; postures which can suggest a particular mood or deity. In keeping with the laws of human anatomy, these associations are worked out on the basis of the distribution of weight and the distance of the feet from each other. There are nine classes of poses, such as *ṛjvāgatasthāna* (the front view) and *sācīkṛta śarīra* (a bent position in profile view), etc.

The term *sthāna* means a particular position of the motionless body. Besides standard *sthānas*, there are *deśī* or regional *sthānas* too. There are six *sthānas* for men and seven for women. A *sthāna* for men is *ālīḍha*. In it the left thigh is motionless in the air and slightly bent. The right foot is stretched forward to a distance of five spans. Both feet are oblique. A *sthāna* for women is *gatāgata* (9.V).

According to *Dhanurveda*, described in *śārṅgadhara-paddhati*, the *sthānas* are eight—*ālīḍha, pratyālīḍha, viśākha samapāda, asamapāda, dardurakrama, garuḍakrama* and *padmāsana*.

The *sthānas* of women in walking and in conversing with others are *āyata, avahittha* and *aśvakrānta*. The *sthāna* will be maintained till the *cārī* begins. Six *sthānas* or postures to be assumed by men are enumerated in *NS* (X, 61-65) are: *vaiṣṇava, samapāda, vaiśākha, maṇḍala, pratyālīḍha* and *ālīḍha*.

(b) voice-registers, one of the paralinguistic qualities enumerated by Bharata under *pāṭhyaguṇa*. The voice with the modulation is produced from the chest, throat and head which is *mandra* (low), *madhya* (medium) and *tāra* (high) respectively. In the lute all the small intervals are used for the musical effect. In the recitation these are not necessary. Only the difference in the voice as grave, medium or high is used. When conversing with a distant person, the voice would be loud; when not far away, the medium; and when near, low. Now as regards the intonation, the speech should be begun in *mandra*, then reaching *tāra*, gradually, should end in *madhya*.

(c) places. According to Varāhamihira (*BS*, L1), places may be auspicious and inauspicious. The prediction is always spatial, according to him.

(d) postures reflect those motivations, attitudes, and intentions that might not have been verbalized. The concept of proximics subsumes variations in posture and distance.

4762 **स्थानक**

Sthānaka : posture. When two friends meet and talk informally they usually adopt similar body postures. If they are particularly friendly and share identical attitudes to the subjects being discussed, then the positions in which they hold their bodies are liable to become even more alike, to the point where they virtually become carbon copies of each other. This is not deliberate imitative process. The friends in question are automatically indulging in what has been called Postural Echo, and they do this unconciously as a part of natural body display of companionship. Whenever a dominant and a subordinate meet, they signal their relationship by their body postures.

The posture that the tribes often adopt standing is the same as can commonly be observed among many other castes in India. They stand, so to day, one foot the other knee being bent so that the sole of the foot may rest against the outer side of the standing leg, the arm on the same side as the bent knee catching hold of a bough or something for steadiness. When not standing in this position, the commonmost posture is to put weight on one foot and keep the other foot relaxed with the knee slightly bent. The feet are changed alternately. The tribes of Chhattisgarh stand to urinate - both men and women.

4763 **स्थानक-मण्डल**

Sthānaka-maṇḍala : type of posture. Different types of postures indicate strength of feeling and underlying mood.

4764 **स्थान-करण**

Sthāna-karaṇa : derives different names from the corresponding *sthānas*.

4765 **स्थान-शुद्धि**

Sthāna-śuddhi : purification of the place (*Kulārṇava*,VI).

4766 **स्थायिन्**

Sthāyin : fixed emotion, the emotion distinguished from its accessories and implied to any *rasa* as love to the erotic *rasa* only. Stable, permanent mood.

Over the centuries, Indian scholars have considered that certain emotions, such as fear, anger, joy and sadness, are more basic emotions, from which most of the others derive.

4767 **स्थायी-भाव**

Sthāyī-bhāva : potential emotion, a basic instinct, a lasting or permanent emotion, dominant state, basic emotion. The eight basic dominant emotive states inherent to human existence which is generated on state and thus transformed, evoke in the audience corresponding *rasa*. Each *sthāyī-bhāva* has its corresponding movement of the face. The eight *sthāyī-bhāvas* are as follows: *rati* (love), *hāsya* (mirth), *śoka* (sorrow), *krodha* (anger), *utsāha* (energy), *bhayam* (fear), *jugupsā* (disgust) and *vismaya* (wonder). These eight emotions may be represented as basic in the following diagram:

Some researchers recognize more. Basic emotions occur at various intensities. Most of us have so many emotions churning around inside us that it would be impossible to analyze them all. Sometimes people express their emotions unconsciously by indirect means. Frown lines on someone's face are often signs of persistent anger or frustration, and yet that person may be unaware of these feelings. Other people walk around with a downturned expression as if they had a permanently an unpleasant task in their mouth. The implied feeling of disgust may not be conscious.

Personality traits are recognizable moves of emotions that characterize how an individual reacts in certain types of situation. Hence, we might say someone who habitually thinks of the future with sadness has a "gloomy" personality, if they generally look to the future with optimism, we say they have bright personality.

Strong emotions are as common today as they ever were in *NS*. People still experience the joys of achievement, possession, marriage, love and children, and the sorrow of parting, illness and death. The survival of emotions in modern society is ensured because they reflect the reality of dangers, losses, pleasures, pains and challenges.

In addition, emotions persist because of the genitic evidence by similar facial expressions of emotion in diverse cultures, by consistent patterns of emotional development and by studies of twins. Thus, if the controlling forces of our emotions are in our genes, emotional changes in whole populations can only occur slowly and over a number of generations. It would take an almost unimaginable change in living patterns and environment to rearrange the gene pools that determine the emotional tendencies of the future generations.

4768 **स्थितावर्ता-चारी**

Sthitāvartā-cārī : type of movement. Foot in *samapāda agratalasañcara*. Lower limbs is *svastika* (crossing) with no distance posture. *Jānu* also cross. *Svastika maṇḍala* similar. One *agratalasañcara* foot is drawn up to cross the other foot and this movement repeated by the other, after separating the two. One foot in *agratalasañcara* dragging on the ground moves across the side of the other foot to form a *svastika* (*NS*, X.15).

4769 **स्थूल**

Sthūla : gross (material, as opposed to mental).

4770 **स्थूलगण्डा**

Sthulagaṇḍā : lady whose cheeks are big, quality of Elephant-lady (*Pañcaśāyaka*, 2.14).

4771 **स्थूल-ग्रीवा**

Sthūla-grīvā : fat neck, quality of a Bull-man (*Ratirahasya*, 3.32-33).

4772 **स्थूल-देह**

Sthūla-deha : gross body.

4773 **स्थूलरदनराजि**

Sthūlaradanarāji : lady whose teeth are strong, quality of the Mare-lady (*Ratirahasya*, 2.13).

4774 **स्थूलस्त्री-रतिलालसा**

Sthūlastrī-ratilālasā : wish to cohabit with the fat woman, quality of the Horse-man (*Anaṅgaraṅga*, 2.29). An anonymous Sanskrit poet has symbolically presented the *ratilālasā* as follows:

> If I could find my lover alone,
> I'd do something unheard of:
> I'd let him absorb me,
> Water soaking into a new earthen jar,
> Making it cool and fragrant.

4775 **स्थूलौष्ठिक**

Sthūlauṣṭhika : lady who has thick lips, quality of the conch-lady (*Anaṅgaraṅga*, 1.17).

4776 **स्थैर्य**

Sthairya : tenacity. One of the temperamental aspects of males. Not moving from one's undertaking relating to the duty, wealth or love, irrespective of its being produced from good or evil, is called *sthairya* (*NS*).

4777 **स्नातक**

Snātaka : literally 'one who has taken the bath'. The return of a student to his paternal home from the teacher's house was signalised or formalised by the rite of *samāvartana* (lit. return) which took place just before his actual entry into his parental abode. Its main feature was a ceremonial bath after which he was known as *snātaka*.

There are various prohibitive rules for a *snātaka*. After the completion of his studies the *brahmacārī*, with the permission of his preceptor, used to take the final *snāna* (bath), which marked the end of that stage of his life. Such a *brahmacārī* was recognized as *snātaka* till he entered the stage of a householder. There are several rules of the nature of prohibitive negations laid down for a *snātaka*. Some of them are as follows: He should not run while it is raining; he should not climb a tree; he should not jump into a well nor he should swim in a river. He should not stake his life in any way. *Aśv. Gṛ. Su.* (III. 9. 6-8) says that the life of a *snātaka* is very valuable because he has taken hardships to complete the course of his studies. Other texts also give such rules (*Vas. Dh. S.*, XII. 25.26; *Gaut. Dh. S.*, IX. 35; *Pār. Gṛ. S.* II. 7.6.; *Śat. Br.*, XI. 3.3.7; *Gobh. Gṛ. S.*, III. 5. 2-20; *Mān. Gṛ.S.*, I. 2.19). To turn to the rules given by *Pār.Gṛ.S.*, the *snātaka* should use the word *vijanyā* and not *garbhiṇī* in the case of a pregnant woman (II. 7.10). He should say *sakula* instead of *nakula* for an ichneumon (*Ibid.*, II); he should say *bhagāla* instead of *kapāla* for a pot-sherd (*Ibid.*, 12); and he should say *maṇidhanus* instead *indradhanus* for the rain-bow (*Ibid.*, 13). It seems, there is an idea of danger attached to the above words. The *snātaka* himself being in a delicate position, the use of these words is inauspicious. Instead of these, he should use words that indicate fullness and prosperity.

4778 **स्नान**

Snāna : bathing. Bathing naked was a sinful activity in ancient India (*Viṣṇu*, LIV. 223; *Yājñavalkya*, III.291). The tribal men and women of Abujhmāṛ bathe nakedly, but they do never bathe together at the same place. There are separate *ghāṭs* for the sexes in India. It is noticed that bathing place for women is generally downstream that of men. (b) bathing for purification. Elaborate rules have been laid down in the *Dharma-śāstras* governing the procedure for bathing, the nature of water to be used, the method to be used by one who is ill or for a woman in her menstrual period, the accompanying ingredients, consequences, restrictions, etc. Bathing once everyday is obligatory on all. It is not allowed at night, except during eclipses, *aśauca*, *vrata*, etc.

4779 **स्निग्धानना**

Snigdhānanā : loving face, quality of the Deer-lady (*Nāgarasarvasva*, 14.5).

4780 **स्निग्धा-भावदृष्टि**

Snigdhā-bhāvadṛṣṭi : a type of *sthāyi-bhāva-dṛṣṭi* suggested in *śṛṅgāra rasa;* a type of *kaṭākṣavasthā;* a sweet glance not far widened, but with eye-balls still, watery and glowing-in with joy; is a love-appealing visual gesture.

4781 **स्नुषा-हस्त**

Snuṣā-hasta : the gesture of a daughter-in-law. If at the end of the *putra-hasta* (q.v), the hand of a woman is held by the right hand; it indicates a daughter-in-law (*AD*, 231-244).

4782 **स्पन्दिता-चारी**

Spanditā cārī : a type of position where thighs cross and the right foot is crossed to a distance of five spans.

4783 **स्पर्श**

Sparśa : touch. In *Mṛcchakaṭikam* (5.46), Vasantasenā finds her lover. She exhibits erotic gestures and Cārudatta displays pleasure at her touch. Rudradeva (1565 A.D. -1596 A.D.) in his *Śyainika śāstram* (II. 18; ed. H.P.Shastri, New Delhi 1982, p.75) has defined the *sparśa* as such : *sparśaḥ kāma itīritaḥ* (touching in reality loving a person). It is a type of sexual touch which gives sensual pleasure leading to sexual arousal and love-making.

This is why in a joint family certain rules of avoidance must strictly be observed. Thus a father-in-law is forbidden to touch his daughter-in-law. An exception may be in sickness when a daughter-in-law has to nurse her husband's father because there is no other woman in the house. An Indian is forbidden to beat his daughter-in-law. If he does so in rage, the society treats him rudely. In Korku-society the village-council will fine him rupees fifteen.

Equally strict are the rules regulating relations between a man and the wives of his younger brothers—equally the same in tribal as well as non-tribal societies. An Indian woman (tribal or non-tribal both) considers the elder brother of her husband like a father-in-law. She is reminded of this during the wedding ceremonies when she has to kneel down before him and touch the ground with her forehead. Elder brothers must never touch the wives of their younger brothers; the same rule applies of course to the wives of the younger brothers. Nor should they ever handover anything to each other directly; they must place the object on the ground or on a cot or grain-bin, but things should never change hands. They must not touch each other's clothes, and women are not allowed to wash the clothes of their elder brothers-in-law. The same rules are observed in relations between a Chhattisgarhi or Korku with his wife's elder sister. It would be an offence against delicacy if a man arranged his lower garment in the presence of the wives of his younger brothers, or if such women appeared before him dishevelled, with heads uncovered, or combing their hair. They may never use the same comb, drink from the same cup, eat from the same plate, sit or lie down on a mat used by the other party.

The great physician Charaka even put forth the view that the organ of touch pervades all sense organs and that they are all 'more modifications of the sense of touch' (*Charaka Saṁhitā, Sūtrasthāna,* XI.32). However, many argued against this view because it contradicts the facts of experience. "If the tactual organ were the only sense organ, it would be able to apprehend all objects, so that colour would be perceived by the blind, sound by the deaf and so on" (Sinha, I, p.20). Another argument put forth against touch being the only single organ is the impossibility of simultaneous perception of colour, sound, etc. Finally, it is pointed out that skin being a *prāpyakarī*, it can apprehend only those objects which can come into contact with it. On the contray, colour and sound can be perceived from a distance. This is probably one of the instances of lively debate in the ancient times. It should be remembered that the whole body is covered with a sensory organ—the skin, which constantly relays messages to the brain. And it performs this function since before a child is born. Touch tells us a great deal about our environment, ourselves, and other people. It is so essential for our health and happiness that babies deprived of it rapidly sicken, and may even die. Indeed, when people feel insecure they often touch themselves as if giving themselves a reassuring hug.

4784 **स्पर्श-तन्मात्रा**

Sparśa-tanmātrā : tactual micro-elements according to the *Sāṁkhya*-process of evolution.

4785 **स्पर्श-दीक्षा**

Sparśa-dīkṣā : also known as *spārśani-dīkṣā*. Initiation by touch (*Kulārṇava,* XIV; *Puraścaryārṇava* V.301; Rāghava on *Śāradātilaka* V. 127-140).

4786 **स्पर्शन**

Sparśana : touching. The first messages we human beings get are touch messages. Our parents kiss, nuzzle, caress, embrace, cuddle, pat and hug us. Communication through touch is not limited to infants or little children of course. We adults get messages from touching people as well as things.

Think of the touching behaviours we use for communication. We shake hands in greeting; women folk seem to use kissing for greetings, we hug—sometimes, some people, under some circumstances. We pat each other on the back, and sometimes we pat another person's behind. Again, it depends on the circumstances, doesn't it? With some people we hold hands. With others, we grasp hands rather than shake them. When we embrace, we may cling to each other. Occasionally, we get slapped—or slugged.

We learn to attach meaning to tactile behaviour, and we learn the norms of our culture that govern touching other human beings. In our Indian culture, touching is usually reserved for intimate personal situations and relationship. We have been conditioned, we have been taught, whom we can touch — and when and where. I think norms may be changing in urban setting, but in the rural areas changes are small and slow.

4787 **स्पर्शनक**

Sparśanaka : a term used in *Sāṁkhya* philosophy for the "skin".

4788 **स्पर्शबोध**

Sparśabodha : concept of touching. The concept of touching behaviour is now fully changed in Indian villages. Most people say that no harm is done if a weaver is touched, and only the most orthodox would deem it necessary to wash their hands afterwards. Touching a Tanner is a more generally acknowledged matter for purification, though it is admitted that many people would not do anything if they were not seen to touch, and some youths maintained that both weavers and Tanners could be touched with impurity. The touch of the sweeper appears tobe the only matter over which it is agreed that action should be taken and that action is taken. Most said that only the orthodox would bathe completely, but that the rest would wash the part of the body which had been in contact and sprinkle water over themselves as a general purification. So touch should not be regarded as the main criterion of separation among Hindus. The concept of pollution is more binding.

4789 **स्पर्शास्पर्श**

Sparśāsparśa : purity and pollution. Before we can attempt to concretize the full structural complexity of the caste system, we must examine the conceptual meaning of purity and pollution. Because of the magico-religious ideas on which the theme the caste-system is based, the reader may find the subject obscure. In fact the whole question of *asparśa* (pollution) is of the greatest importance, and obscure as are some ideas connected with it, it cannot be ignored if we are to elucidate the consequences of magical thought on the psychology of the caste Hindu. It is a common place that Hindu society pays exceptional attention to purity and pollution. The very existence and frequent use of the English word 'untouchability' (*asparśa*) reflects this preoccupation. We know the Hindu attitudes regarding physical hygiene, bodily pollutions, and the compulsive washing habits. However, a distinction must be drawn between customs and systems on which they are based. The idea that opposition of pure and impure can be the form which social distinctions take may appear startling, but it is not unknown in societies besides India's, though less consistently emphasized.

In India proximity to the contaminating factor is thought to constitute a permanent pollution as it is of sufficient intensity. Not only is a person thus placed regarded as in a state of pollution throughout his life; he also transmits the indelible pollution to his children.

Here pollution is both collective and hereditary. At the same time there are degrees of collective and hereditary pollution, which are reflected in the graded status, for example, of specialized castes engaged in polluting work, such as leather-making, barbers, sweapers, and functional attendants. Similarly, there are forms of temporary pollution on which can be overcome by ritual purification, as by sprinkling of water, or a ritual bath, or a temple-rite, a penance, or ingestion of purifying substances. In the daily routine of the individual, pollution is as minutely graded as it is on collective, caste-occupational scale. Again, while every individual is subject to temporary states of relative purity and impurity, this in turn is related to the degree of pollution of everyone else, between one caste and another collectively, and between groups of castes in relation to polar extremes on the pure-impure scales: Brāhmaṇa and untouchable. The network of purity of pollution is thorough, generally consistent in detail within its terms, and permeates every conceivable aspect of life. Nothing is impermeable to pollution: no person; no thing, no act.

4790 **स्पृष्टक**

Spṛṣṭaka : mere touching, touching embrace : "When a man under some pretext or other goes in front of or alongside of a woman and touches her body with his own, it is called *spṛṣṭaka* embrace : *sammukhāgatyām prayojya yāmanyāpadeśena gacchato gātreṇa sparśanam spṛṣṭakam* (*Kāmasūtra,* 2.29). Śriharṣa (*Naiṣadha,* 6.35, 16.63) has described this type of embrace.

4791 **स्पृष्टास्पृष्टि**

Spṛṣṭāspṛṣṭi : touching one another; also known as *Spṛṣṭāspṛṣṭakam.*

4792 **स्पृष्टि**

Spṛṣṭi : touching. Vedic people who liked to touch others and be touched were more talkative, cheerful, socially confident and independent in their thinking than those later Vedic people who touched with certain constraints. They were nevertheless sensitive to social rules about where on the body it is appropriate to touch a stranger, a friend or a member of the family, and in what circumstances. People in modern contact culture, and women who are interacting with women, stand and sit nearer to one another and frequently exchange touches to give reassurance or support or simply to emphasize conversational points.

Taking initiatives in touching gives an impression of personal dominance. For example, your boss will extend a hand in greeting before you. Hitting and pushing express aggression. Slapping on the back in the right circumstances expresses friendliness in the same sexes. A handshake can express an energetic personality if firm, a passive one if limp.

4793 **स्पृष्टिका**

Spṛṣṭikā : touch, contact, haptics, *tadvayasya asmat śarīraspṛṣṭikayā śāpitosi* (*MK,* 3). *Spṛṣṭikā* (the language of touch) falls into the following basic categories in the Sanskrit literature: Professional touch, social touch, friendly touch, loving touch and sexual touch.

4794 **स्पृहा**

Spṛhā (*Bṛhaddevatā* 134-39) : form of speech and thought.

4795 **स्फुरित-पुट**

Sphurita-puta : throbbing of the eyelids; throbbing movement of the eyelids (*NS,* VIII. 106-113), suggests jealousy.

4796 **स्फोट**

Sphoṭa : the idea which bursts out or flashes on the mind when a sound is uttered; the impression produced on the mind on hearing a sound, the eternal sound. *Sphoṭa* is considered to be of eight kinds, viz. *varṇa-sphoṭa, pada-sphoṭa, vākya-sphoṭa, akhaṇḍapada-sphoṭa, akhaṇḍavākya-sphoṭa, varṇajāti-sphoṭa* and *vākyajāti-sphoṭa.* Of these *vākya-sphoṭa* alone is real and the others are unreal. This is the view of grammarians. (b) a capacity (*śakti*) which is manifested through letters and words conveying meaning. The individual letters cannot make known the meaning in case of the word, nor individual words in that of a sentence. Over and above, these sounds or letters or words, there is *sphoṭa,* the essence of the sound or letter or word or the sentence as a whole. Brought into consciousness by different sounds of the word (or the words of the sentence), the *sphoṭa* produces the cognition of what is meant by the word or sentence. This essence of sound is viewed in terms of a monistic metaphysical implication by the followers of *Śabda-brahma* doctrine.

4797 **स्फोटन**

Sphoṭana : putting off relevant sentiment and feelings through appropriate gesture (*NS,* IX, 175).

4798 **स्मर-गृह**

Smara-gṛha : female organ, vagina (*Anaṅgaraṅga,* 1.15-

16). The sexual riddles are interesting in tribal societies which explain the female organ, such as in Muria: "The flat stone itches" means vagina. (b) *kāmaś* epithet of *smara* is also the word for 'memory' in Sanskrit. The pun is often used with irony: when Śiva burns *Kāma* he makes him 'nothing but a memory' (*Bṛhatkathāmañjarī*, 3.346), and *kāma's* house is the female organ which is always reflected in the memory (*Śiva*, 2.2.21).

4799 **स्मरगृहमतिलोमा**

Smaragṛhamatilomā : lady who has a deep secret part which has huge public hair, quality of the Conch-lady (*Ratirahasya*, 1.16-17).

4800 **स्मराम्बु-द्रव**

Smarāmbu-drava : semen. The male sperm cells and the fluid vehicle secreted by the testes and prostate glands respectively.

4801 **स्मित**

Smita : noiseless smile. The most polished form of laughter with slightly widened eyes and a throbbing lower lip. It is the gentlest expression of appreciation of humour and is practised by highly cultured persons of high rank in society. Smile occurs in friendly encounters, pleasant situations, during flirt, as part of the 'embarrassment' syndrome. Ekman's research has identified three main kinds of smile, each denoting a different type of emotion and very similar to ancient Indian scholar's research: the felt smile, the miserable smile and the false smile.

In origin smile is an appeasement gesture. It is the *anubhāva* of *hāsya* (laughter). It represents slightly blown cheeks, elegant glances, teeth not visible.

4802 **स्मितावलोकित**

Smitāvalokita : a type of gentle glance mentioned in *Kādambarī* (p. 226), but this is a more generalized reference.

4803 **स्मृति**

Smṛti : recollection, memory, tradition, authority. The eleventh among thirty-three *vyabhicārī-bhāvas* as enumerated by Bharata. *Smṛti* is the recollection of a past experience called forth by the perception or the idea of an associated or similar phenomenon; it is manifested in the raising of the eyebrows, and the like (*Sāhityadarpaṇa*, 3.162). It is the third stage in love-lorn condition (Nagendra, 1987.164). It is manifested by nodding of the head, looking down, raising up the eyebrows, etc. (b) *Smṛti* is the function involved in reliving past experience. It is the totality of past experience than can be remembered. The memory process is measured by recall, reproduction, recognition and relearning. Patañjali (*Yogasūtra* 1.11) describes memory as not forgetting, not allowing to escape.In his *Bhāṣya* to this *sūtra*, Vyāsa raises the very important question whether memory involves the recall of experience or the recall of the object experienced. In answering this he refers to the concept of *saṁskāra*, subliminal experience. What is remembered may be merely what is imagined as in the case of dream or illusion. In either case memory does not go beyond previous experience. And it depends on the storing of impressions in the mind. So memory refers to the recall of the idea as well as to the recall of the object which gave rise to the idea (*Vyāsa Bhāṣya* I.11).

4804 **स्यन्दिता-चारी**

Syanditā-cārī : a type of body manipulation, both foot in *samapāda* position, five *tālas* apart; both feet used for various *sthānas* like *ālīḍha* and *pratyālīḍha* postures, tense position of the limbs (*NS*, X.24-26; *SR*, VII. 934-35). According to Bharata, "when there is a distance of five *tālas* between the two feet, it is *syanditā*. Abhinava explains (*NS, Ibid.*) that when the left foot is in *sama* position, thigh is motionless and right foot is extended to five *tālas* it is *syanditā*.

4805 **स्याद्वाद**

Syādvāda : a Jain doctrine which is also known as *Saptabhaṅgī*. It is so-called as it holds all knowledge to be only probable. According to it, there are seven different ways of speaking of a thing or its attributes, in accordance with the point of view. There is a point of view from which substance or attribute (i) *syādasti* (is), (ii) *syād nāsti* (is not), (iii) *syād asti nāsti* (is and is not), (iv) *syād avaktavya* (is unpredicable), (v) *syād asti avaktavya* (is and is unpredicable), (vi) *syād nāsti avaktavya* (is and is unpredicable), and (vii) *syād asti nāsti avaktavya* (is not and is unpredicable).

4806 **स्रस्त-स्कन्ध**

Srasta-skandha : shoulder hanging down.

4807 **स्रस्तालसासन**

Srastālasāsana : a type of sitting posture.

4808 **स्वकीया**

Svakīyā : female partner, the valid wife, one's own woman, ones lawful wife; married love. Opposed to *parakīyā*.

4809 **स्वकुल-वर्ण**

Svakula-varṇa : letters belonging to ones own group. There are three other categories of letters, *mitra* (friendly), *udāsīna* (neutral) and *śatru* or enemy (*Prapañcasāra*, III. 70-72).

4810 **स्वगत**

Svagata : The words in the heart are given vent to. It is loud thinking and is one of the parts of *citrābhinaya* (*NS*).

4811 **स्वतःप्रेरित-संकेत**

Svataḥprerita-saṅketa : autonomic signals. Autonomic signals result from physiological changes that are beyond our deliberate and conscious control. Even when we are aware of them we can rarely control them. It is almost impossible to sweat at will, or to make your cheeks go pale. They are not easily concealed in the more powerful emotional situations. These are the actions and other changes resulting from body-stress.

4812 **स्वदन**

Svadana : 'act of tasting' (*RV*). Taste is a sensory modality whose receptors are taste buds on the tongue and in the oral cavity and whose stimuli are substances in solution. There is general agreement that there are four primary taste qualities—sweet, salty, sour and bitter—and that these are mediated by specialized sensory neurons and receptors. (b) The individual's characteristic aesthetic judgments, particularly as these apply to the selection of clothing, reading material, furniture for the home, music and artistic products.

4813 **स्वधर्म**

Svadharma : vocation, calling, specific function, one's own caste duty, one's preordained role.

4814 **स्वधा**

Svadhā : one of the ritual exclamations uttered when making an offering to a deity. These exclamations were regarded as ritual entities and are paralleled by the Greek Goddess Loulo, who was invoked by the iouloi (howls) of Demeter's devotees. Also known as *svāhā*.

4815 **स्वपुष्प**

Svapuṣpa : the first menstrual blood of a newly married woman sacred to Devī. The menstruation fluid figures in sorcery and Tāntric practices. It is said, if this fluid is thrown on the bed of a person, he would turn into an enemy (*Agni* 315.14). The general food of the ghosts is said to be the 'period flow' of women (*Skanda*, VIII.1.222.27).

4816 **स्वप्न**

Svapna : dreaming. It is one of the *vyabhicārī-bhāvas*. In Freudian theory, dreams are held to express unfulfilled wishes, in a disguised form. That is why dreams are considered to be an important guide to the unconscious. Symbolism is a well known disguise, and Freud developed extensive ideas on dream symbolism.

Freud believed that desires and impulses hidden in the unconscious self find an outlet in people's dream. He pleaded great emphasis on sexual imagery because he believed the most important driving force of our personality and the greater cause of inner conflict to be sexual impulses. Any long or sharp object and any tool or weapon he saw as a symbol of penis. All hollow objects—boxes and cupboards, for example, he believed, symbolized the womb.

Walking up or down stairs or ladders symbolized sexual acts. Rooms represented women. Going through a series of rooms represented a visit to a brothel. Landscapes with bridges or tree covered hills symbolized the genitals.

Śaṅkarācārya has defined *svapna* as such : "*jāgṛdavasthāyām yad dṛṣṭam yat śrutaṃ tajjanita-vāsanayā nidrāsamaye yaḥ prapañcaḥ pratiyate sā svapnavasthā*". Śaṅkarāchārya theorizes that dream is a sorting process whereby all the information we have accumulated during the day is assessed and filed away. "The dreaming mind works effectively on finding answers to questions the waking mind can't deal with— 'sleeping on it' can often resolve problems which seem insoluble by day.

There are many hymns in *Atharvaveda* dealing with dreams. There is the concern about the evil dreams. "Sleep, guard us from the evil dream. As men discharge their debt, so we pay for it. Assign them to our foes" (VI.46). Evil dreams are caused by *gṛhi* (complexes), *nirṛiti* (destructive wages), *ābhūti* (unfulfilled wishes), *nirbhūti* (loss of possession) and *parābhūti* (against enemies). The therapeutic procedures adopted are prayer, suggestion, *saṅkalpa*, making up one's mind to get good dreams, or by bathing in sacred rivers, etc.

4817 **स्वप्न-दर्शन**

Svapana-darśana : dreams occupied an important place in everyday existence in ancient India, and it was necessary to wash one's face carefully on arising, so as to ward off their potentially evil influence. And, to regain tranquility of mind it was indispensable to have the dream interpreted as soon as possible, either by a priest or a monk (*Mahāsuppinajātaka*, No. 77, I. p. 187). The importance ascribed to dreams was as great that a whole school of oneiromancy came into being (Renou and Filliozat, *Classical India*, 3 Vols. Calcutta, 1957, I). If the dream was judged baneful, the person who had dreamed it had to offer a sacrifice, make a libation of sesame oil, or even make a substantial gift to the Brāhmaṇas.

Dreams are always symbolic. They are code messages from the other world and only the wise can decipher them. There is a fairly extensive system of dream-interpretation in the tribal regions: (a) If a person in a dream sees the dreadful and unknown men, and women, he thinks that evil spirits will trouble him. (b) If a person is fed in his dreams he thinks that some disease will attack him. (c) If one happens to see performances of marriage in dream, it is believed that some disease of fatal character will inflict him. (d) If someone happens to laugh in his dream, it is supposed that he is doomed. (e) If a sick person is offered milk to drink or looks white corn, he will get rid from the sickness. (f) If onc sees tiger in his dream, he will lose his animals. (g) If a near relative appears in his dream, the next morning the death of the relative is certain. In the case of repeated bad dreams the tribes of Bastar offer sacrifices to their gods and goddesses.

The *Purāṇas* are of the view that dreams reflect the general physical and mental condition of the dreamer. It is said that a person who is very slender, has very thin hair, is unstable, talkative and has irregular hunger, dreams that he is wafted up in the air, he has the *vāta-prakṛti*—predominated by the wind element (*Agni*, 380. 36-37). A person who has become old prematurely is given to wrath, always perspiring, found of sweets, sees bright things in the dream; he is said to have *pitta-prakṛti* bile predominating (*Ibid.*, I., 37.38). A person with firm body, steady mind, full of lustre, having glistening and emollient (*Snigdha*) hair, dreams of clear water; he is said to have *kapha-prakṛti*—phelgmatic (*Ibid.*, I., 38.39). Repressed emotiions, inner change and all kinds of inspiration are connected with our dream lives.

4818 **स्वभाव**

Svabhāva : own-being, essential nature, inwardness, naturalism conceived as the first principle in *Śvetaśvatara Upaniṣad* (1.2). By *svabhāva* is meant the power invariably belonging to material objects, as for instance, the radiation of heat by fire (*Śaṅkara* on *SV. Up.* 1.2). Guṇaratna in TRD says that by *svabhāva* is meant the transformation of objects by themselves. *Mbh.* (XII. 232.19) associates *svabhāva* with the materialistic outlook : *svabhāvam bhūtacintakāḥ*. In modern language, the term *svabhāva* refers to a person's activities, aptitudes and temperament. The choice of occupation has to take into account these characteristics of an individual. Failure and frustration will be the inevitable consequences, harmful to the individual as well as the society, when persons take up work that is not in line with their aptitudes. Mere birth in a group should not determine the choice of occupation. This is the aim of modern development with respect to aptitude testing, vocational guidance and vocational selection.

4819 **स्वयम्भू-कुसुम**

Svayambhū-kusuma : menstrual blood of a maiden.

4820 **स्वर**

Svara : sound; one of the paralinguistic features. *Śruti and svara* are vital elements of a song. The difference between the two lies in the fact that the former has no resonance whereas the latter has it. The number of *śrutis* is twenty-two. They give rise to seven *svaras* called *Sa, Ri, Ga, Ma, Pa Dha, Ni*, in order. These are presented as abbreviations. These seven *svaras* have been taken from the cries of the following respectively. peacock (*ṣaḍja*), *cātaka* bird (*ṛsabha*), goat (*gāndhāra*), *krauñcha* bird (*madhyama*), cuckoo (*pañcama*), frog (*dhaivata*) and elephant (*niṣāda*). *Svaras* are two-fold: *śuddha* (pure) and *vikṛta*. (modified). The above seven are *śuddha*. When a *svara* leaves its own place or the *śrutis* specified for it, and assumes another place or contains other *śrutis*, it becomes *vikṛta*. For example, when *ṛṣabha* assumes for *śrutis* of *ṣaḍaja*, it is *vikṛta*. From the point of view of their relation with a song, the *svaras* are of four kinds, viz. *Vādī, Saṁvādī, Vivādī* and *Anuvādī*. *Svaras* are also divided as *Aṁśa, Graha*, and *Nyāsa*. The trembling of a *svara* is called *gamaka* or *rāga*. The ascent and descent of the seven *svaras* in order are called *mūrchanā*. A group of letters which is the resort of *mūrchanā* etc. is called *grāma*. (b) Accentuation. The principle Vedic texts, primarily the *Saṁhitās* but also some *Brāhmaṇas* are accented. The accents revolve around the *udātta* (raised), the main accent, the position of which is predetermined by the exigencies of grammar. The function of *anudātta* (not raised) is to introduce an *udātta*, whereas the *svarita* (intoned) accomplishes a transition from the *udātta* to an accentless syllable. The series of syllables without accent which often follow the *svarita* are termed *pracaya* (multitude), although the accentless syllable immediately preceding the *udātta* is always the *anudātta*. Two or more *udāttas* may occur consequently. Moreover, a non-*udātta* syllable appearing between two *udāttas* is *anudātta*, not *svarita*. The *Ṛgveda* does not mark *udātta* and *pracaya*, although in transliteration it is customary to designate the *udātta* by the acute sign (') not to be confused with the manner of transliteration the palatal sibilant (s'). The *anudātta* is indicated by a horizontal stroke beneath a syllable, the *svarita* by a vertical stroke above.

Every Vedic word normally is accented and has one *Udātta*. But some words have a double accent (*Bṛhaspati* for example, and others have no accent at all. Among the accentless words are those which are naturally enclitic (certain pronouns and particles) and those which lose accent by their position in the sentence.

A phenomenon occasionally met in the so-called independent *svarita*—a *svarita* not dependent on a preceding *udātta*, which has disappeared as a result of euphonic combination (*sandhi*). The method of accentuation is altered only when an *udātta* follows the *svarita*.

(c) These notes are to be used in different sentiments as follows:

Madhyama and *pañcama* in the Erotic and the Comic; *Ṣaḍaj* and *Ṛṣbha* in the Heroic, the Furious and the marvellous; *Gāndhāra* and *niṣāda* in the Pathetic; and *Dhaivata* in the Odious and the Terrible. Abhinava (*NS*, Vol. II, pp. 385-386) makes clear the use of the seven notes in the recitation. These notes are musical when they are possessed of *rakti* (produced by the specific musical intervals between these notes). These specific distances are not expected in recitation. Only the change of voice to suit the expression is essential. That is why, the manner of utterance as high and low, etc. is clearly defined. (d) The musical notes: are four types according to the principle of consonance or otherwise. They are (i) *Vādī-svara* (sonant), (ii) *Saṁvādī-svara* (consonant), (iii) *Anuvādī-svara* (assonant) and *Vivādī-svara* (dissonant). *Vādin* is the note which is responsible for the effect of the melody. As *vādin* is repeated often, the other notes of the melody-type are used in relation to it, with the respective *śruti* intervals. Consonance and the others are regulated by definite number of *śruti* intervals. (e) In the *Ṛgveda* sound is *svara* and *svana* (frequently of wind, water, rain), the latter equal to Latin *sonus* (sound, noise, voice). Thin, weak voices seem to lack vital energy and do not inspire confidence in others. Quiet voices project a submissive image, and were often admired in women for this reason. Extreme turning up the volume suggests dominance. The speech can be enliven by stressing positive words and phrases to emphasize a dramatic point.

4821 **स्वर-भङ्ग**

Svara-bhaṅga : choking or cracking of the voice. Outburst of deep emotion seems to choke one's throat with tears and the voice becomes coarse. It is the four natural sensation in deep sentiment; also known as *svarabheda* which manifests broken and choked voice.

4822 **स्वर-संक्रम**

Svara-saṃkrama : low progression (Bhāsa, *Bālacarita*, Act. III).

4823 **स्वराज्य**

Svarājya : home-rule. Śivājī first introduced this concept through Rāmdās (1608-1681). Śivājī was fully conscious of his mission as a restorer of Hindu political dignity to its ancient conditions. Accordingly he wanted to go back to the fountain of Hindu culture in the smallest details of his life.

4824 **स्वरूप**

Svarūpa : own form, intrinsic aspect, essential nature.

4825 **स्वसम्मुख-तलहस्त**

Svasammukha-talahasta : palm facing oneself, a type of hand gesture.

4826 **स्वस्तिक**

Svastika : a kind of musical mark on persons or things denoting good luck, a particular symbol, an auspicious mark, the *Oṃkāra* symbol the fire cross, the sun symbol, a symbol, for Buddha and Siddha, the crossing of the arms, the meeting of four roads, a type of village, a sitting posture (*Mānasāra*, XX. 94, 34-41). It was a custom to draw the *Svastika-signs* on the walls on important occasion as today (*Padma*, *Sṛṣṭikhaṇḍa*, 16, 114): स्वस्तिकं प्राङ्गणे ।

4827 **स्वस्तिक-करण**

Svastika-karaṇa : crossed position of either thew hands or the thighs or feet. Hands in feet and both in *svastika.* Static position (*NS*, IV.75-76). It is used in indicating secrecy and avoiding search skillfully.

4828 **स्वस्तिक-चारी**

Svastika-cārī : crossed knees pose, both the knees bent to one side. (Fig. - 4828).

4829 **स्वस्तिक-नृत्त-हस्त**

Svastika-nṛtta-hasta : auspicious dancing hands, a type of hand-gesture in dancing, seen occasionally in sculpture. If the *talamukha* (q.v.) hands are crossed by the wrist in a *svastika* style, it is called the *svastika* (*NS*, IX. 176-197). It is also known as *viprakīrṇa-hasta.*

4830 **स्वस्तिक-बाहु**

Svastika-bāhu : the crossed arm (*NS*, IX. 205-6). Point to a defensive mood. Arms which are more loosely wrapped around the body are providing physical reassurance.

4831 **स्वस्तिक-मण्डल**

Svastika-maṇḍala : a type of posture.

4832 **स्वस्तिक-रेचित-करण**

Svastika-recita-karaṇa : *Recitas* of the hands with arms in *āviddha* (turning inwards). *Svastika* of the feet. The first position of the hands is in *caturaśra* and in the final position they are *haṁsapakṣa* (*NS*, IV. 76-78; IX. 193-220). It symbolizes joy.

4833 **स्वस्ति-वाचन**

Svasti-vācana : the chanting of the auspicious *mantras* at the beginning of any rite. This corresponds to the common Prākṛt expression *sothivāṇa* (*Priyadarśikā*, Act. II) The word designates primarily, the pronouncing of the benediction

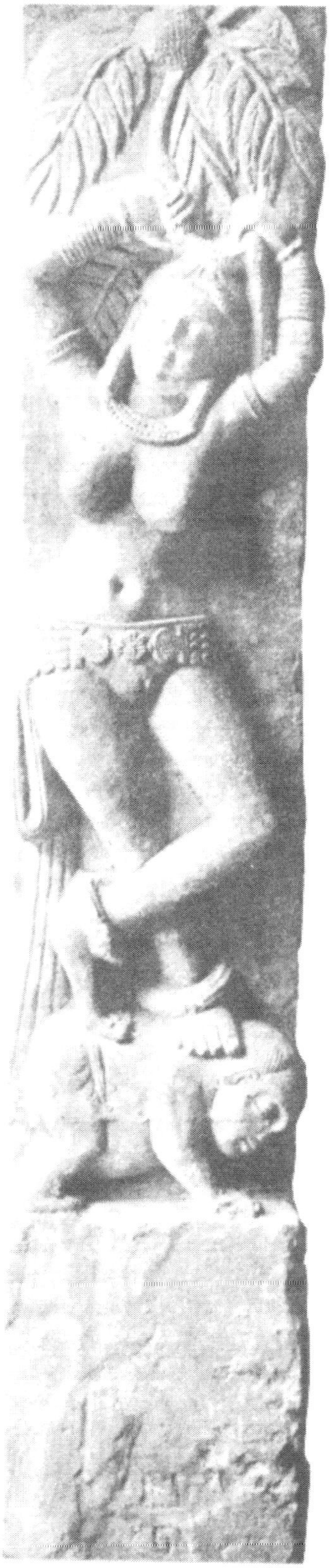

Fig. - (4828)

by a Brāhmaṇa at a religious ceremony (performed particularly by married women) and secondary the gift accompanying it. It is also called *svasti-pāṭha* which means "reciting the welfare *mantras*".

4834 **स्वस्तिक-हस्त**

Svastika-hasta : crossing of hands or arms, both hands gesture. Two *arāla* hands crossing. Indicates crossing of arms at any level of the body. The general movement of *svastika hastas* creates the atmosphere of clouds, thunder and lighthing in *Mṛcchakaṭika* (Act. V). Two palms, either in the *arāla*, or *vardhamānaka* style, are upturned and joined together by the wrist; it is called the *svastika* style. If the style of the *svastika* is separated exhibitingly, it suggests all the ten directions, clouds, the sky, the wood, the ocean, six seasons the earth and any other extensive thing (*NS*, IX. 129-130).

Thus in *svastika-hasta*, the *arāla* hands are upturned and held at the wrist and are placed at the left side. By separating from *svastika* position, it indicates the quarters, clouds, sky, ocean, forest, seasons, earth flood and such other extensive things. This hand is to be used by women.

4835 **स्वस्तिकासन**

Svastikāsana : cross-pose. *Svastika* is the sacred sign of cross of Hindus. Cross is the most pious and sacred symbol of almost all the great religions of the world. *Svastikāsana* is one of those four *āsanas* which are meant for meditational purposes.

Place the left foot between the calf and thigh of the right leg with the heel placed on the groin. The right foot should be placed between the calf and left thigh. Do not lean on one side.

4836 **स्वस्थान**

Svasthāna : The dress of dancers in ancient India. The tight pājāma known as *suthanā* in the dialects of Hindi. It is depicted in the dance scenes at Sārnāth and Deogarh.

4837 **स्वस्थान-चलन**

Svasthāna-calana : the tremor of the eyeballs. Synonymous to *calana*. Only listed in *Bālarāmabharata*.

4838 **स्वस्थासन**

Svasthāsana : a type of sitting posture.

4839 **स्वागत**

Svāgata : a welcome to a hero or a venerated person was a great event, with various preparations. This would be clear from the description of the welcome given to Kṛṣṇa when he returned to Mathurā after defeating Jarāsandha. Flowers were showered on him, bards sang his glory, conches and drums beat the tunes of joy; and the whole city was decorated with flags, canopies, and the streets were sprinkled with water. Women showered on him wreaths, whole grains, curds and fresh sprouts (*Bhāg. P. Uttarārdha*, 50. 36-40).

4840 **स्वाधीनपतिका**

Svādhīnapatikā : having the husband under subjection. A woman who has full control over her husband; a variety of heroine. 'She whose husband does not leave her due to passion, who gets pleasure by coition only' is called *Svādhīnapatikā* (Kalyāṇamalla, *Anaṅgaraṅga*, 10.68). According to Viśvanātha (*Sāhitya-darpaṇa*, 3.99) "*Svādhīnapatikā* is one who feels happy because her beloved always stays by her side and is under her sole control". Radhā of Jayadeva is the same type of woman.

NS calls her *Svādhīnabhartṛkā*. She is a heroine whose husband is by her side as he is attached to her and thus has the great joy of her good luck (*NS*).

4841 **स्वाप**

Svāpa : 'sleep' *Suśr*, defined sleep a state in which we close our eyes, breathing and heartbeat slow down, digestive processes diminish and our brainwaves become progressively longer and slower as they descend from the alpha waves of one to there cycle per second which characterize deep sleep. Positions in sleep shed some light on the personality and also give cues to the amount of stress we are under. Physically, sleep is a state in which we close our eyes, breathing and heartbeat slow down, digestive processes diminish and our brainwaves become progressively longer and slower as they descend from the alpha waves of full consciousness to the delta waves of one to three cycles per second which characterize deep sleep.

4842 **स्वाभाविक-अलङ्कार**

Svābhāvika-alaṅkāra : natural graces. The ten natural graces of women are *līlā* (sportiveness), *vilāsa* (amorous gesture), *vicchitti* (dishabille), *vibhrama* (confusion), *klikiñcitam* (hysterical mood), *moṭṭāyitam* (manifestation of affection), *kuṭṭamitam* (pretended anger), *vibboka* (affected coldness), *lalitam* (elegance) and *vihṛtam* (want of response).

4843 **स्वाभाविका-नासा**

Svābhāvikā-nāsā : natural nostrils; nose in natural position, a type of nose gesture; the natural position of nose indicates the rest and flush of the mind (*NS*, VIII. 123-129). Also known as *svābhāvikī-nāsā*. The nose being touched during a conversation communicates.

4844 **स्वामिनी**

Svāminī : in a play king's wives are to be addressed by servants and attendants as *svāminī*, *bhaṭṭinī* and *devī* (*NS*, XVII. 65-94).

4845 **स्वामी**

Svāmī : O' lord. the crown prince should be addressed as *svāmī*, but other princes as *bhartṛ-dāraka* (*NS*, XVII. 65-94).

4846 **स्वावलम्बनम्**

Svāvalambanam : self-reliance. There is very little emphasis on self-reliance. Transition from infancy to independence is prolonged. A child will continue to sleep with his mother, perhaps with one or two brothers and sisters, for anything up to five years. Similarly, it will be bathed till it is five or six, fed by hand till it is five, and dressed up to the same age. It learns to walk on its own, and learns to talk more by imitation that by precept; children are considered too young for much verbal instruction before the age of five and no attempt is made to build up a model of desired behaviour through long "talks".

4847 **स्वीकृति**

Svīkṛti : assent or promise. The sentence expressing assent or promise listening to (*Aṣṭādhyāyī*, 8.2.99) rule governing a particular accent for a particular period has been suggested by Pāṇini. For Pāṇini, there are certain rules that govern promise-making. They may be propositional content rule, preparatory rules and the essential rule. Searle has concentrated on this aspect.

4848 **स्वेद**

Sveda : prespiration. This is the second sensation or physical manifestation after an outburst of emotion, sexual enjoyment or fatigue. The person feels stunned for a moment and then begins to perspire profusely. It is represented by taking up the fan, wiping off sweat, looking for breeze. (b) In Tāntric ritual, sweat is compared to seed in a negative way: 'The drops of semen of a man who is always excessively attached to women are as unconducive to happiness, as if they were born of sweat' (*Śiva*, 23.55). But the converse is equally true; the drops of sweat of a man of chastity are as productive as seed. The idea of creative *tapas* itself stems from the early Vedic belief in the efficacy of the heat generated by the priest during the ritual, and sweating appears throughout the *Vedas* as a product of yogic activity. Śiva wanders naked, during *tapas*, and when he sheds a drop of sweat from his forehead the Earth nourishes it and raises the child born from it (*Śiva*, 2.3.10.14). The sweat of anger is destructive and creative as the sweat of *tapas* (*Mbh*. XII. 274-45). And of course sweat of lust is particularly creative. The relationship between sweat and seed is apparent in a Bengali tale: After the discharge of semen Śiva sweated and he washed the sweat away with a piece of cloth which he threw away. Out of this sweat a girl was born' (*Padma-Purāṇa* of Narayanadas). There are various references on the motif of perspiration in the Purāṇas:

> खनित्वा तत्र चक्रेण रम्यां पुष्करिणीं हरिः ।
> निजांगस्वेदसंदोहसलिलैस्तामपूरयत् ॥
>
> (*Skanda*, IV. 26.52)
>
> स्वेदाज्जाता सरिद्वरा रेवा (*Ibid.*, V. 2.34.2)

4849 **स्वेदाम्बुकणोपचिता**

Svedāmbukaṇopacitā : lady who sweats a little, quality of the Mare-lady (*Nāgarasarvasva*, 14.6).

4850 **स्वेदु-हव्य**

Svedu-havya : offering sweat as a sacrifice, toiling (*G. Br.* 1.121.6). Perspiration helps to cool an overheated system. Thus, sweating is one of the most noticeable signs of discomfort and rightened nervous tension, and is acceptable in toiling social situations.

4851 **स्वैतु**

Svaitu : going on one's own gait (*CP*, V.41.9); *Śobhanagamanāḥ*.

ह - Ha

4852 **हंस**

Haṃsa : goose, flamingo, a poetical or mythical bird said to be able to separate milk from water; therefore, a symbol of discrimination; the soul as symbolized by the pure white colour of the swan; sometimes used to represent the supreme spirit, swan. Wild ducks and migratory geese symbolized souls journeying towards the moon in the ancient India. (b) a symbolic *mantra* in the form of inhaling *haṁ* and exhaling *saḥ* of breath. *Haṁ* is the male organ and *saḥ* is female principle of creation. (*Kālicaraṇa* or *Ṣaṭcakranirūpaṇa*, XLIII). (c) *Haṁsa* is a fabulous bird of great beauty, that lives on pearls and is often used as symbol of the mysterious invisible life of man:

Rām's *hukumdār* has come
Goose, you must leave the village
The five messengers have come
They have brought the ox-goad
With the goad they beat the soul
They break its sibs and speed it on its way
O jambhaiyā wait a moment
The net of love is spread throughout the world
Let me tie it in a bundle
Then the goose may leave the village.
(Chhattisgarhi-folksong)

4853 **हंसकीलक**

Haṁsakīlaka : a particular posture in coition.

4854 **हंसगामिनी**

Haṁsagāminī : having graceful gait like that of a swan.

4855 **हंसनादिनी**

Haṁsanādinī : an excellent woman :

gajendragamanā tanvī kokilālāpasaṁyuktatā |
nitambe gurviṇī yā styāt sā smṛtā haṁsanādinī ||

4856 **हंसपक्ष-हस्त**

Haṁsapakṣa-hasta : a particular position of the hand, both hand gesture. Horripilation may be shown by the *haṁsapakṣa hastas* (*NS*, IX. 108) and by touching the body. The acceptance of gift is portrayed by a pair of *haṁsapakṣa-hastas* (*NS*, IX. 107) in *Karpūramañjarī* (Act I). It is rarely known to iconography. The palm is raised facing outwards, and very slightly hollowed. The little finger is extended straight and the other three fingers are bent a little forward, while the thumb bends over to touch the centre of the second finger underneath. It is to express the number six, arranging things, a covering and feathers. Three fingers, the fore-finger, the middle-finger and the ring-fingers are stretched straight; the little-finger is up and the thumb is closely joined to other three, all these make the *haṁsa-pakṣa* gesture. The gesture of the *haṁsa-pakṣa* is used to offer water to departed souls, to preserve scent-paste, to receive charity, to feed poor Brāhmaṇs, to embrace, to show a great paralytic pose, to touch, to besmear scent-paste, etc. In addition to them when this gesture is positioned in between the breasts of ladies; it suggests delicate device of young ladies and to touch the chins of affectionate ones, pathos and in cases of some such aesthetic experiences (*NS*, IX.100-103).

4857 **हंसमुखहस्त**

Haṁsamukha-hasta : the thumb is joined to the topmost joint of the middle finger and the hand relaxed. This makes the *haṁsamukha*—hand-gesture which indicates the *jyotiriṅgaṇa* (a firefly).

4858 **हंस-मुद्रा**

Haṁsa-mudrā : gesture of a swan. The *haṁsāsya* hand indicates a swan (*Mirror of Gesture*, pp. 50-51) (b) gesture symbolizing the swan of Vaiṣṇavite cult. The *śikhara*-hand with the thumb up and the little finger stretched indicates the swan (*VD*).

4859 **हंसवक्त्र-हस्त**

Haṁsavaktra-hasta : the swan's beak. The tips of the thumb, the fore-finger and the middle ones are joined together and rest two stretched; make the *haṁsa-vaktra* gesture. This indicates delicacy, slightly loose, light things; which come out easily and in relation to some tender thoughts; particularly with its quivering and sweating tips.

4860 **हंस-समाश्लेष**

Haṃsa-samāśleṣa : embrace of swan experienced by a slender lady (Dāmodaragupta, *Kuṭṭanīmatam*, 581).

4861 **हंसास्य-हस्त**

Haṁsāsya-hasta : single hand gesture (*NS*). *Mirror of Gesture* has it's other variant known as *Mudrākhya*. *Bālarāmabharata* derives it from *Siṁhāsya*. Occurs often in iconography where hands hold attributes. The putting of lamp by Vāsavadattā (*Mṛcchakaṭika*, Act. I)is indicated through the above gesture (*Abhinayadarpaṇa*, 5.155-57). This gesture also indicates an exit from a building (*Mṛcchakaṭika* Act I). Showing the pen for writing and painting is also enacted (*Vikramorvaśīya*, Act II) through this gesture. The palm is raised facing outwards and very slightly hollowed. The little finger is extended straight. The third finger is also extended but bent very slightly, and the first and the second fingers are bent forward to touch the thumb at the tips. It is used to express swan's beak, tying the marriage thread, certainty, drop of water, carrying garlands, a jasmine, fineness, smallness, looseness, lightness, worthlessness and softness.

4862 **हंसोदक**

Haṁsodaka : water purified by the rays of the Sun and Moon (*Dravyaratnamālā*).

4863 **हंहो**

Haṁho : hellow, verily, indeed, of course, then.

4864 **हम्**

Ham : a type of vocative. A low person is to be addressed as *ham* (*NS*, XVII.65-94), equally low persons should address themselves as *ham*. (b) *ham* is the symbol of *Vindu* (the male organ of creation).

4865 **हक्क**

Hakka : the calling of elephants.

4866 **हञ्जा**

Hañjā : a vocative particle used in addressing a female attendant or maid-servant (*Ratnāvalī,* Act III).

4867 **हञ्जिका**

Hañjikā : female attendant, cleroden-drum, siphonantus.

4868 **हञ्जे**

Hañje : this vocative particle, common in Sanskrit dramas, is used especially by a lady in addressing a female attendant or maid-servant (*Priyadarśikā,* Act II). A handmaid is to be accosted by a superior woman with the word *hañje* (*NS*, XVII.65-94); address to a slave-girl.

4869 **हठ**

Haṭha : violence, force, pertinency. *Haṭhāt* forcibly; *haṭhavādika* cārvāka.

4870 **हठयोग**

Haṭhayoga : a kind of *yoga* in *Tantra* in which the mind is forced to withdraw from external objects. *Haṭhayoga* prescribes six purificatory techniques (*ṣaṭkarma*): *netī* (nasal cleaning), *dhautī* (internal cleaning), *bastī* (stomach-washing), *navalī* (abdominal cleaning), *trāṭaka* (gazing for optical nerves) and *kapālabhātī* (purification of the carnal region). All these constitute important techniques of physical hygiene. Thus, *haṭhayoga* is a form of physical exercise for making the body so disciplined as to serve all spiritual purposes (*Haṭhayogapradīpikā,* 1.10).

4871 **हण्डा**

Haṇḍā : a vocative particle used in addressing a female of inferior rank, or by the equals of the lowest caste in addressing each other : *haṇḍe hañje halāhvāne nīcām ceṭīm sakhīm prati.* A low person should be addressed as *haṇḍā* or a low person should de addressed as *hañje* by equally low person (*NS*,XVII, 65-95); used as *haṇḍe*: form of address to a low caste (in drama).

4872 **हत**

Hata : wretched, dejected. *hataka* 'a low person, miserable'. *hata-mūrkha* 'block-headed'. *hata-lakṣaṇa* 'unlucky'.

4873 **हनु**

Hanu : chin. *Hanumūla* 'root of jaw'. A jaw which recedes, and is tucked in towards the neck indicates lack of confidence and occurs when someone is feeling sad, unable to speak up for themselves.

4874 **हन्त**

Hanta : come, look, pray; such as *hanta te kathayiśyāmi* "look I will state".

4875 **हय**

Haya : horse;. *haya-śāstra* 'science of horses'. (b) a Gadabā must not ride on a horse under penalty of being put out of caste. Thurston (*Ethnographic Notes in Southern India*, p.270) gives the following reason for this prejudice: "The Gadabas of Viasakhapatnam will not touch a horse, as they are palanquin-bearers, and have same objection to a rival animal as a cart-driver has to a motor-car". (b) Glasfurd (*Report of Bastar Dependency*, 1860) notes that Gonds had great fear of a horse, on the sight of a man on horseback would put a whole village to flight. Hiralal also experienced the same behaviour among Chāndā Gonds where women picking up *mahua* would run and climb a tree at one's approach on a pony. (Russell and Hirala, II.121).

4876 **हयशिरस्-मुद्रा**

Hayaśiras-mudrā : gesture symbolizing the Vaiṣṇava-deity *hayaśiras.* The alphabetic symbol of '*ikāra*' represents this deity (*VD*). (b) The ring-fingers are to be made curved and placed on the level with the fore-fingers. Then raise the two middle fingers and join them together with thumbs. This makes the symbol of *hayaśiras.* It is also known as *aśvaśiras* (*VD*).

4877 **हरगौरीसृष्टि**

Haragauri-sṛṣṭi : chemical processing of mercury and mica to make the elixir of immortality (Bhattachārya, 1990.67).

4878 **हराश्रम**

Harāśrama : stage of life based on the Śiva sect. The believers of this sect show the *tripuṇḍra* with white ashes according to *Purāṇas.* The *puṇḍra* is a vertical line on the fore-head; and the *tripuṇḍra* has three such lines (*Kūrma,* 2.98-102). The *puṇḍra* is the symbol of the *Kālātman* (time that is the soul of universe), and one who holds the *tripuṇḍra* symbolically holds this universe (*Ibid.,* 103-105).

4879 **हरिणप्लुत-करण**

Hariṇapluta-karaṇa : like the *cārī* of the name, it is derived from the initial position of the *atikrāntā cārī.* There is a jump and then an *añcita* foot is placed at the side. The knees are spread out in *kṣipta* in the final position (*NS,* IV. 143b-144a; X.30, 43).

4880 **हरिणप्लुत-चारी**

Hariṇapluta-cārī : movement of the jumping deer (*NS,* IV. 144). Feet in *samapāda añcita* positions. Initial position of the *atikrāntā cārī.* Jump and sideways movement. *Kṣipta* position of the knees. *Hariṇapluta-karaṇa.* It is also known as *mṛgapluta.* In *Śākuntalam* (Act I), deer is represented not by an actual deer but by a dancer wearing a deer mask, furtively peering and frisking in fright: the movement possibly is the *hariṇapluta* movement (*NS,* IV. 144). Abhinava (*NS, Ibid.*) says that this *cārī* was done by *vidūṣakas* (jesters). Śārṃgadeva (*SR,* IV. 948-49) has termed it as *mṛgapluta.*

4881 **हरिण-मुद्रा**

Hariṇa-mudrā : indication of an antilope. The *mṛgaśīrṣa*-hand indicates an antilope (*Mirror of Gesture,* pp. 49-50).

4882 **हरिद्रा**

Haridrā : *turmeric* is believed to be auspicious in rituals, and is one of the six aspects of Gaṇapati. It is the symbol (along with *navapatra*) of Durgā. Turmeric is also an ethno-medicinal device in village India. (*Agni. P.* 287-28).

4883 **हरिद्रौदन**

Haridraudana : rice boiled with turmeric bits known as *buknī* in Baghelī and used by the female who has given birth to a child. The *Matsya-Purāṇa* (267.26) describes that the female demons (*rākṣasīs*) have an important place in delivery and rice cooked with turmeric is to be offered in the south-east to *vidarī* and then to the mother of the new-born baby.

4884 **हरिश्चन्द्र-हस्त**

Hariścandra-hasta : *Śukatuṇḍa hasta* represents the mythical king Hariścandra (*Mirror of Gesture,* p. 47).

4885 **हर्म्य**

Harmya : attic storey.

4886 **हर्ष**

Harṣa : pleasure. Feeling of joy. One of the *vyabhicārī-bhāvas* as enumerated by Bharata. *Harṣa* is a feeling of joy resulting from the attainment of desired object. In *Mālatīmādhava* (Act I), *Kāntādṛṣṭi* is used for *harṣa.* It is manifested by brightness of the face and the eyes, using sweet words, embracing, horripilation, tears (of joy), stammering, perspiration and the like (*SD,* III. 165).

4887 **हर्षक**

Harṣaka : neck-ornament (*NS,* .I. 61) Abhinava explains it was serpentile in the form हर्षकं समुद्गकं सर्पा दिरूपतया प्रसिद्धम् । It is known as *hasulī* in Baghelī dialect of Hindi.

4888 **हर्षुल**

Harṣula : lover, given to jokes.

4889 **हल-मुद्रा**

Hala-mudrā : the gesture of a plough. "If the thumb is turned up of a curved hand like a grip of a plough, this position exposes the idea of the *hala* (plough). This helps to mature a devout. All the Gods and other divine beings become a *khecara* (one who can move in the sky) and the master of a *cakra* (circle of devouts in the process of the esoteric service)". (*BT*). (b) if the finger of the *kapittha* is curved, it is the *hala-mudrā* which symbolizes a Vaiṣṇava deity (*VD*).

4890 **हला**

Halā : a vocative particle used between females of equal status (*Śākuntalam* Act I; *Priyadarśikā,* Act II). Women friends among their equals are to be accosted by one another with the word *halā* (*NS,* XVII. 65-94); form of addressing a female friend.

4891 **हलासन**

Halāsana : like *sarvāṅgāsana* lie flat on your back, keeping the hand at the sides, palms facing the ground. Raise the legs slowly without the help of hands and do not bend the legs and the trunk. Then slowly lower the legs, folding them over the body until the toes touch the ground. The knees should be straight and close together. The legs and thighs must be in one straight line, with the chin pressing the chest. Breathe slowly through the nose. You can also catch hold of the toes with the two hands. In performing this *āsana,* there should be no jerk and strain. When the *āsana* is over, raise the legs slowly and bring them to the original position lying flat on the ground.

This *āsana* tones up the spinal nerves, muscles of the back, and prevents early ossification of vertebral bones. Various sorts of muscular rheumatism, lumbago, sprain are cured. Obesity and chronic constipation, diabetes, congestion and enlargement of the lever and spleen are also cured by this *āsana*.

4892 **हल्लीस**

Hallīsa : a form of minor drama; *hallīsaka* 'dancing in ring. *hallīsakakrīḍana* 'sporting of one man with the women'.

4893 **हल्लीसक**

Hallīsaka : *hallīsaka* is a form of *uparūpakas*. The *hallīsaka* has been described as the form where there are several women (*nāyikās*) and one man (*nāyaka*) and the women dance in circles (*NS*, Vol I. 437). We find the presentation of *hallīsaka* in *Bālacarita* of Bhāsa.

4894 **हविष्कृत**

Haviṣkṛta : literally it means 'one who separates the grains from the husks'. According to *Taitt Br.* (II. 2.4) it indicates the formula for calling a person. In the case of a Brāhmaṇa it is *ehi* (come hither), for a Kṣatriya *āgahi* (approach), for a Vaiṣya *ādrava* (hasten here) and for a Śūdra *ādhāva* (run hither). Cf. *Śat. Br.* (1.1.4.12), *Āp. Sr.* (1.19.9-10). (b) The comm. on *Āp. Sr.* says that the term means the person who prepares the *havis* and also the formula used to call him. (c) *Jaimini* (III. 2.59) holds that in certain Vedic passages, *haviṣkṛta* indicates an injunction to summon thrice the wife or any other person who separates grains.

4895 **हविष्य**

Haviṣya : oblations made in the morning and evening of cooked food but only such corn as is fit to be offered to fire as *havis* should be used (*Āśv. Gr.* 1.2.1).

4896 **हविस्**

Havis : an oblation of clarified butter or milk or *soma* or grain offered in rituals.

4897 **हसित**

Hasita : smile; free laugh, A polished but free manner of expressing appreciation of humour, with eyes slightly wider and teeth partly visible through the gap between lips. It indicates the superior culture of noble characters (Nagendra, 1967, 63) (b) spontaneous laughter. One of the eight *sāttvika alaṁkāras* added by Viśvanātha to the category of *svabhāvaja alaṁkāras*. "A spontaneous laugh springing from one's rising youth is *hasita* " (*Sahityadarpaṇa*, III.109). (c) laughter occurs in witty situations of humorous, obscence, malicious character, because of great joy, as a part of 'embarrassment' syndrome. I witnessed laughing Hill Maria when the evil *ondorande* pulled the male organ of the Baihā. Hill Maria laughed at the drinking of country made liquor by an Government official which kicked by gulping only one dose. They laugh when someone enquires about their sexual activities. (d) *Hasita* is an *anubhāva* of *hāsa* (laughter) according to *NS*. It represents blooming eyes, face and cheeks, teeth slightly visible.

Smiling is an index of happiness. It is more likely to occur when we are with other people. If you pick up and play with a young baby, your reward will be a smile. A baby seems to be programmed to smile at the sight of a human face, and this reaction first occurs at about eight weeks of age. However, it is equally clear that the way we smile can be changed by our experiences. A quick look around shows us that some people smile much more than others, and all in their own distinctive styles. Children vary too. If they are brought up in an environment where they are not much encouraged to smile, then they simply stop smiling. In fact, in extreme cases, this type of upbringing can lead to emotional apathy and a withdrawal from social contact. (e) Varāhamihira (LXVIII) has symbolized laughter as such: "laughter not accompanied by a convulsion of the body is auspicious; one accompanied by closed eyes belongs to a sinful man; a repeated one to a wicked fellow; and a repetition at the end of one, to a madcap. Cf. the following:

हसितं कम्परहितं नृपाणामन्यथाऽशुभम् ।
असकृद्दोषयुक्तस्य मीलिताक्षस्य चाशुभम् ॥

(f) a woman who shows dimples in her cheeks, while smiling, is declared an unchaste woman by Varāhamihira (LXX. 19):

कूपौ यस्या गण्डयोश्च स्मितेषु निःसन्दिग्धं बन्धकीं तां वदन्ति ॥

Vide the following—

यस्यास्तु हसमानाया जायते गण्डकूपकाः ।
भर्त्तारं हन्ति सा क्षिप्रं नैकत्र रमते चिरम् ॥

Cf. Parāsara

यस्या हसन्त्या दृश्यन्ते कूपकाः गण्डयोर्द्वयोः ।

Vide Halāyudha—

चिबुके कपोलदेशेऽपि कूपिका दृश्यते स्मिते यस्याः ।
विपुलान्वयप्रजातापि जायते सा महाचपला ॥

4898 **हस्त**

Hasta : hand-pose, hand-gesture. Of all the major limbs of a body, two hands of a person demand first recognition, not only in the dramatic art, but in other arts also, especially in Fine Arts and particularly in iconography and sculpture.

After the face-part of a body, hands are the most striking and important limbs of a person; which strike one's own admiration, as to add an extra beauty and spirit to human being. Gestures of the hand, as explicit in the *NS;* are, therefore 64 : *catuṣaṣṭi karā hyete nāmato abhihitā mayā* (*NS*, IX. 17) or 67 according to variance of its recensions.

Gestures of the hand are sixty-four in all, of which, gestures of single hands 24; joined hands 13 and *nṛtta hastas* (dancing hands) 27. Names of the twenty-four single hands are : *patāka, tripatāka, kartarimukha, ardhacandra, arāla, śukatuṇḍa, muṣṭi, śikhara, kapittha, kaṭakāmukha, sūcyāsya, padmakośa, sarpaśīrṣa, mṛgaśīrṣa, kāṅgula, utpala, catura, bhramara haṁsāsya, haṁsapakṣa, sandaṁśa, mukula, ūrṇābha* and *tāmracūḍa.* Names of the thirteen joined hands gestures are as follows : *añjali, kapotaka, karkaṭa, svastika, kaṭaka-vardhamānaka, utsaṅga, niṣadha, dola, puṣpapuṭa, makara, gajadanta, avahittha* and *vardhamāna.* The twenty-seven dancing hands (*nṛtta hastas*) are as follows: *caturasra, udvṛtta, talamukha, svastika, arālakaṭakāmukha, aviddhavaktra, sūcīmukha, recita, ardharecita, uttānavañcitau, pallava, nitamba, keśabandha, latā, karihasta, pakṣavañcitaka, pakṣapradyotaka, garuḍapakṣaka, daṇḍapakṣaka, uromaṇḍalin, pārśvamaṇḍalin, muṣṭikasvastikau, nalinīpadmakośa, alapallava, ulvaṇa, lalita* and *valita.*

The hands are the only parts of the body the uses of which for *nṛtya* and *abhinaya* are separately treated. The *NS* describes *recaka* (rotation) of the *hasta.* The hands can achieve only a restricted movement within the limitation of the wrist and the ankle joint. These hand gestures are broadly classified under the (a) *asaṁyuta hasta* and (b) *saṁyuta hasta.*

There are twenty-four single hand poses and thirteen double hand poses, known as *hasta.* Each has a large number of uses, and while in use, each hand in pose has to be shown differently to indicate different meanings. This is accomplished by changing their position or level and attendant action. These hand poses have increased in number since Bharata and regional texts have added their own special hand poses. For any object, a hand gesture could be devised on the basis of the form of the object, its characteristic activity, or mark, or class. But there are some cautions that an actor should observe: as in life, characters of high status should not indulge in too much gesticulation; middle status characters should gesture moderately; and only lower class characters gesticulate profusely (*NS*, IX. 173).

Secondly, certain situations are acted best with little hand-movement—sorrow, swooning, bashfulness, fatigue, stupefaction, motionlessness, dullness, illness, absorption in thought and penance. Intimate, subtle physical reactions (*sāttvikābhinaya*) are to be employed then, rather than explicit gestures with hands (*NS*, IX. 179-179).

The hand-gesture is the gestures of gestures; the hand is the indication for body. The adage often quoted in Indian dance is: "Where the hand moves, there the eye follows." : *Yato hastaḥ tato dṛṣṭiḥ.*

Gestures of joined and disjoined hands are displayed to give artistic expressions of various dramatic thoughts and aesthetic experiences. In addition to them, an artist is independent to style any gesture in purpose to active success in dance and drama, with the help of bodily actions, signs and its genus, as one's own reasonings allow. Moreover, there are some dramatic gestures current in practice among artists prevalent in local and timely behaviours of people. They should also find due recognition in the dramatic art, though they are not categorically indicated in the celebrated works of the treatise. It is interesting to mark that the *NS* is though appreciated as a scholastic work; yet it is not always in the position to obey the guide lines of poetics and grammar which we suppose is not 'a must' for the technical study in Indian literature. Sentiments, feelings, and dramatic actions always provide scope to devise new ones.

To style gestures in view to give best exposure to the thoughts in women and kings, other gestures may also be styled according to the need of a country, time, direction and appropriation (*NS*, IX. 172-174).

Let us describe now all the actions and functions appropriate to suggest relevant sentiments and feelings. They are (i) *utkarṣaṇa* (drawing up), (ii) *vikarṣaṇa* (reaction), (iii) *apakarṣaṇa* (to draw roughly), (iv) *parigraha* (acknowledgement), (v) *nigraha* (to hold up forcibly, or to punish), (vi) *āhvāna* (to call out), (vii) *nodana* (to direct), (viii) *saṁśleṣa* (to embrace, or to sum up), (ix) *viyoga* (to substract, or to separate), (x) *rakṣaṇa* (to protect, or to maintain), (xi) *mokṣaṇa* (to release), (xii) *vikṣepaṇa* (to throw away), (xiii) *dhūnana* (to thrash), (xiv) *visarga* (to give up), (xv) *chedana* (to cut up), (xvi) *bhedana* (to penetrate), (xvii) *sphoṭana* (to put off), (xviii) *mohana* (to enchant) and (xix) *tāḍana* (to beat) (*NS*, IX. 175).

The movements of hands are generally of three types (i) the *uttāna:* the flat, (ii) *pārśvagata:* the side-traced and (iii) *adhomukha* : the down-facing.

In addition to the above styles of hands, an action may devise such styles of hands and enact such poses and postures appropriate to suggest requisite states and feeling of the mind, befitting to the particular situations as in states of sadness, senselessness, feat, striken by hatred or sorrow, weakness, sleeping, handlessness, motionlessness, drowsiness, inactivity, suffering with diseases or fever, fear-strikened, affected with cold, intoxicated, mad-absorbed in thoughts, austerity, residing in a chilly place, imprisonement, swift-moving, sleep-speaking, breaking things with nails, etc.

There are five movements of hands (palms) in a dance and dramatic performance. They are, (i) the upturned, (ii) the down-turned, (iii) the side-turned, (iv) the facing up, and (v) the down-facing. These five styles of the palm are used in Dance-Drama.

In short, the hand (gesture) should follow the look, the look should follow the mind, the mind should be directed in accordance with the thought, or the (dormant) feeling and when the feeling is heightened to the climax, *rasa* reigns supreme there:

> yato hastastato dṛṣṭir—
> yato dṛṣṭistato manaḥ ।
> yato manastato bhāvo
> yato bhāvastato rasaḥ ॥
> (*Abhinayadarpaṇa*, verse 247).

Mammaṭa (1050-1150 A.D.) cites an example of 'Poetry in Gesture', which a girl-messenger communicates through a suggested word-image to a lover with the help of hands and fingers; that he has the good luck to enjoy the company of his beloved with these limited days, countable with the fingers (say, five or ten); whose both the eyes are as long as her own fore-fingers and her breasts are as developed as they can be indicated by the two full palms of the *padmakośamudrā* (*Kāvyaprakāśa*, second, pp.68). He has also admitted elsewhere that the speech of a side-glance is more potent and meaningful than those of direct words: एद्दहमेत्तत्थिणआ एतद्दहमेत्तेहिं दिऐहिं । अशब्दात्मकनेत्र-त्रिभागावलोकनादिगतत्वेनापि तस्य प्रसिद्धेरिति (*Kāvyaprakāśa*, V.p.242).

Without them dramatic art is barren.

The designator features of hand are well developed in Indian culture. In general 'simple' hand forms such as flat hand, first, or index hand predominate in Indian culture. Extensions of different fingers from the fist can also serve to distinguish one designator from another. In the most common fist appearing among Indian gestures, the thumb lies along the side of the index finger and this finger, although curled, extends slightly to accommodate the thumb. This designator functions as a mime holding something as a pencil or key. A second 'Configuration' in which the thumb protrudes between the index and middle finger, appears in Indian 'intercourse'. The open or flat hand designator frequently appears among modern Indian gestures. Open hand with fingers together, as in 'no' contrasts with open hand and spread fingers in 'five' open hand with fingers together also appears in 'this way', 'stop' and in emblems indicating a source of pain such as 'headache', 'earache' and 'stomach-ache'. A curved open hand with fingers together appears in Indian Muslims 'prayer' and 'give'. As it appears in no minimal pairs, it is probably not emic in Hindi. Indian gesture makes heavy use of the index hand, a closed fist with the index finger extended. This designator appears in 'quiet', 'you', 'one', etc. It contrasts with flat hand in 'intelligence'. Extension of the little finger from the fist appears in one gesture 'thin', which is not a verified emblem. It contrasts with extension of the index finger in 'one'. Included among Hindi designators, then, are the fist, spread hand, flat hand and claw hand. Hindi also employs extensions of the thumb, index middle and little fingers to indicate contrast as well as combination extensions of index and middle, or index, middle and ring fingers.

The hand is very eloquent in the physical gesticulation (*śārīra-abhinaya*). The number of hand poses is sixty-four in all, which is subdivided as the hand poses to be used in dramatic representation and those in dance. The single hand poses are twenty-four and those with both the hands are thirteen. The remaining twenty-seven hand poses are to be used mainly in dance, i.e. in the *karaṇas*, etc. The number comes to thirty according to *SR*. Then three more are treated in *SR*, i.e. *nikuñcaka*, *devīśikhara* and *varadābhaya*. Thus total then comes to seventy.

The experts should use the hand gestures in conformity with the popular usage, taking into consideration the *karaṇa* (movement), *karma* (object), *sthāna* (sphere), *pracārayukti* (appropriateness) and *kriyā* (mode).

4899 **हस्त-कमल**

Hasta-kamala : lotus in hand. It is a symbol of prosperity than poetic embellishment. (b) The *Garuḍa Parāṇa* (1.9.8) says that the hand is the lotus, and the fingers are its petals; the middle of the palm is the pericarp, while the nails are the filaments:

> हस्तं पद्मं समाख्यातं पत्राण्यङ्गुल्यः स्मृताः ।
> कर्णिका तलहस्तं तु नखान्यस्य तु केशराः ॥

4900 **हस्त-कम्पन**

Hasta-kampana : waving of hand. It is at present a non-verbal device of summoning someone, particularly in selling goods.

4901 **हस्त-करण**

Hasta-karaṇa : wrist-joint indicating hand-movement as the most important features. There are four principal styles of the hands applicable especially in a *karaṇa* or a *tāṇḍava* : *apaveṣṭita* (rounding up style of a hand), *udveṣṭita* (outer round up), *vyāvartita* (the contra-round up) and *parivartita* (the external contra round up). *SR* (VII.543) explains the *karaṇa* as the particular movements of the hands resulting in hand gestures expressing various ideas. They are (1) *āveṣṭita*: the fingers beginning with the first finger and gradually turned inwards. The hand moves round with its palm facing the breast (2) *udveṣṭita* : The fingers are gradually turned outwards, beginning with the first finger. The hand moves round, away from the breast (3) *vyāvṛtta* : The same movement is there as in *āveṣṭita* but the fingers are gradually turned with the last finger (4) *parivartita* : The fingers are turned outwards gradually beginning with the last finger.

These hand movements should be used in dance representation accompanying the facial expressions.

4902 **हस्त-गृहीत**

Hasta-gṛhīta : having hands lied down (*Ch. Up.*).

4903 **हस्त-ग्राभ**

Hasta-grābha : graping of the hand of the bride by the bridegroom is the first stage of main marriage rite mentioned in the *Sūtra* texts. "*Hāth men hāth denā*" also means 'to give one's hand in marriage' (Hindi).

4904 **हस्त-ग्राह**

Hasta-grāha : taking by hand; protecting someone; it is known as "*hāth pakaṛnā*" in Hindi. (b) The holding of hand, as in marriage, is a euphemism for a sexual encounter (*Varāha*, 22.8-25). The holding of the right hand of an unmarried women indicated betrothal. Thus, when Śiva goes to Pārvatī in the guise of *brahmacārin* baṭu, and falls downs, he says to her, when she tries to help him by giving a hand, that he would not take her left hand which is unholy. She then gives him right hand, indicating a future marriage (*Skanda*, I. 2.25.4):

सव्यं चाशुचि ते हस्तं नावलम्बामि कर्हिचित् ।

Cf. *Mbh.* (*Ādi* 78.20-23) where Yayāti holds the right hand of Damayantī. Also in *Āpastamba Gr. Su.* (II.4.11) there is the following line in the context of marriage:

दक्षिणेन नीचा हस्तेन दक्षिणमुत्तानं हस्तं गृह्णीयात् ।

4905 **हस्तचटकारोप**

Hastacaṭakāropa : sound produced by thumb and middle finger.

4906 **हस्तचापल्य**

Hastacāpalya : amputation of hand; *hastakauśalam*.

4907 **हस्ततल**

Hastatala : palm of the hand. Throughout the Indian history, the open palm has been associated with truth, honesty, allegiance and submission. Many oaths are taken with the palm of the hand over the heart, and the palm is held in the air when somebody is giving evidence in a court of law; the right palm has a distinct connotation in comparison to the left palm.

In day-to-day encounters, people use two basic palm positions. The first has the palm facing upwards and is characteristic of the beggar asking for money or food. The palm facing downward symbolizes restraint.

4908 **हस्त-ताल**

Hasta-tāla : striking the palms together, clapping the hands.

4909 **हस्त-तुला**

Hasta-tulā : hand-balance, weighing in the hands.

4910 **हस्तदत्तम्**

Hastadattam : given by hand. *Skanda Purāṇa* (I.2.25.41) records that the following things are not to be accepted if given by hand : water, milk-soup (*pāyasam*), alms, ghee and salt :

पानीयं पायसं भैक्ष्यं घृतं लवणमेव च ।
हस्तदत्तं न गृह्णीयात् तुल्यं गोमांसभक्षणम् ।

Hāthādenā is a popular idiom meaning "mark made by the outstretched palm of the hand. Every new implement is marked with the impress of the hand dipped in oil. Before the birth of the child it is also usual for the rural nurse in attendance to dip her hand in oil and make an impression on the wall, and it is supposed by the way the oil trickles down, that she can tell whether the newcomer will be a boy or girl. During a festival towards the end of the year, it is the practice of the women of the herdsmen in Chhattisgarh to go to each house in the village and with red and white paint to make a mark on the wall which bears a faint resemblance to a hand. It is known as *hāthā*. The emblem of the Congress party in India is a 'hand'.

4911 **हस्तदोष**

Hastadoṣa : slip of hand.

4912 **हस्तधारण**

Hastadhāraṇa : warding off a blow; *hastavāraṇam*.

4913 **हस्तधूनन**

Hastadhūnana : shaking hands : *vṛthā te hastadhūnanam*. Though handshake was taboo in the pre-modern India, yet it is now spreading enormously particularly in the urban centres. Now handshake is becoming similar to a signature, in that it has become an integral part of the personality. The purpose of handshake is to create a momentary physical bond between people, which says, 'hello' or 'goodbye' or 'we agree on this."

4914 **हस्तन्यस्त-मुख**

Hastanyasta-mukha : keeping the hand over the mouth (*Megha.*, 2.24); symbolizing anxiety. In *Caturbhāṇi* (p.55) we have हस्तप्रत्यस्तगण्डे प्राशीथिलवलये भिन्ननिःश्वासवक्त्रे ।

4915 **हस्त-पताका**

Hasta-patākā : a small banner (*A*, 4.3.41).

4916 **हस्तपाद**

Hastapāda : the hands and the feet; *na me hastapādam prasarati* (*Śākuntalam*, IV Act).

4917 **हस्त-पुच्छ**

Hasta-puccha : hand below wrist.

4918 **हस्त-पृष्ठ**

Hasta-pṛṣṭha : back of hand.

4919 **हस्त-प्रचार**

Hasta-pracāra : movement of the hand; the general movements of hands are three: (1) *uttāna* (upwards), (2) *adhomukha* (downwards) and (3) *pārśvaga* (sideways). The movements of the hands in different directions are given as five according to other view (*NS*, Vol. II. 70), which is that of Udbhaṭa, as stated by Abhinava. It reads उत्तानोऽधस्तलस्त्र्यस्रोऽग्रगोऽधोमुख एव च । पञ्चप्रचारा हस्तस्य

But Abhinava says that *adhomukha* comes under *adhastala* and *agraga* comes under *uttāna; tryasra* is nothing but *tripārśvaga*. Abhinava explains *uttāna* position, as in the representation of tongue. *Tripatāka* is brought near the face; *pārśvaga* as when the *muṣṭi* is used in the representation of a bow; and *adhomukha* as in the representation of ocean, the use of (*svastika*) hand near the forehead. All the hand movements should be embellished by expressive eyes, eyebrows, and facial colour etc. in performance.

4920 **हस्तप्राप्य**

Hastaprāpya : easily obtainable.

4921 **हस्तं पातयेत् मूर्ध्नि**

Hastam pātayet mūrdhni : placing hand on the head. It is a practice that the *guru* places his hand on the head of the *śiṣya*, which symbolizes initiation. *Garuḍa Purāṇa* (I. 9.8) records :

तं हस्तं पातयेन्मूर्ध्नि शिष्यस्य तु समाहितः ।

(b) In different accounts of Sanskrit literature there is the hand-on-head motif. According to *Skanda Purāṇa* (V. 3.67, 3-76), Kālapṛṣṭha the demon, propitiated Śiva and got a boon. According to it, any person will be turned to ashes the moment Kālapṛṣṭha placed his hand on the farmer's head. After he got the boon, he tried to apply it on Śiva himself. Śiva took resort to Viṣṇu, who took the form of a beautiful maiden, and duped the demon to place his hand on his own head. The moment this happened, the demon was turned to ashes. This is also the popular tale of Bhasmāsura which is not mentioned in any of the Sanskrit *Purāṇas.* According to the *Bhāgavata* (X.88.13), Vṛka, the another demon, propitiated Śiva, and got the boon from him, when he was about to cut his own head. According to the boon, anyone whose head he would touch would die. Having obtained the boon, he desired to try its power on Śiva himself. Hence, Viṣṇu took the form of a boy and stood in the way of Vṛka asking the latter what the matter was. When Vṛka told the fact, the boy laughed and said that the boon was false. He asked him to see it by trying it on his own head, if he wanted. Vṛka touched his own head with his finger, with the result that it immediately burnt off.

4922 **हस्तमुद्रा**

Hastamudrā : hand-gesture. There are thirty-two major hand-positions, twelve hand movements, twenty-four combined hand-positions, and in theory, at least over eighty-eight million minor variations of these something like eight or nine hundred are described in the manuals of the subject. The *hasta-mudrās* of classical dances have about five hundred meanings. These hand-gestures are applied in ritual, dance and occult-symbolism and frequently seen in sculpture.

Touching the partner's head with the hand is a more intimate action which may at first be seen during the encounter of father and the daughter. It manifests a strong bond of trust.

4923 **हस्तमेलनम्**

Hastamelanam : the hand-shake. This appears when a personal bond is absent, weak or there has been a long separation. Now-a-days, it is an expected formality when greeting. It is still limited to the male. A hand-shake can express an energetic personality if firm, a passive one if limp. Also known as *hastabanda* and *hastapīḍanam.* Hand-shake has been ritualized in modern India within the male persons. Specifically, it is in a class of rituals that serves to provide brackets around spate of activity, an occasion, undertaken by several participants, a meeting, a gathering, and encounter. It is still very much restricted to urban setting. Here, the hand-shake makes the beginning of activity, or the period during which there is an increase in joint access. It also can be used at the end of such periods, as an indication that the access gained will extend over the following period of separation, and not be limited to that one occasion. Since there is some amount of regard being contained and conveyed in that offering of access to the self, such behaviour may be designated as "access rituals" (Goffman, *Supportive Interchanges, in Relations in Public,* New York, 1971: 80).

Whereas ritual is a symbolic attestation of respect and regard, the expression and dramatization of such regard is found in ceremonialization. Thus when two peoples shake hands while being introduced a little dance is likely to occur; faces light up, smiles are exchanged, eyes are addressed.

Now-a-days, hand-shake is a sign of access and solidarity, dissimilar to ancient Indian hand-shake meaning to be married. The modern-day hand-shakes serves as an introduction, greeting and farewell.

4924 **हस्तमैथुन**

Hastamaithuna : masturbation. Masturbation is the specialized form of sexual self-contact. Here the use of the hand as a substitute for a partner is obvious enough. This fact makes masturbation into a transparently makeshift alternative to sexual Allo-contact. Because it therefore reflects the unavailabity of a mate and implies the inability to obtain one, it has become associated with shame and unjustly condemned. For those without mates, it provides a perfectly harmless method of relieving sexual tensions and, despite thousands of published statements to the contray, has no damaging effects whatsoever. Officially, of course, it has not always been condemned because it is a poor substitute for copulation. The need for an adult to obtain a pacifying and reassuring sensation by caressing his or her own body has been frowned upon as regressive and immature. Even then this auto-contact behaviour still continues unabated, heavily indulged in by both adult females and adult males.

Masturbation is known as *hathras* in Awadhī. In Bagheli, it is known as *mūnṭh.* Masturbation is widely practised in India, because being the secret society, it is second very best substitute for the real thing. If one cannot get a girl or boy, one masturbates.

4925 **हस्तयुगल**

Hastayugala : the two hands.

4926 **हस्त-रेचक**

Hasta-recaka : hand-movement. (*NS*, IX. 193). Raising up, throwing out, putting forward, turning round and extending the hand, constitute *hasta-recaka.*

4927 **हस्त-लाघव-कला**

Hasta-lāghava-kalā : science of dexterity. One of the 64 arts given in *Kāmasūtra* (1.3.16) also it means magic of hands.

4928 **हस्तलेख**

Hastalekha : handwriting (*Mudrārākṣasa*), We often receive our first impression of someone before we actually meet him, for example by their reputation or from their handwriting—a forward—sloping style might suggest a hurried, impetuous manner, while a neat, legible, upright hand might indicate a calm, methodical and careful person. Thus, when we write or draw we express our personalities almost without conscious control. Although our personal style of writing our words, sentences and notes is unique, however, the value of graphology (the analysis of personality through handwriting) has been demonstrated in Sanskrit literature (b) the first exercise (*Naiṣadha* VII. 15) : *abhūt vidhātuḥ khalu hastalekhaḥ.*

4929 **हस्त-विन्यास**

Hasta-vinyāsa : position of the hands. Certain Hindi idioms convey the meaning of hand-contact, such as : *hāth par gangājalī 'rakhnā* means to make one swear on Ganges water; "*hāth par hāth māranā*" means to join hands in confirmation of a promise; "hāth pasāranā" means to stretch hands, to beg; *hāth thirakānā* means to gesticulate; *hāth joṛanā* means to join both hands in supplication; and *hāth milānā* means shake hands.

4930 **हस्त-वेश्य**

Hasta-veśya : handi work, manual work, labour.

4931 **हस्त-संवाहन**

Hasta-saṁvāhana : rubbing, shampooing (*Megha*, 98), massaging with hands. This kind of massage is called reflexology or zone therapy.

4932 **हस्त-सिद्धि**

Hasta-siddhi : (a) power of touch by hand (*Yukti-dīpikā*, 164. 14-15). One of the six varieties of spiritual powers. In the fourth place, with the loss of the spiritual power of speech or sound, creation was made possible by mere touch of each other with their hands. They used to derive exquisite pleasure from this act. The hands are called the "two chasers of disease" which stroke the patient with a gentle touch (*RV*, X. 137.7 and *RV*, X.60.12). (b) wages. (Fig. - 49320

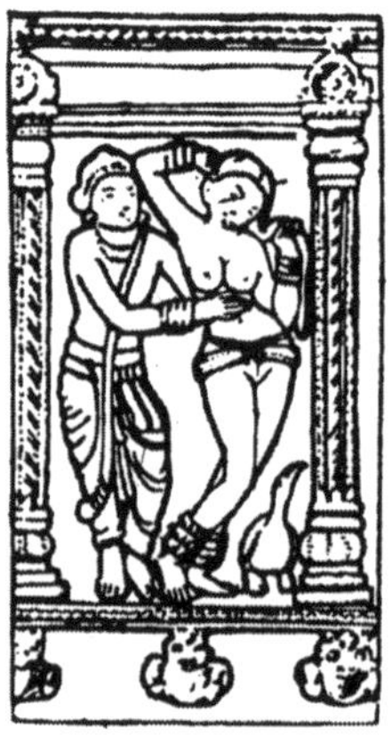

Fig. - (4932)

4933 **हस्त-सूत्र**

Hasta-sūtra : bracelet.

4934 **हस्त-स्वस्तिक**

Hasta-svastika : crossing the hands.

4935 **हस्ताकृतिविज्ञान**

Hastākṛtivijñāna : signs of the hand. Hands like those of a monkey indicates poverty; if the palms are slightly with a dimple, it indicate the person to spend away father's wealth. If the palm is dimpled, it indicates lack of ancestral property; if roundish and hollow, it indicates wealth; if flat it is an indication of generosity; if it is yellowish, it indicates sexual intercourse with a forbidden woman (*Bhaviṣya*, 26. 33-35).

Hands like lotus are appreciated in Sanskrit literature : *karakamala*.

With impure and refuge hands, anything is not to be touched, otherwise Lakṣmī leaves the house (proverb). One should not join one's hands on one's back (*Āpastamba*, II. 5.12.12). Theoretically it is open to attack.

4936 **हस्ताक्षर**

Hastākṣara : signature.

4937 **हस्ताग्र**

Hastāgra : finger, hand below wrist.

4938 **हस्ताभरण**

Hastābharaṇa : ornaments of the upper arm. (a) males : *hastalī* and *valaya*. (b) females : *aṅgada* (arm band) and *valaya* (arm ring).

4939 **हस्ताभिनय**

Hastābhinaya : a comprehensive hand-gesture. The *nṛtya* or *abhinaya* position utilizes for the most part the gesture of the hands. The language of gesture finds its complete articulation in the *hastābhinaya*, where practically are the permutations and combinations of the finger, the palm and the wrist have been worked out and each hand-pose (*hasta*) has been employed as words are in a language. Hand-gestures (*hastābhinaya*) are common technical aspects to Indian sculpture and dancing. They use the same language and many hand-gestures and their symbolic meanings are common to both the arts.

There are three basic movements of the hands : *asaṁyuta hasta, saṁyuta-hasta* and *nṛtta-hasta*. The first two varieties belong mostly to the sphere of finger manipulation and indicate static positions, with a few exceptions where they indicate movement : the *nṛtta-hastas* indicate movement of the fingers for the most part and invariably suggest an arm movement too.

Śārṅgadeva in *SR* lists fifteen positions of the hands in terms of planes, dimensions and direction of the palms and fingers. *Abhinayadarpaṇa* (p.30) lists eleven hands to be used in denoting relationships, such as *dampati* (couple), *mātṛ* (mother), etc. Fifteen hands denote different gods and goddesses (*Ibid.*,26), ten hand gestures indicate ten *avatāras* of Viṣṇu (*Ibid.*, 17; *Nāṭyaśāstra Saṁgraha*, pp. 264-279), nine hand gestures symbolize the nine planets (*Abhinayadarpaṇa*, 33, 250-258; *Nāṭyaśāstras Saṁgraha* pp. 320-329), and four hands denote the four castes (*Abhinayadarpaṇa*, 30, 226-230; *Nāṭyaśāstrasaṁgraha*, 274-276).

4940 **हस्तामर्ष**

Hastāmarṣa : touching with hand.

4941 **हस्तामलक**

Hastāmalaka : anything quite clear, as clear as the fruit Embolic Myrobalan held in the hand, one of the four pupils of Śaṅkara.

4942 **हस्तावलम्बन**

Hastāvalambana : the holding of the hand. The holding of the right hand of an unmarried girl indicated betrothal. Thus, when Śiva goes to Pārvatī in the guise of *brahmacārin*, and falls, he says to her, when she tries to help him by giving a hand, that he would not take her left hand which is unholy. She then gives him a right hand, indicating a future marriage (*Skanda*, I.2.25.41).

4943 **हस्तावसेचन**

Hastāvasecana : hand-water.

4944 **हस्ताहस्ति**

Hastāhasti : hand to hand (fight).

4945 **हस्तिनी (स्त्री)**

Hastinī (strī) : the Elephant-lady. The *Ratirahasya* (1.8-19) explains : "She is an Elephant-lady whose walking style is not attractive, whose feet have elevated fat and uneven fingers, whose shoulder is strong but short, whose hair are red in colour, whose actions are crooked, who is very fat, whose fluid of secret part smells like the rut of elephant, who eats more especially pungent and astringent things, who is shameless, who has drooping and very big lip, who is difficult to attain climax in sex-sport, who has hair even on body, whose secret part is wide, who falters in speech." According to *Pañcasāyaka* (2.14) her limbs are fat, cheeks are big, hair are rough and bluish, lips long, shoulders are strong, breasts are big and hard and joints are defective.

She is cruel, shameless, speaks like an ass, bears an ugly face, gets climax with trouble and her vagina is twelve *aṅgulas* in-depth.

4946 **हस्तेन निर्दिशति**

Hastena nirdiśati : points by hand, indicates (*RV*, X. 119.9) : *iha vā antarikṣe ni dadhāni iha vā dyuloke iti hastena nirdiśati.* This line shows that it was thought during the period of *Ṛgveda* that gesticulation was essential to understand the meaning. Indra says, "Ha! May I place this earth here or there (*iha vā, iha vā*)". These words need gesticulation. Sāyaṇa, the commentator adds the remark points by hand. This indicates that the recitation was accompanied by movements of hand and the like.

4947 **हस्तेन स्पृशति**

Hastena spṛśati : the pat. The paternal action. The pat is a kind of miniature embrace performed by the hand alone, without the involvement of the rest of the body. There are greeting pats, congratulatory pats, comforting pats, loving pats, and plain friendly pats. It is known as *thapkī* in Hindi. Children can be patted on almost any part of the body, but with adults the pat must be confined within the sexes on the hand, arm, shoulder or back, if it is to be neutral in character. Both sexes in India agree that pat is the most friendly and playful behaviour.

4948 **हा**

Hā : a particle expressing grief, dejection, pain as expressed by 'ah, alas'; such as *hā priya* Jānakī (*Uttararāmacarita*, Act III); *hā vatse Mālatī kvāsi* (*Mālatīmādhava*, 10).

4949 **हादिविद्या**

Hādividyā : a Tāntric school which was influential in Kerala and Kashmir. The followers of this school held that their *vidyā* came from a source which was known as *Kāmarājavīja*. *Ha* is the symbol of Śiva after which the school was designated : हकारात् शिवरूपत्वं तद् हादितमतमीरितम् (*Śakti-saṅgama*, Tārā, LVIII.81, from Bhattacharya : 1990 :67)

4950 **हायि**

Hāyi : exclamation used in chanting *sāman* (*MBh.*).

4951 **हार**

Hāra : a string of miniature shrines comprising *kūtas, śālas* and *pañjaras* decorating each story of south Indian *vimāna.*

4952 **हार्धकला**

Hārdhkalā : the sex organ drawn on mystic diagrams. It is also known as *haṃsa-pāda* or *yoni.*

4953 **हाव**

Hāva : any feminine coquettish gesture. This gesture calculated to excite amorous sensation. It is one of the twenty *sāttvika alaṁkāras* of the heroine, as enumerated by Bharata, and the second among the three *aṅgaja alaṁkāras.* When desire for union is betrayed by the movements of the eyebrows and the eyes, it is *hāva* (*Sāhityadarpaṇa*, III.94). The sidelong glances of the maiden to disclose that she is no longer an innocent child. *Hāva* being a developed stage of *bhāva*, its external manifestations are more concrete. *Hāva* manifests itself in the changes of eyes and eye-brows and the *recaka* of neck, indicative of the Erotic sentiment.

4954 **हाव-भाव**

Hāva-bhāva : emotion and grace : *hāvabhāvādi saṁyuktam nartanam*, i.e. 'dancing with emotion and grace'.

4955 **हास**

Hāsa : laughter, merriment. The basic urge of the sentiment of humour (*hāsya rasa*). It causes the mind to expand and is the result of a distortion of speech, face, dress, etc. The distortion may be natural or intentionally affected. Inconsistenly, self-contradiction, queer behaviour, etc. are the main excitants of laughter which is described as light-fold, according to the degree of freedom with which it occurs. Humour, wit, irony, satire, ridicule, etc. are some of its varieties (Nagendra, 1987: 63).

The tribes of India are the cheerful people. The isolation has not saddened their laugh. The Hill Marias laugh at everything.

It was at Irkhabhaṭṭī that they laughed at the way the evil spirit oṇḍoraṇḍe pulls the male organ and they laughed at the cost of Baihā, the big hydrocate man of Irkabhaṭṭi. At Kaccāpāl they laughed because a woman had called her husband and cut a joke that the man would not only come but that a ban was imposed on the nocturnal activity meaning thereby the sexual intercourse. At Kutul, the boys laughed so much that they almost doubled themselves and the source of their laughter was the drinking of liquor by the Tahsil peon who had received a good kick by gulping in only one dose of the Hill Maria liquor.

Again, at Kutul, there was laughter all around when five boys ran after a fowl to catch it. The three Marias accompanying the present writer from Kaccāpāl to Kutul laughed heartily after frightening a bear who was digging for roots. At Handāwāṛā there was a roar of laughter when the present writer wanted to know about the prohibition imposed on sexual intercourse when the crop is in *pendā.* These are only some examples to show that in a Hill Maria village there is always mirth and laughter; no trace of sadness and long faces to be seen anywhere.

Hāsa is the permanent state of comic sentiments represented by throbbing of the lips, the nose and the cheeks, opening of the eyes wide or contracting them, perspiration, colour of the face and taking hold of the side. *Hāsya,* is self-centred when a man laughs himself and is centred in others when he makes others laugh.

The middling and inferior characters should have quick steps in different directions in comic.

A particularly expressive aspect of NV communication is laughter. It involves a massive physiological reaction. The contractions of the facial muscles are the most noticeable. But, in addition, there are many contractions of the diaphragm and abdominal muscles, so that the entire body shakes. As we reach full intensity, our blood vessels dilate and the production of tears increases until we may actually weep with laughter.

Most laughter is a response to humour. Different kinds of humour answer different needs. There are five main kinds: aggressive, sexual, social, intellectual and defensive.

Laughing at ourselves or at the macabre allows us to feel relaxed about situations that would be stressful if taken too seriously. Furthermore, making fun of yourself may disarm those might to attack you.

Research shows that men prefer aggressive and sexual humour, while women are more attracted to intellectual and defensive forms. Introverts choose mainly intellectual, social and defensive humour, whereas extroverts tend to like humour that is aggressive or sexual.

A humorous situation can happen by accident, but unusually humour is created by people who have the special talent of making others laugh. They need a good memory for jokes or creative imagination that allows them to link normally unconnected ideas in funny ways. They also need an assertive personality and enough individuality to make the unconventional connections that most humour consists of.

Laughter is composed of a broad range of gestures and sounds. The softest form of audible laughter is the vocalized smile. Its characteristics: mouth slightly open, lips moderately retracted, slight vocal effects or "chuckles". One can, of course, laugh up one's sleeve—silently, through a slightly open mouth. The corners of the mouth turn up, and the air is ejected in a staccato rhythm from the nose. Psychologists call this "risible sniffling".

4956 **हास-दृष्टि**

Hāsa-dṛṣṭi : a type of *bhāva-dṛṣṭi* enumerated by Bharata. Whatever its form, laughter always begins the same way. Our facial muscles contract, especially the nasal dilator, the risorius and the large zygomatic. The salivary and tear glands are activated, while the other muscles in our body tend to relax and our brain produces endorphines (natural morphines) that sooth pain. Closely akin to tear at first, laughter becomes one of the first fruits of the mother-baby relationship. Parents delighted with baby's first laugh turn themselves inside out trying to keep him laughing : giving him smacking kisses on the tummy, bounching him on a daddy'a knee. At around six months, more ritualized games replace mere touching. Faced with these games, baby gradually abandons passivity for an active attitude: "anticipatory laughter" by which he tries to provoke amusing events.

In adults laughter performs three basic functions: it gives pleasure, tightens group relationships and enables the adult to overcome anxiety.

4957 **हास्य**

Hāsya : the sentiment of humour, the comic sentiment. *Hāsya* is self-centred when a man laughs himself and it is centred in others when he makes others laugh. Abhinava points out that when the others laugh, he also laughs even when he does not see the *vibhāva,* or having seen them suppressed his laughter due to dignity (*NS,* I, p.314). In the verses the *anubhāvas* of *hāsya* are classified into six types : *smita* (gentle smile), *hasita* (smile), *vihasita* (gentle laughter), *upahasita* (laughter of ridicule), *apahasita* (vulgar laughter) and *alihasita* (excessive laughter).

Smita and hasita should be employed in the case of superior characters, *vihasita* and *upahasita* in the case of middling ones and *apahasita* and *atihasita* in the case of the inferior types.

(b) a pleasant, affable attitude.

Its basic instinct is to laugh and merriment. Its excitants are distortion of speech, queer actions, dress, appearance, etc. Bharata has given six divisions of *hāsya* : *smita, hasita, vihasita, upahasita, apahasita* and *atihasita.*

The images of comic sentiment are the various features of a dwarf, a hump backed, a fool, or a buffoon. They should be made ridiculous, curious and oddlooking. Their action and movements are to be made so mocking, mimic and uncommon, that the very look of them would make the people burst into laughter (*VD,* 111.43.4). The *hāsya* is to be represented on the stage by consequents (*anubhāva*) like throbbing of the lips, the nose and the cheek, opening the eyes wide or contracting them, colour of the face and taking hold of the sides. The transitory psychological states in it are dissimulation, indolence, drowsiness, sleep, dreaming, insomnia, envy and the like. It is two-fold : *ātmastha* (self-centred) and *parastha* (centred in others). When one himself laughs, it relates to self-centred comic sentiment, when makes others laugh, it is centered in others. In the view of Bharata this sentiment is mostly to be seen in women and men of the inferior type. To the persons of superior type belong the *smitam* (slight smile) and *hasitam* (smile). To those of middle type the *vihasitam* (gentle laughter) and the *upahasitam* (laughter of ridicule), and to those of inferior type the *apahasitam* (vulgar laughter) and *atihasitam* (excessive laughter).

The humour of the Muria (of Bastar) is probably more fully developed than that of any other tribe in Madhya Pradesh. The *ghoṭul* is the natural school of wit. The constant association of young people forces them to devise many forms of entertainment. The first and most elementary expression of Muria humour is plain people with red ants, creeping up behind someone and clasping muddy hands round his face.

The Muria gets a great deal of fun out of dressing up. At wedding, many people appear in fantastic array. If we turn to verbal wit we find a similar tendency.

Hill Marias have great sense of fun and always keep on laughing.

There are five main kinds of humour according to modern psychologists: aggressive, sexual, social, intellectual and defensive. Aggressive humour is directed toward someone, transforming them into a laughable victim. Sexual humour is directed toward women and allows us to feel relaxed about a topic that makes people anxious. Social humour can smooth relations between groups, reinforce group cohesiveness, or — as in political satire try to influence our perceptions of social realities. Intellectual humour allows us a momentary freedom from the tyranny of logical thinking by allowing up to play with words and concepts. Nonsense humour and puns are good examples. Defensive humour can be black humour, making fun of frightening things such as cancer, bad accidents and death. Another form of defensive humour is self-disparagement. Cracking like parrots, or braying like donkeys, our laughter ranges from a brief snigger to completely uncontrollable belly — laughter where we heave, shed tears, and rock about helplessly.

4958 **हास्य-रसदृष्टि**

Hāsya-rasadṛṣṭi : contraction of two eye-lids in turn with eye-balls slightly moving and visible as those of juggler resulting to the comic sentiment. The two eyelids are contracted by turns and the pupils are moving slightly visible It is to be used to produce laughter.

4959 **हा-हा**

Hā-hā : an expression denoting pain, grief or surprise. It is simply *hā* repeated for the sake of emphasis. *Uttararāmacarita* Bhavabhuti records : *hā hā devi sphuṭati hṛdayam.* (3.38)

4960 **हाहाकार**

Hāhākāra : the cry of *hā-hā*, loud wailing (*Mahābhārata*), general lamentation, wailing.

4961 **हिंसा**

Hiṁsā : violence. It is four kinds according to the Jains; the house-holder is enjoined to abstain from *Saṁkalpī-hiṁsā* or intentional violence, but not from accidental (*gṛhārambhī*), occupational (*udyamī*) and protective (*virodhī*) violence. However, one who has renounced the life of a householder must avoid all the four kinds of *hiṁsās.* (b) In the Vedic texts, though violence as a principle is condemed, the killing of animals is prescribed for sacrificial purposes. *Virodhī hiṁsā* may result into laughter where aggression or violence is inappropriae. Freud writes, 'By making an enemy small, inferior, despicable or comic, we achieve in roundabout way the enjoyment of overcoming him'.

4962 **हिक्का**

Hikkā : hiccups. A hiccup is indicative of omens (*Garuḍa P.,'I.* 60.15). If it comes when facing the east it is greatly advantageous; in the south-east it indicates a grief and trouble; in the south loss; in the south-west grief and trouble; and in the west it indicates the gain of sweets (*miṣṭhānnam);* in the north-west it indicates the gain of wealth; in the north it indicates quarrel, and in the north-east death. (b) neck-line based on the principle of horizontal axes when depicting the movement of the different portions of human-form in sculpture.

4963 **हिक्का-सूत्र**

Hikkā-sūtra : a line passing through the base of the neck. In Indian sculpture, the human figure is divided along the three horizontal *sūtras;* namely the *hikkā,* the *bhadra* and *kaṭi* and each unit moves in an opposite direction to the first. Thus, if the head and hips deflect to the right, the torso deviates to the left. The *hikkā-sūtra* is drawn from the armpit, by the side of the hip and the calf, and terminates on the fifth toe of the foot.

4964 **हिक्किका**

Hikkikā : an indistinct sound, Hiccough. *Mahābhārata* (12.283-55) records : *Śukānāmapi sarveṣām hikkikā procyate jvaraḥ.*

4965 **हिङ्कार**

Hiṅkāra : the sound produced to summon a lady for copulation (*Chāndogyopaniṣad,* 2.12. 1-2).

4966 हित-वचन

Hitavacana : speaking always with a view to mankind (Vātsyāyana). It is also to be noted that the virtues relating to speech constitute one of the specific Hindu contributions to ethical knowledge of the words. Thus in *Mahābhārata* (*Rājadharmānuśāsana-parva,* chapter 109) it is frankly recognised that there are circumstances where truth is falsehood and falsehood is truth and the righteous man in such circumstances prefers the later. It was assumed that the ultimate purpose of speech was the good (*hita*) of mankind. Similarly one should seek to be agreeable as well as truthful, and if the plain blunt truth is likely to wound mortally, it is duty to avoid it or at least take off its edge as far as possible.

4967 हितोपदेश

Hitopadeśa : (a) friendly advice. (b) name of a book of fables.

4968 हिन्दुत्व

Hinduttva : Hinduism. The Muslim scholar and traveller Al-Beruni (quoted from Rawlinson's *India*) wrote of the Hindus of medieval India— "They are by nature niggardly in communicating that which they know, and they take the greatest possible care to withhold it from men of another caste among their own people; still much more, of course, from any foreigner. According to their beliefs, there is no country on earth, but theirs, and no created being beside them has any knowledge of science whatever. Their haughtiness is such that if you tell them of any science or knowledge in Khorassan or Persia, they will think you both an ignoramus and a liar. If they travelled and mixed with other nations, they would soon change their minds, for their ancestors were not so narrow-minded as the present generation is".

This sound observation is true of the generality of the Hindus of the present day. Except those who have broadened their outlook by travel and proper study, the Hindus even now believe that there is little good outside their country and little knowledge outside Sanskrit literature. Ancient Hindus were originators of philosophy, arts and sciences, and they did not consider it derogatory to their national or communal pride to study the literature and scientific achievements of their neighbours and adopt what good could be found in other people. Indian astronomers studied Roman and Greek astronomy, and incorporated what was desirable in these systems into their own, magnanimously acknowledged the sources. Further, from the time of Aśoka (3rd century B.C.) till the Arab expansion under Islam, India was the inspiring source of culture in Asia, and her missionaries, Brāhmaṇs, colonists and adventurers carried Indian religions, social and political institutions, ideals of art and architecture to all Asian countries east of Persia; the admirable part India played in civilising the primitive peoples of South East Asia was particularly important. The Hindus made their cultural empires all over the world.

In medieval times, specially after the Muslim conquest, the cultural expansion of India ceased and her people slid into a narrow conservatism which shut out all outside influences and gradually degenerated into a worship of the past. Hindu thinkers could look only to their dead ancestors for guidance and inspiration. Seclusion and separatism became the watch words of Hindu society. Continued foreign aggression and the fear of annihilation in a hostile world were probably responsible for this extreme conservatism and social rigidity adopted by medieval Hindus. Whatever the causes, the result was not happy. Thought became stagnant and progress reactionary. It is no exaggeration to say that Hindu thought did not far advance from the time of the Muslim-rule.

4969 हिरण्य-गर्भ

Hiraṇyagarbha : the great gift (*mahādāna*) connected with the primitive concept of death and resurrection. (b) The Golden womb. Brahmā is called *Hiraṇya-garbha* in *RV* to denote his creative powers (*RV*. X.121.1). The cosmogenic myth then postulated a golden egg instead of a golden womb (*Śatapatha Brāhmaṇa,* II.1.6.1), and this symbol was replaced in turn by the image of the god of the golden seed, an epithet of Agni and Śiva (*Amarakośa,* 1.58). By the time of the Epic, Śiva was also given the original Vedic epithet of *Hiraṇya garbha,* together with the golden seed (*Mbh.*1) This epithat reveals an optimistic personality. It retains creativity, wisdom and capacity for hard work.

4970 हीनयान

Hīnayāna : one of the major forms of Buddhism, the lower vehicle.

4971 हुंकार

Huṁkāra : the humming sound, the sound of *hum,* also used as *huṁ* or *huṁkāra-vāk*; a type of moaning sound made by the female during sexual act (*Śriharṣa, Naiṣadha,* 18.93). Damayantī produces this sound during coition with Nala. Nayacandra Surī (*Hammīrakāvya,* 7.106) has used the sound "*hum-hum*" uttered by a woman during sex-sport. Dāmodaragupta (*Kuṭṭanimatam,* 155) opines that *Huṁkṛti* is made when a woman is bitten. (b) the sound of Brahmā, the Brahmā derived the fire by his *huṁkāra* into two (*Skanda,* V.1.4.7). According to *Brahma-Vaivarta* (*Prakṛtikhaṇḍa,* 39.81-84) the *hum* sound is indicative of vital breath. The *huṁkāra* is mentioned also in the account of Gaṇapati. It is said that when the head of an elephant was fixed on the body of Gaṇapati, Hari uttered the *huṁkāra* over it; and Gaṇapati was brought back to life (*Ibid. Gaṇapatikhaṇḍa,* 12.22). It is said that an old sage at Avanti created water, earth and fire by his mere *huṁkāras* (*Skanda,* V.11.54.14-24).

4972 **हुतासन-मुद्रा**

Hutāsana-mudrā : in both the hands, if nails are curved down inside the palm-pit and the thumb is joined upturned, it is the gesture of *hutāsana* (*VD*).

4973 **हुम्**

Hum : a particle originally an imitative sound expressing remembrance or recollection; as in *huṁ jñātam;* or interrogation in spells and incantations such as *Oṁ kavacāya huṁ.* An example of paralanguage. (b) he who says *huṁ* to a Brāhmaṇa was supposed to be sinner in ancient India (*Yājñavalkya,* III. 292).

4974 **हुलहुली**

Hulahulī : a kind of inarticulate sound uttered by a woman on joyful occasions, whistling. (b) the shepherds whistle to their flocks to guide them (Hiralal and Russell, III.8).

4975 **हू**

Hū : an interjection of calling of contempt. Cf. Tulasīdāsa : *suni kapi bhālu cale kari hūhā* (*Mānasa,* 6.1.10).

4976 **हृद / हृदय**

Hṛda, hṛdaya : heart, the entire being (sensible and intelligent) soul, self, Brahman.

4977 **हृदय-ग्रन्थि**

Hṛdaya-granthi : knot of the heart.

4978 **हृदय-संवाद**

Hṛdaya-saṃvāda : concord, emotive correspondence. The term has been used by Abhinavagupta in his analysis of the response of a cultured speaker to the aesthetic situation. According to him, in such a situation the cultured spectator does not look upon the dramatic characters with feeling of indifference. On the other hand, there is a correspondence, i.e. a kind of identification, with the situation. Through this emotional identification, he relishes the objective situation on a subjective plane: sympathetic attitude of poet and *Sahṛdaya* known as *vāsanā-saṁvāda* or empathy, feeling of generalization in the art and life as well.

4979 **हृदय-स्पर्श**

Hṛdayasparśa : touching the bride's heart. A marriage rite in which the bridegroom touches her right shoulder and her heart and then touches her navel, mentioned in *sūtra* texts.

4980 **हृदयाग्निः वर्धयति**

Hṛdayāgniḥ vardhayati : passion is gnawing (me).

4981 **हृदयानुबन्ध**

Hṛdayānubandha : attachment of heart.

4982 **हृदयालम्बन**

Hṛdayālambana : touching of the heart; a rite in which the bridegroom touches the heart of the bride after *dhruva-darśanam* (*Śiva,* II.47).

4983 **हृन्मुद्रा**

Hṛnmudrā : when the thumb is taken by the fist, it is called the gesture of the heart (*VD*).

4984 **हृष्टा-भावदृष्टि**

Hṛṣṭā-bhāva-dṛṣṭi : a type of glance in *hāsyarasa.* It is a laugh-suggesting look in which the eyeball is not visible distinctly; but looks winkingly, causing the comic. The glance is moving with slightly bent down, with eyeballs slightly visible, with winking, indicative smile. It is used in laughter.

4985 **हे**

Hē : a vocative particle, 'oh, ho', as in *Gītā* (11.41); '*he yādava he sakhēti'.*

4986 **हेड**

Heḍa : displeasure, wrath (*A,* 1.13.10, 5.6.6).

4987 **हेतु**

Hetu (*NS,* 18. 5-11) : form of speech and thought. (b) also known as *liṅga* and *sādhana.* It is the middle term, the 'reason' or connecting the *sādhya* and the *pakṣa* in the Indian system of logic.

4988 **हेतुवादिन्**

Hetuvādin : a Buddhist sect. They were credited with the view that insight is not meant for the man of the world, and that happiness may be passed on to others (Bhattacharya, 1990.68).

4989 **हेत्वाभास**

Hetvābhāsa : a fallacious reason viz. the erratic, the contradictory, the equal to the question, unproved, and the mistimed. This fallacy is of five kinds according to *Nyāya* philosophy. These are *Savyabhicāra* (irregular middle), *Viruddha* (contradictory middle), *Satpratipakṣa* (counter-balanced middle), *asiddha* (unproved middle) and *bādhita* (sublated middle).

4990 **हेमहस्तिरथ**

Hemahastiratha : a *mahādāna* or great gift. It should be a golden chariot resembling a toy-cart in its entirety and contain small images of certain deities (*Matsya*, CCLXXXII).

4991 **हेला**

Helā : amorous sport or dalliance, passion. One of the twenty *sāttvika alaṁkāras* of the heroine, as enumerated by Bharata, and the third among the three *aṅgaja alaṁkāras*. When the external manifestation of the inner desire is very clear, it is *helā* (*Sāhityadarpaṇa*, III.95). The emotion which depends in the erotic sentiment and expresses itself in graceful movements (*lalitābhinaya*) is called *helā* (*NS*, XXII). *Helā* is the emotion arising out of the Erotic sentiment, expressing itself in graceful movements.

4992 **हैरण्यगर्भी-धारणा**

Hairaṇyagarbhī-dhāraṇā : a *yaugic* achievement which enables a person to turn the heaviest thing into the lightest.

4993 **है-हे-प्रयोग**

Hai-hē-prayoga : employment of the words *hai* and *hē*, while addressing a person from a distance, under the rule : *haihe prayoge haihayoḥ* (Pāṇini, *Aṣṭādhyāyī*, 8.2.85). It is a formula relating to paralanguage. It is also one of the colloquial aspects of Sanskrit.

4994 **हो**

Ho : a low person should be addressed as *ho*; or a low person is to be addressed as *ho* by equally low person (*NS*, XVII.65-94).

4995 **होतृ**

Hotṛ : one of the four major kinds of priests required to perform a sacrifice.

4996 **होतृ-दीक्षा**

Hotṛ-dīkṣā : a form of Tantric initiation in which the *guru* offers *homa* for purifying the six quarters (Raghava on *Śāradātilaka* V. 127-40).

4997 **होम**

Homa : offering oblations, a sacrifice.

4998 **होलाका**

Holākā : spring festival (*Rājat.*), holī : the spring festival : It is precisely in order to prevent *saṁkṣobha* or inversions from occurring in real life that the dominant culture in all traditional societies allows these to be simulated at a regular calendric intervals, and in so far as such a culture is almost invariably mediated by religion, the reversals condoned, in fact enjoined, by it, are acted out as sacred rituals. This is made explicit in the celebration of Holī in the course of which these reversals are acted out with vigour and on a scale as at no other occasion of the same kind. Nothing happens at this festival to upset society in spite of the seemingly radical *bouleversement* of the Holī schedule. The *saturnalia*, the systematic violation of structural distances between castes and classes, the defiance of rules governing interpersonal relationships between members of the family and community, the blatant undermining of private and public morality—all of which feature in this ceremony, add up not to a disruption for the political and social order in the village but to its reinforcement. A great deal of verbal and physical violence, inflicted respectively by abusive speech and actual belabouring by cudgels, takes place on this occasion as all observers agree. But there is no punishment. Its overall effect is the "stressing" not overthrowing of the principle of hierarchy, through reversal, a process whereby it remains the structural vertebra of village life.

The Holī festival is observed by the aboriginals of Maikal Hills mainly as an excuse for a drink and a holiday. It is connected by some of them with the death of Rāvaṇa and its chief feature, the burning of a great pile of wood before dawn, is sometimes believed to represent the burning of the corpse of Rāvaṇa on his pyre. The games and songs that follow represent the rejoicing over the death of an enemy. Eleven months later, Rāvaṇa's death ceremonies are performed at the *chhertā* festival, when the people enjoy a feast called *Ravan-chokni-gato*.

The Holī fire is made of any kind of wood, but should have a *semur* pole standing up in the middle. It is considered very lucky if the wooden triangle on which the cobbler drives his cow-hide can be stolen and thrown on the pile of wood. The pyre must be lit before dawn and, if possible, by a virgin that is, by an unmarried boy. When the fire places up the people watch to see which side it will fall. If not goes to the east, it is considered lucky. The *semur* branch is pulled out and the park removed. Bits of cord are made of the bark, and the boys light these at the fire and burn people with them, crying out that "this will take away your sin".

The Holī fire is regarded as 'virgin fire' and has the magical value.

Later in the day and for several days following the people sing the Holī or *Phāg* songs. They sit very close together in a circle round the drums, they sing with great vigour, clapping their hands and gesticulating. In the remoter villages coloured water is not much used. But the women have the right to catch and beat any man who could not purchase his safety with a small present.

The *Holī* or *Phāg* songs are for the most part coarse and obscene with little poetry.

4999 **ह्लाद**

Hlāda : sound, happiness, joy. Cp. *prayatna-viśeṣajanito varṇavirāme' pyanuraṇana-rūpo varṇāntaroccāraṇe'pi anuvartamāno ghoṣaḥ.*

5000 **ह्लादिनी**

Hlādinī : the blissful *Śakti* of the supreme being symbolised of Rādhā (*Caitanyacaritāmṛta* 1.1.5).

ADDENDA

अ A

5001 अग्रभोजन

Agrabhojana : literally first served with food at a feast; implying a Brāhmaṇa who has read the *Yajur, Sāma* and *Atharva - uedas* (Garg.,226). Brāhmaṇa had societal connotations and dining them first encouraged relaxation.

5002 अङ्कलक्षण

Aṅka-lakṣaṇa : a fire or mark branded on cattle; (b) a rite performed on the New Moon day after the Phālguna Full Moon. The marked conveys a more specified and delimited conception than the unmarked.

5003 अङ्गकर्म

Aṅgakarma : action on the stage are of two kinds. One is to express by the major organs of the body. The other is to express by the minor organs of the body. Head, etc. are the major organs and the eyebrows, etc. are the minor organs. Actions expressed by the major organs are called *aṅgakarma* and those by minor organs *pratyaṅga-karma* (*Agni-Purāṇa*, 341).

5004 अङ्गत्व-बोधक-प्रमाण

Aṅgatva-bodhaka-pramāṇa : according to *Mīmāṁsā*, the list of principles by which one could decide whether there obtains a subsidiary relation or not. They are *śruti* (direct assertion), *liṅga* (indication), *prakarana* (context), *sthāna* (proximity), *vākya* (syntactical relation) and *samākhyā* (designation).

5005 अङ्गुलि-तोरण

Aṅguli-toraṇa : the semi-circular lines drawn across the forehead by Shaivites. They are made of sandlewood powder or the ashes of burned cow-dung; and are usually called *tripuṇḍra.* (b) to crack the fingers at someone is one method of putting a curse on him in central India.

5006 अङ्गुलीय-मुद्रा

Aṅgulīya-mudrā : a finger ring-seal. The seal is engraved with the name of the wearer; and the surface being smeared superficially only with ink.

5007 अजपा

Ajapā : automatic chanting, which cannot be chanted or which is controlled and administered by the inhaling and exhaling of breath. The number of breaths in one day and night is taken to be 21,600 and this inhaling and exhaling of breath is considered an automatic 'chanting'. This automatic 'chanting' goes on from birth to death.

5008 अजहल्लक्षणा

Ajahallakṣaṇā : non-exclusive implication. When the primary meaning of a sentence is not adequate to convey a coherent idea, then the secondary meaning is resorted to. In this case, the primary meaning is not totally rejected, but is retained and added to by the implied meaning, e.g. "The white runs" means that the white horse runs. The primary meaning of "white" is retained, and clarified by adding to it the implied meaning namely 'horse'.

5009 अज्ञातवास

Ajñātavāsa : remaining incognito, said of the Pāṇḍavas, when they remained incognito.

5010 अञ्जन

Añjana : act of anointing an object, especially anointing of axle of a chariot by the newly married girl with clarified butter. (b) Salve or collyrium brought from the *Trikakuda* mountain. The eye-ointment is supposed to give protection against demons and spells, as well as curing jaundice and other diseases (*Atharva Veda*, 4.9).

5011 अञ्जनसिद्धि

Añjanasiddhi : a magical ointment applied to the eyes, power of ointment, one of the magical devices (*Skanda P.* IV.45.13).

5012 अञ्जलिक्रिया

Añjalikriyā : offering the sacred handful of water (Kālidāsa, *Kum.*, 8.154).

5013 अट्टालिका

Aṭṭālikā : upper storey, *aṭārī* in the dialects of Hindi. *Aṭārī* is the loft or upper storey of a substantial village house which occurs in the *Dadariā* songs of Chhattisgarh:

> Above in the loft is my bed
> He climbed up by the ladder
> The *dewar* is playing
> In his *bhaujī's* bed.

It is from this loft that the shy heroine of many a ballad looks down and sees the hero; it is in such lofts, with their comparative remoteness and privacy, that lovers find a convenient meeting-place.

Another song, from a Pankā of Bilaspur, has the same theme:

> In the newly built loft
> you have put your bangles
> Joy-giver, in my loving mind
> You have put delight.

5014 **अतत्वाभिनिवेष**

Atatvābhiniveṣa : paramnesia, or falsification of memory (*Charaka*, 7.5). Literally the term means having faith in what is false, wrong or untrue. So delusion and perversion are also included here. It is attributed to suppression of urges.

5015 **अतिदूरावनतेन**

Atidūrāvanatena : he bent his head far away in order to show his respect for her, indicating that he was inferior to her (*Kādambarī*, p.10). A lowered head is a sign of submission.

5016 **अधिवास**

Adhivāsa : hair-decoration through wreaths, etc. (Kālidāsa, *Raghu.*, 8.118). The powerful symbolism of hair winds its way through thousands of years of Indian history. Perhaps no other part of our anatomy has been subject to so many decorations, changes, substitutions and superstitions.

5017 **अधीतिनी**

Adhītinī : a lady observed in studies (Kālidāsa, *Kum.*, 5.73).

5018 **अधोरत**

Adhorata : lower type of unusual congress practised on the anus. It is mostly prevalent, according to Vātsyāyana, in the southern regions (*Kāmasūtra*, 2.6.49).

5019 **अनपत्यता**

Anapatyatā : being issueless. It was considered to be one of the worst curses by the Vedic Ārya (*Ṛgveda*, III. 54.18), because it was primarily the right of a son to perform *aurdhvadaihika* or the after death rituals of his father (*Śākuntalam*, 6.528).

Childlessness is also a curse among Gonds. If a woman is childless, she should worship *Būṛhādeo* and fast continuously, and then on the termination of her monthly impurity, after she has bathed, if she walks across the shadow of a man she will have a child. It is thus supposed that the woman can be made fertile by the man's shadow, which will be the father of the child. Or she should go on a Sunday night naked to a *Sāj* tree (Boswellia Serrata) and pray to it, and she may have a child. The *Sāj* is the tree in which Būṛhādeo resides, and was probably in the beginning itself the god. Here it is supposed that the woman is impregnated by the spirit of the tree, as Hindu women think that they can be made fertile by the spirits of unmarried Brāhmaṇa boys living in Pīpal trees. Or she may have recourse to the village priest, the *Bhumkā* or *Baigā*, who probably finds that her barren condition is the work of an evil spirit and propitiates him (Russell and Hiralal, III. 84).

5020 **अनवीकृत**

Anavīkṛta : monotonous repetition. If the same word is used time and again in a verse, one finds the monotony irksome.

5021 **अनालम्भुका**

Anālambhukā : a woman in menstruation. A sacrifice is to be carried on by the sacrificer himself; debarring his wife who becomes 'untouchable' on the day of the sacrifice.

5022 **अनुगमन**

Anugamana : the performance of *satī* by a woman whose husband has died in a distant country; a sandal, or any article of his clothes may then represent him. It seems also to have the name of *anumaraṇa*.

5023 **अनुचितार्थ**

Anucitārtha : improper signification. What is not appropriate to the context it is to be avoided. If an expression requiring dignified words is given an undignified colouring, it looks inapt and indecorous.

5024 **अनुधूपवासम्**

Anudhūpavāsam : dying and drying the hair with incense (Kālidāsa, *Raghu.*, 16.239).

5025 **अनुमितिवाद**

Anumitivāda : A theory of poetics ascribed to Śaṅkuka. According to this theory, *rasa* is not produced as an effect, but inferred by the spectators, and inferred feeling is relished by them as *rasa*. Śaṅkuka's works are not extant. His view has been cited by later writers on poetics.

5026 **अनुरक्तचेष्टा**

Anuraktaceṣṭā : amorous gestures, calling gestures, signs of love. Varāhamihira (LXVIII) thinks that 'love arising from sexual desire is revealed by telle-tale blush etc. by exposing the navel, arms, bosoms and ornaments, by retying the garments, by loosening the locks, by twitches and tremblings of the brows, and by side-long glances :

स्नेहं मनोभवकृतं कथयन्ति भावा
नाभीभुजस्तनविभूषणदर्शनानि ।
वस्त्राभिसंयमनकेशविमोक्षणानि
भ्रूक्षेपकम्पितकटाक्षनिरीक्षणानि ॥

Cf. Kasyapa in this regard :

अनुरागस्थिता रक्ता विरक्ता वेशमानिनी ।
मनोदृष्टिनिबन्धेन हृदयेनाकुलीकृता ॥
आकारलिङ्गभेदैश्च ज्ञायते याऽनुरागिणी ।
विक्षिप्तमन्यचित्तत्वं गुरुगेहेऽप्यगोपनम् ॥
आह्लादनं च शब्देन यस्याः सा रागरञ्जिता ।
अतोऽपरा तु या नारी सा विरक्तेति कीर्तिता ॥

Other symbols/signs of love are: a loud clearing of the throat and spitting, loud laughter in the presence of the lover, walking towards his seat or bed (or getting up from her seat or bed and walking towards him), producing sounds with limbs, yawning, asking for trivial and easily available things, embracing and kissing a child, looking significantly at a female friend, casting glances on him when he looks elsewhere, recounting his virtues, and scratching the ears. A damsel who speaks sweetly, spends her own money (for his sake), feels delighted on seeing him, forgets her anger, drowns his faults by extolling his virtues, honours his friends, hates his enemies, feels grateful to him for his good turns, feels miserable when he is away, offers her bosom and lips, embraces him, perspires, and kisses him first, is also to be understood as one deeply attached through her actions :

उच्चैः ष्ठीवनमुत्कटप्रहसितं शय्यासनोत्सर्पणं
गात्रास्फोटनजृम्भणानि सुलभद्रव्याल्पसम्प्रार्थना ।
बालालिङ्गनचुम्बनान्यभिमुखे सख्याः समालोकनं
दृक्पाताश्च पराङ्मुखे गुणकथा कर्णस्य कण्डूयनम् ॥
इमां च विन्द्यादनुरक्तचेष्टा प्रियाणि वक्ति स्वधनं ददाति ।
विलोक्य संहृस्याति वीतरोषा प्रमार्ष्टि दोषान् गुणकीर्त्तनेन ॥
तन्मित्रपूजा तदरिद्विषत्वं कृतस्मृतिः प्रोषितदौर्मनस्यम् ।
स्तनौष्ठदानान्युपगूहनं च स्वेदोऽथ चुम्बनप्रथमाभियोगः ॥

Viśvanātha has presented similar ideas in his *Sāhityadarpaṇa* (III. 140-152). Kaśyapa has also the same reading:

दृष्टिर्निक्षिपते तत्र मनसापि विचिन्तयेत् ।
मूलैर्न रक्षते सा तु चित्रं चित्रपटं यथा ॥
अकस्मात् पुरतो भूत्वा कश्चिदाभिलषति भृषाम् ।
ऊरू नितम्बे नाभी च भूषणानि पयोधरौ ॥
करजैरुत्किरेन्नाभिमनुरागेण रञ्जिताम् ।
जृम्भते ष्ठीवतेऽत्यर्थं वाग्दुष्टानि ददाति सा ॥
कुमारालिङ्गनं चैव दहानैरधरं दरोत् ।
एभिर्विकारैर्विज्ञेया मदनार्ता तु कन्यका ॥
दर्शनाद् हृष्यते या तु मित्रयक्षं च पूजयेत् ।
स्मितं पराङ्मुखं पश्येद् गुणांश्चैवानुकीर्तयेत् ॥

5027 **अनुरागिणी-लक्षण**

Anurāgiṇī-lakṣaṇa : signs of desire and love. According to Guṇapatāka (*Ratirahasya*, 4.25-27), the signs of desire are identical both in women who have already experienced caution and those who have not.

A girl who licks at her lips, whose eyes stay about like fish in water, who wears flowers in her hair, binds it up and then lets it down again, whose breasts show through her clothes, her buttocks likewise—whose girdle keeps slipping however tightly she ties it - all these serve in a woman to make known that she is in love. If she longs for a man, often his face, his good looks, his conversation, his virtues and his affections are praised; and if when he is not present, she delights in hearing news of his acquaintances and his friends - these too are the signs that she is in love.

Anaṅgaraṅga adds further signs by which a man can find out that the woman is attached towards him. They are : (1) when the woman blushes at the sight of the man; (2) when she does not look straight in the face of the man; (3) scratches the earth with toe while standing; (4) uncovers the body on some pretext; (5) laughs without cause; often castes side-glances; (6) when being asked a question, she answers slowly in unaudible voice with smile; (7) when she follows the man while walking on the pretext of some conversation in order to keep his company for a long time; (8) when at the sight of the beloved attracts his attention by loud talks on the excuse of speaking to some other person; i.e. she wants to hide her real intention from the person to whom she is speaking while she wants to draw the attention of her lover; (9) when she makes friendship and repeatedly enquires about many things concerning him, such as who are the women who frequently visit his house; are they beautiful? Whom does he love most? and so on; (10) when at the sight of the lover, she presses her breasts with her hands, cracks her fingers while yawning; (11) when she does not appear before her lover though repeatedly solicited unless she is well-dressed; (12) when she throws playful flowers and similar objects at the lover, laughs for a long time; rubs the palms of the hand or fidgets with the hands; (13) when she goes to the house of the lover on any pretext; when her hands, feet and face perspire at the sight of the lover; (14) the skilled lover, being assured of these signs that the woman is attracted towards him, should without any fear, send a *dūtī* (messenger) to her (*Anaṅgaraṅga* 8.43-48;*Ratiratnapradīpikā*, 7.67.82; *Ratikallolinī*, 41).

5028 **अनुवक्त्र**

Anuvaktra : a form of kiss. In this the husband and wife, while kissing each other as described under *sampuṭa* (i.e.

when both lips of one are taken and pressed between both lips of the other), play with each other's tongue (*Anaṅgaraṅga.* 9.19). It is now known as 'French' kissing or kissing involving the tongue. It combines the exchange of bonding chemicals and the deeply rooted ancestral memories of babyhood.

5029 **अनुवृत्ति**

Anuvṛtti : continuity, repetition. When an aphorism or a part of it is necessary for completing the sense of the following one or more aphorisms, it is said that the first has *anuvṛtti.* This technique is frequently used by Pāṇini to shorten the lengths of the *sūtras* (aphorisms) in his *Aṣṭādhyāyī.*

5030 **अनुव्रजन**

Anuvrajana : to follow some distance, when distinguished visitors or guests return. When some distinguished person comes to one's house, one should lead and the guest should follow; but on return of the guest, one should follow him.

5031 **अनुश्राविक**

Anuśrāvika : matters heard or revealed (pertaining to life hereafter). One cultivates disinterest not only in the object seen but objects or states promised in scriptures such as going to heaven or attaining 'a discarnate state' or dissolution in primordial matter.

5032 **अनुष्ठान**

Anuṣṭhāna : performance of sacred rites (Kālidāsa, *Śāk.* 4.343).

5033 **अनुसन्धान**

Anusandhāna : literal meaning recollection, or recovery or recapturing. It is a term used to explain the mental state of the actor while acting. It is to signify the state of mind in which the actor imaginatively tries to recapture the mental or physical behaviour of the original character and thus identifies himself with him.

5034 **अन्तःपुरिका-वृत्त**

Antaḥpurikā-vṛtta : case-history of the elite-women, description of the women of royal haremy. The women of royal haremy (*ranivās* in Hindi) cannot see or meet any person because they are strictly guarded. They do not have their sexual passions satisfied because the only husband is common to many wives. It is for this reason that they among themselves give pleasure to each other in various ways as follows.

Having dressed the daughters of their nurses, or their female friends, or their female attendants, like men, they satisfy their passions by means of bulbs, roots, or fruits of the form of the penis; or they lie down upon the statues of male figures in which the male organ is visible and erect. Some kings, who are considerate, take certain medicines to enable them to enjoy many wives in one night, simply for the purpose of satisfying the desire of their women, though they perhaps have no desire of their own. Others enjoy only those wives for whom they have a liking, while others take them as the turn of each wife comes, in due course. Some ladies of the royal harem get men into their apartments in the disguise of or dress of women; this is invariably done through their female attendants and daughters of their nurses (*Kāmasūtra,* 6.5. 1-5).

When the king rises from his midday nap, the woman, who is detailed to inform the king regarding the wife who is to spend the night with him, should come to him accompanied through the female attendants of that wife, whose turn may have arrived in the regular course, and of her who may have been accidently possessed over as her turn arrived, and of her who may have been indisposed at the time of her turn. These attendants should place before the king the ointments and unguents sent by each of these wives, marked with seal of her ring; and their names and their reasons for sending the ointments should be told to the king. After this the king accepts the ointment of one of them, who then is informed that her ointment has been accepted and that her day has been fixed.

At festivals and other parties and exhibitions, all the wives of the king should be treated with respect and served with drinks.

But the women should not be allowed to go out alone, nor any woman outside the *ranivās* be allowed to enter it except those whose character is well established. And finally, the work done by king's wives should not be too fatiguing (*Kāmasūtra,* 4.2.55-56; *Kandarpa-Cūḍāmaṇi,* 6.6.1-49).

5035 **अन्यदेश्य**

Anyadeśya : borrowed. The name given to words derived from foreign languages.

5036 **अन्यपूर्वा**

Anyapūrvā : the literal meaning of the word is: *anya* 'another', *pūrvā* 'before'. Any girl who has been given in marriage by word, or if married to another, is called *anyapūrvā.* According to Kāśyapa, these are of seven types and should not be accepted in marriage. Such girls are considered wretched and they ruin the family to which they go. These seven types are: one who has been given to another by word in mind, after celebrating the marriage, after touching water, or just handed over, or after circumambulation, or a daughter born of a mother who had already been married to another.

5037 **अन्वाधेय**

Anvādheya : gift received by a girl subsequent to her marriage, from her parents and husband's families. Such a gift shall go to her offspring, even she dies in the lifetime of her husband (*Manu.*, 9.195).

5038 **अन्वारम्भ**

Anvārambha : 'to seize someone from behind' by the shoulder, by a flap of garment, especially in a processional march which the priests participate; the sacrificer touches the *adhvaryu*, the wife touches the sacrificer, and other relatives touch the wife.

5039 **अन्वाहार्य**

Anvāhārya : rice meant for sacrificial fee for the priests. Literary rice which is supplemented. *Anvāhārya-pacana* is another name of *dakṣiṇāgni* on which *anvāhārya* rice is cooked. *Anvāhārya-sthalī* is a dish on which the said rice is cooked. (b) *anvāhārya* is a monthly *śrāddha* performed immediately after the *piṇḍapitṛyajña*.

5040 **अपथ्य**

Apathya : food-avoidance. Food injunctions to a *yogī*, should not be taken. Such foods are: bitter, sour, saltish, hot, fermented, oily, intoxicating, liquors, fish, meat, oilcakes, garlic, onion etc. All such foods which cause a burning sensation should be avoided. Compare *mitāhāra*.

5041 **अपमान**

Apamāna : insult. Functionally, insult behaviour is designed to have some negative effect on the addressee. That is, at least part of the intended function of an insult is to in some way injure the feelings or lower the self-esteem of the addressee. It may also have functions such as the elicitation of some sort of behaviour from the addressee, but the defining function here is the intended malice.

The central point of our definition, the point that makes the study of insult behaviour particularly productive, however, is that insults are predicated on some shared cultural value. That is, for an insult to perform its malicious function it must make a comment that in some way links the addressee and a cultural value. The structural features of children's insults include, on the stylistic dimension, a hostile and aggressive delivery and, on the content dimension, some statement about the addressee's deviation from a culturally defined value. Insults in India accuse the addressee of deviance from some cultural value. Insult is formulaic in the sense that any number of cultural values can be utilized as content. The formula, can, therefore, be used productively, and the content will always include a value statement.

The most general kind of sequencing in India is that an insult calls for some kind of response. It is almost as if it were a game in which one of the rules is that failure to respond appropriately brings about a loss in points. One of the stylistic features that demonstrates this powerful rule to respond is the rapidity with which responses are made.

5042 **अपरत्व**

Aparatva : spatial and temporal proximity. In *vaiśeṣika*, one of the categories (*padārtha)* is quality (*guṇa*). The 12th quality is *aparatva* and it gives rise to perception of spatial and temporal nearness.

5043 **अपरुद्ध**

Aparuddha : turmoil, anarchy. This term is akin to similar terms like *arājatā*, or *arājatam* or *arājaka*. It can be traced to early texts like the *Atharvaveda* (3.3.4). The distinction between *aparuddha* and *arājatā* is that, whereas the latter indicates a period of no rule, the former points to the attempts of kings, who were expelled from their kingdoms, to regain their rule and to prevent their actual expulsion.

5044 **अपवित्र**

Apavitra : impure. Goṇd's were looked as an impure caste, and were practically in the same position as the Mahārs and Camārs. So they had usually a separate row of quarters and were not permitted to draw water from the village well or enter temples. Their touch defiled and a Hindu did not give anything into the hands of one of the caste while holding it himself, but used to throw it down in from of these impure castes, and took anything from them in the same manner (Russell and Hiralal, III. 17).

5045 **अपहस्तक**

Apahastaka : a type of striking. A kind of striking in love where the lover strikes on the body of the beloved by back of the palm (*Kāmasūtra*, 2.7.3; *Ratiratnapradīpikā*, 6.56).

5046 **अपात्र**

Apātra : impersonal, not the composition of any person. The *Vedas* are said to be impersonal as they were revealed by Ṛṣis and not composed by them. They are held to be eternal and authorities. (b) non-person. We have created, all over the world, a virtually unacknowledged race of people. These people have been called '*apātra*' (non-persons), and are those whose existence we virtually ignore, such as Bhaṅgis, newspaper-sellers and different religious groups.

5047 **अभिघात**

Abhighāta : a type of contact producing sound, striking.

5048 **अभिचार**

Abhicāra : a magical spell for securing some malevolent purpose (*HC*, II). When one wants to spell, a *caru* (oblation of rice) with red powder is sprinkled. Sometimes blood is also sprinkled with *caru.*

5049 **अभिनयवस्तु**

Abhinayavastu : theme presented through acting (Kālidāsa, *Māl.*, 1.29).

5050 **अभिनयविद्या**

Abhinayavidyā : art of acting (Kālidāsa, *Mal.*, 1.14).

5051 **अभिनयाचार्य**

Abhinayācārya : expert in the art of acting (Kālidāsa, *Māl.*, 1.13).

5052 **अभियोग**

Abhiyoga : meeting with the beloved. In case a lover had a meeting with some beloved at a certain place, he should not meet another at the same place (*Kāmasūtra*, 5.2.25). As the bathing-*ghāṭ* of a pond or a river practically gives an outsider the only opportunity of meeting a girl in India', says D.C. Sen (III.209), 'it is quite natural that the place becomes often the meeting-ground of lovers.' In the Bengal ballads there are many charming scenes where the heroine is found alone with her water-pot and is wooed and often won. Sonai and her royal lover meet on a river bank. Chand Binod sees Malua for the first time at a bathing-*ghāṭ*. The washer-maiden Kanchan falls in love with her prince on the bank of a pond. From the window of his palace Shyam Ray sees the Dom girl bathing and never forgets her.

In a Punjabi-song (Temple, *JASB*, LI.195), the lover declares:

> I was going to the watering-place to draw water,
> And my lover met me on the road;
> All my trouble went away altogether,
> And my heart blossomed greatly like a flower.

5053 **अभिवादन-संस्कार**

Abhivādana-saṁskāra : ceremonial greetings, particularly on the marriage ceremony. The aboriginal way of greeting is presented here. Bride and bridegroom sit down under the booth after the *baṛe bhānwar*. Their *susain* sits behind them. A dish of *haldī* is placed before them and a pot of water, and everyone comes in turn for the ceremonial greeting. First they wash their feet, then put a mark of rice and *haldī* on their foreheads with similar offerings of *haldī* to the *mangarohan* and the *kalaśa* pot, and finally give any present that they may have brought. When this continues women break into the wild disordered *Birhā* dance:

> My feet itch for sounding anklets
> My forehead itches for a spangle
> My life itches for a slender girl
> Let me search for her in the bazar.

This is a long and tedious ceremony.

5054 **अभिषेक-दुन्दुभि**

Abhiṣeka-dundubhi : the drum that is beaten at the time of crowning a prince. Bāṇa has indicated (*HC*, IV) that the whole world rejoiced at the birth of Harṣa who was destined to be a great emperor.

5055 **अभ्युत्थान**

Abhyutthāna : getting up to receive. A guest is worthy to be worshipped; to get up to receive the guest is called *abhyutthāna.*

5056 **अमङ्गल**

Amaṅgala : inauspicious. Many things and actions are considered inauspicious and before marriage ceremony, travel and new venture, such inauspicious signs are to be avoided.

5057 **अमावस्या**

Amāvasyā : new-moon-day. The moon is said to be the recipient of a part of the fire from the forehead of Śiva (*Skanda*, 1.2.24.42). On this day moon is said to enter the plants; none is to churn butter on this day; if he does his cattle would die; not to start on a journey on this day; if one does, his ancestors would have to eat sand for a month.

Amāvasyā is also known as *amā*. It is the day of ritual in honour of the manes.

5058 **अमोघपुटिका**

Amoghapuṭikā : small box. According to an account Vasu, the king of the Soma dynasty and the ruler of Jambūdvīpa, was engaged in vanquishing the Mlecchas. He was out of capital for a long while. When his wife, Satyabhāmā, got her menstruation, she sent a message to the king through a parrot. The king got the message. He collected his semen in a small well-built box (*amoghapuṭikā*) and sent it to the capital for the queen, with same parrot (*Skanda*, V.3 97.20-68, *Śiva*, V.44. 10-25).

5059 **अम्बुज-मुद्रा**

Ambuja-mudrā : separate the fingers of the two hands each facing counter-part forming a semi-circle keep half-an-inch distance between the respective fingers and carry on chanting *mantra* invoking desired deity.

5060 **अम्बुवीची**

Ambuvīcī : wetland. *Brahmavaivarta Purāṇa* (1.8.62) records that it is sin to dig it: *ambuvīcī-bhūkhananam.* The *ambuvīcī* stage of earth is believed to be of her menstruation (*Ibid.*, 9.14).

5061 **अयत्न-साध्या**

Ayatna-sādhyā : a woman who is easily gained over. According to *Kāmasūtra*, the characteristics of such a woman are as follows: (1) women who stand at the door of their houses; (2) women who are always looking out in the street; (3) women who sit covering in their neighbouring house; (4) a woman who is always staring at someone; (5) a female messanger; (6) a woman who looks sideways; (7) a woman whose husband has taken another wife without any just cause; (8) a woman who hates her husbands or hated by; (9) a woman who has nobody to look after her; (10) a woman who has not had any child; (11) a woman whose family or caste is not well known; (12) a woman whose children are dead; (13) a woman who is very fond of society; (14) a woman who is outwardly very affectionate to her husband; (15) the wife of an actor; (16) a widow; (17) a poor woman; (18) a woman fond of enjoyment; (19) the wife of a man with many younger brothers; (20) a vain woman; (21) a woman whose husband is inferior to her in rank or ability; (22) a woman who is proud of her skill in arts; (23) a woman disturbed in mind by the folly of her husband; (24) a woman who has married in her infancy to a rich man; (25) a woman who is slighted by her husband without any cause; (26) a woman who is not respected by other women; (27) a woman whose husband is devoted to travelling; (28) the wife of a jeweller; (29) a jealous woman; (30) a covetous woman; (31) an immoral woman; (32) a barren woman; (33) a lazy woman; (34) a cowardly woman; (35) a humpbacked woman; (36) a dwarfish woman; (37) a deformed woman; (38) a vulgar woman; (39) an ill-smelling woman; (40) a sick woman and (41) an old woman (*Kāmasūtra.*, 5.1.51-54).

5062 **अरणि**

Araṇi : a typical Vedic word (*Ṛgveda.*, 1.127.4) for the piece of wood for generating holy fire. For Vedic sacrifices fire was produced by rubbing two pieces of wood against each other (*Kumāra*, 6.101).

5063 **अरण्यपण्डित**

Araṇyapaṇḍita : wise in forest. A foolish person, who can display his learning only in a forest where no will hear him and correct his errors.

5064 **अरण्य-शिष्यपरम्परा**

Araṇya-śiṣyaparamparā : forest disciple-tradition. In the disciple-tradition of Śaṅkarācārya, there is a sub-name *araṇya.* This *araṇya*-tradition was instrumental in the revival of the *Sanātana dharma.* The first forest disciple appointed by Śaṅkarācārya was Padmapāda. Padmapāda had two disciples: *tīrtha* and *āśrama.* (Fig. - 5064)

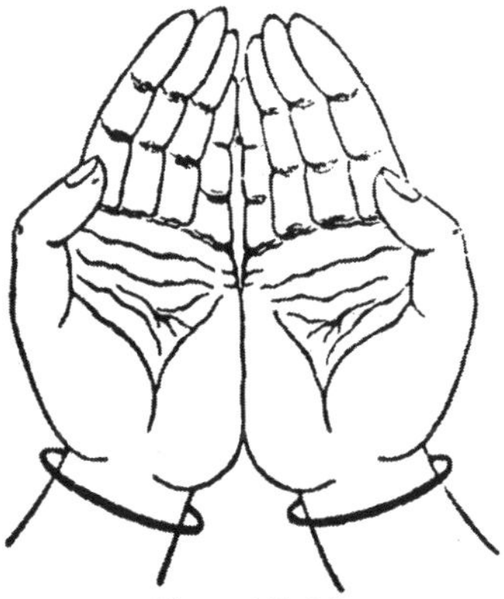

Fig. - (5064)

5065 **अर्घ**

Argha : reception. It is the special emblem of Pārvatī. *Argha* is the cup or circle from which the *liṅga* rises, its cover-edge or rim being the *yoni.* The *argha* or reception ceremony in honour of a bridegroom is performed by his father-in-law. *Argha* is also performed of a newly married couple on their return to the bridegroom's house. It is known as *parghāv* in Bagheli. *Argha* is also performed in honour of the guests.

5066 **अर्थक्रियाकारित्व**

Arthakriyākāritva : the doctrine of casual efficiency, practical efficiency. The power of performing actions and purposes of some kind.

5067 **अर्थक्रियाज्ञान**

Arthakriyājñāna : knowledge attained by practical efficiency.

5068 **अर्थक्रियासिद्धि**

Arthakriyāsiddhi : the fulfilment of any need; the accompaniment of producing any action or event.

5069 **अर्थगौरव**

Arthagaurava : depth in meaning. This is formed in the works especially of Bhāravi.

5070 **अर्थचित्र**

Arthacitra : variegated meaning, striking import meaning. Non-suggestive poetry representing a striking idea conveyed through denotation constitutes this variety which is generally illustrated in single verse.

5071 **अर्थलक्षण**

Arthalakṣaṇa : as opposed to *Śabdalakṣaṇa;* determined by the purpose or need.

5072 **अर्थव्यक्ति**

Arthavyakti : expressiveness, explicit of meaning. Bharata regards expressiveness as natural realistic description of activity in well-known predicates or the capacity to make the content intelligible simultaneously with the hearing of the word. Daṇḍin describes it as freedom from far-fetchedness.

5073 **अर्थव्यत्यय**

Arthavyatyaya : the ancient thinkers enunciated the principle of *arthavyatyaya* to indicate two kinds of changes which generally take place in the connotation of words. The first change is from wide connotation to narrow connotation. For example, the word *kāma* in Vedic terminology is a word with a wide connotation standing in general for desire. But gradually in usage, the connotation narrowed down so that in later times it stood for sex desire in particular. The second kind of change is from a narrow connotation to a wider one. For example, the word *kuśāgra* meant originally the tip of *kuśa* grass. Later on it became widened so that it stood for anything that is sharp.

5074 **अर्थसंशय**

Arthasaṁśaya : doubt about the wealth. When a courtesan is not certain how much a man may give her or spend upon her, this is called a doubt about the wealth (*Kāmasūtra,* 6.6.21).

5075 **अर्थानुपपत्ति**

Arthānupapatti : contradiction of the present perception with a previously acquired certain knowledge.

5076 **अर्वाचीन**

Arvācīna : recent, determinate and indeterminate perception. They are two-fold: *indriyasāpekṣa* (dependent on senses) and *indriya-anapekṣa* (independent of the senses); see *pratyakṣa.*

5077 **अलकचूर्ण**

Alakacūrṇa : powder to polish the hair (Kālidāsa, *Kum* 8.147).

5078 **अलक्षण**

Alakṣaṇa : indefinable, without any sign or mark.

5079 **अलङ्करण**

Alaṅkaraṇa : decoration of mourners which consists of shaving etc.; it also denotes application of collyrium to eyes by women.

5080 **अल्पकाल**

Alpakāla : a short time. *Bhagavad Gītā* defines it as follows, "Take two tender leaves of a lotus and place one on the other. Let a strong man take a sharp needle and thrust it hard at the leaves. The time taken for the needle to pierce one leaf and reach the other is *alpakāla.* "

5081 **अल्पसाध्या**

Alpasādhyā : a woman who can be won over by little effort. Such occasions are: when she is tired after dance, sports; long absence from sexual act; the earlier stages of pregnancy; a month after child-birth; after menstrual flow; when dull or sleepy; when unusually merry and happy; during rainy or spring seasons or on her first sexual experience (*Anaṅgaraṅga,* 4.36-37).

5082 **अवक्षेपण**

Avakṣepaṇa : downward motion.

5083 **अवगुण्ठनवती**

Avaguṇṭhana-vatī : (*Māl,.* V; *Śāk.,* V) or veiled indicates that in Kālidāsa's time there was a custom to cover the face of the bride, in whose case it was an indication of *lajjā.* However, among other women the custom of veil does not seem to be in vogue. The *purdāh* system came to India only later in Medieval period.

5084 **अवपीडितक**

Avapīḍitaka : kissing type. A kind of kissing which is affected by taking hold of the lower lip by two fingers and then after touching it with the tongue, pressing it with great force with the lips (*Kāmasūtra.,* 2.3.11-12; *Kandarpacūḍāmaṇi,* 2.3.13-14; *Ratiratnapradīpikā,* 3.41).

5085 **अवभृत**

Avabhṛta : the bath that was taken at the completion of a sacrifice (*Ṛgveda.,* VIII.93.23) For the bodily purification bath was considered to be very important part of any Vedic ritual. It was taken both in the beginning of a *yajña* and at the end of a *yajña (Raghu.,* 1.12).

5086 **अवमर्दन**

Avamardana : rubbing. In the *Kāmaśāstra,* when the lower part of the female organ is struck, it is called *avamardana* (*Kāmasūtra.*, 2.8.24; *Kandarpacūḍāmaṇi*, 2.8.27).

5087 **अवर्ण**

Avarṇa : blame. For censure there are ten items in *Amarakośa*, of which *jugupsā* and *kutsā* are noteworthy.

5088 **अवर्णक्षेत्रसम्भवा**

Avarṇakṣetrasambhavā : a daughter not born of a wife of the same caste as that of the husband (Kālidāsa, *Śāk.*, 1.62); indicative of the intercaste marriage.

5089 **अवस्थाचतुष्टय**

Avasthācatuṣṭaya : the four periods of states in a man's life: They are *bālya* (childhood up to the age of 15), *kaumārya* (youth, from 15 to 30), *yauvana* (manhood, from 30 to 50), and *vārdhakya* (old age, thereafter). These age limits are given in the *Āyurveda* works.

5090 **अवस्थादशक**

Avasthā-daśaka : the ten stages of love. These according to the writers of poetics are: *abhilāṣā* (longing), *cintā* (anxiety), *smṛti* (recollection), *guṇakathana* (praising), *udvega* (agitation), *pralāpa* (lamentation), *unmāda* (madness), *vyādhi* (sickness), *jāḍya* (stupedity) and *mṛtyu* (death).

5091 **अवाक्यार्थ**

Avākyārtha : a sentence conveying a NV sense; e.g. *tat tvam asi* 'that thou art', according to *Advaita*.

5092 **अविनय**

Avinaya : absence of humility. According to *Manu* (7, 40-41), rulers without humility and propriety of conduct have disappeared with their families from the scene.

5093 **अविवाहित**

Avivāhita : spinster. In the *Mbh.*, a statement regarding spinsters and widows is seen, "Place the meat on the ground and many birds will come to eat it. So also men will gather round the woman who is having no husband" (*Mbh. Ādi.*, 158.12).

5094 **अश्मारोहण**

Aśmārohaṇa : rite of treading on a milestone; while the bridegroom leads the bride thrice round the fire (*agni-pradakṣinā*), he makes her tread on the stone, kept to the north of fire, in each round. He says, "tread on this stone; like a stone be firm. Overcome the enemies; tread the foes down." In Baghelkhaṇḍa region of Madhya Pradesh the bridegroom treads the stone instead of bride.

5095 **अश्वत्थ**

Aśvattha : The pīpal tree. The felling or cutting of an *aśvattha* tree is said to be sinful:

> अश्वत्थं वेधयेद्यो वै एकैकस्मिश्च पर्वणि ।
> मन्वन्तराणि वै तावन्ति रौरवै वसतिर्भवेत् ।।
> (*Skanda.*, VII. 4.39-29).

5096 **अश्वप्रतीक**

Aśvapratīka : horse-symbolism. The horse is not only an object of religious veneration, connected with the ecstatic trance in tribal societies of central India, lucky and pure, but is also has important sexual properties. The stallion scares away the demon of barrenness. In the *Rāmāyaṇa*, Kauśalyā touches a stallion in the hope of getting a son, and a king and queen smell the odour of the burnt fat of a horse with the same purpose. During the *Aśvamedha* the queen lies at night beside the slain sacrificial horse. To the Gond and Paradhān the horse is full of sexual associations. The marriage songs are full of references to the animal, most of them very coarse. It is said that a woman will always be one of the seven kinds of horse - *argal*, which carries its rider quickly to the law-court; *nāngin*, in whose presence wealth soon leaves the home; *tanhī*, which kills its owner; *rikārsin*, with a long tooth, a devil; *jeher*, which kills any companion; *goddā*, which is quarrelsome and cannot be tamed; and *padam*, the lotus horse which has white marks on the legs, and is lucky and auspicious. It is interesting to speculate of gender element in the horse. The open-legged posture of the rider and the rhythmati movement of the horse's body has a sexual undertone.

5097 **अष्टक-बन्ध**

Aṣṭaka-bandha : seated postures of sexual union. If the man and woman sit facing each other, each with one leg extended and the other drawn up; it is the two-footed position (*yugma-pāda*).

If the man sits between the forearms of a woman and takes her repeatedly shaking his thighs, it is the friction (*vimardika*) position, which becomes *mārkaṭika* or the monkey position if she faces the opposite way (*Ratirahasya*, 10.31.32); see also *upaviṣṭa-bandha*.

5098 **अष्टरसाश्रय**

Aṣṭarasāśraya : acting on which eight *rasas* depend (Kālidāsa, *Vikrama.*, 2.42).

5099 **असत्ख्याति**

Asatkhyāti : according to the Buddhist view, there is no objective basis of perception. It is *nirālambana*. This appears to be a statement with reference to delusion and hallucination rather than to illusion. In illusion there is an error in perception. The object is there. But it is wrongly perceived. In delusion and in hallucination there is no object whatever, as, for example, in dream experience. But the thinkers, generally reject this theory as is based on the *śūnyam*, void, hypothesis, viz., that our perceptions have no basis on the analysis of delusion rather than of illusions (Kuppuswamy, 1985, 99).

5100 **असंख्यात-देशकालम्**

Asaṅkhyāta-deśakālam : a condition implying non-limitation by time or place or both in respect of certain payments like debts, sale of goods or merchandise (*Arthaśāstra.*, 3.12).

5101 **असम्भावना**

Asaṁbhāvanā : doubt. Doubt is of two types: doubt about the source of knowledge (*pramāṇa)* which is removed by *śravaṇa* (hearing) and doubt about the object of knowledge (*prameya)* which is removed by *manana* (reflection).

5102 **अहिफेन**

Ahiphena : opium is taken not only by ascetics, but by Ḍhīmar and Ahīr of Chhattisgarh. Its popularity, says Penzer (II. 304), was due to several causes. 'It was looked upon as a cure for diseases, and enabled those who took it to exist on very little food during famines; it was a great restorative, a means of importing strength in any laborious work, and was considered a strong aphrodisiac'. It is an excitant and brings a break into the monotony of village life.

Village opinion is strongly in favour of *gānjā* as superior in its effects 'to any other stimulant':

The gānjā-drinker's wife is happy
The opium-eater's wife lives like a widow
The liquor-drinker's wife cries
My bull comes snorting home.

आ -Ā

5103 **आकर्षणसिद्धि**

Ākarṣaṇasiddhi : a magical power to attract others, control by drawing near (*Skanda,* III.1.18.21-22). Indians place physical altractiveness at the top. This is why the Indian literature has credited them with a long list of other disirable qualities which they may — or may not — possess. The works on dramaturgy assume that an attractive person is also talented, intelligent, happy, sensitive, warm, etc. Tāntric school has not approved this theory. So they stress on the magical power.

5104 **आकल्पसाधन**

Ākalpasādhana : make-up material (Kālidāsa, *Raghu.*, 17.248).

5105 **आकारवर्णश्लक्ष्णता**

Ākāra-varṇa-ślakṣṇatā : delicacy and smoothness in form and colour. *Ślakṣṇatā* is the gender-signal—the physical difference between male and female which enables us to tell each other apart. By emphasizing these signals, we hope to make ourselves more attractive to the opposite sex and have a wider selection of possible mates to choose from (*Ratisarvasva*).

5106 **आकाशदीप**

Ākāśadīpa : sky-lamp. the *ākāśadīpa* is a lamp fixed on a pole and set on higher place; the best is said to be twenty cubits tall, the middle one nine, the lowest one five cubits. It should be such as could be seen by people at a distance (*Skanda*, II. 9.29.103) : **यथा दूरस्थितैर्लोकैदृश्यते ।** It is enjoined to be given from the dark half of Āśvina up to the completion of the dark half of Kārtika (*Ibid*). Every evening the *ākāśadīpa* is enjoined to be lighted. This custom is still prevalent in India.

5107 **आक्षारणा**

Ākṣāraṇā : accusation of adultery (*Amarakośa*). In Halbi (dialect of Bastar), *akhar*-means troublesome.

5108 **आचारलाज**

Ācāralāja : burnt rice strewn on the ceremonial occasions (Kālidāsa, *Raghu.*, 2.23).

5109 **आच्छुरितक**

Ācchuritaka : soft-pressed; a kind of nail-mark, in which the presence of the nail is limited (*Kāmasūtra.*, 2.4.4). When a person presses the chin, the breasts, the lower lip, or the thighs of another so softly that no scratch or mark is left, it it a soft-pressed. It is used in the case of a young girl when her lover shampoos her, scratches her head and wants to trouble or frighten her (*Kāmasūtra*, 2.4.12.13; *Ratirahasya.*, 8.3).

5110 **आत्मदर्श**

Ātmadarśa : mirror (Kālidāsa, *Raghu.*, 7.110); also known as *ādarśabimba* (*Kum.*, 7.121).

5111 **आत्मप्रकृति**

Ātmaprakṛti : self-image, to be given away for peace and prosperity (*Bhaviṣya, Uttarakhaṇḍa,* 185.3). It is the self as the individual pictures it or imagines it to be. The self-image may differ from the true self. Our self-image is the complex impressions we have not only of our appearance but also of our personality traits, our personal history and the profusion of social roles and group affiliations on which our sense of personal identity further depends.

5112 **आनर्तन**

Ānartana : dancing, performed four times by four or eight women, who are not widows, after they have been regaled with food and wine. (b) The Gond often speak of a beloved girl, or even part of her body as 'dancing in their eyes'. A girl may be so beautiful that 'she drags the eyes out of your head':

> You have brought pearly beads
> And tied them in your hair
> But now stop dancing in my eyes
> Or I will tie you round my neck.

5113 **आपानकम्**

Āpānakam : collective drinking. Men and women should drink in one another's houses. Here the men should cause the courtesans to drink and should drink themselves liquors (*Kāmasūtra,* 1.4. 22-44).

5114 **आप्तवाक्य**

Āptavākya : statements of trustworthy persons, the method of learning a language. Here the learning is conscious and deliberate. The growing child learns the meanings of new words by asking his parents, teachers and others.

5115 **आभ्यन्तर-विधि**

Ābhyantara-vidhi : method of obtaining the favour of the beloved girl.

5116 **आभ्यासिकी-प्रीति**

Ābhyāsikī-prīti : affection which is created and developed from intimacy, such as hunting party, religious festivals, sports, musical party, etc. (*Anaṅgaraṅga.*, 4.28; *Ratiratnapradīpikā*, 7.43).

5117 **आमिष**

Āmiṣa : meat (Kālidāsa, *Vikrama.*, 4.93; *Raghu,*. 5.11, 8.114, 14.214, 17.255).

5118 **आम्नाय**

Āmnāya : sacred tradition. Sacred texts handed down by tradition or repetition; hence the *Veda,* (b) regional classification of the Tāntric literature.

5119 **आम्र**

Āmra : mango. The mango is one of the 'royal trees,' of India, sharing this honourable distinction with the pīpal (*ficus religiosia*), the *baṛ* (*ficus Indica*) and the *siras* (*acacia speciosa*). In Indian folklore the child-giving mango is a common theme, and occurs several times in *Folk-Tales of Mahakosal* (Elwin) where references are given. Crooke records a legend that the first mangoes grew in the garden of Rāvaṇa in Lanka and Hanumāna was so delighted with the flavour of them that he threw some of the seeds into the sea and they floated across the channel and took root in Indian soil.

In the Maikal Hills the mango season is a time of excitement and delight :

The dark shadows of the mango grove
What did you say to me
In the mango shadows?
Take me away my love
And make me partner of your life.

Parties of young men and girls go out into the forest and spend days enjoying the most delightful of picnics, eating little except the fresh wild mangoes and drinking the water of mountain streams. Mango leaves strung on a cord are tied round the marriage-booth : the leaves are also used for sprinkling holy water and sometimes for applying *haldī* to bride and bridegroom. Many tribes still celebrate ceremonially the first eating of the mangoes, and it is greatly to be hoped that these beautiful trees will remain free and open to the people forever and not be farmed out to strangers in order to produce revenue for Government.

The mango and other fruits are often used in the tribal regions to describe women friends. The *āmā-dūdh* or mango-breasts are very much admired. It is also a source of delight in Sanskrit literature: *āmram madhuram, mukulam madhuram madhure māse hyakhilam madhuram.*

5120 **आम्रचूषितकम्**

Āmracūṣitakam : sucking a mango fruit is the seventh stage of *auparisṭaka* (q.v) or oral sexual union. When the eunuch puts half of the male organ into his mouth and forcibly kisses and sucks it, this is called sucking of a mango fruit (*Kāmasūtra* 2.9.22). Sucking is an in-born action which takes the form of erotic action. The rewarding contact with the mother during breast feeding is never totally forgotten and is recaptured during the adult life by means of genital sucking.

5121 **आम्रपुष्पभक्षण**

Āmrapuṣpabhakṣana : eating of mango flowers. It should be observed on the first day of the bright half of Caitra; as a worship of Kāmadeva. The small flowers on the mango tree (*baura*) should be eaten (*Smṛtikaustubha,* 519; *Varṣakriyā-kaumudī* 516-17). The intoxicating smell of the flowers hightens the sexual power.

5122 **आरण्यक**

Āraṇyaka : the retreat to the forest. The forest-treatises, so called because they were composed by forest dwellers. At all periods of inner crisis and difficulty, man retreated into the forest to test his own strength and recover the sense of identity with his surroundings. At the moment of spiritual crisis in India, *Upaniṣads* were composed declaring :

In a clean, level spot, free from pebbles fir, and gravel.
By the sound of water and other propinquities
Favourable to thought, not offensive to the eye,
In a hidden retreat protected from the wind,
One should practice *yoga.*
For, smoke, sun, fire, wind
Fire-flies, lightning, a crystal, a moon —
These are the preliminary appearances,
Which produce the manifestation of Brahmā in *Yoga.*
(Trans. R.E.Hume, 1949.398)

'Forest book's were written by mystics who retreated to the solitude of the forest, to wrestle with their inner selves and seek union through Nature with All. 'These high-minded men', (writes the dramatist Bhāsa in *The Vision of Vāsavadattā,*) 'make their home in the forest to escape from the brutalities of town'. Similarly, the Buddhist monks were enjoined to pass a period of time each year (the monsoon months) residing in a place of permanent shelter, preferably in forest caves.

This idea of the retreat to the solitude of nature became one of the most persistent and important traits in the development of Indian culture, owing to the prestige which renunciation conferred; the practice evolved in accordance with the pattern of priestly education of the Brāhmaṇs. The novice withdrew to the forest retreat of his chosen teacher for a period of twelve years or more. The most significant feature of this life, and the one which should be emphasized if the ethos of the forest retreat is to be fully grasped, is that the novice gathered, though *never produced,* food for his *guru.* The ideal of a carefree, simpler pattern of life in which there was no need to engage in hard productive labour for survival, had in itself a profound emotional appeal. Though this needs no further explanation, as it still remains the dream of urban man even in the most industrially advanced societies, it should be rememberd that the co-existence of food-collecting tribes alongside industrious food-producing communities gave to the archaic Indian ideal of the forest retreat a very concrete and specific connotation. The survival of tribal life, with its sense of collective unity, abundantly evident, aroused in the city dwellers ancestral memories of times in the not too distant past when society was not split into antagonistic classes and castes, nor condemned to unremitting labour. The pattern continues to the present day. As many observers have noted, there is a very marked contrast between the caste-ridden Indian village society, with its poverty, its careworn ethos of hard labour on exhausted soil, its tabooridden family relationships, on the one hand, and on the other, a carefree, colourful, joyous, extraverted tribal way of life in the refreshing environment of the forest. But envy for these communities by social misfits in the caste system takes a much stronger form too, as it has since very ancient times: a hankering for the less organized, the less rationalized, even the relatively lawless state. Just as the Dantes, Rousseaus, and Thoreaus of India developed their inner orientation in the forest retreat, so too have Robinhoods found shelter and strength there. The *romanticism* of the *dacoit*, or bandit, and other forms of anarchic social protest, also figure among the components of forest nostalgia. In recent times these types of idealized banditry, 'robbing the rich to pay the poor', have been linked with the cult of 'old gods' and the revalorization of primitive customs. The *ṭhugee*, a celebrated sect of bandits suppressed in the nineteenth century, were worshippers of the aboriginal black goddess of destruction, Kālī. In the ancient period we are dealing with, the contemplative sects who retreated to the forest turned once more to the 'old gods', the mother goddesses, the tree and snake deities of the forest tribes. (b) a person residing in the woods. The seers and people practising penance after renouncing the world and worldly pursuits used to reside in the woods, so that they may meditate for self-realization or unity with gods (*Raghuvaṃśa* 5.15). (c) forest-texts, philosophical treatise. They deal neither with the performance, not the explanation, but with the mysticism and symbolism of *yajña*, and priestly philosophy. At present only four *āraṇyakas* are extant: the *Aitareya*, the *Kauśītaki*, *Taittirīya* and *Bṛhad*.

The hypothesis that tribal dialect has a different base of development from other varieties of Indian languages can be extended to NV communication patterns. That is, NV communication patterns in the tribal culture that are not commonly exhibited by other Indians possibly have their origins in Vedic NV communication patterns. This does not mean that all non-verbal communication patterns of tribal people differ from those of NV. As with language patterns, tribal people share many non-verbal patterns with other Indians. On the other hand, those unique NV patterns of tribal people don't necessarily have to be identical to Indian NV communication patterns in order for them to have an Indian origin. Years and years of separation of tribal people from their Indian culture could have produced alternations in these original NV patterns and separation could have produced entirely new patterns unrelated to NV patterns.

Some support for the hypothesis that tribal NV communication patterns have an Indian base can be gained through observing non-tribals. For example, the non-verbal patterns—specifically, body movement are remarkably similar to those of tribals. Much research to support this hypothesis needs to be done. The purpose of this note is not to establish the link between tribal and non-tribal communication patterns. Instead, the hypothesis is suggested to provide a possible theoretical base to explain the differences between tribal NV communication patterns described here and the NV communication patterns of other Indians.

A second hypothesis is that the isolation of the tribal population from other Indians produced some differences in NV communication patterns within the tribal culture. Perhaps research will establish the validity of both hypotheses— that is, NV communication patterns in the tribal culture could be a result of ancient Indian patterns and also a result of patterns that have evolved out of the indigenous conditions of Indian tribes.

Not every tribal person exhibits every feature in his NV behaviour. However, these features occur with such great frequency in the tribal population that they can be considered patterned behaviour.

In stress or conflict situations, particularly when one of the participants is in subordinate position, tribal people can express with their eyes an insolent, hostile disapproval of the person who is in the authority role. The movement of the eyes is called "rolling the eyes" in the tribal culture.

Another eye behaviour used by many tribes is found in many Indian subcultures. I am referring to the "reluctance" of tribes to look another person (particularly, another person in an authority role) directly in the eye. Reinforcing the avoidance of eye contact is a stance that young tribals take in a conflict situation. Often, in conflict situation tribal youngsters (particularly males) will slowly begin to take a limp stance as the reprimand from the person in the authority role goes on and on. The stance is as follows: the head is lowered, the body becomes extremely relaxed and the tribal stands almost as if he is in a trance. The stance is not taken immediately, but slowly evolves as the reprimand proceeds.

5123 **आरण्यगान**

Āraṇya-gāna : name of one of the four hymn-books of the *Sāmaveda* which are to be chanted in the forest.

5124 **आरति**

Ārati : a ceremony observed to guard against the jealous look. Upon a plate of copper is placed a lamp, made of paste from rice-flour. It is supplied with oil and lighted. Married women (not widowed for, their presence is considered unlucky) hold the plate with both their hands and, raising it as high as the head of the person for whose welfare ceremony is performed, describe in that position a number of circles with the plate and burning lamp.

Sometimes, in place of the rice-lamp, they fill the plate with water, coloured red with a mixture of saffron and other ingredients; and with this describe their circle, raising it as high as the head of a person who is the object of the ceremony.

This ceremony is intended to avert fascination by the eye, and to prevent the accidents which arise out of an evil impression occasioned by the jealous looks of certain persons. This ceremony is common and universal among the Hindus, and especially persons of high ranks, who, being more observed and having more enemies than private individuals, are more opposed to the evil influence of a malevolent or jealous look. Therefore, when such persons appear in the public, the first thing that is done at their homes is to perform the ceremony of *ārati*, as an antidote to the ill-designed looks which may be cast on them or already been cast. For the same reason princes have the ceremony repeated several times in a day (Kauṭilya, *Arthaśāstra* 2.30, 2.32) see *nīrājanā* (Garg, 1992 : 584). cf. *Kañcan thār ārati nānā* (*Mānasa*, 7.9.6).

5125 **आरोग्य**

Ārogya : health. The following verse defines the healthy man :

yasya strīṣu rateśśaktiḥ
jīrṇaśaktiśca bhojane ।
dehe dhika balā śaktiḥ
tasyā rogyam pracakṣate ॥

"One who can well enjoy a wife
Eat well and digest in life.
By whom the physical work's well done—
That one is a healthy one."

Here approach is that muscle tension should be avoided that bright the ill-health.

5126 **आर्जव**

Ārjava : rectitude of conduct. One should behave in a straight-forward manner, both in the states of attachment and detachment. It means uniformity in behaviour towards one's son, friend, wife, enemy as well as one's own self, under all circumstances. (b) It is a technical term in *yoga*. (c) It is one of the expedients, the others were *dāna* (gifts), *anurāga* (affection), and *māna* (honour), by which rulers like Śilāditya VII succeeded in subduing *āṭavikas*.

5127 **आर्थीव्यञ्जना**

Ārthīvyañjanā : sense-based suggestion. In this the reader is incited to read between the lines, as it were, for some different, broader or deeper implication which is conveyed to him by way of suggestion. For example, in the sentence, 'The sun has set', in the mouth of a sage would suggest 'the time for evening prayer', to a cowherd "milking time', etc.

5128 **आलम्बन-विभाव**

Ālambana-vibhāva : fundamental determinant. It is the essential (*ālambana*) or fundamental determinant in a drama or a poem. It consists of such material ingredients as the hero, the heroine, the rival hero and the adjuncts (*DR*, 4.2).

5129 **आवश्यक**

Āvaśyaka : necessary. There are six necessary daily duties to be performed by every Jain. These are *sāmāyikam* (equanimity), *caturviṁśati-stava* (glorification), *vandana* (veneration of the Guru), *pratikramaṇa* (confession), *kāyotsarga* (penance through certain postures of body) and *pratyākhyāna* (refusal of certain pleasure).

5130 **आसक्तप्रेमी**

Āsakta-premī : a lover. A man is said to be sufficiently in love with a woman when his love is disinterested; when he has the same object in view as his beloved; when he is quite free from any suspicion on her account and when he is indifferent to many with regard to her (*Kāmasūtra*, 6.2.73).

5131 **आहार्य-राग**

Āhārya-rāga : exos, sexual union of subsequent love. When two persons come together, while their love for each other is still in its infancy, their union is called the congress of subsequent love (*Kāmasūtra*, 2.10.17). *Āsakti* is the given to physical, romantic and erotic love. Erotic lovers believe in love at first sight for they are strongly influenced by physical attraction. They are very sensual and place a great emphasis on love-making.

5132 **आहुति**

Āhuti : an *oblation* in the performance of a *yajña*. It is an offering of ladleful (*sruca*) of clarified butter into the fire.

उ - U

5133 **उत्थापन**

Utthāpana : rousing up of the god after sleep (*Skanda*, II.2.29.30).

5134 **उद्भव-मुद्रा**

Udbhava-mudrā : symbolic usage in initiatory rites, the symbol for birth. *Guru* considers himself to be Śiva with the *udbhava-mudrā* and places himself symbolically into the heart of the *śiṣya* (*Agni*, 84.50).

5135 **उद्यान**

Udyāna : garden. Special care of the garden is attested from Sanskrit literature. In the context of characteristics of a good house, it is stated that at its left a garden should be nurtured. Everyday in the morning and in the evening, in the hot season and also on alternate days in the cold season, also in the rainy season when the land is yet dry, or gets dry, the planted trees should be watered. The trees also should be sprinkled at the root with cool water prepared from *viḍaṅga* and clarified butter. If the fruit-bearing trees get their fruit ruined, the trees should be sprinkled with cool water prepared from *kulatha, māṣa* (black gram), *mudga* (green gram), sesame, barely, and clarified butter. By doing so they show bumper flowers and fruits (*Agni*, 247. 22-27) :

> वामभागे तथोद्यानं कुर्याद्वासं गृहे शुभम् ।
> सायं प्रातस्तु घर्माप्तौ शीतकाले दिनान्तरे ॥

Likewise the sprinkling (*seka*) of the powder of dried dung of a ram, powder of barley, sesame should be done at the root for seven days. Mango trees are sprinkled with fish-water (*Ibid.*, 30). For date palm and coconut trees sprinkling of salt-water is enjoined (*Ibid.*, 31). Gardening and cooking can also be a form of meditation because they give something outside yourself to concentrate on.

5136 **उपचारयन्त्रणा**

Upacārayantraṇā : formality of getting up. Custom requires that every woman should show respect to her husband by getting up at his approach : **अभ्युत्थानमुपागते गृहपतौ** (*Śākuntalam*, IV.18).

5137 **उपहार**

Upahāra : gifts; *neng* in village dialects, before the bride's people consent to settle down in their camp they demand a number of gifts among the aboriginal tribes. These are known as the *neng* and are demanded at intervals throughout the whole proceedings of marriage. When the bride is to be fed she refuses to eat until she is promised a present. When the people come for *ṭīkā* the Susain refuses to let them do until they are rewarded. When bride and bridegroom wish to enter the house they are prevented by little girls until they bribe them with a gift. So now the bride's party demands cloth for the bride's mother and grandmother and various other presents. Only when these are given they agree to settle down in their camp and to allow the bridegroom's party to anoint the girl with *haldī* and oil. Even now the bride is hidden somewhere and a wrong girl is produced. When at least she is found, the bridegrooms party attempts to feed her with ceremonial bread, but she refuses until they promise to give her ornaments.

The word *neng* covers a social custom and an attitude of mind that is characteristic of Chhattisgarh and Baghelkhand. On all ceremonial occasions— it may be birth, marriage, festival, funeral—certain privileged person, relatives, or officials of the rite, hold up the proceedings and demand a present. Nothing can proceed until the ceremonial tax is paid. This is a fruitful source of dispute in weddings, for on such occasions there are many relatives to be brought off. Here, often the birth of a child, the midwife, barber and washerman refuse to fulfil their proper functions until they are given the proper dues. This is a *neng* , a word of great importance for the understanding of the Chhattisgarhi-Baghelī-mind.

5138 **उलूक**

Ulūka ; owel. Owel is a bird closely connected with sorcery. It is said that if a bone of an owl and that of a cow is dug in at the door of the house of an enemy, the latter is sure to die (*Garuḍa Purāṇa.*, 1.182-17). If faggots from the *Bilva*-tree, smeared with the blood of an owl and that of a black crow are offered into the fire with the names of persons, those persons will have mutual enmity (*Ibid.*, 74) :

> उलूककृष्णकाकस्य बिल्वस्याथ समिच्छतम् ।
> रुधिरेण समायुक्तं ययोर्नाम्ना तु हूयते ॥
> तयोर्मध्ये महावैरं भवेन्नास्त्यत्र संशयः ॥

In villa5ge India these birds are known as the 'priests of the witches': *ṭonhī ka guru.* They are considered extremely unlucky birds and are associated in the minds of the people with misfortune and death. It is considered inadvisable to call aloud at night to anyone by name. The owl will hear the name called and will take to calling that name till the person sickens and dies. A clod of earth or a stone is never thrown at an owl, for it is believed that the owl will take up the stone and drop it in some stream; and as the earth or the stone dissolves in the water, the person who threw it will go into a decline and will die.

5139 **उलूखल**

Ulūkhala : mortar. Crossing a mortar is said to be bad. It is said that where this is strode upon evil spirits arrive (*Mark.*, 50.87).

ऊ - Ū

5140 **ऊर्णवलयिन्**
Ūrṇavalayin : the sacred marriage-thread being worn on a hand which was made of woollen yarn. This sacred thread is mentioned as *Kautuka hasta-sūtra* (Kālidāsa, *Raghu.*, 3.42).

5141 **ऊर्ध्वलिङ्ग**
Ūrdhvaliṅga : ithyphallus, erected penis, ritual retention of semen, avoidance of orgasm, *ūrdhvaretas*, symbolic *coitus interruptus*, and the attribution of magico-religious potency to semen when it is conserved within the body (*Vāmana.*, 22.69). The corpus of yogic tradition includes such related ideas as the 'permanently' chaste ithyphallus, 'storing of semen in the head' and, in its Tāntric form, ritualistic *coitus reservatus* with a consecrated sexual partner. The main principle of these archaic practices (which are still stored to) is that the performance of the sexual act without emission is a means of obtaining spiritual power. These rites are no longer of interest to any but a small minority of Indians, but they are manifestations of widespread beliefs in the need to minimize loss of semen. Day-to-day male preoccupation with the inadvertent loss of semen, pollution rules, and strict regulation in the frequently of intercourse according to the custom's of one's caste, dietary habits designed to check loss of semen but increase its supply and 'recalculation' in the physical system, and the universal idea of 'renunciation' or at least continuence, in the latter half of life all indicate widespread concern with the for head self-torture in physical sexuality for the sake of spiritual salvation.

ए - A

5142 **ऐङ्**
Aiṅ : one of the sounds of *Śāktamantra*. Its *japa* is said to awaken occult power.

ऐ - A

5143 **ऐतिह्य**
Aitihya : tradition. According to *Nyāya*, it is merely verbal testimony or *śabda*. The Paurāṇikas regard it as a valid source of knowledge. Philosophers do not accept it as as valid source of knowledge. It is defined as an assertion which has come down from the past without any indication of the source from which it first originated. It is a means of correct knowledge.

5144 **ऐनेय**
Aineya : posture for sexual union resembling that adopted by the herds of antelopes (*Kāmasūtra.*, 2.6.44).

5145 **ऐभ**
Aibha : Elephant position of sexual union in which the man hold his male organ in his hand and leapes over her, like a bull-elephant, while she lays her brow, face and breasts to the ground and raises her buttocks (*Ratirahasya*, 10.39).

ओ - O

5146 **ओष्ठराग**
Oṣṭharāga : lipstick (Kālidāsa, *Vikrama.*, 4.87) The role of the female lips as labial-mimics is well-known to Vātsyāyana and has often been emphasized by advertisements comploying phallic-shaped objecte approaching the open mouth.

क - Ka

5147 **कच्छ**
Kaccha : known as *kachnī* in Baghelī. The *kaccha* is a portion of the *dhotī*, worn on the portion lower to the navel pit and taken back between the hips and tied at the waist at the back. The usual mode of use was the *pañcakaccha* (*Śiva.*, 13.18).

5148 **कण्टक**
Kaṇṭaka : thorn. The tribal love is compared with the thorn in the following poem :

O Faithless thorn
He has my heart no longer
Yet for his sake I no more see
Mother or brother or any friends
O faithless thorn.

The thorn in this Baigānī *karmā* is a *chhindi* thorn which pricks but leaves no mark. So although the love of the singer's faithless admirer has pricked her and though the wound stings and burns, the thorn does not remain in the flesh or in her mind.

To be pricked by a thorn is considered a bad omen by the Oraon for 'it implies a wound which may mean a loss of blood and a corresponding loss of vitality' (Archer 1907.160). To the Pardhān, however, the thorn is probably simply the sharp prick of desire. The thorn stands for lust in Sanskrit literature:

Lust has no ears; He's sharp as thorn;
And fretful carries hay in its horn (Herrick).

5149 **कदम्ब**

Kadamba : a particular tree called *kadam* in Hindi; *Adina Cordifolia,* hook. It is a tall deciduous tree with cordate leaves, and is distributed throughout India. Its wood is used for building, but the Birhoṛ — and probably other tribes who observe the — *kadambotsava* called *karmā* — must not use it for fuel or in their houses (Roy, *The Birhors,* 383). It is not regarded as specially sacred in Madhya Pradesh or in Bastar, but the *Viṣṇu Purāṇa* describes how Krishna loved to climb it and hide himself in its thick foliage. It was from the *Kadamba* tree (which is the same as the *karmā* in central India) that he leapt into the serpents pool and subdued *kāliya,* the snake king.

Dances with the name of *karam* or *karmā* have been recorded for many different tribes : indeed Dalton (1872.135) speaks of the *karam* dance as 'universal'. He himself describes it as danced by the *kisān,* by the *koirī,* and by the *kol* of Chhotā Nagpur who cut a branch of the *karam* tree, plant it in the dancing ground and dance round it — a ceremony apparently intended to ensure the fertility of the crops. It is a famous dance all over central India except Bastar.

5150 **कदली**

Kadalī : plantain. The plantain is generally regarded as lucky and auspicious in India. Hindus believe it to be the abode of Devī and in North India the tree is worshipped on the last day of Kārtika. The first fruit of the tree should be given to a Brāhmaṇ. In L.B. Days *Folk-Tales of Bengal,* a deserted wife sweeps the earth round a plantain and the tree blesses her. In the Maikal Hills also both Gond and Baiga regard the tree as lucky and use its branches during their marriage ceremonies :

> *Jhir jhir* ripples the stream
> Plantains are growing on the bank
> Your body is like the stalk of a plantain
> Sweet as a divided mango.

In Bastar, however, owing to the fact that the leaves are placed under a corpse while it is being carried out for disposal, the tree is believed to be inauspicious.

5151 **कन्या**

Kanyā : the girl of ten years (*Skanda,* VI.272.47).

5152 **करदर्शन**

Karadarśana : looking at one's own palms. It is auspicious to look at one's own palms when one awakes after sleep, which has been sanctioned by the following *śloka* :

> *karāgre vasate Lakṣmīḥ*
> *karamadhye Sarasvatī I*
> *karamūle sthito Brahmā*
> *prabhāte kara-darśanam II*

5153 **कर्मचाण्डाल**

Karmacāṇḍāla : a brāhmaṇa who is a *cāṇḍāla* by profession (*Skanda,* III. 2.27.3).

5154 **कलहनाशन**

Kalahanāśana : quarrel ends at a holy place. It is said that when Pārvatī was addressed as Kālī (the dark one) by Śiva in joke, she got angry, and there was a quarrel between them. Where the quarrel (*kalakala*) took place, there arose a holy place *Kalakaleśvara* (i.e. Śiva). To set the quarrel at naught, a *kuṇḍa* was created by Śiva. When Pārvatī took bath in it, she was free from the mood of quarrel. Hence the place came to be called *kalahanāśana*:

> एवं हि कलहो जातः शिवगौर्योर्हि यत्र तु ।
> देवस्तत्र समुद्भूतो नाम्ना कलकलेश्वरः ॥
> कृतमग्ने तथा कुण्डं नाम्ना कलहनाशनम् ।
> तत्र कृते व्यास-स्नाने जाताऽकलहिनी प्रिया ॥
> (*Skanda,* V.1.8.8-9)

5155 **कलियुग**

Kaliyuga : Kali age, the present age; one of the four *yugas* (large measure of time). *Kaliyuga* is the last *yuga,* the least virtuous. In the *Kali yuga* the lord is of black colour and the characteristic of this *yuga* is *tamas* (*Skanda,* I. 2.40.173; *Garuḍa,* 1.215.5-37). Some interesting details about the *Kaliyuga* are as follows : Rudra is the god in Kali. the most corrupt is said to be the *Kaliyuga* (present age). In it there is no tendency to study, nor of sacrifice. Everything is topsy-turvy. People having no authority or having less mental faculty. The Śūdras compose *mantras.* It is said that in this *yuga* food-grains would be sold in various country-sides. *Vedas* or gods would be at cross-roads and women would trade for their sexual organs (*Brahma,* 230.11). All sorts of vices are mentioned as being practised in the *Kaliyuga.* It is said that in this age a brother might have sexual relationships with his own sister and the father with his daughter :

> भ्राता भगिनी गन्ता पिता पुत्रीं च वै कलौ
> (*Skanda* II.2.22.45)

An interesting detail of information provided in this context is that at the Kali age men would be of the size of the thumb; and they would prepare their houses in the holes made by rats :

भविष्यन्ति युगस्यन्ति नरा अंगुष्ठमात्रकाः ।
गृहं च तेऽथ कुर्वन्ति बिलैरारवुसमुद्भवैः ॥
(*Skanda,* VI.272.49)

5156 **कविसङ्केत**

Kavisañketa : poetic conventions. See nos. 4415, 4438

5157 **कामवासना**

Kāmavāsanā : libido. The sex instinct, the erotic desire or erotic pleasure, sexuality. Some of the symptoms of libido are as follows: lowered resistance to germs and viruses, jumpy nerves, insomnia, weight loss and exhaustion, reduced resistance to pain, anxiety-ridden sex-life, dry mouth, nausea, bloating, cramps and diarrhoea, high blood pressure, rapid breathing, hair-standing, perspiraion, making mistakes etc.

5158 **कामाग्निद्राविणी**

Kāmāgnidrāviṇī : moistner of sexual organ, Kubjikā is addressed as *kāmāgnidrāviṇī* (*Agni,* 143.15). Sex hormones are reduced.

5159 **कायस्थ**

Kāyastha : a *varṇa,* or profession; keeper of accounts and records or the scribe. Kāyastha is censured by the remark that he did not eat his mother's flesh when in her womb, but that in that act there is not a particle of compassion; the reason is that he had no teeth in that condition (*Brahmavaivarta, Śrīkṛṣṇakhaṇḍa,* 85.136) :

कायस्थेनोदरस्थेन मातुर्मांसं न खादितम् ।
तत्र नास्ति कृपा तस्य दन्ताभावेन केवलम् ॥

(b) Mostly all the tribes of Madhya Pradesh are prejudiced towards Kāyasthas. The Gadbā of Bastar will eat the leavings of other castes and take food from all except the Kāyasthas. They will not take food or water from a Kāyastha (Russell and Hiralal, III.14). Ghasiā caste of Bastar had a peculiar aversion to Kāyastha and did never take food or water from them nor touched a Kāyastha's bedding or clothing. They said that they would never serve a Kāyastha as horse-keeper, but if by any chance one of them was reduced to doing so, he at any rate would not hold his master's stirrup for him to mount. To account for this hereditary enmity they told the following story to Russell and Hiralal (1919, III 31-32) : "on one occasion the son of Kāyastha minister of the Rājā of Ratanpur went out for a side followed by a Ghasia *sais* (groom). The boy was wearing costly ornaments, and the Ghasiā's cupidity being excited, he attacked and murdered the child, stripped him of his ornaments and threw the body down a well. The murder was discovered and in revenge the minister killed every Ghasiā, man, woman or child that he could lay his hands on. The only ones who escaped were two pregnant women who took refuge in the hut of a Gāṇḍā and were sheltered by him. To them were born a boy and girl and the present Ghasiā are descended from the pair. Therefore a Ghasiā will eat even the leavings of a Gāṇḍā but will accept nothing from the hands of a Kāyastha." This story is an instance of the process which has been called the transplantation of myth.

5160 **कालवेदिन्**

Kālavedin : knower of time, a person who can foretell death. A method mentioned in *Śiva Purāṇa* of divination about death is 'the time symptoms from the sound' (V. 25.27-43) and the person who tries this divination is called *kālavedin* and *prāṇavedin* (knower of the vital breaths).

5161 **काषायापरिवीत**

Kāṣāyāparivīta : wearing ochre colour garments. The ascetics generally wear reddish garments to distinguish themselves from the worldly people or householder. It is, therefore, from the times immemorial, Indians who pay a great deal of respect to the ascetics and saints (Kālidāsa, *Raghu.,* 15.277). Every nuance and level of aggression is represented by *Kāṣāya.* From posiive activity to blindly destructive rage from a pleasurable sense of excitement to a definite warning of danger, this especially masculine colour is impossible to ignore.

5162 **काष्ठमौन**

Kāṣṭhamauna : standstill silence. When inner thoughts and feelings are not displayed externally by any gestures, as against *ākāra-mauna* where external form or feature that shows silence but betrays feelings.

5163 **कीटम्**

Kīṭam : dirt in the body. The non-digested food (*kīṭam*) is left in the body in the form of twelve kinds of dirt, namely from the ear, eyes, nose, tongue, teeth, lips, generative organ, the anus, phlegm, perspiration, urine and excreta, in all twelve (*Padma,* 66. 16-21).

5164 **कीलक**

Kīlaka : a mystic word meaning 'pin', associated with a *mantra* (*Skanda,* VI. 262.3).

5165 **कुञ्चिका**

Kuñcikā : bamboo-shoots. It is said that Śiva used to fix bamboo-shoots as an adornment in the left half of his body (*Skanda,* I.21.20-23). It was the *Ardhanārīśvara* form of Śiva.

5166 **कुठार**

Kuṭhāra : axe, of iron for protection of a locality left by

Paraśurāma. It is said that when Paraśurāma (Rāma with the axe) came to Hāṭakeśvara after killing the Kṣatriyas, the Brāhmaṇs there requested him to leave his axe there for their protection. Parāśurāma granted. But instead of keeping the axe as it was, he broke it and prepared an iron-staff from it (*Skanda,* VI. 94.15) :

तेषां तद्वचनं श्रुत्वा रामः शस्त्रभृतां वरः ।
चक्रे लोहमयीं यष्टिं तं भङ्क्त्वा स कुठारकम् ॥

This probably exclaims the practice of offering iron-lances or staffs at holy places, particularly in the tribal areas. The Brāhmaṇas and their followers worshipped that iron-staff as a protective symbol.

5167 **कुतुप**

Kutapa : the time when the sun gets dimmed in the afternoon (*Nārada,* 26.23) :

दिवसस्याष्टमे भागे यदा मन्दायते रविः ।
स कालः कुतपो नाम पितृणां दत्तमक्षयम् ॥

5168 **कुलोपदेश**

Kulopadeśa : family-name (Kālidāsa, *Raghu.*, 7.105).

5169 **कुष्ठ**

Kuṣṭha : leprosy. According to *Padma-Purāṇa* (45.25) the eight types of *kuṣṭha* are the result of speaking bad about the Brāhmaṇs. According to *Skanda-Purāṇa* (VII. 1.278.77), the *kuṣṭha* is of eighteen types.

5170 **कुसुमप्रसाधन**

Kusumaprasādhana : ornamentation of the hair with the help of flowers (Kālidāsa, *Kum,* 4.62).

5171 **कूप**

Kūpa : well. Digging of wells is placed at various places in Sanskrit literature. It is said that digging of wells, from which water could be drunk by men and beasts, eases half of the sins of a person to be destroyed (*Padma, Uttarkhaṇḍa,* 28.2) :

अर्धं पापं संहरन्ति पुरुषस्य विकर्मणः ।
कूपाः प्रकृतयानीयाः सुप्रवृत्तस्य नित्यशः ॥

Khātavana is mentioned as a common name for any dug up place with an idea of storing water, or getting it from springs. A dug-up tank or water-place is extolled, as being useful for various purposes namely washing of clothes, utensils, and other things, also performing the rituals of manes etc. (*Ibid., Sṛṣṭikhaṇḍa.,* 54. 2-10).

Well is also a meeting place of the village women. It is always said that there is no place where a girl looks more beautiful than by wells. Her upright and graceful carriage is emphasized in the following Baiga song when she places a heavy pot on her head:

How sharpely is the pitcher on its stand
How sweet my water-girl down by the well.

5172 **कृच्छ्र**

Kṛcchra : expiation, a type of special vow with varieties such as *mahendra, bhāskara, sāntapana* etc. (*Agni,* 197.16).

5173 **कोकिलबोल**

Kokilabola : The cuckoo saying. When the Gond are discussing a problem and they wish to make matter firm and settled, one of them says as he passes judgement 'This is my *koel bolī*, or my 'cuckoo saying'. Kālidāsa (*Raghu.* 12.39) records it's fascinating voice :

लक्ष्मः प्रथमंश्रुत्वा कोकिलां मंजुवादिनीम् ।
शिवाघोरस्वनां पश्चाद् बुबुधे विकृतेति ताम् ॥

An Oraon poem permits a boy to catapult all other birds but admonishes him on no account to kill a *koel.* W.G. Archer gives an Oraon poem which closely resembles one with the Gondi song :

Kahul kuha, the koel calls
Sitting in the mango branches
Koel, you went away for twelve years
And in the thirteenth year you come
And gladden the grove.

In this poem the grove is the village and the *koel* is a girl returning home after a long stay at her husband's house. The association of the *koel* with the mango tree, another marriage symbol, also in the following Gondi poem is interesting :

Let me come to the mango-grove, my love
Let your *koel* come
Let me come to the mango-grove.

The *koel* or Indian cuckoo is a bird with green bill and a long tail. The female is of a dark green colour with white bands and spotted. The *koel* is often used in Indian village poetry as the symbol of a bride or a lover. According to Vātsyāyana the perfect girl, the Padminī or lotus-girl, has a voice low and musical like that of the *koel.* In Mandla the bird is believed to be very lucky and to foreshadow the coming of a sun or husband, when it cries *uṭh dekh, uṭh dekh,* 'Get up and look'.

Crooke records a proverb which says:

The crow calls on the left
The cuckoo calls on the left
Both are good omens.

The Indian attitude to the cuckoo is more sympathetic than that common in Europe; she is regarded as rather pathetic because she cannot hatch her own eggs and rear her own chicks.

5174 **कोणाघात**

Koṇāghāta : confused sounds of drums and kettle-drums (*Veṇīsaṁhāra*, I.22). *Koṇāghāta* is thus defined :

ढक्काशतसहस्राणि भेरीशतशतानि च ।
एकदा यत्र हन्यन्ते कोणाघातः स उच्यते ॥

There is said to be *koṇāghāta* when thousands of large drums and hundreds upon hundreds of kettle-drums are simultaneously beaten. The word *koṇa* here probably means drums of various kinds. *Koṇāghāta* would thus mean the simultaneous beating of many drums and thence the confused sounds produced by such beating.

Drums and music are everywhere the same. Elizabethan Fletcher makes his trumpets sound 'tara tara tara tara tara' and his drums go 'dum dum'. Hirakhan's 'drum of victory' in central India sounded 'dum dum'. The heroes of tribal songs tremble 'dal dal' or 'thar thar'; the heroines weep 'dhar dhar' and sob 'kalhar kalhar'. They laugh 'gad gad' and an old woman chuckles 'khad khad'.

A sound of great importance to the Gond and Pardhān singer is the musical tinkle of a girl's ornaments, a theme rarely celebrated in Eurpean poetry. But here the *cuṭkī* toe-rings sound 'cuṭuk cuṭuk', the anklets go 'cunur cunur' or 'runjum runjum'— and when a youth hears sweet music, his heart beats 'kudur budur'.

Other sounds are — the splashing of water, 'lijak lijar'; rain falling 'rimik jhimik', or 'rinjhim rinjhim'; a stream rippling 'jhir jhir'. The noise of the churn is 'ghamar ghamar'; of kneading 'gadar gadar', of cooking 'karak karak', of boiling clothes 'radbad radbad'. The beat of the large rice-husker worked by the feet is well represented 'ḍhok ḍhik ḍhok ḍhik'. A litter comes creaking and swinging 'diggi dola' and 'dip dip'.

5175 **कोशकार**

Kośakāra : compiler of a dictionary. There is a legend of a *kośakāra* recorded in the *Skanda Purāṇa* (IV. 33.77).

5176 **कौतुकक्रिया**

Kautuka-kriyā : marriage-ceremony. (Kālidāsa, *Raghu.* 11.168).

5177 **कौतुकवेदी**

Kautukavedī : (*Raghu.*, 7.105) is a term used for a specially prepared place where *vivāhadīkṣā* or the actual marriage ceremony is performed.

5178 **कौतुकहस्तसूत्र**

Kautukahastasūtra : (*Kumāra.*, 7.122) is a term used for a thread worn round the wrist of the bride. This ceremony is still performed.

5179 **कौमुदी-महोत्सव**

Kaumudī-mahotsava : another name of festival of light celebrated in the month of Kārtika. (*Bhaviṣya, Uttarakhaṇḍa*, 140.7).

5180 **क्रियावाद**

Kriyāvāda : action, universal action, interaction. The mere presence of others introduces a degree of control over our demeanor that we do not display when we are alone. We maintain our faces in a moderately expressionless state neither smiling too broadly nor scowling. As we talk, out gait and general body movements are restricted to certain patterns, and we sustain speeds appropriate for the social setting. From strangers we maintain a proper distance and take care not to follow hard on their heels alongside them. Our glances at them are brief and expressionless. No one has taught us these detailed rules of conduct, yet we observe them.

Entering into a conversation with someone similarly involves highly regularized sequences. First there has to be some kind of glance exchange. Only when one knows someone rather well is permissible to side along side to start talking to them without the initial visual permission. This glance is usually followed up with a mutual exchange of smiles, and the person who initiated the encounter is expected to provide the topic of conversation. Our everyday encounters with other people is the study of social interaction which is always in its orderliness.

Gottman (1967:1) offers the following definition of social interaction: 'It is that class of events which occurs during co-presence and by virtue of co-presence. The ultimate behavioural materials are the glances, gestures, positionings and verbal statements that people feed into situation, whether intended or not; Later he distinguished two levels of interaction, co-presence and focused interacion. Co-presence means when people signal through bodily and facial demeanour, the use of space or any other means, their awareness of one another's presence and their accessibility to one another should the circumstances arise. The focused interaction occurs when people gather together and co-operate to sustain a single focus of attention, as in conversation, games, transactions in shops, consultations and a myriad of other social situations.

5181 **क्लीब**

Klība : eunuch. The *Kūrma Purāṇa* (II. 17.4) differentiates between *klība* (eunuch) and *ṣaṇḍa* (a castrated man) and enjoins that a respectable person should not take food from them.

5182 **क्लेश**

Kleśa : afflictions. One of the very important aspect of *Sāṁkhya-yoga* system is the description of five afflictions or *kleśas*, namely, *avidyā* (ignorance), *asmitā* (egoism), *rāga* (attachment), *dveṣa* (aversion) and *abhiniveṣa* (will-to-live) or changing to life (*Yogasūtra*, II.3). The theory of *kleśas* constitutes the very foundation of the *yoga* system. The term *kleṣa* means pain and afflication and what causes it. The theory of *kleṣa* attempts to analyse the underlying and fundamental cause of human misery and suffering and the way in which the cause can be removed effectively.

क्ष - Kṣa

5183 **क्षपणक**

Kṣapaṇaka : a Jain or Buddhist mendicant; seen in dream indicates early death. If ones sees in dream a strong naked Jain or Buddhist mendicant laughing and prattling, he is to die soon (*Mārkaṇḍeya*, 43.18).

5184 **क्षीर**

Kṣīra : a sweet made of rice, milk and sugar and known as *khīr* in Hindi. *Khīr* in the following Gondi poem refers to intercourse (semen) and a resulting pregnancy, the symbolism very common in Sanskrit myths :

He gave her *khīr* for them
With *khīr* he filled her belly.

5185 **क्षुतम्**

Kṣutam : sneeze. To sneeze once is a bad omen, to sneeze twice is good, three times is bad, and so on. A *Pardhān Karma* of Mandla depicts it :

I was going along the road and lost my way;
When I came to the cross-roads I sneezed.
Why did I sneeze when I come to the cross-roads?
O sneeze, why have you stopped me on my journey.
(English rendering)

ख - Kha

5186 **खड्ग**

Khaṅga : sword. Sword symbolizes *māyā* (the magical aspect of Śiva that produces the world) in *Śiva-dīkṣā* ritual (*Agni.*, 81.30). (b) A belief associated with the sword is that one should not see one's face reflected in the (blade of a) sword; one should not touch one's sword or dagger (*kṛpāṇa*) When the mouth is not cleaned after meals; no talk about the price or type of a sword should be entered into; and one should not place one's sword at the head at night when one sleeps :

खड्ग पश्येन्न वदनमुच्छिष्टो न स्पृशेदसिम् ।
मूल्यं जातिं न कथयेत् निशि कुर्यान्न शीर्षके ॥
(*Agni.*, 245.17)

5187 **खञ्जनकलक्षण**

Khañjanakalakṣaṇa : sings of the wagtail bird. Varāhamihira (*BS*, XLV) has depicted four types of this bird : *bhadra, sampūrṇa, rikta* and *gopita*. According to him a wagtail sighted in the following places tends to prosperity : on trees bearing fragrant flowers and sweet fruits, on holy lakes and rivers, on the heads of the elephants, horses and serpents, on temples, gardens and mansions, near cows, cowpens, sacrifices, festivities, etc. When it is seen sitting on a buffalo, camel, donkey, bones, burial grounds, corner of a house, the result would be disastrous and would cause danger. (Fig. - 5187)

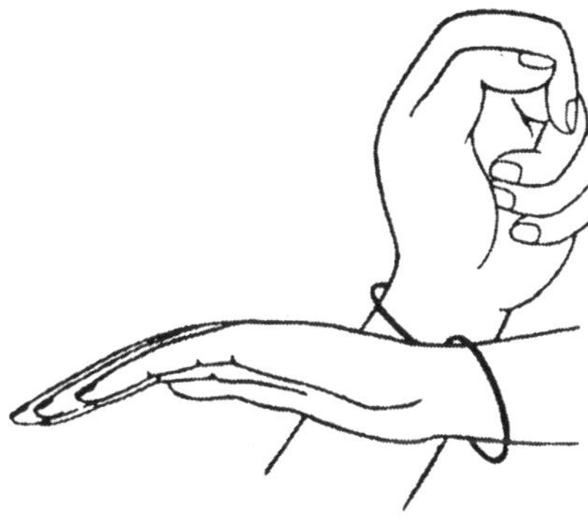

Fig. - (5187)

5188 **खलधान्यम्**

Khaladhānyam : threshing floor. It is considered unlucky for one who has ridden on an elephant to enter a threshing floor, and on the other hand if one who has ridden on a tiger should enter he will bring good luck. The Gonds and Bhumiyās who may capture a young tiger, will lead it around the country amongst the agricultural people, who pay a small fee to have their children placed on the tiger. To enter a threshing-floor with shoed feet is also considered unlucky.

When the grain has been threshed and is awaiting measurement, some branches of the *Baer* tree (*Zizyphus Vulgaris*) is placed on the stacked grain in order to keep off the *Maṭiyā* or goblin who takes away the grain and makes it measure less than was expected. Grain is never measured at noon in the threshing-floor but usually at the morning and evening hours (*JRAS*, 1904.3).

ग - Ga

5189 **गतनासिक**

Gatanāsika : noseless. To accuse a woman of being noseless is a great insult in central India. Sometimes a husband removes the nose-ring, or even cuts off the nose, if a woman taken in adultery. The following *sajnī* song sung in Seoni depicts the same :

> Now he too abuses them
> You noseless, widowed,
> strumpets.

5190 **गन्ध**

Gandha : smell, the subtle element of odour. Shepard class in India deal with the sheep-pen. Owing to their work in cleaning the pens and moving about among the sheep, the women often carry traces of the peculiar smell of these animals. This is exemplified in the saying :

> *ek to gaṛariā, dūsar lasun khāyē tīsar hagī gānṛ*.
> or 'Firstly she is a Gaṇḍariā, and then she has eaten garlic.

The inference being that she is far indeed from having the scent of rose. Yet as a part of spoken language shephard woman's natural scent plays an important part in attracting men. Vātsyāyana has classified the men and women on the basis of heir body smell. Such subtle sexual scents are called *ratāmbu*. Male *ratāmbu* is called androsterone and female copulins. Much like the subtler signals received by our eyes the infomation *gandha* gives is acted upon subliminally.

5191 **गन्धतैल**

Gandhataila : fragrant oil. The *gandhataila* is mentioned by *Matsya Purāṇa* (153.50) :

> कदाचिद् गन्धतैलेन गात्रं अभ्युज्य शैलजा ।

5192 **गरुडशास्त्र**

Garuḍaśāstra : lore dealing with the removal of poison (*Garuḍa*, I.191.1).

5193 **गर्त**

Garta : pit. Pit symbolized the hell in the Purāṇic period as the following *śloka* attests :

> नरकोऽयं महाभाग गर्तरूपेण संस्थितः ।
> (*Brahma.*, 34.67)

5194 **गर्भगृह**

Garbhagṛha : womb-house, symbol of womb.

5195 **गात्रसंस्पर्शलक्ष्म**

Gātrasaṁsparśalakṣma : signals of auto-touch. Varāhamihira in his *Bṛhatsaṁhitā* (LI) has depicted different types of signals of auto-touch which are in a way predictions. Self-touching improves memory according to Varāhamihira, especially on the head, seemingly because it calms us.

5196 **गानविद्या**

Gānavidyā : singing, musical lore, the lore of vocal music is said to have been learnt by Nārada from Ulūka. Among the instructions are that a singer should not make awkward movements of hands, nor should he have anything (eatable) in the mouth nor should he take out his tongue while singing. The singer should not sing with hands raised up, nor with his eye fixed up, nor should he glance at the limbs of his body nor any one particularly (*Liṅga*, II.3.62.63) :

> हस्तविक्षेपभावेन व्यादितास्येन चैव हि ।
> निर्याजिह्वायोगान न गेयं हि कथंचन ॥

When hungry, thirsty or when afraid, a person should never sing, nor in darkness (*Ibid*: 66). (Fig. - 5195)

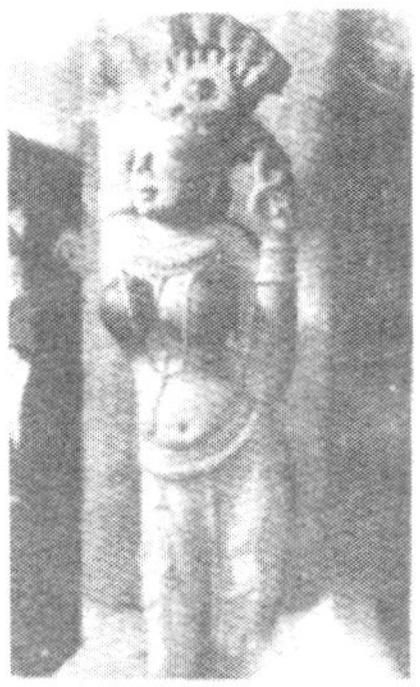

Fig. - (5195)

5197 **गुरु**

Guru : teacher, spiritual teacher, master. The phenomenon of mass Indian loyalty to a *guru* springs from a common source : the dependence physiology rooted in the hierarchical caste system. The elevation of the sage to the status of *guru* at the head of a religious community represents a comparatively large stage in the development of an Indian religious sect from its origin in magic and sorcery. Whether he teaches or not is immaterial, for his charisma itself his sermon. His potency resides in the fact that he does nothing :

he inhabits the zone of nothing, the deeps of silence. If he chooses to talk, the essence of his message is that he can only indicate by language why language cannot say what it cannot say.

Strictly speaking, a *guru* is a man or woman who gives *dīkṣā*, initiation into a sect of renouncers. The *guru*, or *guru*-figure in general, should not be regarded as a kind of inert and passive social mascot. In one sense, he plays a highly positive and active social role. This is his readiness to act as master to his diciple — the *guru-śiṣya-sambandha.*

As long as India continues to be in transition from a sacred to a secular society, the *guru*-figure will remain the model for the Indian charismatic leader, not because India is more or less religious than the supposed advanced cultures, but because the *guru* figure answers a cluster of psychological needs.

5198 **गुरुदक्षिणा**

Gurudakṣiṇā : an offering to the teacher at the end of one's studies. In ancient India, especially in Vedic times, the students used to live in the hermitage with their teachers and after completing their studies and before returning home, they used to offer their teachers whatever best they could afford. Sometimes, it was the demand or wish of the teacher that was to be fulfilled by the disciple. The education being free of charge was considered to be a priceless and sacred gift from the teacher to whom the disciple felt indebted for the whole of his life (Kālidāsa, *Raghu.*, 5.72).

5199 **गोधर्म**

Godharma : behaviour like that of a bull and cow, freedom of food and sex, free sex-relationship. The account of Dīrghatamas who followed the *go-dharma* copulating with his own daughter-in-law is very popular in Sanskrit literature (*Matsya*, 48.81-82). It is said that Dīrghatamas was initiated in *godharma*. According to it there is nothing like a restriction in sex-behaviour, and none is restricted person for sex (*Vāyu, Uttara.*, 35. 54-54). Sexual hospitality is indicated in certain accounts. Thus, one Bhadrāyu is said to have offered his wife Kīrtimālinī to a Brāhmaṇa, who had asked for sex with her on seeing her (*Skanda*, III. 3.14; *Śiva*, III. 27.6-46). In another account, a Brāhmaṇa named Sudarśana figures as allowing his wife to sexually gratify a guest, and advising her that a guest should be offered anything he desires (*Liṅga*, I.30-46). Husband said to the guest :

भुङ्‌क्ष्व चैनां यथाकामं गमिष्येहं द्विजोत्तम ।

Sexual freedom is indicated by another account, where there were certain places open for free sexual acts (*Skanda*, VI. 78.4.25). At those places a regular sexual festival is said to have been going on : (*Ibid.*).

रुद्रशीर्षाभिधाने च प्रचक्रुः सुरतोत्सवम्

5200 **गोपीयूष**

Gopīyūṣa : milk of the newly born cow, known as *peyunsarī* in Baghelī. It is taboo, according to *Skanda Purāṇa* (IV. 40. 9-11), to take milk of a cow in the first seven days of her delivery.

5201 **गोरोचना**

Gorocanā : facial cosmetics (Kālidāsa, *Vikrama* 5.118, *Kum.* 7.119) also known as *rocanā* (*Kumāra*, 7.124).

5202 **ग्रन्थि**

Granthi : knots. In certain rituals cords had to be given knots. The *Aghi-Purāṇa* (78.12.12) mentions ten types of knots such as (a) *prakṛti* (natural, simple). (b) *pauruṣī* (manly). (c) *vīra* (heroic). (d) *aparājitā* (not defeatable). (e) *jayā* (victorious). (f) *vijayā* (specially victorious). (g) *ajitā* (not defeated),. (h) *sadā śiva* (always auspicious). (i) *manomanī* (prone to the mind) and (j) *sarvamukhī* (facing all quarters).

5203 **ग्रहण**

Grahaṇa : eclipse. The cause of the eclipse is that the evil Rāhu eats up the luminaries. Viṣṇu asks his weapon to be on guard. The demon catches them only for a moment. The momentary touch by the demon is called *grahaṇa* by the people (*Bhāg.*, V. 24.2.3). Nothing should be partaken of till the eclipse is cleared.

5204 **ग्रीष्मवेषविधि**

Grīṣmaveṣavidhi : dress-style in the summer season (Kālidāsa, *Raghu.*, 19.273).

च - Ca

5205 **चतुरस्रायन**

Caturasrayāna : palanquin. This was a vehicle in which a person was carried by four persons from one place to another. This vehicle was mostly used by the rich men or the womenfolk of the rich families (*Raghu.* 6., 85).

5206 **चन्द्र**

Candra : moon, not to be seen on the first bright of Kārtika (*Skanda* , II.4.10.22). (Fig. - 5206).

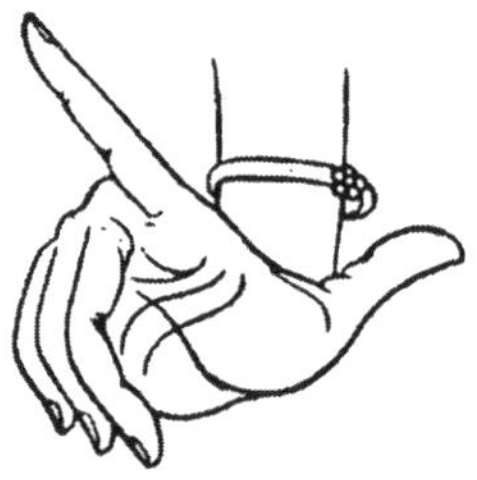

Fig. - (5206)

5207 **चरणराग**

Caraṇarāga : pigment for the feet (Kālidāsa, *Vikrama* . 4.94, *Kum.*, 8.165, *Raghu.*, 19.270).

5208 **चषक**

Caṣaka : drinking bowl (Kālidāsa, *Raghu,*. 7.110).

5209 **चामर**

Cāmara : *caurī* or the fly-whisk consisting of the tail of a yak. It is used during the performance of any worship. *Caurī*-bearers usually shown on the representations of Hindu cult-images. In Gondi society it is the white and black *chauwur*, described as a whisk, it is a sheaf of hair tied to a bamboo stave. Both the hair as well as the stave are sacred objects of great legendary importance. The white *Chauwur* is the emblem of Kali Kalasur Jeitur, whose tale of suffering and persuasion is well-known in the Lingo-legend. The white *Chauwurs* were wrapped in white cloth, and the black *Chauwur* was then placed under a separate leaf shelter (C. Von Haimendorf, p.116).

Chauwur represents a female deity like Sungalturpo. The hair of the *Chauwur* is said to represent the tresses of the female deity. Sungalturpo and Manko are represented by black *Chauwurs.*

To obtain a *Chauwur*, Gond hunters dug pits on the tail of sacred cows; when a god's cow passed, then with one stroke of knife they cut off its tail.

5210 **चारुता**

Cārutā : charm. Kālidāsa defines *cārutā* (charm) as that which causes one to please greatly: प्रियेषु सैभाग्यफला हि चारुता (*Kumāra.*, 5). Charm is an elusive thing, a mysterious quality possessed by a lucky few as Pārvatī. It is not confined to the beauty of the face, figure or even voice, it is a manifestation of ones inner personality. Charm, says Kālidāsa, can be cultivated. To be charming a woman has to make an effort like Pārvatī. One of the most assets of a charming woman is her voice. Pārvatī had the beauty of heaven in her tone. Her voice reflected the beauty of her soul, the loveliness of her mind and the depth of her emotion. She was *mañjubhāṣiṇī.*

A charming woman need not always be very beautiful, but she has achieved an effortless co-ordination of mind and body. Complete self-confidence is her greatest asset. Charm is a combination of glow of health, a soft modulated voice, an easy confident stride, an erect carriage, a radiant personality, intellectual curiosity, integrity and stability of character and finally complete self-assurance.

Charm is the magnet which attracts those around you. It can bind people to you with chains of steel. It is a flower, a fragrance, a magic wand which transforms the ugly into beautiful. Charm is a part of love and its effect on us cannot be over emphasized.

5211 **चूचुकलक्षण**

Cūcuka-lakṣaṇa : signs of nipples (of men). People whose nipples are not raised become attractive and fortunate; while those whose nipples are unequal and long become poor. With stout (hard), muscular and sunken ones they become kings enjoying happiness (*Bṛhat-Saṁhitā*, LXVIII):

> सुभगा भवन्त्यनुद्बद्धचूचुका निर्धना विषमदीर्घैः ।
> पीनोपचितनिमग्नैः क्षितिपतयश्चूचुकैः सुखिनः ॥

See also Prahlāda:

> अदर्शने तु नाडीनां सुखभोजनादिदेश ।
> उत्तुङ्गचूचको भूयादनपत्यश्च दुःखभाक् ॥

5212 **चैत्य**

Caitya : (a) a part of building, holy place (*Skanda*, II.4.7.13-14). (b) a type of building structure built with a thousand stones (*Vāmana*, 2.17.237). (c) the pīpal tree, paid respect (*Vāmana*, 14.52).

ज - Ja

5213 **जत्रुलक्षण**

Jatrulakṣaṇa : signs of collar bones. Varāhamihira (*BS*, LXVIII) has depicted the following signs of collar bones: one who has undulating collar bones becomes cruel; witht hese having many bony knots or sharp joints, poor; with raised ones, enjoyer of pleasures; with sunken ones, penniless; and with stout ones, wealthy." Cf. the same source:

जत्रुभिर्विषमैः क्रूरा दरिद्रा क्रूरसान्धिभिः ।
भोगी चोन्नतजत्रुः स्यान्निम्नैः निःस्वोऽन्यथा धनी ॥

It is to be noted in this connection that according to Vālmīki, who says *gūḍha-jatruḥ* about Śrī Rāma, the collar bone should not be prominent i.e. it should be hidden by muscles.

5214 **जलम्**

Jalam : water. About the cleanliness there is an interesting belief. The half-drunk water from a glass or a container is drunk by corpse or ghosts:

यतः पीतं जलं पुंसामप्रक्षाल्य च यद् भवेत् ।
प्रेताः पिशाचास्तद्रूपं संक्रम्य प्रबन्ति च ॥
(*Skanda*., 1.2.64.11)

It is said that one should not sip water with sandles on, nor while standing in water, nor with turban on. One should not sip with water droped from above, nor with rain-water, nor with standing, nor with water dropped and caught on one palm, nor without the sacred thread, nor while sleeping or sitting with knees forward, nor while speaking, laughing, nor while sounding his fingers, nor while thinking of something else (*Kūrma*., II. 13.10-14).

Water should not be accepted if given by hand, for in that case it is equal to accepting cow's flesh:

पानीयं......हस्तदत्तं न गृहणीयात्
(*Skanda*., 1.2.64.11)

Water given to a thirsty person is highly extolled especially when the summer-sun heats up the earth (*Brahmavaivarta*, 1.17.69).

'A flower', says the Pardhān, 'cannot live without water: nor can a girl', and 'A tree cannot grow without water, nor can love':

This is the way of love
Tie the neck of a pot with cord
Throw it down the well
And bring up water to quench your thirst
It goes down deep
It goes down deep
And brings up water.

5215 **जलाग्नि**

Jalāgni : fire and water. The image of fire placed in water is used throughout Indian mythology to express the control of indestructible excess energy. Although in Western thought water brought to fire usually results in the extinction of fire, in India the fire almost always emerges intact from the combination, merely controlled or transformed, like uranium in which blocks of cadmium have been suspended. The aptness of this apparently anachronistic image of harnessed nuclear energy emerges from two modern ironies: J. Robert Oppenheimer, upon seeing the first atomic explosion, recalled the *Bhagavad Gītā* verses describing the doomsday conflagration, and that the atomic reactor at Trombay in India is in the unmistakable shape of *liṅga* within the *yoni*. The force continues to generate energy, but there is no explosion. Śiva's association with this symbolism may be traced back to an early period. In the *Atharva Veda* (VII.87.1) it is said that Rudra is in fire and water, in the *Brāhmaṇas* (*Śatapatha Brāhmaṇa*, 6.1.1. 1-2) he is born from fire and water. A complex interpretation of these symbols appear in *Śiva Purāṇa* (7.28.3-19). Śiva pleads with Pārvatī to draw him out of *kāma* as out of a fire, to save him with the *soma* of her body (*Kālikā*, 45.117). He seeks relief in the waters of two rivers , which appear as substitutes for Pārvatī as the Ganges does in the Skanda myth (*Skanda*, 6.258.1-4). Pārvatī uses this metaphor to express her passion: 'Even if fire were to become cool, I would not stop loving Śiva; but when, spurned by him, she enters a fire, her ascetic powers make it become as cool as sandlewood paste' (*Śiva*, 2.3.25.69). The concept of the fiery phallus placed in water appears in a dream related by one Agaria: "I made my forge and began to fashion iron tools. A spark fell on me. I got up and waved my hands to put it out. My wife threw water on my penis. 'There is the fire', she cried" (Elwin, 1942.119). This natural symbolism is thus psychologically attested in India, and it is intrinsic in the mythology of the flame *liṅga*. Brahmā instructs the sages to beg Pārvatī to take the form of the *yoni* to receive the *liṅga* and sprinkle the *liṅga* with consecrated water to make it peaceful (*Śiva*, 42.27-32).

This is reflected in actual cult practice: 'The *liṅga* of Mahādeva, a thirsty deity, who needs continued cooling to relieve his distress, must be kept continually moist to avoid drought' (Crooke, 1896.I.76). Although thirst and drought are motifs related to this symbolism, it is primary the lust of the man which must be controlled in this way.

5216 **जातिस्मर**

Jātismara : a person who remembers his former births. The *Skanda Purāṇa* (V.2. 78. 17) relates a tale with conjuring—motif. Lāvaṇyavatī, the daughter of King

Citrasena, remembered her past birth. Another interesting story is that of Ānanda, the son of King Anamitra, who was a *Jātismara* - remembered his former births (*Skanda*, V. 2.33. 5-37).

5217 **जामातृ**

Jāmātṛ : son-in-law (Kālidāsa, *Kum*,. 7. 129).

5218 **जीव**

Jīva : soul, the principle of life, the individual soul as distinguished from the Universal soul, called *puruṣa* in *sāṁkhya* life is the seed, in shape like the flower of *Kadamba* tree:

> जीवं बीजात्मकं ध्यायेत् कदम्बकुसुमाकृतिम्
> (*Agni*, 30.30)

In another place, soul is the trader, who wanders from country to country for the sake of getting the wealth. The individual soul thus arrives in this world, which is like great jungle (*Bhāgavata*, V. 14.2). *Agni-Purāṇa* (60. 19. 23) Symbolizes soul with the thumb.

5219 **ज्ञानपण्य**

Jñānapaṇya : Kālidāsa (*Māl*., 1.20) has used this word contemptuously for a man who imparts education for mercenary motive only.

त - Ta

5220 **तडाग**

Taḍāga : tank. A dug up tank or a water-place is extolled, as being useful for various purposes namely washing of clothes, utensils and other things, also performing the ritual of the means, etc. Hence digging of even one tank is said to be very meritorious, especially in a place where there is scarcity of water (*Padma*., *Sṛṣṭikhaṇḍa*., 54. 2-10).

5221 **तपस्विन्**

Tapasvin : one who has *tapas*, an ascetic.

5222 **तपस्विनी**

Tapasvinī : a female ascetic.

5223 **तपोधन**

Tapodhana : an ascetic. In the works of Kālidāsa we find a live description of forest dwelling ascetics and their pious hermitages. It is no exaggeration if we say that much of sylvan beauty in Kālidāsan literature depends on the word pictures delineated by him of ascetics, their penance groves and the calm, scared and halooed atmosphere prevalent in the woodland dwellings (*Śākuntalā*, 1.14-15; *Raghu*., 1.49-53, V. 6-9, XIV. 76-82; *Kumāra*., III. 41-42).

5224 **तरङ्ग**

Taraṅga : wave. The Gond and Baiga have never, of course, seen the sea but they have opportunities of watching the surface of lake or river stirred into little waves of the breeze, while the passing of the wind over a great field of corn produces waves not unlike those of the ocean. The wave with its swinging movement is a natural sexual symbol and is used frequently in the songs. This symbolism is not unknown to Sanskrit literature. In the *Kathāsaritsāgara* the dancing girl, Sundarī, dances like a wave of the sea of beauty tossed up by the wind of youth. A merchant's lovely daughter, Śikharā, is 'like a wave of the sea of love's insolence' and carries the hero off his feet. Of another girl it is said that 'like a wave of the sea she was full of beauty.'

A poem of Felltham (1661) makes an even more direct comparison:

The waving sea can with such flood that hath stood Bathe some high palace

Far from the main up in the river:

> O think not then but love can do
> As much, for that's an ocean too,
> That flows not every day, but ever.

5225 **तानप्रदायित्व**

Tānapradāyitva : used for producing protracted tone (Kālidāsa, *Kum*., 1.4).

5226 **तित्तिरि**

Tittiri : a kind of patridge, Red-wattled Lapwing, *tītar* in Hindi. According to Muria legend the *tītur* got its name and its cry when at a human marriage the Belosa in charge of all arrangements found she had lost her clitoris (*tītā*). As she was looking for it, she met the bird and borrowed one from her. She promised to return it but never did so; and so now the bird is always saying, 'tītā dē', give me my clitoris.

This *titi* or clitoris - bird is the subject of several folk-tales generally on the lines of a human girl who, finding herself without adequate sexual equipment persuades the bird to lend her its clitoris and never returns it:

> Over you the sun passes like a wave
> In the forest the clitoris-bird is feeding.

5227 **तिथि**

Tithi : days (in a month). Various *tithis* (days) are said to be auspicious for various gods.

5228 **तिलोदकम्**

Tilodakam : water with sesamum. Kālidāsa uses it in the sense of water with sesamum seed offered to the departed.

5229 **तीर्थ**

Tirtha : holy place. In a holy place of great reputation one is required to go on foot, and not in a vehicle (*Skanda*, III. 2. 32. 69): तीर्थे पुरातने पादचारेण गम्यते ।

5230 **तुम्बी**

Tumbī : pumpkin, an interesting variation of the motif of jar in Sanskrit literature. One of the wives of Sagara gave birth to a pumpkin (*Brahma*, 8. 68). A red pumpkin is given with a desire of gaining a son (*Ibid.*, 16. 59).

(b) gourd. A gourd is a favourite symbol of a girl and the tribal people sometimes speak of the *tumā-dūdh* or the breasts that are like gourds. A Lahaki Karmā from Amarkantaka describes the difficulty of a young man unable to get a wife. In ever creeper which represents the village sprawling on its hill, there are many gourds or girls:

> *O ho hai* ? In the middle of the path
> Is a creeper heavy with gourds
> I have searched in every creeper
> Every creeper, but I have found nothing.

5231 **तैलाभिषेक**

Tailābhiṣeka : pouring oil in a continuous line over the head, causing it to stream down, it evades all evils and diseases:

> तैलाभिषेकं यः कुर्यात् (*Skanda* ,V. 1. 21. 25)

The oil *abhiṣeka* motif is common with Hanūmat. It is one of the marriage rites in village as well as tribal India. In Halbi it is known as *tel-ceghnī.*

5232 **त्रित**

Trita : youngest of the three brothers. *Trita* is said to be the youngest of three brothers, the other two being *ekata* and *dvita. Trita* is always a learned man (*Skanda*, VII. 1. 257. 1-32).

द - Da

5233 **दक्षिण**

Dakṣiṇa : south. When a person dies, his head should turned to the south: दक्षिणायां शिरः कृत्वा (*Varāha.*, 187. 98-100), but in living condition he never sleeps turning his head to the south.

5234 **दन्तकाष्ठ**

Dantakāṣtha : twig for washing teeth (*Skanda*, IV. 80. 28).

5235 **दन्तपद**

Dantapada : erotic biting (Kālidāsa, *Kum.*, 8.165).

5236 **दिवस**

Divasa : days. Everyday is said to be symbolic in India. Thus, it is said that gifts on each Sunday, with the worship of the sun secure health in the next birth for ten years; so, it is said, on a Sunday a Brāhmaṇa should be treated with *daśāṅgam ānanam,* i.e. food with ten ancillary services, viz. honour, invitation, giving bath, rubbing his feet, giving clothes to wear, sandal and other applications to his body, clarified butter and *apūpas,* food with six types, betel leaves and *dakṣiṇā* (*Śiva,* 15. 26-28). Monday is special for the worship of Lakṣmī: this is supposed to give wealth. Tuesday for the worship of Kālī and offering of food prepared from black gram and green gram; it is supposed to bestow freedom from diseases. Wednesday is the day for the worship of Viṣṇu with the offering of curds and cooked rice; this is said to nourish the family including sons, daughters, wife and friends. Thursday is marked by worshipping any god, who should be offered milk and boiled rice, and a sacred thread; the result is long life. On a Friday all gods are said to be worshipped for the gain of all enjoyments; and on a Saturday Rudra is enjoined to be worshipped, with the gift of the boiled rice cooked with sesame; the result is the avoidance of premature death (*Ibid.* 14. 11-34). Saturday is a special day for *Śani,* the planet Saturn; and oil is enjoined to be given to the Brāhmaṇa on this day (*Agni,* 280.4): तैलं शनिश्चरे दद्यात् ।

On a Tuesday, new clothes are to be worn; one should start his studies; one should take bath with oil-massage to the body, whereby he would not be blamed by the strength of the planet *Maṅgala* (*Skanda,*V. 2.43. 27).

> नववस्त्रपरीधानं विद्यारम्भं दिने तव ।
> तैलाभ्यङ्गं करिष्यन्ति न च प्राप्तयन्ति ते बलम् ॥

5237 **दिवामैथुनदोष**

Divāmaithunadoṣa : Among all sexual evils, day-time sex and that at the twilights is most censured. *Brahmavaivarta* (I. 34. 44) says that the goddes of wealth leaves such people (also *Śiva*, V. 44.23). According to *Garuḍa Purāṇa* (I. 114.30) morning-sex might cut life. Certain legends employ the motif of day-sex and evening-sex and deplore it. Thus, it is said that when the sage Jamadagni has sexual intercourse with his wife Reṇukā, the sun censured him (*Brahmavaivarta* II. 79. 7-18):

दिवामैथुनदोषो हि वत्त्क वेदो विशेषतः ।

It is said that when Parāśara had sexual union with Satyavatī in the boat in the Gangā, he is said to have created darkness (*Mhb.*, Ādi 63. 70. 83). Kaikasī, the daughter of the demon Sumālin is said to have approached the sage Viśravas in the evening for sexual union. The sage cursed that she would give birth to cruel sons as she approached and insisted on having sex with him at the cruel period (*Skanda*, III. 47. 29): सन्ध्याकालेऽधुना क्रूरे । It is implied that a man could not deny a woman in her period.

5238 **दिवासङ्केत**

Divāsaṅketa : an appointment to meet in certain place by day (Kālidāsa, *Māl.*, IV).

5239 **दीक्षा**

Dīkṣā : purification, consecration, initiation. The earliest reference we have to complete purification rites reveals 'individual' anxiety about bodily margins. This is the Vedic purification or *dikṣā*, whereby the sacrificer prepares himself for the great *Soma* sacrifice. He is separated for purification in a specially constructed hut, as tribes do at present. Dangerous polluting agents are removed by the shaving of hair and cutting of nails. The *Aitareya Brāhmaṇa* (4.7) is explicit in its account of the symbolic nature of this purification: "The bath signifies his conception, the hut is the womb, the garment the amnion, the skin of the black antelope the chorion".

In the *Purāṇas dīkṣā* indicates the primary ritual for admission to a particular order. *Purāṇas* refer to initiation in two ways: (1) one is the regular *upanayana* which is dealt within *Gṛhyasūtras* and *Smṛtis.* (2) another type of initiation is for the *śrauta* rites, which include Vedic sacrifices. The Brāhmaṇa boy is to be initiated in the 8th year of birth or conception, in the 11th year the Kṣatriya, in the 12th year the Vaiṣya; and the upper limit, according to *Agni Purāṇa* (153. 6-7) for all is the 16th year.

Kālidāsa (*Raghu.*, 3.47) has used consecration for religious ceremonies.

5240 **दीप**

Dīpa : lamp. Lamp was placed in a delivery room to ward away evil-powers (*Brahmāṇḍa*, 1.2.27.114). Various types of lamps with oils, wicks and ghee of various kinds are discussed resulting in various gains (*Bhaviṣya, Uttarakhaṇḍa*, 130. 5-37).

The lamp frequently appears in Indian poetry and painting as a love-symbol (Elwin, 1946. 59). In the Punjab ballad of the love of the Princess Chand Karan and Raja Chandarbhan, when the princess prepares to receive her lover *Chatr-mukut*, three hundred and sixty beds are laid in the palace and the swan who arranges the meeting directs:

Light up all the candles,
And pray to the lamps,
Hear Golden Lamps hear my prayer
Today I meet my love, burn all the night.
(*Temple*, II. 92)

Chandainī, the heroine of the Lorik epic, is everywhere called 'the lamp'.

The lamp frequently occurs in the tribal songs of Maikal Hills:

O Mother, what am I to do
With my forbidden love?
The moth does not realise the lamp
Is fire and dies.
* * * * *
O bring back my lighted lamp
Or in a flash I'll send my life away.

The lamp occurs in these songs as a sexual symbol. It is used in the same way in some of the Pahāri paintings of Kangra and Jammu. One of the Mukarni (a sort of riddle) of the ancient Urdu poet Khusron identifies the lamp and the bridegroom:

He passed a sleepless night with me;
But he left me in the morning;
His separation breaks my heart;
Is it the bridegroom? No, friend, the lamp.

The wick, the oil, the bowl of the lamp all have their place in the symbolism. To the modern urban Indian who may never have seen a lamp of the old type, the imagery may not appeal. But it is true and appropriate in village India which still uses the ancient model. A girl is 'pretty as an ornamented lamp'.

5241 **दीपदान**

Dīpadāna : gift of a lamp. Even a chance-virtue amounting to a gift is said to work wonders. Among the *dānas*, the gift of a lamp is said to be important. According to an account, Lalitā, the daughter of the king of Vidarbha gave a lamp to Viṣṇu. Once the lamp, which was about to get extinguished, burnt more brightly due to contact of a she-rat that was chased by a cat. When Lalitā died, she became the favourite of a King, beloved of him among a hundred others, due to the chance - flaring up the lamp (*Agni*, 200. 6.18). There is a myth about the origin of the custom of donating lamps. It is said that once Śiva, concealed himself. Hence the whole world was enveloped in darkness; because the sun and moon, who are the eyes of Śiva, were also concealed. When the gods approached Viṣṇu Nārāyaṇa, the latter asked them to donate lamps. As the gods donated lamps, Śiva came back, and there was light (*Skanda*, V. 1.30. 8-55).

5242 **दीपप्रदान**

Dīpapradāna : the festival Dīpāvalī in honour of Bali (*Skanda*, 1.1.18.53) who churned the ocean whence came out a variety of gems. It is also known as *Kaumudī*.

5243 **दीपमाला**

Dīpamālā : lighting of the oil-lamps arranged in a particular line, arrangement of oil-lamps at temples (*Liṅga*, II. 1. 19-20).

5244 **दीपहर्त्ता**

Dīpahartā : stealing of lamp. The gift of a lamp is extolled by *Agni-Purāṇa* (200. 2.10); and it is said that he who steals a lamp becomes dumb or a dunce, and after death, he goes to hell:

जायते दीपहर्ता तु मूको वा जड एव च ।
अन्धे तमसि दुष्पारे नरके पतते किल ॥

It is also said that one who steals a lamp from a temple suffers after death (*Ibid.*)

5245 **दुर्मन**

Durmana : neurasthemia. It involves timidity, anxiety, nervousness. It may be caused by great strain, anxiety, excessive grief, etc. (*Charaka*, 7.5).

5246 **दुहितृशुल्क**

Duhitṛ-śulka : fee for daughter, bride price. It denotes that the bridegroom had to prove to be worthy of the bride (Kālidāsa, *Raghu.*, 11.166).

5247 **दूतिपद**

Dūtipada : office of go-between (Kālidāsa, *Kum.*, 4.61).

5248 **दूरता**

Dūratā : distance. Distance ranks among the most powerful of all silent messages; so powerful infact, that the amount of distance between communicators can be used as a gauge to measure the type of conversation that is going on, the nature of interpersonal relations, and the purposes of the verbal exchange. Sometimes distance is so powerful that we could get an idea of what was going out in a situation without even hearing a single word. People communicate their status, relationships, and purposes through the way they handle distance. We can observe the distances that characterize everyday events - exchange between strangers, friends, lovers, business associates, working partners, family members. Edward Hall has conducted research that suggests a close link between distance and speech patterns. Hall (1966:126) distinguished, in the case of distance, four zones: zero to $1^1/_2$ feet for intimate; $1^1/_2$ to 4 feet for personal; 4 to 10 feet for social-consultive; and 10 feet and over for public interactions. Hall suggested further that a communicator who violates these implicit distance limits will elicit negative feelings from his addresses. Intimate distances begin with a close phase (the distance of love-making and wrestling, conforming and protecting, where olfactory and thermal sensations are maximal, perception of very fine visual detail (e.g. skin texture) is at its greatest, while large objects (e.g., the head) are blurred and most important, where physical contact is more probable. Speech, interestingly, plays a relatively minor role, given the abundance of other sensory stimulation from other modalities.

At personal distances, visual distortion no longer occurs and thermal perception is effectively diminished, olfaction to a lesser extent. Interactants can reach and touch each other with their extremities, but, at the far phase, only if both extend their limbs.

At social distances most informal business occurs, where the taller of the two interactants can look down at the other. Visual contact is most important to interaction at these distances as gaze aversion is a tantamount to terminating communication.

Finally, public distances, take defensive or socially evaluative actions. Much of the NV communication shift to gesture and body stance.

5249 **दूर्वा**

Dūrvā : name of a grass; its curative and ritual value has been emphasized in various *Purāṇas*. This grass has been mentioned to be auspicious *Ṛgveda* (X. 142.8), where it is said that it should be grown round the house: आयने ने परायणे दूर्वा रोहन्तु पुष्पिणी : ।

Among the daily practice of a person, offering of *dūrvā* into fire is enjoined. (*Vāmana*, 14. 36). The *Bhāgavat* (V. 36) mentions the *dūrvā* as auspicious and apt to be looked every morning.

5250 **देशप्रेम**

Deśaprema : patriotism. In the tribal regions as well as in village India, patriotism is synonymous with regionalism. In Santhālī language, *diṣam dulaṛ* means 'love to the country'. Here is a specimen of the song:

janam diṣam nayo janam diṣam hayre,
rengec reho nayo suluk menak.
janam diṣam nayo rengec nacoge.
enho sores nayo janam diṣam.
janam diṣam nayo bagi kate hayre
eṭak diṣamte calaolen khan
janam diṣam leka bayem namadulaṛ.
beyem nama nayo bayem nama.

Translation:

O' Mother-land? O Mother-land!
In spite of poverty there is peace.
Although my mother-land is poverty stricken,
Still it is better than all.
If one leaves one's mother-land
and makes for a foreign land,
He won't get affection as in his mother-land.
He will not get it, he will not get it.

5251 **दोलनम्**

Dolanam : swinging. Frazer (*The Golden Bough*, 277-85) has studied at great length the interesting subject of the magical use of swinging. Many Gond and Baiga shrines in central India have in front of them tall wooden swings, the seats of which are often studded with sharp spikes. On these priests and magicians swing themselves into a state of trance when they are able to proclaim the will of the gods. In middle parts of Madhya Pradesh the Gond practise the Meghnāth swinging ceremony with the same object. The songs, however, stress the erotic character of the swing as follows:

You always said to me
Ride, ride, ride in my swing
But you never put me
In your swing
Sometimes it was brother's swing
Or he was swinging someone else
But you never put me
In your swing
Sometimes brother swings you
And with your eyes you call him a friend
But you never put me
In your own swing.

It is a point which was noticed by Freud and Havelock Ellis. Havelock Ellis (*The Evolution of Modesty*, 174) says, we do not know on what authority, that in the temples of some parts of central India swings are hung up in pairs, and men and women swing in them until they are sexually excited. It is certainly true that Gond and Pradhān women love a swing and when their husbands are away often make one in their houses. The references in the songs illuminate this practice, which says Havelock Ellis, is one of the six hundred forms of sexual pleasure enumerated by De Sade.

The sexual character of swinging is clearly illustrate in a Pardhān swinging song which is sung by girls as they swing to and fro:

O the Rani swings below and the Raja swings above
What is the pillar made of and how have they made the rope?
Of silver is the pillar made and the rope is made of gold
O the Rani swings below and the Raja swing above.
Swing swing, the Raja wearies; swing swing the Rani
All my body is perspiring, swing swing the Rani
with her cloth she wipes his face, swing swing the Rani
The pillar is dropping and the strings have broken
No longer swings the Rani.

It is perhaps significant that the ancient swing Festival of India was associated with Krishna. At first his image as a baby was rocked in a cradle, but later this was changed to the presentation of the god as a young man accompanied by Radha. That swinging was a very popular pastime in ancient India is attested by numerous representations of the subject in the mediaeval sculptures of Orissa; Vātsyāyana speaks of a swing as a common piece of furniture in every house' (N.K. Basu, 'the Spring - Festival of India', *Man in India*, VII.136).

5252 **दोलारोहण**

Dolārohaṇa : swing festival; also called *dolotsava*. It is celebrated in the month of Phālguna (*Skanda*, II. 2. 43. 1-37). *Dolotsava* is also mentioned in *Padma Purāṇa* (*Pātālakhaṇḍa*, 80.45). It is said to be performed on the 14th bright or on the full-moon-day.

ध - Dha

5253 **धारासार**

Dhārāsāra : custom of pouring the water (*Megha*.). The custom of pouring water from the eaves of a house is confined to marriages in the non-tribal belts; while in tribal areas it is not confined to marriages only. In some Bison-horn Maria villages of Bastar, a girl is given this treatment at the menarche. When her first period is over, the girl bathes and stands below the caves in front of her house. Her elder brother's wife or, if she is married, her husband's sister or elder brother's wife, pours water over her from the roof, and she has to catch some and drink it. In some villages again, if a man marries a widow or another man's wife, the woman must stand below the caves with a *bassia latifolia* leaf on her hand. the *waddai* pours water and rice-beer from the roof, all over her, and after this she can enter her new home. Sometimes rivals are set to stand and water is poured over them, which symbolizes the end of their enmity.

5254 **धावक**

Dhāvaka : rice-pounder, husking ram, rice-husking mill (beam worked by foot); *ḍheki* in rural Hindi. Two kinds of rice-pounders are used in Chhattisgarh. One is a pedal-machine which is worked by two people and is fixed in the ground. One of the workers stands at the pedal end of the machine and works the long wooden pedal with the foot while at the mortar end a woman squats to put the grain into the mortar and clears it when it is ready. The other method of husking the grain is in a mortar usually let into the ground but sometimes made of wood and portable. The grain is then husked with a long heavy pestle of wood with an iron ferrule at one end.

The importance of the rice-husker in the everyday life of the people is seen in the very large number of riddles that are made about it. The *ḍhenkī* is a black bitch that jumps when kicked on the hill, it is 'the man who roars when kicked'; it is 'the man who vomits rice when his bottom is kicked', or 'who parts when you kick his buttocks' or 'who goes on eating no matter how you kick him'. There are many songs about the rice-husker also and the noise made by the *ḍhenkī* when it is being pedalled is represented as *ḍhik-ḍhok*. The rice-husker is generally regarded as lucky among Hindus, for it was one of Baladeva's weapons. During a marriage it is tied to a churning-pole and waved over the bride and bridegroom to make them fertile. The husker is often used by a jester during a marriage as an invitation phallus, probably with the idea of promoting the potency of the bridegroom.

Sometimes when the rains fail, disaster can be averted if a rice-husker is placed upright in a dish. When not in use the husker should always be kept carefully as it would by dangerous to insult it be treading on it or kicking it with the foot.

5255 **धूमवर्ति**

Dhūmavarti : smoke-wick, modern cigarette. Smoking of medicinal substances was prevalent in India during the time of Varāhamihira (505 A.D.). The *dhūmavarti*, which was of various types, was considered a help for preserving health, provided it was used not more than thrice a day (*Bṛhat-saṃhitā*, LXVII). Bāṇa refers to it in the description of king Śūdraka.

5256 **धूलिचित्र**

Dhūlicitra : a form of painting with powders. It is listed in *Śilparatna* (ed. Gaṇapati Shastri, 1992), a Sanskrit text on architecture.

5257 **धौतवस्त्र**

Dhautavastra : *dhotī*, the lower garment (*Śiva*., 13.18).

न - Na

5258 **नकार**

Nakāra : negation. There are six types of negation enumerated in Sanskrit literature:

> *maunaṃ kālavilambaśca*
> *prayāṇam bhūmidarśanam* /
> *bhrukuṭyanyamukhī vārtā*
> *nakāraḥ ṣaḍvidhaḥ smṛtaḥ* //

> "Delaying long and keeping mum when sought,
> And eye-brow-knitting, listening not,
> And looking downward, starting out to go
> Are all as good as saying "NO".

5259 **नखक्षताङ्गी**

Nakhakṣatāṅgī : lady who bears the erotic nails (Kālidāsa, *Ṛtu*., 4. 53).

5260 **नदी**

Nadī : river. *Agni Purāṇa* (155.2) enjoins that one should not cross a river without propitiating the manes and the gods. One should not release dirt in water, nor should one enter water in a naked condition.

In India the use of streams and rivers to symbolize love is, of course, very common. In a remarkable article, 'Studies in the Imagery of the *Rāmāyana*', K.A. Subramanya Aiyar describes the early Sanskrit images used in Vālmiki's epic. He gives the following account of how a river and a woman are intimately connected in the poet's imagination. 'In autumn, we are told, the course of rivers, which exhibit girdles in the form of lines of fishes, is rather slow, like that of women early in the morning when they are weary after the pleasures of love. The sight of a river issuing from a mountain suggests to the poet the idea of a woman slipping off the lap of her lover. In autumn, the rivers lose some of the abundance of water brought to them by the rains and the sand begins to show itself here and there. The poet says it is like shy women exposing their hips hesitatingly in their first unions with their lovers. While describing the sleeping wives of Rāvaṇa it occurs to the poet that some of them are like rivers. In all these images, the water in a river seems to correspond to the flowing clothes of a woman (*JOR*, 1929. 341).

The author refers also to Kālidāsa, where the identification of a river and a woman occurs. 'To him also, lives of fish in a river can represent the girdle going round the waist of a woman and the sandbanks stand for the hips. Ponds in autumn, too, with lines of swans for girdle and lotuses for garland, have the supreme beauty of ornamented woman."

5261 **ननान्दा**

Nanāndā : husband's sister. Amarakirti in his *Nāmamālakośa* has presented the social meaning of the word: न नन्दति भ्रातृजाया यस्यां सत्यां सा ननान्दा 'In whose presence brother's wife is not pleased, she is known as husband's sister'. The relationship between a girl and her husband's younger sister are particularly intimate and tender. A young wife is a stranger in her husband's house; everyone is very critical, she is being tested and criticized all the time; she generally is nervous and afraid of the new family. But two people, beside her husband, console her. One is her *devar*, the husband's younger brother, with whom she has every right to a romantic and humorous connection; the other is her *nanada*, the younger sister who is probably unmarried and a favourite in the house, and to whom she can turn for support and confidence. The *bhāwaj* in turn is specially affectionate to her *nanada* and helps her in her love-adventures. unhappily. This pleasant relationship does not often survive the *nanad's* marriage. The *nanad* now goes to live elsewhere, and her visitior's are - in the opinion of her brother's wife - an economic burden.

5262 **नयनसुख**

Nayanasukha : feasts for eyes; Cf.

gantavyam salilapathā
dṛṣṭavyā madanapūritāḥ rāmāḥ
yadyapi bhavati na lābho
nayanasukhaṃ ko nivārayati.

"You stroll about on riv'rine roads
And glance at girls with love's inroads,
Thus, may be, gain there's none to rise,
But who can forgo feasts for eyes".

5263 **नागरकवृत्ति**

Nāgarakavṛtti : polished manners (Kālidāsa, *Śāk.*, 5.355).

5264 **नाटितक**

Nāṭitaka : dramatising expressions of emotions and sentiments (Kālidāsa, *Śāk.*, VI). (Fig. - 5264)

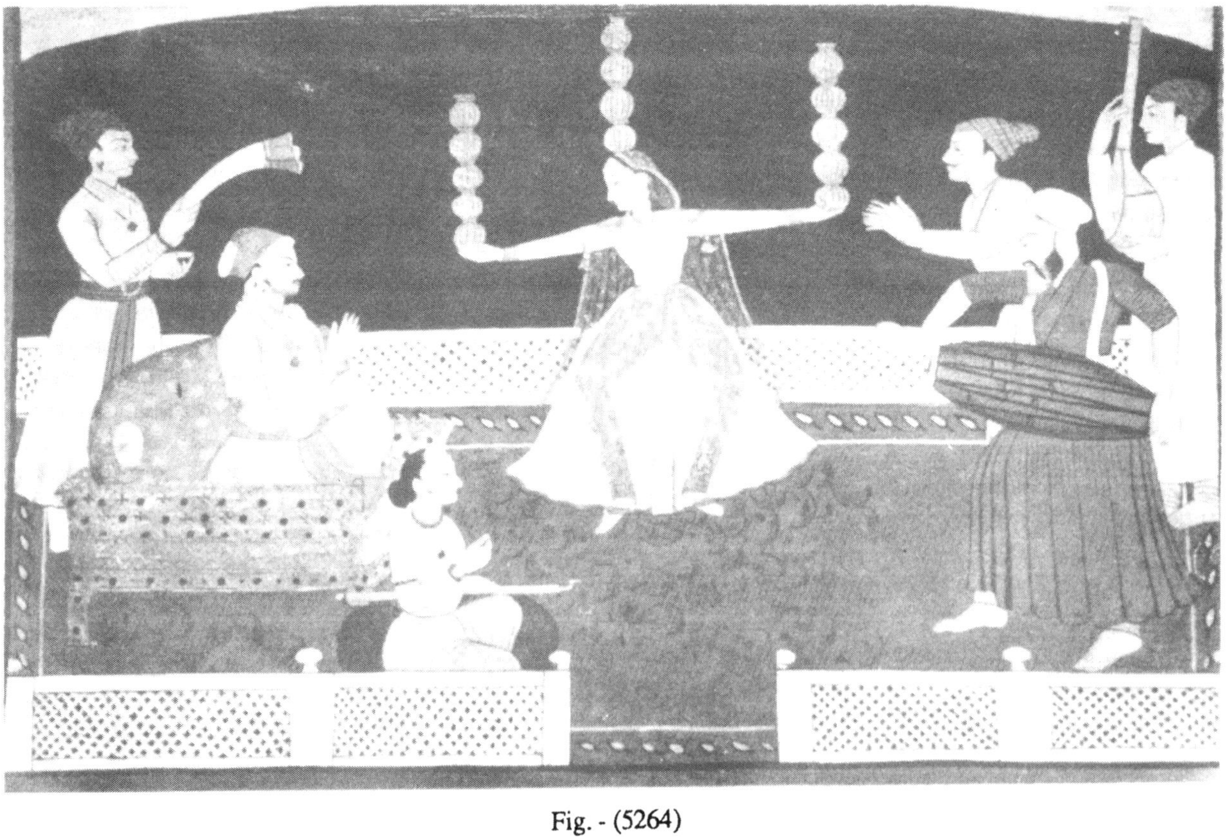

Fig. - (5264)

5265 **नाट्यघात**

Nāṭyaghāta : the blemishes marring the presentation. These *ghātas* are traced to the various sources, but the ones, which are due to actors themselves are endemic to *nāṭya* itself. Unnatural *abhinaya,* erratic movements and gait, forgetting the dialogue or text, faulty pronunciation, speaking timidly, letting the crown fall, fault in music and rhythm are some such flaws (*NS*, XXVII. 24-37).

5266 **नाडिका**

Nāḍikā : water-clock. *kalā, Kṣaṇa* and *nāḍikā* are measure of time (*HC.* VIII). 18 or 15 *nimeṣas* are equal to *kāṣṭhā,* 30 *kāṣṭhās* to a *kalā*, 30 *kalās* to a *kṣaṇa* and 12 *kṣaṇas* to a *muhūrta* which is equal to two *ghaṭikās.* See *Amarakośa.* For a different table and for a water-clock, see *Brahma-Purāṇa* (231. 6-9).

5267 **नारीजीव**

Nārījīva : living by a woman, a profession (*Brahmāṇḍa,* II. 4.8.44).

5268 **निद्राकलश**

Nidrākalaśa : auspicious jars placed near the bed to ward off evil and induce sleep:

> क्रमेण चोद्गते गगनमहापयोधिपुलिने सप्तलोकमङ्गलनिद्राकलशे कुमुदबान्धवे
>
> (*HC,* IV, p. 178)

5269 **निर्मञ्चन**

Nirmañcana : a rite at marriage, said to be for driving away evils. After the marriage, the mother of the bride is said to perform a rite called *nirmañcana* (*Brahmavaivarta, Śrīkṛṣṇakhaṇḍa,* 107, 35).

5270 **निर्माल्य**

Nirmālya : flowers and garlands offered to the deity of the previous day (*Skanda.,* II. 2.38.103).

5271 **निवापाञ्जलि**

Nivāpāñjali : an offering in honour of one's deceased ancestors especially at the time of *śrāddha* ceremony (Kālidāsa, *Raghu.,* 5.69).

5272 **निषेध**

Niṣedha : negative rules, taboo. In the *Kalpa*-tradition and in some of the *Smṛtis,* we come across certain rules of conduct which are prohibitive (*paryudāsa*) or negative (*niṣedha*) in nature. Such a variety of customary abstinences, which according to Marrett, may be called 'negative rites. (*Encl.Of Rel. and Ethics,* Vol. XII. p.183), are also found in the *Gṛhya* as well as *Dharmaśāstra* traditions. Such negative rules are known in the *Pūrvamīmāṁsā* tradition by the name of *niṣedha,* which is defined as *puruṣasya nirvatakam vākyam niṣedhaḥ.* The word *nirvatakam* in this definition implies not only a negation of an act, but has the sense of caution. It is specifically said that such *niṣedha-vākyam* have the purpose of making a person turn away from an action, which is a cause of *anartha* (danger).

This concept of *niṣedha* obtains in a clear-cut manner in the crystallized *Mīmāṁsā*-discipline, where the *niṣedha* (or *pratiṣedha*) sees the probability of an act being done by the natural instinct of man - in the terms of traditional expression when it is *rāgataḥ prāptam.* And, it is negated.

It goes without saying that a fresh study of *niṣedha* would show that quite a few of them had originally the status of the taboo, but this was blurred in due course of time, their place being taken by a promise of boon that would come true in future. This marks the psychological change in the society, that began to care more for the prospective gain, rather than the prick of sin, or the dart from the evil.

5273 **नील**

Nīla : indigo, black or blue colour. It was used in sorcery (*Brahmāṇḍa,* II. 4.41.54). The Brahmahatyā (personified) is believed to wear a black or indigo-नीलवस्त्रधरी भीमा coloured garment - (*Skanda,* II. I. 14.16). The black colour is held to be most inauspicious. It is said that the black or blue-red garment of a woman should be kept away at copulation; but it does not harm on the bed (*Skanda,* IV. 40. 142):

> नीलीरक्तं तु यद् वस्त्रं दूरतः परिवर्जयेत् ।
> स्त्रीणां क्रीडार्थसंयोगे शयनीये न दुष्यति ॥

Both, gift, penance, sacrifice, manes-oblations etc. are fruitless if done with black garment (*Ibid.* 144). The blue or black garment was taboo especially on a *saptamī.* Buddhists belive deep blue is the colour of infinity, and it is often considered to be the ideal colour for contemplation. Indeed, it has been shown that meditation on this colour can reduce blood pressure, breathing rate and lower the pulse rate—encouraging the body to relax.

5274 **नीवारबलि**

Nīvārabali : an offering of a portion of daily wild-rice meal. According to ancient Hindu rituals it is obligatory for every householder to observe the performance of daily five *yajñas* of one is *bhūtabali* i.e. offering of daily meal portions to all creatures. Before taking it, a portion of it is thrown into the air near the house -door (Kālidāsa, *Raghu.* 14. 208).

5275 **नेत्रबन्ध**

Netrabandha : a rite in which the disciples tie a strip of white silk-cloth on the wrist or arm of the preceptor (*Varāha,* 99. 22).

5276 **नेत्रवस्त्र**

Natravastra : eye-strip, famous in Gauḍadeśa (*Skanda* IV. 4.9).

5277 **नेपथ्यविधान**

Nepathyavidhāna : art of make-up (Kālidāsa, *Kum.,* 1.7; *Raghu.,* 14.20). Modern make-up may seem to be sophisticated—but it isn't really very different in essence from ritual tribal adornment. In tribal societies, body decoration reveals an individual's status, gender and often age, for it frequently forms one of the rites of puberty. Elaborate tattoos serve the same function in India. Body piercing is another echo of our tribal past. This kind of body decoration is, like much 'clothing display', one of the way we use ornaments to advertise our wealth, self-image, and place in society. In other words, we're still telling interested observers which tribe we belong to. (Fig. - 5277)

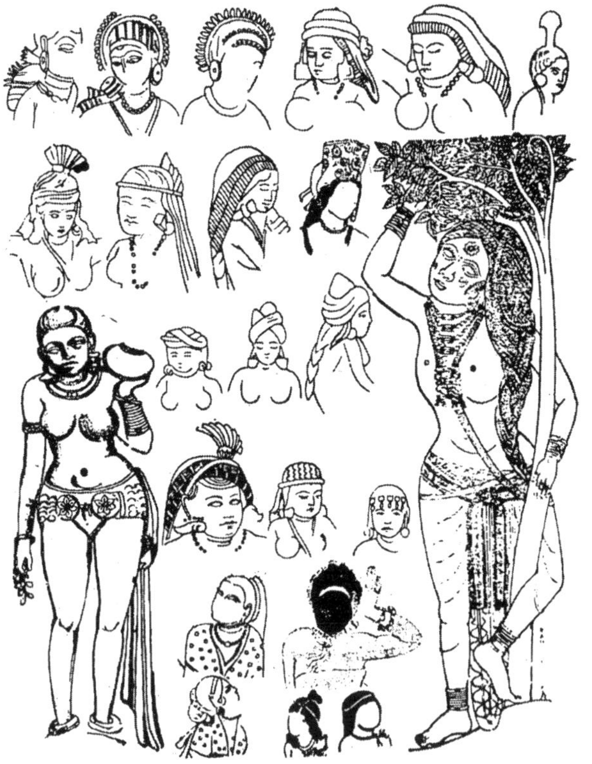

Make-up and dress of olden days

Fig. - (5277)

5278 **नेपथ्यविधि**

Napathyavidhi : art of make-up (Kālidāsa, *Kum.,* 7.125).

प - Pa

5279 **पञ्चकच्छ**

Pañcakaccha : a method of wearing the *dhotī* (lover garment). *Dhotī* was a lower garment with a width from the navel to the feet and above five cubits in length. It was the popular garment with the usual *pañcakaccha,* also known today. This was necessary at rituals (*Śiva. Vidyeśvara Saṁhitā,* 13.18) (b) the Gonds and Halbas tie the cloth round the waist and carry the slack end from the left side behind up the back and over the head and right shoulder; while women of higher castes take the cloth from the right side over the head and left shoulder (Russell and Hiralal, II. 220).

5280 **पञ्चकाष्ठ**

Pañcakāṣṭha : five sticks: a funeral practice; known as *pānc lakaṛiyān* in Chhattisgarhi. There is a custom amongst those who bury their dead known as *pānc lakaṛiyā.* From the name it is undoubtedly originally connected with the practice of cremation. When the grave has been filled in and the mound has been made to mark the spot, those who are present at the burial act each makes five small ball of earh and place them all in a heap at the head of the grave. While doing this Chhattisgarhi address to the deceased and say, "*Jāo mājhī ke kok men avtār leo*" This being interpreted means: "Go become incarnate in some superior human being". Regarding the *pānc lakaṛiyā* practicer it should be noted that it is stated that originally it was the practice of those who attended a cremation to take with them five sticks to place on the funeral pile; this practice seems to have disappeared and the only remains of it, in Chhattisgarh, seems to be this custom at a burial of making balls of earth and calling them the fire sticks.

It is considered meritorious to assist in a burial, and there is a saying that if one could bury a hundred persons, all by himself, he would be made Rājā in the next birth. Another interesting custom in connection with burials is known as *kāndha utāranā.* Those who have carried a bier, after the funeral, each take a clod of earth and with this they will touch first the shoulder, where the bier rested, next the waist, then the knee and finally drop the clod to the ground. They suppose that by so doing they remove from the shoulder the weight of the corpse which would otherwise be left for some time.

5281 **पञ्चध्वनि**

Pañcadhvani : five types of sounds: *Vedadhvani, Vandidhvani. Jayadhvani, Śaṅkhadhvani* and *hulahuladhvani* (made by women folk). These sounds have been enumerated by Tulasīdāsa in his *Rāmacaritamānasa* (1.319.3): *Jaya dhuni bandī bed dhuni maṅgalgān nisān.*

5282 **पञ्चाङ्गाभिनय**

Pañcāṅgābhinaya : acting consisting of five parts; mind, the eye, the eyebrows, the hands and the feet which are used in the pantomimic representation of situations (Kālidāsa, *Māl.*, I). Nīlakaṇṭha quotes:

> कराभ्यां चरणाभ्यां च शिरसा चाभिनीयते ।
> यत्र वस्त्वति विज्ञेया पञ्चाङ्गाभिनयो हि सः ॥

5283 **पटह**

Paṭaha : drums. when a king marches, drums are beaten. Drums announce the march (*prayāṇa*) of a king's army (*HC*, V).

5284 **पट्टबन्ध**

Paṭṭabandha : fillet. It was a mark of great honour. It indicated authority (*HC.*, 313).

5285 **पण्डितकौशिकी**

Paṇḍitakauśikī : a literary lady (Kālidāsa, *Māl.*, 1.5, 1.15, 1.17).

5286 **पतिव्रता**

Pativratā : a faithful wife. Various accounts to extol *pativratā* and to indicate her prowess occur in Sanskrit literature: she used to stop the rising sun (*Padma*, 48. 78), used to die even due to 'false news of husband's death, (*Skanda.*, VII. 3.31. 2-8) etc.

5287 **पदलेप**

Padalepa : ointment for feet, it is for flying through the air (*Agni.*, 81. 20-58).

5288 **पद्मध्वज**

Padmadhvaja : the chariot having the lotus as symbol at Purī (*Skanda*, II. 2.33.2).

5289 **परिभोग**

Paribhoga : amorous sport (Kālidāsa., *Kumāra.*, *Raghu.*,)

5290 **पशुमारण**

Paśumāraṇa : animal sacrifice. Kālidāsa used the word *Iṣṭipaśumāram* in the sense of like the killing of a sacrificial animal; and *paśumāraṇa* in the sense of animal sacrifice.

5291 **पशुयोनिषु मैथुनम्**

Paṣuyoniṣu maithunam : the sexual act with the beasts (*Skanda*, 1.2.41.51, *Nārada*, 14. 125).

5292 **पाण्डर**

Pāṇḍara : white (*Garuḍa*. I. 133.3). In a man white teeth, white clothes, a white turban are admired in the forest regions of India. The following Gondi song expresses the same idea. Women say, 'His turban is white as a mushroom':

> His teeth are white as curds
> His eyes are full of sin
> His face is beautiful as a wild creeper
> His eyes are full of sin
> I am only a bit of cucumber
> He is the ghee
> to make it palatable
> He is the arrow
> But he has not destroyed me
> His arrow has become the pillar of my house.

5293 **पादवन्दन**

Pādavandana : bowing to the feet (*Veṇisaṁhāra*, II).

5294 **पादुकासिद्धि**

Pādukāsiddhi : power due to sandles, one of the magical devices (*Skanda.*, IV. 45.13).

5295 **पानभूमि**

Pānabhūmi : drinking-booth (Kālidāsa, *Raghu.*, 7. 107, 19.268).

5296 **पापभावना**

Pāpabhāvanā : sense of guilt. It is also termed as *manaspāpa* in *Atharva-Veda* (VI. 45): "Whatever wrong we have committed, sleeping or waking, wishing ill of others by disliking them or by slander, may *Agni* take them away from us and keep them far off." It is clearly an expression of sense of guilt. We also find that *pāpa-bhāvana* can be removed by (a) prayer and sacrifice; (b) auto-suggestions; (c) suggestion of the priest; (d) *prāyaścitta* in the form of public confession; (e) hydro-therapy-bathing and sprinkling water; (f) expiatory rites; (g) medicine; (h) amulet and transference.

5297 **पारद**

Pārada : mercury, the symbol of semen. In the funeral rite of the reconstruction of body, mercury is placed symbolically as semen:

> पारदं रेतसः स्थाने
>
> (*Garuḍa*, II. 30.52)

5298 **पार्श्व-पर्यायण**

Pārśva-paryāyaṇa : 'turning of the side' in sleep, a type of ritual during *rathayātrā* (*Skanda*, II.2.29.30).

5299 **पिटकलक्षण**

Piṭaka-lakṣaṇa : characteristics of pimples. Varāhamihira in his *Bṛhat-Saṁhitā* (LII) has devoted a full chapter on the characteristics of pimples on the body. According to him, a white pimple is good for Brāhmaṇs; white and red for Kṣatriyas; white, red and yellow for Vaiṣyas and white, red, yellow and black for Śūdras. He has analysed the effects of pimples on all the parts of the body from head to foot. In the same manner he has classified moles, special marks and hairy circles appearing on the limbs of the human beings.

5300 **पितृक्रिया**

Pitṛkriyā : types of offerings made to the departed ancestor; also known as *pitṛkārya* and *śrāddha* (Kālidāsa, *Raghu.*, 1.45) (b) During the fortnight of the Manes (*pitṛpakṣa*) are two days set apart for the coming of the deceased. The Manes are supposed to visit the homes of their relatives on the date of their decease.

5301 **पिष्टपञ्चाङ्गुलि**

Piṣṭapañcāṅguli : five finger-prints; a marriage ritual in which utensils like mortar, pestle and grinding stones were decked with five finger-prints of turmeric powder (*HC*, IV). The five fingers were dipped in turmeric mixed with water and the mortar and C. were smeared with the finger-marks by way of *maṅgala*. Even now the pestle and grinding stones are marked.

5302 **पीठिका**

Pīṭhikā : platform. It is meant for installing an idol. The *pīṭha* (platform, including the pit) is symbolized as Pārvatī (=vagina). On the platform a white island or erection represents the penis. Round the platform should be vaginal wall (*puram*) with the opening (*gopura*). In the centre is lotus or the *maṇi* (*Skanda*, II. 9.27.1). The platform is of ten types: *sthaṇḍila* (raised), *vāpi* (well-like), *vedi* (alter), *maṇḍala* (circle), *pūraṇa-candra* (like the full-moon), *vajra* (like the shape of a *vajra*), *padma* (lotus-like), *ardhaśaśin* (half-moon) and *trikoṇa* (triangular). All these symbolize vagina.

5303 **पुत्तलिका**

Puttalikā : effigy. *Garuḍa Purāṇa* (II. 30.44) records:

> पश्चात्पुत्तलकः कार्यः सर्वौषधिसमन्वितः ।
> पलाशस्य च वृत्तानां भागं कृत्वा च काश्यप ॥

It is said that when the sage-warrior Paraśurāma visited Kailāsa, he was greeted by beautiful women and boys and girls holding charming images and idols in hands: चित्रपुत्तलिकाकारैः (*Brahmavaivarta,* 1.41.4). Rādhā is said to have seen in her dream the images in the palace dancing and laughing, weeping and singing: सौधपुत्तलिकाः (*Ibid.*, II. 66.17); and when she became ill and fainted, all her attendants tried to protect the toy-images:

> क्रीडापुत्तलिकां काचित् चित्राढ्यां परिरक्षति
> (*Ibid.*, II. 93. 26)

Puttalikās are mentioned also in connection with magic. At the funeral four *puttalās* were kept and burnt along with the body (*Garuḍa.*, II 25, 23-24).

5304 **पुनर्भू**

Punarbhū : woman who had an earlier husband, one whose chastity has been spoiled. Ghosts stay in the house of *punarbhū* (*Skanda.*, VII.1. 167. 36-40).

5305 **पूर्णिमा**

Pūrṇimā : full-moon-day. There is a living tradition of worshipping the *vaṭa* tree on the full-moon-day in the month of Jyeṣṭha, on the part of ladies with their husbands living (*Agni.*, 194.4.8).

5306 **पृष्ठतो मैथुन**

Pṛṣṭhato maithuna : sex from the back, homo-sexuality (*Liṅga*, II. 6.67-69).

5307 **पेषणशिला**

Peṣaṇa-śilā : grindstone. The grindstone and the curry-stone are familiar objects in every Indian house. In Chhattisgarh, the most common grindstone is made of circular stones of the same diameter. The upper stone, which is the heavier of the two, revolves on a wooden pivot which is fixed in the middle of the lower stone. This is sometimes worked by two women, each of them holding the same handle, though often one woman grinds alone. The work is heavy and it is one of the great differences between the life of modern woman, who is not only able to buy four ready made but even bread ready cooked, and the village woman, who has to grind sufficient for a family everyday of her life. Poor women and widows in Chhattisgarh earn a scanty living by grinding for their wealthier neighbours. There are many songs about the grindstone:

> Grindstone is my mother-in-law
> Grinding-peg my brother
> But the silver armlet on my arm
> Is from my husband's earnings.

Most of the riddles are based on the idea that the grindstone is an old woman who eats and eases herself or vomits at the same time. It is, for example, according to the Oraon, 'the women who passes a powdered stool' or 'the old woman who eases herself as she sits'. To the Kharia, it is the woman who vomits ashes or who is always moving about and always easing herself. To the Gond, the grindstone 'eats, runs and vomits all at once'. The Baiga gives a characteristic sexual reference and describes the grindstone as 'the mother who lies still while the father moves about on top of her' or again as 'the sleeping man shaken by a girl. The Oraon again describe the grindstone as 'the cow with one horn that feeds on its master's food' and the Baiga suggests that it is 'a dog that growls when you catch hold of its tail', a reference to that most familiar sound in an Indian village, the roar of the grindstone in a neighbour's house.

Naturally a thing used in such close association with the sacred grain is bound to be lucky. Throughout India great respect is paid to it. 'Part of the earliest form of the marriage ritual consisted in the bride standing on the family grindstone. At the present day she puts her foot upon it and knocks down little piles of heaped grain. It is waved over heads of the pair to scare evil spirits. In Bombay it is said that sitting on a grindstone shortens life, and the Kunbis of Kolaba place a grindstone in the lying-room, and on it set a rice-flour image of a woman, which is worshipped as the goddess, and the baby is laid before it. Such a stone readily passes into a fetish, as at Ahmadnagar, where there is a stone with two holes, which any two fingers of any person's hand can fill, and the mosque where it stands is, in consequence, much respected' (Crooke, II. 166).

At a Kharia marriage also the bride is made to stand on a curry-stone and the husband on a yoke and throughout Chhattisgarh the grindstone is put in front of the bride and bridegroom when they sit for ceremonial greetings during their wedding.

5308 **पौत्री**

Pautrī : grand-daughter. The relationship between an old man and his grand-daughter (both actual and classificatory) in tribal societies are tender and humorous. Marriage between them is permitted and in rare cases occurs, any old man addresses the little girl as his wife, his bride, his lover, and is licensed to make any kind of joke about it. Grandmother and grand-daughter are thus 'co-wives' and they too get a lot of fun out of their relationship, which is based on the idea that they are sisters: it is, of course, quite in order for a man to marry his wife's younger sister.

5309 **प्रकीर्ण मैथुन**

Prakīrṇamaithuna : variations in sex. Those who unite from the back (*pṛṣthato maithuna*) or who indulge in homosexuality, or have sex with beasts, binding them, come under this category (*Skanda*, 1.2.41. 51-52).

5310 **प्रजावती**

Prajāvatī : younger brother's wife (Kālidāsa, *Raghu.*, 14. 210; 15. 219).

5311 **प्रज्ञाचक्षु**

Prajñācakṣu : mental eye (Kālidāsa, *Māl.*, I).

5312 **प्रतिपक्षभावनम्**

Pratipakṣabhāvanam : opposite emotions. What Patañjali (*Yogasūtra*, II. 33-34) called *pratipakṣabhāvanam* is known as *virodhabhāvanā* in Charaka (*Chik.*, 9.86). Excess of eros, grief, fear, rage, delight, envy and greed can be cured by neutralizing it with opposite emotions.

5313 **प्रतिपद्**

Pratipad : the first day of a month; rites are associated with all the *pratipads* (*Agni.*, 176. 1-4).

5314 **प्रतीकवाद**

Pratīkavāda : symbolism. Different domains in the tribal culture evolve their special sets of Vedic or Purāṇic symbolism. Symbolism is frequently associated with the Sanskrit as well as tribal poetry. The symbolism of the songs, which is in some ways their most obvious and important character, is simply the symbolism of everyday set to music. The Gond and Pardhān actually do think and talk in symbols all their lives. A symbol is the readiest cure for embarrassment, and can smooth over a business transaction or a bitch in one's love-making with equal facility. So when the emissaries go on the delicate business of arranging a girl's betrothal, they do not state their purpose directly, but say they have come for merchandise, or to quench their thirst with water, or seek a gourd in which to put their seed.

Similarly, the whole intricate absorbing business of daily love is carried on with symbols. Women by the well ask each other, 'Did you have your supper last night'? 'Are you weary from yesterday's rice-husking?' Men speak of digging up their fields, getting water from the well, entering a house. Not only the solicitations of the seducer but the domestic arrangements of wife and husband cannot be decently conducted without a verbal stratagem.

A good deal of the symbolism is obvious enough, and we get further evidence for its interpretation from dreams, omens and riddles. These interpretations, however, are by no means straightforward. For example, someone dreams of a mango and next day his wife gives birth to a male child: henceforth in that village a mango will stand as the symbol of a boy.

Other symbols are connected with folk-tales and local traditions. Some, which might be expected to depend on obvious sexual associations, actually refer to quite different matters. A girl is symbolised by a bird because she is *pancī*, winged, apt to fly away and desert her lover. She is *canādāl*, gram pulse, which divides in two and reveals the beauty inside. Woman is a cow, not for the obvious reasons, but because women like cows wander scattered across the country-side. When a woman goes to meet a lover, she goes like a cow by devious and secret routes and is never caught; but a man goes directly, like a buffalo, and is soon discovered. It is woman, not man, who appears as a snake in the songs. The conventional phallic meaning is lost beneath an accumulation of legends about the snake-damsel and the poison-maid.

But, of course, a large number of the symbols are just what we would expect and may be paralleled in Western and Chinese poetry as well as in the songs of other Indian tribes.

In Chinese poetry, says Arthur Waley (*The Book of Songs,* London 1937.13), images are used directly. There is no 'as if' or 'like', but the comparison is 'stated on the same footing as the facts narrated. The method of this Chinese poem can be paralleled by many of the tribal poems.

A girl is often compared to a bamboo in the Gondi poetry:

Her hips sway like a young bamboo
Life is only for two days

So is with the Oraon:

On the high hills the bamboo grows
From a bamboo the blue bow is made
The shooting arrows are a spray of water
The gun is fired many rounds.

A girl is a bamboo, says the *Pardhān,* 'because her waist is slender and sways like one'.

One of the most technical devices of the ethnic poetry is its symbolism. This is only an extension into verse of the habits of ordinary life, for people actually do converse all day long in symbols. When a man has daughters to marry he tells his friends that he has *kodon* in his house; when he goes to ask for a girl in marriage he says that he has come for a gourd in which to put his water or for a flower to put in his hair. In Bastar a boy does not ask his girl directly for her favours but begs her to give him some tobacco.

This symbolic method is found everywhere in Indian folk-poetry.

Of Munda-poetry Hoffmann (105) writes: 'The Mundas exhibit a marked predilection for clothing their ideas so completely in similers and symbols always taken from nature as it surrounds them, that an alien might understand every word of a song without as much as guessing what idea the song is meant to convey. Songs of this kind they call *banita kaji,* 'fictions' or '*jonoka kaji,* 'word measures', a piece where the ostensible words are used as a measure or counterpart of something not expressly stated. They will symbolize an idea by translating it into a different order of nature, sometimes in its more striking outlines, sometimes into its details and leave to the listener the task of applying the simile, and of feeling and dreaming himself into the emotion the pest intends to stir up by the picture he presents. Many of these similes are chosen with a genuine poetic instinct and with a correctness which reveals depth of feeling as well as a close and appreciative observation of nature.

W.G. Archer (100) has studied the Oraon method of symbolism with great insight. He describes how Oraon marriage poems use the twin-leaves of an image system - the poems being apparently about objects of nature, but actually referring to aspects of marriage. There are a number of 'clue' poems which reveal what the different symbols mean and thus ensure that the people will always be alive to the method that is used. Sometimes a slight distortion is used to expose the second meaning. A fig tree blossom becomes a girl because its scent spreads for forty miles. A calf becomes a girl because it belongs to the mother and in this way part of the object symbolized is added to the image symbolizing it and the system appears through the distortion. In many poems however there is no distortion and the second level is detected by the employment of pantomimic images.

Wild buffaloes and cobras are equated with opposing relatives because their actions are similar. The action of a bridegroom's party in descending on the girl's house is paralleled in a line of storks descending on a river or a flock of sparrows settling on a tree. A leaping member of the bridegroom's party acts like a frog. The actions of negotiators in closing round a girl resembles bees round a flower and spiders on a web. In these poems the marriage context suffices to show that the images are pantomimic and the accuracy of the pantomime exposes the symbol.

In the poems which relate to the bride and bridegroom the clue remains in the context, but the types of symbol vary more widely. Those of the bridegroom consist either of colour analogies (the green parrot) or power images (the bear, the tiger, the otter). In the case of the bride, certain images are based on the comparison of qualities. Doves, pigeons, wild geese and fish, for instance, possess varying qualities of elegance and speed which resemble the grace or flirtatiousness of a girl; while calves and fawns resemble a girl in their weakness and dependence. Certain other images, such as brinjals, mangoes, figs and bamboos are based on sexual parallels - the connection being either visual or through a fertility power.

In all the poems it is the marriage context - the presence of an audience for a marriage purpose - which enables the images to be used without explanation, and in fact to form the image system. They do not need to refer to the objects they symbolize because the occasion itself makes the audience see them as symbols.

In the Bilaspur version of the *Rasāln* legend there are some remarkable passages where the sexual act is indicated by symbols; unless the reader has the key to the method he can have little idea of what is indicated. Here we find natural objects not only symbolizing the act of life, but providing a sympathetic setting for it.

A very common erotic image is that of cloud and storm - the cloud that covers, the rain that falls, the storm that tosses to and fro - they occur again and again in ethnic songs. The *caumāsā* seasonal songs recorded by W.G. Archer in Patna district are rich in such symbols:

> June is the month of parting, friend
> The sky glowers with gloom
> Leaping and reeling the god rains
> And my sweet budding breasts are wet.
> All my friends sleep with their husbands
> But my own husband is a cloud in another land.

Sometimes the cloud and storm are not directly expressive of the intercourse of lovers but provide a suitable setting for it. Temple (III.225) recorded a vivid poem describing a love-affair between Raja Rasāln and his gardener's wife. There is no manifest expression of the actual encounter of the lovers, but everything is achieved by lament symbols. 'At midnight the rain fell'. The jealous Rani prays that the hut of the gardener's wife may leak. The Raja returns home wet through and the Rani gives him a cold bath.

But Temple's comment on this shows, that he did not grasp the principle of symbolism in Indian folk-poetry. 'It will be observed', he says, 'that there is an allusion to a certain wet night, and all through the long legend of Raja Rasāln there are like mysterious allusions brought into the story in the most inappropriate manner'.

This folk-method of poetry is fully developed in Europe. The symbolism in the East is so much a part of life, so recognized and so easily understood that it naturally dominates its poetry. This is not thc casc in Europe, and those poets who have used symbolism to any considerable extent have often been accused of obscurity.

5315 **प्रदोष**

Pradoṣa : denotes the time just prior to the advent of night and after the sunset: प्रदोषो रजनीमुखम् This period is special to Rudra and Śiva and comes once within a fortnight. It is said, at this time Śiva dances along with the gods in his chamber made of silver in Kailāsa (*Skanda*, III. 3.6.7):

> प्रदोषसमये देवः कैलासे रजतालये ।
> करोति नृत्यं विबुधैरभिष्टुतगुणोदयः ।।

The most important *pradoṣa* is said to be one that comes on a Saturday, and that which comes in the dark half of a month is to be said excellent

> मन्दवारे प्रदोषोऽयं दुर्लभः सर्वदेहिनाम् ।
> तत्रापि दुर्लभतरः कृष्णपक्षे समागते ।।

(*Ibid.*, 5.75)

To sleep at this time is said to be injurious to life (*Ibid.*, 210).

5316 **प्रपा**

Prapā : regular water-booths. Regular waterbooths are enjoined to be arranged, after getting a *pandal* erected on a way by which many people travel in the summer, rainy season or the antumnal season. Water to be given to travellers at such a *prapā* (drinking booth) is also prescribed to be scented with fragrant materials such as *aguru*, and be given along with betel-nuts, betel-leaves and long pepper (*Padma.*, *Sṛṣṭikhaṇḍa.*, 55. 47-48).

5317 **प्रयोगनिपुण**

Prayoganipuṇa : expert in the actual presentation of the dramatic art (Kālidāsa, *Raghu.*, 19.272).

5318 **प्रयोगबन्ध**

Prayogabandha : drama (Kālidāsa, *Vikrama.*, 1.3).

5319 **प्रवासस्थकलत्रवेष**

Pravāsasthakalatraveṣa : dress of the lady during the absence of her husband (Kālidāsa, *Raghu.*, 16. 232).

5320 **प्रसाधिका**

Prasādhikā : a lady expert in make-up work (Kālidāsa, *Kum.*, 7.121; *Raghu.*, 7. 100).

5321 **प्रेम**

Prema : affection, long-enduring, sympathetic love.

5322 **प्रेमवैचित्र्य**

Premavaicitrya : the dual feeling of love. Vaiṣṇava mystics are aware of how both (*saṃyoga* and *viyoga*) ends meet, a state they define as *premavaicitrya:*

> प्रियस्य सन्निकर्षेऽपि प्रेमोत्कर्षस्वभावतः ।
> या विच्छेदधियार्थिः स्यात्प्रेमवैचित्र्यमिष्यते ।।

When in close proximity to the beloved there is a feeling of pain as if out of separation - as a result of the very intensity of love - the state is called *premavaicitrya.* In the state 'the twain (Rādhā and Kṛṣṇa), locked in embrace, shed copious tears, the girls clinging passionately to the lover's neck adds a saltish tang to the nectar of her kisses from tears welling out unbidden. In image after image Kālidāsa (*Meghadūta*) looks forward to fulfilment, every pain relieved by hope that sustains. There is pleasure in fancying that the cold wind from snowcapped mountains in the north carries a touch of the warmth of her body. Separation in love has produced almost identical reaction in every land. In Indian esthetics we have:

न विना विप्रलम्भेन सम्भोगः पुष्टिमश्नुते ।
काषायिते हि वस्त्रादौ भूयान् रागो विवर्धते ॥

5323 **प्रेरक**

Preraka : sender, also known as *preṣaka.* The sender is the source of a message. The sender is the person or persons who produce(s) behaviour that stimulates ideas in a person or persons. The sender is the message-producer, the message-transmitter. The sender responds to some stimulus in terms of his or her conditioned perceptions, fixes on some goal or purpose, has an idea for a message that will accomplish that purpose, chooses symbols for the message, encodes the message, and transmits the message in code.

ब - Ba

5324 **बकवृत्ति**

Bakavṛtti : a *baka* is a symbol of hypocrisy, as it stands on one leg as though deep in meditation and then pounces down upon a fish, known as *bagulā-bhakti* in Hindi (*HC*,III).

5325 **बलि**

Bali : gift of offering from the people to their protector, the king (*Ṛtusaṁhāra,* 1.48).

5326 **बहुभर्तृका**

Bahubhartṛkā : polyandry. Polyandry is indicated to be prevalent among certain castes (*Skanda*, VII.1.29.5.36): The *Skanda Purāṇa* (VII.1.37.19) mentions an *ābhīra* woman having five husbands: *Pañcabhartṛkā.* Vapu, a beautiful woman says to Indra that she is having many husbands, like an *ābhīra* woman: आभीरी त्रिदशाधीश तथाहं बहुभर्तृका ।

5327 **बालविधवा**

Bālavidhavā : child-widow. A child-widow, in her proof of chastity, used to enter the fire. It was thought that her chastity could turn blazing fire into water (*Skanda*, I.2.44.2).

5328 **ब्रह्मयज्ञ**

Brahmayajña : one's own regular study. (*Agni*, 7.10).

5329 **ब्रह्मोदय**

Brahmodaya : poetical riddles. Asking *brahmodaya* was a very ancient practice in India and formed part of the *Aśvamedha*—horse-sacrifice. Just before the actual smothering of the horse, the *Hotṛ* and the Brāhmaṇa began to ask riddles, an exercise in which only they were permitted to take part. This ceremonial use of the riddle is found in many parts of the world, and Frazer (*The Golden Bough*, IX.121) has suggested that it may have originally been adopted at times when for certain reasons the speaker was forbidden to use of direct terms.

Among the aboriginals the custom is found in certain tribes at the beginning of marriage ceremony. In Gond and Pardhān weddings in Mandla, for example, when the bridegroom's representative goes to fetch the bride, riddles are posed and must be answered before he can take her away.

Among the preliminaries to a Birhor marriage there is also a time when riddles are put and answered. When the bride's party comes to the bridegroom's house, hunting-nets are spread for the guests to sit on. When they are seated, the bridegroom's people ask them, 'what did you see on your way here'? The guests reply, "Oh the way, we met with a girl and asked her, where is your father gone?" The girl answered, "My father is gone to catch the rains of the heaven." This meant he had gone to gather thatching-grass. Then we asked her, "where is your mother gone?". The girl answered, "She is gone to take a dead person inside the house." This meant she had gone to transplant paddy-seedlings as a labourer.

The bride's people then say, O friend! a mango tree bore fruit; an old woman told her husband, "Get me the mango by throwing a stick at it" (meaning, get me rice-beer to drink). The old man threw a stick at it and the mango fell and the stick came down on the other side of the tree striking down a deer as it fell (suggesting, let a goat be slain for our entertainment). Men of each party now greet those of the other party and enquire about their health and well-being. Then riddles of a certain type known as *ganamrea bhanita* are asked and solved. For this occasion, five jars of rice-beer were already set abrewing on the return of the three men who had gone to the bride's house for the *Takchanrhi* ceremony. One of these pots of rice-beer is now brought to the court, strained, and distributed to the guests. This is called the fatigue-removing jar' (Roy, The *Birhors*, 1925.159).

In Roy's description of, an Oraon marriage he gives one action as *Khiri Tengna* (propounding riddles). This is the time at which the marriage sermon is given and rice-beer which is called 'riddle-propounding rice-beer' is given to bride and bridegroom, though they must not drink it. The marriage sermon commences with a riddle, but Roy does not make it clear whether during the drinking of the beer riddles are proposed and answered by guests (*Oraon Religion and Custom*, 1928,16).

Thus riddles are being regarded as a measure of the mental equipment and social qualification for the role of husband or wife, i.e. an 'intelligence test'.

The *Dhandā-sailā* songs prevalent in Mahākośala are in the ancient Indian tradition of the wit-combat. Panzer (VI.74) points out that these combats, which sometimes took the form of a series of riddles, were a common feature of entertainments at the courts of Asiatic monarchs.

In Indian fiction there is a rather disappointing account of a wit-combat in Somadeva's *Kathāsaritsāgara* where a learned princess is defeated by Vinītamati. But later this same Vinītamati is himself vanquished in dispute by a Buddhist mendicant. In Pārśvanātha account of Vikrama's adventures as a parrot, there is a well-known series of riddles.

Two types of tale which turn on the hero's solution of a riddle are generally distinguished. In one the hero gains a princess in marriage by this means: in the other a prisoner saves himself from death by setting a riddle that his judges cannot solve. A Gond story from Mandla illustrates the first type of tale, though the heroine is not a princess nor is a marriage the result achieved. Another Mandla story shows how a clever boy redeems a debt by setting the family creditor a riddle he cannot solve.

A considerable collection of Indian riddles, with comment (W.G. Archer, Durga Bhagvat and Verrier Elwin,) will be found in 'An Indian Riddle Book', *Man in India*, XXIII, Part IV.

5330 ब्राह्ममुहूर्त

Brāhmamuhūrta : the period comprising about forty-five minutes prior to the rise of the sun, The *brāhma-muhūrta* is very auspicious for studies or even for birth:

ब्राह्मे मुहूर्ते किल तस्य देवी कुमारकल्पं सुषुवे कुमारम्
(*Raghuvaṁśa*, V.36)

The period is presided over Brahmā, the all-knowing god of the Hindu pantheon.

भ - Bha

5331 भगौष्ठ

Bhagauṣṭha : labia; the folds surrounding the opening of the vagina.

5332 भङ्गा

Bhaṅgā : hemp, cannabis saliva. The abstinence from liquor enjoined by modern Hinduism to the higher castes of Hindus has unfortunately not extended to the harmful drugs, opium, and *gānjā* (*cannabis sativa*) or Indian hemp with its preparation. On the contrary *gānjā* is regularly consumed by Hindu ascetics, whether devotees of Śiva or Viṣṇu, though it is more favoured by the Śaivites. The blue throat of Śiva or Mahādeva (*Nīlakaṇṭha*) is said to be due to the enormous draughts of *bhāng* (a liquor made from the flowers of the hemp plant, commonly drunk with the mixture of sugar and milk with water) which he was accustomed to swallow. The veneration attached to these drugs may probably be explained by the delusion that the pleasant dreams and visions obtained under their influence are excursions of the spirit of paradise. It is a common belief among the primitive people that during sleep the soul leaves the body and that dreams are the actual experiences of the soul when travelling over the world apart from the body. The principle aim of Hindu asceticism is also the complete conquest of all sensation and movement in the body, so that while it is immobile the spirit freed from the trammels of the body and from all worldly cares and concerns may, as it is imagined, enter into the communion with and be absorbed in the deity.

Hence the physical inertia and abnormal mental exaltation produced by these drugs would be an ideal condition to the Hindu ascetic; the body is lulled to immobility and it is natural that he should imagine that the delightful fantasies of his drugged brain are beautific visions of heaven.

In India *bhāng* was regularly drunk by the Rājputs. It is called *hashshāh* in Arabic and the modern word *haśiś* is derived from it.

5333 भजन

Bhajana : rhythmic chanting of religious hymns. It may also include dancing. These sessions of group singing and group dancing may increase the emotionality to such an extent that some of the participants may go into ecstasy. In *bhajana*, members of all castes participate. As Lennoy (1975) remarks with perspicacity, "Hindu society ascribes religious significance both to separation of groups into castes and to the interdependence among those castes. This is universal phenomenon of all religiously oriented societies. The seasonal festival dramatists convey these two facts through religious rapture, ecstatic orgiasticism, trance dancing and art. The festival restores the sense of unity which specialization endangers; this is generally accomplished by a reversal of the customary regulation of daily social interplay and work."

5334 **भार**

Bhāra : weight (of persons). 'A man who weighs half a *bhāra* (i.e. 1000 *palas*) will enjoy happiness; one weighing less than that will become miserable; persons weighing one *bhāra* (i.e. 2000 *palas*), immensely rich; and one weighing a *bhāra* and a half (i.e. 3000 *palas*), an emperor of the whole earth (*Bṛhat-Saṁhitā,* LXVIII).

5335 **भार्या**

Bhāryā : wife. The wife has to be protected; for she has the husband himself born as issue: आत्मा हि जायते तस्याम् (*Mārk.*, 69.35-36). If she is not protected, there is a possibility of mixation of castes (*Ibid.*, 37). Even an unchaste wife is to be protected in the same way as a characterless husband is to be respected:

> पत्यानुकूलया भाव्यं यथाऽशीलेऽपि भर्तरि ।
> दुःशीलापि तथा भार्या पोषणीया नरेश्वर ॥
> (*Mārk.*, 69.59).

This wife is likened to *Prakṛti*, the primeval female creative force. *Prakṛti* gets dejected, defeated and turns away if a woman is disrespected:

> सा च योषित्स्वरूपा च प्रतिविश्वेषु मायया ।
> योषितामपमानेन पराभूता च सा भवेत् ॥
> (*Brahmavaivarta.*, 1.30.16)

Cf. the following verse:

> *kāryeṣu mantrī karaṇeṣu dāsī*
> *bhojyeṣu mātā śyaneṣu rambhā,*
> *dharmenukūlā kṣamayā dharitrī*
> *bhāryā ca ṣādguṇyavatī na labhyā.*

> "The odds, My friend! are one to ten in life
> That one may get a virtuous wife
> Who plays a minister in all affairs,
> In virtuous deeds who helpful fares,
> In household work a maid who's worth,
> In patience equals mother-earth."

5336 **भिक्षापात्र**

Bhikṣāpātra : begging-bowl, *kaṭorī* in Maikal Hills. *Kaṭorī* is a common sexual symbol in the Maikal Hills:

> My heart dwells
> In your beggingbowl.
> Stay, my madman
> Stay a night until
> Our enemy the cock shall crow.

5337 **भिल्लतीर्थ**

Bhillatīrtha : a holy place of the Bhils. A hunter worshipped Śiva here, and offered fresh flesh to him. According to *Brahma Purāṇa* (169) the place is on the bank of Gautamī (Godavari). According to the account recorded here, the sage Veda, a brother of Sindhudvīpa, always worshipped Ādikeśa Śiva at the bank of Gautamī. A Bhilla hunter (*vyādha*) also used to visit that place everyday and worship Śiva with leaves and the offering of flesh. Veda did not tolerate this. One day, as he lay concealed, he heard Śiva talking to the Bhilla. He was very angry. But to his surprise, he saw the next day, a stream of blood coming out from Śiva *liṅga.* He tried to stop and wash it with the help of the sacred grass, earth, cow-dung, etc.; but could not. Soon the Bhilla came. He was sorry and pierced himself with a sharp arrow. Śiva saw it from the *liṅga* and was pleased. As the god wanted to favour the Bhilla, the latter said, "well what is the 'left-over' or that of the previous day may be mine; and the place should have my name". Thus, came the name *Bhilla-tīrtha.* (*Ibid.* 47). This account indicates a subtle controversy between the Vedic worship and the aboriginal. The name of the sage Veda is symbolic. The account also indicates how the original worshipper came to gain a secondary status.

5338 **भिल्ली**

Bhillī : the Bhil-woman. According to *Śiva Purāṇa* (III. 28), Damayantī, the wife of Nala and daughter of Bhīma, the King of Vidarbha, was a Bhil-maiden (*Bhillī*) in her former birth. Her name was *Āhukā,* and she was the wife of Āhuka. They both entertained Śiva, who came as a guest, by offering their lives.

5339 **भूतविद्या**

Bhūtavidyā : one of the aspects of *Āyurveda* dealing with abnormalities of behaviour (*Suṣruta,* 1.1.5). These behavioural disorders were looked upon as having been caused by "sins and transgressions" and they could be cured by *mantras, prāyaścitta,* etc.

Susŕuta (*Sūt.* 1.6-7) defines *bhūtavidyā* as that branch of therapeutics which deals with *graha* (nuroses), *unmāda* (psychoses) and *apasmāra* (epilepsy).

5340 **भूमिदारणम्**

Bhūmidāraṇam : ploughing. The *Bhaviṣya Purāṇa (Madhyama,* 10.1-3) mentions that the ground that is used for a sacrifice should not be even touched by the bullocks:

> या भूमिर्ग्रहयात्रार्थे तन्न वाहैरपि स्पृशेत् ।

In this context we find a logic why the Abujhmāṛiā of Bastar never ploughs his land, instead he burns it for shifting cultivation. The idea behind this custom is that the *bhum* is her mother and tilling symbolizes copulating with the mother and giving birth to Padminī (*Skanda*, II. 1.3.22) or Sītā (the famous heroine of *Rāmāyaṇa*). (b) ploughing symbolizes the Purāṇic meaning in the Gond society. A special method here of obtaining rain is for two naked women to go and harness themselves to a plough at night, while a third naked woman drives the plough and pricks them with a goad. A leather rope is sometimes tied to a plough and harrow, and the boys and girls pull against one another on the rope in a tug-of-war. If the girls win they think that rain will soon come, but if the boys win that it will not (Russell and Hiralal, II. 106).

5341 **भूमिहर**

Bhūmihara : a relation who could be the shareholder of the property (Kālidāsa, *Māl.*, 1.10).

5342 **भ्रातृजाया**

Bhrātṛjāyā : elder brother's wife (Kālidāsa, *Megha*. 9,10); *bhaujī* in Bagheli and Chhattisgarhi. The relationship between *devar* and *bhaujī* is very intimate and tender.

म - Ma

5343 **मणि**

Maṇi : clitoris. Varāhamihira (LXX) prefers clitoris that is hidden. गूढो मणिश्च विपुलां श्रियमादधाति

5344 **मणिपूर**

Maṇipūra : one of the *Ṣaṭcakras* according to *Tantra*. At the navel region is *maṇipūra*, a lotus with ten petals and ten letters. The element is *tejas*, light. The sensations are form and colour. The motor organs connected are of evacuations. *Maṇipūra* is looked upon as the seat of shame, treachery, jealousy, desire, worldliness, aversion and fear - emotions associated with *rajo guṇa*.

5345 **मण्डूक**

Maṇḍūka : frog. The worship of frog is a Vedic method to propitiate it so that it may cause rain. It is still prevalent in the tribal societies. Where there is drought two boys put a pestle across their shoulders, tie a living frog to it with a rag, and go from house to house accompanied by other boys and girls singing:

> *meḍhak bhāī pānī de*
> *dhān kodo pākan de*
> *mor byāh hovan de*

or, 'Brother Frog give rain; let the rice and kodon ripen; let my marriage be held'. The frog is considered to be able to produce rain because it lives in water and therefore has control over the element. The boy's point in asking the frog let his marriage be held is that if the rains failed and the crops withered, his parents would be unable to afford the expense.

5346 **मदात्य**

Madātya : alcoholism. It is discussed by Charaka (24) in detail in one whole chapter. Alcohol is *amṛta*, ambrosia, if taken in small quantities. It promotes life and happiness. When consumed in excess it causes physical and mental disorders.

5347 **मधुकर**

Madhukara : honey-bee. The bee and its honey is widely used in the poetry of the world as a symbol for lover and his love. The English word 'honeymoon' is so familiar that probably most people use it without realizing that imagery that it suggests. Tribal folk uses the bee to create a general atmosphere of love and passion:

> Talk not of love
> For my heart is burning
> The black bee is hiding in my flowers
> And my heart is bursting.

Draydon uses the bee likewise:

> The bees up in honey rolled,
> More than their thighs can hold,
> Lapped in their liquid gold
> Their treasure us bringing.

Herrick, in *The Captiv'd Bee*, uses the same idea of a bee that, going 'to tripple freely in a flower', mistook Julia's lips for it and got 'honey enough to fill his hive'.

In India the theme is used in classical poetry, and there is a beautiful little song in Kālidāsa's *Śākuntalam*, translated by Laurence Binyon:

> In the dusk, as it falls
> On the last golden hour,
> The enamoured maiden
> Takes a honeyed flower,
> A flower the bees kiss,
> Part and kiss, hovering near;
> Its tendrils light as finger-tips
> She twines about her hair.

Some lines attributed to Vidyākara Miśra (*JASB*, XLVIII. 43) employ this symbolism with good effect:

> Lo, there are many bonds
> But none like the binding of the toils of love
> Even the bee, skilled as he is in cleaving timber
> Lies helpless
> Bound in the hollow of a lotus.

Winternitz ('Witchcraft in Ancient India', *The Indian Antiquary*, XXVIII. 81) gives a love-charm from the *Atharvaveda*. The lover should tie to his arm an amulet of licorice wood, saying, 'This plant is born of honey, with honey we do dig for thee. Of honey thou art begotten, do thou make us full of honey. At the tip of my tongue may I have honey, at my tongue's root the sweetness of honey. In my power alone shalt thou then be, thou shalt come up to my wish.... I am sweeter than honey, fuller of sweetness than licorice. Mayest thou, without fail, long for me alone, as a bee for a branch full of honey. I have surrounded thee with a clinging sugarcane, to remove aversion, so that thou shalt not be averse to me.'

The Oraon appear to be fond of songs about bees and honey, where these images have the same meaning as in Sanskrit:

> You planted a *mungā* tree, father
> The *mungā* has spread its branches
> The *mungā* is in blossom
> The bees hum and fly
> They come to suck the honey.

Crooke (*North Indian Notes and Querries*, V. 99) has an interesting note on the folklore of bees. 'In the jungles the people who collect honey think that if the hives are touched, except in the light half of the month, the bees will desert the place and never return. They always ask an astrologer or village sorcerer to select an auspicious time for this duty. All over the world the souls of the dead are supposed to take up their abode in bees and flies. This is the origin of the numerous superstitions connected with these insects.'

But apart from the fact that bees are generally considered lucky, and it is supposed to be very good omen if a swarm settles in or near a house, we do not know how far these ideas are current in India.

5348 **मधूक**

Madhūka : oil from *madhūka* (*mahuā* in Hindi) flowers was prepared for medicinal purposes (*Garuḍa*, 1.174.5). From its flowers liquor is prepared; this is called *mādhvī* in Sanskrit. There is also *madhūkatritīyā-vrata* in bright third day of Caitra. In this *Vrata* images of Śiva and Umā are prescribed to be made and also that of *madhūka* tree. (b) The Gonds and Baigas revere the *mahuā* tree and consider the liquor distilled from its flowers as sacred and purificatory. At a Gond wedding the sacred post round which the couple go is made of the wood of the *mahuā* tree. The Bhatrās of Bastar also use the *mahuā* for the wedding post. Minor caste offences are expiated among the Gonds by a fine of liquor, and by drinking it the culprit is purified. At a Gond funeral one may be seen walking with a bottle or two of liquor slung to his side; this is drunk by all the party on the spot after the burial or burning of the corpse as a means of purification. Among the Korwās and other tribes the Baigā or priest protects the village from ghosts by sprinkling a line of liquor all round the boundary, over which the ghosts cannot pass. At their weddings the Mahārs drink together ceremoniously, a pot of liquor being placed on a folded cloth and all the guests sitting round it in a circle. An elder man then lays a new piece of cloth on the pot and worships it. He takes a cup of liquor himself and hands round a cupful to every person present. For various rites and for offerings to the deities, the Gonds say that the liquor should be distilled at home by the person who offers the sacrifice and not purchased from the Government contractor. Hindus generally make a libation to Devī before drinking liquor (Russell and Hiralal, II. 316-17).

5349 **मधूच्छिष्ट**

Madhūcchiṣṭa : cosmetic for lips (Kālidāsa, *Kum.*, 7.120).

5350 **मध्यमार्ग**

Madhyamārga : middle Path; also known as *Majjhima nikāya*. Hinduism has no 'golden mean'; it seeks the exhaustion of two golden extremes. It was perhaps as a reaction against the extremism that the Buddha called his teaching 'the Middle Path', explicitly rejecting both the voluptuous life which he had known as a prince and the violent asceticism which he had mastered at the start of his spiritual quest. Although the Buddhists also stated the problem explicitly in positive terms, recognizing the merit of both goals, the final choice was a negative one: there are two pleasures, the pleasure of the house-holder and the pleasure of asceticism, but the latter is pre-eminent (*Aṅguttara Nikāya*,1). For the Buddha taught *nirvāṇa* - literally, the extinguishing of flame - while Śiva embodied the flame and danced within it. Hinduism has no use for Middle Path; this is a religion of fire and ice.

5351 **मनोद्रव**

Manodrava : melting of the heart. Love, when developed, becomes *prema*, ardent love. It cannot bear separation from the lover or the beloved. It leads to *manodrava*, melting of the heart. There is intense yearning to be in the presence of the other person. Vātsyāyana was right—for this extraordinary emotion does produce actual physiological secretions in the human body. Love is sickness, love is blind and capricious, say the poets, and who would disagree?

5352 **मनोराग-प्रकाशनम्**

Manorāga-prakaśanam : display of love. the amorous women call the attention of their lovers through different types of amorous signs. Kālidāsa knows that the exposure of the navel is an erotic weapon (*Purva Megha*, XXIX) wielded by amorous dames. There are others:

स्निग्धं दृष्टिपथं विभूषिततनुः कर्णस्य कण्डूयनं
नाभेर्दर्शनमुत्पथं च गमनं बालस्य चालिंगनम् ।
केशानां मुहुर्मुहुर्विवरणं वार्ता च सख्या सह
कुर्युः प्रीतिवशात् स्त्रियः दृष्ट्वा नरं वञ्चितम् ॥

'a fond look, the body gaily decked out, scratching of the earlobes, the exposure of the navel, a deliberate straying from the path, caressing children, constant tugging at the hair, artful speech with her companions - these are amorously performed by a woman at the sight of a man of her heart'.

The stumbling gait of the Nirvindhyā in *Meghadūta* is like the slouch of a wanton: the eddies are deep like the navel of a desirable woman. Tinkling of the girdle is an inviting gesture: and the twists and turn hinting at unwillingness to move on. The cloud would be a fool to reject the advances of such a dear. This is amply illustrated in *Abhijñāna Śākuntalam* in Śākuntalā's artful examination of her toes as if lacerated by the sharp blades of *darbha* grass, disentanging her broken skirt from the branches of a tree, even though it was free. Bharata proceeds in the following way - how should the cluod approach an unwilling woman?

उक्तविशेषणत्रयेण अनुरागाविष्करणं सूचितम् । यदुक्तम् -

कांच्यादिस्वननं भङ्गया गमनं गात्रदर्शनम् ।
यूनः पुरो विदग्धायाः मनोरोगं प्रकाशयेद् ॥

5353 **मन्त्रशास्त्र**

Mantraśāstra : culture of sound. An integral aspect of Vedicism on the aboriginal tribes is *mantraśāstra* - systematic application of magic incantation in ritual. The word is Brahman; the word is Revelation, an icon of the Absolute, *mūrti* - a 'momentary deity'. Words, magical formulae, sacred verses - *mantra* - exist in relation to the divine as the *yantra* to the god; words are machines. The following lines of Sri Aurobindo Ghosh summarize the significance of the word to Hinduism. When the *mantra* falls on receptive ears, he says:

Its message enters stirring the blind brain
And keeps in dim ignorant cells its sound;
The hearer understands a form of words
And, musing on the index thought it holds,
He strives to read it with labouring mind,
But finds bright hints, not the embodied truth.
Then, falling silent in himself to know
He meets the deeper listening of his soul:
The word repeats itself in rhythmic strains:
Thought, vision, feeling, sense, the body's self
Are seized unalterably and he endures
An ecstasy and an immoral change;
He feels wideness and becomes a Power,
All knowledge rushes on him like a sea;
Transmuted by the white spiritual ray
He walks in naked heavens of joy and calm,
Sees the God-face and hears transcendent Speech.
(Aurobindo, *Sāvitrī*, Pondicherry, 1954. 426)

It is worth pointing out in passing that these lines, apart from explaining the concept of *mantraśāstra*, also encapsulate the Indian theory of poetics. Most, but by no means all, Indian poetry is sacred verse for incantation, repetition, 'circulation' in the mind, with or without the aid of music, until it produces the appropriate aesthetic *rasa*, or emotive resonance. While the poetry of the saints is not regarded as *Śruti*, or revealed truth, as are Vedic verses, they aspire to a level of meaning sound which is not far short of *mantra*, the word as 'momentary deity'.

5354 **मंत्रोक्षण**

Mantrokṣaṇa : to sprinkle with sacred water rendered pure through the utterance of sacred *mantras* (Kālidāsa, *Raghu.*, 5,73).

5355 **मन्मथ-लेख**

Manmatha-lekha : love-letter (Kālidāsa, *Śāk.*, 3,253).

5356 **मयूर**

Mayūra : peacock. *Kāma* (sex) is often said to ride upon a peacock, which is the form that the 'Blue-necked One' (Śiva) assumes when he swallows poison (*Skanda*, 5.2.14. 2-30), and the peacock is also the vehicle of *Skanda*.An obvious sexual symbol, the peacock is a recurrent motif in Indian erotic painting and poetry. (Fig. - 5356)

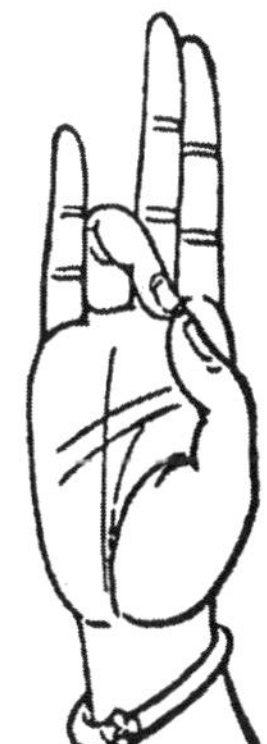

Fig. - (5356)

The peacock has not very good reputation in Europe, for its cry is supposed to be a warning of death, and it is usually associated with the deadly sin of pride. For example, in Middle English literature the priest may be described as 'proud as a peacock' or a lover maybe 'as any peacock proud and gay'. But in Indian songs the peacock is a living picture of colour, beauty and movement. It is the bright plumage and the dancing that is remembered. Even the fishing float made from its feathers is supposed to be so attractive to the fish that the word is used as a symbol for a lover.

In traditional Indian mythology the peacock is represented as suffering from the heat and delighted with the first drops of rain. The peacock is supposed to watch the lightning flashing in the clouds which prophesy that its sorrow will soon be at an end. Its feathers get ruffled if it is taken near poison. Used in magic the feathers are a potent demon-scarer. The aboriginals also use peacock feathers as a symbol of gods, as personal decoration and often carry bunches of them during their dances. The peacock, therefore, is an apt symbol for expressing the delight and vitality of a man's beloved.

5357 **महिषी**

Mahiṣī : she-buffalo. A woman who is faithless to her husband, or who has sexual relationship with more men is termed *mahiṣī*, and a person who desires sex with her is termed *Māhiṣika* (*Skanda*, IV. 40.92):

> महिषीत्युच्यते नारी या स्याद् व्यभिचारिणी ।
> तां दुष्टां कामयेद्यस्तु स वै माहिषिकः स्मृतः ॥
> (*Skanda*., IV. 40. 92)

5358 **माता**

Mātā : mother. (b) small-pox, etc. Diseases of this group are all associated with *mātā* or Mother, the Devī or goddess of these diseases. Those who have been attacked by the disease, and have recovered, are said to have been wedded by the *Mātā: Mātā usko bihāyā hai.* It seems probable that this expression arose from the resemblance of one attacked by the disease to the bride or bridegroom covered with turmeric and oil during the marriage ceremony (*JRAS*, 1904.2).

5359 **माता-पिता**

Mātā-pitā : mother and father, parents. All holy places are said to centre round the mother or the father:

> तत्र गङ्गा गया तीर्थं तत्र पुष्करमेव च ।
> यत्र माता पिता तिष्ठेत् पुत्रस्यापि न संशयः ॥
> (*Padma, Bhūmi*., 62.68-69)

5360 **मार्गोपदेशक**

Mārgopadeśaka : guide (*Veṇīsaṁhāra*, III).

5361 **मास**

Māsa : month. The months are of two types - *saura* (Solar) and *cāndra* (Lunar). There are taboos as to days and months. The Hindus will not shave themselves on certain days. Others observe not the days but the dates in this particular context. During the fifteen days of the *pitṛ-pakṣa* or the fortnight of the Manes, a Hindu will never be shaved. A woman will not put on new bangles during this same period. In the month of *Jyeṣṭha* , May-June, it is against the custom of the people in Chhattisgarh to perform the marriage ceremony of a first born son - the *jyeṣṭha putra.* A pundit tells me that the restriction applies only when a *jyeṣṭha putra* is wedded to *jyeṣṭha putrī.* But the common people have narrowed down the restriction and make it apply to the marriage of every first born son, whether married to a firstborn daughter or not. It is the self-imposed restriction placed on themselves by the people themselves.

5362 **मुखचूर्ण**

Mukhacūrṇa : facial powder (Kālidāsa, *Raghu*,. 9.137). Historically, face and body paint had magical, mystical links with spirits and gods. People pointed themselves before any ritual sometimes make-up was also used to pretect lower-lids-the delicate part of the body.

5363 **मुसल**

Musala : pestle. Crossing a pestle is said to be bad (*Mārk.* 50.87). The pestle is a must in a delivery room (*Ibid.*, 105). there is a queer account of a pestle being born from the stomach of Sāmba which brought about the total destruction of the race of Yādavas (*Brahma.*, 210. 6).

In the tribal world, the rice-husker has magical significance. It is waved round the heads of bride and bridegroom during a marriage. Crooke (II. 191) has an interesting note on its use. 'In Bengal, it is worshipped when the child is first fed with grain. And there is a regular worship of it in the month of Baisakh, or May. The top is smeared with red lead, anointed with oil, and offerings of rice and holy dūrvā grass are made to it. The worship has even been provided with a Brahminical legend. A Guru once ordered his disciple to pronounce the word *Ḍhenk* at least one hundred and eight times a day. Nārada Muni was so pleased with his devotion, as he is the patron deity of the rice-pounder, that he paid him a visit riding on one, and carried off his votary to heaven."

5364 **मूत्र**

Mūtra : urine. In the Purāṇic as well as tribal myths, urine is basically creative. The Gond legend of creation explains that "From Mahādeva's urine numerous vegetables began to spring up. Pārvatī ate of these and became pregnant and gave birth to eighteen threshing floors of Brāhmaṇa gods and twelve threshing floors of Gond gods. All the Gonds were scattered in the jungle (Russell and Hiralal, III. 50).

5365 **मूर्धजराग**

Mūrdhajarāga : hair-dye. In the opinion of Varāhamihira (*Bṛhat-Saṁhitā,* LXXVII) people with grey hair should add one item i.e. dying the hair, to their daily routine. One with grey hair need not wear fine clothes. He records:

> स्रगन्धधूपाम्बरभूषणाद्यं न शोभते शुक्लशिरोरुहस्य ।
> यस्मादतो मूर्धजरागसेवां कुर्याद्यथैवाञ्जनभूषणानाम् ॥

'As garlands, perfumes, fine clothes, ornaments and the like do not shine in a man of grey hairs, one ought to use hair-dyes, just as one does collyrium for the eyes and ornaments'. He has also given the method of preparing of the hair-dye:

> लौहे पात्रे तण्डुलान् कोद्रवाणां शुक्ले पक्वाँल्लोहचूर्णेन साकम् ।
> पिष्टान्सूक्ष्मं मूर्ध्नि शुक्ताम्लकेशे दत्वा तिष्ठेद्वेष्टयित्वार्द्रपत्रैः ॥
> याते द्वितीये प्रहरे विहाय दद्याच्छिरस्यामलकप्रलेपम् ।
> सञ्छाद्य पत्रैः प्रहरद्वयेन प्रक्षालितं कार्ष्ण्यमुपैति शीर्षम् ॥

'Cook the grains of *Kodrava* (*Paspalum Scrobiculatum*) in sour gruel or vinegar in an iron vessel; grind them well with iron dust and make the fine paste. After washing the hair with sour gruel (or vinegar) apply this paste to the head. Then, covering the head with green (juicy)leaves, remain for six hours. Thereafter remove the paste from the head and apply a paste of myrobalan (*Emblica officinalis*). Cover it again with green leaves and retain it for another six hours. On being washed, the hair will become black.' Dark men are often thought of as more manly, desirable and dependable. Sanskrit literature frequently makes a dark-haired man the dashing hero.

5366 **मूषक**

Mūṣaka : rat, mouse. The eating of rat's flesh is a common practice amongst the tribes and the lower castes. Since the pastime of children is often the remains of the earnest life-work of adults in an earlier stage of culture, this practice of eating rats seems to point back to the time when rates formed a staple article of food amongst the people. Even now, in times of scarcity, the people of Chhattisgarh have been known to live on field rats when they were obtainable. (*JRAS,* 1904. No.1.2). I am told that rat's flesh is considered fattening and is given to emaciated children and to cattle in order that they may put on flesh.

5367 **मृगया**

Mṛgayā : hunting. It is important to note that Kālidāsa (*Śāk.,* 2.127, 131, 134, 135, 142; *Raghu.* 9.130, 142; 10.196) appreciates hunting in almost those very terms in which it is appreciated by Kauṭilya (*Arthaśāstra,* VIII.3). But *Manu* (VII. 47) counts hunting not only among the *Kāmajanya* faults of a king but also among the worst defects. As *Manusmṛti,* being the prevalent law-book of the Indian society, had certain additions made to it in the passage of time, it might have been influenced by the Buddha and Jain ideas, which condemned the killing of animals and eating of meat. But Kālidāsa certainly belongs to an age when meat was eaten freely.

5368 **मृष्टक**

Mṛṣṭaka : lit. kneaded, to waggle the buttocks, *maṭakānā* in Hindi. *Maṭakānā* is a common trick of the Pankā comedian and the weaver in the following song adopts this method of amusing his wives and encouraging them to do better work:

> Brother, who will set the warp?
> Riding on an elephant I set the warp
> As I am sitting I waggle my buttocks
> I make my first wife through the shuttle.

Maṭakko is an expression used of a flirtatious girl who walks about with hips swinging.

5369 **मैथुनीसृष्टि**

Maithunī-sṛṣṭi : creation by intercourse. Marriage of Śiva is contrasted with the illicit sexuality of Brahmā: Śiva enters into a regular marriage for the sake of *Maithunīsṛṣṭi,* whereas Brahmā emits his energy at the sight of Sārasvatī or Sāvitrī or Śatarūpā (Agrawal, 1964. 99).

5370 **मोहनगृह**

Mohanagṛha : room employed for the amorous play (Kālidāsa, *Raghu.,* 19. 276).

य - Ya

5371 **यक्षकर्दम**

Yakṣakardama : an unguent. It is said to be prepared in the following way : two parts of saffron, two of musk (*mṛgamada*) three of sandal and one of camphor (*Skanda.,* IV.80.43,45).

5372 **यथेच्छसि तथा कुरू**

Yathecchasi tathā kuru : do as you thinkest best (*Gītā* XVIII.63). Arjuna is asked to reflect upon the teaching. He is not asked to accept anything merely on the basis of the prestige of his teacher. He is asked to think on his own the implications of the teaching. Secondly, he is asked to choose for himself the action he desires to pursue in the light of his own reflection. Neither blind faith nor total surrender to the dictates of the teacher is required. The teacher is only a counsellor. The final decision is left to the individual.

5373 **यभ माम्**

Yabha mām : fuck me. In *Atharvaveda* (XX.136.11), a great nude man with matted locks is pursued by a great nude woman who says that her limbs are burning with desire as if with a forest fire and begs him, 'Eat this dish of boiled rice and fuck me.' This incidence is the first mention of nudity symbolizing sexuality. The obvious erotic connotations which are mingled with the ascetic practice of nudity may be traced back to the above mentioned *Atharvaveda* hymn. Scratch the surface of Vedic civilization, and you'll find that we all have a good deal in common.

5374 **यमदीप**

Yamadīpa : light for Yama. On the previous day of *dīpotsava* (i.e. on the 13th dark), one offers (or kindles) in the evening the *Yamadīpa* whereby untimely death is avoided :

आश्विनस्य सिते पक्षे त्रयोदश्यां निशामुखे ।
यमदीपबलिं दद्यात् अपमृत्युर्विनश्यति ॥

(*Skanda.*, II.4.9.20)

5375 **यष्टिका-कर्षण**

Yaṣṭikā-karṣaṇa : the pulling of the stick, a type of game which is a sort of tug-war. It was a game played in the month of Kārtika during *Bali-pratipadā*. The *yaṣṭikā* (actually a rope as tough as stick) is freshly prepared out of the grass called *kāśa* and *kuśa*. It should be then carried to the gate of a temple, or the gate of a royal palace or at a place where four roads meet. On one side it should be held by the princes, and on the other by people of low *varṇas*. Both groups should be strong and of equal number. At the back of either group, as they stand holding the *yaṣṭikā*, there should be lines dance at a distance. This is the goal to which each group is to drag the other one. When this is done, both groups should start pulling each other. The group which drags the other to the line at its own back is declared victorious. In this game the group comprising the low *varṇa* should win, so that, thereafter, the year is gained by the king :

प्रतिपत्पूर्वविद्धैव यष्टिकाकर्षणे भवेत् ॥

(*Skanda.*, II.4.10.64)

कुशकाशमयीं कुर्यात् यष्टिकां सुदृढां नवाम् ।
देवद्वारे नृपद्वारेऽथवा नेया चतुष्पथे ॥

(*Ibid.*, 66)

तामेकतो राजपुत्रा हीनवर्णास्तथैकतः ।
गृहीत्वा कर्षयेयुस्ते यथासारं मुहुर्मुहः ॥

(*Ibid.*, 67)

समसंख्या द्वयोः कार्या सर्वेऽपि बलवत्तराः ।
जयोऽत्र हीनजातीनां जयो राज्ञस्तु वत्सरम् ॥

(*Ibid.*, 68)

उभयोः पृष्ठतः कार्या रेखा तत्कर्षकोपरि ।
रेखान्ते यो नयेत्तस्य जयो भवति नान्यथा ॥

(*Ibid.*, 69)

The *yaṣṭikā* is therefore kept by the king as sign of victory :

जयचिह्नमिदं राजा विदधीत प्रयत्नतः

(*Ibid.*)

This game was played in the first bright of Kārtika; and the Dīpāvalī extends here. This day is called the *Bali-pratipadā* in honour of the demon king who gave away all his kingdom to Viṣṇu Vāmana—when he had promised three steps, and who traversed the heaven and earth with his two steps and gave his third step on the head of Bali. The *Purāṇa* enjoins that on this day an idol of Bali is to be prepared with dung in the courtyard, and curd should be placed before it (*Skanda.*, II.4.10.15). It is said that whoever stands before the idol in whatever form, gets the same form for the whole of year, hence one should perform auspicious rites. In the morning *Govardhana* is to be erected and worshipped; and in the night the dice-game should be played. The above game is associated with this day.

5376 **यात्रासंकेत**

Yātrāsaṅketa : travel-signals. Whenever a Gond is about to start on a journey or on some purpose and if a dog by chance or a jackal cries in his front he thinks something wrong will happen. If the cry of jackal is heard from behind, his purpose will be well saved. If someone happens to sneeze in the advent of journey, the journey will either be abandoned or postponed.

5377 **यूप**

Yūpa : a sacrificial post, *Yūpa* was an important part of *Vedikā* erected to fasten the animal of sacrifice (*Raghu.*, 1.44).

5378 **योगिनी**

Yogini : woman following a Tantric cult. The names of the *yoginīs* in Sanskrit literature originated various tribal social customs and even totemistic surroundings. They are said to be sixty-four in number, and are to be worshipped with flesh and wine etc. (*Skanda.*, VII.4.22.29-31).

5379 **योग्री**

Yogī : *Yogin.* One who practices *yoga. Yogī* is *jogī* in village India. A *jogī* often symbolizes a lover in the songs. The term is not altogether complimentary, for it implies that a man's love is as unsettled and transitory as a wandering mendicant. But it may also mean that a man has become restless as *jogī* because he cannot win his love. The following *Suā*-song depicts the same theme:

> To which hamlet has the *jogī* come, *bhaujī* ?
> Where has he made his camp ?
> He has come to the Ḍhīmar's hamlet, *bhaujī*
> O how I long to see him
> *Tari O nāna O de mor nāna*
> *re Suā tari nāwawa nāna.*
> From the swing the girl comes down
> Let us go to bathe in the lake
> From the curtain the maid comes out
> Take warm water with you
> I will go away with the *jogī*
> Take my cloth from the basket
> comb my hair, put on my ornaments
> Don't tell my father and mother or they kill me
> The *jogī* has come to the courtyard
> The maid has come out of the house
> O with this *jogī* I will run away
> Good-bye, good-bye, my parrot
> If I live, I will come to see you
> If I die, it is the same sorrow throughout the world
> The *jogī* went ahead, the maid behind, parrot
> He is going to his country, parrot
> The maid goes behind him.

5380 **योग्यता**

Yogyatā : compatibility. The two or more words can convey a meaning only when they are not in consistent with each other or one another. A word such as fire and sprinkling of water and burning will not convey any sense. So, for the words to form a sentence and give rise to some meaning, they should be compatible with each other (one of the conditions of a sentence).

5381 **रक्षाकरण्डक**

Rakṣākaraṇḍaka : a thread placed around the neck of a child to protect against evil spirits (Kālidāsa, *Śāk.*).

र - Ra

5381 **रक्षाकरण्डक**

Rakṣākaraṇḍaka : a thread placed aroundthe neck of a child to protect against evil spirits (Kālidāsa, *Śāk*)

5382 **रतिमात्र**

Ratimātra : 'mere' love-play, i.e. intercourse without ejaculation.

5383 **रथयात्रा**

Rathayātrā : chariot-fair. The famous *rathayātrā* of Bastar is an offshoot of the chariot fair at Purī. *Bhaviṣya Purāṇas* (*Brahma.* 18.3-14) records that it is celebrated in the month ot Āṣāḍha. The chariot is drawn by people from the three *varṇas*, but never by a Śūdra (*Ibid*).

Here chariot is symbolic of the cosmos. It is said that the chariot stands for the earth, the wheels indicate the sun and the moon, the carriers represent the *Vedas;* and the charioteer represents Brahmā:

> रथं पृथिवीं विजानीयात् रथाङ्गे चन्द्रभास्करौ ।
> वेदानश्वान्विजानीयात् सारथिं पदमसम्भवम् ।।
> (*Śiva.*, V.51-64)

5384 **राम-राम**

Rāma-rāma : It is the rural and tribal form of greeting. In Madhya Pradesh. *Johār* is more old-fashioned, but still common among wilder tribesmen, specially in Bastar. The following English-rendering of the *Suā*-song may be presented as a specimen of this greeting:

> The dweller on the hill, parrot
> Is sitting on the mango branch
> Take a message, parrot
> Take a message to my mother in her country
> Give father *Rām-rāmosā*
> Say *Johār* to mother
> Your daughter is away in a foreign land
> Do not weep for her, mother
> But the parrot flew away
> And sat on a tamarind branch.

5385 **राशि**

Rāśi : sum. In Bhopalpatnam (Bastar) in cases of important purchases such as that of a cow or a bullock or the like the number seven and nine are avoided, i.e. one would not purchase a bullock for a full some of rupees seven or nine. He would pay some paise more or less.

5386 **रिङ्गण**

Ringaṇa : crawling of infants (*Amarakośa*). Infantile locomotion in a prone position by means of the arms pulling the body forward as the legs or knees push. This we can observe in the locomotive behaviour of Bharata in *Śākuntalam.*

5387 **रुत**

Ruta : animal call (*Amarakośa*).

5388 **रुदितम्**

Ruditam : (a) signs of the weeping of men. 'Weeping which is soft, tearless and without wretchedness, is auspicious for men; whereas one that is rough, abject and accompanied with copious tears is disastrous to them :

> रुदितमदीनमनश्रु स्निग्धां च शुभावहं मनुष्याणाम् ।
> रूक्षं दीनं प्रचुराश्रु चैव न शुभप्रदं पुंसाम् ॥
> (*Bṛhat-Saṁhitā*, LXVIII).

The ability to weep is uniquely human form of emotional response. The idea that having a good cry can do women good is a very old one. And now it hes scientific validity. When someone has had a shock, is very stressed, or in a lot of pain the natural response is to cry.

5389 **रोचना**

Rocanā : it was used to ward off evil spirits. It was bright yellow pigment prepared from the urine or bile of a cow or found in its head. It was auspicious (*HC*, II).

5390 **रोटिका**

Roṭikā : wheat-bread. The soft wheat-bread is a sexual symbol in the following Gondi song meaning vagina. Oil is also very much symbolized for the fluid :

> How can I go into the inner room ?
> My anklets sound *chunur chunur*
> The wheat-bread is soft
> The oil drips from it
> O lover, eat, and you will be content
> My anklets sound *chunur chunar.*

The picture here is of a youth who goes to visit his lover in her own house. She gives him his supper and he begs her to go with him into the inner room which with its grainbins and darkness is a very common place for the meeting of lovers.

ल – La

5391 **लकुलीश**

Lakulīśa : the ithyphallic *Yogī.* The emblem of *lakulīśa* is the 'large club'. The significant signs and gestures of this *Yogi* were provoking and indecent and he belonged to the Pāśupata sect. He used to speak improperly (*Pāśupatasūtra*, III.16-17). Other elements, such as the cutting of the *Liṅga* and its extension to heaven and hell, are familiar from the Sanskrit tradition.

5392 **लक्ष्य-लक्षणभाव**

Lakṣya-lakṣaṇabhāva : relation implying identity (Sadānanda, *Vedāntasāra*).

5393 **लप**

Lapa : to speak. In *Amarakośa*, derivatives of *lapa* (speak) form an interesting series. They are *ālāpa* (dialogue), *pralāpa* (nonsense), *anulāpa* (chatter), *vilāpa* (bemoaning), *vipralāpa* (contradiction), *saṁlāpa* (discussion), *supralāpa* (agreeable speech, well-said) and *apalāpa* (denial).

5394 **लब्धवर्ण**

Labdhavarṇa : literate, a person versed in letters (Kālidāsa, *Raghu.*, 6.87).

5395 **लब्धवर्णभाज्**

Labdhavarṇabhāj : a person who respects scholars (Kālidāsa, *Raghu.*, 11.160).

5396 **लवण**

Lavaṇa : salt. Salt is not accepted if given by hand (*Skanda.* IV.40.114). It is said that weighing against salt gives beauty of form (*Ibid.*,V.1.8.67-69). The *vānaprasthin* should not take salt, and if they desire it should be 'salt made by himself : **स्वयं कृतं च लवणम्** (*Skanda*, IV.41.6). There is general belief that it is unfortunate to spill salt. One who does this will in *Pātāla loka* gather up each pinch of salt with his eyelids. It is also considered inadvisable to hand salt to a friend or neighbour in the bare palm of hand, for this will cause enmity between the parties concerned. Salt is therefore received, not in the bare palm but in a cloth or vessel.

5397 **लाक्षणिक**

Lākṣaṇika : allegorical, being a symbolic narrative. Allegory is a particularly different form of literary composition because its author seeks to communicate on two levels : One, the direct or the concrete, which embodies a romantic or heroic tale or both rolled into one, and the second, a more abstruse or abstract plane whereupon he aspires to concentrate on a deeper and subtler message reflecting his view of life. It resembles a tight-rope walk because the slightest lapse in organization of the various ingredients, in its meaningfulness on the two planes, shatters the whole fabric of the composition and renders the narrative lame and incapacitated. In Sanskrit, the most important allegorical dramas are Kṛṣṇa Mishra's *Prabodha-Candrodaya* (11th cent.) and Appashastri Rashivadekar's *Adharma-Vipāka* (20th cent.). In these dramas symbolic figures appear as characters.

Allegory in Sanskrit literature can be seen as a systematic, structural kind of symbolism. It is a narrative which is not simply a narrative; it is a TEXT which has a level of meaning other than the superficial one. It can be seen to be a kind of extended *lakṣaṇa* (metaphor). Here narrative level is not as significant as the analogical level or meaning. In some works (*Prabodha-candrodaya*) can be found one device, but in other works (*Adharma-vipāka*) the different one. *Adharma-vipāka* is an satirical allegory of the political situation of the beginning of the 20h century.

5398 **लावक**

Lāvaka : quail, the *lāvā* in Halbi. Tribes call it as a jealous bird. The female quail is believed to be possessed by the fear that her husband will be going to other women and is always *gudur-gudur*. When she lays eggs "she makes him sit on them or he might go to another women forgetting his own children".

The quail is very common is tribal folksongs. The following Gondi song picturizes it :

The quail calls in the stream
On the banks of the lake it cries
Burnt is the oil-seed
Burnt is the grass of last year
In the middle of the forest the quail calls
And the Raja comes and bears the quail calling
On the bank of the lake
The house is of mud
The door of cotton-wood
Milk-sweet of the brown buffalo
Is being cooked
The Raja comes hastily
But all he hears
Is the quail calling on the bank of the lake.

The quail is greatly relished by the Gond and Baiga for food. These birds are said to be great lovers and always feed near one another. If one of them is found missing, they all cry out, come together, look at each other and then continue feeding. A common refrain in the *Karmā* song runs 'The quail calls on the brow of the hill'.

5399 **लिम्बुक**

Limbuka : lemon, *Citrus Medica*. 'Lemon' is a simile for th breasts in Amarkantaka :

He saw ripe lemons on her tree
How could he control his hunger ?

But the above is not a very common one, for lemons are not common in this region.

5400 **लोह**

Loha : iron. Believed to be inauspicious in the ritual-meal, nothing should be offered in iron-plates or vessels (*Skanda*,I. 206.39) :

न आयसेन च पात्रेण तद् वै रक्षांसि भुंजते ।

Iron is associated with demons, and is believed to be produced from their body (*Bhaviṣya*, 138.35.36). Iron is associated with poverty (*Ibid, Pratisarga* 8.99) : दारिद्रं लोहरूपिणम् । Iron is said to be special to the planet Śani (saturn). In a magical act a needle of the iron is said to be used. Iron is also a protective measure (*Skanda*, VI. 94.15).

व - Va

5401 **वंश**

Vaṁśa : bamboo. Bamboo image is very much common in the tribal poetry. A girl is often compared to a bamboo :

Come, boys, and let us play
Life is only for two days
Take whichever girl you like
Life is only for two days
Her hips sway like a young bamboo
Life is only for two days.

The use of bamboo is also found among Oraon:

On the high hills the bamboos grow
From a bamboo the blue bow is made
The shooting arrows are a spray of water
The gun is fired many rounds.

A girl is bamboo, say the Pradhān, 'because her waist is slender and always like one'.

In the Santhāl folk-tale a bamboo grows out of the grave of a girl who has been murdered, and from it a *Jogī* makes a flute of great sweatness. Bamboos are often used in the construction of marriage-booths and small bamboo lids are placed below the bride and bridegroom when they sit for the ceremonial greeting of their relatives.

The Gond and Baiga indeed personify the bamboo as a girl, as Basmoti Kaniā or Bās Kaniyā. Basmoti Kaniyā fed the little Nangā Baiga with her milk and gave him a golden axe. According to one story Nangā Baiga and Nangā Baigin were born under a clump of bamboos. It was from the shavings of a bamboo that mankind were born. A curious tale about the origin of the seed allots to the bamboo an obvious sexual function. Nangā Baiga was taking seed to the forest and on the way met Basmoti Kaniyā the bamboo and asked her to keep the seed with her for the night. She put all the seed in her belly, and in the morning Nangā Baiga cut the bamboo and, leaving the head and feet behind, carried the belly, full of seeds to his clearing. Another version is that Basmoti turned herself into a bamboo for shame when her own father gave her seed.

5402 **वक्तृतात्पर्य**

Vaktṛtātparya : knowledge of the intention of the speaker.

Viśvanātha, the author of *Bhāṣā-pariccheda,* adds a fourth requisite in a sentence. The favourite illustration given is the sentence *saindhavam ānaya.* The sentence has two meanings, 'bring salt' and 'bring a horse'. It is true that the sentence has all the three requisites. Still it is the knowledge of the intention of the speaker, that enables one to understand whether it is the salt or the horse that has to be brought.

5403 **वक्त्रलेप**

Vaktralepa : make up of the face, facial make-up. *Garuḍa Purāṇa* (I. 169) has presented certain ingredients for facial makeup. Their components are as follows: (a) *lodhra* (saffron), *mañjiṣṭhā, kāleyaka,* barley, rice, *yaṣṭimadhu,* pounded and applied. (b) red sandal, *mañjiṣṭhā, lākṣā, karṣaka; yaṣṭimadhu* and saffron together powdered and applied.

5404 **वधू**

Vadhū : bride (Kālidāsa, *Śāk.,* 5.389; *Kum,.* 3.48). *Vadhūbandhu* (*Śāk,.* V) was used for the relations of a bride. Kālidāsa (*Kumāra.,* VII) has depicted Pārvati as a bride in the following lines :

> Stepped from her bath, gowned in the whitest silk,
> She was ready to be a bride as the land is ready
> Just after rain has washed it and, freshened, it bears
> A million blossoms of kāśa for a raiment of white.
>
> Her lips a little parted, stain on the lower,
> Leavings of wine, a smear of red and trembling
> To speak of desire, a filling fruit, not quite
> In its deepest hue, but splitting with so much sweet.
>
> Putting her bridal ornaments right, she seemed
> A young vine just now coming to blosson, seemed
> A young night filling its sky with stars, of a river
> Of autumn bearing a rush of migrant birds.
> The mirror gave back her white silk dress;
> But also gave back the foaming shore
> Of the milky sea, an exultant tide;
> Gave back the autumn full of the moon.
> (Vātsyāyana and Miśra, 1983.105-6)

5405 **वनभजन**

Vanabhajana : forest songs. The *Dadariā* or *Sālho* as they are called in Chhattisgaṛh, are the true *ban-bhajan* or forest-songs. They are sung by the people at work in field or forest, by groups of girls on their way to a bazar, by travellers resting by the fire at night. Young lovers sing them to each other, and many a proposal has been made and elopement arranged in verse. At weddings, the two parties sing them against one another competitively; while they are singing boys and girls throw rings to each other and exchange gifts of tobacco and betel. The *Dadariā* can also be used as taunt-songs; at one time notorious criminal, in whose activities English had ventured to interfere, never passed their house without singing at the top of his voice a selection of obscene and insulting *Dadariā.*

These are the most spontaneous and original of the songs. There is great corpus or floating reserve of *Dadariā* verse, on which boys and girls draw according to their knowledge and their fancy. But they also often improvise, a task which is facilitated by the rather cheap and easy rhymes that are in fashion.

The music is always fresh and thrilling, with a lilt, a joy, an excitement that never stales. The songs are sung very loudly, at a high pitch; they are the radio messages of the aboriginal. They are usually sung antiphonally; one verse of a *Dadariā* expects an answer.

5406 **वर्णविचारक्षमा**

Varṇavicārakṣamā : the literary lady (Kālidāsa, *Vikrama.,* 5.105).

5407 **वर्तमान**

Vartamāna : present. The work in the present is hailed in a Sanskrit verse :

> *gate śoko na kartavyo*
> *bhaviṣyam naiva cintayet* /
> *vartamānena kālena*
> *vartayanti vicakṣaṇāḥ* //
>
> "Wail not for what is past,
> Talk not of future too thou hast,
> Sagacious men I say
> Work in the present night and day."

5408 **वर्धनी**

Vardhanī : broom-stick (*Agni,* 27.3). Sticks taken from a broom are used for the magic purpose and there is generally an idea that the broom sweeps poverty and disease out of the house. Brooms are collected and taken to the boundary by the tribes at ceremonies for the purification of a village. It is known as *bohrāni* in Bastar.

To the aboriginals of Chhattisgaṛh, the broom is primarily something that wipes away refuse. For this reason brooms are carried out of the boundary of the village and hung up there as a sign that poverty and disease has been swept away. Sometimes sticks from the special brooms made of *chir* grass are used in divination. The magician takes two or three of these sticks and measures them over and over again with his hand.

Brooms are also used by the people at the time of husking grain or grinding wheat. The housewife sweeps away the chaff and gathers together the grain with the broom which thus becomes something of a sacred implement on account of its association with the grain. For this reason there is a certain belief in a broom being lucky or at least infected with some kind of magical power. A broom, for example, should never be left standing upright in a house as this might lead to a quarrel between husband and wife. It is unlucky to see a broom early in the morning but, on the other hand, if the grass used in a broom is burnt and the smoke allowed to enter the nostrils of a newly-born child it will do it good.

At the Holi festival a special broom is made of *chir* grass and hung up in a cotton tree.

5409 **वस्त्र**

Vastra : garment. A garment is said to increase life; the contrary is, that a person without a proper garment would be losing his years:

> वस्त्रं आयुष्करं विदुः (*Śiva*, XV.48)

It is enjoined that the garment should not be washed after bath, at a holy place such as river; it should be carried to a well or straight home for washing (*Ibid.* 19):

> नद्यादितीर्थस्नाने तु स्नानवस्त्रं न शोधयेत् ।
> वापीकूपगृहादौ तु स्नानादूर्ध्वं नयेद् बुधः ॥

A dirty cloth, or one without ends (*daśa*) was taboo: वर्ज्यं च मलिनं वस्त्रं दशाभिश्च विवर्जितम् (*Ibid.* 164)

What you wear, and when you wear it, affects everyone who sees you. Personality, political inclinations, occupation, sexuality and even religion are suggested by what you wear. And whether you like it or not, your clothes make a strong visual statement about how you see yourself. In his book *Style in Costume*, James Laver described clothes as "the furniture of the mind made visible."

5410 **वातावर्त**

Vātāvarta : whirl-wind. All over India whirl-winds are supposed to be caused by evil spirits (*bhūt*). It is known as a 'knot in the wind'. Tylor has truly said, "what is poetry to us was philosophy to early man." (also see *JRAS*, 1904.2).

5411 **वामाचार**

Vāmācāra : the 'left-hand' or orgiastic path of the *Tantras*.

5412 **वायस**

Vāyasa : crow. The crow is a very natural symbol of the human beings in whose company it lives so intimately. Even in a village where there is little waste and little enough to get for food, the grows gather round and lodge in any neighbouring tree. The crow is regarded in Mandla as a learned bird, probably on account of its wonderful eyesight. It is supposed to know all about the surrounding:

> Every evening
> The crows sit talking
> But my Raja
> Without a word
> Left me
> Without a word
> Every evening
> The crows sit talking.

It is unlucky, however, to see a crow sitting on the back of a pig, nor should one see a crow bathing as one is about to start on a journey. If a crow says 'rāo' there will be a quarrel in the house, or bad news will come. But if it says 'cāo' it is lucky. It is lucky also to see two crows feeding each other.

Crooke classes the crow with the cuckoo and the Jay as a news-bearer. If a crow flies a short distance and hops about on the roof or near the house, it is sign that the master is coming or that news of him may be expected.

5413 **वासित**

Vāsita : animal call (*Amarakośa*).

5414 **विक्षिप्त**

Vikṣipta : distracted (mind). The symptoms of a distracted mind are grief, mental distress, tremor of the body, irregular breathing etc. (*Vyāsa-Bhāṣya*, I.31). To overcome this concentration, some particular subject is prescribed (Ibid, 1.32). Further, in order to overcome the distraction which normally arises in social relations, one is asked to cultivate friendliness (*maitrī*) toward those who are happy, compassion (*karuṇā*) towards those who are misery, gladness (*muditā*) towards those who are virtuous and cooperation and indifference (*upekṣā*) towards those who are non-social (Ibid, 1.33). This shows the awareness of the significant part played by proper social relations in the promotion of mental health.

5415 **विज्ञापय / विज्ञाप्यताम्**

Vijñāpaya/vijñāpyatām : be informed or told (*Mālatīmādhava*, I). When a person in an inferior position a addresses or says something to a person in a superior position, the verb *vijñāpaya* is used; and when one in higher status says something to a person in a lower status, *ājñāpaya* is used (without there being any idea of actual request or command). The former (*kah do*) and the latter (*ājñā den*) are still used in Hindi in the same sense.

5416 **विनय**

Vinaya : moderation. *Vinaya* is often equated with moderation which is already a virtue in matters of eating (Manu, II.57). Moderation is often equated with social indifference towards praise and blame (II. 161). Those who are affluent are recommended not to show off their wealth (III. 125).

A monarch was expected to learn modesty and discipline from the wise (VII. 39). Control over greed, lust and anger was always considered a virtue (VII. 49). The control of the senses with the help of one's reason is invariably emphasized (II. 96). What could be called 'good manners', like not producing unnecessary noise by clapping and shouting even when one is excited, are strongly recommended by *Manu* (IV. 64). At one place Manu recommends that a beast of burden like a horse should never be excessively whipped (IV. 68). Manu, strangely, appears to be unusually harsh in so far as behaviour towards one's enemy is concerned (IV. 144).

5417 **विन्यस्तवामचरण**

Vinyastavāmacaraṇa : to plant one's left foot on another's head is symbolical of utterly humiliating him (HC. II).

5418 **विपरीतख्याति**

Viparītakhyāti : malobservation. The *Nyāya-vaiśeṣika* theorists assert that in illusion, there is malobservation. This is also called *anyathākhyāti*. The object is seen as something shining. However, it is not grasped as a mere conch-shell (*Śukta-rajata*). It is grasped as "something shining". On the basis of memory, the shining piece is perceived as silver. So there is a confusion here of some object that is seen, with some object that is remembered. The *Mīmāṁsā* and the *Sāṅkhya* schools explain illusion as *ākhyāti*, non-grasping of the properties of the object seen (Kuppuswamy, 1985.98).

5419 **वियोनौ मैथुनम्**

Viyonau maithunam : an abnormal sexual act in which a woman is not united in the normal way (*Skanda*, 1.2.41.57).

5420 **विरक्तचेष्टा**

Viraktaceṣṭā : indications of disaffection. The following are the indications of the disaffection of a woman : "A frowning face (*bhrukuṭīmukhatva*) from her lover, forgetting the good turns done by him, indifference, not being pleased with anything offered, kindness toward his enemies, harsh words, shaddering on touching or seeing him, assuming arrogance, not preventing him from going away, wiping off the month after being kissed, going to bed first and getting up last" (*Bṛhat-Saṁhitā*, LXXVIII). Cf. Kaśyapa .

दृष्ट्वा न दृश्यते मूढा स्पृष्ट्वा दूर्वचनं वदेत् ।
रतिकालावगूढा तु चुम्बिनी मार्जयेन्मुखम् ॥
सुप्ता विबुध्यते पश्चाच्छयने तु पराङ्मुखी ।
विरक्ता सा स्मृता नारी वर्जनीया प्रयत्नतः ॥

5421 **विरक्ता-प्रमदा**

Viraktā-pramadā : disgusted woman. Varāhamihira (LXVIII) warns the men to examine carefully whether the damsels are disgusted with them, because the king Vidūratha was murdered by his own queen with a weapon concealed in her tresses, and that the king of Kāśī by his disaffected queen with her anklets smeared with poison. In this manner, women, when they are disgusted with one, bring about dangers amounting to death. What is the use of enumerating other troubles ? These two instances of female treachery are alluded to by Kāmandaka and later by Bāṇa in the *Harṣacarita*. In ancient times kings used to have many queens in their harems. It may happen that at times some of the beautiful queens are agents of foreign powers for bringing about the king's downfall. Kāmandaka has also warned the people :

नहि देवीगृहं गच्छेत्मीयात्सन्नि वेशनात् ।
अत्यन्त वल्लभोऽपीह विस्रब्धाः स्त्रीषु न व्रजत् ॥

5422 **विरहाख्यान**

Virahākhyāna : songs of sorrow, widely known as *birhā* in central India. These *birhā* songs are used indifferently at marriages or funerals, though there is little in their subjects to connect them with either. The word *birahā* is said to mean 'sorrow'; and the songs are used by the Gond and Baigā while a bridegroom takes a girl to his house and after the feasting on the tenth day celebrations of a death. The singers stand in a group and sing quickly and very loudly; then the song stops and the drums begin and they dance, each alone, bending down and hopping about with great vigour :

There is no thunder in the sky today
Nor the clouds driven to and fro
I know, I know
It was a dry cloud thundered
Fie on your earthen pot
That breaks at the first touch of water.

A girl has broken her water-pot down by the stream, and when she gets home she has to face an angry and sarcastic mother-in-law. The song accuses her of breaking the pot during a struggle with a man (dry thunder) and at the first touch of water (intercourse).

5423 **विलोचन-लक्षण**

Vilocana-lākṣaṇa : signs of the eyes. "People become wealthy with eyes similar to the petals of a lotus; very opulent and powerful, with those that have red corners; immensely rich with those coloured tawney like honey; sinners with feline eyes; thieves with round and crooked ones as well as with those resembling the eyes of the deer; cruel with squint eyes; commanders of armies with elephantine ones; wealthy with deep ones; learned with those resembling blue lines. The eyes whose pupils are extremely black will be pulled out. Broad and thick eyes make a minister; green ones lovely and fortunate; and large ones enjoyer of vast wealth and pleasures of life" (*Bṛhat-Saṁhitā*, LXVIII). Śrīrāma, according to Vālmiki, was *raktāntanayanaḥ*. Vide the following :

समे गोक्षीरवर्णाभे रक्तान्ते कृष्णतारके ।
प्रसन्ने च विशाले च स्निग्धे चैवायते शुभे ॥
अतसीपुष्पसङ्काशे भवेतां यस्य लोचने ।
भूपतिः स तु विज्ञेयः समुद्रवचनं यथा ॥
व्याघ्रचक्षुर्धनैर्युक्तः कर्कटाक्षः कलिप्रियः ।
बिडालहंसनेत्राश्च भवन्ति पुरुषाधमाः ॥
मयूरनकुलाक्षाश्च नरास्ते मध्यमाः स्मृताः ।
न श्रीस्त्यजति सर्वत्र पुरुषं मधुपिङ्गलम् ॥
आज्यपिङ्गलनेत्राश्च राजानो भोगसंयुताः ।
रोचनाहरितालाश्च गजपिङ्गा धनेश्वराः ॥
बलवन्तो गुणोपेताः पृथिव्यां चक्रवर्तिनः ।
तप्तहाटकवर्णाभे भवेतां तस्य लोचने ॥

5424 **विवाहदीक्षातिलक**

Vivāhadīkṣātilaka : *(Kumāra.)* is used for the mark of pigment on the forehead of the girl to be given in marriage. This ceremony is still performed. (7.122).

5425 **विवाहनेपथ्य**

Vivāhanepathya : the costume to be worn on the wedding day (Kālidāsa, *Māl.*, V).

5426 **विवाहयज्ञ**

Vivāhayajña *(Kumāra.7.122)* : is used for *marriage*, and indicates that the marriage of a daughter was considered to be a *Yajña.*

5427 **विवाहवेष**

Vivāhaveṣa : dress during the time of marriage (Kālidāsa, *Māl.*, 4.68).

5428 **विशुद्धि चक्र**

Viśuddhi-cakra : one of the *Ṣaṭcakras* in Tantra. In the throat region is *Viśuddha* with sixteen petals and on these petals are the vowels. The element connected with it is *ākāśa*, the sensation is hearing and the motor organ is the mouth which produces speech. The *Viṣuddha-cakra* makes the person become merciful, gentle, steady, modest and self-controlled. He will become free from greed, malice, pride and other anti-social tendencies.

5429 **विशेषण-विशेष्यभाव**

Viśeṣaṇa-viśeṣyabhāva : relation between two words which qualify each other, signifying a common object (Sadānanda, *Vedāntasāra*).

5430 **विश्रब्धालाप**

Viśrabdhālāpa : confidential (*Veṇīsaṁhāra*, II)

5431 **विहगगीत**

Vihagagīta : bird-lore. The bird-lore follows the usual lines : some of the birds are associated with the erotic adventures of historic lovers, others with the personage of Hindu mythology. The fidelity of birds to each other is often held up as a warning and inspiration to less contact human partners : The *cakka-cakki* birds, for example, remain together like the two parts of a grindstone. Curiously, they are said to have 'no children till they are very old'. The expression *Sārus-joṛī* given to a devoted husband or wife is derived in Chhattisgaṛh from the well-known love of the *Sārus*-crane for its mate :

Without its mate
What great sorrow for the crane !
Only if Fate demands
Will it ever live solitary
When it is left alone
It weeps at midnight.

5432 **वृक्षारोपण**

Vṛkṣāropaṇa : planting trees. It is considered both meritorious and exciting to plant trees. The Gond or Pardhān who does this generally has a great desire to perpetuate his name, and looks forward to a prosperous old age. In the following poem the old men who planted mango and tamarind trees in his youth finds himself jealous of the vigour of their fresh green leaves and compares it to the lack of strength and life in his own limbs :

How young I was
When I planted the mango
And the tamarind
And still her leaves are full of life
But there is none in my old body.

5433 **वेदी**

Vedī : a sacrificial platform. The construction or erection of a *vedī* required the strict and proper observation of certain rules of measurement and laying of bricks etc. (Kālidāsa *Śākuntalam* 3.182, 4.30, 3.255; *Raghu.*, 5.79).

5434 **वैद्य**

Vaidya : medicine-man; his sight is inauspicious (*Vāyu.*, 91.2.45).

5435 **वैश्वानर**

Vaiśvānara : the fire within the human body, digestive fire.

5436 **व्यक्तिवाद**

Vyaktivāda : the word signifies only a particular individual and not the class, a view advanced by certain psycholinguists in India. Only individual cows exist. The class is incorporeal and motionless. Only individuals are corporeal and moving. A collection of cows, is a collection of individual cows. Further, they show that qualities can exist only in individuals. There are white cows and black cows. The quality refers to the particular cow. (*Nyāya*-theorists).

5437 **व्यंजनहारिका**

Vyañjanahārikā : remover of sex-mark. The evil power named *vyañjana-hārikā* is said to trouble a maiden. She cuts the *vyañjana* (sex-mark; menstruation) in the case of a maiden who gets married without paying funeral homage or proper respect to her (dead) mother (*Mārkaṇḍeya*, 50.82.100).

5438 **वृद्ध-व्यवहार**

Vṛddha-vyavahāra : use of words by elders. The close relationship between the word and its meaning is due to social transmission—socialization. As the grammarians put it, the use of sentences in the imperative mood helps us to observe the action of the child who brings the object specified by the word. It is agreed by the grammarians, *Mīmāṁsakas* and *Nyāya-vaiśeṣikas* that the first and fore most method of learning the meaning of words is not of observing the use of language in actual life. This is the way in which the child picks up a language. It is through *āvāpa*, using the word in a given context and *udvāpa*, using the word in a different context, by the process of assimilation and elimination that meanings of words are picked up. Words and their meanings thus, are primarily picked up in actual usage. Secondarily, they are picked up through *kośas* or lexicons (Kuppuswamy, 1985, 139). Grammarians as well as logicians agree that the best method of learning a language is that of observing the use of knowledge in actual life. Children learn the language by this direct method.

5439 **वृषली**

Vṛṣalī : one who leaves her own bull i.e. husband. *vṛṣalī* is one who leaves her own *vṛṣa* (bull) and goes to another 'bull' with sexual desire :

> स्ववृषं या परित्यज्य परवृषे वृषायते ।
> वृषली सा हि विज्ञेया न शूद्री वृषली भवेत् ॥

श - Śa

5440 **शब्दगुण**

Śabdaguṇa : sky or space, because every sound is produced in space, without space there cannot be any sound. Hence the quality of space element is sound (Kālidāsa, *Raghu.*, 13.190). Hall (1966) described three kinds of spatial organization: fixed feature, semifixed feature, or informal space. Fixed feature space refers to arrangement of environmental space such as houses, rooms, even cities and towns. Semi-fixed feature are such immovable objects as a table, chairs and the like. Informal space pertain to interpersonal distance, which is of primary interest in proximics. This all comes under the *āhārya* category of *Abhinaya* in the Bharata's schemata.

5441 **शाकुनम्**

Śākunam : omens. The subject of omens in *Bṛhat-Saṁhitā* (LXXXVI) receives unusual attention of Varāhamihira (505 A.D), in that he devotes eleven chapters to its various ramifications. According to him this is a very ancient discipline that has been handed down right from Indra, Bṛhaspiti, Śukra and many sages like Parāsara, Garga and Bhāradvāja. We find in all branches of Sanskrit literature ample evidence for people's faith in omens, which are generally observed when a person goes on a journey.

Omens are of various kinds as those caused by beings that are rural, wild, acquatic, terrestrial, atmospheric, diurnal, nocturnal and diurnal nocturnal. The sex of the creatures was taken into consideration in respect of their cry, gait, look and utterance which act as omens:

> ग्रामारण्याम्बुभूव्योमद्युनिशोभयचारिणः ।
> रुतयातेक्षितोक्तेषु ग्राह्या पुंस्त्रीनपुंसकाः ॥

(Varāhamihira, *Ibid.*)

5442 **शापास्त्र**

Śāpāstra : a missile of curse, whereby an ascetic could destroy or harm his teaser to protect himself against his wicked acts (Kālidāsa, *Raghu.*, 15.283).

5443 **शालिगोपी**

Śāligopi : a lady looking after or protecting paddy crop, rice being the principal diet of the people in early India (Kālidāsa, *Raghu.*, 4.20).

5444 **शास्त्र**

Śāstra : a text book, particularly of sacred law.

5445 **शिखाबन्धनविद्या**

Śikhābandhanavidyā : art of hairdressing (*Vikrama.*, 2.32).

5446 **शिरः कण्डूयन**

Śiraḥ-kaṇḍūyana : scratching the head. *Skanda-Purāṇa* (1.2.40.236) records that women in Kali-age are said to be scratching their head: शिरः कण्डूयनतत्पराः ।

5447 **शिरः जानुनि**

Śiraḥ-jānuni : head on the knees, a sitting posture. There is a custom inauspicious for a pregnant woman to sit with head on her knees. This fact is clarified by the *Brahmāṇḍa Purāṇa* (II. 3.5.49). Diti requested her husband Kaśyapa to favour her with a son. Once at mid-day Diti was overpowered by sleep, and slept placing her head on the knee with her hair falling on feet:

> मध्यमे प्राप्ते दिवाकरे
> शिरः कृत्वा तु जानुनि
> केशान् कृत्वा तु पादस्थम् ।

Now, it is said that whatever is below the navel pit is impure. Indra saw that in that position she was impure. He entered her womb through her vagina.

5448 **शिरसि आघ्राय**

Śirasi-āghrāva : smelling on the head (*Veṇisaṁhāra*, IV). The *Gṛhyasūtras* mention the rite of the smelling of the son's head. Thus *Āśv.Gr.S.* refers to this rite and says that the father having returned from a journey, should smell the head of the son thrice. The *Purāṇas* are replete with references to the smelling of the head of the younger ones, especially the son, by the elders (*Bhāg.*, IV. 9.44; *Skanda*, V. 213). Smelling on the head appears to be due to the belief that it is *uttamāṅga* (the best parts of the body) and due to the fact of the practice of blessing a person on the head. But in the origin, smelling does not appear to be restricted to the head. It may be of interest to note in this connection that when Viṣṇu brought the earth out from water, in his boar-incarnation, he is said to have placed her on his lap and smelt her mouth (*Skanda.*, II. 1.94)

5449 **शिरसि चुम्बनम्**

Śirasi cumbanam : kissing on the head. The father when leaving the house on a journey used to kiss his son on the head (*HC*, IV).

5450 **शुभदिन**

Śubhadina : lucky days.

The life of the aborigines of Bastar is not free from superstitions. Particular days are lucky for particular purposes; but for the worship of spirits, demons, gods and goddesses all days are considered lucky. Towards Bhopālpaṭnam Thursday and Sunday are generally considered lucky for purposes in connection with marriage and for the purposes of agricultural operations of all kinds. Thursday, Friday and Sunday are considered lucky towards Kuakonda Pargana of Dantewara tahsil for commencing sowing. Monday, Tuesday and Wednesday; and for commencing ploughing their fields. Monday Tuesday and Thursday and for the grain, Friday for commencing reaping, Monday, Tuesday and Thursday are considered lucky. With witches and charmers Sunday is lucky.

5451 **शून्य**

Śūnya : the void, the zero it does not mean negation. The most important Indian symbol of the *coincidentia oppositorum* is the zero. While in mathematics zero means 'naught', for the Indian thinker the zero or *bindu* - 'dot', 'semen' - is an unlimited entity, the productive point of potentiality. Zero and *nirvāṇam* are both called *Śūnyam*, the void, which means 'excessive', 'swollen'. Heimann calls zero the *No*—or *All-figure*, 'the only mathematical symbol which extends beyond the every temporary value'. In other words, by reason of its *coincidendia*, the zero refers to a plane higher that of empirical reality, of the flux of things, while signifying the point where empirical reality dissolves into transcendental reality. Both void and *plenum*, it subsumes the plus and the minus signs. Similarly, *nirvāṇa* is called 'the whole'. Any attempt, therefore, to equate *nirvāṇa* with negation, or to take the flat off the zero idea, is unwarranted. Rather, the zero should be regarded as the matrix of negative and positive, the fulcrum, the hub of the wheel.

The concept of *Ātman*, or essence of self, is the correlative of zero in the various mystical systems. In Tāntrism, the *bindu* is equated with semen, not in a reductive, 'nothing but' sense, but as the empirical substance which can transform a man into a godlike being. But common to all the philosophical applications of the zero idea is the tendency, exemplified by the Tāntric attempt to 'store' semen, to associate the lalent power of the irreducible minimum with self-containment, completeness, consistently perfect continence (*brahmacarya*). The man who fully comprehends the mystry of the zero is the man who has reduced himself to zero - the ego-less monad suspended in the stratosphere of the void which, under normal conditions, would asphyxiate ordinary mortals. In other words - weakness is power.

5452 **शूर्प**

Śūrpa : winnowing-basket, winnowing-fan. Winnowing baskets are supposed to be seats of ghosts (*Skanda*, VII. 1.167.108). It was a taboo to stride over the winnowing basket in the evenings (*Brahma*, 124.56). Evils are said to frequent where people are in the habit of tossing the winnowing basket (*Mārk.*, 51.92). If the winnowing basket is touched with the nails, it may cause lack of lustre (*Skanda*, VI, 22.26). Image of Lakṣmī was placed on it and worshipped (*Matsya.*, 80.15.27). The winnowing-fan, everywhere in the tribal regions, is associated with magic. In the Maikal Hills it is used by the Guniā for divination. The winnowing-fan is one of the most important of domestic implements. It is used by men for winnowing grain at harvest time. Women must not touch it then, but they can use it at all other times. They clean the grain with it before husking and again clean the husked grain before cooking. The winnowing-fan makes a very convenient open basket in which chillies, *haldī*-roots, salt and many other things are temporarily placed for use in the kitchen. The refuse of the house is swept into an old winnowing-fan and partly because it is used for this purpose it is taken along with the broom to the boundary at the ceremonial purification of the village. When a child is born, rice is put in a winnowing-fan. This is covered with a cloth and the child is laid on it. At a marriage when bride and bridegroom are bathed they are fanned with a winnowing-fan possibly with the hope that all the unlucky chaff in their lives may be blown away. Finally when a woman dies her winnowing-fan is taken and placed by her pyre or on the grave.

This is quite enough of itself to make the winnowing-fan sacred but there is another cause. It is used as a sort of planchette by the Guniā magician. In Chhattisgarh the Guniā puts rice in the winnowing-fan and rubs his hands over it in a rhythmic circulation, muttering charms as he does so until the god comes upon him. Dalton (218) records that at a Santhāl funeral, towards evening it is customary for a man to take his seat near the ashes with a winnowing-fan, in which he tosses rice till a phrensy appears to seize him, and he becomes inspired and says wonderful things.

The Oraon also use the winnowing-fan as a 'sort of divining rod to conduct the person holding it to the door of a man most fitted to hold the office of a village priest' (*Ibid.*, 247).

5453 **श्वास**

Śvāsa : sighs, breath. As an aspirate from the living body, the breath was associated with the creation of new life. Thus it is said that when Brahmā was thinking deeply about creation, he released a deep sigh; from it was born the spring season (*Śiva*, II. 8. 37). Uneven breathing may be signal of insincerity. Correct posture aids breathing.

ष - Ṣa

5454 **षट्चक्र**

Ṣaṭcakra : the six bases of meditation according to *Tantras*. The entire design of *cakras* is based on the concept of lotuses at the various centres of the body. On the petals of these lotuses are the fifty letters of the Sanskrit alphabet. The design is intimately connected with the notion of five elements.

स - Sa

5455 **संवत्सर**

Saṁvatsara : a year, division of time. Two *ayanas* form a *saṁvatsara*. They are the *uttarāyaṇa* and *dakṣiṇāyaṇa* (*Varāha*. 20.5).

5456 **संहार-मुद्रा**

Saṁhāra-mudrā : name of a *mudrā* in breathing, a position of palms indicating 'taking in' (*Agni*, 155.4), the position of hand indicating collection and taking breath in (*Agni*. 83.7).

5457 **सङ्केतगृहम्**

Saṅketagṛham : a rendezous, a place where lovers meet by appointment (Kālidāsa, *Māl.*, V).

5458 **संग्रह**

Saṅgraha : collection. In *NS* (1.14) it is a technical term meaning the collection of topics and concepts which, together, describe a subject in its totality. Bharata takes up the *saṅgraha* of *nāṭya* at the beginning of the sixth chapter. His *saṅgraha* has ten topics (VI. 10).

5459 **सजीवीकरण**

Sajīvīkaraṇa : infused with life, the ritual of infusing the books with life. *Agni-Purāṇa* (63. 13-15) records that when the manuscript is complete, it should be placed on an auspicious seat (*bhadrapīṭhika*) to the northeastern quarter, placed on auspicious designs. The author should keep the manuscript to be reflected in a mirror and cause it to sprinkle with water from holy jars:

दर्पणे पुस्तकं धृत्वा सेचयेत् पूर्ववत् घटैः (*Ibid.*, 17)

After that he should place the new script on a bed. Alongside it, or upon it, he should place the *Puruṣa Sūkta* (*RV*,X. 90) or a *Veda* (*Ibid.*): न्यसेत्तु पौरुषं सूकत्तं वेदाद्यं तत्र पुस्तके । The script is, then to be infused with life with a ritual called *Sajīvīkaraṇa*, after smelling the *caru;* he should worship elders and feed the brāhmaṇs (*Ibid.*, 19). Then the manuscript should be taken round the city in a chariot or an elephant. Then it is placed in the house or in a temple; and it should be worshipped:

रथेन हस्तिना वापि भ्रामयेत्पुस्तकं नरैः ।
गृहे देवालयादौ तु पुस्तकं स्थाप्य पूजयेत् ॥
(*Ibid.*, 20)

It should be covered with cloth. While reading it, the reader should keep in mind the place of the word.

5460 **सन्देश**

Sandeśa : message (*Megha*). A message is any sign or group of signs capable of being interpreted meaningfully. In other words, a message is something that stands for or represents ideas. A message is something that has significance for people; that is, they attach or attribute meaning to it. *Amarakośa* defines it as सन्देशवाग्वाचिकं स्यात् । *Sanjīvanī* on *Meghadūta* (*Pūrva*) calls it *vārta* and *vācikam*.

Messages are made of signs, which are things that stand for something else: *sandiśyamāna vastūni* (*subodhā* on *Meghadūta*). Things that signify point to something beyond themselves; they represents things or ideas or events other than themselves. Signs could be objects or signs or marks—anything that stands for something else. And it is signs that messages are made: संदेशः संवाद (*Ibid.*)

In Sanskrit speech communication, the word *sandeśa* has been used in three senses. In fact, there are three messages involved: the message in the mind of the sender (i.e. Yakṣa), the message transmitted by the sender (i.e. through *Megha*), and the message received and interpreted by the receiver (i.e. Yakṣiṇi). Thus, a message is a piece of information encoded by a speaker/writer as addresser into a linguistic form or code and transmitted via the medium of speech or writing along a channel to an addressee who decodes it.

5461 **सन्धि**

Sandhi : joints. Varāhamihira (LXVIII) has given effects of the joints - 'one who has a well developed body is termed 'Fleshstrong', and possesses learning, wealth and handsome features:

उपचितदेहो विद्वान् धनी सुरूपश्च मांससारो यः ।
सङ्घात इति च सुश्लिष्टसन्धिता सुखभुजो ज्ञेया ॥

(b) compromise. Bṛhaspati says that when the plaint and the answer have been produced before the court and the suit has commenced, the court can make a compromise between the two parties, just as two pieces of redhot iron can be welded together. (c) Euphonic combination of final and initial letters. (d) juncture of the day and night. (e) structural divisions in a drama.

5462 **सपापता**

Sapāpatā : sinfulness. It is a common idea in the forest region of Madhya Pradesh that sin or sorrow or a quarrel turns the skin black. A *karmā* of Mandla has the same theme:

You have bathed in the river,
And you are standing on a rock to dress.
But your beautiful body has turned black,
For sin always turns the body black.

5463 **सपिण्डीकरण**

Sapiṇdikaraṇa : a ritual performed for the dead person. This ritual elevates the 'dead' (*preta*) to the status of the 'manes' (*pitṛ*). The three vessels here have significance in the fact that always three ancestors in degrees are invoked at the ritual, the performer being the fourth (*Matsya*. 18.18).

5464 **सभ्य**

Sabhya : member of an assembly, cultured, assessor. (b) Apart from the chief judge, there were some *sabhyas* in the court of justice. According to Nārada the *sabhyas* should be honourable men of tried integrity who are competent to discharge the duties, who can bear the burden of the administration of justice like good bulls. They should be acquainted with sacred law and rules of prudence, and be noble veracious, and impartial (*Nārada Smṛti*, III. 4-5). Persons who are ignorant of the customs of the country, atheists, those forbidden by the *śāstra*, insane, hot-tempered, greedy, or distressed should not be appointed as *sabhyas* (Bṛhaspati Smṛti, 1.64).

5465 **समनाम**

Samanāma : (a) bearing the same name is a mark of close relationships and it is known as *sahnāv* in Baghelkhand. It is considered highly improbable that there will be immoral relationship between those who are closely related by name. Public opinion on this subject is that it is considered improper for a man to marry a woman who bears the name of his mother, sister, aunt, etc. In fact, I think that on no account would a marriage be arranged, between those who bear the names of near relatives. Parent's names are never given to children. (b) homonym.

5466 **समानाधिकरण्य**

Samānādhikaraṇya : relation between two words having the same meaning (Sadānanda, *Vedāntasāra*).

5467 **सम्पुट**

Sampuṭa : a form of kiss. 'when both lips of one are taken and pressed between both lips of the other' (*Anaṅgaraṅga*, 9.19).

5468 **सम्भोगचिह्न**

Sambhogacihna : signs of the enjoyment of coition. Sanskrit classics as well as tribal poetry portray parallel images of the signs of coition. The following Bhili folksong indicates that the woman has attained sexual pleasure:

> 'O my darling daughter,
> How did you muddy yourself so?'
> "Father dear, my leg did slip,
> And hence I got so dirty."
> 'And how did you tear your *oṛhnī* ?'
> "When I went to pluck berries,
> My *oṛhnī* got caught in the bushes."
> 'And how did you tear your petticoat?'
> "While playing ball with my friends,
> My petticoat did tear in the melee'.
> 'And how has the sweet look of innocense
> Fled from your lovely face to-day?'
> "In the wild days of mid-summer
> These things happen, father dear!"

The second type of Bhili love-song reveals the signs of coition:

> My new wife is very smart
> When she goes to the river for water, she meets her lover.
> When he pulls her down, some of the water spills out of her pots.
> I ask, "Foolish woman, why this delay?"
> "You fool!" She resorts, "don't you know it takes a lot of time
> To clean out the water-hole?"
> "How did you break the water-pots?"
> "While lifting them, they broke."
> "Who broke the straps of your bodice?"
> "While lifting the water-pots, they broke".
> "How is there so much dust on your clothes?
> "I was caught in a dust-storm,
> "That is why I am so dusty."
> "How could the pots break, then?
> "Why do you ask me the same thing again and again."

5469 **सविकल्प**

Savikalpa : determinate perception. It was recognised that two distant stages of perception take place, viz., *nirvikalpa* (indeterminate stage) and *savikalpa*. Determinate perception is based on memory, recognition, and such other non-perceptual processes. It involves a knowledge of the genus to which the perceived object belongs and its specific qualities which distinguish it from the other objects of the same class.

5470 **सहस्रारचक्र**

Sahasrāracakra : the thousand-petalled lotus in the brain. It hangs with its head downwards. It has in it potentially all the powers and all the *guṇas*. When one goes beyond and meditates on the *sahasrāra*, the thousand-petalled lotus, all nescience (*ajñāna*) and delusion (*moha*) are destroyed. He attains the *svarūpa*, his real form. He is pure consciousness and pure bliss.

5471 **साधारणीकरण**

Sādhāraṇīkaraṇa : universalization, a theory in the field of Indian aesthetics elaborated by Bhaṭṭa Nāyaka. While the ordinary emotional experience is characterized by time, space, causing event or person, a sense of personal involvement, etc., the aesthetic expression is freed from all such limitations. It is this freedom from limitation that makes the experience universalistic. This makes the underlying emotion common to all people. It makes it an impersonal and disinterested delight. The aesthetic experience is a liberated and liberating experience. So it is self-fulfilling. It does not generate other desires. The joy is untainted by the needs of everyday life.

5472 **सार**

Sāra : substances in the body. Living beings have seven vital substances in their body, viz. fat, marrow, skin, bones, semen, blood and flesh:

> सप्तभवन्ति च सारा मेदोमञ्जात्वगस्थिशुक्राणि ।
> रुधिरं मांसं चेति प्राणभृतां तत्समासफलम् ॥
> (*Bṛhat-Saṁhitā*, LXVIII).

In Āyurveda these are called *dhātus*.

5473 **सिद्धान्न**

Siddhānna : *sadhaurī* in the Chhattisgarhi and Bagheli dialects of Hindi, a birth practice. Before the birth of the first born child, at the seventh month (?), it is customary for the women's nearest relatives to prepare some specially tasty dishes and bring them to the house of the woman who is expecting that she may partake of them. The more wealthy will bring along pieces of clothing also, and these will be presented to the woman. The food brought at this time to the woman who is expecting is called the *sadhaurī*. This word may also be connected with the word "*Sādh* " meaning desire and may have some connection with the *dohada* (see). Thus, *sidhaurī* or *sadhaurī* is a little ceremony intended to satisfy the cravings. The woman is visited by her mother, on her brother, who brings seven of food: she sits in her mother's lap and is ceremonially fed in Chhattisgarh.

5474 **सुख**

Sukha : pleasure. *Gītā* (II. 14-15) records that pleasures and pains arise through contact with objects and so, it is said one should be the same in pain and pleasure. *Gītā* (XVIII. 36-39) describes three kinds of *sukha* as follows; (a) the *sattva*, that which springs from clear understanding and is like poison at first and like nectar at the end; (b) the *rajasa*, that which arises from the contact of senses and their objects and like nectar at first, but like poison at the end; and (c) the *tamasa*, which deludes the self both at the beginning and the end, arising as it does from sleep, sloth and negligence.

5475 **सुरतोत्सव**

Suratotsava : sexual festival. The *Śiva-Purāṇa* (II. 51.27) mentions an erotic festival as was conducted by the people of the Asura king Bāṇa. The day of the festival is mentioned as the 12th bright of Kārtika and Māgha (*Ibid.*, 58). It is also said that on one of these two days Pārvatī got Śiva as husband, the custom being that whosoever would touch a maiden, fasting on this day, in the dead of the night, would be her husband (*Ibid.*, 59).

Another festival is that of Pañcālikeśa, a yakṣa (*Vāmana*, 6. 52-53); and it comes in the month of Caitra. It is said whosoever touches Pañcālikeśa (i.e. the idol) at that time gets excited-may the person be a male or female, young or old. People are said to sing, dance and sound musical instruments, making all sorts of sounds and bring merry in this festival. Pañcālikeśa is said to have been a *gaṇa* (attendant) of Śiva and Śiva himself is said to have been bestowed upon him this honour of a festival in his name:

> गायन्ति नृत्यन्ति रमन्ति यक्ष वाद्यन्ति यत्नादपि वादयन्ति ।
> तवाग्रतो हास्यवचोभिरक्ता भवन्ति ते योगयुतास्तु ते स्युः ।
> (*Vāmana*, 6.53)

Kālidāsa (*Ṛtu* 4. 48) has depicted *suratotsava* in detail.

5476 **सुवासिनी**

Suvāsinī : women, having their husbands living, played an important part in various festivals. They were invited at various functions. They were called, as now, *suvāsinaī* (*Agni*. 247. 30). *Suvāsinīs* were invited at various functions. They were respected and worshipped. The gifts given to them include cloth, saffron, coconut and sandal. They should be given collyrium for applying it to the eyes, betel-nuts and *sindūra* to be applied at the parting of the hair on the head (*Padma*, *Sṛṣṭikhaṇḍa*, 29. 196-203). In a festive occasion in respect of the goddess Lalitā, the *suvāsinīs* are enjoined to be worshipped, with the accompaniment of songs and instrumental music. They should be offered red clothes and red flowers, and *sindūra* should be applied to them on their heads (*Matsy*, 61. 20).

5477 **सूतिका**

Sūtikā : a brāhmaṇa woman kept as mistress in a Brāhman's house; undesired act, food at her hands is also censured (*Vāmana*., 15.27).

5478 **सृष्टि**

Sṛṣṭi : creation. According to *Manu* (1.29) creation ordains the future course of objects created. The social order itself is a creation by the Lord. Manu is not one of those who think that the social order came into existence as a result of human decision (1.21). The Lord created a King for the protection of the whole creation (VII. 3). Punishment too was created by the Lord (VII.14).

Incidentally the creation of man and woman is referred to elsewhere and they were created to reproduce (IX.96). One of the *ślokas* (1.29) says that the qualities assigned to the different creatures in the beginning clung to them spontaneously. If this is true then the scope for improvement, particularly in the human sphere, is impossible.

5479 **सैकतवेदिका**

Saikatavedikā : house of sand which children built on the sandy banks of rivers or rivulets (*Kumāra*., 1.11).

5480 **सौन्दर्य**

Saundarya : beauty. Kālidāsa (*Kumāra*., III) has a specific concept of beauty when he visualizes Pārvatī. *The Indian Poetic Tradition* (102) renders those lines as follows:

Spring has given her jewels -
Ashoka whose red has taken the
heart out of ruby, *Karṇikāra*.
Essential gold drawn from pure gold alone.
Sindhuvāra, more white than pearl is white.

> A little slower because of the full of her breasts,
> Her garment the hue of sunrise, she's much like a vine,
> Swaying as it might sway, a little bent down
> By the comely weight of blossoms bunched in its leaves.
>
> That girdle of saffron blossoms needs tying again,
> How can she stop it from sliding with hips so smooth.

And round. It isn't a girdle at all; the Love God
Has left her an extra string of His bow, Just in case.

The bees found her mouth like the *Vimba*, a red
More sweet for her breathing across it; and, fearful,
She drove them time and again from her face
By a flick of the lotus she playfully held.

5481 स्तनौ गृहीत्वाऽधरपानम्

Stanau gṛhītvādharapānam : drinking lips (kissing) while holding breasts. A curious expiation performed by Parāvasu (*Skanda.*, VI. 197. 22).

5482 स्त्रीरत्न

Strīratna : gems of women. Varāhamihira enumerated the following excellences known as 'gems of women':

स्त्रीणां गुणा यौवनरूपवेषदाक्षिण्यविज्ञानविलासपूर्वाः । स्त्रीरत्नसंज्ञा च ....

(*Bṛhat-Saṁhitā*, LXVIII. 13)

The excellences of women are youth, beauty, charming dress, favourable attitude, knowledge of the arts of winning man's affection, graceful gait and the like. In Bhāsa's *Svapnavāsvadatta* are come across such excellent qualities in the characters of Vāsavadattā and Pādmāvatī are the best examples.

Every group of things and beings has its gem according to the dictum:

जातौ जातौ यदुत्कृष्टं तद्रत्नमिति कथ्यते ।

Cf. also Vyāsa:

यस्य भार्या शुचिर्दक्षा मिष्टान्नप्रियवादिनी ।
आत्मगुप्ता भर्तृभक्ता सा श्रीरित्युच्यते बुधैः ॥

5483 स्त्रीव्याधि

Strīvyādhi : feminine diseases (for men). Varāhamihira (LXVIII) enumerates certain women which may be permanent diseases for men by the term *strīvyādhi*. The concept of *strīvyādhi* is similar to Kālidāsa's: यान्त्येव गृहिणीपदं युवतयो वामाः कुलस्याधयः which must have been in the mind of Varāhamihira while writing the particular verse.

5484 स्थितप्रज्ञ

Sthitaprajña : the person with steadfast wisdom (*Gītā*). A person with steadfast wisdom is one who is untroubled by sorrows and pleasures. Joys and sorrows will always be there in every human being. The characteristic of a well-developed personality is that he is unaffected by feelings of pleasure and pain that result from the success or failure of his undertakings. Secondly, he is not moved by the emotions of passions, fear and rage - *vītarāgabhayakrodhaḥ*. Thirdly, he draws away his mind from the object of his senses. Does this mean that his sense organs, perceptual and motor, are unaffected? No. He is rather like the sea which always receives the waters from the rivers overflowing. Things affect him, but he is unaffected by them (*Gītā*, II. 54-72).

5485 स्नेह

Sneha : affection, love, oil.

Mattavilāsaprahasana (10) believes that the word for oil also signifies love or affection with the underlying current:

False is the tale, my love, that once the flame
From Śiva's third eye burned to ash the frame
Of Kāma, nay his body, through that heat
Melted to oil, which now inflames our hearts.

Kāma's effect upon all of Śiva's subjects is a form of revenge against Śiva: 'Kāma has disturbed the world, the creation of Śiva, making woman his weapon, as if recalling Śiva's enmity' (*Kālikā*, 52. 111). (b) gloss is to be observed in five things, viz. speech, tongue, teeth, eyes and nails. If all these are glossy, men will be blessed with sons, wealth and attractive features; whereas if these are rough or dry, they will be poor:

स्नेहः पञ्चसु लक्ष्यो वाग्जिह्वादन्तनेत्रनखसंस्थः ।
सुतधनसौभाग्ययुताः स्निग्धैस्तैर्निर्धना रूक्षैः ॥

(*Bṛhat-Saṁhitā*, LXVIII)

(c) a broad class of mental processes, including feeling, emotion, moods and temperament.

5486 स्मरदशा

Smaradaśā : symptoms of passion. Vātsyāyana describes in detail the ten symptoms of being struck by Cupid:

नयनप्रीतिः प्रथमं चित्तसङ्गमस्ततोऽथ संकल्पः ।
निद्राच्छेदस्तनुता विषयनिवृत्तिस्त्रपानाशः ।
उन्मादो मूर्च्छामृतिरित्येताः स्मरदशा दशैव स्युः ॥

of the ten symptoms enumerated above, starting with 'fond glances', insanity (*unmāda*) ranks eighth in intensity. The world of lovers is mostly peopled by lunatics. The types of love have been divided into six categories in the western erotics—and most loving relationships contain elements of each: eros, storge, mania, ludus, pragma and agape. The body's response to passion is as follows: The heart beats faster, the breathing rate increases, perspiration increases and the five physical senses are sharpened.

5487 स्वन

Svana : male-voice according to Varāhamihira (*BS*, LXVII).

The following characteristics of the voice occur in the *Bṛhat-Saṁhitā:* "Persons become monarchs, if their voice is similar to the sound of elephants, bulls, a group of chariots, drums, tabors, lions or clouds. They become unhappy and poverty-stricken, if their voice is broken, rough or like that of a donkey". Vide Garga:

> गम्भीरो दुन्दुभिः स्निग्धो महाश्चैवानुनादवत् ।
> इति स्वरगुणान्पञ्च समुद्रः प्राह तत्त्ववित् ॥
> एभिरायुर्यशो विद्या मानं सौख्यं धनागमः ।
> वाहनानि सुता नार्यो राजभोगागमास्तथा ॥
> भिन्नो जर्जरितश्चैव मिर्मिणो गद्गदस्तथा ।
> क्षामस्वरस्तथैवोक्ताः समुद्रेणाभिनन्दिताः ॥
> स्वयमेभिः कलिक्रोधलोभमोहतमोरजः ।
> नैर्घृण्यमभिमानं च पारुष्यं शाठ्यमेव च ॥

5488 **स्वनित**

Svanita : the rustle of leaves or silks (*Amarakośa*).

5489 **स्वर्ण**

Svarṇa : gold. To the people of India the word 'gold' awakes memories of the Golden Age now sunk to iron, of the days when monarchs handled gold *mohurs,* of exquisite fabled ornaments of the precious metal. Gold has always had a high place in the poetic imagination of India. Winternitz (*IA*, 1899.79) describes how in ancient times, 'At the first feeding to a child, it was made to taste honey and milk from a golden spoon. Gold was frequently used at auspicious rites by the ancient Hindus, and was also worn as an amulet for long life. "The gold which is born from fire, the immortal, they bestowed upon the mortals. He who knows this deserves it; of old age dies he who wears it." It seems to me highly probable that the auspiciousness of gold is due to its supposed origin from fire. "The seed of Agni (Fire)" is a frequent designation of gold. As fire could not be worn as an amulet, gold was used instead'.

In popular folk-song, gold and silver images recur continuously and to my mind at least, with invariably successful effect: The Chhattisgarhi folk sings:

> By day she is the sun
> By night the moon
> My lovely girl is gold
> Fresh from the Sonār's house
> Golden her teeth
> But she is hard to win
> As the gold *mohur* to find.

The *karmā* singer would add a refrain:

> What is the nutmeg made of
> What colour is the pear?
> The nutmeg is silver
> The pear is gold.

5490 **स्वाधिष्ठान**

Svādhiṣṭhāna : one of the *ṣaṭcakras* in Tantra. Above the genitals is *svādhiṣṭhāna* with six petals and six letters. The element is *āpa,* water. The sensation is taste. The motor organs are the hands. The *svādhiṣṭhāna cakra* is the seat of sexual feelings, lassitude, stupor, cruelty, suspicion and contempt. It is also the seat of credulity, disdain, delusion and false belief. Meditation on it destroys lust, anger, greed, delusion, pride, envy and facilitates the acquisition of knowledge (Woodroffe, 1952).

ह - Ha

5491 **हस्तस्पर्श**

Hastasparśa : touch with hand. The king Agnivarṇa in *Mālatimādhava* (IV) describes: "When I actually touched her with my hand (*Ibid.,* III. 102), इति हस्तेन गृदीत्वा उत्थापमति । my hair stood on its end as I was thrilled with delight." Also compare *Vikrama.* (I. 11). In erotic poetry, the standing of hair on end is considered to be the first sign of love, produced by the first bodily touch. It is a type of sexual touch which gives sensual pleasure leading to sexual arousal and love-making.

5492 **हीरक**

Hīraka : diamond. The singers of the folksongs have rarely seen a precious stone, but like the following Gondi song they talk about it:

> The drums are beating
> The singers are calling
> The Sunflower Queen has begun the dance.
> What would she will bring for her house?
> What would shall we bring for the beams?
> What would shall we bring for the verandah?
> Gold we bring for the pillars
> Silver we bring for the beams
> Diamonds we will bring for the verandah
> Where the Sunflower Queen is dancing.

Unlike the aboriginals living in the neighbourhood on a palace in erstwhile Indian State, the Gond and Baiga of the remote Hills did not even had the opportunity of observing from afar the bejewelled insignia of royalty. Yet references to the diamond, the ruby and the pearl are common in their songs and folktales. Motilāl, of the pearl Boy, is common name and a Pardhān hero is called Hīrāman kṣatrī, the Diamond Warrior. 'A woman', says a proverb, 'is diamond because she gives you one'.

The use of these symbols is probably a poetic convention (*kavi-samaya*) that has been acquired from wandering Hindu minstrels or has come down in the traditions of the ancient Gond kingdoms. The five precious things of Hindu story are gold, diamond, sapphire, ruby and pearl (Penzer, IX. 23). In *Kathāsaritsāgara* a beautiful woman is described as having a waist like a diamond and ruby-coloured feet (*Ibid.*, VIII. 248). Penzer (*Ibid.*, VII. 8) quotes a story from Bernhard Julg about the Diamond Kingdom of Central India, through apart from the name the story has nothing to say about jewels. Such references are frequent throughout the whole range of Indian literature and have affected the poetry of other tribes. There is, for example, an Oraon song:

Come and visit us, brother
With your diamond girl
In the morning, brother
With your diamond girl.

(Archer, *The Blue Grove*, 38)

The imagery is obvious and natural, as for example in Drummond's *Madrigal*:

The ivory, coral, gold,
O breast, of lips, of hair,
So lively sleep doth show to inward sight.

What is remarkable here is its use by people to whom the objects of comparison are so unfamiliar.

SUBJECT INDEX

A

B

C

E

F

G

H

I

J

K

L

M

N

O

P

Q

R

U

V

W

Y

Z